The New York Times
Film Reviews
1973-1974

The New York Times
Film Reviews
1973-1974

The New York Times & Arno Press/New York 1975

Contents

Foreword

In 1970, THE NEW YORK TIMES FILM REVIEWS (1913-1968) was published. It was a five-volume set, containing over 18,000 film reviews exactly as they first appeared in The Times.

The collection was accompanied by a sixth volume, an 1,100 page computer-generated index, which afforded ready access to the material by film titles, by producing and distributing companies, and by the names of all actors, directors and other persons listed in the credits.

Further volumes appeared in 1971 and 1973 reproducing the reviews that were printed in The Times during the years 1969-1970 and 1971-1972; the present volume carries the collection through 1974. The same type of index as originally conceived was incorporated into the 1969-1970, 1971-1972 and the present volume.

New compilations will be published periodically to keep the collection constantly updated.

BEST FILMS

Articles listing the best and award-winning films published in The Times appear at the end of each year's reviews. These include the awards of the Academy of Motion Picture Arts and Sciences and the "best films" selections of The New York Times and the New York Film Critics.

The New York Times
Film Reviews
1973

Film Shorts Yield Slice of Americana

AMERICAN DREAMS AND NIGHT-MARES: "Love It/Leave It," by Tom Palazzolo, running time: 14 minutes; "The End of One," by Paul Kocela, edited by Staney Vogel, running time: seven minutes; "Honeymoon Hotel," by Tony Ganz and Rhody Streeter, running time: three minutes; "Cruel and Unusual Punishment," by Charles F. Bailey, running time: 15 minutes; "The Chromium Horse," by Bart Goldberg and Norman Seider, running time: 10 minutes; "Beauty Knows No Pain," produced, directed and photographed by Elliott Erwitt, edited by Geof Bartz, running time: 25 minutes. At the Whitney Museum of American Art, Madison Avenue at 75th Street.

By VINCENT CANBY

A nice little old lady sits in a child's swing. She isn't wearing tennis shoes. In fact, she isn't wearing anything if you don't count the flower painted on her waist. In Chicago, police practice the use of tear gas. A plump, middle-aged man named Bernie welcomes us to a honeymoon hotel that has heart-shaped bathtubs and round beds.

In Texas, Gussie Nell Davis, who wears harlequin glasses and seems to exercise her face by smiling, talks about the values she instills in the girls who become Kilgore College Rangerettes: loveliness, poise and dependability. Somewhere else we watch as the state legally executes a terrified little man by hanging him.

Whether you like them or not, these are some of the scenes you'll probably carry away from the Whitney Museum's vivid and tough new program of six short films collectively titled "American Dreams and Nightmares."

•

Taken together, they suggest that America may collapse into mumbling witlessness in about five minutes. This is a legitimate suggestion from concerned social critics, people whose business is raising hell about society's sanctified idiocies. It may not, however, be an opinion shared by each of the film makers represented in the Whitney show.

Short films of this sort are terribly impressionable. They acquire moods and attitudes from the things that surround them. Thus the dominant theme of "American Dreams and Nightmares" — that America the Beautiful has become rotten and grotesque — gives to "Beauty Knows No Pain" an effective malignance I didn't notice when I first saw it last year in a commercial theater.

On a program with the beatifically bland "The Trial of the Catonsville Nine," Elliott Erwitt's 25-minute documentary, about the care and training of a group of majorettes, seemed rather sweet and sad. Here the rigors the girls so willingly endure look like the preparations for a national lobotomy.

Tom Palazzolo's 14-minute "Love It/Leave It," which he describes as a Chamber of Commerce film, opens the program and sets its tone. It's a montage of exhibitionism (nude beauty contests, parades, professional wrestling) intercut with shots of people (Gov. George C. Wallace) and things (riots, the White House), about which there's no doubt what our associations should be. As social criticism, it's facile, but as film-making it's riveting.

Paul Kocela's seven-minute "The End of One" shows us seagulls going out of their small minds with delight at a huge garbage dump, cross-cut with shots of one very ill bird staggering off to die alone down the beach. Although I don't have much feeling one way or the other for a seagull, I did wonder why the film maker photographed rather than helped it.

"Honeymoon Hotel" is a funny, short (three-minute) anti-commercial for some place called Cove Haven, and "The Chromium Horse" is a

sober-sided appreciation of an overage boy who loves his Harley-Davidson as life itself.

•

The most effective film on the program is Charles Bailey's 15-minute, black-and-white "Cruel and Unusual Punishment," perhaps because it makes no attempt at irony, no attempt to hide its feelings about capital punishment. Correction officers, penologists, professional executioners talk about their business, some quite matter-of-factly.

One executioner thinks it's odd that the condemned men always sit on the edge of the electric chair's seat, "so you have to sort of skooter them back onto the chair." Others, including Gov. Milton A. Schapp of Pennsylvania, are passionate in their loathing. Says one penologist after witnessing an execution: "You are no longer outside the system . . . You assume a degree of community guilt." Which is, more or less, the point of "American Dreams and Nightmares."

1973 Ja 5, 14:2

Screen: Tangled Motives

'Spider's Stratagem' at the New Yorker

"The Spider's Stratagem," which has opened at the New Yorker Theater, was shown at the ninth New York Film Festival. The following excerpts are from Vincent Canby's review, which appeared Sept. 18, 1970, in The New York Times.

"The Spider's Stratagem" is an elaborate, theatrical plot uncovered by the son of a murdered anti-Fascist hero, 30 years after the murder, when he is called back to his father's town for the dead man's former mistress. In a series of curious, dreamlike encounters with the mistress and with the men who were his father's comrades, the young man discovers that his father had been a traitor to what seems to have been a comic opera plot on Mussolini's life.

Much more than his "Partner," which was shown at the 1968 New York Film Festival, Bernardo Bertolucci's "The Spider's Stratagem" recalls the Stendhalian world of his best film,

The Cast

THE SPIDER'S STRATAGEM, directed by Bernardo Bertolucci; screen-play (Italian with English subtitles) by Mr. Bertolucci, Edoardo de Gregorio and Marilu Parolini, based on a story by Jorge Luis Borges; director of photography, Vittorio Storaro; produced by Giovanni Bertolucci for R.A.I. At the New Yorker Theater, Broadway and 88th Street. Running time: 97 minutes. This film is classified GP.

Athos Magnani Jr. .... Giulio Brogi
Athos Magnani Sr. .... Giulio Brogi
Draifa .... Alida Valli
Costa .... Tino Scotti
Gaibrazzi .... Pippo Campanini
Rasori .... Franco Giovanelli
Sailor .... Allen Midgette

"Before the Revolution," which also had to do with self-deception, political action compromised and motives almost hopelessly tangled. The settings, too, are similar, provincial towns that seem to be millions of miles from where the real action is taking place.

The film's color photography is extraordinarily lovely for, like the conspirators within the film, Bertolucci has a weakness for the purely theatrical effect. Of the players, I particularly liked Alida Valli, as the aging mistress, a tough, lean lady who lives in a style fitting an impoverished princess, but who walks around, barefooted and untidy, like a peasant.

1973 Ja 6, 21:1

The Program

CINE-DANCE: IMAGING by Fred Aronow, 6 minutes; CIRCLES II by Doris Chase, 12 minutes; EARTH SONG by Bob Cowan, 25 minutes; THIS IS MY BODY by Grover Dale, 6½ minutes; FILM WITH SEVEN DANCERS by Jill Demby and Paul Halpern, 7 minutes; ALMIRA by Nancy Kendall, 20 minutes; 9 VARIATIONS ON A DANCE THEME by Hilary Harris, 13 minutes. At the Film Forum, 256 West 88th Street. Jan. 5-7, 12-14, 8 P.M.

By ROGER GREENSPUN

Most serious dance films, except the very best, become a contest between dance and film in which, if we are lucky, dance wins. Of course, the very best dance films, like George Stevens's sublime "Swing Time" and Hilary Harris's excellent "9 Variations on a Dance Theme," prove that movies sometimes can be a genuine synthesis of the arts. But the proposition still holds, and I think it is amply demonstrated by the seven short films in a program called "Cine-Dance," which opened last night at Film Forum. "Swing Time" isn't on the program, naturally, but Hilary Harris's film is. And it may be taken as a standard by which everything else stands or falls — mostly falls.

•

"9 Variations" features the dancer Bettie de Jong, alone, in practice leotards, in a tight, bare room. Each brief variation, to music by McNeil Robinson, begins with Miss De Jong on the floor and continues through movements of greater or lesser elaborateness, until she again subsides to the floor. The whole thing takes 13 minutes. It is a very severe but by no means simple film, and its great virtue — in addition to the beauty of Miss De Jong's dancing — is in its marvelously supple and tactful program of montage and camera movement, continually meeting and matching the dancer as if fulfilling a choreographic pattern of its own. "9 Variations" seems a genuine collaboration, and in its own very seemly way it is ravishing.

Both "Film with Seven Dancers" by Jill Demby and Paul Halpern and Grover Dale's "This Is My Body" attempt a similar unmediated confrontation between camera and dancer (or dancers), but with smaller ambitions and much less success. "Film with Seven Dancers" at least offers the pleasurable interplay of several graceful young bodies. Grover Dale's movie offers Grover Dale.

I very much preferred Doris Chase's "Circles II," which uses dancers, the Mary Staton Dance Ensemble of Seattle, but uses them primarily as elements in a rich, semiabstract movie in which

postproduction work is almost as important as the lovely rolling and dancing with circles (in fact, sculptures by Doris Chase) that takes place in front of the camera. "Circles II" is colorized into soft monochromatic pastels as beautiful as anything of the sort I've seen in the movies.

Bob Cowan's "Earth Song" and Nancy Kendall's "Almira" attempt expanding the dance —into a kind of cinematic pantheism for "Earth Song" and into dramatic narrative for "Almira." Both are too long and fairly ridiculous. "Earth Song" overwhelms its dancer (Tandy Beale) with images of the land and the sea, and flowers and fish eyes and rhinoceros hide (I think) and the whole catalogue of obligations that the metaphoric dance of life nowadays calls forth.

The heroine of "Almira," who is probably insane, alternately walks and runs away from the torments of her life—to a beach, where she dances for a while, before wandering off into the water. Gay Delanghe, a most exciting dancer, plays the heroine, and while she actually does dance—briefly, between flight and suicide — "Almira" looks wonderful, as film can look in the service of another art.

1973 Ja 6, 22:1

The Cast

LITTLE MOTHER (advertised under the title "Mother"), produced and directed by Radley Metzger; screenplay by Brian Phelan; director of photography, Hans Jura; editor, Amedeo Salfa; associate producer, Ava Leighton; distributed by Audubon Films. Running time: 92 minutes. At neighborhood theaters. This film has been classified R.

Marina .... Christiane Kruger
Pinares .... Siegfried Rauch
Umberia .... Ivan Desny
Riano .... Mark Damon
Cardinal .... Anton Diffring
Annette .... Elga Sorbas

By VINCENT CANBY

The easy availability of hard-core pornography in so many conventional motion-picture theaters has had the odd effect of beaching the old-fashioned, soft-core, sex-exploitation film, the sort of movie beyond which (it used to be regularly exclaimed) it will be impossible to go.

As we've learned, it's always possible to go further than the last film, to show a little more and to enjoy it a little more. The result is that a movie of the primitive order of "Deep Throat" is a box-office smash while Radley Metzger, a serious director of an earlier though never very serious kind of sex-exploitation film ("The

---

1

Lickerish Quartet," "Therese and Isabelle," etc.), is more or less hounded into respectability.

Perhaps checkmated is a better term. I'm not sure where Metzger wants to move next, or whether he can move at all. However, it's apparent with "Little Mother," a very lightly fictionized biography of the late Eva Perón, that his ambitions are alive and essentially respectable.

It's not that Metzger's films are more respectable today—they've always been respectably made—but we see them with consciences anesthetized by real porn. When he shows us a shower scene in which Marina, the Eva Peróne character played by Christiane Kruger, stands on one side of the glass curtain with her lover on the other side, caressing the outlines of her body, the old titillation has gone and a snicker has taken its place. Metzger's thoughts about sex as a political weapon intrigue us for maybe 10 seconds.

Even more peculiar is an old-fashioned orgy sequence in which the women are nude and the men wear bathing trunks—which suggests that Metzger's fictionized Argentina carried the double-standard to lengths only imaginable by a movie.

The fleshy fantasies being so mild, we are forced to take Metzger's new film as seriously as he does, which puts something of a strain on us, and it.

"Little Mother" is the odd, typically Metzgerian mixture of opulence (camera work, color, sets, costmues) and poverty (writing, acting), all of which somehow suits the Eva Peron legend without doing justice to it.

Brian Phelan's screenplay covers the last weeks of Marina's life, after she has learned she has cancer and while she schemes for, among other things, her husband's re-election as dictator of the never-named country and her own canonization. The movie is filled with so many flashbacks that at times it stumbles over them, even when they are almost subliminal. The story outline is, however, simplicity itself: how a poor but beautiful little radio actress rose to the top, her ambitions rising too, from a lust for lust and money to a lust for political power and, finally, for sainthood.

The real-life story of Juan and Eva Perón is so fascinating that one aches for "Little Mother" to be better than it is. The effect of Phelan's screenplay is to reduce extraordinary melodrama of politics and power to ordinary melodrama of murder, spite and wilfulness, which just happens to have an entire country as its locale rather than a few barrooms, bedrooms and kitchens.

•

The good things in the film include Christiane Kruger

(Hardy Kruger's daughter), who manages to look very much like Eva but who has the class of Grace Kelly, which Eva never had. Most especially the look of the entire film is right, even though it was shot in Zagreb, Yugoslavia. It's the sort of film in which you can believe the buildings, the drawing rooms, the motorcades, the demonstrations in front of the presidential palace, even the passion and fury of its heroine. The dialogue, however, is sometimes comically bad, and most of the supporting actors, including Siegfried Rauch, who plays Marina's dictator-husband, are inept.

"Little Mother" is schizoid. It looks intelligent and talks like an idiot—to such an extent that I'm sure one of these days Metzger will make a first-class film, when and if he gets a good screenplay and hires actors with the same care he usually gives to the hiring of actresses.

1973 Ja 6, 25:1

The Ten Worst Movies Of 1972

By VINCENT CANBY

THIS is the week to be churlish, to turn that smile upside down. To encourage a kind of cab driver-grumpiness and to nourish unfair biases. To use blunt instruments on sinners. To be negative in as decisive a way as possible. To be insincerely alarmed and saddened by second-rateness. To cite failure wherever found. To be, above all, frank, letting the chips fall where they may.

It is the time to say, straight out, that almost every non-musical film that Barbra Streisand has ever made would have been more interesting with another actress. To declare Charles Bronson the winner of the award given annually to the actor who has succeeded in appearing in two or more of the year's dumbest movies (Terence Young's "The Valachi Papers" and Michael Winner's "The Mechanic"), and to cite Mr. Winner for having directed another of 1972's more rotten efforts, "The Nightcomers," in which Mr. Winner modestly took it upon himself to tell us

everything that Henry James, after some deliberation, decided not to tell us about the events that occurred before those in "The Turn of The Screw."

•

It's never easy to compile a list of the 10 worst films of the year. There always are considerations. No movie directed by Billy Wilder will ever be allowed on the list, even if it seems as bitterly archaic as "Avanti." "Butterflies Are Free" is foolish, sentimental stuff, but that, after all, is just what everyone loves about it. "Child's Play" doesn't work, but it has a superior performance by James Mason, and "The Effect of Gamma Rays on Man-in-The-Moon Marigolds" has its heart in the right place.

You simply cannot hate a horror film ("The Night of The Lepus") in which a mother explains to her small daughter the hormone shots being given to a pair of rabbits: "We're trying to make Jill a little more like Jack, and Jack a little more like Jill." Peter Ustinov's "Hammersmith Is Out" was, over the long haul, a disaster, but it offered us occasional glimpses of Elizabeth Taylor giving a real performance—being tough, dim-witted, funny and beautiful — and though Richard Burton was not good in it, he recouped all with his splendid work in Joseph Losey's "The Assassination of Trotsky."

No matter how bad a film by Sam Peckinpah is — and both "Straw Dogs" and "The Getaway" are pretty bad—you simply cannot put a Peckinpah film on the list. He's too good a director, even when the films don't work. Last year, in addition to seeing his "Straw Dogs" and "The Getaway," we also saw his "Junior Bonner," which was very good indeed.

The following films, listed in no particular order, are my list of the 10 worst films of 1972, or, more accurately, the 10 films I remember best with malice:

Mary, Queen of Scots, directed by Charles Jarrott; screenplay by John Hale. Vanessa Redgrave plays Mary more by size than with emotion (she looks beautiful and huge) and Glenda Jackson plays Elizabeth with a good deal of intensity, yet what I recall about this film most vividly is its complete lack of urgency. It's a Christmas card sale in January. The dialogue often has the desperate ring of improvisation. Mary, to the dissolute Darnley: "You disgust me!" Darnley to Mary: "I disgust you!" So it goes.

Young Winston, directed by Richard Attenborough; pro-

duced and written by Carl Foreman, based on "My Early Life: A Roving Commission," by Sir Winston Churchill. "Young Winston" is one of those movie biographies in which a character asks the great-man-to-be: "What's ever to become of you?" Because young Winston has a fairly good idea of what's to become of him, and we know for sure, the point of the movie has to be an interpretation of that knowledge. According to Carl Foreman, young Winston grew into the great Sir Winston because his mum was a London toast, and his dad distant and syphilitic. The movie makes a great call on our affection for the indomintable old cuss, and it's so confident that it presents, as a climax, Winston's first major appearance before Commons at the age of 27, when he makes a passionate plea for a sane fiscal policy. It has all the charm and grace of a report by the keeper of the exchequer.

The Man, directed by Joseph Sargent; story and screenplay by Rod Serling, based on the novel by Irving Wallace. According to a long-popular myth, some movies are so bad they're good. If it's possible, though, I doubt it, you might describe "The Man" that way. James Earl Jones plays a black Senator who suddenly becomes the President of the United States when the ceiling in a 600-year-old palace falls on a lot of powerful heads during a summit conference in Frankfurt, Germany. It may be some indication of the film's narrative drive that, during the rest of "The Man," I kept wondering why the ceiling fell rather than getting involved with the new President's battles with red-neck Congressmen, his advisors, the members of the Black Caucus, and his daughter, who just hangs around the house sneering at her old man for not being militant enough. The dullness of the drama, and the fuzziness of its thinking, evoke the magic of the Eisenhower Years.

The Public Eye, directed by Carol Reed; screenplay by Peter Shaffer, based on his play. Mia Farrow plays an American waif, though she is actually an armor-plated anti-intellectual, married to a nice, respectable London accountant (Michael Jayston) who doesn't share her passion for horror films, sunsets, dolphins, ice cream and Franco Zeffirelli's "Romeo and Juliet." It takes Topol, who gives what is positively the year's worst performance as a lovable private detective, to reunite the couple. The film spends so

much time sight-seeing around London you might reasonably wonder if it was financed by BOAC.

Portnoy's Complaint, directed by Ernest Lehman; screenplay by Mr. Lehman, adapted from the novel by Philip Roth. "This is my life, doctor, my only life," Alex Portnoy (Richard Benjamin) shouts at his analyst, "and I'm living it in the middle of a Jewish joke!" Under Ernest Lehman's spectacularly clumsy direction, Philip Roth's great Jewish joke has turned terribly unpleasant. Because the movie looks as pretty as a Prell commerical and as prim as a Sermonette, Roth's hugely funny, dirty, first-person narrative becomes embarrassingly crude and show-offy. It proves once again that there are some things that simply cannot be filmed — The Yellow Pages, The Bible, "Remembrance of Things Past," most film reviews and "Portnoy's Complaint."

A Place Called Today, directed and written by Don Schain. This is my sentimental choice as the most horrible film of the year, one of the two soft-core porn films of 1972 that starred Cheri Caffaro (Mrs. Don Schain) as a singularly unqualified enchantress, a role that amounts to a kind of character part for her. The film also has to do with a furiously complicated and crooked election campaign involving a crooked black politician, a crooked white politician, and a pretty white revolutionary (Lana Wood) who obviously divides her time equally between participating in politics and applying eye make-up.

The War Between Men and Women, directed by Melville Shavelson; screenplay by Mr. Shavelson and Danny Arnold, suggested by the writings and drawings of James Thurber. This was undoubtedly the year's most peculiarly mixed-up comedy, about a cartoonist (Jack Lemmon) who's going blind and tries to keep it a secret from the decent woman (Barbara Harris) who loves him. Another hilarious character is a little girl who stutters. The cartoonist is loosely based on Thurber himself, but Shavelson and Arnold seem to have confused the Thurber wit with the humor of W. C. Fields, to the disadvantage of all. The biggest Shavelson-Arnold coup: an endorsement of the film by Mr. Thurber's widow.

Trouble Man, directed by Ivan Dixon; screenplay by John D. F. Black. This stands out as one of the worst black rip-off films of the year because so many good people were involved in it, including Ivan Dixon, the director, and Robert Hooks, the star who plays, though without a great deal of conviction, another black supercat.

Savage Messiah, directed by Ken Russell; screenplay by Christopher Logue, based on the book by H. S. Ede. No list of the most awful films of the year would be complete without something by Ken Russell, even a comparatively placid drama such as "Savage Messiah," which is all about the strange (platonic) affair between Henri Gaudier-Brzeska, the French sculptor who died in World War I at the age of 24, and Sophie Brzeska, the Polish woman twice his age whose name he added to his own. If it's nothing else (and it isn't), "Savage Messiah" is a Golden Treasury of Definitions of Art. Among other things, we learn that "art is alive" and that "art is above sex," which, I suppose, is a kind of definition.

. . . . And Hope To Die, directed by René Clément; screenplay by Sebastian Japrisot, based on a novel by David Goodis. The cast is headed by Robert Ryan, Jean-Louis Trintignant, Lea Massari and Aldo Ray and the story is about some underworld characters in Montreal and more than that ye need not know. Just remember the title and, if you have to, break your leg to avoid seeing it.

The Trial of The Catonsville Nine, directed by Gordon Davison; screenplay by Father Daniel Berrigan and Saul Levitt, based on the play by Father Berrigan. An object lesson in piety as a dramatic fallacy, "The Trial of The Catonsville Nine" sets out to celebrate a real-life event of courage and commitment and effectively embalms it in tableaus so full of self-congratulations that you're likely to wind up questioning your original admiration for the nine. The acting is uniformly dreadful. At a period when the war news has been so grim, the failure of this film seems just that much more grievous.

1973 Ja 7, II:1:8

The Cast

DR. PHIBES RISES AGAIN, directed by Robert Fuest; screenplay by Mr. Fuest and Robert Blees, based on characters created by James Whiton and William Goldstein; original music composed by John Gale; produced by Louis M. Heyward; distributed by American International Pictures. Running time: 89 minutes. At neighborhood theaters. This film has been classified PG.

Dr. Phibes	Vincent Price
Biederbeck	Robert Quarry
Vulnavia	Valli Kemp
Diana	Fiona Davis
Captain	Peter Cushing
Mrs. Ambrose	Beryl Reid
Lombardo	Terry-Thomas
Ambrose	Hugh Griffith
Inspector Trout	Peter Jeffrey
Waverly	John Cater
Hackett	Gerald Sim

By VINCENT CANBY

To recapitulate: when we last saw him (in "The Abominable Dr. Phibes," released here in 1971), the abominable Dr. Phibes was climbing into his well-appointed London tomb. The soundtrack orchestra was playing "Over the Rainbow," and the doctor was preparing to await—in a state of suspended animation—that perfect conjunction of the moon with the other planets before rising again.

You may also remember that the doctor, a vaudevillian whose artistic sensibilities are stuck in the 1930's, had earlier been driven mad by the death of his wife, Victoria, in an automobile accident that had, in turn, left him horribly disfigured. He has to eat and talk through a tube in his neck. Even worse, when he moves about in society he must wear a plastic mask that makes him look rather like Vincent Price.

●

As we pick up our story in "Dr. Phibes Rises Again," Dr. Philbes is rising again, on an elevator from his tomb, to book passage to Egypt for himself, the body of Victoria and for his slave Vulnavia, there to search for the underground elixirs that will awaken Victoria and bestow upon them both eternal life.

"Dr. Phibes Rises Again," which opened yesterday at neighborhood theaters on a bill with "Blacula," makes the usually dumb mistake of aspiring to be camp. Mysteriously, a lot of it works, probably because Robert Fuest, the director, knows just how long to hold an effect before it wilts.

You should like a quick shot of the doctor, who really is Vincent Price, dancing with Vulnavia to the tune of "You Stepped out of a Dream," on the foggy, lonely deck of the liner Elsinore that's taking them to Alexandria. Or the shot of them dining otherwise alone, atop an Egyptian sand dune, under a tent that might charm Fellini. "Vulnavia," says the doctor as he discreetly picks a tiny bone out of the tube in his neck, "you've done wonders with the local fish."

Or some of the other lines: "You can't just go charging into someone else's mountain. This isn't Hyde Park!" says the idiot London police inspector, who's followed Phibes to Egypt, to his idiot assistant, who wants to storm Phibes's underground hideout. The settings are indescribably garish, an homage to the modernistic, 1930's movie-theater décor that reached its zenith with Radio City Music Hall. Robert Quarry, who plays Phibes's archenemy, and Fiona Davis, as Quarry's mistress, read their lines in clipped, elegant, deadpan fashion, in an appreciative parody of Noël and Gertie in "Private Lives."

I also liked the idea that a man, murdered by Phibes aboard ship, might wash ashore in a bottle.

●

The movie, written by Fuest and Robert Blees, an old Hollywood hand, has such respect for fantasy that it never gets bogged down in explanations. A lot of it is not funny, including guest appearances by Terry-Thomas and Beryl Reid, but a lot of it shows a real awareness of style that is usually absent in the work of people who set out to exploit camp.

1973 Ja 11, 35:1

The Program

IMAGINE, directed and edited by John Lennon and Yoko Ono; a Joko films, Inc., Production. Running time: 70 minutes. At the Whitney Museum of American Art, Madison Avenue and 75th Street.

With: John Lennon, Yoko Ono, Dick Cavett, George Harrison, Fred Astaire, Jack Palance and Jonas Mekas.

By ROGER GREENSPUN

The private lives of culture heros, like the private lives of most of us, normally offer a richer field for gossip than for enlightenment. "Imagine," the somewhat autobiographical new movie by John Lennon and Yoko Ono, doesn't mean to be gossip, nor even enlightenment, but rather a kind of meditation on how a couple view their privacy. Since the privacy of John and Yoko is very close to publicity, I suppose they may be excused a certain penchant for public demonstration in the ways they view how they live, what they think, what they feel—above all, what they feel about each other.

So ther are scenes showing John and Yoko strolling together down romantic tree-shaded pathways; John and Yoko dancing through lower Manhattan, John and Yoko gazing at John and Yoko The War Is Over posters, John and Yoko writing "John loves" and "Yoko loves" in the sand. One sequence, an outdoor beautiful-people party, looks a lot like a Jonas Mekas home movie. And when the main titles come on (at the end) it turns out to be a Jonas Mekas home movie. Mekas is fully credited, as is the animator, Carmen D'Avino, and several editors, and three separate production crews in England, the United States and Japan. But the mood is very intimate; just a different kind of intimacy from what we're used to.

It is an intimacy that has room for brief celebrity appearances by Jack Palance, Fred Astaire, Dick Cavett and others; and that summons up elaborate visual fantasies tuned to the music of John (from "Imagine") and Yoko (from "Fly"), which occupies most of the soundtrack. Sometimes the fantasies include the celebrities (but who is more celebrated than John and Yoko?); more often, just the magic couple—and perhaps a stray servant or two—being in love.

John and Yoko play chess—in a summer house, on a tiny island, in a little lake, on a huge estate—and she vamps him, and he eats her chess pieces. On a dark city street, Yoko cruises, and John approaches; they go off together into some iniquitous den—which looks rather like the main entrance to the Plaza Hotel.

●

Many of these sequences use Yoko Ono as a sex object, not really her best role, and many of them mean to be funny. On the whole, they fail. For all its elaborate production and its technical expertise, "Imagine" is the soul of amateurishness. Even its stabs at humor seem a kind of eager self-parody, covering for what is indeed a massive self-indulgence.

I saw "Imagine" in a screening room in 35mm. The Whitney Museum, where it opened yesterday, is showing it in a 16mm. copy—with, I should assume, the usual loss in picture quality.

1973 Ja 13, 17:1

The Cast

THE FIRST CIRCLE, directed by Aleksander Ford; screenplay by Mr. Ford, based on the novel by Aleksandr I. Solzhenitsyn; editor, Carl Lerner; director of photography, Wladyslaw Forbert; music composed and conducted by Roman Palester; produced by Mogens Skot-Hansen; distributed by Paramount Pictures. Running time: 98 minutes. At the Fine Arts Theater, 58th Street near Lexington Avenue. This film has been rated R.

Gleb Nerzhin	Gunther Malzacher
Simochka	Elzbieta Czyzewska
Volodin	Peter Steen
Clara	Vera Chekova
Ruska Doronin	Ole Ernst
Rubin	Ingolf David
Bobynin	Preben Neergaard
Professor Chelnov	Preben Lerdorff Rye

By VINCENT CANBY

"The First Circle" is a very sad film. Not because of the austerity of its place and time (a special Soviet prison camp for scientists in the late 1940's), nor because hopelessness would seem the only rational philosophy under a tyranny as effective as Stalin's. Rather it's because the movie is such a wan and ineffectual testament to the novel it is based on, as well as to the life and career of its extraordinary author, Aleksandr I. Solzhenitsyn, the 1970 Nobel Prize-winning Soviet writer.

●

Aleksander Ford, the 64-year-old Polish film maker who wrote and directed the film, has a reputation for serious work that goes back to the late 1920's. Mr. Ford, who left Poland in 1968 to live in Israel, has also lived and worked in the Soviet Union, leading one to believe that "The First Circle" would, at least, look and sound right. But it doesn't.

It's an international mess. It was filmed in Denmark, mostly with what I assume to be Scandinavian actors, who apparently mouthed English dialogue that was later dubbed in a variety of accents, some so alarmingly American that the way the actors say their lines makes what they say sound even worse, like the dialogue in a Hollywood prison melodrama of the 1930's.

"We can make you talk if we want to," the camp superintendent says to a prisoner who the government wants to have invent "the absolute encoder." Or (with a snarl): "We'll shoot you like a dog. You'll never get away!"

The absolute encoder, which sounds as if the movie wanted to talk like Flash Gordon, is a device ordered by Stalin so that no one can bug his telephone conversations. Its also the peg around which the melodrama proceeds, in lurching starts and fits, introducing us to various inmates and, through flashbacks, to their earlier lives.

By trying to cram so much of the 580-page novel into a film of conventional length, Mr. Ford has gotten hold of practically nothing. A lot of events and characters are there, but the tremendous range of experience and emotion is gone. So are the novel's sense of heroisin, of history, of magnificent mission. Instead, awkward actors stand about in costumes in which they don't seem overly at ease, being photographed in the blunt, bright reds and greens and blues that I associate with Denmark's soft-core porn features, playing, essentially, good guys and bad guys with an often ludicrous solemnity.

●

Even though they fail as films, some adaptations of great novels may work to the extent that they excite that they excite enough curiosity to send one to the novel itself. "The First Circle," which opened yesterday at the Fine Arts is such a clinker it just might shrivel the interest of anyone unfamiliar with Solzhenitsyn's work. The effect, though not the intent, is anti-intellectual—and it's fairly unforgivable.

1973 Ja 13, 17:3

What Makes 'Poseidon' Fun?

By VINCENT CANBY

ARK movies are easy to describe: a group of assorted characters (two of each is the accepted way) are put aboard an ocean liner, in an airplane, or maybe on a bridge that clearly looks unsafe to us but to no one within the film. In short order (the shorter the better for this sort of thing to be successful), the bridge collapses, the ocean liner starts sinking, or the airplane threatens to crash (though two out of three times it doesn't), which is the easiest way to explain survivors in Ark Movies about airplanes, most air crashes being so fatal. This is also the factor that makes Ark Movies about airplanes seem such gyps.

The technology and the ingenuity of survival are what fascinate us in Ark Movies, especially survival after some spectacularly dreadful sequence of events that has effectively eliminated all of the non-speaking roles and all of the other not-quite-anonymous actors, leaving us with a small group of featured performers and one or two stars to figure things out against odds that must, ultimately, be surmountable. Some of which may explain why I found Ronald Neame's "The Poseidon Adventure" such innocent, earnest entertainment as it satisfied a certain lust for classic form, although I'd been thoroughly bored by "Airport," the movie to which it can be too glibly compared. "The Poseidon Adventure" puts the Ark Movie back where God intended it to be, in the water. Not flying around in the air on one engine or with a hole in its side.

*

I can think of no really good Ark Movies, films that one might go back to see a second time, yet I see them all, usually sooner than later—"Airport," "The High and The Mighty," "A Night to Remember," "Titanic," "Phone Call From A Stranger." I'm not at all sure that such senior or pre-Ark movies as Stanley Kramer's "Ship of Fools" wouldn't have been better if his liner had run into a submerged object early on, or that George Cukor's "Dinner at 8" wouldn't be still more vivid in my memory if something cataclysmic had interrupted all of the elegant chatter and back-biting.

This may sound as if I have a peculiar affection for disaster, at least on the screen. Perhaps I do. I also have affection for the kind of special effects that are so beautifully executed in "The Poseidon Adventure" and make the film so much fun, even when the screenplay (by Stirling Silliphant and Wendell Mayes, based on Paul Gallico's novel) is burrowing into some new foolishness with all of the intensity of a mad mole digging through soap chips.

When, early in the film, we see the S.S. Poseidon, en route from New York to Athens, plowing through a Mediterranean gale, the combination of model liner and studio-made (I assume) high seas is so effective that one applauds the ferocity while acknowledging the fakery. When, a little later, a few minutes after midnight on New Year's Eve as the Poseidon is steaming between Gibraltar and Sicily (I think, but the film is fuzzy on its navigation), the ship is walloped by a 90-foot wave and turns over, hull-up, the movie delivers all of the details of disaster that could possibly be promised by even the most hyperbolic ad campaign.

It seemed apparent from the audience with which I saw the film last Sunday afternoon at the National Theater (it's also playing at the Beekman) that a lot of the people had been pre-sold by the television commercials. One little boy sitting in front of me was anticipating the big wave (supposedly caused by the collapse of a section of sea floor north of Crete) almost from the film's first frame. "Here it comes!" he announced during the initial gale sequence. But it didn't. "Here it comes!" he announced again at the height of the carefree New Year's celebrations aboard the Poseidon. This time he was right.

As any student of Ark Movies knows, disaster strikes most effectively at carefree moments. We know what's going to happen. They don't. Which is very much a part of the simple pleasures afforded by such fiction.

The pleasures are simple, and have little to do with characterization or acting, or such techniques as the split screens with which George Seaton tried to jazz up the old-fashioned nonsense of "Airport." "The Poseidon Adventure" has no first-magnitude stars on the order of Burt Lancaster and Dean Martin, no first ladies of the theater like Helen Hayes, no particularly topical problems (abortion)—all of which contributed to the dogged fatuousness of the Seaton film. It tried to put on airs, to act above its station, which is that of upper low-brow fiction. "The Poseidon Adventure" makes no such mistakes.

Its stars (Gene Hackman, Ernest Borgnine, Red Buttons, Carol Lynley, Roddy McDowall, Stella Stevens, Shelley Winters) and its so-called co-stars (Jack Albertson, Pamela Sue Martin, Arthur O'Connel, Eric Shea "and Leslie Nielsen as The Captain") are all relentlessly second-magnitude, which is no reflection on their talent, but rather an acknowledgement that most of them are names who, with the possible exception of Hackman, don't mean a great deal at any box office. There is also something very second-magnitude about the characters they play—a sweet old Jewish couple (Albertson and Miss Winters) on their way to Israel, a hard-headed cop (Borgnine) and his wife (Miss Stevens), who is a former prostitute, a swinging preacher (Hackman) who sees poverty in conventional prayer, a lonely little haberdasher (Buttons), and so on and so forth.

The screenplay offers some of the most uncomfortably maudlin if obligatory death scenes you're likely to see all this year, and my favorite line (out of a 1972 movie) directed to God: "We don't want You to fight for us. Just don't fight against us!"

*

It's the kind of movie in which earnest enemies become admiring friends and in which simple pleas for understanding touch cold hearts, all the while as the small group of survivors of the Poseidon disaster struggle to make their way upwards into the bowels of the ship and, they hope, freedom, after the ship has capsized.

The simple pleasures of "The Poseidon Adventure" are mostly technical and, I suspect, not at all simple to effect. The interior, pre-capsize scenes of the film were shot aboard the Queen Mary, now in Long Beach, California, and it's the old Queen's innards, especially its first-class dining room, that are carefully recreated in studio mock-ups of the upside-down liner. The sequence in which the ship rolls over is seen almost entirely from the point-of-view of the passengers in the dining room, and it's a smashing bit of photographed, simulated chaos, of gradual fright and then sudden panic, of extras dropping from the floor to ceiling, while the film's stars and co-stars survive, as you know they must.

Shortly after this big scene, you stop worrying about acting and writing and logic and probability. You simply enjoy the engineering feats of the moviemakers, which are so effective that they touch even outrageous things with credibility. Last week the audience at the National actu-ally applauded a bit of business by Shelley Winters that, in another, less spectacular film, would have had me asking for my money back. I'm beginning to think that when Miss Winters, who can be a very good comedienne, wants us to know she's acting, she just eats a lot. Perhaps I'm being unreasonable. The audience clearly adores her, to such an extent that at one point, when it appeared the character might be having a heart attack, a lady in my row cried out with concern: "Aw, come on, Shelley!" If they are nothing else, Ark Movies are what the trade calls, with justification, audience pictures.

1973 Ja 14, II:1:6

HOW DO YOU PHOTOGRAPH A CRY OR A WHISPER?

By JOHN BARROW

"WHEN a director dies he becomes a photographer." So said John Grierson, the late British film critic and pioneer of the documentary form, of the Josef von Sternberg-Charlie Chaplin 1926 film, "A Woman of the Sea." He went on: "If one cannot by taking thought add a cubit to one's stature, one can no more by great gifts of photography add power to a feeble story."

And too often today we endure such deceit, practiced in the name of artful photography, using the jiggle of the hand-held camera, the sudden and dramatic magnification of the zoom lens, the perspective distortion of the wide-angle or telephoto lens, the intentional softening and perpetual pulling of focus —all with the aim of making us think that something of substance is up there on the screen, when, in fact, it is empty.

All films are photographed, yet in so few does photography contribute anything essential. Cinematographers, when they talk of their craft, talk like technicians, reminiscing about the problems they had stringing a zillion lights in a forest grove or clamping their cameras to helicopter struts and so on. Rarely do they mention the script or the director's conception as something which might inform their method.

All of which brings us to Ingmar Bergman's "Cries and Whispers." Much will be written and spoken of this profound film — of Bergman's puritanism. of the powerful performances of Liv Ullmann, Ingrid Thulin, Harriet Andersson and Kari Sylwan. But something must be said as loudly of the film's photography, for rarely, if ever, has photography been used so dramatically (not spectacularly, as, say, in the films of David Lean, for one) as in this film — to the point where the film has a fifth star. That star is light.

*

It is not surprising that light has attained top billing under the direction of

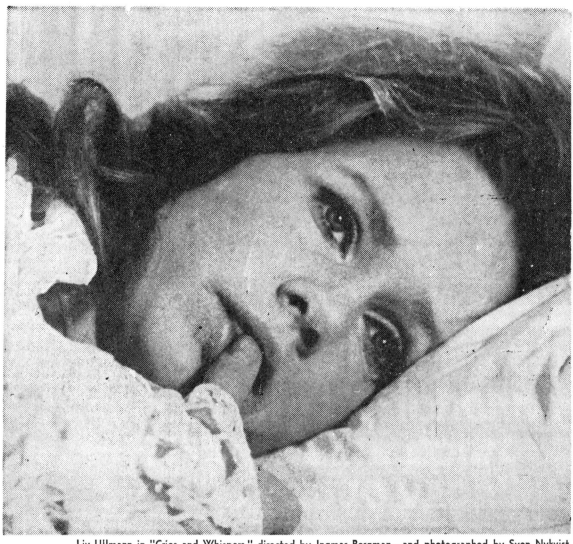

Liv Ullmann in "Cries and Whispers," directed by Ingmar Bergman—and photographed by Sven Nykvist
"Bergman does not so much film his people as confront them, searching for some chink in their armor"

and only on rare occasions may it participate in the action." So reticent are the movements in "Cries and Whispers" that they only become evident in repeated viewings: At times the camera waltzes, as when the sisters and the maid bathe the dying Agnes; at times it does a *kermesse*, as when they rush to Agnes in the night or when Maria flees from the touch of the dead Agnes's hand; at times it moves almost in sympathetic aid of the characters, as when Agnes's body is straightened and covered.

*

And just as significant are the effects that Bergman and Nykvist attain within the frame of a static camera — not in the perfection of composition (that is the still photographer's art), but in the dynamic potential that resides in every shot of this sort. As when Agnes's dead hands rise into the frame to touch Maria's face, seen in close-up, they have managed to make us always aware of the importance of what is *not* seen; the close-ups do not isolate, any more than any of the characters can isolate themselves from their ineluctable tragedy.

Throughout "Cries and Whispers," one sees traces of painterly influences — touches that remind of Renoir, Monet, Velasquez, Mary Cassatt, Whistler, Rubens, Kasper David Friedrich, Vermeer. That is not to imply that the collaborative art of Bergman-Nykvist is imitative, that they are merely using the technical tools of film to mimic a higher art. What they have done is beyond technique; it is art itself, and of a very high order. In that lies the film's significance; that the celluloid has been transfigured as is a painter's canvas.

To alter Grierson, when a director lives, he becomes a painter.

1973 Ja 14, II:13:1

Sven Nykvist, for just as Bergman loves Liv Ullmann, so Nykvist, Bergman's long time cinematographer and friend, loves light. (It is unfortunate, since as cinematographers go Nykvist is one of the better known, that none of the first heat-of-the moment reviews of the film mentioned his name and that the newspaper ads spell it wrong.)

"Light is a passion for me," Nykvist wrote in the April, 1972, issue of American Cinematographer. ". . . It is as important as the lines the actors speak or the direction that is given to them.... Light is a treasure chest that is largely unexplored and that, once properly understood, can bring a wider dimension to the medium and a greater appreciation to the audience. . . . People must do more than see a motion picture. They must have a feeling for it, and my experience has told me that they appreciate and are held spellbound by a certain mood that is created for them by the proper utilization of light. That is the key to it all. That is what it is all about."

*

And Bergman's script calls for — yes, demands — such an attitude. In the treatment of "Cries and Whispers" that appeared in a recent issue of The New Yorker, Bergman wrote, "When constructing them (the interiors), we must bear in mind the possibilities of creating the lighting conditions we desire—dawns that don't look like dusk, soft firelight, the mysterious indirect light on a day when it is snowing, the gentle radiance from an oil lamp. The torment of a bright, sunny autumn day. A solitary candle in the darkness of night, and all the restless shadows when someone wrapped in a wide peignoir hurries through the big rooms."

All that is there (though the location weather did not provide snow) and more: The brilliance of a priest's gold cross against his black coat, the mockery of warm sunlight falling across the face of a woman about to die ("My cruelest dreams," Bergman writes, "are flooded with unbearable sunlight."), the unutterable reds—of the walls and carpets and of blood. And yet there are no pyrotechnics, no tricks; the palette is small, the permutations enormous.

Cinematography involves more than light, though; it involves decisions as to focal lengths of lenses, camera movement, what will be encompassed in the frame. Here, too, Bergman and Nykvist have elevated the technique to a new high; they have made a film of which each and every frame could hang in an art gallery.

The most evident weapon in their arsenal in "Cries and Whispers"· is the close-up, in which perhaps as much as a third of the film is shot. "The close-up," Bergman wrote in a recent issue of Film Comment, "if objectively composed, perfectly directed and played, is the most forcible means at the disposal of the film director."

And forcible they are, though not by dint of numbers, but because Bergman uses his camera as a scalpel; he does not so much "film" his people in close-up, as he does confront them, staring at them, searching for some chink in their impenetrable armor, asking for some sign, some clue, some gesture, that will explicate their viciousness, their tenderness, their insipidity.

For all the close-ups, the film is never static; yet its rhythmic vitality is not achieved through the editing so much as through the dynamics of the camera. Not that it is in perpetual motion: "In order to give the greatest possible strength to the actor's expression," Bergman has written, "the camera movement must be simple, free and completely synchronized with the action. The camera must be a completely objective observer

The Cast

DEATH OF A JEW, directed by Denys de la Patelliere; screenplay by Vahe Katcha and Mr. de la Patelliere; director of photography, Alain Levent. Produced by Films Copernic for Trans America Film Corporation; released by Cine Globe, Inc. At neighborhood theaters. Running time: 98 minutes. This film is certified PG.
Shimon .... Assaf Dayan
Mehdaloun .... Akim Tamiroff
Kassik .... Jean Claudio

By ROGER GREENSPUN

With a title like "Death of a Jew," you almost don't need a movie. And in Denys de la Patelliere's "Death of a Jew," which opened yesterday at neighborhood theaters, you almost don't have one. What you do have is an incredible story, told in moving pictures, about a tender relationship between an old Arab police inspector (the late Akim Tamiroff) and a young Israeli spy (Assaf Dayan). The newspaper ads quote one critic as saying that the story "can be appreciated by Arabs as well as Israelis." And I am afraid that an ecumenism at just that level of naiveté, is what "Death of a Jew" is all about.

5

Shimon, the Israeli spy, is captured deep inside some unidentified Arab country, and, to make him reveal his contacts he is turned over to the police. When all else fails, even the evil technology of the police chief (Jean Claudio: "It's not a question of courage; it's a question of voltage." Sneer.), the old inspector, Mehdaloun, gets his licks.

•

Mehdaloun hopes to replace Shimon's silence with a gregarious will to live, and thus to talk (so as to stay alive); and to this end he sets about corrupting him with kindness. He plies Shimon with gifts; rooms him in his own apartment; takes him eating, drinking, whoring; and grows so fond of his enemy that he begins calling him "my son."

It is all to no avail. Shimon remains tight as a clam. But, irony of ironies, Mehdaloun falls prey to his own scheme! And he is left at the last, entering his dotage, with a new gregarious will to live—not to mention extravagant tastes for room service, vodka straight and compliant Scandinavian blondes.

All this is not quite as stupid as it may seem in the abstract. Anyplace *but* the Middle East (and perhaps North and South Vietnam) it might have furnished a movie plot. A friend, intelligent and much too kind, has suggested analogies all the way from Claude Berri's "The Two of Us" to Bergman's "Persona." Personally, I am put more in mind of certain Shirley Temple movies; but any plot idea that has floated so far must have some buoyancy to sustain it.

•

Assaf Dayan and Akim Tamiroff have been highly engaging actors, but they are both pretty dreadful here. The film is in English, which Tamiroff speaks with a Yiddish accent (somewhat unsettling, under the circumstances), and which all the others speak as if they had learned it at school in France. Denys de la Patalliere, ("Taxi for Tobruk," "Marco the Magnificent") directs as if he hadn't learned anything at all. "Death of a Jew" is the kind of film that seems to advance from scene to scene not by any inner necessity, but rather because everybody at a particular time in a particular place finds himself at a loss for what to do next.

1973 Ja 18, 47:1

IF I HAD A GUN, directed by Stefan Uher; screenplay (Czech with English subtitles) by Milan Ferko and Mr. Uher, based on the novel by Mr. Ferko; director of photography, Vincent Rosinec; music, Ilja Zelienka; produced by Slovak Film Studio Bratislava Kolba; distributed by Ajay Film Company. Running time; 90 minutes. At the First Avenue Screening Room Theater, at 61st Street. This film has not been classified.

Boy .... Marian Bernat
Friend .... Josef Graf
Father .... Ludevit Kroner
Mother .... Emilia Dosekova
Girl .... Hana Grissova

By VINCENT CANBY

New York is the greatest city in the world for seeing all kinds of movies, but it's also the toughest for a movie to survive in. The competition for audience attention is so fierce that, unless a film is a smash hit, it is, almost instantly, a smash flop. The costs of theater operations and advertising are huge. Even with the price of tickets at first-run theaters between $3 and $4 each, most films, including many of the successful ones, lose money on their initial engagements.

It simply doesn't pay to open the offbeat American film or the unknown foreign film that can hope for a mixed press at best. A few brave souls do buck the system—most notably, Dan Talbot, owner of the New Yorker Theater on the Upper West Side. Add now the name of Associated Independent Theaters' First Avenue Screening Room, at 61st Street.

The new 200-seat house, which opened yesterday with Stefan Uher's 1971 Czechoslovak film, "If I Had a Gun," has an announced policy of showing what are euphemistically called difficult films—most of them local premieres —for engagements of one week each. The idea is to keep the overhead low and the quality high, in order to provide Manhattan audiences with the opportunity of seeing films that might otherwise be missed even in this city, the best of all possible movie-going worlds.

The intent, which is noble, is gently and honorably defined in the Screening Room's first attraction, a small, mostly comic memoir of a 15-year-old boy in a Czechoslovak village during the last months of the Nazi occupation. The film is full of memories, including at least one that is not entirely happy: the World War II period recalls so many other films made in Eastern Europe in the postwar, prethaw, Stalinist years, when the only safely noncontroversial subject was the German occupation. More specifically, it recalls other Czechoslovak films made before Alexander Dubcek's brief, brilliant Prague Spring.

Like Ivan Passer, Milos Forman and Jiri Menzel in their early work, Stefan Uher, the 42-year-old director of "If I Had a Gun," speaks around and through a screen of official blandness. He has not, admittedly, packed his film with coded messages, with disguised slices of political or social satire. However, the sort of humaneness and wit that the film deals in are muted but real reminders of other freer times and places.

"If I Had a Gun" is the story of Vlado (Marian Bernat), an intelligent, cheerful boy whose fantasies—which

we share in the film's funniest moments—eventually overtake the reality of the humdrum life in his village. Near the occupation's end, Vlado's comic dreams of heroism and vengeance are realized, though with the addition of the kind of terror and sorrow we usually eliminate from our dreams of glory.

The film is not, however, especially sad, though its fine, short-focus, black-and-white photography would seem to evoke that mood in this era when almost everything is shot in color. Instead, it has the elegiac tone of a diary that is being read years after the events recorded and that makes no particular differentiation between the tragic and the comic, which time has somehow made equally important.

Thus Mr. Uher—quite consciously, I assume—devotes no more time or emphasis to a sequence in which Vlado and another younger boy are caught, in youth's equivalent of *flagrante delicto,* spying on two older girls who are bathing, than he does to the film's melodramatic, penultimate sequence. Memory has sealed but not erased the original feelings of trauma and desperation.

In the film's final lines, Vlado recalls that after the liberation he and his friends returned to school: "They said we had been lazy too long." Among other things, "If I Had a Gun" is about the remarkable resiliency of children in ordinary as well as extraordinary situations. The film, the work of a director new to Manhattan, deserves the protection and the care of the Screening Room.

1973 Ja 19, 23:1

The Program

ALLIANCE FOR PROGRESS, directed by Julio Luduena; screenplay (Spanish, with English subtitles) by Mr. Luduena; director of photography, Juan Carlos Ciravegna; produced by Mr. Luduena. A Tricontinental Film Center release. At the Film Forum, 88th Street, west of Broadway, Jan. 19-21 and 26-28 at 8 P.M. running time: 108 minutes. This film has not been classified.

By ROGER GREENSPUN

"Alliance for Progress," a fictional radical political film, opened yesterday at the Film Forum. Its director, a 27-year-old Argentine named Julio Luduena, has described his approach, and I think he is worth quoting, in part:

"The camera chooses the worst possible position, the actors the worst possible style, the story-telling the worst possible simplicity, the chosen scenery the worst possible alternative, the editing the worst possible solution. Rhythm doesn't exist . . ."

I don't think he has succeeded with this entirely. In places, he has clearly come

up with only the next-to-worst solution. But by and large he has stuck pretty well to his intentions, and as a program for film-making, they clearly have limitations.

•

They aren't the only limitations to "Alliance for Progress," which deals with revolution and counterrevolution in some unspecified Latin-American country. The characters aren't characters. They aren't even types. They are their names: the Businessman, the General, the Priest, the Student, the Syndicalist, the Artist, Miss Middle Class and USA—a quite stunning young woman, who is very powerful, very evil, and who wants to grind up cities into foundation stone to build superhighways for which she would sell cars of her own manufacture. One or two people do change (for example, Miss Middle Class joins the revolution, when she has to), but everybody else is immutable until death and sometimes beyond.

Luduena's camera placement belongs in a class of its own — though occasionally parodying other radical film stylists: Glauber Rocha, and especially Jean-Luc Godard. The camera sits above and slightly apart from the

action, as if in the first balcony of a small theater. I can't think of a less natural camera angle, even when the tops of people's heads aren't cut off (as they often are), and I assume that Luduena couldn't either. But when he wants to, when the Businessman seduces Miss Middle Class or when soldiers sadistically torture a captive revolutionary to death, his camera becomes intimate and agile enough — just enough to remind you of the kind of movie that "Alliance for Progress" does not mean to be.

Why all this should work as well as it does, it is difficult to say — largely because the ordinary terms of praise obviously don't apply. Sometimes the film is gruesomely funny, sometimes—as when viewing USA's network of superhighways — it is oddly poignant. More often it is neither. But it is so impudent about technique and so casual about its radicalism that it achieves a kind of frumpy chic. "Alliance for Progress" is nothing if not the product of a very sophisticated cinematic intelligence, though not a very experienced one. Where it will go is anybody's guess. At some point, Luduena may accept the greater and more interesting risk of trying to make a movie and trying to make it good.

1973 Ja 20, 37:4

What Are We To Think of 'Deep Throat'?

By VINCENT CANBY

TRYING to write honestly about pornographic films is like trying to tie one's shoe while walking: it's practically impossible without sacrificing stride and balance and a certain amount of ordinary dignity, the sort one uses with bank tellers who question a signature. Almost any attitude the writer adopts will whirl around and hit him from the other side. The haughty approach ("It's boring") has long-since been suspected as evidence of a mixture of embarrassment and arousal. The golly-gee-whiz style ("They've gone as far as they can go!") is patently untrue, while to make fun of pornography is to avoid facing the subject at all. To call it a healthy development is another vast oversimplification that refuses to acknowledge that it may be fine for some people, and quite upsetting for others.

Then, too, to suggest that pornography degrades the audience as well as the performers assumes a familiarity with all of the members of all audiences that I, for one, do not have. It even ignores what little evidence I do have about the production of the films. Not long ago, a director of several porno films, a seriously bearded young man with an interest in Cinema, told me he was never aware of any of his performers feeling degraded. "They do it because they enjoy it and because it's an easy way to make money—I think in that order. They're also exhibitionists. The camera turns them on. The women as well as the men. Sometimes, at the end of the day, they don't want to stop."

It's difficult to write honestly about pornographic films, but it's getting easier, largely, I think, as a result of all of the publicity given to "Deep Throat," including the recent, widely covered Criminal Court trial here to determine whether or not the film is obscene. With an early assist ("The very best porn film ever made") from Al Goldstein, the editor of Screw Magazine who isn't exactly stingy with his superlatives (a few months later he was quoted as saying that " 'Bijou' tops 'Deep Throat' "), "Deep Throat" has become the most financially successful hard-core pornographic film ever to play New York. According to Variety, which now regularly reviews porno films as a service to the film trade and gives weekly box-office reports on their business, "Deep Throat," made in Florida on a budget of $25,000, has grossed more than $850,000 at the New Mature World Theater here since it opened last June. (The New Mature World Theater is, incidentally, the former World Theater, on 49th Street near Seventh Avenue, which, in its old immature days, used to play films like "Open City" and "Shoe Shine.")

For reasons that still baffle me, "Deep Throat" became the one porno film in New York chic to see and to be seen at, even before the court

case, even before Earl Wilson wrote about it.

When I went to see it last summer, mostly because of the Goldstein review, I was so convinced of its junkiness that I didn't bother writing about it. Still uncertain, I went back to see it again last Sunday. The large afternoon crowd sat through what seemed like at least a half-hour of porno trailers (which may be better pornography than narrative features since they're nothing but climaxes), plus Paul Bartel's fairly amusing, non-porno short, "The Naughty Nurse," as well as an old Paramount cartoon, a G-rated, absolutely straight, violence-without-sex cat-and-mouse thing, in order to experience the dubious achievements of "Deep Throat," which runs 62 minutes. Although the audience last Sunday was a good deal more cheerful and less furtive than the one with which I first saw it, the film itself remains junk, at best only a souvenir of a time and place. I'm sure that if "Deep Throat" hadn't caught the public's fancy at this point in history, some other porno film, no better and maybe no worse, would have.

As for "Deep Throat," its pleasures — its powers to arouse — are not inexhaustible, or, at least, they are very exhausted once one gets over the wonder and surprise at the accomplishments of its heroine, Linda Lovelace. The frame of the film — Linda's search for sexual fulfillment once she learns that fellatio is her thing — provides little room for the kind of satire that some critics have professed to see in the movie. Its few dumb gags, not including a rather funny title song, cannot disguise the straight porno intent of what has been reported to be the film's "seven acts of fellatio and four of cunnilingus."

At the risk of sounding like the usual bored critic (which I certainly wasn't the first time around), I must say "Deep Throat" is much less erotic than technically amazing. How does she do it? The film has less to do with the manifold pleasures of sex than with physical engineering.

It's possible — but only if one really tries — to make "Deep Throat" sound more significant than it is. You can argue that Linda in her way is a kind of liberated woman, using men as sex objects the way men in most porno films are supposed to use women. But that's straining to make a point that is very debatable. You can also argue, as Arthur Knight did at the trial here, that Linda and her friends show us that there's more than one way to have sex. It's almost as if he saw the film in the position of a missionary.

All of these arguments can be made — and, I suppose, they should be made — to defend the film against censorship laws that are, academically speaking, wrong. I say academically because I'm about to put myself in a corner that can't be reasonably defended: the laws are wrong but the film isn't worth fighting for. The necessity to prove a film totally without redeeming social value in order to get an obscenity conviction is, to my way of thinking, absurd. Everything created in this era — good, bad and pornographic — is or will be of social interest (my definition of social value), hence it's rather idiotic to have adults arguing this point back and forth in court. Expert witnesses, who defended "Deep Throat" against the charges made possible by fuzzy laws, wind up, in effect, by acknowledging the validity of the laws. In defending the film the way they do, they become parties

to the foolishness of the established order.

They've been co-opted, which is, I understand, the only way to fight the laws, but I think they might have second thoughts about attempting to prove their points by citing "Deep Throat" as "more professional, more cleverly and amusingly written" than others. Professor Knight even went on about the "clarity and lack of grain" in the photography.

We are living on the other side of the looking glass. Bad films are correctly defended for the wrong reasons. "Deep Throat" is described in terms that would not demean Henry Miller.

What may be worse, the film is prompting a whole new flood of inexpert, very biased writing about pornography, including this piece and other rather tortured articles elsewhere. The New York Review headed its recent contribution "Hard to Swallow," and at least two writers I've read have made bad puns on the fact that while most people are curious about porno films, they're too yellow to see them, in reference, of course, to the Swedish film of 1969 that a lot of hysterical people said was pornographic and went as far as films could go. Both claims turned out to be false.

The only possible way to write about porno films, I suspect, is to be so autobiographical that the reader gets a fair idea of the sexual orientation of the writer, of his each little quiver during the showing of the film. This, however, makes necessary a kind of journalism that few of us are equipped to practice well. When it isn't practiced well, we are apt to get the dopey film critic-confessionals that reverse the usual way of doing things. They intrude the critic's privacy upon the public.

1973 Ja 21, II:1:1

'The Poseidon Adventure's' Treatment Of Women Is All Wet

By ALJEAN HARMETZ

"THE POSEIDON ADVENTURE" aims no higher than being a submerged "Airport," a mid-ocean "The Guns of Navarone." But I find it hard to cluck indulgently that Hollywood will be Hollywood and, after all, what do the clichés matter when there is all that lovely water for the characters to drown in.

I do not know whether "The Poseidon Adventure" is really worse than the decades of similar pictures I have sat quietly through or whether, without my suspecting it, the Women's Liberation Movement has raised my own consciousness. But there were barely 10 minutes of the film that did not vastly offend me.

At the beginning of "The Poseidon Adventure," a sturdy 10-year-old boy makes his way through a storm to the bridge of the S.S. Poseidon. When we first meet his 17-year-old sister, her only concern is that he won't be presentable at church services if he doesn't take a bath. Among them, the four female characters who burrow their way upward in an attempt to escape the sinking ship manage to embody almost every stereotype with which Hollywood has labeled women during the last three decades except the gun moll.

*

If the six men who join them in their climb do not stray far from cliché either, there is the subtle difference that the male clichés are, for the most part, positive ones. There is the maverick minister, a leader of men (Gene Hackman); the decent steward, uncomplaining despite his smashed leg (Roddy McDowall); the resourceful young boy (Eric Shea); the passive husband who finds the courage to go on (Jack Albertson); the timid health fanatic who becomes a man during his ordeal (Red Buttons); and the thoroughly obnoxious

police detective who at least has the virtue of a bullheaded physical strength (Ernest Borgnine).

In contrast, Carol Lynley must stumble through the whole picture in such a state of neurotic shock from the death of her brother that she cannot even rouse herself in the face of death and must be saved several times by the timid hypochondriac at the risk of his own life. Pamela Sue Martin, the adolescent girl, reacts to her peril by falling into puppy love with the strong minister. Stella Stevens is an ex-prostitute, tough as a three-year-old hen but undoubtedly golden-hearted, who lacks sense enough to take off her five-inch platform heels while climbing up slippery metal ladders. And Shelley Winters, hidden somewhere beneath the 35 extra pounds the director is said to have required her to gain for the film, is a Jewish grandmother given to sentimentalizing everything and preferring at one point to die rather than to crawl through a pipe because she is "a fat lady."

*

Only once during the one hour and 58 minutes of this saga of guts and determination is a woman allowed to behave with either dignity or courage. After being roundly patronized and ridiculed by the men for her presumption, Shelley Winters is allowed to make an underwater rescue of Gene Hackman. But she is promptly punished for her exertion by dying of a heart attack. Almost nowhere else in the film is a woman allowed to help or work together with a man, although the men are constantly risking their lives to help the women.

It is not that the women in the film are unnecessary to the men. They are prized possessions, and those men whose women die immediately collapse. But although they are as valuable as solid gold watches, the women are not human. In the first scene after the tidal wave that turns the Poseidon upside-down, a metal Christmas tree must be dragged as quickly as possible across the ceiling of the Grand Ballroom. No woman lends a hand. Even the strongest of them huddle in a corner, waiting passively for men to provide them with a means of escape. Nor do they then see that they cannot climb the tree to the next deck encumbered with the long skirts. The men must tear the skirts from them. They then must be pulled, pushed, coddled and babied through every inch of the one-hour climb that follows.

*

From the beginning—in which fun is made of Stella Stevens' seasickness—to the end—when the manly young boy prefaces his underwater swim by saying of his older sister, "I can swim three lengths under water in our swimming pool, but Sis can only swim two' —"The Poseidon Adventure" degrades its female characters. What is most appalling is that those connected with the film probably didn't even do it deliberately. Their attitudes and dialogue are simply borrowed from a tradition that includes the Hollywood movies of their own childhoods.

The ads for "The Poseidon Adventure" ask, "Who will survive?" Hopefully, none of the female stereotypes that "The Poseidon Adventure" offers.

1973 Ja 21, II:13:6

There's a Cop-Out in The 'Sandbox'

By ROSALYN DREXLER

IN "Up the Sandbox," Barbra Streisand plays the role of Margaret, a fantasy ridden, day-dreaming housewife and mother who spends her days at the sandbox with her children, escaping into wild mind-trips. Her husband is a history professor totally absorbed in his work, who ostensibly has no need for fantasies. They all live in an upper West Side apartment full of toys, books, pillows, art and other possessions demonstrable of the daily life well lived.

Into this seemingly innocent nest of twigs and feathers a few worms begin to wriggle, and under the unused wings an itch develops. This is not a serious disease, since it is confined to the skin alone and can be cured by hourly immersion in the running stream of life

Margaret truly loves her family; the movie opens with the joyous physicality of children being bathed, and later read to. There is a closeness of husband and wife: sexual playfulness as well as minor irritations common to all relationships. Imposed on this naturalism, on this example of the absurdity and beauty of just being alive, a "political"

platform is added from which a number of current and popular concerns are aired. Margaret finds herself pregnant for a third time! Question: should she have an abortion, or (this question mine) should she continue dreaming tabloid-type dreams instead of acting on them?

Should she (this question mine) wait 20 years until she is in her 50's (a romantic, liberating age?) only to find there is no place to fulfill herself since there is nothing she can do, and this includes prostitution, waitressing, saleswork, or even housework, all of which require both strength and a great deal of professional finesse.

Although Margaret makes some motions in the direction of enlightenment and freedom, one has the feeling that—with her Neanderthal mentality—she will never amount to more than an all-purpose perpetual dustmop.

Margaret has three friends whose purpose in the movie is to voice (superficially) ideas now prevalent in the women's movement. FRIEND 1: "I suppose you say thank you when he does the dishes."

FRIEND 2: "To be a good mother, you've got to eat ———."

FRIEND 3: "The best mothers maintain their identity." One does not hear conversation, one hears research—dull extrapolation by a scriptwriter with a tin ear.

Now, although "Up the Sandbox" purports to examine Margaret's changing role in relation to her husband, children, political reality, racial problems—anything and everything that touches upon herself and the rest of the world—it becomes a clumsy reaffirmation of the notion that staying at home and having babies is the best thing for a woman to do, especially if her husband "generously" likes babies and is willing to give her one day a week off. The husband (David Selby), just another pretty face in a poorly written role, says: "Honey, our children will be a credit to the world . . . they'll make it less crazy." Maybe they will, but he does not notice that his wife is getting more crazy. When dreams become more satisfying than real life, something has to give.

It is symptomatic that in the fantasies that interrupt Margaret's everyday existence, women appear as her enemies: husband stealer, militant powerhouse, mother, tribal goddess, doctor. In Anne Roiphe's book, Margaret does not fantasize going to an abortion clinic, but in Paul Zindel's screenplay, she does. The clinic is filmed as a kind of horrible limboland housing countless women, all waiting to rid themselves of unwanted fetuses...no one speaks...the quiet is ominous...the female doctor is made to look like a monster . . . the husband arrives and, wonderful man that he is, struggles with the forces of evil (the doctor and the nurses) for the return of his pregnant wife! The hospital table breaks free and with Margaret still on it, freewheels back to the sandbox where children are playing...and a chorus of angels is heard. This sentimental, male-imposed fantasy is unliberating and tacky, the very lowest point of the movie.

However, politics aside, Irvin Kershner, the director, is often really excellent: I loved his direction of a family get-together on the occasion of Margaret's parents' 33rd wedding anniversary. During this party, a relative is shooting home movies, the lighting is blinding, and so-called normal behavior becomes abnormal or forced. The actors perform within a performance: they realize that movies—home movies—are for posterity, a reservoir of information, a cheerful record.

There is a variation of the pie-in-the-face routine as Margaret imagines shoving her mother's face into an elaborate anniversary cake, after which they tussel on the floor, with the father cheering Margaret on. If only all problems could be handled by slapstick, with each of us expert in pratfalls, exploding cigars, and magic umbrellas that would suddenly lift us out of harm's way.

Jane Hoffman as the mother (she also played Mommy in Albee's "The American Dream") is an intelligent and funny actress who has mastered her craft. John C. Becher, as the father, is also fine, as is Paul Benedict, who plays a comic anthropologist. Barbra Streisand is Barbra Streisand (love her or leave her) trying to be ordinary, but being beautiful.

*

The rest of the cast, a few hundred if one is to count the Somburu Tribe of Kenya which pops up in a dream sequence, do their thing well too. But so what! "Up the Sandbox" is to the women's movement what "The Strawberry Statement" was to the student revolution, a rip-off giving lip service to authentic concerns but copping out in the end. It concludes in typical Hollywood starry-eyed wonder as the husband asks Margaret on her day off: "Where are you going?" and she answers: "I don't know, but it's such a beautiful day it doesn't matter." She drives off into the sunlight, sitting in the back of a cab as if it were the saddle of a magnificent white stallion. Note: The more the meter ticks away, the more she'll have to pay. She'll wish she had known where she was going

1973 Ja 21, II:13:1

UNDER MILK WOOD, directed by Andrew Sinclair; screenplay by Mr. Sinclair, based on the play by Dylan Thomas; director of photography, Bob Huke; music, Brian Gascoigne; editor, Willy Kemplen; executive producers, Jules Buck and Hugh French; a Timon Films, Ltd., production; distributed by Altura Films International. Running time: 90 minutes. At the East Side Cinema, Third Avenue near 56th Street. This film has been classified PG.
First Voice .... Richard Burton
Rosie Probert .... Elizabeth Taylor
Captain Cat .... Peter O'Toole
Myfanwy Price .... Glynis Johns
Mrs. Pugh .... Vivien Merchant
Mrs. Ogmore-Pritchard .... Sian Phillips
Mog Edwards .... Victor Spinetti
Second Voice .... Ryan Davies
Gossamer Beynon .... Angharad Rees
Mr. Waldo .... Ray Smith
Polly Garter .... Ann Beach
Mr. Pugh .... Talfryn Thomas
Lily Smalls .... Meg Wynn Owen

BY VINCENT CANBY

"Under Milk Wood" is the kind of film project that carries failure within it almost proudly, as if to be over-

whelmed by literacy were a mark of distinction, even though a fatal one.

Dylan Thomas, the Welsh poet who died in 1953, originally conceived "Under Milk Wood" as a radio play, a poetic, plotless memory of life in a tiny Welsh seaport that is evoked through narration and short, occasionally brilliant gusts of comedy, drama and dreams.

●

Although he originally thought of it as something to be listened to, or read, Thomas went on to adapt the play for the stage where, however, it's never quite as satisfactory as many people think it should be, apparently reasoning that the stage needs words and these Thomas provides — by the bushel basket.

Too many words, perhaps, for the stage. Too many words, I'm convinced, for the screen. It's not simply the quantity of words, though. It's also their ornateness. They overflow the ears and get into the eyes. Great clouds of them everywhere, like swarms of big soft gnats. They won't stop, and they make the job of the film adapter almost impossible.

This business of finding screen images to match those in Thomas's text can be, at best, redundant. At worst, banal, misleading or wrong. "To begin at the beginning," says the First Voice (Richard Burton), a sort of composite narrator, guide and angel of death who conducts our tour of Llareggub, "it is spring, moonless night in the small town. . . ." What we see, however, is night so awash in moonlight that we could, if we wanted, read the small type that guarantees a vacuum cleaner for a year.

A little later he continues: "It is night, dumbly, royally winding through the Coronation Street cherry trees, going through the graveyard of Bethesda with winds gloved and folded, and dew doffed. . . ." Can any ordinary screen images equal those? Not easily.

When Burton urges us, the members of the audience, to look into "the blinded bedrooms" to see "the glasses of teeth, Thou Shalt Not on the wall, and the yellowing dickeybird-watching pictures of the dead," there's not much for the camera to do but to try desperately to keep up with the language—but the language wins.

●

Some of the dozens of characters we meet do come fitfully alive: Mrs. Pugh (Vivien Merchant), a dainty, purse-lipped, dry-fingered bitch whose husband (Talfryn Thomas) meekly fetches her breakfast and dreams of putting ground glass into her omelette; Mrs. Ogmore-Pritchard (Sian Phillips), who sleeps with the ghosts of her two husbands and fears

Richard Burton in "Under Milk Wood"

strangers breathing all over her chairs; Polly Garter (Ann Beach), the town's gentle-spirited whore who can't help having babies because she loves them.

Less successful, perhaps because he has to handle so many words, is Peter O'Toole, ordinarily a fine actor, as the old, blind Captain Cat. O'Toole's readings are so perfectly rhythmical, his wind so magnificently controlled for long eruptions of words without pause, that he almost put me to sleep.

Whenever sleep threatens, however, there is the spectacle of Elizabeth Taylor, a wonder to behold though she doesn't seem directly connected to Wales. She does a short, sort of lie-in, as opposed to walk-on, as Rosie Probert, the whore out of Captain Cat's youth who now is buried in the Llareggub graveyard. "I've forgotten that I was ever born," she tells us toward the end in a lovely Thomas line that recalls the greater simplicity and economy of Thornton Wilder's "Our Town."

•

Burton's readings are fine, especially when you close your eyes. Nothing that Andrew Sinclair, the director, chooses to show us does more than complement the text, which often means literalizing it, making it seem smaller, less mysterious, more postcard - picturesque than need be. When Burton tells us that we can hear the dew falling, I had a small panic that Sinclair would show us even that, though he doesn't.

Gone is any sense of discovery of language, which, when Thomas was working

well, could make one feel very young again, almost drunk with surprise and pleasure. The problem is all those pictures. In a way, Thomas did to words what booze did to him. He shook them up, liberated them, twisted them around so that they took on, if only momentarily, a higher order of meaning. The camera has the presence of a sober-sided friend. It interrupts most of the poet's flights of fancy.

"Under Milk Wood" opened yesterday at the new East Side Cinema, on Third Avenue near 56th Street.

1973 Ja 22, 20:1

The Cast
THE FLAVOR OF GREEN TEA OVER RICE, directed by Yasuiiro Ozu; screenplay (Japanese with English subtitles) by Mr. Ozu and Kogo Nada; director of photography, Yuharu Atsuta; produced by Shochiku/Ofuna Films; distributed by New Yorker Films. Running time: 115 minutes. At the Quad Cinema 3.
Husband ....Shin Saburi
Wife ....Michiyo Kogura
Niece ....Kuniko Miyake
Boyfriend ....Koji Tsuruta
Former Soldier ....Chishu Ryu

By VINCENT CANBY
Donald Richie, the Japanese-film expert, tells us that the late Yasujiro Ozu took meticulous care in his choice of settings, especially the small details that, according to Mr. Richie, were always intended to emphasize character rather than environment. This is true, but the passage of time has added an environmental significance to the details originally picked to give dimension to character.

In Ozu's 1952 film, "The Flavor of Green Tea Over Rice" (another Ozu title to challenge Western patience even when his film does not), the environment that Ozu more or less took for granted, since he always made his films in their own time, seems now to play a more interesting—or at least more obvious part—in the drama.

•

All of the Ozu films we have seen in this country ("Tokyo Story," "Late Spring," "End of Summer," "Floating Weeds") have been social comedies, but they have been told entirely in terms of character. More than any of these other films, "The Flavor of Green Tea" looks as much like a social history as it does a classic Ozu work.

The movie, which opened yesterday at the Quad Cinema 3, is essentially a comedy, what the Japanese call a tsuma-mono, or wife film, about an upper-middle-class marriage, one that has been arranged in the old-fashioned way and now is falling gently apart as the childless couple approach middle age.

She (Michiyo Kogura) gives every indication of being a rather mean-spirited snob. Among other things, she sleeps apart from her husband in an awful American-style bedroom that seems to be constructed entirely of chintz.

However, he (Shin Saburi) gives every indication of being as thickheaded and boring as she says he is.

That is, at the beginning. The revelation—the surprise —of the film is not that they are eventually reconciled, but that they become such appealing characters, touched by a kind of nobility.

•

As important as the revelations of character—to me anyway—is the casual picture of the world in which they occur. I am not sure if it is factually true, but I have the impression that more of this film is set in public places, that is, locations outside the home that is the emotional center of any Ozu film, than in the films of his released here earlier.

What we see of Japan in 1951 and 1952 defines the time in a fashion I am not sure I would have been as aware of had I seen the film in 1952.

It is a world only seven years removed from Hiroshima. Nobody in an Ozu film seems directly affected by the American occupation, but the American influence is everywhere, in second-hand clothes, in cigarettes, in the liberation of women.

The world of this film is more geographically open than those of the other Ozus, but the economy of narrative and technique is practically quintessential. Ozu never wastes our interest on connecting scenes if we can take them for granted. When he does show us a man proceeding, say from one office to another, it becomes im-

portant, perhaps as an acknowledgment of time lost or as a sort of film equivalent to the white space between the chapters in a novel.

No one shrug or sigh or smile is more or less dispensible than another gesture, which explains why minor characters are so important in Ozu films.

•

One of the funniest and most moving scenes in "The Flavor of Green Tea" is the scene in which the operator of a pinball parlor (Chishu Ryu) talks gloomily about his success. "This is trash," he says in effect. "It degrades the national spirit," and then he goes on to remember, as if with nostalgia, the beautiful nights during the war in Singapore.

•

"The Flavor of Green Tea" is not great Ozu. There are times—especially in its sub-plot about a girl who refuses traditional wedding arrangements—when it is almost formula comedy.

No true Japanese formula comedy, however, would punctuate its climactic reconciliation scene, set in the kitchen that the wife is discovering for the first time, with the image, seen only out of the corner of the camera eye, of a can of Wesson oil.

1973 Ja 25, 51:6

INNOCENT BYSTANDERS, directed by Peter Collinson; screenplay by James Mitchell, from the novel by James Munro; director of photography, Brian Probyn; editor, Alan Pattillo; composer, John Keating; musical director, Phillip Martell; produced by George H. Brown; presented by Sagittarius Films; released by Paramount Pictures. At the Cinerama Theater, Broadway and 47th Street; 86th Street Twin 2, west of Lexington Avenue; 59th Twin 2, east of Third Avenue and neighborhood theaters. Running time: 111 minutes. This film is classified PG.
John Craig................Stanley Baker
Miriam Loman.........Geraldine Chaplin
Loomis..................Donald Pleasence
Blake....................Dana Andrews
Joanna Benson.............Sue Lloyd
Andrew Royce..........Derren Nesbitt
Aaron Kaplan..........Vladek Sheybal
Omar....................Warren Mitchell

By ROGER GREENSPUN
Paramount Pictures has provided film critics with an unusually detailed plot synopsis for its "Innocent Bystanders." I've read the synopsis and I've seen the picture, and I still don't know exactly what is going on, or why, through perhaps 60 per cent of Peter Collinson's new movie, which opened yesterday at local theaters. The confusion is probably intentional and not entirely unprofitable. But it results less from the extraordinary complexity than from the general inconsequence of everything that happens in the film.

•

"Innocent Bystanders" is a spy thriller, reminiscent of the nostalgia-drenched late 1960's, about an over-age British secret agent (Stanley

Baker) who has to bring back alive one Kaplan, a brilliant Russian scientist, now defected and living modestly as a goat herder in Turkey. Opposed to Baker are his boss (Donald Pleasence), his young replacements (Sue Lloyd and Darren Nesbitt), a chief American secret agent (Dana Andrews), a conniving Turkish hotel keeper (Warren Mitchell), and an organization of Russian Jews who don't like Kaplan. Baker must also deal with his own self doubts and with a hostage, an innocent bystander (Geraldine Chaplin) who is not what she seems.

Indeed, nobody is what he seems. Everybody either has a cover or is a cover—which doesn't much matter, because "Innocent Bystanders" is the sort of movie in which shooting enemies in one scene become drinking companions in the next, without changing sides, and for no better reason than that the screenplay calls here for bullets and there for booze.

The actual film-making is never quite as pleasantly casual as the screenwriting (by James Mitchell, from a novel by James Munro). Peter Collinson ("The Penthouse," "Up the Junction," "The Italian Job," etc.) is noted for a ponderously flashy technique. But despite its involvement in his silly cinema of obtrusive montage, improbable camera angles and forced perspective, "Innocent Bystanders" may well be Collmovie.

Almost everything in the movie seems to come from some other movie—from "One Day in the Life of Ivan Denisovich," from a whole generation of hard-nosed disillusioned spy films, perhaps even from "North by Northwest," with its own elusive Mr. Kaplan. Stanley Baker's characterization owes a lot to James Bond and a little to Richard Burton, and although not one of his better roles, it allows him enough dignity at least to keep his reputation intact.

•

But Geraldine Chaplin's performance is so reticent and so appealing as to constitute a small personal triumph. She is saddled with the movie's dumbest sequence (restoring Baker to his long lost masculinity, just by holding hands with him) but she is also granted its only moments of quiet intelligence. She fills these moments with a delicate intimacy that contrasts with everything else in the film and that really does suggest a reservoir of feeling to oppose the lives around her that are wasted in mere action.

1973 Ja 25, 51:6

PRISON GIRLS, directed by Thomas DeSimone; written by Lee Walters; music by Christopher Huston; produced by Nicholas D. Grippo and Burton Gershfeld; 3-D Film Technology and color by Pacific Film Industries; released by United Producers. Running time: 84 minutes. This film has not been classified yet. At the Penthouse Theater, Broadway and 47th Street; 59th Street Twin I, east of Third Avenue and the 86th Street Twin I, west of Lexington Avenue.
With: Robin Whitting, Maria Arnold, Angie Monet, Lisa Ashbury, Tracy Handfuss, Ushie Digard, Jamie McKenna, Illona Lakes, Carol Peters and Claire Bow.

The "Prison Girls," who broke into the Penthouse and a couple of other theaters yesterday, vividly illustrates this observer's conviction that soft-core pornography can't be much of a help either to serious penology or dedicated thrill-seekers. These "girls" and their varied guys have been filmed in color and a 3-D process labeled Optivision, which requires wearing Polaroid glasses in the tradition of "The House of Wax" and "The Stewardesses" and which makes viewing this amalgam of simulated sex, frontal nudity, four-letter words and ersatz plottting a good deal more of a chore than necessary.

•

The story line, to coin a phrase, involves the effects of a distaff psychiatrist's idea to help rehabilitate her "girls" via furloughs from life behind bars. So, we have a succession of the ladies making it back for short-term reunions with a pimp, a bank robber on the run, a brother-in-law and gang rape in a garage, a rich dilettante who dotes on body painting and a husband who thaws his erstwhile frigid wife. The ladies, for the record, are nobly endowed and who plays whom isn't listed and doesn't matter. With the encumbrances of a one-D script and this 3-D process, they're likely to generate more headaches than kicks.

A. H. WEILER.

1973 Ja 25, 51:6

FIVE SHORT DRAMAS: THE MAN WHO KNOCKED ME DOWN by Philip Shafer, 11 minutes; **A GAME OF CATCH** by Stephen Witty, adapted from a short story by Richard Wilbur; 8 minutes; **WHAT FIXED ME** by Tom Rickman, 20 minutes; **KETTLE OF FISH** by W. Boon Collins, Bill Terry, O. .B. Lewis, Dave Connel and Clio Vias, 15 minutes; **THE ODYSSEY OF GLORIA TWINSON** by Dick Bartlett, written by Mr. Bartlett and Ray Loring, 30 minutes. At the Whitney Museum of American Art, Madison Avenue and 75th Street.

By ROGER GREENSPUN

There must be poets whose life's ambition is to write short poems. And there have been great composers whose ultimate masterpieces were art songs, four or five minutes long. But nobody aspires to make short movies, especially short fiction movies, if he can make long ones instead. Short movies usually come at the beginning of a film maker's career, when he lacks money and needs experience, and they are a kind of apprenticeship, or schooling, in which he learns the potentials of his craft.

Taken at this level, the program of five short movie dramas that opened yesterday at the Whitney Museum is very good and honorable and promising work. None of the films is brilliant, or very polished, or especially innovative. But at the same time, they are all intelligent, and lucid, and technically idiomatic — while avoiding the easy symbolism and pretentiousness of effect that seems the curse of the medium and a particular temptation to young directors.

I suppose the greatest virtuosity, at least in concept, belongs to Philip Shafer's "The Man Who Knocked Me Down," which consists entirely of a single 11-minute take from the viewpoint of a subjective camera that goes out for a walk, gets knocked down by a madman on a Greenwich Village street, and then has to listen to his plans for reshaping the world. The concept works very well, partly because John Bottoms plays the madman with enough variety to sustain the film's concentration and partly because Shafer knows just how seriously to take his visual trick.

Stephen Witty's "A Game of Catch," a kid's fantasy, and W. Boon Collins's "Kettle of Fish," an adult's slice of unnerving reality, are dramatically the least assuming of the films. Neither seems wholly realized as a movie, though "Kettle of Fish," another Village confrontation, deals pleasantly with its large cast of slightly drunken, vaguely dispirited characters.

"What Fixed Me" is the most ambitious of the Whitney movies. Filmed by Tom Rickman in Kentucky, it attempts to occupy the mind of a sensitive boy, son of a brutish backwoods preacher and of a young mother who dies trying to escape from the father. It is a rather literary film, complete with a cautionary folk song ("Old Dan Tucker") on the sound track, but good at building a frame of mind out of the process of storytelling.

Dick Bartlett stars his own stepmother, Mary Bartlett, in "The Odyssey of Gloria Twinson" as the contented, supernaturally ordinary middle-aged proprietor of a small town gift shop. It is her ne'er-do-well novelist sister Renata (Ann Priest) who messes things up for Gloria, moving in with her, drinking, bitching, and repeatedly playing her tape-recording of their late father's last coughs and death rattle.

Renata eventually takes off to do her own thing — cause a scandal, as it happens — and Gloria begins to think she would like to do her own thing too, if only she could figure out what that might be. Gloria and Renata really are originals. And so is Dick Bartlett, whose manner of dry deadpan humor is as good a style for the short dramatic film as any I've seen.

1973 Ja 26, 42:1

LIFE STUDY, directed by Michael Nebbia; screenplay by Arthur Birnkrant, based on a story by Mr. Nebbia; director of photography, Mr. Nebbia; editors, Ray Sandiford and Sidney Katz; music composed and arranged by Emanuel Vardi; produced by Mr. Nebbia. Running time: 99 minutes. At the First Avenue Screeening Room Theater, at 61st Street. This film has not been classified.

Angelo Corelli .... Bartholomew Miro Jr.
Myrna Clement .... Erika Peterson
Angela .... Ziska
Adrian Clement .... Gregory D'Alessio
Gus .... Tom Lee Jones
Grandma .... Rosetta Garuffi
John Clement .... Anthony Forest
Peggy Clement .... Yvonne Sherwell

By VINCENT CANBY

Nothing works the way it should in "Life Study," Michael Nebbia's all-too-vulnerable love story about Angelo Corelli, a moody young Italian-American boy who wants to make movies "about the way things are," and Myrna Clement, who, at 17, is rich, eccentric, lonely and pregnant, though not by Angelo.

Myrna falls in love with Angelo at first sight, when he walks into her uncle's painting class at the New York Art Students League. It's a measure of the imagination of Myrna (and of the film) that she immediately sees Angelo as a knight in shining armor—and that Mr. Nebbia insists that we see it too.

The way is thus immediately prepared for a film that attempts to honor squareness but ends up by demonstrating it.

•

Angelo has these flat-footed, conveniently coherent dreams that establish the fact that he blames his father for his mother's death in childbirth, nine months after Angelo caught them making love. As Angelo is riddled by Roman Catholic guilt and keeps a plastic Jesus on the dashboard of his convertible, Myrna fights against the burden of her WASPness. "Daddy," she says on the telephone, "Why don't you follow Christ's example and give away all your money?" Myrna, who is always a bit cute, becomes intolerable when given access to a telephone. She calls Angelo late one night to ask, "Isn't it awful about Abelard?"

Mr. Nebbia, the director, and his screenwriter, Arthur Birnkrant, present Angelo and Myrna straight, without humor. They obviously feel affection for a girl who'd say, seriously, that she wants to be married "in a meadow, by a river, facing the rising sun, at dawn." If they cared more, however, they might have given the girl the wit to recognize that if it's dawn, the sun had damn well better be rising.

•

Bartholomew Miro Jr. plays Angelo. Erika Peterson is Myrna, and a girl named Ziska is the worldly model who represents the flesh opposed to Myrna's spirit. I haven't the faintest idea if any of them can act.

"Life Study," which opened a week's engagement yesterday at the First Avenue Screening Room, pretty much defines the purposes of the new theater—perhaps too well. It is neither good enough nor strong enough to compete in the commercial market.

However, it is the first directorial effort of Mr. Nebbia, whose talent as a cinematographer ("Alice's Restaurant") should earn him the right to fail publicly as a director.

1973 Ja 26, 42:4

The Cast

TRICK BABY, directed by Larry Yust; screenplay by Mr. Yust, T. Raewyn, A. Neuberg, based on the novel by Iceberg Slim; director of photography, Isadore Mankofsky; music by James Bond; produced by Marshal Backlar and James Levitt; distributed by Universal Studios. Running time: 89 minutes. At the DeMille Theater, Seventh Avenue and 47th Street, and Juliet 2 Theater, Third Avenue and 83d Street. This film has been rated R.

White Folks .... Kiel Martin
Blue Howard .... Mel Stewart
Dot Murray .... Dallas Edward Hayes
Susan .... Beverly Ballard
Cleo .... Vernee Watson
Morrison .... Donald Symington
Phillips .... Don Fellows
Felix the Fixer .... Tom Anderson

By ROGER GREENSPUN

I don't know what you might expect from a movie title like "Trick Baby." But what you get is the story of a pair of engaging con men who lie themselves to their glory and to their doom, during a couple of fateful days in the grimier reaches of Philadelphia. Directed by Larry Yust, and essentially the work of not terribly well-known talents, "Trick Baby" opened yesterday at the DeMille and Juliet 2 Theaters.

Both Blue Howard (Mel Stewart) and his young companion White Folks (Kiel Martin) are black, but only Blue looks it. White Folks, son of a white father and a black mother, is so white that he can pass—mainly as one Johnny O'Brien — and passing is the essence of his game. Folks plays white and Blue plays black—oppressed black — and their victims, their marks, play at economic exploitation with greater or lesser degrees of racist venality.

•

"We got them squeezed between us . . . With your complexion and my brains, the sky's the limit," boasts Blue, the prospect of a $90,000 inner-city real estate con almost as certain for him as tomorrow's breakfast. But a little later, with the mob after his head, and tomorrow's breakfast likely to be a last meal, if he lives that long, he pulls another con—a rather beautiful one, and just for a night's lodging—and confesses that he still needs his calling: "Lying takes my mind off my troubles."

Despite the crudity of its racial stereotypes, especially its white racial stereotypes, "Trick Baby" seems most interesting in its understanding of race relations—which I assume are at issue in the friendship, almost love, between Blue and Folks. Folks really is white. The film says he's black, and he manages a few soulful turns of phrase, but your eyes and your ears tell you he's white. At the movies, that is all you have to go on. The point is that relations between Folks and Blue are absolutely normal, not very competitive, resilient, and rich in a kind of mutual professional appreciation. The playing of the cons is funny, but very restrained, and the two con men seem to demonstrate viability—however precarious it may be.

•

There are enough things wrong with "Trick Baby" to fill a bad review, and yet I think it deserves a good one. Half its characterizations are absurd (the female leads, Beverly Ballard and Vernce Watson, suffer particularly) and the other half are very fine. Much of the spoken rationalization is nonsense, but the physical action is often very true, not especially violent, but exciting.

Larry Yust indulges in too much flashy sound montage and in the obtrusive cross-cutting into sequences that seems the curse of the newer movies. But he and Isidore Mankofsky have a lovely sense of place and perspective for the camera frame and, in the slums of Philadelphia, a bleak and fascinating cityscape in which to exercise it.

1973 Ja 27, 15:1

The Cast

LIMBO, directed by Mark Robson; screenplay by Joan Silver and James Bridges, based on a story by Miss Silver; director of photography, Charles Wheeler; editor, Dorothy Spencer, music, Anita Kerr; produced by Linda Gottlieb; a Universal-Filmmakers Group production, distributed by Universal Pictures. Running time: 112 minutes. At the Festival Theater, 57th Street near Fifth Avenue. This film has been rated PG.

Sandy Lawton .... Kate Jackson
Mary Kaye Buell .... Kathleen Nolan
Sharon Dornbeck ...... Katherine Justice
Jane York .... Hazel Medina
Alan Weber .... Russell Wiggins
Phil Garrett .... Stuart Margolin
Margaret Holroyd .... Joan Murphy
Joe Buell .... Michael Bersell
Kathy Buell .... Kim Nicholas
Pete Buell .... Ken Kornbluh
Julie Buell .... Laura Kornbluh

By VINCENT CANBY

If it has nothing else — and Mark Robson's "Limbo" hasn't — you might at least expect topicality of a film about the problems facing wives of American servicemen who are either missing in action in Vietnam or prisoners of war. By using something less than the sheerest art, Robson manages to make this story ("torn from today's headlines," we are told) resemble any number of dreadful World War II tearjerkers.

"Interestingly, however, "Limbo" does demonstrate the impotency of so much of the liberal opposition to the war that is now, apparently, coming to an end.

Robson is, I take it, a liberal. He certainly was back in the late nineteen-forties when he directed such films as "Champion" and "Home of The Brave."

In that optimistic time, political and social issues were clear cut. War against bigotry was simply an extension of the war against Hitler. It was cosily patriotic. The good, voting liberal had not yet had to wrestle with the unruly, rising consciousnesses of all sorts of impatient groups, with, for example, the new black philosophy that says to hell with integration, we'll do it by ourselves.

A lot of liberals lost heart in the nineteen-fifties and sixties. It is not fun being ridiculed by the people you had always wanted to protect. Robson, for reasons of his own, has devoted most of his later career to big-budget nonsense on the order of "Peyton Place," "Von Ryan's Express" and "Valley of The Dolls." Watching "Limbo," you can speculate why.

●

The mind that made it is, I suspect, outraged by the war but seems afraid to say so. It is as split in mood as a lot of other people may be split in their sympathies — feeling sorrow for the American P.O.W. fliers, yet overwhelmed by fury with those who continued to go on bombing missions.

The liberals protested but mostly with a politeness born, I think, out of memories of World War II, and even Korea, when wars were declared and the stakes were easy to define. There is a similar liberal sort of politeness in 'Limbo," which is as obvious in its narrative structure and physical look as in anything that anyone says.

The screenplay, by Joan Silver and James Bridges, set on an Air Force base in Florida, is about three wives who are three points of view, good, bad and all mixed-up.

The good wife (Kathleen Nolan) is middle-aged, Catholic, the mother of four, faithful to her husband and angry about the war.

The bad one (Katherine Justice) is rich, beautiful, Southern, an all-out patriot and so spoiled that she refuses to believe the eyewitness report of her husband's death.

The confused one is Kate Jackson, married only two weeks before her husband's departure, and now hopelessly in love with a nice, honorable, out-of-work space technician.

●

The situations are real enough, but Robson entombs them in a lot of bogus domestic complications, photographed and acted in a simplistic romantic style that denies any sense of real topicality and urgency. If Vietnam were a war like any other (which it is not), there might be a small point to this approach.

Only occasionally does the film seem to be about a special, very confused moment in history, but Robson tends to flub these moments too, as in the sequence in which three American wives visit the North Vietnamese embassy in Paris. He opens the sequence with some nice old chop-chop music that 40 years ago used to identify a stock shot of wicked Shanghai.

Robson's heart is in the right place, but his movie is unimaginative, phony and ineffectual. It opened yesterday at the Festival.

1973 Ja 27, 17:1

Erotic or Exotic?

By VINCENT CANBY

BERNARDO BERTOLUCCI'S "Last Tango in Paris" is a beautiful, courageous, foolish, romantic and reckless film and Bertolucci is like the diving champion, drunk on enthusiasm, who dares dive from the high board knowing well that the pool is half empty. The stunt comes off, but the dive is less grand than we might expect from what we've heard and read, and especially from what we know of Bertolucci. I mention this at the outset because the film is being so overpraised (and overpriced) that many disappointed people may be reluctant to indulge its failures, thus to miss its achievements, which are considerable.

"Last Tango in Paris" is the movie romance of the 1970s, at least of that portion of the 1970s we have seen so far. It carries its ideas of love and sexuality not to the limits of conceivable time, but to the limits of last year—the era of Norman Mailer, Germaine Greer, "J," airplane goggles, porno films and revolutionary semantics. It's not the film's boldness that shocks, amuses and fascinates us, but its topicality, which, when we stumble upon it in films, has the practical effect of a vision of the future—movies, which take up to two years to make, being usually and fundamentally out-of-date. It's a movie for the breathless weekly news magazines that discover, analyze and embalm trends when the trends are still in nascent states.

It's what in the 1960s (a decade not great for jargon) would have been called, lamely, a Now film. It's so Now, in fact, that you better see it quickly. I suspect that its ideas, as well as its ability to shock or, apparently, to arouse, will age quickly. This is not true, I think, of the superlative production by Bertolucci, nor of the extraordinary performance by Marlon Brando who, following his fine, sentimental triumph in "The Godfather," now plays a role that does not simply identify him with his own time, as did his roles in "A Streetcar Named Desire" in the 1940s and "On The Water-

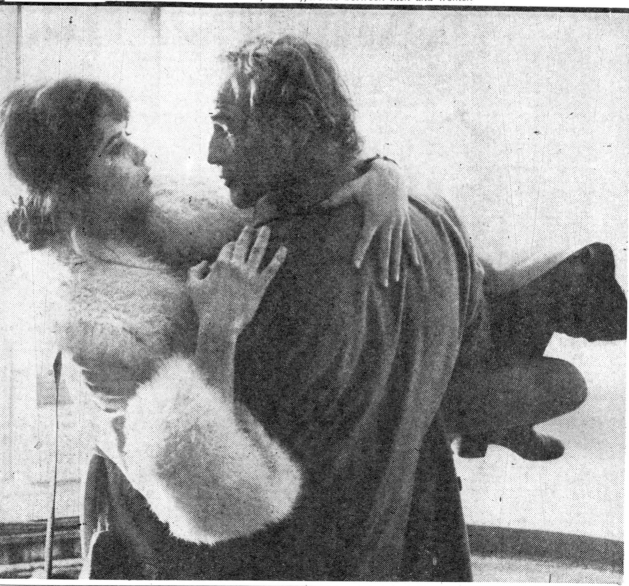

Marlon Brando and Maria Schneider are lovers in "Last Tango in Paris." Thursday, Trans-Lux East.

"Riotous, furious, frenzied celebrations of the difference between men and women"

front" in the 1950s. It also makes him a Pop spokesman, tough, irreverent, mocking, as well as an incurable sentimentalist, a guy who still thinks it's possible to exorcise nothingness by embracing it, who chooses exile in a super-fascist state of mind where the only love allowed is sexual.

The original screenplay, by Bertolucci and Franco Arcalli, is about Paul (Brando), a middle-aged American living in Paris who, when we first meet him, is not quite on his last legs, though close to it. His wife, a French woman, the owner of a second-rate pension, has just committed suicide with a razor (Paul calls her a "fake Ophelia drowned in the bathtub"). In a despair that I, for one, never really believe, he sets up an apartment with a 20-year-old girl named Jeanne (Maria Schneider) who agrees to meet him there for afternoon encounter sessions. The ground rules: they will not tell each other their names, who they are, what they do. The outside world will be forgotten, he says, as they explore and test and refine what may be discreetly labeled the Sexual Experience.

Jeanne, a pretty, would-be liberated, middle-class girl, engaged to a marvelously self-absorbed movie nut (Jean-Pierre Léaud), who is making a cinema vérité film about her, is the first one to rebel against the format. She falls in love with Paul, or thinks she does, as he systematically instructs her in variations on sexual experience (sex is violence, it says here) that are comparatively new in conventional theatrical films, though they cannot possibly be new to anyone who has read any novels in the last fifty years or seen a few of the porno films that,

I'm beginning to think, may turn out to be the art form of the 1970s. (The sex scenes, not so incidentally, simply extend the limits of the sort of prudery that conventional films have always practiced. The sex is, of course, simulated. Only Jeanne is seen nude, front view, full-figure, while Brando, more often than not, is wearing his pants while making love to Jeanne. This is not important to the film, but only to its reputation as a breakthrough movie, which it isn't.)

*

However, the finest things about "Last Tango in Paris" are these scenes, riotous, furious, frenzied celebrations of the differences between men and women. Oddly enough, I found them more funny, occasionally more embarrassing, even more philosophical, than erotic. The intensity of Brando's anger and humor, and the desperation with which he sets out to insulate himself from the world through this affair are very special to behold. His language—crude, witty, magnificently vulgar — and the stories that tumble out in the form of random monologues are unlike anything we've ever heard on the screen before. It sounds tough as hell, which explains, I think, why the film's full-blown, almost old-fashioned romanticism goes unnoticed.

Paul is, first and foremost, a romantic hero, one of almost 19th-century Gothic proportions. Like Mr. Rochester, he has a secret locked

away in a vault (one that Bertolucci would perhaps have been wise not to open). It's not that Paul is a nonbeliever in romantic love; he believes too well. He knows its punishments and rewards, which he affirms by attempting to disremember them.

In spite of all the simulated sex, everything in the film is touched by exotic fancy, including the very availability of the apartment that Paul and Jeanne happen to meet in, an absolutely smashing flat in Passy, the sort with his and hers wash basins in the bath. It's made to seem in need of a little paint, and there are rats, but housing in Paris is scarce and I don't know anybody living there who wouldn't give a large ransom for worthless furniture to be able to take over one like it.

The easy availability of Jeanne to the aging Paul is also wish-fulfillment of the most romantic kind. They chance to meet, exchange a few mild insults, and in less than five minutes they're furiously fornicating standing up, fully clothed, then rolling around on the floor, finally to be hugely exhausted and satisfied. It's every respectable traveler's time-passing fantasy, on IRT subway, Fifth Avenue bus or trans-Atlantic plane: wouldn't it be interesting, if. . . .?

The look of the film, too, is pure romance — lots of dusky, autumnal golds and blue-grays, long, graceful camera movements, scenes shot through frosted glass or

against fractured mirrors, and a soundtrack that carries music on the order of a high-class, though not classical, Muzak. When Bertolucci scores one of Paul and Jeanne's encounters with what sounds like a Hawaiian love song, you know he must be kidding. Or is he?

I don't think he is. The shape of the film is ironic—as Jeanne falls coolly out of love with Paul, he finally confesses his love for her, giving up his romantic defenses by giving her his name, age, occupation, etc. How does he declare himself? "Anyway, you dummy, I love you!" The film goes suddenly feeble. The secret apartment recalls a theme from Rodgers and Hart ("A Small Hotel"). Paul's wife is revealed to have been a calculating, willful bitch whom he loved so hopefully that he tolerated her cheerfully acknowledged affairs with other men. Not even Brando's performance, nor the general vitality of the film, can carry the scene in which Brando must sit beside his wife's bier and alternate rage with tears of lamentation over her unfaithfulness, his love for her and the mystery of her suicide. (It's also very bad judgment to show the woman, whom we never see in life and who, in death, looks like nothing more interesting than a dress extra.)

The film-as-a-failed-meringue is most peculiarly revealed, however, in one of the last encounter sessions between Paul and Jeanne.

Jeanne tells Paul she has found a man to make her love him. Paul taunts her about the idiocy of such dreams. Better get used to isolation, he says in effect, then he goes on angrily:

"No, you're all alone. And you won't be able to be free of that feeling until you look death in the face. I mean that sounds like bull—and some romantic crap. Until you go right up into the —— of death, till you find the womb of fear, maybe then you'll be able to find him."

*

Bertolucci attempts to underscore this warmed-over, reversed, into-the-jaws-of-death metaphor by making it actual. Paul tells Jeanne to get the scissors and pare the nails on two fingers of her right hand, then to explore him anally. It's not the physical action that's banal, but the motivating emotions. Somehow the intensity of the feelings, which until that moment have been real, turn as fake as the sex we've seen.

We'd believed in Paul, and in the character created by Brando, but the film's revealed mysteries let us down.

They aren't grand enough for violence and humiliation and the intimacies we've been asked to share until then. Behind the raised consciousness of "Last Tango in Paris," there's a little bit of the simplistic foolishness of "Love Story," which people thought was old-fashioned but was topical enough to make a zillion dollars. "Last Tango," touted as something completely new, will, I predict, make a zillion dollars for the very same reason.

To be crudely commercial about it, the film will also be helped by the fact that at the

Trans-Lux East, where it opens next Thursday, the price of admission will be $5 a seat at every performance. The only other straight dramatic films to get away with those prices are the porno films. I have reservations about the ultimate point of the film, but "Last Tango in Paris," which I first saw and reviewed at the 1972 New York Film Festival, is too fine to be associated with the porno junk, even if only through the cost of tickets.

1973 Ja 28, II:1:1

A Bouquet for 'Marigolds'

By STEPHEN FARBER

THERE are a lot of little things wrong with Paul Newman's movie of "The Effect of Gamma Rays on Man-in-the-Moon Marigolds," some of them attributable to Alvin Sargent's screenplay and some deriving from Paul Zindel's original play. It is easy to pick at details — overstated or contrived moments, irrelevant transitional scenes, some crudely-drawn minor characters. Yet the film as a whole is powerful and affecting. Sargent and Newman have made some miscalculations, but they have succeeded in liberating the material from the confines of the stage, and they have intelligently refashioned the play, retaining its best qualities—the insights into character, the strong sense of family—and eliminating some of its melodramatic excesses.

Zindel's central character, Beatrice Hunsdorfer (Joanne Woodward), is a frowzy, badly-used middled-aged moth-

"It puts some honest feeling back into American movies"

er of two teen-age girls: Ruth (Roberta Wallach), an epileptic, and Mathilda (Nell Potts), a gifted science student. Living on a million memories and a million get-rich-quick schemes, Beatrice recalls the neurotic, nostalgia-drugged heroines of Tennessee Williams and especially William Inge. At first these echoes are distracting, but "Marigolds" has surprises of character and mood. It is hard where you expect it to be soft, almost obscenely funny when it should be grim, strangely moving during some of the most manic stretches.

The film is especially bold in its introduction of black comedy in the treatment of Nanny Annie (Judith Lowry), the cast-off old woman who lives as a boarder in the Hunsdorfer house. Instead of wringing pathos from the neglect of the aged, "Marigolds" sustains an original comedy of the grotesque; Beatrice's abusive jokes about Nanny's senility represent a classic form of survival humor. In a daring, fully successful shift of mood, the film slips from a very funny scene of Beatrice telling Nanny's fortune to Ruth's harrowing epileptic fit, startlingly effective because it is introduced so casually and forgotten so quickly.

As a director Newman resists the obvious, and he has the decency never to push us. He never *explains* the characters; he respects their secrets, and he can demonstrate their paradoxes. Tough, brassy, assured women like Beatrice and Ruth have profound concealed wounds, while the shy, sensitive Mathilda, who might seem certain to be the first casualty of this crazy household, is in fact the strongest of the three—untouchable in spite of everything she witnesses.

"Marigold" freezes the complex tensions of family life. It is at moments almost unbearably painful, a savage record of frustrated, cruel symbiotic relationships. Ruth has inherited Beatrice's pragmatic common sense approach to life, and sarcasm is a bond of bitter-

ness between them. Sometimes their intimacy is more desperate; Beatrice's disordered life has scarred Ruth, and now Beatrice does what she can to take care of Ruth and shield her from nightmares. In the sunlight their roles are reversed. Trapped by the values of her peer group, Ruth is ashamed of her mother's slovenliness, mocks her in front of her classmates, and takes advantage of Beatrice's vulnerabilities to destroy her spirit. The cycle is inescapable: Mother and daughter slash at each other and then tentatively heal each other's wounds.

With Mathilda, both Beatrice and Ruth are slightly uneasy. Her talents set her apart from them, and their natural instinct is to put her down, though they are secretly proud of her too; they can see that she alone redeems their wasted lives. In the cluttered, ramshackle house that imprisons them, the moods change like quicksilver; for in spite of everything tearing them apart, they *are* a family. There is one lovely brief scene on the porch, a moment of reverie when mother and daughters imagine opening a tearoom with Nancy as cashier.

*

"Marigolds" is a modest movie of character, and it is not intended as a major social statement. Still, what gives the film special importance is that it concerns women living without men—alone, abandoned, defeated, but

determined not to surrender. All of them are doing what they can to survive —even old Nanny Annie, who achieves a kind of dignity in silence. Beatrice has the classified ads and a resilient imagination to keep possibilities open, and the afflicted Ruth has some of her mother's unexpected resources: she is touchingly intense as she practices baton-twirling in her overgrown backyard. Only Mathilda will escape unscathed, but none of them indulges in self-pity. Although far from a radical feminist manifesto, "Marigolds" is one of the most sympathetic films about women to come out of Hollywood in recent years.

The actresses help to build this sympathy for the characters. As Ruth, Roberta Wallach performs a neat balancing act. She vividly recalls the hard, shallow, boy-crazy girls we all knew in high school, but she never condescends to the character; and she handles the pyrotechnics with impressive control. The role of Beatrice gives Joanne Woodward a chance to show her range. Cast against type as a loud, frumpy shrew, she plays the more flamboyant scenes with a wonderful comic zest that her faded Southern belle and spinster roles never tapped.

In the quiet moments, when her brassy facade suddenly falls away, she reveals Beatrice's outrageous sense of humor for what it is—a defense against despair. One silent expression mingling

fear, maternal compassion, helplessness, and self-disgust as she comforts Ruth after her convulsions is as shattering a bit of *film* acting as anything I've seen in the past year. Woodward supplies depth as well as flair; it is a superb performance.

In the end, however, the film belongs to Nell Potts (the Newmans' daughter), who plays Mathilda. Child actors are notorious camera hogs, and maybe no one but a father would have trusted a young actress enough to let her give such an understated, unsentimental performance. Paul Newman knows that Mathilda doesn't need our sympathy, and he never has Nell Potts play for it. She stays aloof; her coolness and imperturbability are what seem amazing. When Beatrice comes to school drunk on the night of the science awards, Ruth is ashamed, but Mathilda can look straight at her mother without judging her and without feeling sorry for herself. Absolutely confident of her own worth, she is beyond bitterness; she seems to understand and accept everything.

*

"Marigolds" is a tribute to the endurance of children, and although some of her dialogue about mutations is too heavily symbolic, Nell Potts communicates an unshakable inner strength. In the final scenes, after a series of crises that could break many adults, she achieves a sense of serenity that is mysterious, stirring, marvelous.

With movies growing more and more brutal, it is gratifying to find a film that offers a subtle emotional experience. "The Effect of Gamma Rays on Man-in-the-Moon Marigolds" is riddled with imperfections, but it puts some honest feeling back into American movies. Right now that's a rare achievement.

Stephen Farber, film critic, is author of "The Movie Rating Game."

1973 Ja 28, II:13:1

Joanne Woodward, right, acts the frustrated mother of Nell Potts and Roberta Wallach in "The Effect of Gamma Rays on Man-in-the-Moon Marigolds"
"It concerns women living without men—alone, abandoned, defeated, but determined not to surrender"

The Program

WOMEN ARTISTS AS FILMMAKERS, PART ONE: WOMEN'S LIBERATION IN THE ARTS by Lil Picard, 10 minutes; ALMIRA by Nancy Kendall, 20 minutes; THE TRANSFORMATION OF PERSEPHONE (scene from Orpheus Underground) by Silvianna Goldsmith, 10 minutes; SELF PORTRAIT by Maria Lessnig, 5 minutes; PAINTING by Patricia Sloane, 5 minutes; CIRCLES II by Doris Chase, 13 minutes; ALCHEMY BLUES by Olga Spiegel, 10 minutes; EPISOLE ON THE EDGE by Frances Alenikoff, 4 minutes; PARALLAX by Rosalind Schneider, 20 minutes. At the New York Cultural Center, 2 Columbus Circle.

By ROGER GREENSPUN

Relations between the fine arts and the movies have always seemed uncomfortable at best. And when practitioners, or mere students of the fine arts take up the movies, the results may be good or they may be a form of high-minded or opportunistic intellectual slumming.

I get this feeling—a sinking feeling—just from looking at some of the titles of papers read at the College Art Association's Friday morning session, "Film History as Art History," titles like "The Iconography and Iconology in 'Citizen Kane,'" or "Hogarth as a Source for 'Tom, Tom, the Piper's Son.'" And I get the same feeling from a large part of what I saw in the first of the Women Artists as Filmmakers programs, which opened yesterday as part of the "Women Choose Women" show at the New York Cultural Center.

•

For some reason, the most beautiful film by a woman artist, perhaps by any recent artist, Nancy Graves's "Izy Boukir," is not included, though some very insignificant work is. Lil Picard's "Women's Liberation in the Arts," Patricia Sloane's "Painting," Frances Alenikoff's "Episode on the Edge" scarcely seem to exist as movies, though the makers use film and, therefore, I suppose, explore the medium. Olga Spiegel, with "Alchemy Blues," on the other hand, seems already at home in the medium and capable of doing rather lovely things with it. "Alchemy Blues" is an animated abstraction, full of drops and blobs and spills of color that it proceeds to organize into a complex and exceptionally lively order.

Maria Lessnig's "Self Portrait," a five-minute cartoon accompanying an interior monologue, is probably the least pretentious of the films, and Rosalind Schneider's "Parallax" is surely the most pretentious. "Parallax" uses dancers engaged in a kind of shadowy, slow, cosmic grope, and it repeats its images in three distinct projections separated in time. I don't know what is gained by this technique, except screen space, and Miss Schneider's movie seems dull in each of its manifestations.

•

Silvianna Goldsmith's "The Transformation of Persephone" is a magical, flashback narrative about the abduction and rape of Persephone in the underworld. Persephone apparently enjoys her rape, which changes her into a goddess (greatly in the manner of Jean Cocteau) spouting pomegranate seeds and pulp. The film has the look, the boldness, and some of the appeal and uncertainty of avant-garde moviemaking of a decade or so ago.

Two of the more ambitious films, Nancy Kendall's "Almira" and Doris Chase's "Circles II," both dance films, have been reviewed here within the last few weeks. Both gain from a second viewing, and "Circles II" emerges as the best work in the Women Artists as Filmmakers program.

1973 Ja 29, 25:1

The Cast

SHAMUS, directed by Buzz Kulik; written by Barry Beckerman; director of photography, Victor J. Kemper; music, Jerry Goldsmith; film editor, Walter Thompson; produced by Robert M. Weitman; released by Columbia Pictures. At Loews State 2, Broadway and 45th Street, and Loews Cine, Third Avenue at 86th Street, and neighborhood theaters. Running time: 99 minutes. This film is classified PG.

McCoy	Burt Reynolds
Alexis	Dyan Cannon
Colonel Hardcore	John Ryan
Lieutenant Promuto	Joe Santos
Dottore	Georgia Tozzi
Hume	Ron Weyand
Springy	Larry Block
Bolton	Beeson Carroll
The Kid	Kevin Conway
Bookstore Girl	Kay Frye

By ROGER GREENSPUN

"What are you doing in the tub?"

"I'm taking a bath."

"Taking a bath with your clothes on?"

"Saves on laundry bills."

It's a joke; a rotten joke to be sure; but a joke anyway. The shamus, McCoy, isn't really taking a bath. He was worked over by some hired thugs the night before, and in the tub is where his pal Springy finds him the next morning — ready for jokes, ready for punches, for kisses, for just about anything, in Buzz Kulik's "Shamus," a game but not especially good movie that means to put the private eye back into some kind of current relevance.

•

The attempt has been made often enough before. But this time it is made with a mixture of contemporary satire and knowing nostalgia that keeps proving itself more interesting than the movie it is supposed to support. Just possibly, the private eye, that last refuge of unfettered consciousness, is a less immortal pop-culture hero than some would like to imagine. When "Shamus" goes back to "The Big Sleep," and it goes back quite openly, it can parody certain personages—the beautiful bookstore girl behind glasses; General Sternwood in his hothouse—but it can't really capture people, or what they stand for in a society that is, like any society, a system of deep and necessary interdependencies.

Thus, Marlowe, in "The Big Sleep," could be not just the eyes but also the conscience of his world, as McCoy cannot, because in "Shamus" there is nothing to which a conscience can attach itself. People aren't more wicked. They are more brutal, but if anything less wicked. The case that McCoy breaks, the plot of the icy millionaire, Hume (Ron Weyand), to export government arms illegally, may be fraught with danger; but is is given its meaning by the dopey Col. C. C. Hardcore (John Ryan), who sells off surplus tanks as if they were used cars, and so it becomes another one of the film's game but rather lame little jokes.

As the tough and artful shamus, Burt Reynolds has both a dramatic role to play and a public image to live up to; and I think he does better with the former than the latter. I'm not sure how you *would* play an insatiable lover in a PG-rated movie that has you rolling out of your bed of passion each morning still wearing your boxer shorts, but Reynolds plays it for bemused embarrassment—which is not bad, considering the options.

In some respects, appreciative, oddly courteous, Reynold's relations with his women—especially with the innocent Alexis (reasonably managed by Dyan Cannon)—are the closest "Shamus" comes to approximating the circle of moral good fellowship that films like "The Big Sleep" erect against the corrosive mists of the studio-created night.

The approximation isn't close enough, and "Shamus," which is full of appealing New York locations and much inventive action, ultimately amounts to little more than the kind of situation melodrama that the movies these days offer for excitement. On this level it is workmanlike, well-paced, modest, sometimes scary, and sometimes genuinely funny. It opened yesterday at Loews State 2 and Loews Cine and other neighborhood theaters.

1973 F 1, 41:1

STEELYARD BLUES, directed by Alan Myerson; screenplay by David S. Ward; directors of photography, Laszlo Kovacs and Stevan Larner; editor, Robert Grovenor; music, Nick Gravenites, with special contributions by Paul Butterfield; produced by Tony Bill and Michael and Julia Phillips; distributed by Warner Brothers. Running time: 92 minutes. At the Beekman Theater, Second Avenue at 65th Street. This film has been rated PG.

Iris	Jane Fonda
Veldini	Donald Sutherland
Eagle	Peter Boyle
Duval	Garry Goodrow
Frank	Howard Hesseman
The Kid	John Savage
Black Man in Jail	Melvin Stewart
Zoo Official	Richard Schaal
Police Captain	Morgan Upton

By VINCENT CANBY

"Steelyard Blues" is an appealing movie if only because all of the people connected with it seem so utterly convinced that they are making a Third World film disguised in the shape of an eccentric caper comedy. I like its earnestness, its brow furrowed with mission.

It reminds me of the little boy who covered himself with vanishing cream and then walked through a dinner party in the fond belief he was invisible. He was not, nor is the essential, simple-hearted evangelism of "Steelyard Blues," which does have, as a matter of fact, some bright things in it.

•

There is an early, pre-credit sequence in which Veldini (Donald Sutherland), serving time for larceny, is confronted by a marvelously self-assertive black inmate who asks whether Veldini is dangerous, rather in the way you might ask someone if he's from St. Louis. "Yes," says Veldini, a little uneasily. "I'm dangerous."

"I been dangerous since I was 14," says the black man cheerfully. "By the time they lost my records, I'd killed eight guys, at least. . . . You pretty tough kid, but you ain't dangerous."

Sutherland, playing a sad-faced, gentle, demolition-derby driver, gives the impression of someone who's too thin because his passion will not let him rest. He hasn't time for proper meals while he works on plans to wreck every car manufactured in America between 1940 and 1960. His impossible dream: a giant demolition derby involving not just passenger cars, but dump trucks, school buses, pick-up trucks, delivery vans, trailers, campers and, at the finale, mobile homes.

He is, of course, the visionary loser who, by the definition of this film, is a positive force for true freedom and justice. So too is Iris (Jane Fonda), a $100-a-night hooker who does not know she's being humiliated until she's beaten up by the police at the direction of the district attorney (Howard Hesseman). He is not only an occasional customer but also Veldini's brother.

•

Like Iris and all the others who come under Veldini's mad revolutionary spell, Eagle (Peter Boyle) hasn't any passion of his own. Eagle is a schizoid, out-of-work circus man ("there's not much call for human flies these days") who hasn't a thought one way or the other about the yoke of the automobile economy.

Intuitively, he recognizes Veldini's genius, and, through him, he worships the spirit of liberation. In "Steelyard Blues" liberation is represented by a plan to raid a Navy yard to steal an electrical circuit that, in turn, will allow the innocents to fly off to a better world in a refurbished PBY of World War II vintage.

Alan Myerson, whose credits include work with San Francisco's improvisational satire group, The Committee, and Chicago's Second City, directed the film. He clearly has a sense of humor, but the movie often is totally confused in ways that can be credited to either the directing or writing.

Different shots within a single scene do not match. When comedy goes thin, the volume of the rock score (actually a very good one) on the soundtrack is raised to such a fierce level that it sounds like a radio in the projection booth. It has to have no relation to the movie.

It may be because Miss Fonda's and Sutherland's soberly humanitarian left-wing political views are so well known that they lend a heaviness to "Steelyard Blues" that it would not have if we were not so aware. I doubt it, however. They are two performers I admire very much, but this film, which may be up to their politics, is not up to their talents. Their presence gives it more importance than the material warrants.

"Steelyard Blues," which opened yesterday at the Beekman, is the sort of caper comedy in which you cannot even take the graffiti ("Off the pigs," says a penciled inscription in a jail cell) without suspecting a lot of ponderous premeditation.

1973 F 1, 41:1

Films by Women

The second package of short subjects by women film makers-artists presented yesterday at the New York Cultural Center graphically illustrates that many of the eight contributors offer a good deal less than meets the eye or mind. The creative drive is obvious in all the shorts but only a few, unfortunately, seem worthy of the effort expended.

List as this viewer's favorite, "Wake Dream," an 8-minute color and sound combination of colleges, posters, varied found objects and live-action by Alida Walsh, a sculptor-teacher, that is imaginative and forceful in making antiwar statements. Miss Walsh's use of sacred and modern music enforces a subtly persuasive work.

•

"Dissolve," a 20-minute subject by Tina Girouard and Susan Harris, sculptors, implements its title artistically by the deft use of camera in the frieze-like dissolving and dual images of two nude female dancers. Phyllis Mark, a kinetic sculptor, is equally effective with "Abstraction/Refraction," a 5-minute study of prismatic images through transparent forms.

The changing dots, ectoplasmic shapes and electronic music of Lillian Schwartz's "Mutations," which has been shot with the aid of computers and lasers, makes for a small but eye-catching view of the potentials of the new techniques. However, Martha Marbles's 3-minute look at bubbling water, "Camino Real" appears to be largely an exercise in self-indulgence. And the same might be said of "Swamp," a 6-minute exploration of weeds, reeds and marsh to nowhere under the auspices of Nancy Holt and Robert Smithson.

•

Perhaps the most pretentious (and longest subject) is "Pierre Vallieres," Joyce Wieland's 30-minute focus, in the literal sense of the term, on that former Quebec separatist revolutionary expressing opinions on Quebec minorities, women's liberation and other topics. The camera never leaves the area of Vallieres's lips and teeth in what is not, in effect, a film, but a stultifying lecture.

Joan Jonas's "Vertical Roll," which employs what seems to be a television screen out of control as background for fragmentary figures—arms, legs, torsos—is at best merely disturbing. All the women, such as Miss Jonas, are to be commended for a serious approach to movies but only a few of them represented here are artists as film makers.

A. H. WEILER.

1973 F 1, 41:1

The Cast

PRIVATE PARTS, directed by Paul Bartel; screenplay by Philip Kearney and Les Rendelstein; director of photography, Andrew Davis; film editor, Morton Tubor; music by Hugo Friedhofer; produced by Gene Corman; released by Metro-Goldwyn-Mayer. At the First Avenue Screening Room, at 60th Street. Running time: 87 minutes. This film is classified R.

Cheryl Stratton	Ayn Ruymen
Aunt Martha Atwood	Lucille Benson
George Atwood	John Ventantonio
Reverend Moon	Laurie Main
Jeff	Stanley Livingston
Judy	Ann Gibbs
Mike	Len Travis
Mrs. Quigley	Dorothy Neumann

By ROGER GREENSPUN

Innocent but eager, young runaway Cheryl Stratton means to explore her aunt's seedy Los Angeles hotel no matter what stands in her way. Neither the creaking doors, nor the footsteps in the hall that scare her half to death each night, nor Aunt Martha's prudent warnings, nor even the 110-volt charge of electric current intended to keep idle fingers from Aunt Martha's master key ring, will deter her.

And so she roams the corridors of the dim old place, little dreaming that her girlfriend's boyfriend (who came to find her) has been fed in pieces to the hotel furnace, or that her girlfriend (who came to find the boyfriend) is already decomposing between trays of developer and wash in the basement darkroom of a strange, intense photographer named George.

Indeed, it is George who draws Cheryl on, with his soft, disturbing eyes and his half anonymous gifts of black leather and silky nothings for her to wear. And it is George who spies on Cheryl — to her knowledge and rather to her pleasure — from behind the secret peephole in the bathroom wall.

•

Cheryl, George, Aunt Martha, the girlfriend, the boyfriend, the crazy Mrs. Quigley and the wicked Reverend Moon — all of them live, and some of them die, in "Private Parts," a movie by Paul Bartel, which opened yesterday at the First Avenue Screening Room. Bartel is a young director whose previous short films have shown a genius of title ("Secret Cinema," "Naughty Nurse") not entirely matched by their content. "Private Parts" is no triumph, but it does mark a giant step forward toward the successful blending of precocious perversity and satiric good sense that seems the fated direction of his career.

Bartel really has a theme — the willful annexing of one personality by another—a scary and potentially serious theme that at the movies tends to make its way more profitably into the horror film than any other genre. The hapless heroine of "Secret Cinema" finds herself unconsciously starring in somebody else's movie, shown to

Ayn Ruymen

selected audiences in weekly installments. The not-so-hapless heroine of "Private Parts" dresses or undresses for a part (the film's title, of course, contains a pun) that she does not begin to comprehend until she is literally trapped in the Feudian intricacies of its motivation.

•

Attempting to make all this funny as well as frightening, Bartel succeeds in some details and fails in others. But the attempt, even when it isn't quite working, is a good deal more interesting than most. With Ayn Ruymen as the beautiful Cheryl and Lucille Benson as her protective aunt (also a photographer, a specialist in attending funerals and snapping the moment when the spirit escapes the body) he has been fortunate in getting good performances from perfect types. Not all the film's nonsense is under imaginative control, but most of it is.

"Private Parts" is at least a hopeful occasion for those of us who love intellectual cinema and at the same time care for the menacing staircase, for the ominous shadow, for empty rooms shuttered against the light of the afternoon.

1973 F 2, 16:1

Vincent Canby saw "Last Tango in Paris" for the first time at the New York Film Festival last October. His review of it appeared Oct. 16, 1972. He saw it a second time, as is his custom with important films, before its commercial opening yesterday at the Trans-Lux East at Third Avenue and 58th Street. In a second evaluation, written for the Sunday Arts and Leisure section Jan. 28, he developed a number of points touched on in the original review. Following are excerpts from both reviews, the earlier first.

The Cast

LAST TANGO IN PARIS, directed by Bernardo Bertolucci; screenplay in French (with English subtitles) and English by Mr. Bertolucci and Franco Arcalli; director of photography, Vittorio Storaro; music, Gato Barbieri; editor, Mr. Arcalli; produced by Alberto Grimaldi, for release by United Artists. Running time: 125 minutes. This film has been classified X. At the Trans-Lux East Theater, Third Avenue and 58th Street.

Paul	Marlon Brando
Jeanne	Maria Schneider
Tom	Jean-Pierre Leaud
Prostitute	Giovana Galetti
Rosa's Mother	Maria Michi

The feelings of love, anguish and despair that erupt all over the place in Bernardo Bertolucci's new film, "Last Tango in Paris," are so intense, so consuming, that watching the film at times comes close to being an embarrassment.

"Last Tango in Paris" is all about romantic love, but its expressions are the sometimes brave, sometimes wildly foolish-looking Lawrentian gestures of an intense sexual passion that goes as far as it can and then collapses, in physical and emotional exhaustion. The movie is sad, but it's also hugely funny, occasionally when it doesn't mean to be.

The film is about Paul (Marlon Brando), a middle-aged American of obscure antecedents who has been living in Paris for seven years with his wife, the beautiful patronne of a second-rate hotel. When the film opens, the wife has just committed suicide and Paul is coolly setting up an apartment with a girl whose name he does not want to know, whose feelings he does not want to hear, for afternoons of pure, absolutely free sexual encounters.

•

A most willing partner (and victim) is Jeanne (Maria Schneider), a pretty, comically independent girl who, on her hours off, returns to her mother, the widow of an Army colonel, and to her fiancé (Jean-Pierre Léaud). The latter is a movie nut in the process of starring Jeanne in a cinéma vérité film.

The center of the film is composed of the extraordinary Paul-Jeanne encounter sessions, during which she, at first, demands to know more about him, after which the tables slowly turn. Little by little Paul reveals himself as the widower of a woman he loved in spite of her other lovers, freely admitted and even discussed.

"Last Tango in Paris" is most affecting when it's most ambiguous, cross-breeding tragic melodrama with elegant satire. When, eventually, Paul tries to explain himself, and the despair that drove him into the affair with the girl, the movie goes so surprisingly banal that not even Bertolucci's magnificently rich physical production, or Brando's courageous performance can make it seem as important as we want it to be.

I use the word courageous carefully. For Brando, like Bertolucci, has pulled out all the stops without fear of looking absurd, as when, toward the end, he runs drunkenly through a proper Paris dance hall pursuing the frightened girl, whom he has admitted to himself he now loves.

Bertolucci's courage is expressed in his undertaking a film of such poetic ambitions and being as successful as he has been. After the success of the comparatively conventional "The Conformist," he might easily have preferred to play it safe. He hasn't. He has made a film that, on one viewing, leaves me somewhat cool—and determined to see it again.

Bernardo Bertolucci's "Last Tango in Paris" is a beautiful, courageous, foolish, romantic and reckless film and Bertolucci is like a diving champion, drunk on enthusiasm, who dares dive from the high board knowing well that the pool is half empty. The stunt comes off, but the dive is less grand than we might expect from what we've heard and read, and especially from what we know of Bertolucci. I mention this at the outset because the film is being so overpraised (and overpriced) that many disappointed people may be reluctant to indulge its failures, thus to miss its achievements, which are considerable.

"Last Tango in Paris" is the movie romance of the 1970's, at least of that portion of the 1970's we have seen so far. It carries its ideas of love and sexuality not to the limits of conceivable time, but to the limits of last year —the era of Norman Mailer, Germaine Greer, "J," airplane goggles, porno films and revolutionary semantics. It's not the film's boldness that shocks, amuses and fascinates us, but its topicality.

It's what in the 1960s (a decade not great for jargon) would have been called, lamely, a Now film. It's so Now, in fact, that you better see it quickly. I suspect that its ideas, as well as its ability to shock or, apparently, to arouse, will age quickly. This is not true, I think, of the superlative production by Bertolucci, nor of the extraordinary performance by Marlon Brando who plays a role that does not simply identify him with his own time, as did his roles in "A Streetcar Named Desire" in the 1940's and "On the Waterfront" in the 1950's. It also makes him a Pop spokesman, tough, irreverent mocking, as well as an incurable sentimentalist.

•

The finest things about "Last Tango in Paris" are the set scenes, riotous, furious, frenzied celebrations of the differences between men and women. Oddly enough, I found them more funny, occasionally more embarrassing, even more philosophical, than erotic. The intensity of Brando's anger and humor, and the desperation with which he sets out to insulate himself from the world through this affair, are very special to behold. His language—crude, witty, magnificently vulgar —and the stories that tumble out in the form of random monologues are unlike anything we've ever heard on the screen before. It sounds tough as hell, which explains, I think, why the film's full-blown, almost old-fashioned romanticism goes unnoticed. In spite of all the simulated sex, everything in the film is touched by exotic fancy.

The look of the film, too, is pure romance — lots of dusky, autumnal golds and blue-grays, long, graceful camera movements, scenes shot through frosted glass or against fractured mirrors, and a soundtrack that carries music on the order of a high-class, though not classical, Muzak. When Bertolucci scores one of Paul and Jeanne's encounters with what sounds like a Hawaiian love song, you know he must be kidding. Or is he? I don't think he is.

The film's revealed mysteries let us down. They aren't grand enough for violence and humiliation and the intimacies we've been asked to share until then. Behind the raised consciousness of "Last Tango in Paris" there's a little bit of the simplistic foolishness of "Love Story," which people thought was old-fashioned but was topical enough to make a zillion dollars. "Last Tango," touted as something completely new, will, I predict, make a zillion dollars for the very same reason.

1973 F 2, 20:1

A GROUP OF EXPERIMENTAL FILMS: ICE by J. J. Murphy, 9 minutes; IN PROGRESS, by J. J. Murphy and Ed Small, 20 minutes; ASPECTS OF THE HILL PART I: THE HILL by Naomi Levine, 12 minutes; PROJECT ONE (OP PRINTER) by Dave Lourie, 14 minutes; MR. PELICAN (OP PRINTER) by Robert Lange, 16 minutes; THE REPEATER by Stacy Keach, 17 minutes. At the Film Forum 256 West 88th Street.

By ROGER GREENSPUN

All the short movies in the program that opened yesterday at the Film Forum make some gesture toward elaborating concepts implicit in the nature of film, concepts having to do with its existence in time and the quality of its images. Some of the elaborations are ambitious indeed. It is, therefore, ironic that at least in this instance, simplest is best—not through any sacred esthetic prohibition against fooling around with film, but because J. J. Murphy's and Ed Small's "In Progress" is the loveliest, most idiomatic, most responsive work in the program.

"In Progress" is a 20-minute time-lapse movie recording the passage of the days and seasons from September through May on a bit of landscape photographed on an Iowa farm. The camera doesn't move (though there are two or three slightly different locations) and it is so nearly passive that at one point frost is allowed to form on its lens, and at another the dew turns its image into a glamorous haze. "In Progress" really proves nothing except that it has a subject worth sustained contemplation. The film provides an access to such contemplation, and its beauty—including its ravishing variations of color within the natural blues and greens, grays, blacks, whites and reddish browns — is in large part the beauty of the subject in view.

Stacy Keach's almost one-man show (written, directed and acted by, though Judy Collins sings and collaborated in writing the song on the soundtrack) has previously been shown on television. A combination of fictional narrative and poetic documentary about being in prison, it exploits certain editing techniques, mainly to break up the screen into pointedly expressive kinds of space. I think it is an awful movie, affected, needlessly fancy, full of poses instead of perceptions.

Each of the remaining films —J. J. Murphy's "Ice," Naomi Levine's "Aspects of the Hill Part I," David Lourie's "Project One," and Robert Lange's "Mr. Pelican" — offers rewards, and yet none of the rewards seem quite to validate the ingenuity or effort put into making the movie. "Ice" is a film rephotographed through a slab of ice, so as to emerge as a source of colors and patterns of pulsating light.

Both the Lange and Lourie films were made with an optical printer (another, highly flexible means of rephotographing a movie), and both achieve the look of grainy instant profundity that seems the hallmark of optically printed film. I like the effect better in the dramatic context of "Project One" than in the West Coast seascape of "Mr. Pelican," but both movies deserve a second look.

"Aspects of the Hill Part I," subtitled "The Hill," is at its best when it is about a hill, or a couple of trees, or a lot of people flying kites. And it is at the worst when it imposes on these images a soundtrack consisting of experimental questions and non-answers. In making it, Naomi Levine has raised some problems about the relations between film and feeling, but she has not begun to settle them.

1973 F 3, 19:1

JUNK IN JANUARY

By VINCENT CANBY

JANUARY is the month for wallflower movies, for things that couldn't obtain bookings during the usually profitable Christmas-New Year's week. They often are films that have been hanging around for a while, sometimes for years. It may not be true, but I have the feeling that no film ever really opens in January. It suddenly shows up—like a bill. The following is a consumer's guide to last month's films, some of which may still be playing. These are not all of January's films by any means, but those that I remember for one reason or another, in no special order of importance or pique:

"Dr. Phibes Rises Again." If you saw the original rise of Dr. Phibes in "The Abominable Dr. Phibes," you know that he is a seedy old vaudevillian (Vincent Price) who goes mad after an automobile accident that leaves his wife beautiful but dead and the doctor disfigured but alive. Even if you didn't see the first film, you'll soon know that because a large chunk of the sequel is devoted to recapitulating these facts in the breathless manner of old movie serials. The new film, which opened as a supporting feature to "Blacula," follows Dr. Phibes to Egypt in the company of the body of his wife and the body of his slave, Vulnavia, who acts like a girl trained by Bobby Clark. She not only can cook, get ship reservations and tune the doctor's voice box (he has no larynx), she is lovely and unflappable. The movie, about a search for an ancient Egyptian Geritol formula, displays a good deal of wit in its amused affection for awful movie styles of the 1930's.

"The Flavor of Green Tea Over Rice." One doesn't exactly leap out of bed at seven and knock over little old ladies at eight to be the first in line to see a new (in this country) Ozu film. One goes gradually, as to a chiropodist late in the afternoon, after the film's been running a while, perhaps in the second or third week. Ozu films don't tease you into seeing them. They're like Siamese cats: they pretend not to care and then demand complete attention. "The Flavor of Green Tea Over Rice," made in 1952, the year before "Tokyo Story," is, in outline, a formula domestic comedy about a middle-class, middle-aged marriage going on the rocks, just as the husband's about to fly to Uruguay (Uruguay? yes) on business. In Ozu's care, the story becomes surprisingly heroic and sad, not because anything dreadful happens but because everyone seems to grow resigned with such self-awareness and little fuss. You have to get in sync with "The Flavor of Green Tea." Ozu shows us so many things in every frame that unless you're willing to look, you might as well forget it. Not great Ozu, but very good. In Japanese with English subtitles.

*

"Little Mother." This is Radley Metzger's handsome-looking, not-quite-sexposé of the lives and loves of Eva Perón, called Marina Pinares by his screenwriter, Brian Phelan. The script is bad but the production looks great, especially Christiane Kruger (Hardy Kruger's daughter) who displays a good deal more class than the real-life character ever did—maybe too much. Metzger shot the film in Zagreb, which is a long way from Buenos Aires, and the odd part about it is that the settings work. The film also works to the extent that it sent me burrowing through two different biographies of Eva Perón to try to find out what Phelan had made up, oversimplified or ignored. A fascinating film is still there, somewhere.

"The First Circle." A sincere child's introduction to the novel by the Nobel Prize-winning Soviet author? Not at all. It was written and directed by 64-year-old Aleksander Ford, the highly regarded Polish Communist filmmaker who worked in Russia during World War II, more or less founded the Communist film industry in Poland after the war, and left his country in 1968 in protest against the rising anti-Semitism. The Solzhenitsyn novel is long, passionate, complex and stirring. The movie is short, simple and dull, badly acted by a Scandinavian cast who speak (in dubbed American) lines that are, at best, synopses of ideas and feelings. It was photographed in Denmark in a style so unimaginative and artificial that even real snow looks fake. It probably wouldn't be worth worrying about except that it's likely to turn off some people who haven't yet gotten to Solzhenitsyn.

*

"Under Milk Wood." Text by Dylan Thomas. Pictures (direction, that is), by Andrew Sinclair. Acted by Richard Burton, Peter O'Toole, Elizabeth Taylor, Glynis Johns, Sian Phillips, Vivien Merchant, Victor Spinetti and a large number of Welshmen, mostly quite well. Thomas's robust, sentimental, plotless recollection of a night and a day in the continuum of a tiny Welsh seaport needs conventional pictures the way Times Square needs voice-over narration. Sometimes the film reaches a kind of accord with the text, so that you can still, at least, hear the words. Mostly the images interrupt the text. It's quite difficult to listen to what's being said when you're trying to figure out how Miss Taylor, impersonating a small-town Welsh whore, applies all that eye shadow. With a brush? A spray gun? With her left foot? Then, too, there are odd additions to the text by Sinclair, including a sequence in which Burton and Ryan Davies, as the film's two narrator-tour guides, have their way with a girl who is supposed to be another of the port's easiest marks, though from her clothes and style she looks more like a London model whose Jaguar broke down en route to a castle for a weekend. Buy a recording, if there is one, and if you have to.

*

"Limbo." Mark Robson, the director ("Champion," "Home of The Brave," "Peyton Place," "Valley of the Dolls," etc.), tore this one from the headlines, says a publicity release on behalf of a drama about the problems facing the wives of American servicemen who are either missing in action in Vietnam, or prisoners of war. After tearing it from the headlines, he and his writers seem to have studied World War II movies for clichés that have little or no relation to what the Vietnam war has meant to the American people. Robson, one feels, is outraged by the war but too polite to say so. Everything about the movie recalls a simpler, sweeter time—the casting of types, the sunny color photography, even the music. When one of Robson's Viet wives is feeling sentimental about her marriage, she listens to Jo Stafford. Jo Stafford, for heaven's sake! If I remember correctly, she's on the original soundtrack recording of the Mindoro invasion.

January was not a completely forgettable month, though. New York got a new, small (200-seat), first-run theater whose stated policy is to present off-beat American films and not easily exploitable foreign films for engagements limited to one-week each. Of the two films I've seen to date, one (Stefan Uher's Czechoslovak "If I Had A Gun") was very pleasant and unassuming and the other (Michael Nebbia's independent American film, "Life Study") was not-so-hot. The policy is a good one and I hope it can be supported, by the films as well as by the public. The house is small, functional and comfortable. It's called the First Avenue Screening Room and is at 61st Street.

1973 F 4, II:1:6

The Cast

THE WORLD'S GREATEST ATHLETE, directed by Robert Scheerer; written by Gerald Gardner and Dee Caruso; director of photography, Frank Phillips; film editor, Cotton Warburton; music, Marvin Hamlisch; produced by Bill Walsh; presented by Walt Disney Productions and released by Buena Vista Distribution Company Inc. At Radio City Music Hall, Avenue of the Americas and 50th Street. Running time: 92 minutes. This film has been classified G.

Coach Archer	John Amos
Nanu	Jan-Michael Vincent
Gazenga	Roscoe Lee Browne
Milo	Tim Conway
Jane	Dayle Haddon
Landlady	Nancy Walker
Maxwell	Billy DeWolfe
Leopold	Danny Goldman

By A. H. WEILER

"Life is not so simple. You have got to make the dream happen," says John Amos, the black college coach in "The World's Greatest Athlete," in a serious moment during a series of concocted competitions in which he is a loser. Well, the dream does happen in this farce, which has landed at the Radio City Music Hall, fresh from Walt Disney's dream factory. But it's a dream that is more often simple-minded than simple and generally as hilarious as finishing fourth in the mile run.

It should be stressed, however, that this ribbing of the Tarzan myth runs a good, clean course that should grab all red-blooded sports fans up to and including the 14-year-old group. It might be added that everyone—from coach Amos to Jan-Michael Vincent, in the title role, athletically tries without much success to make all this good-natured nonsense funny.

One gets the feeling very soon that all concerned are involved in what appears a series of random gag situations. The athletes of Merrivale College depicted here can't avoid tripping over their own feet, which, for no convincing reason, drives our coach to go on an African safari. There he discovers the answer to his dream. And that is Jan-Michael Vincent, as the young, long-haired, blond, muscular Nanu, orphan son of missionaries, who may speak only pidgin English but can run, jump and throw like Jim Thorpe.

There are many extracurricular complications, of course, such as Nanu's pet tiger and Roscoe Lee Browne, who plays Nanu's suspicious, Zambian witch doctor-godfather. Both show up at Merrivale. Tim Conway, as the fatheaded assistant coach, is momentarily turned into a tiny Tim by the angered witch doctor. And then there is Dayle Haddon, the pretty tutor, who adds romance to the course.

As Merrivale's one-man team, Nanu sets records in everything from the 100-yard dash to the pole vault. However, Mr. Vincent and the rest of the cast good-naturedly do their things with speed but little discernible style, all under the uninspired direction of Robert Scheerer.

Mr. Vincent, although laconic, is a handsome figure of an athlete. His coach, Mr. Amos, is spirited and willing and gives the impression that he knows he's kidding, while Mr. Conway as his assistant is properly energetic and woebegone but not really funny. Even Howard Cosell makes a guest appearance, joshing his own, authentic verbose delivery as a sports broadcaster.

"It's kind of hard saying good-by to 'The World's Greatest Athlete,'" coach Amos intones when our hero finally decides to return to Zambia. But it isn't, really.

1973 F 5, 25:1

Burt Kennedy Western Keeps It Traditional

By ROGER GREENSPUN

If tone and attitude were enough to sustain a movie, then Burt Kennedy's "The

John Wayne and Ann-Margret

The Casts

THE TRAIN ROBBERS, directed and written by Burt Kennedy; director of photography, William H. Clothier; film editor, Frank Santillo; music by Dominic Frontiere; produced by Michael Wayne; released by Warner Bros. At the Criterion Theater, Broadway at 45th Street and neighborhood theaters. Running time: 92 minutes. This film is classified PG.

Lane ....John Wayne
Mrs. Lowe ....Ann-Margaret
Grady ....Rod Taylor
Jesse ....Ben Johnson
Calhoun ....Christopher George
Ben Young................Bobby Vinton
Sam Turner...............Jerry Gatlin
Pinkerton Man........Ricardo Montalban

Train Robbers," which opened yesterday at neighborhood theaters, would rank among the best-sustained movies in recent months. Except for a bitter, unnecessary, and rather stupid plot twist at the end, it is so full of understanding, fellowship and reconciliation, that the air of good feeling pervading it almost seems sufficient reason for its being.

I don't think that tone and attitude are quite enough to sustain a movie, or that an air of good feeling can take the place of meaningful dramatic action. But as an exercise in pleasantness, "The Train Robbers" is an interesting addition to the late history of the traditional unpretentious Western.

At this stage, at least in the Burt Kennedy films ("Hannie Caulder" is a recent, also very interesting, example), the Western takes place in the West—not a place really, but a few buildings and much countryside occupying a state of mind.

John Wayne and some long-time buddies — notably Ben Johnson and Rod Taylor —band together to help Ann-Margret, a voluptuous, hard-drinking but virtuous widow, recover the half-million dollars worth of gold that her husband, a burglar, long ago stole and then hid in some Mexican desert. Only she

knows where. The object isn't the gold; it's the $50,000 reward money and also a chance that Ann-Margret's little son can preserve his honor among his playmates in grammar school.

You may begin to see what I mean by good feeling. The feeling is enhanced by the companionship, the growing intimacy and trust within the little band. And it is intensified from without by a menacing group of hard-riding horsemen, also after the gold, and by a mysterious stranger (Ricardo Montalban) who observes everything from the sidelines, like a nonsensical ironic fate.

The turns of the story are mostly predictable and not very important. But the turns of conversation among the friends around the campfire are full of good memory and decent conviction, and it is for this that "The Train Robbers" seems to exist.

The cast is for the most part quite lovely, led by a gentle Wayne, too old for romance but not for regrets, and well supported, most happily for me, in fine restrained performances by Ben Johnson and Rod Taylor.

1973 F 8, 36:3

CARRY ON DOCTOR, directed by Gerald Thomas; screenplay by Talbot Rothwell; produced by Peter Rogers; released by American International Pictures. At neighborhood theaters. Running time: 95 minutes. This film is classified PG.

Francis Bigger ....Frankie Howerd
Charlie Roper ....Sidney James
Doctor Tinkle ....Kenneth Williams
Mr. Barron ....Charles Hawtrey
Doctor Kilmore ....Jim Dale
Sandra May ....Barbara Windsor
The Matron ....Hattie Jacques
Chloe Gibson ....Joan Sims
Nurse Clark ....Anita Harris
Mavis Winkle ....Dilys Laye

I can't wholly resist a movie comedy that comes billed as "the greatest medical discovery since laughing gas," or one that has characters with names like Doctor Tinkle and Mavis Winkle, or that takes the plunge into sexual innuendo with exchanges like:

"I dreamt about you last night, nurse."

"Did you?"

"No, you wouldn't let me!"

This isn't to say that "Carry on Doctor," which opened yesterday at neighborhood theaters, isn't pretty resistible. It is rather a matter of how you happen to feel today about the tradition of noisily overstated British humor to which it belongs. Today, I feel unresistant.

"Carry on Doctor" is one of a series of British comedies ("Carry on Camping" was the last I saw here) directed by Gerald Thomas and featuring more or less a single cast playing different roles from film to film but occupying, if you will, the same existential situations.

Thus Kenneth Williams (Dr. Tinkle) is forever the

oily villain aided by the enormous Hattie Jacques (The Matron) who at some point will let her hair down and slip into something more comfortable and, much to her leader's disgust, declare her love for him.

The appetites and irritations of Frankie Howerd and Sidney James (here, a couple of hospital patients) will remain unchanged no matter what their ages, as immutable as the uplift to Barbara Windsor's (Nurse Sandra May's) bosom.

In the hospital their manner is no different from anywhere else. And their comic acting style—a kind of fast burn twice repeated—loses no emphasis and gains no subtleties. Of course the hospital's chief surgeon has St. Vitus's dance, and of course the principal items of medical equipment are the bedpan and the urine bottle.

There is nothing in the arsenal of mere movie criticism to combat this, and any mere movie critic would be an idiot to try. Furthermore, I find I rather like the plucky attachment of Nurse Clark to the resident Dr. Kilmore, and the clumsy middle-aged romance across the wards between Ken Biddle and Mavis Winkle.

ROGER GREENSPUN.

1973 F 8, 36:3

The Cast

BLACK CAESAR, directed, written and produced by Larry Cohen; director of photography, Fenton Hamilton; film editor, George Folsey, Jr.; music by James Brown; released by American International Pictures. At the Cinerama Theater, Broadway at 47th Street, the RKO 59th Street Twin 2 Theater, east of Third Avenue and the 86th Street Twin 2, west of Lexington Avenue. Running time: 92 minutes. This film is classified R.

Tommy Gibbs ....Fred Williamson
Joe Washington ....Phillip Roye
Helen ....Gloria Hendry
Mr. Gibbs ....Julius W. Harris
Cardoza ....Val Avery
Mama Gibbs ....Minnie Gentry
John McKinney ....Art Lund
Rev. Rufus ....D'Urville Martin
Alfred Coleman ....William Wellman Jr.

"I'm trying to break into the business at the top," a smiling assured Fred Williamson says before becoming the "Black Caesar," who crashed into the Cinerama and other theaters yesterday. Despite the fact that he reaches the top temporarily and given the film's lip-service to social injustices, this "Black Caesar" is essentially black bad guys against white bad guys in gory warfare that evolves more as exploitation than as clear, convincing exposition of man's inhumanity to man.

One can't avoid the feeling that Larry Cohen, the writer-director-producer, has stacked his melodrama largely for black machismo and constant carnage. As a youngster, our hero is already working for Harlem gangsters and venial white cops, one of whom maims him. So, before you can utter one of the many

pithy epithets used in the script, he is grown up, wise in the ways of the white underworld and blasting away at the Mafia-like type on his way to the top.

Our man, of course, snatches the books of the syndicate, which gives him the power he needs. And, of course, there's blighted romance with Gloria Hendry, a sultry nightclub singer, and confrontations with his heartsick mother (Minnie Gentry) as her estranged husband (Julius W. Harris) before the mob starts striking back.

Mr. Williamson, who led the slave revolt in the recent "The Legend of Nigger Charley," this time is equally imposing, tough and unflappable—if not as dignified—as the "Black Caesar," who seems to be subject to some of the shocks as well as the fate of the original Caesar. And the performances are as obvious as the program blurb which proclaims him "the cat with the .45 caliber claws."

He's plagued, for example, by Art Lund, as the blatantly bad cop who gave him his first traumas and now, as the Commissioner and still gangland's pal, plots his downfall. Miss Hendry, as his girl, falls in love with his best friend (Michael Jeffrey) and is forced to set him up for the kill. And, as noted, Mama and Papa don't like him either.

Mr. Williamson, in short, can't be blamed for the plot contrivances that hinge mostly on action and bloodshed. "Black Caesar" may have been shot in fine colors in Harlem and elsewhere but its bullet-filled contents are unrelievedly black and white.

A. H. WEILER.

1973 F 8, 36:3

BARON BLOOD, directed by Mario Bava; written by Vincent G. Fotre; music by Les Baxter; produced by Alfred Leone; released by American International Pictures. At neighborhood theaters. Running time: 90 minutes. This film is classified PG.

Alfred Becker ....Joseph Cotten
Eva Arnold ....Elke Sommer
Karl Hummel ....Massimo Girotti
Peter Kleist ....Antonio Cantafora
Fritz ....Alan Collins
Police Inspector ....Humi Raho
Christine Hoffman ....Rada Rassimov
Herr Dortmundt ....Dieter Tressler

There's more to Austria than gemütlichkeit and Mozart. There's also "Baron Blood," one of the dual horror entries that alit at local houses yesterday to illustrate that a flight to Austria isn't absolutely necessary.

The "Baron," in short, is a dastard who'd been cursed into haunting his Devil's Castle by a witch he immolated 300 years before. And when resurrected, somewhat witlessly by his handsome, contemporary descendant, Antonio Cantafora, with the reluctant aid of the local, gorgeous castle expert, Elke Sommer, the ghostly hob he raises is mostly ersatz.

The revived "Baron" seems to be suffering from terminal

leprosy and bleeding and is good for a mild shock or two. But when he appears in the guise of a seemingly crippled tycoon who buys the castle, he's only a bland, avuncular villain as played by Joseph Cotten.

Under Mario Bava's pedestrian direction, the concocted creaking, screaming, gory murders and Miss Sommer's frightened racing through dark passageways largely add up to spectral schlock.

A. H. WEILER.

1973 F 8, 36:3

The Cast

PULP, directed and written by Michael Hodges; director of photography, Ousama Rawi; editor John Glenn; producer, Michael Klinger; released by United Artists Corporation. At the First Avenue Screening Room, at 60th Street. Running time: 96 minutes. This film is classified PG.

Mickey King	Michael Caine
Preston Gilbert	Mickey Rooney
Ben Dinuccio	Lionel Stander
Princess Betty Cippola	Lizabeth Scott
Liz Adams	Nadia Cassini
Miller	Al Lettieri
A Mysterious Englishman	Dennis Price

By ROGER GREENSPUN

I know I'm wrong, but it feels as if every week for the last six months at least one new imitation private-eye movie has opened in New York City. They all haven't been awful. But I don't see what the profit is (except for the profit from salable nostalgia) in parodying a genre that more or less lived by grace of self-parody even in the classical noon of its warmest heyday.

There is certainly not much profit, even at this stage of the nostalgia business, in making an actor up like Humphrey Bogart and giving him a bit movie role in which he must ask what that bird is ("It's a Maltese Falcon"). And yet that is typical of what happens in Michael Hodges's "Pulp," which opened yesterday at the First Avenue Screening Room.

•

"Pulp" pits Mickey King (a bit up from Sam Spade?), writer of dirty novels, against a determined band of rich sportsmen who will stop at nothing, even murder, to keep him from ghost-writing the incriminating autobiography of one Preston Gilbert, former movie star, ex-Mafia man, currently living in raucous seclusion with his mother, his mistress and his bodyguard on the island of Malta.

The plot, which is somewhat better than the movie it occupies, is full of incredible complications and clever conceits—like an international hired gunman who between hits teaches literature at Berkeley. But it is also a plot that is painfully aware of its origins, all its origins, perhaps on the assumption that anything is better if you can guess where it came from.

You can guess where most everything comes from: the cast—Mickey Rooney, Lionel Stander, Lizabeth Scott — partly out of the nineteen-thirties and forties; the characters — imitation Bogart, Cagney, and the like—out of those pop-culture objects now made icons; the moods and tensions, out of the collective depths of the film *noir*. But all this is better recollected, or revived, not reworked. And "Pulp" has no very interesting passions to match its ideas or its several dozen memories. For all its intricacy, intrigue and physical action, it is a curiously detached—almost somnolent—movie.

•

There is nothing really in the performance of Michael Caine, as Mickey King, to dispel the drowsiness, and nothing much in the deliberate, often intentionally gimmicky, direction of Hodges. I suspect that this is a very personal project for Hodges (previously responsible for "Get Carter"), but his personality seems to have been engaged only in disparate parts.

Much of the soundtrack for "Pulp" is given over to King's interior monologue, full of color of the "He had eyes like bloodshot oysters" variety. But by some cruel trick of electronic reproduction, all the other voices are weak, unresonant, difficult to hear —as if picked up by a soundman working across the street, on somebody else's movie.

1973 F 9, 32:1

The Cast

THE HARDER THEY COME, directed by Perry Henzell; screenplay by Mr. Henzell and Trevor D. Rhone; editor, John Victor Smith; photography, Peter Jassop, David McDonald and Franklin St. Juste; produced by Mr. Henzell; released by New World Pictures, Inc. At the New Embassy Theater, 46th Street and Broadway. Running time: 93 minutes. This film is classified R.

Ivan	Jimmy Cliff
Elsa	Janet Barkley
Jose	Carl Bradshaw
Pedro	Ras Daniel Hartman
Hilton	Bobby Charlton
Detective	Winston Stona
Preacher	Basil Keane

By A. H. WEILER

Reported to be the first feature filmed by Jamaicans in Jamaica, "The Harder They Come," which landed at the Embassy yesterday, is striking proof that a good many of the natives are far removed from the carefree vacationer's sun, surf and daiquiris. If it isn't particularly polished in its acting or melodrama, this focus on an aspiring young black singer's short, unhappy life seems as honest as its depiction of the seamier practices of some of the islanders. The authentic settings in Kingston and its environs have been captured in the vivid colors dear to visitors.

•

Perry Henzell, the 36-year-old, white producer-director-co-scenarist and a professional in the commercial and documentary film fields, has achieved a sort of cinéma vérité approach to his story. The film deals with a country boy who is hurt by the minister he works for, the producer of his first and only hit record and the marijuana traffickers who hustle him until, in desperation, he becomes a gunslinger who ends up as a martyred folk hero.

It must be stressed that the film is not all that grim. The heavily accented dialogue, while technically English, is, on most occasions, tough to follow, and Mr. Henzell and company helpfully have provided copious English subtitles, which amusingly makes this one of the rare, if not the first of English-language films with English subtitles.

Jimmy Cliff, a noted exponent of the native rock-like Reggae music, is natural and energetic in his movie debut as the ill-starred singer-gunman. And, naturally, he makes good use of his talents with the titular song, as do others with the supersyncopated Jamaican rhythms and spirituals of the film's score.

•

Credit for equally unvarnished portrayals should go to Janet Berkley, as a minister's ward who loves him; Ras Daniel Hartman and Carl Bradshaw, as marijuana dealers; Bobby Charlton, as the graspingly tough record tycoon, and Winston Stona, as a detective in cahoots with the "grass" traders.

The largely amateur cast of black performers and their producer-director may be involved in basically simple action fare in "The Harder They Come," but they also leave a slightly disturbing, documentary impression of the darker side of the sunny Jamaica.

1973 F 9, 32:3

SNOWBALL EXPRESS, screen play by Don Tait, Jim Parker and Arnold Margolin, based on "Chateau Bon Vivant," by Frankie and John O'Rear; directed by Norman Tokar; produced by Ron Miller for Walt Disney Productions; presented by Buena Vista. At neighborhood theaters. Running time: 84 minutes. (This film is rated G.)

Johnny Baxter	Dean Jones
Sue Baxter	Nancy Olson
Jesse McCord	Harry Morgan
Mr. Ridgeway	Keenan Wynn
Chris Baxter	Kathleen Cody
Richard Baxter	Johnny Whitaker
Wally Perkins	Michael McGreevey
Miss Wigginton	Mary Wickes

What could be more square —or welcome—at the moment than a pleasant Disney movie, the old-fashioned, family kind? "Snowball Express" fills the bill very nicely. What it lacks in wit it has in wholesome, hearty chuckles. Add to this some nice, snowy backgrounds and slope activity in the Colorado ski country.

Last but not least, it has a genuinely winning little family front and center, including Dean Jones, Nancy Olson (as Papa and Mama), Kathleen Cody and little Johnny Whitaker. They're New Yorkers who pull up stakes, head west and turn an old Gothic mansion that they inherited into a bustling ski lodge.

•

There are few surprises, including maintenance problems, a helpful old miner (Harry Morgan), a wily banker (Keenan Wynn) and plenty of broad, pratfall gags involving the business of skiing (obviously using experts).

There is a picturesque climax of a snowmobile race that would have been more impressive minus the cliff-hanging gags. But the pacing is generally easy, under Norman Tokar's direction, and the playing is genial. That old darling, Mary Wickes, finally comes to the rescue of the Baxter family like the cavalry.

As for the four charming Baxters themselves, you can't beat a family like this. The new picture, which opened Wednesday in neighborhood theaters, is double-billed with a revival of the animated "Lady and the Tramp," an old Disney delight. Anybody interested in family entertainment?

HOWARD THOMPSON

1973 F 9, 32:3

The Program

EMITAI, directed and written by Ousmane Sembene, in Wolloff, an African language, with English subtitles; photography by Michel Remaudeau; editor, Gilbert Kiboine; produced by Paulin Soumanou Vieya; released by New Yorker Films. At the Fifth Avenue Cinema, at 12th Street. Running time: 103 minutes. This film has not been classified.

With: Ibou Camara, Ousmane Camara, Joseph Diatta, Dji Niassebanor, Sibesalang, Kalifa as the villagers; Robert Fontaine as the Commandant; Michel Renaudeau as the Lieutenant, and Pierre Blanchard as the Colonel.

By ROGER GREENSPUN

All the feature films of Ousmane Sembene have opened locally, generally to quite favorable reviews, and yet I doubt that he is known to more than a handful of the most devoted and adventurous moviegoers. The reason isn't far to seek. Sembene —50 years old and a novelist as well as a film maker—is Senegalese, and Senegal is his subject. You look for Senegal in the National Geographic, not in a movie theater. Or if you do look for it in a movie theater, you expect danger, ritual sacrifice, tom-toms, faces hidden in the treetops—the traditional matter of darkest Africa.

"Emitai," Sembene's latest movie, has all that — the ritual sacrifice, the tom-toms, the danger—but with the difference that it approaches everything from the point of view of the faces hidden in the treetops. At one point in "Emitai," native warriors ambush a small detachment of French colonial troops (also natives), and the absolute ineffectualness of massed spears against a few well-placed rifles should lay to rest the memories of a good many delicious terrors during Saturday afternoons at the movies.

The film takes place near the beginning of World War II, and the troops have been sent to seize 50 tons of harvested rice in a little village from which they have already impressed the able-bodied young men—to serve in the army of Marshal Petain.

The villagers don't exactly need the rice; it is to be used in religious ceremonies, not for sustenance. And the French don't really need it either. Halfway through the movie, deGaulle replaces Petain, the above-ground battles are ended, and so is the demand for overseas food. But everyone remains inflexible, and the story of "Emitai" continues to a fatal standoff in its bitter conclusion.

I don't mean to suggest that Sembene doesn't take sides; he does, and of course he is not pro-French. But his stronger interest is in the life of the village; in the difficult, slightly hostile, relations between the men (who conduct the ceremonies) and the women (who seem to do the work); and in the relations between the men and the gods, who sometimes appear when summoned and sometimes don't, who generally give their worshipers a hard time, and who generally are given a hard time in return.

Just before the village chief dies—from French rifle wounds — he utterly renounces the gods, wherupon he is gotten up for a marvelous funeral, so he may rest with them in eternity. This juxtaposition is typical of the spirit "Emitai."

•

It is a cool, balanced, proportionate spirit, affectionate but unillusioned, and wonderfully suited to the intricacies (and the idiosyncracies) of the subject matter. Sembene does not grab you; he engages you. Much of the time he photographs his action in the middle distance —not for the sake of distance but for the sake of an inclusiveness that keeps surprising you with its ironic sophistication.

"Emitai" isn't a very complicated movie—in the abstract, little more than a tragic vignette. But for its purposes it is very complete; and considerate of the puzzles faced by its gods, its victims and its killers.

"Emitai" opened yesterday at the Fifth Avenue Cinema.

1973 F 10, 22:1

The Cast

LADY CAROLINE LAMB, written and directed by Robert Bolt; director of photography, Oswald Morris; music by Richard Rodney Bennett; produced by Fernando Ghia; released by United Artists Corporation. At the Fine Arts Theater, 58th Street between Park and Lexington Avenues. Running time: 123 minutes.

Lady Caroline Lamb	Sara Miles
William Lamb	Jon Finch
Lord Byron	Richard Chamberlain
Canning	John Mills
Lady Melbourne	Margaret Leighton
Lady Bessborough	Pamela Brown
Miss Milbanke	Silvia Monti
George IV	Ralph Richardson
Duke of Wellington	Laurence Olivier

By ROGER GREENSPUN

In 1812, in the midst of the extraordinary success of "Childe Harold," Lady Caroline, wife of William Lamb, Lord Melbourne, met and promptly fell in love with the poem's author, Lord Byron. At first excited and later embarassed by the indiscreet ardor of the flamboyant Caroline, Byron found his own passions waning. In 1813, there was a rupture, and in her first novel ("Glenarvon," 1816), she included a satiric portrait of Byron.

But years later, when she encountered the poet's funeral procession, she was mentally affected. She died in 1828, never fully recovered according to some, from the passionate attachment that made her famous.

•

"England expected an affaire," reads the ad copy; "Caroline gave them history." But all the claims for Robert Bolt's new movie to the contrary, it would be fairer to say that England probably expected nothing much, and Caroline at least gave them (in my dictionary) an affair. Robert Bolt gives us a bit of history—that is, he gives us a corner of the National Portrait Gallery, including Canning (John Mills), George IV (Ralph Richardson) and the Duke of Wellington (Laurence Olivier, in one of his noses). And he also gives some of that intimate historical wisdom on which he has so auspiciously built a career: "I am not a fool of history," says Wellington.

"Napoleon was," answers Caroline (she has gone to spend the night with him, I mean Wellington, for reasons somewhat obscure).

"I mastered him!"

"You will be remembered for it."

"Thankee." (long pause)

"Napoleon will be remembered for himself"!

In characterizing a film like "Lady Caroline Lamb," I am tempted to go on quoting lines. Let me give in to the temptation:

"He writes like a housewife on the verge of the vapors." (Hostile—male—reaction to Lord Byron).

"He does not mean to write like Alexander Pope!" (Lady Caroline to the defense, neatly mentioning the one poet Byron would in fact mean to write like.)

Despite its intimations of authenticity, "Lady Caroline Lamb" is less fact than fiction, with a plot that reads somewhat more like "Ryan's Daughter" (original screenplay by Robert Bolt) than like the true history of Lady Caroline. This would be perfectly acceptable if it weren't that the story Bolt tells is so much less fascinating than the story he ignores, and if he were able to give his story some form beyond the rhetoric of theatrical phrase-making that reduces the text of the movie to an endless succession of curtain lines.

•

As Lady Caroline, Sarah Miles (Mrs. Robert Bolt) very much looks the part—at least from the one portrait, of Caroline in page's costume, that I have seen. Her pallor is perhaps too waxen, her manner too distracted, but her performance seems to be reaching for a character not realized in the film. Richard Chamberlain is an absurd Byron, but John Finch is a very reticent and feeling William Lamb—forced to do and say many uninteresting things.

Robert Bolt directs (here, for the first time) in the same style in which he writes with the result that every scene, every grouping, every decision behind the camera or at the editing table is immediately effective and ultimately gratuitous. The settings are sumptuous, the costumes lavish, and the productions glossy to a fault. "Lady Caroline Lamb" is to cinema what the coffee-table book is to literature: a heavy but insubstantial irrelevancy. It opened yesterday at the Fine Arts Theater.

1973 F 12, 24:4

The Casts

A REFLECTION OF FEAR, directed by William A. Fraker; screenplay by Edward Hume and Lewis John Carlino, based on "Go to Thy Deathbed" by Stanton Forbes; director of photography, Laszlo Kovacs; film editor, Richard Brockway; music by Fred Myrow; produced by Howard B. Jaffe; released by Columbia Pictures. At neighborhood theaters. Running time: 89 minutes. This film is classified PG.

Michael	Robert Shaw
Anne	Sally Kellerman
Katherine	Mary Ure
Marguerite	Sondra Locke
Julia	Signe Hasso
McKenna	Mitchell Ryan
Hector	Gordon Devol

and

THE CREEPING FLESH, directed by Freddie Francis; screenplay by Peter Spenceley and Jonathan Rumbold; director of photography, Norman Warwick; music by Paul Ferris; editor, Oswald Hafenrichter; produced by Michael Redbourn; released by Columbia Pictures. At neighborhood theaters. Running time: 92 minutes. This film is classified PG.

James Hildern	Christopher Lee
Emmanuel Hildern	Peter Cushing
Penelope	Lorna Heilbron
Waterlow	George Benson
Lenny	Kenneth J. Warren

By ROGER GREENSPUN

With so much celebrated acting talent in front of the camera — Robert Shaw, Mary Ure, Sally Kellerman, Signe Hasso — with Laszlo Kovacs as cinematographer behind the camera, and with a screenplay partly by Lewis John Carlino, one might have expected something good. At the very least, one might have expected a more interesting failure than "A Reflection of Fear," which opened Friday on a double bill in neighborhood theaters.

"A Reflection of Fear" deals with the horror attendant upon a delicate, rich and strange teen-age girl (Sondra Locke) whose secluded life is upset by the arrival of her estranged father (Mr. Shaw), who wants to divorce her mother (Miss Ure) so he can marry his mistress (Miss Kellerman). Horrible things happen — and if you want to guess why, I'll mention that the girl has a deep-voiced friend, a doll named Aaron. "Life," as somebody remarks, minutes before being done in, "is so full of changes."

Sondra Locke has a virtuoso role, and I guess she is impressive, and Sally Kellerman is downright good. But "A Reflection of Fear" has been so ponderously paced and fatally overdecorated (with symbolically "meaningful" decoration) that performances can't count for much. No mere actor is allowed in the way of the crystal or the chinaware. And there is such density of atmospheric haze that half the film looks as if it had been photographed through a jellyfish.

Much more fun, and also pretty fancy, is the second half of the double bill, Freddie Francis's, "The Creeping Flesh." Peter Cushing and Christopher Lee play brothers, scientists, both mad, but one is good and the other bad. There is a scary 3,000-year-old skeleton and some spooky lunacy, but the story mainly has to do with evil, which Christopher Lee has located under a microscope, like a disease germ, and for which he means to develop an antidote.

•

"The Creeping Flesh" thus belongs to the grand tradition of "Doctor, the serum! Thank God, we didn't use it on a human being!" But the doctor has, of course, just pumped quite a lot of it into the right forearm of his beautiful and virtuous young daughter.

1973 F 13, 25:5

The Cast

SAVE THE TIGER, directed by John G. Avildsen; written and produced by Steve Shagan; music scored and conducted by Marvin Hamlisch; director of photography, Jim Crabe; editor, David Bretherton; executive producer, Edward S. Feldman; a Filmways-Jalem-Cirandinha production, distributed by Paramount Pictures. Running time: 100 minutes. At the Tower East Theater, Third Avenue near 72d Street. This film has been classified R.

Harry Stoner	Jack Lemmon
Phil Greene	Jack Gilford
Myra	Laurie Heineman
Fred Mirrell	Norman Burton
Janet Stoner	Patricia Smith
Charlie Robbins	Thayer David
Meyer	William Hansen
Rico	Harvey Jason
Ula	Liv Von Linden
Margo	Lara Parker
Jackie	Eloise Hardt
Dusty	Janina

By VINCENT CANBY

Harry Stoner (Jack Lemmon), a Los Angeles garment manufacturer, lives in a Tudor mansion in Beverly Hills where, in cold dawns, heated swimming pools steam ominously, like tanning vats. He sends his daughter to a Swiss finishing school, drives a limousine equipped with a telephone and has a wife who suggests that he see a certain Dr. Frankfurter to cure his nightmares. "Hypnosis is the thing," she says.

If not hypnosis, Harry is in great need of something, including money. To finance his disintegration into middle age, he juggles the books of Capri Casuals and isn't adverse to acting as a pimp for an important client. "Dammit!" says Harry when the client has a heart attack just before the big fashion show, "we should have gotten the order up front!"

•

In desperation, Harry puts out a contract to burn down one of his factories. The arsonist, a fastidious professional, reassures Harry that he has set 15 major industrial fires in three years and only had five firemen overcome by smoke. "Each received a citation," the arsonist says, adding, "but this is a matter of technology, not morality."

"Save The Tiger," written by Steve Shagan and directed by John G. Avildsen ("Joe," "Cry Uncle"), is not a very good movie but it's a rather brave one, a serious-minded examination of some of the least interesting aspects of the failed American dream. It's not really the sort of thing a producer would expect to make $10-million with.

Although both Mr. Avildsen and Mr. Shagan are aware of how all the people and places should look and sound, their film is relentlessly unmoving, largely, I think, because life for Harry Stoner is less a series of lost confrontations with conscience which might be moving than an inventory of the small affronts that are the consequences of his failures.

Harry feels very badly about all the things he has to do, and people are often quite nasty to him. A parking-lot attendant is rude. Some small boys in the park won't let him play ball with them. He comes to think upon the 1940's as a kind of Golden Age when it was possible to have courage, to affirm moral stances. Harry mourns the oblivion of Lou Gehrig, Joe Penner, Henry Wallace. He loathes monster jets and plastic baseball diamonds.

Harry feels so absolutely rotten, in fact, that "Save The Tiger" seems intentionally to sentimentalize his self-pity, as if that would somehow upgrade the feeling into true passion. It doesn't. It results in a film that is, at heart, as soft as Harry—and as soft as the sequence in which he spends the night with a sweet Sunset Strip waif who tells Harry, among other poetic things: "I saw this piece in National Geographic, about how lions and tigers always return to places of remembered beauty...."

The unfortunate thing is that although people often do talk such nonsense, most solemnly, the movie itself deals in the same kind of sentimentality. In spite of very good performances by Mr. Lemmon, who projects a lightweight bitterness that is a sad fact of homogenized American culture, and by Jack Gilford, who plays Harry Stoner's morally stricken partner, "Save The Tiger" never succeeds in disassociating itself from the self-pity it details. The film opened yesterday at the Tower East.

1973 F 15, 53:1

WATTSTAX, directed by Mel Stuart; cinematography by Roderick Young, Robert Marks, Jose Mignone and Larry Clark; concert photography by John Alonzo, David Blewitt, Robert Grant, Hal Grier, Roy Lewis, Howard Morehead, Joe Walcotts; editors, David Newhouse and David Blewitt; produced by Larry Shaw and Mel Stuart; a Stax Films-Wolper Pictures presentation, distributed by Columbia Pictures. Running time: 102 minutes. At the Criterion Theater, Broadway at 44th Street; Orpheum Theater, 86th Street and Third Avenue, and Columbia I Theater, Second Avenue at 64th Street. This film has been classified R. With: Richard Pryor, The Dramatics, The Staple Singers, Kim Weston, Jimmy Jones, Rance Allen Group, The Emotions, The Bar Keys, Albert King, Little Milton, Johnnie Taylor, Mel and Tim, Carla Thomas, Rufus Thomas, Luther Ingram, Isaac Hayes and others.

By VINCENT CANBY

"Wattstax" is the 102-minute filmed record of the seven-hour concert sponsored in Los Angeles last August by the Stax Organization, a black recording company based in Memphis, and the Schlitz Brewing Company, the (I assume) mostly white manufacturers of the beer that made Milwaukee famous. The concert was the climax of the seventh annual Watts Summer Festival, which marks the Watts riots of 1965.

The proceeds from the $1-a-person ticket sales went to the Sickle Cell Anemia Foundation, the Martin Luther King Hospital in Watts and the budgets of future Watts summer festivals. All of the performers at the concert were Stax employes.

•

I mention these fascinating details because they explain something about the look and feel of the film, which are those of a slick souvenir program rather than of a motion-picture documentary on the order of "Woodstock," a film that assumed the shape of the event recorded. "Wattstax" seems to have evolved the other way around.

I don't mean that the film is in any way fake; it just has the air of something too carefully laid out in advance. It's so busy being glossy and optimistic that it doesn't even allow its performers time to create on screen a measure of the excitement they might have created in person.

More than two dozen solo performers and groups appear on the bandstand in the middle of the Los Angeles Memorial Coliseum, but few of their turns are allowed to build to any sort of emotional climax. Instead, the flim keeps cross-cutting to less-than-incisive interviews with various Watts residents, survivors of the riots and architects of its future, who discuss, among other things, blues (one man says he can get them over his car).

It may be because of this film context that the concert appears to have been a good deal less than exciting, though a number of good performers turn up, including Carla Thomas, the Staple Singers, Johnnie Taylor and Isaac Hayes.

•

The only moments worth noting are provided by Richard Pryor, the actor ("Lady Sings the Blues") and comedian who, apparently, never got near the concert. He is seen in a casual, very funny interview, seemingly shot in a nightclub, talking about his childhood and doing bits and pieces of routines that are both witty and sad, such as the one about the ex-con who fails to get unemployment insurance just because he can't find a job as a license-plate presser.

The rest of the film is prefab. It opened yesterday at the Criterion, Orpheum and Columbia I Theaters.

1973 F 16, 17:1

The Program

A NEW CONSCIOUSNESS: BIRTH FILM by Susan Kleckner (35 minutes); JUDY CHICAGO AND THE CALIFORNIA GIRLS by Judith Dancoff (25 minutes); JOYCE AT 34 by Joyce Chopra and Claudia Weill (29 minutes). At the Whitney Museum of American Art, Madison Avenue and 75th Street.

By ROGER GREENSPUN

"A New Consciousness,' which opened yesterday at the Whitney Museum, is a program of three medium-length documentaries by and about young women actively concerned with the quality of their lives in their families, their homes, their professions—which are by and large the arts. One of the three movies, Susan Kleckner's "Birth Film," wasn't available for my screening (I am assured it will be in the show), but Judith Dancoff's "Judy Chicago and the California Girls" is interesting, and Joyce Chopra's and Claudia Weill's "Joyce at 34" is lovely enough to justify anybody's program of documentary films.

•

The subject of Miss Dancoff's film is a course given at Fresno State College by Judy Chicago (the artist Judy Gerowitz, who changed her name to Judy Chicago), which teaches women the new consciousness partly by means of exaggerated dramatic role-playing. "Will you help me do the dishes?" asks the girl playing the girl. "Help you do the dishes!" shrieks the girl playing the man, who then delivers an explanation of relations between the sexes that has nothing to do with romance.

Miss Chicago's methods are strident—for the purpose of exposing roles as roles—but her manner is good-humored, and her sensibility is quite pleasantly ebullient. She seems nowhere more herself than when arguing against Ti-Grace Atkinson and in favor of a happy marriage, which she happens to have and feels is worth preserving.

Joyce Chopra also has a happy marriage — to the writer Tom Cole—and a profession—as film maker—and she has a baby, right at the beginning of "Joyce at 34." For the next several months she nurses the baby, travels between Boston (her home) and Brooklyn (her parents' home, directs a movie and admits that she loves the first but doesn't want a second baby.

I don't know any of Miss Chopra's films, but I do know some by her co-director, Claudia Weill (bits from "Sesame Street" and a short study called "This is the Home of Mrs. Levant Graham"), and they are very fine, but not as fine as the relaxed, wonderfully revealing clutter of "Joyce at 34." The collaboration has been rich and, I should think, totally satisfying.

•

This is not a feminist film, though clearly aware of feminist positions, but it is a film about people of three generations and many loyalties and ambitions, and many ways of accommodating to life. It sees life as a complex and viable continuum—and that insight is perhaps as close to ecstatic perception as the documentary film can get.

1973 F 16, 17:2

The Program

HIPPODROME HARDWARE by Red Grooms, photography by Peter Hutton and Rudy Burkhardt, 45 minutes; PAINTING AND SCRATCHING ON FILM by Al Jarnow, 3 minutes; VISOR, by Mr. Jarnow, 3 minutes; ROTATIONS by Mr. Jarnow, 3 minutes; THE OWL AND THE PUSSYCAT by Al and Jill Jarnow; CIRCLES I by Doris Chase; GANGLION ROTUNDA SERIES I by Lowell Bodger, 6 minutes; 41 BARKS by Eli Noyes, 1 minute; IN A BOX by Mr. Noyes, 5 minutes; THE BIRTH OF THE BIG MAMOO by Jody Silver, 6 minutes; ONE MAN'S LAUNDRY by Fred Aranow and George Griffin, 17 minutes. Friday, Saturday and Sunday and Feb. 23 through Feb. 25 at 8 P.M. At the Film Forum, 256 West 88th Street.

By ROGER GREENSPUN

Red Grooms's new movie (completed this week) "Hippodrome Hardware" opened yesterday at the Film Forum in the company of 10 short animated films by other hands, of greater or lesser skill.

"Hippodrome Hardware" runs for 45 minutes and it contains, just for starters: a purple cow, a shooting star that rides a bicycle, a man wintering on an iceberg, an enormous folding ruler that moves by its own volition, three carpenters carrying tools bigger than they are, a flying robin as large as a young girl (who plays her), and Her Majesty the Goddess of Carpentry—a 10-foot-tall giant who throws flowers representing builders' supplies out to the audience at a "happening."

The happening, presided over by a clumsy clown named Ruckus (Mr. Grooms) and attended by an audience partly real and partly a construction of Mr. Grooms's imagination, is at the center of the film—though it's difficult to say what is the center of a work that seems to have randomness as its principle of organization. Some of "Hippodrome Hardware" is mechanistic abstraction, and it looks like the work of Stuart Davis. Some is semi-pointillist animation, and it looks like comic-book Seurat. But most is a private dream beset by a benign giganticism and it looks like nothing in this world except the art of Red Grooms.

That it isn't as good as much of the art of Mr. Grooms is at least partly because film, even animated film, is a different medium from painting or sculpture and because the camera sees everything, even the most fantastic pop-art cutouts, with a kind of literalness not imposed by the human eye. "Hippodrome Hardware" never quite transforms its elements into a movie. But as a visual record and a compendium of wild ideas, it has undeniable fascination.

The rest of the Film Forum program contains one rather long, very ambitious, satiric fictional cartoon—"One Man's Laundry" — and nine much shorter works.

I didn't greatly like "One Man's Laundry," though it is technically skillful, because I don't greatly credit animated satire. The kind of animated whimsey contained in some of the films of Eli Noyes and Al and Jill Jarnow is more fun—and it is more fun than the changing perspective studies in Al Jarnow's "Visor" and "Rotations," or in Lowell Bodger's "Ganglion Rotunda Series I."

•

Jody Silver's lovely, ferocious, pastel-colored creation fantasy, "The Birth of the Big Mamoo," is one of the high points of the program. But the highest point for me is Doris Chase's "Circles I," which involves the use of a computer and consists of nothing more than sets of thin gleaming circles moving in combination through—usually black — space. Restrained elegance isn't a common movie virtue, but it is Miss Chase's, and I am won by it completely.

1973 F 17, 39:1

"Tout Va Bien," which opened yesterday at the New Yorker Theater and the Fifth Avenue Cinema, was shown at the 10th New York Film Festival. The following excerpt is from Roger Greenspun's review, which appeared Oct. 11, 1972, in The New York Times.

The Cast

TOUT VA BIEN, directed by Jean-Luc Godard and Jean-Pierre Gorin; screenplay (French with English subtitles) by Mr. Gorin and Mr. Godard; photography by Armand Marco; editor, Kernout Peitier; produced by Jean-Pierre Rassam for Lido Films/Empire Films. A New Yorker Films Release. Running time: 95 minutes. At the Fifth Avenue Cinema, Fifth Avenue and 12th Street, and the New Yorker Theater, Broadway and 89th Street. This film has not been classified.

He	Yves Montand
She	Jane Fonda
Factory Manager	Vittorio Caprioli
Delegate	Jean Pignol
Frederic	Pierre Ondry
Genevieve	Ilizabeth Chauvin
Lucien	Eric Chartier
Leon	Yves Gabrielli

Jane Fonda plays She, an American correspondent in Paris, and Yves Montand plays He, her French husband, who used to write scripts for New Wave movies and now makes television commercials. One day She, on assignment, and He, along for kicks, are trapped in a workers' take-over of a sausage factory. The factory, shown as a large multilevel construct with cutaway rooms, halls and stairways (perhaps purposely, like the famous Jerry Lewis set for "Ladies' Man"), contains a boss, straw bosses, a shop steward, assembly-line men oppressed by the bosses, and women oppressed both by the bosses and the assembly-line men.

Everybody explains his position, and the boss is made a fool of, and by the time they leave the factory He and She have been radicalized to the point that they begin to see their lives not as isolated activities but as a unified whole—a whole that must be understood politically.

The factory is one great image of our society and later in the film there is another, a supermarket so enormous it might well be another factory. Jean-Luc Godard photographs the supermarket by tracking his camera back and forth in a straight line in front of the checkout counters while goods are bought, a French Communist party author hawks a book, young activists break in and a minor riot ensues.

Godard has been using a slow, deliberate, horizontal camera movement at least as far back as "Contempt" (1963), and by "La Chinoise" (1967), an early film of political education, it had become a dominant part of his visual rhetoric. It is a very good way of turning rhythm into mere repetition, and of stringing out an environment as a succession of discrete but boringly similar elements.

•

This is a way of treating film as linear argument rather than as comprehensive vision. And though it is full of ideological demonstrations, it makes very few discoveries—as if the text had all been written and it were only necessary for people to work themselves around to the right opinions now.

1973 F 17, 39:1

The Cast

LOVE YOU ROSA, written and directed by Moshe Mizrahi; produced by Menahem Golan; executive producer, Yoram Globus; director of photography, Adam Greenberg; film editor, Dov Hoenig; music, Dov Seltzer; presented by Peter Gettinger and Oliver A. Unger of Leisure Media, Inc. At the Little Carnegie Theater, 57th Street, East of Seventh Avenue. Running time: 84 minutes. This has not been classified.

Rosa	Michal Bat-Adam
Nessim	Gabi Otterman
Eli	Yosef Shiloah
Rabbi	Avner Chezkiyahu
Jemila	Levana Finkelstein
Nessim, grown up	Moshe Tal
Nessim's mother	Elisheva Michaeli

Although it is inspired by Old Testament law, "I Love You Rosa," the Israeli-made nominee for an Oscar that arrived at the Little Carnegie yesterday, happily doesn't exude the mustiness of a period piece. Despite a slow, measured pace and a soap opera note or two, this gentle but perceptive examination of a decidedly unusual affair that happens to be set in Jerusalem of the eighteen-eighties is as sentimental as genuine love and as up to date as the women's liberation movement.

In dealing largely with an 11-year-old Jewish boy's love for his young, widowed sister-in-law, Moshe Mizrahi, writer-director, sticks to his theme and avoids religious or distaff proseletyzing. He is a refreshingly professional craftsman who allows a viewer his own judgments.

His story, unfolded mostly through a flashback, derives from the tenets in Deuteronomy on the duty of a man to marry his brother's widow as well as those involving the widow's rights if she's refused. Mr. Mizrahi's sentimentality may be obvious but his deft use of his material and his principals is sensitive and multifaceted.

His hero, even under ancient law, is too young to marry, but he jumps at the chance to live with the sister-in-law he adores despite the opposition of his family and the taunts and attacks of friends and neighbors. And, as the drama's strongest character, the resolute widow is maternally understanding in her affection, even in the face of the community's heated criticism. When he does make love to her as a young man, a love she obviously reciprocates, she nevertheless rejects him as a husband. Eventually, he unselfishly releases her from her religious commitment. Women's liberation? She, in turn, in a somewhat sidsy finale, does choose to marry him.

Michal Bat-Adam, a dark-eyed, brunette beauty she also appears as a shriveled grandmother in the opening and closing sequence), is markedly persuasive as the stalwart Rosa who adamantly waits and achieves her rights and desires. Gabi Otterman is diffidently natural as the boy confused by love, sexuality and unbending religious requirements. And competent supporting players, among them Avner Chezkiyahu, as a compassionate rabbi, and Yosef Shiloah as the widow's suitor and the boy's employer, help enhance the bittersweet romance.

Color cameras have vividly captured ancient Jerusalem, and English subtitles make the Hebrew dialogue lucidly plain. "I Love You Rosa" may have evolved as naive, mawkish folklore but Mr. Mizrahi's polished handling of his cast and subject makes them come alive in a simple, subdued and knowledgeable portrait.

A. H. WEILER.

1973 F 17, 39:2

You See Yourself in 'Heartbreak'

By STEPHEN FARBER

THE REVIEWS touting "The Heartbreak Kid" as a "human" comedy do not give audiences a fair idea of what they're in for, and when I recently saw the film for a second time, part of the audience was noticeably puzzled and disappointed. It is indeed a "human" comedy, but not in the sense the word is ordinarily used by reviewers; it's not warm or tender or affectionate, though it is an unflinching, mercilessly accurate portrait of human awkwardness and cruelty. Audiences see themselves on the screen, and they don't like what they see.

Working from a Bruce Jay Friedman story, Neil Simon has written a screenplay that is unlike anything else he has done; free of gags and compromises, this acid satire is easily his best piece of writing. And with her second feature, Elaine May becomes a major American director. The unusual thing about this comedy is that it has no focus for audience sympathy or identification. Everyone is treated with the same savagery: Lenny Cantrow, the sporting goods salesman who discards his bride on his honeymoon; Lila, the sweetly trusting, bovine bride; Kelly Corcoran, the teasing, sexy, shallow coed queen from Minnesota; her bigoted, mulish father, and her polite, bubble-brained mother. The only distinctions in this world are between the fools and the rats.

Many people probably expect "The Heartbreak Kid" to be more like "The Graduate"; unconsciously, they still associate Elaine May with her ex-partner Mike Nichols. Actually, the two films do have a good deal in common, beginning with Charles Grodin's resemblance to Dustin Hoffman. Both comedies take off from the style of a Nichols-and-May revue, and both uncover some of the perverse obsessions of affluent middle-class America. Even the plots are similar: In both "The Graduate" and "The Heartbreak Kid" the hero meets the girl of his dreams at a very inconvenient moment — while involved with another woman; after extricating himself from the first relationship, he furiously pursues and eventually wins his storybook princess. But in "The Heartbreak Kid" the victory is more than slightly ambiguous.

*

The larger difference is that "The Heartbreak Kid" has none of the sentimentality that ruined "The Graduate." Mike Nichols pandered to the young audience, treating the two earnest, anguished, goody-goody lovers as the heroes of a corrupt world. Luckily "The Heartbreak Kid" isn't about soulful, "sensitive" youth; the kids in this movie are hard, selfish, stupid, just like the adults. Elaine May sees exactly what's in her characters, and she never makes false claims for them. "The Heartbreak Kid" is her hard-edged "Graduate," and I think it's everything "The Graduate" should have been—not a soft caramel optimistic comedy, but a comprehensive, fully-achieved, dark satiric vision.

*

Simon and May have created a wittily-detailed world (down to the CCNY pennant on Lenny's wall), and they are in control of the social tensions implicit in the story: Mr. Corcoran's anti-Semitism is subtly established without being belabored; and we can imagine a whole Portnoy-like history for Lenny on the basis of his compulsive pursuit of Kelly, his *shiksa* golden girl. The advantage of Elaine May's understated, oblique style is that we become *involved* in interpreting the carefully-planted hints.

The only problem is that purposeful ambiguity is very close to confusion. The film's one significant failure is in the characterization of Kelly. We can accept her flirting with Lenny; but when we are asked to accept a more serious attachment between them, her motives are impossible to decipher.

With Lenny and Lila, however, the director makes very few miscalculations. These two losers are achingly vivid. In my predominantly Jewish high school in Cleveland, I *knew* Lenny and Lila; after seeing this movie, I feel I *know* what became of them. Lenny in particular is a brilliant creation. This Jewish go-getter, too open to hide his aggressiveness, transcends ethnic stereotype; he's the prototypical male egotist. A classic kind of American hustler and climber.

Almost the first time we see Lenny he is admiring himself in the mirror. His fastidious wardrobes — including several sets of matching swim trunks and shirts—are beautifully observed. Not many movies have been so ruthless in exposing a *man's* vanity; that's one of the special perceptions Elaine May, as a woman, brings to this material. Lenny's narcissism is an overwhelming form of blindness; he loves himself too much to be objective, and he really believes in his own goodness. Even telling a blatant lie, he manages to be self-righteous. A master at rationalization, he has an endless store of homilies and euphemisms to let himself off the hook. When Lila complains about how little time he has spent with her since their wedding, Lenny replies patiently, "Honey, it's not the amount of time you spend with somebody, it's how the time was spent." Lenny has the hustler's special gift for putting everyone else on the defensive.

Besides, Lenny is a walking embodiment of "stick-to-it," never-say-die American gumption; he's plucky, determined, aggressive, resilient in adversity, and a fighter when the odds are against him. He always gets what he goes after, but does he truly know what he wants? His entire identity is assumed; his ideas are all second-hand, all equally disposable. At the end he tries to impress the Midwesterners by regurgitating the platitudes he picked up in a newspaper editorial on ecology. But he's played himself out. Sitting alone at his second wedding reception, Lenny wonders what he's doing in this WASP ice palace. For just an instant his energy flags, and he seems lost and pathetic. Appalling as he is, he's essentially as much a victim as poor Lila—a victim of false expectations and empty dreams, a slave to his society's conventions.

*

If the film questions American initiative and WASP ideals, it reserves its most searching, devastating questions for the traditional movie myths of romance. In most movies love is the characters' ultimate goal, their noblest aspiration, the solution to all dilemmas. "The Heartbreak Kid" begins and ends with a wedding; but unlike the typical Hollywood comedy, it mocks the emptiness of the ceremony.

Lenny and Lila don't know anything about each other when they get married, but they think they're "in love." On their way to Miami Beach they sing with forced exuberance, aping media models of the happy newlyweds. "The Graduate" crooned of the glories of love—parsley, sage, rosemary, and thyme; "The Heartbreak Kid" exposes the bankruptcy of middle-class romance. At both of Lenny's weddings the same two songs play in the background—the simpy Bacharach-David "Close to You" and the Coca-Cola tune "I'd Like to Buy the World a Coke." It is a biting touch: in America romantic ballads and advertising jingles are indistinguishable.

Charles Grodin comforts Jeannie Berlin, the bride he's decided to dump, in "The Heartbreak Kid"

"He drops her as if he were returning her under a 60-day guarantee"

The lovers in "The Heartbreak Kid" are hypnotized by the images of romance merchandised in TV commercials. Even in their mating games they can't break out of the patterns prescribed by the consumer society.

Romantic courtship is seen as a middle-class initiation rite; it has no higher, loftier meaning. Marriage is a transaction or an investment, not a spiritual union. Lenny drops his first wife as if he were returning her under a 60-day guarantee. With Kelly the dividends are more inviting; she holds the key to yachts and mountain cabins—a WASP dream of elegance. Lenny doesn't realize he's status-seeking; he sincerely believes he's in love, but he's pursuing an illusion. Love itself is an illusion in "The Heartbreak Kid." This film retains its skepticism right to the end.

Some people will try to dismiss the movie's anti-romantic satire by saying that Lenny, Lila, and Kelly are too shallow to know the true meaning of love. But how often is "love" anything more than the mixture of sex, social ritual, acquisitiveness, gamesmanship, and media-programed dreams that this film identifies? The movies have defined "love" for us—in impossibly exalted terms—and "The Heartbreak Kid" sets out to redefine it. At first the film seems to be a slight, narrow satire about people to whom we can feel comfortably superior. Gradually that sense of superiority disintegrates, as we recognize the delusions we share with the characters.

Maybe I haven't made it clear that "The Heartbreak Kid" is a very funny movie; but it is a comedy with something on its mind. The uncomfortable questions it poses cannot be laughed away.

Stephen Farber is a critic and author of the book "The Movie Rating Game."

1973 F 18, II:1:1

The Cast

LOLLY-MADONNA XXX, directed by Richard C. Sarafian; screenplay by Rodney Carr-Smith and Sue Grafton, based on the Grafton novel, "The Lolly-Madonna War;" music, Fred Myrow; director of photography, Philip Lathrop; editor, Tom Rolf; producer, Mr. Carr-Smith, distributed by Metro-Goldwyn-Mayer. Running time: 103 minutes. At the 59th Street Twin East Theater, 59th Street near Third Avenue. This film has been classified PG.
```
Laban ..................... Rod Steiger
Pap ...................... Robert Ryan
Roonie Gill Lolly-Madonna
                         Season Hubley
Thrush ................... Scott Wilson
Zack ..................... Jeff Bridges
Skylar .................. Timothy Scott
Hawk ...................... Ed Lauter
Finch .................... Randy Quaid
ChicLie ............... Katherine Squire
Elspeth ................. Tresa Hughes
Villum ................... Paul Koslo
Ludie .................... Kiel Martin
Seb ...................... Gary Busey
Sister E ............... Joan Goodfellow
```

By VINCENT CANBY

"Lolly-Madonna XXX" is a disaster, but I can't tell whether it's because hillbillies make rotten metaphors or because Richard C. Sarafian has made a rotten movie. The film was photographed in the Tennessee hills, and its cast includes Rod Steiger, Robert Ryan, Jeff Bridges, Season Hubley and a lot of other people who play characters with names like Laban and Pap and Ludie and Seb and Lolly-Madonna.

Its high-minded intention: to demonstrate the futility of war in terms of a feud between the Feather family and the Gutshalls, which begins with some fussing over a piece of land and climaxes in the sort of fighting in which people really get their heads blown off. I assume Mr. Sarafian and his screenwriters thought they were making a film about Vietnam without making a film about Vietnam, which is the weasel way of dealing with Great Issues.

Had the story about the Feathers and the Gutshalls any dramatic or emotional intensity of its own, it wouldn't be necessary to mention Vietnam. But "Lolly-Madonna" is so absolutely spineless, it can't even be consistent about its characters, some of whom come straight out of old Esquire cartoons and some of whom are apparently sophisticated enough to argue scruples vs. principles. The result is what W. C. Fields, describing a particularly ghastly mixture of free lunch ingredients, once called a moulage.

•

Mr. Sarafian, the director of "The Vanishing Point" and "Man in the Wilderness," has done better things, as has the co-author, of the screenplay, Rodney Carr-Smith, who worked on "Bartleby." Perhaps the blame should be put on the editor—I don't know. I am sure, however, that "Lolly-Madonna" (which is a signature, not a film rating) opened yesterday at the 59th Street Twin East I Theater and it's indefensible on any level.

1973 F 22, 30:1

CHARLOTTE'S WEB, directed by Charles A. Nichols and Iwao Takamoto; story by Earl Hamner Jr., based on the book by E. B. White; music and lyrics by Richard M. Sherman and Robert B. Sherman; produced by Joseph Barbera and William Hanna; a Hanna-Barbera-Sagittarius production, distributed by Paramount Pictures. Running time: 94 minutes. At Radio City Music Hall, Avenue of the Americas at 50th Street. This film has been classified G.
```
            Voices
Charlotte ............. Debbie Reynolds
Templeton ............... Paul Lynde
Wilbur .................. Henry Gibson
Narrator ................ Rex Allen
Mrs. Arable ............ Martha Scott
Old Sheep ............. Dave Madden
Avery ................ Danny Bonaduce
Geoffrey ............... Don Messick
Lurvy .................. Herb Vigran
The Goose ........... Agnes Moorehead
Fern Arable ........... Pam Ferdin
```

By VINCENT CANBY

Some years ago when it was announced that henceforth all children's records would be made of unbreakable plastic, a friend of mine —a father with a special hatred for the nursery rhyme orchestrated and sung—predicted madness for parents and illiteracy for children.

"I could always count on the kids breaking the records faster than we could buy them," he said. "Now they'll accumulate . . . by the roomfuls. Imagine entire collections of Mother Goose! They'll forget how to read."

I always remember how parents and children survived that technological breakthrough when I see a film like "Charlotte's Web," Hanna-Barbera's animated feature based on the funny, sad, lean novel that E. B. White wrote for children—and for anyone else interested in the elements of style in the English language. Parents will survive it, and so will their children.

"Charlotte's Web" is not really bad in the way that the archy and mehitabel film was bad. It's not a distortion. It's just a big, bland-looking cartoon feature with a musical score by Richard M. Sherman and Robert B. Sherman that sounds like any number of other Sherman scores ("Mary Poppins," "Chitty-Chitty Bang Bang").

The music and the pictorial style, which seems to be a blend of early Grant Wood and late Max Fleischer, are exceedingly uninteresting, but though they blunt the precise effects of Mr. White's prose, they don't obliterate them. Probably enough of the original feeling is left to prompt the child of elegant taste to look into the book for himself, to read pure White and to look at the scratchy, rather harried, utterly charming Garth Williams illustrations.

Earl Hamner Jr., who wrote the screen play, has followed the original so closely that it's still possible to be moved by the story of Charlotte, the spider who devotes her entire life (one spring, summer and fall) to saving the life of Wilbur, the stout-hearted pig who would otherwise have been turned into ham, bacon and pork chops.

Charlotte's method is the word. As Wilbur preens on the ground below, Charlotte calls attention to him by weaving "SOME PIG" into her web above. Later she writes "TERRIFIC," then "RADIANT," though she's not convinced that Wilbur's action is as radiant as that of the detergent whose box supplied the inspiration.

"Charlotte's Web" is about friendship, vanity, love, birth and death, all of the things, in fact, that make life worth living, even in a barnyard. While the film version is told principally in terms of syrupy songs and pictures, enough of the text remains to occasionally please the curmudgeon.

There is, for example, the healthy cynicism of old Templeton, the rat (whose personality is perfectly projected in the voice of Paul Lynde). "Play? Play?" Templeton screams in answer to Wilbur's invitation. "I'm a glutton but not a merrymaker!"

The one sequence in which music, pictures and original property come to some kind of happy accord is the one in which we follow Templeton's night-long debauch on soggy spun sugar, old franks, watermelon and corn cobs at the county fair.

•

For most of the rest of the time, we have to compromise. Fern, the little girl who adopts Wilbur when he is first born, has apparently been drawn to look like the adult Julie Andrews with very short arms and legs. The animals are somewhat more attractive, though styleless, and Charlotte has remarkably blue eyes for a movie spider. The major voices are supplied by Debbie Reynolds (Charlotte), Henry Gibson (Wilbur) and Agnes Moorehead (The Goose).

"Charlotte's Web" opened yesterday at Radio City Music Hall. I have very mixed feelings about most of it, but not its ending, which are the closing lines of Mr. White's book: "She was in a class by herself. It's not often that someone comes along who is a true friend and a good writer. Charlotte was both." It's difficult to hate anything with such style, even if it's borrowed.

1973 F 23, 18:1

Wilbur the pig and friend

PAYDAY, directed by Daryl Duke; screenplay by Don Carpenter; editor, Richard Halsey; music by Ed Bogas; produced by Martin Fink and Mr. Carpenter; released by Cinerama Releasing Corporation. At the Forum Theater, Broadway at 47th Street; Juliet 2 Theater, Third Avenue and 83d Street, and the Murray Hill Theater, 34th Street east of Lexington Avenue. Running time: 103 minutes. This film is classified R.
```
Maury Dann ............... Rip Torn
Mayleen Travis ........... Ahna Capri
Rosamond McClintock .... Elayne Heilveil
Clarence McGinty .... Michael C. Gwynne
Bob Tally ................ Jeff Morris
Chicago ................ Cliff Emmich
Ted .................. Henry O. Arnold
```

By ROGER GREENSPUN

The pursuit of that ultimate all-American pop-culture artifact, the road movie, continues. And it is not likely to be delayed for long by the emergence of "Payday," an account of two nights and a day in the life of one Maury Dann, a country-and-Western singer journeying not too successfully up from Alabama to Nashville.

To appreciate the road movie, or the spirit of the road movie, you must refine your sensibilities—until you become a connoisseur of main streets, motel rooms, roadhouse parking lots, and of the dawn rising warmly over superhighways in the Southeast. To such taste "Payday" offers some nourishment—perhaps too much. In other respects it is very thin.

•

Indeed, a feeling very close to exhaustion, a kind of psychic emptiness, pervades the film. Maury Dann arranges play dates, bullies his entourage, hunts quail, visits his feeble pill-popping mom, picks up one girl and drops another, gets into real trouble with the cops, and drives off into the morning—on the lift from one dose of amphetamines too many. It should mean something, or say something about a quality of life ("quality of life" is surely the film's subject); and yet it all seems unrealized, unrelated — like illustrative material for a movie not yet made.

To some extent this stems from a screenplay that seems curiously unattached to its material. But Daryl Duke's direction is a good deal less forceful than it needs to be, and though he clearly has some feeling for the atmosphere of the road, his approach to dramatic events ranges from hopeful uncertainty to downright miscalculation.

•

Rip Torn seals off the character of Maury Dann—a compound of meanness, gentleness, opportunism, enthusiasm and desperation—as if covering an inner complexity that he never quite persuades us he possesses. The two girls, Ahna Capri and Elayne Heilveil, are pretty awful. This leaves the locations, all in Alabama, and very nice, and a collection of authentic-seeming minor players. It is probably a function of what's wrong with the movie that its happiest moments are provided by Michael C. Gwynne, who plays Maury Dann's business manager, and plays him for simple efficiency.

"Payday" opened yesterday at the Forum, the Juliet 2 and the Murray Hill theaters.

1973 F 23, 22:1

The Program

TEN PERSONAL FILMS: PESCADOS VIVOS by Susan Felter, 21 minutes; TRANSPORT by Amy Greenfield, 6 minutes; GOOGOLPLEX by Lillian Schwartz, 6 minutes; SPECTRUM IN WHITE by Lois Siegel, 11 minutes; BIRD by Sharon Hennessey, 1 minute; WHAT I WANT by Sharon Hennessey, 10 minutes; RED by Mary Feldhaus-Weber, 5 minutes; SWEET DREAMS by Freude Bartlett, 3 minutes; WOMEN AND CHILDREN AT LARGE by Freude Bartlett, 10 minutes; THE DIVINE MIRACLE by Diana Krumins, 6 minutes. At the Whitney Museum of American Art, Madison Avenue and 75th Street, through Feb. 26.

The "personal films" section of the Women's Film Festival that opened yesterday at the Whitney Museum leaves no doubt that their talents are varied. And, if a majority of the nine shorts shown ("The Divine Miracle" by Diana Krumins was not ready for showing at a preview) are more personal than fascinating, the program does illustrate a fair proportion of artistry.

This artistry is vividly evident in Mary Feldhaus-Weber's "Red," which, in five minutes and fine color, transforms Little Red Riding Hood into a tender, imaginative reflection on the bittersweet beauties and loneliness of childhood.

•

Similarly, the 10-minute "Women and Children at Large" by Freude Bartlett, celebrates woman, through a complex of images such as happy, dancing, pregnant nudes or innocent, beautiful babies, in cogent, poetic style. However, her three-minute, "Sweet Dreams," a collage of babies, dolphins and unrelated outdoor scenes, evolves as a series of unfinished impressions.

This viewer also found "Googolplex," the six-minute computer-made compilation of swiftly-moving geometric patterns by Lillian Schwartz, and the 11-minute "Spectrum in White" by Lois Siegel, who used constantly changing lines and abstract shapes scratched on negative film, to be inventive, eye-catching examples of technical professionalism.

"Pescados Vivos," by Susan Felter, the longest (21 minutes) entry, employs a wide assortment of techniques (slow motion, stop motion and the like) to achieve, in black and white and color, a good deal more variety and ideas than one can assimilate. Despite all the apparent effort, an observer is left with the impression that simply capturing people and animals in states of animation is this study's major goal.

Amy Greenfield's six-minute "Transport" is notable for its good color photography. But one is hard put to relate to the meaning of four youths struggling up a beach with a seemingly lifeless body, which constitutes all the action.

Sharon Hennessey, who crystallizes a moment of movement and some emotion in the one-minute "Bird," is merely static in her 10-minute "What I Want." The spectacle of a continuous shot of a young woman reciting a vast catalogue of her desires from wanting a husband to being herself, is neither fervent nor funny, but merely stultifying. Happily, however, what some of the other women film makers in this conclave want is expressively projected.

A. H. WEILER.

1973 F 23, 22:2

The Program

TEN FROM YOUR SHOW OF SHOWS, directed by Max Liebman; written by Mel Tolkin, Lucille Kallen, Mel Brooks, Tony Webster, Sid Caesar, and Mr. Liebman. Produced by Mr. Liebman. A Walter Reade Organization, Inc., release. Running time: 92 minutes. At the Festival Theater, 57th Street at Fifth Avenue. (This film has been rated G.) With Sid Caesar, Imogene Coca, Carl Reiner, Howard Morris, Louis Nye, Dorothy Patten, Jack Russell, Eleanor Williams, Ray Drakely, Swen Swenson, and Ed Herlihy as the narrator.

By ROGER GREENSPUN

Even the picture quality adds to the effect. Low contrast, a little distortion at the edges, 16-mm. kinescopes blown up for the theater screen—and looking like old movie history or a message from Marshall McLuhan. It isn't movies; in the early nineteen-fifties it was a way of avoiding movies, of staying home Saturday nights to have your mind eroded by television for a change. Probably you were watching Sid Caesar and Imogene Coca in "Your Show of Shows," and probably you knew how lucky you were.

But if you've forgotten, and need to be reminded, or if you haven't forgotten, and want to be reminded anyway, or if you are just too tragically young for the proper memories, you can recoup your losses and enrich your life with "Ten From Your Show of Shows," a selection of skits captured in glorious gray-and-white and presented at the Festival Theater.

•

Not all the skits are of equal value. They range, I should say, from magnificent to merely very good. A couple are rather famous: "From Here to Obscurity," the tempestuous story of a boxing bugler and a babe on a beach in Hawaii; or "The Clock," in which a great Bavarian town clock goes curiously out of whack, much to the discomfort of the life-size figures that strike the hours.

"The Clock" is pantomime, as are several of the skits in whole or in part, and it is pantomime of a marvelously clear, economical and expressive sort. Thus, a silent movie take-off, "The Sewing Machine Girl," is not only heartbreakingly funny, but it also complements the acting styles and sentiments it parodies. In "The Sewing Machine Girl," Imogene Coca eventually dies and flies up to heaven (on wires), but before dying she does a little whirling Dervish dance of consumption that may be the most surprising thing in silent movies before or after the coming of sound.

Miss Coca has her celebrated leer, and her dignity—always wounded but still game against any incursion. Sid Caesar has his face—soft, pliable, continually supporting a stoicism beyond its powers—and he has his roles. In one skit he is a fastidious German general with a "geschmutzed monocle." In another he is a great Viennese specialist, a space scientist, suffering through an airport interview: "Professor, what is the most important problem in space today?" "Closet space. Drawer space is really something, but closet space is the worst!"

That's not just a joke; it's the key to an important world view.

•

Another key is what happens to the poor sap (Sid Caesar) who finds his past unfolding on the real-life TV tearjerker "This Is Your Story." Not only is he confronted with his long-lost aunt, the kindly old hometown fireman, and his favorite uncle, Goopy. But also the fireman ends up in his arms, the aunt crawling over his back and Goopy, hanging onto one leg, crying his very eyes out.

Such a glorious muddle of bawling humanity does more than gladden the soul. It leads me to think that on certain Saturday nights "Your Show of Shows" may have been the laughter of the gods.

1973 F 24, 17:1

He and She and Godard

By VINCENT CANBY

No matter how austere and didactic and boring his revolutionary films may be from time to time, Jean-Luc Godard has maintained his genius for titles—which may be the real clue to the well-being of this most passionate and nervy and irritating of artistic temperaments. Work backward from "Vladimir and Rosa," through "Wind From the East," "One A.M.," "Le Gai Savoir," "La Chinoise," "Two or Three Things I Know About Her" and "Vivre Sa Vie," all the way to "Breathless," using the original French titles or their English translations, and it would be difficult to tell exactly when Godard became converted by the Radical Left, when he elected to make only revolutionary teaching films for audiences of an ever dwindling number of supporters.

Yet as the poetry remains in his titles (it's less difficult to renounce an income, a wife or even an ideology than it is to shuck off a particular talent), the poetry also remains in the films as a signature that cannot be easily disguised by any amount of production chaos ("One Plus One"), Marxist mannerisms ("Wind From the East"), or collaboration ("Vladimir and Rosa," made with his young political mentor, Jean-Pierre Gorin). The poetry is something immutable. It can't be used up or denied. It remains constant even while the body and the mind that contain it suffer all sorts of physical and spiritual ravages. It separates the great directors, who, I admit, can make awful films, from the competent directors, who often make some of the excellent ones.

*

"Tout Va Bien" (freely translated as "Just Great") is his newest film (written and directed in collaboration with

Gorin), and although I like the title immensely, it might have been better as "Un Film Comme Les Autres" (which I would translate as "A Film Like Any Other"), the only problem being that Godard squandered that title on an apparently impossibly aggressive, political lesson-film shown here just once, with a garbled English soundtrack, at Philharmonic Hall in December, 1968. "Tout Va Bien," which had its local premiere at last year's New York Film Festival, is now playing its initial commercial engagements at the New Yorker Theater on the upper West Side and at the Fifth Avenue Cinema in the Village.

It's not really a film like any other, but it does recall the pre-radicalized Godard, the Godard who was experimenting with revolution (aimlessly, he seems now to think) with films like "Two or Three Things" and "La Chinoise," before the Paris riots in May, 1968. Actually its casting style goes even further back, to 1963, when he made a film, "Le Mepris" ("Contempt") with such stars as Bardot, Piccoli and Palance.

"Tout Va Bien" stars Jane Fonda and Yves Montand, who are — in spite of their loudly proclaimed leftist (but hardly radical) political views — symbols of the bourgeois film industry on which Godard turned his back five years ago.

It is Godard's first revolutionary film for the bourgeoisie and, unless audiences are more indulgent than I credit them to be, it may well be his last. Although I find Jane Fonda most appealing (and very funny) as a solemn American political correspondent who becomes radicalized after being trapped over night in a strike in a Paris sausage factory, I suspect that most people who go to movies would prefer to see her as the unhappy hooker for which she won her Academy Award.

"Tout Va Bien" is two stories, sort of. It's about the making of a movie these days—about the things you have to put into it, supposedly, to attract the conventional audience—and it's about She (Miss Fonda) and her lover, He (Montand), a former New Wave director who has chosen to step out of that rat race and, instead, to make television commercials. The dramatic line, such as it is, is one of self-discovery.

He and She find themselves prisoners at the Salumi sausage factory where she has gone to interview the manager on the problems facing management today. They are caught when the Maoists usurp a nice, genial, one-hour work-stoppage, planned by the conservatively Communist C.G.T., and turn it into a leaderless rampage. The sit-in describes the workers' frustrations in mostly comic actions. The plant manager is locked in his office and not allowed to go to the bathroom. The personnel files are destroyed. One woman striker argues with her husband over the telephone: "You'll have to heat it yourself . . . You stayed at your factory during your strike. . . ." Another woman paints her nails. Occasionally they revive themselves with a revolutionary song.

As the actions describe the frustrations, typical Godardian monologues define them—some are broadly funny, some pious and just a little foolish. All, however, are photographed with that particular Godard eye for finding beauty in the most banal shapes and colors. If red and yellow were the predominant colors of "Weekend," dusky blues, and greens and beiges of the sort Braque used, are the colors of "Tout Va Bien."

To the extent that Godard has any interest in allowing us emotional involvement with He and She (Him and Her?), "Tout Va Bien" is both moving and witty, but these are qualities that slip through in just three or four scenes.

In two sequences, one shot at a TV studio and another at a Paris construction site, Montand, talking directly to the camera, describes the weariness with which he came to direct his fiction films and how he finally preferred to make commercials, which allow him to participate in the system without hypocrisy.

When, at last, he was offered his chance to direct a David Goodis novel he'd always cherished (a rather nasty reference to Truffaut's "bourgeois" adaptation of Goodis's "Shoot The Piano Player"), he says he no longer cared. It's not necessary that you believe the character (characters in Godard have always been slightly implausible and unreal in any conventional way), you believe the passions expressed, you believe Montand, and you believe the world in which Godard, at the beginning, has so carefully set his film, a world, he has told us, in which "farmers are farming, workers are working and the middle classes are middle classing."

Miss Fonda has some equally fine moments near the end when, after She and He have been freed from the sausage factory, they sit having breakfast in their flat, the liberated She now furious with He who, though politically aware, remains impossibly chauvinistic where she's concerned. When we last see He and She, each is, says the narrator, rethinking himself in historic terms.

"Tout Va Bien" looks a lot like the earlier Godard films (the opening of the breakfast scene mentioned above is taken directly from "Vivre Sa Vie), and it talks the committed radical line of the most recent films. Though it does both with great style and a surprising amount of humor, it's neither the look of the film nor its politics that I find most fascinating about Godard at this point. Rather it's his courageous and quite mad persistence in trying to evolve a film form to match the intensity of his political and social concerns. In the last five years he's tried to do without everything except, perhaps, film itself. He got rid of the narrative, actors-as-performers, and anything resembling emotional suspense—all techniques of the bourgeois cinema that, he thinks, have helped enslave the capitalist world. The results have been films that have bored almost everybody, most especially the masses that he would politicize.

"Tout Va Bien," with a few graceful if minor concessions to conventional cinema form, shows Godard getting ever closer to a new kind of film that makes most other politically and socially concerned movies seem like sentimental garbage.

Take, for example, "Save The Tiger," the new Jack Lemmon film directed by John G. Avildsen and written by Steve Shagan, about the decline and fall of a Los Angeles garment manufacturer played by Lemmon. I've no doubt that Avildsen, Shagan and Lemmon are very concerned about the moral breakdown of a system that supposedly allows a once-nice guy (Lemmon) to juggle books, to pimp for clients and to employ arsonists in order to continue his existence in a rotten world. Yet their method (realistic, full of attempts to engage our sympathies, and full of references to simpler, more decent times past) is to bathe real horrors in the kind of self-pity that precludes meaningful action. When we go to see movies like "Save the Tiger," we're invited to watch the spectacle of decadence. We aren't—heaven knows—asked to do anything. We aren't even asked to think very much, just to feel sorry for a poor slob who made it big and feels lousy about all the rotten things he has to do to stay on top.

This is the kind of cinema that Godard sneers at, rightly, I think. And although I find his politics as muddled and self-indulgent in their way as the sentimentality of "Save The Tiger," I admire Godard's willingness to use his talent so extravagantly, so recklessly, in the pursuit of a goal that may forever elude him. "Tout Va Bien" is a film of true political importance, whether you believe its politics or not.

1973 F 25, II:1:1

Why Is the Co-Eatus Always Interruptus?

By JOHN SIMON

LUIS BUNUEL'S "The Discreet Charm of the Bourgeoisie" presents me with a critical poser. Here is a film that has received rave notices from all reviewers, top to bottom, and is doing well with local audiences; yet I consider it absolutely worthless. Why?

The film operates on two levels: as an essentially realistic yet satirical portrait of the French bourgeoisie, and as a series of dreams and visions constituting a surreal plane. Not only does the film strike me as a failure on each of these levels, it does not even manage to benefit from contrasting or dovetailing the two. I submit that Buñuel, who has made some splendid and some dismal films, is now an old, exhausted filmmaker, and that his besetting sins of lack of discipline and indulgence in private obsessions have gotten quite out of hand.

To begin with the satirical-realistic level: satire must, at the very least, be funny. But "Bourgeoisie" is either groaning under old, obvious jokes or coasting along barren stretches of mirthless nastiness. A sextet of rich and decadent bourgeois, including one ambassador from the imaginary Latin American country of Miranda, enjoy eating copiously and well. Yet, for one reason or another, their meals get interrupted. Let's call this the co-eatus interruptus theme.

For example, they come to dinner at their friends' house on the wrong day and must leave. They go, instead, to a country inn, but find in an adjoining alcove the dead proprietor's body awaiting the undertaker, and so decide to leave. Or they go, of an afternoon, to a fashionable café-restaurant in Paris and, successively ordering tea, coffee and hot chocolate, are told by the returning waiter that the place is out of each. So they leave.

Where is the joke or satire in that? No decent restaurant is ever out of all beverages, so the scene does not correspond to some ludicrous reality. But what about satiric-comical heightening? Does the scene, by indirection or hyperbole, succeed in ridiculing fancy restaurants? Or their waiters? Or their clientele? None of the above. Does it, then, make some sardonic point about French society? Not at all. Is it funny? No, only preposterous. In another scene the group sits down to dinner only to be interrupted by some officers, who are to be billeted with them and whose maneuvers have unexpectedly been moved ahead. Dinner is delayed while the hostess improvises additional food and tables, and the meal is about to start again. But now the other mock army attacks prematurely, the officers must leave, and we get an interruptus within an interruptus. Absurd, yes; funny, no.

Fernando Rey, Delphine Seyrig and Jean-Pierre Cassel play eccentric dinner guests in "The Discreet Charm of the Bourgeoisie"
"Bunuel is an old, exhausted filmmaker and his private obsessions have gotten quite out of hand"

And not meaningful either. What do these and other such scenes tell us? That the French bourgeoisie likes its food and takes it seriously, and hates to be thwarted in its enjoyment of it. So what? The Italian bourgeoisie is just as keen on eating, and so is the German and Austrian, and any other you care to name, with the possible exception of the English and American. But is this telling us anything new or enlightening or needful of iteration? What is so hilarious about people rattling off names of dishes or holding forth on the best way to make dry martinis? Nothing; yet from the way audiences are laughing you'd think the ushers were passing out laughing gas.

With interrupted eating comes also interrupted sex, the archetypal interruptus. A husband discovers his wife on the verge of adultery with his good friend the ambassador; or guests arrive for lunch just as the host and hostess feel so amorous that they must have instant intercourse—so they must climb out of the window and have it in the bushes. This is not only juvenile prurience, it does not even make satirical sense: if these solidly married bourgeois can still pant for each other so at high noon, all is not lost. Where the blood stirs, there is hope.

But where is the satire, where the joke? Two people greedily pawing each other at an inopportune moment? Compared to that, a man slipping on a banana peel is Wildean wit and Swiftian satire.

*

On the surreal plane, the equivalent to the interruptus is the shaggy-dog story. In a sense, a dream is always over too soon, before the punchline of fulfillment can set in. But Buñuel shaggy-dogifies his dream or fantasy sequences in every possible way. A young lieutenant pops up from nowhere and relates a childhood vision in which his dead mother and her murdered lover appeared to the boy. They tell him that the dead and bloody man is his real father, and that the evil man he lives with is merely the killer of that true father. At the ghosts' urging, the boy poisons his pseudo-progenitor. He has had an unhappy childhood, says the lieutenant, and departs, never to be seen again.

Another man, a sergeant, is brought on to recount a dream of his. It is full of weird goings-on in a necropolis photographed and edited as in cheap horror movies; the events signify nothing meaningful or related to anything else in the film. The sergeant is asked to tell also his "train dream," but there is no more time for this. He has to leave, and we are left with a shaggy dog within a shaggy dog.

Again, a police commissioner we neither know nor care about has a dream about a bloody sergeant, allowing Buñuel to bring on yet another bloody corpse (the film is awash with blood, but you don't hear any of the antiviolence critics denouncing this one!) and to have a sado-comic scene in which the police torture a young rebel by means of an electrically charged piano, which, so to speak, plays him, and from

which, suddenly, an army of cockroaches pours out—a shaggy-roach story.

Why should we care about the dreams of supernumeraries? A dream becomes interesting in relation to the waking personality of the dreamer, but if he remains a passing blank, of what concern are his grotesque dreams to us? Yet even the principals' dreams remain in this film unrevealing, unfunny, unconvincing. It would seem (as Buñuel has more or less admitted) that some of those dream episodes were originally intended as strange but real events—as, for example, in "The Milky Way"—but that the filmmaker lost his nerve and explained the thing away as dreams within dreams.

Typically, we'll see a character wake up after a grotesque dream, and another, equally grotesque, sequence begins. Then a second character is seen waking up, and he tells us that he dreamed both foregoing sequences, that even the first dream was dreamed by him, the second dreamer. Yet the protagonist of the second dream was really a third character, whose dream that should have been. If this doesn't make sense to you reading it, don't worry—it won't make sense viewing it, either.

The shaggy dogs spill over into the waking sequences. There is one in which an elderly peasant woman promises to tell a bishop why she hates the gentle Jesus, but is whisked off before she can do so. Again, the police commissioner receives a phone call from the minister of justice to release his prominent prisoners. Why? he asks.

The minister explains, but the noise of a low-flying jet obliterates the explanation. Asked for a repeat, the minister wearily obliges, but another jet interferes. The frustrated commissioner passes the order on to his sergeant, who also requests an explanation. As the commissioner answers, the radiator pipes drown out his words—shaggy upon shaggy upon shaggy dog.

All the humor is pathetic. A bishop is summoned to give absolution to a dying old man. He turns out to be the gardener who, years ago, killed the bishop's parents who employed and tormented him. The bishop absolves the old man, then shoots him dead—another blood-spattered corpse. And people laugh at this! But they'll laugh at anything. We first glimpse the bishop innocently walking up to a front door to ring the bell; in the audience, hearty laughter. Why? Surely they have seen a soutane before, and the churchman is not walking on his hands or backward or hopping on one foot.

*

Then there is a visual refrain, a periodically repeated shot of the six main characters walking down a highway. This is no one's dream or vision and may be an auto-*hommage* to Buñuel's own "The Milky Way," in which a highway was the connecting metaphor. Here, however, the three or four recurrences of the shot with incremental variations tell us no more than that our bourgeois sextet is trudging down the road of life with a different expression on each face. So what else is old? To resort to grandiose symbolism in order to say what plain narrative has already conveyed (and what, anyhow, is self-evident) is arrant pretentiousness.

Coitus or co-eatus interruptus and the shaggy-dog story are the two faces of the same debased coin. They are an impotent old man's cacklingly sadistic interference with his own fictional characters, and an exhausted mind's failed search for meaningful conclusions. Buñuel is merely rehashing his earlier and better films (themselves often enough marred by incoher-

ence), without the fascinating love-hate or righteous indignation that informed them. We knew what was assailed in "Los Olvidados" or reduced to absurdity in "Simon of the Desert." In "The Discreet Charm of the Bourgeoisie" we have not so much a shaggy as an old dog, unable to learn new tricks or even adequately recall old ones.

This latest Buñuel film is a haphazard concatenation of waking and dream sequences in which anything goes, and which would make just as much, or just as little, sense if they were put together in any other disorder. Since there is no plot and the characters are just pawns—oily businessman, dissembling diplomat, spaced-out debutante, haughty matron, frivolous wife —able performers are reduced to striking permanent attitudes and hoping they will add up to performances. The talented Delphine Seyrig, for instance, opts for one unrelieved smirk from beginning to end.

Why, then, such slavish adulation, placing the film on every Best List from high to low? Buñuel is a Grand Old Man— antifascist, anticlerical, antibourgeois— well into his seventies and still swinging. Secondly, he is European and has been through all those prestigiously arcane cults like surrealism, dadaism, fetishism, sadomasochism, and can provide nothing so shallow but that it is somehow chockful of profundities. Thirdly, his films are in a foreign language and must contain subtleties submerged in the subtitles. The reviewers, like good Pavlovian dogs, salivate away at the ring of Buñuel's name.

Audiences, in turn, have the unanimous rapture of the critics and all those awards to rely on. Dogs multiply: shaggy begets shaggy, Pavlovian conditions others into Pavlovians. "Dr. Strangelove," a satire that did have meaning, predicted the world's end by hydrogen bomb. This Buñuel bomb merely ushers in the end of common sense in movie appreciation.

John Simon is the author of "Ingmar Bergman Directs," published recently by Harcourt Brace Jovanovich.

1973 F 25, II:13:1

tive morality is only dimly, if fervently, projected.
A. H. WEILER.

1973 F 26, 28:1

The Program

CHILDHOOD II, a documentary directed by Martin J. Spinelli, photographed by Ken Basmajian and produced by Richard M. Gibson. Produced and released by Posttape, Inc. At the First Avenue Screening Room, at 61st Street. Running time: 85 minutes. (This film has not been classified.)

The released tensions of adults, psychological and sexual, that are recorded in a group-encounter feature, "Childhood II," are the primary value and appeal of this documentary, even though the revelations aren't especially surprising. The new picture at the First Avenue Screening Room is one of the better group-encounter movies of about six released so far, ranging in quality from fair to very good indeed.

●

This first offering from a new company, headed by Martin J. Spinelli, the director, and Richard M. Gibson, the producer, is marked by care, dignity and purpose. Some of the film's flaws would seem to stem partly from the therapy itself. The session participants and their director, photographed during a weekend experience at Mays Landing, N. J., are totally nude.

Nudity may be considered essential to loosening tongues and inhibitions, as the group director initially reminds the clustered adults, but some discreet body posturing does indicate a slightly self-conscious awareness of the camera. Furthermore, with the group shifting to an indoor pool for more self-revelations, the photography indulges in some obtuse, psychedelic effects. Add some jivey music. The film doesn't need a note.

●

The homestretch is, best, back on the parlor carpet, as one stricken young woman discloses a father-rejection obsession hinging on a sexual incident from early childhood. This affords genuinely fine, stimulating viewing. So do the candid, clear-eyed utterances of an interracial couple called Angela and Jim.

Although it does cover fairly familiar terrain in trailing other sessions on films, this is a worthy movie that may do good where such therapy is needed.
HOWARD THOMPSON

1973 F 26, 28:1

By VINCENT CANBY

Bud Yorkin's "The Thief Who Came to Dinner" is about a bored young computer analyst named Webster (Ryan O'Neal) who chucks the

The Cast

THE THIEF WHO CAME TO DINNER, directed by Bud Yorkin; screenplay by Walter Hill, based on the novel by Terrence L. Smith; director of photography, Philip Lathrop; editor, John C. Horger; music, Henry Mancini; producer, Mr. Yorkin; a Bud Yorkin-Norman Lear production, distributed by Warner Brothers. Running time: 105 minutes. At the Loews State 2 Theater, Broadway at 45th Street, and the Beekman Theater, Second Avenue at 65th Street. (This film has been classified PG.)
Webster .... Ryan O'Neal
Laura .... Jacqueline Bisset
Dave Reilly .... Jill Clayburgh
Jackie .... Warren Oates
Henderling .... Charles Cioffi
Deams .... Ned Beatty
Zukovsky .... Austin Pendleton
Dynamite .... Gregory Sierra
Ted .... Michael Murphy

straight life to become the best adjusted, most successful jewel thief in Houston, nicknamed the chess burglar because of his fondness for leaving chess pieces at the scenes of his crimes.

In the course of his upward movement Webster falls perfectly in love with an amused society girl (Jacqueline Bisset), befriends the sober-sided insurance investigator (Warren Oates) who tries to trap him and causes the nervous breakdown of The Houston Chronicle's chess editor (Austin Pendleton). Webster suffers a superficial gunshot wound at one point.

It would be difficult to name any contemporary film with less sense of consequence than "The Thief Who Came to Dinner," yet it's this quality that gives the comedy its buoyancy even when its sense of humor fails. It's the quality of a lot of old Hollywood comedies that one is inclined to remember as being funnier than they were simply because they were cheerfully mindless of awful possibilities.

It's also the quality that Peter Bogdanovich almost exhausted himself to achieve in "What's Up, Doc," and while "The Thief Who Came to Dinner" is not so funny, Yorkin, the director ("Start The Revolution Without Me"), and his screenwriter, Walter Hill, haven't tried so hard.

The film, however, has been carefully cast—the principal roles as well as the supporting characters. By being almost too beautiful to be either true or good, O'Neal and Miss Bisset further remove the comedy from the sort of reality in which jewel thieves are probably hopeless neurotics. Both Oates and Pendleton are maniacally serious about themselves and therefore extremely funny, as are Ned Beatty, as a Houston jewel fence, and Jill Clayburgh, as O'Neal's first wife, who, remembering how bored she was with O'Neal as a computer analyst, wants to return to the man who has become a jewel thief. "I was short-changed," she says curtly.

"The Thief Who Came to Dinner," which opened yesterday at Loew's State 2 and the Beekman, is no avalanche of hilarity, but it respects a kind of comic make-believe that is rare in movies these days. You can like it without laughing a lot.

1973 Mr 2, 22:1

The Cast

THE PRIEST AND THE GIRL, a Brazilian film (Portuguese with English subtitles) written and directed by Joaquim Pedro de Andrade; photography by Mario Carneiro; music by Carlos Lira; produced by Luis Carlos Barreto; released by New Yorker Films. At the Quad Cinema 3, 13th Street between Fifth and Sixth Avenues. Running time: 87 minutes. This film has not been classified.
Priest .... Paulo Jose
Girl .... Helena Ignez
Old Man .... Mario Lago
Druggist .... Fauzi Arap

Taken as a modern parable, the Brazilian drama "The Priest and the Girl," which arrived at the Quad Cinema recently, is as mildly disturbing and fascinating as a faintly remembered legend. But it is a good deal more effective in its sharp focus on a distant but picturesque area and its depressed, little-known simple people than in its thematic clashes between sacred and profane love, temptation and native mores.

Joaquim Pedro de Andrade, the writer-director represented here last year by the picaresque adventure "Macunaima," is recounting in "The Priest and the Girl,"

which he made in 1966, a moody saga of a dedicated young country padre drawn into an affair with a pretty, apparently nubile girl and the dour, brooding villagers who harass them in their sad liaison.

●

The film was reportedly controversial in Brazil. But an American viewer finds it difficult to relate to the tragedy except on its obvious terms. One can see that the priest, played in properly anguished style by Paulo Jose, is torn between his churchly mission to love all mankind and the physical love literally thrust upon him. But the affection demanded by the girl, portrayed feelingly, if naively, by Helena Ignez, is only vaguely realized.

She has been, it turns out, "the woman" of her jealous, elderly, domineering stepfather, portrayed laconically by Mario Lago, who has been keeping the moribund mining village alive as its major shopkeeper and buyer of the

few diamonds panned. And she has also been adored by the Milquetoast druggist, Fauzi Arap, who bleats intimations of her intimacies with the village's previous priest, now dead.

●

One is inclined to wonder at the truth of her plea for love and protection when she sobbingly says to the confused young priest, "I love only you." Their ensuing flight from the village, her seduction of the priest (artistically underplayed), their return home and their expulsion and pursuit by the villagers are, one supposes, meant to be meaningful, but the impact is only slight.

Mario Carneiro's stark photography etches, in memorably beautiful blacks and whites, the sparse village and the rolling hills and the streams of the Minas Gerais mining country. But the implied commentary on the trials of a priest under the strictures of the church, natural passions and primi-

EROTICISM AND EXPLOITATION; CHARLIE COMPANY by Nancy Edell (10 minutes); DIRTY BOOKS by Linda Feferman (17 minutes); TAKE OFF by Gunvor Nelson (10 minutes); GAME by Abigail and Jonathan Child (45 minutes). At the Whitney Museum of American Art, Madison Avenue and 75th Street.

By ROGER GREENSPUN

There are two wrong ideas you might have about the film program called "Eroticism and Exploitation" that opened yesterday at the Whitney Museum. First, noting the title, you might expect some eroticism and exploitation—which of course would be wrong. Second, noting that all the films in the program were made by women (with one male co-director), you might expect feminist outrage—which would also be wrong.

"Eroticism and Exploitation" consists of four clever, ironic, thoughtful, amused and sometimes amusing short movies about sex. Only one, Linda Feferman's "Dirty Books," strikes me as very good. But all are interesting—and happily free from the rhetorical poses that afflict most serious films on the subject.

Gunvor Nelson's "Take Off" comes closest to ordinary, in terms of outrage and exploitation. A girl named Ellion Ness strips, coyly, flamboyantly, all the way down, until there is nothing left to take off except her hair, both legs, breasts, head, both arms—leaving her torso a particle of matter taking off into intergalactic space.

Only the intensity of Miss Nelson's technique (she is among the best of the West Coast independent film makers) justifies the material, and I don't think the justification is sufficient.

●

In Nancy Edell's "Charlie Company" a procession of fanciful, or fantastic, or nightmarishly distorted erotic animated figures moves across the screen from right to left into what I take to be the backside of the American consciousness. Oddly, the implicity of the idea is in the end more moving than the richness of the imagery. But that imagery is impressive and, often enough, shocking.

"Game," by Abigail and Jonathan Child, deals by way of documentary, reverie and staged situations with a whore named Tina and her pimp, Yogi Slim. Both are black, articulate, attractive, gentle, perhaps only mildly self-deceived. Tina likes her life for all its problems ("You live nice—but it's a hassle"), but worries about the future. Yogi practices yoga (he is very good) and meditates on the past.

Both see themselves engaged in a struggle for survival, which they interpret as a game of much skill and some danger, and which they choose to enjoy. Something about the contrast between the private thinking of Yogi and Tina and the many nighttime shots of street hustling touches me—like an emblem for the miserable contradictions of any New York career, which is what "Game" is all about.

●

The career contradictions in "Dirty Books" are a little more on the surface. Ellen Frank (played by the film maker, Linda Feferman) lives by writing sexy novels under the name of Frank Ellen and worries about getting down to her own work. She also worries about boyfriends ("He *sounds* like he eats macrobiotic food"), about her middle-class family, who don't know her secret, and about whether to drop everything and take a job in San Francisco.

It is a portrait of the pornographer as a nice Jewish girl, a typewriter in the kitchen and fellows on the telephone and it suggests exactly the playful irony of a sophisticated, good-humored intelligence musing over home movies.

1973 Mr 2, 23:1

The Program

BIO/AUTOBIO: TURNIP by David Woods, 31 minutes; IT IS THERE AND WE ARE HERE. THIS IS SOME TIME AGO by Theodore Spagna, 51 minutes; at the Film Forum, 256 West 88th Street. Today and tomorrow and Friday through next Sunday at 8 P.M.

By ROGER GREENSPUN

Both of the two medium-length movies that opened yesterday at the Film Forum deal with biographical material. Both attempt to develop a form in which to render observed personality on film. But any resemblance between them ends right there.

At its simplest, Theodore Spagna's "It Is There And We Are Here. This Is Some Time Ago" is a parallel study of a 97-year-old man (the director's grandfather) and a 28-year-old designer, thinker and man of several worlds. The younger man resists self-definition, and the film tends to see his life as fluid—sometimes ridiculously fluid. The older man has obviously never worried about self-definition. He is contented and fulfilled. But the film sees his life as measured and constrained; not unhappy, but tied to the limited rituals of an old man's routine.

●

But, like its title, "It Is There And We are Here. This is Some Time Ago" is never very simple. Upon its subjects it imposes itself—its cameramen, its sound crew, even its main titles, which keep unfolding on the screen periodically throughout its 51-minute length. It is thus a film about making a film about two men at vastly different stages of life. And it is also a film that means to be governed by the attitudes and actions of its subjects, to find its methods in terms of how, and even where they live.

From time to time, this is an interesting method, especially as the old man repeatedly discovers and leaves behind him cameras and the like, strategically stationed in the maze of doors and corridors that define his existence. But more often it is an overbearing method (though expertly handled), too intricate for its insights or for the depth or quality of feeling it conveys.

●

In a different way, a similar problem afflicts David Woods's "Turnip," an autobiographical memoir in which the film maker speaks of his childhood (in England), his hatred of his father and his youthful courtship of a girl he briefly loved with tender innocence. The courtship is illustrated mainly through country maps; the unhappy childhood, mainly through old photographs and family snapshots. Woods is very bitter about his father, a rigid man who apparently beat his children, but the pictures he shows are in themselves so defenseless, so nostalgic or so neutral that the bitterness falls back upon the narrator—and we are left with a stronger image not of a vicious parent but of an uncommonly vindictive son.

1973 Mr 3, 18:1

Caesar Conquers— And Coca, Too!

By VINCENT CANBY

"TEN from Your Show of Shows" is a collection of 10 sketches originally seen on Max Liebman's "Your Show of Shows," the extraordinary 90-minute, Sid Caesar-Imogene Coca Saturday night television series that began in 1950 and went off the air four years later when the partners split, the production costs rose and sponsors became scarce.

Caesar and Miss Coca, who each had what were described as 10-year million dollar contracts with the National Broadcasting Company, eventually left the network and their contracts—she in 1955 and he in 1957. Liebman went on to produce more shows for NBC, as well as for the Columbia Broadcasting System, and audiences remained in front of their television sets watching other things, as if nothing important had happened. Caesar and Miss Coca were never long off-screen and they co-starred again briefly, but things were never the same again—for them or for television.

"Ten from Your Show of Shows," which is now at the Festival Theater, is a 35-mm enlargement of 16-mm kinescopes owned by Caesar and Liebman (N.B.C. reportedly having junked its prints), and edited by Caesar and Liebman.

It's a hugely funny program. It's also a bit disorienting, as if you had looked through a spy glass into the past and found a sort of reasonable facsimile of the present, a land where time has had a stop, even though life cycles in television are only slightly less swift than the speed of light. With the obvious exceptions of a sketch that parodies Fred Zinnemann's film version of "From Here to Eternity" (called "From Here to Obscurity" in the sketch), and one that has a high old time with the early, noncelebrity version of "This Is Your Life," there is hardly anything in the collection to connect it with the late Truman-early Eisenhower years in which "Your Show of Shows" flourished.

●

I assume that Liebman and Caesar deliberately picked sketches that could be easily appreciated by audiences not yet born 20 years ago, but their choices have a curious secondary effect. While they confirm our memories of Caesar and Coca as two of our most brilliantly comic television performers, they also confirm our suspicions that commercial American television is—and has always been—doomed to placidity, not only by the rating wars but by the frantic pace with which shows must be produced, and by the voraciousness with which the public consumes the performers and their material.

The sketches in "Ten from Your Show of Shows" have been taken from more than 100 programs produced on a weekly basis during the show's four-year run. This is not equivalent to 100 theatrical features, but it represents a tremendous amount of creative time and energy, almost as much, I suspect, as went into the film careers of such teams as Abbott and Costello, Martin and Lewis, Powell and Loy, and Dressler and Beery.

The wonder is not that Caesar and Coca and "Your Show of Shows" folded after four years, but that it lasted as long as it did while maintaining such a high order of comedy, which, according to this compilation, had less to do with what Caesar and Coca did than with how they did it.

The Caesar-Coca sketches are often difficult to describe because, essentially, they're never about very much. One of my favorites is a fancy musicale that Caesar interrupts because everything he does seems to be wired for high-fidelity sound. He innocently cracks his knuckles and it sounds like an eight-car collision. He crosses his legs and it is as if a redwood tree had split. He shakes his head and 80 pieces of silver seem to be sliding around in a steamer trunk.

＊

In a pantomime sketch Caesar, Coca and two other performers are the life-sized figures in a Bavarian clock that goes madly, progressively to pieces every hour on the hour. Such a sketch is not about mechanization, any more than the Rockettes are about mechanization. It is beautifully lunatic fantasy, realized with such comic precision that the manner becomes the subject. This is equally true of the sketch in which Caesar, as a poor slob, goes into a movie theater to relax, chewing his two packs of gum and simultaneously eating his popcorn, only to find himself the innocent victim of a lovers' quarrel between Carl Reiner and Miss Coca, who combines the most fearful qualities of a George Price wife with those of the Lucy of "Peanuts." The only parody that works both as parody and as a comedy in its own right is "The Sewing Machine Girl," which, like Sandy Wilson's "The Boy Friend," has a sweetness that transforms what in other, heavier hands would be camp.

These are the film's highlights. Less successful in varying degrees are a couple of sketches that depend largely on Caesar's gifts for dialect and doubletalk, a sketch in which Miss Coca tries to hide the fact that she's smashed up her husband's car and something called "Big Business," a chaotic board meeting that may or may not have been prompted by the television success of "Patterns."

Unlike Jackie Gleason, who is a much more versatile actor than he usually cares to show us, and unlike Milton Berle, whose great popularity on television was simply a part of a career that was already well in progress, Cae-

Sid Caesar in "Ten From Your Show of Shows"
"He gave new standards to TV comedy"

sar's greatest moments have all been on television where he's seen in comparatively short takes. In films such as "Mad, Mad, Mad, Mad World" and "The Busy Body," and on stage in "Little Me" — all more or less legitimate projects, full-length book shows—Caesar's intelligence and his technical facility show through the comic disguises. He never appears to lose himself in what he's doing, and it may be that it's this quality of always seeming to be a little outside the part he's playing that makes him so great in sketches (which, being short, demand that kind of perspective) but destroys what might be called his straight performances.

Watching "Ten from Your Show of Shows" it occurred to me that we—his admirers —are being indefensibly sentimental either by ruing Caesar's lack of real success elsewhere or by finding his post-"Show of Shows" TV performances something less than the earlier performances. The truth of the matter is that as he gave new standards to TV comedy, his television success shaped his talent and his performing personality.

Caesar was too restless an actor to assume the single continuing identity that can carry comedians as different as Woody Allen and Bob Hope through the lean years that might follow the fat—

and that gave Chaplin and Keaton a continuing context for isolated gags. After that great burst of creative energy on "Your Show of Shows," Caesar was repeating himself in his subsequent television work. Repeating himself without much discipline. And since his sketches were never that brilliant, our familiarity with how he did them blunted their effect.

"Ten from Your Show of Shows" is a souvenir of a remarkable time in television's development, and just a bit saddening. In an earlier show business era, the amount of work that Caesar accomplished would have occupied a lifetime. It occupied Caesar less than a decade. Bland, relatively placid personalities are the ones who survive on television. They don't give away too much too quickly. They don't get on your nerves when they aren't in top form, probably because, as with Ed Sullivan, it's not easy to tell the difference between top form and bottom. With Caesar there's never any doubt.

1973 Mr 4, II:1:4

The Cast

BAXTER! directed by Lionel Jeffries; screenplay by Reginald Rose, based on Kin Platt's novel "The Boy Who Could Make Himself Disappear"; music composed and conducted by Michael J. Lewis; director of photography, Geoffrey Unsworth; editor, Teddy Darvas; produced by Arthur Lewis; an Anglo, EMI and Group W Films production, released by National General Pictures. Running time: 100 minutes. At the 68th Street Playhouse, Third Avenue at 68th Street. This film has been classified PG.
Dr. Clemm .... Patricia Neal
Roger Tunnell .... Jean-Pierre Cassell
Chris Bentley .... Britt Ekland
Mrs. Baxter .... Lynn Carlin
Roger Baxter .... Scott Jacoby
Nemo .... Sally Thomsett
Mr. Rawling .... Paul Eddington
Mr. Baxter .... Paul Maxwell

By VINCENT CANBY

"Baxter!" is a sincere, quite solemn film about the breakdown of a teen-age boy who has a speech defect. Roger Baxter (Scott Jacoby) cannot say his r's, a psychic disability he sports as if it were a service ribbon commemorating the most epic squabbles of his uninterested parents. When they are divorced and his mother (Lynn Carlin) moves from California to London with Baxter in tow, the boy goes steadily to pieces.

•

"Baxter!" was directed by Lionel Jeffries, the English actor-turned-director ("The Railway Children") and written by Reginald Rose, who was responsible for a lot of those scripts ("Twelve Angry Men," among others) that made the nineteen-fifties seem the golden age of television drama, at least in retrospect.

"Baxter!", cut down to 60 minutes, might very well look fine on the small screen with the short focal distance. However, there is not enough in Mr. Rose's screenplay to sustain the 100-minute running time of the film, to justify the punctuation of the title or to support the fancy audiovisual effects that the director employs to dramatize poor Baxter's collapse into anxiety and catatonia.

Mr. Rose writes good sardonic dialogue and all of the film's best moments are rather nasty ones. "It was pretty neat," Baxter tells his bored mother after the divorce, "being the only kid in Beverly Hills whose mother and father lived in the same house."

Mr. Rose's point—that children need parental love and understanding—is made early, and then again and again and again. I suppose it can't be made too often—except in a film.

All of the performers are most attractive, though they haven't much to do. Patricia Neal, especially, seems wasted in the very small role of a speech therapist who will probably be the one eventually to rescue Baxter. Young Jacoby projects a nice skepticism, which, in less cheerless circumstances, would probably be very comic.

"Baxter!" opened yesterday at the 68th Street Playhouse.

1973 Mr 5, 23:4

The Cast

SLITHER, directed by Howard Zieff; screenplay by W. D. Richter; director of photography, Laszlo Kovacs, editor, David Bretherton; original music, Tom McIntosh; produced by Jack Sher; a Talent Associates-Norton Simon, Inc., production, distributed by Metro-Goldwyn-Mayer. Running time: 97 minutes. At the Coronet Theater, Third Avenue at 59th Street. This film has been classified PG.
Dick Kanipsia .... James Caan
Barry Fenaka .... Peter Boyle
Kitty Kopetzky .... Sally Kellerman
Mary Fenaka .... Louise Lasser
Vincent J. Palmer .... Allen Garfield
Harry Moss .... Richard B. Shull

By VINCENT CANBY

One week after he has been let out of prison after serving two years for car theft, Dick Kanipsia (James Caan) is ready to go back in. Clearly prison is sanity's sanctuary. The straight world has been occupied by lunatics.

First off, there is the assassination attempt when persons unknown storm the farmhouse where Dick is visiting a former prison mate. Dick, an aging athlete, has the sweet, uncomplaining resilience of the none-too-bright but things like that worry him. So, too, does the kindly truck driver who gives him a ride and then, for no apparent reason, threatens to break his arm.

•

The most baffling creature, however, is Kitty Kopetsky (Sally Kellerman), who offers to give him a lift to the beach and proceeds, among

other things, to hold up a lunch counter. Kitty, a pill-popper, confides: "There's this battle going on inside me. The forces of evil against the forces of light." She pauses, then adds with a beatific smile: "I'll swing with the winner."

All of this is just the beginning of "Slither," a comedy-melodrama about America going to the madhouse in mobile homes, or specifically, about a cross-country trailer chase by Dick, Kitty, and Mr. and Mrs. Henry Fenaka (Peter Boyle and Louise Lasser) to locate what someone describes as "wealth beyond your wildest dreams." Actually it's $312,000 (which is not quite beyond my wildwere embezzled seven years earlier by Barry Fenaka and Dick's now-dead prison friend.

For almost three-quarters of the way (which is about one-quarter of the way further than most films of this sort), "Slither" is as funny and bizarre as it means to be. A sort of wet-blanket of reason eventually is thrown over the narrative when W. D. Richter, who wrote the original screenplay, feels compelled to supply explanations for a lot of the perfectly illogical events we've accepted earlier. Until then, "Slither" is a most entertaining, thoroughly anarchic morality play about an innocent who wakes up to find that his land has been taken over by greedy but mostly ineffectual body-snatchers.

Because few American comedies are ever bothered by such visions, I may have enjoyed "Slither" somewhat more than is warranted by the bright but inconsistent material. The movie is the first directorial effort of Howard Zieff, who is credited as the man who thought up those comic Benson & Hedges TV commercials, which, one might think, would be no guarantee that he could make a feature film as good as this one. As short as they are, however, commercials do depend on a sense of timing and casting, both of which are obvious here.

Miss Kellerman, Mr. Boyle and Miss Lasser do the sort of thing they've done before, though better, but Mr. Caan ("The Godfather"), one of our best young leading actors, is a real surprise as the Candide-like ex-con. He is funny and dim without ever being dumb, which, for most actors, is as difficult as playing Lear.

"Slither" opened yesterday at the Coronet Theater.

1973 Mr 8, 32:2

By VINCENT CANBY

Ludwig II became king of Bavaria in 1864, at the age of 19, and more or less misruled until he was certified

Helmut Berger and Romy Schneider

LUDWIG, directed by Luchino Visconti; story and screenplay by Mr. Visconti and Enrico Medioli, with the collaboration of Suso Cecchi D'Amico; executive producer, Robert Gordon Edwards; director of photography, Armando Nannuzzi; film editor, Ruggero Mastroianni; music by Robert Schumann, Richard Wagner and Jacques Offenbach; released by Metro-Goldwyn-Mayer. At the 59th Street East Twin 2 Theater. Running time: 173 minutes. This film is classified R.

Ludwig .... Helmut Berger
Elizabeth of Austria ..... Romy Schneider
Richard Wagner .... Trevor Howard
Cosima von Bulow .... Silvana Mangano
Father Hoffman .... Gert Frobe
Durcheim .... Helmut Griem
Queen Mother .... Isabella Telezynska

insane, three days before his suicide in 1886. He was not a good man. Like A. A. Milne's King John, Ludwig had his whims and ways, only a few of which have put posterity in his debt: he was Richard Wagner's friend and patron through thick and thin, and he was responsible for the construction of some of Bavaria's maddest castles, including the spectacular Neuschwanstein. Yesterday's fiscal scandal is today's tourist attraction, but Ludwig was mostly a rotter.

It's this aspect of Ludwig that seems most to fascinate Luchino Visconti, the great Italian director whose preoccupation with things Germanic is resulting in films of progressively less importance.

"The Damned" (1969), as operatic as it was, was a hugely effective evocation of a civilization's collapse as detailed in the terrible deeds of a Krupp-like munitions family. Visconti's adaptation of Mann's "Death in Venice" (1971) failed, but it failed with such consistent intelligence that one was always aware of a system of ideas within it.

"Ludwig," which opened yesterday at the 59th Street Twin 2 Theater, is opera buffa that doesn't know it. Visconti and his writers give us the story of Ludwig's reign (or, at least, the outline of it) in a manner that is meant to be grand but actually is just a frantic inventory of what historians usually call his excesses— his rather superficial appreciation for art and architecture, his love of sweets (which resulted in his teeth falling out) and especially his love affairs with a series

of grooms, actors and other pretty fellows.

Visconti has been such an intelligent film maker in the past that it's difficult to believe that "Ludwig" could be quite as bereft of ideas as it is. Is it about kingship? About the genesis of the Second Reich under the domination of the Prussian dynasty? About family? I don't think so. All of these things are touched upon at one point or another, in the almost three hours of running time, but always in what would be called telephone scenes in a contemporary drama—the sort of get-it-over-with scenes designed to give us necessary information as quickly as possible.

Mostly "Ludwig" consists of the spectacle of Ludwig (Helmut Berger) getting more and more depraved, from the early scenes in which he delays his coronation to drink champagne from a goblet (in movies about depravity, people always drink from goblets, not glasses) to those in which he spies on one of his grooms bathing nude in the castle lake, until, toward the end, there's a full-scale, though fairly lethargic orgy. We've seen most of these things done better in other Visconti films.

It may be one of my biases, but movies about royal personages, usually trike me as being essentially comic. It has something to do with a lot of ordinary folk trying to act like royals, and usually succeeding in looking only like stage extras. The royals in "Ludwig" all seem a little second-rate, even Romy Schneider, who plays Ludwig's cousin, the Empress Elizabeth of Austria, with whom he thinks he is sort of in love. It also has something to do with the rhythm of drama in which so much emphasis is placed on the arrivals and departures of royal carriages, on entrances up grand staircases and on people walking regally through doorways.

These things give "Ludwig" an air of self-importance that it doesn't deserve, any more than it deserves the almost nonstop Wagner and

Schumann on the soundtrack. The images can't compete.

There is one interesting performance in the entire film. Trevor Howard makes a rather British Wagner, but he is a profoundly interesting combination of self-absorption, craftiness, genius and vision. Because everyone else acts as if trying to make an impression during the eruption of a volcano, the comparative understatement of Howard's performance rivets the attention.

1973 Mr 9, 27:1

The Cast

THE HERO, directed by Richard Harris; screenplay by Wolf Mankowitz, from an original story by Joseph Gross; film editor, Kevin Connor; music, Johnny Harris; produced by John Heyman and Mr. Mankowitz; released by Avco Embassy Pictures Corporation. At the First Avenue Screening Room, at 60th Street. Running time: 97 minutes. This film is classified PG.

Eitan .... Richard Harris
Nira .... Romy Schneider
Nimrod .... Kim Burfield
Yasha .... Maurice Kaufman
Weiner .... Yossi Yadin
Chairman .... Shraga Friedman

By ROGER GREENSPUN

Forty years old, fading star of the Tel Aviv soccer team, not much to show for a life of hard play except slowed reflexes, rich in feelings, of course—and frustrations—but with nothing you could call a brain, he marshals his meager resources to face his greatest crisis: his Last Big Game. He is pursued by his past and haunted by his future. His fans are fickle, his apartment's a mess and his car won't go.

He is Eitan, played by Richard Harris and the subject of Mr. Harris's "The Hero," and I've only begun to list his problems. Perhaps the biggest is Nira (Romy Schneider), beautiful sculptor with a burgeoning career and a fine new car. Eitan loves Nira, and after six years of courtship still doesn't know what to do about it. But his worst problem may be the littlest: Nimrod (Kim Burfield), a kid from a kibbutz who lives for soccer and idolizes Eitan. He is a constant reproach. While Eitan drowns his sorrows in vodka Nimrod refuses ice cream cones—so as not to break training.

Anyone familiar with the tradition of the Last Big Game can supply the rest: the careless friends, the callous owners, the fears of age against the demands of youth. It all comes too easily, a kind of prepackaged drama with the fatal distinction that not only is the story formula, but the emotional response must be formula as well.

As a director, and as an actor, Mr. Harris isn't about to deny himself indulgences. His performance is full of too many emphases, appeals to sympathy, expressions of imprecise rage. But his movie is equally mannered. And it is simply the nature of the medium that it can survive

an excessive performance better than a gratuitous camera angle or a passage of lyrical slow-motion intended to force a feeling.

When Eitan faces his team's managers (he is being offered a contract that will effectively put him out to pasture) he sits on a low stool in the center of an almost bare room—like Joan of Arc before the ecclesiastical court at Rouen. A crooked gambler who bribes him to throw the game (you thought you'd escaped that?) materializes out of the shadows, and tempts Eitan with a convertible that almost glows in the dark. But the game itself is thrown away in a confused mess of fancy editing, and whatever might have shown the meaning in

an athlete's life is lost in an attempt to make cinematic points.

Through this movie, as through so much of her mature career, Romy Schneider moves like a bemused enigma, beautiful, mysterious and unexciting. The boy, Kim Burfield, is an accomplished actor—but he is directed very broadly, for a style to match Mr. Harris's. But there are no career predictions to be made from "The Hero." Though it opened here only yesterday at the First Avenue Screening Room, it is not a new film, and it played at European festivals three years ago under the name "Bloomfield."

1973 Mr 9, 27:2

'Payday' Doesn't Shortchange You

By PETER SCHJELDAHL

"PAYDAY" is a brilliant, nasty little chrome-plated razor blade of a movie superficially about the last 36 hours in the life of a country-western singer. On a deeper level, it is a film about certain forms of American striving and desperation, a "road picture" that is not, for once, a sentimental odyssey, but rather a clear-eyed study of people whose lives are linked to the road, how they behave and what becomes of them. Its clarity is what makes it so extraordinary. It is a work of such dead-honest realism that it is hard to know how, except as a kind of literal truth, to take it.

The common reservation of "Payday's" admirers so far — and the grounds on which its detractors have dismissed it — is that it fails to establish a bond with the audience, that it fails to transcend its materials. This is a valid objection, I think, so long as it is advanced gently. For the excellence of "Payday" occurs on a level quite separate from that of conventional drama.

It is a work constructed with all the discipline and flair a good scenarist, good director and good cast can supply, but a work, informed by a kind of ethical commitment to factuality close in spirit to the best cinema verité. It neither exalts nor condescends to its characters, people whose nervous vitality and emotional isolation combine to give "Payday" its rough and ultimately harrowing tone.

"Payday" tells the story of Maury Dann (Rip Torn in what may be the performance of his career), a third-magnitude country star, piano-wire tense at the end of a long road tour in Alabama. Subsisting on whisky and amphetamine, running afoul of everyone around him, he is a sitting duck for the disaster that triggers his destruction. It is not a tragic tale, because the tie between Maury Dann's compulsive, reckless character and his downfall is not felt to be a necessary one — he simply has a run of bad luck at a bad time. But it is a deeply believable tale. Maury Dann is the opposite of "legendary," a real, suffering man in a warped but recognizable world.

We get to know Maury Dann's scrabbling existence by rote, his sordid dealings and fugitive pleasures. He is a star. This entitles him to a Cadillac, a hard-eyed manager and a dog-loyal driver-bodyguard to smooth the rough spots, all the women he wants and the adoration of white, Southern, working-class people. He accepts all these things, not cynically so much as indifferently, as his due. Meanwhile he claws and chisels, abasing himself when he has to, to keep the bubble from bursting and landing him back in the poverty from which he came.

"Payday" was made with a smooth blend of professional and amateur actors. Some of its characters, like Maury Dann's preposterous pill-popping wreck of a mother (Clara Dunn) and food-obsessed driver-bodyguard (Cliff Emmich), are broadly drawn, but

Pop star Rip Torn eyes groupie Elayne Heilveil, as his mistress, Ahna Capri, fumes in "Payday"
"A real, suffering man in a warped but recognizable world"

not one of them sounds a false note. Groupies, journeyman musicians, cops, a bullying disk jockey, an aspiring songwriter and miscellaneous citizens who faultlessly contribute their one or two lines —taken together, they flesh out a social milieu depicted, if not with love, at least with a passionate eye for its vagaries. And some of them — notably Elayne Heilveil's Rosamond, a breathless, anxiety-prone ingenue groupie — are unforgettable, real American originals.

In raising the issue of cinema verite, I do not mean to suggest that "Payday" affects a documentary tone. It is, on the contrary, slickly shot and edited almost, but not quite, to a fault. But there is a profound undercurrent of cinema-verite savvy in the work of scenarist Don Carpenter and director Daryl Duke. (Duke once worked for the Canadian Film Board, an outfit justly famed for its advancement of the documentary form.) For one thing, there is a canny "real-time" development of episode in "Payday," a refusal to be punchy and elliptical that lets an unhurried, absorbing rhythm assert itself. There is plenty of plot, but no insistence on it; events in the film have the random, distracted air of events in life.

Which brings us to Rip Torn, whose Maury Dann is the center and catalyst for all the film's events. His performance is one of those incarnations so complete they make one fear for an actor's future career; he virtually disappears into the role. Torn's kinetic presence, wired-in sexuality and frequent Incredible demon glee are simply perfect. The effect is impressive — awesome, even — rather than involving. We are not meant to identify with Maury Dann, only to watch as he careens increasingly out of control and rages, finally, over the brink. The film tells us to spare our pity. Dann was dealt a winning hand and he blew it. *Sic transit.*

"Payday" is a study in morality without a moral, except maybe that speed kills. (Its graphic demonstration of what too much amphetamine does to the mind and body is salutary.) It shows what can happen to people in whom a horror of poverty and boredom has occluded reason and empathy. Along with this goes a suggestion that things could not be otherwise, that the hero-worship that connects Maury Dann to his constituency of plain folks is based not mainly on his music (of which we get few examples) but on the illusion of a common condition, a shared experience of life.

That the country star has wealth and mobility which his fans lack is not supposed to make a difference; they admire him for living the way they would if they got the chance. The human costs of maintaining this tawdry mutual pretense are acknowledged by no one. "Payday," a work of devastating realism, tots them up to the last digit.

1973 Mr 11, II:13:7

is preparing him for his sacred initiation as brother to the rattlesnake (and to talk like a medicine show Confucius). Among other bits of wisdom Billy Jack pronounces throughout the film is the answer he gives a young Indian boy who wants to be his apprentice in the forthcoming ceremony.

"In order to be an apprentice," he reminds the boy, "you have to strip yourself of your greed and your ego trips."

There is something of Sgt. York about Billy Jack, who is described as a war hero (an ex-Green Beret) who hates war, and something of both Tonto and the Lone Ranger. He is, of course, half-Indian and he has an uncanny knack for showing up at the scenes of rapes, lynchings, etc., usually, but not always, just in time. "How do you get in touch with Billy Jack?" the sheriff of the town asks the school mistress. "We contact him, Indian-style," she says. "We want him and he comes."

I rather like the fact that he sometimes comes on his horse, sometimes on a red motorcycle. The movie, however, is not about Billy's means of transportation. It's about his mysticism. In the rapture of a vision, Billy reminds the students watching his initiation that "heaven is not out there. The Great Spirit, the Messiah and the Christ are not out there. They are right here!"

This is the sort of thing that is enchanting the "Billy Jack" audiences, who, if they continue to grow, may eventually discover Kahlil Gibran. Billy carries with him at all times a little pouch containing an owl's feather, a kernel of sacred corn and (I think) some snake teeth. "It's my power," he says at one point. Like Samson's hair, someone explains. Among other things it allows him to be shot and lose a lot of blood and yet to look nothing worse than fatigued.

Almost all great legends utilize supermen who are inspiring as examples of human possibility but a little scary as instruments of virtue and vengeance. To see "Billy Jack" as an optimistic vision of an America in which all races and political points of view are eventually reconciled (which is what one critic has done) carefully avoids acknowledging the means of that reconciliation. Billy Jack is no repository of wisdom and no great humanist either. He is a comic strip character with delusions of philosophic grandeur.

The one admirable quality the film exhibits is sincerity,

Why Has 'Billy Jack' Made So Much?

By VINCENT CANBY

ONE of the most financially successful films of the last two years is a drama called "Billy Jack," a passionately muddle-minded contemporary Western about a half-breed Indian named Billy Jack and the members of the "freedom school" he protects from small-town bigots who hate pacifists, pot smokers and long-haired weirdos.

The film, which is now at the Plaza Theater, originally opened in New York July 28, 1971, to mostly bored reviews. Although it didn't last long in New York, it went on to become one of America's most popular films, exhibiting the sort of appeal that has people coming back again and again to see such disparate things as "The Godfather," "The Sound of Music," "Deep Throat" and "El Topo." As of last week,

"Billy Jack" had earned approximately $10,000,000 in the United States and Canada, more than "Bedknobs and Broomsticks," "Nicholas and Alexandra" or "Frenzy," to name just three films to which it bears absolutely no resemblance.

*

"Billy Jack" is saying something to somebody. That's clear enough. What it's saying is something else — and I'm not at all sure that it's quite as hopeful as a lot of critics have recently found it to be. The one thing that is hopeful about the film is that it found a public with very little initial help from either its distributor or from the critics, who are supposed to make or break films although they monitor taste more often than they mold it.

The sentiments of "Billy Jack" are pure. They're also brainbendingly dumb. As I watched the film for the first time at the Plaza the other day, it seemed to me that its effect was to exploit innocence and violence in ways that overrate the power of the first and underrate the complexity of the second, which is just the sort of thinking that contributed to the smug ineffectualness of so much of the opposition to the Vietnam war.

In fits and starts, "Billy Jack" presents itself as a modern legend, as a youth-scene movie and as one of those films that pretend to celebrate life while indulging the ratty behavior of its various villains. Most peculiarly, it shows pacifists to be effective only when there's a kindly, gun-toting Big Brother in the wings to protect them.

All of which may be just what was intended by Tom Laughlin — I've no way of knowing. Mr. Laughlin wrote the screenplay with his wife, Delores Taylor, directed the film, and plays Billy Jack opposite Miss Taylor, who gives the film's only interesting performance as the mistress of the freedom school. Miss Taylor is not exactly the combination of Moreau and Signoret that the ads suggest, but she performs with the kind of monotonous intensity that sometimes transforms lack of technique into the representation of real emotion.

As written and acted by Laughlin, Billy Jack combines the most convenient talents of at least a dozen superheros and demigods. He lives, we are told on the soundtrack, in some ancient Indian ruins with a holy man who which is not to be confused with an indefensible naivete. It's apparent in the choice of subject and in the characterizations, especially in Miss Taylor's performance.

"Billy Jack" is Mr. Laughlin's third film as writer-director, the two earlier being "The Proper Time" (1960), about college students and what used to be called "premarital relations" (not reviewed by The New York Times as far as I can find), and "The Born Losers" (1967), a cycle film that some people I respect honor as the best of its kind (for whatever that is worth). Mr. and Mrs. Laughlin obviously aren't the sort of people who are obsessed with filmmaking to the exclusion of everything else. They cared enough about the education of their own children to found and run the first Montessori school in Los Angeles. Something of that kind of concern shows through "Billy Jack" even when it's being most aggressively, irritatingly simplistic.

1973 Mr 11, II:1:3

The Cast

WHITE SISTER, directed by Alberto Lattuada; screenplay (in Italian with English subtitles) by Iaia Fiastri, Alberto Lattuada, Tonino Guerra and Ruggero Maccari, story by Mr. Guerra and Mr. Maccari; director of photography, Iafio Contini; music by Fred Bongusto; film editor, Sergio Montanari; produced by Carlo Ponti; released by Columbia Pictures. At the Columbia I Theater, 64th Street and Second Avenue. Running time: 96 minutes. This film is classified R.

Sister Germana .... Sophia Loren
Annibale Pezzi ...... Adriano Celentano
The Chief Physician .... Fernando Rey
Guido .... Juan Luis Galiardo
Libyan Brigadiere ....Luis Marin
Dr. Arrighi .... Giuseppe Maffioli
Dr. Filippini .... Sergio Fasanelli
Sister Teresa .... Pilar Gomez Ferrer
Sister Caterina ...... Patrizia de Clara
Lisa .... Teresa Rabal
Martina .... Valentine

By ROGER GREENSPUN

No doubt it comes from seeing too many of the wrong old movies, but from a title like "White Sister" I expected something slightly tropical, mildly mysterious and vaguely erotic. I should have known better. There have been White Sisters on film before—two, in fact: Lillian Gish in 1923 and Helen Hayes in 1933—and though their stories haven't much to do with Sophia Loren in the nineteen-seventies, they, like she, were nursing nuns.

•

Expelled from her African home and duty by the revolutionary government of Libya, Sister Germana (Miss Loren) is assigned to a hospital in Italy—where, immediately, she takes charge. It is a happy-go-lucky hospital, unusual, and with two doctors, two lay nurses, two orderlies, a cook, several hundred patients, and Sophia Loren.

Miss Loren controls the wards, keeps the records, tastes the food, supervises the nurses and assists in the operating room. She is without peer and without competition—*except* from one patient, Annibale Pezzi (Adriano Celentano), atheist, communist and amorous young malingerer who wants to run the hospital his way. It is immediately obvious that he and she will fall in love.

Each in his own way, Annibale and Sister Germana, are forces for good. And from the combination of two such forces—at least in a movie like "White Sister"—there can come only supergood.

Beyond a spell of pouting for Annibale and a bit of heartbreak for Sister Germana, there is not much relief from the goodness, though a hospital always provides emergency cases, terminal cases, hair-breadth recoveries and malpractice mortalities—the whole day-to-day life-and-death routine of the place to make up for real dramatic action.

•

Annibale and Sister Germana have a momentary spiritual union maybe, but no affair. Once they hold hands and, under extenuating circumstances, they kiss (she is devout, but no prude). But the general aura of sentimental piety is never dispelled, not even by the presence of Sophia Loren.

For those who feel, as I do, that if there were no cinema Sophia Loren would be sufficient reason for inventing it, "White Sister" will offer very little more than a beautiful but unanimated mask of their heroine.

Adriano Celentano, a good actor (scarcely known here), is made to portray a kind of sullen rough-edge cuteness. And Fernando Rey, as the hospital's chief of staff, plays straight the quality of distinguished gentleness that he has so brilliantly parodied in the films of Luis Buñuel.

•

Alberto Lattuada directs down for drama and up for emotion with a sometimes-appealing innocence. When a young man expires in a hospital bed to the accompaniment of violins and cellos, and a heavenly choir (I swear) just at the moment of his passing over—it seems less like film than like archaeology, like unearthing the world's oldest cliché, long dead but with its heart still gamely beating.

"White Sister" opened Saturday at the Columbia I Theater.

1973 Mr 12, 38:1

Musical 'Tom Sawyer' Is at Radio City

By VINCENT CANBY

Mark Twain's "The Adventures of Tom Sawyer" is not the great American novel that "The Adventures of Huckleberry Finn" is, but it is the great American book for boys, especially those who grow up in a rural Middle West where one has to manufacture the kind of local history and folklore that boys in the East, South and Far West take for granted.

In the Middle West there are no houses that George Washington ever slept in, no memorable Civil War battlefields, no real mountains, much less any with snow on them year round. In Illinois, there's a town named Cairo, but it's pronounced "Care-oh," and one drive through it should be enough to shrivel any boy's fantasies about ancient Egypt, King Tut's tomb and mysterious Pharoinic curses.

There were once great Indian civilizations in the Middle West, but they have long since vanished, leaving behind a few arrowheads and some burial mounds whose archeological importance has only recently been recognized. Until I read "Tom Sawyer," at the age of 9 or 10, I was convinced that we Middle Westerners had been short-changed.

"The Adventures of Tom Sawyer" is both a story set in its own time (the 1840's) and a middle-aged man's recollections, not of the way growing up ever was in Hannibal, Mo. (which Twain calls St. Petersburg in the book), but of the way any boy worth his salt in imagination would have had it.

Summer is perpetual, friendships are forever, and misconduct of the most minor sort, such as playing hooky, is immensely satisfying. Most adults are tolerable and, in crises, loving. Boredom with swimming, camping and other children's games is periodically broken by extraordinary adventures involving the kind of melodrama (murder, among other things) that allows the boy to be the man he longs to be.

All of these qualities are beautifully evoked in the new film version of the Twain classic that opened yesterday at Radio City Music Hall. This "Tom Sawyer," with music and lyrics by Richard M. Sherman and Robert B. Sherman, who also adapted the screenplay together, is contemporary Hollywood performing at its best, capturing the essentials of a unique work in such a way that even the occasional show-business tone and look become a form of genuine appreciation.

I've never been a great booster of the Sherman brothers, but their work here is first-rate, especially the screenplay that remembers the feelings of the childhood-that-should-have-been without condescension or overwhelming sentimentality. Even their songs are attractive, particularly a three-part title song in which Tom's Aunt Polly (Celeste Holm) and his cousins Sid and Mary express their various reservations about Tom, and a jolly paean to the art of doing absolutely nothing ("Freebootin'"), sung by Tom, Huck Finn and Muff Potter.

The film is so good that it just about recoups the reputation that Arthur P. Jacobs, its producer, lost with the dreadful "Dr. Dolittle." It is also further evidence that Don Taylor, the actor-turned-director, is a film maker of special intelligence. Not only does the film cover most of the classic "Tom Sawyer" incidents (the whitewashing of the fence, Tom and Huck's sudden appearance at their own funeral, the climatic cave confrontation with Injun Joe), but it also introduces lots of other things that are almost equally nice.

There's a very funny schoolroom scene in which Henry Jones, as Mister Dobbins, the master, explains the Crusades in a manner that reminds me of Robert Benchley at work. The film's big production number—the Hannibal holiday picnic—is show biz Americana, and exhilarating. Taylor never holds a scene or a song longer than it can sustain itself, which is most welcome in the final sequence in which Tom and Becky Thatcher are pursued by the evil Injun Joe. The film's terrors are no more terrifying than an enjoyably short nightmare.

Johnny Whitaker has a few too many adult mannerisms to be completely convincing as Tom, but he looks right and he has the sort of spirit that a musical needs. Miss Holm is a lovely, romantic memory of all kind aunts and Warren Oates is, again, fine as the drunken, sweet-natured Muff Potter. Jeff East may be a little too clean and well-scrubbed as Huck, but that's the sort of film it is.

It's also the sort of film that looks right in its houses, landscapes, weather. Taylor shot the film entirely on location in Missouri, and the results are enormously pleasing. The Middle West is not, after all, such a barren place. It has beauty that both the book and the film recognize with enthusiasm.

1973 Mr 15, 28:1

The Program

SOLEIL-O; written and directed by Med Hondo; photography by Francois Catonne; songs and music by Georges Anderson; animation by Pro Santini and Jean-Francois Languionie; produced by Gray Films in French with English subtitles and released by New Yorker Films. Running time: 104 minutes. At the Olympia Theater, Broadway and 107th Street. This film has not been classified.

With: Robert Liensol, Theo Legitimus, Gabriel Glissand, Gregoire Germain, Mabousso Lo, Bernard Fresson and Giles Segal.

"Soleil-O," which opened yesterday at the Olympia Theater, is sharply direct about some of the darkness that has enveloped immigrant, African blacks in France, particularly in Paris.

In his first film, the young, black Mauritanian stage actor-director Mel Hondo makes a pitiable and often dramatic outcry even if his dramatization of injustices is open-ended and inconclusive.

Mr. Hondo is presenting the sad, frustrating existences of his black brother workers in an alien country through the experiences of one educated, gentle immigrant from Mauritania.

While his obvious anger seems biased on occasion, he is meticulous in stressing that white employers and other citizens are fearful of the ever-increasing numbers of black people in France, who were "only a handful" in 1946 and are in the hundreds of thousands now.

If he is elliptical in his use of symbolism and a stream-of-consciousness approach, his total portrait, like the film, is stark black-and-white. A white entrepreneur blandly outlines the need for work aptitude tests to the tall, bearded, young hero at the beginning of his quest for a better life in Paris.

But the civil, religious and educational principles inculcated in African blacks by French colonialists are, however, of little help in qualifying them for jobs in present-day Paris.

The anomaly of people adrift is projected through the cold attitude of wary employers (and union leaders), menial jobs, lack of housing and varied forms of racism. Mr. Hondo, it must be underlined, also is unsparing in his view of black officials in their own country who, it says here, are merely giving the expatriates little but official doubletalk.

One assumes that behind all the symbols, Mr. Hondo is looking for salvation that might come from the precepts of Malcolm X and other black revolutionaries whose portraits we glimpse toward the end of his film.

Mr. Hondo and Robert Liensol, who plays the leading role forcefully and naturally, and the others in his cast of blacks and whites (simply listed by their proper names), have not solved the problem or come up with a prospective solution to it.

But they and, particularly, Mr. Hondo, whose imagery tends to be arty and disjointed, have given us a drama that remains disturbingly vivid. A. H. WEILER.

1973 Mr 15, 55:3

The Screen

Satyajit Ray's "Days and Nights in the Forest" began a commercial engagement yesterday at the First Avenue Screening Room, at 60th Street. The Indian-made import was previously shown here once as an entry in the New York Film Festival in 1970. A review by Howard Thompson deemed the feature "a rare, wistful movie that somehow proves it's good to be alive."

The "subtle, perceptive and serene" drama depicts the vacation involvement of "four youngish pals from Calcutta" with a nearby family in the Palamau woods. Expert photography evokes a tranquil setting and frames a small cast, all of whose members perform effortlessly, with good English titles. "But it is the light brush strokes of the director that give the picture its flow and substance, Chekhovian to look at but Ray at heart."

1973 Mr 15, 29:1

The Cast

FEAR IS THE KEY, directed by Michael Tuchner; written by Robert Carrington, after a novel by Alistair MacLean; director of photography, Alex Thomson; music, Roy Budd; film editor, Ray Lovejoy; produced by Alan Ladd, Jr. and Jay Kanter; released by Paramount Pictures. At the DeMille, Juliet I and neighborhood theaters. Running time: 103 minutes. This film is classified PG.

John Talbot .... Barry Newman
Sarah Ruthven .... Suzy Kendall
Vyland .... John Vernon
Jablonski .... Dolph Sweet
Royale .... Ben Kingsley
Ruthven .... Ray McAnally

By ROGER GREENSPUN

An action movie that generally manages to deliver some action and is almost always as good as it pretends to be (however modest its pretensions) must be allowed some excellence by its own scale of values. That is the scale, the only proper scale, to apply to Michael Tuchner's "Fear Is the Key," a minor, rather satisfying entertainment that opened yesterday at neighborhood theaters.

It is based on an Alistair MacLean novel, and like "Puppet on a Chain," the last Alistair MacLean novel seen on film here, it has a little of the look and something of the feel of a James Bond thriller—but cheaper, more threadbare, with fewer gadgets and more nerve.

This doesn't necessarily make for better movies, but it should make for different expectations. People seem to wear the same clothes all through the film. They chase economy cars, shoot from smaller arsenals. And sometimes second best, like virtue, is its own reward.

•

So the film seems to need its locations—the flat Louisiana coastline, the offshore oilfields, the sumptuous rain-swept mansion (this last shot in England)—for use rather than just for exotic appeal. There is a car chase, ingenious, obligatory, overlong and rather dull, but there are also the tidal swamps, the mostly empty roads receding into a distance that make up in atmospheric emotion for what the story lacks in sense.

The story, an incredible intrigue enacted by one John Talbot (Barry Newman) to revenge the murder of his wife and child and at the same time make the world safe for Western monetary systems, is sufficient for the movie but not for critical examination. It is enough that it provides some dangerous encounters and the particular kind of good-guy heroics that have become trade.
Barry Newman's stock in
No matter where he is courting danger ("The Salzburg Connection," "Vanishing Point") Newman always seems vaguely out of place. I've about decided that "out of place" is really where he belongs, and that he is not so much the hero as a fantasist (city-bred, nice Jewish boy, good-looking though a trifle cross-eyed) seeking heroism.

•

When he goes "Aaargh," near suffocation underwater in the film's climax, he is almost pure comic book—which is already a kind of sophistication, though perhaps not so intended. It is in terms of such comic-book sophistication that he meets the villain, Vyland (John Vernon), and will one day court the heroine, Sarah Ruthven (Suzy Kendall), waiting for him topsides with her oil-rich dad.

We never really put away childish things, and when we pick them up from time to time it may be well that we can do it with games as gracefully innocuous as "Fear Is the Key."

1973 Mr 15, 55:6

The Cast

LOST HORIZON, directed by Charles Jarrott; screenplay by Larry Kramer, based on the novel by James Hilton; music by Burt Bacharach; lyrics by Hal David; director of photography, Robert Surtees; editor, Maury Winetrobe; produced by Ross Hunter; released by Columbia Pictures, Running time: 15Ŧ minutes. At Loews State Theater, Broadway at 45th Street, and Tower East Theater, Third Avenue near 72d Street. This film has been classified G.

Richard Conway .... Peter Finch
Catherine .... Liv Ullmann
Sally Hughes .... Sally Kellerman
Sam Cornelius .... George Kennedy
George Conway .... Michael York
Maria .... Olivia Hussey
Harry Lovett .... Bobby Van
Brother To-Lenn .... James Shigeta
High Lama .... Charles Boyer
Chang .... John Gielgud

By VINCENT CANBY

To a small boy in 1937, Frank Capra's film adaptation of James Hilton's "Lost Horizon" did not seem as naive as it did the last time I saw it, four or five years ago, but it remains an example of romantic Hollywood filmmaking at its best. It has the style of Ronald Colman, the wit of Robert Riskin (its screenwriter) and its sets, costumes and special effects are superb. In those days, there was virtually no place or thing that could not be reproduced bigger than life on any Hollywood backlot.

One can even accept the Capra film's rather smug, ostrichlike attitudes toward world problems, if only as a souvenir of the decade that gave us, among other things, the Reichstag fire, Munich and World War II. Shangri-La — Hilton's secret Tibetan valley where poverty, illness and age are unknown and the only excesses are those of moderation — is an almost perfect expression of the wishes of a very specific time — one that is long-since past, at least to me.

•

Not so to Ross Hunter, the producer ("Airport," "Imitation of Life," "Magnificent Obsession") who has devoted a lot of his career to trying to preserve the glamour that once was Hollywood's by ransacking its old movies. With his updated, musicalized remake of "Lost Horizon," which opened yesterday at Loews State I and the Tower East Theaters, Hunter persists in his mad if harmless mission with the fanaticism of someone trying to build sandcastles at the water's edge.

This "Lost Horizon," with Peter Finch at the head of a not-quite-all-star cast, is a big, stale marshmallow, notable, perhaps, in that most of it was filmed in and around Hollywood at what is reported to have been a rather large budget. Money apparently doesn't go very far in Hollywood these days, for the film, in addition to packing all of the dramatic punch of a Moral Re-Armament pamphlet, is surprisingly tacky in appearance.

•

When we aren't seeing the magical valley of Shangri-La in long-shot as something painted through trick photography, we see it in close-up as a couple of seedy backlot sets, one of which, the High Lama's palace, looks like Pickfair remodelled as a motel. The old Hollywood craftsmanship is as dead as the arch attitudes and philosophizing of Larry Kramer's screenplay, which replays most of the memorable moments of the original film, with sometimes hilarious results.

"I am Chang," says John Gielgud, his eyes slightly taped for an Oriental effect, but you are not meant to snicker. "Can this be the skin of a 100-year-old woman?" asks 20-year-old Olivia Hussey who plays the remarkably well-preserved Maria, whom we all wait to turn into an ancient peanut once she goes beyond the Shangri-La pass.

The most hilarious moments, however, are the original contributions of Hunter, Charles Jarrott, his director, and Hermes Pan, who choreographed some of the great Astaire-Rogers musicals but is out of his element here.

•

With the exception of Bobby Van, who plays a second-rate comic who is hijacked to Shangri-La along with Finch, the British diplomat, nobody in the film can dance very well, not the chorus boys (featured in a pricelessly ill-suited number celebrating the joys of fatherhood) nor poor Sally Kellerman, who plays a Newsweek correspondent fed up with life. It's extraordinary how Miss Kellerman successfully maintains her appeal even while failing as a singer and dancer. Dancer? What she does is try to keep time.

The second-rate auspices just about destroys everyone in the film, with the possible exceptions of Finch, Van and Michael York. Liv Ullmann, who is the world's most beautiful woman when photographed by Ingmar Bergman, is stiff and uncomfortable as a Shangri-La school mistress. Charles Boyer, as the High Lama, dressed in a sheet, looks like the ghost of Hamlet's father emerging from a steam-bath. And how long has it been since you've seen the soul of a dying man depart through a window? You'll see it again here.

•

The music written by Burt Bacharach is often pleasant, but it's too sophisticated for both the movie and the lyrics, written by Hal David. The lyrics, when not silly, have a way of attracting attention to the ersatz nature of the entire enterprise. "Look inside yourself," Miss Ullmann sings to Finch, "that's where the truth always lies." The conjunction of truth and lies hardly seems accidental in a film that sets out to recall a kind of filmmaking now lost, but succeeds only in denting pleasant memories.

1973 Mr 15, 58:1

The Program

LEACOCK, a retrospective of documentary films by Ricky Leacock; "Canary Island Bananas" (1935), 12 minutes; "Primary" (1960), 30 minutes; "A Happy Mother's Day" (1963), 26 minutes; "Chiefs" (1968), 18 minutes; "Queen of Apollo" (1970), 12 minutes. At the Film Forum, 256 West 29th Street, today and tomorrow, and next Friday through Sunday, † 8 P.M.

By VINCENT CANBY

The extraordinary growth of television in the nineteen-fifties and the concurrent development (mostly by independent film makers) of lightweight camera and sound equipment, changed not only the fortunes of a number of documentary film makers but also the look and sound of their films. Instructive, bossy voice-over narration became increasingly rare as the films came to speak for themselves, through their subjects. It's called Cinéma vérité abroad, direct cinema here.

Although commercial TV producers were never the most adventurous of bosses, they commissioned a lot of material of great political and social interest, including many films that they eventually chose not to show, for one reason or another.

•

These are some of the things touched upon in the new Film Forum show, "Leacock," a retrospective of five films by Ricky Leacock, who is one of America's most accomplished practitioners of direct cinema (along with D. A. Pennebaker, Albert and David Maysles, Frederick Wiseman and Canada's Allan King). The show is hardly definitive, even of Leacock's work, but it reminds us of the achievements of the new documentary, along with some of the questions of ethics that the form prompts.

The program, chosen by Leacock, begins with a straightforward, completely conventional, pre-direct cinema documentary, "Canary Island Bananas," which Leacock made on his father's banana plantation in 1935. He was then 13 and a film maker whose talent was weighted down only by the solemnity of his age.

The remainder of the program is devoted to more recent, more typical work: "Primary," Leacock's 30-minute version (which he prefers) of the 54-minute film covering the Hubert H. Humphrey-John F. Kennedy contest in Wisconsin in 1960; "A Happy Mother's Day" (1963), a jaundiced look at the efforts of the city fathers of Aberdeen, S. D., to turn the first-month birthday of the Fischer quintuplets into a civic promotion; "Chiefs" (1968), made in collaboration with Noel Parmentel Jr., a report on a convention of police chiefs in Honolulu and "Queen of Apollo" (1970), about a New Orleans debutante who becomes more queenly than Jacqueline Kennedy (one of the participants in "Primary") during her reign as queen at a Mardi Gras ball.

Taken collectively, the films are a remarkable record of a time and place, of how people look and sound, of their attitudes, hopes, prejudices, fears and blind spots. The montage is vivid and funny and (I suspect) meant to be always a bit scary, whether Leacock is showing us a couple of nuns pushing in to take snaps of the Fischer family on parade in Aberdeen or a salesman pitching American policemen on the versatility of a new, "nonlethal" type of buckshot shell.

•

The montage is fascinating, though it is not necessarily complete and not without its biases, which is not particularly disturbing at first if, like me, your biases coincide with the film maker's.

One begins to wonder, eventually, if such committed film-making — for example, making absolute fools out of the police chiefs — is enough. Did, by any chance, the policemen convening in the shadow of Diamond Head ever discuss the problem of police corruption? According to the film, they spent their time trying out new weapons, singing fraternally, giggling at their wives, learning the hula and listening to speeches upholding the police action at the 1968 Democratic convention.

At his best, which is much of the time, Leacock functions not as a wide-eyed reporter but as a critic whose responsibility is to his own conscience.

1973 Mr 17, 17:1

The Cast

THE VAULT OF HORROR, directed by Roy Ward Baker; screenplay by Milton Subotsky; director of photography, Denys Coop; editor, Oswald Hafenrichter; produced by Max J. Rosenberg and Mrs. Subotsky; released by Cinerama Releasing Corporation. At the Penthouse, 86th Street Twin 1 and Murray Hill theaters. Running time: 86 minutes. This film is classified R.

Rogers ....Daniel Massey
Donna ....Anna Massey
Maitland ....Michael Craig
Alex ....Edward Judd
Sebastian ....Curt Jurgens
Inez ....Dawn Addams
Indian Girl ....Jasmina Hilton
Fakir ....Ishaq Bux
Critchit ....Terry-Thomas
Eleanor ....Glynis Johns
Moore ....Tom Baker
Diltant ....Denholm Elliott

By ROGER GREENSPUN

If there is, as I believe, a natural hierarchy in horror films — then to the top rises the vampire movie, and at the very bottom creeps the scary omnibus vignette film, especially the scary vignette film with comic undertones. An example of the last, "The Vault of Horror," opened yesterday at three local theaters.

Actually, "The Vault of Horror" contains a brief vampire story, called "Midnight Mess" (that title happens to be the cleverest thing in the movie), that makes the mistake of equating vampirism with sustenance rather than sex. The hero of "Midnight Mess" (Daniel Massey), a thorough rotter who becomes dinner before his tale is done, meets each night with four other gentlemen to recount the dream, so he thinks, of his own violent demise.

The others do likewise, with miseries ranging from burial alive to a fatal rage for order. Everyone pretty much deserves his death (I'm not sure about Terry-Thomas, who merely wants his house kept neat), and everyone gets it through one of those ironic twists of fate so dear to the soul of 10th-rate mystery fiction.

Several distinguished performers — Anna Massey, Michael Craig, Dawn Addams, Glynis Johns, among others — appear in the film, and none is ever quite so bad as the material warrants.

•

Except for the tacky optical effects in an episode called "This Trick'll Kill You," where you can see the invisible wires supporting an unsupported vertical Indian rope, the film displays a surface proficiency that keeps suggesting better things. The director, Roy Ward Baker ("A Night to Remember," "Five Million Years to Earth"), has made good movies in the past. But toward "The Vault of Horror" he displays a reticence approaching fastidiousness, which may be the cover for a well-concealed but very honorable distaste.

1973 Mr 17, 17:1

I Won't Tango, Don't Ask Me

By GRACE GLUECK

IF, as my male filmgoing friends assure me, there is such a thing as a "woman's picture," i.e., one that plays up to the romantic sexual fantasies of housewives, then "Last Tango in Paris" can surely be regarded as its male counterpart — the perfect macho soap opera. From the film's beginning, when its he-man heel-hero, Paul, engages a compliant Parisian playgirl, Jeanne, in a genital collision, through the very end, where Jeanne reacts to his aggressions with a violence that metaphorically expresses her own sexual rage, its fantasies comfortably reinforce the misogynist stereotypes that have always enabled men to regard women as something less than emotional peers.

•

We'll get back to that in a minute. But first, some recap for those —and they've got to be hermits—who have managed to remain unaware of "Tango's" story line. The setting of this Bernardo Bertolucci-Marlon Brando collaboration is Paris; its two protagonists are Paul, a handsome but aging expatriate loser of 45, and Jeanne, a sexy bourgeoise of 20, whose physical endowments we get to know intimately during the picture's course. (Not Paul's, however; in keeping with the conventions of art and pornography in the Western world, the camera focuses frequently and frontally on Jeanne in her birthday suit, while allowing Paul — who, granted, has less youthful a body —to keep his clothes on for almost every sexual occasion. When he's naked, it's all soft-focus.)

At the film's beginning, Paul spots Jeanne on the street and follows her to an apartment house, where he manages to station himself beforehand in a flat she inspects for rental. After some preliminary stalking, the two, as mentioned, engage head-on in a powerful sexual encounter. Appetites whetted, they embark on a game plan: they will meet at the apartment for sex only, avoiding all reference to their outside lives. This stylized — well, tango — is led, of course, by Paul. And it is he who is free to break the step, revealing fragments of his barren emotional life with the depth of a Holden Caulfield while abruptly dismissing any attempts on Jeanne's part to give voice to hers.

The film follows Jeanne and Paul through three days of sex- (not love-) making in the apartment, with digressions to their outside preoccupations.

During the course of those, we discover that Paul is in a state of shock and rage over the suicide of his faithless wife, an inscrutable femme du monde with whom he shared the proprietorship of a seedy hotel — the same hotel in which his wife openly shared the bed of a lover; and that Jeanne has a fiancé, a sweet young film freak, for whom she is also less a woman than an object (he is, in fact, making a movie of her life and keeps her constantly on camera).

In the apartment, masochist Jeanne takes sex from sadist Paul as, in his hostility, he dispenses it. And often (as in the now famous butter-and-sodomy scene) it hurts. (Male fantasy: Women may protest, but they really wallow in rough handling; it's good for their souls.) At one point in the throes of aging adolescence, Paul bids Jeanne insert her fingers in his anus to explore a notion he has about death; at another, he dangles a dead rat before her horrified face. But he has his tender moments: in one, he gives Jeanne a bath with a paternal condescension that might suit a 3-year-old. (Male fantasy: Treat women as little girls; it fulfills their need for protection.)

•

Purged of his grief after three days, Paul fails to show at the flat. Jeanne decides that the frolic is ended; she'll marry her nitwit moviemaker. She leaves the apartment, only to encounter Paul on the street. "It's over," she tells him, but — Surprise! Our feckless antihero is smitten, panting now to reveal all of the Real Self he's held back. (It turns out in his case that more is even less.) With the same delicatesse he has used so far to avoid probing Jeanne's real feelings, he lays on her a heavy declaration of love — going so far, in fact, as to intimate marriage. But Jeanne refuses and runs off. Paul pursues her to a tango palace, where a dance contest is in progress. (Heavy on the symbolism, Bertolucci uses the elegant, stylized steps of the tango and its frozen postures to suggest a totentanz, a dance of death.)

As they sway in drunken parody among the dancers, Paul once again declares his yearning for Jeanne, but she, her wishes and desires still ignored, is unrelenting. The sex spree is over. Again she takes off, and again is pursued by Paul, up and into her mother's apartment. Panicked, she takes out a gun, a symbolic equivalent to the sexual weaponry Paul has used with her, and shoots him as he attempts to embrace her. With a gallant self-mockery that is pure Brando, he strolls out onto a balcony and dies, having the aplomb first to remove his chewing gum and fix it firmly to the railing.

•

Holding the smoking gun, Jeanne rehearses her story for the police: "I didn't even know his name. He followed me on the street. He tried to attack me." The rage that led to the shooting is motivated, but again the act itself is focused on Paul, a confirmation of his bad luck as a born loser. And what Bertolucci is really saying is (male fantasy): See what happens when you strip yourself bare for a woman?

If the film can't really be accepted as an erotic one, it is still less valid —heaven help us —as a drama about man-woman relationships. Brando's and Bertolucci's dislike of women is intense: it's not only Jeanne whose character they fail to develop in the film. Every woman the camera touches is similarly shortchanged: Paul's bad wife (whom we only see as a waxen corpse laid out in a hotel room); an ugly cliché of a French prostitute who visits the hotel with a client; the mindless bourgeois mothers of both Jeanne and Paul's wife; even the slightly demented black concierge who gives Jeanne the key to the flat. No, the film is a one-actor vehicle, a tour-de-force whose star is involved in a constant—albeit inventive—projection of the life and roles of Marlon Brando.

Yet "Tango" is being hailed—and not just by Pauline Kael, who ought to know better—as a "breakthrough." I think I see why. All unaware, it comes closer than any "romantic" film I've seen to exposing woman's real sexual status.

1973 Mr 18, II:1:1

'Slaughter Hotel' to Young 'Tom'

By VINCENT CANBY

ACCORDING to a critic's notebook, it was this sort of week:

Monday, March 5. At breakfast I was stopped short again by a newspaper ad for a film called "Slaughter Hotel." "See The Slashing Massacre of 8 Innocent Nurses!" the ad screamed. "Slaughter Hotel...A Place Where Nothing Is Forbidden!" Does that really sell tickets? If so, to whom? The Times, at my suggestion, had not bothered to review the film when it opened at the Penthouse Theater. This morning I began to wonder if I was wrong. Perhaps we should monitor more films of this type, which, if they're like "Last House on The Left," deal in knifings, hackings, choppings and complete dismemberments with the sort of resolute earnestness that stag films devote to sex.

*

In the afternoon, a press screening of "Slither," opening at the Coronet Theater. It is a cheerfully erratic, very American comedy written by W.D. Richter and directed by Howard Zieff, neither of whom have ever made a feature before. Richter and Zieff, a graduate of television commercial production, seem to be making a film about the meutal and moral health of the society for which most television programing is invented. Everybody in the movie is a monomaniac about something. Everyone except Dick Kanipsia (James Caan), a trusting car thief who gets out of prison after serving a two-year stretch and immediately finds himself on a treasure hunt in the company of (1) an amphetamine freak (Sally Kellerman), (2) an embezzler (Peter Boyle) who has a passion for mobile homes, and (3) the embezzler's loving wife (Louise Lasser). Dick's reasonable puzzlement is the fixed point on which the comedy depends. The narrative runs low on invention towards the end, but it is written, directed and performed with an unusually perceptive comic intelligence. Not a bad Monday, not a bad way to start the week.

*

Tuesday, March 6. This morning the papers again carried the ads for "Slaughter Hotel," as well as one for a double bill of "Twitch of The Death Nerve" and "The Blind Dead," opening tomorrow. "Diabolical! Fiendish!" says one ad. "The Ultimate Tolerance Test for Violence!" The ad also featured a picture of a girl with what appears to be a scythe at her neck. Not included are the names of the distributors, the producers, the directors or the actors.

Wednesday, March 7. Luchino Visconti's "Ludwig" was screened. At last. The film had been scheduled to open two weeks ago but was postponed at the last minute because Visconti had not finished re-editing it. When it was shown in Hollywood several weeks ago, it ran 186 minutes and Variety reported that the director was going to eliminate 30 minutes. He actually took out 13. The film would be intolerable at any length. Visconti has made some fine films in the past ("Senso," "Rocco and His Brothers," "The Damned," among others), but he seems to have lost his bearings in this era of screen freedom. In the manner of a lapsed celibate trying to make up for lost time, he has begun to indulge his interest in corruption with embarrassing enthusiasm. There is something essentially prissy in his attitude.

"Ludwig" is the story of King Ludwig II of Bavaria (Helmut Berger), who reigned from 1864, when he was 19, until he was certified insane in 1886. In passing, Visconti touches on Ludwig's patronage of Wagner and his passion for building magnificent castles on the Rhine, but the director is most interested in showing us Ludwig's physical and emotional decline. However, the movie is so muddled that you might get the idea that all his teeth fell out because he was homosexual, rather than a candy addict. "Ludwig" takes its royalty and their problems more seriously than the rest of us are likely to. "Rulers such as us," says the Empress Elizabeth (Romy Schneider) of Austria, "have nothing to do with history. We are only display, unless someone makes us important by assassinating us." Which may or not explain why Ludwig goes so thoroughly to pot, having his way with this groom and that, winding up at an orgy that looks like an all-boy cookout. Trevor Howard is interesting (and terribly English) as Wagner, but everyone else behaves as if he were a dress extra in grand opera.

*

Thursday, March 8. In Philadelphia for a noontime television show and, while having breakfast, I watched one of the station's quiz shows on a color set. Was it just this set, I mused to a waitress, or has color television reduced everything in the real world to either blue or orange?

Friday, March 9. This has been a day without sunlight. From 2:30 P.M. until 5:01 P.M. I watched Ross Hunter's remake of "Lost Horizon" with music by Burt Bacharach and lyrics by Hal David. It probably did cost a lot of money, but money doesn't go too far in Hollywood these days and "Lost Horizon" looks surprisingly tacky. The hills surrounding the lamasery at Shangri-La look very Southern California, as does the architecture of the High Lama's palace. The Bacharach music is too good, too sophisticated, for David's lyrics and the movie that contains it. Larry Kramer's screenplay makes the mistake of repeating familiar bits of dialogue (or reasonable facsimiles of same) and even key camera movements from the classic Frank Capra 1937 film, with the result that the movie becomes unintentionally funny in important moments. A big-screen imitation of the Late Late show. The all-star cast includes Peter Finch, Liv Ullmann, Olivia Hussey, Bobby Van, Sally Kellerman and John Gielgud. Kellerman and Gielgud should sue.

At 6 P.M. I slipped into the Penthouse Theater to see "Slaughter Hotel," which turns out to be not about a hotel but an expensive nursing home outside Rome (the film is Italian and English-dubbed) specializing in highly-strung neurotics, all women. One patient gets put into an iron maiden, another is shot with a crossbow, a third is sliced up with a sword. In addition there's some lesbian hanky-panky, a lot of complete nudity and buckets of splattered blood.

The audience accepted it all mutely.

There were, I'd estimate, about two dozen people in the theater, including a couple with their two children, aged approximately 7 and 9.

On leaving the Penthouse, I grabbed a hot dog and went over to 42d Street to see "Twitch of The Death Nerve" and "The Blind Dead" at the Harris. I knew if I didn't go immediately I never would. Like "Slaughter Hotel," these are two imports that have been dubbed into English, and they are terrible. The 42d Street audience, however, almost made them bearable, since they accepted the films as being the ridiculous fantasies they are. "Twitch of The Death Nerve" (R-rated, Italian) is not easy to sit through, however, even when the audience laughs. Absolutely everybody is murdered, on-screen, by hanging and drowning, but mostly by ax.

"The Blind Dead" (PG, Spanish-Portuguese) has to do with some undead medieval knights who emerge at midnight to suck what blood they can find. They are something less than terrifying, though, looking rather like monks in sugar-frosted habits. It may be harmless enough, but I'm not sure that "Slaughter Hotel" and "Twitch of The Death Nerve" are.

Like the American-made "Last House on The Left" they are such vivid spectacles of pointless, mindless cruelty that I could almost suspect them of political subversion, though to what end, I'm still undecided. Do they further corrupt the common folk, thereby hastening the end of the old order? Do they preach social anarchy? Or, perhaps, do they numb the mind in such a way as to create a citizenry so apathetic it becomes powerless in its disinterest?

*

Saturday, March 10. At 9 A.M. I arrived at Radio City Music Hall to see a preview of "Tom Sawyer," only to find that the location had been changed to the Rivoli. It was less than 12 hours since I'd crawled out of the Harris Theater and I was thinking that in this direction awaited madness. No time to indulge my own dreams. Always someone else's and usually of an inferior nature.

I sat toward the rear of the Rivoli orchestra, looking, I'm sure, glum, as did a lot of the parents accompanying the children. Said a father to his small daughter: "Remember, I gave up a tennis game for this. It'd better be good." She seemed apprehensive. Further front, one woman was putting on nail polish. The lights dimmed and there was an overture of the Richard M. and Robert B. Sherman score (this is a musical adaptation), and it sounded very familiar. When the film began, however, it was quickly apparent that this "Tom Sawyer," adapted as well as scored by the Sherman brothers and directed by Don Taylor, is a first-class hit. It manages to capture, in 1973 show biz terms, a lot of the feelings that I associate with the book, which, of course, is not very 1973 show biz. It's like the first day of summer when you're about 9 or 10, and it's so good that I'll write about it later.

1973 Mr 18, II:1:6

The Cast

TWO PEOPLE, directed by Robert Wise; written by Richard De Roy; director of photography Henri Decae; music by David Shire; film editor, William Reynolds; produced by Mr. Wise; released by Universal Studios. At the Baronet, 59th Street and Third Avenue. Running time: 100 minutes. This film is classified R.

Evan Bonner	Peter Fonda
Deirdre McCluskey	Lindsay Wagner
Barbara Newman	Estelle Parsons
Fitzgerald	Alan Fudge
Gilles	Philippe March

By ROGER GREENSPUN

"There's no time. There's no time for *any* of this."

"Almost eight hours. Some people don't ever have eight hours."

And so together they begin to waste those eight hours hand and hand, strolling down the dark and deserted boulevards past all the tourist attractions of Paris. Pausing before Notre Dame she grows bitterly philosophical: "By the time you get out, that may have become a parking edifice!" But eventually they do get to bed, and, through a night of blurred-focus passion, they make love. And if she does not say "I never knew it could be like this," it is perhaps only because she could never be heard over the welling up of the music — the music that follows them everywhere on plucked and bowed strings and sounds nothing like so much as total submission to the last three bars of the "Summer of '42" theme.

●

They have come to Paris —he, she and the background music—from Marrakesh, and they are bound for New York. They are the central elements in Robert Wise's "Two People," a very silly movie that opened yesterday at the Baronet Theater. He is Evan Bonner, high-principled Vietnam war deserter returning home to face the music (not this music, some other music). She is Deirdre McCluskey, high-fashion model and daughter of a West Virginia coal miner (what else?), returning home to her little illegitimate son, to at least $100,000 a year and to a life that has lost its meaning. Naturally, they fall in love.

●

I am tempted to hang the movie with quotations from its dialogue — which would be unfair. It is really equally bad in all departments. It may even be most aggressively awful when its people stop talking and take the train from Marrakesh to Casablance or the plane from Casablanca to Paris (first class all the way) or just watch the streets from their hotel rooms. There has never been such appreciation for the poetry of Paris traffic patterns, and in general the esthetic program behind "Two People" seems to be: When in doubt, travel.

●

Estelle Parsons plays a supporting role as a fashion editor accompanying Deirdre, and, though conventionally brittle, her performance comes closer to suggesting two sides to a person than does any other characterization in the movie. As Deirdre, Lindsay Wagner, a newcomer, is pretty and solemn. But a tendency for her facial expressions to disintegrate into grimaces (perhaps occasioned by the lines she must speak) makes it difficult to accept her quality. Peter Fonda, as Evan Bonner, seems greatly withdrawn to some inward meditation—a strategy, I believe, not of performance but of self-defense.

Separate units are credited with filming in North Africa, in Paris and in New York City. But "Two People" is remarkably of a piece—not with the consistency of a movie director like Robert Wise, but rather with the consistency of something cooked up from the same package of synthetic soup.

1973 Mr 19, 46:4

PAINTERS PAINTING, a documentary feature produced and directed by Emile de Antonio; sound and editing, Mary Lampson; camera, Ed Emshwiller; distributed by New Yorker Films. Running time: 116 minutes. At the Fifth Avenue Cinema, Fifth Avenue at 12th Street.
With: Willem de Kooning, Helen Frankenthaler, Hans Hoffman, Jasper Johns, Robert Motherwell, Barnett Newman, Kenneth Noland, Jules Olitski, Philip Pavia, Larry Poons, Robert Rauschenberg, Frank Stella, Andy Warhol, Leo Castelli, Henry Geldzahler, Clement Greenberg, Tom Hess, Philip Johnson, Hilton Kramer, William Rubin, Robert Scull, among others.

By VINCENT CANBY

In the past, Emile de Antonio has made some fine documentaries, including "Point of Order" and "Millhouse," each a scathing, highly biased attack against someone or something. His newest film, "Painters Painting," represents a change of

mood. It's a great big, cheerfully uncritical hug of a movie about a subject he adores, the contemporary New York art scene and the people who make it hustle.

Watching it is like being at a cocktail party. Robert Rauschenberg is there. Andy Warhol is there (with Brigit Berlin taking Polaroid snaps of him). Jasper Johns is there. As are Barnett Newman and Henry Geldzahler and Kenneth Noland and Frank Stella and Larry Poons. Robert Scull and Ethel are there, looking pleased and modest and just slightly uncomfortable, as if waiting for the next attack by the philistines who refer to him as the taxi tycoon when he is really the Lorenzo di Medici of pop.

The movie is mistitled. It should be called "Painters Talking." Although we do see Larry Poons ripping a large color-filled canvas off his studio floor, and although we see old still pictures of the late Jackson Pollock at work, most of the movie is devoted to the painters talking about themselves and their work.

A few make more sense: Jasper Johns, Willem de Kooning, Andy Warhol (at least, he smiles a lot and looks genuinely modest). At one place or another, some basic points are made about the various trends in American art that followed abstract expressionism. Much of it, however, is cocktail party conversation. Says Barnett Newman: "Esthetics are for me what ornithology is for birds."

Mr. Rauschenberg says that to be an abstract expressionist one had to have time to feel sorry for oneself. He doesn't and didn't. Mr. Stella says that the kind of contemporary painting he represents is designed, among other things, to keep the viewer from "reading" the painting, and to make it difficult for critics to describe and thus difficult to carry out their function.

A lot of "Painters Painting" is funny (intentionally), some of it is boring (unintentionally) and a great deal of it is somewhat less informative than is absolutely necessary. Hilton Kramer, art editor of The New York Times, is given rather short shrift when he tries to trace the European roots of American abstract expressionism. In the festive context of the rest of the film, his attempt amounts to a social mistake.

I would assume that Mr. de Antonio has some opinions (not entirely favorable) about the parts played in the New York scene by various art dealers and curators. You wouldn't know it from "Painters Painting." It all looks like a warm, lovable rat race, even though one in which the stakes can be tremendous. Leo Castelli, the dealer, smiles benignly as he tells of the Jasper Johns that was bought for $2,000 and could be sold today for $200,000.

Mr. de Antonio has been

an observer of the scene for years, and is obviously as fond of the artists as he is fascinated by their work, which has been beautifully photographed in color and black and white by Ed Emshwiller, who is a first-class film maker in his own right. "Painters Painting," which opened yesterday at the Fifth Avenue Cinema, looks great. Like so much contemporary painting, however, it involves too much talk.

1973 Mr 20, 30:1

●

The Cast

GODSPELL, directed by David Greene; associate director, John-Michael Tebelak; screenplay by Mr. Greene and Mr. Tebelak, based on the stage production as conceived and directed by Mr. Tebelak; music and lyrics by Stephen Schwartz; director of photography, Richard G. Heimann; editor, Alan Heim; produced by Edgar Lansbury; released by Columbia Pictures. Running time: 103 minutes. At the Columbia 2 Theater, Second Avenue at 64th Street. This film has been classified G.
Jesus .... Victor Garber
John Judas .... David Haskell
Jerry .... Jerry Sroka
Lynne .... Lynne Thigpen
Katie .... Katie Hanley
Robin .... Robin Lamont
Gilmer .... Gilmer McCormick
Joanne .... Joanne Jonas
Merrell .... Merrell Jackson
Jeffrey .... Jeffrey Mylett

By VINCENT CANBY

In filling in some of the narrative gaps in the Gospel according to St. Mark, St. Matthew took pains with the chronology, which, if you read him closely, makes it seem as if Jesus, on the day after He delivered the Sermon on the Mount and effected three healings, was in such good form that He made two lake crossings, healed five more people and held several lengthy discussions.

It is this quality of nonstop busyness that is one of the chief assets of "Godspell," both of the Off Broadway musical (still running at the Promenade Theater on upper Broadway) and of the film

adaptation that opened yesterday at the Columbia 2 Theater. Especially of the film.

●

This update of—and variation on—the Gospel according to St. Matthew is less a celebration of the life and teachings of Christ than it is a celebration of theater, music, youthful high spirits, New York City locations and the zoom lens. The movie amounts to one long, breathless production number (some of whose parts are considerably less effective than others), as well as a demonstrations that, in films, what is said is often less important than how it's said.

"Godspell" pretty much reduces the story of Jesus to conform to a kind of flower-child paranoia that was probably more popular three or four years ago than it is today: the only way to survive in this world is to drop out of it, which, if you think about it, effectively reverses Jesus' instructions to the disciples.

That, however, is to mistake what I, at least, understand "Godspell" to be all about. It's not about religion or philosophy but show business, and its frame—the life and death of Jesus re-enacted in contemporary Manhattan and environs — is hardly more than a gimmick to allow the show's authors to help themselves to some lovely original material never protected by copyright.

At its worst, "Godspell" exalts a kind of simplicity and sweetness that are often the disguises of fierce anti-intellectualism. Luckily, the film constantly betrays itself through its highly sophisticated show-biz manners. Jesus is not simply the androgynous circus clown He looks to be. As played by Victor Garber, He's a tireless hoofer and a most engaging minstrel man. One of the finest production numbers

I've seen in years is the exuberant and ironic "All for the Best," which Jesus and John the Baptist (David Haskell) sing and dance all over New York, highlighted by a marvelous soft-shoe done in front of the Bulova Watch sign overlooking Times Square.

After a certain point, all of Stephen Schwartz's music begins to sound the same, but there is a momentum in its pacing that carries us over the monotony. Almost every member of the cast has his or her moment of glory at screen center. I think particularly of Robin Lamont, a beautiful honey blonde, who sings "Day by Day," and of several hugely funny parables acted out by virtually the entire company.

John-Michael Tebelak, who is credited with having "conceived and staged" the Off Broadway show, is credited as associate director of the film, and David Greene as its director. I have no idea who did what, but the movie has the look of something shot by Richard Lester in an evangelical frame of mind. Ordinarily, this sort of fractured style is something I can easily resist, but it is the only way, I suspect, that "Godspell" could be made to work on film.

●

Every song number is an amalgam of splintery shots against dozens of New York locations, and a lot of them are both funny and beautiful. I can't remember another film that seems to have caught the way New York appears on a lot of hot summer days, when its jagged outlines are softened by a golden smog. The atmosphere may be lethal, but it's also incomparably romantic.

I have some of these same feelings of ambivalence about "Godspell." I like its music, its drive and its determination, even when it's pretend-

David Haskell, left, and Victor Garber dancing above Times Square in "Godspell"

ing to a kind of innocence and naiveté that I never for a second believe.

1973 Mr 22, 52:1

The Cast

FIVE FINGERS OF DEATH, directed by Cheng Chang Ho; screenplay by Chiang Yang; cinematographer, Wang Yung-lung; music by Wu Ta-Chiang; produced by Run Run Shaw; released by Warner Bros. At Loews State 2, Broadway and 45th Street, Loew's Orpheum, 86th Street at Third Avenue and neighborhood theaters. Running time: 104 minutes. This film is classified R.

Chao Chih-hao	Lo Lieh
Sung Ying Ying	Wang Ping
Yen Chu-hung	Wang Chin-Feng
Han Lung	Nan-Kung Hsun
Meng San-yeh	Tien Feng
Okada	Chao Hsiung
Meng Tien-hsiung	Tung Lin

By ROGER GREENSPUN

A kind of film new to most local audiences, a karate movie called "Five Fingers of Death," written by Chiang Yang, directed by Cheng Chang Ho, and produced in Hong Kong by Run Run Shaw, opened yesterday at neighborhood theaters.

The hero, Chao Chi-hao (Lo Lieh), a promising student of the martial arts, enrolls in the school of Sun Hsin-pei (Fang Mien), where he is first put to menial tasks like scrubbing floors and chopping firewood — with the sides of his bare hands, of course. But soon he proves his worth, and Sun entrusts him with the secrets of the Iron Fist, a technique that should win him the All-China Karate Tournament.

He does win, despite the vile trickery of a rival karate master, and the film's end sees him firm in the love of his hometown sweetheart, Sung Ying Ying (Wang Ping), and dispatching his enemies bodily into several inches of solid brick wall—by means of the Iron Fist method, which he has learned to use for all it's worth.

To those who will complain that I've given away the ending, let me point out that I've thoughtfully omitted the middle and that there is more than enough plot in "Five Fingers of Death" for everyone to share. But plot isn't what the movie is all about. It is all about fighting — kendo and judo, but mainly karate and in several styles. It is bloody and rather flashily spectacular — normally pitting one good guy against 20 bad guys, all armed to the teeth with knives, and with predictably happy results.

I don't know much about karate, but I know what I don't like. And the karate in "Five Fingers of Death," for all its slow-motion high leaps, its grunts, its whooshing fists, has the look of the bottom of the barrel. It is all too extravagant, too gratuitously wild—as if composed for show rather than for attack, defense or any real purpose.

●

It is entirely possible, perhaps intentionally possible, to take the film as a joke. It has been dubbed into inappropriate English, and it is funny enough, say, when a character named Wan Hung-chieh accosts the beauteous Yen Chu-hung after her recital of traditional Chinese music with "Hi there? I love the way you sing." But humor at this level palls very rapidly; laughing *at* a movie is never fun for long.

The net effect of "Five Fingers of Death" is to make me appreciate all the more the stylishness, the solemnity, even the gore, of all those doom-ridden Japanese samurai dramas that used to open so regularly a year or so ago at the Bijou.

1973 Mr 22, 54:3

LOVE, directed by Karoly Makk; screenplay (Hungarian with English subtitles) by Tibor Dery; photography by Janos Toth; music by Andras Mihaly; editor, Gyorgy Sivo; produced by Mafilm, Studio 1, Budapest. An Ajay Films release. Running time: 92 minutes. At the First Avenue Screening Room, First Avenue and 61st Street. This film has not been classified.

Old Lady	Lili Darvas
Luca	Mari Torocsik
Janos	Ivan Darvas

"Love," which opened yesterday at the First Avenue Screening Room, was shown at the 10th New York Film Festival. The following excerpt is from Roger Greenspun's review, which appeared Oct. 2, 1972, in The New York Times.

"Love" tells the story of a young Hungarian woman whose husband has been arrested by the secret police and who eases the last months of her ancient bedridden mother with the fantastic tale that her son is in America seeing to the completion and premiere of his own motion picture.

In her youth, the old woman was used to some wealth and frivolous luxury, and to maintain the appearance of wealth and luxury, the daughter-in-law gives up her time, her energy, and most of her material possessions. "Love" thus deals not only with several kinds of love, but also with a history of heroic, exceptionally skillful devotion.

●

Sustaining the illusions of middle- and upper-class old folk has been the concern of many Eastern European movies over the years. But I find "Love" unique, not because it breaks new ground, but because it has such superb appreciation of emotions and responses already understood.

Subtle, rich, reserved, even elegant, it is a beautiful movie. Although never sentimental, it is about sentiment and also about a code of values. Surrounded by her books and mementos,

propped and somewhat pampered on her bed, the old woman all but dreams her life away. A great and intelligent beauty in her youth (and, as played by Lili Darvas, a greatly refined beauty in old age), she relives her past and imagines the present as if it were the past; she asks after her doctor—so she may discuss Goethe with him in German.

Meanwhile, her son, serving 10 years for his politics, sits in prison. And his wife scrimps and patches, humors the old woman and puts the best face possible on the seeping ruin of her own life. An actress named Mari Torocsik plays the wife, a marvelously controlled and complete characterization, with an open-eyed and by no means uncomplaining gallantry.

Ultimately the wife and the mother-in-law have everything in common — even to jealousy in their love for the same man — but they share nothing so much as a standard of conduct and of feeling that I should want to call aristocratic, and that is one of the loveliest manifestations of romantic imagination I have seen on the screen.

●

Hungarian movies sometimes look like a demonstration of everything you could possibly learn in film school. Karoly Makk's direction of "Love" is also full of technical resourcefulness, but a resourcefulness fully in the service of the drama, and therefore not assertive of its own virtuosity. It is a deeply proportionate film, and it earns its insights, its feelings and, finally, its happiness.

1973 Mr 23, 22:1

The Cast

THE CRAZIES, directed by George A. Romero; screenplay by Mr. Romero; based on an original script by Paul McCollough; director of photography, S. William Hinzman; editor, Mr. Romero; music by, Bruce Roberts; produced by A. C. Croft; a Cambist Films Release. At the Forum Theater, Broadway and 47th Street; UA East Theater, First Avenue and 85th Street, and the UA Eastside Cinema, Third Avenue between 55th and 56th Streets. Running time: 103 minutes. This film is classified R.

Judy	Lane Carroll
David	W. G. McMillan
Clank	Harold Wayne Jones
Colonel Peckem	Lloyd Hollar
Artie	Richard Liberty
Kathie	Lynn Lowry
Dr. Watts	Richard France
Woman Lab Technician	Edith Bell
Major Ryder	Harry Spillman

By VINCENT CANBY

The citizens of Evans City are in a fix, but they don't know it. The Army plane that recently crashed nearby was carrying some deadly bacteria that have poisoned the water supply. The symptoms of the illness: uncontrollable giggles followed by madness and probably death.

Thus begins "The Crazies," an inept science-fiction film from George A. Romero, the Pittsburgh man who established himself as the Grandma Moses of exurban horror films with "The Night of the

Living Dead," a movie whose stark, primitive style has made it into a classic of low camp.

●

Like that earlier film, "The Crazies" was shot near Pittsburgh with a bunch of actors who perform with the kind of hysterical enthusiasm I haven't seen in 30 years, not since viewing a grade-school production of "Six Who Pass While the Lentils Boil," in which one young actor fell off the stage into the orchestra pit.

The film's real subject is not bacteriological weaponry, or the idiocies of the military, but the collapse of a community presented as a spectacle, prompted when the Army moves to quarantine Evans City without explaining what's wrong.

The soldiers, who wear gas masks all the time (though the poison is in the water supply), shoot the citizens on sight. The citizens begin shooting soldiers on sight. Here and there, people go mad. A priest immolates himself, and the Army commander shouts: "You must get the President on the phone! We've got to get a nuclear weapon over that town!" The scientist who developed the bacteria despairs: "Jesus Christ! This is so random!" Toward the end, his beautiful lab assistant quietly asks: "Just how would you rate our chances, doctor?"

●

The film opened yesterday at the Forum, the UA Eastside Cinema and the UA East Theater.

1973 Mr 24, 20:1

'Tom Sawyer'

By VINCENT CANBY

MARK TWAIN once described "The Adventures of Tom Sawyer" as "simply a hymn, put into prose form to give it a worldly air." The new musical version, adapted by Robert B. and Richard M. Sherman, who also wrote the score together, may be just a little too worldly for some people. About half of the songs supplied by the Sherman brothers might—with different lyrics and orchestrations—have turned up in any number of other, considerably inferior Sherman musicals from "Mary Poppins" to "Charlotte's Web." The small, ageless boy who plays Tom—Johnny Whitaker—is a TV veteran, as well as a Disney graduate, and it shows. He looks right, but he has a practically Merman-like drive to please and the mannerisms of someone trying to time his actions to match a canned laughtrack.

Yet with all of the worldliness of this "Tom Sawyer," there remains the memory of a perfect innocence that is very much the sense of Twain's "The Adventures of Tom Sawyer." It's a memory prompted more by longing than by fact, and it's very much a part of the Hollywood movie tradition from which "Tom Sawyer" is derived. Carry that tradition back far enough and you'll run into the earliest Our Gang comedies, which were never about the way childhood ever was, but the way Mack Sennett and *his* gang knew that it should have been.

Most of the movies that have come out of this tradition, and most of the child actors who became stars in them, have been awful. It is to the credit of the Sherman brothers and Don Taylor, who directed "Tom Sawyer," that they've made a film that manages to evoke the fears, joys, triumphs and disasters of childhood within a tradition that usually deals in forced anthropomorphism, insisting that children act like small-scale humans with hormone deficiencies.

There have been few intelligent American films about childhood—certainly nothing on the order of Vigo's "Zero de Conduit" or Truffaut's "The 400 Blows" or even Reed's "The Fallen Idol," and there have been few performances by children in American films to match those in any number of European films. Offhand, I can think of only Richie Andrusco in Morris Engel's "Little Fugitive" and isolated moments of Margaret O'Brien in Vincente Minnelli's "Meet Me in St. Louis." It's not that European children are naturally better actors, nor that European directors are better at directing children. Rather it has to do with the fantasy-feeding function (then as well as now) of American films aimed at mass audiences, as opposed to the more idiosyncratic aims of the better European directors, who probably sent their children to see American films on Saturday afternoons.

Twain's "Tom Sawyer," as marvelous as it is, is essentially Saturday afteroon fiction, at least compared to "The Adventures of Huckleberry Finn," which was published in 1884, eight light-years after the appearance of "Tom Sawyer." The two novels share authorship and character names, but fundamentally they have little else in common. "Tom Sawyer" is a timeless lark in a Hannibal, Missouri, remembered as Eden but called St. Petersburg. Tom is, at heart, a rather impossible little superman masquerading as a normal boy who plays hookey, beats up boys who wear clean clothes, tells small lies at his own convenience, worships women as creatures from another planet, captures villains and, generally, goes from triumph to triumph, improving a world that isn't so terrible to start with.

*

The Huck Finn of the later novel is someone who barely survives, and the novel itself is an adventure in a world of greed, hunger, violence and arbitrary cruelty, in which even the buffoonery is never as innocent as it seems. To enjoy what the Shermans and Mr. Taylor have accomplished in "Tom Sawyer" is to remember that they weren't making "Huckleberry Finn," but a kind of pageant glorifying an idealized time (boyhood) and place (the American Middle West in the first half of the 19th century). This they do with such immense verve and great high spirits that they effectively transform a tradition without ever breaking with it.

The look of the production has a lot to do with the film's success. Mr. Taylor shot the film entirely on location in Missouri, mostly in and around the village of Arrow Rock, which serves as Hannibal, and on the Missouri River, which doubles nicely as the Mississippi. Everything is a little bigger, brighter, more colorful than life, but that's the way a pageant should

be. Houses are roomy and spotless (the only shabby thing is the fence Tom must whitewash). Trees are perfect for climbing and the weather remains ideal. It is such a lovely spot that it doesn't seem at all odd that people might express themselves in song, nor that the big holiday picnic—which precedes the cave confrontation of Injun Joe with Tom and Becky Thatcher—should turn into a huge, exuberant production number. By golly, it really would have been good to be alive then!

With the exception of Joshua Hill Lewis, who plays Tom's tattle-tale Cousin Sid with a very funny, pudgy sort of pushiness, all of the younger actors give standard though never horrid performances. The old folk, however, are fine, including Celeste Holm as Aunt Polly, Warren Oates as Muff Potter, and Lucille Benson as the Widow Douglas, the foolish lady whose mission in life becomes the reformation of Huck Finn.

Although the Shermans' screenplay eliminates most of Twain's philosophizing about Tom's not-too-deeply hidden virtues, it retains the identify of Injun Joe, played by Kunu Hank, as "that murderin' half-breed."

Twain was full of all kinds of prejudices that today would be insupportable, but Injun Joe, the outcast, is not one of them. He is a man with an evil heart, and that's all there is to it, though the film does make a case for how he got that way. Mostly, the people in the film are exactly the way they are because God made them so.

"Tom Sawyer" has little truck with psychological complexities and contradictions. It is as direct an expression of faith as "Rock of Ages," which the Hannibal citizens —in one of the film's best moments— sing at Tom and Huck's funeral with a little more gusto than the apparent grief of the occasion should properly allow.

1973 Mr 25, II:1:2

Is This 'Tiger' Dangerous?

By STEPHEN FARBER

"SAVE the Tiger" is the kind of preachy, pessimistic social drama that used to be considered box-office poison, and almost every studio had turned it down before Paramount decided to gamble on the script. The gamble has paid off; "Save the Tiger" looks like one of the first commercial successes of 1973. Audiences seem to sit still for the soul-searching speeches, and it would be pleasant to report that this film's success represents a new maturity in the moviegoing public. In truth, the movie is as muddled and chickenhearted as most Hollywood "problem" pictures. Then why has it caught on? What accounts for its mass appeal?

*

Writer-producer Steve Shagan (clearly this film's *auteur*) and director John Avildsen have set out to make a harsh, incriminating study of greed and corruption in America. No one, however, goes to the movies to be insulted, and I doubt that "Save the Tiger" would have found such an appreciative audience if it were really the blistering assault on American materialism that some critics have acclaimed. The film begins very well, with several vivid, convincing scenes of an American businessman at work. But something goes wrong as the film continues; the focus blurs, the "Tiger" loses its teeth. Although the movie retains a surface verisimilitude—thanks to Jack Lemmon's deeply felt performance and Avildsen's shrewd, fluent direction—the ideas are not really under control.

Lemmon's performance is just about flawless, but the character of Harry Stoner — a middle-aged Beverly Hills garment merchant on the verge of bankruptcy—is misconceived. Shagan and Avildsen understandably wanted to avoid another caricature of the tired businessman; but they have added so many "humanizing" touches that the characterization is torn apart by the inconsistencies. One keeps wondering how such a sensitive, articulate man ever ended up in the brutal garment business. It isn't easy to believe in a pantsuit manufacturer with a taste for Billie Holiday and a concern about Malcolm, Medgar, and Mylai.

*

Only a couple of scenes have the proper harshness: when Harry is pimping for a potential buyer, or a little later — in the movie's best moment — when he stands over the same buyer, who has collapsed from a heart attack, and pitilessly labels him a "casualty." Those moments are the exception, however; most of the time Harry suffers nobly. He's anguished because he knows he's not living up to the sublime aspiration of his youth, but we are supposed to believe that there's still poetry in his soul. Harry is kind and understanding with almost everyone; he even forgives the hooker who fouls up an account. A compulsive, driven businessman might

have disturbed moviegoers. Tender, compassionate Harry flatters the audience; he's the silent majority's finest image of itself, and that's where the evasions in "Save the Tiger" begin.

Because Harry is the most sympathetic character on screen, and because he is expert at rationalizing everything he does — and because we never see the consequences of his office immorality—the film ends up justifying his position. To keep his company afloat, Harry has already doctored the books, and he is now planning to burn down his secondary factory in order to collect the insurance. He rationalizes his immorality by saying "there are no more rules" in America: "Everybody dances around the law."

Although Harry's partner Phil (Jack Gilford) attacks this view, Shagan gives Harry all the good lines, and he makes Phil such a hypocrite that we can't take his scruples very seriously. Phil is perfectly willing to take money from the Mafia, while Harry's determination to remain independent of the mob is clearly a point in his favor. And Harry's reasons for setting the fire are not simply mercenary. He's genuinely concerned about his employes. "To keep people working—is that a criminal act?" he asks. At the very end, when he clinches the deal with the arsonist, he is careful to make sure that Phil will never be implicated. Even as he plans a major felony, Harry is so unselfish that he retains our sympathy.

*

The fire itself takes place offscreen—after the movie is over. If we actually saw people injured in the fire, the ending would have a very different impact. But even if there are no injuries, the fire will put a whole factory of people out of work. Clearly Harry is not so concerned about his employes as he pretends. The filmmakers seem unaware of that irony; they gloss over Harry's hypocrisy. Here is the situation at the end of the film: Harry is planning to set a fire that won't injure anybody, collect from an insurance company that is probably crooked in its own right, in order to keep himself and a lot of other people working. Put in those terms, does it sound so terrible? Harry's logic is very seductive, and although Shagan may have meant to show how easy it is to rationalize corruption, he hasn't really dramatized any alternatives; he hasn't dissociated his own view from Harry's with nearly enough force. As a result, the film seems to vindicate the hero's jungle ethics.

In the last analysis "Save the Tiger" is a post-ITT, post-Watergate movie, an apology for corruption. At a time when almost every day's headlines raise new doubts about the credibility of big business and government, "Save the Tiger" doesn't urge us to protest corruption; implicitly it encourages acquiescence. This smugly cynical film says that corruption is so deep a part of American life that it's futile to try doing

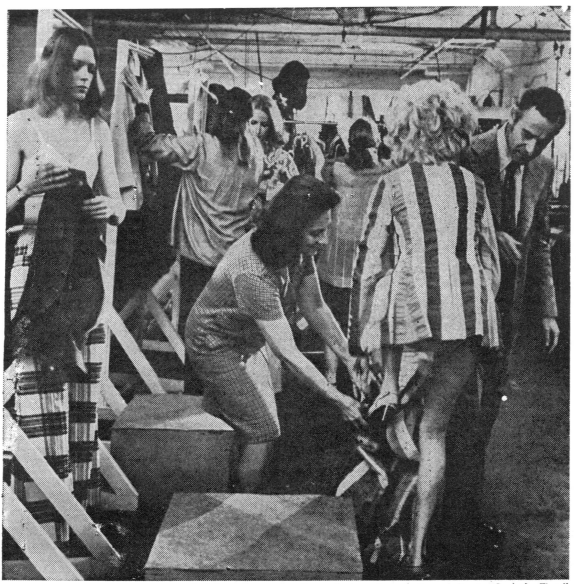

Jack Lemmon, a garment manufacturer, inspects the new line in "Save the Tiger"
"One keeps wondering how such a sensitive, articulate man ended up in the brutal garment business"

The Cast
SUCH A GORGEOUS KID LIKE ME, directed by Francois Truffaut; screenplay (French with English subtitles) by Jean-Loup Dabadie and Mr. Truffaut, based on the novel by Henry Farrell; director of photography, Pierre William Glenn; music, Georges Delerue; editor, Yann Dedet; executive producer, Marcel Berbert; a Les Films du Carosse production, released by Columbia Pictures. Running time: 98 minutes. At the 68th Street Playhouse, Third Avenue at 68th Street. This film has been classified R.
Camille Bliss ....Bernadette Lafont
Murene ....Claude Brasseur
Arthur ....Charles Denner
Sam Golden ....Guy Marchand
Stanislas Previne .....Andre Dussollier
Clovis Bliss ....Philippe Leotard
Helene ....Anne Kreis
Isobel Bliss ....Gilberte Geniat
Florence Golden ....Daniele Girard
Prison Secretary ......Martine Ferriere
Marchal ....Michele Delahaye
Schoolteacher ....Annick Fougerie
Old Prison Guard .....Gaston Ouvard
Alphonse ....Jacob Weizbluth

By VINCENT CANBY

When Stanislas Previne (Andre Dussolier), a conventionally shy young sociologist, arrives at the prison to gather material for his thesis, "Criminal Women," the matron tries to dissuade him from interviewing Camille Bliss. Instead, the matron suggests that he talk to the inmate who cut her men victims into pieces or to the inmate who strangled men with one hand. Stanislas persists, and the haughty matron says of Camille: "She's just a tramp."

The matron's absolutely right. Camille (Bernadette Lafont) is brassy, vulgar, talks in clichés, is not strikingly pretty and not in the first bloom of youth, but she possesses several other qualities that drive some men wild.

Like poor tubercular Mildred in "Of Human Bondage," Camille is so intensely self-absorbed that the selfishness amounts to a sexual challenge. Most important, perhaps, Camille has a smashing figure, one that seems to have little relation to the bird-brain that directs it, a figure that looks particularly great in slips and unbuttoned blouses and is seemingly impervious to assaults by men or time.

François Truffaut's newest comedy, "Such a Gorgeous Kid Like Me," is the story of Camille's wild rise to fame and fortune as a singing star of absolutely no talent, in a world that cares less for performance onstage than for achievements off. Camille's rue to success is littered with corpses, including those of her father and her mother-in-law and one marvelously manic suitor (Charles Denner), a rat exterminator who had known from the age of 9 what he wanted to be.

Camille doesn't consider herself a murderer. She just sets up situations that can — if she's lucky — result in certain disadvantages to others.

"Such a Gorgeous Kid Like Me" is a very curious and disappointing movie. It has wit, but it's not very funny. It is too schematically predictable ever to be surprising

anything about it; it doesn't really matter if you cheat because everyone else is cheating too. Maybe Shagan has spent too much time in Hollywood.

Then again, millions of people outside the movie industry must respond to this cynical reasoning. How else can you explain Nixon's landslide victory? It isn't that Americans didn't believe the evidence of scandal and duplicity in Washington; they didn't *care*. "Save the Tiger" is another expression of a society that has learned to live with dishonesty.

The nostalgia engulfing the film helps to cushion the audience from moral concern. In "Death of a Salesman" Arthur Miller made it clear that Willy Loman's nostalgia falsified and obscured the true sordidness of his past. Shagan, on the other hand, shares Harry Stoner's nostalgia; he really seems to believe that America was purer during the forties. The film treats Harry's reveries —about the Second World War and baseball—with maudlin sentimentality. At the conclusion Harry astonishes some Little Leaguers by throwing a baseball over the fence, boasting, "I thought you

ought to see it just once." The implication is that today's middle-aged failures were tigers in their time.

*

In the most curious scene, Harry recalls that he used to stand at attention whenever he heard the national anthem, and he complains, "Now they're making jockstraps out of the flag." Shagan yearns for the innocent, blind patriotism of the forties; he takes American ideals at face value.

Throughout the film, the values of Shagan and Avildsen prove to be simplistic and highly questionable. Harry and Phil meet the arsonist in a porno movie theater in downtown Los Angeles. Presumably the setting is meant to symbolize the moral rot of contemporary America — though to some of us the more open acceptance of pornography is a sign of health, not sickness. Shagan uses the porno theater for its old associations with sin. (Couldn't Harry have contacted the arsonist at a G-rated movie?)

In this movie, freedom is symbolized by a wandering hippie girl — who else?

—and for a "positive" moral image Shagan has dredged up one more noble peasant in the form of a wise old Jewish tailor. We know he's virtuous because he loves his wife and is contemptuous of a homosexual designer. Shagan's "moral vision" usually turns out to be nothing more than conventional puritanism. His reliance on cliché disqualifies him as a moralist; he doesn't have the fiercely original way of seeing that distinguishes a true moral artist.

"Save the Tiger" is one of those important bad movies that catch the pulse of the country, the frustrations of the times. Shagan and Avildsen cannot bring any kind of order to the highly charged material, but their confusions are remarkably revealing. The film is part of the nostalgia boom, and a helpless affirmation of the new mood of political apathy and cynicism. A work of art stirs doubts; "Save the Tiger" stills them. This is a Nixon Era movie, an emblem of the moral evasions of the seventies.

1973 Mr 25, II:13:1

except in minor details. Its woefully comic attitude toward the triumph of secondrateness is not of an especially interesting order. Nor, I suspect, does it come naturally to Truffaut, whose films — even the so-called failures like "The Soft Skin," "The Bride Wore Black" and "Mississippi Mermaid" — posses a poetic complexity seldom achieved by other directors' successes.

In the entire film, there are just two scenes that are worthy of anything in his earlier films: a moment that is almost shocking in its suggestion of recognizable feeling, when Stanislas takes his leave of Camille in prison, where he's been taping her story and falling in love with her, and another, purely comic moment toward the end when a scholarly 10-year-old film director refuses to let strangers look at his unedited "rushes."

•

I have such admiration for Truffaut's intelligence that I can't believe that perhaps what I take to be failures in "Such a Gorgeous Kid like Me" might not be his purposeful decisions. Bernadette Lafont, who was in Truffaut's first short film, "Les Mistons," is a singularly uninteresting actress. She's sort of horsy and loud, incapable of anything resembling a small gesture. But then (I think to myself), perhaps that is just the quality he wanted—in order to make Camille's triumph that much more grotesque.

The decision may be intellectually correct, but it squashes the comedy, which is not especially inventive to start with. It also puts a burden on the actors who play Camille's victims, only one of whom, Denner, catches the exuberant spirit of the piece, which is too often simply frenzied. One of Truffaut's great talents, especially evident in "Shoot the Piano Player" and "Stolen Kisses," is his way of parsing any mood into its components of comedy, tragedy, put-on and poetry. "Such a Gorgeous Kid Like Me" is a single comic mood, repeated with variations, shrilly.

1973 Mr 26, 55:1

MONEY, MONEY, MONEY, directed and written by Claude Lelouch; photographed by Jean Collomb; music by Francis Lai; a G.S.F. Presentation, distributed by Cinerama Releasing. At the Paris Theater, 58th Street west of Fifth Avenue. Running time: 115 minutes. (This film is rated "R.")

Lino	Lino Ventura
Simon	Charles Denner
Jacques	Jacques Brel
Charlot	Charles Gerard
Aldo	Aldo Maccione
Juarez	Jean-Louis Bunuel
Ambassador	Andre Falcon
Johnny	Johnny Halladay

Claude Lelouch's "Money, Money, Money" is such a bright, clever comedy-satire that the writer-director can be forgiven toward the end, when he almost beats the horse — his joke — to death. This is a sly, funny picture, but nothing like Lelouch's lyrical "A Man and a Woman" — whose sessiness and visual punctuation of slapstick outride patches of arid blandness and a fade-out when he simply pelts us with his point.

It goes like this. Why shouldn't present-day pirates, banding together in Paris, pluck profit from a chaotic society jangling with ideologies, causes and trends? Materialism, spelled money, is at the root, and this is what the five knaves go after, with brash success and a few ironic snags.

The first part of the picture is the most freshly inventive, with the blithe crooks converging, careening around in cars (Mack Sennett-style), heisting a corporation safe (in the neatest trick of the year) and kidnapping a pop singer, then an ambassador.

This last stunt, overlapping a plane hijacking, involves the men with a bearded South American revolutionary, whose ideals are acutely hitched to the value of a dollar. This is the sharpest section but blandness sets in until Lelouch whisks the story and tone into broad, breezy comedy. The ending is a nimble surprise. If only Lelouch had let go.

Technically, the movie is first-rate. As the brazen, carefree culprits, Lino Ventura, Charles Denner, Jacques Brel (toothsomely alive and well), Charles Gérard and Aldo Maccione are amusing indeed. So is most of the new, subtitled import at the Paris Theater.

HOWARD THOMPSON

1973 Mr 26, 56:2

The Program

AM A DANCER, directed by Pierre Jourdan; narration written by John Percival; produced by Evdoros Demetriou; presented by Sam Lang and J. Arthur Elliot in association with EMI Film Productions Limited; released by Cinevision Films, Ltd. Running time: 93 minutes. At the Ziegfeld Theater, Avenue of the Americas and 54th Street. With Rudolf Nureyev, Margot Fonteyn, Carla Fracci, Lynn Seymour, Deanne Bergsma.

By ANNA KISSELGOFF

Rudolf Nureyev — onstage —is both magnificent beast and great classicist. It is this animal quality held in check by superb discipline that makes hs performances so exciting. No other ballet dancer has this tension of leashed power straining against schooled excellence.

Yet this is not the Nureyev you will see in "I Am a Dancer," a firm that attempts to show his versatility in four types of ballets, but perversely ignores the base upon which his reputation rests.

For ultimately Nureyev will be remembered not only for the high technical standard of male dancing he brought to the West from Russia in 1961, but as a great classical dancer in the 19th century ballet classics.

Something of the excitement Nureyev can bring to these old ballets flickers through the last minute of this film. He is seen leaping around the stage in a performance of the Royal Ballet's "Sleeping Beauty." All the splendor and brilliance of the classical ballet tradition is there and Nureyev is part of it.

This is what Pierre Jourdan, the French director of this French-British production, fails to demonstrate, perhaps because he does not really understand the one full ballet and three excerpts in which he presents Nureyev so uncharacteristically.

The first sequence is from "La Sylphide," an 1836 Romantic ballet by the Danish choreographer Auguste Bournonville, in which Nureyev and Carla Fracci, one of today's best Sylphides, establish no rapport whatsoever. "La Sylphide" has only recently entered Nureyev's repertory, and it was perhaps unwise to record him in a Bournonville ballet. This is a delicate work that depends on image more than on virtuosity, and the camera wrongly stresses footwork over atmosphere.

A more tedious ballet, paradoxically, provides the film with moments of great interest. Nureyev, now quite anxious to move into the modern-dance field, is seen rehearsing a duet with Deanne Bergama from "Field Figures," by the contemporary American choreographer Glen Tetley, and he brings to it an overwhelming physicality. Of course, all this huffing and puffing is unnecessary, but his refusal to spare himself or his body is absolutely fascinating.

There is a hint of what makes Nureyev Nureyev in the complete filmed version of Sir Frederick Ashton's "Marguerite and Armand." Yet Ashton is too good a choreographer to be judged by this schmaltzy reworking of "Camille," and Nureyev and Dame Margot Fonteyn, acting and dancing their hearts out, have more to offer in ballet than hand-wringing and cape-flinging. Having chosen a literary ballet, the film underscores its weakness by providing it with narration.

In the fourth sequence, Lynn Seymour and Nureyev appear to be greeted with canned applause in dancing the grand pas de deux of "Sleeping Beauty" on an empty stage ordinarily filled with other dancers. This was Mr. Jourdan's chance to show Nureyev at his best. But the resplendence of a famous ballet showpiece is destroyed through a shabby and dark setting.

•

The dance sequences are linked by offstage glimpses of Nureyev, replete with the nonsense non-Russians say about Russians (for instance, the idea that Nureyev's international bookings can be traced to the nomadic instinct of his Tartar ancestry). Nothing is to be gleaned about Nureyev's personal life here, but he does seem to be a regular fellow in Fonteyn's and Ashton's presence.

There is one wonderful flash of spontaeity as he clears a way among his fans by swatting them with a long-stemmed rose. Nureyev is one of those people who make the world more interesting than it often is. Even a bad film about him can't all that bad.

"I Am a Dancer" opened yesterday at the Ziegfeld Theater.

1973 Mr 29, 41:1

PHEDRE, directed by Pierre Jourdan; text (French with English subtitles) by Jean Racine; director of photography, Michel Kelber; editor, Genevieve Winding; produced by Nicole Stephane. A coproduction of Ancinex Films du Valois and Galba Films; distributed by Altura Films International. Running time: 90 minutes. At the First Avenue Screening Room, at 60th Street.

Phedre	Marie Bell
Theramene	Jean Chevrier
Theseus	Jacques Dacqmine
Hippolyte	Claude Giraud
Aricie	Tania Torrens
Ismene	Claudia Maurin
Panope	Jean-Noel Sissia
Oenone	Mary Marquet

By VINCENT CANBY

Pierre Jourdan's adaptation of Racine's "Phèdre," with the French text translated by English subtitles taken from William Packard's alexandrine translation, is surprisingly interesting and unhackneyed for a film devoted to a kind of drama so completely at odds with what films are supposed to be about.

Seventeenth-century French neoclassic drama requires a certain discipline even when you watch it in a legitimate theater, where the uncomfortable seats and bad sight lines help keep you awake. In a movie house, I would have expected instant sleep.

This "Phèdre," which opened yesterday at the First Avenue Screening Room (which has alarmingly comfortable seats and very good sight lines), is a graceful homage to a play and a style of performance that, under less attractive circumstances, might have reduced me to the kind of acute, uncontrollable high spirits I sometimes experience at the opera, when the tenor can't get his arms around the soprano.

Marie Bell, who has been a star of the Comédie Française, of her own theater and of French films for longer than I can remember, comes to us as the unhappy Phèdre, tragically in love with her stepson, Hippolyte, in the full bloom of what has alsions expressed in verse from which all easily identifiable passion has been distilled—are so intelligently embraced that Miss Bell's age and theatrical mannerisms are less an intrusion than a means of emphasis.

Racine's theater deals in emotions almost as if they were abstract principles. It asks us to think first, feel later. Everything about this production directed by Mr. Jourdan (brother of the actor Louis Jourdan) invites such a ready long passed middle age.

Yet the artificialities of the film—from its Poussin-like painted backdrops to its preoccupation with grand pasdistancing of response. The effect, if you can overcome an initial resistance, is soothing and reassuring, as if you'd been taken away from time.

•

The camera glides about the colonnaded interior of Theseus's palace with a kind of discreet insistence that we pay attention. Only occasionly does it move in for tight close-ups or take one of those ladder-high positions from which birds and movie cameras view the world. Mostly, however, the camera, the sets, the costumes and the actors are simply instruments used in the cause of the playwright, so designed as not to interfere with him grossly.

At this point, Miss Bell is somewhat too majestic to be entirely convincing, even at the center of a tragedy of intellect, but she is a living landmark not easily denied. With the exception of Tania Torrens, a beautiful, truly young woman who plays Aricie, the real love of Hippolyte, all of the other actors seem a bit seedy, which may or may not reflect their inability to adapt to film a florid acting style that isn't all that interesting today, even on the stage.

1973 Mr 30, 34:1

The Program

THE BROTHERS KUCHAR: THE SUNSHINE SISTERS by George Kuchar, running time 35 minutes; five short films by Mike Kuchar, **VARIATIONS**, 15 minutes; **TALES OF THE BRONX**, 16 minutes; **ABODE OF THE SNOWS**, 10 minutes; **AQUA CIRCUS**, 10 minutes; **FAR AWAY PLACES**, 10 minutes. At the Film Forum, 256 West 88th Street. Today and tomorrow, and next Friday through next Sunday at 8 P.M.

By ROGER GREENSPUN

At a certain period in the history of the American independent cinema, the brothers George and Mike Kuchar occupied a position of special, almost unique, importance. This was a time, about 10 years ago, when it began to seem to many that perhaps there wasn't anything outside the mainstream except, say, the solemnity of Marie Menken, Ray Wisniewski, or Gregory Markopolous with "Twice a Man." So you can imagine the thrill of learning that all the while, in the pastoral seclusion of the Bronx, two young fellows were laboring at a wholly new kind of art film with such adventures in 8-mm. cinema as "I Was a Teenage Rumpot," "Lust for Ecstasy," "A Town Called Tempest" and "The Naked and the Nude."

To indicate a healthy new direction just the titles were enough (actually, I never got to see the movies), and when George Kuchar really burst into the 16-mm. big time with "Hold Me While I'm Naked" (1966), there was dancing in the streets off lower Second Avenue, and at last a line at the box office. The Technicolor story of a sincere but lecherous independent film maker from the Bronx who tries for artistic purposes to get his leading lady to undress — and fails — "Hold Me While I'm Naked" still lives in happy memory and, excites the question sometimes whispered in New York alleyways: "What ever happened to the Kuchar brothers?"

Well, they've moved to San Francisco, where they teach and make movies, and a program of their more recent work — five short films by Mike Kuchar and a longish one by George — opened yesterday at the Film Forum. I'm afraid it isn't a very good program.

Mike's "Tales of the Bronx," which owes much to "Hold Me While I'm Naked" (including Donna Kerness, its sumptuous star), is the most enjoyable of the lot, but adds nothing very new to the tragedy of inept lust that is its theme. The other Mike Kuchar films are all more or less straight — poetic fantasy or semiabstraction or filmed essay. For a while, near the start of "Abode of the Snows," a movie about timeless Nepal, I hopefully thought, leave it to Mike Kuchar to see the humor in a Nepalese rice terrace. But he didn't see the humor; he saw what everybody else has seen, and for a talent that has deserved to be called rare, that isn't enough.

George's "The Sunshine Sisters," the story of two San Francisco girls with problems, attempts to refine the particular blend of garish sentiment and ridiculous intensity that has been a Kuchar specialty from the beginning. The heroine, Sara Cartwright — dying from a nameless disease, three months behind in her rent, plagued alternately by corpses in the bathtub and young men who rape her — is surely a viable figure for screen comedy. But in dealing with the story the director has somehow lost the ambiance, or never found it —perhaps because the West Coast men are too strong, the women too weak, the neuroses learned but not lived through. As a friend who taught at San Francisco

State once remarked: "California is O.K., but it's 3,000 miles from the ocean."

1973 Mr 31, 41:3

The Cast

THE MACK, directed by Michael Campus; screenplay by Robert J. Poole; director of photography, Ralph Woolsey; film editor, Frank C. Decot; music by Willie Hutch; producer, Harvey Bernhard; released by Cinerama Releasing Corporation. At the Cinerama Theater, Broadway at 47th Street and the 86th Street Twin 2 Theater, west of Lexington Avenue. Running time: 110 minutes. This film is classified R.
Goldie .... Max Julien
Hank .... Don Gordon
Slim .... Richard Pryor
Lulu .... Carol Speed
Olinga .... Roger E. Mosley
Pretty Tony .... Dick Williams

By VINCENT CANBY

"The Mack" is a very noisy, very exploitative black film about the rise and the peaceful retirement of a pimp who, according to the film's program notes, is known in West Coast street language as a mack, an apparent corruption of "mec" of French argot.

When Goldie (Max Julien) gets out of jail, he finds that his brother has become a militant black nationalist, that his middle-class mother still wants him to go to church on Sundays, that two crooked, psychotic white cops hope to put him back in jail, and that the only thing he can do is pimp. "I'm going to be the meanest mack there ever was!" Goldie vows. He then adds: "They're going to talk about me the way they used to talk about Jesus."

That doesn't make much sense, but nothing does in this essentially sentimental melodrama. The screenplay by Robert J. Poole uses lines that seem to have been saved from a sophomore's notebook. "Truth," says a white cop, "is pimples, garlic and armpits." Says Goldie to a hooker whom he'd known when both were children: "I thought you'd become a nurse or a lawyer or something heavy." Or, and this is my favorite wisdom of the week: "A pimp is only as good as his product—and his product is women!"

Even as action melodrama of a "Shaft" sort, the film is inept, so confused that it occasionally it seems surreal. Plot elements bump into one another like air bubbles in a mostly empty stomach. I suspect the film isn't even very honest about the profession it glorifies. We're asked to believe that Goldie, with five girls out hustling on what looks like Skid Row, could clear $3,000 a day.

●

Max Julien seems vaguely uncomfortable impersonating another fantasy-fulfil-

ling movie superblack, but he's genuinely funny in a couple of scenes with Richard Pryor, a first-rate comedian who plays his sidekick. Michael Campus directed the film in a manner that suggests that much of the time he must have sat in his canvas chair, afraid to look.

1973 Ap 5, 51:2

The Cast

COME HAVE COFFEE WITH US, directed by Alberto Lattuada; screenplay (Italian with English subtitles) by Tulio Kezich, Mr. Lattuada, Adriano Baroco and Piero Chiara, based on the novel by Mr. Chiara; music by Fred Bongusto; produced by Maurizio Lodi-Fe; an Altura Films Release. At the First Avenue Screening Room, at 61st Street. Running time: 90 minutes. This film has not been classified.
Emerenziano Paronzini ... Ugo Tognazzi
Tarsilla .... Milena Vukotic
Fortunata ....Francessca Romana Coluzzi
Camilla .... Angela Goodwin
Caterina .... Valentine

By VINCENT CANBY

Alberto Lattuada's 1970 Italian comedy, "Come Have Coffee With Us," which opened yesterday at the First Avenue Screening Room, has a terrible title and it pursues — for more time than the subject may deserve — a phobia that is seemingly shared by all Italian men over the age of 40. That is, that a middle-aged man's sexual satisfaction is quite as dangerous as the coronary it will lead to.

Are Italian men—for all of their eyeball-rolling when a pretty girl walks by a sidewalk cafe, and for all of their appreciative pinches in crowded buses—so guilt-ridden that only death can offer true relief? It would seem that way according to the subcategory of Italian comedy to which "Come Have Coffee With Us" belongs. It's not something that most American men think much about, possibly because we are being constantly reassured of our inexhaustible energy by everything from television commercials to porno films.

Yet even if the fear does lurk somewhere within us, it's probably not the reason that "Come Have Coffee With Us" seems quite as funny as it does, or, for that matter, why Marco Ferreri's "The Conjugal Bed" and Pietro Germi's "The Climax" also were so amusing (some years ago). The reason, principally, is Ugo Tognazzi, a fine, very comic actor who, for approximately 20 years now, has been defining the pitfalls of middle-aged passion so eloquently.

As in the Ferreri and Germi films, the really ageless Mr. Tognazzi is again impersonating a man whose desires are bigger than his ventricles. This time he plays a petty tax official, assigned to a small town in southern Italy, where he decides to settle down as the husband of a well-to-do but no long-

er young bourgeoise and finds himself also the lover of his two equally over-age sisters-in-law. It all works beautifully until his roving eye falls on the unattended serving girl.

●

The idea is not terribly funny, but Mr. Tognazzi, and the small town setting provided by Mr. Lattuada, are. The actor is a model of what I can describe only as a thoroughly masculine but dainty self-assurance, whether he is carefully placing a toothpick in an ashtray (after cleaning one ear and one fingernail) or pompously explaining to the three sisters, on an early meeting, how an old war wound has left him with a troublesome (but not incapacitating) deviated

rectum. The three women are so smitten that not even a stroke cools their devotion.

The sisters are admittedly grotesque (especially the tall one with a huge mole at the side of her mouth), and Mr. Lattuada treats them with a certain comic awe, if not fear. Never for a moment do they suspect their capacity to wound with love. This fantasy, I should emphasize, is not only a man's, but also an Italian man's, and all objections should be directed to him in Rome, where, according to my fantasy, he is at this very minute, sitting in a cafe enjoying the passing parade and the exquisite guilt pangs the parade prompts.

1973 Ap 6, 28:1

About Miss Jones And Mr. Oscar

By VINCENT CANBY

IT'S too easy to be critical of this year's Academy Awards telecast to make it much fun, even in a week otherwise highlighted by the opening of an absolutely ridiculous new porno film, "The Devil in Miss Jones," which a lot of people, who should have known better, seem to have been conned into finding a breakthrough movie. Ever since "Last Tango in Paris," finding breakthrough movies has virtually become an epidemic. Sometimes two or three in a week. It reminds me of fleebus, the curious virus that swept through Bob & Ray's Skunk Hollow some years back and caused its victims to walk as if they were sitting down.

The Oscar show probably doesn't hurt films (except, possibly, on the night of the telecast itself), but it would take a rather large stretch of the imagination to think that it could generate an interest in any but one or two winners, and maybe in some movies that can now only be seen on television either at 4 in the morning or 4 in the afternoon.

One certainly got this drift when Robert Wagner and Natalie Wood, publicly together again for the first time since their remarriage, turned up on the platform to deliver the award for best documentary. Imagine wanting to be the Debbie and Eddie of 1973, when the original Debbie and Eddie were such flops in 1957.

*

Perhaps we shouldn't ask that Hollywood look forward, but at least there should be some point in backward glances that, with two exceptions, only reminded us of all the boredom that we and Hollywood have survived. It was sort of nice seeing that Greer Garson and Merle Oberon don't yet need wheelchairs, but Laurence Harvey is, unfortunately, not far enough removed in time to evoke anything resembling affection. A few snickers, at best.

The appearance of Connie Stevens was a big fat tribute to 1966 (the year she made "Way...Way...Out," and how many non-Jerry Lewis fans remember that one?), and asking Angela Lansbury to star in one of the production numbers was apparently an insult that no ambitious actress would dream of acknowledging. But then I'm one of those people who remember Miss Lansbury's singing of "Yellow Bird" in "The Picture of Dorian Gray" as a highpoint of movie-going in the Paleolithic era. I've never understood how she could continue to be so charming to the community that would buy her Broadway show ("Mame") and give it to someone else (Lucille Ball) to make as a movie. Actors are inscrutable, and probably desperate.

Not so the producers of the Oscar show. They are positively bent on destroying themselves in as public a way as possible. Why in heaven's name would they otherwise insist on trotting out so many television personalities (if that is not a contradiction in terms) to act as presenters? Why would they insist on having us witness the very folksy spectacle of Richard Walsh, the president of the International Alliance of Theatrical Stage Employes, presenting a special Oscar to Charles Boren, the vice president of the Association of Motion Picture Producers, the man who helped Hollywood—are you ready—negotiate the five-day week? The five-day week! Good grief! There still must be someone around out there who had a hand in eliminating the 40-hour day. Hollywood, for all of its political troubles in the 1940's, has never been a crucible of radical socialism. Ask not what your country can do for you but what you can grab for yourself. That's the era we're now in so I suppose a tribute to these two ancient, thoroughly domesticated labor experts could be interpreted as a kind of legitimate poetic license.

*

So too could Frank Sinatra's remarks when he presented the Jean Hersholt Humanitarian Award to Rosalind Russell. If my ears were not filled with bubble gum, I seem to remember his saying that Roz, when she first arrived in Hollywood and even before she unpacked her make-up case, had rushed off to cheer up people at tne Jewish old folks home. I can now hear one elderly lady who says, not rudely but with desperation: "Please, I don't want to be cheered up. I just want to take a nap."

What Hollywood really thinks of the rest of us was spilled by Candy Bergen, a beautiful, intelligent, funny girl who went to the University of Pennsylvania and reportedly gives her father Edgar the screaming meemies because she is so liberal and free-thinking. Candy explained that the score for "Limelight," originally released in 1952, was eligible for consideration for a 1972 Oscar because the movie had not previously been released "in this country." On the West Coast, "this country" obviously means Los Angeles. Well, in New York we tend to think one falls into a bottomless pit once one ventures past Newark.

*

There were two nice things in the show: the "Limelight" award and the montage of clips from Edward G. Robinson films. I also rather liked Marlon Brando's rejection of his award, through Sasheen Little Feather, though the point might have been more

honorably made had Brando himself done the rejecting.

There were some younger people on the show, but they all seemed old or tired or, like Glen Campbell and Raquel Welch, younger people with unmistakable connections to the elderly, right-wing tradition of what movies are supposed to be. Where, for example, were the real stars of today, Paul Newman, Dustin Hoffman, Robert Redford, Ron O'Neal, Linda Lovelace?

On second thought, Linda really isn't a star in any conventional sense. Because she doesn't act as much as perform, her ties are closer to vaudeville than to films.

*

Much closer to vaudeville too is the week's most overinflated porno film, Gerard Damiano's "The Devil in Miss Jones," which, because it's not badly photographed and points such a dismal moral, has been described as bridging the gap between real movies and porn. It's also being taken as "serious," I suspect, because its star, "Georgina Spevlin," is a rather plain looking woman of not easily determined age. Her body is not bad, but her expression is that of a mean hooker. Miss Spevlin plays Miss Jones, a virgin-spinster who commits suicide in the first reel and finds herself awaiting shipment to hell, not because she's done anything bad but because she has committed suicide. The film thus might be classified as the first porn movie suitable for adult Roman Catholics. But not really. The film shows reformist tendencies when Miss Jones receives a chance to return to earth to earn her sentence of eternal damnation. (Would Calvin approve?) As Miss Jones poetically puts it, she wants to be enveloped in lust. Now I ask you: When was the last time you ever heard someone you took seriously use the word lust for anything but comic purposes?

Cut then to earth, or what the film's idea of earth is: a bedroom that looks like a guest room in middle-class Westchester, a bathroom that could be in someone's summer house near Woodstock (the tub is rusty), and a couple of other small locations, including a bed covered (handily) with clear plastic. In what Variety's reviewer solemnly calls "a breathtakingly erotic odyssey," Miss Jones then makes it with one man, with one woman, with two men, with one man and another woman, with a snake and, on several occasions, with herself with the help of the contents of a bowl of fruit.

*

She finally finds herself in a cubicle in Hell with a man who has no interest in sex, in a finale that Variety ecstatically reports "takes Jean-Paul Sartre's 'No Exit' to a logical and surprisingly mor-

alistic extreme." I might have thought that Hell, certainly Sartre's Hell, was beyond qualification, the way "unique" is.

Until I read the reviews for "The Devil in Miss Jones" I would have been prepared to testify that as far as I know, plain old porn movies are probably harmless for adults. Now I'm not so sure. They seem to be warping the minds of some critics. Maybe they've seen too many. After a while the tendency is to seize on any slight variation, usually a variation that contradicts the erotic intent, to deny essential junkiness.

"The Devil in Miss Jones" is not entirely without its comic aspects, including the piety of the reviews. It's also the first film I've ever seen that seems to equate sexual indulgence with nail polish. When we first see Miss Jones, the virgin, she isn't wearing polish. Toward the end, her nails have been painted a deep spinach-green.

1973 Ap 8, II:1:7

Let the Boys in the Band Die

By ARTHUR BELL

BLACK used to be Hattie McDaniel with a feather duster and Stepin Fetchit polishing the rump of a racehorse and Bill "Bojangles" Robinson in spic and span livery tapping up and down the mastah's staircase with little colonel Shirley. Gay used to be Franklin Pangborn as a prissy florist and Eric Blore as a primping butler and Erik Rhodes as a flouncy dress designer whom Ginger Rogers spurned for Fred Astaire in "The Gay Divorcee."

The Hattie McDaniel stereotype went with the 30's, and with the 50's came the black revolution and the evolution of a new consciousness. Hollywood became careful. No longer a shuffle or a yowsah for an easy laugh. Black servitude died and the silver screen gave birth to social films which instilled a sense of black identity in the 60's, which in turn begat the current cycle of blaxploitation films starring Richard Roundtree and Jim Brown as the foremost cats giving the orders.

But gay is something else. Our revolution came late, in 1969, but our stereotypes continue and our screen image is alive and sick and in need of an euthanasic ending and a liberated beginning.

*

In "Pete 'n' Tillie," for instance, Erik Rhodes lives in the body of René Auberjonois, but minus the flair and garble-tongued innocence that were Rhodes' hallmark. Now the humor is catty, with a touch of sanctimonious compassion thrown in, making Auberjonois both false and

Harvey Jason, as a homosexual fashion designer, is criticized by his boss, Jack Lemmon, in "Save the Tiger"
"Why not gay godfathers and gay heartbreak kids and gay sleuths?"

unfunny. He is the token homosexual, a well-groomed swizzle stick in a cocktail party world, who suddenly turns sympathetic because he proposes marriage to Carol Burnett after her long heterosexual liaison with Walter Matthau has hit the rocks.

"Pete 'n' Tillie" is stereotypical of the progression of films of the late 60's and early 70's, written, produced, and/or directed by homosexuals who have not been willing to come out of the closet or by heterosexuals who are either unconscious of what they're doing or homophobic enough to want to perpetuate the age-old stereotype that gay is bad, a stereotype equivalent to black is ugly, and one which the gay movement is working to obliterate.

About a year ago, I attended a screening of "J. W. Coop." Cliff Robertson, who made the film, was present to answer questions from the audience. During the course of the film, one scene stood out. Coop, a staunch defender of the rights of blacks, chicanos, hippies, Indians and aging ranch hands, beats up on some white guys after they've cast a racial slur on his black friend. The beating takes place in a men's lavatory and when the cops come, Coop responds with a cutesy remark to the effect that he had been solicited and his red-blooded duty was to preserve his male honor.

The scene was very quick, very in-passing, yet very out of character considering Coop's other right-on attitudes. Questioned about this inconsistency, Robertson replied that it had not occurred to him that someone would interpret the scene that way and he'd be more sensitive to such situations in the future.

A lack of consciousness on Robertson's part? Sure. But I wonder about the recent put-down cracks in "Shamus" and "Up the Sandbox" and the rationale that prompted screenwriter Alvin Sargent to include a short scene in "The Effect of Gamma Rays on Man-in-the-Moon Marigolds" in which Joanne Woodward yells "You homo" at her neighbor because the man has rejected her advances (and why did director Paul Newman choose to show this particular film clip on the Dick Cavett Show when he and star-wife Joanne Woodward appeared?).

Granted, the remark is within the psychological framework of the pathetically frustrated mother played by Miss Woodward. But did it add a new dimension to her character? The remark was not made in Paul Zindel's play, from which the film was adapted. So one wonders, was it a lack of awareness to include it in the film or did the "Marigolds" people choose to throw one more poison dart at a popular unpopular subject?

Another example of homophobic neurosis can be found in the aging ex-movie star that Sylvia Miles plays in "Heat." When informed of her daughter's lesbian tendencies, Sylvia goes berserk. From her mouth spews a barrage of ugliness that caused a gay liberationist at the Lincoln Center Film Festival showing to state to a panel of "Heat" experts, including Miss Miles and director Paul Morrissey, "I thought the film went out of its way to grossly underline the actress's anti-gay hangups when there were so many other ways you could have depicted her frustrations."

*

Practically every other film that dribbles from the sound stages these days has a "Heat" or "Marigolds" anti-homosexual reference — or a dipsy depiction of a homosexual character or an offensive secondary homosexual theme. In addition to the character played by René Auberjonois in "Pete 'n' Tillie," recent gay film gentlemen include the simpering benefactor of "Savage Messiah" and the grossly effete gentleman who watches a boxing match with Sarah Miles in "Lady Caroline Lamb." Both are gay equivalents of Stepin Fetchit at his "Yowsah, ma'am" low.

Homosexuality is the secondary theme in "Play It As It Lays." A handsome stud of a movie star tells Tuesday Weld to "dump the fags." A couple of reels later, one of the "fags," Tony Perkins, noshes a couple of handfuls of Seconals and dies in Tuesday's arms, because that's the way it is when you're depressed and talented and suppressed and suffering from an overpossessive mother, a mockery of a marriage to Tammy Grimes, and too much money. Homosexuals have to end up unhappily or, better still, dead.

*

Then there's "Lolly Madonna XXX." The daughter of Robert Ryan's hillbilly clan chances upon two of the rowdier members of rival Rod Steiger's family. The boys are in the woods and they're in a playful mood and one of them, Ed Lauter, dresses up in ladies' clothes and minces and swishes out his Ozark mountain fantasies of faggotry. The young woman taunts him: "You look like a . . . queer." To prove otherwise, Lauter rapes her.

But put-downs of homosexuals in movies are not confined to males. A special smarmy exploitation award goes to the gratuitous lesbian scene in "The Valachi Papers." Out of nowhere, the promiscuous girl friend of an organized crime figure is caught by her boss's henchman in a compromising position with another girl. The henchman's reaction to the situation is one of shock and disgust.

A steady diet of this fodder causes gay radicals to take up arms and gay inverts to stay in their closets and gay isolationists — with only the movies and television as nourishment — to consider suicide and gay activists to picket and make loud noises to stop this emotional destruction.

My least favorite depiction of a gay character among the current movies is the fashion designer played by Harvey Jason in "Save the Tiger." The man is temperamental, egotistical, one-dimensional and he's pitted against a lovely, sympathetic old garment-district cutter, who is symbolic of the good old ways. Designer and cutter argue, and cutter tells boss Jack Lemmon, "I can't be in a playpen with fairies."

In gay liberation circles, we play a game called "switch." Switch the designer to a black man, leave the cutter white, substitute "niggers" for "fairies," and would a director still dare to shoot the movie that way?

*

As long as filmmakers continue to be closed in by their unliberated attitudes, films will continue to repress millions of homosexuals. Yes, occasionally a breath of fresh air sweeps the screen: the enlightened relationship between Murray Head and Peter Finch in "Sunday Bloody Sunday," the healthy bisexuality projected by Michael York in "Cabaret," the delicious chess expert of Austin Pendleton in "The Thief Who Came to Dinner." But it's rare.

What would I like to see? Films in which homosexuals are treated as fully developed human beings. Films in which homosexuals are an integral part of the plot and not camp objects of scorn. Gayploitation films, eventually, where an updated Eric Blore — a hero who carries with him a scent of untainted sweetness — is the cat on top of the heap. Gay films that aren't about "the pain of homosexuality." Gay godfathers and gay heartbreak kids and gay sleuths, as well as originals from our own developing culture. Films that might be provocative and entertaining and fine.

A pipe dream? I don't think so. The movement is laying the foundations, but Hollywood isn't building yet. It's time the creative brains realized that the boys in the band are dying. But as long as the media play the sickee game, homosexuality will linger as a disease. How long before the films give birth to a new and healthier baby?

Arthur Bell is a writer and a founder of the Gay Activists Alliance.

1973 Ap 8, II: 15:1

The Cast

BROTHER SUN, SISTER MOON, directed by Franco Zeffirelli; original story and screenplay by Suso Cecchi D'Amico, Kenneth Ross, Lina Wertmuller and Mr. Zeffirelli; songs composed and sung by Donovan; director of photography, Ennio Guarnieri; editor, John Rushton; produced by Luciano Perugia; distributed by Paramount Pictures. Running time: 121 minutes. At the Coronet Theater, Third Avenue at 59th Street. This film has been classified PG.

Francesco .... Graham Faulkner
Clare .... Judi Bowker
Bernardo .... Leigh Lawson
Paolo .... Kenneth Cranham
Silvestro .... Michael Feast
Giocondo .... Nicholas Willatt
Pica .... Valentina Cortese
Pietro di Bernardone ..... Le Montague
Bishop Guido .... John Sharp
Pope Innocent III ...... Alec Guinness

By VINCENT CANBY

Franco Zeffirelli's "Brother Sun, Sister Moon" is the sort of movie that tries to make poverty look chic, and almost goes broke in the attempt.

It's the splendiferously costumed, fancily photographed (through rain, smoke, mist or muslin, whenever possible), multimillion-dollar, near-musical life of Giovanni Francesco Bernardone (1181-1226), the cloth merchant's son who later became St. Francis of Assisi. The title is taken from Francis's "Canticle of Creatures," and it could be worse, since Francis had a way of referring to everything as his "brothers" or "sisters," including his illnesses. These he called his "sisters" and on their part he once begged the pardon of his "brother ass the body."

●

Like Roberto Rossellini, who sought the essence of St. Francis more in fable than in fact, Zeffirelli makes no special claims to historical accuracy. However, unlike Rossellini, whose "Flowers of St. Francis" is a film of sweet purpose and simplicity, Zeffirelli has made a big, absurd doodad, a movie that confuses simplicity with simple-mindedness and that makes saintliness look like an extreme form of Asian flu.

When Francis comes down with it, he gets feverish, hallucinates, goes off into a long coma and then wakes up as a Good Person. We know this because he spends a lot of time weeping for the underprivileged, giving away his daddy's yard goods and hanging out with birds, bees and flowers.

●

The screenplay, written by Zeffirelli with three other people who should be nameless but aren't (see listing), opens with Francis's return from the war with Perugia and his vow to follow the life and teachings of Christ covers the years that finally culminate with the recognition of what was to become the Franciscan order by Pope Innocent III.

In a film that isn't exactly devoid of unintentionally funny moments, this last sequence is a standout, when the sack-clothed Francis and his little band of barefoot followers confront Innocent III in a St. Peter's throne room so photographed as to look like a set from a "Ziegfeld Follies." Francis's philosophy consists entirely of assorted cribs from the Gospel according to St. Matthew, which Francis hurls around the throne room as if they were thunderbolts instead of familiar quotations. The Pope is so impressed he falls on his knees in front of Francis, at which point we suddenly recognize Innocent III as old Alec Guinness, wearing his famous Fagan beard but not the controversial nose.

●

Guinness and Valentina Cortese (who plays Francis's mother) are the only familiar actors in the film. Graham Faulkner (Francis), Judi Bowker (Clare) and the men who play Francis's followers are all young English actors making their film debuts. They are noteworthy only in that they share a prettiness that is barely distinguishable from the landscape's.

Although Zeffirelli has a fondness for posing Francis in attitudes suggested by Christ on the cross, he downplays the visions to, literally, one blink—of the eyes of a statue. Zeffirelli makes Francis seem such a bland sort of fellow that we spend most of the time looking at the scenery, the auroral photographic effects and the costumes, which were also the chief attractions of the director's hugely popular "Romeo and Juliet."

The film is scored to a point that makes your teeth hurt with awful songs ("Birds are singing sweet and low/ From the trees that gently grow . . .") by Donovan, sung by him on the soundtrack in a role I assume to be God's.

1973 Ap 9, 48:1

CLASS OF '44, directed and produced by Paul Bogart; screenplay by Herman Raucher; director of photography, Andrew Laszlo; editor, Michael A. Hoey; music, David Shire; distributed by Warner Brothers. Running time: 95 minutes. At the Sutton Theater, 57th Street, east of Third Avenue. This film has been classified R.

Hermie .... Gary Grimes
Oscy .... Jerry Hauser
Benjie .... Oliver Conant
Fraternity President..... William Atherton
Marty .... Sam Bottoms
Julie .... Deborah Winters

By VINCENT CANBY

"The little bird has scratched at the window," says the girl who looks like Ann Rutherford in cap and gown, "for nature has told him it's time to go." It's June, and Hermie, Oscy and Benjie, the three friends of Robert Mulligan's "Summer of '42," are graduating from their Brooklyn high school to face not the terrors 'of a world at war but those of a sequel gone suddenly, hopelessly flat.

The only things worth attention in "Class of '44" are the period details—the cars, the billboards, the haircuts, the songs, the suits and dresses and shoes, all soberly researched and reconstructed as if they were artifacts for Colonial Williamsburg. But because nothing much happens with these props, "Class of '44" seems less like a movie than 95 minutes of animated wallpaper.

The new film takes Hermie (Gary Grimes) and Oscy (Jerry Houser) to college (Benjie joins the Marines),

where Hermie falls in love while Oscy provides the comic relief by, among other things, installing the town whore in his fraternity house for one busy night. The boys have intimations of mortality, and there are jokes about making out, but "Class of '44" has about as much relation to what growing up was like then (and may still be now) as did the Henry Aldrich radio series of that period.

The screenplay is by Herman Raucher, who also wrote "Summer of '42." Those were the good old days, I assume we're supposed to say, but the good old days in "Class of '44' seem incredibly unimportant and Hermie and Oscy essential clods, fellows who've most likely grown up to be legendary bores on their respective Thursday night bowling teams.

Paul Bogart directed the film, which opened yesterday at the Sutton Theater.

1973 Ap 11, 41:1

Screen: New Directors

◀ Foreign Works at the Modern Art Have Political or Social Themes

By ROGER GREENSPUN

Surely by accident, and not by programing design, each of the last four films in the New - Directors/New - Films series at the Museum of Modern Art deals with a decision made for some kind of political or social commitment. The causes range from fascism (Juraj Herz's "The Cremator") to anarchy (Claude Faraldo's "Themroc"), but the movies share a tendency to replace dramatic development with thematic or historical demonstration. For this they pay a high price.

The Czechoslovak "The Cremator" was made in 1968, and so is not a new film. But, like its director, it is new to us. The central character, a Mr. Kopfrkingl, is the director of a fancy crematorium, happy in his work, who finds that almost without his wishing it the spirit of his times (the very late nineteen-thirties) is propelling him toward the peak of his career: directorship of a super crematorium with massive ovens and all the necessary bodies to burn in them.

Kopfrkingl's story, how he feels rising within him the power of his one drop of German blood, how he finally solves the problem of his beloved half-Jewish wife and quarter-Jewish children, is treated with a blend of intelligent theatrical irony and inflated film technique that is so typical—and so typically the limitation—of East-European cinema. But Kop-

frkingl himself, played by Rudolf Hrusinky, with the face of a gently demonic Charles Laughton and the manner of a malevolent Herbert Marshall, is a creation of considerable interest.

I suspect that almost everything outside the film is more interesting than what actually gets into Paul Leduc's "John Reed: Insurgent Mexico." It is an account of a famous journalist's involvement with the revolutionary forces of Pancho Villa under Gen. Tomas Urbina that began as a magazine assignment and became a process of personal radicalization.

Leduc obviously means to keep his film low key—at which, alas, he more than succeeds. But he seems also to claim for it a quality of authenticity—partly by way of soft sepia-tone photography, like the reproductions in old photo-journalism—that it never earns. The pseudo-documentary style of "John Reed" isn't a style at all, but rather an affectation hopefully overlaid upon a flaccid, didactic, fairly conventional treatment of political biography.

Shinsuke Ogawa's "The Peasants of the Second Fortress" really is documentary, 2½ hours of it, dealing with a 1971 struggle by farmers to stop the construction of a Tokyo airport on their land. The movie has a characteristic look, the look of the

wet gray spring during which it was filmed, and it is sometimes very beautiful. More often it is dull.

Ogawa's uncanny selectivity in photographing the actual combat between peasants and riot police (like a medieval battle staged by Kurosawa at his best) contrasts with his seemingly total indulgence of every random conference among the peasants, to produce a movie that appears always at odds with itself.

Because it uses big stars, and because it is the most ambitiously imaginative, I suppose place of honor should go to Claude Faraldo's "Themroc," though I do not much like it as a movie. Themroc, a Parisian laborer, gets bounced from his job one day. He goes home, seals off his room in his mother's apartment, breaks open the outer wall, and begins living like a happy caveman, making ardent love with his kid sister and feeding himself on roast policeman, captured during nighttime raids in the city streets.

There is much more to the movie than this, but not enough to hide the earnest propagandizing behind its fantasy—which, for all its daring, might have come from a Stanley Kramer slightly high on pot. But the real pleasure comes from the performances. In "Themroc" some speak a nonsense language, while everyone else merely makes noises or acts in mime—and it is fun to watch Michel Piccoli, so often the fastidious hero of boulevard romances, cope with a role in which he can only grunt and groan, and to see Béatrice Romand of "Claire's Knee," as the kid sister, a part that enforces total silence. In fact they both do very well.

One further film, "Kodou," by the Senegalese director Ababacar Samb, arrived in an unsubtitled print. Because I do not understand its language, I do not think it proper to review it at this time.

1973 Ap 11, 39:1

The Cast

SCARECROW, directed by Jerry Schatzberg; produced by Robert M. Sherman; screenplay by Garry Michael White; director of photography, Vilmos Zsigmond; editor, Evan Lottman; music, Fred Myrow; distributed by Warner Brothers. Running time: 112 minutes. At the Cinema I Theater, Third Avenue near 60th Street. This film has been classified R.

Max	Gene Hackman
Lion	Al Pacino
Coley	Dorothy Tristan
Frenchy	Ann Wedgeworth
Riley	Richard Lynch
Darlene	Eileen Brennan
Annie	Penny Allen
Mickey	Richard Hackman

By VINCENT CANBY

Max and Lion (full name: Francis Lionel) are classic drifters. Cut loose from their lower-middle-class backgrounds, for various, prob-

ably neurotic reasons, they float across the face of America with all of the resolution of a couple of cheerful mongrels checking out the bushes, trees and lampposts on any new street that happens to cross their field of limited vision.

They never quite get where they're going, which, I suspect, seems more poetic and tragic to the makers of a movie like "Scarecrow" than it does to the Maxes and Lions of real life. It's the moving around, not the getting anywhere, that counts.

For most of "Scarecrow"— for as long as the movie doesn't intrude on their essential aimlessness — Max (Gene Hackman) and Lion (Al Pacino) are two marvelously realized characters.

Max, a big, near-sighted clown with a bad temper, has just finished an extended stay in San Quentin for assault. He's always a bit cold, which is why he wears a half-dozen layers of long johns, shirts and sweaters. He wants to open a carwash in Pittsburgh—not because he knows Pittsburgh but because that is where his savings account happens to be.

Max is not without a kind of sloppy sex appeal. When he enters a cocktail lounge, a female barfly named Darlene issues an invitation by screaming: "Shut the door, you big dope! You're letting all the smoke out!"

Max neither loves nor trusts anyone until he meets Lion, an ex-seaman hitching his way from California to Detroit to see the wife he deserted six years before and a 5-year-old child who may be either a boy or a girl. He doesn't know—which is why the present he carries is a lamp. A lamp, he figures, is a suitable way to avoid the issue.

The friendship of Max and Lion, as they lurch across the United States, with time out for a visit with Max's sister Coley (Dorothy Tristan) in Denver (as well as for a month's stay on a Denver Honor Farm), is genuinely moving and funny. It all goes decisively wrong when Jerry Schatzberg, the director, and Garry Michael White, who wrote the screenplay, decide to saddle the pair with a poetic vision that suddenly makes everything needlessly phony.

This doesn't come as a complete surprise. There have been hints earlier in the picture that Schatzberg and White want to impose their own sensibilities on Max and Lion. The hints are in the title (Max and Lion and all of the other drifters are life's scarecrows) and in the spectacularly beautiful landscapes, photographed by Vilmos Zsigmond, through which Max and Lionel move, unaware (though we aren't) that they are in the world as it

might be seen by Peter Hurd. No amount of time and no expenses have been spared to obtain the right light.

The hints are also there in the supporting performances, which aren't bad, just too busy. There is a definite limit on the number of nose-wipings on sleeves, speeches said with mouths full and elegant burps that any movie can contain before it begins to turn back on itself, like parody. Which is too bad because both Hackman and Pacino are fine and so many of the early, character-setting scenes are so accurate.

I assume that Schatzberg and White wanted somehow to ennoble Max and Lionel, but they sentimentalize them in ways rigidly avoided by both John Huston's "Fat City," and Barbara Loden's "Wanda," two other films about a similar kind of sad, almost national witlessness. "Scarecrow" opened yesterday at the Cinema I.

1973 Ap 12, 56:1

The Cast

BOOK OF NUMBERS, directed by Raymond St. Jacques; screenplay by Larry Spiegel, based on the novel by Robert Deane Phaar; film editor, Irv Rosenblum; director of photography, Gayne Rescher; produced by Mr. St. Jacques; released by Avco Embassy Pictures. At the DeMille Theater, Broadway and 47th Street. Running time: 80 minutes. This film is classified R.

Blueboy Harris	Raymond St. Jacques
Kelly Simms	Freda Payne
Dave Greene	Phillip Thomas
Pigmeat Goins	Hope Clarke
Makepeace Johnson	Willie Washington, Jr.
Eggy	Doug Finell
Kid Flick	Sterling St. Jacques
Blip Blip	G. L. Williams
Billy Bowlegs	D'Urville Martin

By ROGER GREENSPUN

For reasons I can only guess at, "Book of Numbers" seems a lovely title for a movie. And neither the title, nor its quality, is wasted on Raymond St. Jacques's film about the adventures of two benevolent entrepreneurs who bring the numbers game to the grateful black population of El Dorado, Ark., sometime in the nineteen-thirties.

Before their story is over, the younger man finds a sense of purpose and a marvelous girl, the older finds the means to an act of heroism he had never imagined, and El Dorado finds a whole new interest in such simple pleasures as learning the number of the hymn the pastor wants them to sing in church on Sunday.

This is a lot to expect from the numbers game, and "Book of Numbers" doesn't expect it with too much seriousness. The film has all the standard accouterments of crime melodrama, including real danger and real death. But its spirit comes mainly from its music—background music, blues and spirituals, dance tunes—

rather than from the requirements of melodramatic plotting. That may be why it moves with such efficiency and agility (there is almost nothing wasted in its mere 80 minutes of running time), why it spends no energy on examining profundities where none exist, why the faults of some parts never really threaten the success of the whole.

I don't mean to make "Book of Numbers" sound like a perfect movie, which it surely isn't. But it does seem an uncommonly well-balanced movie, intelligently directed, very cleverly edited (by Irv Rosenblum), with an air of real enjoyment in what it is about.

The characters are all stereotypes of greater or lesser intricacy — which is what they ought to be. The situations are fairly predictable, though no less exciting for all that. And life itself, as the movie sees it, is just enough show-biz so that cardboard characters can run through it as it were on railroad tracks—and still maintain the illusion of exceptional grace and freedom.

•

The cast, headed by Mr. St. Jacques (the numbers chief), Philip Thomas (his protégé), and Freda Payne (the girl) is expert and very attractive. Sometimes they seem to be having more fun with their material than the screenplay strictly allows—an agreeable kind of excess. In a supporting role, Hope Clarke plays a knowing charmer with the wonderful name of Pigmeat Goins and she is so outrageously good that if I had to see the movie again, she would be reason enough.

"Book of Numbers" opened yesterday at the DeMille Theater.

1973 Ap 12, 59:1

THE CHALLENGES, A TRILOGY: Part I directed by Claudio Guerin; Part II directed by Jose Luis Egea; Part III directed by Victor Erice. Script (Spanish with English subtitles) by Jose Hernandez Miguel; film editor, Pablo G. del Amo; music by Luis de Pablo; photography by Luis Cuadrado; distributed by Dean Selmier. At thet First Avenue Screening Room, at 61st Street. Running time: 96 minutes. (This film has not been classified.)
With Francisco Rabal, Dean Selmier, Anuncion Balaguer and Teresa Rabal (Part I); Mr. Selmier, Alfredo Mayo, Julia G. Caba, Barbara Deist and Fernando S. Polack (Part II); Mr. Selmier, Julia Pena, Daysl Granados and Luis Suarez (Part III).

By ROGER GREENSPUN

"The Challenges," which opened yesterday at the First Avenue Screening Room, consists of three dreadful vignettes, filmed in Spain, each featuring a young American named Dean Selmier, who acts nasty.

In the first vignette he is an American Air Force officer who plays at seducing a rich Spanish girl, plays at seducing her mother and then gets boffed to death with a baseball bat by her unsympathetic father. In the second vignette, he is a hippy traveling through Spain with his girl friend on the way to India. Both of them are speared to death by a rich landowner, whom they have vilely humiliated. In the third vignette, he is a well-to-do drifter, heavily into personal machismo, who explodes some dynamite to demolish himself, his beautiful wife and a pleasant couple of hitchhikers — apparently in despair over his own incurable impotence.

Except for Francisco Rabal, the father in the first vignette, none of the other performers are likely to be known here. I assume that most of them are Spanish; many of them seem to be very good. Three separate directors are credited for "The Challenges." But from the homogeneously out-of-date stylishness of the film they have produced, they must all have misspent their youths in the same movie theater, soaking up the collected works of Michelangelo Antonioni.

1973 Ap 13, 48:2

The Cast

STATE OF SIEGE, directed by Costa-Gavras; produced by Jacques Perrin; executive producer, Max Pelevsky; screenplay (French with English subtitles) by Franco Solinas and Costa-Gavras; music, Mikis Theodorakis; director of photography, Pierre William Glenn; editor, Francoise Bonnot; a Reggane Films and Cinema 10 production, distributed by Cinema V. Running time: 120 minutes. At the Beekman Theater, Second Avenue near 66th Street. This film has not yet been classified.

Philip Michael Santore . . . Yves Montand
Captain Lopez . . . Renato Salvatore
Carlos Ducas . . . O. E. Hasse
Hugo . . . Jacques Weber
Este . . . Jean-Luc Bideau
Mrs. Santore . . . Evangeline Peterson
Minister of Internal Security: Maurice Teynac
Woman Senator . . . Yvette Etlevant
Minister of Foreign Affairs Harald Wolff
President of Republic . . Nemesio Antunes
Deputy Fabbri . . . Andre Falcon
Fontana . . . Mario Montilles
Lee . . . Jerry Brouer

By VINCENT CANBY

Costa-Gavras's "State of Siege" is a riveting film and possibly an inflammatory one. It oversimplifies recent history, but raises so many complex and important moral questions that to attack it for oversimplification may be just a discreet form of rationalization, of looking the other way.

The screenplay by Franco Solinas, who wrote "The Battle of Algiers," is based on the kidnap and murder of Dan. A. Mitrione in August, 1970, in Montevideo, Uruguay. Mr. Mitrione, an Italian-born American, the father of nine children and a former police chief in Richmond, Ind., was an official of the United States Agency for International Development assigned as an adviser to the Uruguayan police. Officially he was an expert in traffic control and communications, and in this capacity he had earlier been an adviser to the police in Brazil and the Dominican Republic.

On July 31, 1970, Mr. Mitrione and the Brazilian consul in Montevideo were kidnapped by the Tupamaros, a group of Marxist-oriented, urban guerrillas who demanded the release of 150 political prisoners. The Uruguayan Government declined, and 10 days after his kidnapping, Mr. Mitrione was executed by the Tupamaros who, until then, had mostly refrained from violence in their efforts to discredit the Government and what they called its repressionist policies.

Much of the world was appalled, as it was by the Black September massacre at the Tel Aviv Airport, by the killing of the Israeli athletes in Munich and by the more recent murders in Khartoum.

After Mr. Mitrione's murder, information began to be published here and abroad that suggested that Mr. Mitrione's specialty was not necessarily traffic control and communication, but internal security, more specifically, antiguerrilla warfare, with close associations to those responsible for the systematic torture and liquidation of the revolutionary opposition.

Among the many questions raised by "State of Siege" is one relating to the film maker's responsibility to stick to the truth of an event even when it might be inconvenient. The Solinas screenplay changes the names of the principals (I suppose releases would be hard to get from those alive) and only indirectly alludes to the Uruguayan setting (the film was actually shot in Salvador Allende's Chile). It very carefully never puts the Mitrione character (named Philip Michael Santore in the film and played by Yves Montand) at the scene of any tortures, but the inference — very loud and very clear — is that Mitrione-Santore was a major architect of those policies.

Thus to the extent that Costa-Gavras and Solinas suggest that the A.I.D. man was secretly involved in the internal affairs of a foreign government, the film is a rationalization of a terrorist act. However, in its biased but elegantly cool way, it's much more than that. It's an examination of an event first, then of national policies that led to that event (including the United States' historical role as Big Daddy in Latin America through economic programs that help others to help themselves as well as our industry), and lines of responsibility.

•

Finally, it's an examination of our capacity to be shocked, a capacity that may have begun to run out with the disclosures about the Bay of Pigs, so that now, when we read the stories about the International Telephone and Telegraph Corporation and Chile, we are as much inclined to laughter as we are to grief or even to surprise. We shrug and ask ourselves, in effect, what will they do next? Self-interest carried to the limit is no longer evil, or a matter for review by one's conscience, but a kind of dumbfounding rascality, a high form of scalawaggery.

What makes "State of Siege" so harrowing is not that it is all true (I'm not in a position to know), but that it could be true, and all of us could be responsible. This is more important, I think, than carping over details of the film, over the fact that no effort is made to define the inflationary economic conditions in Uruguay that first prompted the press censorship and other repressive measures that, in turn prompted the revolutionary opposition.

•

Strictly as an example of film-making, "State of Siege" is exceptionally shrewd. Although we have no doubt what the outcome of the narrative will be, Costa-Gavras and Solinas maintain our interest at what is sometimes called (in admitted desperation) a fever pitch. Through the kind of rapid cross-cutting made familiar in both "Z" and "The Confession," they manage to make straight exposition hugely dramatic.

Will or won't the police find the kidnapped officials? Cut to the Uruguayan legislature where a report is being read concerning the existence of "an uncontrollable and autonomous organization" within the national police. Cut to the rebels' interrogation of Montand, cut to . . . cut to. . . . The movie's pace is unrelenting, and it wasn't until I saw it the second time that I recognized the essential monotony of the techniques.

Most shrewd is the casting of Montand, who, because he is Montand, evokes sympathy for a character who remains at best sincerely wrongheaded, at worst a fuzzy villain. Were this American played by an American actor, the film might well be insupportably antagonizing.

"State of Siege," which opened yesterday at the Beekman, also raises the question about what the American Film Institute was up to when it first booked the film to open its new Washington theater at the Kennedy Center. It should have been apparent to anyone who had seen it that "State of Siege" would ruffle a lot of people in Washington, but then to cancel it, as was done last week, suggests incompetence of an order as scary as outright censorship.

1973 Ap 14, 39:1

The Program

NEW AMERICAN CINEMA: THE MAGIC BEAUTY KIT by Ira Wohl, 15 minutes; **JEFFREY** by Rick King, 14 minutes; **KISS MY LIPS, ARTCHIE,** by Ron Lieberman and Salvatore Bovoso, 20 minutes; **FRANK FILM** by Frank Mouris, 9 minutes; **OPENING/CLOSING** by Kathleen Laughlin, 4½ minutes: **THE FLIGHT OF ALEXANDER MAXIMILIAM TUMONT SENAT OHM OLIVER,** by by Vincent Grenier, 16 minutes; **BUSBY PASSES THE ACID TEST** by Marc Stone, 10 minutes. At the Film Forum, 256 West 88th Street, April 13-15, 20-22, 8 P.M.

By ROGER GREENSPUN

One of the most pleasant possibilities of the new, relatively unassertive documentary movie has nothing to do with the truth it tells, but rather with the chance it offers to spend some time together with a sensibility you might find congenial. I felt this last year at a Whitney Museum showing of "Co-Co Puffs," Ira Wohl's charming film about a drum lesson. And I felt it all over again with "The Magic Beauty Kit," another Ira Wohl documentary, and the first work in a program called "New American Cinema," which opened Friday at the Film Forum.

•

It is a fairly simple movie. A cosmetics salesman demonstrates his products to a group of Long Island housewives by making up a woman from the audience, and transforming her into a creature of quite extraordinary beauty before their eyes. In fact, he succeeds. But the context of the success—the drab audience; the salesman's easy patter; the subject's awareness of her own life, which is not so awful but lacks the means to support romantic illusions —makes it not less real but terribly fragile, an expression of vulnerable joy, which seems Wohl's special, very privileged insight.

The other special work in the program is a 9-minute collage-animation by Frank Mouris. It is called "Frank Film," and it consists wholly of a breathtaking succession of images—of TV sets, babies, watches, birds, chairs, lips, meals, and on and on—crossing and filling the screen in response to a narrtor's meditation on all the things that have interested him in his life. It is both funny and touching — and exhilarating and handsome to look at.

Kathleen Laughin's fantasy upon washing-machine doors, "Opening-Closing," is also handsome, but not so interesting. And the same seems true of Marc Stone's "Busby Passes the Acid Test" — a colorized reprinting of a dance number from "Gold Diggers of 1935," which doesn't need the treatment.

•

"Kiss My Lips, Artchie," by Ron Lieberman and Salvatore Bovoso—an elaborate recreation of a transvestite's world by way of words and images of Jackie Curtis—only sometimes with a mixture of sadness and gaiety, illuminates its subject. But Rick King's study of a 16-year-old spaced-out drifter, "Jeffrey," is as lucid and as terrifyingly dispassionate as is the boy himself in detailing the personal wasteland in which he lives.

One last film, Vincent Grenier's "The Flight of Max-imiliam Tumont Senat Ohm Oliver," a poetic fantasy of high pretensions and low achievement, belongs not in this program but on the shelf.

1973 Ap 15, 59:1

Falling in Love With 'Love'

By VINCENT CANBY

"LOVE," the Hungarian film directed by Karoly Makk, is very special—precise and moving and fine-grained—and unless you make a point of getting to it within the next several days, you may well miss one of the best films of the year to date. In a season in which excellence has been as rare as snow, it's difficult to understand why "Love" should be leading such a gypsy life. It's now at the Art Theater in Greenwich Village, where it moved from the Beekman, where it played briefly following its initial one-week engagement at the First Avenue Screening Room, where it opened five months after its local premiere at last year's New York Film Festival at Lincoln Center. It still hasn't taken New York by storm, and perhaps it shouldn't. I'm almost inclined to feel protective towards it, as if a lot of people crowding in on it would in some way be an act of rudeness. Which is to deal in a kind of sentimentality that the film consistently avoids. It's also to mistake the respect "Love" shows for its characters for cinematic weakness.

"Love" is the 13th feature film to be directed by Mr. Makk, who is 47 and, as far as I can learn, has never before had a film in commercial release here. It's an adaptation of two novellas by Tibor Dery, one of Hungary's best known writers, and it is, much of the time, a two-character, one-set film, though it covers an extraordinary range of things—psychological, social, political—with a directness and simplicity one seldom finds in a film. The movie image usually conveys too much information, through too many standard details, to allow for the degree of precision one finds in "Love," and otherwise only in the best prose.

A very old lady (Lili Darvas), whose great beauty hasn't faded but only slightly receded into fine, fragile bones, lies in bed, her life draining away in little fits and starts, sustained by books, old photographs, and memories that cut across one another like telephone wires that mix up yesterday's conversations with ones that took place 50 years ago. Mostly she is sustained by her daughter-in-law, Luca (Mari Torocsik), who seems to be an entirely different sort of woman, tough, caustic, pretty in the square way of the social realists.

Luca visits the old lady daily, bringing flowers she can't afford and, whenever she feels up to it, letters written to the old lady by her son, Janos (Luca's husband).

Janos, the letters reveal, is in New York completing a film that will open a new, 16,000-seat theater (with an airport on top), to be attended by the President's widow and her best friend, Queen Wilhelmina, the Soviet foreign minister and the Queen of Greece. Right now, he says, he can't send any presents because he won't be paid until the film is completed, and besides, if he sent presents his mother would just have to pay duty. In the meantime, he reports, his life goes on. He's moved from his 100th floor apartment at the Waldorf-Astoria into a more convenient palace protected by six Secret Servicemen.

The setting of "Love" is Budapest and the time is late in the Stalinist era, and Janos is not in America but only one year into a 10-year term in a political prison. The old lady frets that she won't live to see Janos's return and Luca points out roughly that the doctor has said she'll probably live to be 100. The old lady has bad days and good, and Luca, whom the old lady calls "the young girl," never is entirely certain of how many of the lies the old lady believes.

Luca's love for the old lady is a furious confusion of respect, tenderness, love for her husband, sexual frustration and anger at what her life has been reduced to. The more lies the old lady believes, the more outrageous Luca makes the next ones. When the maid cautions her about them, Luca says curtly that the old lady *wants* to believe them.

The tallness of the stories is just one measure of the younger woman's passion. There are others. She says at one point that she feels the way she did when, as a child, she got lice in her hair and her mother shaved her head. It took a year for the hair to grow out.

When the old lady is having a good day, Luca asks her to tell a story she's told dozens of times before, how, when the family was very hard up and had to live in one room, the old lady, then a young mother, told her two sons to turn their faces to the wall when she undressed. One son, later killed in a war, used to peek. Janos didn't.

"Janos was always honorable," says the old lady. "That's why you wanted me to tell the story, isn't it? He may have one or two affairs when he's away from you, but he'll always come back. . . ." And she remembers—in a confidence that her age makes immensely rueful—her own single infidelity, with a man who may or may not be one of the figures we occasionally see on the screen as her mind goes ricocheting between memory and dream within little pockets of the present.

Miss Darvas has, to date, received the major portion of the critical praise, but both she and Miss Torocsik are splendid, and so completely complementary that it's almost impossible to tell where one performance leaves off and the other begins. These are not isolated performances, not from each other, nor from the film itself, which recalls the best work of Satyajit Ray in the seemingly effortless way that Makk moves between objective and subjective points of view and creates a world dense with feeling, with echoes, aural and visual, of past and present.

The film has the air of something so modest that it's well along before one begins to recognize it as the tour de force it is. For me that moment comes when Makk suddenly, somehow, makes us all aware of the curious, not always unpleasant experience of serious illness, when days get muddled with nights, when lights snap on apparently in the afternoon, when solicitous people appear and immediately disappear as if erased by the blink of an eye. The ruts of memory collapse, and there is nothing left to care about.

Were "Love" anything less than a tour de force it would probably be too sad to endure, but although it's moving, it's also hugely satisfying. Some years ago Chabrol wrote that "there is no such thing as a big theme and a little theme, because the smaller the theme is, the more one can give it the big treatment. The truth is, the truth is all that matters."

1973 Ap 15, II:1:7

Will Kids Get Caught Up In 'Charlotte's Web'?

By DEBORAH JOWITT

DURING the fifties, when I was a professional babysitter (seven nights a week and all day Saturdays and Sundays), I must have read aloud E. B. White's "Charlotte's Web" a hundred times. Which was O.K. by me. Kids loved it, and so did I. The plot—as probably everyone knows—concerns the efforts of Charlotte, a barn spider, to save her friend Wilbur, a young pig, from being butchered. To this end, she weaves into her web words in praise of Wilbur (e.g. "some pig"). Her dicta are accepted as miracles by the farm community, and eventually her plan pays off.

But "Charlotte's Web" is about much more. It's about the cycle of birth-growth-death, about gullibility and the power of the written word, about prejudices and the sort of friendship that cuts through them, about opportunism and selflessness, about childhood in rural, pre-TV America. The prose is fresh and lean. Garth Williams's illustrations and wonderfully appropriate—strong, clumsy, uncolored shapes outlined in scratchy pen-and-ink lines.

Now "Charlotte's Web" has been made into a full-length animated film by Hanna-Barbera, Sagittarius Productions. All connected with the movie profess, even show, admiration for White's book. But they also betray (not unnaturally) itching palms and terror at the specter of a displeased GP.

Oh, sure, scriptwriter Earl Hamner Jr. has used a lot of the book's stylish dialogue; and the scenery and characters look enough like those in the original Williams drawings not to offend youthful purists. But the animation style, the addition of a musical score, the careful, almost timid insertion of ingredients that baked up success for films like "Cinderella" and "Mary Poppins" have subtly altered "Charlotte's Web." The movie is perfectly palatable, bland "family" entertainment. Children who like Wonderbread will love it. For the rest . . . well, White's prose may provide enough pungent apple butter to keep them interested.

The book's pace has been tightened, but at the same time the story has been bloated by inappropriate comedy bits, barnyard production numbers, and soggy sentiment (". . . and she didn't even say goodbye!" sob). Has our thinking been so shaped by Disney and musical comedy conventions that we automatically love seeing Zuckerman's farm seething with choruses of animals swaying in unison to the chirpy songs provided by Richard M. and Robert B. Sherman (of "Mary Poppins" fame)?

Doesn't it strike anyone as odd that Debbie Reynolds, who speaks for Charlotte, belts out "Chin Up" so heartily that you'd think Wilbur's friend was a cow, instead of a spider whose voice White characterized as "thin, but pleasant"? And what about the addition of

A tearful Fern hugs Wilbur goodbye in "Charlotte's Web," now at local houses
"Visually, it's as smooth and pretty as a lollipop, but . . ."

Geoffrey, a maverick gosling? O.K., we get another baby animal to love, plus a boost for that old "runts are the greatest" message, but doesn't Geoffrey's presence undermine Charlotte's role as Wilbur's only companion?

Surely, some children will object to the hackneyed image of Henry Fussy as a mother-dominated, violin-playing kid, who apparently turns into a "real boy" when he breaks his glasses. (Didn't this go out with early Betty Grable flicks?) And I'd think quite a few wou'd hate a Fern Arable (the untidy and imaginative eight-year-old of the book) who looks like a squashed-down Barbie doll, given to prim poses and apparently wearing lipstick. Charlotte, a difficult female to deal with, emerges looking not unlike a blue Loretta Young with eight legs. But that's O.K., I guess.

*

Maybe only adults will choke on the treacly title song, which is delivéred by an invisible chorus while the screen fills with glittering webs and foggy blue shapes reminiscent of the "Ave Maria" sequence in "Fantasia." Maybe only a few will be offended by "There Must Be Something More." Obviously aimed at the teen-love ballad market, it struck me as downright peculiar when sung by a little girl to a pig.

To be fair to the Sherman brothers, there is one terrific, well-motivated musical number—"A Veritable Smorgasbord." In it, the snide rat, Templeton, goes on a dream binge in a deserted fairground. The audience screams with gleeful revulsion as towers of glop vanish into his mouth and he performs a mad ballet in the debris.

Visually, the film is as smooth and pretty as a loHipop. Years of innovative work in the short-subject cartoon field don't seem to have had much impact on this traditional pop style. People and animals have a neat cut-out look; black lines indicate creases and hollows. Backgrounds, on the other hand, are often soft, shaded, more luscious in texture. Within their chosen style, the animators are wonderfully skillful, of course. They can suggest curmudgeonly hauteur in the twitchings of an old ram's mouth and brow, or warmth and mildness by the puckering of wrinkles on a man's face.

I'm prepared to read "Charlotte's Web" to my own baby another couple of dozen times, but I'll hire a babysitter to take him if he wants to see the flick.

1973 Ap 15, II: 13:6

HOW TASTY WAS MY LITTLE FRENCH-MAN, directed by Nelson Pereira dos Santos; screenplay (French and Tupi, Indian dialect, with English subtitles) by Mr. Dos Santos; camera, Dib Lutfi; produced by Mr. Dos Santos and Luis Carlos Barreto; released by New Yorker Films. At the Fifth Avenue Cinema, at 12th Street. Running time: 80 minutes. (This film has not been classified.)
Frenchman ....Arduino Colasanti
Girl ....Ana Maria Magalhaes
Chief ....Ital Natur
With Eduardo Embassahy, Manfredo Colasanti and Jose Cleber

By ROGER GREENSPUN

Anybody confronting a film with a title like "How Tasty Was My Little Frenchman" has a right to know what it is about. Well, it happens to be about eating a Frenchman—though that's not all. And even that isn't quite the simple gastronomic thrill the average moviegoer may have come to expect from his celluloid cannibalism.

In the coastal wilds of 16th-century Brazil, a French soldier (Arduino Colasanti) escapes his officers—only to be captured first by the Portuguese and then by a tribe of man-eating Indians. Mistaking him for one of their mortal enemies, the Portuguese, the Indians decide to kill him for his crimes and then to eat him for his powers. But first he is given a long period of relative privilege, enjoying a young Indian wife (Ana Maria Magalhaes) and counseling the tribal chief (Ital Natur). This period is the central concern of the film.

●

But it is not the only concern. "How Tasty Was My Little Frenchman" means to be a meditation on the past and perhaps the future of Brazil—ironic, often comic—and it mixes fictional drama with allusions to economic, social and religious history. In portraying its Indians, it exercises great care (there is an elaborate Indian village, which looks for all the world like a superb, animated textbook reconstruction), and if they sometimes suggest too much the noble savage, they at least represent an attempt at verisimilitude.

The verisimilitude, of course, is something of a joke. The Indians are middle-class white Brazilians (ordinary men and exceptionally beautiful, young women) stripped down and reddened up for the occasion. "How Tasty Was My Little Frenchman" is the first absolutely non-exploitative (not nonerotic) movie I have seen to require almost total nudity from its cast, both sexes. Everyone is very convincing, but not always so convincing as to dissociate daily life in a 16th-century Indian village from just having an awfully good time.

●

But in the last analysis the film isn't all that funny, and it doesn't really mean to be. A very uneven work, its best passages are among its most

serious—especially one sequence near the end, when the Indian wife describes for her captive husband the ritual that is to be his death. Half-dancing, sometimes smiling, sometimes almost crying, she re-creates on a barren place—a huge rock by the seashore—all the elements and emotions of a complex and fateful drama. It is a lovely performance, and, in its respect for space and movement, it seems very close to the spirit of classic cinema.

"How Tasty Was My Little Frenchman," which was directed by Nelson Pereira dos Santos, opened yesterday at the Fifth Avenue Cinema.

1973 Ap 17, 34:1

The Cast

THE NELSON AFFAIR, directed by James Cellan Jones; produced by Hal B. Wallis; screenplay by Terence Rattigan, based on his play "A Bequest to The Nation"; director of photography, Gerry Fisher; editor, Anne V. Coates; music, Michel Legrand; distributed by Universal Pictures. Running time: 118 minutes. At the Fine Arts Theater, 58th Street, near Lexington Avenue. This film has been classified PG.
Lady Hamilton ....Glenda Jackson
Lord Nelson ....Peter Finch
Captain Hardy ....Michael Jayston
Lord Minto ....Anthony Quayle
Lady Nelson ....Margaret Leighton
George Matcham Jr. ....Dominic Guard
George Matcham Sr. ....Nigel Stock
Catherine Matcham ..Barbara Leigh-Hunt
Lord Barham ....Roland Culver

By VINCENT CANBY

If English history could be reduced to the size of an owl, Hal B. Wallis would undoubtedly stuff it.

As it is, the veteran producer has been doing something on that order, but in bits and pieces, in his recent films. First "Anne of a Thousand Days," then "Mary, Queen of Scots," and now "The Nelson Affair," all made with such pure-hearted humorlessness that they might be expected to win Mr. Wallis a knighthood, that is, if he had not had the frightfully bad taste to be born in Chicago and to remain an American.

"The Nelson Affair," adapted by Terence Rattigan from his play "A Bequest to the Nation," is so thoroughly genteel that it is perhaps best seen before having afternoon tea. The film is Mr. Rattigan's conception of the last days of the scandalous affair of Lord Nelson, the hero of the Nile, and Emma, Lady Hamilton, who was born Amy Lyon (any time between 1761 and 1765) the daughter of a blacksmith, was painted by Romney, Reynolds and Hoppner, and once in 1941, was enchantingly portrayed by Vivien Leigh (in "That Hamilton Woman").

●

Mr. Rattigan ("The Winslow Boy," "Separate Tables") writes period dialogue in the manner of someone regurgitating the cadences of a 19th-century schoolgirl's diary. "I have a fever of the blood," says Nelson, who has been at sea two years, to a friend, "and you, as well as anyone, know its name." "He's made these mutinous dogs love him," a subordinate says of the admiral. "I expect a perfect hero to be a perfect saint," his mopey nephew wails when he learns that Nelson and Lady Hamilton actually are lovers.

The playwright's style is so insidious that it even makes the great lines of history sound more foolish than they need to. When Nelson, just before the great battle of Trafalgar, orders that "England expects that every man will do his duty," it comes out like solemn Rattigan. Nelson's dying words, spoken to his flag captain, become near-camp: "Take care of Lady Hamilton . . . Kiss me, Hardy."

Peter Finch plays Lord Nelson with a reserved passion that seems intelligently thought out but is not terribly interesting to watch, while Glenda Jackson seems to go at Lady Hamilton from the opposite direction. As written by Mr. Rattigan, this Lady Hamilton is long in the tooth and aware of it. Miss Jackson is rather fun to watch, awaking with a hangover, burping pleasantly while drinking her first brandy of the day and telling anyone who chances by to bug off. It is an all-stops-out performance, but one that is defined by the quality of the material. So, too, is Margaret Leighton's, the abandoned Lady Nelson.

•

The film was directed by James Cellan Jones, whose background is in television, in some rather handsome English settings, and in some elaborate mock-ups of naval ships of the period. The movie makes reference to only one of Emma's children (she had four) and leaves it to a closing title card to tell us what finally happened to her after Nelson's death. The good old Encyclopedia Britannica puts it more poetically: "She died in Calais in distress of not in want on Jan. 15, 1815.

1973 Ap 19, 52:1

The Cast

SCORPIO, directed by Michael Winner; screenplay by Gerald Wilson, from a story by David Rintels; produced by Walter Mirisch; released by United Artists Corporation. At the Rivoli Theater, Broadway and 49th Street; UA Eastside Cinema, 85th Street and First Avenue; the Trans Lux 85th Street, at Madison Avenue and neighborhood theaters. Running time: 114 minutes. This film is classified PG.

Cross .... Burt Lancaster
Laurier .... Alain Delon
Zharkov .... Paul Scofield
McLeod .... John Colicos
Susan .... Gayle Hunnicutt
Filchock .... J. D. Cannon
Sarah .... Joanne Linville
Pick .... Mel Stewart

By ROGER GREENSPUN

Just possibly there may be something in Michael Winner's "Scorpio" that you have never seen at the movies before. But then I think it fair to ask where have you been hiding yourself for the last 10 years, as spy melodramas have come and gone, and double agents have multiplied, selling their secrets but saving their souls—for whatever tragic, trendy, ironic fate awaits them at the end of the sordid alleyway that the rest of us call life.

Set in Vienna, Paris, suburban Georgetown and other fleshpots of the world, "Scorpio" pits C.I.A. agent Cross (Burt Lancaster) against his boss McLeod (John Colicos), while between them stands Laurier (Alain Delon), hired assassin, the Scorpio of the title, hired by McLeod to kill Cross—who happens to be the closest thing he ever had to a best friend, and who also taught him everything he knows about the hired-assassination business.

•

What Cross wants to do is go off and relax with his wife Sarah (Joanne Linville), and what Laurier wants to do is go off and relax with his girl Susan (Gayle Hunnicutt—in this movie all the men have only last names and the women have only first names). But there remains the problem of the contract on Cross's life, and why it is there. The situation sounds like elemental anguish, except that in "Scorpio" nobody stops long enough to feel anguish—and so it all becomes merely elemental, or elementary, if your critical facilities are so disposed.

The dialogue consists mainly of aphorisms. Actually, the aphorisms come only from Cross and from Zharkov (Paul Scofield), Cross's Russian counterpart and a pal from the old days when we could all be anti-Fascists together. Everybody else gets told what to think. But the aphoristic style, combined with Winner's unwavering visual instinct for crushingly obvious detail, helps to push "Scorpio" out of low dullness into vertiginous absurdity. This is almost enough to save the movie from suffocating in its own cliché's.

There are people who take Winner seriously ("The Jokers," "Chato's Land," "The Mechanic," etc.), but I doubt if anyone could take "Scorpio" seriously, and that is the best I can say about it. Sitting in the theater, begrudging every minute and yet slightly hoping it would not end, I am caught in the moviegoer's age-old agony, between heart felt derision and guilty delight.

"Scorpio" opened yesterday at neighborhood theaters.

1973 Ap 19, 52:1

CHARLEY-ONE-EYE, directed by Don Chaffey; screenplay by Keith Leonard; photographed by Kenneth Talbot; music by John Cameron; produced by James Swann; presented by Paramount Pictures. At the New Penthouse Theater, Broadway and 47th Street, and the R.K.O. 86th Street Twin One Theater, at Lexington Avenue. Running time: 110 minutes. (This film is rated "R.")

Black Man .... Richard Roundtree
Indian .... Roy Thinnes
Bounty Hunter .... Nigel Davenport

"Charley-One-Eye" is a chicken, the ephemeral pet of a crippled, monosyllabic Indian who is held captive by a fierce, babbling black man, a fugitive, in a deserted church in the desert (supposedly the Southwest). This is a starkly simple but static and obvious allegory, spurting violence and suggesting the fatalistic bondship of two social outcasts.

Richard Roundtree and Roy Thinnes play the leads—only a few others appear—with a burning intensity matching the sun-parched locale (actually Spain). The picture is slow, heavy and stacked, but it makes a point and holds to it. It opened yesterday at the New Penthouse and R.K.O. 86th Street Twin One.

HOWARD THOMPSON

1973 Ap 19, 52:1

LOVE AND PAIN AND THE WHOLE DAMNED THING, directed and produced by Alan J. Pakula; screenplay by Alvin Sargent; editor, Russell Lloyd; director of photography, Geoffrey Unsworth; music, Michael Small; distributed by Columbia Pictures. Running time: 110 minutes. At the Regency 72d Street, and Columbia I Theater, Second Avenue at 64th Street and other theaters. This film has been classified R.

Lila Fisher .... Maggie Smith
Walter Elbertson .... Timothy Bottoms
Duke ...... Don Jaime de Mora y Aragon
Spanish Gentleman ...... Emiliano Redondo
Dr. Elbertson .... Charles Baxter
Mrs. Elbertson .... Margaret Modlin
Melanie Elbertson .... May Heatherley

By VINCENT CANBY

"Love and Pain and the Whole Damn Thing," directed by Alan J. Pakula and written by Alvin Sargent, is most of the time such a funny and eccentric romantic comedy that you have to excuse the attack of Anglo-Saxon ethic that finally overwhelms it.

Despite almost everything written by Colette, despite the experience of even Benjamin Franklin, popular American and English fiction writers persist in spreading the gloomy word that the conjoining of an older woman and a younger man is a near-mortal sin, usually punishable by death. It may not be so in life (Mary Pickford and Buddy Rogers made a go of it), but the audiences for which Hollywood thinks it is making its films (if not the film makers themselves) are afraid to believe otherwise.

This is what's wrong with "Love and Pain," which is about the thoroughly revivifying love affair of an English spinster in her late 30's, Lila Fisher, who's supposed to be plain, although she is played by the spectacularly engaging Maggie Smith, and a troubled, asthmatic American college boy, Walter Elbertson (Timothy Bottoms). The setting is Spain, which, in summer, becomes a giant, open-air museum and parkland to be overrun with organized tours by bus and bicycle.

Their meeting is not auspicious. Walter, taking the seat next to Lila on a bus, inadvertently squirts her with his breath-freshener and then allows her to sit on his Mounds bar—but they both seem to be neurotic messes at the start.

•

Lila is running away from Bournemouth, where she lives with two elderly aunts and lodgers who must be propped up in their baths and who misplace their teeth in the piano. Walter's background is also forbidding. His father has won a Pulitzer Prize for a book called "The Identity of Man," and his sister can build her own cellos.

Lila and Walter are clearly made for each other, and the film is charming so long as it focuses on the details of their growing love and need for each other. Miss Smith, who was so fine in "The Prime of Miss Jean Brodie" and somehow completely out of step with "Travels With My Aunt," is again magnificent (and magnificently funny), whether locked in a ladies room and crying out a dainty, plaintive "por favor" (read from a phrase book), or putting off an ardent Spaniard, who tries to seduce her with birdcalls. "I'm not too familiar with birds," she says with a mixture of hautiness and desperation. "I have a fish."

Mr. Bottoms, the hero of "The Last Picture Show," is equally funny and believable, full of wonder at the intensity of purpose (and intensity of clichés) that Lila awakens in him. It is something of a breakthrough for him when he finds himself saying, quite seriously: "We have to smile in the rain and be cheerful losers."

"Love and Pain" was photographed in front of, around and through somewhat more scenery than is absolutely necessary, and it eventually goes to soap suds, but that happens late. In the meantime, you can enjoy two of the most intelligently comic performances of the year so far.

1973 Ap 20, 14:1

The Cast

CIAO! MANHATTAN, written and directed by John Palmer and David Weisman; edited by Robert Farren; camera, John Palmer and Kiell Rostad; music by John Phillips, Richie Havens, Kim Milford, Skip Battin and Kim Fowley; released by Maron Films, Ltd. At the First Avenue Screening Room, at 61st Street. Running time: 90 minutes. This film is classified R.

Susan .... Edie Sedgwick
Butch .... Wesley Hayes
Mummy .... Isabel Jewell
Geoffrey .... Geoff Briggs
Paul .... Paul America
Charla .... Jane Holzer
Dr. Braun .... Roger Vadim
Mr. Verdecchio .... Jean Margouleff

By ROGER GREENSPUN

For people who, like myself, came to the cinema of Andy Warhol in the mid-nineteen-sixties, there was no way and indeed no need to separate the films from the young woman who was their principal subject and who gave them their fragile, vague, but rather distinguished glamour. "Poor Little Rich Girl," "Vinyl," "Beauty II"—to a greater or lesser degree they are the personality of Edie Sedgwick, the most characteristic, the most important, though by no means the most durable of Warhol's female superstars.

I saw her occasionally, at openings and receptions, and she looked as she was supposed to look—fabulous legs, silver-dyed hair, enormous deep brown eyes—but almost shockingly more beautiful than any description had allowed and with a presence, a vibrancy that was certainly not apparent in the Warhol movies. After she left those movies (supplanted by Ingrid Superstar, Nico, Viva, all with an eminence that seemed to depend more on publicity than on personality) and generally dropped out of view, there were reports about mental hospitals, stories of massive drug abuse. In the summer of 1971 she married a young California student. And in the autumn of the same year she died, at the age of 28, from an overdose of sleeping pills.

•

A little of the best and much of the ruin of Edie Sedgwick's life (there was never really a career) have found their way into "Ciao! Manhattan," a curious movie by two young film makers, John Palmer and David Weisman, that opened yesterday at the First Avenue Screening Room. The movie takes its start from Sedgwick material shot in 1967 for an unfinished film, to have been called "Ciao! Manhattan," by Genevieve Charbin and Chuck Wein. The original film, a fantasy about a mysterious plot to spy on and control New York's Beautiful People, was to have starred Miss Sedgwick and the Warhol superstar Paul America.

The present movie carries the fantasy to California, with Susan (Miss Sedgwick) housed in a drained swimming pool on the grounds of her nutty mother (Isabel Jewell), living on drugs, shock treatments and the memory of past triumphs, and overseen by a disgruntled guardian named Geoffrey (Geoff Briggs) and a dumb Texan named Butch (Wesley Hayes). "Ciao! Manhattan" actually is Butch's story, and it is through his eyes that we see Miss Sedgwick destroying herself in her own special "Sunset Boulevard." How much is real and how much is acted I don't know. I suspect that most of the worst is real, though Miss Sedgwick may have thought she was acting, and it is no fun to watch.

At bottom "Ciao! Manhattan" is cruel exploitation—though the film is dedicated to Miss Sedgwick's memory, an ultimate indignity. The Warhol movies were also exploitation, and also very cruel—but they were in contact and even in sympathy with their subject, their victim, in a way the Palmer-Weisman film is not.

1973 Ap 20, 15:1

"HIGH PLAINS DRIFTER"

Callie Travers (Mariana Hill) is indignant. Having so successfully caught the eye of The Stranger (Clint Eastwood) that he has carried her into the livery stable and had his way with her (with her cooperation), she complains to the sheriff: "Isn't forcible rape in broad daylight still a misdemeanor in this town?"

It is not, and has not been for some time, not since the good citizens of the little frontier community of Lago banded together to murder their former sheriff, an honorable man who had wanted to reveal that the town's mining company was on Government land.

"High Plains Drifter," with Eastwood as director as well as star, is part ghost story, part revenge Western, more than a little silly, and often quite entertaining in a way that may make you wonder if you have lost your good sense. The violence of the film (including a couple of murders by bull-whipping) is continual and explicit. It exalts and delights in a kind of pitiless Old Testament wrath.

However, it is also apparent that neither Ernest Tidyman, who wrote the screenplay, nor Eastwood are taking themselves too seriously. Eastwood's characterization of The Stranger, who settles God's score with Lago, is a high parody of the soft-featured, brutal Man With No Name he played in those bitter Sergio Leone Westerns. Tidyman's dialogue is funny, and the physical setting— some weatherbeaten shacks on the edge of a body of water that looks like a dead sea—is startlingly beautiful.

Eastman, who earlier directed "Play Misty for Me," has also surrounded himself with a group of good supporting actors, including Verna Bloom, Mitchell Ryan and a 65-year-old midget named Billy Curtis.

VINCENT CANBY.

1973 Ap 20, 21:1

"SOYLENT GREEN"

New Yorkers certainly have problems these days— graffiti, income tax, the Yankees — but nothing like the horrors due in 2022 as depicted in "Soylent Green," which arrived at local thea-

ters yesterday. To begin with, the Gotham of 2022 teems with 40-million citizens; overpopulation and its concomitant horrors aside, the erosion of the environment is such that there's little to eat other than "Soylent Green" which, we're told, is synthesized from plankton. Unfortunately, the script, direction and the principals involved in this struggle for survival often are as synthetic as "Soylent Green."

There is, of course, every reason to view the next century with some fear. But "Soylent Green" projects essentially simple, muscular melodrama a good deal more effectively than it does the potential of man's seemingly witless destruction of the earth's resources.

Charlton Heston, as a harried detective investigating the murder of Joseph Cotten, a bigwig in the dictatorial Soylent Company (whom we see only fleetingly), is aided by the late Edward G. Robinson in his last role as an aged, wise, suspicious researcher, who remembers the good old days of steaks and the like. And, finally exposed by a bewildering succession of hungry citizens, overcrowded streets, fancy pads and the resident, luscious lasses (called "furniture" here) of the rich few, is the awful truth about the secret ingredient of "Soylent Green."

We won't reveal that ingredient but it must be noted that Richard Fleischer's direction stresses action, not nuances of meaning or characterization. Mr. Robinson is pitiably natural as the realistic, sensitive oldster facing the futility of living in dying surroundings. But Mr. Heston is simply a rough cop chasing standard bad guys.

Their 21st-century New York occasionally is frightening but it is rarely convincingly real.

A. H. WEILER

1973 Ap 20, 21:1

The Cast

GANJA & HESS, directed and written by Bill Gunn; director of photography, James E. Hinton; film editor, Victor Kanefsky; music by Sam Waymon; produced by Chiz Schultz; released by Kelly-Jordan Enterprises, Inc. At the Playboy Theater, 57th Street between Avenue of Americas and Seventh Avenues. Running time: 110 minutes. This film is classified R.

Dr. Hess Green............Duane Jones
Ganja Meda...............Marlene Clark
George Meda...............Bill Gunn
Rev. Luther Williams......Sam Waymon
Archie ....Leonard Jackson
Girl in Bar...............Candece Tarpley
Dinner Guest..............Richard Harrow
Queen of Myrthia..........Mabel King
Dr. Green's son...........Enrico Fales
Pimp ....Tommy Lane
Woman with Baby...........Tara Fields

By A. H. WEILER

As a black-oriented, contemporary horror study, "Ganja & Hess," which arrived at the Playboy yesterday, is dedicated to what is obviously meant to be a serious theme. The artistry for which it strives, however, is largely vitiated by a confusingly vague mélange of

symbolism, violence and sex.

●

Bill Gunn, the talented black writer ("The Landlord," etc.), who makes his debut as a screenwriter-director with "Ganja & Hess" (in which he also appears), leaves a compassionate viewer with a pressing need for fuller explanations. He is recounting in decidedly clouded, episodic style, the Grand Guignol-like adventures of a black anthropologist (Duane Jones), who, after killing his neurotic associate (Bill Gunn) in a sudden fight, becomes immortal and addicted, for some arcane reason, to a passionate yen for blood.

Our plagued researcher also takes up with his late assistant's willing, amorous widow, Ganja (Marlene Clark). And, between bouts of lovemaking and angst, he manages to satisfy that gory compulsion through a series of murders (a prostitute, her pimp, etc.) before freeing himself by death (with the aid of a friendly minister) of

his addiction.

Mr. Gunn's elliptical approach to the sanguine subject is ineffectually arty and does little to conceal the film's accent on blood and nudity. As an actor, he is merely given to pointless philosophizing. As our latter-day Dracula with a chauffered Rolls-Royce, Duane Jones robs a bloodbank between slayings and sex, which must be a new wrinkle in this genre. But he is, essentially, a dour, laconic type who rates little sympathy.

●

Dressed or nude, Miss Clark is an arresting presence as the enamored Ganja. Also, she occasionally invests an unbelievable character with style and humor. "Everybody is into something," she calmly replies when Mr. Jones asks her if she thinks he's "psychotic." whi Which is about as funny and rational as "Ganja & Hess" ever gets to be.

1973 Ap 21, 19:2

'Siege': An Angry Muckraker

By VINCENT CANBY

JOURNALISM, most honorably, pursues truth through an inventory of available facts, while fiction seeks truth in essences. When journalism and fiction overlap, the result can be the utter foolishness we see in much of the New Journalism, including the New Television in which the personality of the reporter sits atop the story being covered like an elephant lounging on a toadstool. Or the result may be the more heady confusion of the fictional documentary.

The difficulty presented by Costa-Gavras's films — "Z," "The Confession," and now the fascinating and provocative "State of Siege" — is that although they have their roots in journalism, and although they look and sound like journalism and adopt journalism's dispassionate tone, they are, first of all, fiction of an essential sort.

"State of Siege," which is at the Beekman, is an angry muckraker of a film that, for all of the documentation offered to support its truth, succeeds in being truthful or not largely because of what we bring into the theater with us. Not because of the facts necessarily (not many of us can qualify as experts on Uruguayan politics, or as experts on United States policies in Latin America), but because of the feelings and bias-

es with which we automatically respond to the film.

Journalism and fiction overlap in "State of Siege" in ways that are most disturbing, but whether or not the inferences drawn from its facts are true, the desperation and the moral and intellectual poverty of the world it shows us unquestionably are. You don't have to know anything about Uruguay. Remember the Bay of Pigs and the speed with which a phrase like "credibility gap" became jargon for night club comedians and ad men. Remember Watergate, I.T.T. and Chile, or even having your eardrums pierced by a passing transistor radio on which someone was singing sorrowfully of "vee-nuus in bloo jeans" — and meaning it.

"State of Siege," written by Costa-Gavras and Franco Solinas, the man who earlier collaborated with Gillo Pontecorvo on the screenplays for "The Battle of Algiers" and "Burn!", is about an event, the kidnap and murder of Dan A. Mitrione in Montevideo, Uruguay, three years ago. Mitrione, an Italian-born American and a former police chief in Richmond, Ind., was a member of the U. S. Agency for International Development assigned to the Uruguayan police, supposedly as an expert in traffic control and communications.

After his execution by the

Tupamaros, a band of Marxist-oriented urban guerrillas that had unsuccessfully sought the release of 150 political prisioners, stories began to appear here and abroad that linked Mitrione to the stepped-up antiguerrilla activities of the Uruguayan police. Specifically, he was connected to what one official Uruguayan report called "an uncontrollable and autonomous organization" within the police that specialized in the systematic torture and liquidation of the revolutionary opposition.

Costa-Gavras's technique hasn't advanced very far beyond the souped-up "Dragnet" style of "Z" — with suspense created by a lot of breathless cross-cutting, by the continual use of the zoom lens in or out, by the kind of shrewd pacing tricks that are the movie equivalents of the way sensational stories are presented in tabloid newspapers. "State of Siege" also lacks a protagonist of the sort that made "The Confession" so moving. Yet, cinema art or not, slanted or not to make its points, it raises political and moral questions of special interest to us in this time and place.

I couldn't care less that the film comes out of the European intellectual tradition of anti-Americanism, or that a comparable film about France would probably have difficulty getting released there. (Four years after "The Battle of Algiers" had won the first prize at Venice, it still hadn't been commercially released in Paris.) I'm sure these things will be mentioned in an effort to discredit "State of Siege," but they only confuse the issues presented by the film.

That they are legitimate issues is simply confirmed by the foolishness of the American Film Institute, which first planned to show the film as one of the opening attractions at its new theater in the Kennedy Center in Washington, then canceled it, supposedly because the film rationalizes political assassination. All of which suggests incompetence on the part of the institute, if not censorship.

There is no doubt where the film's sympathies are — the Tupamaros are mostly young, handsome, intensely sincere intellectuals who would like to avoid violence, while the establishment people are either elderly and overfed American puppets or career fanatics with a taste for sadism that, in turn, prompts the violence by the revolutionaries.

In the middle, presented more or less as his government's sincerely wrong-headed, church-going, family-loving dupe, is the Mitrione character, named Philip Michael Santore in the film and played by Yves Montand.

To the extent that "State of Siege" assigns a romantic, selfless purpose to the revolutionaries, and shows them cornered, rendered impotent (because of the work of the American "adviser"), the film does offer reasons for their execution of Mitrione/Santore — which would be frivolous rationalization were the role played by anyone less sympathetic than Montand. It also shows the government people feeling cornered by the Tupamaros, but the balance of the sympathy is so overwhelmingly in favor of the revolutionaries that the film becomes something more than a mere comparison of legal violence with illegal violence, as has been suggested.

Curiously enough, although its biases weaken the drama, they do not discredit the point of the film, which has to do with the real nature of U.S. aid to all foreign countries and the manner by which national self-interest can evolve into repression, terror and torture thousands of miles away at what might be called the local level.

Among other things, the film asks if this must be the way of the world and, if not, what we are going to do about it. Most important to me, it wants to know whether we can be outraged by duplicity, corruption, violence and torture, even when they're presented as methods for maintaining not just law and order abroad, but the standard of living at home.

These are not things that are very pleasant to think about. The essence of the film is a little embarrassing, like an encounter with one of those eccentrics who wander around Times Square carrying hand-lettered placards advising us not to put our faith in our Cadillacs. It's not enough to answer that one doesn't own a Cadillac, or to rejoice in the revelation that the old buzzard carrying the placard was driven to his beat in a Fleetwood. There is truth in "State of Siege" and it is shaming.

This is why I'm inclined to go along with the flashy style of the film, which, I assume, will provide it with a sizable audience, and why I don't mind the simplification of facts and conditions. I do have reservations about the Costa-Gavras method of overlapping journalism and fiction, by helping himself to history and then changing names, and sometimes chronology, but not making use of the freedom of fiction. It may be that such freedom would get in the way of the truth he's interested in. It might also be that it would allow him to make a film as great as the issues he likes to raise.

In the meantime, he is making very practical films. Jean-Luc Godard, who once described a particular horizontal pan shot as a political statement, has gone on to make beautiful truly political films that speak to hardly anyone. They're small, privately printed volumes of poetry. Costa-Gavras makes movies as if he were putting together a Page One and wanted every copy of this particular edition to sell out on the newstand.

1973 Ap 22, II:1:4

'To Be Free'

By VINCENT CANBY

"To Be Free" is a very bad, very self-indulgent first feature written, directed and produced by Ned Bosnick, a native of Pittsburgh who is reported to have studied film at the University of California at Los Angeles under the great Jean Renoir.

It's a humorless psychological fantasy about a girl named Carole (Barbara Douglas), a sort of pretty Barbra Streisand type, who goes to see a psychiatrist because she can't enjoy sex with her fiancé, Bruce, although Bruce has, in Carole's words, "unlocked my love balloon." Thinking that Carole may be afraid of pregnancy, the doctor suggests birth control. Says Carole primly, but with all of the conviction of Bea Lillie impersonating Goldilocks: "My religion doesn't permit me."

The plot, such as it is, is not too different from that of "Deep Throat," but what didn't work very well in a porno comedy is even less effective as the basis of an apparently seriously intended drama. The movie obviously used up a good deal of money and while I was watching it, I was reminded of the difficulty that Mr. Renoir has had in recent years in trying to raise financing to make films. Such an awareness tends to transform boredom with Mr. Bosnick's lack of talent into militant impatience.

1973 Ap 27, 27:1

AND NOW THE SCREAMING STARTS, directed by Roy Ward Baker; screenplay by Roger Marshall; director of photography, Denys Coop; editor, Peter Tanner; produced by Milton Subotsky and Max J. Rosenberg; released by the Cinerama Releasing Corporation. At the Forum Theater, Broadway at 46th Street and the Juliet 2 Theater, Third Avenue and 83d Street. Running time: 87 minutes. This film is classified R.

Doctor Pope .... Peter Cushing
Henry Fengriffen .... Herbert Lom
Doctor Whittle .... Patrick Magee
Charles Fengriffen .... Ian Ogilvy
Catherine Fengriffen .. Stephanie Beacham
Maitland .... Guy Rolfe

As horror wholesalers, the production team of Milton Subotsky and Max J. Rosenberg do little to enhance the creepy legend or spooked stately mansion movie genre with "And Now the Screaming Starts." Their latest consignment from Britain, which landed at the Juliet 2 and Forum Theaters yesterday, may have a few shocks, but they're not enough to overcome a padded plot and the mounting feeling that the screaming is being done for the wrong reasons.

Stephanie Beacham, as the pretty, full-bosomed but timorous 18th-century bride of Ian Ogilvy, the handsome lord of Fengriffen manor, tips the bloody mitt at the start when she observes that the house "filled my nights with horror." And before you can say "Long live the King!" the screen is filled with dire implications, bloody-eyed specters at the windows, a crawling, severed hand and five corpses, to send our now-pregnant heroine screaming out of her wits.

It's not ungallant to note that Herbert Lom, as the late grandfather of the bridegroom, was the dissolute baronet who brought the curse down on the Fengriffens when he violated a local woodsman's bride and lopped off the hand of the frenzied bridegroom, who then puts the hex on future Fengriffens.

Miss Beacham is decorative even when screaming. Ian Ogilvy, as her worried husband, Patrick Magee, as the family's kindly doctor, Geoffrey Whitehead, as the woodsman's strange grandson, and Guy Rolfe and Rosalie Crutchley, as Fengriffen retainers, are simply dour or frightened as they stretch the mystery.

•

Peter Cushing, however, adds a singular bright note to the dark proceedings directed in somber, largely measured style by Roy Ward Baker. He has apparently beaten Dr. Freud by about a century as the genteel specialist in the "distress of the mind" called in to aid our obviously distressed heroine. As the script says a good deal of "torment is caused by the written word, not fact."

A. H. WEILER

1973 Ap 28, 21:1

The Program

DYN AMO, directed, photographed and edited by Stephen Dwoskin; based on a stage play by Chris Wilkinson; music by Gavin Gryers. At the Film Forum, 256 West 88th Street. Running time: 120 minutes. This film has not been classified.

WITH: Jenny Runacre, Pat Ford, Catherine Kessler and Linda Marlowe.

By ROGER GREENSPUN

During the last week Stephen Dwoskin's "Dyn Amo" has been screened at the Millenium Film Workshop, has been the subject of a Cineprobe at the Museum of Modern Art and has received its New York theatrical premiere —last night, at the Film Forum. For a 16 mm. feature, that means touching almost all bases at once. Given the film's subject matter, it is easy to see why.

•

Mr. Dwoskin, a young American who makes films in Britain, has based "Dyn Amo" on a London theater piece, "Dynamo," by Chris Wilkinson. There is a single setting: a small stage containing a double bed covered in sleazy satin in front of a large window frame through which shine incandescent stars. A tough tired blonde enters and slowly strips. Then a second girl, a vivacious brunette, strips and acts out a sexual fantasy for some man, presumably a customer. Next, a third girl, young, pretty, apparently very vulnerable, also strips — out of a tawdry chambermaid costume. She is inept and unwilling, and the camera concentrates on her frightened eyes. At last a fourth girl appears, as if in a trance, dancing before four sullen young men who eventually take hold of her, undress her, bind and gag her, variously assault her (exactly how, the movie leaves fairly vague), and leave her alone to her tears and trembling lips.

Each episode deals with conventional and highly conventionalized sexual use of women. In the first two episodes the women emerge rather exultant; in the last two, they are utterly humiliated. The film's interest is in personal exaltation and humiliation — and surely not in the mechanics or pressures of human desire. "Dyn Amo" thus exploits exploitation, which is a nice trick if you can do it. I am not sure that this film does.

•

Mr. Dwoskin's film runs for two hours, about half of it devoted to the final episode. There is music — a kind of hurdy-gurdy solemn music — but no speech except for a few loud nonsense syllables from two of the men. The camera is sometimes stationary, sometimes nervously active, but almost always concerned with isolating a gesture, a look, a fragment of an action. It is in such gestures, looks, fragments, that "Dyn Amo" tries to discover meaning — a rich, elusive theater profoundly beneath its obvious erotic theater — and in this it succeeds precisely in inverse proportion to its ambitions. Thus the first episode, with the tough stripper, is the best because it is the least complete, the least "acted," the most demanding of sympathetic interpretation.

All but one of the girls are actresses (the one who isn't, Pat Ford, the second girl, has the lightest role), and their tears are stage tears, not real, and I do not know to what degree Mr. Dwoskin has taken account of this while attempting to probe emotion. In any case, an air of futility does settle upon "Dyn Amo" — though it remains one of the most fascinating, one of the most boring and one of the most excruciatingly obsessive new movies to deserve to be called avant garde in a long time.

1973 Ap 28, 21:1

The Cast

WEDDING IN WHITE, directed by William Freuet; produced by John Vidette; screenplay by Mr. Fruet, based on his stage play; director of photography, Richard Leiterman; music, Milan Kymlicka; editor, Tony Lower; a Dermet Productions film, distributed by Avco Embassy Pictures. Running time: 103 minutes. At the Little Carnegie Theater, 57th Street east of Seventh Avenue. This film has been classified R.

Jim .... Donald Pleasence
Jeannie .... Carol Kane
Mary .... Doris Petrie
Sandy .... Leo Phillips
Jimmie .... Paul Bradley
Billy .... Doug McGrath
Sarah .... Christine Thomas
Dollie .... Bonnie Carol Case

By VINCENT CANBY

William Fruet's "Wedding in White" is a good, tough, clear-eyed Canadian film about a working-class family and the sweet, dim-witted, 16-year-old daughter, Jeannie, who finds herself "in trouble" (the euphemism she favors) after a singularly quick and joyless seduction by her brother's best friend.

The time is midway through World War II, when being in trouble meant instant disgrace, especially to a father like Jeannie's, a hard-working, hard-drinking, narrow-minded man who would say that boys will be boys but that the girls who do are whores. His solution: marry Jeannie off to his best friend Sandy, a robust Scot of about 60 who is a drunk.

•

"Wedding in White" is the sort of domestic drama that most playwrights and film makers botch, either because they determinedly explain away the characters as sociological phenomena, as in another Canadian film, "Goin' Down the Road," or because they invest the characters with inclinations to doggedly banal self-analysis. People in plays like Robert Anderson's "I Never Sang for My Father" and Frank Gilroy's "The Subject Was Roses" tend to talk about themselves as if they were not there, and to conceptualize problems that in life, arguing by the kitchen sink, remain specific.

Mr. Fruet, who wrote the screenplay for "Goin' Down the Road," directed "Wedding in White" and adapted the script from his stage play. The dialogue is so faultless that even the slang defines the era as much as the skirt lengths and the automobiles. "My dad would crown me if I did that," Jeannie says at one point. More important, never does the writer-director allow his characters to talk above their station, to describe the overview that we in the audience can see for ourselves.

•

"Wedding in White" is not really tragic, nor is it as bleak as it might sound. It is a closely observed chronicle of one family's life, moving and funny and a little scary, full of unexpected stoicism and the kind of boozy jocularity that can suddenly erupt into violence. It is also marvelously well acted.

Donald Pleasence is Jeannie's dad, "a top-notch bowler and a triple-threat man at darts," who also manages to suggest the existence of evil in the most commonplace of personalities. Jeannie's mother is played by Doris Petrie, a Canadian actress of unaffected beauty and great discretion of gesture. Also fine are Paul Bradley and Doug McGrath (the born losers of "Goin' Down the Road") as, respectively, the soldier son and the best friend who so casually gets Jeannie into trouble.

At the center of the film, looking oddly like a Jan van Eyck subject transplanted to a land of five-and-tens and drug stores, is Carol Kane, whose Jeannie is someone obviously destined to go through life with nothing ever fitting.

When her father brings home a second-hand dress for her to wear to the wedding she doesn't want, Jeannie's first thought is to call her friend Dollie, as if she had just received a birthday present. The world, the passions of others, her clothes, even her masses of frizzy reddish hair, are too big for her, and her brain is too small.

"Wedding in White" opened yesterday at the Little Carnegie.

1973 Ap 30, 26:1

YOU'RE LYING, a Swedish film with English subtitles, directed by Vilgot Sjoman; produced by Goran Lindgren for Sandrews; released by Grove Press, Inc. At the First Avenue Screening Room, at 61st Street. Running time: 110 minutes. This film is not classified.
Lasse .... Stig Engstrom
Bjorn .... Borge Ahlstedt
The Mother .... Siff Ruud
Vilgot Sjoman .... Himself

Whatever their subjects, the feature films of Vilgot Sjoman—"I Am Curious (Yellow)," "I Am Curious (Blue)" —tend to share a common form: the not-exactly documentary. In "You're Lying,"

which was made in 1969 and opened this week at the First Avenue Screening Room, the form persists, though with changes. "You're Lying" begins as a straight documentary about the Swedish penal system, becomes a fictionalized documentary about a young man who is not rehabilitated in Swedish prisons, and ends as a psychological study about what seems almost a symbiotic relationship between a prisoner and the imprisonment he cannot quite bring himself to escape.

As a documentary, "You're Lying" intends to expose Swedish prisons. Much of this may be lost on American audiences, for whom the lot of the Swedish prisoner —considerable privacy, personal freedom, leave privileges, etc.—will probably look like summer camp.

The prisoner in question is Lasse (Stig Engstrom), a would-be artist, a would-be writer, a well-developed alcoholic who steals a bit to keep in booze. Lasse is the special concern of Bjorn (Borge Ahlstedt), a young art teacher who respects Lasse's talent, who writes newspaper pieces protesting his imprisonment and who tries to provide for him when he does win parole. But he is beyond providing for, and he breaks parole and returns to jail, leaving behind him broken promises, personal abuse and bitter memories. The indictment of the prison system has turned into an indictment of a man for whom there is, in a sense, no imprisonment absolute enough to satisfy him.

Though the later parts of "You're Lying" are much more interesting than the earlier parts, Sjoman is so deadly earnest about everything in his movie (and about his own involvement as a film maker) that he treats the drama as if it were an illustrative annex to the documentary. This is manifestly unfair.

Sjoman has shot "You're Lying" largely in close-up. Indeed, he is the kind of director who cannot achieve distance without suggesting alienation—and though this may be right for his subject, it is a real limitation in the experience of seeing the film. This is too bad, because "You're Lying," possibly despite its intentions, is a work of some integrity.

ROGER GREENSPUN.

1973 My 5, 25:3

FISTS OF FURY, directed by Lo Wei; screenplay by Mr. Wei; cinematography by Chen Ching Chu; produced by Raymond Chow; released by National General Pictures. At neighborhood theaters. Running time: 103 minutes. This film is rated R.
Chen .... Bruce Lee
Mei .... Maria Yi
Mi .... Han Ying Chieh
Mi's Son .... Tony Liu
Prostitute .... Malalene
Chen .... Paul Tien
With: Miao Ke Hsiu, Li Quin, Chin Shan and Li Hua Sze.

Perhaps it is because his male cousins begin disappearing—mysteriously and forever—two by two. Perhaps it is because he discovers that the blocks of ice have plastic bags frozen into them, bags full of a suspicious white powder. But for whatever reason, young Cheng does come to realize that things are not right at the old icehouse down by the river, where he and his cousins have been working.

So he breaks a solemn vow to avoid fighting and stay out of mischief. Once that happens, all hell breaks loose. All hell breaking loose is the reason for "Fists of Fury," another karate movie from Hong Kong, which opened recently at neighborhood theaters.

Set in Bangkok, with trucks and buses running just across the street, "Fists of Fury" nevertheless presents an absolutely primitive moralistic melodrama — and the incongruities between setting, costume and action are the sum of its fairly minimal charm.

•

The fighting is energetic but not so terribly violent. The cast is sullenly attractive the way that the casts of American teen-age gang movies used to be 20 years ago. The background music seems wholly the work of electronic synthesizers — as does the miserably dubbed English dialogue.

ROGER GREENSPUN.

1973 My 5, 25:3

DEEP THRUST, directed by Heang Feng; produced by Raymond Chow; a Golden Harvest (Hong Kong) production and a Hallmark Pictures presentation; released by American International Pictures. At neighborhood theaters. Running time: 88 minutes. This film has been rated R.
With: Angela Mao, Chang Yi, Pai Ying, June Wu and Anne Liu.

"Deep Thrust," one of the latest Chinese-made features bristling with "martial arts" that appear to be fighting for the local popularity of, say, chow mein, is decidedly a departure from the norm of the genre.

Its most feared kung-fu and karate expert is a pretty, if lethal, little miss, who can grimace and shout and chop and kick any dozen male experts into a gory mess single-handedly before you can say "Gung Ho!"

Neither Hallmark Pictures, which imported it from Hong Kong, nor American International, the distributors, have come up with either writing credits or character listings for the unfamiliar cast.

•

It does not much matter, "Deep Thrust," a title, we suspect, that was not dreamed up in the Orient, has been dubbed into colloquial English that is often unwittingly funny. And, the adventures of our indestruc-

tible heroine who, we can only assume, is Angela Mao, are either simply muscular or unintentionally comical.
A. H. WEILER

1973 My 5, 25:3

AN AUTUMN AFTERNOON, directed by Yasujiro Ozu; screenplay (Japanese with English subtitles) by Kogo Noda and Mr. Ozu; director of photography, Yushun Atsuta; editor, Yoshiyashu Hamamura; music, Takanobu Saito; produced by Shizuo Yamanouchi; a Shochiku Company film, distributed by New Yorker Films. Running time: 113 minutes. At the Fifth Avenue Cinema, Fifth Avenue at 12th Street. This film has not been classified.
Shuhei Hirayama .... Chishu Ryu
Michiko Hirayama ...... Shima Iwashita
Kazuo Hirayama ... Shin-Ichiro Mikami
Koichi Hirayama .... Keiji Sada
Akiko Hirayama .... Mariko Okada
Shuzo Kawai .... Nobuo Nakamura
Mobuko Kawai .... Kuniko Miyake
Susumu Horie .... Ryuii Kita

By VINCENT CANBY

"An Autumn Afternoon," which opened yesterday at the Fifth Avenue Cinema, is Yasujiro Ozu's last film, completed shortly before his death in 1963 at the age of 60. Whether or not this great Japanese director knew he was dying of cancer while he was making the film, "An Autumn Afternoon" is such a completely realized example of the Ozu art that it seems impossible he did not intend it to be a kind of testament.

What Ozu left us is not a style of film-making. That style is so unmistakable that anyone who dared imitate it would risk exile to a faculty position at an obscure institution for film education. He left something a good deal more important, an appreciation of the possibilities of all films.

•

Although Ozu's films are realistic — they're usually about relationships within upper middle-class families — they evoke emotions not only through identification but also through methods more commonly associated with music and other non-representational forms of art, through rhythms and patterns that express the essence of things.

Ozu's titles are impossible to keep straight, and one should take care not to confuse "An Autumn Afternoon" with "Late Spring," which he made in 1949 and which was released here last midsummer (July).

Both films, however, are about aging widowers hanging on to only daughters who have reached marriageable age. There is possibility for even further confusion since Ozu's favorite actor, the lean, handsome, deliberate Chishu Ryu, plays the father in each film.

Though the films overlap in important ways, "An Autumn Afternoon" is more benignly contemplative and more beautiful than the earlier work. And never for a minute does one mix up its awareness of man's lonely state with anything on the order of pity.

•

Like all of the late Ozu films, "An Autumn Afternoon" is about the accommodations we make, not necessarily to get ahead in the world but simply to get along in it with a certain amount of dignity intact. For the aging Chishu Ryu, this is the acknowledgement that his 24-year-old daughter is not, indeed, the mere child he has called her, but a woman who must live her own life apart from him. For the daughter, it is the acknowledgement that she has lost the man she wanted to marry and must settle for someone else.

Ozu treats these matters coolly, without sentimentality, keeping them at the middle distance at which he photographs them. Yet Ozu's middle distance allows for a kind of metaphorical deep focus. The images are full of odd and disturbing details that often have a kind of delayed-action effect.

When, near the end, we see the daughter, a sweet, spirited, very 20th-century girl, dressed in her elaborate, traditional wedding costume,

Chishu Ryu

it seems, at first, that Ozu is indulging himself: the very prettiness of the bridal dress conveys a sense of impending damage. Nothing that fragile can survive. Yet Ozu's characters are not fragile. They do survive, and often with a good deal of humor.

In one of the nicest sequences iin the film, Ryu, a former naval officer, runs into the man who had been his chief petty officer during the war. They get drunk together and the man, now plump and not entirely dissatisfied with his life as a mechanic, allows himself to speculate on what would have happened had Japan won the war: "We'd be in New York—the real thing—and the blue-eyed ones would be wearing wigs and chewing gum while plucking their samisens!"

•

In "An Autumn Afternoon," the old culture is giving way—as old Ryu is—to time and inevitable change. Ryu's elder son and his wife are scrambling for refrigerators, vacuum cleaners, golf clubs and white leather handbags. There's nothing particularly cheering about that, but it is possible, Ozu seems to suggest, to face these changes without despair. Despair would not just be bad form. It would guarantee defeat that might otherwise be held at bay.

"An Autumn Afternoon," which was shown for one performance at the first New York Film Festival in 1963, is a profoundly simple, profoundly moving film.

1973 My 8, 39:1

The Cast

HITLER: THE LAST TEN DAYS, directed by Ennio de Concinni; screenplay, Mr. de Concini, Maria Pia Fusco and Wolfgang Reinhardt (English screenplay adaptation by Ivan Moffat), based on "The Last Days of the Chancellery" by Gehard Boldt; director of photography, Ennio Guarnieri; music, Mischa Spoliansky; editor, Kevin Connor; a co-production between Wolfgang Reinhardt Productions, Ltd. London, and West Film, Rome, distributed by Paramount Pictures. Running time: 106 minutes. At the Criterion Theater, Broadway at 45th Street, and 86th Street East Theater, 86th Street between Second and Third Avenues. This film has been classified PG.

Adolf Hitler .... Alec Guinness
Hauptmann Hoffmann .... Simon Ward
General Krebs .... Adolfo Celi
Hanna Reitsch .... Diane Cilento
Field Marshal Keitel .... Gabriele Ferzetti
Eva Braun .... Doris Kunstmann
Josef Goebbels .... John Bennett

By VINCENT CANBY

"Adolf," Eva Braun says to Hitler at one point during their last 10 days in the Berlin bunker, "you really *are* the most incredible person. . . ."

The film is called "Hitler: The Last Ten Days," and it seems to be factually correct in all major matters. H. R. Trevor-Roper, the British historian and author ("The Last Days of Hitler"), has given it his seal of approval. As a historial re-enactment, however, "Hitler" is about as exciting as a high-minded, parent-approved comic book about the adventures of James Watt and his steam engine.

•

It's only when the screenplay makes its little stabs at what I take to be fiction that it becomes at all interesting and, quite often, dimly funny. As when Eva, just before biting her cyanide capsule, becomes upset because it is apparent that Adolf doesn't give a hang about what happens to the citizens of Berlin, then being laid low by the advancing Soviet Army.

"Maybe I never knew you," she says with a tear in her eye. It's the sort of realization that in a cartoon would be indicated by the appearance of a light bulb over her head.

It is possible that Eva did have such second thoughts. She was in love with Hitler but she wasn't the world's biggest brain. Yet the quality of the speculation in "Hitler" is not worthy of what we know and feel about the subject. The speculation is small and routine. It is as if Ennio de Concini, the Italian director who also wrote the Italian screenplay with Maria Pia Fusco and Wolfgang Reinhardt (son of Max), which was then adapted into English by Ivan Moffat, had set out to transform the banality of evil into a film style.

The rise of the Third Reich is one of the most fascinating stories of all time, and its collapse one of the most thoroughly satisfying, supplying, as it does, the fundamental dramatic needs for irrevocable revenge and retribution. The written accounts of these events—by Shirer, Speer, Trevor-Roper, Toland and others—never cease to fascinate, even when the prose gets as gummy as a Sunday supplement's. It is curious, then, that a fairly serious-minded film should be so superfluous.

One principal reason seems to be that no film can possibly present the accumulation of details and facts that make something like Shirer's "The Rise and Fall of the Third Reich" so riveting. It can present only a pictorial view of things and a selection of details.

In "Hitler: The Last Ten Days," it is almost impossible to keep the people straight, with the exception of Adolf (Alec Guinness), Eva (Doris Kunstmann) and maybe the Goebbelses. The film doesn't seem to have been directed, or acted, as much as cast, in the waxworks sense. Actors play individual characters not because they are actors but because they resemble the people in life.

•

Sometimes, however, they look very wrong. Adolfo Celi looks awfully Italian as General Krebs. Guinness looks right as Hitler, and that's about all—but then Hitler may be an impossible role. Almost anything even a good actor does with such a role risks prompting a certain amount of unintended hilarity. (There are times when Guinness's Hitler reminded me most of Jack Benny.) Those of us who knew Hitler from contemporary newsreels could, I suspect, respond only to a completely fictional character, not one pictured, as Guinness is, in a supposedly objective way. Miss Kunstmann is more successful, probably because we know less of Eva, and most of the other people are news pictures and studio portraits that have come to vogue life.

The film covers the period from April 20 through May 1, 1945, and takes place mostly in the bunker under the Chancellery. For anyone unfamiliar with how Hitler got there, the film supplies a sort of "the story to date" outline of Hitler's rise and World II behind the opening credits.

1973 My 10, 57:1

The Cast

L'AMOUR, directed by Andy Warhol and Paul Morrissey; story by Mr. Warhol and Mr. Morrissey; executive producer, Mr. Morrissey; editors, Lana Jokel and Jed Johnson; director of photography, Mr. Johnson; music, Ben Weisman; distributed by Altura Films International. Running time: 90 minutes. At the UA Eastside Cinema, Third Avenue near 56th Street. This film has been classified R.

Michael .... Michael Sklar
Donna .... Donna Jordan
Jane .... Jane Forth
Max .... Max Delys
Patti .... Patti D'Arbanville
Karl .... Karl Lagerfeld

By VINCENT CANBY

"L'Amour," the newest chapter in the continuing series of Andy Warhol-Paul Morrissey soap-opera putons, takes the Factory gang to Paris where Michael (Michael Sklar), a rich American, represents his father's firm, the Watkins Bathroom Deodorant Company. Michael is head over heels in love with Max (Max Delys), a street hustler who looks like a French version of Joe Dallesandro. Michael, however, is fond of Jane (Jane Forth), a self-described American high-school dropout who has come to Paris to model with her best friend Donna (Donna Jordan), who would sort of like to marry Michael so they could legally adopt Max.

This is a film unafraid to ask questions. Will Michael find happiness with Max? (No.) Will Max find satisfaction with Jane? (Not really, since Jane says she gets more excited buying make-up.) Is this sort of thing funny? (Only intermittently.)

•

Were there fewer demands for one's attention, "L'Amour" might be worth sitting through for the occasional comic moments, such as Michael's big renunciation scene with Max ("I'm growing older, Max. . . ."), which leaves Michael so shaken that all he can do is crochet. Michael, however, is but a poor, hairy substitute for Sylvia Miles, who handles this sort of comedy better. There is also a nice title song, sweetly sung from time to time by Cass Elliot, and a rather pretty scene where everyone roller skates around the Palais de Chaillot. It looks like a high-fashion layout gone a bit looney.

These things simply are not funny or important enough to compete with late-night talk shows, a new album by the Carpenters, the Watergate scandal, kung-fu movies, dining at Blimpie's, and a number-one best seller by Jacqueline Susann. We live in a time and place in which first things must come first.

"L'Amour," which opened yesterday at the UA Eastside Cinema, is so wan it makes one remember "Trash" and "Women in Revolt" as robust classics of their kind.

1973 My 11, 26:1

THE P.O.W., directed and written by Philip H. Dossick; director of photography, Benjamin Gruberg; edited by Philip H. Dossick; music by Martin Egan and Neal Goldstein; produced by David Mlotok and Jane Dossick; a Philip H. Dossick production. At the First Avenue Screening Room, at 61st Street. Running time: 82 minutes. This film has not been classified at this time.

Howie Kaufman .... Howard Jahre
Rudy Craig .... Rudy Hornish
Wendy Craig .... Wendy Messier
Manuel .... Manuel Sicart
Marcia .... Marcia Davis
Shelley Kaufman .... Shelley Kaplan
Patty .... Joanna Lee Dossick

By ROGER GREENSPUN

Howie Kaufman, the hero of Philip Dossick's good but poorly titled "The P.O.W," is a young New York veteran of the Vietnam war, permanantly disabled by a wound that has left him paralyzed from the waist down. The film picks him up shortly after his discharge from the hospital, and it leaves him, a few weeks later, at the end of a party given in his honor by several of his friends. Nothing too dramatic happens in between. Howie renews acquaintance with a girl he used to know, attempts two — unsuccessful — job interviews, sets up housekeeping in his own one-room apartment; and without too much hope and without despair he begins to settle into a life of limited and difficult options.

"The P.O.W." sounds like documentary, and it looks like documentary, but it is actually fiction. Howie is played — quite beautifully — by a lawyer named Howard Jahre, and he is supported by a group of mainly nonprofessional actors who, for the most part, simply use their own first names in becoming characters in the movie. There are also a pair of documentary film makers who are doing a movie about Howie. Most of the footage we see is supposed to be theirs. This device may seem confusing and rather precious in the abstract. In practice it is very useful.

Useful — not profound, in the sense of making a movie about the act of making a movie. But the documentary framework provides the film with a method, and it allows a degree of detachment, coolness, objectivity toward the hero, which might very well be felt as cruelty in the context of conventional dramatic fiction. "The P.O.W." is remarkably free from excess rhetoric, either for pathos or irony. And that freedom, which suggests a considerable artistic intelligence, is not the least of the film's virtues.

The little rhetoric there is comes by way of clips from some of President Nixon's most self-congratulatory speeches about the unwinding of the Vietnam war. The speeches furnish a contrast not only in sentiment but also in style, and it comes as something of a shock to realize that Mr. Nixon is the only older person in the movie. Everyone else is young — middle class, very decent though fairly ordinary — but young. There are no parents with hang-ups or wise counselors with advice. Howie must make his way among his peers — and the sense of equality promotes a kind of levelheadedness that for me is a source of real delight.

If I have made it sound like a triumph of filmmaker's strategy, that's the kind of movie "The P.O.W." is. You don't go out smiling from a movie about a paraplegic. But you may go out admiring the skill, the tact, the instincts of a new director who has made an impressive debut.

"The P.O.W." opened yesterday at the First Avenue Screening Room.

1973 My 11, 30:1

THE OFFENCE, directed by Sidney Lumet; screenplay by John Hopkins; produced by Denis O'Dell; director of photography, Gerry Fisher; editor, John Victor Smith; distributed by United Artists. Running time: 114 minutes. At the Festival Theater, 57th Street near Fifth Avenue. This film has been classified R.

Johnson .... Sean Connery
Cartwright .... Trevor Howard
Maureen .... Vivien Merchant
Baxter .... Ian Bannen

By VINCENT CANBY

Sidney Lumet's new film, "The Offence," takes place in a suburb of London, not an old suburb but one of those barren new suburbs still in the process of development, where lawns fade into scrubby fields that don't give one a feeling of space as much as emptiness, of vacant lots awaiting overnight transformation into bleak, middle-income housing blocks.

The time (probably winter) and the place perfectly reflect the unacknowledged despair contained in almost every frame of this harrowing story, which seems to be about the search for a man who's been luring little schoolgirls into culverts and then raping them.

"Seems" is the proper word because, about halfway through, one becomes aware that the film is not about a manhunt. Rather it is a psychological striptease, about a tough, hard-drinking, hard-headed detective.

For some time before the start of the film, Detective Johnson (Sean Connery) has been cracking up, remembering (even if against his better will) the way that suicides have looked when he has found them, the way a murdered child's arm dangled through the slats of a crib, the awkward position of a woman who had been tied to a bed and tortured to death. Other men put these things out of their minds. Johnson cherishes them.

●

As it progresses, "The Offence," for all its elaborate setting of scene and for all its introduction of subsidiary characters (beautifully played by Trevor Howard and Vivien Merchant, among others), sort of gets smaller and smaller, instead of bigger. The entire film, it turns out, exists for a single sequence, a brutal station-house confrontation between the detective and his prime suspect (Ian Bannen), between a lower-class psychotic and a middle-class neurotic, between a closet sadist and an admitted masochist. In a sense, they are lovers, made for each other.

It's highly theatrical — perhaps just a little too highly theatrical for the more or less realistic context — but it's been staged by Lumet for maximum effect. The revelations explode predictably, like the ingredients of a 24-hour cold capsule, but the dramatic impact is real while one is watching it. Connery and Bannen are so fine, and the feelings prompted so intense, that I wouldn't be at all surprised if the sequence could stand on its own, as if it were a one-act play. Everything that has gone before seems to have been so much vamping for time.

●

Some of the things that have gone before also tend to detract from this climax. Since it's so clear to the audience that Detective Johnson has long since come apart, it's difficult to understand why the men who work with him haven't recognized the fact. That may be splitting hairs. "The Offence" has one big, carefully worked out, dramatic moment, which is more than most movies have these days.

1973 My 12, 19:1

The Cast

THE HARRAD EXPERIMENT, directed by Ted Post; screenplay by Michael Werner and Ted Cassedy, based on the novel by Robert H. Rimmer; director of photography, Richard H. Kline; music by Artie Butler; produced by Dennis F. Stevens; released by the Cinerama Releasing Corporation. At the Baronet Theater, 59th Street at Third Avenue. Running time: 95 minutes. This film has been classified R.

Stanley Cole	Don Johnson
Harry Schacht	B. Kirby Jr.
Sheila Grove	Laurie Walters
Beth Hilyer	Victoria Thompson
Philip Tenhausen	James Whitmore
Margaret Tenhausen	Tippi Hedren

By ROGER GREENSPUN

If I can believe the promotional material floating around, almost all the adults in North America who read anything have read Robert H. Rimmer's novel "The Harrad Experiment." The remaining half-dozen of you need only know that it concerns a special Eastern college, Harrad, where a super-bright group of special students live in a co-ed dorm with the express purpose of sharing meaningful sexual experiences.

The book came out in 1966, and it was supposed to be prophetic. To an extent it was prophetic. Many Eastern college students do live in co-ed dorms now. The last group I heard of (college to be nameless) the girls were complaining that the boys had retreated to one part of the dorm and were plotting some nineteen-seventies version of panty raids.

Nothing like that happens in the book; all the students are much too busy discovering themselves and exploring the miracle (I think I've got the prose right) of one another. Nothing like that happens in the movie that has just been made from the novel either; the students are all too busy working out lasting monogamous relationships. Despite the splendid opportunities offered, Ted Post's "The Harrad Experiment" isn't even soft-core pornography; it is something more like soap opera with a little frontal nudity. This is the kind of movie in which never does flesh touch flesh without a choir of dulcet strings on the soundtrack to sanctify the meeting.

●

But into any bowl of mush a little sweetener may fall. The goodness in this case comes not from the students — a handsome though unexciting lot — but from their mentors, the kindly pipe-sucking, Nietszche - quoting Dr. Tenhausen (James Whitmore), and his lovely wife, Margaret (Tippi Hedren). Whether jointly conducting their class in human values, protecting academic standards ("Thank God, you screened Valerie Latrobe! I shudder to think what she might have done to Harrad. And she did so *well* on the writtens . . ."), or advising students of the need to disrobe for the 7:30 yoga seminar—they are the spirit that guides the school. They are so uncommonly, solemnly, unintentionally funny that they almost justify seeing "The Harrad Experiment," which opened yesterday at the Baronet Theater.

1973 My 12, 19:1

The Cast

THEATER OF BLOOD, directed by Douglas Hickox; screenplay by Anthony Greville-Bell; produced by John Kohn and Stanley Mann; music, Michael J. Lewis; director of photography, Wolfgang Suschitzky; editor, Malcolm Cooke; distributed by United Artists. Running time: 104 minutes. At the Rivoli Theater, Broadway at 50th Street, and other theaters. This film has been classified R.

Edward Lionheart	Vincent Price
Edwina Lionheart	Diana Rigg
Peregrine Devlin	Ian Hendry
Trevor Dickman	Harry Andrews
Chloe Moon	Coral Browne
Oliver Larding	Robert Coote
Solomon Psaltery	Jack Hawkins
George Maxwell	Michael Hordern
Horace Sprout	Arthur Lowe
Meredith Merridew	Robert Morley
Hector Snipe	Dennis Price

"Theater of Blood" is an extremely cheerful horror film about Edward Kendall Sheridan Lionheart (Vincent Price), the world's worst Shakespearean actor, who sets out to take his revenge on London's drama critics by murdering each in the rococo style of one of the plays featured in Lonheart's final and, apparently, most dismal repertory season.

Thus Meredith Merridew (Robert Morley), who dyes his hair lavender and speaks of his miniature poodles as his little dears, finds himself on a bogus TV show called "Dish of the Week," eating an uncommonly tasty meat pie made out of — well — I shouldn't give away the plot of "Cymbeline." A critic, Trevor Dickman (Harry Andrews), is invited to take part in a sort of Living Theater production of "The Merchant of Venice," playing an Antonio who really does give up a pound of flesh. It's his heart and it's the suggestion of the people who made this film that critics' hearts, when exposed, steam like dry ice.

"Only Lionheart," scoffs another critic, "would have the temerity to rewrite Shakespeare."

Anthony Greville-Bell, the screenwriter, and Douglas Hickox, the director, are hard pressed to maintain this nicely slapdash humor through nine murders, but they have the aid of some of England's most attractive character actors, including Robert Coote, Arthur Lowe and Dennis Price. Best of all, they have the extraordinary Diana Rigg, who does turn up in the oddest places.

Miss Rigg plays Lionheart's beautiful, faithful daughter, a Cordelia who stands by dad through thick and thin, assisting at amputations, drownings, stabbings and what-not, sometimes disguised as a mustachioed motorcyclist in shades, sometimes as Marilyn Monroe, sometimes as herself. Miss Rigg is an actress of such wit that she succeeds in being both funny and legitimately moving, especially when Price is occupying screen-center, horrendously over-acting with her loving approval.

VINCENT CANBY.

1973 My 12, 19:1

Screen: Festival Shorts

The package of nine short subjects from this year's Ann Arbor Film Festival, which opened Friday at the Film Forum, illustrates, as have previous selections, the serious intentions, if not the over-all artistry, of their independent moviemakers. If some of the entries, which run from 3 to 26 minutes each, are largely vague personal exercises, at least four are forceful enough to make the show worth viewing.

The most striking is "6344", the longest offering. Even though its locale is undefined, this color depiction by Joseph Pipher and several associates of the corny songs, memories and anecdotes of the aged occupants of an old house (at No. 6344) destined for the wreckers, gently stirs the heart and mind. Despite its basic sadness, its drama and emotion are projected with professional polish and a large helping of humor.

●

In oblique, improvised style, a chance roadside pick-up of a hitchhiking girl in "Autostop" is developed by Roberta Cantow into a touching evocation of the bittersweet fantasies of the girl and the bearded, seemingly ailing motorist who's grasp-

The Program

ANN ARBOR FILM FESTIVAL: CORRESPONDENCE by Bob Mathes, 3 minutes; ZOMBIES IN A HOUSE OF MADNESS by Michael Anderson, Paul Jacobs, Saul Landau and Bill Yahraus, 4 minutes; BEST OF MAY by Jay Cassidy, 4 minutes; ASSASSINATION RAGA by Max Crosley and Lawrence Ferlinghetti, 13 minutes; SEPTEMBER 11 by Marion Caiori, 12½ minutes; THOUGHT DREAMS by Barbara Linkevitch, 3 minutes; AUTOSTOP by Roberta Cantow, 15 minutes; 6344 by Joseph Pipher, 26 minutes; INSIDE DOUBT by Michael Rudnick and Rock Ross, 6½ minutes. At the Film Forum, 256 West 88th Street, May 11-13 and 18-20, 8 P.M.

ing for momentary affection.

In similarly effective fashion, "Assassination Raga" brings home the tragedies of John F. and Robert F. Kennedy, the Rev. Dr. Martin Luther King Jr., Gandhi and Malcolm X through the poet Lawrence Ferlinghetti's dirgelike laments and the complementary musical background of doleful, twanging sitars. And giggles are generated through the satiric invention of "Inside Doubt," created by Michael Rudnick and Rock Ross, as animated vegetables take their revenge on an unsuspecting young homemaker.

●

The efforts of the group point to a pleasant potential for the future of these film makers, who are obviously in love with the medium.

A. H. WEILER

1973 My 13, 59:1

'Have You Seen Shu Lately?' 'Shu Who?'

By VINCENT CANBY

THE following memo, submitted by my secretary last week, is reprinted in its entirety:

"'Fist of Fury' was released in New York last November. That was its original title in Hong Kong. It will be reissued here later this year under the title 'The Iron Hand.' 'Fists of Fury' (note the plural), which is now playing at local theaters, was called 'The Big Boss' in Hong Kong. These two films are not to be confused with each other or with 'Deep Thrust—The Hand of Death,' also from Hong Kong and also playing locally now, or with 'Five Fingers of Death,' which opened in New York last March and which elsewhere has had various titles employing the word 'Boxer.'"

I've been aware that karate has been in fashion for some time, ever since that afternoon several years ago when, stranded between planes, I lay beside a hotel swimming pool in San Juan, a kapok pillow over my eyes, and listened to a group of weight-conscious women go through their daily lessons:

"No, Sandra, you've got it all wrong. You're supposed to start from the position of humility.'" "That *was* 'the position of humility,' wasn't it Estelle?" "It looked like 'the awareness position' to me." "Estelle can't tell the difference between the awareness position' and 'the reverent position.'" "Shut up, Sandra, I'll tell Fred . . ."

*

It was not only much less tiring than deep knee

bends but also much more fun, especially when the p.a. system was blasting the transplanted palm trees with rhumba L.P.s.

Then it was plain old Japanese karate. Today, if the movie box offices of the world are any indication, karate has given way to kung fu, which is described as the "older Chinese style of karate" by Bruce Tegner, the author of 25 books on the subject, including one in my possession that was published by the Thor Publishing Company of Ventura, Calif.

According to Variety, there hasn't been such a comparably profitable movie fad since the early days of the Italian Western about 10 years ago. According to Samuel Z. Arkoff, the head of American International Pictures, a company that ought to recognize a trend when it bumps into one (with films like "The Fall of The House of Usher," "I Was a Teenage Frankenstein," "Beach Blanket Bingo," "Blacula" and now "Deep Thrust"), kung fu movies began as a local phenomenon in Hong Kong a couple of years ago, began to win audiences in Latin America two years ago, and in the last year have scored remarkable financial successes in Europe, especially Italy and Germany.

*

They are now here, and the two I've just seen, "Fists of Fury" and "Deep Thrust," make the worst Italian Westerns look like the most solemn and noble achievements of the early Soviet cinema.

"Fists of Fury" stars Bruce Lee, a Chinese-American who is now apparently the Mr. Big of Hong Kong, and it has a plot that wouldn't have taxed one episode of a 15-chapter Flash Gordon serial.

Bruce, who looks a good deal like Alain Delon with a lot of bee stings that make him seem plump, arrives in an unidentified oriental seaport city to work with his cousins in a factory that makes ice. He falls in love with his pretty, virginal cousin, Chow Mein, but gets into trouble when his cousin, Shu, mysteriously disappears. "Have you seen Shu lately?" Bruce asks a girl who sells lemonade on what appears to be a deadend street. "Shu who?" she answers.

*

The dubbed English-language script is obviously meant to be funny, though it doesn't have a patch on Woody Allen's "What's Up, Tiger Lily?" More important, the audience with which I saw it at the National Theater on Times Square accepted it straight, as a non-stop series of kung fu encounters between Bruce and the bad guys, the owner of the ice plant and his henchmen, smugglers of packets of narcotics inside cakes of ice.

Like the Bruce Lee film, "Deep Thrust — The Hand of Death," returns the action movie to its cradle, although there is one slight variation. The most accomplished kung fu artist in the film is a woman out to avenge her sister who was loved, and then left pregnant. However, it's soon clear that "Deep Thrust" has less to do with Women's Lib than it has to do with ancient male fantasies about dominating dragon ladies. The true villain of the piece is another woman who says to one of her servants, who has been bettered in a kung fu match with the heroine: "God damn you! How could you lose to a lousy girl?"

Neither film makes any attempt to be dramatically coherent. Instead they present a series of purposely fantastic and outrageous kung fu-karate demonstrations in which one person takes on anywhere between one dozen and three dozen opponents at a single session. The fights are staged rather like production numbers in old-fashioned musical films, with long-shot and overhead shots intercut with close-ups of the mayhem and time out for specialties, including, it seems, the use of trampolines. At least, that's the only way to explain how some of the kung fu artists are able to appear to jump over seven-foot walls from standing positions.

*

The fights begin in more or less classic manner, with the opponents facing each-other with bare hands. When a villain pulls out a knife, a club, a chain, or a sword, the hero is forced to even matters, to resort to the same tactics. Curiously, though the films seem to have contemporary settings, no one thinks to carry a gun. This hardly means that the films are less violent than our occidental action films. The paint flows like blood as hatchets are implanted in chests, knives in backs, or, as in "Deep Thrust," one fighter is able to stick three fingers through the stomach of his opponent.

The movies are pure bloody spectacles in which the issues fought over have hardly any relation to the intensity of the fights themselves. Kung fu movies are to cinema what roller derbies are to theater.

Why the popularity at this point in history? There may be a clue in a line in a poster outside the Trans-Lux West, where "Deep Thrust" is playing.

"The strong," says the ad, "bend before the clever and the quick."

*

Few of us can maintain the fiction that we're strong. It's too easy to be proven false. We can, however, take refuge in the wish that we're clever and quick. Kung fu and karate have finally, irrevocably, replaced old Charles Atlas and his promise to make the world safe for all ninety-pound weaklings. With a little training, we can all become our own secret weapons, and we don't have to add much weight.

This, I would guess, is a major reason for the international success of these films, and maybe even for the success of the current kung fu TV series, called, naturally, "Kung Fu" (though the one installment I saw recently had less action than an average David Susskind show).

Everybody is fearful. Everyone would like to have a weapon, which may be why Mr. Tegner, in his kung fu manual, quite carefully disassociates himself from what are probably the prime reasons for the popularity of kung fu today.

"A teacher of physical education," says Mr. Tegner, "feels repugnance, and rightfully so, when he is told that kung fu training prepares one to kill his adversary with a mere poke of the finger at the right time of day. His objections are social, moral and anatomical."

It's difficult to know at this time what social moral and anatomical outrages may be perpetrated by this newest of film fads, but it is certain to be with us for a while. About a dozen more kung fu films are due to be imported within the year if the market holds up. In Bangkok, I'm told, some far-sighted Italian and Chinese producers have already joined forces to make what might be called the first of the post-kung fu films, in which a Mediterranean-based strong man, a Hercules-type who is big but probably not too clever or quick, meets and is matched against a kung fu artist. National sensibilities being what they are, it sounds like a film that will have to be shot with two different endings.

1973 My 13, II:1:5

Just a Locker Room Fantasy?

By STEPHEN FARBER

MOVIES about male friendships touch something in the fantasy life of Americans. That is the only explanation for the commercial success of "Scarecrow" (written by Garry Michael White, directed by Jerry Schatzberg), a tedious, pretentious, ultimately dishonest saga of two down-and-out rovers adrift in Middle America.

A crude, boisterous, violent Max (Gene Hackman) hopes to open a car wash in Pittsburgh; shy, awkward, sensitive Lion (Al Pacino) is on his way to Detroit to visit the child he has never seen. They meet while hitch-hiking in California, decide to become business partners, and set out across the country together. The film obviously owes more than a minor debt to "Midnight Cowboy." Max and Lion, like Joe Buck and Ratso Rizzo, are a Mutt 'n' Jeff who approach each other warily, have a few squabbles, but eventually find the only stability they have ever known through their deepening relationship; their shabby lives are redeemed when they learn to care about each other. Unfortunately, the redemption comes too late; at the end, an unexpected catastrophe separates them.

Although it is a much clumsier film, "Scarecrow" shares "Midnight Cowboy's" sentimentality, and its stridency. There are a lot of subjects Hollywood filmmakers can handle with skill and even insight, but it seems that simple, ordinary life is no longer one of them. Jerry Schatzberg, like John Schlesinger, can't help patronizing the artless characters, presenting them with a superior kind of "passion" that actually denies the characters' individuality and their full humanity.

Elia Kazan was one director who could illuminate the inner lives of in-articulate, uneducated, poverty-stricken people; his best characters engaged us because the complexity of their drives kept them mysterious and inviolate. In "Scarecrow," by contrast, Max and Lion have no depth, no mystery; they only have tics — colorful little eccentricities — and their secrets are exposed in the first five minutes. After that, you can only laugh at them or feel sorry for them; they're fashionable movie losers, and that's all they are.

*

The minor characters in "Scarecrow" are even more crudely drawn caricatures of hicks and sluts, while the visual details caught by the camera are the clichés an urban outsider would pick out — the bucket of Kentucky Colonel Fried Chicken, the frying pan bubbling over with grease, the cluttered, weedy backyard, the girl with pink curlers in her hair and a crucifix on the wall. To emphasize Max's coarseness, Schatzberg shows him burping over his beer. The whole film belabors the obvious; it makes no discoveries, and it has no respect for its low-life characters.

Because he doesn't understand the world of drifters, slatterns and ex cons, Schatzberg imposes a fake visual poetry. All the arty landscapes — the blue-black skies, the golden fields, the red-streaked sunsets and sunrises — are there to pump significance into a shallow, underwritten script. Vilmos Zsigmond is a talented cameraman, but his self-conscious cinematography is wrong for this movie; the stately chiaroscuro tableaux betray a slick sophistication that destroys any possibility of confronting Max and Lion on their own terms.

*

After directing three films, Schatzberg still hasn't learned much about his craft. He's still a fashion photographer composing beautifully-framed images that might look impressive on a calendar or a postcard; but they aren't *moving* pictures. And although Hackman and Pacino both have good moments, they play much too broadly, without the attention to nuance that has marked their best work.

Beyond the failures in acting and direction, what makes the film insufferable is its dumb, dreamy celebration of male camaraderie. "Scarecrow" is in a long tradition of popular movies about male partners—from "Boom Town" and "Of Mice and Men" through "The Professionals," "Butch Cassidy and the Sundance Kid" and "Husbands." These gruffly tender male love stories delight audiences who want to retreat into reveries of summer camp, locker room and Army barracks, the rugged world of adventure on the open road or the high seas.

Women play a small role in these masculine fantasies, and when they do appear, they're little more than mattresses. In "Scarecrow" Max and Lion are living an early adolescent dream, where two buddies share the purest kind of love, and women are seen as sexual diversion or as the violators of a beautiful friendship. The sad thing is that the filmmakers seem to share the heroes' stunted views. The portrait of Lion's ex-wife, for example, is hysterical and overdrawn; she is heartless enough to pretend that their child is dead, thus precipitating Lion's final breakdown. In fact, the only woman in the movie who might have been something more than a Dumb Dora or a bitch—Max's sister Coley (played by the gifted Dorothy Tristan)—is inadequately developed.

In one of the slyest scenes in Woody Allen's "Everything You Always Wanted to Know About Sex," two semi-naked jocks appeared in a TV commercial to sell a gooey hair tonic; the advertising parody proceeded predictably until the fade-out, when the two all-American athletes embraced passionately. In taking locker room camaraderie to its logical conclusion Woody Allen should have exploded the Hemingway idealization of masculine friendship. But some myths seem indestructible.

*

Allen, along with Freudian critics, could have a field day with "Scarecrow," a movie filled with homosexual motifs—Max and Lion dancing together, Max referring to Lion as "my wife," etc. —that seem completely unconscious on the part of the writer and director. But the filmmakers go out of their way to deny the sexual undercurrents. The only purpose of a ridiculous, protracted, sensational prison episode — in which a sadistic homosexual attacks an astonished Lion — is to underscore the boyish innocence of Max and Lion's relationship. The filmmakers want to make absolutely certain that no one in the audience mistakes Max or Lion for a homosexual. It could be that they protest too much.

Perhaps Schatzberg and screenwriter White set their Hemingway idyll in a lower-class world — a world they have little feeling for — because they hoped a gritty, seedy milieu would somehow confirm the heroes' masculinity, and obscure the sexual ambiguities. But Max has spent six years in prison, and Lion five years in the Navy—two of the most overtly homosexual subcultures in America; how can we believe in their naivete?

*

Like "Midnight Cowboy," "Scarecrow" evades the most obvious implications of its theme. Of course, if the two buddies in these locker-room fantasies ever had a sexual relationship, the films would disturb and threaten all the men in the audience who despise homosexuals and yet secretly believe that their relationships with their fraternity brothers, drinking cronies, or bowling partners are the noblest in their lives, deeper and truer than any relationships they have with women. American men yearn for the breezy, undemanding liaisons of a 12-year-old's life; they want to flee the threat of deeper involvement.

Recent movies like "Carnal Knowledge" and "Deliverance" have begun to demonstrate some of the limitations of male camaraderie. And a few meaningful films have been made about nonsexual male friendships — "Jules and Jim," for example, or Benton and Newman's "Bad Company," where the characters are sharply defined and the complexities of the relationship are honored; those two films acknowledge the profound tensions in a real, organic friendship.

"Scarecrow" is no more than a mindless exaltation of the sacred, privileged bond of two buddies. White and Schatzberg are the latest victims of a prevalent American disease, the Peter Pan syndrome; but aren't there a few filmmakers who want to grow up and make honest movies about *adult* relationships, heterosexual or homosexual? Caught somewhere in between, these maudlin, juvenile fantasies of Boy Scout puppy love have been taken too seriously for too long.

1973 My 13, II:13:1

The Cast

THE DAY OF THE JACKAL, directed by Fred Zinnemann; screenplay by Kenneth Ross, based on the novel by Frederick Forsyth; produced by John Woolf; director of photography, Jean Tournier; editor, Ralph Kemplen; music, Georges Delerue; distributed by Universal Pictures. Running time: 142 minutes. At the Loews State 2 Theater, Broadway at 45th Street, and Loews Orpheum Theater, 86th Street near Third Avenue. This film has been classified PG.
The Jackal .... Edward Fox
Colonel Rolland .... Michel Auclair
The Minister .... Alan Badel
Inspector Thomas .... Tony Britton
The President ...... Adrien Cayla-Legrand
The Gunsmith .... Cyril Cusak
Caron .... Derek Jacobi
Lebel .... Michel Lonsdale
The Forger .... Ronald Pickup
Colonel Rodin .... Eric Porter
Colette .... Delphine Seyrig
Mallinson .... Donald Sinden

By VINCENT CANBY

Except for its downbeat ending, Fred Zinnemann's thoroughly competent film version of "The Day of the Jackal" might lead one to believe that the life of a professional political assassin involves almost as much ground travel to and from airports as does an airline pilot's — but the assassin's work is much better paid.

The Jackal, the code name for the assassin played by Edward Fox, a man reported to have murdered both Trujillo and someone cryptically identified as "that fellow in the Congo," is hired by a group of former French Army officers, furious over the loss of Algeria, to assassinate President Charles de Gaulle. The fee: $250,000 down and another $250,000 on completion.

Frederick Forsyth's novel, which has been written for the screen by Kenneth Ross, belongs to a very special subcategory of fiction — one that leaves me cold but apparently fascinates two out of every three people in the Free World who can afford to buy adventure novels in hardback editions.

Because history has tipped us off that no one ever did assassinate De Gaulle, the suspense of the novel and the film must depend on our wondering just how the assassin is going to fail. This preordained failure also allows us to hope rather tentatively for his success. We can identify with him in a way that we certainly would not allow ourselves with an Oswald or a Ray.

"The Day of the Jackal," which opened yesterday at the Loews State 2 and Orpheum Theaters, devotes itself entirely to this question of how — how the assassin operates and how he is ultimately caught.

It is virtually encyclopedic in describing the assassin's preparations, which involve a lot of flying back and forth between London, Paris, Vienna and Rome. We watch him doing research in libraries, ordering false identify papers, and buying specially made weapons as well as over-the-counter hair dyes. The details are minutely observed and, to me, just a bit boring. I keep thinking that although it could have happened, in this case it didn't.

Zinnemann's way with this material is cool, sober and geographically stunning (the film was shot all over Europe at what looks to be a huge cost). Where Hitchcock would have made it funny, Zinnemann plays it straight (and perhaps dull), allowing himself only that margin of humor provided by the bureaucratic style of the good guys (cops and government functionaries), so that the funniest line of the film comes when someone says of De Gaulle: "At 10 he rekindles the eternal flame."

Edward Fox is a very natty-looking assassin, a role that requires a lot of walking around, getting in and out of cars, and puffing on cigarettes, but not much acting. In the supporting cast are some of the best actors in England and France, including Michel Lonsdale as a French supercop and Delphine Seyrig as a bored baroness whom the assassin encounters en route to his date with destiny.

I've no doubt it will be a smash.

1973 My 17, 53:1

The Cast

PAPER MOON, directed and produced by Peter Bogdanovich; screenplay by Alvin Sargent, based on the novel, "Addie Pray," by Joe David Brown; director of photography, Laszlo Kovacs; editor, Verna Fields; a Directors Company presentation, distributed by Paramount Pictures. Running time: 102 minutes. At the Coronet Theater, Third Avenue near 59th Street. This film has been classified PG.
Mosses Prap .... Ryan O'Neal
Addie Loggins............ Tatum O'Neal
Trixie Delight............ Madeline Kahn
Deputy Hardin............ John Hillerman
Imogene.................... P.J. Johnson
Floyd..................... Burton Gilliam
Leroy..................... Randy Quade
Widow Huff.............. Dorothy Forster

Most American movies of the nineteen-thirties took the Depression for granted. Occasionally Hollywood made socially conscious films but the general run of screwball comedies and gangster melodramas was primarily designed as escapist entertainment. They were less about the life and hard times of the period than unselfconscious souvenirs of them.

This is the basic difference between something like "Little Miss Marker (19-34)," which unleashed Sirley Temple upon Franklin Delano Roosevelt's America, and "Paper Moon," Peter Bogdanovich's new comedy that opened yesterday at the Coronet. "Paper Moon," like the early Temple film, is about a kid and a con artist, an alliance that only someone who had never seen a movie could call "unlikely" (a term used to describe it in the publicity material).

●

Bogdanovich and his screenwriter, Alvin Sargent, who adapted Joe David Brown's novel, have set out to make a bittersweet comedy that is both in the style of thirties movies and about the thirties. They evoke the time (1936) and the place (rural Kansas and Missouri) so convincingly that their rather sweet formula story seems completely inadequate, even fraudulent.

The adventures of Moses Pray (Ryan O'Neal), who deals in small, essentially harmless swindles (like selling back to a bootlegger the bootlegger's own booze), and Addie (Tatum O'Neal), who may or may not be Moses' illegitimate daughter, do not measure up to all of the period details with which the film is stuffed — marvelously tinny old recordings, old cars, old radio programs, including snatches of Jack Benny and Fibber McGee and Molly. These are things that a real film of the period hardly notices. Here they stick out a mile.

Bogdanovich loves old Hollywood movies, and his love is infectious. In "What's Up,

Doc?" he was surprisingly successful in updating at least a half-dozen of Hollywood's favorite comedy styles. "Paper Moon," however, is oddly depressing instead of what is usually called heart-warming.

Laszlo Kovacs's black-and-white photography doesn't recall some nice little studio picture but "The Grapes of Wrath" with its gigantic, sorrowful landscapes. Also, Bogdanovich's use of prairie faces in subsidiary roles keeps nudging the movie into a category in which it is not at all comfortable. The film never makes up its mind whether it wants to be an instant antique or a comment on one.

I suspect these reservations will strike many people as superfluous since "Paper Moon" also contains two first-class performances by O'Neal and his 9-year-old daughter. The actor moves easily between his roles as star and as straight-man for Tatum, a charming, tight-lipped little girl who has — and this may well sound absurd—the quality of a teeny-weeny Joanne Woodward. I also very much liked Madeline Kahn's very broad characterization as a carnival kootch girl and Burton Gilliam's as a small-town lecher.

VINCENT CANBY

1973 My 17, 53:1

The Cast

THE SOUL OF NIGGER CHARLEY, directed by Larry G. Spangler; screenplay by Harold Stone; story by Mr. Spangler; director of photography, Richard C. Glouner; edited by Howard Kuperman; music by Don Costa; produced by Mr. Spangler; released by Paramount Pictures. At the Penthouse Theater, Broadway and 47th Street and the 86th Street Twin I Theater, West of Lexington Avenue. Running time: 109 minutes. This film is classified R.

Charley	Fred Williamson
Toby	D'Urville Martin
Elena	Denise Nicholas
Sandoval	Pedro Armendariz Jr.
Marcellus	Kirk Calloway
Ode	George Allen
Colonel Blanchard	Kevin Hagen

By A. H. WEILER

Despite lip service paid by "The Soul of Nigger Charley" to freedom and dignity, its ex-slave hero and his followers and the unregenerate post-Civil War Confederates out to destroy them, are, for the most part, good black guys shooting it out almost constantly with bad white guys.

As in last year's "Legend of Nigger Charley," to which this is a sequel, the fictions occasionally intrude on the bloody action. How did those vicious Southern renegades manage to set up a domain in Mexico complete with slaves? Where did the freed slaves they slaughtered in a nearby American village come from?, etc.

•

The need for fuller explanations aside, Charley, again played coolly and with muscular determination by Fred Williamson, the handsome former football star, is able to surround himself with an amazing variety of black and Mexican aides to free the slaves held by the murderous Kevin Hagen and an unbilled "General Hook" and set up a new black community below the border.

There is Pedro Armendariz Jr. and his Mexican banditos, who are happy to help for friendship and money. There is the massive George Allen, who is handy with a bow and arrow because his mother was an Indian, and there is the comely but ill-fated Denise Nicholas (of TV's "Room 222"), who has lost her heart to Charley. And there are those freed slaves who have lived with white Quakers; Kirk Calloway, the black, orphaned youngster protected by Charley, and D'Urville Martin, Charley's indestructible sidekick from "Legend," still around as his trusty right arm.

As noted, there is a romantic scene or two and a few verbal outbursts against blatant bigotry. Essentially, however, gunfire, not characterization, is the order of the day.

1973 My 17, 54:1

The Cast

ADIEU PHILIPPINE, directed by Jacques Rozier; screenplay (French with English substitles) by Mr. Rozier and Michel O'Glor; photography by Rene Mathelin; edited by Monique Bonnot and Claude Durand; music by Jacques Deniean; produced by Unitec France; released by New Yorker Films. At the New Yorker Theater, Broadway and 88th Street. Running time: 111 minutes. This film has not been classified at this time.

Liliane	Yveline Cery
Juliette	Stefania Sabatini
Michel	Jean-Claude Aimimi
Pachala	Vittorio Caprioli
Horatio	Davide Tonelli

By ROGER GREENSPUN

One by one, over the years, from "Les Bonnes Femmes" to "L'Amour Fou," the lost films of the French New Wave have made their appearance in New York. You could still program a sizable festival from what is left to be seen (work by Chabrol, Astruc, Melville will do for starters). But it seems especially ironic that perhaps the most agreeable, and surely one of the loveliest, of all New Wave movies, Jacques Rozier's "Adieu Philippine," made in 1961, should have had to wait so long. It opened yesterday at the New Yorker Theater.

•

"Adieu Philippine" was not a commercial success in Europe, and Rozier, now in his forties, has been able to make only one feature film since. But when it came out, Eric Rohmer and Jacques Rivette classified it a masterpiece; and a still from it (two smiling girls in bathing suits) graced the front cover of the superb "Nouvelle Vague" issue of Cahiers du Cinéma. To a degree it was valued for what seemed a prophetic newness in the wedding of cinéma-vérité techniques to a fictional subject. For one reason or another — mostly personal pleasure — I've seen "Adieu Philippine" half a dozen times at screenings since the early nineteen-sixties, and it remains a beautiful movie; important not for its technique but for its expression of a lyrical sensibility rare enough in any decade.

•

The title refers to a French kids' wish-granting game and "phillipine" means "sweetheart." The sweetheart in question, Michel (Jean-Claude Aimimi), works in television, mainly pushing cables away from moving cameras — a job at which he is none too successful. One day he picks up a pair of teen-age girls (Vveline Céry and Stefania Sabatini) and casually begins to romance them both in his time off and eventually through a beachcombing vacation in Corsica. There is a comic subplot — actually very funny — about a crooked producer of TV commercials (Vittorio Caprioli). But there is no main plot to speak of — except the progress of a casual affair, the passage of relaxed time, and in the distance for Michel, national service and, presumably, the Algerian War.

Inevitably "Adieu Philippine" deals with an end to innocence, or the encroachment of time, or whatever happens in a young person's life to signify the frailty of wishes against the demands of necessity. Both the girls fall in love—just as Michel is called up. He is left with nothing of love but a long, overwhelming, harborside farewell. For the movie, which is awkward in its greetings, is magnificent in its good-byes — and, given its rich romanticism, that may be the best clue to its meaning.

•

Typically, the most beautiful moments in "Adieu Philippine" are not its events but its interludes. The two girls walking along a succession of Paris streets, tracked at eye level by the camera, and virtually orchestrated with the rhythm of a tango on the sound track. One of the girls (Miss Céry), on the evening of Michel's departure, dancing by herself for a while in a perfect evocation of the seriousness of desire. Or the departure itself, set to music, like so much of the movie, Michel on the boat to Marseilles, the girls ashore; in a breathtaking passage that by the simplest means creates a deep and subtle visual correlative for what it means to take one's leave.

In a sense, Rozier's is a cinema of privileged moments — moments that account for its success and generate its poignancy.

1973 My 17, 56:4

MEMORIES OF UNDERDEVELOPMENT (Memorias del Subdesarrollo), directed and written (Spanish with English subtitles) by Tomas Gutierrez Alea, based on the novel by Edmundo Desnoes; director of photography, Ramon Suarez; editor, Nelson Rodriguez; music, Leo Brower; produced by the Instituto Cubano del Arte e Industria Cinematograficos; distributed by Tricontinental Film Center. Running time: 104 minutes. At the First Avenue Screening Room, at 61st Street. This film has not been classified.

Sergio	Sergio Corrieri
Elena	Daisy Granados
Noemi	Eslinda Nunez
Laura	Beatriz Ponchora

By VINCENT CANBY

The time is 1961, not long after the Bay of Pigs, and Sergio (Sergio Corrieri), the hero of Tomas Gutierrez Alea's superb Cuban film, "Memories of Underdevelopment," moves through Havana as if he were a scuba diver exploring the ruins of a civilization he abhorred but cannot bear to leave. The world he sees is startlingly clear. It is also remote. The sounds he hears are his own thoughts.

"Everything happens to me too early or too late," says Sergio, an intellectual in his late 30's whose critical faculties have effectively rendered him incapable of any action whatsoever. After his estranged wife and his mother and father have fled to Miami, with the other bourgeosie, he thinks he will write the novel he has always thought about, but then Sergio's standards are too high to allow him to add to the sum total of civilization's second-rateness. He finds himself blocked.

Perhaps if the revolution had happened earlier, he tells himself, he might have understood.

Sergio makes half-hearted little efforts to maintain his old ways. He picks up Elena (Daisy Granados), a pretty, bird-brained girl who wants to be an actress, and he tries to educate (he says "Europeanize" her. He takes her to art galleries and buys her books but her brain remains unreconstructed and birdlike. "She doesn't relate things," he tells himself. "It's one of the signs of underdevelopment."

He takes Elena on a sightseeing tour of Hemingway's house. "He said he killed so as not to kill himself," Sergio remembers, looking at some mounted antlers. "In the end he could not resist the temptation."

Even suicide is beyond Sergio. All he can do is observe, much of the time through the telescope on the terrace of a penthouse apartment he must give up, sooner or later.

•

"Memories of Underdevelopment," is a fascinating achievement. Here is a film about alienation that is wise, sad and often funny, and that never slips into the bored and boring attitudes that wreck Antonioni's later films. Sergio is detached and wary, but around him is a hurricane of life.

Gutierrez Alea was 40 when he made "Memories" (in 1968), and he is clearly a man, like Sergio, whose sensibilities are European. Yet unlike Sergio, and unlike the director of "Eclipse" and "Red Desert," he is so full of passion and political commitment that he has even been able to make an essentially pro-revolutionary film in which Castro's revolution is observed through eyes dim with bafflement.

•

The result is hugely effective and moving, and it is complete in the way that very few movies ever are. I haven't read Edmundo Desnoes's original novel (published here in 1967 as "Inconsolable Memories"), but I like the fact that Desnoes apparently likes the film that, in his words, had to be "a betrayal" of the book to be a good film. Gutierrez Alea, says the author, in the film's program notes, "objectivized a world that was shapeless in my mind and still abstract in the book. He added social density. . . ."

"Memories of Underdevelopment" was one of the films scheduled to be shown here last year at the aborted Cuban film Festival. It finally opened yesterday at the First Avenue Screening Room where it will play one week and then, I hope, it will move to another theater for the long run it deserves.

1973 My 18, 28:1

The Cast

EXTREME CLOSE-UP, directed by Jeannot Szwarc; screenplay by Michael Crichton; photography, Paul N. Lohman; music by Basil Poledouris; produced by Paul N. Lazarus III; released by National General Pictures. At neighborhood theaters. Running time: 82 minutes. This film has been classified R.

John Norman	James McMullan
Tom	James A. Watson Jr.
Sally	Kate Woodville
Sylvia	Bara Bynes
Equipment Salesman	Al Checco

By ROGER GREENSPUN

Here it is only mid-May, and already we have the most pointless movie of the year.

John Norman, the hero of "Extreme Close-up," a TV newsman doing a series on invasion of privacy, gets secretly hooked on the personal surveillance equipment rented for his show, starts spying on people more or less at random, and then falls into voyeurism — virtually as a way of life.

•

All this sounds deceptively like the beginning of a movie, and while watching the first half hour of it I kept expecting something original to happen — like Norman's discovering a wife murderer while peering through a telescope in his apartment's Rear Window. But nothing of the kind happens.

What does happen is that Norman, a girl-watcher from way back watches girls more closely. Then he watches couples, and finally he watches himself and his own wife — in a mirror — while they make love. He doesn't see much—about up to the level of very timid old-fashioned peeping-Tom pornography. And since he is always being found out, and humiliated, in his spying, "Extreme Close-up" revives the nervous formula of alternating lust and shame that I thought the nineteen-sixties sexual revolution had, thankfully, gotten rid of.

•

Eyes glued to his superpower sniperscope; ears plugged into his super-directional midget microphone, Norman (James McMullan) is an intriguing image and even an interesting idea. But there are no other ideas in the movie.

"Extreme Close-up," which was written by Michael Crichton ("The Andromeda Strain," "Terminal Man," etc.) and directed by Jeannot Szwarc, opened Wednesday at neighborhood theaters.

1973 My 18, 33:3

The Cast

DIRTY LITTLE BILLY, directed by Stan Dragoti; story and screenplay by Charles Moss and Mr. Dragoti; director of photography, Ralph Woolsey; film editor, Dave Wages; produced by Jack L. Warner; released by Columbia Pictures. At the Columbia 1 Theater, Second Avenue at 64th Street; the Forum Theater, Broadway at 46th Street; and neighborhood theaters. Running time: 93 minutes. This film is classified R.

Billy Bonney	Michael J. Pollard
Berle	Lee Purcell
Goldie Evans	Richard Evans
Ben Antrim	Charles Aidman
Catherine MaCarty	Dran Hamilton
Henry MaCarty	Willard Sage
Jawbone	Josip Elic

Credit the team headed by Stan Dragoti, the television commercials director who is making his movie bow with "Dirty Little Billy," with giving us a realistically raw view of the beginnings of the Billy the Kid legend. Unfortunately, Billy, floundering in a search for roots in sleazy, muddy Coffeyville, Kan., and the vicious or callous unwashed types he's involved with remain largely vague, unresolved figures brawling and killing on a primitive landscape.

Billy, who is portrayed by Michael J. Pollard in smiling, almost witless fashion, revolts against the hard farm life forced on him by his stepfather. Thereafter he's befriended by the town badman, Richard Evans. Lee Purcell, as Evans's prostitute girlfriend, initiates Billy into one aspect of manhood. Eventually, Coffeyville's puritanical element, led by Charles Aidman — who, for unexplained reasons, is dallying with Billy's mother—drives Billy and his pal out of town after gunning down the hapless Miss Purcell.

Our callow hero, once inept with guns, uses them with bloody effect to protect his friend in a final shootout with a gang of thieving renegades. And, one

may assume, Billy the Desperado now emerges fullblown as he happily packs his six-shooters and trudges off into the sunset with his mentor.

The look of an authentic period and place is captured in the dirt, sloppy roads, rickety buildings and tattered itinerants who never owned fancy 10-gallon hats, spurs or chaps. And the unremitting struggle for survival is also starkly spotlighted, especially in a couple of brutal fights staged without glorification of the principals.

"Dirty Little Billy" projects an unvarnished picture of the Old West, even if the contributions of the script and the dour Charles Aidman, the misused Lee Purcell and the rough Richard Evans are unconvincing. And one is inclined to agree with a confused Billy when he asks, "What's all this rushing about for?"

A. H. WEILER

1973 My 19, 28:1

The Cast

THE MATTEI AFFAIR, directed by Francesco Rosi; story by Mr. Rosi and Tonino Guerra; screenplay by Mr. Rosi and Mr. Guerra in collaboration with Nerlo Minuzzo and Tito de Stefano; editor, Ruggero Mastroianni; music, Piero Piccioni; produced by Franco Cristaldi; a Cinema International Corporation presentation; released by Paramount Pictures. At the Little Carnegie Theater, 57th Street, east of Seventh Avenue. Running time: 118 minutes. This film is classified R.

Enrico Mattei	Gian Maria Volonte
Journalist	Luigi Equarzina
McHale	Peter Baldwin
2d Journalist	Renato Romano
Minister	Franco Graziosi
Engineer Ferrari	Gianfranco Ombuen
Official of Inquiry Commission	Elio Jotta
Mrs. Matei	Edda Ferronao
Bertuzzi	Luciano Colitti

By ROGER GREENSPUN

In the time between the end of World War II and his death in 1962, Enrico Mattei put together an industrial-service complex that was at the very least instrumental in shaping Italy's postwar economic boom. Based on the discovery of abundant natural gas in the Po Valley, but extending to chains of service stations and hotels, to deals with Arabian oil countries, with the Soviet Union and potentially even with China, Mattei's work served neither his own gain nor a private corporation, but rather the national Government—which his enemies asserted he more or less openly controlled.

•

Mattei had enemies enough, and on an international scale, for his power, his ambition, his corrosive energy, and for such outrages to the prerogatives of private enterprise as actually lowering the price of gasoline through economies effected by a state-owned monopoly. And when he died, in the crash of his private airplane, there was some question whether he died by accident or by carefully concealed design.

The mystery of Mattei's life and death, and of the investigation following the death, is the subject of Francesco Rosi's "The Mattei Affair," co-winner of the Grand Prize last year at Cannes, which opened yesterday at the Little Carnegie Theater. It is a subject not too unlike the life and death of Orson Welles's Charles Foster Kane, or of the famous Sicilian bandit who is the elusive hero of Rosi's own fine early movie, "Salvatore Giuliano" (1961).

Elusiveness was virtually the key to "Salvatore Giuliano," and, in a simple but excellent stylistic stroke, Rosi photographed usually from a distance and from the back. I'm not at all sure that elusiveness is the key to Enrico Mattei, though I think that Rosi rather wishes it were, and is sometimes at a loss in treating a figure so aggressively interested in explaining himself. "The Mattei Affair" seems scrupulously accurate at least to the events of its hero's life, and fairly often—as when Mattei demonstrates an offshore oil-drilling rig or inspects his gas stations or hotels—it resembles an awkwardly dramatized biographical documentary.

But occasionally it comes brilliantly alive. When Mattei battles over an elegant lunch with an American oil magnate, or when, on the last day of his life, he addresses the cheering people of a Sicilian town and then, one by one, each of his associates begs off flying home with him—the "Mattei Affair" suggests the superb movie it does not finally become. Such sequences owe a good deal to the acting talents of Gian Maria Volonte, who complicates the character of Mattei, sometimes refining him, sometimes broadening him, sometimes pushing him into a public-relations caricature of the industrial visionary, which he must also have been.

•

The film's time ranges at will from Mattei's emergence in 1945 to the investigation of his death still continuing in 1970—but it centers on a day in autumn of 1962, as it keeps returning to the field outside Milan where the bits and pieces of its hero are being collected for burial. In themselves these remains are nothing. And as emblems for the life that preceded them and the intrigues that follow, they do not seem to have the power to crystallize Francesco Rosi's potent magic or to vitalize this immensely honorable but unsuccessful movie.

1973 My 21, 40:1

The Cast

A DOLL'S HOUSE, directed by Patrick Garland; screenplay by Christopher Hampton, based on the play by Henrik Ibsen; produced by Hillard Elkins; director of photography, Arthur Ibbetson;

editor, John Glen; music, John Barry; distributed by Paramount Pictures. Running time: 95 minutes. At the Fine Arts Theater, 58th Street near Lexington Avenue. This film has been classified G.

Nora Helmer	Claire Bloom
Torvald Helmer	Anthony Hopkins
Dr. Rank	Sir Ralph Richardson
Kroqstad	Denholm Elliott
Kristine Linde	Anna Massey
Anne-Marie	Dame Edith Evans
Emmy	Stefanie Summerfield
Ivar	Mark Summerfield
Bob	Kimberly Hampton
Old Woman	Daphne Rigg

By VINCENT CANBY

Henrik Ibsen wrote his drama about the liberation of Nora Helmer, "A Doll's House," in 1879. It was first produced in an English translation in London in 1889, and by the time George Bernard Shaw was reviewing a London revival in 1897, he felt compelled to say something to the effect that since we now accept Ibsen's once-radical ideas about women's rights, we can turn our attention to the achievements of the drama itself.

Shaw, who called Ibsen a greater dramatist than Shakespeare, did not want people fussing about the possibility of the play's seeming dated.

Shaw need not have worried. "A Doll's House," according to the new film adaptation that opened yesterday at the Fine Arts, only dates in second-rate productions. This version, starring Claire Bloom in as classic an interpretation as is possible within the limits of film, is not only a first-rate production but also theater of amazing ferocity.

•

The film has its origins in Christopher Hampton's adaptation, which was directed by Patrick Garland and starred Miss Bloom on Broadway two years ago. Except for several brief excursions outside the Helmer house,

which, I suppose, are obligatory in any film adaptation, this production sticks to the original time and text with fidelity.

Mr. Hampton and Mr. Garland, who also directed the film, evidently appreciate the fact that Ibsen, after all, knew what he was doing, and that their job was not to alter, update or rearrange drastically, but to give it the best interpretation that intelligence and a certain amount of money can make possible. There are no desperate attempts to tie-in to contemporary feminist movements, nor is there any use of the sort of contemporary jargon that would—more quickly than anything else perhaps—have made the play into an antique.

The locus of the film remains the comfortably middle-class (and probably overheated) drawing room of the Helmer house, in a small city in Norway over a Christmas weekend. In spite of the excursions outside, the film largely succeeds because (in addition to the fine performances) we experience, along with Nora, the sense of physical confinement, something that comes naturally in a one-set play and is likely to be lost when a one-set play is opened up.

•

The sense of physical confinement is also absolutely necessary if we are to believe the play's theatrical progression, actually a sort of emotional avalanche that overtakes Nora, Saturday's toy wife who becomes Monday's liberated woman. Ibsen's plots are so finely made, and his scenes so tightly constructed, that the slightest tampering can shatter them.

Anthony Hopkins and Claire Bloom

At this point the story of "A Doll's House" is so familiar that I find myself thinking of this production almost as if it were made up of arias and set pieces.

Thus, it seems as if Miss Bloom starts off slowly so as to have heights still to attain in her final confrontation with her husband, Torvald, played by Anthony Hopkins with such decency that the husband is less an unfeeling prig than a sincerely wrong-headed lover.

•

At first simply beautiful and single-mindedly silly, Miss Bloom evolves with the play itself, and with very classy support from among others, Denholm Elliott as the fidgety, not really dishonorable blackmailer, and from Sir Ralph Richardson as Dr. Rank, the family friend who is dying of congenital syphilis. Anna Massey is equally fine in the generally impossible role of confidante to Nora. Dame Edith Evans is as much a symbol of English theater as she is the ancient nurse of Nora, but that's all right too.

My one reservation about the film is also a form of praise: one never forgets for a moment that this is a photographed play. It has to do with the way Mr. Garland uses his camera, cutting back and forth, for example, between a medium close-up of Nora and one of Torvald, in the final scene. The camera too often seems to be meddling in things when it should be content to stand back and let us make up our minds where we want to look next.

1973 My 23, 38:1

The Cast

A WARM DECEMBER, directed by Sidney Poitier; written by Lawrence Roman; director of photography, Paul Beeson; editors, Pembroke Herring and Peter Pitt; music, Coleridge-Taylor Perkinson; produced by Melville Tucker; released by National General Pictures. At the National Theater, Seventh Avenue at 43rd Street and 86th Street East Theater, at Third Avenue. Running Time: 103 minutes. This film is classified PG.

Matt Younger .... Sidney Poitier
Catherine .... Esther Anderson
Stefanie .... Yvette Curtis
Henry Barlow .... George Baker
Myomo .... Johnny Sekka
George Oswandu .... Earl Cameron
Marsha Barlow .... Hillary Crane

By ROGER GREENSPUN

He is tall, masterly, sweet, gentle, and very mysterious. She is tall, masterly, sweet, gentle, elusive, and very mysterious. He is ardent but she is stand-offish: "His love, Her December," as the ads so poetically say. She has a reason; she doesn't look it, but she is going to die. Sidney Poitier's "A Warm December" is the latest in the grand tradition of non-disfiguring incurable-illness movies. But there is a twist. He and she are black, and the illness now is sickle-cell anemia.

You might call it a breakthrough, but then you might call anything a breakthrough. This is merely a breakthrough into a timelier version of the ultimate rare blood disease, but one denied to Bette Davis and Ali MacGraw and all other fading ladies until now. The real reasons for "A Warm December" (besides a good cry) are kindness to children, homely virtues, sentimental sex, touristy travel and unforgettable personality. It is like opening some impossibly typical transcendentally awful issue of Reader's Digest.

•

Poitier directs himself as Matt Younger, an American in London, and Esther Anderson as Catherine, a beautiful African in London, strangely meeting with Arabs, Israelis, Russians, Chinese, fierce-seeming black men with tribal markings and a collection of very proper middle-aged Englishmen.

Matt has come to England to relax and race his motorbike and show his daughter Stefanie (and us) some of the sights. Catherine is there with her uncle the ambassador. She too is an ambassador of sorts, but she has a secret — which I've mentioned. Matt also has a secret — which I won't mention except to note that it begins by seeming as serious as Watergate and ends by looking like an international conspiracy to feed free lollipops to kids.

Everything in "A Warm December" tends toward the ordinary. Free at last to do what she wishes, Catherine cries "May I cook? — and wash dishes, and make beds, and fuss around with Stefanie . . ." so as not to waste her precious hours any more on mere champagne and caviar.

For the romance in this game Sidney Poitier, now almost 50 years old, is a little past his prime. It seems especially cruel that he, such a good actor, should suffer one of his silliest roles in his own movie. Miss Anderson, a strikingly beautiful woman who wears clothes as if she were the reason they matter. How she might do if given the opportunity I cannot say. But she is rather breath-taking at rising above the lack of opportunity in this movie, and she is clearly an actress to watch.

"A Warm December" opened yesterday at the National and 86th Street East theaters.

1973 My 24, 53:1

The Cast

PAT GARRETT AND BILLY THE KID, directed by Sam Peckinpah; screenplay by Rudolf Wurlitzer; produced by Gordon Carroll; director of photography, John Coquillon; editors, Roger Spottiswoode, Garth Craven, Robert L. Wolfe, Richard Halsey, David Berlatsky and Tony de Zarraga; music, Bob

Kris Kristofferson, left, and James Coburn

Dylan; distributed by Metro-Goldwyn-Mayer. Running time: 106 minutes. At the New Embassy 46th Street Theater, Broadway at 46th Street, East 59th Street 1 and 2 Theaters, 59th Street near Third Avenue, and Loews 83d Street theater, Broadway at 83d Street. This film has been classified R.

Pat Garrett .... James Coburn
Billy the Kid .... Kris Kristofferson
Sheriff Kip McKinney .... Richard Jaeckel
Mrs. Baker .... Katy Jurado
Lemuel .... Chill Wills
Governor Wallace .... Jason Robards
Alias .... Bob Dylan
Alamosa Bill .... Jack Elam
Paco .... Emilio Fernandez
Sheriff Baker .... Slim Pickens
Cody .... Elisha Cook
Mr. Horrell .... Gene Evans

By VINCENT CANBY

The passage of time often means something more than the mere annoyance of wrinkles and baldness. It can result in mortgage foreclosures, the exhaustion of love and total physical and mental decay. There is, however, a limit to the number of occasions it can be effectively invoked to excuse the wobbly if violent melodrama in Sam Peckinpah's new film, "Pat Garrett and Billy the Kid."

"Us old boys ought not to be doing this to each other," an aging outlaw says during a barroom gunfight with Pat Garrett, the desperado turned lawman. The outlaw then adds: "There aren't too many of us left." Someone else later observes that "the time for outlaws and drifters is over."

•

The time is 1881 and, at least according to Peckinpah's "The Wild Bunch," there were outlaws and drifters still carrying on as late as 1913. This is not terribly important in itself, only to emphasize the surprising phoniness of his new endeavor, which sounds like an album called "The Worst of Bob Dylan." Mr. Dylan not only appears in the film, sort of hesitantly, as a retarded hanger-on to Billy the Kid but he also wrote and sings the soundtrack score, which does not include "The Times They Are a-Changin'." The music is so oppressive that when it stops we feel giddy with relief, as if a tooth had suddenly stopped aching.

Peckinpah has recently directed some fine films ("The Wild Bunch," "The Ballad of Cable Hogue," "Junior Bonner") and some not so fine ("Straw Dogs," "The Getaway"). The mushy pretensions of "Pat Garrett and Billy the Kid" suggest either that he has begun to take talk about his genius too seriously (it can happen to the best) or that he has fallen in with bad company.

I prefer to believe the latter, though it's impossible to know who the bad company might be. The editors? No fewer than six names are credited with having cut the film. More probably it's the screenwriter, Rudolf Wurlitzer, the novelist whose first screenplay, "Two Lane Blacktop," was judged to be so perfect that Esquire magazine nominated the film as the movie of 1971 when the year had got only to April.

•

"Pat Garrett and Billy the Kid" has the manner of something written for Peckinpah by a writer who'd seen "The Wild Bunch" and vowed to give the director an important script, something worthy of his talents. Instead, Mr. Wurlitzer has come up with what is apparently an unconscious parody of the Peckinpah concerns for fading frontiers, comradeship and machismo.

In outline the story is not bad. It's about the search undertaken by Sheriff Pat Garrett (James Coburn) for his long-time saddlemate and best friend, Billy the Kid (Kris Kristofferson). Pat is getting old and wants to live to a good age, but Billy is only 21, which raises questions about how old Billy was when they started riding together. Fourteen?

What's worse, they talk like an endangered species, such as the whooping crane. "It feels like times have changed," Pat says to Billy when he warns his friend he's becoming a sheriff. "Times," says Billy, "not me." Lines like these pretty much define the scope of the performances of Coburn and Kristofferson.

There are a few, good, eccentric moments in the film, such as Billy's escape from the Lincoln jail in New Mexico and an encounter between Pat Garrett and another sheriff (Slim Pickens), who wants to survive only long enough to get out of the territory.

There also are a lot of very good actors in the cast, including Richard Jaeckel, Chill Wills and Jason Robards, who plays Lew Wallace, then Governor of New Mexico and a recent author ("Ben-Hur").

The film is mostly a bloody mess of card games, gunfights and camaraderie, so peculiarly edited that it is difficult to follow a story that is a good deal less complex than "Remembrance of Things Past." This universe is so out-of-order that even the gunfights seem mysterious: there is no real relationship between how a man aims his gun and who he hits.

1973 My 24, 53:1

The Cast

EMPEROR OF THE NORTH POLE, directed by Robert Aldrich; screenplay by Christopher Knopf; executive producer, Kenneth Hyman; producer, Stan Hough; director of photography, Joe Biroc; editor, Michael Luciano; music, Frank De Vol; released by 20th Century-Fox. Running time: 120 minutes. At the Rivoli Theater, Broadway at 49th Street, and the Columbia 1 Theater, Second Avenue at 64th Street. This film has been rated PG.

A-No. 1 .... Lee Marvin
The Shack .... Ernest Borgnine
Cigaret .... Keith Carradine
Cracker .... Charles Tyner
Hogger .... Malcolm Atterbury
Policeman .... Simon Oakland
Coaly .... Harry Caesar

By VINCENT CANBY

Robert Aldrich's "Emperor of the North Pole" is a fine, elaborately staged action melodrama set mostly on the freight trains and in the hobo jungles of the American Northwest during the Great Depression.

It's about bindle stiffs and tramps and a psychotic trainman named The Shack, a man who keeps order with a chain in one hand and a hammer in the other, thus becoming known, not surprisingly, as "the meanest conductor alive." To those of you who have always thought of conductors as a docile breed—their worst fault being an occasional inaudibility when coming into East Hampton (or was that Amagansett?)—the film will be an exposé not without its silly moments. I admit I found it most entertaining.

"Emperor of the North Pole" is a king-of-the-hill movie. It sees all life in terms of physical self-assertion, in terms of beating the other guy, not because there is anything valuable to win, but rather because if you don't win you lose, and when you lose, you're nothing. Absolute zero. It is a game a lot of small boys play all their lives. It is also one that's been overloaded with metaphysical associations in fiction romanticizing mountain climbing, bull fighting, boxing and big-game hunting, but never, as far as I can remember, the bumming of freights.

•

Christopher Knopf, who wrote the original screenplay, is not without his impulses to set "Emperor of the North Pole" in a larger, more meaningful context, but usually he resists them. More important, he has created almost perfect action-movie characters, people who can't bore us with their earlier histories because they don't have any. They exist solely within the time and the action of the film itself. When it stops, they vanish, but we have had a sensational ride.

With his last film, "Ulzana's Raid," and this new one, Aldrich clinches a claim to being the best director of this kind of film now at work. This is not because he plays down to a lower class of film but because he takes it seriously enough to get splendid performances from his actors and to stage the action sequences with a dizzying vividness and accuracy. Compare the technical proficiency of the various fights that Aldrich has staged here, a lot of them aboard moving freight cars, with the lethargic, dumbly bloody gunfights in Sam Peckinpah's "Pat Garrett and Billy the Kid." It's no contest.

Boiled down to its irreducible minimum, which is not difficult, the story of "Emperor of the North Pole" is about the vow of A-No. 1 (Lee Marvin), a jaunty, aging hobo, acknowledged by his peers to be the champion of champions, to ride the freight captained (or conductored) by The Shack (Ernest Borgnine), from somewhere or other to Eugene, Ore. Nobody has ever successfully freeloaded The Shack's train and, indeed, even before the title credits, we are treated to the sight of one of The Shack's hobo victims.

•

The suspense of the film (which is so hugely violent that its PG rating is a mystery), is unrelenting and the performances first-rate, including that of Keith Carradine, a son of John, as a loudmouth kid to whom Marvin tries to teach the rules of the road. The only ludicrous thing in the film is a song sung behind the credits. It tells us, if my notes do not deceive me, that "a train's not a man, and a man's not a train, for a man can do things a train never can."

1973 My 25, 23:1

The Cast

HAPPINESS, a silent film written and directed by Alexander Medvedkin; photographed by Gleb Trolanski; music by Modest Mussorgsky; produced by Moskino Kombinat; presented by New Yorker Films, at the First Avenue Screening Room, at 61st Street. Running time 70 minutes. This film has not been classified at this time.
Khmyr .... Piotr Zinoviev
Anna .... Elena Egorova

By ROGER GREENSPUN

Alexander Medvedkin, born in 1900, occupies a minor place in the history of Russian cinema, mainly for the production of documentary and propaganda films, beginning in 1927 and extending into the nineteen-seventies. Roger Manvell's International Encyclopedia of Film credits Medvedkin with three features, all made in the thirties. The earliest of these, "Happiness," opened yesterday at the First Avenue Screening Room.

The film's very existence became general knowledge only two years ago, when it had its premiere in Paris. The present version carries French titles translated into English (though made in 1934, "Happiness" is silent) and a musical sound track given it in France.

"Happiness" is a comedy, and it owes a good deal to the techniques of American silent film comedy, especially Chaplin, whom it quite openly imitates. But it is also a very Russian movie, and its story of a poor peasant farmer who sets out to find happiness and instead finds a purse full of money and all the attendant troubles, could, at least to begin with, be outright folk tale. But before it is over it has passed through the exigencies of at least one four-year plan, and many complications have been introduced into the plot, by no means for the best.

The peasant, Khmyr, has a little farm, a stalwart wife, Anna, a stubborn polkadotted horse, and a host of greedy enemies. These include the Church, the state (old order), the military, the aristocracy, and all the forces of capitalistic nonproduction. A kulak, a rich peasant, guides these enemies, and he survives, a figure of more than natural power, into a new order that sees evil brought low and the peasantry triumphant—though at the price of eternal vigilance. Somehow Khmyr doesn't make the transition. The education of Khmyr, sometimes a charmingly slapstick education, is the action of the movie.

•

There are a number of pleasant conceits in "Happiness" — magic food that finds its own way into your mouth (a gift that enables the kulak to eat not only well but also effortlessly), a walking granary, the polkadotted horse whose mind is its own and is better than its master's. But even the pleasantest conceits turn out to be better in theory than in practice, and too often the film suffers for its willingness to subordinate comic ideas to political ideology. In a movie that starts out with the philosophic question "What is happiness?" it seems more than a disappointment to discover that happiness may be driving a tractor on a collective farm.

Like so many Russian films, "Happiness" is visually stylish and inventive. It is never especially funny, though it is rather moving in its will to be funny. Its premiere is valuable enough for adding to our knowledge of a great national cinema.

1973 My 25, 24:1

The Cast

LET THE GOOD TIMES ROLL, directed by Sid Levin and Robert Abel; director of photography, Robert Thomas; executive producer, Charles Fries; produced by Gerald I. Isenberg; supervising film editor, Sid Levin; a Metromedia Producers Corporation Production; a Cinema Associates Film; a Richard Nader Production; a Columbia Pictures release. At Loew's State I, Broadway and 45th Street and Loew's Tower East, 72d Street and Third Avenue. Running time* 99 minutes. This film is classified PG.
WITH Chuck Berry, Little Richard, Fats Domino, Chubby Checker, Bo Diddley, the Shirelles, the Five Satins, the Coasters, Danny and the Juniors, the Bobby Comstock Rock and Roll Band, Bill Haley and the Comets and Richard Nader.

By VINCENT CANBY

"Let the Good Times Roll" is an engaging, technically superior concert film that recalls music of the nineteen-fifties, mostly through two recent concerts in Detroit and New York that featured some of the stars of the fifties who have survived into the seventies. The style of the film is world's-fair avant garde: lots of split-screen stuff that allows us to see what the stars looked like then, alongside what they look like now.

In its noisy and frantic way, "Let the Good Times Roll" is most reassuring. Hair is longer if sometimes thinner, sideburns have sprouted and waistbands have gotten wider. Little Richard has openly embraced androgyny. Yet time has been largely kind to Bo Diddley, Chuck Berry, Bill Haley, Fats Domino, the Shirelles and the others, none of whom have probably been recorded on film to better advantage.

•

Sid Levin and Robert Abel, who directed the movie, have a good deal of fun associating musical numbers with people and events of the fifties. Thus as Danny and the Juniors are giving us a replay of "At the Hop" or Chuck Berry is doing "Maybellene," another part of the screen may be reminding us of Elvis, of Castro, of James Dean, of Jonas Salk, of "I Was a Teen-Age Werewolf" or of the Eddie-to-Debbie-to-Lizz parlay.

It doesn't go very deep,

and if you didn't know there had been a Korean war, "Let the Good Times Roll" wouldn't tell you. The film also contains some (what I take to be) unintentional social comment. The members of the audiences at the recent concerts—who appear to be 99 per cent white—give the black-power salute to the performers, most of whom are black. The lack of blacks in the audiences seems to suggest that there are no black memories of the nineteen-fifties, although black performers were stars.

•

The music of the decade, which marked the emergence of rock as a true pop form, is less interesting in itself (at least, as reflected by the film), than for the liberating effect it had on the music and the performers who followed in the sixties. If it hadn't been for the fifties, there probably would have been no Beatles, no Stones, no Grateful Dead. We might still be seeing strangers across crowded rooms on enchanted evenings and wondering if there wasn't more to music and to life in general.

1973 My 26, 18:1

'This Is Cinerama' Returns, but Not Quite

"This Is Cinerama," the first of five hugely successful Cinerama travelogue features originally opened at the Broadway Theater in New York on Sept. 30, 1952. It has now returned to the Ziegfeld Theater in New York with ads proclaiming: "The last time you saw a show like this one, it was this one!" Not quite.

The original Cinerama process was a variation on the three - negative Polyvision process used by Abel Gance in 1927 for parts of his spectacular film, "Napoleon." Cinerama then employed three interlocking 35 - mm projectors to throw a single panoramic image onto a deeply curved screen. The resulting pictures, only slightly

marred by the lines where the negatives overlapped, were of amazing clarity and brilliance. The width and depth of the screen also provided a heightened sense of audience participation, fully exploited in the first Cinerama program by such marvelous gimmicks as putting the cameras on a roller coaster and in airplanes.

The program now at the Ziegfeld is the same "This Is Cinerama" we first saw. The screen still is deeply curved but a large portion of the pictorial quality has been lost. The three 35-mm. negatives have been squeezed onto a single 70-mm. negative. The lines are still there, but image definition is often poor, as is the color quality in certain sequences. At the performance I attended, even the multitrack, magnetic sound system often had a small, tiny ring, although I'm told it's virtually the same sound system originally used.

The contents of the film are, as they always were, pure camp, especially the visit to Cypress Gardens and a sequence featuring the Vienna Boys Choir ("The lads have just been rounded up hastily —from games in backyards," Lowell Thomas, the host-narrator, tells us without too much conviction.)

People who remember the original presentation will be disappointed, but small uncritical children should still get a kick out of the roller coaster and airplane sequences.

VINCENT CANBY.

1973 My 25, 25:1

The Program

VAMPIR, a film by Pedro Portabella, photography, Manuel Esteban; a Films 59 Production; distributed by Roninfilm. At the Film Forum Theater, 256 West 88th Street. Running time: 75 minutes. This film has not been classified.
WITH Christopher Lee, Herbert Lom, Soledad Miranda, Klaus Kinsky, Jack Taylor, Maria Rohm and Fred Williams.

By ROGER GREENSPUN

Slowly the brides of Dracula rise from their coffins. Their long hair flowing, diaphanous gowns scarcely concealing the soft contours of their bodies, they advance. Over the cold stone castle floor they glide. Past massive arches, gothic windows, between rows of arc-lights, through mazes of cables, before a tracking camera they move into what is certainly the strangest — and one of the best — vampire movies in recent years.

Not quite a vampire movie; a movie upon a vampire movie. Pedro Portabella made his "Vampir" on the sets and locations, essentially in the midst of the filming of "The Nights of Dracula," a real vampire movie by Jesus Franco. Filmed in Spain in 1971, with a cast led by Christopher Lee and Herbert

Lom, "The Nights of Dracula" purports to be a fairly accurate adaptation of the Bram Stoker novel.

It will be released here under the title "Count Dracula," and it may be worth seeing. "Vampir" isn't an accurate adaptation of anything — except, perhaps, its own moods — and is so distinctly worth seeing as to be almost mandatory, for anyone who fancies the material.

"Vampir" plays with that material and complicates and redefines it. Thus we see

Count Dracula pause to joke with the camera crew (Portabella's camera crew) before lying back on his ancestral earth, where he will be safe against the coming daylight. But not long before we have seen a fog machine slither through the underbrush, transforming a Spanish forest into Transylvanian fantasy by an act that is more lovely and more unsettling than the final effect it produces. "Vampir" is not a scary movie. But it is serious in a way that is not inconsistent with rational good humor — a seriousness that has always been among the usually unrealized) potentials of the horror film.

Portabella is engaged not in a documentary so much as in a meditation upon the act of film-making. His people—Jonathan Harker, Mina Murray and the others — are both more and less than their characters, and his sets are never more mysterious than when being revealed as canvas flats behind the ancient moss-grown facades. There is no speech except a brief account of Dracula's death, read by Christopher Lee near the end, and natural noises — creaking doors, crashing thunder, and the like — become, by unnatural repetition, a kind of patterned sound beyond the needs of any drama.

In one sequence, Professor Van Helsing (Herbert Lom) alone in his study feverishly pores over tomes of vampire lore, while elsewhere at the same time upon the soft white neck of Lucy Westenra appear the ominous twin puncture marks — fashioned by a team of make-up men. Movies have always lived by the desirable confusion of illusion and reality, and "Vampir" begins an exploration, and an appreciation, of the basic elements in that confusion.

"Vampir" opened yesterday at the Film Forum.

1973 My 26, 27:1

GIRLS ARE FOR LOVING, directed and written by Don Schain; director of photography, Howard Block; music by Continental Distributing. At the DeMille Theater, Broadway and 47th Street. Running time: 95 minutes. This film has not been classified.
Ginger McCallister..........Cheri Caffaro
Clay Bowers...............Timothy Brown
Ronnie St. Clair...........Jocelyn Peters
James L. Whitney 3d.....Scott Ellsworth
William Henderson.......Fred Vincent
Mateo.................Robert C. Jefferson

"Girls Are for Loving" is the third awful soft-core porn film made by Don Schain about Ginger McCallister (Cheri Caffaro), an F.B.I. person who, in spite of a good figure, a lot of eye make-up and a fondness for bikinis, comes across as only slightly less butch than other F.B.I. persons. The story is about a blackmail plot involving international trade secrets, and it takes place on slopes in the Catskills and the Virgin Islands, whose police, the film reveals, use electric shock torture, apparently legally.

Miss Caffaro sings and dances, which is a mistake, and tries to pronounce the word sensuous, which is difficult since she recites so many of her lines through clenched teeth.

VINCENT CANBY.

1973 My 26, 19:1

The Cast

SWEET JESUS, PREACHER MAN, directed by Henning Schellerup; screenplay by John Cerullo, M. Stuart Madden and Abbey Leitch; director of photography, Paul E. Hipp; music by Robert G. Orpin; produced by Ralph T. Desiderio; released by Continental Distributing. At the DeMille Theater, Broadway and 47th Street. Running time, 95 minues. This film has not been classified.
Holmes Lee..............Roger E. Mosley
Martelli................William Smith
State Senator Sills.......Michael Pataki
Eddie Stoner............Tom Johnigarn
Joey.....................Joe Tornatore
Sweetstick...............Damu King
Beverly Solomon..........Mark Gibbs
Deacon Greene............Sam Laws

As the latest black-accented, shoot-'em-up adventure, "Sweet Jesus, Preacher Man," which opened at local houses yesterday, has two unusual, if decidedly dubious, attributes. Its tough, black killer-hero hides behind the cloth and the pulpit to ply his bloody business and neither the whites nor the blacks involved receive or are worth much sympathy.

Roger E. Mosley, the largely glum, if unflappable, muscular "hit man" and "preacher" here, is working for the white, Los Angeles gang chief (William Smith) to control his rackets and the white state senatorial candidate (Michael Pataki). But our "Preacher Man" soon learns there's millions, not thousands, to be snatched, if he double-crosses his boss and takes over that proposed urban redevelopment program.

The staccato, colloquial and often four-letter dialogue as well as Henning Schellerup's uninspired direction, concentrate on obvious fights, militants, chases and bloodletting, rather than on the implied injustices, such as the murder of a couple of innocent black youngsters by a pair of trigger-happy white cops.

The cast is, for the most part, kept too busy dodging either white or black gangs to register any appreciable emotion other than occasional anger. As both the hit man Holmes and "Preacher Man" Lee, Mr. Mosley, may be given minor credit for being a blatantly venal type who displays a cool superiority toward both the black and white establishments. "The Lord giveth and he also can taketh away," he cynically quips as he rakes in some spoils. But "Sweet Jesus, Preacher Man," like some previous entries in this gory genre such as "Trouble Man" and "Black Gunn," has very little to give.

A. H. WEILER.

1973 My 26, 27:2

FILM PRIZES GIVEN AT HILTON FETE

Nontheatrical Festival Hails 'Three Robbers,' Cartoon

Prize winners of the 15th annual American Film Festival were announced last night at the closing banquet of the five-day assembly at the New York Hilton Hotel. Winners were selected from 36 categories with more than 250 entries. The festival is sponsored by the Educational Film Library Association.

The Emily Award, named for the festival founder, Emily Jones, was given to the highest rated movie, "The Three Robbers," an animated children's film.

"Watersmith," was cited in the experimental category. "Tidikawa and Friends," a documentary on New Guinea, won in the category of anthropology and ethnology. "To Be Young, Gifted and Black," a television feature on the late playwright Lorraine Hansberry, won in the performing arts category.

Among the other winners were "It's Your Heart" (Physical Health), "Tokyo—the 51st Volcano" (Technology and Society), "About Sex" (Sex Education) and "New View of Space" (Science).

The John Grierson Award, a $500 prize for young documentary film makers, went to Martha Coolidge for "David: Off and On."

1973 My 27, 37:1

CANNES VOTE CAST FOR ACTORS, LOVE

'Scarecrow' and 'Hireling' Cited for Stars, Themes

Special to The New York Times
CANNES, France, May 26— One of the winners at this year's Cannes Film Festival was titled, "Film of Love and Anarchy."

And in the best movie tradition, the festival that ended Thursday chose love.

The festival jury, with Ingrid Bergman presiding, awarded its grand prix to "Scarecrow" from the United States, and "The Hireling" from Britain. Both deal with types of love peculiar to their respective countries.

In these and most of their other selections, the jury seemed to favor modest success over ambition, personalities over politics, sentiment over satire, feeling over form, smugness over audacity—and,

indeed, actors over directors. The official acting prizes went to Joanne Woodward for "The effects of Gamma Rays on Man-in-the-Moon Marigolds" (directed by her husband, Paul Newman) and to Giancarlo Giannini for his performance as the would-be-assassin of Mussollini in the Italian "Film of Love and Anarchy" (directed by Lina Wertmuller).

The jury also cited for outstanding performances Gene Hackman and Al Pacino for "Scarecrow" (directed by Jerry Schatzberg) and Sarah Miles "The Hireling" (directed by Alan Bridges).

There was no prize for best director.

Other major awards were the following:

Grand Jury prize: "The Mother and The Whore" ("La Mamam et la Putain"), written and directed by Jean Eustache.

Special Jury prize: "The Wild Planet" ("La Planète Sauvage"), an animated film by Roland Topor and René Laloux.

Best First film: "Jeremy," written and directed by the American documentarist Arthur Barron.

Best Short Subject: "Balablok," a Canadian animated film by Bretislav Pojar.

Special Jury Award for Short Subject: "1812," a collage film by the Hungarian animator Sandor Reisenbuchler.

The awards covered only a small number of the 24 features in competition. Others, such as François Truffaut's "La Nuit Americaine," Joseph Losey's "A Doll's House" and Alejandro Jodorowsky's "The Holy Mountain," were shown out of competition to enthusiastic reaction.

1973 My 27, 37:3

This Is Cinerama —Or Is It?

By VINCENT CANBY

"THIS IS CINERAMA," the first feature program in what was once a giant, three-negative film process, has returned to New York where it originally opened Sept. 30, 1952, becoming such an immediate box-office hit that it made Wall Street investors careless with their money and prompted Hollywood technicians, who hadn't been very busy since receiving sound, to take another look at what God (and His representatives on earth) had wrought.

However, the film that is now playing at the Ziegfeld Theater is not quite the same "This Is Cinerama" that caused the sensation at the Broadway Theater 20 years ago. The program itself is the same — including the roller coaster ride, the snatch of a performance of Handel's "Messiah" by the Long Island Choral Society, the sightseeing in Edinburgh, Venice and Cypress Gardens, and the climactic air tour of the United States, all more or less chaperoned by Lowell Thomas (on screen and soundtrack) in a fashion that lays more stress on the cheeriness of existence in Mr. Thomas's America than on real facts. "Crater Lake!," Mr. Thomas exclaims as the Cinerama plane flies over the deepest lake in North America. "Its bottom has never been found!" (Its bottom must have been found by somebody since the Encyclopedia Britannica says Crater Lake, Ore., is 1,932 feet deep, while the Americana says it's 1,983 feet deep.)

What has happened to the Cinerama process in two decades is a kind of technological equivalent to what's happened to certain aspects of American living. In many ways it's become simpler, but it's also become a little shabbier. Cinerama has been perfected and perfected and perfected until it's become something less than it first was in the early 1950s, when lots of people expected it to revolutionize movies. After all that original hubbub, which prompted the introduction of now-almost-forgotten processes like CinemaScope and VistaVision, movies are somewhat better visually and aurally, and they are certainly wider, but that's about all.

The original Cinerama process, invented by Fred Waller and first used by the United States armed forces to instruct aerial gunners during World War II, involved the use of three interlocking projectors projecting three separate 35-mm film strips onto a deeply curved screen covering an arc of 146 degrees. As long as the process made use of three different negatives, the resulting picture was always slightly marred by lines where the images overlapped, and by a color imbalance among the three images, but it provided a brilliance of image definition never matched before or since, as well as a remarkable sense of audience participation because of the effect on our peripheral vision.

This Cinerama process was a gimmick, and a marvelous gimmick, one that returned movies to what they are by that original definition: movies. Movies needn't always be movies. They can also be films, film or, at their intellectually fanciest, cinema, but movies also are important, not as literature, but as vicarious thrills, allowing us to experience sensations that we can otherwise safely experience only in dreams.

"This Is Cinerama" and the four subsequent Cinerama features released through 1958 were all basically journalism of a sort that would look square even in the pages of the National Geographic. As travelogues, however, they were superb. When we flew into Cairo in "Seven Wonders of the World" (1956), we saw Cairo as we'd never be able to see it on a commercial flight (unless we were in the pilot's cabin) and certainly not as we'd see it in a conventional film.

In one panoramic sweep of amazing clarity, we saw not a blur of a portion of a city, but the relationship of the entire city to the Nile, to the pyramids at Giza, to the great desert itself, which just suddenly begins were the irrigated green ends.

In these three-panel Cinerama films, we landed jet fighters aboard aircraft carriers, shot rapids in India, and bobsledded down Alps in Switzerland. They were immense fun even when Mr. Thomas might be droning on about "the sublime mysteries" of one Asian temple or another, or preparing us for a "great scoop," the Milan Opera's presentation of the triumphal march from "Aida" (which turns out to look a good deal like the opening of New York's Festival of San Gennaro with a slightly oriental flavor).

The three-panel Cinerama films were expensive to shoot and expensive to show, and the two attempts to make conventional narrative films in the process—"The Wonderful World of The Brothers Grimm" (1962) and "How The West Was Won" (1963) —quickly proved that three panels were two too many, and that the huge screen had the effect of inhibiting a narrative instead of enhancing it.

After a certain amount of work, Cinerama came up with a single-negative process, in fact a single-strip, 70-mm process, which is better, more flexible for story-telling, but never can compete with the definition and clarity of the pictures provided by three 35-mm images locked together.

The version of "This Is Cinerama" at the Ziegfeld currently is the original three-negatives printed down to fit into a 70-mm frame. The

lines (which never really bothered me) are still there, but the picture and color quality have deteriorated to such an extent that the movie sometimes doesn't look as clear as an ordinary 35-mm picture. Indeed, at the presentation I attended last week, even that portion of the film in which Mr. Thomas is introduced in 35-mm black-and-white looks to have been shot about the same time as those portions of "The Great Train Robbery" he shows us. It also seems as if a certain amount of important pictorial information at either side of the screen has been chopped off, Equally important (or disappointing) was the quality of the sound in much of the presentation.

One of the most innovative aspects of the original Cinerama show was its introduction of seven-track magnetic sound ("we call it— 'stereophonic sound,'" Mr. Thomas says portentously, and the long-stereo-oriented audience at the Ziegfeld laughs). There are speakers in the auditorium at the Ziegfeld, but the quality of sound reproduction behind the screen sometimes seemed surprisingly tinny.

*

There were other unintentional laughs at the performance I saw. Early in the film, Mr. Thomas tries to explain persistence-of-vision. "If it were not possible," he says, "the movie you are looking at would only be a

blur." Which, at that point, it was.

The passage of time has not been kind to Mr. Thomas's narration. When the Cinerama plane flies over Washington and he says something patriotic about the Pentagon, the audience boos. It then cheers wildly when he introduces the concluding section of the film with the once-innocent line: "Now for a climax! A culmination!"

A lower order of fakery has replaced the beautiful illusion of the original presentation. The Ziegfeld has no real curtains to mask the screen, and instead projects the image of a curtain on the screen at the beginning of the show and between the

acts.

Even with these imperfections, especially the poor picture quality, the show does offer a greater sense of audience participation (if you sit in the center of the orchestra) than you'll probably get in most other movies these days. At the end of the show's first half, just after the Milan Opera's presentation of the march from "Aida," when the word "Intermission" was flashed on the screen, a woman sitting in front of me turned to her husband and asked: "Is that for them or us?"

1973 My 27, II:1:1

'If We Understood Bergman, We'd Stone Him'

By RONALD FRIEDLAND

WE see John Schlesinger's "Sunday Bloody Sunday" and we know it is a good film. Its miseries are clear, inescapable, familiar. We see it a second and third time and it holds up. Still, there is a revealing flaw. In a world of motives, the motiveless young man, who is loved by both a divorcée and a middle-aged bachelor, seems a mere construction. He is too artificially placed in the center as a device allowing the others to react. He is given a veneer of ambition, but this doesn't sufficiently account for his lack of commitment. We ask, why do these people do these things? And we expect an answer.

We see Peter Bogdanovich's "The Last Picture Show" and we sense an honest pathos. There is a dry, gritty truth to the movie. But it falters characteristically at the end. The retarded boy is run over by a truck. The insensitive men of the small Texas town, conditioned by their class and nation, crowd around angrily, unmoved by the boy's death. We know this situation isn't truthful. The picture has stiffened into political caricature. The reaction of the men is too patly fascistic, too predictable, too easily judged and dismissed.

Still, there is Sam, a good man who manages to retain his humanity in a world that refuses to acknowledge value. The pool hall which he owns is his immediately identifiable symbol. It provides temporary comfort, allows communion of a sort. When he

wills it to Sonny, along with his vision of charity, we recognize the customary use of symbol and theme.

Yet there is the itch of sentimentality here, as with the final scenes of "Sunday Bloody Sunday." Although the characters are original enough, the form and the behavioral concepts are familiar. They elicit the usual response from us. We leave the theater disturbed, but also in some way satisfied. These movies do not jar us.

These are sociological, psychological films. We are what we are because of our society, because of the history of our relationships from birth. Change the society, seek psychiatric help, and we can realize what we really are. In these movies, virtually every character has an explanatory context. Peter Finch, in "Sunday Bloody Sunday," has a domineering, middle-class Jewish mother and a weak father; Glenda Jackson has been shaped by fear of her father's rejection, has anxieties about her role as a woman.

It is all real and believable. Such films handle things which are ordinary but complex as well. They do not go any further.

*

There is another film, Ingmar Bergman's "Cries and Whispers," which defines the others. When we see it, we know we are in another dimension, the dimension of myth. Bergman knows that the specific society makes no difference. Money, furniture,

servants, life in the woods, on the farm, in a Marxist utopia, cannot solve the loneness and doubt fostered by death. Psychology cannot help here. Bergman's film, like "Sunday Bloody Sunday" and "The Last Picture Show," appears to be realistic. It attends to words and gestures and the surface patterns of life. But Bergman deliberately misuses the traditional techniques of representation. His realism is of another kind. Kafka's castle and courtroom are also minutely drawn, a perfect photograph of hell. Beckett's rooms and forests are excruciatingly detailed, authentic portraits of indescribable despair.

Bergman employs, but contradicts, the usual language of story. There are flashbacks. We are used to the device. Karin is having dinner with her husband. Their marriage is sterile, banal, a charade. The scene appears to be a memory of what really happened. Karin tips over a glass and it shatters. She plays with a fragment of the glass and carries it to her bedroom. We have a recognizable symbol. Her marriage is shattered. Her life, as well. We register the meaning and file it away.

*

But that sharp piece of glass continues to bother us. Karin may cut herself, but we sense this possibility doesn't really account for our fear. The jagged edge will cut something, but it will cut deeper than we can endure. It terrifies us in an unfamiliar

way. When Karin finally thrusts the broken glass deep within herself, then goes to her husband and smears her most intimate blood across her face in a gesture of ultimate negation, we know this is not a flashback. This memory does not come from biography, but from a more primal place, beyond sociology, beyond the psychoanalytic.

The allegory of the visit of the two sisters and the servant Anna to the dead Agnes also resembles what we have seen before. A conventional dream-fantasy, the test of love which Agnes herself will win. We can interpret this seemingly straightforward literary method in the usual manner—until the final frame is held: Agnes caught curled like a child in Anna's arms. It is the power of love. A lesser artist than Bergman would leave it at that. It completes the allegorical meaning.

But something frightening, dissonant, disrupts that familiar concept. Anna is maternal, protective; but there is also something dreadful in her possessiveness. Anna wants Agnes dead. She wills it. Only in death can there be perfect love. And if that is the desire of love, what is left to any of us?

In the final scene, we see Anna reading through Agnes' diary. Again, we are tempted to apply the usual interpretation. Anna has been offered any item of Agnes' she wants. But, with apparent selflessness, she refuses anything of value. Her choice of the diary at first seems appropriate because it fits our definition of love.

Bergman knows that the choice is maudlin and sentimental. He takes such sentiment and dissects it. This is not the ordinary scene of the beloved recalled by the lover. Anna has become Agnes. In possessing her diary, she possesses—now with absolute control — that woman's life. The essence of Anna's concern is her own empty existence which must be filled, even at the expense of the loved one. Agnes dead is the perfect fulfillment.

＊

We assume "Cries and Whispers" has come full circle. The only person who can truly understand Agnes' message of happiness is Anna, the one who has sacrificed unselfishly for her. As the diary is read, we listen to Agnes' final declaration. It is uplifting. Agnes sees joy where her sisters cannot. Through her suffering, she finds a peace unknown to the more beautiful and exuberantly healthy.

Another filmmaker would leave it at that. Bergman does not. Anna's deathly use of Agnes' banal joy reveals it for what it is. It is, like Anna's Bible, what she needs to believe. What we all need to believe, because we cannot support anything more.

The ending is not happy. It is perhaps the most despairing, the most arid conclusion to any film. Bergman offers a grim choice: Agnes' sentimental, self-deceiving happiness, fed by her immense self-concern, her parisitic use of the others, or Anna's supreme triumph, a static exploitation of another's death.

Ultimately, "Sunday Bloody Sunday" and "The Last Picture Show" are comforting. Not because their people learn to accept despair, but because their despair is so familiar. We accept it too easily. We have seen it in the same form so many times before. It disturbs us but passes away.

Bergman refuses to give such comfort. If we were to recognize Bergman's work for what it is, what it forces us to see, we would stone him, drive him away with howls of execration. Perhaps the only proper review of "Cries and Whispers" is silence.

1973 My 27, II:11:1

The Cast

By VINCENT CANBY

The skies are cloudless and serene. The sense of timeless-

ness is disturbed but not shattered by the noise of an occasional jet fighter plane en route to some unknown destination. Below, in a tiny Bavarian farming community, there flourishes a kind of primal, interlocking cruelty that has no connection with time.

The village idiot boy, unloved by his mother ("dumbness is more expensive than college," she says), beats up smaller children. An old man with a wooden leg, ostracized by the pious villagers for his liaison with a widow, seduces the village whore but will not pay her the amount due. An exhausted drudge of a mother, a field worker from sunup to sundown, refuses to acknowledge her homosexual son who, in his turn, refuses to acknowledge that he's the father of the village whore's expected child while he goes on the make for the idiot boy. Each victim has his victim.

The title of "The Hunters Are the Hunted," the first feature film by Peter Fleischmann, a 36-year-old German director, says it all, which is a major problem when you put accurate titles on parables. If the parable can be reduced to a title, then the rest of the parable is unnecessary or, as in the case of "The Hunters Are the Hunted," it becomes a kind of perverse celebration of the things it abhors. Its motives become suspect, especially when it is apparent that some of its horrors are made horrible through the act of film recording.

In following the fate of one pig from knock-out blow and throat-cutting to sausage meat, as the film does in one long sequence, "The Hunters Are the Hunted" is making less of a comment about criminal cruelty, collective guilt and Nazism than it is exploiting our natural queasiness at watching a pig being disemboweled. People and pigs are fundamentally different (pigs cannot make movies, among other things), and to suggest anything else, as the film seems to do, is to befuddle things, to confuse issues that must be clear if man is somehow to improve his condition.

●

When I first saw this Fleischmann film at the 1969 Cannes Film Festival, where it was shown under the English title of "Hunting Scenes in Bavaria," I was impressed by the director's skill in his use of both professional and amateur actors and in creating a kind of Boschian landscape. Four years later, the skill is still evident but the result now impresses me more as a largely theoretical cartoon than as the sort of haunted, human vision that an artist such as Goya created in a desperate effort to exorcise his nightmares.

The film opened yesterday at the New Yorker Theater.

1973 My 31, 48:4

The Cast

By ROGER GREENSPUN

Janis Roswick, who has the lead, of sorts, in William Richert's documentary, "First Position," is an 18-year-old New York girl who hopes to become a dancer.

She is pretty, a little plump, not noticeably graceful except when dancing, and resolutely middle class.

Her public life is the round of "classes" (beginner, advanced beginner, intermediate and upward) that fill the days of any ballet student in this city. Her private life is a happy family outside Manhattan, a shared apartment in town, romantic interests in another student (Daniel Giagni) and an introspective diary in which she keeps account of these important years in her emotional and spiritual development. "My pink stage is slowly becoming deep cranberry red . . ." she writes. She isn't kidding.

Janis has in superabundance the capacity for awe at herself that seems the identifying characteristic of bright young people native to New York City.

But "First Position" isn't about Janis only. It is also about her boyfriend (not really; they're both too shy), whose life outside the dance includes training to be a clerk-typist in the National Guard. And it's about other students: a clever, ironic man who loses out in Janis's affections, and a talented but insecure boy who finally goes home to Florida to become a bagger in a supermarket—after almost succeeding at ballet school in New York.

●

The school itself (the American Ballet Theater School, though its identity isn't too important) we know mainly through the qualities of some of its teachers—the vigorous Valentina Pereyaslavec, and Leon Danielian, severely crippled by arthritis, who spends most of the movie in a wheelchair. For an image of personal presence, Danielian's taking command over a dance class, even from a wheelchair, will do until something pretty spectacular comes along.

From time to time the film cuts to passages from the recent Ballet Theater production of "Petrushka"—almost the only formal dancing in the movie.

"Petrushka" is in costume, but danced in a semi-darkened classroom rather than on stage. Given the ballet and the setting, the effect is chilling and oddly dispirited. This is what we see of suc-

cess in the film's terms. It isn't glamour; it's more like loneliness and a vague fear.

●

And it is emblematic of what raises "First Position" above the level of sensitive slice-of-life documentary—to provide a vision of what lies just beyond, say, the winning self-assertion of Janis's diary, the classroom discipline, or Danielian's personal bravery.

Temporary victories against time, they lead finally to a lovely expression, of defeat, and that is how they are understood in this very good movie.

"First Position" opened this week at the First Avenue Screening Room.

1973 Je 2, 19:1

A 'Doll,' a 'Kid' and an 'Emperor'

By VINCENT CANBY

HERE are some further thoughts on three new films that have little in common except the acetate stock they are printed on:

"A Doll's House," directed by Patrick Garland from Christopher Hampton's adaptation of the play by Henrik Ibsen. All of us have had to weather so many second-rate Ibsen productions that we can be excused if we anticipate a new Ibsen revival with slightly less excitement than we bring to the payment of a telephone bill. "A Doll's House" was written in 1879 and if it were only about women's rights, it would have died a long time ago, not because women's rights are no longer an issue (they are) but because issue-dramas disintegrate as quickly as newsprint.

This film, made in England with a few (a very few, happily) exterior shots photographed in Norway, is more or less an extension of Mr. Hampton's adaptation, starring Claire Bloom and directed by Mr. Garland, which was done on Broadway two years ago. It is an absolutely first-rate recording of a theatrical experience that never was. Although Miss Bloom stars once again as Nora, the supporting cast is new: it now includes Anthony Hopkins as Torvald, Sir Ralph Richardson as Dr. Rank, Denholm Elliott as Krogstad, Anna Massey as Mrs. Linde and Dame Edith Evans as the old nurse. They are brilliant and a theatrical experience is just what it is. Never does one forget that this is a photographed play, but the play is a classic that is enriched by an awareness of theater manners. Which is ironic, considering that Ibsen was put down by the philistines of his own day for being so dully realistic.

Mr. Garland's camera sometimes gets too close to the characters, as if it had leapt over an orchestra pit and in-

sisted on getting between the actors like an over-eager autograph hunter. Too many scenes are broken up with alternating cuts from one performer to another and back again. On stage they'd be seen simultaneously within the proscenium frame. But that's a minor annoyance considering the quality of the performances and the progression of events that Mr. Garland's cast makes so vivid and ferocious.

Miss Bloom's Nora is beautiful and complex, having something of the too-intelligent mistress about her at the beginning. She is vaguely aware of her role-playing as bird-brained wife, though she doesn't want to recognize it, which makes her eventual liberation more comprehensible and more moving.

There is—somewhere near the center of the film—an Ibsen scene the likes of which I've never seen before, though I've sat through more revivals of "A Doll's House" than I want to remember. It's when Nora briefly considers the idea of borrowing the money from old, dying Dr. Rank to pay off the blackmailer. It is late afternoon. Nora and the doctor are alone in the drawing room. The lights haven't yet been turned on, and Nora has been teasing Dr. Rank with glimpses of a stocking she'll wear with a fancy dress costume.

In a moment of childish ruthlessness, Nora challenges the doctor to do something for her, which the doctor then wrecks by declaring his love. Nora is furious. Dr. Rank has not played fair by declaring this intimacy. The way Miss Bloom and Sir Ralph play the scene, it becomes both erotic and a turning point in Nora's education. His declaration forces her to acknowledge to herself, for the first time in the play, exactly the game she's been playing not only with the doctor, but also with her husband. In effect it's the practical beginning of the last act.

Superior performances like

these make the filmed "Doll's House" more explicit and more mysterious, which is just a fancy way of saying more human.

"Pat Garrett and Billy The Kid," directed by Sam Peckinpah from an original screenplay by Rudolph Wurlitzer. The question to ask is: what happened? One might have thought that the story of the last days of Billy The Kid, who is finally hunted down and shot by his old friend, Pat Garrett, the former badman-turned-sheriff, would have been perfect Peckinpah material. Perhaps it was a little too perfect.

Throughout the film there are little bits and pieces of very good scenes, the only problem being that we've seen them all before in other Peckinpah films. The opening sequence, set in the outlaws' lair in the ruins of old Fort Sumner, is less an evocation of the legendary West than a steal from the opening of "The Wild Bunch." Bored badmen sit around in the sun shooting the heads off chickens. The chickens are surprised. The children are fearful, at least for a while. In Peckinpah's scheme of things you know they'll be doing the same soon enough.

*

Pat (James Coburn) and Billy (Kris Kristofferson) know that time is running out for them, as it always is for people in Peckinpah's best films ("The Wild Bunch," "The Ballad of Cable Hogue," "Junior Bonner"). The difference between Pat and Billy and the characters in the other films is that Pat and Billy and their buddies have a way of talking about nothing else, or so it seems.

Even the casting of Bob Dylan in a supporting role, as a sort of retarded hanger-on to Billy, overstates this point. It was Dylan, after all, who wrote "The Times They Are A-changing." Unfortunately, however, he sings a lot of new junk on a soundtrack that won't shut up.

Coburn is a good, straight, tired Pat Garrett but Kristofferson is an odd choice to play the Billy The Kid of myth. He looks awfully soft and tubby for a guy who's supposed to be spending so much time on the run. Instead, he looks more like a fellow who's fond of drinking double-thick malteds and reading good books. The supporting cast is made up of some of the best character actors around, including Chill Wills, Slim Pickens, Richard Jaeckel, Gene Evans, Katy Jurado and Elisha Cook.

Jason Robards (Cable Hogue) does a funny walk-on as Lew Wallace, who was then (1881) the Governor of the territory of New Mexico. "These fabulous, rainy New Mexico evenings," muses the Governor at one point. "They bring us closer to the vast design of things." Or something like that. It's funny because it's the way we like to think the author of "Ben Hur" might have talked—which he was.

*

In my daily review of the film, I suggested that perhaps Wurlitzer's screenplay was responsible for the mess of the film. Someone I respect—someone who knows Wurlitzer—later raised strong objections. He'd read the original script, he said, and it was great. He thought that maybe Peckinpah hadn't followed it too closely. I've no way of knowing and withdraw the insinuations. Six editors are credited with having cut the film, which has the continuity of cole slaw.

"Emperor of The North Pole," directed by Robert Aldrich, from an original screenplay by Christopher Knopf. This is not the sort of movie for most people who read film reviews on Sunday. It's an almost pure action melodrama, set in the American Northwest during the Great Depression, about the greatest hobo of his day, A-No. 1 (Lee Marvin), who attempts the impossible: to hitch a free ride into Eugene, Ore., on freight train No. 19, whose conductor, The Shack (Ernest Borgnine), is known throughout hobo jungles as "the meanest conductor alive."

It's not exactly "Cries and Whispers," but it's superior moviemaking of its kind, about characters who exist entirely in terms of the physical action in which they are involved. When you come down to it, this is the way most people do live their lives, though possibly the action is more often concerned with getting to and from supermarkets, dentists, used car lots, etc., than with endurance tests, even on the Long Island Railroad.

People who are allergic to comic book blood-and-gore should stay away, as should people whose stomachs rebel at soundtrack songs like "A Man and A Train," which tells us that "a train's not a man, and a man's not a train, for a man can do things a train never can." Its message: that a train must stop when it runs out of steam, but that a man can keep going on his dream. The lyrics are by Hal David, who also did the lyrics for "Lost Horizon."

Borgnine hasn't much opportunity to be anything except extremely mean, going after the hobos, as he does, armed with hammer and chain, but Marvin is richly comic as the heroic A-No. 1 and Keith Carradine, a son of John, is appropriately impossible as a brash young guy named Cigaret to whom Marvin says: "I'm going to tell you once, kid, and no more. You got it in you to be a good bum." It has to do with what your goals are.

The action, much of it beautifully staged on top of moving freight cars, is full of outrageous challenges, impossible predicaments and improbable escapes. It runs two hours and it seems half as long as "Pat Garrett and Billy The Kid," which runs an almost endless 106 minutes.

1973 Je 3, II:1:3

If You Expect James Bond, You're in for a Shock

By STEPHEN FARBER

IN return for starring in his final James Bond movie, "Diamonds Are Forever," Sean Connery won from United Artists an agreement to finance any two movies of his choosing; the only condition was that the movies be brought in for less than $1-million each. "The Offence" (written by John Hopkins, directed by Sidney Lumet) is the first of the films, and it must be one of the most relentlessly bleak and dour movies ever released by a major American studio. Now the problem is finding how to promote it. United Artists seems to have already given up; the movie recently opened here without warning and closed just as suddenly two weeks later.

A compelling chronicle of the crack-up of a British police detective hunting a child molester, "The Offence" makes no concessions to the audience or the studio executives—no gags, no sensational thrills, no romantic interest, no facile, convenient explanation for the horrors we are asked to contemplate. This film, in other words, has integrity —the hardest commodity to market these days.

*

At moments one may wish there were a few concessions to the audience—not a softening of Hopkins's harsh vision, but a more ruthless cinematic reshaping of it. The script sometimes betrays its stage origins. A couple of long confrontation scenes bog down in overly florid speeches; dialogue like "filthy, slimy, swarming maggots in my mind, eating my mind" is embarrassingly self-conscious and bombastic.

It may be that Lumet has underestimated the power of his images. As Detective-Sergeant Johnson (Connery) drives home from the station after brutally beating the suspect he has been questioning, there is a shattering wordless flashback sequence in which he recalls a series of grotesque deaths—murders, accidents, suicides—that he discovered during 20 years on the force. This hypnotic montage sequence captures the experience of living on the edge—the growing absorption in death and perversion that has finally deranged Johnson. Then, in the next scene, Johnson describes those deaths to his wife (Vivien Merchant), and although the long stream-of-consciousness aria is very well recited by Connery, it seems totally superfluous. After such eloquent pictures, the words can only seem redundant and anti-climactic.

In the last analysis, however, these miscalculations can be overlooked; "The Offence" is sometimes too shrill, but it has a fierce honesty that distinguishes it from all the other police movies in vogue today. What makes this film unique is the psychological depth with which it dissects a cop's inner life, his secret fantasies and obsessions. Neither a glib anti-police tract nor a belligerent hymn to Law and Order, "The Offence" records a detective's anguish as he perceives his close symbiotic relationship with the killers, sadists and psychopaths he hunts.

Detective-Sergeant Johnson is a "good cop," devoted to his work, concerned about the innocent, unusually sensitive to everything he sees; but his tireless dedication to justice has become inseparable from a morbid, lascivious identification with the criminals he pursues. The film would be more comforting if we could construct a neat Freudian case history to account for Johnson's breakdown; then we could dismiss him more easily. Hopkins refuses to provide a single, clearcut explanation, but his point is that no one can trade so exclusively and so compulsively in death without becoming more and more attached to the underworld he is supposed to scourge. Just as the pornographer and the censor share the same obsessions, at some point the fantasies of the criminal merge with those of his persecutor.

In the film's climactic scene, Johnson's interrogation of a man who may or may not be a child molester, their identities are interchangeable. Speculating about the suspect's psychological history, Johnson reveals his own sexual frustration; and as he excitedly recounts the details of the rape, he participates in it viscerally. The suspect (Ian Bannen), who is masochistically stimulated by Johnson's bullying, recognizes the bond that they share, and taunts him seductively: "Nothing I have done can be half as bad as the thoughts in your head. There's nothing I can say that you haven't imagined."

As he confronts the obscene truth about himself, Johnson comes apart; his frustrations explode, and he finally acts on his sadistic fantasies, attacking the suspect in a murderous rage. All distinctions between cop and criminal dissolve in that one moment of violence.

It seems that in this electrifying scene Hopkins wants to move beyond the police milieu to make a larger statement about the heart of darkness in all men. You may or may not accept that final leap, but the dramatic conflict is so precisely drawn that the abstractions never overwhelm the action. Like all good movies, "The Offence" draws us into a vividly detailed world—one of those ghastly new towns outside London, a luminous tomorrowland stranger and more ominous than anything a science fiction writer could invent.

But the plastic Utopia is not quite complete. Ladders and pieces of canvas still clutter the antiseptic police station.

Bulldozers have been abandoned in the muddy fields adjacent to the ultra-modern apartment blocks. This juxtaposition of slime and sterility could be said to visualize the film's theme of the precariousness of civilization, but the symbolism isn't forced; the images are completely naturalistic, and at the same time, eerily surreal. Lumet and his brilliant cinematographer Gerry Fisher summon up a magic night landscape that has the poetry and terror of a dream.

The visual style of "The Offence" mirrors the protagonist's obsessions. The distortions are barely discernible at first, but the normal, every-day rational perspective is always slightly blurred. When Johnson patrols a school, we share his disorientation; we cannot quite distinguish the police decoys from the voyeurs, the innocent bystanders, or the possible criminals.

A little later, discovering the raped little girl in the woods, Johnson approaches her furtively, struggles with her to calm her, and starts nervously when the other police flashlights close in on him. Nothing needs to be said; we understand his fearful identification with the rapist, his uneasy, guilty complicity.

Structured in a complex cyclical fashion, "The Offence" suggests a recurring, spiraling nightmare. The images convey Johnson's tension, bewilderment, and growing sense of isolation. The subtle soundtrack—dislocating echoes of a children's song, construction drilling, distant footsteps—and Harrison Birtwhistle's haunting electronic score heighten the hallucinatory mood.

*

Lumet understands his medium. The whole film is beautifully made, and Connery's startling performance provides the dramatic momentum. He has a powerful presence—his physical movements are those of a caged but dangerous animal; and his characterization is rich in shadings. Connery has given strong performances in the past (particularly in two other films directed by Lumet—"The Hill" and "The Anderson Tapes"), but his performance in "The Offence" has a depth of feeling that will amaze people who still associate him with James Bond.

Lumet's extraordinarily sensitive work with actors has been one of his acknowledged talents from the start of his career, but in his control of the purely visual elements of film he has grown more and more accomplished. Unfortunately, Lumet is at this point one of our most underrated directors; he is out of fashion both with auteur critics (who prefer cruder, more reactionary police movies) and highbrow critics (who would probably rave about "The Offence" if it were dubbed in French).

During the last few years, Lumet has been exceptionally unlucky. His all-star film of "The Seagull" failed to find an audience. "The Appointment," a fascinating subjective film about romantic obsession, starring Anouk Aimée

and Omar Sharif, was never even released in America until a mutilated version showed up on television last year. When his projected film of "The Confessions of Nat Turner" was canceled weeks before shooting was scheduled to begin, that might have been the end of his career. He finally did two straight commercial movies, however — the slick, entertaining "Anderson Tapes" and the clumsy, hokey "Child's Play"—in order to keep working.

Lumet began his career by taking chances—in live television and in films like "Twelve Angry Men," "The Fugitive Kind" and "A Long Day's Journey Into Night." Now, at a time when most directors are playing it safe with violence or nostalgia, it is gratifying to see that Lumet is still taking chances.

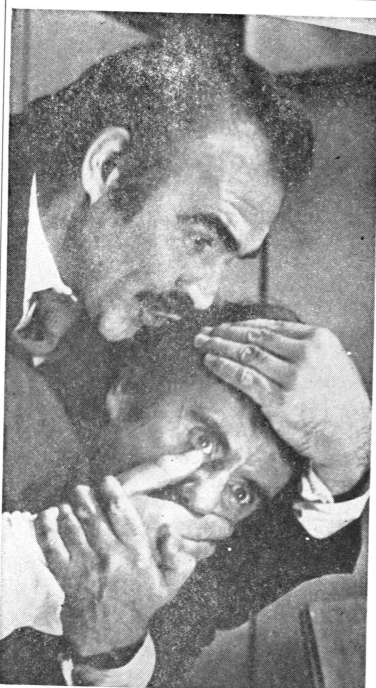

Sean Connery, as a deranged cop, brutally interrogates Ian Bannen, a suspected child-molester, in Sidney Lumet's "The Offence"
Have their identities become interchangeable?

"The Offence" is not a complete success, and I don't think anyone can watch it without some impatience. Still, it is exciting to see a talented director and actor test themselves against challenging material. "The Offence" may not be a movie for everybody; but it is an important and memorable film, and it deserves the attention of serious moviegoers — an embattled species in danger of becoming extinct.

1973 Je 3, II:11:1

The Cast

ELVIS ON TOUR, directed and produced by Pierre Adidge and Robert Abel; director of photography, Robert E. Thomas; editor, Ken Zemke; distributed by Metro-Goldwyn-Mayer. Running time: 93 minutes. At the 59th Street Twin 2 Theater, 59th Street east of Third Avenue, and other theaters. This film has been classified G. With: Elvis Presley, Jackie Kahane, Kathy Westmorland, The Sweet Inspirations, J. D. Sumner and the Stamps Quartet, Vernon Presley and others.

By VINCENT CANBY

A natural spin-off of the rock concert tour is the rock concert tour film, at which Pierre Adidge and Robert Abel ("Mad Dogs and Englishmen," "Let The Good Times Roll") are such experienced hands that I suspect they were inhibited by the magnitude of their latest subject, Elvis Presley. Or perhaps—dare I say?—his minitude.

•

The movie is called "Elvis on Tour" and it purports to be an intimate portrait of Elvis as he revealed himself on recent tours, while performing onstage and while getting on and off airplanes, on and off buses, and in and out of limousines. Strip away the storybook myth and—lo—there is a storybook myth underneath: a nice, clean-cut, multimillionaire pop idol who is, offstage, hard-working and friendly and something less than a riveting personality.

The essential blandness of the offstage Elvis has the effect of diminishing the impact of what we see of the onstage performances, which are presented with a lot of fancily photographed and edited split-screen frills that ultimately suggest that Elvis is much duller to watch than to hear.

Whether this is his fault or the fault of the moviemakers, I don't know. It is quite apparent that Mr. Adidge and Mr. Abel are treating him with the kind of respect that French television used to reserve for the formal appearances of De Gaulle. The camera never catches him in a truly candid moment. Close-ups do not reveal anything but, rather, they enshrine an ideal, like an official photograph of a President or a Pope.

•

Compared with "Mad Dogs and Englishmen," which chronicled the American concert tour of Joe Cocker in a way that reflected Cocker's tumultuous talent, "Elvis on Tour" seems almost stately. Elvis himself looks vaguely ill at ease in his baby blue (or scarlet), rhinestone-studded Batman costume, not really formidable enough to be announced (as the film does) with the first several bars of "Thus Spake Zarathustra."

The film opened yesterday at the East 59th Street Twin 2 Theater and other theaters.

1973 Je 7, 54:1

3 Documentaries From China Examine a History

THE CHINESE FILM FESTIVAL consisting of 3 documentaries: 2100 YEAR OLD TOMB EXCAVATED; HISTORICAL RELICS and ACUPUNCTURAL ANAESTHESIA; presented by Tai Ming Enterprises, Sino-American Exports-Imports, Inc., and China Trade Corporation; produced in China. Running time: 130 minutes. This film has not been classified at this time. At the Festival Theater, 57th Street at Fifth Avenue.

By ROGER GREENSPUN

The three Chinese films that opened yesterday at the Festival Theater were all made during the last year, obviously for foreign consumption. Each has an English-language narration—not too perfectly spoken—and each has a fairly obtrusive didactic purpose. There is nothing, say, of the quality of life so marvelously sensed in Michelangelo Antonioni's recent television study of China. But there is a good deal to be learned from movies that have such fascinating material at their disposal.

Two of the films deal with archeological discovery. "2100 Year Old Tomb Excavated" is an account of the Han Dynasty Tomb discovered—with considerable publicity — two years ago, which yielded a woman's body in a remarkable state of preservation and a superb collection of funeral objects, household utensils and painted silk panels. "Historical Relics Unearthed During the Great Proletarian Revolution" is also largely concerned with tomb finds: Han Dynasty bronzes, gold-wired jade burial vestments; gorgeous silks that were at about the time of Christ already being traded overland to the Eastern Mediterranean cities of the Roman Empire.

The films are immensely appreciative of their splendors, and at the same time suspicious of them. No glory of the ancient past is without its revolutionary lesson

—historical, by way of Marx and Engels, and moral, by way of the great proletarian revolution. Thus, an excavation exposes "not only the extravagance and debauchery of the ruling class" (bronze drinking cup) "but also the cruel exploitation of the people. From the fantastic jade burial suits (as terrifying a *momento mori* as any I've seen recently) we learn only of "the wisdom and back-breaking labor of the toiling masses."

●

A similar feeling for class struggle gets into the third film, "Acupunctural Anaesthesia," which sees acupuncture, part of a traditional, cooperative people's medicine in victorious combat with genera anesthesia, the revisionist medicine of certain scornful big-city doctors. But the film's actual demonstrations—almost painless

removal of tonsils, a uterus, a lung, a brain tumor, all with the aid of a few properly placed electrically agitated needles—are very convincing. Throughout an operation everybody smiles, especially the patient, who of course remains conscious and is expected to encourage his surgeon.

Thus we see a brain-tumor patient, his scalp already cut back, urge his doctor to continue, drilling through his skull so as to attack the tumor, the enemy within. I should feel better about freedom of choice in this kind of collectivism if I could also see what might happen to a patient, his scalp already cut back, who urges his doctor to stop. But it is otherwise difficult to fault an anesthetic technique that allows you to swallow mandarin orange sections rather than gas during your operation.

1973 Je 8, 46:1

FUNERAL PARADE OF ROSES, directed and written (Japanese with English subtitles) by Toshio Matsumoto; produced by Mitsumu Kudo; director of photography, Tatsuo Suzuki; music, Joji Yuasa; editor Toshie Iwasa; a Matsumoto production, distributed by Grove Press. Running time: 95 minutes. At the First Avenue Screening Room, First Avenue at 61st Street. This film has not been classified.
Eddie .... Peter
Gonda .... Yoshio Tsuchiya
Leda .... Osamu Ogasawara
Guevara .... Toyosabura Uchiyama
Tony .... Don Madrid
Eddie's mother............ Emiko Azuma

By VINCENT CANBY

Eddie, the transvestite hero of Toshio Matsumoto's 1969 Japanese film, "Funeral Parade of Roses," keeps up a brave but frankly fake front.

While his lover, Gonda, has a post-breakfast cigarette, Eddie frets with his hair. "Do you like it up or down?" he asks Gonda, who is the manager of Tokyo's Club Genêt, where Eddie works as a B-boy. Gonda

likes Eddie with hair up or down, but he has a ferocious mistress named Leda, who's jealous of Eddie and threatens to tell the cops about Gonda's drug trade.

Eddie is young, beautiful and in love, but his story is messier than the plots of a half-dozen Bette Davis films. "I feel as if life left me behind some time ago," he says.

He keeps having these visions. Well, they aren't truly visions. The're more like flashbacks. As a child, Eddie murdered his mother and her lover with a carving knife. That was extremely messy and led to a certain period in jail, which was no fun at all.

●

The one stable factor in Eddie's life is Gonda, but when you read in the ads

that "Funeral Parade of Roses" is "a modern reworking of the Oedipus myth," you are given a major clue as to who Gonda actually is. When Eddie finds out, it's back to the old carving knife.

Like Eddie, who wears make-up, wigs, miniskirts and false eyelashes, which are as thick as the brushes in a carpet sweeper, the movie spends most of its time trying to disguise its identity. "Funeral Parade of Roses" is a mopey soap opera made by someone who has seen too many better movies.

Matsumoto uses speeded-up action, reverse-negative photography and "in" movie jokes that the subtitles invariably get wrong, as in a reference to "Jonas Mecas." Time is splintered for no ap-

parent purpose and individual sequences are introduced by title cards that say such things as "all doors are already open."

The film shows us an underworld of male prostitutes, pimps and drug pushers that looks comfortably middle-class, not much more desperate than Saturday at a country club. As literature, "Funeral Parade of Roses" is closer in spirit to something like "A Stolen Life," in which Bette Davis played twins, than it is to the work of Genêt, whose name the film uses in vain.

"Funeral Parade of Roses" opened yesterday at the First Avenue Screening Room.

1973 Je 8, 47:1

Mary's Poppin' Up Again

By VINCENT CANBY

AS of the first of this year, "Mary Poppins," Walt Disney's 1964 musical adaptation of the P. L. Travers stories had earned approximately $31,000,000 in the United States and Canada. The film was voted five Academy Awards, including one for Julie Andrews as the best actress of 1964, and it was so popular that it even inspired its own tiny backlash: bumper stickers announcing "Mary Poppins Is A Junkie," which may or may not have been prompted by a song in the Oscar-winning Sherman Brothers score to the effect that "a spoonful of sugar helps the medicine go down."

"Mary Poppins" is now back at the Radio City Music Hall, one of the few reissues ever to play that giant (6,000-seat) theater, accompanied "on the

great stage" by a 50th birthday salute to Walt Disney Productions. Since I am apparently one of the few people who was alive in 1964 who missed seeing the film during its original release, I made a field trip to the Hall one afternoon last week, not without some risk to limb and sanity.

*

From the looks of things, "Mary Poppins" may be about to make another $31,000,000. Not that every seat was occupied when I entered the auditorium. There were lots of bald spots here and there, but every time I started to sit down in one, a cross voice would whisper in the twilight: "It's taken! It's taken!" I later estimated that at no time during the film and the stage show were there less than 2,000 children either on their way to or from the bathrooms. The aisles were aswarm, a

single file up, a single file back, creating a gentle, constant drone. It was like being inside a huge beehive.

Because I'd not seen the film earlier, I can't say fairly whether or not the movie holds up, only that the entire Music Hall program, which runs for approximately three hours, is old-fashioned capitalism run gloriously amok. It's the American Dream inflated like a balloon, but not to the point of bursting. Let Costa-Gavras expose United States imperialism as he sees it in "State of Siege." Let Dalton Trumbo beat us over the head with artificial moral equations about war in "Johnny Got His Gun." Let Tom Laughlin and Delores Taylor define one sort of counterculture in "Billy Jack." Everything they're reacting against, one way and another, is delightfully and explicitly detailed in either the Music Hall film

or the stage show.

First the film. Others have long noted that nurses occupy a privileged place in the sexual fantasies of American males. One friend of mine says it's because of the impression they give that they wear nothing under their uniforms. The "Mary Poppins" film, which is, of course, based on the work of an English novelist and set in London (though the time has been pushed back from the thirties to the Edwardian era), takes that adult American fantasy and somehow renders it comprehensible to children.

Miss Andrews's Mary Poppins is Mummy, Daddy, God, Doris Day and the Wizard of Oz all rolled into one. She's not a nurse but a nursemaid (in London: a nanny). She is stern, bright, listens to reason (but she is also enraptured by nonsense), and she can talk to dogs. She sings with a purity that is absolutely enchanting and quite expected, since Mary Poppins is, by her own admission, practically perfect. Also, she is almost completely sexless. Well, not completely sexless, but in none of her relations with men does she give her two small charges the slightest cause for jealousy. To top it all off, she can fly, and we all know what *that* means!

*

She comes into the lives of the Banks children flying, and she leaves them by simply taking off, umbrella open and not a hair out of place. In between, she chaperones them through several demonstrations of levitation, which, as I take it, are the equivalents of the sane sex talks every child of my generation never got from his parents.

"Mary Poppins" thus presents an idealized picture of a childhood that no child ever had, with the result that the child, not having had it, grows up frustrated to become the imperialist, righteous, hard-hatted, wrong-headed, self-serving mess that Costa-Gavras and others so painstakingly and humorlessly expose.

These curmudgeons may be right. Certainly Robert Stevenson, the director of "Mary Poppins," as well as of such things as "The Love Bug" (which is nothing less than a romance about a Volkswagen) and "Son of Flubber," has never shown himself to be overly concerned with the world's evident ills. It isn't simply that in "Mary Poppins" he propounds the possibility that man (as well as woman and child) can escape, at will, into a universe of animated drawings, nor that he allows us to believe that Mary Poppins can actually slide *up* a bannister.

He goes further. One of the highpoints of the film is a confrontation between young Michael Banks (Matthew Garber), who is probably about six, and the president and the directors of Michael's father's bank. When Michael refuses to deposit his tuppence, it causes a run on the bank that almost ruins it.

You might think that Stevenson would use this sequence to give a plug to the Federal Reserve system, or to some such supervisory government body, but no. Although "Mary Poppins" makes a few gestures that poke fun at materialism, and at money-grubbing, it can be said to endorse only a sort of harmless, childish insolence. It is solidly pro-economic success and administrative advancement. As a result of Michael's behavior, Michael's father is fired, but he then is rehired by the bank and made a vice-president. Bad manners, according to "Mary Poppins," pay. So does greed.

Edwardian London, even the Edwardian London suggested by the film's beautifully stylized sets, was not exactly a promised land with a boiled chicken and a sweet on every table. It was a city of terrible extremes of poverty and wealth. Yet for whom does the film shed its tears? For the bloody pigeons! The reason that Michael has his confrontation with the bankers is that he wants to use his tuppence not to invest in the Suez Canal (the movie more or less tolerates this bad judgment because of Michael's youth), but to buy crumbs to feed the pigeons that befoul the steps of what looks to be St. Paul's.

*

Of more contemporary interest is the film's attitude toward air pollution, which it treats much in the way that "Super Fly" treated cocaine and "The Mack" treated prostitution. It makes pollution not only picturesque, but as romantic as morning mist. When Mary Poppins, Bert (Dick Van Dyke), the Banks children and the chorus of chimney sweeps go into their spectacularly choreographed (and danced) roof-top ballet, "Mary Poppins" takes a firm stand in favor of filthy air.

No wonder this country is falling apart. The least the Disney people could have done would have been to have the Sherman Brothers write one of their dumber scores, instead of a quite charming one that became the prototype for a lot of boring ones they wrote later. They could have cast Angela Lansbury or Carol Channing or someone equally inappropriate as Mary Poppins, in-

stead of Miss Andrews, who was always cut out for the role, right down to the line of her jaw. They could have made the children a mite more horrid.

What the Disney people failed to do, the Music Hall seems trying to make up for in the stage show.

I suppose this is really what I meant when I described the experience as capitalism run amok. The Hall's stage presentation comes across as a kind of live-action annual report, a stock prospectus in Snow White-drag.

There are a lot of adult actors dressed up in Goofy costumes, in rabbit costumes, in Mickey Mouse costumes. In the musical numbers there's a great emphasis on wishing as political method. I don't particularly care that the master of ceremonies is inclined to introduce the individual acts with phrases like ". . . and now, without further ado," but the plugs for Disneyland and Disney World are eventually oppressive.

*

It's as self-perpetuating in its way as is the capitalism that is defined by a Costa-Gavras character as the purpose of the Alliance for Progress. The stage show celebrates the corporation that successfully financed movies like "Mary Poppins" that allow the corporation to successfully finance other films for which the corporation will be celebrated, I'm confident, on its 75th and 100th birthdays.

1973 Je 10, II:1:6

The Cast

THE HIRELING, directed by Alan Bridges; screenplay by Wolf Mankowitz, based on the novel by L. P. Hartley; produced by Ben Arbeid; executive producer, Terence Baker; music, Marc Wilkinson; director of photography, Michael Reed; editor, Peter Weatherley; a World Film Services-Champion production, released by Columbia Pictures. Running time: 108 minutes. At the 68th Street Playhouse, Third Avenue at 68th Street. This film has been rated PG.

Leadbetter .... Robert Shaw
Lady Franklin .... Sarah Miles
Cantrip .... Peter Egan
Mother .... Elizabeth Sellars
Connie .... Caroline Mortimer
Mrs. Hansen .... Patricia Hogg

By VINCENT CANBY

"The Hireling," Alan Bridges's film version of the L. P. Hartley novel, is about England in the nineteen-twenties, about county aristocracy, about the cruelties of a class system that Hartley (who also wrote "The Go-Between") remembers with an outrage so tempered that it often seems a kind of fondness.

Lady Franklin (Sarah Miles) is recovering from a mild breakdown she suffered

following the loss of her husband, a young Tory Member of Parliament for whose death she feels vaguely responsible. She was at a party when it happened. It? Probably a heart attack, though we never learn exactly. Lady Franklin wears sensible shoes and cardigans that droop almost to the floor. She doesn't much care what she looks like, but she knows she must take hold.

In a hired limousine, a magnificent old Rolls-Royce, which takes her from the clinic to her mother's house in Bath, Lady Franklin engages the chauffeur in small talk. She talks to the back of his head, to one eye seen in a mirror. She tells him that people say things to one another but rarely make contact. He answers "yes, my lady," because it's his style and because his customers are always right.

When they arrive at her mother's and Leadbetter, which is the name of the chauffeur, gets out to open the door for Lady Franklin, the camera suddenly looks at him for the first time. Leadbetter (Robert Shaw) is not just the back of a head, an eye and a uniform. He is a singular man, youngish, handsome, polite and, above all, calculating. Lady Franklin has been so invigorated by the depth of their communication that she engages Leadbetter to take her on a series of afternoon drives.

Thus begins "The Hireling," which is about the recovery of Lady Franklin and the misunderstanding that develops between the lady and the chauffeur. It's all very cool and precise and, to me, anyway, a bit less than entirely engrossing. The characters in Wolf Mankowitz's screenplay simply aren't very interesting, despite a calm, intelligent performance by Miss Miles and an almost diabolical one by Shaw who, not really tragically, aspires to love above his station.

●

For Lady Franklin's benefit, the unmarried Leadbetter fabricates a complete family for himself, with stories about two small children and a wife named Frances who looks at lot like her ladyship. Lady Franklin, in turn allows Leadbetter to think she fancies him. She insists on riding next to him in the front seat. She draws him out about his business as well as family affairs, and she even lends him money so that his Rolls won't be carried off by creditors.

"The Hireling" is very good in individual scenes, in the look of its landscapes, in its observation of manners and especially in its refusal to overexplain narrative details. However, by effectively re-

Sarah Miles

ducing the conflicts within the English social order to a misunderstanding, it becomes not only silly but grossly misleading.

●

The excellent supporting cast includes Peter Egan, as an ambitious young Liberal politician, who succeeds with Lady Franklin without half trying; Elizabeth Sellars, as Lady Franklin's mother, who is as self-absorbed as Lady Franklin will one day be, and Caroline Mortimer, as Egan's cast-off mistress.

"The Hireling," which opened yesterday at the 68th Street Playhouse, shared the grand prize at this year's Cannes Film Festival with an American film, "Scarecrow."

1973 Je 11, 45:1

them as per instructions in his correspondence-school mortician's course. It is also the story of a hotel dick named Rick (David Bailey), and his lovely lady, Lisa (Tiffany Bolling), and the marvelous old monstrosity (Hotel del Coronado, in San Diego) where Rick detects and Lisa entertains and Jason clears away the customers.

What distinguishes "Wicked, Wicked" from all other recent psychopathic-killers-loose-in-rambling-old-hotels movies is its gimmick. "A unique projection process" according the distributor, which calls it Duo-Vision. Duo-Vision is in fact nothing more than split-screen unremittingly applied, as in "Chelsea Girls" and "Dionysus in '69," but never before with such winning simplicity of intention.

By means of Duo-Vision we see: 1. two things at once, 2. two points of view on any one thing at once, 3. present action and flashbacks to past action at the same time, and 4.—when there isn't much else going on—a pop-eyed woman who plays spooky music on a big theater organ. Obviously, a big hotel full of rooms and corridors is a natural for multiple-screen projection. But not quite so obviously, the effect of such projection is to defuse the action.

When you can see both the distant, stalking killer and his intended victim at the same time you have more activity but less anticipation—and consequently less suspense. And the lifting of suspense, which in most such movies functions as an annoying burden upon the audience, is a very real advantage.

"Wicked, Wicked" thus emerges as an oddly pleasant movie about which there is not too much good to say. Everybody is likable—even the killer, who, like most amateur embalmers in movies for the last 10 years, owes a bit to Hitchcock's Norman Bates. And everybody is at least professionally competent.

●

There should always be a place for the low-budget hotel movie, where the same six extras as guests continually crisscross the lobby and enjoy the show in the supper club, and where everything, from room service on up, has the attractively casual air of making do with the needs and opportunities of the moment.

"Wicked, Wicked," written, produced, and directed by Richard Bare, opened yesterday at neighborhood theaters.

1973 Je 14, 56:1

The Cast

WICKED, WICKED, written, produced and directed by Richard L. Bare; director of photography, Frederick Gately; film editor, John F. Schreyer; music by Philip Springer; a Richard L. Bare-William T. Orr Production; released by Metro-Goldwyn-Mayer. At neighborhood theaters. Running time: 97 minutes. This film has been classified PG.

Rick Stewart .... David Bailey
Lisa James .... Tiffany Bolling
Jason Gant .... Randolph Roberts
Sergeant Ramsey .... Scott Brady
Hank Lassiter .... Edd Byrnes
Dolores Hamilton .... Diane McBain
Manager .... Roger Bowen
Lenore Karadyne ..... Madeleine Sherwood
Genny .... Indira Danks
Hotel Engineer .... Arthur O'Connell

By ROGER GREENSPUN

Titles tell you nothing. Just on the surface, "Wicked, Wicked" sounds like a slightly misbehaving nineteen-fifties sub-deb. Actually, it is the story of Jason (Randolph Roberts), a poor confused lad who works in a huge California resort hotel where he occasionally slices up the guests (preferably good-looking younger blondes) and then pieces their bodies back together, secretly preserving

The Cast

O LUCKY MAN! directed by Lindsay Anderson; screenplay by David Sherwin, based on an idea by Malcolm McDowell; produced by Michael Medwin and Mr. Anderson; music and songs, Alan Price; director of photography, Miroslav Ondricek; editor, David Gladwell; a Memorial-Sam production, distributed by Warner Brothers. Running time: 166 minutes. At the Cinema I Theater, Third Avenue near 60th Street. This film has been classified R.

Mick Travis ....Malcolm McDowell
Monty, Sir James Burgess ....Ralph Richardson
Gloria, Mme. Paillard...Rachael Roberts
Mr. Duff, Charlie Johnson, Dr. Munda ....Arthur Lowe
Patricia ....Helen Mirren
Tea Lady ....Dandy Nichols
Sister Hallett, Usher...Mona Washbourne
Dr. Millar, Prof. Stewart ....Graham Crowden
Chairman, Prison Governor..Peter Jeffrey
Mrs. Ball, Vicar's Wife...Mary MacLeod
Welfare Lady ....Vivian Pickles
Captain, Dickie Belminster ....Michael Medwin

By VINCENT CANBY

Mick Travis (Malcolm McDowell), at heart, is literature's classic innocent. He is wide-eyed and tireless, and he is possessed by such sweetness of temper that arbitrary cruelties go unrecognized. Instead, unpleasant shocks are absorbed by an optimism that serves him as a kind of ship's fender, protecting him on all sides.

However, unlike Candide, even unlike Evelyn Waugh's Paul Pennyfeather, Mick would hardly qualify for citizenship in any but the most haphazardly administered state of grace. Mick wants to succeed and he is willing to try just about anything to do it. His completely unfounded belief that he can succeed, that he will overcome all obstacles, becomes the badge that certifies his innocence. It is a second-rate sort of badge, like something out of a cereal box, and a second-rate sort of innocence, quite in keeping with the second-rate morality of the times we live in.

•

"O Lucky Man!", the new English comedy directed by Lindsay Anderson (his first since "If . . .") and written by his "If . . ." collaborator, David Sherwin, chronicles the adventures of Mick from his humble beginnings as a trainee-salesman at Liverpool's Imperial Coffee Company, through various good fortunes and outrageous disasters, until, at the end, Mick has a kind of Zen illumination. A light bulb goes on inside his head. He smiles broadly: He is, after all, alive.

Mick has hobnobbed with international tycoons, scientists and politicians, and he's been double-crossed by all. He has also been nursed (quite literally) with the milk of human kindness by a vicar's wife. He has been thrown into jail for simply wanting to succeed ("And you failed!" says the furious judge), and he's been rehabilitated ("Did you know you have eyes like Steve McQueen?" asks a kindly warden).

•

He has been seduced by a rapacious landlady, abandoned by a beautiful London debutante, tortured at an atomic research center (in the name of national security) and beaten up by vagrants he would have helped.

"O Lucky Man!" clearly has a number of things on its mind, but as a movie, it is a very mixed bag.

Because Mr. Anderson is much more bold and free as a director than Mr. Sherwin is inventive as a social satirist, "O Lucky Man!" always promises to be much more stimulating and funny than it ever is. Staying with it through its almost three-hour running time becomes increasingly nerve-racking, like watching superimposed images that never synchronize. The result does not match the ambition of the intention. The wit is too small, too perfunctory, for the grand plan of the film and the quality of the production itself.

Every member of the cast—headed by McDowell, Ralph Richardson, Rachel Roberts, Arthur Lowe and Helen Mirren—is superb, and there is something surprisingly appealing (both to one's theatrical sense and to the dramatic unity of the film) in having lots of the actors turn up in different roles throughout the chronicle.

The real star, however, is Alan Price, best known here for "The Animals," who wrote the film's fine score and sings at various intervals during the movie, either on the soundtrack or in scenes shot in a recording studio. The songs, which more or less punctuate the individual chapters of Mick's odyssey, provide the wit and sense of surprise that are lacking in Sherwin's screenplay. It is funny when Price sings cheerfully, "Sell, sell, sell—sell everything you stand for"—when Mick starts out on the road, since Mick, quite obviously, stands for very little.

•

The score exhibits real irony about the ghastly indecencies that Sherwin so ponderously tries to ridicule. In this day and age, for those of us who have grown up with the truly epic visions of film makers like Buñuel and Chaplin, it's hardly enough for a film to qualify as "serious" or "important" by pointing out to us the excesses of capitalism, the awesomeness of technology gone mad, or even that poor people can act like beasts, just like rich people.

A more disturbing proposition by far would be a film that might suggest that rampant capitalism and technological madness could possibly succeed, by some terrible fluke, in fulfilling their promises. That is something that would force us to rethink the clichés we liberals live by. "O Lucky Man!", which opened yesterday at Cinema I, is a kind of homage to those clichés.

1973 Je 14, 58:1

The Cast

THE LAST OF SHEILA, directed and produced by Herbert Ross; screenplay by Stephen Sondheim and Anthony Perkins; executive producer, Stanley O'Toole; director of photography, Gerry Turpin; editor, Edward Warschilka; music, Billy Goldenberg; distributed by Warner Brothers. Running time: 120 minutes. At the Sutton Theater, 57th Street east of Third Avenue. This film has been classified PG.

Tom ....Richard Benjamin
Christine ....Dyan Cannon
Clinton ....James Coburn
Lee ....Joan Hackett
Philip ....James Mason
Anthony ....Ian McShane
Alice ....Raquel Welch

By VINCENT CANBY

"The Last of Sheila." directed by Herbert Ross from an original screenplay by Stephen Sondheim and Anthony Perkins, is an old-fashioned murder mystery that has been dressed up fit to kill and set aboard a fine, white-hulled, teak-decked Mediterranean yacht of the sort that souls have been sold to obtain.

The characters are Hollywood types who, by this time, must be as familiar to any woman who has ever spent a minute under a hair dryer as they are to people who read The Hollywood Reporter: the sadistic producer, the down-and-out director, the flesh-peddler (talent agent), the sex symbol, the ambitious writer, and so on. They are beautiful but edgy people, the kind who greet good jokes with a rating ("That's beautiful") rather than laughter. For these people even casual conversation can be a form of competition. The wisecrack is the weapon.

•

For as long as it runs, "The Last of Sheila" is also a good deal of fun, like one of those tricky, after-dinner party games that always seem dreary in advance but then somehow turn out to be more amusing than one had any right to expect.

The movie is, quite literally, a game, one that has been set up by the producer (James Coburn) who, on the first anniversary of his wife's mysterious hit-and-run death, invites six friends for a week's cruise off the coast of southern France. Any one of the guests, it turns out (as it must in this sort of thing), could have had a motive for doing in Sheila, which is the name of the producer's wife as well as of the yacht.

The format of the cruise is as strict as that of a television quiz show. Each guest has been given a slip of paper with a guilty secret written on it, a secret, it further turns out (as it must) that actually applies to one of the guests, though not the one who holds the paper. One is an alcoholic, one a child molester, one a homosexual, etc. They are, in short, just folks, and by the end of the week the host plans not only to have exposed each of them, but also to have his murderer.

I'm not a great after-dinner game person and I must admit that at various points in "The Last of Sheila" my mind wandered from the clues, even though it's difficult to avoid noticing them. They are only slightly less inconspicuous than would be snowshoes around a swimming pool.

Since I'm told that Sondheim and Perkins are serious game people, I assume that the plot, if run backward, would make sense. More important to me was the generally festive air in which all this genteel mayhem takes place, as well as the rather charming, Agatha Christie manners that are observed. As plot points are explained, people get themselves drinks from the bar. If someone is murdered, the pall of gloom lasts for a maximum of five minutes.

No one takes himself seriously and the characters are a colorful though not a very nice lot. Beautiful people, after all, haven't got time to be nice.

Most colorful is Dyan Cannon who plays the talent agent for all that the wisecracks are worth ("My mouth is so dry they could shoot 'Lawrence of Arabia' in it" or "I hate my luggage more than life itself"). It's not wit, but it's funny, and she gives a very good, very comic performance.

The others are also good, especially Richard Benjamin and Joan Hackett (as the writer and his wife) and James Mason (as the failing director), but the essential bitchery that makes the film work is provided by Miss Cannon and by all of the Sondheim-Perkins inside references—to things like pool maintenance, Joyce Haber and Hammer Films — which really are not too inside for us ordinary people to get.

Perhaps the best thing about "The Last of Sheila," which opened yesterday at the Sutton, is that it never tries to convince us that its characters are not having fun. They enjoy having money, or having access to it. It makes murder, as well as life, more interesting.

1973 Je 15, 24:1

'Red Psalm,' a Jansco Film, Starts Run

By ROGER GREENSPUN

"Red Psalm," which opened yesterday at the First Avenue Screening Room, was shown at the 10th New York Film Festival. The following excerpt is from Roger Greenspun's review, which appeared Oct. 2, 1972, in The New York Times.

Miklos Jansco's "Red Psalm" takes place at an indeterminate time on an open field where a group of peasants confront and, in the long run, symbolicallv conquer a group of soldiers and landed aristocrats. Thus there are political issues at stake—though for Hungary of the nineteen-seventies, I should think, exceptionally safe ones—but I'm not sure they matter much. In "Red Psalm," as in Jansco's movies generally ("The Round-up," "The Red and the White," etc.), the point is not what things are, but what they look like.

On one level things look pretty good. The cast is made up mostly of handsome young men and beautiful young women, and some of the young women undress from time to time in a kind of solemn masque of eroticism. The color is lush, the movements are graceful and the camera work — a Jansco trademark—is spectacular.

•

According to the film magazine Sight and Sound, "Red Psalm" contains only 26 shots. An ordinary movie of this length (88 minutes) would contain several hundred shots. To make up the difference, the camera moves and people move back and forth and in large or small circles, and I suppose it is right to say—as everybody says—that a Jansco film as not so much directed as choreographed. Actually, it looks to me less like choreography than a cross between eurythmics and close-order drill.

It is difficult to pinpoint the reasons for the incredible monotony of so much vigorous activity, but surely one reason is that nothing happens in "Red Psalm" except for the benefit of the camera. That may sound like any movie, but actually it is like no movie (except another Jansco movie) and is virtually a negation of the whole, necessary relation of cinema to life.

1973 Je 15, 28:1

The Cast

SUPER FLY TNT, directed by Ron O'Neal; screen play by Alex Haley, from a story by Sig Shore and Mr. O'Neal; photographed by Robert Gaffney; produced by Sig Shore; presented by Paramount. At the Criterion Theater, Broadway and 45th Street, and the Juilet 1 and 2, Third Avenue and 83d Street. Running time: 88 minutes. This film is rated "R".

Priest ....Ron O'Neal
Dr. Lamine Sonko ....Roscoe Lee Browne
Georgia ....Sheila Frazier
Matty Smith ....Jacques Sernas
Jordan Gaines ....Robert Guillaume
General ....Minister Dem

Coming after a fast, colorful movie like "Super Fly," a follow-up called "Super Fly TNT" is a wet firecracker. Long on talk and short on action, this juiceless bundle comes close to being super dull. It opened yesterday, with Ron O'Neal repeating the protagonist role and also directing.

Most of the time Priest, the reformed, cocaine pusher from Harlem simply slouches around Rome, as a tired, cynical expatriate, trailed by the loving Sheila Frazier, from the first film. He plays poker. Occasionally, the couple ride past Roman landmarks. Priest finally lets himself be persuaded to fly off to Africa on a gun-running mission for a small, oppressed country, and the picture ends just when it should be starting.

●

The Africa of the climax is a feeble, low-budget simulation, with some brief, standard, travelogue footage, as Mr. O'Neal is yanked off a plane and sadistically beaten in a room that could be anywhere.

One thing stands out like a small, personal lighthouse. This is the excellent performance of Roscoe Lee Browne—strong, dignified and piercing—as an impassioned African revolutionary. His patient recruiting in Rome of Mr. O'Neal, who often looks bored to death, takes most of the picture. Sharing that patience requires real indulgence.

HOWARD THOMPSON

1973 Je 16, 13:1

The Cast

INTERVAL, directed by Daniel Mann; screenplay by Gavin Lambert; produced by Merle Oberon; photography by Gabriel Figueroa; edited by Howard S. Deane; music by Armando Manzanero and Ruben Fuentes. A co-production of Euro-American Films Corporation and Churubusco Studios, Mexico; an Avco Embassy release. Running time: 84 minutes. At the 34th Street East, 34th Street near 2d Avenue. This film has been rated PG.

Serena Moore .... Merle Oberon
Chris .... Robert Wolders
Armando Vertiz .... Claudio Brook
Fraser .... Russ Conway
Broch .... Peter von Zerneck

BY ROGER GREENSPUN

"Married?"

"No"

"Never?"

"Not yet!" . . . sigh . . . And so Serena Moore (Merle Oberon), as tremulous as any girl, parries the charming but too insistent German restaurateur who rescued her from her stalled car and has already fallen in love with her on the short drive from nowhere to the Mayan ruins at Chichen-Itza. She has come to the Yucatan, Serena Moore, in search of peace. And she has brought with her a gold-framed Romantic landscape painting, a 5 million-year-old fossil fish ("to put me in perspective"), a change of wardrobe for every occasion, and an unquenchable thirst for life.

"It's so beautiful here," she exclaims, forging her way through a tropical rain forest, "only one thought on its mind—to grow!"

Who could resist a lady like that? Nobody. Not the helpful German, nor the old rake at the bar, nor the handsome stranger on the beach, nor the teen-age boy on room service—but, always graciously, Serena refuses them. Until Chris. Tempestuous, passionate, young, it is the vagrant artist Chris (Robert Wolders), also in search of peace, who awakens Serena's dormant fire and provides the occasion for "Interval," the story of a woman who finally stops running from love. The film opened yesterday at the 34th Street East Theater.

It is one of those ecstatic affairs, full of wonder and discovery, and yet it doesn't work. Perhaps Serena is just too fine, too sensitive. Perhaps it is something else. There is a problem, a silent traveler with Serena on her journeys, which I wouldn't bring up if the movie didn't keep bringing it up—in whispers: "The age thing." Though it is the last thought on his mind, and though you could never tell from looking at her, at some point Chris has to admit that Serena is—well—"over 40."

●

But truth to tell, Merle Oberon is well over 60, and from time to time it shows. "Are you a statue or are you real?" asks Chris, marveling at her beauty. You can't always say. Such uncanny freedom from wrinkles has not been achieved without a certain cost, and at this stage in her career Miss Oberon seems to have only two or three facial expressions left. Consequently, she acts mainly with her eyes, and with a small shake of her shoulders, which may be spunk, but which is never quite appropriate for the emotion of the moment. There was never such a movie for observing its leading lady from the back of the head.

●

There probably was never such a movie for anything. As performed by Miss Oberon, directed by Daniel Mann, written by Gavin Lambert, with a musical score by Armando Manzanero and Ruben Fuentes that flows over everything like detergent back-up, the tragic tale of Serena Moore in "Interval" provides the first genuinely funny comedy of the year.

On the scale of awfulness, it is almost sublime, better than "Pope Joan," nearly as good as "The Great Waltz." A few movies like this can last you for a lifetime.

1973 Je 16, 13:1

The Cast

JONATHAN, directed by Hans W. Geissendorfer; screenplay (German with English subtitles) by Mr. Geissendorfer; camera, Robby Muller; editor, Wolfgang Hedinger; music, Roland Kovac; production company, Iduna Films; presented by New Yorker Films. At the New Yorker Theater, Broadway and 88th Street. Running time: 103 minutes. This film has not been rated.

Jonathan .... Jurgen Jung
Josef .... Hans Dieter Jendreyko
Count .... Paul Albert Krumm
Thomas .... Thomas Astan
Lena's Mother .... Ilse Kunkele
Lena .... Eleonore Schminke
Professor .... Oskar Von Schab
Eleonore .... Ilone Grubel

Hans W. Geissendörfer's "Jonathan," which opened yesterday at the New Yorker Theater, was first seen here last year when it was the most entertaining—if not exactly the best — of the movies in the excellent New German Cinema show at the Museum of Modern Art. It is a vampire movie (Jonathan Harker, you may remember, is the principal narrator in Bram Stoker's "Dracula," an exceptionally classy vampire movie, and the distributor is billing it as the first anti-Fascist film of its kind.

None of this gets so seriously into "Jonathan" as to spoil the fun. But when Professor Van Helsing complains (to a meeting of 19th-century Transylvanian student activists) that "the power of these blood suckers increases every day," you can bet he's at least two-thirds of the way into political metaphor.

But the quality of imagination behind the film is generally much better than this. You can see it in such inventions as the malicious dwarf who lives in the forest outside Count Dracula's estate and who collects the paraphernalia — crosses, wooden stakes, old sprigs of garlic — of fearless vampire killers who came before our hero, Jonathan, and failed. And you can see it in the disciplined troop of ethereal little girls who attend the vampires — not the brides of Dracula (they are there also), but perhaps the bridesmaids, or even the first communicants. For this Count Dracula, an anti-Christ of parts, not only takes blood but also gives it too — from a wound in his side which, with infinite sadness, he offers to the lips of his victims.

●

Nothing else quite matches that gesture. Nothing ever matches the ritual of the first voluptuous kiss in any vampire movie, and "Jonathan" is especially canny—though very restrained—with the erotic potential of its material. But the whole film is invested with a kind of solemnity that is sometimes terrifying (though never cheaply shocking) and sometimes silly, but that, on balance, makes it the most beautiful-looking vampire movie I have seen.

Geissendörfer's camera glides — almost floats — through extremely long takes orchestrated to marvelously florid sequences of pans and tracks. The cast is huge (there is ultimately a veritable plague of vampires, and they decimate whole villages), the settings are unusual and very sumptuous. "Jonathan" doesn't really make movie history. But it substantially adds to one of the oddest and grandest traditions of recent popular art.

ROGER GREENSPUN.

1973 Je 16, 13:1

The Cast

COFFY; written and directed by Jack Hill; produced by Robert A. Papazian for American International Pictures. Music composed and conducted by Roy Ayers. At the Penthouse, 47th Street and Broadway, and the R.K.O. 86th Street Twin I, 125 East 86th Street. Running time: 91 minutes. This film is classified R.

Coffy .... Pam Grier
Brunswick .... Booker Brashaw
King George .... Robert DoQui
Carter .... William Elliott
Vitroni .... Allan Arbus
Ramos .... Ruben Moreno
Aleva .... John Perak
Omar .... Sid Haig
McHenry .... Barry Cahill

As the obviously sexy, black heroine of several recent black-oriented, gory and, naturally, sexy shoot-'em-ups, Pam Grier again is tougher than the opposition as the titular "Coffy," which crashed into the Penthouse and 86th Street Twin I Theaters yesterday. And, if it can be called a switch, she plays a nurse who operates on bad scenes, bad guys and dolls, with explicit dialogue, but almost never in an operating room.

Despite a good deal of lip service against the evils of drugs and the like, there's a maximum of footage devoted to exposing Miss Grier. She is plagued by problems. Her kid sister is hooked on drugs, so she uses a shotgun to dispatch a pusher. Then there's that bigtime white hood, Allan Arbus, who's muscled in on Robert DoQui, the black pimp and pusher. And there's Booker Bradshaw, her boyfriend and a politico in cahoots with the gang lords and cops who've maimed her admirer, William Elliott.

What happens? She kills them all off, including her two-timing lover. All of which leaves a viewer with the happy thought that she now can get back to nursing and away from films like "Coffy."

A. H. WEILER

1973 Je 16, 13:3

The Cast

THE LEGEND OF HELL HOUSE, directed by John Hough; screenplay by Richard Matheson, based on his novel "Hell House"; director of photography, Alan Hume; editor, Geoffrey Foot; music, Brian Hodgson and Delia Derbyshire; produced by Albert Fennel and Norman T. Herman; released by 20th Century-Fox. At neighborhood theaters. Running time: 93 minutes. This film is classified PG.

Florence Tanner ...... Pamela Franklin
Ben Fischer .... Roddy McDowall
Dr. Chris Barrett .... Clive Revill
Ann Barrett .... Gayle Hunnicutt
Henley .... Peter Bowles
Rudolf Deutsch .... Roland Gulver

"The Legend of Hell House," unfolded at local theaters yesterday, brims with "psychic phenomena" that, a foreword insists, "are not only very much within the bounds of possibility but could well be true." Perhaps. But it's an unconvincing legend on screen despite this sober note and a pseudo-scientific approach to ghouls, poltergeists and the like. And if John Hough, the director, and his small, willing cast maintain mild tension during their harried visit to this haunted "hell house," the few chills they provide are of little help.

The gloomy Victorian pile in question was once owned by a mysteriously departed, evil munitions tycoon, who filled it with those psychic phenomena. Now, it appears, Roland Culver, as another British millionaire, has acquired that specter-filled manse and hired a group of experts, including Roddy McDowall as a dour "physical medium," to check the dire legend for answers on survival after death.

One member of the group, Clive Revill, as a physicist who scoffs at ectoplasm, night noises and survival after death, is, however, convinced there are forces in the mansion and has a slew of scientific gadgets to destroy them.

Call it fairly standard procedure — the screams, seances, poltergeist's flying crockery and a couple of killings. But the young, decorative Pamela Franklin, as a "mental medium, and Gayle Hunnicutt, as the physicist's well-endowed wife, add an unusual, titillating facet to this film genre when they occasionally serve as sex objects for those dastardly ghouls. The rampaging spirits, however, are hard to believe, and we must agree with the realistic, unflappable Clive Revill when he exclaims: "It's impossible, I can't accept this."

A. H. WEILER

1973 Je 16, 14:5

'PAT GARRETT AND BILLY THE KID'

What you see on screen...

By ALJEAN HARMETZ

THERE are half a dozen things wrong with Sam Peckinpah's "Pat Garrett and Billy the Kid." Bob Dylan's lyrics sound silly and a century out of place. Dylan himself, in his acting debut, is saddled with a character who calls himself Alias. ("Alias what?" "Just Alias.") When asked who he is, Dylan replies, "That's a good question." Other such portentously symbolic moments are strewn throughout the film, rocks on which both characters and audience stumble

Yet "Pat Garrett and Billy the Kid" may very well be Peckinpah's best film. The classic Peckinpah themes of sadness at the death of the West and anger at the confined and mechanistic civilization that replaced it have here been deepened into something approaching Greek mythology. Whoever the real 21 - year - old killer William Bonney and the real outlaw turned lawman Pat Garrett were, they were not these victims of fate and hubris riding their separate ways through empty landscapes to adobe ruins. Beneath a somewhat shallow intellectualizing is an emotional power that sweeps one along with it. It is not on an intellectual level that the picture works but on an emotional one.

The story is simple. Pat Garrett, an old friend of Billy the Kid who now wears a star, has been sent to drive Billy out of New Mexico, or, failing that, to kill him. Billy is incapable of running away.

But the emotional underpinnings of the story are not that simple. Garrett tells Billy that the West is growing old and he wishes to grow old with it. Yet James Coburn's ambiguous Garrett appears to be driven by more Freudian furies than self-interest. When the final killing is done, he takes the same gun with which he has shot Billy the Kid and destroys his own image in a mirror.

Kris Kristofferson's Billy ("Times change. Not me.") is simpler—smiling as he kills just as he smiles at the incredible thought of being killed. This good-natured Billy enjoys killing, just as he enjoys a good whore and a good horse. (As an actor, Kristofferson is good. Coburn is something more. Minus the *cleverness* with which much of his work has been afflicted, it is perhaps his best performance.)

It is no accident that the film is titled "Pat Garrett and Billy the Kid." They are well-matched antagonists, this mercurial Billy with his capacity for pleasure and this dark, compelling Garrett dominating the web in which he is trapped by the rich, faceless civilized men who have hired him.

*

Director Peckinpah has always had an obsession with dying. In "Straw Dogs" and "The Getaway," the obses-

sion was turned to superfluous, disgusting, sadistic violence. In "The Wild Bunch," death was used as a wild and bloody catharsis. In "Pat Garrett and Billy the Kid," dying is a subtle form of art. The dead are everywhere. They mount like snowdrifts, grotesque red flowers of an arid plain. And yet the dying is not extraneous. Like death in legends, it has been fated; and nothing can change its logical necessity. Dying is a somber ritual, lovingly embraced, almost sexually fulfilling.

Billy's own death is almost a seduction. He has risen,

barefoot and shirtless, from the bed of a virginal whore. Garrett's bullet penetrates his white flesh without, seemingly, wounding him or causing him to lose even one drop of blood.

And the best scenes in the picture focus on an aging sheriff who—wanting only to be well-fed and comfortable —is forced into what he knows will be his last battle by Garrett's implacable will. As the sheriff, mortally wounded, turns his back on the battle in the oppressive red and black twilight that overlays most of the film, he walks deliberately toward a

river that might well be Archeron flowing into the Underworld.

*

Peckinpah's emphasis on children—so prominent in "The Wild Bunch," where they imitated the savage games of their elders—is almost oppressive in "Pat Garrett and Billy the Kid." These children are less primitive as, golden-haired and giggling, they innocently play with the tools of death. In scene after scene, they stand at the sidelines and absorb the lessons they are inadvertently taught. The picture opens with Billy and his friends killing chickens they have pinioned for target practice. A moment later, hungry Mexican children steal the chickens their elders have slaughtered in their ritual competition.

And Peckinpah's fingers are busy smoothing the raw wood of a child's coffin in the one-minute scene he has reserved for himself as a coffinmaker at whose side Garrett rests before forcing himself to the film's final shooting. "You finally figured it out," Peckinpah says. "Well, go on. Get it over with."

In an ordinary sense, the words are meaningless. Garrett has certainly not just figured out where Billy is, since he has spent most of the film avoiding his former friend. Half of the men who have died are victims of Garrett's refusal to pursue Billy and of Billy's hubris in refusing to run to safety in Mexico. If this Garrett has figured anything out, it is that what he is about to do is a necessity forced upon him by time and fate and his own character.

In the confrontation between a man who will compromise and a man who can not, at a time when adaptation offers the only chance of survival, lies the film's enormous and disturbing power.

"MY baby is maimed," says Sam Peckinpah of 15 minutes MGM has removed from "Pat Garrett and Billy the Kid." Peckinpah's contract with MGM gave him control of the film for two previews. After that, it was the studio's turn.

"After the first preview, it was obvious that some trimming was necessary," says the film's producer, Gordon Carroll. "Audiences were restless."

"Previews!" says Peckinpah. "There were no previews for paying audiences. The previews were held at MGM by invitation only and they had more armed guards around the studio than Watergate. They allowed me to bring 22 people, members of my family only. They wouldn't allow me to bring my crew or Jason Robards or Henry Fonda." Nor were any press allowed. The only critics to see early footage of the film were Jay Cocks of Time and Pauline Kael of The New Yorker, whom Peckinpah sneaked into a projection room to see a rough, unscored cut.

The biggest chunk of film removed is a prologue and epilogue in which Garrett is assassinated some 19 years after he has killed Billy the Kid. Garrett's assassination formed the frame of the movie while the central story became a flashback. ("Although the prologue was my idea originally," says Carroll, "an idea that Sam overjoyously latched on to, it became clear that audiences were confused by the way we executed it. Sam intercut it with the rest of the picture, added freeze frames to it and titles.")

Other sequences removed from the film include a scene between Pat Garrett and his wife; the entire character of the rancher Chisum who hires Garrett, played by Barry Sullivan; a scene in which the villainous Poe, who has been sent to accompany Garrett to make sure Garrett does his job of killing Billy, shows his villainy and cowardice by roughing up a pair of miners. Severely trimmed are whorehouse ribaldry and a hysterically religious deputy who threatens Billy.

*

"The heart of the film is missing," says Peckinpah. "I mean the motivations of the people." He is, he says, suing MGM. And he voices particular anger at the redubbing of the music to make Bob

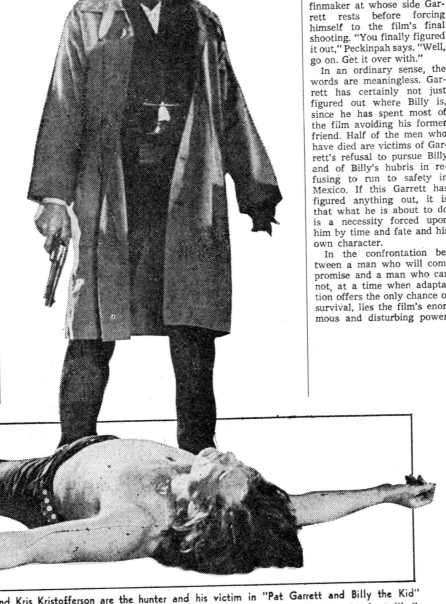

James Coburn and Kris Kristofferson are the hunter and his victim in "Pat Garrett and Billy the Kid"
"This may very well be Peckinpah's best film"

Dylan's lyrics omnipresent throughout the film. "I only had Dylan sing twice, but Gordon Carroll obviously wants to sell a Bobby Dylan album."

Peckinpah is careful to say nothing negative about the finished film. "I have not seen it—nobody invited me to see it—and my contract forbids me to say anything bad about the picture or I lose my points [percentage of profits]. They tell me it's a good film. Maybe. But at two hours and two minutes, it was sensational, the best film I ever made."

Rudolph Wurlitzer, the author of the script, is ambivalent. "I liked Sam's cut better," he says hesitantly. "It was flawed and the pace of the film was too slow, but I liked it better because it was more resonant." He adds, "It was probably less commercial. But I think the prologue and epilogue worked. And MGM cut a lot of individual lines that didn't really shorten the picture but just reduced its meaning."

—ALJEAN HARMETZ

1973 Je 17, II:13:4

How the West Was, and How Elvis Is?

By VINCENT CANBY

IT is probably impossible for seriously commercial American filmmakers ever quite to fulfill promises—made in their advertisements—to give us the truth behind the legend, or behind what a copywriter for "Elvis on Tour" calls the storybook myth. It's not because Americans are reluctant to expose truths. Debunking is an especially appreciated American art, one that is often rewarded with so much money, as well as with so much fame, that no film producer in his right mind would hesitate to do it if he possibly could. The truth is that he can't. It has something to do with the nature of popular American films, and with the manner in which we look at them.

As soon as something is reproduced through film, it becomes not just larger (and sometimes smaller) than life but also captured in time. It is different from you and me. It seems to have a call on a kind of immortality. This process has become so automatic with us today that we don't even require the use of film. How else to explain the star status, the aura of mystery, that television confers on reporters who don't do their own leg work, on weather forecasters who can't tell whether it's raining, even on people who sell remedies that might possibly, at best, offer temporary relief for mild cases of psoriasis?

The televised hearings may bring the facts of Watergate into every home, but they also spread a feeling of enchantment over them. We look at them through a curtain of red herrings. We are as impressed by the poise and by the looks of someone as we are by the possibility that perjury may have been committed. We watch the hearings as if they were a marvelous movie, some-thing beyond the wildest dreams of an Emile De Antonio or a Costa-Gavras. They are instant myth.

*

So too are a couple of recent movies that pretend to strip away old myths, only to find others underneath.

"Dirty Little Billy," a first feature directed by Stan Dragoti, written by Dragoti and Charles Moss (both of whom are successful ad men), wants to show us what the West was really like, and it does this with such earnest purpose that it creates another myth. The film's intentions are interesting, the physical production is stunningly squalid and Michael J. Pollard is spectacularly runty in the title role, that of a very young, androgynous Billy The Kid who literally wanders his way into legend through mud up to his knees.

It is a reflection of the method of the film that although we never see it rain in Coffeyville, Kansas, where most of the story is set, Coffeyville's main street is always up to here in a mucky mixture of earth and water. But that's okay. So are the little bits of character data that have as much to do with earlier films about Billy The Kid as with this supposedly new conception.

"Not many people know this," says Billy, trying to impress his friend Goldie (Richard Evans), "but I almost killed a guy in New York . . . with a brick." It's funny, not because Pollard is particularly funny, but because it's a comment on all of those other, romantically driven Billy The Kids we've seen played by Robert Taylor, Paul Newman and Kris Kristofferson (in Sam Peckinpah's current "Pat Garrett and Billy The Kid").

Dragoti's recollection of the West is probably as honest in many of its details as any recollection ever seen on the screen. For one thing, the marksmanship is terrible. People shoot at each other but miss most of the time. The guns were no good. "I tell you, Billy," Goldie says at one point, "these goddamn things are not only undependable, but they're inaccurate!"

"Billy The Kid Was A Punk," the ads proclaim, and "Dirty Little Billy" confirms this so enthusiastically that it winds up substituting for the heroic Billy of earlier movies a Billy who is so witless that he becomes a new kind of hero, the sort of legend that any kid who's ever knocked over a subway candy dispenser can identify with.

I have no idea whether this is a Good or Bad Thing, but it may possibly be that Dragoti hasn't destroyed a legend but simply broadened its base. He's made it less elitist, more accessible, more in tune, I should think, with younger audiences of today than are the middle-aged visions of Peckinpah that worry about questions of personal freedom, choice and compromise.

Pollard's Billy has hardly a thought in his head. He's a New York City kid dumped, against his will, onto a bleak Kansas farm—a guy without much in the way of mental and physical resources, who stumbles into the prairie low life for no apparent reason except that it's there.

"Dirty Little Billy" has so many good things in it that one wishes Dragoti had exercised a little more discipline over Pollard, whose mannerisms become quickly monotonous, and over his own tendency toward overstatement. It's one thing to suggest that people living in prairie hamlets seldom got a chance to bathe but quite another to have all of the extras made up to look as if they'd been working in a coal mine. As I remember it, prairie dirt is more beige than burnt cork, anyway.

The most curious thing about "Dirty Little Billy," however, is not that Dragoti has demystified the legend of Billy The Kid, but that he has —probably unintentionally— substituted one kind of myth for another. This West is bleak, dumbly violent, boring, economically depressed, hard to find enough food in, but still, in an odd way, it's romantic.

"Elvis on Tour" calls itself an intimate portrait of Elvis Presley, and was made in the course of several recent concert tours across the country. It was put together by Pierre Adidge and Robert Abel, who were among those responsible for the very lively and funny "Mad Dogs and Englishmen," the Joe Cocker concert tour film.

"Elvis on Tour" gives us an opportunity to watch large sections of individual concerts, which are okay, and then takes us behind the scenes so that we can watch Elvis flying, driving and busing to and from the concert halls, which isn't very interesting at all. The movie strips away the storybook myth to find underneath a private person who is indistinguishable from the public one, except for the fact he dresses with somewhat less flamboyance.

This could be the truth but the film remains unconvincing. If it is true, then the stolid, nicely mannered Elvis we saw in all those dozens of Hal Wallis quickies is no more or less real than the actor who played the roles. "Elvis on Tour" suggests that at this point in Presley's long and successful career, there is no "real" Elvis left. The person and the image have become one. For better or worse the camera has sanctified him.

1973 Je 17, II:1:1

The Cast

BLUME IN LOVE, directed, written and produced by Paul Mazursky; director of photography, Bruce Surtees; editor, Donn Cambern; released by Warner Brothers. Running time: 115 minutes. At Loew's Tower East Theater, Third Avenue near 72d Street. This film has been classified R.

Blume .... George Segal
Nina .... Susan Anspach
Elmo .... Kris Kristofferson
Arlene .... Marsha Mason
Mrs. Cramer .... Shelley Winters
Analyst .... Donald F. Muhich
Hellman .... Paul Mazursky
Cindy .... Erin O'Reilly
Gloria .... Annazette Chase

By VINCENT CANBY

Paul Mazursky's "Blume in Love" is an oddly affecting comedy about a successful Los Angeles divorce lawyer named Blume (George Segal) who is hopelessly in love with his ex-wife, Nina (Susan Anspach). Nina is pretty and almost painfully thin, and she approaches her social work, her yoga and her status as a newly liberated woman with such humorless determination that it's difficult to understand what Blume ever saw in her. That, however, is very much a part of the mystery and the mood of the comedy.

The air is chilly, but the sun is warm as Blume wanders around Venice, mostly around the Piazza San Marco, remembering what happened in Southern California in more or less chronological sequence. Not always. He remembers his honeymoon with Nina in Venice before he remembers their meeting at a fund-raising party for lettuce pickers. He even remembers things he didn't see, such as Nina's first encounter with Elmo (Kris Kristofferson), an out-of-work musician who seeks welfare aid from Nina and winds up living with her.

•

Blume is at loose ends, which is virtually the style of a film that is composed of flashbacks. Blume is haunted, sometimes hilariously, by memories of Nina, by memories of his own postdivorce impotence and his visits to an analyst (the same analyst who was in "Bob & Carol & Ted & Alice"), and by memories of life in Southern California.

More than anything else, perhaps, "Blume in Love" is a Southern California movie, to such an extent that Mazursky can't resist the temptation to recall Visconti's film version of "Death in Venice" as a rueful background gag while Blume wanders through Venice. It's not terribly funny, but it somehow seems appropriate to Mazursky, a very bright flim maker who seems torn between a desire to be hip and a need to ridicule the kind of fraudulent hipness he identifies with life in Southern California.

There has been this contradiction in all of Mazursky's films so far—in "I Love You, Alice B. Toklas," which he wrote in collaboration with Larry Tucker, as well as in "Bob & Carol" and "Alex in Wonderland," both of which he directed from scripts written with Tucker.

"Blume in Love," his first solo effort as writer, director and producer, strikes me as being by far his most interesting film to date, a little too self-absorbed and smart-mouthed for its own good, like Blume, but intelligent and full of healthy disrespect and energy.

These are also the qualities of Segal's performance as Blume, the sort of man who takes terrible risks for things that aren't worth risks. The divorce, for example, is prompted by the fact that he was caught when, instead of taking his secretary to a motel for an afternoon affair, he took her to his house. Blume's life is full of such suicide substitutes.

•

Miss Anspach's Nina, who begins as such a touchy character, eventually becomes conventionally sweet, not, I suspect, because Mazursky really understands her but because the film has a conventionally comic shape. Kristofferson, so ill at ease in Peckinpah's "Pat Garrett and Billy the Kid," is most relaxed and debonnaire as the musician, and Mazursky himself is extremely funny as Segal's uptight law partner.

I also very much liked Shelley Winters in the brief role of a fearful wife who wants a divorce as well as the house, the children, the beach house, the Jaguar and *all* the money.

"Blume in Love" is a restless, appealing, sometimes highly comic contemporary memoir. It opened yesterday at the Tower East.

1973 Je 18, 37:1

The Cast

SHAFT IN AFRICA, directed by John Guillermin; written by Stirling Silliphant, based upon characters created by Ernest Tidyman; director of photography, Marcel Grignon; film editor, Max Benedict; music by Johnny Pate; produced by Roger Lewis; released by Metro-Goldwyn-Mayer. At the Cinerama Theater, Broadway at 47th Street, and R.K.O. 86th Street Twin 2, west of Lexington Avenue. Running time: 112 minutes. This film is classified R.

John Shaft	Richard Roundtree
Amafi	Frank Finlay
Aleme	Vonetta McGee
Jazar	Neda Arneric
Wassa	Debebe Eshetu
Sassari	Spiros Focas
Perreau	Jacques Herlin

By ROGER GREENSPUN

When Gordon Parks's "Shaft" opened here two years ago, Vincent Canby praised it in the Sunday New York Times for recalling an almost lost tradition: the good Saturday night movie. A lot of people must have agreed. We are now into the third installment of John Shaft's adventures. But if the original "Shaft" was Saturday night, the latest sequel, John Guillermin's "Shaft in Africa," has become by some benign process, inescapably Saturday afternoon.

•

It is still good—quite surprisingly good—fairly violent and very sexy. But it is less daring, less ethnically sophisticated, more antiseptic, more comfortably middle-class. Having left his West Village pad, Shaft now lives in a luxury high-rise at the corner of Fifth Avenue and Eighth Street. It is here that representatives of an emergent African nation begin to persuade him (kidnap is a better word) to use his unmatchable talents to break up a sinister ring smuggling cheap illegal labor out of Africa and into the factories, the construction sites, the road gangs of Paris.

So Shaft leaves his native wilderness (Manhattan) and is spirited to Addis Ababa, where he sets out on a mission that seems designed to benefit French labor unions more than black workers—though a certain dimness in the plotting has never bothered movies of this nature. Shaft will pose as an ignorant job-seeking tribesman and go the whole route, by foot, by camel, by ship and by truck, to unmask the master criminal behind this 20th-century black servitude.

As Shaft, Richard Roundtree remains among the most attractive of recent movie actors. As an African tribesman he looks about as indigenous as, say, during the nineteen-thirties heyday of filmed colonialism, Ralph Richardson might have looked if gotten up with blackface in order to infiltrate the Fuzzy Wuzzies. In either case, you give up authenticity in favor of more dramatic virtues.

•

Of the two women in Shaft's current life, Vonetta McGee, here the daughter of Shaft's employer, the Emir of Kemant, is a well-known, well-admired personality. Neda Arneric, an exciting, very young Yugoslav actress, plays Jazar, a sensuous beauty with a taste for everybody, including Shaft, who makes her happy before she dies.

She is the mistress of Amafi (Frank Finlay), the smugglers' leader, and her death occasions a brief and curiously gentle exchange of regrets between him and Shaft—the kind of gallantry that sometimes enters action movies and complicates them in surprising and wholly gratifying ways. Mr. Guillermin's direction has never pleased me before, but I like it here for its economy, its generally serviceable professionalism.

"Shaft in Africa" opened yesterday at the Cinerama and RKO 86th Street Twin 2 theaters.

1973 Je 21, 53:1

The Cast

A TOUCH OF CLASS, directed and produced by Melvin Frank; screenplay Mr. Frank and Jack Rose; music, John Cameron; songs, George Barrie and Sammy Cahn; director of photography, Austin Dempster; editor, Bill Butler; a Joseph E. Levine and Brut Productions film, distributed by Avco Embassy. Running time: 105 minutes. At the Baronet Theater, Third Avenue near 59th Street. This film has been classifed PG.

Steve Blackburn	George Segal
Vicki Allessio	Glenda Jackson
Walter Menkes	Paul Sorvino
Gloria Blackburn	Hildegard Neil
Wendell Thompson	Cec Linder
Patty Menkes	K. Callan
Martha Thompson	Mary Barclay
Night Hotel Manager	Nadim Sawalha

By VINCENT CANBY

Steve Blackburn (George Segal) is an American insurance executive living in London with his wife and two children. Vicki Allessio (Glenda Jackson) is a high-voltage young Englishwoman who successfully pirates Paris fashions for New York's Seventh Avenue. She has two children but is separated from her Italian husband who lives in Milan. "He'd send me money for the children," she says, "if I sent him money for the cars."

Steve and Vicki meet in a manner that Hollywood writers used to call cute. He's playing softball in the park and almost tramples her son trying to catch a fly ball. Steve and Vicki trade rebukes and after two more meetings, they are preparing to have an affair in Marbella. "It'll probably do us both a world of good," says Steve, although he throws his back out of joint on their arrival in Spain and the next night they are throwing lamps at each other while a comic desk clerk is pleading: "Is this any way to treat a hotel?"

•

Melvin Frank's "A Touch of Class" is a very patchy movie—enormously funny in bits and pieces and sometimes downright dumb. When the material matches their intelligence, Segal and Miss Jackson are extremely funny lovers, as on their first night when they find themselves lying in bed, each on his (or her) "wrong" side, arguing about how they will change locations with a minimum of fuss.

There are also some fine farcical scenes more or less dedicated to the proposition that maintenance of a love nest is, at best, full of peril. On one occasion, after Steve has left his house telling his wife he is going to walk the dog, he returns home unaccompanied. In a transport of illicit joy he has left the dog with Vicki.

Steve and Vicki obviously are perfectly matched, sharing not only the star billing of Segal and Miss Jackson, but also a common fondness for the excitement to be found in periodic domestic rough-house. Steve's wife (Hildegard Neil) seems to be a frigid bore and Vicki's life alone is certainly unrewarding. They were made for each other.

However, Mr. Frank, who directed the film, and his collaborator on the screenplay, Jack Rose, will not let the characters alone. They keep forcing them into awkward attitudes. To set up the kind of laughs the film wants, the Segal character is asked to behave like such an idiot he wouldn't know second gear from third, which has the effect of turning Miss Jackson's Vicki into a wisecracking shrew.

The problem, I suspect, is that "A Touch of Class" is a remodeled comedy out of the nineteen-forties, when it was written in Hollywood (in the old Production Code) that adultery was tabu. Adultery must not be consummated, but it was O.K. as long as it was being constantly interrupted. It's not adultery that gets interrupted in "A Touch of Class," but the natural instincts of two supposedly sophisticated people.

•

This may be taking "A Touch of Class" more seriously than most audiences looking for easy laughs will care to. Others may share my feeling that there is something contradictory about a contemporary comedy that wishes to tell us that adultery is simply not worth the effort, even though the partners are so clearly in love. The ending is not sad, only a bit fraudulent.

Somehow I expect more of a movie that can contain a desperately funny defense of an American mother who, though the family was not rich, saw to it that her children always had fresh grapefruit in winter and were the first on their block to own electric blankets.

1973 Je 21, 52:1

Five Premieres Held at Little Carnegie

By ROGER GREENSPUN

A brief festival of new Russian movies—five feature-film premieres, a kids' film, and a revival of Andrei Smirnov's "Byelorussian Station" —played last week at the Little Carnegie Theater in a program meant to tie in with Leonid I. Brezhnev's visit to the United States. The films are scheduled for further showings in this country, possibly for commercial distribution. Two have been dubbed into English; the rest, mercifully, are subtitled.

They are presented as representing a cross section of recent Soviet film making. I suspect they do represent certain aspects of popularly accepable Russian film making, and for people whose idea of the Soviet cinema has been formed by "Potemkin," "Alexander Nevsky," "The Lady With the Little Dog" or even "Ballad of a Soldier," the new movies may come as a discouraging surprise.

Consider the story of Aleksei Sakharov's "In His Right Place": Semyon, a young engineer, gets himself elected chairman of his collective farm. He believes in much work and no wasted time. He does not believe in smoking, drinking or miniskirts—and neither does the film. He proposes many changes with a view to modernizing the collective. At first the older people oppose him, but eventually they see the light, and the young chairman succeeds.

•

Or consider the story of Oleg Bondaryev's "The Stepmother": When Pavel, who maintains and operates machinery on a collective farm, learns that a woman he was once in love with has died—leaving behind a little girl who is, in fact, his daughter —his good wife, Shura, agrees to take the child in and to become her stepmother. At first the child is mistrustful and withdrawn; but eventually Shura's goodness and maternal warmth win her over, and the stepmother succeeds.

I've left out a lot. The films are full (but not too full) of humanizing and individualizing details. Some of the performances—such as Tatyana Doronina's as the plump, good-natured, perpetually flustered, slightly dim-witted stepmother—are very expert. But despite the details and the performances, these are films of an almost numbing simplicity. They are exactly the "realism" that might do for edification in some ideally placated society. And compared with other East European cinemas—compared with what we have seen over the last few years, say, from Yugoslavia, from Hungary, even from Bulgaria—they are film making at a kindergarten level of cultural awareness and dramatic sophistication.

Two of the Russian movies are escapist entertainment. Vladimir Motyl's "White Sun of the Desert" is a picaresque adventure, involving the heroic exploits of a Red Army soldier in the insufficiently socialized wilds of Turkestan. Leonid Gaidai's "Ivan Vassilyevich Changes His Profession" suggests what might happen if, by means of a time machine, Ivan the Terrible were suddenly to find himself in 20th-century Moscow, while two 20th-century Muscovites were taking Ivan's place in medieval Russia.

●

With the kind of madcap comedy idea that withers the imagination even before it hits the screen, "Ivan Vassilyevich" is of interest mainly for its director's unflagging devotion to the assumption that rapid-motion photog-raphy is always funny, for the graffiti that show up on Moscow apartment-building walls (extensive, but still pre-aerosol-spray-can) and for the intimations of luxury in middle-class urban life. Convertibles, cameras, tape recorders, black-market transistors—the film is a small-scale homage to conspicuous consumption.

The best of the films also ostensibly the most official—a long semidocumentary called "The Taming of Fire." Written and directed by Edward Smirnov and Miss Doronina (the stepmother is also a scenarist), it concerns a pioneering space scientist who suffers a heart attack and then, hovering between life and death, immediately has a 2-hour-and-20-minute flashback covering the entire history of Soviet rocket development from the beginnings to the present.

●

There are interesting sidelights, such as the shooting down of Francis Gary Powers's U-2 spy plane in 1960, or the exploding of a Soviet nuclear bomb (justified on the grounds, more or less, that the Americans already have it, and the only language those people understand is force). But the movie really comes alive with its rocketry and with its exotic and marvelously theatrical—and, I assume, authentic—space hardware.

Unfortunately the dialogue is English-dubbed, and, through the universal alchemy of dubbing studios, it has been transformed into 50 per cent non sequiturs. But from what I can make out, "The Taming of Fire" is not wholly enamored of state science or hard work or success. It even sees its great scientist (quite well played by Kirill Lavrov) as something of a dedicated monster and all of Moscow's honors as a rather paltry substitute for life. In the context of Soviet cinema week, this seems like the stirring of some real air to breathe.

1973 Je 23, 18:1

'State of Siege' Speaks 'A Warning to Us All'

By THEODORE C. SORENSEN

COSTA-GAVRAS'S "State of Siege" is a provocative, disturbing film that will shake most viewers out of their slumbering indifference to Latin America and make them think. For that reason alone, it is worth seeing. Although it relies too heavily on blatant oversimplification to be a great film, it is nevertheless an important one.

To be sure, it is not the subtlety or complexity of Costa-Gavras's characterizations that requires one to think. The most somnolent viewer will have no trouble determining that nearly everyone on the side for which it is clearly intended he root is, if not literally wearing a white hat, unfailingly eloquent, efficient, youthful and idealistic, while those wearing the figurative black hats are nearly all rich, self-righteous, cynical, aging and power-hungry.

*

No shades of gray, no lingering doubts or exceptions intrude. The urban guerril-las who seize an American A.I.D. official in a violence-ridden Latin-American nation feel free to murder him, and the police and government forces who seek his return feel free to murder them. With the possible exception of one wise old reporter-narrator, there is no one in the middle, no one to suggest that urban guerrillas may be as brutal and terroristic as the police department's unofficial execution squad, no one to suggest that the Alliance for Progress and A.I.D. might, for all their imperfections, have done some good, or that Latin-American resentment of the United States would rightly and greatly increase, not diminish, if all United States aid and investments were ever in fact to be withdrawn — which the film implicitly favors.

Nevertheless, "State of Siege" cannot be dismissed as nothing more than crude propaganda. However irrationally the film makes the leap from A.I.D. to the

Jean-Luc Bideau, as a guerrilla leader, is blocked by soldiers in Costa-Gavras's "State of Siege"
"President Kennedy would have disagreed with much in the picture, but I think he would have liked it"

torture of political prisoners, a more valid underlying message remains: namely, that United States policy toward Latin America over the last decade has in fact placed too much emphasis on "internal security" and not enough on social security; that we have all too often lined up behind a corrupt elite and against those protesting the paternalistic power of our corporate enclaves, and that our broken promises on trade and our distorted priorities on aid have contributed to the ugly hunger and poverty in the southern half of this hemisphere that breed the very kind of resentment and violence that Costa-Gavras has so chillingly portrayed.

In fact, bitter feelings against this country, its foreign policy, its foreign economic policy and its leadership are not confined to the young or the radical left in Latin America, as the viewer of this movie might assume. Nor is the resultant danger confined to villainous officials. Like most Americans, the kidnapped and ultimately executed A.I.D. police instructor was not a cruel or greedy right-winger who knowingly abetted the suppression of human values. Nevertheless, it was upon him that the rage of the oppressed ultimately and inevitably — however unjustifiably — fell; and as this nation's continued neglect of Latin America helps build an atmosphere for violence throughout that region, this film is a warning to us all.

*

Unfortunately, its effects may be contrary to its intent and only worsen the situation its creators deplore. By romanticizing the nobility of those who murdered the A.I.D. official, "State of Siege" may only encourage some youthful fanatics to believe that such tactics are a true measure of their commitment to political and social change; and that, in turn, can only increase extremism among the hard-pressed governments trying to cope with them.

I am not one of those who read into the film a justification for political assassinations. On the contrary, the film made it clear to me that violence on both sides is wholly futile. When one A.I.D. police instructor is senselessly killed for no advantage, another promptly takes his place. When one student revolutionary is murdered by the government's unofficial "death squad," another promptly takes his place. Nevertheless, the invitation by Costa-Gavras to cheer for the murderers of the A.I.D. official — instead of grieving for his widow and children — may inspire similar misdeeds among the fervent.

Additionally, by implanting in other impressionable minds the notion that all Latin-American governments and their military officials are corrupt and incompetent, the film may only reinforce the North American attitudes of condescension and contempt that have so long characterized much of our governmental, business and public thinking about Latin America. By grouping proud and highly developed Latin-American cultures with far less mature societies

Theodore C. Sorensen, former Special Counsel to President Kennedy, practices law in New York City.

on other continents merely because they are all poor and nonindustrialized, and by lumping the best in Latin-American leadership, both civilian and military, with the worst, we have in the past justified every kind of exploitation, intervention and discrimination by United States interests. The film's scathing portrayal of the besieged government (presumably Uruguay) may unfortunately increase those patronizing tendencies.

Finally, the film is likely to add to the enemies of an overseas assistance program that already has more handicaps than it deserves. I have viewed firsthand some of the schools, hospitals, homes and resource development projects made possible by the Alliance for Progress and it will take more than a film to persuade me that A.I.D. in Latin America has been principally involved in teaching torture and assassination.

But one insidious result of the Watergate affair is the temptation it offers to believe the worst about every government agency. If the C.I.A. is involved in raids on psychiatric records, if State Department cables are loaned out to falsify the history of the assassination of President Diem in Vietnam, if the Acting Director of the F.B.I. is burning documents, who among us in the general public can say with assurance what A.I.D. or Bebe Rebozo or David Eisenhower may have been up to?

None of these drawbacks, it should now be clear, justified the removal of the film as a premiere offering by the American Film Institute at the John F. Kennedy Center in Washington. I am certain that was a well-intended action badly understood. But if one such intention was concern for the ideals of President Kennedy, in my opinion it was misplaced. He would have disagreed with much in the picture, as he did with countless films, books, articles and other expressions of opinion and history that he consumed so consistently. But I think he would have seen "State of Siege," thought about it and, on balance, liked it.

1973 Je 24, 15:1

'O Lucky Man!' Ran Out of Luck

By VINCENT CANBY

WRITERS of movie scripts shouldn't keep diaries, or, if they do, they should not allow them to be published for at least 50 years.

David Sherwin's screenplay for "O Lucky Man!", which has been published in England by Plexus, contains a diary by Sherwin that explains the genesis of the project (an idea by Malcolm McDowell) and describes the trials and tribulations of the writer in the self-important tones that only the best diarists avoid. Sherwin reveals himself as a writer being pushed beyond his capacities by the director, Lindsay Anderson, who had earlier directed the Sherwin screenplay for "If . . ."

This, I'm sure, is not the way Sherwin sees it. He sounds eternally grateful to Anderson for having had the pluck to see him (Sherwin) through the long process by which McDowell's funny little germ of a story, about a trainee-coffee salesman who wanted to be a pop singer, was stretched into social satire of supposedly epic proportions. In Sherwin's finished screenplay the trainee-coffee salesman has become a classic innocent named Mick Travis (McDowell) whose over-riding desire to succeed leads him into disastrous adventures in the worlds of business, international finance, science and even social welfare.

*

"O Lucky Man!," which is now at the Cinema I, looks as if it should be great and one keeps wanting it to be great. It has been beautifully photographed by Miroslav Ondricek, the Czech cinematographer who did "If . . .," and given a kind of cabaret-film form by Anderson,

who without making a big deal out of it, separates the various episodes by cutting to a black screen (which becomes a kind of harmless death threat), or by occasionally cutting to the recording studio where Alan Price, the composer-singer, and his back-up men are recording the film's score. More than any other single element in the film, this score, including the title song and a number called "Poor People," realizes the cool sarcasm and wit that never are fully evident in the screenplay.

*

The cast is not large, but everyone (McDowell, Ralph Richardson, Rachel Roberts, Arthur Lowe, Helen Mirren, Dandy Nichols and the others), is marvelous, especially those who reappear throughout Mick's adventures as different characters. In the theater this practice of having actors double or triple in roles is usually a means to hold down the costs of a large cast. Here, in addition to permitting us to enjoy the various humors of people like Richardson and Lowe, it also serves to unify a narrative that sprawls as if sprawling were a noble end in itself.

In his diary, Sherwin recalls that Anderson read the first 20 pages of the screenplay, then called "Coffee Man," and found it "too mini and naturalistic." There follow discussions in which are mentioned works like "Heaven's My Destination," "Amerika," "Pilgrim's Progress" and "Candide," which eventually leads to the following quote of Anderson:

". . . .to make it epic, to give it an epic quality, a view of society, it ought to be quite separate things (Mick) tries, thinking each time that this is going to

be marvelous, this is the answer, then when it collapses he tries something new — so each time we see a completely different section of life. This would be epic. . . ."

In an interview in The Times of London, Anderson is quoted as describing the proposed story about the trainee-coffee salesman as a "genre comedy" and then commenting that the epic "is a form which hasn't been attempted very much recently—middle class artists lack the confidence for it."

The evidence presented by "O Lucky Man!" is that they may lack the confidence because it's bloody difficult to bring off. Among other things, it presents very special technical problems for the writer since there is usually only one continuing character and each new episode means the introduction of new people who have to be immediately identifiable. There isn't time for buildups. It's like writing a dozen blackout sketches. If half of them are only so-so, then the whole review probably fails.

*

More important, the form demands not only wit but a sense of mission, the sort displayed by Shaw in his drama reviews, when he knew what kind of plays he wanted to write to reform the world. Middle-class artists don't lack the confidence necessarily. They lack the fanaticism of reformers committed to extreme and shocking positions.

The social satire in Sherwin's script is essentially as chatty (and familiar) as his diary account of giving birth to the screenplay:

"31st July, 1971. Go down on the train with Lindsay to Hythe—to spend the weekend working. On the train he reads the first draft for the first time, groaning and closing his eyes.

"'It's terrible,' he says.

"Then he comes to three blank pages.

"'What's this?'

"'It's the scene on the roof. Mick and the girl. It's a complete blank—I can't think of anything. It's totally unreal. I can't write it.'

"'You'll just have to this weekend or we'll pack in the film.'"

They did not, of course, pack in the film. Sherwin plowed on, writing with no special rage or conviction. The nearest thing to a political idea in the film is a slogan painted on a London wall: "Revolution is the opium of the intellectuals." Which is less an idea than a gag.

*

Actually one of Sherwin's best scenes — according to

the published screenplay—was eventually cut out of the film. It's a scene in which Mick, lately released from prison where he was sent for having failed at being successful, tries to talk a haggard housewife out of committing suicide. Full of optimism as usual, he reads to her: "Life is mostly froth and bubble/"Two things stand like stone/"Kindness in another's trouble/"Courage in your own." She goes on about her business, which is the cleaning of her apartment. "My husband has to find the place looking nice," she says. "I won't have him saying I did wrong at the end."

Yet this scene, like all of the film's best moments, is closer to what I think Anderson means by genre comedy than it is to epic comedy. With the exception of the sequence in which Mick, as private secretary to a tycoon played by Richardson, witnesses a business deal between the tycoon and the corrupt president of an emerging African nation, the content of the satire is either too small or too banal for the form of the film. Among other things, the movie discovers that court justices may be closet masochists, that casual torture of innocents can be excused because of national security interests, and that the have-nots of the world can be just as cruel as the haves.

Anderson, in a preface to Sherwin's published screenplay, talks about "intuitive choices" he made when he was shooting "O Lucky Man!", especially in connection with the choice of actors to reappear in different roles. Anderson is an intuitive director, yet it's schematicism that inhibits the film, to an even larger extent than it did "If. . ."

The very fact that he and Sherwin felt called upon to name their hero Mick Travis indicates a desire to impose a certain program of intellectual responses upon the movie. Mick Travis was the name of the schoolboy-revolutionary played by McDowell in "If. . .," and there seems to be absolutely no reason to recall him in the new film except to establish connections that are of no value whatsoever.

According to Sherwin's diary, it was Anderson who prompted the transformation of the story of the trainee-coffee salesman ("something small-scale") into its present epic form, the sort of film that's much more interesting to talk about than to sit through, and that often winds up getting reviewed for its intentions instead of its accomplishments. Anderson is a fine director, a quirky and bristly sort of artist, but one of these days I'd like to see him work again in the comparatively small scale he handled so beautifully in "This Sporting Life."

1973 Je 24, II:1:3

THE FRIENDS OF EDDIE COYLE, directed by Peter Yates; screenplay by Paul Monash, based on the novel by George V. Higgins; produced by Mr. Monash; director of photography, Victor J. Kemper; editor, Pat Jaffe; music, Dave Grusin; distributed by Paramount Pictures. Running time: 102 minutes. At the National Theater, Broadway at 44th Street, and Cinema 11 Theater, Third Avenue near 60th Street. This film has been classified R.

Eddie Coyle	Robert Mitchum
Dillon	Peter Boyle
Dave Foley	Richard Jordan
Jackie	Steven Keats
Scalise	Alex Rocco
Artie Van	Joe Santos
Waters	Mitchell Ryan
Sheila Coyle	Helena Carroll

By VINCENT CANBY

Peter Yate's "The Friends of Eddie Coyle," adapted by Paul Monash from the George V. Higgins novel, is a good, tough, unsentimental movie about the last days of a small-time Boston hood.

Eddie Coyle (Robert Mitchum) is a guy who knows his place. Once he didn't. Once he bought some guns for some associates, and when the guns were traced to those associates, the associates of the associates took Eddie aside and broke all the knuckles on one hand. There was nothing personal. Eddie could undetrstand how they felt.

Now Eddie is getting old, not like most movie gangster heros, with grandeur, but with desperation. He's facing a two-year sentence in New Hampshire for driving a truck that carried stolen whisky. He has no money in the bank and his wife and children will probably have to go on welfare.

•

Eddie was never one to think big. He let the other guys do that. He buys stolen guns for the guys who pull the bank jobs, and at night he goes home to the wife and kids or, sometimes, to a hockey game.

Eddie is not very imaginative, and he's not a tragic hero, but as played by Mitchum he has wit and a certain dignity. In the end, even the dignity is taken away from him.

"The Friends of Eddie Coyle" is so beautifully acted and so well set (in and around Boston's pool halls, parking lots, side-streets, house trailers and barrooms) that it reminds me a good deal of John Huston's "Fat City." It also has that film's ear for the way people talk—for sentences that begin one way and end another, or are stuffed with excess pronouns. "What you don't know, it don't bother you," a friend might say to Eddie.

Unlike "Fat City," however, "The Friends of Eddie Coyle" is interested in plot and narrative suspense. The film splits its attention between Eddie, as he slowly evolves into a stool pigeon in an effort to stay free, and the more or less conventional caper movie sequences that show us how to rob a bank. Mr. Yates ("Bullitt") is so good at this sort of thing that it's probably difficult to resist putting it in.

There's nothing wrong with it, but it does diminish the impact of Eddie's story, which could have been quite special.

Giving Mitchum excellent support are Peter Boyle, as a bartender who deals in larceny and contract murder on the side, and Richard Jordan, as a young detective who looks deceptively soft, talks much like the hoods he is tracking, and is genuinely fascinated by the game he must play with them.

The detective's manner with Eddie is direct, absolutely straight, but he is always pushing him. "You help uncle, uncle will help you," he tells Eddie. It's fairly typical of everything that's wrong in Eddie's life, that when he decides to turn in several associates he is 12 hours too late. Someone else squealed before he could.

"The Friends of Eddie Coyle" opened yesterday at the National and Cinema II Theaters.

1973 Je 27, 68:1

The Cast

CHARLEY AND THE ANGEL, directed by Vincent McEveety; screenplay by Roswell Rogers, based on Will Stanton's "The Golden Evenings of Summer"; produced by Bill Anderson for Walt Disney Productions; presented by Buena Vista. At the Guild Theater, 33 West 50th Street, and Quad I Theater, 13th Street between Fifth Avenue and the Avenue of the Americas. Running time: 93 minutes. (This film is rated "G.")

Charley Appelby	Fred MacMurray
Nettie Appleby	Cloris Leachman
The Angel	Harry Morgan
Ray Ferris	Kurt Russell
Leonora Appleby	Kathleen Coty
Willie Appleby	Vincent Van Patten
Rupert Appleby	Scott Kolden
Sadie	Barbara Nichols

By HOWARD THOMPSON

"Cinderella," the cartoon-revival half of a current Walt Disney package, is far and away the better part of yesterday's double-bill at the Guild and Quad I Theaters. Wise parents will time it so that the youngsters see this treat first. The new live-action comedy, "Charley and the Angel," can be taken as a tame, friendly caboose.

The only real fun, judging by audience squeals at the Guild, is the finale, involving some wildly-flapping old flivver cars, as Fred MacMurray tries to rescue his two young sons from gangster-bootleggers. The kids loved this careening chaos. Otherwise, they had to settle for spurts of familiar trick photography, as a natty "angel" popped in to remind Mr. MacMurray, a stodgy business man, that he wasn't getting any fun out of life.

Otherwise, nothing much happens. The picture, set in the Depression years, has a mildly diverting facade of nostalgia in costumes, tunes and those fine, tacky old cars. Mr. MacMurray, by now a Disney veteran, is front and center, unremittingly wide-eyed.

Little sparkle or wit is accorded as appealing a family as any papa could wish. But Cloris Leachman as his wife, Kathleen Coty, Vincent Van Patten and little Scott Kolden do pleasantly by humdrum material. The same goes for Harry Morgan as the wry visitor from above, young Kurt Russell and, very minutely, Barbara Nichols.

Master Kolden wedges in on bright, morning-after breakfast line after Mr. MacMurray is picked up, sipping lemonade, during a mild-looking roadhouse raid by police. "Hey, Pop," he chirps, "how was it in the clink?" The rest, until that chase, is pretty much milk and crackers.

1973 Je 28, 58:1

The Cast

LIVE AND LET DIE, directed by Guy Hamilton, screenplay by Tom Mankiewicz; camera, Ted Moore; editors, Bert Bates, Raymond Poulton and John Shirley; music, George Martin; produced by Albert R. Broccoli and Harry Saltzman; presented by United Artists Corporation. At the United Artists East Theater, First Avenue and 85th Street; the Rivoli Theater, Broadway and 49th Street and the 49th Street East Theater at Third Avenue. Running time: 121 minutes. Rating: PG.

James Bond	Roger Moore
Doctor Kananha	Yaphet Kotto
Solitaire	Jane Seymour
Sheriff Pepper	Clifton James
Tee Hee	Julius W. Harris
Baron Samedi	Geoffrey Holder
Leiter	David Hedison
Rosie	Gloria Hendry
"M"	Bernard Lee

By ROGER GREENSPUN

Torchlight. Voodoo drums. Dark bodies writhe in the mounting frenzy of some unspeakable tropical rite. Suddenly a door is flung open and framed within it stands a beautiful white girl held captive by two monstrous black men. Her filmy white gown scarcely covering the soft contours of her body, she is dragged — protesting — to a crude scaffold and there is tied fast.

As if by signal, the ranks of jeering celebrants open and there advances an executioner, laughing, stomping, hideously costumed. He holds a poisonous snake in his outstretched hands, a snake whose bite is destined for the smooth young bosom. . . .

•

Whatever the quality of this little scenario, you must admit that to stick it into a movie these days takes nerve. Merely to make a new adventure movie in which all the bad guys are black and almost all the good guys are white, and which includes in its climax the (near) sacrifice of a (recent) virgin—takes nerve.

Nerve, and certain insolence toward public pieties, and a lot of canniness about just what level of sophistication its audience is up to—all of them qualities that have characterized the James Bond movies since the beginning, 10 years ago, and that abundantly characterize the latest, Guy Hamilton's "Live and Let Die."

There are now eight Bond movies, and though they are the work of many different talents (Hamilton has directed two previously: "Goldfinger" and "Diamonds Are Forever") they do represent a recognizable tradition in which the whole—or the memory of the whole — seems to be greater than the sum of the parts.

The plots tend to flow into each other—one scheme after another for controlling all the money in the world—changing their elements to fit changing anxieties (in "Live and Let Die" the evil is a heroin monopoly operating out of some Caribbean island kingdom with pipelines into New York City and New Orleans), but remaining the same in essence.

And always there is a woman waiting to be converted by the power of sex. In "Live and Let Die" she reads the Tarot pack to tell fortunes for the enemy. James Bond's card keeps coming up "Lovers," though she thinks she is hoping for "Death."

There are three chases (four, if you stretch a point), including one by car and motorboat that gets so complicated it allows for character development. One actor, Clifton James, who appears only during the chase, gets fourth billing in the cast list. The names above Mr. James's do not seem so impressive. Roger Moore is a handsome, suave, somewhat phlegmatic James Bond—with a tendency to throw away his throw-away quips as the minor embarrassments that, alas, they usually are.

As Solitaire, to whom the cards speak truth only so long as she remains a virgin, Jane Seymour is beautiful enough, but too submissive even for this scale of fantasy. Yaphet Kotto (Dr. Kananha), a most agreeable actor, simply does not project evil.

However, I could list compensating virtues by the score. There is a marvelous escape from an alligator farm (deadly reptiles are rather a motif in this movie), a superb collection of grotesque ways of killing, and a fine sense of pace and rhythm. "Live and Let Die" has been especially well photographed and edited, and it makes clever and extensive use of its good title song, by Paul and Linda McCartney.

1973 Je 28, 56:1

The Cast

PLAYTIME, directed and produced by Jacques Tati; screenplay (English, French, German, Japanese) by Mr. Tati; directors of photography, Jean Badal and Andreas Winding; editor, Gerard Pollicand; a Spectra Film production, distributed by Continental Films. Running time: 108 minutes. At the Festival Theater, 57th Street near Fifth Avenue. This film has not been classified.

Mr. Hulot	Jacques Tati
Young Stranger	Barbara Dennek
The False Hulot	Marc Monjou
The Architect	George Faye

By VINCENT CANBY

"Playtime," which opened yesterday at the Festival Theater, is Jacques Tati's most brilliant film, a bracing reminder in this all-too-lazy era that films can occasionally achieve the status of art.

"Playtime" is a gloriously funny movie about a Paris so modern it does not yet exist, a Paris composed entirely of streets like our Avenue of the Americas, hemmed in by efficiently beautiful glass-and-steel towers in which, if we are quick about it, we may see momentary reflections of Sacre Coeur, the Arch of Triumph or the Eiffel Tower.

It is a city inhabited almost entirely by tourists and their shepherd-guides who are spreading a terrible pox among the natives. It is not an immediately fatal disease but it makes everyone behave with the kind of frigid competence affected by airline stewardesses and reservation clerks.

Not even nuns are immune. Their heels click importantly as they glide across marbleized floors. A receptionist—a man so ancient that he could be a veteran of Verdun—operates a complex of computer buttons designed to announce a visitor's arrival in an office building. The old man does his best and the machine bleeps and gurgles successfully. It is the world of Kubrick's "2001" without the metaphysics and without Richard Strauss.

•

"Playtime," which was made in 1967 and is only now being released in this country, is Tati's most free-form comedy to date, as well as his most disciplined, even more so than "Traffic," which was made in 1971 but was seen here last winter.

It is virtually three major set pieces, or acts. The first act is set at Orly Airport, where we pick up some American tourists who arrive in a single, all-expenses-paid clump. The second is more or less devoted to a trade fair, where the tourists cross paths with Tati's Mr. Hulot.

The last act, a kind of neon-lit Gotterdammerung—is set in a posh nightclub whose opening night turns into the sort of chaos that civilizes. Everything goes wrong, including the air-conditioning, but in going wrong, life is somehow restored to the tourists as well as the natives.

You may well recognize the shape of the film, which is a variation on the favorite comedy theme about the family that inherits a lot of money, tries to put on fancy airs, loses it soul, and only finds itself again when the fortune is taken away.

However, it is not the shape of the film or its cheerful philosophy that are important. Rather it is the density of the wit. It is the gracefulness of the visual gags that flow one into another, non-stop, in a manner that only Tati now masters.

Mr. Hulot is still the nominal focal point of the comedy, particularly in the trade-fair sequence, but he is less in evidence in "Playtime" than in any other Hulot feature. The film is even further removed from character than was "Traffic." It observes not persons, but social clusters, in a manner that serves curiously to humanize group action and response instead of to dehumanize the individual.

•

However, don't waste time analyzing "Playtime" too much. It can easily withstand such critical assaults, but they serve to distract attention from the film's immense good humor, from, for example, the closing sequence that shows us a Parisian traffic circle that has been turned into a giant lazy Susan, serving, among other things, the sacred cause of inefficiency.

In addition to everything else, "Playtime" is a reckless act of faith—by Tati in himself. He photographed it in 70-mm (though it is being shown here in 35-mm), and he invested not only huge amounts of time in it, but also his own money. As anyone connected with films can tell you, this is certifiable madness.

The movie business is supposed to exist so that people other than its artists can lose their shirts in it, thereby to gain things that are called (by those who can use them) tax-loss carry-forwards. I hope "Playtime" will make Tati very rich so that at some future time he can use a tax-loss carry-forward.

1973 Je 28, 57:3

40 CARATS, directed by Milton Katselas; screenplay by Leonard Gershe, based on Jay Allen's stage play adapted from a French play by Barillet and Gredy; produced by M. J. Frankovich; director of photography, Charles B. Lang; editor, David Blewitt; music, Michel Legrand; distributed by Columbia Pictures. Running time: 109 minutes. At the Radio City Music Hall, Avenue of the Americas at 50th Street. This film has been classified PG.

Ann Stanley	Liv Ullmann
Peter Latham	Edward Albert
Billy Boylan	Gene Kelly
Maud Ericson	Binnie Barnes
Trina Stanley	Deborah Raffin
J. D. Rogers	Billy Green Bush
Mrs. Margolin	Nancy Walker
Mr. Latham	Don Porter
Mrs. Latham	Rosemary Murphy
Mrs. Adams	Natalie Schafer

By VINCENT CANBY

"40 Carats," which opened yesterday at Radio City Music Hall is Jay Allen's Broadway comedy recycled as a movie, the sort in which you could put the world's greatest actors and not even miss them. The blandness of the project renders everyone invisible.

Liv Ullmann plays Ann Stanley, a Manhattan real-estate agent with a pool-playing daughter of 17 (Deborah Raffin), a madcap mother (Binnie Barnes) and a charming ex-husband (Gene Kelly) who acts in TV pilots and coffee commercials. Ann is successful and tranquil but unfulfilled.

•

On a holiday in Greece, Ann meets personable, presentable Peter Latham (Edward Albert) when her car breaks down in front of a view of the Gulf of Saronikos. Peter, 22, offers her a lift on his motorcycle. Ann refuses, pointing out she is 36. Instead, he gives her some ouzo, which, strangely, she has never heard of, even though she has been junketing around Greece for weeks. One thing leads to another, and Ann and Peter spend an idyllic night together on the beach.

Back in Manhattan, Peter wants to marry Ann. She refuses. She's lied to him, she admits. She's not 36 but 38, well, actually 40? The way Ann vacillates, you get the idea she sees herself as a female Humbert Humbert. Should she or should she not? Will love triumph? "Don't think of them as years," suggests her charming ex-husband, "but carats. You're a multi-careted, blue-white diamond!" As one drama critic said of the play with admiration, the movie doesn't cop out.

•

It doesn't do much of anything. It just sits there, like a piece of expensively upholstered furniture.

The women wear a lot of fancy gowns and trade wisecracks, only one of which, spoken by that fine comedienne, Nancy Walker, made me laugh. Gene Kelly gives the impression that he might still be as charming as we all remember him in "Singing in the Rain." Edward Albert, who made his debut in "Butterflies Are Free," has a very spruce appearance.

Miss Ullmann, however, is utterly lost. This marvelous actress, the world's most beautiful woman in Bergman's "Cries and Whispers," looks like a 33-year-old frump, not a 40-year-old beauty. She is, I suspect, constitutionally incapable of dealing with this sort of nonsense in anything except the rather somber manner of a concerned night nurse in a charity ward. It seems she wants to help but she can't.

Milton Katselas directed the movie and Leonard Gershe wrote the screenplay. They've succeeded in disguising the fact that it is basically a stage play, but not the fact that the material is hopelessly dumb.

1973 Je 29, 14:1

OPERATION LEONTINE, directed by Michel Audiard; screen adaptation and script (French with English subtitles) by Mr. Audiard; photography by Georges Barsky; produced by Alain Poire; released by Audio Brandon Films. At the First Avenue Screening Room, at 61st Street. Running time: 85 minutes. This film has not been classified.

Leontine	Francoise Rosay
Rita	Marlene Jobert
Fred	Andre Pousse
Charles	Bernard Blier
Casmir	Robert Dalban
Ruffin	Paul Frankeur
Tiburce	Claude Rollet

By ROGER GREENSPUN

Michel Audiard's "Operation Leontine," which opened yesterday at the First Avenue Screening Room, is a heavily artificial comic-caper movie about an aged French queen of crime (Françoise Rosay) who temporarily leaves her retirement to outwit, outmurder, and outsteal all the hottest talent in Paris—including her own fast-thinking, two-timing young niece (Marlene Jobert). There is a story behind all this, but it is of no account, and since the film doesn't care about it, neither shall I.

What the film does care about is some not terribly exalted notion of cinema style—or stylishness—which it does its endless, agonizing, suffocating, unfunny best to exploit. In the early nineteen-sixties it was fashionable among second- and third-rank French directors to make movies that were archly self-conscious of the medium, and it is to this tradition, 10 years out of date, that "Operation Leontine" belongs. It is the kind of film in which characters spend almost as much time talking to the camera as they do to each other—thus presuming on a bond of audience sympathy that has not been earned and therefore does not exist.

Michel Audiard is well-known as a writer (not director) of popular film comedies, and François Rosay's career covers literally the entire history of the French sound film—so there is a degree of professionalism in "Operation Leontine" that seems to belie the absolute dullness of everything that shows on the screen. But the dullness is real and the professionalism, a waste. Movies at precisely this level make me long for fresh air and sunlight, and perhaps immersion in the 19th-century novel.

1973 Je 29, 17:1

THE MAN WHO LOVED CAT DANCING, directed by Richard Sarafian; screenplay by Eleanor Perry, based on the novel by Marilyn Durham; produced by Martin Poll and Mrs. Perry; music, John Williams; director of photography, Harry Stradling Jr.; editor, Tom Rolf; distributed by Metro-Goldwyn-Mayer. Running time: 114 minutes. At the Trans-Lux West Theater, Broadway at 49th Street, and East 59th Street Twin 1 Theater, 59th Street east of Third Avenue, and other theaters. This film has been classified PG.

Jay	Burt Reynolds
Catherine	Sarah Miles
Lapchance	Lee J. Cobb
Dawes	Jack Warden
Crocker	George Hamilton
Billy	Bo Hopkins
Dub	Robert Donner
Iron Knife	Larry Littlebird
The Chief	Jay Silverheels

Richard Sarafian's "The Man Who Loved Cat Dancing" is set in the post-Civil War West and is about a former Army officer-turned-train robber (Burt Reynolds) who was once married to an Indian girl named Cat Dancing. Hence the title. It's also about the high-born lady (Sarah Miles) whom he apparently liberates when he teaches her how to cook and make love.

Most of the movie is a desultory chase: the officer-gentleman-train robber, the woman and some outlaws (including Jack Warden) in the lead, pursued by a sherif (Lee J. Cobb), the woman's husband (George Hamilton) and a posse. When one of the lesser outlaws gets fresh with Miss Miles, Jack Warden kicks him in the groin. When Mr. Warden rapes Miss Miles, Mr. Reynolds shoots him in the groin. When Miss Miles asks Mr. Reynolds why two people fall in love, he answers: "I dunno. I suppose it's like two drops of rain that fall together and become one."

The film's poetry is as numbing as its violence.

"The Man Who Loved Cat Dancing" is, indeed, a kind of festival of incompetence. Each shot is held slightly too long or too short, and is somehow off-center. Each performance is uncertain, like something seen in an early rehearsal. Even the Indians look fake, including good old Jay Silverheels, who is real.

The screenplay, based on Marilyn Durham's novel, is by Eleanor Perry ("David and Lisa," "Diary of a Mad Housewife"), who can do much, much better.

VINCENT CANBY.

1973 Je 29, 17:1

When Muni Wore Chains and Bogart Wore a Black Hood

By CHARLES HIGHAM

ON Wednesday, we'll be celebrating the Fourth of July, and so will the Museum of Modern Art— with a showing of Jimmy Cagney's rousing 1942 movie, "Yankee Doodle Dandy." But there will be more than patriotism on MOMA's mind that day, for "Yankee Doodle Dandy" is just one of 207 films made by Warner Brothers to be screened between July 4 and Nov. 18 in honor of the studio's 50th birthday.

The classic musicals, the epics and biographies, the crime and war pictures will all be heavily represented, and it will be possible to trace the evolution of the great Warners stars: Davis and Muni and Stanwyck, Blondell and Robinson and Cagney, Astor and Flynn and Francis, Jolson and Keeler and Powell, Lupino and Garfield and De Havilland, Bogart and Bacall and Sheridan.

Charles Higham is the author of "The Warners Saga: History of a Great Studio," to be published by Charles Scribner's Sons in 1974.

And there'll be the chance to see, or re-see, the unforgettable Warners moments: Robinson gasping, "Mother of Mercy, is this the end of Rico?" as he is gunned down in "Little Caesar"; Cagney pushing the grapefruit into Mae Clark's face in "Public Enemy"; Paul Muni murmuring "I steal," when he's asked how he manages to survive in the final, overpowering scene from "I Am a Fugitive From a Chain Gang"; Bacall whispering huskily to Bogart in "To Have and Have Not," "If you want anything, just whistle." Tough, acrid, with the bite of a neat Scotch-on-the-rocks, the Warners flavor is unmistakable.

*

The studio was at its greatest in the Depression; while other studios peddled glossy escapism, Warners came to grips with social problems, portraying a country down on its luck, desperate, greedy. Warners even provided a musical, "Golddiggers of 1933," which told it like it was: Al Dubin and Harry Warren drew their great song about out-of-work war veterans, "Remember My Forgotten Man," from their memories of the breadline after they had served in World War I. Daringly for the time, a black singer, Etta Moten, was shown taking up the lyrics initially spoken by Joan Blondell, propped Fannie Brice-ishly against a lamp post.

Warners' impressive cycle of social protest films was initiated in the spring of 1932, when Jake Wilk of the studio's story department in New York bought the rights to Robert Elliott Burns's book, "I Am a Fugitive From a Georgia Chain Gang!" It was passed on to Jack Warner and Darryl F. Zanuck in Hollywood, and they immediately decided to make it as "I Am a Fugitive From a Chain Gang" with Mervyn LeRoy—who had done "Little Caesar"—as director.

Ghost-written by Burns's brother, who also wrote the introduction, the book was a ferocious attack on prison atrocities in the Deep South, the apparently true account of a man who had been a prisoner in Georgia, worked on a chain gang for several months, escaped, lived an honorable life, and re-turned to jail on condition he would be pardoned—a promise on which the authorities immediately reneged. Burns escaped again, and, protected by his brother—a clergyman—he went into hiding in New Jersey.

Warners' story department assigned the script to Sheridan Gibney, a Broadway playwright in his early twenties, who wrote it with the producer, Hal Wallis. Robert Burns, given the complete protection of a studio security blanket, came to Hollywood and worked with Gibney for five weeks, filling him in on details of Georgia prison life not covered in the book. Terrified of being recaptured, Burns used an assumed name and hid in a hotel under armed guard. When a crime film was being shot on a lot adjoining the writers' building where Gibney and Burns worked day and night, Burns—horrified by the sound of gunfire and police sirens—cowered against a wall until Gibney reassured him that it was "only a movie."

Gibney returned to New York to work on a new play; he says he was

Paul Muni has his chains checked in "I Am a Fugitive From a Chain Gang," to be shown Aug. 14 at the Museum of Modern Art as part of a retrospective of Warner Brothers films.
"The film established Warners' claim that it was providing genuine social commentary—aggressive, liberal, effectively reformist"

dismissed by Zanuck when he refused to come back to Hollywood for rewrites, and other scenarists worked on the material. The result was as powerful a condemation of Georgia prison procedure as the book had been. It was brilliantly played by Paul Muni as Burns and reached a far greater audience than the book had.

According to Gibney, Muni's famous last line, "I steal," was almost cut out of the film. Gibney says Hal Wallis felt that it would be too strong for audiences. But Zanuck returned from a trip to Europe, overruled Wallis, and forced the scene in.

*

Gibney claims that the shot of Muni being swallowed up in darkness as the final line is uttered was in the script; Mervyn LeRoy says that it came about by accident when a convenient power failure took place while the sequence was being shot in downtown Los Angeles. The distribution of credit for a major achievement is always subject to fierce controversy in Hollywood, but the brilliance of "I Am a Fugitive From a Chain Gang" is due chiefly to LeRoy, whose direction of the chain gang scenes, the escape sequence and the final, stunning fade-out has an electricity unaffected by time.

*

After the picture opened, there was so widespread a public outcry that chains were removed from prisoners throughout Georgia. At the same time, various Georgia officials let it be known that no employe of Warners would be permitted to cross the state line; the state of Georgia sued the company for defamation, and two Georgia prison wardens jointly lodged their own suit for libel. To prevent a lengthy legal battle, all of these cases were settled out of court.

"I Am a Fugitive From a Chain Gang" was a huge success and established the studio's claim that it was providing genuine social commentary—aggressive, liberal, effectively reformist.

Another important social protest film of 1933 was "Wild Boys of the Road," powerfully directed by William Wellman, a study of homeless youths in the Depression which some critics felt all too clearly resembled the Russian film, "The Road to Life," directed two years earlier by Nikolai Ekk.

In 1935 Hal B. Wallis—who had succeeded Zanuck as production chief in 1933—set in motion a new social drama, "Black Fury." Jake Wilk had bought a story called "Jan Volkanik," by Judge M. A. Musmanno, based on a case in which Musmanno had been a prosecuting District Attorney. It involved a miner who had been beaten to death by strike-breaking police in Imperial, Pa., in 1929. Another Wilk property, a play called "Bohunk" by Harry S. Irving, formed the basis of other incidents in the script by Abem Finkel and Carl Erickson.

Made at the time of extensive coal strikes, "Black Fury" was violent, topical, and brilliantly directed by Michael Curtiz. Paul Muni was magnificent as the ignorant Hunky miner Joe Radek.

But the picture ran into censorship trouble and was banned in several states, including Pennsylvania itself. Paradoxically, however, it was criticized by left as well as right-wing elements. The left-wing press complained that "Black Fury"—made at a time when organizing by the C.I.O. was in the ascendant against very heavy odds —unfairly portrayed union members as stubborn bargainers and the easy prey of sinister outside agitators. To them, the message of "Black Fury" was that labor should slow down and make fewer demands of management.

But even the most urgent left-wing critics of "Black Fury," including William Troy in The Nation, admitted that the film was an extraordinary piece of craftsmanship.

Two years later, in 1937, Warners again made a distinguished contribution to the mode in "Black Legion," directed by Archie Mayo. On May 23, 1936, headlines around the country announced the arrest in Detroit of seven members of the Black Legion—a fascist organization centered in the Middle West—for the murder of Charles A. Poole, a 32-year-old W.P.A. worker. Subsequent investigations led to the life imprisonment of 11 members of the Black Legion and the disclosure of a massive organization of xenophobic, sometimes highly placed hooligans who had begun their infamous career of pillaging and murder and burning the homes of foreigners in 1931 after their parent body, the Ku Klux Klan, rejected them because they wore black hoods instead of white. Although several of the ring-leaders were still at large (some 3,000,000 members were estimated to exist) and possibly dangerous, the writer-producer Robert Lord prepared a story for Hal Wallis which severely attacked Legion activities.

Adapted by Abem Finkel and William Wister Haines, "Black Legion" was marvelously handled by Mayo, particularly the scenes in which the members of the Legion gathered in their sinister hoods, against a background of flaring torches, to whip their victims or initiate a new member as a servant of "God and the Devil." Humphrey Bogart further developed his growing reputation as an actor with his compelling performance as a pathetic stooge of the Legion, a dumb factory worker given a sense of spurious power after his indoctrination. The character was based on Dayton Dean, Legion executioner, who turned State's evidence. The film greatly assisted in the stamping out of the Legion in the late 1930's, and further established Warners as a great reformist studio.

That same year, Warners attacked the racial prejudices of the Deep South in Mervyn LeRoy's remarkable "They Won't Forget," based on a book which reworked the facts of the Leo Frank lynching case. Once again, the portraits of the characters were unsparing: Claude Rains's bigoted attorney and Allyn Joslyn's hustling re-

porter were cruelly, acutely drawn in the fine script by Robert Rossen and Aben Kandel.

The Thirties were also notable for the cycle of biographies directed by William Dieterle which attacked various forms of corruption in an historical context. These included "The Story of Louis Pasteur," an onslaught on rearguard practices, "Dr. Ehrlich's Magic Bullet," which, as well as dealing in the defeat of syphilis, exposed flaws in medical attitudes, and "White Angel," the story of Florence Nightingale, who was shown fighting Victorian medical authorities. The most important film of the cycle, "The Life of Emile Zola," contained a fierce attack on military regimes in its story of Zola's struggle for the freedom of the unjustly imprisoned Alfred Dreyfus, while somewhat tentatively dealing with the crucial fact of Dreyfus's Jewish birth and his persecution by anti-Semites.

Also in 1937, Jack Warner learned from his close friend President Roosevelt that the F.B.I. had begun uncovering a Nazi spy ring in the Eastern states. With Roosevelt's approval, and without the knowledge of J. Edgar Hoover, Warner sent a contract writer, Milton Krims, to New York to work with the F.B.I. special investigator Leon G. Turrou. Disguised as a Nazi, Krims appeared at German - American Bund meetings while Turrou prepared a series of articles for the New York Post. Hoover dismissed Turrou from the F.B.I. at once when he heard that he had breached the G-Man's oath by working with Krims and offering his findings to the public. Turrou then came to Hollywood and collaborated with Krims for weeks, using photographs he had obtained from F.B.I. files. When the famous spy trials opened in New York in 1939, Krims attended them.

The film which grew out of this exhaustive research was "Confessions of a Nazi Spy," directed by the passionately anti-Nazi Anatole Litvak and starring Francis Lederer, Paul Lukas and — in one of his strongest performances—Edward G. Robinson as Turrou. Once again, Warner's had sailed into a storm. George Gyssling, German Consul in Los Angeles, fought for the film's cancellation, the German Government lodged protests in Washington, and the film was banned in four countries. Finally, the German-American Bund sued Warners for $500,000. The case was dropped, however, when Fritz Kuhn, former head of

the Bund and the instigator of the suit, was jailed for misappropriating Bund funds.

The dynamic, if occasionally melodramatic, movie was a commercial flop; despite the widespread publicity accorded the spy trials, the public found the events depicted in "Confessions of a Nazi Spy" wholly unconvincing. Like other Warners films of the period, it was clearly ahead of its time. Warner did not dare venture another boldly political film until "Mission to Moscow" nearly four years later.

But when World War II broke out in 1941, the studio swiftly prepared movies to instill pro-war fervor in the public. Errol Flynn appeared in a series of adventures — ironically, in view of the fact that he was an Army reject on the grounds of ill health —including "Desperate Journey," "Northern Pursuit," "Edge of Darkness," and the notorious "Objective Burma," which was withdrawn from exhibition in England when public and critics alike condemned it for omitting any reference to the key British role in the Burma campaign. Other films, made at Roosevelt's express request, were "Action in the North Atlantic," "Air Force," and "Destination Tokyo." The emphasis was heavily on the Air Force in many of these films because General "Hap" Arnold was a close friend of Jack Warner's. Most of these pictures were ridiculous, heavily sentimental and overly emphatic in their patriotism, but they proved to be of value in a time when the American public needed effective propaganda films.

*

More serious, at least in intent, was "Mission to Moscow," based on the memoirs of Ambassador Joseph B. Davies, which Warners made in 1943, again at the request of Roosevelt. Howard Koch wrote the script, Michael Curtiz directed with his customary flair, and the sets were constructed under the careful supervision of Davies himself. Walter Huston was cast as Davies, Manart Kippen as Stalin, while lawyer Dudley Field Malone developed his well-known dinner-party turn as Winston Churchill. This technique of portraying living personalities had been previously employed by Warners in "Confessions of a Nazi Spy," in which Martin Kosleck was a memorably fanatical Joseph Goebbels.

The moment "Mission to Moscow" was released, it ran into the kind of criticism Jack Warner had dreaded. Although Bosley Crowther, in The New York Times, saluted the film as "clearly the most important picture on a political subject any American studio has ever made," he went on to object to its glamorized picture of Soviet society and to question its historical accuracy. Particularly, Crowther challenged the film's blunt assertion that the Trotsky group had plotted the overthrow of Soviet Russia with the Nazis and the Japanese. The Times also published an intense denunciation of the film written by John Dewey and Suzanne La Follette, the chairman and the secretary of the International Commission of Inquiry into the Moscow purge trials. Howard Koch wrote a spirited reply, and the controversy raged for weeks.

Westbrook Pegler also violently criticized Warners for having made "Mission to Moscow," and the Hearst press joined the attack, while Illinois state attorney George F. Barrett, among others, demanded a boycott.

Like "Confessions of a Nazi Spy," "Mission to Moscow" was not a great success at the box office. Four years later, during the House Un-American Activities Committee hearings in Washington, Warner was to be seriously embarrassed by the reminder that he had made "Mission to Moscow" at all. The times were changing. Social comment in films was clearly suspect. Warner and his studio soon abandoned their zeal for movies that dared to be political.

1973 Jl 1, II:9:1

The Cast

OKLAHOMA CRUDE, directed and produced by Stanley Kramer; written by Marc Norman; director of photography, Robert Surtees; music, Henry Mancini; editor, Folmar Blangsted; distributed by Columbia Pictures. Running time: 108 minutes. At Loew's State I, Broadway at 45th Street, Orpheum Theater, 86th Street near Third Avenue, and Columbia I Theater, Second Avenue at 64th Street. This film has been classified PG.

Mase	George C. Scott
Lena	Faye Dunaway
Cleon	John Mills
Hellman	Jack Palance
Marion	William Lucking
Wilcox	Harvey Jason
Wobbly	Ted Gehring
Massive Man	Cliff Osmond

By VINCENT CANBY

"Oklahoma Crude" is Stanley Kramer's least solemn movie since "So This Is New York," the very funny but financially unsuccessful adaptation of the Ring Lardner novel that marked Kramer's debut as a film producer in 1948 (and is still one of my favorite comedies). It is less solemn than even "It's a Mad, Mad, Mad, Mad World," that behemoth of a slapstick comedy, which Kra-

mer directed as well as produced. In the context of such Kramer works as "Guess Who's Coming to Dinner," "On the Beach" and "Judgment at Nuremberg," his new film is virtually a tonic, but maybe I'm letting myself get carried away.

"Oklahoma Crude" is Stanley Kramer, the director-producer, working very hard —doing his damndest, as a matter of fact—to entertain us with the kind of fiction that Edna Ferber used to write with such an easy touch that cliché was gentled into something approaching true style.

The story is set in the great Oklahoma oil fields some time before World War I, when American free enterprise was the purest form of piracy. The characters include a headstrong, tempestuous beauty named Lena (Faye Dunaway), who looks ravishing in long johns, trainman's boots and a dirty face, and who hates men; Lena's father, Cleon (John Mills), a charming ne'er-do-well; and an oil field drifter named Mase (George C. Scott), who signs on for cash to help Lena fight the Pan-Oklahoma oil trust (which wants to take Lena's well away from her) but who stays on when he falls in love with her.

Marc Norman's original screenplay (which was later turned into a novel) is not exactly wall-to-wall with surprises, but part of the appeal of such fiction is the anticipation of scenes we know to be obligatory, such as the one in which Lena admits that, after all, she is a woman. It is also necessary that someone important to the plot be killed in the showdown fight with the villains, and that, just when all hope has gone, the gusher be brought in with a whoop and a holler and with everyone standing around the rig getting marvelously drenched in the sticky stuff. Suspense is never a matter of what, but of who and when.

•

The variations that "Oklahoma Crude" works on the familiar formula are largely the work of Scott. It is a broadly comic performance, beginning with lots of double takes, protestations of offended dignity and expressions of horror at the thought of violence, even though we know that the character will turn out to be true blue and brave, or Scott would not be playing it. The performances of Miss Dunaway, Mills and Jack Palance, who plays the chief oil company villain, are more conventional but still quite classy under the ordinary circumstances.

Kramer's approach to sheer entertainment, as it is to important and timely subjects, is rather plodding if not truly solemn. Moments of high spirits and good humor are not particularly convinc-

ing, and there is such a fondness for shots of beautiful sunrises that I suspect he wishes the movie had more than just a message about the value of individual integrity. Still, compared to his other recent films, "Oklahoma Crude" comes very close to being refreshing, a medium-big and brawling adventure film.

1973 Jl 4, 8:4

The Cast

DIARY OF A SHINJUKU BURGLAR, directed by Nagisa Oshima; screenplay (Japanese with English subtitles) by Tsutomu Tamura, Mamoru Sasaki, Masao Adachi and Mr. Oshima; photographed by Yasuhiro Yoshioka and Seizo Sengen; edited by Mr. Oshima; produced by Masayuki Nakajimi. Released by Grove Press, Inc. Running time: 94 minutes. At the First Avenue Screening Room, First Avenue and 61st Street. This film has not been classified.

Birdey Hilltop	Tadanori Yokoo
Umeko Suzuki	Rie Yokoyama

and

Moichi Tanabe, Tetsu Takahashi, Kei Sato, Fumio Watanabe, Mitsuhior Toura, Kara Juro and the Situation Players.

By ROGER GREENSPUN

Except for "Boy," introduced at the seventh New York Film Festival, the work of Nagisa Osima (born 1932) is scarcely known here — though the film histories place him among the most important younger Japanese directors, regularly comparing him to Jean-Luc Godard, his near contemporary and an obvious influence on his style. Another Osima film, "Diary of a Shinjuku Burglar" (1969), opened yesterday at the First Avenue Screening Room. I should say that Oshima is certainly influenced by Godard—especially in medium - distance shots. In long shots he is more often influenced by Michelangelo Antonioni. But in close-ups and in almost everything else he seems firmly and not too appealingly himself.

•

The burglar (Tadanori Yokoo), who, under duress, admits that his name is Birdey Hilltop, steals books — good books—from a Tokyo bookstore. A girl (Rie Yokoyama), who says she's a clerk, catches him and turns him in to the boss. The boss doesn't care about the thefts and doesn't really believe the girl works for him, but he takes an interest in the young people anyway and attempts to straighten out their sex lives.

That is what the movie is all about—straightening out their sex lives—though incidentally it touches on a great many other things as well. For example, just as Birdey and his girl finally do straighten out their sex lives (she simulates hara kari using a little of her own blood, which happens to be the key to Birdey's heart) all hell breaks loose with a student riot in the Shinjuku section of Tokyo. That's how

the movie ends.

But before it ends, Birdey and his girl have been through a variety of bizarre experiences that range from visits to an analyst (who analyzes transference of sexual roles and wants them to undress), to imitation rape (which turns out to be real when some onlookers get their signals crossed), to participation in a dramatic happening produced in a style that seems to combine traditional noh with guerrilla theater.

Some of the experiences are funny, as when the would-be lovers go to a pleasure house where attendants on the roof manufacture a rain shower timed just to the moment of passionate surrender. More often, the experiences are very dull, with an air of having been produced only for purposes of demonstration. Like the more recent Godard, Oshima's is a highly didactic cinema.

1973 Jl 6, 7:1

But unlike any Godard, it seems imprecise—and possibly less concerned with the quality of its thoughts than the momentary effectiveness of its images. The result is a high-powered sterility in the midst of much energetic busyness.

•

"Diary of a Shinjuku Burglar" has been photographed mostly in black and white, occasionally in color, and always with the sort of modish disjointedness that makes of the shock cut what the terrible zoom lens is to a different and less intellectual practice in movie making. I shouldn't want to dismiss Oshima on so little evidence, but I don't see that he has brought very much to this film beyond a skillful eye, a close familiarity with his betters and a lot of not very interesting ambitions.

1973 Jl 6, 7:1

Bravo, Chaplin! Bravo, Tati!

By VINCENT CANBY

CHARLIE CHAPLIN'S "Monsieur Verdoux," made in 1947, and Jacques Tati's "Playtime," made over a period of years and completed in 1967, are two of the greatest screen comedies of all time and they are now in first-run theaters here. For "Monsieur Verdoux," the engagement at the Paris makes a return. The Tati film, which is now at the Festival Theater, is being seen in New York for the first time, apparently because the distributor was not terribly enthusiastic about it when the film was acquired four or five years ago, especially after it was rather poorly received in its native France.

In addition to the quite mixed critical reception each film received in its own time, "Monsieur Verdoux" and "Playtime" share one other thing in common: although they are comedies of the highest order, by filmmakers who, in the past, have had us rolling in the aisles with bellylaughs, both are comparatively rigorous and demanding. Each has its marvelous bellylaughs, but if great comedies are measured by the number of laughs they contain, then Laurel and Hardy's "Way Out West" is better than either—and as fond of "Way Out West" as I am, I must say that it isn't in a league with either the Chaplin or the Tati.

"Playtime" is Tati's fourth feature but his fifth to be released in the United States—"Traffic," made in 1971, having been released last winter. "Playtime" is his chef d'oeuvre, his testament, his grandest gesture, the basket with all of his eggs in it. Like "Jour de Fete," "Mr. Hulot's Holiday," "Mon Oncle" and "Traffic," it is a film composed of minute detail, but of so many that are so odd and seemingly random

and glorious, that it's almost as difficult to describe accurately as a Jackson Pollock painting. It all seems to have happened at once or, at least, in the time it takes to watch it. It didn't, of course. It's the result of almost nine years of work and is such an accumulation of Tati observations that probably only the 70-mm frames, in which the film was originally photographed (though it's being

shown in 35-mm here), are big enough to present Tati's special visions properly.

All of which brings me to the business of the demands that the film makes upon the audience. Tati photographs everything in a medium or a long shot. Seldom does he use close-ups to focus our attention on specific details. "Playtime" is a succession of wide-angle views of a world in which we must make decisions as to where we'll look and what we'll look at. So much is going on simultaneously that the results, while rewarding, also are somewhat exhausting. It is a little like trying to watch the three rings at the Barnum & Bailey Circus, but at the circus the activities quite often cancel each other out.

*

Every Tati sequence is composed of interlocking elements so that the eye, if relaxed and unharried (I was about to say, unafraid), will generally find Tati's rhythm —and with special pleasure for having discovered that rhythm for itself. For this reason, I suspect that "Playtime," of all of Tati's films, will be the most taxing for a small child. Not that children can't delight in any number of individual things in the film, but children tend to see the small details and overlook that major design. They are the ones who, at the circus, may be more fascinated by the sanitation men who come in immediately after the animal act to scoop up the tiger droppings than they are by the latest troupe imported from Bulgaria: a family of six that, for the first time in this country, performs a quadruple somersault-twist from a high-wire bicycle to the paws of a chimpanzee hanging by its feet onto a trapeze.

"Playtime" is less a series of laughs than a series of supremely ebullient smiles in appreciation of the foolishness, humanity, self-deceptions and beauty of the world around us. It is not, I think, about the drabness of modern manners, about conformity or even about the inhumanity of modern architecture. Manners, conformity and architecture are used, rather, as props in Tati's particularly cheerful, invigorating comedy, the subject of which—to make it sound more pretentious than need be—is the possibility of survival without tears and without psychic scars.

*

The film can be roughly divided into three acts, all set in a Paris so modern that it does not yet exist in life except in isolated corners of the real Paris. It's a Paris composed entirely of glass and steel office buildings of the sort that in the last five years have transformed our Avenue of the Americas into the world's biggest, longest, most magnificent reflecting pool. We see glimpses of the old Paris—the Paris whose vistas were designed by Baron Haussmann at the bidding of Napoleon III—in reverse images of Sacre Coeur, the Eif-

fel Tower and the Arch of Triumph, which are simply reflections on the face of Tati's fictitious Paris.

The first act takes place at Orly Airport, where we pick up a group of American tourists on their arrival on an all-expenses-paid sight-seeing tour. The second act is set at a trade fair, at which the tourists cross paths with Tati's Mr. Hulot. The last act celebrates the opening of a dreadfully modern Parisian nightclub when the tourists, Mr. Hulot, odds and ends of the haute monde and assorted drunks and misfits all come into singularly funny conjunction as the opening night goes dreadfully wrong.

The film ends with an almost surreal epilogue in which we follow the tourists in their bus out of Paris at dawn: they admire the gracefulness of the activity at a filling station, and they thrill as they see themselves reflected in a louvered window whose motion makes it seem as if they are on a ferris wheel. The bus that leaves Paris in the morning speeds along the eight-lane highway ("The street lights are just like ours!" one tourist has said with admiration at the beginning) and arrives at Orly at midnight. Time, in "Playtime," is as wild as the soundtrack. Time hasn't to do with reality (ordinarily it takes half an hour to drive from the center of Paris to Orly), but with the meaning of experience. The tourists are worn out. They feel as if they've been in Paris for weeks instead of something like 24 hours.

Tati's use of sound in "Playtime" is extraordinarily funny, whether he employs sound effects such as footsteps, dialogue (spoken primarily in a mixture of French, English and German, which render subtitles unnecessary), or music. One of my favorite Tati sequences of all-time, which lasts only a few seconds, features some great Dixieland accompaniment to the sight of five men carrying a huge piece of plate glass, as they start, stop and lurch in time to the music.

*

"Playtime" has no real hero, though Mr. Hulot is very much in evidence—in the flesh and in a couple of look-alikes who are, in effect, his reflections. Mr. Hulot is a focal point, but not a point of identification. Mostly the film engages us in the manner that an ant palace does, by total spectacle, though it is much, much funnier. I don't want to give away the superb gags, but I will say that among the things that delighted me most were the

solution to the problem of how to keep a drunk standing upright at a bar (stand him inside the legs of an upturned barstool) and a sequence at a trade fair booth promoting soundproofing (the slogan: "Slam Your Doors in Golden Silence").

"Playtime" is nothing less than a brilliant film.

So, too, is "Monsieur Verdoux," but to appreciate its brilliance it's necessary, I suspect, to see it in the context of Chaplin's career, and particularly in the context of the evolution of The Tramp. Andre Bazin (who, with James Agee, was one of the few intelligent defenders of the film when it came out) notes correctly that Verdoux, the Bluebeard, is The Tramp turned inside out, which gives the film a fascination and importance to us now that make superfluous all quibbling about the profundity of its social philosophy. It's not a modest film,

which I think is one of the things that must have troubled critics most when they first saw it. Chaplin plays a saint of sorts, which was all very well when the Chaplin character was a tramp, but this became intolerable when essentially the same character was revealed to be economically successful, articulate, dapper and an absolute whiz with the ladies, all of which Chaplin was. He shouldn't have had the bad taste to remind us of this—or so the argument seems to have gone—while trying to communicate some of his deepest feelings.

*

After Bazin and Agee, I don't think I'm qualified to add anything to the film's defense. I would like to urge people to see "Monsieur Verdoux" in connection with the entire Chaplin career, however, and then to be thoroughly charmed by the comic interludes that are as

funny as those in any of his films. I'm not thinking only of the Martha Raye sequences, which are special and which everyone remembers quite easily anyway (the idea of her going boating in silver fox furs is inspired), but of others, such as Verdoux's impetuous courtship of Isobel Elsom when he first meets her. He clutches a rose to one nostril, minces outrageously and apologizes: "You must pardon me. I'm all disheveled." He is, on the contrary, the perfect dandy, lacquered from head to toe, his eyes practically illuminated with stage make-up. Only Chaplin would have had the audacity to find material for a moral fable in himself, in the stock market crash, in the depression, as well as in the rise of Mussolini and Hitler and the beginnings of World War II.

1973 Jl 8, II:1:1

Rock Saves a Bad Movie

Alan Price, the composer of "O Lucky Man's" rock songs
"A three-minute title song of wit, clarity and honesty"

By LORAINE ALTERMAN

IF Lindsay Anderson's "O Lucky Man!" proves anything, it's that contemporary rock music can save films as well as the conglomerates that own the film companies. Last year, the record division of Warner Communications outgrossed the film division and it's a safe bet that Warner Bros. Records could make more money from the "O Lucky Man!" soundtrack LP than the movie company will from the film itself.

The film's songs and music, written and performed by veteran British rock musician Alan Price, skillfully get across a message in about 25 minutes (the length of the LP) that Anderson belabors in nearly three cliché-infested hours. The only fresh idea in the film is the way Anderson has used the music almost as if it were a Greek chorus, to explain and connect what is happening in this saga of a young man in search of his fortune. At key turning points in the action, Anderson cuts from the story to Price's group (Price, keyboards and vocals; Colin Green, guitar; Dave Markee, bass; Clive Thacker, drums) in a rehearsal hall, performing songs that reflect what's happening to our hapless hero.

The story, based upon an idea by the film's star Malcolm McDowell, is a heavyhanded reworking of "Candide" or "A Cool Million." McDowell portrays an ambitious young man named Travis, so incredibly naive for

1973, when youth has been suckled on mass media, that he must have been raised in a Himalayan monastery. At first, armed with an engaging smile, he attempts to make a bundle legitimately as a coffee salesman, but he instantly smacks up against every cliché in the cynics' handbook —corrupt cops, randy middle-aged women, government Commie hunters and mad doctors grafting human heads on the sheeps' bodies in the name of science. (One can only muse wistfully about what Woody Allen could have done with that one.)

Venturing farther into the land of stereotypes, Travis gets picked up by Alan Price's rock group, which now enters the film's action, and gets thrown to its groupie. Back in the band's sixties flower-power pad, Travis discovers the groupie is actually the daughter of an immensely rich but heartless industrialist. With visions of money dancing in his blue-blue eyes, Travis cons his way into a job as the industrialist's assistant only to take the rap when the government gets wise to a crooked deal. After his release from prison and some new adventures, chance makes him a movie star and the film ends with the entire cast rocking and rolling on the set on the final day of shooting.

If you can stay awake through this adolescent hodgepodge of fumbling black comedy and simple-minded anti-establishment propaganda, the message is that no matter what we do, or even think we can do to get ahead in life—whether we follow the right path or the wrong, the Calvinist or the hedonist —it's all a matter of luck whether we end up on the top or the bottom of the heap.

But Price's title song tells us this in less than three minutes and moreover tells it with wit, clarity and honesty. Musically rocking but not raucous, the song has that immediate rhythmic impact that makes contemporary music so powerful. Price is filmed in a rehearsal hall performing the title song behind the beginning credits and reprises a second version during the final cast party. Even though this isn't a musical in that the actors aren't singing and dancing, the music, not the action, really ties the film together. What makes director Anderson look so silly is that the music doesn't need the film at all to convey his philosophy.

All of Price's music is free of pretense and brimming with energy — two qualities that elude Anderson. Take, for example, Price's song "Justice." Anderson clobbers

us over the head illustrating the venality of modern-day justice. He pictures a judge retiring to his chambers, stripping down to red bikini underpants and having his secretary flog him. Such a scene could perhaps outrage those people not shocked by the Watergate swamp, but to me it is merely arch. Price's "Justice," sung in his earthy manner, passes on succinctly the view that "only wealth will buy you justice." The light-heartedness of Price's music and his cool, smiling manner further emphasize the intent.

Despite the presence of such fine actors as McDowell, Ralph Richardson and Arthur Lowe, "O Lucky Man's" redemption lies only in the exposure it will give to Price who has been absent too long from the music scene here.

*

Still, Anderson's way of utilizing contemporary rock in "O Lucky Man!" is an innovative switch on the more traditional ways the music enters Sam Peckinpah's "Pat Garrett and Billy The Kid" as background music and "Let The Good Times Roll" as the star attraction.

Peckinpah's film not only has new songs by Bob Dylan, but also gives the grand guru of contemporary songwriting a featured role and co-stars another current music idol, Kris Kristofferson. This standard Peckinpah tale of rugged individualism confronting its last frontier doesn't have enough action or vitality to sustain interest for very long. But Dylan fans will undoubtedly pile into the theaters to hear two new songs from their hero who has been playing hermit for several years and to see him in his debut acting assignment. (Columbia is releasing the soundtrack LP.)

"Billy's Song," the title tune Dylan wrote, is a straightforward, folk-style explication of the film's story of Pat Garrett, outlaw turned lawman, hunting his old buddy Billy the Kid. The song warns Billy to look out because Pat doesn't dig Billy's freedom. Actually, Kristofferson, who plays Billy, said it a lot more cogently in his hit of a couple of years ago, "Me And Bobby McGee," with that line about "freedom's just another word for nothing left to lose."

The other song Dylan contributed to this film is "Knockin' On Heaven's Door." Quite honestly, I wasn't sure if it was a second song when I saw the film. I can understand Dylan's importance to current music, but I've never really been able to appreciate him as an artist. Everything sung in that drawling, nasal voice sounds the same to me.

Dylan's presence as a member of Billy's gang is most distracting. Even riding a horse, Dylan can't be anything but Dylan, just as Cary Grant is always Cary Grant. Looking more like a 15-year-old Hassidic student from Williamsburg than an outlaw, Dylan is extremely self-conscious about his acting. His greatest moment comes when Garrett, played by James Coburn, forces him to read the labels on cans of food and Dylan drones out "beans, salmon, string beans" in that monotone he parlayed into gold records. One worries whether this represents his range as an actor.

Rock music itself has been the subject of films like "Woodstock" and "Gimme Shelter," but never have I seen it presented so dynamically as in "Let The Good Times Roll," which shows rock greats like Bo Diddley, Chuck Berry and Little Richard performing in Richard Nader's Rock and Roll Revival shows. Imaginative and versatile camera work as well as the use of split and multiple screen images make the actual live performances as exciting as they are in a concert.

But what makes the film more than a mere concert presentation is the clever intercutting of newsreel, film and television footage from the fifties. More than a nostalgic look at the great originators of rock and roll, it evokes the real beginnings of the youth pop culture that blossomed in the sixties and caused so much social change. Perceptive directors Sid Levin, Robert Abel and Pierre Adidge also capture revealing glimpses of the stars in their dressing rooms. There's a scene in which Bo Diddley cooks up a batch of fried chicken in an electric skillet and explains to the people around that he learned to do this beause in the old days black performers would be sent to the back doors of restaurants where they'd get a cheese sandwich with a side of ptomaine. The soundtrack album on Bell Records includes some of this dialogue.

"The Graduate," "Easy Rider," "A Hard Day's Night," "Shaft" and "Super Fly" are some of the films that have scored with contemporary music in recent years. With the young audiences more attuned to the glamour of rock stars rather than movie stars —and there are few of the latter around today anyway —filmmakers are eager to cash in. They know that the film business has fallen behind the record industry in profits and they must realize that it's the energy of rock that captivates under-35 audiences.

At the same time, recording artists want very much to meet the creative challenge of another medium and Ringo Starr, Neil Young and top record producer James William Guercio have made films to be released in the next few months. Although some stuffy squares shown in "Let The Good Times Roll" prayed for rock and roll to die in the fifties, it's certain that the seventies will see it become even more common in movies —a medium that used to be America's favorite form of entertainment.

1973 Jl 8, II:8:1

The Cast

CAHILL, UNITED STATES MARSHAL, directed by Andrew V. McLaglen; screenplay by Harry Julian Frank and Rita M. Fink, based on a story by Barney Slater; produced by Michael Wayne; director of photography, Joseph Biroc; music, Elmer Bernstein; editor, Robert L. Simpson; a Batjac production, distributed by Warner Brothers. Running time: 102 minutes. At neighborhood theaters. This film has been classified PG.

Cahill	John Wayne
Danny Cahill	Gary Grimes
Lightfoot	Neville Brand
Billy Joe Cahill	Clay O'Brien
Mrs. Green	Marie Windsor
Struther	Morgan Paull
Brownie	Dan Vadis
MacDonald	Royal Dano

By VINCENT CANBY

The air must be cleared. The truth can no longer be covered up—no matter who is hurt. Someone must state the facts: John Wayne has reached the awkward age, which, in his case, is an official 66. When Shirley Temple became 12, there were those who said her career was over. She was too old for repeats of "The Little Colonel," but not yet old enough for politics. However, she survived, as I am sure Wayne will, but how is anybody's guess.

●

Certainly not in things like "Cahill, United States Marshal," a tacky Western of drowsy pace in which Wayne plays the title character, a tough old law officer whose two sons, Danny, 17, and Billy Joe, 12, assist in robbing a bank when dad—as is his wont—is away chasing badmen. The lads, whose mother is dead, feel deprived of dad's company.

It's not outrageous that Wayne should play a United States marshal or that he should be the father of two such young sons (though someone felt obliged to insert a line into the script to the effect that "we had our children late in life"). What has become increasingly difficult to accept is Wayne's peculiar physical presence.

Unlike most people as they age, Wayne is not shrinking and shriveling, nor is he becoming in any way decrepit. Instead, he is swelling up like

John Wayne

a balloon. He is not only getting bigger and rounder, he is also getting visibly lighter. He sort of floats through this movie with no heft whatsoever. He gets shot several times, and stabbed once, but he seems less indestructible than puncture-proof, automatically and wondrously self-sealing. He is a plastic man.

●

'Cahill, United States Marshal' was directed by Andrew V. McLaglen and written by Harry Julian Fink and Rita M. Fink. Perhaps recognizing the new limitations of their star, they spend a good deal of time trying to turn a conventional Western into a children-in-peril movie. Danny (Gary Grimes) and Billy Joe (Clay O'Brien), basically decent kids, of course, are terrorized by the robbers they once helped, in situations borrowed from "Tom Sawyer" freely but without wit or true sentiment.

In addition to Wayne and the boys, the cast includes George Kennedy, who plays a clean-cut, nicely mannered badman, and Neville Brand, who plays Wayne's sidekick, a half-breed Indian and an excellent tracker who talks like a social worker. "You got a bad feeling about your Paw," he tells young Danny, "because he's not home every night." A line like that would have sent Huck Finn hooting back to the raft. Danny, however, begins to melt.

1973 Jl 12, 46:1

PRISON GUARD, directed and written by Ivan Renc; produced by Novotny-Kubala; presented by Filmaco, the Film of America Corporation. At the First Avenue Screening Room, at 61st Street. Running time: 90 minutes. (This film has not been rated.)

Pepa	Jiri Hrzan
Mother	Vera Tichanokova
Mary	Helene Verschurova
Cervinka	Karel Mares

By ROGER GREENSPUN

I guess there is some virtue in confounding expectations, no matter how ineptly or on whatever level. And so I guess there is some virtue in "Prison Guard," a fairly inept Czechoslovak movie about Pepa, a shy young prison guard, who is kind to his prisoners, sweet to his mother, good to his neighbors—but who gets his kicks in private by secretly beating up his little pet dog. Not all his kicks; he also has a special fantasy life. He daydreams that he is a lonely lighthouse keeper, tending his lamp, smoking his pipe, peering into the endless moonlit sea to search for mariners in distress.

The dog-beating separates Pepa from his fellow men. But the lighthouse-keeping takes him right into the center of town, where he climbs the church tower, a make-believe lighthouse, while everybody else thinks he simply wants to get closer to the ringing bells. From time to time, the bells are rung by Mary, the aged sexton's beautiful halfbreed ward. (I don't know how you get halfbreeds in Czechoslovakia, but you do.)

Pepa falls in love with Mary and proposes, and she accepts because there is nothing better for her. This is the fateful decision that shoots to pieces Pepa's well-ordered round of prison, lighthouse, doting mom and most unhappy dog.

"Prison Guard" is set in the nineteen-twenties, in a small provincial town, but it is never really localized in time or place. Both its fantasy and its reality are highly idealized and the quality of benign satiric observation that so wonderfully characterized the best Czechoslovak film-making a few years back—say, by Ivan Passer and Milos Forman—is here pushed into an assertion of the grotesque in everyday life. Thus Pepa (pretty well played by Jiri Hrzan) is a bungling idiot with his prisoners and a sullen monster with his dog—and never enough of a human being in between to make it matter.

The town itself is grotesque—everyone plays with a Yo-yo in his free time—and the prison is not so much a place of detention as an image of stupid bureaucracy, where the doors are mostly left open and the warden mystifyingly governs, as if he were an early reject from a Kafka novel. If none of this comes together in any meaningful way, it may be because "Prison Guard" looks like the ambition to make at least three kinds of movie—without the reason or the passion for even one movie to justify its way.

"Prison Guard," written and directed by Ivan Renc, opened yesterday at the First Avenue Screening Room.

1973 Jl 13:19:1

Ape family

BATTLE FOR THE PLANET OF THE APES, directed by J. Lee Tompson; screenplay by John William Corrington Joyce Hooper Corrington, based on a story by Paul Dehn and characters created by Pierre Boulle; produced by Arthur J. Jacobs; music, Leonard Rosenman; director of photography, Richard H. Kline, editors, Alan L. Jaggs and John C. Horger; an Apjac International production, released by 20th Century-Fox. Running time; 86 minutes. At the New Embassy Theater, Broadway at 46th Street, the Juliet 2 Theater, Third Avenue at 83d Street, and other theaters. This film has been classified G.

Caesar	Roddy McDowall
Aldo	Claude Akins
Lisa	Natalie Trundy
Kolp	Severn Darden
Mandemus	Lew Ayres
Virgil	Paul Williams
Lawgiver	John Huston

By VINCENT CANBY

"Battle for the Planet of the Apes," is not great, but it is appealing and a bit sad. It is the fifth and reportedly the last chapter in the fantastically successful series of films inspired by Pierre Boulle's novel "Planet of the Apes" (total domestic earnings to date of the first four films: $33,450,000).

The time is now A.D. 2670, not long after the cataclysm in which ape rebelled against man and virtually, all civilization was melted into atomic slag.

According to the Lawgiver (John Huston), an ape Moses in a shoulder-length bob who narrates the beginning of the film, a few neurotic human mutants still live in the sewers under the lump that was once Manhattan, while the apes have set up a cheery commune not far away. Their children attend open-air classes taught by a human slave, and everyone lives in airy, rattan-furnished tree houses, the sort that any 20th-century human kid would flip over.

The commune is called Ape City, but it looks more like an ape Shangri-la, set in an ape Sherwood Forest and presided over by an ape lama who calls himself Caesar (Roddy McDowall), husband to Lisa (Natalie Trundy) and

father to little Cornelius (Bobby Porter).

According to the old Lawgiver, Caesar was sent to earth to bring peace and goodwill to ape and human alike. According to the story by Paul Dehn, no such entente can long endure.

I am told that the plot of "Battle for the Planet of the Apes" more or less brings the story back to the start of the original "Planet of the Apes" (1968), but I can no longer be sure. In my mind the titles of the sequels ("Beneath the Planet of the Apes," "Escape From the Planet of the Apes," "Conquest of the Planet of the Apes") have become as detached from the stories themselves as the titles of Evelyn Waugh's novels or Ozu's films.

It makes no great difference. All of the "Ape" films are alike, and yet each is a little different. The common theme (surprisingly pessimistic for this kind of entertainment): ape and man must live in harmony—but they never will. At the end of "Battle for the Planet of the Apes," after yet another confrontation between ape and man (quite small-scale, in terms of film logistics), we see a statue of the venerable old Caesar. He successfully fought off an attack by the human mutants and put down an attempted revolt by an ape junta, but still the statue weeps.

J. Lee Thompson, who directed the earlier "Conquest of the Battle of the Apes," will not win any awards for "Battle," but the film's simplicity defuses criticism. The chimpanzee and orangutan make-up remains remarkable, and the lines are occasionally bright and funny. There are far worse ways of wasting time.

1973 Jl 13:19:1

In 'Live and Let Die,' the Bad Guys Are Black

By VINCENT CANBY

IN "Live and Let Die," the James Bond novel that Tom Mankiewicz has had the good sense to rewrite almost completely for the screen, the late Ian Fleming introduces Mr. Big, the villain of the piece, in exposition presented in the form of the following dialogue:

"'I don't think I've ever heard of a great Negro criminal before,' said Bond. 'Chinamen, of course, the men behind the opium trade. There've been some big-time Japs, mostly in pearls and drugs. Plenty of Negroes mixed up in diamonds and gold in Africa, but always in a small way. They don't seem to take to big business. Pretty law-abiding chaps, on the whole, I should have thought.'

"'Our man's a bit of an exception,' said M. 'He's not pure Negro. Born in Haiti. Good dose of French blood. Trained in Moscow, too, as you'll see from the file. And the Negro races are just beginning to throw up geniuses in all the professions—scientists, doctors, writers. It's about time they turned out a great criminal. . . .'"

"Live and Let Die," which was published in 1954, is filled with casual prejudices that today seem dumbfounding, especially that reference to Mr. Big's being a bit of an exception because he's not pure Negro. Mr. Big, says Fleming, has an advantage over most Negroes because he possesses a good dose of French blood and was trained in Moscow, presumably (I think that Fleming would have thought) the same Moscow that would have embraced a man on the order of Paul Robeson. Even Fleming's use of the word "dose" to describe French ancestry says something about what the English novelist fears about the free-loving French (loose-livers?).

*

"Live and Let Die," the novel, is a true period piece, though not necessarily of the 1950's. Its snobberies are turn-of-the-century while its plot—some nonsense about buried Jamaican pirate treas-

ure that's being used to finance Soviet espionage activities in the United States —goes back even further, to Robert Louis Stevenson, desperately updated.

James Bond, the movie rather than novel hero, who was first acted by Sean Connery and has been taken over by Roger Moore in "Live and Let Die" with no visible ill effects, is still very much a figure of the more conservative 1960's when "Dr. No," the initial film in the Bond series, was released. He's a natty though hardly a mod dresser. His haircut couldn't possibly have offended the late J. Edgar Hoover and his language is remarkably free of the sort of expletives that aren't allowed on prime-time television.

Yet, in several ways, "Live and Let Die" is more liberated, more uninhibited, less uptight than any number of contemporary fantasy-feeding black films like "The Mack" and "Cleopatra Jones."

Tom Mankiewicz, who wrote the screenplay and virtually a whole new plot for "Live and Let Die," Guy Hamilton, who directed the film, and Albert R. Broccoli and Harry Saltzman, who produced it (as they did seven of the eight earlier Bond films), have created a most unusual entertainment. "Live and Let Die" is certainly not a black film—though it is black-oriented in a way that no earlier Bond film was—and it must be labeled more or less right-wing, if only because it doesn't have any easily identifiable political or social concerns in its head. I say this perfectly aware that in Mankiewicz's new plot Bond's mission is to destroy a huge heroin-smuggling operation, based not on Jamaica (though the film was partially photographed there) but on a fictitious Caribbean island named San Monique. However, Bond carries out his duties as unencumbered by ideology as a plumber. It's his job and he does it for the good life it affords him. Similarly, the villains in the film, all of whom are black, are motivated principally by personal gain.

This may not be a surprising virtue to find in a film as earnestly dedicated to the pleasure principle as "Live and Let Die," but it's a refreshing change from most black exploitation films, which tend to be sensational garbage wrapped in piety, and from white "message" films, which tend to be pious garbage wrapped in sensation.

Even though its gags and one-liners (especially those having to do with Bond's prodigious sexual prowess) are stunningly obvious (but sometimes funny, in the way familiar old vaudeville routines are funny), the film's point of view is so civilized that it renders most prejudices ridiculous by royally ingoring them.

It appreciates the style, wit and cleverness of Mr. Big (Yaphet Kotto), though it never patronizes him. Black and white are equally matched throughout the film (even in the credits, which, if I remember correctly, divide their attention between **a beautiful white dancer** and a beautiful black dancer), but the purpose of the film is not to promote equality. The film simply reflects it as if there were no question about the matter. This, too, is fantasy, perhaps, but it seems to me to be a lot healthier than fantasies about black or white supercats who pretend to be socially conscious.

Just how civilized the film is, I think, is reflected in the fact that it is able to exploit, in a single coherent narrative, sinister Caribbean voodoo rites, a crooked black island dictator, a sense of real black brotherhood, the supremacy of James Bond at almost everything, and a red-neck Louisiana sheriff who, as played by Clifton James, becomes one of the funniest characters you'll probably see on screen all year.

This last I find particularly startling, for it wasn't very long ago (say as long ago as "Easy Rider") that this character was a figure of almost mythical dread. He couldn't be treated comically. Our liberal sentiments wouldn't allow it. Today he can be. And we can have a black villain matching wits against a white hero without immediately seeing it in terms of a social or political confrontation.

In its odd, off-hand sort of way, "Live and Let Die" **turns old stereotypes inside out.**

However, I don't want to put you off "Live and Let Die" by overstressing its social importance. It's pop entertainment, carefully calculated to amuse as many people as possible, black as well as white, and thus to make fortunes for everyone connected with it. It thus honorably carries on the tradition established in the earlier Bond films (on two of which, "Goldfinger" and "Diamonds Are Forever," Hamilton and Mankiewicz also collaborated successfully). The titles, plots and gadgets are now beginning to run together, but the intelligence of the series remains highly distinctive.

1973 Jl 15, II:1:6

The Cast

SIDDHARTHA, directed and produced by Conrad Rooks; written by Mr. Rooks, based on the novel by Hermann Hesse; director of photography, Sven Nykvist; editor, Willy Kemplen; released by Columbia Pictures. Running time: 86 minutes. At the Columbia One Theater, Second Avenue at 64th Street, the Eighth Street Playhouse, west of Fifth Avenue, and other theaters. This film has been classified R.

Siddhartha .... Shashi Kapoor
Kamala .... Simi Garewal
Govinda .... Romesh Sharma
Kamaswami .... Pincho Kapoor
Vasudeva .... Zul Vellani
Siddhartha's son .... Kunal Kapoor

By VINCENT CANBY

For those who don't believe, no explanation will be satisfactory. For those who do believe, no explanation is necessary.

Is that from "The Song of Bernadette"? "Going My Way"? "The Secret Storm"? No matter. It's pretty much the way I feel about Hermann Hesse's "Siddhartha," the fable about a young Brahmin's search for wisdom and spiritual peace written by the Nobel Prize-winning German author and poet who died in 1962 at the age of 85.

One either accepts "Siddhartha" with rapture, in the kind of ecstasy that is Novocaine to thought, or one throws up. I say that immediately because it has a great deal to do with my reactions to the simple, solemn film version that Conrad Rooks has made in India, and that opened here yesterday at the Columbia One and other theaters.

●

"Siddhartha," originally published in 1922, was first translated into English in the early nineteen-fifties and for the last four or five years has been one of the bigger things in American paperback publishing. Its popularity, on college campuses and off, especially with drop-outs, is awe-inspiring, a little depressing, and probably as foolish to fight as a musical adaptation of "Love Story" by Rod McKuen. It's the one book to be read by people who don't read books.

Although Hesse has been incorrectly heralded as the prophet of the drug culture, his novel's aggressive anti-intellectualism, enunciated in dime-store prose-poetry, provides comparable escape from social and political responsibility. Don't think, it says, feel. Knowledge can be taught, it says, but wisdom must be experienced. (To which I would add, like death.) Don't try to do anything about the mess in the world around you, find your own peace and to hell with everyone else (unless, of course, they can find *their* peace simultaneously).

Mr. Rooks's film is a fairly faithful adaptation of Hesse's fable, the product of a journey to India undertaken by the author a half-century before the Beatles and Mia Farrow had even booked passage. The time is a mythical past and the conflict is one that continues throughout Hesse's work. Flesh battles spirit to a mystical draw, to the revelation that all things are one: youth, age, sin, grace, life, death, stones, tadpoles.

●

Siddhartha (Shashi Kapoor), accompanied by his lap-dog friend Govinda (Romesh Sharma), leaves his father's house to find wisdom with a troupe of traveling holy men. He learns how to meditate, how to fast, but wisdom eludes him. He seeks out the Gotama Buddha, and learns only that wisdom cannot be taught. He turns to what is called — if only in fiction of this sort — the pleasures of the flesh.

Siddhartha becomes the lover of the beautiful courtesan Kamala and, at the same time, a successful merchant. But still — are you ready? — he knows he is missing something. He chucks it all and finally, with the aid of an old boatman, he finds what he is seeking in the river as a metaphor of life.

These are more or less the highpoints of the story that Mr. Rooks and his cameraman, the usually celebrated Sven Nykvist, have photographed with a kind of photogenic but plodding piety. Mr. Rooks has resisted any temptation to employ the fractured style of his first film, "Chappaqua," and instead has made a small-scale "Ten Commandments" for flower children.

The Gotama Buddha is photographed from the back or the side, the way Jesus and United States Presidents are photographed in movies in which they have tiny parts. There are lots of shots into the sun, which create halos, and there is one love scene that is mostly between a couple of presumably nude silhouettes. Toward the middle you know Siddhartha is getting fed up with earthly pleasures when, at a banquet, he tosses aside a bunch of grapes

If the film does nothing else, however, it does expose Siddhartha's ultimate wisdom to be nothing much more profound than a technical device. When, as an old man he tells Govinda to look into the river and see the cycle of life, we see what Govinda sees. What is it? Plain old superimposition of images. Heck. D. W. Griffith knew how to do this.

1973 Jl 19, 31:1

The Cast

SCREAM BLACULA SCREAM, directed by Bob Keljan screenplay by Joan Torres, Raymond Koenig and Maurice Jules; story by Miss Torres and Mr. Koenig; director of photography, Isadore Mankofsky; editor, Fabian Tordjman; produced by Joseph T. Naar; a Samuel Z. Arkoff Presentation; released by American International Pictures. At the Criterion Theater, Broadway at 45th Street and the Juliet II Theater, Third Avenue and 83d Street. Running time: 96 minutes. This film has been classified PG.

Mamuwalde .... William Marshall
Lisa .... Pam Grier
Justin .... Don Mitchell
Willis .... Richard Lawson
Denny .... Lynn Moody
Maggie .... Beverly Gill

By ROGER GREENSPUN

Blacula, when last we saw him (late last August, in point of fact), had met his end on the roof of a power station. Undone by morning, as often happens to vampires, he had been reduced to no more than a bag full of bones in the first feeble rays of the smog-filtered Los Angeles sun.

Now those bones are made to rise again. Brought back to undeadness through the meddling of a dissident Southern California voodoo priest, Blacula is again condemned to walk the earth—in "Scream Blacula Scream," which opened yesterday at the Criterion and Juliet II Theaters, and which is not, as the title might suggest, too much fun for anybody.

●

Blacula never asked for his fate anyway. Originally Mamuwalde, a distinguished African prince, he had been bitten—and renamed—by Count Dracula as long ago as the 18th century. His current incarnations among jive-talking West Coast dudes and their ladies are not greatly to his taste, and despite some involuntary spreading of his habit (he creates at least six new vampires in the first half hour of the movie), his only real interest is to get himself back where—and when—he came from. To this end he enlists the aid of Lisa, a non-dissident voodoo priestess of high repute ("When it comes to voodoo, Lisa has more natural power than *anyone* in the last 10 years.")

That's really all the movie is about. Mamuwalde's torment, Lisa's efforts, and, of course, the knuckle-headed failure of the local cops to admit that there are vamires among us. And that simply is not enough. Despite all its blood-letting, "Scream Blacula Scream" fails for lack of incident, weakness of invention, insufficient story.

The director, Bob Kelljan, has at least the shadow of an idea—that the vampire's curse really is a curse, all pain and no pleasure, and is as miserable for the vampire as for his victim. In William Marshall (Mamuwalde) and Pam Grier (Lisa) he has two good performers—powerful, ironic, potentially rather complicated. But he hasn't enough for them to do. It is as if the movie had completed filming without their ever having developed the shooting script.

But I'll bet there will be another chance for Blacula. I get that feeling from a movie that determines the only cure for vampires to be a wooden stake through the heart—and then leaves its principal antagonist suffering from nothing more than a very pesky chest pain.

1973 Jl 19, 31:1

THE ADVERSARY (PRATIDWANDI), directed by Satyajit Ray; screenplay in Bengali (with English subtitles) and English by Mr. Ray, based on a story by Sunil Ganguly; directors of photography, Soumendu Ray and Purmendu Bose; editor, Dulal Dutta; music, Mr. Ray; produced by Nepal Dutte and Ahim Dutta for Priya Films; distributed by Audio Brandon Film. Running time: 110 minutes. This film has not been classified at this time. At the First Avenue Screening Room, at 61st Street.

Siddhartha .... Dhritiman Chatterjee
With: Krishna Rose, Joyshree Roy, Kalyan Chatterjee and Debraj Roy

"The Adversary," which opened yesterday at the First Avenue Screening Room, was shown at the 10th New York Film Festival. The following excerpt is from Vincent Canby's review, which appeared Oct. 9, 1972, in The New York Times.

For a number of reasons, a Satyajit Ray film doesn't demand our immediate attention in the way that a Buñuel or a Bergman or a Godard does. A Ray film carries no guarantee to shock. Its characters are too involved in one form or another of daily survival to fret about metaphysical matters. It won't outrage us. Regarded in India as the most un-Indian of Indian film directors, he is, to us, quintessentially Indian.

This has to do with the rhythm of his films and with Ray's vision of Indian life, which is anything but exotic or sensuous. His male characters, especially, seem at first somewhat timid, dressed in their occidental clothes that hang on them like the hand-me-downs from someone else's civilization.

"The Adversary" is about such a man, a former medical student named Siddhartha who shares a crowded Calcutta flat with his widowed mother, an uncle, a pretty younger sister with a fairly well-paying job, and a younger brother, who is supposed to be a student but who apparently spends most of his time working for revolutionary causes.

Siddhartha is caught betwixt and between. He seethes with rage about social injustices, about economic corruption, but he is powerless to express it. The best he can do is act rudely at job interviews. "Do you like flowers?"

he is asked by a prospective employer at the botanical gardens. "Not unconditionally," says Siddhartha. "Who was Prime Minister at the time of independence?" the employer goes on. "Whose independence?" the young man answers.

"The Adversary" is about Siddhartha's taking hold of himself when he falls in love and after he has endured a series of small but awful humiliations. These have the effect of making him accept his individuality, and of increasing his awareness of the fact that to be a part of a generalization, as humanity is a generalization, is not necessarily defeat.

"All people are the same," he tells his girl at one point, meaning that one body is much like another as far as bones, muscles, nerves and arteries are concerned. "Not exactly alike," says the girl. Men and women are different. Temperaments are different.

"The Adversary" moves so quietly, with such seeming politeness to jaded film senses, that it takes a while to realize that for all its somberness it's a particularly moving comedy. The methods are so conventional, they seem reserved, but the director's sensibility is profoundly compassionate.

1973 Jl 20, 14:1

White Plains. And there's the rationale that comes to a would-be adulterer in his sleep: extramarital sex is no more offensive to God than double-parking.

•

According to this rationale, if we lived in a society in which men wore gloves and women wore earmuffs, the big deal would be getting the earmuffs off.

Greenburg's wit is not exactly side-splitting, but it's amusing and cheerful in the fashion of a true anecdote recounted at a neighborhood picnic.

The film was directed by Robert McCarty, whose first feature this is, and written by Greenburg, based on his novel "Chewsday." It's an East Coast "Bob & Carol & Ted & Alice" about two couples who spend a horrendous vacation together in a rented house on Martha's Vineyard. Being Greenburg people, they have none of the ersatz chic or flair of their West Coast counterparts. Marvin and Laura and Stanley and Mandy are square. They are nice but they are so square it hurts.

In the course of the vacation — mostly rain, cold, fog, cocktail parties and sheer boredom—Marvin and Mandy develop a full-sized

yen for each other. First it's Mandy who wants to "do it" (which is the term they use). Then Marvin wants to do it, and Mandy doesn't. Finally, when their respective mates are out of the house, they decide to give it a try.

"I'm used to a lot of foreplay," says Mandy. "Tney only went antiquing," says the desperate Marvin, "not to Europe!"

In this kind of fiction, nobody ever really does it. In fact, the very idea that they have thought about it ultimately strikes them with terror. Virtue is served, not because anyone has any particular scruples but because Marvin and Laura and Stanley and Mandy are so fearful and — dare I even whisper it? — boring. Their libidos are as tiny as their imaginations.

•

The cast includes Carmine Caridi (Marvin), who sometimes looks like Elliot Gould and sometimes like Bob Downey; Andrew Duncan (Stanley), Cynthia Harris (Laura) and Lynne Lipton (Mandy), who plays what on the Coast would be the Goldie Hawn role.

The film opened yesterday at the Beekman Theater.

1973 Jl 21, 21:4

The Cast

BADGE 373, directed by Howard W. Koch; written by Pete Hamill; director of photography, Arthur J. Ornitz; edited by John Woodcock; music by J. J. Jackson; produced by Mr. Koch; released by Paramount Pictures. At Loews State I Tehater, Broadway at 45th Street Loews Cine, Third Avenue at 86th Street, and neighborhood theaters. Running time: 115 minutes. This film has been classified R.

Eddie Ryan	Robert Duvall
Maureen	Verna Bloom
Sweet William	Henry Darrow
Scanlon	Eddie Egan
Ruben	Felipe Luciano
Mrs. Caputo	Tina Cristlani
Rita Garcia	Marina Durell
Frankie Diaz	Chico Martinez
Gigi Caputo	Louis Cosentino

By ROGER GREENSPUN

As you might guess from the title, "Badge 373" is a police melodrama. According to the distributors, Paramount Pictures, it is based on the "real-life career" of a former New York City detective, Eddie Egan — whose real-life career has been the basis of movies before this.

I suspect it is also based just a bit on some real-life fantasies. Eddie Egan is featured in the movie not as himself — a suspended New York cop named Eddie Ryan —but as a police lieutenant— Scanlon — who might have been the real-life Eddie's boss. Pete Hamill, the reporter who wrote the screenplay, also shows up. He plays a sympathetic reporter named Pete.

•

These performances, especially the lackluster one by Eddie Egan, provide an aura of amateurishness for "Badge 373," an aura that neither Robert Duvall, as the cop Eddie, nor Verna Bloom, as his girl Maureen, nor Henry Darrow, as the villainous Sweet William, does anything at all to dispel.

Sweet William, who may very well be the worst-written role in recent movies, is a Harvard - educated Puerto Rican who quotes Gide; makes his living from whores, drugs and contraband machine guns; and occupies a secret sumptuous book-lined palace hidden inside a wholesale meat plant right on the edge of the Hudson River.

This last location introduces an intentional unreality, in contrast to the unintentional unreality of everything else in the movie—as if the people who made "Badge 373" were unsure whether they wanted to rip off "The French Connection" or "Dr. No."

The former more than the latter, I should think. The movie is full of gratuitous authenticity (the vehicle in its inept big chase sequence is a 14th Street crosstown bus), with fears and prejudices right off the city streets. All the evil is perpetrated by Puerto Ricans, either innocent but violent revolutionaries who run around shouting "Puerto Rico Libre!" or the uninnocent but equally violent nonrevolutionaries who manipulate them. Against such forces, Eddie the hard-nosed cop

The New York Times
Eddie Egan

has only the instincts of his personal bigotry to guide him. And invariably the instincts of his personal bigotry turn out to be right.

There is absolutely nothing to praise in "Badge 373" —from Howard Koch's helpless direction to the dumpy performances by all the cast —but Pete Hamill's screenplay has at least the interest of its overblown prose (Sweet William gets all the lines; nobody else can manage much more than monosyllables) and its curiously devious intentions.

•

At some level, the screenplay means to make use of racial prejudices, expressing them but not endorsing them, and enjoying a free ride through current anxieties that ought to be worth something at the box office. This strategy fails completely. The potential tragedy of conflicting cultures becomes the exploitation of one and the debasement of the other. And unless you care to hate Puerto Ricans (or Irish cops) I don't see how the movie can have anything for you.

"Badge 373" opened yesterday at the Loews State I, Loews Cine and neighborhood theaters.

1973 Jl 26, 43:1

'Oklahoma Crude' Gains Honors at Moscow Fete

The Cast

I COULD NEVER HAVE SEX WITH ANYONE WHO HAS SO LITTLE REGARD FOR MY HUSBAND, directed by Robert McCarty; screenplay by Dan Greenburg, based on his novel "Chewsday"; produced by Gail and Martin Stayden; director of photography, Jeri Sopanen; editor, John Carter; theme music, Joe Liebman; distributed by Cinema 5. Running time: 86 minutes. At the Beekman Theater, Second Avenue at 65th Street. This film has not been classified.

Marvin	Carmine Caridi
Stanley	Andrew Duncan
Laura	Cynthia Harris
Mandy	Lynne Lipton
The DeVrooms	Gail and Martin Stayden
Herb	Dan Greenburg

By VINCENT CANBY

Dan Greenburg is a very funny writer ("How to Be a Jewish Mother"), and there are some funny lines and bits of business in "I Could Never Have Sex With Any Man Who Has So Little Regard for My Husband," a title so long that it seems intended as a bit of business in itself. It's the sort of movie you're supposed to start laughing at just from seeing the ads. You could also call it a cocktail party movie: it's funnier to be told about than to sit through.

There is, for example, a husband's righteous statement: "I haven't looked at another woman since I've been married. . . . That's 11 months now." Or there's the darling object someone finds in an antique shop: an ancient picture postcard of a shoe factory sent by a man in Newark to his brother in

MOSCOW, July 23 (AP) — The American movie "Oklahoma Crude" by Stanley Kramer shared first place for feature films today with Soviet and Bulgarian entries at the eighth Moscow International Film Festival.

Announcement of the winners came shortly before the closing ceremonies of the two-week festival, which has been dominated by films from Communist and third-world countries.

Mr. Kramer, a frequent exhibitor at the Soviet festival, was specially cited for "humanist contribution to the development of the world cinema."

The American film, set in the Oaklahoma oilfields in 1913, is the story of how "two persons win a moral victory over the despotism of business and force," reported a reviewer for the Defense Ministry newspaper, Krasnaya Zvezda.

Also receiving gold prizes in the feature category were "That Sweet Word Liberty" by Vitautas Zalakiavicus of Soviet Lithuania and "Love" by Bulgara's Lyudmil Staikov.

The Italian film "Pinocchio," starring Gina Lollobrigida, won the first-prize gold medal in the children's classification judged by adults.

A separate jury of Moscow children, however, voted the American film "Tom Sawyer" by Don Taylor the No. 1 entry.

Two films on environmental protection, Denmark's "The Sun Is Red" and Britain's "Undercurrents," shared first place in the popular science category.

With some 90 countries entered in the competition and more than 50 prizes and diplomas handed out, there were far more winners than losers at the festival.

The Moscow organizers of the show created three special award categories unknown in Western film festivals.

A Yugoslav film, "Sutjeska," captured the "best anti-Fascist" award, the Mexican production "Those Years" was named the 'best anti-imperialist" film, and Italy's "Matteoti Assassination" was voted the "best political" movie.

1973 Jl 24, 28:3

The Cast

DEAF SMITH & JOHNNY EARS, directed by Paolo Cavara; written by Harry Essex and Oscar Saul; director of photography, Tonino Delli Colli; editor, Mario Morra; music by Daniele Patucchi; produced by Joseph Janni and Luciano Perugia; released by Metro-Goldwyn-Mayer. At neighborhood theaters. Running time: 91 minutes. This film has been classified PG.

Erasmus (Deaf) Smith	Anthony Quinn
Johnny Ears	Franco Nero
Susie	Pamela Tiffin
General Morton	Franco Graziosi
Hester	Ira Furstenberg
Hoffman	Renato Romano

"Deaf Smith & Johnny Ears," the Italian-made, English-language horse opera shot in Spain that clattered aimlessly into local houses yesterday, is as limp an example of the so-called "spaghetti Western" as has turned up in recent memory.

Anthony Quinn and Franco Nero are the titular heroes who stop Franco Graziosi, as a would-be dictator, from taking Texas from President Sam Houston in 1836. They are ineffectually involved in an ersatz adventure that is neither as explosive or as funny as most movies in the genre it tries to emulate or lampoon.

•

The gimmick here, if you have not already guessed, is Mr. Quinn playing a deaf-mute whose "ears" are supplied by his tough sidekick, Mr. Nero. As a veteran movie vaquero, Mr. Quinn is properly saddle-weary and weatherbeaten in a floppy sombrero and a worn, dusty Prince Albert frock coat. He is also handy with his fists, sticks of dynamite, a Gatling gun and rudimentary sign language. UnUfortunately, neither he nor the action has much to communicate to a willing viewer.

Mr. Nero, handsome if unshaven, projects an overacted machismo that is pointless, especially when it is channeled toward comedy that rarely registers and Pamela Tiffin is merely naive

Associated Press
Anthony Quinn

as a pouting, babyish blond prostitute. "Deaf Smith & Johnny Ears" also has a couple of scenes in an ornate bagnio seemingly inspired by Toulouse-Lautrec, but they are no reason to visit this simulation of frontier Texas.
A. H. WEILER

1973 Jl 26, 43:1

THE MACKINTOSH MAN, directed by John Huston; screenplay by Walter Hill, based on Desmond Bagley's novel, "The Freedom Trap"; produced by John Foreman; director of photography, Oswald Morris; editor, Russell Lloyd; music, Maurice Jarre; distributed by Warner Brothers. Running time: 100 minutes. At the Loews State 2 Theater, Broadway at 45th Street, and Loews Orpheum Theater, 86th Street near Third Avenue. This film has been classified PG.
Rearden ....Paul Newman
Mrs. Smith..........Dominique Sanda
Sir George Wheeler........James Mason
Mackintosh.................Harry Andrews
Slade ....Ian Bannen
Brown ....Michael Hordern
Soames-Trevelyan...........Nigel Patrick
Brunskill ....Peter Vaughan
Judge ....Roland Culver
Taafe ....Percy Herbert
Jack Summers................Robert Lang
Gerda ....Jenny Runacre

By VINCENT CANBY

John Huston's new film, "The Mackintosh Man," is an espionage melodrama torn from the headlines—20 years late.

It's about a secret agent (Paul Newman), employed by British intelligence to capture a master spy who—it turns out quite early on—is an influential Member of Parliament, a law-and-order Tory (played with great charm by

Paul Newman

James Mason) who rants on about complacency and permissiveness and the ebbing of traditional values.

The trap requires a lot of planning (some of it so cryptic as to be intentionally comic), several carefully manufactured false identities, a spectacular prison break and locales that shift from London to Ireland to Malta (though the editing is so odd you may not be immediately aware that a shift has been made).

"The Mackintosh Man" is, technically, an espionage melodrama, but it strikes me more as a memory movie. It's not *about* memory, heaven knows. Nothing so fashionable. Rather it seems to have been made *from* memory, recalling, as it does, Burgess and MacLean; the cold war and especially cold war movies, every possible variant on which has already been made, including the post-cold war movie like "Scorpio" (about spies who no longer care).

The screenplay by Walter Hill, adapted from Desmond Bagley's novel, "The Freedom Trap," has very little to do with character and motivation and everything to do with the incidents and the mechanics of the spy trade. All of which seems to inhibit Huston's talents as a director, as well as those of most of his actors. They must express themselves entirely in terms of physical action and expository dialogue that, here, aim for complexity and arouse only confusion.

•

Part of this confusion may be the result of the soundtrack. Three-quarters of the way through the film I was ready to admit that wax had

impaired my hearing. That is, until Dominique Sanda, who also plays an intelligence agent, reading aloud from a newspaper reported that a reception would be held for diplomatic and "shersh dig-nah-TREES," which turned out to be her way of saying "church dignitaries."

"The Mackintosh Man" may have you sitting on the edge of your seat from time to time. More often, I suspect, you'll be cupping a hand to an ear.

The film opened yesterday at the Loews State 2 and Loews Orpheum theaters.

1973 Jl 26, 44:1

The Cast

BLOOD OF THE CONDOR, directed by Jorge Sanjines; screenplay (Quechua and Spanish with English subtitles) by Oscar Soria and Mr. Sanjines; produced by Ricardo Rada; director of photography, Antonio Eguino; A Ukamau Limitada production, distributed by Tricontinental Film Center. Running time: 74 minutes. At the First Avenue Screening Room, First Avenue at 61st Street. This film has not been classified.
Ignacio ....Marcelino Yanahuaya
Paulina ......Benedicta Mendoza Huanca
Sixto ....Vicente Salinas

By VINCENT CANBY

Jorge Sanjines's "Blood of the Condor," reportedly the first Bolivian feature film to be commercially released in this country, is like a lot of mid-20th-century revolutionary art that has its roots in the guilt-ridden middle classes of underdeveloped countries.

Its story—an exposé of how American aid workers systematically (and secretly) sterilized Indian women to prevent a nonexistent population explosion—is a curious mixture of primal passion and second-hand sophistication. Its sincerity is apparent, but its methods sometimes ludicrous.

The film is about Ignacio and Paulina, a Quechua Indian couple who find themselves unable to have further children after their first three have died of a plague. After Ignacio and other male members of his village castrate the two American doctors, Ignacio is summarily shot, and he dies, not directly of the wounds, but because Paulina and his brother Sixto cannot raise the 700 pesos necessary to buy blood for a transfusion.

•

Mr. Sanjines bites off many more issues than can be conveniently chewed in 74 minutes of screen narrative: American imperialism disguised as foreign aid, the practice of birth control as effective genocide, the population explosion, the exploitation of Bolivia's Indian majority by its white and mestizo minorities and the

desperate efforts of the Quechua Indians to maintain some kind of cultural identity.

The style of the film is both poetically plain (in the performances and the handsomely bleak black-and-white camerawork) and film-school fancy. Mr. Sanjines cuts back and forth in time in a way that would seem careless if one did not suspect he had been influenced by European film makers of the late nineteen-fifteen and sixties.

The marvel of "Blood of the Condor" is not its art but that the film could have been made at all in a country with so little in the way of a film heritage and with such unstable political régimes.

Mr. Sanjines, now 37 years old, was the founder-director of the Bolivian Film Institute in 1965, but was removed from that position (the institute was closed) a year later because the Government considered his first feature (also Bolivia's first) "too negative." "Blood of the Condor" was made in 1969, under the liberal Torres government that was overthrown in 1971. Since then, the director has been living in exile in Peru.

"Blood of the Condor" opened a one-week engagement yesterday at the First Avenue Screening Room. It hardly packs the wallop of "State of Siege," but unlike that film, which looks at Latin America through European eyes, it is a genuine homemade article. It is a firsthand statement that cannot be easily dismissed.

1973 Jl 27, 19:3

The Cast

THE LAST AMERICAN HERO, directed by Lamont Johnson; written by William Roberts, based on articles by Tom Wolfe; director of photography, George Silano; film editor, Robbe Roberts; music, Charles Fox; produced by Mr. Roberts and John Cutts; released by Twentieth Century-Fox Corporation. At neighborhood theaters. Running time: 100 minutes. This film is classified PG.
Elroy Jackson Jr..........Jeff Bridges
Marge ....Valerie Perrine
Mrs. Jackson....Geraldine Fitzgerald
Hackel ....Ned Beatty
Wayne Jackson ....Gary Busey
Elroy Jackson Sr..........Art Lund
Burton Colt ....Ed Lauter

By ROGER GREENSPUN

Lamont Johnson's "The Last American Hero" has a source in an Esquire article Tom Wolfe wrote several years ago about a stock-car racer and automobile customizer named Junior Johnson. The source isn't very close, however, and the film, with its hero, Junior Jackson (Jeff Bridges), hasn't too much to do with the subject of Wolfe's famous article. It hasn't too much to do with the mystique of automobile racing either — though it is full of automobiles and races. It does have to do with human

relations, with the choice between a private and a public life, with the meaning of imprisonment, with the ways in which a souped-up hot rod is like a Carolina moonshiner's still.

•

Junior's dad (Art Lund) makes the moonshine. Really committed to his trade, by now almost friends with the revenue agent who keeps tossing him in jail, he is a man of great character and gentle sadness whose way of life is pushing him into an extreme of privacy literally hidden down inside his native earth. Junior's spirit of independence, equally fierce, has no such luck. In a sense he must rise, taking nothing with him — not his friends, not even his own car — as success encloses him in its own forms of isolation.

The outline of this progress is conventional. But the terms developed for it in "The Last American Hero" are serious and rich and sometimes very beautiful.

Strictly for its car racing, the film isn't so exciting. But you might say the same for Howard Hawks's stock-car movie, "Red Line 7000" (1965), which from this distance begins to look like one of the important films of the last decade. But Hawks did care about the world of the drivers and their women, and he used car racing to express the stoical pessimism typical of his later work. Johnson withdraws from all that, to concentrate on individual solutions and moments of personal exploration. In this he is aided by stunning performances from Bridges, from Lund, from Geraldine Fitzgerald as Junior's mother, from Ed Lauter as the factory-team manager to whom Junior must finally sell himself, from Valerie Perrine as the girl for Junior — and for any other driver in the circuit.

•

Miss Perrine — known only, and rather spectacularly, for her performance in "Slaughterhouse Five" — has an interesting role. Quite obviously cast as the fickle prize of fame, she becomes humanly more appealing as she is revealed to be more tawdry, more helplessly disloyal — to just about everybody, even herself. "The Last American Hero" is a film of many regrets but no great bitterness. And its freedom from easy ironies and from any kind of condescension is one clue to its value.

The movies of Lamont Johnson ("The McKenzie Break," "The Groundstar Conspiracy," etc.) continue to impress me for their intelligence, their good B-movie toughness, their care and grace in performance. "The Last American Hero" opened yesterday at neighborhood theaters. That means that it may not be around long — and it is worth seeing.

1973 Jl 28, 16:1

The Cast

HAIL TO THE CHIEF, directed by Fred Levinson; original story and screenplay by Larry Spiegel and Phil Dusenberry; produced by Roy L. Townshend; executive producer, Norman W. Cohen; director of photography, William Storz; music, Trade Martin; editor, Robert DeRise; distributed by Cine Globe, Inc. Running time: 85 minutes. At the Playboy Theater, 57th Street east of Seventh Avenue. This film has been classified PG.

President ....Dan Resin
Secretary of Health....Richard B. Shull
Attorney General..........Dick O'Neill
Rev. Jimmy Williams.....Joseph Sirola
First Lady.............Patricia Ripley
Tom Goodman...............Gary Sandy
Vice President........Willard Waterman

Willard Waterman as the Vice President

By VINCENT CANBY

"No more Congress!" shouts the President of the United States. "No more Supreme Court! Just me!"

The President, who looks a lot like Bob Newhart and is played by another seriously comic actor named Dan Resin, can barely contain his old-fashioned, down-home joy. Sufferin' catfish! He can now give full rein to his paranoia, so that the Attorney General is able to warn that "the Commies and their dupes" (pronounced "doopays") "will have to go elsewhere for their revolution."

The President's extravagant fancies, expressed in the uniforms he has chosen for his special guard (a mixture of toy soldier and Storm Troop), are mirrored in the Attorney General's way of overdressing the language.

•

"Hail to the Chief," which opened yesterday at the Playboy Theater, is quite a remarkable political satire even though it's never so funny as you want it to be. It wobbles between moments of good, low buffoonery (the President's walking cheerily into a Cabinet meeting unaware of the piece of toilet tissue stuck to one shoe) and overstated outrage (when his secret police massacre all hippies and flower children in slow motion).

Rather, the film is remarkable because it was made three years ago, when few of us understood what was really going on in Washington, when all anyone had to

go on were do-it-yourself psychiatric profiles.

The lunatic prophesies of "Hail to the Chief" project Presidential paranoia beyond self-righteous explanations for the scuttling of constitutional rights (which is called "Presidential flexibility") to elaborate schemes of political assassination — which may or may not be one of the reasons it has taken the film so long to find a distributor.

The movie fits the mood of much of the Watergate testimony, but it does so only periodically, in passing, as it moves from adolescent gags to serious concerns and back again. The truth of the matter is that Watergate on television is funnier, more dumbsounding, sadder and much more instructive than "Hail to the Chief" (or probably any movie) could ever hope to be.

Fred Levinson, who directed the film and whose background has been in television commercials, and Larry Spiegel and Phil Dusenberry, who wrote the story and screenplay, are essentially funny men. Although the over-all design of their satire is hardly grand, some individual moments are most genial. I especially liked a White House reception where we see guests tearing into an American flag made out of red and black caviar, and the President's testy response when someone reminds him of the intentions of the founding fathers when they wrote the Constitution. "What did Benjamin Franklin know about nuclear capability?" he says. "He had a hard time just getting his kite up."

•

Mr. Resin is fine as the mad, no-longer-buttoned-down President. The supporting cast, comprising mostly New York actors, includes Richard B. Shull, as a well-meaning Secretary of Health, Education and Welfare; Willard Waterman (once the Great Gildersleeve) as an idiotic Vice President, and Joseph Sirola, as a pious, right-wing Southern evangelist.

It wouldn't be fair to say that truth has overtaken the satirical fiction of "Hail to the Chief." Things aren't that bad yet. Instead, truth has flattened the satire, making it seem slightly misshapen, as if a Metroliner had run over a penny.

1973 Jl 28, 16:1

Mason—Better Than Ever?

By VINCENT CANBY

IN THE better films of the better directors—Hitchcock, Rohmer, Truffaut, Mankiewicz, Kubrick, to name just a few who come to mind for no particular reason—it's difficult to tell where the work of the director (or the screenwriter) leaves off and that of the actor begins. A good film is all of a piece. It's an entity. It has no seams. It's possible for the critic to describe such a film, to try to communicate its effect as accurately as possible, and to give some idea of what it means, but the critic can get into trouble when he tries to distribute blue ribbons. He may even feel a little silly, as I sometimes do. It's like pinning the tail on the donkey.

Not having any idea of precisely who did what, the critic can find himself paying tribute to (or blaming) someone who wasn't even on the set when a film was made.

Film acting—or as someone has called it, film behaving—is subject to so many variables, from direction, writing, lighting and editing to the line of a jaw or of a thigh (which evoke subterranean responses probably best not analyzed) that I sometimes am reduced to calling a performance good, bad, indifferent or excellent —but more or less blindly.

Not always, but often enough to make me realize that for film actors the reading of reviews must be about as essential as the study of calculus. The new Dan Greenburg comedy, "I Could Never Have Sex With Any Man Who Has So Little Regard for My Husband," has some funny lines in it but it is, over the long haul, a cheerful bore: a frumpy East Coast version of "Bob & Carol & Ted & Alice." Are the four new (to me) actors in it any good? I haven't any idea. They aren't terrible, certainly, and each has his moments, but the quality of the film pretty much defines the

performances.

Lots of us, I suspect, make the mistake of confusing a performance with a role, especially with the kind of small, colorful roles that were so carefully cast, mostly with non-professionals, in John Huston's "Fat City" last year. Were these people great actors? I doubt it. But the roles were beautifully written and someone had the great good fortune to find people to play them who, for one reason or another, were able to project the sense of the roles as written. Sometimes they did it just by looking right and by being properly photographed.

*

Liv Ullmann, so fascinating in Bergman's films, registers with all of the impact of boiled ham on white bread in the Hollywood-made "Lost Horizon" and "40 Carats." Is this her fault? Does it mean she's really a lousy actress? Probably not. Yet it makes us re-evaluate some of the things we've thought about her in the past. For one reason or another, Dyan Cannon seemed hopelessly ill-at-ease in Otto Preminger's "Such Good Friends," which otherwise is one of Preminger's best films; but she is very funny, and very much at ease, in Herbert Ross's "The Last of Sheila."

I can't quite believe that means that Miss Cannon has suddenly learned how to act. I assume that the same intelligence was at work in both films, but for reasons over which she might not have had complete control, she comes off splendidly in one film and as a kind of blank spot in the other.

There are, of course, exceptions, performers who remain somehow inviolate no matter how tawdry the circumstances in which they happen to find themselves. Mostly these are the so-called stars, people like Steve McQueen and Paul Newman and Robert Mitchum, whose professional personalities tend to distract attention from their talents as actors. When they make good films, we accept the

quality of their performances as a matter of course. When they show up in junk, their reputations aren't damaged,

James Mason
Always superb

even though their contributions may not be particularly interesting. They manage to remain aloof from the disaster around them.

All of which brings me to the point of this piece: James Neville Mason who, at age 64, is no longer the leading man he once was though he remains a star and one of the most consistently interesting actors in films today. I have no idea if he is actually a *better* actor now than he was in the early 1950s. He was awfully good then (in "Julius Caesar," "A Star Is Born," "Five Fingers"), though he was known less as a good actor than as an eccentric personality. It may be that today he is wiser, more nonchalant—I have no way of knowing. What is apparent is that seeing him in two current first-run films that are not of classic caliber, "The Last of Sheila" and John Huston's "The Mackintosh Man," is like running unexpectedly into an old friend who turns what would have been a dull dinner party into a thoroughly enjoyable evening, not by remaining aloof but by using his intelligence, wit and experience, and by allowing himself to become as completely involved as possible.

Neither role offers him the opportunities he had in "Lolita," (which was a magnificently funny portrait of seedy desperation) or even in "Child's Play" (in which he played a totally unsympathetic victim), but Mason gives the two films unexpected dimension. He does nothing so vulgar and flashy as to walk off with the films. He doesn't steal them. Rather, by creating characters that command attention, he gives the other characters in the films importance they do not deserve under the circumstances.

In "The Mackintosh Man," which, as melodrama, ranks somewhere between Huston's "The Kremlin Letters" and "Beat The Devil" (at least it's almost as confusing as "Beat The Devil," if not as funny), Mason has what amounts to a disposable role, that of a platitudinous Tory M.P. who is really an arch-traitor to the crown. It's disposable because the character is not on the screen long enough to be identified in any way whatsoever, except as a first-class nasty. He's not a person but

a plot function. Mason, however, gives the role a presence that carries over into the scenes in which he doesn't appear. We remember him, we wonder what makes him tick (even though the screenplay doesn't) and we are always aware that there is a mind at work.

In "The Last of Sheila," Mason is cast as Philip, a once successful film director now reduced to directing television commercials, preferably with the small, pre-pubescent girls with whom he is obsessed. The trouble with Philip, it seems, is that

in the past he has let his obsession rule his head, which got him into trouble and (though the screenplay doesn't come out and say so) seems to be responsible for his present low estate in the Hollywood hierarchy. Stephen Sondheim and Tony Perkins, who wrote the script, thus manage to recall one of Mason's greatest roles, Humbert-Humbert, though the recollection doesn't have much to do with the story at hand, which is a whodunit. Mason could just as well be playing a crooked dentist for all the difference it makes to the

plot.

All of which is beside the point. Mason invests the character with a kind of self-mocking, rueful courage (which is not in the screenplay as far as I can tell) and his technical assurance allows him effortlessly to reel off great convoluted chunks of exposition of the sort without which no whodunit can be said to have been brought to a climax.

*

For some time I'd been thinking that Mason was be-

coming a better, more interesting actor with the passage of time. Having recently reseen "Lolita," "North by Northwest" and "Georgy Girl," it now occurs to me that he has always been superb. It's just that because so many of his recent films have been less than great, it's easier to recognize his contributions. He is, in fact, one of the very few film actors worth taking the trouble to see, even when the film that encases him is so much cement.

1973 Jl 29, II:1:3

Who Murdered Sheila? It's Worth Finding Out

By STEPHEN FARBER

WHEN Hollywood was a boom town, the studios had a knack for turning out lively, unpretentious genre movies. During the present nostalgia craze filmmakers are trying to recapture the spirit of those old movies, but they can't find the secret; most of the new pictures are mechanical reproductions of vintage Hollywood schlock. An exception is "The Last of Sheila," a stylish, literate, marvelously entertaining diversion in the classic tradition of the good-bad movie. It combines two hardy but unfashionable genres—the whodunit and the Hollywood expose, "And Then There Were None" crossed with "The Bad and the Beautiful."

Six silver-screen personalities, each hiding a guilty secret, are invited to spend a week on the yacht of a wealthy producer.

One of them is responsible for the hit-and-run death of the producer's wife a year earlier, and you know that the parlor games they play will eventually turn sinister. The filmmakers honor all the hoary thriller conventions — the wind howling through the rafters of an abandoned monastery, the morning-after-the-murder interrogation by an amateur sleuth, the telltale clues and the false confession—and their distinctive brand of acid humor freshens the clichés. The script by Stephen Sondheim and Anthony Perkins is a dazzling technical achievement; Herbert Ross's direction is slick, energetic, and professional; and most of the performances are first-rate.

"The Last of Sheila" shares "Sleuth"'s fascination with aristocratic gamesman-

ship, but it has a dizzyingly complex puzzle plot that makes "Sleuth" seem like a nursery story. In today's thrill-seeking, blood-hungry market, the authors have taken a chance creating a murder mystery that depends on ratiocination instead of sensations. The film demands close attention moment by moment, but your attention is rewarded; the labyrinthine plot is unraveled with exemplary lucidity. Sondheim and Perkins play fair, and anyone who follows the clues can solve the puzzle along with the characters. There are no loose ends, no red herrings; the logic is impeccable. Some thrillers may have had more surprising denouements than "The Last of Sheila," but not many have been as beautifully crafted.

The smooth storytelling flair demon-

Joan Hackett, as an unstable Hollywood wife, tries to defend herself in "The Last of Sheila"
"The evil in this story isn't banal; the murderer is truly fiendish"

strated by Sondheim, Perkins and Ross may be underestimated, but most moviemakers have lost the ability to tell coherent stories. Routine genre movies like "Scorpio," "Shamus," and "Hickey and Boggs" can't keep their stories straight; they are hopelessly muddled, unintelligible.

This incompetence has given the whodunit a bad name, but the genre has been out of fashion in literary circles for many years. In 1944, in an essay called "The Simple Art of Murder," Raymond Chandler attacked the artificiality of the Conan Doyle—Agatha Christie—Dorothy Sayers school of detective fiction and praised Dashiell Hammett for taking "murder out of the Venetian vase and [dropping] it into the alley." "The Last of Sheila" is in the Agatha Christie Venetian vase school, and the problem, as Chandler understood, is that it isn't really possible to believe in the superhuman brilliance of the murderer. No one could possibly foresee all the accidents and contingencies that the intricate plot depends on; he would have to be a clairvoyant as well as a tactical genius.

Still, it is probably this unreality which gives the drawing room mystery its special appeal. Raymond Chandler is a better writer than Agatha Christie, and his stories are much more realistic; but hers are in a strange way more terrifying. The reason, I think, is that they deal in extremes of evil. We know that most murders are sordid and clumsy, committed on impulse, by desperate people with very ordinary, petty motives.

The murders in "The Last of Sheila" are also committed for mundane rewards—money and sex—but the diabolical cunning of the murderer takes us beyond the mundane into a darker, more frightening realm. The evil in this story isn't banal; the murderer is truly fiendish, and although we may find the plot implausible, that idea of evil teases the imagination. Modern psychology and sociology offer explanations for murder, but can the act of murder ever be fully explained or understood? The paradox of "The Last of Sheila," and of all good mysteries, is that while it celebrates the triumph of reason, it also hints at the existence of hellish, irrational forces. The murder itself can be "solved," but the deeper mystery of human behavior is not so easily solved.

In his essay Chandler complained that drawing room mysteries are so involved in problems of logic that they never get around to creating characters or building atmosphere. But in "The Last of Sheila" the plot derives its logic from the characterizations. Setting the whodunit in the celluloid kingdom was a stroke of inspiration. Hollywood hustlers are some of the world's master games players. Their killings are usually only financial, but it isn't hard to believe that their guile gives them an aptitude for deadlier sports.

The denouement is esthetically as well as logically pleasing. The underlying question posed by this film is: Who is likely to be the most ruthless, crafty, coldly opportunistic and ambitious personality in the movie colony—the loudmouth agent, the sadistic producer, the has-been director, the young screenwriter trapped in the rewrite syndrome, the manufactured sex goddess, or her grasping manager husband? The answer may surprise you, but I think it is close to the mark. I salute Sondheim and Perkins for their very astute understanding of corruption in today's Hollywood.

*

Although the characters are almost all selfish and vicious, they are singularly charming. Inside-Hollywood movies always set out to expose the rot beneath the glitter of tinseltown, and end up glamorizing their monster characters. One watches their intrigues in horrified fascination, as if they were an exotic species of poisonous snakes. The characters in "The Last of Sheila" have no depth, but they are vivid gargoyles.

And for once, the all-star casting adds to the pleasure. James Coburn shows his choppers, and goes all the way with his own brand of gleeful malevolence. Richard Benjamin finally breaks free of the Portnoy stereotype and demonstrates his range and intelligence. James Mason has already proved that he can play just about anything; in this kind of elegant high comedy role he is unsurpassable — wonderfully, subtly sardonic. As the high-powered agent, Dyan Cannon plays a much broader kind of bitchery, but she is wonderful too —earthy, exuberant, and almost innocent in her maliciousness.

Best of all is Joan Hackett, one of the most attractive and gifted actresses this country has ever produced. Her career has never taken off as it should have—maybe because the complex, demanding roles she deserves simply aren't being written for women in American films. Although her role in "The Last of Sheila" doesn't challenge her, the skill with which she *creates* a character—an edgy, unstable, vulnerable but generous Hollywood wife—offers a lesson in the art of screen acting.

"The Last of Sheila" is a trifle, utterly without redeeming social value, but everything has been thought out, right down to the ironic use of Bette Midler's "Friends" over the end titles. And there's something to be said for craftsmanship at that high level. Many of the new genre movies are drenched in sentimentality and fake romanticism; they want to have "heart," but they're just mindless and manipulative. "The Last of Sheila" is the opposite: it's completely heartless, but it has a brain. It doesn't beg for sympathy for its unsavory characters; it stays ice cold, and it never insults the audience's intelligence by going soft. Taken on its own terms, this is an honest and immensely satisfying movie.

1973 Jl 29, II:7:1

DISNEY ON PARADE, starring Mickey Mouse and his friends. Produced and directed by Michel M. Grilikhes; choreography by Marc Breaux and Dee Dee Wood; costumes by Bill Campbell; character costume design by Bill Justice; musical supervision by Paul Weston.
WITH: Mickey and Minnie Mouse, Goofy, Pluto, Donald Duck, Pinocchio, Gepetto, Jiminy Cricket, The Blue Fairy, Mary Poppins, Herbie the Love Bug, Liver Lips, Henry, Big Al and Wendell Bear. At Madison Square Garden through Aug. 26.

By A. H. WEILER

Criticizing "Disney On Parade," which opened its fourth annual, 40-performance stand yesterday afternoon at Madison Square Garden is tantamount to hating ice cream, flowers, Mary Poppins or kids. And practically every youngster or parent or even a curmudgeon of an appraiser could not help but appreciate the cheer generated by the host of performers in the Garden's vast arena.

The mixture is, of course, essentially the same as before. The large cast, beautifully costumed as animated Disney characters and dancers, perform the show's version of variations on some noted Disney movies with excerpts from the actual films flashed on an immense overhead screen.

The cheering, chanting youngsters, as noted, were proof that the familiar can be fun. And, Michael Grilikhes, the producer-director who has been with it all from the beginning, has kept the show moving briskly with the aid of Marc Breaux and Dee Dee Wood, the husband-and-wife choreographers, who also know their business, having done the same for the films of "Mary Poppins" and "Sound of Music."

Mickey Mouse, Pluto, Goofy, Donald Duck and company scurry and dance about in most of the numbers, but this year's top attraction is Mary Poppins, who descends by wires and other engineering tricks from the Garden's ceiling to delight the small and larger fry. The strains of the likes of "Chim Chim Cheree" and other standard ditties got foot-stomping responses, too.

This viewer happened to like a sparklingly choreographed sequence involving the "Codfather" and other fish cavorting and dancing in a marine nineteen-twenties nightclub out of "Bedknobs and Broomsticks."

Pinocchio's adventures with other unruly boys on Pleasure Island and especially a tricked-up Model T and a Volkswagen (with eyelids and a flapping mouth), which chase Goofy up to the Garden roof (via those mechanical aids) also got whoops of enjoyment from the kids.

A nearby 10-year-old from Ozone Park, Queens, who admitted to the name of Alice played no favorites. "I enjoyed everything," she said contentedly. Her father, equally pleased, smiled and noted, "Everybody wants to be a kid occasionally." This "Disney On Parade" pleasantly helps to turn that trick.

1973 Ag 1, 49:3

The Cast

JEREMY, directed and written by Arthur Barron; director of photography, Paul Goldsmith; film editor, Zina Voynow; music, Lee Holdridge; produced by George Pappas; released by United Artists Corporation. At Loew's Tower East, 72d Street and Third Avenue. Running time: 90 minutes. This film has been classified PG.
Jeremy Jones............Robby Benson
Susan Rollins..........Glynnis O'Connor
Ralph Manzoni...............Len Bari
Cello Teacher.........Leonardo Cimino
Susan's Father............Ned Wilson
Jeremy's Father..........Chris Bohn
Jeremy's Mother............Pat Wheel

By ROGER GREENSPUN

Well over two years ago, when "Love Story" first began making everybody connected with it rich and famous, there was a lot of talk about a romantic revival—or a revival of romance—in movies. We were about to face the legions of the children of "Love Story." The offspring never materialized —or if they did, they were so pale that you couldn't see them.

But now there is one, full blown, blushing and very unashamed—a genuine "Son of Love Story." Its name is "Jeremy," and it opened yesterday at Loews Tower East.

It's a smaller movie than its sire, and, of course, much younger. The scene is not Harvard/Radcliffe, but something like sophomore-year High School of Music and Art. The boy is Jewish, middle-class, a musician—a cellist. The girl is gentile, middle-class, a dancer.

Their problem is not how to get married and live together, but rather, how to work up nerve enough to say hello to each other in public. And when they do, and when they finally acknowledge that they are in love, it is not the Grim Reaper Death who ends the tale. It's her dad, who yanks her off to Detroit with him, on his way to a better job. "Jeremy" is touchingly awkward, pleasantly sad. It is not exactly a desperate movie.

•

However, it is a movie of rather heavy calculation, indulging almost every cliché available to young love in Manhattan—the city at night, rainy afternoons, the camera floating over Park Avenue, or looking up through the sun-dappled leaves of Central Park. Like the advice of Jeremy's wise old cello teacher (e.g. "The music expresses life! Play it that way."), they deal not so much with experience as in preordained states of mind.

But in the long run "Jeremy" is less committed to its clichés than to its kids. It may be dull about the glamour of the city strets, but about the agony of calling up a girl for the first time just to make a date it is right on target. It specializes not in tragedy, but in a kind of bittersweet discomfort — which is true and moving, in spite of all the efforts to jack up its appeal.

•

An aura of not-quite professionalism surrounds "Jeremy," generally saving it from its own slickness, and validating a number of decent, tentative performances like that of Glynnis O'Connor as the girl, Susan.

As Jeremy, Robby Benson faces the problem of any clever kid playing a klutzy kid—bright, sensitive, original, and rather a jerk—and I think he handles it admirably. I don't know how com-

Robby Benson and Glynnis O'Connor

plete an 'actor he'll be one day, but in this performance he virtually shapes everything that matters in the movie.

Arthur Barron is the writer and director of record for "Jeremy," but there has been notice given in the trade press to an assertion by Joseph Brooks, a New York film and TV music composer, that the movie is in some measure his. I can't pretend to sort out the claims—not too unique in the busines of movie making—but it seems fair to suggest that in whatever proportion, both men were involved in the authorship of the film.

1973 Ag 2, 28:1

Skip "The Boy Who Cried Werewolf," the standard, slapdash half of a new horror double bill that includes something called "Sssssss" (as in snake). There is some amusing business in "Werewolf" toward the end, as the thrashing werewolf (Kerwin Mathews) tangles with a bunch of Jesus Freaks. Bob Homel, who plays the leader, also wrote the picture.

See "Sssssss," a ss-surprise. Were it not for the lurid, starkly flapping windup, this would be recommended in toto as a gripping, quietly imaginative haircurler. It is the only movie fiction I have ever seen that sustains a scholarly, informative attitude toward the world of snakes. This aspect is fascinating and chilling, as a gentle old venom researcher, Strother Martin, putters around with cobras and pythons in a country lab. His aides are his daughter and a smitten student.

That's the set-up, adroitly blended into a low-budget canvas of small-town characters and a visiting carnival by Hal Dresner's script (from a story by the producer, Dan Striepeke) and by Bernard L. Kowalski's direction. About midpoint, the effective color and music subtly signal that something perfectly horrible in the human department is also uncoiling on the doctor's premises.

Toned down, without the final fireworks, the picture would have emerged as a real sleeper for thriller fans, who should catch it anyway. It's certainly original. Mr. Martin does well, so does young Dirk Benedict, but the best are Jack Ging as a sheriff and Heather Menzies, a perfectly charming daughter. As for those snakes—Oooooo.

HOWARD THOMPSON

1973 Ag 2, 31:1

As a potentially inspirational saga that respects the awesome truth that generated it, "Maurie," now at Loews State and Cine Theaters is, unfortunately, rarely moving as drama. The heroism, tragedy and friendship of Maurice Stokes, the black basketball star destined to die, and his white teammate, Jack Twyman, formerly of the Cincinnati Royals, evolves on screen with largely soap-opera effects.

Fans, of course, will recall that Stokes was incapacitated and hospitalized after a head injury, and Jack Twyman selflessly spent 10 years raising the many thousands of dollars for the attempts to rehabilitate his friend before he finally succumbed three years ago.

But Daniel Mann's direction is uninspired, and the script by Douglas Morrow, who won an Oscar for another story stemming from the sports world, "The Stratton Story," has not effectively transplanted much of what was real and affecting in the Stokes-Twyman story into touching movie terms.

His principals are characters obviously injured by the fates, but they are rarely equal to the shattering true circumstances into which they have been plunged.

Further explanations are called for from the script that doesn't develop its characters completely and seems pointed mostly toward tear jerking. Bo Swenson as Twyman, is sincere and stalwart in his devotion as Stokes's official guardian and Bernie Casey is dignified as the stricken Stokes.

Janet MacLachlan is pretty and unassuming as his persevering girl, and Stephanie Edwards is natural as Twyman's understanding wife. But as a dramatization of unusual, affecting real human drama, "Maurie" only occasionally stirs the heart or mind.

A. H. WEILER

1973 Ag 2, 31:1

By A. H. WEILER

John Milius, the 29-year-old enfant terrible who wrote and directed "Dillinger," appears to be confused in his loyalties in this latest focus on the legendary Public Enemy No. 1, which opened at the Cinerama and other houses yesterday. His gangsters are larger, funnier and fuzzier than life as obviously monstrous killers. But they also leave the impression of having been slightly martyred as they are just as monstrously mowed down by G-men and others.

In making his debut as a director, Mr. Milius gives us a "Dillinger" that is fascinating for its speed, action and firepower. But as character studies of decidedly interesting types out of explosive history, "Dillinger" shoots blanks most of the time.

A viewer is frequently reminded of the likes of "Bonnie and Clyde" and "The Wild Bunch" as Dillinger and company rob banks and get shot up in dashes across the Depression countryside in vintage cars to vintage music "We're in the Money," etc.) on a gory road that ends in Dillinger's bloody finish outside that Chicago movie house in 1934.

There is, however, no full explanation of why or how Dillinger or the others took that path. They often seem to be caricatures rather than real characters. "I sure am happy. I just want to steal people's money," says Dillinger in an observation indicative of some of the film's surface, tongue-in-cheek dialogue.

As depicted in scenes shot in and around Enid, Okla.,

Warren Oates

members of his gang (Pretty Boy Floyd, Baby Face Nelson, et al) are callous but equally happy in their work. "This just isn't my day," says one of the fleeing mobsters before he is killed. And slaughter is the order of the day as they are cut down in their pastoral hideout, Little Bohemia, by G-men led by the gang's nemesis, the cigar-smoking Melvin Purvis, who also serves as the off-screen narrator.

The Dillinger portrayed by Warren Oates is tough and homespun, if little else. He can push Baby Face Nelson around. He is sentimental about visiting his folks, and he is roughly affectionate with his girl, but the full character of the man or gangster rarely emerges.

Ben Johnson comes across more vividly as the indomitable Purvis, who longs for the kind of recognition Dillinger gets. Michelle Phillips (formerly with the singers the Mamas and the Papas) is mildly effective in her debut as Dillinger's ever-loving girl. And, like most of the principals, Cloris Leachman, as the "lady in red" informer who helped trap Dillinger, is hardly on screen long enough to impress a viewer.

"Dillinger" does capture the look of the nineteen-thirties, but its violence dominates the scene and the players, who remain largely undefined figures on a bloody landscape.

1973 Ag 2, 31:1

By ROGER GREENSPUN

With two growing kids, a loving wife who nevertheless likes to spend money and a public that seems to have called it quits on reading, Claude (Claude Berri) doesn't need much persuading to close down his bookstore and, on a successful friend's advice ("Proust or 'Positions,' a book's a book"), to reopen it as a sex shop.

So he finds himself—this small, quiet, balding Parisian —the chief proprietor in a world of potency pills, personal vibrators, leather goods and specialized magazines catering to a number of preferences and peculiarities that are 90 per cent news to him.

His horizons expand—into one embarrassment after another—with a wife-swapping dentist (Jean-Pierre Mariello) and the dentist's swappable wife (Nathalie Delon), at a group-sex night spot, on board a Mediterranean cruise sponsored by a love club, with his father-in-law and mother-in-law, as companions. Here, through the entire course of a petit-bourgeois *Walpurgisnacht*, he never does quite manage the infidelity it seems his social obligation to commit.

These adventures, an hour and a half of them, make up Claude Berri's "Le Sex Shop" —a French name, like "Le Drugstore" — which opened yesterday at the Fine Arts Theater.

As a nonfan, from way back, of Claude Berri ("The Two of Us," "Marry Me! Marry Me!"), I was interested in seeing how he would treat material not as susceptible to the sentimental sweetness that has been his trademark and, for me, his greatest liability. On the whole, he treats it very respectfully.

But he hasn't really dropped the sweetness. He has only modified it to encompass sadism, masochism, fetishism, voyeurism, old men who like young girls and young girls who like other girls — the whole sexual revolution that is greeted by some with rage, by others with delight and by Claude Berri with a kind of gentle, sympathetic tolerance.

This may sound like transcendent virtue, but it is not. Berri's cinema, never sharp enough for satire, is also never exalted enough for transcendence. If you were to reduce Blake's "everything that lives is holy" to something like "everybody is ultimately a nice guy," you would have a reasonable formula for the drabness of Berri's film.

●

There are moments of real pleasure in "Le Sex Shop." There are a lot of really marvelous girls, including Juliet Berto as the wife, Beatrice Romand as the sex-shop salesgirl and the excellent Nathalie Delon. As a type, Claude Berri must be just what he wanted in a leading man—though I wish he had better ideas for what to do with himself, how to turn himself into the deadpan comedian he isn't but apparently means to be.

The X rating that accompanies this film is an absurdity—based on a few bared breasts, one (simulated) position, 10 vibrators and a chastity belt. "Le Sex Shop" may deal in the Devil's merchandise, but its soul is as pure (too pure) as the driven snow.

1973 Ag 3, 16:1

'Loops' Peeps Into 25-Cent Pornography Machines

"Loops," according to the ads, shows and tells all about "one of America's most shocking subcultures," the one where you plunk in a quarter, hunch over a machine and hope for the best. Or worst. Which is it?

They must be kidding. This feature squint at pornography in production couldn't be duller or less revealing; ditto the comments by the participants in this new feature, which ar yesterday at the First - Avenue screening room.

There is nudity, continual giggling on all sides, a chatterbox director and very obvious simulation of sex, as a twitchy cinéma-vérité camera bobs around to project a stamp of authenticity.

●

In quest of something, the picture even drops in some cinema soap-opera scenes as the glib young director-producer (the star of "Loops") has a verbal tug of war with his wife.

What's his real ambition? The young porno impresario would like to "pop over to London and shoot Thomas Mann's story 'Disorder and Early Sorrow' with Ralph Richardson and a cast of thousands." Thousands of what?

One porno queen, a pretty blonde, attributes her new career to her escape from "middle-class morality, ya know?" This, her new line, is "cool, ya know?"

Her leading man, interviewed as he uses the studio-office dartboard, at least has a sense of humor. His candid personal résumé and philosophy, much of it unprintable, is at least original. Otherwise, as a purposeful probe of sizzling cinema, "Loops" is thin, cold turkey.

HOWARD THOMPSON

1973 Ag 3, 19:1

The Cast

THE NEPTUNE FACTOR, directed by Daniel Petrie; written by Jack DeWitt; director of photography, Harry Makin; music, Lalo Schifrin; editor, Stan Cole; produced by Sanford Howard; released by 20th Century-Fox. At neighborhood theaters. Running time: 98 minutes. This film is classified G.
Commander Blake..........Ben Gazzara
Leah Jansen.............Yvette Mimieux
Dr. Andrews............Walter Pidgeon
Don (Mack) Mackay....Ernest Borgnine
Captain Williams........Chris Wiggins
Bob Cousins.........Donnelly Rhodes
Norton Shepherd...Michael J. Reynolds

By ROGER GREENSPUN

With the subtitle "An Undersea Odyssey" and with a musical score that sounds as if it might have been written by a brother-in-law of Richard Strauss's chambermaid, "The Neptune Factor" isn't exactly shy about claiming its parentage. Like many other claims of parentage, this one should be taken with a grain of salt.

What "The Neptune Factor" is really about is a search and rescue mission to save three aquanauts trapped by an undersea earthquake on the ocean floor somewhere off the coast of Nova Scotia. Down, down the rescuers descend — Ben Gazzara, Yvette Mimieux, Ernest Borgnine and Donnelly Rhodes — led by the faintest ray of hope (and rather forcibly pushed by Miss Mimieux, who plans to marry one of the aquanauts), until at last....

●

Until at last they plumb the nethermost ocean depths and enter what I do believe is an oversized tabletop aquarium. Gargantuan goldfish, enormous sea horses, earth-shaking lobsters, man-eating softshell crabs — from every side the terrors of the sea approach them, torment their submersible craft, the Neptune, until at last....

Until at last — they either find their colleagues, or they don't. Anyone willing to sit through 90 minutes of this in order to find out probably does not really know and shouldn't have his suspense ruined. My own pleasure in "The Neptune Factor" begins and ends with the miniature photography — as nutty as anything I've seen in recent movies — and with the eliciting from Ben Gazzara, as the steely leader of the mission, Comdr. Adrian Blake of Atlanta, what may be filmdom's most confidently unconvincing Southern accent.

Directed by Daniel Petrie, "The Neptune Factor" is largely the work of Canadian film makers. It opened yesterday at neighborhood theaters.

1973 Ag 4, 19:1

'Graffiti' Ranks With 'Bonnie and Clyde'

By STEPHEN FARBER

SUPERLATIVES are dangerous, but sometimes hard to resist. George Lucas's "American Graffiti" is easily the best movie so far this year. Beyond that, I think it is the most important American movie since "Five Easy Pieces"—maybe since "Bonnie and Clyde." The nostalgia boom has finally produced a lasting work of art.

"American Graffiti" opens a little uneasily, with an overdose of fifties camp: waitresses on roller skates at Burger City, double chubby chucks and cherry Cokes, snowball at the sock hop, the classic pop songs, from "Rock Around the Clock" to "Teen Angel," and the exotic lingo — "cooties," "boss," "bitchin'," "bod," "dork." For the first few minutes, the trivia threatens to get out of hand; one expects another "Summer of '42," or a "Grease" on wheels. But the movie deepens as it goes along. Its definitive, remarkably resonant portrait of adolescence transcends all generation gaps. On a budget of just over $700,000, and on a very tight shooting schedule — 28 days (28 nights, to be precise) — Lucas has brought the past alive, with sympathy, affection, and thorough understanding.

The film actually takes place in 1962, in Modesto, California, on the night before two high school graduates are scheduled to set off for college in the East. There is no conventional "story"; the movie has a freer musical rhythm, interweaving the adventures of four teen-age boys as their paths crisscross during the night. Lucas uses all the resources of the medium to build his mosaic of impressions of small-town life.

The soundtrack has a special importance. A nonstop stream of fifties music, punctuated with fragments of a disk jockey's crazy freeform monologue, accompanies all the action. The radio is these kids' lifeline, and by keeping it in the background of almost every scene, Lucas mesmerizes us right along with the characters. The music releases our own memories, and gives an emotional charge to everything on screen.

Great films absorb the audience in a distinctive world, and the garish night world of "American Graffiti" is vividly detailed, sometimes claustrophobic. But the film represents more than a technical triumph. The stunning screenplay by Lucas, Gloria Katz and Willard Huyck is rich in characterizations, full of wit and surprise. First im-

Sun-Drenched 'Lady Ice'

Donald Sutherland and Jennifer O'Neill Star

To put Jennifer O'Neill, Donald Sutherland, Robert Duvall and Patrick Magee into a movie and come up with nothing must take some kind of ability — though not the kind of ability you would search out too often at your neighborhood theater, which is where Tom Gries's "Lady Ice" has opened.

Duvall, a Miami police inspector, merely walks through his part. Magee, a big-time Miami sports-car dealer, merely squeezes a few more drops of self-pitying rage — like something left over from his role in "A Clockwork Orange." As for Miss O'Neill, as Magee's daughter and Miami's most important trader in hot diamonds; and Donald Sutherland, as the happy-go-lucky insurance investigator who tracks her down — well, they mainly smile a lot and look very healthy. But the look of health—dewy tan for Miss O'Neill; blue-eyed bronze for Mr. Sutherland — might have been poured out of a bottle. So might everything else in "Lady Ice," which carries the American feature movie a bold step closer to the condition of a Florida orange-juice commercial.

I'm not really opposed to synthetics, however, and

Lot of Smiling, but Not Much Communicating

every so often, when it gets far enough away from its characters, "Lady Ice" takes on the mute, appealing pathos of a travel poster. But when it gets close to its characters—even to the spectacularly beautiful Miss O'Neill — who talk without communicating and touch as if without ever making contact, it gives up everything to the development of a plot that makes no sense and the intimation of a lifestyle that you couldn't keep fresh even under Saran Wrap.

Everything in the film leans to the conventional—the sex, the violence, the thrills, the anger, the cool. Some nice conventional movies have been made in this way. But "Lady Ice" never discovers how the conventions live, only that they die, and so it becomes kind of a sun-drenched, breeze-swept, palm - laden, sea-sparkled reminder of lost delights and failed powers.

ROGER GREENSPUN.

1973 Ag 3, 19:1

pressions can never be trusted. For example, John Milner (Paul Le Mat), the car freak who carries his pack of Camels rolled up in the sleeve of his T-shirt, could be a caricature of a greaser, but his sweetness and vulnerability keep undercutting his belligerent pose; he's the town Galahad, the protector of the weak and the helpless.

All the characters burst out of stereotype; they seem to have an independent life, and by the end they are so real that it's painful to leave them. The whole movie is brilliantly cast and performed.

Ronny Howard and Cindy Williams are high school sweethearts at a 1962 sock hop in "American Graffiti," the film due next Sunday at the Sutton.
Its portrait of adolescence transcends all generation gaps

Lucas's technical flair was already visible in his first movie, "THX-1138," but his work with the actors in "American Griffiti" is a revelation. His gifts are prodigious; at 28 he is already one of the world's master directors.

Lucas has an interesting sense of social history. Set at the tail end of an era, the film freezes the last moment of American innocence. In 1962 the kids in Modesto still drive fifties cars, listen to fifties music, and pattern themselves after fifties culture heroes — James Dean,

Connie Stevens, Sandra Dee. It's as if they were trying to make time stand still. They can't know how radically the country will be shaken and polarized by the cataclysms of the next few years; but they do have an intuitive sense that their culture is disintegrating. "The whole strip is shrinking," the dragstrip champion Milner complains forlornly. "Five or six years ago it used to take a couple of hours and a whole tankful of gas just to make one circuit." A little later he dismisses the Beach Boys' new brand of surfing rock: "Rock and roll's been going downhill since Buddy Holly died."

The transience of this world regulated by Ozzie and Harriet is always implicit, and the titles at the end of the film make the point explicit — probably overexplicit. That sense of impermanence gives the comedy its undercurrent of pathos. Everything seems precious because we know it can't last. "American Graffiti" conveys the feeling of a dream about to dissolve. The whole movie was shot at night, and Lucas and Haskell Wexler (credited as "visual consultant") create a dream landscape; the cars glide through the darkness in a strange, hallucinatory parade.

It seems as if several years are compressed into one night — a series of comic, terrifying, romantic adventures that represent the most hypnotic possibilities of small-town life. The film isn't meant to be a naturalistic record; it's a carnival fantasy, a pageant of wonders, seen through the eyes of kids who don't want to leave. The class president, Steve (Ronny Howard) breaks up with his steady girlfriend (Cindy Williams), but they reunite at dawn. On this charmed night even the awkward, creepy boy nicknamed Toad (Charlie Martin Smith) can pick up a bouffant kewpie doll (Candy Clark) in his borrowed Chevy, and although he does everything wrong, he manages to win her anyway. Luckily for him, she thrives on disasters; she can accept anything but a routine evening.

Curt (Richard Dreyfuss), the sharpest of the teen-age quartet, is still trying to decide whether to go East to college, or stay at the mediocre junior college in town; the town has a strong hold on his imagination. On his last night he gets picked up by a gang of hoods, the Pharaohs, and although he almost gets killed carrying out their horrifying ultimatums, he proves himself to them and wins the

chance to take part in their blood initiation. He even discovers a woman of mystery cruising main street — a blonde in a white '56 Thunderbird who whispers "I love you" as her car passes his, and then disappears.

This shadowy woman in white embodies the magical promise of the familiar world. Cruising through town one summer night, a boy can see his old friends, meet glamorous or dangerous new people, experience just about everything — love at first sight, break-up and reconciliation, felonious assault, a hairbreadth escape from a fiery death — from the sublime to the ridiculous. Why would anyone want to leave?

Yet in spite of everything that happens, nothing really happens. You feel stimulated by the drive through town, and you also feel trapped in the circle; there's no way out. For all the charm of this world, there is pain in it too — the constant pressure of testing yourself against the challenges of the tribe, the cruelty of adolescence at a time when behavior was regimented. The street is enchanted by night, transformed in the spectral glare of headlights. In the morning, everything looks smaller, drabber.

Toward the end of the movie, the comedy is displaced by a growing sense of wistfulness and melancholy. Even Milner, the king of the road, feels strangely depressed by dawn, as he walks away from his latest victorious drag race. "I was losing. He had me, he was pulling away from me," he tells the blindly idolatrous Toad. The triumphs that this world offers no longer satisfy Milner; he is nagged by a feeling of failure, the fear of time slipping away from him. He knows that his only future is in the car graveyard he haunts. One day his shiny yellow deuce coupe will be junked right on top of the legendary '41 sedan he never had a chance to race.

*

For Curt the night ends with a visit to the Wolfman (played by the real Wolfman Jack), the disk jockey on the outskirts of town. To the kids, the Wolfman is Modesto's most exotic, resplendent culture hero. Some people say he broadcasts from a plane that never lands; others believe he lives in Mexico. But when Curt goes inside the radio station, he finds only a kind, befuddled man eating a Popsicle from a broken-down refrigerator. The Wolfman who stirs the town's imagination is a fictional character; the real Wolfman is a ragged Wizard of Oz, the great pretender.

This encounter clinches Curt's decision to leave his childhood wonderland. At last he knows that the emerald city is a mirage.

But when Curt finally does leave town, we feel deeply torn — saddened by what he must sacrifice, relieved that he is breaking away. Somehow the sense of melancholy seems stronger. This emotionally complex film retrieves the exuberance of a carefree moment of youth, but by the end it is suffused with a feeling of lost opportunities, shattered possibilities. You feel sad for the kids who stay, equally sad for the boy who leaves. No decision is the right decision. Everybody loses. That blonde in the T-bird is still on the highway as Curt's plane takes off, tantalizing, elusive, unattainable; she will always be the one that got away.

The ambiguity of this film disturbs whatever preconceptions one brings to the theater. I don't happen to share the current nostalgia for the fifties — a period of apathy, complacency, and anti-Communist hysteria — but I found myself irresistibly drawn to the world created in "American Graffiti." That's because the film is free of special pleading. It acknowledges the insularity of the fifties, but it also recalls the innocence and the sense of community — the shared language, music and humor that contributed to the last authentic national folk culture. The kids who left home in 1962 didn't know they were embarking on a journey across centuries. We have to contemplate their innocence with mixed emotions.

In thinking about the past, one almost always distorts it — either sentimentalizing it or indicting it by applying the standards of the present. "American Graffiti" takes us *inside* the gaudy, swollen universe of the fifties; it sees the period whole, without settling for easy judgments.

The film has the spirit of rock music — bold, confident, colloquial, casually lyrical, unpretentious but evocative; it is a tribute to the beauty of American graffiti. Although it is a highly personal film, drawn from Lucas's own experience (he grew up in Modesto and was graduated from high school in 1962), it has the universality of the greatest popular art. Part of the experience of moviegoing is private — dreaming in the dark; but the best movies create a fragile community of dreamers.

That is why movie houses are still on occasion the true churches of the twentieth century. On the streets everyone is isolated, but sometimes when the lights go down in the theater, the current that races through the house overwhelms all differences, dissolves all barriers. "American Graffiti" connects with an audience in a way that few movies ever have.

The only thing that worries me is the thought of all the exploitative fifties nostalgia pix that this movie may spawn. "American Graffiti" happens to reflect the public's yearning for the innocent contentment of the fifties, but the special excitement of the film is that it takes us beyond nostalgia — into a *rediscovery* of the past, and of memories that might have been lost forever. For those of us in Lucas's generation, watching "American Graffiti" is like going home; it's a primal experience, and the deeply conflicting feelings that it stirs cannot possibly be resolved.

1973 Ag 5, II;1:4

JESUS CHRIST SUPERSTAR, directed by Norman Jewison; screenplay by Melvyn Bragg and Mr. Jewison; based on the rock opera by Tim Rice, with music by Andrew Lloyd Webber and lyrics by Mr. Rice; produced by Robert Stigwood and Mr. Jewison; a Universal presentation. At the Rivoli Theater, Broadway and 49th Street, the Murray Hill, 34th Street at Third Avenue, and other showcases. Running time: 108 minutes. (This film is rated G.)
Jesus .... Ted Neeley
Judas .... Carl Anderson
Mary Magdalene .... Yvonne Elliman

By HOWARD THOMPSON

Broadway and Israel meet head on and disastrously in the movie version of the rock opera "Jesus Christ Superstar," produced in the Biblical locale. The mod-pop glitter, the musical frenzy and the neon tubing of this super-hot stage bonanza encasing the Greatest Story are now painfully magnified, laid bare and ultimately parched beneath the blue, majestic Israeli sky, as if by a natural judgment.

The producers of this Universal release could, of course, have taken the easy way and simply photographed the stage original, which simulates the last seven days of Christ. Boldly, at least with high box-office hopes, they have tried for a natural, cinematic flow, with the good earth underfoot and an encircling camera doing the rest. It doesn't work, not even with a perspiring cast clambering around crags and caves, grimacing soulfully and singing their heads off.

•

They sing well and almost continually some 28 numbers. But their bizarre garb, ranging from Ali Baba to platinum-blond transvestite, is a far-out put-on that signifies the rigging of the whole enterprise, as on stage. (The disciples' garb is toned down. A thin, blue-eyed Jesus wears white sackcloth.) Toward the end, amid a tediously staged, even anti-climatic Crucifixion, the color camera splashily cuts in some plain, hotsy-totsy hoofing.

Before that, the prisoner Jesus is mocked by a fat, roguish Herod in a revolting song-and-dance straight out of Minsky's and what looks like leftover footage from Fellini's "Satyricon."

Even so, the movie, which churns and flaps like a stranded road show, does have some interesting aspects. One is the brilliant opening, the "overture," as a busload of players arrives to make the film, in the film-within-a-film format, which the director Norman Jewison (also co-producing) and Melvyn Bragg have briefly bracketed to Tim Rice's stage book.

Mr. Jewison also achieves some nice pictorial composition and texture, although he fared infinitely better on location (Yugoslovia) with "Fiddler on the Roof." An enraged Jesus purging the Temple (here a flea-market) makes a strong scene. Even stronger is another with Jesus overcome by a clawing, cave rabble. The director has elicited sturdy performances from Ted Neeley in this role and from Carl Anderson, a black actor who portrays Judas. The nub of the story seems, in fact, to be merely leadership rivalry between Jesus and his betrayer.

Yvonne Elliman does well, again, as Mary Magdalene with the best-known song, the torchy ballad "I Don't Know How to Love Him." Bob Bingham is a properly ominous Caiaphas, with Barry Dennen, Larry T. Marshall and Joshua Mostel in other key roles.

•

The onslaught of music by Andrew Lloyd Webber (to Mr. Rice's lyrics), with bits and pieces of everything since rock started rocking, is haunting, deafening. It pours from the loudest soundtrack in years. Brace your ears.

The movie, like the play, has already drawn preopening protests, including charges that its stress on Jews as killers of Jesus might provoke anti-Semitism. And some Christians may construe the picture as blasphemous.

To this viewer, a gaudy rock rhinestone has now shriveled so transparently that by contrast it makes the Greatest Story seem greater than ever.

1973 Ag 8, 28:1

The Cast

HEAVY TRAFFIC, an animated film written and directed by Ralph Bakshi; cinematography, Ted C. Bemiller and Gregg Heschong; film editing, Donald W. Ernst; music by Ray Shanklin and Ed Bogan; characters created by Mr. Bakshi; produced by Steve Krantz; released by American International Pictures. At the Penthouse Theater, Broadway and 47th Street; 86th Street Twin 1, west of Lexington Avenue, and 59th Street Twin 1, east of Third Avenue. Running time: 76 minutes. This film has been classified X.
Michael .... Joseph Kaufman
Carole .... Beverly Hope Atkinson
Angie .... Frank De Kova
Ida .... Terri Haven
Molly .... Mary Dean Lauria
Rosalyn .... Jacqueline Mills
Rosa .... Lillian Adams

By ROGER GREENSPUN

In the glass top of a pinball machine the figures start to materialize, like emanations from the mind of a player obsessed with a game that can only end in "TILT." They strut, creep, hobble out into the squalid streets — these characters whose passing miseries, become the substance of "Heavy Traffic," Ralph Bakshi's animated movie, a cruel, funny, heartbreaking love note to a city kept alive by its freaks, and always, always dying.

There is Michael, the shy young cartoonist, fed by his Jewish mother, prodded by his Italian father whose chief ambition is to make it big with his bosses in the Mafia. There is Shorty, the legless bar bouncer, hopelessly in love with the gorgeous black barmaid, Carole, whom Michael also loves, and courts with gift cartoon strips from afar. The drag queen Snowflake looks for true affection, but chases brutal boy friends, who always find him out. Everyone tends toward tragedy, with gobs of tears, and sometimes buckets of blood—like the stoical godfather whose head is riddled with bullets, and *still* he finishes his plate full of spaghetti.

Not everyone's ending is so conclusive. For example, when Rosalyn Schecter, the freckle-faced neighborhood seductress, falls off a tenement roof top (victim of a small miscalculation in Michael's fumbling attempt to lose his virginity), she never hits the ground. She is saved halfway down by a clothesline, where throughout the picture she remains, totally naked, somewhat embarrassed and upside down, hanging by a big toe.

Bakshi's subject is really the city, New York City, the sum of his many characters' lives, and yet desolate, depopulated. Generally it looks as if news of some impending disaster had reached everybody in time to leave New York deserted—except for the creatures in the movie, who live together in the shadow of a doom they don't understand but somehow express. At one point Michael goes to the movies, and he sits utterly alone in a cavernous Broadway theater while on the screen, in actual film clips, Harlow stars with Gable in "Red Dust." It's like always being haunted by the ghost of

yourself, a familiar, unshakable terror.

Bakshi's sources range from Alfred Hitchcock to Edward Hopper (both very openly quoted) and his resources seem almost limitless. Often he places his cartoon characters over photographed back-projection footage of the city at night — some of it very old, like a seamy memory of the nineteen-fifties. The characters themselves, the drawings, are rich, vigorous, full of comic-book vitality and exaggeration. People who felt that his earlier feature, "Fritz the Cat," merely debased a cherished original, can now judge Bakshi's development of his own material. I think that development is as brilliant as anything in recent movies—as brilliant, and in its own improbable way, as lovely and as sad.

"Heavy Traffic" opened yesterday at the Penthouse and the 86th Street and 59th Street Twin 1 theaters.

1973 Ag 9, 30:1

WHITE LIGHTNING, directed by Joseph Sargent; screenplay, William Norton; director of photography, Edward Rosson; film editor, George Nicholson; music, Charles Bernstein; produced by Arthur Gardner and Jules V. Levy; released by United Artists Corporation. At the Trans-Lux West, Broadway at 49th Street; the 34th Street East Theater, east of Third Avenue, and the Juliet I Theater, Third Avenue and 83d Street. Running time: 101 minutes. This film has been classified PG.
Gator McKlusky .... Burt Reynolds
Lou .... Jennifer Billingsley
Sheriff Connors .... Ned Beatty
Roy Boone .... Bo Hopkins
Dude Watson .... Matt Clark
Martha Culpepper ...... Louise Latham
Maggie .... Diane Lad
Big Bear .... R. G. Armstrong

"White Lightning," which opened yesterday at neighborhood theaters, is a fairly awful movie that keeps producing good things—scenes, performances, moments of insight—that seem connected to better ideas than anything suggested in the film's larger intentions. There are enough of those good things so that I shouldn't mind seeing more work directed by Joseph Sargent, or written by William Norton, or featuring such performers as Jennifer Billingsley, Ned Beatty or Matt Clark.

In form, "White Lightning" is straightforward revenge melodrama. Gator McKlusky (Burt Reynolds), a convicted Arkansas moonshiner, is let out of prison so he can help establish evidence for a Federal case against a particularly evil and law-breaking small-town sheriff (Ned Beatty). But Gator has his own reasons, the sheriff's killing of his college-student kid brother mainly because the boy wore his hair long and espoused good government, and he means to get more than evidence.

•

For reasons that I'm sure are clearer to the producers than they are to me, half of this action involves endless car chases, which are a

crushing bore. The other half involves human relations—between Gator and the wild girl (Miss Billingsley) he is attracted to, between Gator and the helpless whisky runner (Matt Clark) he makes use of—and sometimes these are very interesting indeed.

Burt Reynolds may by now have a bare-chest clause in his contract, because you see a lot of his bare chest—for example, in flirtation scenes with Miss Billingsley where you don't see any of hers. What you do see of her is a rather complex and subtle characterization of a girl more vulnerable than she seems. In fact, all the local types, like Matt Clark, Bo Hopkins, or R. G. Armstrong (all in the moonshine business) are more complete and more resilient than the situation strictly demands.

Ned Beatty makes of Sheriff Connors one of those bland phlegmatic manifestations of evil that have from time to time been such a specialty of the South as shown in American movies. And there are sequences involving him — some of the best take place inside the sheriff's office — that seem unexpectedly intricate and cleverly paced, and on the way to rather exciting film making. ROGER GREENSPUN.

1973 Ag 9, 30:2

NIGHT WATCH, directed by Brian G. Hutton; screenplay by Tony Williamson, with additional dialogue by Evan Jones, based on a play by Lucille Fletcher; produced by Martin Poll, George W. George and Barnard S. Straus; a Joseph E. Levine and Brut Productions presentation. At the Radio City Music Hall, Avenue of the Americas and 50th Street. Running time: 99 minutes. (This film is rated PG.)
Ellen Wheeler .... Elizabeth Taylor
John Wheeler .... Laurence Harvey
Sarah Cooke .... Billie Whitelaw
Inspector Walker .... Bill Dean
Mr. Appleby .... Robert Lang
Tony .... Tony Britton
Dolores .... Rosario Serrano

Elizabeth Taylor, and about time, has got herself a good picture and a whodunit at that. More than one Music Hall patron seemed to be stumbling from the first showing of "Night Watch" yesterday in stunned delight at the windup, a gorgeously brazen, logical swindle.

Seldom, at least recently, has a mystery carpet-yanking been so effective, especially after a familiar suspense set-up that seems to be carelessly shedding red herrings. This is the one about the rich, jittery wife who howls murder about the empty old house next door. She says—or thinks—she has seen two bloodied corpses, at intervals, through the window.

•

Well, has she? Or is she cracking up? There is much solicitous tiptoeing around the frenzied Miss Taylor—a bit too much—by her stockbroker husband, Laurence Harvey, and her best friend, Billie Whitelaw. A snippy, garden-digging neighbor, Robert Lang, handles a spade most ably. An unctuous psychiatrist drifts in, as does an airy cook and a caustic, impatient police inspector.

All this seems fairly old stuff, with an insistent Miss Taylor clearly about to pop her cork, with outside help. Something else pops, and you'll never guess what unless you saw Lucille Fletcher's original play starring Joan Hackett.

The Broadway hit had a swank, one-set, Manhattan town house and a larger, more raffish gallery of suspects. Tony Williamson's adaptation trims the cast to a handful, and shifts the locale to luxury digs in London.

With fewer people under close camera scrutiny, beautiful color photography and Miss Taylor agonizing in some dazzling Valentina finery, it's easy to play a smug Sherlock. But the glossy intimacy only deepens the surprise of the climax, a hair-raising stalk in the house next door, yeastily directed by Brian G. Hutton.

Miss Taylor churns up a fine, understandable lather of nerves. Mr. Harvey is properly sleek, Miss Whitelaw makes a peppery parrot, and Mr. Lang is neat. The deliciously cunning postscript may make you feel like a perfect fool. Once in a while it's fun.

HOWARD THOMPSON

1973 Ag 10, 26:1

GORDON'S WAR, directed by Ossie Davis; screenplay by Howard Friedlander and Ed Spielman; produced by Robert L. Schaffel; presented by 20th Century-Fox. At the National Theater, Broadway and 44th Street, and other houses. Running time: 90 minutes. (This film is rated R.)

Gordon .... Paul Winfield
Bee .... Carl Lee
Otis .... David Dowling
Roy .... Tony King
Spanish Harry .... Gilbert Lewis
Luther .... Carl Gordon

In "Gordon's War," four black veterans of Vietnam wage fierce personal battle, using Army tactics, against drug channelers in Harlem. What, indeed, could be more admirable? This is a worthy film, whose format and substance—a black theme dramatized for practical, constructive purposes — remain exceeded by its goal.

⬤

The picture is tough, fast, moves in a straight line with no sideline fiddling but with pungent humor and vividly jabs the crime-ridden underbelly of Harlem. The sharp direction of Ossie Davis catches the argot, the flavor and the sinister ambiance of the area. And Mr. Davis stages a wingding of a car-motorcycle chase near the end.

But the picture is inconclusive, far from profound, and the urgency of the theme has been overly simplified to fit the action. Only in the first part of the script is there character probing, as Paul Winfield (of "Sounder") broods over the ad-

diction of his dead wife and recruits his three pals for personal and moral vengeance. A real uptown dope purge, says somebody, "would take an army."

These four—Carl Lee, David Dowling and Tony King are the others—do very well on their own. Fiercely, methodically, the good guys nail the bad guys, with comparative ease. No policeman or detective, black or white, ever appears. At the fade-out, which simply hangs in mid-air like a warning, four white business executives are lined up as the culprits. "Gordon's War" is well-fought but definitely not the drug war to end them all.

HOWARD THOMPSON

1973 Ag 10, 26:2

VISIONS OF EIGHT, directed by Milos Forman, Kon Ichikawa, Claude Lelouch, Juri Ozerov, Arthur Penn, Michael Pfleghar, John Schlesinger and Mai Zetterling; music, Henry Mancini; film editor, Robert K. Lambert; produced by Cinema V. At the Cinema I Theater, Third Avenue and 60th Street. Running time: 105 minutes. This film has not yet been classified.

By ROGER GREENSPUN

"Visions of Eight," which opened yesterday at Cinema I, is an attempt by an international group of eight mostly well-known directors to deal with individual aspects of last summer's Munich Olympic Games. The attempt was surely doomed to failure. In a film of this kind there is no way of dealing with the event that shaped the 20th Olympiad—or deprived it of all shape: the killing of 11 members of the Israeli team.

That event does figure, by way of fairly inappropriate montage, in John Schlesinger's otherwise lovely meditation on the running of the marathon. And it hangs like a pall over Avery Brundage's farewell remarks inviting everybody to the 1976 Olmpics. Once admitted (as Brundage seemed unwilling to do), it cannot be integrated in the context of a movie that only wants to be thoughtful, funny, satiric or poetic.

But "Visions of Eight" fails in more immediate ways, largely because several of the eight didn't have such interesting visions. Arthur Penn and Kon Ichikawa do not so much film as analyze, respectively, the pole vault and the 100-meter dash. You don't see a race or a jump; you see the way the flesh bunches on a runner's face or the curve a pole makes in rising. Everything is slowed down to the speed of "poetry in motion."

By contrast, almost everything is speeded up in Milos Forman's satiric vignette intercutting the decathlon with shots of musical groups, ranging from some sort of cowbell band to a full-scale performance of Beethoven's Ninth Symphony. Nobody escapes the witless humor,

Ludmilla Tourischeva

and Forman, usually a fine director, has turned in the worst sequence in the film.

⬤

Not everything is this bad. Claude Lelouch's study of the losers shows some athletes in real pain, some merely befuddled (like competing swimmers staring in disbelief at the retreating form of Mark Spitz) and has at least the virtues of canny documentary.

And there are parts of Mai Zetterling's sequence on weight-lifting. or the West German Michael Pfleghar's tribute to women in the Olympics, in which concentration on athletic performance overcomes the impulse to fancy film-making and results in work of real quality.

Pfleghar devotes a few minutes to a very young Soviet gymnast, Ludmilla Tourischeva, both standing by herself and working on the uneven parallel bars, and those are perhaps the most beautiful, least assertive, moments in the movie.

I also liked the long closing sequence to "Visions of Eight," which is uncredited, but which I understand is largely the work of John Schlesinger. As for so much of the rest, it seems to forget that it is the privilege of the modest art of film to find the meaning of things just in the way they are seen to be.

1973 Ag 11, 25:3

'Jeremy' —A Big 'Little' Movie

By ROSALYN DREXLER

LAST year I saw a wonderful documentary on the emotion-packed subject of birth and death. The film was unusually sensitive to nuance: an unspoken thought, a spoken thought, a gesture, facial expressions. Objects — hospital beds, trays of food, medical machines (the still-life of a still life)—filled the screen the way they filled the lives that depended on them. We the viewers felt a sense of intimacy, though the camera did its best not to invade privacy, or to presume upon relationships that had sprung up naturally during the filming.

Arthur Barron, the guiding spirit behind that movie, has now written and directed a movie about love called "Jeremy." It is in the style of a documentary, and as honest and sympathetic a story about young love as I've ever seen. "Summer of '42" was a fake (impure commercial inroads treading a young man's mind; even the record he and the woman of his dreams danced to was the movie's theme music, not a song of the period) compared to "Jeremy."

Love is about as embarrassing a topic as death in our present day culture, the victim of overblown sentiment and hidden despair. Love has been swept under the carpet as if it were a dusty assortment of crumbs, roaches, bent nails, and cat hair; love that once was fresh, lively, straight, and attached to the blood-nourished skin of dreams. People who fall in love suffer the same misunderstanding from those who are not in love as dying people suffer from those who are not immediately on the way out. There is a quality of truth in really loving that is akin to death: the sharing of one's life breath, life thought, lifetime . . . the avoidance of pretense, the freedom to just "be." Love is cliché (so is death) but it is our familiarity with it that enables us to empathize with "Jeremy."

Morning. We are in a room. The camera caresses a cello, glides across its bow, travels from wall to wall pausing for a portrait, books, a chess set, photos of racing horses, a basketball. It touches everything we would if our eyes were closed and we had to get around in uncharted territory. Quiet. A boy is asleep. One feels tenderness for the sleeping child; for his beauty and innocence, his

Rosalyn Drexler is a critic and the author of "Home Movies."

imminent awakening. Jeremy (Robby Benson) is a gifted and privileged boy of 16; he plays cello, is an athlete (although he walks like a klutz off the court), scholar (straight A's, though he does his homework while listening to rock through earphones), lover of pizza, W. C. Fields fan, and also has a special talent for handicapping the horses (though he never bets. He prefers spending the money on books and records).

Jeremy is not into girls, hypocrisy, or verbosity (he is easily tongue-tied and often his jaw goes slack, which gives the erroneous impression that he is a goof). The girl he meets, Susan (Glynnis O'Connor), is a new girl at his school. He first has a mind-blowing sight of her as she practices a dance exercise in an empty classroom. She is more than his equal in sincerity, talent, and need. Need of course is most important. She is someone who has not been able to make friends easily.

Jeremy is a dog walker, and we see him in Central Park holding the leashes of five dogs of assorted breeds. He reads the dogs a poem (". . . she was a phantom of delight . . ."), to which the dogs listen with dignified inattention, as would any captive audience in need of a translator. The funny (poignant) scenes proliferate from the first phone call that Jeremy makes to Susan, with a list of things to say on his lap, to his enactment of a race he has with an unsuspecting pedestrian, which he wins after whipping himself to an imaginary finish line with a folded newspaper.

Susan plays sober straight woman to Jeremy's antics; she reveals herself by speaking of her childhood, by listening well, by her enjoyment of the sweet things in life: being with someone you love, walking, breathing, dancing, talking. Jeremy's awkwardness does not put her off: "I knew you were someone special when I heard you play," she says to him.

✶

As they spend more time together, they fall deeply in love. That love is consummated one afternoon in Jeremy's room; it is very moving because it is so natural, so hoped for, and so innocent. Music throughout the picture is simple and appropriate: ". . . Before the rivers run dry, let's be kind to one another . . .", the lyrics go. Excellent advice for fish, but when the rivers run dry, human beings can walk or run to the nearest shore, which is what happens when

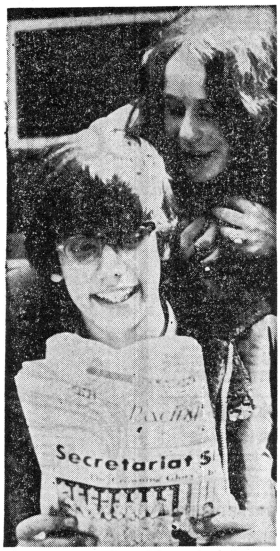

Robby Benson and Glynnis O'Connor play the teenage lovers in "Jeremy," now at Loews Tower East.
"A plunge into youth's rites of passage"

Susan's father (Chris Bohn) decides to go back to his old job in Detroit. The kids have barely had time to be "kind" to each other before they must part.

*

Robby Benson is funny, enthusiastic, and intelligent; able to play scenes as if they were entirely spontaneous. It is his presence that gives "Jeremy" its most attractive quality, a kind of wholehearted plunge into youth's critical rites of passage. His best friend, Ralph (Len Bari), who is slightly more experienced than Jeremy, advises him on boy-girl matters, playing the role with genuine good humor. And Glynnis O'Connor, who has never acted before, gives an inspired performance as the bittersweet Susan.

The adults in "Jeremy" are bit players predictably involved in their own affairs: ambition, jobs, social events. Most of their conversation is

either cautionary — everybody gives Jeremy advice on almost everything—or boring: a discussion at the dinner table between Jeremy's father and his mother (Pat Wheel) about the color some new tiles should be (the choice is between orange and avocado), or, oracular: as in the case of the cello teacher (Leonardo Cimino) who tells Jeremy, "You don't have to be great, not everybody can be great."

Perhaps in the world of upper middle - class youth, adults do appear solely as rigid enacters of predetermined behavior, taking bows only for moving the plot along (while their own lives remain static), but this is changing too, and though it is Jeremy's movie, I would have liked to see (something I know exists) adults with a spark of unconventional life. However, "Jeremy" is a movie I want to see again, with son, daughter, husband, friends. We know that

"little" movies can be better than "big" ones. This is a BIG "little" movie.

P.S. Two important questions: 1) What gestures have you made on behalf of grace and shared tenderness? 2) Would you like to begin all over again?

1973, Ag 12, II:1:2

'Blume'

By ALLEN McKEE

AT a recent sneak preview in San Francisco of Paul Mazursky's new film "Blume in Love," an evening of entertainment evolved into an intriguing confrontation of social ideologies as the predominantly white, upper-middle class, liberal audience found itself irresistibly involved with an irreverent satire of white, upper-middle class liberal life. The effect was something like a David Frye performance at the White House.

Bearded and braided, affluently casual, young and young in spirit, the audience had been wooed into a receptive temper by the preceding film, "Scarecrow," a funny and endearing tale with Gene Hackman and Al Pacino as two luckless drifters bumming their way across an America of photogenic banality. It is the perfect film for liberal sensibilities, combining, as it does, a gritty lowlife realism with the romance of lovable eccentricity, so that we may admire the immutable human spirit even as we lament the futility of life in general.

A fashionably grim and brutal ending provides the touch of tragedy that grants "Scarecrow" its resemblance to a localized "Waiting for Godot" (Godot in this case represented by a carwash in Pittsburgh). When the movie was over and the house lights went up, a kind of blissful melancholy blanketed the audience. People were quiet and smiling. Everyone was warmly, deliciously sad.

*

Mazursky's film began in an atmosphere of communal acceptance. The appearance of Kris Kristofferson's name in the opening credits occasioned some scattered applause, and while the initial segments of "Blume in Love" were well received, one sensed that the laughter was coming from individual pockets in the audience, pockets surrounded by a growing air

of defensiveness. Mazursky's sharp, if affectionate, satire seemed directed at the very people he was trying to reach; it was disorienting, like a slightly derisive giggle in the middle of a kiss.

Paul Mazursky is one of the few original talents to emerge in the American film industry in the last few years. Working within the studio hierarchy as both writer and director, he has managed to impose a distinctively personal style on slick, commercial material, transcending the soap-opera origins of films like "Bob & Carol & Ted & Alice" and "Alex in Wonderland" with pointed ensemble acting and a perceptively comic approach to suburban morality. He is that rarest of Hollywood mutations—a mercenary with style.

*

"Blume in Love" is Mazursky's first fully-realized film. The director's presence, while unmistakable, is the presence of a filmmaker too confident in the strength of his story to rely on obtrusive stylistic tricks. With unblinking accuracy for the nuance of comfortable desperation, "Blume in Love" traces the emotional, sexual and psychological development of one Stephen Blume (played with well-groomed ferocity by George Segal) as he flippantly divorces his wife Nina (Susan Anspach) only to discover that he is still in love with her, obsessively in love, so much so that he sets out to win her back from the amiable, freeloading musician Elmo (Kristofferson) with whom she has begun a new life.

The movie takes place in a world of yoga classes and psychiatric sessions, swingers and social workers, money and pot and stylish informality — an environment that affects Mazursky's characters almost as much as they affect each other, so that the collapse of Blume's marriage becomes ultimately attributable not only to the human inadequacies of husband and wife, but to the fundamental emptiness of their lifestyle. They're unhappy and they don't know why.

*

Mazursky handles all of this with uncompromising honesty, but his affection for the sufferers is always apparent. Blume comes across as a likable faker certain only of his love, while Nina in trying to peel away the layers of reflex hypocrisy that have smothered her self-esteem, is seen as a woman involved in a noble endeavor with slightly silly results.

Only the musician Elmo impresses us as totally genuine. A kind of professional victim, he passively allows life to lap over him, devoting his energies to simple survival. Kristofferson's incomparable smoke-and-cider voice betraying no trace of the pain he has felt.

The thing that makes "Blume in Love" an assaulting experience for liberal audiences is the way that it plays on the audience concept to scramble reactions that have become unconsciously standardized. In showing and ridiculing the way that people use clothes and art and sex as indications of status, the film in effect is catching the audience red-handed, because moviegoing itself has become a socially revealing activity.

The modern film audience exists not as a self-contained group entity, not even as a congregation of individuals; it exists as a network of interacting personalities responding to and *for* each other, as well as to the screen. Going to the movies has become more than an amusement. It has become a sociological event at which one may advertise one's intellectual and cultural status without fear of being labeled an exhibitionist.

People who laugh uproariously at the corny lines in old dramatic films, who hiss at the end of "Last Tango in Paris," who chuckle knowingly at any reference in a film to marijuana are essentially performing for their dates, their friends, or the other people in the audience. They are assuming a posture that immediately places them on a certain social and intellectual plane — that of sophisticate, or renegade or fellow grass enthusiast.

I have always experienced an involuntary cringe upon hearing people applaud after a film. Since the actors and director are not present to acknowledge the response, it seems unavoidable to conclude that the applause is directed toward the rest of the audience, a kind of cultural clarion, a proclamation of status. One wonders how long the applause would last if, at its inception, the projectionist, ushers and concession girl were to mount the stage for a few discreet bows.

"Blume in Love" sabotages this kind of facile status identification by gaining audience acceptance with its commercial polish, even as it needles the concepts and truisms that its audience takes for granted. When Mazursky makes fun of psychoanalysis, the people in the audience who are themselves psychia-

Susan Anspach and George Segal, a divorced couple, continue to battle, catching drifter Kris Kristofferson in the middle, in "Blume in Love"
"When the film is over, there are as many different reactions as there are people in the theater."

trists or under analysis don't know how to respond. When group sex is ridiculed, those who are no strangers to group sex are suddenly vulnerable. It is not enough to assume a superior air and ignore it, because the satire is accurate. To respond too self-consciously is to be implicated.

"Blume in Love" strips an audience of its status. By inviting introspection, it smashes that sociological network of interaction and turns the viewer into an isolated personality. When the film is over, there are as many different reactions as there are people in the theater.

Emerging from that San Francisco preview, it was this diversity of response that impressed me most. A couple who had been sitting in the next row argued all the way out of the theater: the girl thought it was a "lovely film," while her companion—bearded and worldly—pronounced it "pure corn," presumably because the hero is reunited at the end, however tenuously, with the woman that he loves. The same man had responded blissfully to "Scarecrow," in which Al Pacino's attempt to

contact the mother of the child he has never seen is met with a vicious rejection that drives him into catatonic shock—an indication perhaps that a contrived kick in the stomach is essentially more sophisticated than an honest reaffirmation of joy. Hell is so fashionable when you're literate and young.

"Blume in Love" succeeded that night in shattering the homogenized complacency that had been created by "Scarecrow." People left grumpy or elated or confused, but they all left *affected*. Not many movies appeal to us so individually. In severing the umbilical connection between an audience and its status, Mazursky has turned film viewing into the vital and personal experience that it all too seldom is.

1973 Ag 12, II:11:1

The Cast

AMERICAN GRAFFITI, directed by George Lucas; written by Mr. Lucas, Gloria Katz and Willard Huyck; editors, Verna Fields and Marcia Lucas; directors of photography, Ron Eveslage and Jan D'Alquen; music coordinator, Karin Green; produced by Francis Ford Coppola; released by Universal Pictures. At the Sutton Theater, Third Avenue and 57th Street. Running time: 110 minutes. This film has been classified PG.

Curt	Richard Dreyfuss
Steve	Ronny Howard
John	Paul Le Mat
Terry	Charlie Martin Smith
Laurie	Cindy Williams
Debbie	Candy Clark
Carol	Mackenzie Phillips
Disk Jockey	Wolfman Jack
Bob Falfa	Harrison Ford
The Pharaohs	Bo Hopkins, Manuel Padilla Jr., Beau Gentry

By ROGER GREENSPUN

At dusk the cars begin to congregate. The drivers, kids in their teens, meet and greet and happily insult one another. A few couples, going steady, may pair off. There is a high school dance, but there is also the lure of the main street to cruise up and down, exchanging pleasantries, looking for dates, for excitement, an impromptu race, even a little danger. Every radio in town is tuned in to Wolfman Jack with his line of eerie patter and all the latest hits — "Sixteen Candles," "The Book of Love" . . . It is early in the fall of 1962, somewhere in northern California.

•

Two of the boys, Curt Henderson and Steve Bolander, headed East to college, are uneasy at the prospect. John Milner, champion drag racer, is 22—old enough to know he's headed nowhere, except up to the neon-lighted circle of Mel's Drive-In and perhaps

down to the stillness of the automobile graveyard at the edge of town. Those are roughly the perimeters of George Lucas's "American Graffiti," which examines that much of America as it lives for about 12 hours, from an evening to the following morning.

A lot happens. Steve (Ronny Howard) breaks up and makes up with Curt's sister Laurie (Cindy Williams). A younger boy, Terry, (Charlie Martin Smith) borrows Steve's Chevy, picks up a dizzy blonde (Candy Clark) for a night of horrendous misadventures, all greatly to her pleasure.

John (Paul Le Mat) enters the climactic drag race of his career. Curt (Richard Dreyfuss), the local intellectual, is almost inducted into the Pharaohs, the town gang. But Steve is following a vision, an elusive girl in a white Thunderbird who may have whispered "I love you." He never finds her. But when, in the morning, he takes off (via Magic Carpet Airlines), a white T-bird heads East on the road below. It is the only car we ever see leaving town.

"American Graffiti" exists not so much in its individual stories as in its orchestration of many stories, its sense of time and place. Although it is full of the material of

fashionable nostalgia, it never exploits nostalgia. In its feeling for movement and music and the vitality of the night —and even in its vision in white—it is oddly closer to some early Fellini than to the recent American past of, say, "The Last Picture Show" or "Summer of '42."

It is a very good movie, funny, tough, unsentimental. It is full of marvelous performances from actors (especially Candy Clark, Richard Dreyfuss and Cindy Williams) hardly known for previous screen credits. But for me its excitement comes at least partly from its indication of what may be a major new career.

George Lucas, 28 years old, has made one previous feature. It is a good science fiction film, "THX 1138," about a closed, tranquilized future society, controlled by mysterious broadcast voices, and from which there is almost no escape. For all its apparent differences, "American Graffiti" really presents the obverse of that world— now beneficent, familiar; but also closed, tuned in to mysterious voices, and offering almost no means of escape.

•

The ways in which they are like each other are fascinating, and very much in keeping with the kinds of continuity the best directors have sustained from film to film. And somehow the persistence of an idea, reshaped and re-examined, gives me even greater joy than the specific pleasures of "American Graffiti."

"American Graffiti" opened yesterday at the Sutton Theater.

1973 Ag 13, 21:1

COPS AND ROBBERS, directed by Aram Avakian; screenplay, Donald E. Westlake; director of photography, David Quaid; editor, Barry Malkin; music, Michel Legrand; produced by Elliott Kastner; released by United Artists Corporation. At the Criterion Theater, Broadway at 45th Street, the 68th Street Playhouse, at Third Avenue and UA Eastside Cinema, Third Avenue and 55th Street. Running time: 89 minutes. This film is classified PG.
Tom .... Cliff Gorman
Joe .... Joseph Bologna
Paul Jones .... Dick Ward
Eastpoole .... Shepperd Strudwick
Secretary .... Ellen Holly
Patsy .... John Ryan
Bandell .... Nino Ruggeri
Mary .... Gayle Gorman

By ROGER GREENSPUN

One of the minor occupational hazards of reviewing lots of movies is that after a time you have seen so much conventional junk you begin to forget the possibility of conventional excellence. If anybody had told me even a week ago about a funny, exciting, semi-plausible, exceptionally intelligent caper movie, I would not have believed him. I'd have been wrong. "Cops and Robbers," despite its title, and despite the slightly dumb-dumb ad campaign that is introducing it, is all those good things and more. It is uncommonly well acted. And it is the first movie in a long time to understand, rather than merely to exploit, its New York City locales.

●

The perpetrators are a pair of cops named Tom and Joe (Cliff Gorman and Joseph Bologna), hard-working and only sporadically corrupt. Though tied to pregnant wives, the Long Island Expressway and plastic swimming pools in the backyard, they dream of better, or at least richer, things. They make plans. They make contacts; and they learn that the current preference in stealable items is bearer bonds, worth 20 cents on the dollar for anyone looking to increase his assets by $2-million overnight. So, on a day when lower Manhattan is distracted by a ticker-tape parade honoring the first astronauts to land on the moon, Tom and Joe take one small step against Wall Street, a giant step for themselves — as they commit, rather by accident, the perfect crime.

Even the best of caper films is likely to be a fragile structure, and "Cops and Robbers" is no exception. If you press it, it will break. But I don't think you will want to press it. At moments

of implausibility it becomes very funny. For every bind it gets itself into it discovers wonderfully exhilarating means of escape. It has the only chase sequence — something involving much of Central Park plus the 86th Street crosstown bus — worth looking at in the last 50 American movies. And for casting, down to the smallest role, it comes fairly close to inspiration.

●

Both Cliff Gorman and Joseph Bologna give totally authentic comic performances. A little bewildered, cautious, with a kind of unsteady cool, they seem to embody the spirit of—let's say —urban free enterprise in modern society.

Aram Avakian is probably best known for having directed a heavy, sporadically moving adaptation of John Barth's "The End of the Road." "Cops and Robbers" is a less ambitious project, but a very much better movie; an auspicious continuation in a young film maker's career. "Cops and Robbers" opened yesterday at several local theaters.

1973 Ag 16, 40:1

The Cast

THE LONG DARKNESS, directed by Kei Kumai; screenplay (Japanese with English subtitles) by Keiji Hasebe and Kei Kumai, story by Tetsuro Miura; photographed by Kiyomi Kuroda; executive producers, Masayuki Sato and Hideyuki Shino; distributed by Toho International Company, Limited. At the Elgin Theater, Eighth Avenue and 19th Street. Running time: 120 minutes. This film has not been classified.
Tetsuro .... Go Kato
Shino .... Komaki Kurihara
With Yasushi Nagata, Kinzo Shin and Kaneko Iwasaki

By ROGER GREENSPUN

"The Long Darkness," which opened the current Japanese film series at the Elgin Theater yesterday, is a long, solemn, ponderous modern love story set in Tokyo and in parts of northern Japan. It has a happy ending, but all the rest of it is very, very sad.

Tetsuro, a handsome but over-age college student, meets Shino, a beautiful but virtuous saki-shop waitress and falls in love with her. Tetsuro's home life has been difficult.

After his oldest sister killed herself in remorse for loving an unsuitable man, his second oldest sister killed herself because she blamed herself for her sister's death. Tetsuro's oldest brother, finding these deaths intolerable, disappeared. But it was not until the next oldest brother ran away with the family fortune that Tetsuro's father suffered the stroke that left him almost a vegetable. Now he lives in the north, frugally, with his wife and daughter, Tetsuro's sole remaining sister, who has some unspecified dread disease that makes her wear

dark glasses and feel self-conscious.

●

Tetsuro considers his family history — well — special, and he is diffident about mentioning it to Shino. Her family, on the other hand, has been destitute since her father lost his shooting gallery (now turned into a house of prostitution) and moved into a temple where he lives as a pauper and where Shino's younger brother makes straw brooms.

Undone by drink, the father eventually dies. Tetsuro witnesses the death, the first natural death he has ever seen. Somehow this makes him confident enough to want to go ahead and marry Shino—who, I forgot to mention, is already engaged to another man, a rich businessman she doesn't love and who isn't good enough for her anyway.

●

That pretty well sums up the background. I haven't left much space for the foreground, but I don't see that it greatly matters, because the foreground is so given to covering up or explaining the background. As drama, "The Long Darkness" is largely exposition up until the last 10 minutes. That may be the meaning of its title.

All the performances are bearable, except for Go Kato, as Tetsuro, who looks and, alas, acts like a Japanese Gregory Peck, and is unbearable. Kei Kumai's direction imitates some of his betters—including Yasujiro Ozu —and comes down heavily on studied pictorial composition, without ever finding a style to express its intentions. It is smooth, professional seeming, but very dull. Considering the rococo miseries of the plot, the direction consists essentially of missed opportunities.

1973 Ag 18, 26:1

The Cast

HAPPY MOTHERS' DAY, LOVE GEORGE, directed by Darren McGavin; screenplay by Robert Clouse; director of photography, Walter Lassally; film editor, George Grenville; music, Don Vincent; produced by Mr. McGavin; released by Cinema V. At the New Embassy Theater, 46th Street and Broadway, and the Plaza Theater, 58th Street, east of Madison Avenue. Running time: 90 minutes. This film is classified PG.
Cara .... Patricia Neal
Ronda .... Cloris Leachman
Eddie .... Bobby Darin
Celia .... Tessa Dahl
Johnny .... Ron Howard
Crystal .... Kathie Browne
Piccolo .... Joe Mascolo
Ron Howard .... Simon Oakland

Anybody who has seen half a movie in his life will instantly recognize that a title like "Happy Mothers' Day, Love George" has to indicate gothic horror. In this case, coastal gothic horror, as young Johnny (Ron Howard) returns to the New England fishing village of his childhood, in search of a father he has never known.

It is one of those towns where everyone seems to have a skeleton in the closet. Actually, a skeleton in the closet would be a blessing. This town has two skeletons on the beach (under the beach, to be precise), a corpse in the master bedroom, another corpse in the summer house's upstairs bathtub, two more in guest rooms, a third in the overgrown front yard, a fourth fresh-killed in the garage, and still another fouling up the nets in the nearby fishing grounds. There may have been more. I didn't notice.

Johnny never finds his father — mainly because his father, what is left of his father, can be found only at low spring tides during a strong offshore wind. But he does find his mother (Cloris Leachman), and his aunt (Patricia Neal), the local downat-the-heels aristocrat, who is also his father's widow. Eventually he finds the identity of the murderer, an identity that should keep you guessing for at least the first six minutes of the movie.

"Happy Mothers' Day, Love George" makes use of several distinguished performers. Cloris Leachman was seen to better advantage in "Last Picture Show." Ron Howard is currently seen to better advantage in "American Graffiti." And Patricia Neal may be seen to better advantage any time in Maxim Coffee television commercials.

●

In this, his first directorial assignment, Darren McGavin has come up to just about the level of his material, which is very low. The locations, actually in Nova Scotia, are predictably lovely. There is some sense of place (the great gift of the provincial horror movie), but no sense of purpose, or of a reasonable inevitable doom.

"Happy Mothers' Day, Love George," opened yesterday at the Plaza and New Embassy theaters.

ROGER GREENSPUN.

1973 Ag 18, 26:1

The Cast

ENTER THE DRAGON, directed by Robert Clouse/ screenplay by Michael Allin; produced by Fred Weintraub and Paul Heller in association with Raymond Chow; photographed by Gilbert Hubbs; music by Lalo Schifrin; presented by Warner Brothers. At the Loew's State 1 and Loew's State 2, Broadway and 45th Street, Loew's Cine, Third Avenue at 86th Street and Loew's Orpheum, 86th Street at Third Avenue. Running time: 98 minutes. (This film is rated R.)
Lee .... Bruce Lee
Roper .... John Saxon
Williams .... Jim Kelly
Han .... Shih Kien
Su-Lin .... Angela Mao Ying
Mei Ling .... Betty Chung

Although they have made a mint at the American box office, those bone-crunchers from China — adventures pegged on karate, hapkido, kung fu and judo—were essentially shoddy productions.

Now Hollywood has muscled into the act, dispatching a unit to Hong Kong and vicinity. The result is "Enter the Dragon," opening yesterday at four theaters. Now brace yourself.

The picture is expertly made and well-meshed; it moves like lightning and brims with color. It is also the most savagely murderous and numbing hand-hacker (not a gun in it) you will ever see anywhere. Indeed, toward the end the musical score simply stops—or gives up—as three secret agents pulverize their way out of a sinister island fortress.

Arms, legs and necks snap like kindling, and the predominantly young audience cramming Loew's State 2 yesterday applauded, laughed and ate it up. Anyone over 30 will have plenty to think about.

●

But the real surprise is that this caboose cash-in was made so well, unlike its imported predecessors. The story is a bit reminiscent of James Bond's "Dr. No," with a renegade fiend (same white cat and minus one hand) running an island fortress and a spectacular school in "martial arts." Just as obviously, the three tough agents invading the place are white (John Saxon), black (Jim Kelly) and yellow (Bruce Lee).

Yet from the opening (a stunning evocation of Hong Kong, centering on the harbor), the crisp dialogue of Michael Allin's script and the pounding pulse of Robert Clouse's direction spur the action forward without an ounce of fat.

On an adventure level, the performances are quite good. The one by Mr. Lee, not only the picture's supermaster killer but a fine actor as well, is downright fascinating. Mr. Lee, who also staged the combats, died very recently. Here he could not be more alive.

HOWARD THOMPSON

1973 Ag 18, 26:1

The Cast

ELECTRA GLIDE IN BLUE, directed by James William Guercio; screenplay, Robert Boris; story, Mr. Boris and Rupert Hitzig; director of photography, Conrad Hall; edited by Jim Benson, John F. Link 2d and Jerry Greenberg; music, Mr. Guercio; produced by Mr. Guercio; released by United Artists Corporation. At the Coronet Theater, Third Avenue at 59th Street. Running time: 113 minutes. This film is classified PG.
John Wintergreen .... Robert Blake
Zipper Davis .... Billy (Green) Bush
Harve Poole .... Mitchell Ryan
Jolene .... Jeannine Riley
Willie .... Elisha Cook

By ROGER GREENSPUN

For a long time now the ads have been everywhere. Ads for a movie, yet they feature not the movie but a man. "An American Movie by a New Director. James William Guercio." And there has been a picture of him, James William Guercio, a modestly heroic picture of a young man in bold leather boots—movie director's boots—but with tousled hair and downcast eyes. He is like a different Joseph von Sternberg, a secretive Cecil B. DeMille. But a lot of money has been spent to make him very, very public.

•

The movie behind the image, "Electra Glide in Blue," also became public, yesterday, when it opened at the Coronet Theater. Under different intentions, it might have made a decent grade-C Roger Corman bike movie—though Corman has generally used more interesting directors than Guercio. It is in fact a murder mystery, in which a higher-principled Arizona motorcycle cop discovers the death of an old recluse and, against all odds, finds out who killed the man and why. Upon this slender plot is grafted lots of excess cinema, and a really unfair share of meaning.

Guercio, a 27-year-old music producer who has never made a movie before, has chosen to specialize in the mid-body shot—mostly between the collarbone and the upper thigh—and so he comes down heavily on belt buckles, gun holsters, shirt buttons and the like. When he raises his sights to the istance (and it usually seems to be the distance) he sees the sky, the scrubland and the unending road—the far-sighted equivalent of such close-up details as belt buckles or shirt buttons.

When he just looks at what is going on in front of his eyes he sees very ordinary or very embarrassing things: a crudely staged bike chase, or the confessions of a demoralized bar girl in what looks and sounds like a second-year acting exercise in drama school.

•

The girl, played by Jeannine Riley, probably suffers more than anyone else from the ambitions of the film. But Elisha Cook, who must project senility as the murder victim's only friend, fares almost as badly. And Mitchell Ryan, a fascistic plainclothes detective, and Billy (Green) Bush, a bike-crazy cop, are also pushed into caricatures without any centers.

The weight of the film rests on Robert Blake, as John Wintergreen, a little cop whose sense of decency continually betrays his own self-interest. The tragedy—irony, really—of his career is the film's message. It is a trite and ordinary message, and nothing Blake does to try to render his character complex can quite shake it off. He remains a very decent actor, stranded in what is surely the most strangely inflated movie of the season.

1973 Ag 20, 21:1

The Cast

SWORD OF VENGEANCE, directed by Kenji Misumi; screenplay by Kazuo Koike; distributed by Toho International. At the Elgin Cinema, Eighth Avenue and 19th Street. Running time: 83 minutes. (Not submitted for rating.
The Samurai ...... Tomisaburo Wakayama
The Girl .... Tomoko Mayama
The Child .... Akihiro Tomakawa

By HOWARD THOMPSON

Moviegoers familiar with those imported samurai dramas know that the best can be strong, towering works of art. The one showing through Monday, "Sword of Vengeance," in the Elgin Cinema's current Japanese festival is only fair stuff.

The color is good, naturally. Sword-hacking and grunting abound. This time continual flashbacks compound an Occidental unfamiliarity with medieval, intramural customs, along with puzzling references and names that casually dot the English titles (much of it white-on-white, as usual).

The plot seems a rather milling business, as a fugitive samurai assassin hits the road, carrying his baby son, and hacking down opposition until a wily lord hires him for murder. He also befriends a fallen woman, who trails after the two of them as the picture ends.

If this sounds familiar, it should. Using the American West, John Ford has done far better with these staples—the manly, misunderstood outcast, the appealing infant and the tarnished belle. Here, with no particular imagination or flair, Kenji Misumi directs a blunt melodrama accordingly.

Tomisaburo Wakayama is the brooding, dangerous hero. Akihiro Tomikawa makes a cute infant, oblivious to it all and probably better off. As the prostitute, Tomoko Mayama is so pretty and bright-eyed that it's too bad she didn't have more to do.

"Sword of Vengeance" may be a swinger, but it's all been swung before—over in Japan and here, too.

1973 Ag 24, 18:1

With Joy in Its Own Violence

By JOHN SIMON

"ELECTRA GLIDE in Blue" is the kind of film that splits the movie audience into two camps: those who thrive on vivid images, eruptions of cleverly orchestrated violence, outbursts of raucous humor, and generous dollops of rock music; and those who want a film also to have a point of view, a meaning—not a message, mind you, not moralizing, just an aesthetic and moral sensibility that informs it. This may, though it need not, mean younger versus older viewers; it certainly means coasting versus thinking ones. It also means those who will love "Electra" versus those whose respect is outweighed by reservations.

James William Guercio, the 27-year-old pop musician and entrepreneur whose first film this is, seems to have a genuine flair for directing movies. I say "seems to" because persistent rumors from the Coast have it that the film is largely the work of Conrad Hall, its distinguished cinematographer, who has long been announcing his urge to break into directing. Hall has an impressive reputation as a cameraman—whether for the stark blacks and whites of "In Cold Blood," or the often thoughtful, always noteworthy, yet sometimes too flashy use of color, as in "Cool Hand Luke," "Fat City," and, most daringly, in "Tell Them Willie Boy Was Here." However that may be, "Electra Glide in Blue" is conspicuously, even if not entirely, a cinematographer's picture.

The plot concerns the life and death of a determined, plucky little Arizona motorcycle policeman, John Wintergreen, only 5 feet 4 inches and a bit of a joke among his colleagues (and a bit of an improbability, too; I doubt if the Arizona police force admits such heroic coplets), who dreams of bigger, or at least better, things: dumping the Electra Glide, the motorcycle to which his posterior is achingly wedded, and graduating from issuing traffic tickets to the homicide division. There the uniform is an understated version of Duke Wayne, and one drives about in cars and uses one's head.

*

Unfortunately, when John's keenness does get him into Homicide—the mighty detective, Harve Poole, having taken him on as his driver—he proves to be more virile than Harve, something that rancorous giant with gonads of clay cannot forgive. So John is soon back on his motorcycle, once again a conscientious, lowly cop, neither giving nor asking favors. Just once, though, he does a hippie a good turn, and pays the supreme price for his kindness.

What characterizes the film, however, is surely not this often unconvincing plot, but certain ingenious cinematic strategies. First of these is the extreme close-up, used almost obsessively in the early parts of the film. So we see a pair of hands elaborately preparing and committing a suicide while also frying pork chops on a stove; after the fatal shot goes off, the same hands jolt us by proceeding to cut up the chops. Here the extreme close-up is used for shock value: the hands must have been a murderer's, not a suicide's.

Elsewhere, when John is putting on his police uniform and gear, and the camera virtually rubs, catlike, against black leather, nuzzles a set of zippers cracklingly shut, drools over a gun and its holster, the oppressive but also impressive closeness suggests fetishism. But whose? Not John's, for he is fed up with this job and uniform; later, in a similar sequence, when the camera itemizes and hugs a detective's outfit John gets into, the ecstasy is, believably, his. Here it ominously seems to be the filmmakers'.

Again, in a poolroom sequence, the fanatical close-ups are there purely for the love of textures, shapes, sensuous surfaces, and the drama of the poolroom's chiaroscuro: the sudden fields of light and realms of murk through which a face glides. This is strikingly lovely, but a sheer cameraman's bubble bath, without any structural significance. During that very scene, John and a pal are discussing their dreams, which are totally unrelated to what is going on; nor is there any irony intended, e.g., "Look what beauty these fellows are overlooking!" The scene, like so many others, suggests a poem whose individual metaphors clash with the movement and purpose of the whole: concettismo of the most flagrant sort.

*

The second favorite device of the film is to begin an episode suddenly, out of context and not at its beginning, so as to keep us nervously guessing who is who or what is what. While this is an effective way of generating suspense—filmmakers have been known to waste much precious time on expendable establishing shots—there comes a point where the spectator feels unduly manipulated. Especially since Guercio, who is a great one for antitheses, is equally fond of giving us a protracted panoramic shot of an empty Arizona landscape, and only after a minor eternity, out of nowhere (and usually with a telephoto lens) letting the action erupt on it.

Vehement contrasts of all kinds are favored: cutting from very quiet to very noisy scenes, from dazzlingly lit ones to others shrouded in darkness, from extreme close-ups to extreme long shots. Or the other way round. All very well, until it begins to look repetitious, schematic, manipulative. How many times, for instance, can Harve, the towering heavy, be seen in a low-angle shot, his features blotted out by shadows, with only a sinister penumbra outlining his face?

The trickiness becomes an ostentatious end in itself—as when John is seen walking off, in superimposition, both toward and away from us; or when a mournful passage of time is rendered by a series of over-opulent slow dissolves—panoramic shots of Monument Valley in every darkening hue from orange through lavender to purple. Most self-conscious is the wholly gratuitous device of having the film, near its conclusion, go from black-and-white to sepia to color; then, at the very end, reverse the procedure: from color to sepia to black-and-white. Why?

All of which is not to say that "Electra" has no virtues. Thus Guercio and Hall know how to make a point in strong visual terms, as when the camera pans along a lineup of tall helmeted policemen being inspected and casually hits a lacuna: instead of a whole face, we see only the tip of a helmet—little Johnny's. Or, more elaborately, they will switch from a trompe l'oeil background—painted, photographed, or even featuring plaster figures—to the real thing, which it oddly resembles or differs from, and so create significant irony or dislocation.

Yet when, to convey loneliness, some immense, Astrodome-like convention hall becomes the scene of a nocturnal soliloquy of Wintergreen's—with a wordlessly munching old Negro janitor added for gratuitous melancholy—we become painfully aware of the straining after effect.

Such things would be more bearable if (1) the Robert Boris screenplay did not indulge itself in clichés like the supercop who is overcompensating for sexual impotence, or the hard yet pathetic waitress who, chasing after Hollywood rain-

Robert Blake, a motorcycle cop, makes it to Homicide in "Electra Glide in Blue"
Does it really try to understand where hatred and murder come from?

bows, ended up a tough yet touching floozy and delivers the usual defiant-but-tearful autobiographical monologue; (2) the film did not so complacently exploit previous filmmaking—e.g., John Ford's Monument Valley backgrounds, Sam Peckinpah's slow-motion deaths, the senseless and haphazard killings of "Easy Rider"; and (3) there were some sort of deeper purpose to the whole thing.

To be sure, the film postures as if there were; it even ends with an interminable and obstreperous "concert" of a song by Guercio, which redundantly asks how much longer war and bloodshed must continue. But the movie does not really try to understand, except in gross platitudes, where hatred and murder come from; it does not even generate much sympathy for the cops and hippies who torment or kill one another.

What you do feel strongly is the film's joy in its own violence. Thus before the big, bloody motorcycle chase begins, everything stops and goes silent; then the soundtrack bursts into delirious rock music, as if to say "Now the fun begins!" and we're off to thrills, spills and killings. Perhaps "Electra Glide in Blue" is its own, albeit inadvertent, best answer: the violence will go on as long as a movie can so revel in it.

1973 Ag 26, II:1:5

BANG THE DRUM SLOWLY, directed by John Hancock; screenplay by Mark Harris, based on his novel; director of photography, Richard Shore; film editor, Richard Marks; music, Stephen Lawrence; produced by Maurice and Lois Rosenfield; released by Paramount Pictures. At the Cinema I Theater, Third Avenue and 60th Street. Running time: 98 minutes. This film has been classified PG.

Henry Wiggen ....Michael Moriarty
Bruce Pearson ....Robert de Niro
Dutch Schnell ....Vincent Gardenia
Joe Jaros ....Phil Foster
Katie ....Ann Wedgeworth
Mr. Pearson ....Patrick McVey
Piney Woods ....Tom Ligon
Holly Wiggen ....Heather Macrae
Tootsie ....Selma Diamond
Team Owners ....Barbara Babcock,
                        Maurice Rosenfield
Ugly Jones ....Andy Jarrell
Bradley Lord ....Marshall Efron
Red Traphagan ....Barton Heyman

By ROGER GREENSPUN

Except for some updating, and minimal plot simplification, John Hancock's "Bang the Drum Slowly" is a remarkably faithful rendering of the well-known baseball novel that Mark Harris wrote in 1955. It is one of those rare instances in which close adaptation of a good book has resulted in possibly an even better movie.

The story is simple enough. Bruce Pearson, a kid from Georgia and a catcher of no great quality for the New York Mammoths, is dying of Hodgkin's disease, incurable but, in his case, not yet debilitating. Nobody knows except his roommate and one friend, Henry Wiggen, and it is Henry's job not to tell—especially the team manager, Dutch Schnell—so that Bruce can play baseball through the last season that is left him on earth.

Henry leads the league in pitching, and sells insurance and writes books on the side. Everybody admires Henry and calls him "Author," except Bruce, who calls him "Arthur" — because he's a little too dense to get the name straight.

•

The film is more Henry's than Bruce's — Henry's and Dutch Schnell's. Henry conceals; Dutch wants to reveal. A rough diamond with a heart of coal, Dutch is the game, and the team, and the world series bid. Henry must learn — lots of things, like why he is devoting his life to easing the end of his dopey

roommate. But Dutch, though he hires a private detective to answer the same particular question, already has a vast store of general knowledge to hand.

Some of the film's greatest moments consist of his imparted wisdom, in certain locker-room speeches, like the "When I die the newspaper will write in their headline 'The Son of a Bitches of the World Have Lost Their Leader'" speech, or the "Go ahead you old Baltimore fly" speech—consisting largely of buzzing fly noises, all simultaneously translated into Spanish for the benefit of the Mammoths' Cuban third baseman.

Vincent Gardenia, a wonderfully professional New York stage actor who has had a fairly minor career in film, plays Dutch with a belligerent comic diligence that should constitute any director's dream performance. In his way, Michael Moriarty as Henry — clever, cautious, skilled at keeping secrets from himself—is almost as good.

And all the rest of the cast, from Robert de Niro, as Bruce, down to the least consequential team members who only stand and get photographed, seem to have been assembled out of a love for placing the right kinds of people in dramatic situations —a love that proves all over again that it is just as possible to make a movie in front of the camera as in the lab or the editing room.

John Hancock's background is mainly in the theater (he has had one previous feature: an entertaining but very mixed-up horror film called "Let's Scare Jessica to Death"), and that background shows to stunning advantage. We are not so used to performance — as opposed, say, to "presence" — in movie acting. But if Hancock pros-

Michael Moriarty

pers, as he should, we may get used to it. This will be everyone's good luck.

"Bang the Drum Slowly" (the title comes from the cowboy song "The Streets of Laredo") is ultimately a lament for the dying. But since that includes all of us, it would be unseemly to shed too many tears. Henry Wiggen doesn't cry; he peddles life insurance. And once he forces the Mammoths to sign a contract tying himself to Bruce — a necessary gesture, in a sense, accepting death—then he is free for the play of wits and character, the comedy, that takes up most of the film.

It's a gentle comedy; not gutless, but kind. Even Dutch Schnell is allowed his moments of second-rate decency. And since the Mammoths win the pennant and the series that year, everybody ends up happy — except Bruce, who ends up dead. The juxtaposition is ironic, but not too ironic.

Henry resolves never again to be brutal to people; but that was not his problem in the first place. If you want a major statement on man's fate, you'd better try another movie. This one pretends to no more insight than it has honestly earned. Its chief quality is not its pathos, but its beautiful, perhaps heroic, tact.

"Bang the Drum Slowly" opened yesterday at Cinema I.

1973 Ag 27, 35:1

The Cast

THE DAY THE SUN ROSE, directed by Tetsuya Yamanouchi; screenplay (Japanese with English subtitles) by Hisayuki Suzuki and Kunio Shimizu; original novel by Katsumi Nishiguchi; produced by Nihon Eiga Fukko Kyokai; released by Shochiku-Eihai Company, Ltd. At the Bijou Theater, 209 West 45th Street. Running time: 123 minutes. This film has not been classified.
Shinkichi .... Kinnosuke Nakamura
Kuma .... Toshiro Mifune
Ayame .... Shima Iwashita
Akamatsu .... Yunosuke Ito

"The Day the Sun Rose" is an anti-samurai drama dealing with class struggle in 16th-century Japan. Beset on the one hand by poor rioting farmers, and on the other by rich overlords and their treacherous samurai retainers, the merchants and artisans of Kyoto scarcely know where to turn. Where to turn happens to be to the side of the poor rioting farmers, aided by the rice-carrying mounted coolies (led by Toshiro Mifune). Once united, the poor and the middle classes are invincible—aided by the mounted coolies—and despite overwhelming opposition, they are able to reinstate the Gion Festival, expressing in music and pageantry the people's aspirations.

•

A romantic subplot accompanies the march of public events. The plot shows how young Shinkichi (Kinnosuke Nakamura), a dyer by trade and leader of the Kyoto artisans, learns from Ayame, a beautiful flutist, how to play the Gion Festival music. Without the music there can be no festival. Shinkichi and Ayame fall in love.

The daughter of an outcast gardener, Ayame compensates for her bitter and humble lot by affecting a new and ever more dazzling change of kimonos for every scene in which she appears. It isn't enough. Not content with her kimonos, her musical talent or even with Shinkichi, she needs reassurance:

"You think I'm beautiful?"
"Yes."
"You know nothing about me, so you think I'm beautiful." (They have been kissing ardently for some time.) "If you really knew me you'd think that I was ugly . . ."

This is all in subtitles, of course. But it doesn't read like a Japanese movie. It reads like a West Side psychodrama, or like Elaine May celebrating the triumph of rejection fantasies over the wish for success in interpersonal relations.

"The Day the Sun Rose" opened yesterday at the Bijou.

ROGER GREENSPUN.

1973, Ag 30, 26:3

THE STONE KILLER, directed by Michael Winner; screenplay by Gerald Wilson, from the book "A Complete State of Death" by John Gardner; director of photography, Richard Moore; film editor, Frederick Wilson; produced by Mr. Winner; released by Columbia Pictures. At neighborhood theaters. Running time: 95 minutes. This film is classified R.

Torrey	Charles Bronson
Vescari	Martin Balsam
Lorenz	David Sheiner
Daniels	Norman Fell
Mathews	Ralph Waite
Armitage	Eddie Firestone

By ROGER GREENSPUN

Anyone suspected of liking a Michael Winner movie may be assumed guilty until proven innocent. Since there is no way in which I can be proven innocent, I might as well confess to liking Winner's latest, "The Stone Killer," very much indeed. It is an uncommonly nonsensical cops-and-crooks movie set in New York, Los Angeles and the desert between. It opened yesterday at neighborhood theaters.

A revenge plot, a fantastic scheme using especially trained Vietnam veterans to eliminate everyone responsible for the great 1931 murders that changed the power structure of the Mafia, is the basis of "The Stone Killer." Masterminding the scheme is one Vescari (Martin Balsam), a kind of super-Godfather with infinite patience for revenge. "I have waited 42 years . . .," he exclaims, his voice resonant with weariness. But so far as I can see, there was no reason for his waiting 42 years, except that they did not get around to making the movie until 1973.

The delay, it so chances, puts Vescari smack up against a cop named Torrey (Charles Bronson), the stone killer of the title. Ostensibly a desperate character, Torrey is in fact only desperately good. He upholds minority rights, shuns extramarital sex (he is no longer even married), and never shoots dead anyone who has not tried to shoot him dead first. But he also never misses, so he has a bad reputation.

Charles Bronson

The antagonists never actually meet. To a large extent, the real interest in "The Stone Killer" rests in subordinate characters—hired assassins, ancient junkies, young creeps, down to a dwarf perched on a seedy hotel's registration desk. In such picturesque details, Winner is obviously recalling his predecessors in the genre, but I

think he recalls them honorably. He has at least put a lot of favorite devices into a film that moves with great energy and with an over-all economy to control its small-scale flamboyance.

Michael Winner's recent career ("The Mechanic," "Chato's Land," etc.) has created at least a few loyal supporters, and I think I begin to sense why. With a strange combination of vulgarity and technical elegance, a feeling for when to cut away from an action or a face—whether by accident or design—"The Stone Killer" keeps turning into exciting cinema, crude, often funny, and sometimes quite brilliantly idiomatic. It may come as close to inspired primitivism as we are likely to get in the movies these days.

1973 Ag 30, 26:3

THE TALL BLOND MAN WITH ONE BLACK SHOE, directed by Yves Robert; screenplay (French with English subtitles) by Mr. Robert and Francis Veber; photography, Rene Mathelin; editor, Ghislaine Desjonqueres; music, Vladimir Kosma; produced by Mr. Robert and Alain Poiré; distributed by Cinema V. At the Paris Theater, 58th Street west of Fifth Avenue. Running time: 90 minutes. This film has been classified PG.

François	Pierre Richard
Milan	Bernard Blier
Toulouse	Jean Rochefort
Christine	Mireille Darc
Maurice	Jean Carmet
Paulette	Colette Castel
Perrache	Paul Le Person

By ROGER GREENSPUN

An obsession with repetition, with a mechanical continuation of gesture, seems to characterize French movie comedy from the greatest down to the very worst. It is as if everyone felt that if one man making a funny face is good, then six men making the same funny face are better; as if each comedy film director were consciously illustrating points in Bergson's famous essay on laughter.

I felt this more often than I might have wished during Yves Robert's "The Tall Blond Man With One Black Shoe," which opened yesterday at the Paris Theater. While sometimes a very funny movie, it keeps settling for academic demonstrations of comic ideas and devices. The demonstrations are clever and highly professional. But if the film never fails embarrassingly it also rarely attempts any exhilarating or even very interesting risks.

The tall blond man (Pierre Richard) is a musician, a symphony violinist, who is chosen at random by the head of a secret service organization (Jean Rochefort) as a sacrificial decoy to trap a subordinate (Bernard Blier) hungry for his job. The trap works, but not in the ways intended. The tall blond man never discovers his role. Secret agents die like flies around him, and his ignorance is bliss — with the

added bliss of a particularly beautiful agent (Mireille Darc) who falls in love with him.

Pierre Richard plays the tall blond man along a rather thin dividing line between the dead-pan, slightly comic and the almost ordinary. Since the film's basic running gag depends upon a misreading of every innocent thing he does, Richard's characterization seems exactly right. Even his face (he looks like a skinnier, more antic Gene Wilder) contributes, and some of the best moments don't do much more than show him in a series of candid snapshots.

But the film that surrounds him, the whole intrigue plot, too often offers the mechanics of comedy without the effect.

The people in the film, which is set in a modern glass and chrome Paris, grow almost indistinguishable from one another, lost into the world they manipulate. Since that world is not too different from the world of Jacques Tati's great "Playtime," recently seen here, it is worth noticing the difference between a comic vision that keeps discovering individualities, and one in which individualities very nearly disappear from view. In "Playtime," even the inhuman city falls happy victim to the bungling humanity of its people. But in "The Tall Blond Man" the people begin to recede — to become types, devices: cool, cold, predictable and unreal.

1973 Ag 31, 10:1

The Cast

LAKE OF DRACULA, directed by Michio Yamamoto; executive producer, Fumio Tanaka; produced by Toho Company, Limited. At the Elgin Theater, 171 Eighth Avenue. Running time 82 minutes. This film has not been classified.

Akiko	Midori Fujita
Sacki	Choei Takahashi
Natsuoko	Sanee Emi

By ROGER GREENSPUN

Do you want to know how vampires came to Japan?

The historians of the Toho Company explain it: "Since even vampires, when not working at sucking blood, probably enjoy sexual activity, they doubtless foster offspring, albeit illegitimate ones. Dracula himself would have been no exception. It was thus during the early years of this century that one of Dracula's bastard sons made his way to Japan, liked it, settled down."

He settled into a tatty old Transylvanian castle smack in the middle of modern Japan, near a lake called Fujimi, which is the Lake of Dracula, which is the title of a new movie directed by Michio Yamamoto and released by Toho. It opened yesterday at the Elgin.

If the idea of a Japanese vampire movie seems intriguing, "Lake of Dracula" leaves that idea all but untouched. The actors are Japanese, but the clothes, the conventions, the architecture — especially the architecture — are all carried over from the West. I've never seen such a movie for creaking doors, footsteps on the stairs and all the other paraphernalia that have so much to do with shock and so little to do with the deeper and more delightful forms of terror.

Dracula himself—actually the great-grandson of Dracula, victim of some particularly goofy sort of curse that produces vampires only every third generation—is almost pure animal. He doesn't seduce; he growls. His eyes light up like bicycle reflectors — which I think they possibly are.

Akiko (Midori Fujita), the girl he wants to get his teeth into, is at the same time chased by the vampire and accused of paranoia by her fiancé (Choei Takahashi), a young physician who reduces every fear to Freud.

Between the predator and his prey there stands nothing much except some tangled forest, a thunderstorm and the previously mentioned doors and stairways. It is as if the whole mystique of repulsive attraction were being reduced to a collection of studio props. After "Jonathan" and "Vampir," and even the "Count Yorga" movies and "Blacula," we vampire lovers are used to something better.

1973 S 1, 14:3

The Cast

SLAUGHTER'S BIG RIPOFF, directed by Gordon Douglas; written by Charles Johnson, based on a character created by Don Williams; director of photography, Charles Wheeler; film editor, Christopher Holmes; music by James Brown and Fred Wesley; produced by Monroe Sachson; released by American International Pictures. At the Cinerama Theater, Broadway at 47th Street and the 86th Street Twin II Theater, west of Lexington. Running time: 94 minutes. This film is classified R.

Slaughter	Jim Brown
Duncan	Ed McMahon
Reynolds	Brock Peters
Kirk	Don Stroud
Marcia	Gloria Hendry
Joe Creole	Richard Williams
Burtoli	Art Metrano
Noria	Judy Brown
Crowder	Russ Marin

By LAWRENCE VAN GELDER

"Slaughter's Big Ripoff" belongs to the class of movie that seems to offer itself for judgment in terms of body count, quarts of gore expended, variety of weaponry, number of panes of glass shattered, excellence in portrayal of death throes and destruction of automobiles.

It tempts the viewer to subtract points for a flaccid thigh on a bikinied extra in the background or a bald tread on the tire of a car sinking under water after hurtling off a cliff with the hero and his girl inside.

For what counts is the surface of things and by no means their substance. On the level of relationship to reality, inner logic, nuance of character and even sufficient morality to distinguish the good guys from the bad (except in the realm of drugs, which Jim Brown, as Slaughter, deftly spurns) such movies as these make no pretense toward achievement.

But even within its own terms, as latter-day cinema of sheer entertainment concocted out of conspicuous violence, facile sex, with-it locales and a theme of vengeance pitting a loner against the mob and crooked cops, "Slaughter's Big Ripoff" must be adjudged third-rate.

It has the conceit to virtually ignore its hero's past —something of an affront to those who did not see "Slaughter," the first in what promises to be a series of these films—and the willingness to sacrifice its pacing to a long, aimless scene of Jim Brown's driving through the night while the mandatory rock tune performed by the singer James Brown takes over.

As the story of how Slaughter wreaks vengeance on Duncan (Ed McMahon), the mob boss whose killer missed Slaughter while doing in some of Slaughter's friends, "Slaughter's Big Ripoff" falls short of inventiveness of plot and originality of style, but Richard Williams, as a pimp named Joe Creole, does seem to be having himself a good time.

"Slaughter's Big Ripoff" opened yesterday at the Cinerama and 86th Street Twin II theaters.

1973 S 1, 14:3

"DILLINGER" AND "BANG THE DRUM SLOWLY"

By PETER SCHJELDAHL

"DILLINGER" and "Bang the Drum Slowly" are two new movies that could not be more unlike in style. The former is a bright and crackling celluloid comic book, a gleeful fantasia of gangster mayhem, and the latter is a chuckly and wet-eyed idyll about baseball players, a sort of "Love Story" in pinstripes. What they have in common is, first, that both are clearly products of the "nostalgia craze" that is still upon us (soon, one imagines, to be nostalgic for itself) and, second, that each is as perfect a piece of mindless entertainment as one could wish for in a steamy summer.

The esthetics of movie death—bullets snapping through the air and gouts of blood leaping joyfully from tumbling bodies—have been brought to such sophistication in recent years that further refinements hardly seem possible. But director John Milius has actually come up with enough refinements to earn his "Dillinger," despite its lack of explicit sex, a solid "R" rating. It's really something. The exclusion of unaccompanied teen-agers cannot be pleasing to Milius, the 29-year-old screenwriter of such other macho trips as "Jeremiah Johnson" and "The Life and Times of Judge Roy Bean." For the fantasy of "Dillinger" seems to be aimed directly at the solar plexus of the pubescent male imagination, calculated to dizzy the young mind with visions of gory grandeur.

To less excitable moviegoers, "Dillinger" offers the attractions of a high-gloss epic style and a nice sense of dirty fun. Produced by American International Pictures, it is the distilled essence of the AIP film: fast and florid and trashy as all hell. It differs from previous AIP bloodbaths in being even emptier of substance and at the same time a far harder and shinier article. AIP wizard Robert Corman's "The St. Valentine's Day Massacre" and "Bloody Mama" (about the Ma Barker gang) were full of Gothic psychologizing touches that were enjoyable but tended to muffle the action. Not so with "Dillinger," which is flat-out crazy behavior and carnage.

What makes "Dillinger" like a comic book is its intense self-consciousness on the level of myth. Milius's crooks—Dillinger, Pretty Boy Floyd, Baby Face Nelson and other all-stars, gloatingly described at one point as a "super-gang"—are cut out of archetypal cardboard, as is their FBI nemesis Melvin Purvis. Warren Oates and Ben Johnson, as Dillinger and Purvis, don't act their roles so much as swagger through them, egomaniacal monsters endeavoring to out-mean-and-ugly each other. Purvis smokes "ciggarrs" over the riddled corpses of his quarry because those cigars were the gift of a murdered G-Man. Why he gets a kick out of this you don't ask. And all you need to know about Dillinger is contained in one line: "I'm just about the best bank-robber they ever had, and boy am I happy!"

"Dillinger's" machinery of period cues, old-timey music, intercut stock footage and lyrical interludes is familiar stuff, done neither better nor worse than in a half-dozen films since "Bonnie and Clyde" defined the rural gangster opus. What is extraordinary, as I've said, is the finesse of the shoot-outs and glory-dying, a nuance or two beyond even Sam Peckinpah. And there is one scene, of the gang trapped in

a roomy mansion raked by FBI gunfire, that is one of the most beautiful action sequences I've ever seen, a symphony of splintering wood, crashing glass and hysterically scampering figures in voluminous, smoky interiors. Whether we owe the splendor of this sequence to Milius or to cinematographer Jules Brenner I don't know, but it's a zinger.

There are no comparable esthetic satisfactions in "Bang the Drum Slowly," directed by John Hancock with the kind of pacing that makes you anticipate commercial breaks. But then, has there ever been a movie about baseball that was esthetically satisfying? Hollywood has always had a convincing way with bloody gun duels, but I have yet to see a baseball film in which the game looked real. This may be because baseball is, in effect, a rival art form with spatial and temporal conventions all its own; attempts to represent it on film invariably make it seem obscure and pointless. In any case, "Bang the Drum Slowly" falls down on the field and picks itself up in locker rooms, hotel rooms and bars.

What elevates it is mainly a deeply humorous performance by Robert de Niro as Bruce Pearson, an earnest, painfully dumbbell catcher for the pennant-bound New York Mammoths who is doomed to die of Hodgkin's Disease at season's end. De Niro, who bears a striking resemblance to Jughead, may be destined to replace Dustin Hoffman as our foremost portrayer of wacky, guileless dolts. Michael Moriarty plays narrator Henry Wiggen, star pitcher for the fictional Mammoths and Bruce's bosom friend, in finely laconic, decent style. (Whoever thought of making the character of Wiggen a ringer for real-life Tom Seaver of the Mets deserves credit for a delightful coup.) As gravy, there are a lot of very funny people in minor roles.

The script of "Bang the Drum Slowly" was written by Mark Harris from

his own 1956 novel. It suffers a bit now from having been ahead of its time in the fifties as a work of jock literature. Revelations of profane locker-room carryings-on no longer warrant the prestige accorded them by Harris. Even more serious is all the Runyonesque dialogue Harris has not seen fit to update—contraction-free phrasing on the order of "Do not be mad," each syllable hit with the impartial emphasis of a metronome. One feels sorry for Vincent Gardenia, who, as Mammoths' manager Dutch Schnell, is given any number of speeches quaint enough to make your ears ache.

The sentimentality of "Bang the Drum Slowly" is a matter of taste. Pathetic Bruce, too dumb to have any feeling about his imminent death beyond vague stirrings of resentment, will leave some people's heart-strings untugged. And the movie's fond view of ballplayers as a

bunch of big, lovable kids—relieved now and then by flickers of healthy cynicism in the narration—may cloy. But, after all, team feeling is largely a sentimental phenomenon, and this story of the mutually transforming effects of a relationship between a dying catcher and his team seems basically sound. A surrender to it is nothing to be ashamed of.

When I saw "Bang the Drum Slowly" at a large screening, noses were being blown toward the end. I shudder to imagine the audible reactions to "Dillinger" of your average Manhattan neighborhood crowd—pretty bestial, probably. Both, however, are bona fide nights at the movies, guaranteed to scratch where you itch and to leave you happily unimproved.

1973 S 2, II:7:1

The Program

LADY KUNG-FU, directed by Huang Feng; photography, Li Yu Fang; produced by Raymond Chow; released by National General Pictures. At neighborhood theaters. Running time: 99 minutes. This film is classified R. With Angela Mao, Carter Hunning, Pai Wing, Han Jae, Wei Ping Ao, Nancy Sit and Terio Yamane.

By LAWRENCE VAN GELDER

Aficionados of the recent wave of martial-arts movies can take comfort in the knowledge that the latest arrival, "Lady Kung-Fu," displays adequate reverence for the form they first knew and loved.

That is by no means to lavish praise on the form itself. But it does serve as assurance that "Lady Kung-Fu"—like "Fists of Fury," for example — accelerates through provocation of the good people to increasingly violent confrontation and the ultimate visitation on the principal villains of what Winston Churchill liked to call condign punishment.

●

What this means is that they wind up dead after a showdown battle with the most skillful of the good people — in this case, Angela Mao, the sole survivor among the three young partners who open a kung-fu school and earn the enmity of a Japanese-run judo academy.

Such plot as there is serves merely as a vehicle for the escalation of violence, but it should be noted that in this instance there are elements of dispute over the merits of kung-fu as against judo; and over the extent of Japanese influence in a China that no longer exists.

Miss Mao, according to her publicity, is a martial-arts expert and certainly does justice to the physical demands of her role. But her role—like the others—is a caricature of a character. "Lady Kung-Fu" abounds with caricatures: a cackling chief villain, a smug and homicidal head judo instructor and an assortment of henchmen given to portrayals of gibbering cowardice at the first signs of misfortune.

Where it counts—in the reproduction of all the thwacks, whooshings and bone crackings attendant on the violence—the soundtrack of "Lady Kung-Fu" is fine. It fares much more poorly in the delivery of the dubbed dialogue. But in films like these, that hardly seems to matter.

"Lady Kung-Fu" opened yesterday at neighborhood theaters.

1973 S 6, 43:1

The Cast

SASUKE AGAINST THE WIND, directed by Masahiro Shinoda; screenplay (Japanese with English subtitles) by Yoshiyuki Fukuda, based on a novel by Koji Nakada; photographed by Massao Kosugi; music, Mitsuru Takemitsu; produced by Shizuo Yamauchi. At the Bijou Theater, 45th Street, west of Broadway. Running time: 99 minutes. This film has not been classified.
Sasuke Srutobi .... Kohji Takahashi
Mitsuaki Inamura .... Mutsuhiro Toura
Okiwa .... Misako Watanabe
Jinnai Horikawa .... Seiii Miyaguchi
Yashiro Kobayashi ... Yasunori Irikawa
Genba Kuni .... Minoru Hotaka
Sakon Takatani .... Tetsuro Tanba
Omiyo .... Jitsuko Yoshimura

Any assessment of "Sasuke Against the Wind" distills itself inevitably into a balancing of the movie's magnificent black and white photography, its spectacle and its sense of period against the utter chaos of its plot.

Unfortunately for this Japanese film, which opened yesterday at the Bijou, the scales are tipped well over the borderline of failure by the weight of the incomprehensible plot.

●

It is a medieval spy and murder melodrama whose chaos is capped when the hero is rescued by means of a character previously unknown to the audience, a feat of illogic roughly comparable to ending a James Bond movie with a deus ex machina in the form of John Shaft.

The difficulty of keeping pace with the story is compounded by a set of subtitles

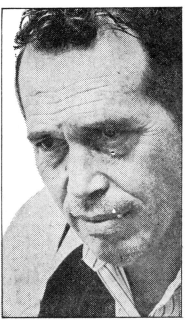

Warren Oates as "Dillinger"
"A bright and crackling celluloid comic book"

that are infested with distracted typographical errors. It really is too bad, because visually "Sasuke Against the Wind" has moments of great beauty, for which credit is due to the director, Masahiro Shinoda,

and the photographer, Masao Kosugi.

•

The hero, Sasuke, a "ninja," or samurai spy of ambiguous character and a fundamentally pacific dis-

position despite the number of deaths he figures in, is given a commanding presence by Kohji Takahashi.

But neither the moody photography nor the combat nor the costumes can compensate for a story that

seems not to share their commitment to plausibility.

LAWRENCE VAN GELDER

1973 S 6, 43:1

instincts that are almost congenital and with strident, exclamatory speech and frenetic arm-waving.

Returning to American films, we may ask what relation there is between the above qualities and the life depicted in, say, Steve Shagan's "Save the Tiger," a film with a more than tangential connection to Jews. The movie's strategy is to sweep the audience through a one-day synopsis of Jack Lemmon's angst-filled life as quickly and flashily as possible. Along the way there are heavy intimations that the film's ambience is Jewish (which makes sense, since it deals with a Los Angeles garment manufacturer). For one thing, Lemmon's guilt-ridden partner, Jack Gilford, comes across Semitically in every conceivable way—appearance, mannerisms, intonation, etc. For another, Lemmon's head tailor, William Hansen, is pure Delancey Street. Pouring forth his Sholem Aleichem-type wisdom, speaking a Yiddish-inflected English, he seems like a man who is still awaiting an exit visa from the Yiddish Art Theater.

And what are we to make of Jack Lemmon, trying to squeeze his unmistakably WASP presence into an apparently Jewish persona? An outrageously bad fit, even in an industry that has produced such remarkable misalliances as John Garfield playing a Mexican soldier, Boris Karloff as a Chicago gangster, and Frank Sinatra as a sensitive writer. To this gallery of preposterous matchups, add Jack Lemmon as the son of a poor immigrant who ran a small store on New York's lower East Side.

There are no casting errors in "The Heartbreak Kid," the Elaine May-Neil Simon collaboration that has earned so much praise and money this year. It is difficult to imagine actors better suited to their roles than Charles Grodin and Jeannie Berlin as a couple of Jewish newlyweds from New York and Eddie Albert and Cybill Shepherd as a WASP banker and his daughter from the Midwest. The problem here, however, is that the parts themselves are cramped little molds, which the actors are unable to enlarge.

The worst of these is the bride, a cruel compendium of every unpleasant trait that has ever been associated with Jewish girls — particularly from New York. As seen by Simon and May (there is no auteurish friction between screenwriter and director evident here, rather an awful complicity), Lila is noisy, vulgar, demanding, insanely

'Blume' and 'The Heartbreak Kid' — What Kind of Jews Are They?

By ROBERT F. MOSS

UNTIL quite recently it has been one of the abiding paradoxes of the American cinema that in an industry where Jews have been a major source of talent, creative and entrepreneurial, Jewish culture—particularly in its contemporary American context — has been a very minor source of subject matter. Prior to World War II, it is difficult to find a Hollywood film that deals even marginally with this topic. Of movies that come readily to mind, what is there besides "The Jazz Singer" (in which the Jewish milieu, though fairly authentic, is too maudlin to be taken seriously)?

The postwar spirit of tolerance and brotherhood brought "Crossfire" and "Gentleman's Agreement" (both 1947), two famous treatments of a previously taboo subject, anti-Semitism. But, ironically enough, these films were too busy attacking anti-Semitism to bother dealing with Semites themselves; the few Jewish characters in them are strictly peripheral—Gentiles dominate the action.

Then, in the decade of the 1960's, after a relatively fallow period, came films like "Come Blow Your Horn," "The Apartment," "The Detective," and "No Way to Treat a Lady," which, to one degree or another, deployed a collection of stereotypes that had been around since "Abie's Irish Rose," especially the "Jewish mother" figure. Also revived was the by-now dormant "Gentleman's Agreement" tradition, in which sermons on religious tolerance took the place of drama and personifications of Jewish goodness and Jewish wisdom wandered around pretending to be real flesh and blood. The chief representatives of this second tradition were "Exodus" and "Ship of Fools." There was some attempt to break new ground

in "The Pawnbroker" and "Goodbye, Columbus"; but the former was vitiated by its sledgehammer tactics and the latter by its reliance on caricatures that were cruel without being penetrating—and which were rather cheap besides (a charge that could be made against the Philip Roth novella as well).

By the late 1960's a pro-Semitic vogue had taken hold of the country, probably fostered by the ascendancy of Jewish novelists in the last 20 years and by Israel's spectacular victory in the Six-Day War. In the movies, actors like Zero Mostel, Elliott Gould and Barbra Streisand began to establish themselves as international celebrities, not by suppressing their Jewishness, but by exploiting it. Why not? Suddenly it was "in" to be Jewish.

*

Which brings us to 1973 and a few of the recent efforts at doing something artistically significant, or at least entertaining, with Jewish American life. In "Blume in Love," the new Paul Mazursky film, George Segal, who is attempting with mulish persistence to recapture his ex-wife's affections, shows up one day at her front door with lox and bagels. This incident, along with the names assigned to the two leads, is the only indication that they are supposed to be Jewish.

There is, of course, no reason why a director has to comment on the uniquely Jewish aspects of a Jewish character, but in the case of "Blume in Love" the omission is puzzling. Segal's name, Stephen Blume, coyly hints at a composite of Joyce's Stephen Dedalus and Leopold Bloom. The preciosity seems particularly intentional in the light of the film's plot—mostly Blume's interminable efforts at wooing his former wife. True, Joyce's hero in "Ulysses" is not divorced, but

one of the major dimensions of the book is Bloom's gnawing alienation from Molly and his struggle to overcome it. Moreover, Bloom's status as a Jew is symptomatic of his larger alienation from parochial, tradition-bound Dublin and Joyce emphasizes it accordingly, demonstrating considerable familiarity with Jewish culture. The discrepancy between Joyce's Bloom and Mazursky's Blume is indicative of a bigger, more troublesome gap: the vastly greater thoroughness and profundity with which Jewish life has been treated by American novelists (e.g., Bellow and Malamud) as compared to American filmmakers.

Naturally, these remarks raise the question of just what constitutes Jewishness. What is the nature of this ethnicity that novels have caught and films have not?

Before setting forth any specifications, a cautionary note is in order. Any ethnic

"definition" carries with it the danger of violating the uniqueness of the individuals it describes; they spill out in all directions and cannot be satisfactorily penned up within the confines of a single, generally applicable analysis. Still, there are patterns that, on balance, are more characteristic of one group than another. In the case of Jews, a fair-minded observer does have to note a high degree of family solidarity; an achievement-oriented outlook (at a WASP country club the conversation is apt to be about golf scores; at a Jewish club it will be about whose son got into Harvard, whose didn't); a high degree of scholastic aptitude; a generally outreaching and aggressive approach to life (the less complimentary term is "pushy").

Moving from a legitimate paradigm to a distasteful stereotype, it is also common to associate Jews with guilt and anxiety, with mercenary

Robert F. Moss is an assistant professor of English at Rutgers University who often writes on film.

Jeannie Berlin and Charles Grodin, the ill-matched bride and groom in "The Heartbreak Kid"
She is "a cruel compendium of every unpleasant trait ever associated with Jewish girls"

possessive, impossibly overbearing and grimly committed to pre-marital virginity. In short, a Jewish princess of unmistakably lower middle-class origins.

Beyond the strictly Jewish elements in this poor pincushion of a character, Lila has still other sins (of an ethnically neutral variety, one assumes), such as caroling away compulsively in a reedy, tone-deaf voice and covering her face with particles of food at lunch. This latter scene, one of the most offensive in a deeply offensive film, asks us to accept, in an adult of average intelligence, table manners that would be believable only in a retarded child. We recoil from all this, it should be stressed, not because the portrait of Lila is wholly inaccurate in what it tries to say about her "type," but because it says these things in such a loud, coercive, uncharitable manner that it's impossible to accept her as a credible human being.

When Simon and May have

finished burying Lila under every kind of abuse they can think of, they have the audacity to dig her up and offer her to us suddenly in her last scene as a figure of Chaplinesque poignancy, pathetically unable to guess that her husband is trying to dump her. This is the big "Academy Award scene," set in an expensive Florida restaurant, where overwriting, overacting and overdirection all come together in one excruciating mess.

*

Lenny Cantrow, the miserable bridegroom, is intended to be likable and so, since Simon and May are obviously unable to find much to praise in Jewish culture, he is rendered less Semitic than Lila. His looks are not definitively Jewish, as hers are, and of the characteristics associated with Jewish men, he has only a few—chiefly aggressiveness (though only in its romantic-sexual manifestation) and a

tendency to raise his voice.

Herein lies the film's most arrant dishonesty: it simultaneously stacks the deck against Lila and in favor of Len. Behind all the fancy attempts at social commentary, at juxtaposing two different cultures, is an old-fashioned romantic comedy and the filmmakers are taking no chances on alienating or disenchanting the audience by bringing it excessively close to reality. Hence, Lila is, by Hollywood standards, homely, while Lenny is, by the same standards, rather a pretty boy, not too far from the John Garfield-Tony Curtis image. In addition, where Lila is harsh, he is charming; where she is dull and obtuse, he is clever and inventive; where she is all abrasiveness, he is all personality.

Although Lenny is made to look pretty good in contrast to his grotesque wife, it's still not clear how he casts such a spell on his WASP goddess Kelly, that she marries him. There is a school of thought which holds that Gentile women are often attracted to Jewish men.

Whatever the accuracy of this theory, it could certainly use more of a workout than it's gotten in the American cinema. The only attention it receives in "The Heartbreak Kid"—a movie which is ostensibly resting right on top of it—is in the indication that Lenny's liveliness and unflagging, Mountie-like pursuit of Kelly set him off from her bland WASP boyfriends.

For the most part, however, Simon and May bypass the issue of Jewish appeal in favor of standardized Hollywood comedy. It is difficult to locate the wit and intelligence in this movie that so many reviewers were able to spot. The sensibility behind it seems strictly "show biz."

*

"Blume in Love," "Save the Tiger" and "The Heartbreak Kid" illustrate, in their various ways, Hollywood's failure to deal with the cultural roots of the very people who built it, who shaped it and gave it substance. Ironically, the closest approximation to a successful cinematic treatment of Jewish American life is "The Angel Levine," made

in 1970 by Jan Kadar, a Czech immigrant who could hardly speak English. "Levine" went unhailed, unseen and, in many quarters, unnoticed, but it has infinitely more integrity and sensitivity to its subject than an overblown hate letter like "The Heartbreak Kid." Despite an uneven script, poor photography and Zero Mostel, the movie manages to bring its central characters, an elderly, impoverished Jewish couple of European background, miraculously to life. "Levine" succeeds because of the informed compassion and quiet warmth of Kadar's direction and of Ida Kaminska's performance, a characterization that, for once, justifies the old clichés, "radiant" and "glowing." "Blume in Love," "Save the Tiger" and "The Heartbreak Kid" show that not only has there been no advance since 1970 in dealing with the Jewish experience in this country, the movement has been distinctly retrograde.

1973 S 9, II:1:3

George Segal, right, as "Blume in Love," tries to give Susan Anspach, his ex-wife, a letter. Kris Kristofferson watches. *Nothing besides a taste for lox and bagels—and his name—to mark Blume as a Jew?*

BATTLE OF OKINAWA, directed by Kihachi Okamoto; written (Japanese with English subtitles) by Kaneto Shindo; produced by Sanezumi Fujimoto and Hiroshi Haryu; director of photography, Hiroshi Murai; music, Masaru Sato; a Toho Company production, distributed by Min-On of America. Running time: 149 minutes. At the Elgin Cinema, Eighth Avenue at 19th Street. This film has not been classified. With: Keiju Kobayashi, Yuzo Kayama, Tetsuri Tamba, Tatsuya Nakadai, Mayumi Ozora.

By VINCENT CANBY

With "Battle of Okinawa," which opened yesterday at the Elgin Theater, Japanese film makers continue to explore the limited dramatic possibilities of the not-quite-documentary historical feature that Darryl F. Zanuck exploited so successfully in "The Longest Day," and then virtually annihilated in the boredom of "Tora! Tora! Tora!"

The film covers a period of approximately one year, beginning in the summer of 1944, when the Japanese high command decided to prepare the island for possible American invasion, and following through the invasion itself and the terrible hill-by-hill, cave-by-cave fighting that came after. Kihachi Okamoto, the director, uses some old newsreel clips (which become wildly distorted by the CinemaScope lens) and efficiently restages most key scenes, though in rather more massive detail than a non-military student may be interested in.

The most curious thing about the film is its difficult-to-define point of view. It seems to have reservations about the miltary men who denied adequate protection to Okinawa, and it seems to be very pro-Okinawa, one-third of whose population was slain in the fighting.

Yet "Battle of Okinawa" gets so wrapped up in showing examples of the terror—the slaughter of soldiers and the mass suicides of civilians—that the spectacle of the carnage overwhelms any pity. The movie keeps saying in effect: "Look at what these people endured," but the images are those of conventional make-believe gore. They are not good enough.

1973 S 12, 41:1

'Jealousy,' a Japanese Triangle Film, Opens

By LAWRENCE VAN GELDER

Given the ingredients of first-rate psychological mystery, "Jealousy," a Japanese film that opened yesterday at the Bijou Theater, manages to deliver no more than soap opera — and unexceptional soap opera at that.

Its promising beginning poses the question of how a young business executive with a wife, a small child and apparently a record of marital fidelity came to commit suicide in the company of a previously uknown mistress, who survives her own effort to die with him.

And "Jealousy" proposes to answer the question by having the widow take on a new name and a job as a hostess in the luxurious businessmen's bar run by the mistress.

With these elements as a springboard into a possibly illuminating unraveling of character and mystery, "Jealousy" plunges into the creation of an assortment of triangles.

The wife-husband-mistress triangle alone would have sufficed, but audiences are also given other triangles involving the husband's sister, the husband's boss, the wife's new lover and the mistress.

No particular respect for the delights of puzzle-solving accompanies the dispelling of mystery. And as for revelation of character, there is no indication of a master hand at work.

The director, identified as Sadanaga Katahisa, has a fondness — bordering on addiction — for the close-up. He fills the screen with faces, foreheads and eyes, and when he tires of that, he turns to lingering shots of tropical fish, birds, liquor glasses, sunsets and lemons being sliced. Only those possessed of saintly empathy could accept them as valid symbols of anything except a good idea gone wrong.

1973 S 13, 60:1

'Heavy Traffic' and 'American Graffiti'—Two of the Best

By VINCENT CANBY

RALPH BAKSHI'S mostly animated feature, "Heavy Traffic," is American graffiti of a very high and unusual order, a tale of a young New York City pilgrim named Michael, half-Italian, half-Jewish, ever innocent, and his progress through a metaphor that is nowhere near as dreary as it sounds: the pinball machine called Life. It is a liberating, arrogant sort of movie, crude, tough, vulgar, full of insult and wit and an awareness of the impermanence of all things.

Most of George Lucas's "American Graffiti" takes place inside, on top, underneath or within spitting distance of cars — Fords, VWs, Chevies, Citroens, Pontiacs—in which the teenagers of one small American city, on a late summer's evening in 1962, are cruising Main Street out of boredom and in their obsession with movement. "American Graffiti" is about heavy traffic of the most troubling kind: young lives going nowhere in particular but with a debonair manner, a good deal of humor and a lot of decent feelings. The doom that is on-screen almost constantly in Bakshi's film is never manifest to Lucas's teenagers, but it lies in the road ahead.

It is one of the confusing coincidences of the current season that the titles of two of the most interesting films (two of the best, really) to open here this summer could easily be interchanged. A good title is like that. It has its own life and mystery that make it almost infinitely adaptable. However, there's no need to worry about the confusion in these two titles — you should see both films — unless you're under 17, in which case you might want to sue. Bakshi's "Heavy Traffic" is rated X, not because it's pornographic in any way but because it employs the small gestures and words of obscenity to make its rude statement about the quality of what might be dangerously described as the New York City Experience.

The opening of the film sets its mood as the screen goes from a live-action Michael, playing his pinball machine, to the animated world that lies just beyond reality. Michael, a would-be "underground" cartoonist, asks "What makes you happy? Where do you hide? Who do you trust?" And the voice carries over as two ancient jazz musicians in terrible repair meet while foraging through a garbage can: "Tilt city. Pinball alley. Blinking lights. Shot to hell. — it all. Let's get a jug . . ."

With a poet's freedom (including the freedom from the fear he might be making an ass of himself), Bakshi conducts his misery-house tour of the quintessential modern metropolis, a New York City inhabited entirely by undesirables, junkies, whores, crooked cops, crooked union leaders, Mafia soldiers, craven dads, mad moms. The only two innocents are Michael and Carole, the pretty, no-nonsense black bartender who is also beloved by Shorty, the legless bouncer at her bar.

Bakshi's first feature, "Fritz The Cat," was criticized by purists for the liberties he took with a favorite underground comic strip. Now he has created his own world in "Heavy Traffic," which at its best moments is as nutty and bleak and beautiful as some scenes out of early Henry Miller, with whom Bakshi shares the inability to be entirely glum in the face of disaster.

Michael's home life is a horror, but it's also horribly funny as his mom, whose eyes glow magenta in the dark, rails about her marriage to a goy ("Marry a Catholic, they said. No divorce, they said. Some luck," she says) and at one point tries unsuccessfully to murder her drunken lout of a husband, a Mafia pier boss named Angie. "That's one," she says as she turns on the gas and gets Angie's head and shoulders inside the oven, apparently meaning that she might also like to get rid of Michael because he won't eat.

"Heavy Traffic" wouldn't be much fun, however, if it were nothing more than an inventory of horrors. The fascination of "Heavy Traffic" is the way the horrors are turned inside out, most often for laughs but occasionally for reflections on love and loss. There is a most peculiar, most moving sequence in which Michael runs into his mom at a cheap Manhattan dance hall. She's being drunk and disorderly (her left breast just won't stay inside her dress) and then she glides off into a sodden reverie in which she's confronted by real photographs out of a not-quite-forgotten childhood.

There's also a very funny and sad rooftop encounter Michael has with a deranged old black man named Moe, who tells Michael cheerfully that he has come up to the roof to kill Michael's pigeons. Says Moe, who is suddenly sad: "I ain't there. Everybody plays like he's there. But they ain't there . . ."

Everyone in "Heavy Traffic" seems to think he's there or that he knows how to get there, including Snowflake, the transvestite who inevitably picks up the kind of rough trade who will beat the hell out of him when the truth is revealed. Even Michael and Carole think they know how to get there, which for them is California, a plan that is cruelly interrupted because if there's one thing Angie hates more than the idea that his son is a virgin, it's the idea that his son is sleeping with a black girl.

Bakshi's background images, which often mix animation with photographs and with well-known paintings (an Edward Hopper, for example), brilliantly evoke a New York that spans the 1930s to the 1960s. Even though the time seems always immediate, when Michael sits alone in the top balcony in some now long-removed Loew's picture palace, he is watching an actual clip from the Clark Gable-Jean Harlow film, "Red Dust" (1932).

In "Fritz The Cat," Bakshi's characters were animals. Here they are cartoon humans who, in themselves, are not very interesting to look at. They are the heritage of decades of Terrytoons and Looney Tunes and Max Fleischer work that never measured up to the Disney creations. (Michael in "Heavy Traffic" reminds me of the bland-faced hero of Fleischer's feature-length "Gulliver's Travels"). Yet this very ordinariness of the characters' looks, plus Bakshi's use of the most familiar sort of cartoon prerogatives (an assassinated Mafia godfather can continue to eat his spaghetti even though he is full of see-through bullet holes), are part of what I take to be a serious attempt to use the commonplace stratagems of one era to mock the nightmares of the era that came after.

"Heavy Traffic" may well turn out to be the most original American film of the year.

"American Graffiti" is such a funny, accurate movie, so controlled and efficient in its narrative, that it stands to be overpraised to the point where seeing it will be an anticlimax. Some of the things that make it so effective are things that have been rigorously left out of it — the sort of sentiment and melodrama that can ease one through second-rate movies that have nothing else going for them.

The first-rate screenplay, written by director Lucas with Gloria Katz and Willard Huyck, tells us everything we want to know about its teenagers entirely in terms of one night's action that has as its focal point Mel's Burger City Drive-in, whose waitresses work on roller skates. To the teenagers of "American Graffiti," Mel's

Burger City occupies more or less the same place that Nick's Bar had in the lives of the picturesque misfits of Saroyan's "The Time of Your Life." There is an important difference, though. Nick, the bartender-as-priest, was always on hand to tend the needs of Saroyan characters. There is no Mel at Mel's Burger City, at least no Mel that we or the teenagers ever see. They are on their own.

There is an awful lot of 1960s nostalgia in "American Graffiti," especially in period songs on the soundtrack, but it never corrupts the discipline of the film or cheapens the sorrows of its characters, all of whom, in one way or another, are haunted by the passage of time. Most of them are 17. However, as one boy says to another: "You can't stay 17 forever." He's referring to a friend of theirs named John, the town's champion drag racer who, at 22, is still out cruising Main Street on Saturday nights as he did five years ago. What the boy wants to say is that you *can* stay 17 forever, but that doesn't mean you won't age like everyone else, and that life won't pass you by.

Hardly any parents or adults figure in "American Graffiti," which confines itself to one night and to the teenagers' own views of themselves. Two of the boys are due to leave for college in the east the next morning. One wants to go. The other is apprehensive about leaving the nest. Another boy, who finds it impossible to make out with Mel's Burger City's easiest mark, borrows a friend's Chevy and immediately becomes a Lothario of sorts. In one of the funniest individual sequences I've seen in any film in months, this fellow finally acquires a bottle of hard stuff (bourbon) demanded by his date, a blonde named Debbie who thinks she looks like Sandra Dee.

Like most of the best movies, "American Graffiti" keeps its focus short. Its aims are specific, not general, certainly not epic, but because it achieves its aims so well, there may be a temptation to overload the film with an importance that can kill spontaneous appreciation of it. The performers, most of whom are new to me, are marvelous: Richard Dreyfuss, Ronny Howard, Paul Le Mat, Charlie Martin Smith, Cindy Williams and Candy Clark. Miss Clark you may remember as the girl who conned Jeff Bridges into marriage after he deflowered her in "Fat City."

1973 S 16, II:1:1

The Cast

LE RETOUR D'AFRIQUE (Return From Africa), directed by Alain Tanner; written (French with English subtitles) and produced by Mr. Tanner; directors of photography, Renato Berta, Carlo Varini; music, J. S. Bach; a Group Five (Geneva) and Filmanthrone, NEF (Paris) production, distributed by New Yorker Films. Running time: 108 minutes. At the 8th Street Playhouse, 8th Street West of Fifth Avenue. This film has not been classified.
Françoise...............Josee Destoop
Vincent.............Francois Marthouret
Emilio......................Juliet Berto
Girl..................Anne Wiazemsky

By VINCENT CANBY

Movies about people in the dead-center of boredom are usually difficult to sit through. Boredom is contagious. It is the Asian flu of the arts. Given half a chance, it leaps off the screen to ravage the audience. At $3 to $5 a ticket, it is cheaper to stay home to search for flyspecks on the ceiling of a room that has not seen a fly in years.

Alain Tanner, the Swiss director of "Charles—Dead or Alive" and, most notably, "La Salamandre," makes films about people who come perilously close to that numbing, anesthetizing dead-center, but escape it, not always for their own good. This is the source of Tanner's comedy, which, in his new film, "Le Retour d'Afrique," is intelligent, humane and just a tiny bit irrelevant, at least to someone who does not share the feeling that he is being overwhelmed by the boredom of life in Switzerland today.

Vincent (François Marthouret) and his wife Françoise, (Josee Destoop) are young, in love with each other, and thoroughly fed up with their roles as witnesses to great endeavors in other parts of the world, more specifically, the Third World. They live quite comfortably in Geneva, where he works as a gardener and she as an attendant in an art gallery. At night they go to movies with their friends and afterward have ponderous discussions about film, its meaning and its mission. But Vincent and François don't want to watch. They want to do.

At last Vincent comes to a decision: They must either have a baby or immigrate to Algeria, which is the nearest Third World country they can reach (and the only one where they have a friend to help them get settled). Since Françoise flatly refuses to have a baby, they make preparations for Algeria. They give up their jobs, sell their car and their furniture, and say good-by to their friends, only to have their contact in Algeria cable them at the last minute not to come, that things are not working out there.

"Le Retour d'Afrique" (Return from Africa) is about the emotional return of Vincent and Françoise to Geneva after spending two weeks holed up in their empty apartment as ersatz exiles, hiding from their friends to whom Vincent had grandly explained their emigration by saying: "I don't want to suffocate in my own fat."

•

Much more, perhaps, than Tanner realizes, "Le Retour d'Afrique" is a very Swiss sort of movie. It has no great highs or lows. It is efficient, and it keeps wanting to be funnier than Tanner can quite allow it to be, as if the natural high spirits of Vincent and Françoise would somehow diminish their importance.

Far from diminishing their importance, the few scenes in which we see Vincent and Françoise behaving with something on the order of exuberance give them and the film a striking identity. Otherwise, "Le Retour d'Afrique" is too muted, too gray, like the photography that was apparently designed to make Geneva look like the world's dullest suburb that Tanner thinks it is.

The performances are attractive, especially those of Miss Destoop, who has a lot of the quality of Cher Buono, when Cher plays it straight, and of Juliet Berto, as a moody and funny Spanish exile in Switzerland.

I suspect that the principal problem with "Le Retour d'Afrique" is its screenplay, which Tanner wrote himself. It is never strong enough to prevent the boredom and futility experienced by Vincent and Françoise from seeping into the experience of watching the film. It opened yesterday at the 8th Street Playhouse.

1973 S 17, 41:1

The Cast

HIT! directed by Sidney J. Furie; screenplay by Alan R. Trustman and David M. Wolf; produced by Harry Korshak; music, Lalo Schifrin; director of photography, John A. Alonzo; editor, Argyle Nelson; distributed by Paramount Pictures. Running time: 134 minutes. At Loews State 2, Broadway at 45th Street, and Loews Orpheum Theater, 86th Street at Third Avenue. This film has been classified R.
Nick Allen .... Billy Dee Williams
Mike Willmer .... Richard Pryor
Barry Strong .... Paul Hampton
Sherry Nielson .... Gwen Welles
Dutch Schiller .... Warren Kemmerling
Ida .... Janet Brandt
Herman .... Sid Melton

By VINCENT CANBY

Sidney J. Furie, the Canadian-born director who made a couple of good, concise films early in his career ("The Leather Boys," "The Ipcress File"), now seems to be turning out movies as if they were yard goods. His "Lady Sings the Blues," which had the good fortune to star Diana Ross, ran almost two and a half hours and still never got around to telling the real story of Billie Holiday.

His new film, "Hit!," is a caper movie that was apparently designed as escapist entertainment, though by the time it enters its third hour you may well think you've been trapped. It isn't easy to leave a movie after you've invested that much time and money in it, no matter how foolish it is. You have a right to know how it turns out.

•

"Hit!" has a screenplay credited to Alan R. Trustman ("The Thomas Crown Affair") and David M. Wolf, but it looks very much like the sort of movie that was made up as it went along to match its landscapes (Los Angeles, Seattle, Marseilles).

The story, for what it's worth, is about a black Federal agent (Billy Dee Williams) who, after his teenage daughter is killed by drugs, takes it upon himself to recruit, finance, train and transport to France a small band of private American citizens willing to assassinate the nine leaders of a Marseilles drug syndicate.

Although the movie is about order outside law, it lacks even the offensive political purpose of something like Don Siegel's "Dirty Harry." It's a movie out for kicks, but the kicks are so implausible, so humorless, so

without redeeming style and wit, that to sit through it is to give oneself a false low.

•

In addition to Williams, the cast includes Richard Pryor, Gwen Welles, Paul Hampton, Warren Kemmerling, Janet Brandt and Sid Melton, who are the members of Williams's very unlikely gang. Miss Brandt and Melton, for example, play a nice little old Jewish couple who go along on the assassination trip as a way of thanking Uncle Sam for giving them a second chance. Miss Brandt slices the throat of her victim. Melton shoots his two targets in the chest and face.

"Hit!" opened yesterday at the Loews State 2 and Orpheum Theaters.

1973 S 19, 38:3

SAVE THE CHILDREN, directed by Stan Lathan; narrative written and spoken by Matt Robinson; editors, George Bowers and Paul Evans; produced by Mr. Robinson; executive producer, Clarence Avant; released by Paramount Pictures. At the Apollo Theater, 253 W. 125th Street; Beekman Theater, 65th Street at Second Avenue, and the Criterion Theater, Broadway at 45th Street. Running time: 123 minutes. This film is classified G.

With: Marvin Gaye, the Staple Singers, the Temptations, the Chi Lites, the Main Ingredient, the O'Jays, Isaac Hayes, Zulema, the Rev. Jesse Jackson, the Cannonball Adderly Quintet, the Push Mass Choir, Albertina Walker, Loretta Oliver, the Rev. James Cleveland, Bill Withers, Curtis Mayfield, Sammy Davis Jr., Roberta Flack, Quincy Jones, Gladys Knight and the Pips, Jerry Butler, Brenda Lee Eager, the Ramsey Lewis Trio, Nancy Wilson, the Jackson Five, Jackie Verdell and Dick Gregory.

"Save the Children," the movie spinoff (and theme) of last year's Black Exposition conducted by Operation PUSH (People to Save Humanity) in Chicago's Amphitheater, has the virtues of being forthright, unabashedly emotional and entertaining. And, if two hours of more than 30 black artists doing their musical things occasionally seem repetitive, the heart and craft of the performers (and speakers, including the Rev. Jesse Jackson, head of PUSH) project enough soul and meaning to captivate viewers.

The name "acts," who contributed their services to "Save the Children," now at the Criterion, Beekman and Apollo Theaters, constitute enough talent to fill a month of Sundays on the stage of Harlem's Apollo Theater. And they neatly complement the intercut arts, crafts and commerce displayed at the Exposition as well as the footage of Chicago's blacks, their churches, schools, slums and playgrounds.

Credit Stan Lathan, the director; Matt Robinson, the producer, and George Bowers and Paul Evans, the film's editors, with making "Save the Children" move briskly and with considerable impact in promoting

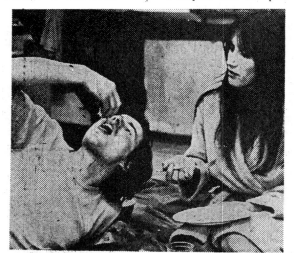

François Marthouret, left, and Josee Destoop

the hope for the future of its "Children." But it is really the performers in this teeming "cast" who make this bulging package of jazz, blues, rock, gospel, ballads and honest proseletyzing a gratifyingly varied and persuasive entertainment.

A. H. WEILER

1973 S 19, 40:2

The Cast

LA GRANDE BOUFFE (The Big Feast), directed by Marco Ferreri; screenplay and adaptation, Mr. Ferreri and Rafael Azcona; dialogue (French with English subtitles), Francis Blanche; produced by Jean Pierre Rossau; editors, Claudine Merlin, Gina Pignier; directors of cinematography, Mario Vulpiani and Pascuale Rachini; music, Philippe Sarde; a Mara Film-Capitolina production, released by ABKCO Films. Running time: 125 minutes. At the Little Carnegie Theater, 57th Street east of Seventh Avenue. This film has not been classified.

Marcello	Marcello Mastroianni
Ugo	Ugo Tognazzi
Michel	Michel Piccoli
Philippe	Philippe Noiret
Andrea	Andrea Ferreol

By VINCENT CANBY

Marco Ferreri, the Italian director whose "La Grande Bouffe" ("The Big Feast") opened at the Little Carnegie yesterday, is best known here for three films: "The Conjugal Bed" (1963), in which an eager 40-year-old bridegroom becomes a fatality, the victim of his lusty young wife's sexual appetites; "The Ape Woman" (1964), about a wretched lady covered with hair like a sheepdog's fur, and "The Man With the Balloons," about a fellow who is so obsessed with finding out how much air a balloon contains that he goes crazy and commits suicide.

These comedies now turn out to have been only warm-ups for "La Grande Bouffe," which so infuriated a number of Italians at this year's Cannes Film Festival that they insisted that Ferreri was not really Italian but French, which is the nationality of the film. It also fascinated a number of other people who weren't turned off by the spectacle of vomit and excrement. At the end of the festival the film was awarded the International Critics' Prize.

"La Grande Bouffe" is about four charming, middle-aged men who meet in a villa near Paris to spend a gourmet weakend to end all gourmet weekends. They are Marcello (Marcello Mastroianni), an airline pilot; Ugo (Ugo Tognazzi), a grand chef de cuisine; Michel (Michel Piccoli), a television producer, and Philippe (Philippe Noiret), a judge.

Early in their extraordinary revels they are joined by three pretty whores—who become quickly bored by all the eating and leave—and by a lovely, plump school teacher named Andrea (Andrea Ferreol), who stays on to eat and eat and eat, and to tend each man in his time. It soon becomes evident—although it's never stated explicitly—that the four men have joined in a suicide pact: they have decided to dine themselves to death.

"La Grande Bouffe" is not a successful film—it allows for too much pretentious, doomy interpretation. But if you can stand its almost childlike fascination with bodily functions and, toward the end, malfunctions), and the sight of food being eaten, slurped, sucked and stuffed, it is sometimes very funny in the robust bad taste of a joke about a flatulent bishop.

I say this perfectly aware that a lot of people will find "La Grande Bouffe" as disgusting as it sounds, and that there will be others who insist on seeing it as a solemn metaphor about the collective suicide of the bourgeoisie. Metaphors are an unfortunate Ferreri hangup. One of the four pactees in "La Grande Bouffe" meets his end slurping a pink gelatin dessert, sitting under a tree that once was a resting spot for Nicholas Boileau, the 17th-century poet and critic who advised prudence, moderation and common sense in all things.

•

If "La Grande Bouffe" were no more than a metaphor, or if it was meant as serious contemplation of a world's end, it would be intolerable; one of the most decadent films ever made.

It does, however, have a surface life of its own. It is vulgar vaudeville on an epic scale, beautifully performed by four of Europe's finest comic actors, as well as by Miss Ferreol, who shares her hosts' obsession with the food which, from time to time, is either equated with sex or confused with it.

Ferreri's preoccupation with the grotesque eventually grows tiresome. In the audience latent ulcers stir. But much of the time "La Grande Bouffe" works as a guilt-ridden fantasy of horrendously comic proportions. Its most weighty statement: "I ate too much."

1973, S 20, 64:3

ARNOLD'S WRECKING CO., directed by Steve De Souza; screenlay by Mr. De Souza; cameraman, Sam Virgoglini; music, Laurel Brothers/Blackstone/Solomon; produced by Otto G. Stoll 3d; released by Cine Globe, Inc. At the First Avenue Screening Room, at 61st Street. Running tim: 85 minutes. This film has been classified PG.

Arnold	Mike Ranshaw
Kenny	Steve De Souza
Rollo	Eddie Henderson
Mae	Shirley Kauffman
Officer Ace	Byron Schauer

A motion picture called "The Story of Dope" opened yesterday at the First Avenue Screening Room. It is a concise and well-observed pastiche of self-congratulatory industrial films in general and an impudent take-off on that coffee commercial in which El Exigente determines the future of growers by bestowing his favor on their crop. Only in this case the crop is marijuana.

Unfortunately, "The Story of Dope" is a film within a film, and to see it one must endure "Arnold's Wrecking Co.," a sophomoric celebration of marijuana and youthful smarts at the expense of an assortment of cartoon characters who might as well be wearing labels identifying them as Typical Jewish Mother and Stupid Corrupt Pig Cop.

The Arnold of the title is a preposterously straight and inept youth who comes to Philadelphia for a summer visit to his cousin Kenny, is forced to smoke marijuana, becomes an instant convert to its pleasures and proceeds to turn pusher. But he is a pusher on a mammoth scale, using the techniques and technology of big business in a concern he calls Arnold's Wrecking Co.

The idea reads better than it plays, and one need not look far for the culprit. The movie is directed by Steve De Souza from a screenplay by Mr. De Souza. The part of Kenny is played by Steve De Souza. The rewards of self-indulgence are to be found in "The Story of Dope"; the excesses are all too visible in "Arnold's Wrecking Co."

LAWRENCE VAN GELDER

1973 S 21, 48:1

Another Samurai Slice of Life

Out of the enmities loosed in 19th-century Japan by Western insistence on an end to its isolation, the director Masahiro Shinoda has fashioned another of his vexing samurai dramas.

Entitled "The Assassin," it opened yesterday at the Bijou, where another of Mr. Shinoda's films, "Sasuke Against the Wind," also played recently. What the two films share is a striving for epic quality and success mainly in sowing confusion. What redeems them both is their arresting and moody black-and-white photography (by Masao Kosugi).

On its most basic level, "The Assassin" is a recounting—mainly through flashbacks and flashbacks within flashbacks—of the downfall of Hachiro Kiyokawa, a farmer's son turned samurai possessed of an unusual sword that he believes has marked him for greatness.

To those who know him, Hachiro, played by Tetsuro Tanba, is an enigma. Is he a wanton killer or a man who fights only when necessary? Is he loyal to a shogunate too impotent to resist the pressures of foreigners or is he loyal to the xenophobic imperial forces? Is he an idealist or a self-seeking schemer? Trustworthy or dishonest?

Mr. Shinoda seems better at posing such questions than at resolving them with equal clarity and artistry on the scale of drama in which he is working.

LAWRENCE VAN GELDER

1973 S 20, 64:4

The Cast

GET TO KNOW YOUR RABBIT, directed by Brian De Palma; screenplay by Jordan Crittenden; produced by Steve Bernhardt and Paul Gaer; director of photography, John Alonzo; editor, Peter Colbert; music, Jack Elliott; distributed by Warner Brothers. Running time: 92 minutes. At neighborhood theaters. This film has been classified R.

Donald Beeman	Tom Smothers
The Terrific-Looking Girl	Katharine Ross
Mr. Delasandro	Orson Welles
Mr. Turnbull	John Astin
Paula	Suzanne Zenor
Susan	Samantha Jones
Vic	Allen Garfield

By VINCENT CANBY

Brian De Palma's "Get to Know Your Rabbit" was made three years ago; yet it did not arrive in New York until Wednesday, and then with less advance word than usually accompanies the opening of a Broadway shoe store. This casual treatment is unfortunate since De Palma ("Greetings," "Hi, Mom") is a very funny filmmaker. He's most funny, so far, anyway, when he's most anarchic, and "Get to Know Your Rabbit," though somewhat inhibited by conventional form, has enough hilarious loose ends and sidetracks to liberate the film from its form.

In outline, it's the story of a nice, clean-cut market analyst named Donald Beeman (Tom Smothers), who one day walks out of his office in the Los Angeles headquarters of Servo-Temp, Inc., to be a tap-dancing magician. It's Donald's aim to become perfectly seedy, which doesn't amuse his girl very much, especially when he comes home with the rabbit that's been issued to him at class. "It doesn't suit you," she says crossly, and then remembers how nice he looked with his attaché case colored burnt umber.

•

Donald's path to Perfect Seediness is littered with lunatics, some more desperate than others, like the airline pilot who, before each flight, climbs to the top of a tree and refuses to come down. "It's just butterflies," says a stewardess to a kindly fireman who wants to help. "If you can get him down now, he can still make the 10:52 flight to Detroit."

There's a depressed brassiere manufacturer (Allan Garfield), who dreams of finding a girl, someplace, somewhere, who appreciates a good, medium-priced bra. There also are old Mr. Delasandro (Orson Welles), who teaches Donald how to become a seedy, tap-dancing magician; Katharine Ross, a small-town girl who comes to worship Donald's lack of talent, and John Astin, a former executive at Servo-Temp whom Donald finds on Skid Row, clutching a wine bottle and a knapsack containing his dearest possessions (a matching pen-and-pencil desk set).

•

Tom Smothers makes a very cheerful, optimistic novice, though his Donald is never a pushover for the con artists he meets. When Mr. Delasandro, after graduating Donald magna cum laude, asks the young man if he would like to consider himself Mr. Delasandro's spiritual son, Donald thinks a minute, then says no.

Movies that promote the importance of non-conformity are almost always fraudulent or, what's worse, they're sentimental. "A Thousand Clowns" is a case in point. "Get to Know Your Rabbit" largely avoids those pitfalls, and with a great deal of comic exuberance. It also reinforces my expectation that De Palma will one day make a really fine American comedy.

1973 S 21, 49:1

The Cast

THE SPOOK WHO SAT BY THE DOOR, directed by Ivan Dixon; screenplay by Sam Greenlee and Melvin Clay, based on novel by Mr. Greenlee; produced by Mr. Dixon and Mr. Greenlee; music, Herbie Hancock; director of photography, Michael Hugo; editor, Michael Kahn; a Bokari, Ltd., film, distributed by United Artists. Running time: 102 minutes. At the De Mille Theater, Seventh Avenue at 47th Street, and Juliet 2 Theater, Third Avenue at 83rd Street. This film has been classified PG.

Dan Freeman	Lawrence Cook
Dahomey Queen	Paula Lawrence
Joy	Janet League
Dawson	J. A. Preston
Do-Daddy Dean	Paul Butler
Stud Davis	Don Blakely
Pretty Willie	David Lemieux
General	Byron Morrow
Carstairs	Jack Aaron

By VINCENT CANBY

In "The Spook Who Sat by the Door," Dan Freeman (Lawrence Cook), a mildmannered, bespectacled, black social worker who seems to know his place, allows himself to become the token by which the Central Intelligence Agency becomes integrated.

There is, of course, no thought of ever sending Dan into the field. Black men, otherwise invisible, have a tendency to be conspicuous as spies. They stand out. Dan is kept around the home office where he says "yes, sir" and "no, sir," and escorts sightseeing parties through the nonclassified sections. That, however, is just one side of Dan.

•

The other side is Dan Freeman as the superblack nationalist. After Dan has learned everything that the C.I.A. has to teach him about guerilla warfare and weaponry, he returns to Chicago to orgnize a black revolution that, at the end of the film, is about to bring white America to its knees.

Like Dan Greenlee's novel, on which it is based, "The Spook Who Sat by the Door" is a difficult work to judge coherently. It is such a mixture of passion, humor, hindsight, prophecy, prejudice and reaction that the fact that it's not a very well-made movie, and is seldom convincing as melodrama, is almost beside the point.

The rage it projects is real, even though the means by which that rage is projected are stereotypes. Black as well as white.

Mr. Greenlee, who adapted his novel for the screen with Melvin Clay, and co-produced the film with Ivan Dixon, the director, couldn't care less about convincing white audiences of anything except black anger. The white characters are even more idiotic than can easily be explained by their roles as C.I.A. officials and United States Senators. The blacks are either poetic proles or members of the corrupted black middle class.

•

"This is not about hating white folks," Freeman says as the black revolution is about to begin. "This is about loving freedom enough to fight and die for it."

In spite of what Dan Freeman says, the film equates the two. "The Spook Who Sat by the Door" stacks its cards, and in doing so, it raises black consciousness by trivializing several hundred years of black neglect.

1973 S 22, 18:1

Crime Not Only Pays, But It's Funny, Too

By VINCENT CANBY

WHILE television thrives on unimportance, some of it less trivial than the rest, moviegoers have become increasingly stern about the unimportant film, not the bad film but the good, entertaining - for - as - long - as - it - takes - to - watch movie that, afterwards, disappears from the memory with the completeness of rain sinking into a desert. I'm not talking about unimportant schlocky movies, some of which, like "Cleopatra Jones," achieve financial rewards by meeting some contemporary needs or by being a part of some particular fashion.

I have in mind two specific movies, both farces and both charming in rather different ways, which opened here in August and which, to be blunt about it, should probably win no awards anywhere, although they should amuse vast numbers of people. They are Aram Avakian's ebullient "Cops and Robbers," about a couple of New York cops who become robbers simply because they're fed up, and Yves Robert's French-language "The Tall Blond Man With One Black Shoe," a funny spy movie with no foreign intrigue whatsoever.

Each of us has his own definition of what movie entertainment should be. There's the creep who says "I don't want to *think*, I want to be *entertained*," as if movies were hamburgers, to be consumed through the mouth. There's the kind of person who is entertained by film used as an instrument for social and political consciousness-raising, and there is always the buff who can be in joyous transport for weeks remembering a particular tracking shot in "Juarez." In view of the tremendous competition for our attention, one is hard-put to defend good-but-unimportant films. Seeing them will not change our lives, but (according to my definition) they have wit, style, even some ideas, though the ideas need not be brand new. They never insult the intelligence, either ours or those of the filmmakers.

"Cops and Robbers" is another caper movie (sigh), and it may be that by this time it's impossible for any caper movie, no matter how bright it is, to overcome completely our fatigue with the form. Thus starting several hundred yards behind "Go," Aram Avakian, the director,

and Donald E. Westlake, who wrote the screenplay, have succeeded admirably in almost catching up.

Avakian, the film editor who made his directorial debut with a thoroughly mixed up and pruned down film adaptation of Barth's "The End of The Road," gives us hints now and then that he wants his new film to make An Important Statement about urban life, but most of the time he allows the characters to do the talking, which is mostly about the happily liberated greed of two nice New York cops (Cliff Gorman and Joe Bologna), suburban family men who decide that there must be something better than commuting daily to tend to Manhattan's problems.

How the two men successfully bring off a Wall Street heist of $10-million in negotiable bonds, and manage to outwit the Mafia, becomes the material for marvelously plausible farce that includes one of the best chase sequences I've seen in three months (which is about as long as I care to remember most movie chase sequences).

The movie stumbles from time to time. There are a couple of sequences that mean to show us some of the horrors of New York City life, but while the horrors are real, the sequences overmotivate the cops' decision to go crooked. In the kind of rollicking, wise-talking farce that "Cops and Robbers" does best, people can be cruel, stupid and venal, but they shouldn't get hurt too badly.

"The Tall Blond Man With One Black Shoe" is up to its ears in corpses at the end, but that's the sort of farce it is. Death is not forever in this kind of movie. It's more a way of making an exit. One of the reasons the film is so funny is that each character in it has been drained of a sense of humor, like Francois (Pierre Richard), the young violinist-hero who, when someone nails his shoes to the floor outside his Munich

hotel room (he'd hoped to have them shined), simply puts on the two nearest shoes that fit and returns to Paris that way. Solemnly. Francois is a fine comic figure, affable, gentle-natured and incapable of the kind of deviousness that everyone else in the film traffics in.

•

The movie is concerned with espionage for its own sake. Francois, unknown to him, is chosen by the head of a French intelligence agency to act as a decoy to trap the agency's over-zealous second-in-command, a fierce rabbit of a man named Milan (Bernard Blier), who persists in trying to run the agency himself.

The comedy of "The Tall Blond Man With One Black Shoe" depends entirely on misunderstanding, and since Milan is able to bug Francois' day-to-day activities with hidden microphones, and sometimes with hidden television cameras, the opportunities for misunderstanding are quintupled. "He's flushing the toilet," says one of the agents monitoring Francois' apartment. "I wonder what that means." Milan scans Francois' biography and comments grimly: "A normal life. . . . The perfect cover."

*

Mireille Darc plays a pretty blond agent who has been assigned to spy on Francois and winds up falling in love with him (but not before he has somehow, innocently, managed to catch her hair in the zipper of his pants). She and Blier are probably the only people in the film you'll recognize, but the cast is excellent even when the story falls rather heavily into the deep end of foolishness.

You may especially like Jean Carmet, a short, wide-bottomed man who plays Francois' best friend, the husband of a woman who thinks she's madly in love with Francois, whom she attacks in his apartment every free

afternoon. It's the husband's curious experience to be riding a bicycle across Paris and to come upon a florist's delivery truck, from the inside of which he hears the voice of his wife making love to another man. The florist's delivery truck is, of course, the "cover" for the agents who are listening to the goings-on in Francois' apartment.

Well, it isn't comedy of the highest order, but most of it is thoroughly winning.

*

It isn't easy to make a good unimportant movie, as Sidney J. Furie demonstrates in his newest film, "Hit!" a caper movie about a couple of United States narcotics agents—one black, one white—who, on their own time, set out to bust the top drug people in Marseilles in a day of multiple assassinations. The movie is not only a stupid rip-off on "The French Connection," it seems positively spendthrift. It runs for well over two hours (though it never does get around to explaining a number of important plot points) and it was shot on location in California, Washington and France with such seriousness that you expect the reality of the locations to rub off on the film itself. It doesn't.

"Hit!" unravels at such a ponderous pace that it might even prompt thinking by people who don't want to think at the movies: the loose ends of the narrative don't entertain, they irritate. They make you want to talk back to the screen, or leave the theater.

Because each of us has his own definition of what entertainment is, I suppose "Hit!" could well be someone else's idea of a good unimportant movie. But then there are some people who read Jacqueline Susann for fun, some people who read her enviously, to find out what the secret of her financial success is, and some who look to her prose for Rules to Live By.

1973 S 23, II:1:6

Brother Caring for Brother

By MARY E. MEBANE ("LIZA")

BOTH "Gordon's War" and "Cleopatra Jones" are important films. They are remarkably accurate in reflecting the mood, the ambience, the sensibility of the seventies in black communities across the nation. Such an accurate reflection is startling, for movies are many months in preparation and by the time the moviegoer puts his money down, he gets to see what was the going thing—two or three years ago.

"Gordon's War" and "Cleopatra Jones" are also revolutionary films, though each in a different way.

Unlike the recent films "Shaft in Africa" and "Super Fly TNT," which reflect the thinking of avant-garde black intellectuals of the period circa 1965-1970, when there was a strong identification with Africa, the Motherland — the afro, the dashiki, Swahili — in the belief that such an identification was the most effective answer to white racism in the United States, "Gordon's War" and "Cleopatra Jones" portray a different mood: far from concentrating on

sters and is weakening the social fabric of family and community. Both films deal with that fact of life in the inner cities, one in Los Angeles, the other in New York.

On the surface, "Cleopatra Jones" is about a black distaff James Bond who drives a fancy car equipped with a submachine gun in the door, wears smart clothes, is a karate expert, and travels all over the world as a United States secret agent, destroying the poppy wherever it is found, before it can get to the United States and enter some luckless individual's arm.

Underneath, however, there is the story of black people loving and helping each other—in many ways. In contrast to the first wave of black films, such as "Shaft" and "Cotton Comes To

itation center in Los Angeles. Though they are shown embracing, they are not shown undressed. They are a compatible pair, each doing in his own way what he can to stem the tide of drugs in the inner city, she as a secret agent, he as a drug abuse counselor. To show that human feeling is not the exclusive province of the "good guys" even Doodle Bug and Tiffany, the black gangster and his girlfriend, show affection for each other.

There is brother caring for brother as the counselor watches over a young man who is undergoing withdrawal pains, and warmth and respect between the generations as Cleopatra goes to her

about what they are going to do — some day; they have a plan, carefully thought out, carefully escalated, and they put it into effect—with deadly results.

"Gordon's War" is a revolutionary picture in that it is a how-to-do-it picture, a plan for community action. First, it says, gather intelligence on drug pushers, then harass the small-time operators, next smash the drug factories, and then seek out the suppliers. The picture is realistic in that the fourth step is incomplete at the end—they do not yet know who "Mr. Big" is, but Gordon is alive and one has reason to believe

In "Gordon's War," Paul Winfield, right, holds Harlem drug pusher Joseph Lacosta captive with the aid of fellow Vietnam veterans David Downing and Carl Lee.

Africa, they deal with the problems of black folk in the United States.

"Gordon's War" and "Cleopatra Jones" reflect the mood of the seventies in another way: they show strengths in the black communities, unlike such recent films as "Super Fly," "The Mack," "Trick Baby" and "Black Caesar," all of which accurately portray the weaknesses in the black community, but which give a grossly distorted picture because weakness is all that is portrayed.

A major problem facing the black community is drug abuse—mainly the hard drugs, heroin and cocaine — that is destroying the lives of many young-

Harlem," which showed the relationship between men and women as being either perfunctorily physical or hostile — "Shaft's Big Score" actually opened on an explicit bedroom scene; "Super Fly" had a naked bathing scene; "Black Caesar" had a scene in which a black woman was beaten and sexually assaulted by Black Caesar—this film, "Cleopatra Jones," portrays the relationships between black men and black women as supportive and lasting.

*

The heroine has a stable, warm relationship with the head of a drug rehabil-

old neighborhood to seek out Mrs. Johnson, whose two sons, both karate experts, help her uncover some wrongdoers.

Though personal love plays a part in "Gordon's War"—it is love for his dead wife, the victim of a drug overdose, that enrages Vietnam veteran Gordon Hudson—it is concern for the whole Harlem community that sets him in action. And it is the action—a war against drug peddlers—that makes this picture revolutionary. For Gordon and the men from his old Vietnam company take the law into their own hands, without calling on the police. They do not dream

that he will continue his search. It is also realistic in that it shows the underworld community fighting back once it is threatened; one of Gordon's men is killed.

But the first two operations are a call to action by the citizenry: everyone in inner cities can gather intelligence, and there are thousands of ex-service personnel who are quite capable of "harassing the hostiles."

This could easily be a picture where life follows art.

1973 S 23, II:13:6

The Cast

HARRY IN YOUR POCKET, directed by Bruce Geller; written by James David Buchanan and Ron Austin; director of photography, Fred Koenekamp; film editor, Arthur L. Hilton; music, Lalo Schifrin; produced by Mr. Geller; released by United Artists. At the Forum Theater, Broadway at 46th Street; the Festival Theater, Fifth Avenue and 57th Street; the Riviera Theater, Broadway and 96th Street and neighborhood theaters. Running time: 103 minutes. This film is classified PG.

Harry .... James Coburn
Ray .... Michael Sarrazin
Sandy .... Trish Van Devere
Casey .... Walter Pidgeon
Fance .... Michael C. Gwynne
First Detective .... Tony Giorgio
Second Detective ...... Michael Stearns
Francine .... Sue Mullen

By LAWRENCE VAN GELDER

The peripatetic world of pickpockets has provided the producer-director Bruce

Geller, who gave television audiences "Mission: Impossible" and "Mannix" with the material for a promising debut in feature films.

"Harry in Your Pocket," playing at the Forum and Riviera theaters, is a film of many pleasures, not the least of which is the thoroughgoing professionalism that sets up its goals — good performances, eye-catching settings, absorbing story—and achieves every one of them with clean precision.

•

Below the glossy surface of things, this is also a film

with something to say about crime and morality, jealousy and loyalty, youth and age and the pleasures of craftsmanship in a world where everyone wants to start at the top and no one wants to serve an apprenticeship.

For those who know nothing of the art of picking pockets, the movie is a kind of a vocational school and a type of Berlitz school. The vocational school offers an education in the techniques of picking pockets— the work of cannons (master pickpockets), steerers (victim spotters) and stalls (who distract victims). From the Berlitz comes a

language of kicks (pockets) and holding (retaining possession of a poke, or wallet.).

The teachers are James Coburn as Harry, the cannon whose first law is "Harry Never Holds"; Walter Pidgeon as the steerer, and Michael Sarrazin and his girl friend, Trish Van Devere, who hire on with the two old pros as stalls.

Mr. Coburn covets not only cash and credit cards but Miss Van Devere. Mr. Sarrazin covets Mr. Coburn's skills and success; Mr. Pidgeon covets cocaine and immortality of a sort, and Miss Van Devere—well, without her, things would

be a lot less interesting.

For all its polish, there is a bittersweetness to "Harry in Your Pocket" and moments reminiscent of "The Hustler" and "The Cincinnati Kid." You'll come away from it checking your pockets, but not because it has taken your money without giving good entertainment in return.

1973 S 24, 39:1

The Program

INSIDE WOMEN: LIVING WITH PETER by Miriam Weinstein, 22 minutes; THOUGHT DREAMS, 3 minutes; GOODMAN, 12 minutes; TRACES, 14 minutes, all by Barbara Linkevitch; APPROACHING MARA by Susanne Szabo Rostock, 12 minutes; DIANE by Mary Feldhaus-Weber, 29 minutes. At the Film Forum, 256 West 88th Street. Friday through Sunday, 8 P.M.

"Under the collective title "Inside Women" or "Portrait of the Artist as a Young Woman," a program of six short films ranging from the surreal to the documentary ushered in the fourth season of the Film Forum last weekend. The program will be repeated next weekend.

As a unit, the program is never less than interesting, frequently dazzling and well worth a visit from anyone with serious interest in film as art, and with genuine curiosity about what talented independent film makers are doing.

Individually, the quality ranges from the tentative and self-conscious, as in the case of Miriam Weinstein's "Living With Peter," to the fully realized combination of sight, sound and sensitivity that elevates "Diane," Mary Feldhaus-Weber's exploration of an actress's life, to a memorable level of accomplishment.

Moving away from the documentary approach, Barbara Linkevitch's "Traces" and Susanne Szabo Rostock's "Approaching Mara" exhibit their artistry through the use of color and impression. Two short, surreal works in black and white by Miss Linkevitch round out the program.

The Film Forum is supported by the New York State Council on the Arts and the National Endowment for the Arts. In this case, both have spent their money admirably.

LAWRENCE VAN GELDER

1973 S 24, 39:2

The Casts

THE MAN CALLED NOON, directed by Peter Collinson; screenplay by Scot Finch, based on the novel by Louis L'Amour; director of photography, John Cabrera; music, Luis Bacalov; produced by Euan Lloyd; released by National General Pictures. At neighborhood theaters. Running time: 97 minutes. This film is classified R.

Noon .... Richard Crenna
Rimes .... Stephen Boyd
Fan .... Rosanna Schiaffino
Judge Niland .... Farley Granger
Peg .... Patty Shepard
Janish .... Angel Del Pozo
Bayles .... Howard Ross
Henneker .... Jose Jaspe
and

TRIPLE IRONS, directed by Chang Cheh; screenplay by I. Kuang; cinematographer, Kung Mu-to; editing, Kuo Ting-hung; musical director, Chen Yung-huang; production supervised by Run Run Shaw; released by National General Pictures. At neighborhood theaters. Running time: 99 minutes. This film is classified R.

Pa Chiao .... LI Ching
Lei Li .... David Chiang
Feng Chun-chieh .... Ti Lung
Lung I-chih .... Ku Feng
Chen Chen-nan .... Chen Hsing
Chin Fen .... Wang Chung

Perhaps it's chauvinistic but the West wins over the East in the double dish of ersatz adventures, "The Man Called Noon" and "Triple Irons," that are playing in local theaters. But it's a minor triumph since the manufactured action in both is aimed largely at producing gore rather than persuasive logic or artistic excitement.

There are no karate chops in "Triple Irons," the Oriental martial-arts exhibition turned out in Hong Kong and dubbed into English. Its small distinction is David Chiang, as a one-armed, handsome hero, who is the handiest man around with two swords. And, to the accompaniment of comic-book dialogue, grunts, grimaces and scores of corpses, he finally dispatches Ku Feng, the bandit-villain and master of those destructive triple iron bars that cost him his arm in the first place. Even with a pretty heroine, Li Ching, around, a visit to this familiar, bloody kung-fu country isn't necessary.

•

"The Man Called Noon," filmed on rugged, Spanish mountain locations, is fairly successful in maintaining some mystery, as Richard Crenna, its amnesiac, gunfighter seeks to find his true identity and a hidden fortune.

Under Peter Collinson's brisk direction, the chases, fights and shootouts are serious and practically continuous. But the equally serious characterizations cry for fuller explanations.

•

Farley Granger, as a bearded, scheming judge, who, like Patty Shepard, is out to grab that fortune, and Rosanna Schiaffino, as the well-endowed heroine who aids and loves Mr. Crenna, may be occasionally effective but they are rarely as large as life.

Mr. Crenna is fairly convincing in an underplayed performance that makes him as much an intellectual as a gunslinger. "I get the feeling," he muses at one point in his search, "that I've been here before." That wise observation generally could apply to both "The Man Called Noon" and "Triple Irons."

A. H. WEILER

1973 S 25, 37:1

SISTERS, directed by Brian De Palma; screenplay by Mr. De Palma and Louisa Rose, based on a story by Mr. De Palma; produced by Edward R. Pressman; music, Bernard Herrmann; director of photography, Gregory Sandor; editor, Paul Hirsch; distributed by American International Pictures. Running time: 92 minutes. At the Penthouse Theater, Broadway at 47th Street, R.K.O. 86th Street Twin 1 Theater, 86th Street near Lexington Avenue, and 59th Street Twin 1 Theater, 59th Street east of Third Avenue. This film has been classified R.

Danielle Breton .... Margot Kidder
Grace Collier .... Jennifer Salt
Joseph Larch .... Charles Durning
Emil Breton .... Bill Finley
Philip Woode .... Lisle Wilson
Mr. McLennen .... Barnard Hughes
Mrs. Collier .... Mary Davenport
Detective Kelly .... Dolph Sweet

By VINCENT CANBY

Grace Collier (Jennifer Salt) has several problems. She writes for a Staten Island newspaper that isn't as interested in news as it is in civic promotion. She has a mother who wants her to get married. "The Cunningham girl," her mother says one day, "is engaged. He's a doctor. Well, he's really a veterinarian, but all the animals are owned by wealthy people." Grace's biggest problem is the Staten Island policeman who refuses to believe her when she says she saw a man murdered in an apartment across the way.

•

This is pretty much the beginning of Brian De Palma's "Sisters," a good, substantial horror film with such a sense of humor that it never can quite achieve the solemnly repellent peaks of Roman Polanski's "Repulsion." Never, however, does it become the sort of Nancy Drew detective tale it otherwise resembles, at least in outline.

At the center of the story is a lovely French-Canadian girl named Danielle Breton (Margot Kidder), one of a pair of separated Siamese twins. Danielle, like so many young women in horror stories of this sort, has a terrible guilt complex about sex, and it is in her apartment that Grace thinks she saw a man repeatedly stabbed, then write "help" on the window in his own blood.

The screenplay, by Mr. De Palma and Louisa Rose, cuts back and forth between Grace's investigation of the murder, with the help of a persistent though none-too-bright private detective, and Danielle's story, quite stunningly presented through news film and drug fantasies that take the narrative place of flashbacks.

Mr. De Palma, best known for his anarchic comedy ("Hi, Mom," "Get to Know Your Rabbit"), reveals himself here to be a first-rate director of more or less conventional material that has associations not only with "Repulsion" but also with Hitchcock's "Psycho." The "Psycho" associations are unfortunate, since they tip one important plot point sooner than is absolutely necessary.

•

The performances are fine, especially Miss Kidder's as the loony twin whom we first meet when she's doing a walk-on on a popular television quiz show called "Peeping Toms," which, like so many of Mr. De Palma's comic fancies, is just terrible enough to become a reality.

An intelligent horror film is very rare these days. "Sisters," which opened at three theaters yesterday, is just the thing to see on one of those nights when you want to go to the movies for the old-fashioned fun of it.

1973 S 27,44:4

Finnish Film Festival

Titta Karakorpi and Aarno Sulkanen in one of the festival films, "Under the Northern Star."

By PAUL GARDNER

Just try telling someone that you're off to a festival of Finnish films and the response is likely to be, "Did you say *finished* films?"

Although film has become an international art, it's still hard to imagine that such countries as Brazil, Nigeria and, yes, Finland, have small film industries of their own. To let filmgoers here know that Finland is not just the country of saunas and Sibelius, the library at Lincoln Center and Cinema Dimensions, a distribution company, are presenting, through Saturday, 13 Finnish films in the library's museum.

In recent years, the only Finnish director to emerge with any recognition was Jorn Donner, and most of his films have been Swedish productions. His bubbly sex comedy, "To Love," starring Harriet Andersson, was shown several years ago at the New York Film Festival and then had a modest run here. Donner's worldly film, influenced by Ingmar Bergman's light comedies, had a kicky champagne spirit.

Change Is Sought

I remember "To Love" because it aroused my curiosity about Finland—and the Finnish movie industry. Donner is not included in the festival. The sponsors understandably wanted to introduce other directors. His presence was missed.

"There's a lot of talent in Finland," says Richard Anobile of Cinema Dimensions, "but the films are not considered commercial on foreign markets." He's right, but he hopes to change the situation with Finnish-American co-productions.

The grand old man of Finnish theater and films is apparently Edvin Laine, whose three-hour epic of Finnish history, "Under the Northern Star," opened the festival and will be shown again this week. The color, widescreen film, based on a popular Finnish trilogy, might be described as Finland's "Gone With the Wind."

With a big cast in interweaving stories covering two generations, "Star" shows the plucky nation's suffering and stumbling progress—from a grand duchy of Russia to independence and civil war. Like a Cecil B. DeMille pageant, the canvas is almost too cumbersome, the characters are cardboard and yet, despite elements of operatic kitsch, the director knows how to build suspense and pathos while giving a thumbnail sketch of Finnish history.

Old-Fashioned Personality

His plot devices are old-fashioned, but you have to admire the unabashed sentiment of his last shot: a bedraggled soldier returning home in the howling rain. Obviously there was a personality behind this work, which I did not feel at all in the two other "modern" movies I saw.

"Worker's Diary" by Risto Jarva deals with contemporary life in Finland, which rises like a glassy skyscraper on the edge of a primeval forest. It touches, but only blandly, the monotony—and isolation—in the marriage of a clerical secretary and her husband, a factory foreman. It's almost as if the director were embarrassed by the bleakness of his material.

"Green Widow," by Jaakko Pakkasvirta, is a suburban housewife who finds relief from her philandering, boorish husband with a mini-affair of her own. The mad housewife, ably played by Eija Pokkinen, is the sort of striking Finn who usually runs to Paris—one of the exotic Left Bank Lapps.

But this "Green Widow" is strangely repressed. The social mores reflected in her life are related to yesterday, to the late nineteen-fifties. I refuse to believe that the ultimate Finnish decadence is a marijuana cigarette smoked in the late afternoon.

My impression from these films is that the Finns have resources. What they really need is boldness—and cinematic vision.

1973 S 27, 44:1

The Cast

THE SLAMS, directed by Jonathan Kaplan; written by Richard L. Adams; director of photography, Andrew Davis; editor, Morton Tubor; art director, Jack Fisk; music, Luther Henderson; sound, Bill Kaplan; wardrobe, Jodie Tillen; produced by Gene Corman; a Penelope Productions, Inc., picture; released by Metro-Goldwyn-Mayer. At the Cinerama, Broadway at 47th Street, and the R.K.O. 86th Street Twin No. 2 Theaters. Running time: 91 minutes. Rated R.

Curtis Hook .... Jim Brown
Iris Daniel .... Judy Pace
Stambell .... Roland "Bob" Harris
Jackson Barney .... Paul E. Harris
Capiello .... Frank de Kova
Glover .... Ted Cassidy
Macey .... Frenchia Guizon
Sergeant Flood .... John Dennis

"I can always take care of myself," Jim Brown assures his mother just before starting a stretch in "The Slams" for heisting $1.5-million, which everyone, including "the syndicate," in that titular California prison wants.

There's no need to worry, mama. Our black, tough hero has been successfully taking on all comers as a top full-back and in 15 muscular movies before this one smashed into the Cinerama and R.K.O. 86th Street yesterday. And the results are about as unusual as a television rerun of a hard-fought football game.

The now all too familiar clashes involving black and white machismo are here, including explicit, colloquial dialogue, fights between cons, bloodshed and a prison break as Mr. Brown keeps the whereabouts of the loot secret from Frank de Kova (the incarcerated mob boss), Roland Harris (the black prison guard captain), the black and white inmates and even the warden.

Mr. Brown is his normal stoic but rough self as he finally escapes to that Caribbean sanctuary with the loot and his girl, Judy Pace.

"While they're making it," he remarks smugly, "we're taking it." But "The Slams" doesn't give the viewer much more than gory, explosive action.

A. H. WEILER

1973 S 27, 45:1

The Cast

THE SCARLET CAMELLIA (GOBEN NO TSUBAKI), directed by Yoshitaro Nomura; screenplay (Japanese) with English subtitles) by Masato Molda, based on the novel by Shugoro Yamamoto; photography by Ko Kawamato; music by Yasushi Akutagawa; art direction by Takashi Matsuyama and Chiyoo Umeda; produced by Shiro Kido. At the Bijou Theater, 209 West 45th Street. Running time: 117 minutes. This film has not been rated.

Oshino .... Shima Iwashita
Kihei Musashiya .... Yoshi Kato
Osono .... Sachiko Hidari
Gen. Maruumeya .... Elli Okada
Aoki .... Go Kato

On the landscape of old Japan, Yoshitaro Nomura, the director, has sown the seeds of a 20th-century psychological murder story and reaped a harvest of teary melodrama in "The Scarlet Camellia," which opened yesterday at the Bijou.

It's the kind of movie you don't see much around here any more, with footprints in the snow, convenient rains, autumn leaves swirling in a prison courtyard and a weepy girl — with consumption — as its focal point.

Unfortunately, Oshino, played by Shima Iwashita exhausts patience and sympathy long before she graduates from the adolescent moralizing that has prompted her to incinerate her sluttish mother, skewer several of that woman's lovers with silver hair pins and condemn her true father to shame, madness and the suicide of his wife. All this is by way of making up to her stepfather for the suffering he put up with at the hands of her mother.

Visually, it is all very lovely, but at .ottom it promises more than it can deliver.

LAWRENCE VAN GELDER

1973 S 27, 45:1

The Cast

DEADLY CHINA DOLL, directed by Huang Feng; screenplay by Ho Jen; cinematography, Li Yiu-tang; editor, Chiang Lung; music by Joseph Koo; assistant director, Chou Hsiao-pei; sets designed by Tsao Nien-lung; make-up, Siao Hsin-mei; produced by Andrew G. Vajna; A Panasia Film Production; released by Metro-Goldwyn-Mayer. At neighborhood theaters. Running time: 94 minutes, Rated R.

Chin Su-hua .... Angela Mao
Pai Chien .... Carter Huang
Han Fei .... Yen I-feng
Hu Szu .... Nan Kung-hsun
Chin .... Ke Hsiang-ting

Angela Mao, the Billie Jean King of Kung-fu films, came back to town again yesterday in another Wimbledon of mayhem.

Distinguishable from its predecessors principally by means of its title, "Deadly China Doll" pairs Miss Mao once again with Carter Huang, in competition against opium smugglers and hijackers. The outcome is never in doubt.

Suffice it to say that Miss Mao seems to have suffered no loss of skills since last seen here a couple of weeks back in "Lady Kung Fu." The stunning backhands, forehands, drop shots and overheads are all there, as well as that particular contribution of the martial arts films, the sternum crunch.

The dialogue and most of the performances are as deadly as the principals. Miss Mao works very hard, and one only hopes that, like Miss King, she earns equal pay.

LAWRENCE VAN GELDER

1973 S 27, 45:1

The Cast

FROM THE MIXED-UP FILES OF MRS. BASIL E. FRANKWEILER, directed by Fielder Cook; screenplay by Blanche Hanalis, based on the novel by E. L. Konigsburg; produced by Charles G. Mortimer Jr.; director of photography, Victor J. Kemper; editor, Eric Albertson; music, Donald Devor; a Westfall production, distributed by Cinema 5. Running time: 105 minutes. At the Radio City Music Hall. This film has been classified G.

Mrs. Frankweiler .... Ingrid Bergman
Claudia .... Sally Prager
Jamie .... Johnny Doran
Saxonburg .... George Rose
Mr. Kincaid .... Richard Mulligan
Mrs. Kincaid .... Georgann Johnson
Schoolteacher .... Madeline Kahn

By VINCENT CANBY

When Fielder Cook's "From the Mixed-Up Files of Mrs. Basil E. Frankweiler" opens, we see 12-year old Claudia Kincaid (Sally Prager) running through the New Jersey wood, finally coming to rest hugging a tree. Claudia is a restless romantic. She wants to be Lady Guinevere. Any movie that defines an adolescent's restless romanticism in terms of tree-hugging is, I have found, usually a fake.

Little girls hug cats, sometimes fatally. They hug dogs, horses, gerbils and, if allowed, they would probably hug parakeets, opossums, lions, tigers and polar bears. Little girls will hug almost any kind of creature, as long as it breathes and is soft to the touch. Trees are an adult fancy.

•

It's not an accident that Claudia hugs a tree. "From the Mixed-Up Files of Mrs. Basil E. Frankweiler" is one of those G-rated movies about children, not as they are but as they appear in television commercials for things like peanut butter and potato chips. They play out adult dreams in adult gestures.

Claudia and her 10-year-old brother Jamie (Johnny Doran) run away from home and take up residence in the Metropolitan Museum of Art, where Thomas Hoving's ever-alert guards somehow never come upon them, even though the children clatter through the halls and exhibition rooms at all hours of the day and night. They are horribly stanch youngsters. They bathe nightly in the pool in the cafeteria (with their underwear on) and regularly change their socks.

Somewhere along the line, they come upon a movie plot of sorts: they will authenticate the origins of a statue that has been attributed to Michelangelo. These children are not only clean, they are also scholarly.

Their investigation leads them eventually to the home of Mrs. Basil E. Frankweiler, described as a wealthy recluse, who is played in the film's last 25 minutes by Ingrid Bergman wearing a white wig and long black dress of the sort usually worn by the male lead in "Charley's Aunt."

The screenplay by Blanche Hanalis is based on E. L. Konigsburg's novel, which, I am told, is immensely popular among fourth-graders. There may also be some interest in the fact that a large portion of the film was shot in the Metropolitan, with the museum's cooperation.

I guess this gives the movie some quasi-educational status, which is the only status it deserves. It opened yesterday at the Radio City Music Hall.

1973 S 28, 25:1

The Cast

DAY FOR NIGHT (La Nuit Amercaine), directed by Francois Truffaut; screenplay (French with English subtitles) by Mr. Truffaut, Jean-Louis Richard and Suzanne Schiffman; executive producer, Marcel Berbert; director of photography, Pierre-William Glenn; editors. Yann Dedet, Martine Barraque; music, Georges Delerue; a production of Les Films du Carrosse (Paris) and P.I.C. (Rome), distributed by Warner Brothers. Running time 116 minutes. At the New York Film Festival at Fisher Hall, Lincoln Center. (Opens Oct. 7 at the Festival Theater, 57th Street near Fifth Avenue.) This film has been classified PG.

Ferrand .... Francois Truffaut
Julie .... Jacqueline Bisset
Alphonse .... Jean-Pierre Leaud
Severine .... Valentina Cortese
Alexandre .... Jean-Pierre Aumont
Lilianna .... Dani
Stacey .... Alexandra Stewart
Bertrand .... Jean Champion

By VINCENT CANBY

Movie-making is a strange business, says Severine (Valentina Cortese), an actress who steadies her nerves by sipping champagne on the set of "Meet Pamela," a rather tacky melodrama being made within François Truffaut's exhilarating new comedy about movie-making, "Day for Night."

"As soon as we grasp things," says Severine, "they're gone."

In one way and another, almost all of Truffaut's films have been aware of this impermanence, which, instead of making life and love seem cheap, renders them especially precious.

•

Worthy adventures are risky; they are headlong plunges into the unknown. Whether they end with a shotgun murder ("La Peau Douce"), middle-class boredom ("Bed and Board") or total isolation ("Jules and Jim") is not so important as the acceptance of the gamble itself. The quality of an experience cannot be measured by its duration or its end. Longevity is for redwood trees.

The original French title of "Day for Night" is "La Nuit Americaine," which is what French movie makers call the method by which a scene shot in daylight is made to look like night through the use of filters. "Day for Night" is a hilarious, wise and moving chronicle about the members of a crew who come together for seven weeks at the Victorine Studios in Nice to manufacture a movie, an illusion that is, for the period of its production, more important than life itself.

•

They include Ferrand (Truffaut), the director who observes at one point that making a movie is like a stagecoach trip through the old West ("At first you hope for a pleasant trip. Then you simply hope to reach your destination"); Julie (Jacqueline Bisset), the beautiful Hollywood star of the film within; Alphonse (Jean-Pierre Léaud), a nice, nut-brained young actor preoccupied by movies and women, in that order; Alexandre (Jean-Pierre Aumont), the aging male lead of the film within, and Severine (Miss Cortese), Alexandre's co-star and former mistress, who is genuinely pleased for Alexandre when he reveals plans to settle down with his new young male lover.

"Day for Night" is Truffaut's fondest, most compassionate film, and although it is packed with references to films and film people (Welles, Vigo, Fellini, Buñuel, among others) and although it is dedicated to Lillian and Dorothy Gish, it's not a particu-

Jacqueline Bisset and Francois Truffaut, director, in a scene from the movie, "Day for Night."

larly inside movie. That is, it has great fun showing us how movies are made, how rain and snow are manufactured, how animals are directed (or not), how acts of God can affect a script, but its major concerns are people working at a profession they love, sometimes to the exclusion of everything else.

The movie people are different from you and me, Truffaut seems to say, but only in the intensity of their passions and in constantly having to differentiate between reality and its various reflections. Romantic alliances are always shifting. Infatuation is mistaken for love (and, for a moment, it may really be love). Severine becomes hysterical after fluffing half a dozen takes because the make-up girl is doubling as a maid in a brief scene. "In my day," she screams, "make-up was make-up, and an actress was an actress."

The performances are superb. Miss Cortese, and Miss Bisset are not only both hugely funny but also hugely affecting, in moments that creep up on you without warning. It's no accident, I suspect, that the only characters who come close to being either evil (the jealous wife of the film's production manager) or uninteresting (Julie's doctor husband) are nonmovie people. In "Day for Night," Truffaut is looking at the world from inside a glorious obsession: everyone outside looks a little gray and dim.

•

"Day for Night," which begins its commercial engagement Oct. 7 at the Festival Theater, was the opening attraction of the New York Film Festival last night at Lincoln Center. Never has the festival been so appropriately begun.

1973 S 29, 22:1

The Cast

QUE HACER, directed by Saul Landau, Nina Serrano, Raul Ruiz; screenplay by Mr. Landau, Miss Serrano and Mr. Ruiz; director of photography, Gustavo Moris; second unit camera, Richard Pearce; edited by Bill Yahraus; music by Country Joe McDonald; produced by James Becket and Saul Landau. A Lobo Films Production. Distributed by Impact Films, 144 Bleecker Street, Cinema. Running time: 90 minutes. Rated R.
Suzanne McCloud .... Sandra Archer
Martin Bradford .... Richard Stahl
Hugo Alarcon .... Pablo de la Barra
Simon Allelo .... Anibal Reyna
Osvaldo Alarcon .... Lucho Alarcon
Padre Eduardo .... Jorge Yanez
and
ALLENDE, produced and directed by Saul Landau and Haskell Wexler. Spanish with English subtitles. Running time: 30 minutes. Not rated.

By LAWRENCE VAN GELDER

The recent events in Chile, culminating in the death of the Marxist President, Salvador Allende Gossens, and the imposition of military rule, lend a special poignancy to an unusual and engrossing new film called "Que Hacer" ("What's to Be Done").

Mordant, self-aware, freighted with sensitivity toward Chile's problem, wary of caricature, disposed toward consciousness of human fallibility, it is a deft blend of fiction and documentary set in the tumultuous days leading up to the election of Dr. Allende in 1970.

Although its bias is clearly pro-Allende—its villains are militant rightists, an American foundation representative who talks about "matrices" and, especially, a mysterious American engineer who is most certainly a C.I.A. man—it leaves unresolved the question of precisely what it means to be a revolutionary.

On the documentary level, "Que Hacer" makes its points about Chile and its problems through the faces and voices of its people, the flimsiness of their hovels and the hardship of their lives, in a landscape possessed of mineral and agricultural riches and studded with the billboards of American industry.

On the fictional level, it delineates political argument through a revolutionary returned from Cuba, a Communist legislator living in luxury, his terrorist son, the American engineer, a revolutionary priest and a girl working for the Peace Corps.

The performances by a cast of unfamiliar faces are restrained and appropriately despairing. The mordant commentary comes from occasional glimpses of the film crew itself and particularly from the presence and singing of Country Joe McDonald.

The work of Saul Landau, who produced this film and served as one of its directors, also includes an earlier, well-received documentary on Fidel Castro. "Que Hacer" will remind some audiences of the Costa-Gavras films, "Z" and "State of Siege," although it is less blatantly emotional.

It shares the bill with a 30-minute documentary interview with Dr. Allende, with Mr. Landau asking the questions. History will render its eventual judgment, but at least in this film, Dr. Allende emerges as a compassionate leader who "thought that man should have a different dimension."

The films opened yesterday at the Bleecker Street Cinema.

1973 S 29, 22:1

Rape—an Ugly Movie Trend

By ALJEAN HARMETZ

THE women lie with their thighs forced apart. Their bare buttocks scrape against polished wooden floors, kitchen tables, the scrub grass of arid plains, snow-filled hollows in the high mountains.

Rape is the new Hollywood game. There is supernatural rape ("The Legend of Hell House," "The Exorcist"); incestuous rape ("The Damned"); multiple violations of one woman's body ("Man of La Mancha," "Lolly Madonna XXX" and the still unreleased "The Little Sparrow"); rape ardently enjoyed by the victims ("The Getaway," "Blume in Love," "Straw Dogs.") There is stylized rape ("Pat Garrett and Billy the Kid," "A Clockwork Orange"); strongly implied rape ("Frenzy"); and even, in one old-fashioned instance, rape as a fate worse than death ("Enter the Dragon").

To my 10-year-old son, just emerging from the cocoon of Disney in which we had carefully wound him, there is also PG rape as the way in which men deal sexually with women ("Billy Jack," "The Man Who Loved Cat Dancing"). He seems unperturbed by the brutal way in which men press their bodies against frightened flesh. But the attack between the thighs is only an extension of the bullet between the eyes, the karate chop between the cervical vertebrae, the knee to the groin.

But I am more than a little perturbed.

At least 20 films during the last two years served rape to their audiences. In almost none of those films has the rape been more than a plot point, a quick way of getting from here to there —of motivating a distraught husband or lover to kill rapists. Often, it has been less. In "Pat Garrett and Billy the Kid," the only reason for the naked Mexican woman pinioned beneath a wagon on a vast, arid plain was Sam Peckinpah's desire to set a bloody scene across which Billy could stumble. In "Blume in Love," an unmarried ex-wife must be made pregnant by her ex-husband.

*

Once a woman has been raped, the film no longer concerns her. Half the time, she is dead. Whether she is dead or not, the rest of the film focuses on her husband, brother, or lover as he rushes to avenge her. She is a victim not only of the rapist in the film but of the writer of the film who has used the violation of her body to juice up his script. Her rape is merely a device to provide a male hero with a course of action.

There are a few exceptions. Although Blume is the hero of "Blume in Love," his ex-wife's reaction to her pregnancy is an integral part of the remaining third of the film. And "Billy Jack" offers a deep and terribly sad account of the way in which a woman must try to come to terms with her violated body. Delores Taylor—who also helped to write the script of "Billy Jack"—is allowed to show the almost physical injury to her spirit caused by her rape. She is also allowed to show the equally deep injury caused by being unable to cry out her rage. Self-contained, mature, unhysterical, she must bury her pain in fear of the violence of Billy Jack's response if he learns of her rape.

The antithesis of "Billy Jack" is "The Man Who Loved Cat Dancing." Sarah Miles is a fluorescent sex object to nearly every man who stumbles across her path in the film. She barely avoids being raped by a drunken Bo Hopkins and a whole band of Indians before Jack Warden finally manages to shove past the defenses of Victorian undergarments and crinoline skirts. Screenwriter Eleanor Perry has publicly denounced the rape. "I thought she would defend herself; she would not be raped. But the director and my co-producer thought otherwise. The rape scene is in the film. One of the men told me, 'Well, rape turns some men on.'"

The rape is in no sense necessary to the film. Sarah Miles submits when Jack Warden threatens to kill Burt Reynolds if she does not. Since Reynolds is sleeping in another building and has several guns stacked next to his bed, it seems that he would be better protected by a shrill scream. Even unwarned, he manages to kill Warden when, after the rape, Warden lunges in to kill him. As soon as Warden is killed, Burt Reynolds, Sarah Miles, and "The Man Who Loved Cat Dancing" pay no further attention to what has happened. Earlier in the film Miss Miles has shown far more concern over the stains on her pretty dress. Now, tit for tat and on with the business of making love and climbing mountains.

No such fluffy and casual treatment occurs in the two recent films which include homosexual rape. In "Scarecrow," Al Pacino's rape is so costly to his personality that it takes only one more blow of fate to turn him into a catatonic schizophrenic. In "Deliverance," the brutal and humiliating rape of a baby-soft fat man is as painful on a human level to every member of the audience— male or female—as it is to the character. Raped men are allowed anguish. Raped women are ignored.

The men who finance and distribute movies disavow the rapes in the films they finance and distribute. Says Warner Brothers' head of production, John Calley, whose studio has—pure accident, Calley insists —released eight or nine of these rape-infested films, "I don't know that there's a rational explanation for it. It just happens that a number of the films we decided to make have this element. There's no dark subtext. I don't sit around saying, 'Hey, guys, I found another one.'"

*

Calley adds that "We mainly act as a financing and purchasing agent. We respond to what's submitted, and this is what has been submitted." Since most of the films with rape scenes have been "extremely successful at the box office," Calley can anticipate the submission of more scripts with similar scenes.

MGM's articulate vice president in charge of production, Daniel Melnick, although equally puzzled by the mushrooming rapes, is honest enough to speculate that "it has something to do with the fantasy life of the men who make movies. They seem to want to believe that at some point the woman stops struggling and starts moaning, that all women really love it, really want to be raped."

Paul Mazursky, who does not disavow the rape in "Blume in Love"—a picture that he wrote and directed —says, "I don't consider it a rape scene. The girl is, on some level, permitting it to happen."

*

There may be some justification for Blume's ex-wife being aroused while being raped by her ex-husband. There is no justification for the women of Sam Peckinpah's films panting like animals in heat. Peckinpah's last three films have included rapes. Although the Mexican woman spreadeagled under a wagon in "Pat Garrett and Billy the Kid" was an unwilling victim, Sally Struthers, as the morcnic wife of a veterinarian in "The Getaway," found true happiness at the hands of a bank robber. And Susan George, as the wife of Dustin Hoffman in "Straw Dogs," maneuvered herself into being raped by her ex-boyfriend.

"Rape turns men on." It is a new cliché for screenwriters. And one producer guesses hopefully that maybe "Rape turns women on, too."

Not exactly. On a recent sunny afternoon in Sun Valley, Idaho, women drift out of a movie theater one by one. The Brut Film Festival—which is open to the public—is showing "The Little Sparrow." On the screen, surrounded by artistic snow, an Indian girl is being raped in brutal and painstaking detail by at least five white men. The women—a middle-aged housewife, a couple of teen-age girls, a tanned and very rich lady—sit on the steps waiting for the scene

to be over. One is outraged, one merely annoyed, by what is happening in the darkness inside. They sit and talk in the sunlight and none of them makes the effort to go back and see the end of the picture.

*

Is it finally, then, another battle between men and women—an undeclared war between the men who make movies and their male allies shifting restlessly in the darkness on one side and, on the other, the women who see themselves mirrored as objects and victims? Perhaps. One thing, at least, is certain. Some of the films are the ripest garbage, others pedestrian but earnest, still others arrogantly brilliant. Yet almost all share the contemptuousness of a male-directed camera that focuses lovingly on female helplessness.

"We give the people," says one producer, "what they want to see."

1973 S 30, II:1:4

Jim Bouton Bangs The Drum, Loudly

By JIM BOUTON

I SAW "Bang the Drum Slowly" twice and both times there were a lot of sniffles in the audience. This is embarrassing. Right after the movie you have to walk out into broad daylight past a huge crowd waiting to get into the next showing. "Hey, look, there goes Jim Bouton, he's crying." Actually I had something in my eye both times. The waiting crowd studies your face to see whether you liked it. I liked it. (Advertisers please note: Do not use, "Jim Bouton says . . . 'I liked it.'" Reviewers always include a couple of lines that they know will appeal to advertising blurb writers. Here's mine: "Deeply moving, superbly cast," or "A simply marvelous cinematic experience," or combine both. Thank you.)

I had heard good reports about "Bang the Drum Slowly" but I was still expecting the worst because it was a baseball movie and we all know about baseball movies. Remember those terrible—

Jim Bouton, former pitcher for the New York Yankees and author of "Ball Four" and other books about baseball, is a sportscaster for WCBS-TV.

now wonderful camp—"Babe, Gehrig, Stratton Strikes Out Fear" movies, where the actors dressed up in baseball suits and looked like they were throwing with the wrong hand and said things like, "Tell it to me straight, Doc, is it strike three?" and "C'mon, Lefty, fire that old apple in here," and then they'd limp off into the sunset? Most folks thought those movies were just corny, but baseball players had a special laugh over all the obvious mistakes.

Basically, "Bang the Drum Slowly," adapted from the Mark Harris novel, is a story about a marginal catcher named Bruce Pearson, the butt of everyone's jokes, who suddenly becomes one of the boys when his teammates discover that he might die at any moment from a rare disease.

I admit that sounds like another corny old baseball movie. But most people, especially baseball players, will not laugh at "Bang the Drum Slowly." It seems too real. Too many details are perfect. The general manager negotiates a pitcher's contract by remarking how well the other pitchers are throwing. The star pitcher's wife is Midwestern, pretty and pregnant. There's talk about having an airline stewardess

as a girlfriend. The manager is named Dutch and says things like, "Never mind the facts, give me details," and he worries that the clap, an occupational hazard, will spread right around his infield. The third-base coach says things like, "Hey . . . now . . . hmm." Not, "C'mon, Sluggo, hit it a mile," but "Honn . . . now . . . hey . . . bay." Perfect. Any third-base coach who ever hollered anything coherent would never make it past spring training, and if he ever hollered "C'mon, Sluggo . . ." he'd be fired right in the coaching box.

There were some minor mistakes in "Bang the Drum Slowly." For one thing, too many players sang the National Anthem; there wasn't enough yawning and scratching. And at one point the catcher's friend, Henry Wiggen, says, "He's dying and you mustn't tell Dutch." Now no ballplayer in the history of baseball ever said "mustn't." Also, there was not enough swearing throughout, and none of the really "good" words were used. The most obvious mistake was when someone suggested asking the Baseball Commissioner for help. The idea that a Baseball Commissioner could be of any help is not believable.

There was one part I first thought was a mistake or was there because it was a low-budget movie. But I liked the effect and realized it was probably intentional. You see the tarpaulin being pulled over a rainy field in the Washington, D. C., stadium. Cut to the locker room and players singing about death —the song is "The Streets of Laredo"—and looking at "doomed" Bruce Pearson. Now cut back to the tarp-covered field, only it's not Washington this time but Yankee Stadium. The idea being that it's raining on this catcher's life no matter what town they're in.

The thing that makes the movie is that the actors look like real ballplayers, not only when they're on the field playing but, more important, when they're not playing. Athletes have a way of standing or sitting — a certain graceful confidence or cockiness—that becomes noticeable only when it's not present. Director John Hancock went out and got actors who have spent some time in a jockstrap, and it paid off.

How real was the story? Reviewers *must* ask these questions. The idea of ballplayers hanging close with a dying teammate seemed genuine while I sat and watched the movie. Then on my way out I heard two

women say they didn't think guys on a baseball team would be so sweet to another player just because they knew he was dying. I thought about that, and you know something? The two women were right.

The dying catcher says, "Probably everybody would be nice to you if they knew you was dying." True. But not for half a baseball season, unless you *looked* like you were dying. Once the shock of first hearing about it had worn off—and if you looked healthy like the catcher, Bruce Pearson, did—there would be jokes right up until the day you suddenly conked off.

That's because baseball players, like many athletes, are crude/honest about life's tragedies. That's their style. It's partly a hero's natural insensitivity to the outside world, but mostly it's a way of facing the tough realities of their own lives. Boredom and tension and being tested every day and half the time failing while everyone watches.

The athlete's mocking humor has been compared to soldiers' humor, soldiers being another band of men who deal with boredom and tension and failure that in their case can mean death. Maybe that's why when baseball players get sent to the minors they call it "dying." A player just released from the team walks out of the manager's office and says, "I died." During the spring training cutdown, players walk around the locker room and say, "Who died today?"

Such "deaths" take the pressure off a swollen spring roster. One man's death means another man's life. Law of the Jungle. When the doomed catcher, Pearson, stays on the roster, another catcher, Piney Woods, must be sent down. And in a line I've heard before in locker rooms, Piney Woods says, "Maybe somebody will drop dead up here and open up a slot for me." I've also heard a ballplayer jokingly ask his roommate, "If you get released, can I have your sweatshirts?"

In baseball that mocking humor, which in the movies is called "ragging," has no boundaries. A man with a complexion problem is called "pizza face." A rival player hollers to Jim Piersall, "Hey, crazy, they coming to get you with a net today?" A limping traveling secretary is called "gimp" to his face. The midget P.R. man for the Atlanta Braves is playfully hung up on a hook in a closet. On the Yankees we had a left-handed pitcher whose right arm was with-

Robert DeNiro in "Bang the Drum Slowly"
At last, a good movie with a baseball theme

ered from childhood polio, and during pre-game warmups sometimes the whole team would be imitating his awkward bent-arm catch. And he enjoyed it.

That might be healthy. The unspeakable is shouted and laughed at. Lenny Bruce understood that. But, my wife says, what about a guy who was actually dying? Well, there's a fellow in the big leagues right now who's reported to have leukemia. I don't know for sure, but I wouldn't be surprised if the players call him "Luke."

So the story is corny and the players' reaction to death may not be quite true, but "Bang the Drum Slowly" works because of the details and mostly because of the marvelous performances by Robert DeNiro as Pearson, the dying catcher, and Michael Moriarty as his friend Henry Wiggen, the pitcher. Before the movie was shot, DeNiro asked me what he could do to prepare for the part. I told him to read a wonderful book called "Ball Four" and spend two weeks riding the buses with some minor league team down South. Now I ask you, who ever heard of DeNiro before he came to me for advice? The best thing DeNiro learned was to talk while chewing tobacco and to spit it without getting it all over himself, which is something most real ballplayers have not mastered.

Moriarty as pitcher Henry Wiggen has the clear, open, blue-eyed face of a young 20-game winner who'd use his "contacts" to sell life insurance in the off season. I liked Dutch, the manager, played by Vincent Gardenia, because he seemed like a combination of Casey Stengel and Danny Murtaugh with a little Joe Schultz thrown in. After one of Dutch's clubhouse soliloquies, a lady sitting behind me said, "Strange man." She should've heard Joe Schultz.

I think "Bang the Drum Slowly" is an excellent movie, but it could be I've waited so long for a good movie with a basball theme that I'm not a fair judge.

1973 S 30, II:1:1

The Cast

RITORNO, directed by Gianni Amico; screenplay by Gianni Amico and Enzo Ungari with Dominica Rafele; produced by Paola Cortese. At the New York Film Festival. Running time: 85 minutes.

Francesca	Llaria Occhini
Andrea	Luigi Diberti
Clara	Laura Betti
Adriano	Paolo Brunatto

Gianni Amico's "Ritorno" is set thematically near the soulless wasteland of Michelangelo Antonioni, whose beautiful but emotionally dried-up couples embark on a search into their past that reveals the arid desert of their lives. Their experiences, which expose desensitized nerves, are painfully cathartic.

In "Ritorno" a handsome married couple, on the verge of being bored with each other, suddenly leave Rome one night and drive through an ominous thunderstorm to the husband's family several hours away. A telegram had arrived announcing that his father was dying. Now, wordlessly — and fearfully — they race the shadow of death.

But their homecoming is a surprise; the withered father is very much alive. No one knows who sent the wire. As they attempt to find the answer from discarded lovers, disillusioned friends and relatives who only want to eat, they realize the trip is a preview of death. They will have to make it again, soon.

A provocative situation quickly becomes dulled by the mushy influence of another director, Claude Lelouch. "Ritorno" focuses on billowing storm clouds, radiant meadows and simmering afternoon sunlight — external textures.

The puzzled, windswept couple have about as much depth as a cup of espresso. Their accidental remembrance of youth past is never more meaningful than the excessively used pleasantry, "Ciao."

The film stops being a prosaic postcard for only a brief moment, when the unforgettable Laura Betti, as the husband's demented old flame, sends a wickedly sensuous venom stinging across the landscape. Her gothic villa frightens the husband away. If his "return" has any truth worth pursuing, it probably remains hidden there.

PAUL GARDNER

1973 O 1, 44:3

KID BLUE, directed by James Frawley; written by Edwin Shrake; produced by Marvin Schwartz; director of photography, Billy Williams; editor, Stefan Arnsten; music, Tim McIntire and John Rubinstein; distributed by 20th Century-Fox. Running time: 108 minutes. At the New York Film Festival at Lincoln Center.

Kid Blue	Dennis Hopper
Reese Ford	Warren Oates
Preacher Bob	Peter Boyle
Sheriff (Mean Bob) Simpson	Ben Johnson
Molly Ford	Lee Purcell
Janet Conforto	Janice Rule
Drummer	Ralph Waite
Mr. Hendricks	Clifton James
Old Coyote	Jose Torway

By VINCENT CANBY

"Kid Blue," which was shown at the New York Film Festival at Lincoln Center Saturday night and again yesterday evening, is an American Western set at the turn of the century in the tiny but go-getting Texas town of Dime Box, about a train robber named Kid Blue (Dennis Hopper), who tries unsuccessfully to go straight.

Rampant capitalism, in the form of the town's Great American Ceramic Novelty Company, and Puritan morality, as defined by Sheriff ("Mean Bob") Simpson (Ben Johnson), eventually force Kid Blue again to take up the life of crime at which he never was any great shakes in the first place.

•

"Kid Blue" is the sort of movie that is likely to sound a lot better than it really is. It's nice to hear about a Western that begins, as "Kid Blue" does, with a carefully planned train hold-up that doesn't even succeed in stopping the train. Inept bandits are usually funny. So are bogus preachers and the innocence of solid citizens who don't recognize a high-class whore when they meet her.

Yet "Kid Blue" is never very funny or provocative. It tries too hard. It's too insistent. Like the performance of Mr. Hopper (who is getting a bit long in the tooth to play naifs with much conviction), "Kid Blue" is a heavily mannered work, with little or no sense of the spontaneous gaiety that one got from time to time in Eliot Silverstein's "Cat Ballou."

One has the feeling that James Frawley, the director, and Edwin Shrake, who wrote the screenplay, are good-hearted but essentially humorless men, incapable of constructing any kind of comfortable bridges between the film's would-be comic and melodramatic sequences. When Warren Oates, as Kid Blue's best friend, starts to talk admiringly of "the old-time Greeks" who went bare of clothes, one cringes in the anticipation of the about-to-be-delivered folksy wisdom, with which the movie is unspontaneously stuffed.

•

"Kid Blue" is a well-meaning, liberal, anti-fascist Western, dressed up with some good performances by Peter Boyle, Lee Purcell and Janice Rule. But it's not a very good movie.

1973 O 1, 45:2

The Cast

A TEAR IN THE OCEAN, directed by Henri Glaeser; screenplay by Mr. Glaeser and A. P. Quince, from a novel by Manes Sperber; cinematographer, Claude Lecomte; music by Joseph Lemovitz with traditional themes interpreted on violin by Ivry Gitlis; produced by Mr. Glaeser; a Syn-Frank Enterprises, Inc., presentation; released by Levitt-Pickman Film Corporation. At the Plaza Theater, 58th Street, east of Madison Avenue. Running time: 86 minutes. This film has not been rated at this time.

Edi Rubin	Alexandre Stere
Bynie	Dominique Rollin
Roman Skarbek	Armand Abplanalp
Rabbi	Henri Glaeser
Yanouch	Dominique Zardi
Mendel	Jacques Brafman
S.S. Commandant	Frantz Wolf
Jadwiga	Diane Lepvrier

Jewish resistance to the Nazis in Poland needs no stressing now as a heartbreaking, indelible testament to courage and faith. But if the likes of the 1943 Warsaw ghetto uprising has become familiar in films, "A Tear in the Ocean," the French feature that had its local premiere at the Plaza yesterday, is disturbingly different as an exposure of men's minds (both Jew and Pole) under extreme stress.

•

Henri Glaeser, who produced, directed, helped adapt and appears in this dramatization of a novel by Manes Sperber, is more concerned with the terrible decisions his principals must make than with guerrilla action. Even though there is enough gunfire and bloodshed here to make this more than just a tract, the heart of the matter is whether the Jews of Wolyna will cling passively to their beliefs in the face of callous, godless invaders or resist as men fighting oppressors.

However, this is multifaceted, philosophical drama dominated by the convictions of its beleaguered characters. There is the flinty performance of Alexandre Stere, as a tough, singleminded Austrian Jewish doctor determined to save Wolyna's ghetto dwellers. And there is Armand Abplanalp, as a Polish count and the leader of his own resistance group, who is his friend and quite ready to help him.

But some of the villagers choose not to fight and are mowed down, among them a revered rabbi, played with dignity and reserve by Mr. Glaeser. Others, including Dominique Rollin, as the rabbi's dedicated, frail but fearless teen-age son, follow the doctor and join the compassionate count's underground guerrillas. However, peasant Poles resent these newcomers, unlikely warriors all, because they feel their fight is for Poland and not for Jews. It's a smoldering situation that, after a successful ambush of a Nazi platoon, erupts with tragic results.

•

Mr. Glaeser, who shot his color film in 1971 on strikingly autumnal locations in Alsace, purposely leaves unanswered the gnawing question: whether resistance in fictitious Wolyna, like the actual bloody Warsaw uprising that followed it in time, was no more effective than the titular "tear in the ocean."

Like the performances and the philosophies that are translated in lucid English subtitles, "A Tear in the Ocean" is both effective and provocative.

A. H. Weiler

1973 O 1, 45:2

The Cast

HISTORY LESSONS, directed by Jean-Marie Straub; screenplay by Mr. Straub and Daniele Huillet; produced by Straub-Huillet, Janus Film and T.V. American distributor, New Yorker Films. At the New York Film Festival. Running time: 85 minutes.

Mummlius Spicer	Gottfried Bold
Young Man	Benedikt Zulauf
Peasant	Johann Unterpertinger

After seeing Jean-Marie Straub's short feature on Nazism, "Not Reconciled," Susan Sontag said that she wanted to kiss the screen. I doubt that this latest work, "History Lessons," will arouse quite the same response, but Straub, a political exile from France who lives in Germany and Italy, is a director who clearly stirs passionate feelings among cinéastes.

His reputation here comes directly from the film festival and Dan Talbot of the New Yorker Theater, who has acquired his films despite their scant commercial appeal. Intensely political and self-consciously intellectual, Jean-Marie Straub is becoming a cult director who gets those kisses—and also boos.

•

"History Lessons" may well be the festival's most teasingly irritating film. It is impossible to like—even for many dedicated Straubists. Half the press audience walked out of "Othon," his adaptation of a Corneille drama, a few years ago at the festival, and it was more comprehensible than "History Lessons," Straub's austere version of a Brecht novel about Julius Caesar.

The camera seldom moves. Mostly it stays slightly behind the head of a young man as he drives his sports car aimlessly through the streets of Rome, a modern city suspended in an ancient world.

The young man's function is almost that of a detective in a philosophical thriller. He searches out elderly Romans — a banker, a lawyer, a peasant — who remember Caesar. As their garlanded past blends into his transistorized present, he pieces together a Brechtian-Marxian-Straubian viewpoint on history.

The interviews are long tedious monologues, in which the static figures speak almost expressionlessly in German, a language that sounds very curious amid sunburnt Italian settings. But German also has a harsh, didactic quality that provides another Straubian juxtaposition.

Jean-Marie Straub deliberately alienates his audience. He defies traditional concepts of the medium just as minimal art in the nineteen-sixties went against prevailing sculptural ideas and as the music of Philip Glass ignores accepted theories of composition today.

With "History Lessons," he further tests his audience—with a film that is coldly anticinema.

PAUL GARDNER

1973 O 1, 45:2

ILLUMINATION, directed by Krzysztof Zanussi; written (Polish with English subtitles) by Mr. Zanussi; executive producer, Jerzey Buchwald; director of photography, Edward Klosinski; editor, Urszula Sliwinska; music, Wojciech Kilar; produced by TOR unit for Film Polski. Running time: 92 minutes. At the New York Film Festival at Lincoln Center.

Franciszek	Stanislaw Latallo
Malgorzata	Malgorzata Pritulak
Agnieszka	Monika Dzienisiewicz-Olbrychska
Doctor	Edward Zebrowski
Patient	Jan Skotnicki

"Illumination" is the fourth feature film by Krzysztof anussi, the Polish director whose "Family Life" was well received at the 1971 New York Film Festival, but its concerns are those grandly fundamental ones of an artist's first work.

The film devotes itself to the pursuit of life's meaning undertaken by a solemn young university student who opts to major in physics in order to learn "unequivocal things." When the study of physics fails to provide him with answers, Franciszek (Stanislaw Latallo) elects to work in a hospital devoted to neurosurgery. "Why," he asks a doctor friend, "do we invade the soul's material bases?"

For a while, Franciszek even contemplates the contemplative life of a hermit in a monastery. At last, just as his own body has physically peaked, shortly before his 30th birthday, a professor tells him there are no absolute truths in any science. There is only the possibility of understanding a little more.

Although Zanussi's techniques, which mix fiction with documentary footage, are intelligent, "Illumination" manages to become increasingly banal as its hero zeroes in on compromise: marriage, fatherhood, the acceptance of his own mortality. This, I assume, is his "illumination," which is a kind of arid joke on the Augustinian doctrine.

"Illumination," which was shown at the New York Film Festival Saturday evening and again last night, is lovely to look at and almost impossible to know, partly because the subtitles don't seem to do justice to the Polish text. At least, I hope they don't.

VINCENT CANBY

1973 O 1, 45:3

Jane Fonda and David Warner in Joseph Losey's film of "A Doll's House"

The Cast

A DOLL'S HOUSE, directed by Joseph Losey; screenplay by David Mercer from Michael Meyer's English translation of Henrik Ibsen's play; director of photography, Gerry Fisher; editor, Reggie Beck; music by Michel Legrand; art director, Eileen Diss; costume designer, John Furniss; makeup, Bob Lawrence; produced by Mr. Losey; a World Films Services presentation; released by Tomorrow Entertainment, Inc. At the New York Film Festival, Alice Tully Hall. Running time: 103 minutes.

Nora .... Jane Fonda
Torvald .... David Warner
Dr. Rank .... Trevor Howard
Kristine Linde .... Delphine Seyrig
Krogstad .... Edward Fox

By NORA SAYRE

A psychologist once remarked: "After your namesake slammed the doll's house door, I bet her first words were 'Oh God, I've forgotten my keys!'" This suggestion inspired some embattled evenings. If that cynic had a clue to Nora's key ring, there were two possible interpretations. Some of us agreed that she might eventually need her keys to collect a few papers crucial to divorce. But of course the opposition claimed that she would hate her new freedom — hence the keys would be necessary for rushing back and locking herself in.

It was quite like fighting about the end of Henry James's "Portrait of a Lady." Well before the feminism of recent years, many women were convinced that Isabel Archer was going to leave her husband for good, while numerous men insisted that she was far too conventional and masochistic to dump her bad marriage. At any rate, those who believe that Nora would have returned to her particular prison will lose out to Jane Fonda and Joseph Losey: when this Nora leaves, it's forever.

Since we have two flawed versions of "A Doll's House" this year, it's exasperating to have to choose between the sets of mistakes that were made. Hillard Elkins's production is dignified, intelligent and as respectful as a tour of a renovated cathedral. Claire Bloom plays Nora with such austerity that most of the play's emotional punch is lost. And there are some mangling cuts that simply muck up the characters' motives.

Meanwhile, both movies have diminished an ingredient essential to Nora's nature: her immense powers of denial—the refusal to recognize a chain of consequences, to actually acknowledge what's happening or about to happen. Ibsen carefully fueled her naïveté with this quality. Then, there was the impact of watching her grow and shed the trait that was almost as crippling as convention. Both Patrick Garland and Losey have obscured that childish blindness—perhaps because both actresses are over 12. The directors were wise to shun the fluffy, twittering Noras we've seen before. But they sacrificed the immaturity Ibsen gave her so that she might outgrow it.

However, expansions can be even more destructive than cuts. The Losey script by David Mercer has been fattened with feeble lines and even short scenes that the old genius didn't write. Also, some passages, such as Kristine Linde's reunion with Krogatod and Nora's tarantella, have been intercut. So the dramatic momentum is butchered. Although we can sympathize with a filmmaker's urge to escape one single indoor setting, and it's always nice to have an excuse for shots of snow—especially if you can sling in a sleigh or two—most of these tricks merely weaken a tightly written play.

Of the two pictures, Losey's is the more ferociously flawed, and yet I recommend it over the other: for Jane Fonda's performance. Beforehand, it seemed fair to wonder if she could personify someone from the past; her voice, inflections, and ways of moving have always seemed totally contemporary. (She may not smoke, but in "Klute" and elsewhere she sounded like at least two packs a day. No disrespect intended: the characters she usually plays are apt to be under severe pressures.) But once again she proves herself to be one of our finest actresses, and she's at home in the eighteen-seventies, a creature of that period as much as ours.

Dancing or laughing or worrying, eating macaroons, skating or suffering, Miss Fonda brings an emotional range to the part that Claire Bloom didn't: here is the ringing gaiety and the energy that the role demands. She can also be innocent without seeming stupid or silly—which is a traditional bear trap in this play.

Actresses in tight-laced 19th-century waistlines often tend to wear their hands on their hips.

But Miss Fonda does it with a difference: even her liveliest gestures are tempered by constricting clothes. However, she flirts at a minimum, though she wheedles well when she has to. Still, it's regrettable that the movie omits her impulse to seductively show her stockings to Dr. Rank; the absence of that telling detail leaves a gap like a yanked tooth.

Nora's habit of lying was played down in the Bloom version, and that made the character too noble. But it's exhilarating to watch what Fonda does with this reflex: she projects a person who is able to believe her own lies —such as pretending to have earned cash that she actually borrowed. And the contrasts between the private and the public self are beautifully drawn: Nora puts on her jolly act for others, then allows herself to release anxiety when she is alone. There is also the extreme poise that is summoned by profound nervousness: only a flicker of the fingers betrays the tensions within.

Gradually and subtly, we are given a portrait of Nora as a political prisoner—one who hasn't ever tasted the air outside the walls. And Miss Fonda is such a sensitive actress that we can even see the ideas taking root—as when it occurs to her to try to milk money from Dr. Rank (Trevor Howard, very good), and when she quietly makes the moment-to-moment discovery that her marriage is worthless, that the time for departure has come.

David Warner as Torvald and Edward Fox as Krogstad both overact, and Delphine Seyrig walks through the role of Kristine (which Anna Massey did so well) as though she yearns to be back in a luxuriant comedy by Truffaut or Buñuel. Thus, many of Ibsen's intentions have been squelched or stomped on—apart from one magnificent piece of casting. "A Doll's House" was shown last night at the New York Film Festival. This production has been sold to the American Broadcasting Company, and will be seen on television this season.

1973 O 2, 54:1

The Cast

ReJEANNE PADOVANI, directed by Denys Arcand; screenplay by Jacques Benoit and Mr. Arcand; photography, Alain Dostie; editor, Mr. Arcand and Marguerite Duparc; music by Gluck and Walter Boudreau; sound, Serge Beauchemin; executive producer, Marguerite Duparc-Lefebvre; a Cinak Cie Cinematographique Ltee. Production. At the New York Film Festival. Running time: 90 minutes.

Vincent .... Jean Lajeunesse
Rejeanne Padovani ...... Luce Guilbeault
Jean-Leon Desaulniers ..... Roger Lebel
Dominique Di Muro ..... Pierre Theriault
Helene Caron .... Frederique Colin

As a sobering drama, "Réjeanne Padovani," shown last night as the Canadian feature entry at the New York Film Festival, is, like its venal principals, fascinating but imperfect.

Corruption among its effete, influential Canadian wheeler-dealers, politicos and their ruthless hirelings is made shockingly obvious but it remains as an indictment of characters who are sometimes undefined and shadowy. In essence, "Réjeanne Padovani" evolves as an intermittently vivid illustration of truths that more often strike at the mind rather than the heart.

Denys Arcand, its 32-year-old director and a newcomer to the United States movie scene, maintains a good deal of suspense as his group of bigwigs dine at the plush Montreal home of Jean Lajeunesse on his completion of a superhighway. He, like the governmental minister, the mayor, their assistants, wives and secretaries as well as their police and bodyguards dining in the servants' quarters, are obliquely exposed as urbane, suave or rough, direct men and women callously on the take or on the make.

Unfortunately, Luce Guilbeault, as the ill-fated, estranged wife of the builder, who turns up pleading to be reunited with her children after a long liaison with another man, is not entirely convincing in her motivations. If she provides a strong portrayal as the only decently emotional individual in an otherwise nefarious crew, Mr. Arcand also indicates the power, lust and money drives that propel the others in that cynical crowd.

As the cool, polished tycoon, Mr. Lajeunesse is there with payoff gifts to his guests who helped him steal millions, as well as their muscle men. He loves his kids and he is ready to dally with one of his willing guests while looking the other way as his wife faces her doom. And the fatuous mayor, the minister and the builder's tough strongarm man, Pierre Theriault, among others in a large cast, make the going rough for inquiring reporters, potential demonstrators and the gangster opposition.

Although its French dialogue is made plain by English subtitles, "Réjeanne Padovani" presents a grim picture of corruptors whose acts are more explicit than their feelings. The film will be shown again tomorrow night.

A. H. WEILER

1973 O 2, 56:3

The Cast

MEAN STREETS, directed by Martin Scorsese; screenplay by Mr. Scorsese and Mardik Martin; produced by Jonathan T. Taplin; executive producer, E. Lee Perry; director of photography, Kent Wakeford; editor, Sid Levin; distributed by Warner Brothers. Running time: 110 minutes. At the New York Film Festival at Lincoln Center. This film has been classified R.

Johnny Boy .... Robert De Niro
Charlie .... Harvey Keitel
Tony .... David Proval
Teresa .... Amy Robinson
Michael .... Richard Romanus
Giovanni .... Cesare Danova
Mario .... Victor Argo
Joey .... George Memmoli

By VINCENT CANBY

No matter how bleak the milieu, no matter how heartbreaking the narrative, some films are so thoroughly, beautifully realized they have a kind of tonic effect that has no relation to the subject matter. Such a film is "Mean Streets," the third

Martin Scorsese, right, directing Cesare Danova, left, and Harvey Keitel in a scene for "Mean Streets," set principally in New York's Little Italy.

feature film by Martin Scorsese, the once-promising young director ("Who's That Knocking at My Door?" and "Boxcar Bertha") who has now made an unequivocally first-class film.

•

"Mean Streets; which was shown last night at the New York Film Festival in Alice Tully Hall, has a lot in common with "Who's That Knocking at My Door?", Scorsese's first feature released here four years ago. It is set almost entirely in New York's Little Italy, where Scorsese grew up. Its hero is a second-generation Italian-American, a young man whose nature is a warring mixture of religious guilt, ambition, family loyalty and fatalism.

Charlie (Harvey Keitel) is a nice, clean-cut petty hood, a sort of trainee-executive in the syndicate controlled by his Uncle Giovanni (Cesare Danova), an Old World gangster full of cold resolve and ponderous advice ("Honorable men go with honorable men"). Charlie makes collections for his uncle and aspires to take over a restaurant whose owner is deeply in debt to Giovanni.

Early on, however, it's apparent that Charlie is not quite ruthless enough to succeed in the Lower East Side territory that defines his world. He has made the mistake of falling in love with Teresa (Amy Robinson), an Italian-American girl who has epilepsy and is therefore out of bounds. He also feels almost maniacally responsible for Johnny Boy (Robert De Niro), Teresa's simple-minded brother who traffics with loan sharks, suicidally.

When Charlie tries to flee the territory, with Teresa and Johnny Boy, crossing over the bridge to Brooklyn

in a borrowed car, the results are predictable. It's as if an astronaut had decided to take a space-walk in a gray flannel suit.

"Mean Streets," which has a screenplay by Mr. Scorsese and Mardik Martin, faces its characters and their world head-on. It never looks over their shoulders or takes a position above their heads in order to impose a self-conscious relevance on them. There is no need to. It is Scorsese's talent, reflected in his performers, to be able to suggest the mystery of people and place soley in terms of the action of the film.

This may seem simple but it's one of the fundamentals of filmmaking that many directors never grasp. Bad films need mouthpieces to tell us what's going on.

"Mean Streets," which was shot entirely on its New York locations, unfolds as a series of seemingly caual incidents — bar-room encounters, pick-ups, fights, lovers' quarrels and small moments of introspection—that only at the end are seen to have been a narrative of furious drive.

De Niro ("Bang the Drum Slowly") has an exceedingly flashy role and makes the most of it, but Keitel, modest, honorable and doomed, is equally efective as the hood who goes right, and hates himself for his failure.

"Mean Streets" will be screened at Alice Tully Hall again this evening. It opens its commercial engagement at the Cinema One Theater on Oct. 14, and deserves attention as one of the finer American films of the season.

1973 O 3, 38:1

The Cast

WHAT?, directed by Roman Polanski; screenplay by Gerard Brach and Mr. Polanski; produced by Carlo Ponti; executive producer, Andrew Braunsberg; music, Claudio Gizzi; directors of photography, Marcello Gatti and Giuseppe Ruzzolini; editor, Alastair McIntyre; distributed by Avco Embassy Pictures. Running time: 112 minutes. At the Coronet Theater, Third Avenue at 59th Street. This film has been rated X.

Alex .... Marcello Mastroianni
The Girl .... Sydne Rome
Owner of The Villa ...... Hugh Griffith
Administrator .... Romolo Valli
Priest .... Guido Alberti
Stud .... Giancarlo Piacentino
Zanzara .... Roman Polanski
Jimmy .... Roger Middleton

By VINCENT CANBY

Roman Polanski's "What?" is an X-rated nonsense comedy about a Goldilocks manqué, a wide-eyed American girl on the loose in Asia and Europe, and her specific adventures among some mad characters she meets when she takes refuge in an Italian seaside villa to escape three would-be rapists.

The girl, played by a new actress whose name is improbably spelled Sydne (conventionally pronounced "Sidney") Rome, has hair that looks like an elaborate taffy dessert. She also has a terrible time keeping her clothes on, try as she will. When they aren't torn off in usually friendly struggles, they are stolen while she sleeps. Sometimes she's reduced to wearing a dinner napkin. Sometimes she just gives up and wears nothing, but she is never daunted. Nobody in the villa notices.

•

In addition to a body that invites constant assaults, like Everest, the girl possesses the kind of optimistic American purpose that pioneered the West, invented the light bulb and developed frozen food. She is as curious, unflappable and self-assured as a favored child and, as she is ravaged by the world, so does she ravage it. When she finally departs the villa, at least one of its inhabitants has expired

sheer joy of contemplating her.

"What?", which opened yesterday at the Coronet Theater is a male chauvinist pig sort of comedy. It is not consistently inspired in its lunacy, but it is so totally without redeeming social value that it should be protected and, from time to time, cherished, as when a grumpy maid attempts to clear the air of flies and mistakes and aerosol can of shaving cream for Fly-Tox.

Anarchic comedy is a form that continues to challenge Polanski even though neither he nor his script collaborator, Gerard Brach, succeeded in their earlier "Cul-de-Sac" or "The Fearless Vampire Killers." Perhaps, like verse drama, it's become one of those things that need only to be attempted to succeed in partial measure. It can be fun to watch the try.

•

Occasionally Polanski and Brach seem to want to introduce a system of surreal disorder to the girl's adventures in the villa, but I doubt that they really much care beyond presenting us with an Alice trying to comprehend an X-rated Wonderland. Among the inhabitants are Marcello Mastroianni, playing a former pimp with a sense of honor and a passion for sado-masochistic games; Hugh Griffith, the villa's ancient owner, once a great collector of art, now a man who prefers the object to its artistic image, and other assorted odd balls, including Polanski himself.

The girl, the villa and the performances are beautiful enough to bridge those sequences when the film, like its heroine, seems searching for explanations that will never be found.

1973 O 4, 57:1

The Cast

LA RUPTURE (The Breakup), directed by Claude Chabrol; screenplay (French with English subtitles) by Chabrol, based on a novel by Charlotte Armstrong; produced by Andre Genoves; director of photography, Jean Rabier; editor, Jacques Gaillard; music, Pierre Jansen; a Belgian-French-Italian co-production by Les Films la Boetie, Euro International and Cinevog Film. Running time: 125 minutes. At the New York Film Festival at Lincoln Center.

Helene................Stephane Audran
Paul Thomas.........Jean-Pierre Cassel
M. Regnier..............Michel Bouquet
Mme. Regnier........Marguerite Cassan
Charles Regnier......Jean-Claude Drouot
Mme. Pinelli............Annie Cordy
M. Pinelli..............Jean Carmet
Elise Pinelli..........Katia Romanoff

By VINCENT CANBY

Claude Chabrol has reportedly described his 1970 melodrama, "La Rupture" (The Breakup), as belonging to his Fritz Lang period, which may be one of its virtues as well as one of its difficulties. The film, which was shown at the New York Film Festival at Lincoln Center last night, will be shown there again tonight.

At least I find it difficult to sit comfortably through a movie in which innocence and virtue are so hopelessly imperiled that it takes nothing less than a fairly arbitrary plot device to straighten things out.

"La Rupture," with a screenplay adapted by Chabrol from a novel by Charlotte Armstrong, has so many beautiful things in it that I'm tempted to suspect some terrible weakness in myself, rather than the film, for the feeling of depressed impatience it left. Perhaps not.

•

Perhaps one should be impatient with a film that opens with a brutal sequence in which a father beats up his wife and attempts to smash the brains of his 4-year-old son. Later on, the film treats us to the spectacle of a retarded teen-age girl, who has been kidnapped and drugged by the villain, being shown pornographic films and seduced by the man's mistress.

It's not that newspapers don't contain stories of worse horrors, but that Chabrol, who is not a frivolous film maker, allows these things to be put in the service of a rather frivolous end. That is, our entertainment.

I realize that in saying this I'm also testifying to the film's effect, which is torturous. But then I found Lang's "Human Desire," which is a much tougher film, much easier to endure. "La Rupture" is the story of a woman trapped in such circumstances that even her decency and trust can be used as weapons against her.

When Hélène, played by the extraordinarily gifted Stéphane Audran, attempts to leave her husband, a part-time writer and full-time junkie, her wealthy father-in-law attempts to discredit her morals in order to obtain custody of his grandson. The father-in-law, played by Michel Bouquet (who, like Miss Audran, has become an important contributor to Chabrol's films), employs Jean-Pierre Cassel to frame Hélène, but the attempts are so clumsy that the film, though emotionally harrowing, is plausible only as an arid statement about the possibility of evil.

•

Within this frame, which I found difficult to accept, "La Rupture" contains some true Chabrol achievements, especially the sense of locale (Belgium, which is seen as the suburb to the rest of the world), and the performance by Miss Audran. About halfway through the film, she delivers a monologue about Hélène's marriage that is one of the most moving things I've seen this year. It may be difficult on any realistic level to accept Miss Audran as the barmaid she is supposed to be, but the stunning quality of her beauty and personality become a kind of personification of Chabrol's cool concerns, which, otherwise, have no recognizable human shape.

There is also another problem with the frame of the film: the disadvantages and indignities are piled so thickly on the poor heroine that one knows early that the film is obliged to offer her vindication. Otherwise it has no shape. That her vindication is achieved at a high price isn't surprising or touching enough to transform the melodrama of "La Rupture" into tragedy.

1973 O 5, 19:1

Trio by Brakhage Is at the Film Forum

In his "Pittsburgh Trilogy," which opened yesterday at the Film Forum (not to be confused with the current Film Festival), Stan Brakhage sends the lens of his camera rooting across the landscape of his subject matter like a pig's snout in search of truffles of truth and meaning.

And so swiftly does it move, and so frequently does it turn away from what it has seen, littering the screen with fragments, that in the end one suspects that it has found nothing.

The subject matter of these three silent avant garde documentary films — "Eyes," "Deus Ex" and "The Act of Seeing With One's Own Eyes" — is, respectively, the police, a hospital and a mor-police, a hospital and a morgue.

It is possible to respect Mr. Brakhage's disdain for sound as a logical byproduct of the purity of his commitment to the camera as his medium of expression.

But it is also possible to question whether an almost frenetic but passively imaginative use of the camera constitutes the exercise of an artistic intelligence. Basically, these films are overlong and repetitive without cumulative effect and studded with fragmentary images — part of a shoulder, a hand, a thumb, a hand holding a cigarette, a hallway, a portion of a corpse.

There is less here than we want to know about the subjects and more than we want to know about Mr. Brakhage's exercises in his chosen medium.

A note of caution: A portion of the second film and all of the third are not recommended to the squeamish. "Pittsburgh Trilogy" may be seen tonight and tomorrow at 8 P.M. and again next Friday, Saturday and Sunday at the same time.

LAWRENCE VAN GELDER

1973 O 6, 17:4

The Cast

THE MOTHER AND THE WHORE (La Maman et La Putain), directed by Joan Eustache; screenplay (French with English subtitles) by Mr. Eustache; photography, Pierre L'homme; editors, Mr. Eustache and Denise de Casablanca; executive producer, Pierre Cottreli; production companies; Elite Films, Cine Qua Non; Les Films du Losangeand Simar Film, V. M. Productions. At the New York Film Festival at Lincoln Center. 215 minutes.

Marie .... Bernadette Lafoni
Alexandre .... Jean-Pierre Leaud
Veronika .... Francoise Lebrun
Gilberte .... Isabelle Weingarten
and Jacques Renard, Jean-Noel Picq, Jessa Darrieux, Marinka Matuszewski, Genevieve Mnich and Berthe Grandval.

By NORA SAYRE

Time-traveling can be demoralizing — when you're going in reverse. Watching "The Mother and the Whore," you find that you're back in the movie-sludge of the nineteen-fifties, when a number of mediocre French films focused on sub-Sagan characters: numb, semi-paralyzed creatures who hardly had the calories to drag themselves through the day. Then, boredom was a hip disease — and it all comes rushing down the spout of memory when Jean-Pierre Léaud explains that he lives "in a world where people are old at 17." Jean Eustache's picture, which was shown last night at the New York Film Festival, is so reminiscent of those mossy productions that you start wondering if nothing has been learned about movies, about acting, about men and women. The discoveries of the last decade have been erased. Or else the sixties never happened: you were just hallucinating.

It's been claimed that the movie explores all the possible relationships between men and women — which seems like an invitation for a sackrace to the nearest crematorium. Léaud has two girlfriends: Bernadette Lafont and Françoise Lebrun. He talks. They listen. The usher says you can't smoke. It takes three and a half hours to state that women are unpredictable and that men are easily depressed. There's a bale of boastful talk about sex but not much of it. Finally, Miss Lebrun has hysterics, Léaud asks her to marry him, she says yes and throws up. Now you can smoke.

●

But this movie won the Grand Prix and also the International Critics Prize at Cannes. Before we all take sanity tests, let's examine the fantasies afoot. The director has said that we won't be able to distinguish between the mother and the whore. He's wrong about that. While both women are made to be incredibly passive, Bernadette Lafont is permitted a bit of gumption when she's jealous—an emotion that turns Léaud on. (He gets jealous himself.) When a woman is jealous, it must mean that she's possessive, therefore a mother: by definition a figure to be needled and punctually defied and, finally, left. A

mother is someone to escape —when she's not changing spiritual diapers. "The whore" is simply a woman who has had a lot of sex. At first, she says she likes it, later she calls it sordid; ultimately, she has to repent.

Perhaps there's meant to be a whiff of grim maternity in her character: because she's a nurse who gives anesthetics. By implication, a nurse is supposed to cure everything, to heal all wounds. Françoise Lebrun is acutely severe, precise— thus evoking Léaud's childhood attraction to hospital nurses. He thought them alluring because they seemed cold and hard, impervious to pain. She asks if he's ever seen a pair of lungs, adding that they're pretty because they're pink.

Toward the end, Miss Lebrun has one long drizzling aria of remorse—about the futility of sex without love. It's her only opportunity to act; otherwise, both women are allowed to alternate rapt but blank stares with faint, indulgent smiles, while Léaud lectures about nothing. (Miss Lafont gets a chance to throw up too, but very quickly. Léaud's monologues are spiced with maxims intended to knock us sideways. Such as: "In the long run, the phonier you are, the further you go." (Holden, you should be with us at this movie.) Or: "My only dignity is cowardice." And: "Women always belong to their rescuers" — such as their abortionists.

It's worth worrying about Léaud these days — as to whether he can do his best for directors other than Truffaut. Godard and Bertolucci have already brought out the aridity that also withers his persona in "The Mother and the Whore," and it's rather sad to see this dour, fatigued appearance so soon after hugely enjoying his skill in Truffaut's "Day for Night." But all we learn from his performance in this movie is that his right nipple twitches violently when he's dialing a phone.

All in all, it's tempting to mail the director a list of complaints as long as his movie. What possessed him to use slow dissolves when we yearn for quick cuts? Or to give us a tour of the inside of a refrigerator or lessons in putting records on turntables or how to make a call? And occasionally, when Eustache builds toward a scene that might be almost interesting—in which these weary people might have to cope with one another — he leaves it out. The program notes report that he "now hates most films." So this picture may be his vengeance on the apes who like them. But perhaps he was paying homage to Gore Vidal's Myra Breckinridge, who had "a radical theory" that "boredom in the arts can be, under the right circumstances, dull."

1973 O 6, 17:1

Night or Day, Truffaut's the One

By VINCENT CANBY

WHEN we are children we build sandcastles and snow men and marionette theaters. We have electric trains we can wreck at will without serious damage to any lives, limbs or trains. We play make-believe games that give us power over the uncertain universe, which, otherwise, rules our lives without knowing we exist. In these things we bring reality to its knees so it can see us. Some children grow up to paint, to sculpt, to make constructions of aluminum and barbed wire, to write stories and novels and plays, to create movies.

One of the propelling impulses still is the need to make ordered and comprehensible a world that is disordered and incomprehensible. It's not the only impulse but it is an important one, and it has always seemed to me that one of the most moving aspects of the work of any artist is this ability to continue to function when, deep down, he must suspect an ultimate futility.

This suspicion is apparent throughout the best work of Francois Truffaut, whose newest and most exhilarating comedy, "Day for Night" (original French title: "La Nuit Americaine"), was the opening attraction at the 11th New York Film Festival at Lincoln Center and will begin its commercial engagement at the Fine Arts Theater here today. It's not the final disposition of things that is important, Truffaut's films keep saying, but the adventures and the risks en route, the mad and often doomed challenges that are accepted in living.

In "Bed and Board," the fourth and, according to Truffaut, the last of his semi-autobiographical films about Antoine Doinel, Antoine's wife Christine, the lovely, sweet representative of a middle class that Antoine envies without quite being able to become a part of, turns on Antoine with fury. "I'm not like you," Christine says. "I hate what is vague . . . illusory. I hate the ambiguous. I like what is clear-cut."

"La Nuit Americaine," which is what French filmmakers call the technique by which, through the use of filters, a scene shot in daylight is made to look like night, is Truffaut's love letter to people who, for one reason or another, choose to live their lives halfway between reality and illusion. It's the highly comic and affecting chronicle of the members of a movie crew who gather at the Victorine Studios in Nice to make what looks to be (at least, from the bits we see of it) a sudsy romantic melodrama about a young wife who falls tragically in love with her father-in-law.

On its surface, "Day for Night" is a very inside movie, decorated with references to dozens of movies and moviemakers, packed with behind-the-scenes information about how movies are made, how technicians manufacture rain and snow, how stuntmen crash cars without suffering fatalities themselves, how bits and pieces of seemingly disconnected footage are finally put together to make an intelligible whole.

It is full of marvelous anecdotes about moviemaking, some dramatized, some simply recounted, like the story of an actress who, after attending the preview of her first film, asked with surprise: "Did I do that? All I remember is the waiting."

In "Day for Night," Truffaut is emulating two earlier artists he admires a great deal, Balzac and Hawks, each of whom in his own way was fascinated by the details of a profession, which, in turn, could express the essence of a character. If "Day for Night" were simply about how movies are made, however, it would be no more than a pleasantly frivolous film, charming in its details, perhaps, but as easily forgotten as a successful soufflé. It is, I think, a great deal more than that since this profession, which Truffaut happens to know best, also happens to be an almost perfect metaphor for life as Truffaut seems to see it in his films.

Beautifully expressing one of the essential thoughts of the film is a line spoken by Severine (Valentina Cortese), a once-popular Hollywood actress who has returned to Europe to live and to play roles like that of the middle-aged mother in "Meet Pamela," which is the title of the film-within-the-film. After a party celebrating her last day of shooting, Severine says of moviemaking: "As soon as we grasp things, they're gone." Which, I suspect, is also the way a lot of non-movie people may feel about their lives.

"Day for Night" is about seven weeks—the time allotted to the production of "Meet Pamela" by the American backers of the film—in the lives of the members of the crew, including Ferrand (Truffaut), the director of the film within, a man who wears a hearing aid and is obsessed with movies; Julie Baker (Jacqueline Bisset), the Hollywood actress imported to play the title role in "Meet Pamela"; Alexandre (Jean-Pierre Aumont) who, like Severine, is a refugee from an earlier Hollywood career; Alphonse (Jean-Pierre Leaud) who, as the young leading man of "Meet Pamela," is a kind of grotesque extension of Antoine, so self-absorbed that he's the last one on the set to realize that the girl he thinks he loves, Lilianne, the script girl, played by Dani, is having quickie affairs with almost everyone who has five minutes free.

The film uproariously details the minutiae of temperament and disaster in the course of the production, which becomes a sort of lifetime. Everything is as temporary as the sets, as illusory as a prop candle that has an electric light hidden inside. Everything is obviously disguised, a substitute for reality, or a reflection of it. Real-life dialogue is transformed into the art of the film within. When Julie is discussing her role in "Meet Pamela" at a press conference on her arrival in Nice, she explains the plot of the film within by saying that the heroine falls in love with her father-in-law when she realizes that her husband is just a so-so reflection of the father.

For all of its inside details, "Day for Night" seems to me to be less about moviemaking than about a way of facing the conundrum of human existence. A candle may turn out to be fake, life-long friendships may simply be temporary alliances, and what seems to be love may only be infatuation or simply a cheering gift, a one-night stand. Art may be actual experience, ransacked and reformed. This awareness, however, need not diminish the quality of the experience or art. It can, in fact, enhance it. To deprecate it is to deprecate the grand possibilities of life itself.

I don't want to freight "Day for Night" with too much drug-store philosophy. It's such a buoyant, charming film, though, I fear that its wisdom, and the clear eye with which it regards some of life's more troubling aspects, will be overlooked.

1973 O 7, II:1:4

The Program

ISRAEL WHY, directed by Claude Lanzmann; screenplay (French, English, Hebrew, German and Russian with subtitles) by Mr. Lanzmann; photography, William Lubtchansky and Colin Mounier; editors, Ziva Postec and Francoise Beloux; production companies: Stephan Films, Parafrance, Compagnie d'Enterprise et de Gestion, Laboratoire Vitfer and Biderman. Running time: 185 minutes. At the New York Film Festival at Lincoln Center.

By NORA SAYRE

Soldiers in a grove of orange trees; American visitors exclaiming delightedly over Jewish products in a supermarket; a grizzled ex-Berliner singing Communist songs from the nineteen-thirties: "Rosa Luxemburg, we want to hold your hand"; children scrambling down a chalky hill to shout greetings at some Israeli Black Panthers; Arabs being frisked at a border, their hands raised meekly in the air; many old people — so many canes, limps, parched faces with seamed smiles.

Ranging from scholars to policemen and construction workers, encompassing a spectrum of nationalities, "Israel Why," the excellent documentary shown yesterday at the New York Film Festival, stresses the diversity of a society that seethes with as much complexity as ... America itself. Of course there's a different batch of contradictions. But we have to recognize a kinship with a pot that didn't melt.

This is a film that all kinds of Americans should see immediately: between the news bulletins, during and after the events of this very week.

Meanwhile, let's congratulate an immensely honest explorer; the director Claude Lanzmann, who calls his movie "subjective reportage." It's clear that, as a French Jew, he loves Israel and is also highly critical of it. And he refuses to pretend that this is an unemotional subject. He's said that he didn't seek to make a political picture. Yet he knows that almost any aspect of life in Israel is hinged to politics. The result is a deeply engrossing and moving three hours, with very fine camera work to boot.

In the tradition of Ophuls's "The Sorrow and the Pity," Lanzmann has used a giant chorus of voices to articulate the gut responses and conflicts of Israelis. Many of his interviewees didn't—and could not—agree with one another. But among the themes that recurred was the longing for peace, which many expressed most powerfully.

The people Lanzmann filmed certainly weren't war-like. Yet most also said that while there is war, they must and want to participate. And there's an emphasis on identification with the army: pride in the military, pride in the self that belongs to it, plus respect for the education it bestows. However, one young woman stated that the older generation was sacrificing the younger people of Israel—by demanding that they die for their country.

But quite a few also said that "if there were peace," they'd be willing to give back some of the territories. Others argued: "Give them Sinai, then they'll want Jerusalem. Would you give Paris to the British?" One man remarked that Israelis who weren't especially religious would have an easier time yielding territory and living within smaller boundaries than those who believed the land was theirs by divine right.

Although training is depicted, the film suggests that the authority of orthodox religion is waning in Israel—while, at the same time, identification is waxing. Another man said, "Israel was formed because the Jewish religion was weakening—like most religions."

Meanwhile, loyal Israelis discussed the dangers of insularity and isolation. It's explained that not being able to cross borders casually makes it difficult to see others' points of view. And peril at the borders is never forgotten: "It's a basic Jewish truth, to be in danger—not only at our own borders, but almost anywhere."

•

The movie also examines the situation of the Soviet Jews and the fact that many don't feel welcome in Israel. A wan young Russian couple are driven toward their future home in Arad. As great pleated folds of the desert, brilliant waterscapes and swirling green hills rush past the car's windows, those of us who don't know Israel see it for the first time through the Russians' eyes. They themselves look hopeful, cautious, slightly abashed.

The husband asks to stop at the Wailing Wall; he stands quietly with one hand upon it, overwhelmed by seeing and touching it for the first time. Afterward he says, "I haven't been here for 2,000 years." When they glimpse their new city—and we're struck by the bleakness of the raw buildings—they smile hugely and say they never knew it would be so beautiful.

A month later, the Russians are bitterly packing for departure. They look healthier but miserable. The man says, "I thought this was a country of Jews, and that here I'd be a real Jew, and everyone calls us Russian, Russian, Russian." He thinks that Israel is like the Soviet Union, partly because he feels pressured to say he likes it—and also that it's capitalistic. (Elsewhere, a few debate whether socialism or capitalism will win out in Israel. But no one makes a rousing conclusion.)

The Russian feels that he should have gone to America. But apparently, the couple stayed after all.

Words like "Russia" or "America" or "Israel" used to provoke a stock response from those of other nations, since political occurrences were automatically assumed to echo the public will. But surely one of the lessons of this last decade is that most governments don't represent all of their citizens. And "Israel Why" demonstrates that some of the people of Israel don't personify their foreign policy.

1973 O 8, 40:1

The Program

BEN-GURION REMEMBERS, directed by Simon Hesera; produced by Mr. Hesera and Alan Kay; written by Michael Bar-Zohar and Mr. Hesera; distributed by Lawrence Friedricks Enterprises. Running time: 85 minutes. At the Festival Theater, Sixth Avenue at 57th Street, the Little Neck in Queens and the Town East in Middletown, N.J.

"Ben-Gurion Remembers," in which Israel's elder statesman discourses on his life and career, took on special and unexpected poignancy yesterday as Arab and Israeli armies battled again over a country he so devotedly helped put together. At one point, indeed, he reminisces with other Jewish leaders about crucial decisions and battles, as newsreel shots sketch out Israel's 25-year history.

The result is an anniversary tribute to Israel and a good, thumbnail refresher course in history. But it is the personal exchanges of Mr. Ben-Gurion with such colleagues as Golda Meir, Moshe Dayan, Abba Eban and Zalman Shazar — wise, warm and wryly amusing — that make this movie so winning. As they recount sad, turbulent times, even noting personal dissensions, they reflect the detachment of key people who had significant jobs to do.

The film takes the former Premier from Jaffa, where he landed from Russia, to the sites of the Six Day War. These scenes have been directed unpretentiously but effectively by Simon Hesera. Mr. Ben-Gurion interestingly postscripts some footage of his visits with American leaders, including a deferential young Richard M. Nixon.

Of a smiling Dwight D. Eisenhower, he says, "A good man but I wouldn't have voted for him." Of John F. Kennedy: "Such a boy and one of their best Presidents."

Near the film's end, Mr. Ben-Gurion is shown in his home library, in the desert kibbutz where he has retired, discussing his memoirs. And at the fade-out, and the most moving thing in this admirable close-up, the old man and a young Israeli boy talking together, cross a field toward the horizon.

HOWARD THOMPSON

1973 O 8, 40:4

The Program

THE SECOND GUN, a documentary adapted and directed by Gerard Alcan, based on the investigation by Theodore Charach; produced and edited by Mr. Alcan; music, Travis E. Pike; produced by Mr. Charach and Mr. Alcan; released by National General Pictures. At the Trans-Lux East Theater, Third Avenue and 58th Street. Running time: 110 minutes. This film has not been classified.

Some seeds of doubt that Sirhan B. Sirhan was the sole assassin of Robert F. Kennedy that terrible day in 1968 have been developed into an arbor of testimony, allegations and accusations in "The Second Gun," which opened on Sunday at the Trans-Lux East. And, if Theodore Charach and Gerard Alcan, producers of this feature-length compilation of color and black-and-white interviews, re-enactments, newsreels and photographs, are not conclusive in their contentions, their insistent presentation does accentuate those doubts.

Mr. Charach, a radio and television journalist reportedly on the scene of the killing in Los Angeles's Ambassador Hotel, who spent five years in gathering his material, and Mr. Alcan, a writer-film maker who joined him in 1970, do not dispute the fact that Sirhan fired his gun directly at Mr. Kennedy, facing him. But the bulk of their material strongly suggests that a second gunman behind the Senator fired the bullet that actually killed him.

While the slayer is not named, an array of witnesses and researches contribute to their implication that justice still needs to be done. Thane Cesar, a private security guard behind Mr. Kennedy, admits drawing his gun, for example. And William W. Harper, a ballistics expert, and Dr. Thomas F. Noguchi, the coroner, among others, indicate that not one but two guns were involved.

In addition, the Los Angeles police, its ballistics man and legal and Federal agents who participated in the investigations leading to the ultimate conviction of Sirhan are criticized for, among other matters, alleged irregularities in testimony and suppression of evidence. But it must be noted that some members of the participating establishment are permitted to state countervailing views too.

"The Second Gun" evolves as serious and generally low-keyed pleading for further investigation and fuller explanations of the tragedy. But it gives the effect of sitting through a lengthy, diffuse, often static trial that tends to confuse, rather than prove, the case argued by the obviously dedicated producers. A viewer is still left with the feeling that the alleged evidence here is not nearly enough proof beyond a reasonable doubt that justice was blind.

A. H. WEILER

1973 O 9, 43:1

The Program

LAND DES SCHWEIGENS UND DER DUNKELHEIT (Land of Silence and Darkness), directed and produced by Werner Herzog; narrated (German with English subtitles) by Rolf Illig; director of photography, Jorg Schmidt-Reitwein; editor, Beate Mainka-Jellinghaus. Running time: 90 minutes. At the New York Film Festival at Lincoln Center. With: Fini Straubinger.

Werner Herzog's "Land des Schweigens und der Dunkelheit" ("Land of Silence and Darkness"), which was shown at the New York Film Festival at Lincoln Center last night (and will be repeated tomorrow night), is described in the festival's program as "a film that speaks up for life, warmly and movingly."

Only someone who has not seen any other Herzog films ("Even Dwarfs Started Small," "Fata Morgana") could accept this bland appraisal without flinching. Herzog speaking up for life, warmly and movingly? He may speak up for life, but it's through an acknowledgment of outrages, often lovingly inventoried. Herzog is not a simple film maker. The emotions evoked by his films are never easily categorized, nor, I think, are they meant to be.

"Land of Silence and Darkness" is no exception. It seems, at its beginning, a rather conventional documentary about the efforts of a middle-aged German woman named Fini Straubinger, who went blind at 15 and deaf at 18, to help other blind-deaf people. Fini travels around Germany doing good with alarming self assurance.

Her cheery efforts are most easily appreciated by people who've gone deaf and blind later in life, after they've had the use of those two senses. Later on, we see the efforts fail totally with people who've been born blind and deaf, since theirs is a world incomprehensible to even a do-gooder with Fini's energy and optimism. This is the note that concludes the film, which is not exactly the philosophy of "The Sound of Music."

Herzog is fascinated by grotesques, which he makes us see as object lessons in a perverse universe. A key to the irony with which Herzog invests this so-called warm and moving subject is contained in the film's title. As Fini tells us in the course of the movie, the deaf are not even allowed the comfort of silence: the head is full of strange buzzing and cracking sounds. The eyes, though incapable of seeing, are continually assaulted by lights, shadows and colors. Total darkness is a sighted person's poetic conceit.

Herzog, one of the most talented of the new young German film directors, will one day make a movie that's as interesting to sit through as to argue about later. "Land of Silence and Darkness" is not it.

VINCENT CANBY.

1973 O 9, 43:1

JUSTE AVANT LA NUIT (Just Before Nightfall), directed by Claude Chabrol; screenplay (French with English subtitles) by Mr. Chabrol, based on the novel, "The Thin Line," by Edward Atiyah; produced by Andre Genoves; director of photography, Jean Rabier; editor, Jacques Gaillard; music, Pierre Jansen; a French-Italian co-production by Les Films La Boetie, Columbia Pictures and Cinegai, distributed by Columbia Pictures. Running time: 107 minutes. At the New York Film Festival at Lincoln Center.

Helene Masson .... Stephane Audran
Charles Masson .... Michel Bouquet
Francois Tellier .... Francois Perier
Jeannot .... Jean Carmet
Dominique Prince .... Dominique Zardi
Cavanna .... Henri Attal
Bardin .... Paul Temps

By VINCENT CANBY

Marriage is a joke, according to nightclub comedians who possess no great amount of imagination. Claude Chabrol, the French director who has a lot of imagination, and whose elegant, witty "Juste Avant La Nuit" ("Just Before Nightfall") was shown at the New York Film Festival at Lincoln Center last night (and will be repeated there tonight), goes substantially further. If an ordinary marriage is a joke, he says, what appears to be a perfect marriage may be a cosmic jest.

This is one way of describing Chabrol's lovely "La Femme Infidèle," released here in 1969, as well as "Juste Avant La Nuit," which is about the problems of poor Charles (Michel Bouquet), a successful Paris advertising man, the husband of the incomparable Hélène (Stéphane Audran), the father of two healthy, spoiled children, and the possessor of a suburban house so modern, so full of corners, split-levels and glass that any drinking except for medicinal purposes is impractical.

As the film opens, Charles is matter-of-factly throttling the life out of his beautiful mistress, the wife of his best friend, François (François Perier) who is also his architect. The soon-to-be-late mistress, an enthusiast of sado-masochism, has goaded Charles into strangling her, though she didn't mean for him to go all the way.

Did Charles intend to kill her? Probably not, though we are never sure. Charles gets away with murder easily enough. When the dread news of her death arrives, he is able to share Hélène's surprise and to console the not-terribly-bereaved husband, who acknowledges that he and his wife went their own ways. Says François: "We weren't like you and Hélène." The only thing Charles cannot escape is his own need to be punished.

He must confess to Hélène, who is pained for a moment and, being the perfect wife, she consoles him. François is equally reluctant to be an instrument for retribution. "Listen," he says as if talking about a bit of bad luck on the golf course, "we've known each other for 25 years. What happened was a nightmare. Nobody is guilty in a nightmare."

"Juste Avant La Nuit," like so many Chabrol films, eventually becomes too schematic for my taste, but early on the scheme has so many ambiguous twists and turns that the film continues to provoke the memory long after one has left the theater.

The relationship between Charles and Hélène is especially complex. They maintain that precarious balance sometimes achieved by two loving, intelligent people who deny each other nothing except true intimacy. It is significant that although we see Charles in passionate connection with his mistress (murder, I assume, is passionate), there is never any hint of sex between him and Hélène. When such intimacy is denied, Chabrol suggests, the results can be disastrous. They can also be extremely entertaining.

On the scale of recent Chabrol films, "Juste Avant La Nuit" is somewhere below "La Femme Infidèle" and "Le Boucher" but above "La Rupture," though the latter is a much more ambitious film. This one is a comedy of a high, intelligent and dark order, full of scenes of charming domestic accord (family meals, Christmas celebrations, in-law visits) casually punctuated by a close-up shot of a mouse making a fatal lunge at the cheese in a mousetrap.

1973 O 9, 42:1

The Cast

ANDREI RUBLEV, directed by Andrei Tarkovsky; screenplay (Russian with English subtitles) by Andrei Mikhalkov-Kontchalovsky and Mr. Tarkovsky; director of photography, Vadim Youssov; editors, N. Beliaeva and L. Lararev; music, Viatcheslav Ovtchinnikov; a Mosfilm production, distributed by Columbia Pictures. Running time: 146 minutes. At the New York Film Festival at Lincoln Center.

Andrei Rublev .... Anatoli Solonitzine
Kirill .... Ivan Lapikov
Daniel the Black .... Nikolai Grinko
Theophane the Greek .. Nikolai Sergueiev
The Simpleton .... Irma Raouch
Boriska .... Nikolai Bourliaiev
The Grand Duke .... Youri Nasarov

By VINCENT CANBY

Andrei Rublev (circa 1360-1430) is the Russian monk who is credited with having liberated Russian icon painting from Byzantine traditions of severity and estheticism to create a distinctly Russian art, warmer and more poetic than the work that came before. His life, of which only the most general details are known, is the take-off point for the massive, oddly elliptical Russian film that was shown last night at the New York Film Festival at Lincoln Center and will be shown there again tonight.

"Andrei Rublev" has had a curious history. Verifying facts about it is only slightly less difficult than authen-ticating some of the paintings that have been attributed to Rublev.

This much is known: the film, which was being shown privately in Moscow in 1967, was presented out of competition at the 1969 Cannes Film Festival by the owner of the French distribution rights but against the official wishes of the Russians, who reportedly felt that one of its themes—the artist trying to make sense within a brutalizing world—had embarrassing contemporary parallels.

When it was shown at Cannes, the film was almost three hours, although it was said to have been cut. Last night at Alice Tully Hall, the running time was 2 hours and 26 minutes. This should be pointed out, I think, to explain the certain disadvantage under which we must judge it. How much of the film's highly praised free form is the intention of the director or simply a result of an editor's itchy fingers? I'm not sure.

The film I saw was free in narrative form, all right, but almost DeMille-heavy in style. This is most apparent in the huge spectacle scenes that show us the Tartars pillaging and raping with great, old-fashioned gusto ("I saw a town," one Tartar chief explains to another, "and couldn't resist"), and, at another point, drop Andrei into the midst of a pagan orgy where, it seems, he suffers a fate more provocative than death. That is, for a monk.

The film is presented in a series of separate chapters, or panels, not unlike those in an iconostasis, that especially Russian collection of icons (developed in Rublev's day) that form a screen between the sanctuary of a church and the nave. In some panels Andrei (Anatoli Solonitzine) is barely visible, a minor character; in others he is in the foreground although he is seldom more than the passive recorder of the events around him, as we are.

In this fashion, I assume, we are meant to share the passions, sorrows and doubts that shaped the artist, but since there always seems to be more going on in the head of the film's director than in the head of the man playing Andrei, the system did not work for me. I wondered, for example, how the director got a horse to fall down stairs. Was the horse hurt? That sort of question takes precedence over questions of esthetics.

Andrei Tarkovsky, the director whose "My Name Is Ivan" was released here in 1963, spares us most of the usual movie-nonsense talk about art and the artist, and he never once shows us Andrei's trying to decide whether to use blue paint or green. He also has created a couple of impressive individual sequences, including the preparations for, and casting of, a giant church bell, and the opening sequence in which Andrei witnesses the desperate revels of a group of peasants who have taken refuge in a barn during a storm.

Unfortunately, Tarkovsky also has a particularly Russian eye for movie lyricism, which is not very interesting: a fondness for sun-created halos, rain, snow, rushing streams and air filled with dandelion fluff, all those clichés that more frequently evoke the moviemaker's fatigue than his poetic sensibility.

However, I hedge my comments in the knowledge that I've not seen the film that Tarkovsky made. This "Andrei Rublev" says not much more about the trials of the artist than does Truffaut's "Day for Night," which manages the feat without any impalings and with no dandelion fluff.

1973 O 10, 43:1

The Cast

DISTANT THUNDER (Ashani Sanket), directed by Satyajit Ray; screenplay (Bengali with English subtitles) by Mr. Ray, based on the novel by Bibhuti Bhusan Bannerji; director of photography, Soumendu Roy; editor, Dulal Dutta; music, Mr. Ray; executive producer, Mrs. Sarbani Bhattacharya. Running time: 100 minutes. At the New York Film Festival at Lincoln Center.
Gangacharan .... Soumitra Chatterji
Ananga .... Babita
Chhutki .... Sandhya Roy
Dinabandhu .... Gobinda Chakravarty
Biswas .... Romesh Mukerji

By VINCENT CANBY

The Bengali countryside is almost heavy with color, with golds, yellows, umbers, and especially with the greens of the rice fields. The village is tranquil. Caste is observed. It is part of the order of things. Occasionally groups of airplanes are heard overhead, but they are as remote as the war that, according to a village elder, "the king is fighting with the Germans and the Japanese." One villager reports the Germans have captured Singapore, but he is corrected. It's the Japanese who have captured Singapore, the man is told.

Aside from a shortage of kerosene, the war, at first, doesn't seem to have much effect on the villagers in Satyajit Ray's fine, elegiac new film, "Distant Thunder" (Ashani Sanket). The movie, which has the impact of an epic without seeming to mean to, was shown last night at the New York Film Festival at Lincoln Center. It will be presented there again tonight.

"Distant Thunder" has all sorts of connections with Ray's great Apu Trilogy—its village setting, its leading actor, Soumitra Chatterji, who played the title role in "The World of Apu," and its source material. The new

film, like the Apu Trilogy, is based on a novel by Bibhuti Bhusan Bannerji. It is, however, very different from those early films.

It is the work of a director who has learned the value of narrative economy to such an extent that "Distant Thunder," which is set against the backdrop of the "manmade" famine that wiped out 5 million people in 1943, has the simplicity of a fable.

Though its field of vision is narrow, more or less confined to the social awakening of a young village Brahmin and his pretty, naive wife, the sweep of the film is so vast that, at the end, you feel as if you'd witnessed the events from a satellite. You've somehow been able to see simultaneously the curvature of the earth and the insects on the blades of field grass.

•

"Distant Thunder" is about Gangacharan (Mr. Chatterji), the only Brahmin in his village, a solemn and rather pompous young man who accepts the responsibilities as well as the privileges of caste. As teacher, physician and priest he looks forward to the material rewards due him. When Ananga, his wife, asks him if he really can ward off cholera through spells, for which neighboring villagers will pay him handsomely, he replies that, in addition to the spells, he will pass on to the villagers from his hygiene encyclopedia.

As the war-induced rice shortage becomes increasingly acute, the tranquillity of the village is destroyed. Life-long trusts are betrayed. Civil order falls apart. At the same time, the famine prompts some remarkable instances of love and compassion. The self-assured Gangacharan, who wears black-rim spectacles and carries a black umbrella, is at first angry when his wife proposes that she go to work to earn rice for them. Then he says quietly: "If we have to humble ourselves, it's best we do it together."

•

As the scramble to survive humiliates some of Ray's characters, it ennobles others, including Gangacharan who, towards the end, has begun to question the social system that he has always accepted as given and right. In the context of the film, this is a revolutionary conversion, and a most moving one.

Ray has chosen to photograph the film in rich, warm colors, the effect of which is not to soften the focus of the film but to sharpen it. The course of terrible events seems that much more vivid in landscapes of relentless beauty.

1973 O 12, 32:1

CARRIAGE TRADE, a 60-minute, silent compilation of travels, home movies and documents by Warren Sonbert. At the Whitney Museum of American Art, Madison Avenue and 75th Street.

"Carriage Trade," which arrived yesterday for a week's stand at the Whitney Museum of American Art, leaves the kaleidoscopic impressions caught from a jet, not a carriage, speeding across the globe with momentary, unscheduled stops at exotic and familiar places. There is no doubt as to the beauty of the images in this latest offering in the museum's New American Filmmaker series, but these are flashing vignettes that titillate the eye but rarely remain long enough to engage the mind.

Warren Sonbert, who spent some six years traveling, shooting, compiling and editing his 16-mm. color and black-and-white footage of "home movies and documents" into an hour-long, silent feature, has succeeded in achieving what he calls "varied displaced effects."

Thus, his journeys from Broadway to Afghanistan, Turkey, India, Egypt, among other areas, have quickly passing, individual but not general, visual impact. Arab camel riders on a desert follow pleasingly pastoral views of waving flowers. The Music Hall's Rockettes prance by as rapidly as an English wedding scene or bathers in the Ganges, or gondolas on the Grand Canal, or a pretty American girl smoking a cigarette or traders in an Indian market place.

As a cinematic diarist, Warren Sonbert admits in a program footnote that his editing does not stress any particular place or people. "It's all just there," he says. It is indeed. And while "Carriage Trade" makes for a slightly dizzying but colorful and far-ranging trip, it also illustrates the talents of an acutely perceptive and artistic film maker.

A. H. WEILER

1973 O 12, 33:1

The Cast

THE BITTER TEARS OF PETRA VON KANT (Die Bitteren Tränen Der Petra Von Kant), directed by R. W. Fassbinder; screenplay (German with English subtitles) by Mr. Fassbinder; from the play by Mr. Fassbinder; photography, Michael Ballhaus; music, Verdi, the Platters and Walker Brothers; production company, Tango-Film (Filmverlag der Autoren). At the New York Film Festival, Lincoln Center. Running time, 119 minutes.
Petra von Kant ...... Margit Carstensen
Karim Thimm .... Hanna Schygulla
Marlene .... Irm Hermann
Gabriele von Kant .... Eva Mattes
Sidonie von Grasenabb.. Katrin Schaake
Valerie von Kant ...... Gisela Fackelday

By NORA SAYRE

"My heart is sore as if it had been stabbed": that kind of imagery may pass in Germany, but stab-wise New Yorkers know that wounded hearts don't lounge around, they go to Bellevue. Even those who love pain will be frustrated by "The Bitter Tears of Petra von

Kant," shown last night at the New York Film Festival.

Throughout, the cruelty creaks and the sobs sound forced — you might call it sawdust suffering. Petra (Margit Carstensen), a successful fashion designer, plays slavemaster to her secretary, barking out orders— "Get my shoes!"—in a style that fails to match Joan Crawford's in "The Best of Everything."

The slave winces with mute gratitude until their stable relationship is disrupted by a younger woman. Then the secretary's typewriter clatters with agitation while Petra seduces the newcomer. You can see the next scene coming like an avalanche: there's going to be a role reversal here. So Petra becomes a slave to the sulky model who says she needs men "from time to time" and soon returns to her husband.

In response, Petra gets sloshed all over a white fur floor, stamps on her antique tea set, announces that she'd like to die, to sleep . . . (no, she's not going to dream), and ruins her own birthday party. Hung over, she resolves to be nicer to her secretary, who exits at once—apparently appalled by even a hint of kindness.

•

"Bitter Tears" almost contributes to film history—it's like an anthology of movie chestnuts culled from the last 50 years. It would be even more enlightening if the director (R. W. Fassbinder) had been born in the eighteen-nineties instead of 1945. Still, we get a flood of lavish facial expressions from silent movies. The actresses grin or smoulder extravagantly, heave their shoulders high in poignant shrugs. There's also the old gimmick of peering intently into a mirror while making a long slow speech about the past.

And obviously, Mr. Fassbinder thinks that women flirt like mastodons. Every gesture, each glance, any

phrase is freighted with significance—e v e n "Would you . . . like coffee" or "I used to like . . . mathematics." And eyes have to freeze between the simplest of sentences. But my favorite relic from bad old pictures is the (deeply emotional) monologue delivered by someone, who has her cheek pressed against the upper back of the lucky listener, while the latter stares into space. This occurs three times in the movie, surely a record for the shoulder blade as amplifier.

All the right props are present—a Siamese cat, bald-headed unclothed mannequins, a quasi-Renaissance mural of far-flung nudes more wigs than you ever saw at a demolition sale, plus seasonable slave clothes: metallic breast cups, throttling gold collars, a bare back with a latticework of chains. And there's traditional wisdom, too, such as: "A woman has her trumps, but she has to play them." Or, "Where terror reigns, mankind is puny." And, "Everyone needs consolation."

•

Clearly, the director was awash in his fantasies about lesbianism. He worked hard on decadence (gin at breakfast, fur on anything,) and strugged to create a lush, weird setting for inevitable remorse. He wants the audience to remember how terribly unnatural this all is. Hence, his women look like no one you'd ever meet, and he has filmed them under lighting that makes them look pastier and stranger than anyone encountered by flashlight in a sewer.

Despite a few lines like "Woman must fight for her place in this world," don't let it be rumored that this is a liberated movie. Instead, it should be regarded as a chronicle of blunders that film-makers have repeated throughout the decades.

1973 O 13, 26:3

Down 'Mean Streets'

BY VINCENT CANBY

AMERICAN moviemaking can't be in such a sorry state after all, not when it can produce three films by new directors as gifted and as particularly American as Ralph Bakshi ("Heavy Traffic"), George Lucas ("American Graffiti") and Martin Scorsese ("Mean Streets"). Each of these films is the director's second or third feature, which is worth emphasizing in an era and an art in which a man's debut is likely to be his entire career. Making movies is expensive—even cheap ones. The film industry is notoriously impatient with promising beginners. They had better deliver the goods in a hurry or it's a quick hustle out a back door into an alley called oblivion. The first films of each of these directors—Bakshi's "Fritz The Cat," Lucas's "THX-1138" and Scorsese's "Who's That Knocking at My Door?" and "Boxcar Bertha" — were respectfully received but, with the exception of "Fritz The Cat," they caused no great stir with the public. Thus it is encouraging that the directors somehow managed to go on.

I'm especially impressed with "Mean Streets," which was shown at the New York Film Festival at Lincoln Center 10 days ago and opens today at the Cinema I Theater. It's a tough, vivid melodrama set in New York's Little Italy about a nice young second-generation Italian-American named Charlie (Harvey Keitel), a punk whose instincts are fatally decent. Charlie is trapped in a tiny world that is on the lower East Side geographically, but whose manners and morals are a jumble of things accepted here and other things handed down from over there. Charlie is not the sort of guy to use Kleenex. He carries big old-fashioned handkerchiefs that you know have been carefully washed and ironed by his mother.

I'm impressed because although "Who's That Knocking at My Door?," which took place in the Little Italy of "Mean Streets," showed a lot of technical expertise and sensitivity, neither the expertise nor the sensitivity was remarkable. It looked like the work of someone who had studied his film-school lessons and had done about as well as he could, but that would be that. The difference between Scorsese's first feature, full of poetic pan shots and other visual equivalents of purple prose, and his third, "Mean Streets," is the difference between an undergraduate's notebook and a novel written by someone who has learned that the best stories are not told, they are evoked.

When I saw "Mean Streets" I didn't know that Francis Ford Coppola, himself a successful young director-writer, who was instrumental in the production of "American Graffiti," was also a Scorsese booster. Yet I was aware of similarities between the two films, which may not have anything to do with Coppola. Both films make use of a narrative form that is no less effective, no less full of suspense, for being free of a

conventional story line and the kind of exposition usually needed to explain that story line.

Like "American Graffiti," Scorsese's new film, written by the director and Mardik Martin, takes place in a present that tells us all we need know about the past and, probably the future. At the center is Charlie, on the surface a flashy dresser and a self-assured favorite of his Uncle Giovanni (Cesare Danova), a syndicate boss for whom Charlie makes collections.

Charlie, however, is riddled with guilts he probably couldn't explain if he tried. His self-assurance is wood that termites have lived in.

His off-screen mom and the off-screen priests have left him convinced that he is unworthy, a fear that the on-screen Giovanni aggravates by questioning the sort of people he goes around with. Giovanni suggests that Charlie drop the two persons who are most important in his life, the girl he loves, Teresa (Amy Robinson), an Italian-American girl who would be acceptable but for the fact she is an epileptic,

and her cousin, Johnny Boy (Robert De Niro), a simpleminded neighborhood tough, given to blowing up mail boxes and borrowing money from loan sharks he has no intention of repaying.

The heart of the film is the responsibility that Charlie feels for the suicidally irresponsible Johnny Boy. It's a George-and-Lenny relationship transplanted from Steinbeck's "Of Mice and Men" country to the lower East Side.

*

Scorsese's method is deceptively oblique. "Mean Streets" starts off as harmlessly as a Little-Italy version of "Marty": a bunch of the guys horsing around—Charlie, Johnny Boy, their friend Tony (David Proval), who runs a bar—not going anywhere in particular, not worried about much. Slowly, however, we become conscious that the boredom in Charlie's world is simply a gentle disguise for fear.

Friendships are constantly tested by short, furious tempers. Even love is denied. Johnny Boy lies to Charlie, the one man in the world who cares about him, and says "I swear on my mother . . . . I swear on Jesus Christ." Charlie, afraid of what his uncle will say, refuses to commit himself to Teresa, who has more courage than Charlie does. The violence that erupts in the film seems a logical consequence of these denials and subversions.

"Mean Streets" is full of stunning sequences, including a casual assassination in the men's room of Tony's bar when an ambitious kid who wants to get in good with the mob shoots a drunk who has in some way insulted a local don. There is another sequence at Tony's, a welcome home party for a local boy back from Vietnam, which is one of the most mysteriously sorrowful moments in any recent American film.

The look, language and performances are so accurate, so unselfconscious, so directly evocative, that they provide "Mean Streets" with the momentum and suspense that one usually associates with more conventional narratives, movies about prison breaks, bank heists, and such. Will they? Won't they? In "Mean Streets," the question has to do with survival.

Scorsese photographed most of "Mean Streets" in and around Little Italy, a lot of it in barrooms and pool halls where the colors are juke-box primaries. He depends—perhaps a little too much—on the picturesqueness of the quarter's San Gennaro Festival, but maybe I object to that only because I'm so used to second-rate films that employ sight-seeing as a substitute for drama. "Mean Streets" is a decidedly first-rate film, a film that continually reinforces its various themes with gestures taken from life rather than cinema.

At one point in the movie, Charlie takes Johnny Boy into a cemetery late at night to try to talk some sense into him. He's furious and Johnny Boy is being purposely opaque. Before they sit down, each takes out his handkerchief and places it daintily on the gravestone so as not to get city dirt on the seat of his trousers. It's the kind of thing that someone who depends on Kleenex would never think of doing.

1973 O 14, II:1:1

'The Grande Bouffe'

By FOSTER HIRSCH

FOUR men spend a weekend eating themselves to death in a grim, overdecorated mansion: the conceit has the imprint of an allegory by Buñuel, the echo of wild house parties in Italian movies of a decade ago, the teasing metaphysics of a "Last Year at Marienbad." Four men tied to a brotherhood pact that tests endurance — the premise is also a kinky Continental variation on "Deliverance."

Marco Ferreri's "The Grande Bouffe" trips over prize-winning foreign films of the sixties, tickles us with memories of Fellini and Resnais and Buñuel, of Antonioni and claustrophobic chamber works by Bergman. But the movie's greatest debt is not to the preceding era's prestigious portraits of European decadence but to the laws of the universe — the ways of the world — as the porno movie sees them. Ferreri's is a porn epic in the grand manner, a mordant, chilling, hilarious dirty movie that, for sheer audacious lubricity, out-tangoes "Last Tango in Paris" and almost gives the devilish Miss Jones a run for her money.

Like "Last Tango," "The Grande Bouffe" derives added shock value from the presence of stars: it's not Linda Lovelace, but respectable people like Marcello Mastroianni and Ugo Tognazzi taking the chance of their careers, letting loose, talking dirty, abandoning themselves to the urges of the unleashed libido.

Ferreri has set out with a fierce will to challenge audience sensibility, and his Rabelaisian romp establishes new levels of raunchy foul taste in art house — as distinct from 42d Street — porn movie fare. In manner and matter, Ferreri is working on a level that the makers of "Deep Throat" could not — and would not — aspire to, but his movie's lifelines are decidedly pornographic.

The first law of the true-blue porn movie is the tyranny of the flesh: we don't see the characters in "The Grande Bouffe" otherwise occupied than at the feast, their one obsessive, consuming goal the constant satisfaction of the senses. Locking themselves away from the world in a mausoleum of a house and shedding civilized restraints, Ferreri's cardboard figures are participants in a porn-movie banquet, questers in search of absolute freedom. At their

Foster Hirsch is the author of "Elizabeth Taylor," a critical study of the actress's films, to be published next month by Pyramid.

Andrea Ferreol and Philippe Noiret are participants in a weekend orgy of food and sex in Marco Ferreri's film, "The Grand Bouffe"

"The movie tests our limits of shockability"

non-stop weekend orgy, food and sex are available in unlimited supply, and as with the Linda Lovelaces and Felicity Splits of the blue-movie screen, too much is not enough for these celebrants. Once embarked on an orgy of tasting and touching, they are powerless, imprisoned rather than liberated by the spirit of Dionysus.

*

There's no joy at Ferreri's table; their passions and appetites spent, the revelers have no place to go. It's the presence of melancholy and death in the face of a sensational bacchanal that distinguishes Ferreri's feast of carrion from its lowbrow cousins. Characters in porn movies are evaluated with regard to their sexual prowess and their freedom from guilt, and they are never more than temporarily unhappy: more frequent and more intense sex can solve any passing malaise. But here, the pleasures of the flesh are but harbingers of the coffin, and Ferreri's pestilential houseparty is, finally, a warning, an exemplum, an inverse appreciation of bourgeois restraint.

Porn people, those guiltless joy-seekers, may inspire our envy and ignite our lascivious fantasies, whereas Ferreri's party-makers have only our pity, and our disgust. In porn, and in "advanced" movies of the sixties such as "La Dolce Vita," say, or "L'Avventura," decadence and dissipation are chic, inviting; the houseparty in "The Grande Bouffe" is entirely without glamour. You'll remember in "La Dolce Vita" the character of Paola the Innocent who represents the possibility of a higher and finer life than the one Marcello slips into. Here, Marcello has no options — he's sunk, irretrievably, in a swamp of self-indulgence.

*

The movie entertains no visions of romance or purity. The eaters have nothing beautiful to look back on, having left behind — in the world outside their death-trap — crummy, undistinguished lives. Stripped now of the final vestiges of self-respect, they devote themselves to total self-abasement. (And the women who are their companions in degradation are in every way their moral equals.)

Adapting the audacious lawlessness of the porn movie to his Swiftian demolition of untrammeled appetite, his parable, as many critics have read it, of the collapse of modern society, Ferreri has arrived at a tantalizing blend: the dirty movie with the heart of an impassioned medieval moralist. The director has the puritan's inevitable fascination with sin and corruption: he's titillated by what he shows us, but he's repelled, too — and it's that moralistic disapproval, that unconcealable sense of shock, that separates his work, for all its salacious preoccupations, from that of the true, unstricken pornographers.

*

Morality aside, "The Grande Bouffe" is a liberatingly funny pitch-black comedy. Ferreri assaults us. You're bound to be caught off guard by the overheated outhouse humor, the bloated, fetid atmosphere, the absorption with vomit and excrement, the colossal disrespect for human anatomy. Like pornography, it turns us (whether we're willing or not, and if we pay our porn-movie price of $5 we certainly ought to be willing) into voyeurs and accomplices. It appeals to our prurient curiosity at the same time that it disdains erotic indulgence. The movie tests our limits of shockability: how much can you take, Ferreri seems, combatively, to be asking. His theme is the folly of moral anar-

chy, but Ferreri himself holds back: he is a strict, even severe director who allows not one arty shot or lyrical moment to intrude onto his bleak canvas. Slowly, carefully, his film builds, snaring us by its opposing tensions. Porn brushed with intense moral vigilance, the movie keeps turning on itself, proffering and withdrawing erotic titillation, discovering laughter and terror in the retreat from social restraints.

One of the most tantalizing dissonances is the work of the superb actors, who keep insinuating real pathos and depth beneath the gaudy surfaces of their dirty-cartoon-strip characters: one lost, soulful look from Marcello, one hurt glance from Andrea Ferreol (the actress who plays, unforgettably, the concupiscent schoolteacher who outlasts them all), and the eaters who are bent on turning themselves into trash become momentarily sympathetic — real people that we feel can still be "saved." Convulsed by laughter that chokes, we're depleted by movie's end, having been through a cathartic, unlovely experience: the orgy as death-kit.

1973 O 14, II:15:1

The Cast

BADLANDS, produced, written and directed by Terrence Malick; directors of photography, Brian Probyn, Tak Fujimoto and Stevan Larner; editor, Robert Estrin; a Pressman-Williams presentation. Running time; 95 minutes. At the New York Film Festival at Lincoln Center.
Kit .... Martin Sheen
Holly .... Sissy Spacek
Holly's Father .... Warren Oates
Cato .... Ramon Bieri
Deputy .... Alan Vint

By VINCENT CANBY

The time is late summer at the end of the nineteen-fifties and the place a small, placid town in South Dakota. The streets are lined with oak and maple trees in full leaf. The lawns are so neat, so close-cropped, they look crew-cut. Kit Carruthers (Martin Sheen) is 25, a garbage collector who fancies his cowboy boots and his faint resemblance to James Dean. Holly Sargis (Sissy Spacek) is 15. Until she meets Kit, she hasn't much interest in anything except her dog and her baton, which she practices twirling in her front yard.

In Terrence Malick's cool, sometimes brilliant, always ferociously American film, "Badlands," which marks Malick's debut as a director, Kit and Holly take an all-American joyride across the upper Middle West, at the end of which more than half a dozen people have been shot to death by Kit, usually at point-blank range.

•

"Badlands" was presented twice at Alice Tully Hall Saturday night, the closing feature of the 11th New York Film Festival that began so auspiciously with François Truffaut's "Day for Night." In between there were a lot of other films, good and bad, but none as provocative as this first feature by Malick, a 29-year-old former Rhodes Scholar and philosophy stu-

dent whose only other film credit is as the author of the screenplay for last year's nicely idiosyncratic "Pocket Money."

"Badlands" was inspired by the short, bloody saga of Charles Starkweather who, at age 19, in January, 1958, with the apparent cooperation of his 14-year-old girlfriend, Caril Fugate, went off on a murder spree that resulted in 10 victims. Starkweather was later executed in the electric chair and Miss Fugate given life imprisonment.

"Badlands" inevitably invites comparisons with three other important American films, Arthur Penn's "Bonnie and Clyde" and Fritz Lang's "Fury" and "You Only Live Once," but it has a very different vision of violence and death. Malick spends no great amount of time invoking Freud to explain the behavior of Kit and Holly, nor is there any Depression to be held ultimately responsible. Society is, if anything, benign.

This is the haunting truth of "Badlands," something that places it very much in the seventies in spite of its carefully recreated period detail. Kit and Holly are directionless creatures, technically literate but uneducated in any real sense, so desensitized that Kit (in Malick's words at a news conference) can regard the gun with which he shoots people as a kind of magic wand that eliminates small nuisances. Kit and Holly are members of the television generation run amok.

They are not ill-housed, ill-clothed or ill-fed. If they are at all aware of their anger (and I'm not sure they are, since they see only boredom), it's because of the difference between the way

The Cast

THE OPTIMISTS, directed by Anthony Simmons; screenplay by Mr. Simmons and Tudor Gates, based on the novel "The Optimists of Nine Elms" by Mr. Simmons; director of photography, Larry Pizer; film editor, John Jympson; music by Lionel Bart; produced by Adrian Gaye and Victor Lyndon; released by Paramount Pictures. At Radio City Music Hall, Avenue of the Americas and 50th Street. Running time: 110 minutes. This film is classified G.

Sam .... Peter Sellers
Liz .... Donna Mullane
Mark .... John Chaffey
Bob Ellis .... David Daker
Chrissie Ellis .... Marjorie Yates
Ellis Baby .... Katyana Kass

By LAWRENCE VAN GELDER

Before proceeding to review "The Optimists," which opened yesterday at the Radio City Music Hall, there are a few confessions I feel obligated to make.

I am an unabashed Anglophile.

I have been carrying on a torrid love affair with London for 18 years and expect it to endure for the rest of my life.

I have recently been thinking about trying to lay my hands on some recordings of old English music hall tunes.

Having said all that, I can now comfortably go on to say that I wallowed with porcine delight in "The Optimists." Its principal ingredients are an old busker (street entertainer) with a head full of music hall songs and jests, a couple of slum children and their poverty-calloused parents, a pair of dogs and London itself.

●

A little bit of it is the London of tourists—the West End; but much of it is London south of the river, the London of Thames-side garbage dumps, looming power stations, squalid housing erected some 80 years ago and the new council flats that are the hope of a more comfortable life for thousands of people. And the director of photography Larry Pizer, has caught it all, and more, with a loving eye.

On the level of story, "The Optimists," with songs and music by Lionel Bart, is the sort of old-fashioned excursion into sentiment that ought to warm the hearts of parents in search of that elusive piece of merchandise that goes under the name of good family entertainment.

Peter Sellers, with a wardrobe of old music hall clothes, a talented but aged dog named Bella and a pram he pushes around London, plays the lonely, idiosyncratic old busker. And commendably, he submerges himself sufficiently in the part to allow old Sam to have a life of his own.

David Daker and Marjorie as a London schoolgirl recruited for her role, is pure enchantment as the elder of the two children (John Chaffey plays her little brother) who befriend the busker and learn from him a little bit about the magic of life.

David Daker and Marjorie Yates are letter-perfect in the thankless roles of the parents too busy surviving to worry about magic.

"People like you bring kids into the world, don't know what they're all about," Sellers says. On that subject, this film succeeds better than most.

1973 O 19, 58:1

I. F. STONE'S WEEKLY, a documentary directed, photographed, produced and edited by Jerry Bruck Jr. Narrated by Tom Wicker. Running time: 62 minutes. At the First Avenue Screening Room. First Avenue at 61st Street. This film has not been classified.

I. F. Stone, in the movie of the same name

By VINCENT CANBY

It's only 62 minutes long. It was photographed in black and white with a religious austerity. It has no theme music. It is a documentary, and its title sounds like something glimpsed on an index card at the Public Library.

Yet Jerry Bruck Jr.'s "I. F. Stone's Weekly," which opened yesterday at the First Avenue Screening Room, is such a thorough delight it left me feeling the way other people said they felt after seeing "The Sound of Music." That is, quite high.

●

I should admit that "The Sound of Music" depressed me. It evoked civilization's imminent collapse. It made me think of the Chinese Communists and suspect that they'd be taking us over sooner rather than later.

the ferocious conscience of American journalists and those American citizens who would listen to him in person or who subscribed to his newsletter, which he started in 1952 and finally folded in 1971, when he moved his often dumfounded prose to the New York Review of Books.

"I. F. Stone's Weekly" is no dopey paean to a great man. Supplemented by a modest, informative commentary spoken by Tom Wicker, the film presents Izzy Stone straight, with all his eccentricities and enthusiasms intact, in interviews, in public speeches and even walking down to the corner to stuff a week's issue into the post box.

We listen to Izzy describe a hilarious early confrontation with the Atomic Energy Commission (about underground testing), requiring

What was the use of thought or reason? Our minds have already turned into mashed potatoes.

Or have they?

Not, I think, as long as Isadore Feinstein Stone is on the American scene, passionately exposing the fallacies, double-talk and ignorance of the various rascals in Government, elected, appointed or there simply because of being someone's friend.

I. F. Stone, now 66, has been a maverick all his life, a Communist anarchist in his youth, once described as "a strident voice of illiberalism" by Spiro T. Agnew, and now self-defined as a counter-revolutionary.

Through it all, he has been

him to make a visit to some seismology experts in the Commerce Department's Coast and Geodetic Survey. "They were so glad to see a reporter. I don't think they'd seen a reporter since there was a tremble from Mount Ararat, when Noah's Ark landed."

He describes the danger for Washington correspondents who become pals with statesmen ("You begin to understand there are certain things the public ought not to know"). He talks about his own lean years as a blacklisted reporter and the genesis of his weekly, through which he taught all the rest of us how to find stories within stories, through inconsistencies, through information inadvertently made public but unnoticed by other reporters.

The film brilliantly succeeds in communicating Stone's near-obsessive interest in truth and his optimism. The war in Vietnam, he suggests, and the survival of the Vietnamese people through years of bombing have re-established "the primacy of man in an age of technology."

Toward the end Stone tells a group of students: "I really have so much fun I ought to be arrested." There is more to that statement than sentimental fondness for his profession. A cub reporter, he says, may get so excited covering a big fire that he forgets that something really is burning.

●

As Jerry Bruck Jr. is lucky to have a subject as dynamic as Stone, so is Stone lucky to have a young film maker as persistent and as obsessed, in his way, as Bruck. "I.F. Stone's Weekly" has been three years in the making, on a shoestring, and in bits and pieces. The result is a rare film, a fitting tribute to a man who never gives up.

1973 O 19, 52:1

The Cast

CHARLIE VARRICK, directed and produced by Don Siegel; screenplay by Howard Rodman and Dean Riesner, adapted from the novel "The Looters," by John Reese; director of photography, Michael Butler; music, Lalo Schifrin; editor, Frank Moriss; executive producer, Jennings Lang; distributed by Universal Pictures. Running time: 111 minutes. At the Loews State 2 Theater, Broadway at 45th Street, and Loews Orpheum Theater, 86th Street near Third Avenue. This film has been classified PG.

Charley Varrick .... Walter Matthau
Molly .... Joe Don Baker
Sybil Fort .... Felicia Farr
Harman Sullivan .... Andy Robinson
Maynard Boyle .... John Vernon
Jewell Everett .... Sheree North
Mr. Garfinkle .... Norman Fell

By VINCENT CANBY

An intelligent action melodrama is probably one of the most difficult kinds of film to make. Intelligence in this case has nothing to do with being literate, poetic or even reasonable. It has to do with

movement, suspense and sudden changes in fortune that are plausible enough to entertain without challenging you to question basic premises. If you start asking whether such-and-such could really have happened, or if so-and-so would have in a certain way, the action film falls apart.

It also falls apart when it has the distasteful philosophical underpinnings that Don Siegel last year gave his "Dirty Harry." The vigilante justice favored by that film made the violence truly shocking. There are no such problems with Siegel's new movie, the entertaining robbers-and-robbers action melodrama called "Charley Varrick," which opened yesterday at the Loew's State 2 and the Orpheum.

●

Charley Varrick (Walter Matthau) is a former air-circus pilot, supposedly turned legitimate crop duster, who makes his living robbing small banks in the Southwest.

By some dreadful fluke, when he and his associates stick up the bank in Tres Cruces, N. M., they get away not with the modest $15,000 or $20,000 they expected, but with more than three-quarters of a million dollars. The neat, unassuming little bank turns out to be a way station employed by the Mafia when it sends Las Vegas gambling money out of the country to be laundered.

There is a lot of violence in "Charley Varrick"—so much that I'm staggered by its comparatively benign PG rating. Yet its violence is less a disturbing reflection of any recognizable world than an essential part of the choreography of action melodrama in a make-believe world.

The fun in "Charley Varrick" is not sadistic, though there are cruel moments in it, but in watching Charley attempt to outwit both the cops and the Mafia. The casting of Matthau in this key role helps tremendously. Though Charley is tough enough to walk away from his wife's death (after the initial holdup) without showing much emotion, the character is inhabited — maybe even transformed — by Matthau's wit and sensitivity as an actor. If the role were played by someone else, "Charley Varrick" would be something else entirely.

With the exception of Charley and a sheriff, played by Norman Fell, who is pretty much a straightman, everyone in the movie is to a greater or lesser extent rotten: Charley's greedy young assistant (Andy Robinson), the Mafia hit man (Joe Don Baker), the owner of the Tres Cruces bank (John Vernon) and a photographer, very nicely played by Sheree North, who specializes in making fake passports on short notice.

Siegel has decorated the movie with a lot of colorful

bit characters including a chatty, sex-obsessed old woman, but the action sequences give the film its content as well as style. The duel between a high-powered automobile and an ancient biplane at the end of the movie is what it's all about.

1973 O 20, 27:1

The Program

YEAR OF THE WOMAN, directed and written by Sandra Hochmann; produced by Porter Bibb; directors of cinematography, Claudia Weill and Juliana Wang; editor, Patricia Powell. Running time 80 minutes. At the Fifth Avenue Cinema, Fifth Avenue at 12th Street. This film has not been classified. With Sandra Hochman and others.

It's one thing to be the invisible "I" in a poem or a novel. It often takes courage. It's quite another thing to hire a camera crew and photograph yourself tap-dancing in front of the White House, which Sandra Hochman, a recognized poet and novelist, has done in "Year of the Woman." That takes chutzpah.

The feature film, which is now playing at the Fifth Avenue Cinema, is described variously as a satire and a fantasy, but it's mostly Miss Hochman's silly, self-indulgent semidocumentary about feminist activities at the 1972 Democratic National Convention in Miami.

Miss Hochman, who apparently considers herself a force for raising women's consciousnesses, sees hardly anyone except herself in this montage of interviews and dopey fantasy sequences, with a supporting cast including Liz Renay, Florynce Kennedy, Art Buchwald, Warren Beatty, Shirley MacLaine, Gloria Steinem, Shirley Chisholm, Norman Mailer, Bella Abzug and others.

Everyone gets used. The cause of women isn't served, it's purloined.

VINCENT CANBY.

1973 O 20, 27:2

Niblock and Benning

Two of the five movies in a program of experimental works by Phil Niblock and James Benning are beauties —not a bad batting average. The pictures make up the new 100-minute program at the Film Forum, 256 West 88th Street, showing at 8, this weekend and repeating next Friday through Sunday.

Mr. Niblock's "Thir Film and Music One" (43 minutes) freezes microscopically in fragmented close-ups of nature, such as a twig, crystalline rocks in a brook or shadowy trees. As the camera glues hard, nature itself supplies the movement and impact, whether rushing water, shifting light or scudding clouds. These images, even-

tually pulsating with an inner life of their own, simple majesty.

●

What may drive you up the Film Forum wall is the picture's music, or the sound, which is one long, ear-splitting drone. After 43 minutes, you may wonder if a mule had sat on a bagpipe.

Mr. Niblock's less impressive "The Magic Sun" (17 minutes) sustains ghostly effects by photographing some musicians, Sun Ra and His Solar Arcestra, in black-and-white high-contrast stock. Then we're back to that drone again with "Animals" (16 minutes), a thoughtful but random look at different species, some of them simply staring curiously into the

camera. No wonder. Animals —what about 'em?

●

Mr. Benning's beauty is "Time And a Half" (17 minutes), strong, searching and striking as it wordlessly documents a machinist's workaday life, his sexual fantasies and his environment. The face of the subject, John Krieg, is a plastic revelation. The natural, abstract soundtrack hits home.

Mr. Benning's "10-NINE-8-7-Six-5-4-3" (7 minutes) shows a tomato on a plain background. The focus blurs, there it is again, then more blurring. Say, what is this? But hold on a few minutes for the finale, a splattering pip. Logic wins.

HOWARD THOMPSON

1973 O 20, 27:2

Movie Murders

By STEPHEN FARBER

PEOPLE who never go to movies are always complaining about the abundance of sex on screen, but the truth is that almost no major American films have dealt seriously and intensively with adult sexual relationships or changing sexual mores. Even before the recent disastrous Supreme Court decision, there were no American movie equivalents of "Last Tango in Paris" — or even of Claude Berri's comedy, "Le Sex Shop."

In the area of violence, however, American moviemakers have taken full advantage of their new freedom. It is difficult to think of a sadistic embellishment that has been overlooked. When the repressive Motion Picture Production Code collapsed in 1966, violence was no longer regulated, and crime no longer had to be punished in every film. After 30 years of hypocrisy, it was a relief to see comedies like "The Thomas Crown Affair," "There Was a Crooked Man" and "The Hot Rock," in which thieves were finally allowed to get away with the loot.

Murderers, like thieves, no longer have to be punished, so filmmakers have an opportunity to create more honest, mature studies of crime. The disturbing thing about many recent movies is that murder is not simply unpunished; it is positively celebrated.

In American movies about war, murder was always rationalized, and there have been plenty of movies — westerns and thrillers — in which heroes killed to defend themselves. But the new films aren't about self-de-

fense; they are about cold-blooded murder, what the courts call first-degree murder, methodically plotted and executed. In the last couple of years, movies have exalted the ingenuity of a professional assassin ("The Mechanic"), and the deep gratification of revenge ("High Plains Drifter," "Badge 373," "White Lightning"). One of these revenge melodramas ("The Cowboys") concerned young boys mastering the art of slaughter. Lovers have cemented their relationship by killing together ("The Getaway," "The Man Who Loved Cat Dancing"). We have even been asked to see murder as a desirable solution to social problems ("Gordon's War," "The Spook Who Sat by the Door," "Hit!").

In these movies the characters rarely feel the slightest remorse for the murders they commit. "Bonnie and Clyde" may have encouraged us to identify with killers, but we were never allowed to forget the horror of violence. In the new movies there's no horror, no pain, no guilt, no concern. Murder has become utilitarian, insignificant, even fun.

Two new melodramas illustrate just how far movies have gone in making murder palatable. Don Siegel's crafty, engrossing crime caper "Charley Varrick" is the story of a smalltime bank robber in the Southwest who unwittingly knocks over a bank that serves as a drop for Mafia money, and walks out with $750,000. The rest of the movie shows how he eludes the Mafia, eliminates all obstacles (including one of his partners), and eventually makes off with the fortune. He is not directly re-

sponsible for all the deaths in the movie, but he does murder his last pursuer — a Mafia hit man — before riding happily into the sunset. Because the hit man is an even more rotten character than the bank robber, we're supposed to applaud the murder and walk out smiling.

"Charley Varrick" expresses the new movie morality: The characters are all thieves, killers, con men; even a crippled old man in a wheelchair is a crooked opportunist. Fair enough; although some of these characters are very crudely drawn, the film could have been a tough, cynical portrait of a completely amoral world — like an earlier, more abrasive Siegel movie, "The Killers" — if it had kept the same distance from all the characters.

But the film is soft at the center. Charley Varrick is seen as a lone entrepreneur against the system; he calls himself "last of the independents," and the film treats him as a charming, iconoclastic American maverick. A very sentimental scene near the beginning begs for our sympathy by demonstrating Charley's loyalty to his dying wife. And the casting of Walter Matthau contributes to this glamorization. One's first reaction is that Matthau is miscast, but Siegel obviously wanted a lovable hero. What's insidious about the movie is not that the central character is a killer, or even that a killer is rewarded, but that a very ruthless murderer is played as a cute, wisecracking rascal.

Irresponsible as it is, "Charley Varrick" is a Sunday school parable compared to "Hit!", perhaps the most blatant advocacy of murder ever filmed. The plot recalls "The Dirty Dozen": A brutal, cynical government agent rounds up a group of private citizens — each with a lethal specialty — and trains them for a mission of murder; they are to wipe out the nine top people in the heroin syndicate in Marseilles. The hero's teenage daughter died of a heroin overdose, and several of the others have lost members of their family on account of drugs; they take their revenge by going after the people at the top. (Applying their logic, someone who had had a relative killed in an automobile accident might decide to murder the president of General Motors.)

Some critics, afraid to confront the moral implications of "Hit!", have tried to dismiss it as technically incompetent. In fact, it's a very clever, proficient piece of factory-style moviemaking. It may be preposterous, and routinely directed by Sidney

J. Furie, but on its own terms the movie works; the audience is carried along by it. The ribald street humor — mainly provided by Richard Pryor — is seductive, and the Mission Impossible format (no matter how often it is used) guarantees a certain amount of excitement. And although the script seems to have been assembled from market research, rather than written, it touches all bases. Among the squad of killers are two blacks, an overzealous white cop (for the "Dirty Harry" audience), a hip university professor and a bright Barnard girl turned junkie (for the youth audience?), even — in one of the script's crazier conceits — a comical old Jewish couple who happen to be ex-cons.

The leader of the commando unit (played by the charismatic Billy Dee Williams) epitomizes the ruthless, amoral style of today's movie heroes. In enlisting his team members, Williams uses every vicious trick to whip them up to kill. He takes Richard Pryor to the prison where the junkie murderer of his wife is incarcerated, allows him to beat the helpless man to a bloody pulp, then pulls him off and whispers seductively, "You want to kill somebody? I'll give you the right people to kill."

He entices the Barnard girl by promising her a life supply of heroin if she joins the team. In an older movie, if a hero were trying to enlist the help of a drug addict, he probably would have promised to cure her. Maybe the makers of "Hit!" think that the cure of an addict would be square; they would probably defend their cruel approach as more "honest." The Billy Dee Williams character is one of the most repellent sadist heroes ever to appear in a major movie, though some people may be afraid to call him a fascist because he's black. The filmmakers, who are white, are cynically exploiting the Black Is Beautiful mystique to silence objections to murder.

Another rationale for the nine murders in "Hit!" is the decadent life-style of the French syndicate leaders. The filmmakers obviously didn't think dope dealing was quite enough to validate murder, so they decided to give the victims extra vices: One is a homosexual, another a lesbian, a third enjoys two girls in bed, another is a fat glutton, etc. According to this primitive movie shorthand, unconventional sexual preferences and even bad table manners are equated with evil. The assumption is that lesbians and gluttons are something less than human, and therefore disposable. When the Barnard girl expresses some qualms about killing, another member of the team tells her, "There's nothing to it. We're killing some pigs, that's all."

The audience seems to accept the premises and identifies with the American killers. When I saw the film, the full house laughed delightedly and even cheered the brutal, perfectly executed murders in the final reel. Maybe they believe that this is the way to solve the drug problem. In the last scene the hero seems to be advising the American government to follow his example and set up more murder squads.

To suggest that the murder of nine or even 209 kingpins could stop the drug traffic is not only immoral and irresponsible, but idiotic as well. Individual suppliers can always be replaced. The drug traffic will continue as long as there is a demand for drugs, and this is the crucial point that the film evades. It never acknowledges the true sources of the drug problem — racism, poverty, the degradation of urban life in America. It must be comforting for people to believe that those profound social problems can be swept away by simple, brutal direct action.

Critics like to squawk about violence in movies, so I should make it clear that violence per se isn't the issue here; it's the attitude toward violence. There has always been a lot of violence in good as well as bad American movies, but the belligerent celebration of murder is something new. These movies are not simply violent; they're sadistic.

I don't know what impact these movies have on viewers. There still isn't any reliable evidence about the effect of films on audiences, and it would be dangerously glib to talk of influences that one one can accurately determine. But that doesn't mean the movies can be dismissed as "mere entertainment." The cynicism and amorality of current American movies may seem predictable in the post-Vietnam, post-Watergate era; the vigilante tactics of movie heroes reflect a society in which the illegal activities of burglars and plumbers enjoy the sanction of top government officials.

What is less predictable — and more troubling — is the movies' contemptuous disregard for life, the ghoulish, bloodthirsty savoring of murder. Has Hollywood judged the public correctly? Are we getting what we want? Is murder the only thing that sells?

The Movie That Made The Festival Memorable

By VINCENT CANBY

KIT, 25, wearing blue jeans, a T-shirt and a panama hat, drives the big Buick sedan across the prairies towards Montana. Beside him on the front seat is Holly, 15, who is on the verge of being pretty though she still looks something like a cookie that hasn't yet been baked. The country is so flat you think Columbus was wrong. To pass the time, Holly reads aloud from a movie magazine. "'Rumor: Frank Sinatra and Rita Hayworth are in love. Fact: Yes, but not with each other.'"

Kit and Holly have a good laugh at that one. It's one of the things that Kit likes about Holly, her sense of humor, as well as the fact she can play the clarinet. Meanwhile Holly, on the soundtrack, has let us know that she's getting tired of their rootless wandering. "The world," she says, as if dictating her true story to Adela Rogers St. John, "was a faraway planet to which I could never return." She can, of course, and she eventually does return. But there are complications.

Starting in their home town, a peaceful little South Dakota village in late summer, Kit and Holly have left behind them a trail of dead bodies, including that of Holly's father, a sign painter who so objected to Holly's going around with Kit, a garbage man, that he shot Holly's pet dog.

＊

There are also the bodies of three men who found Kit and Holly's hideout, just outside town, the body of Kit's friend, a nice old rummy who worked on the garbage truck with Kit, and those of a young man and woman whom Kit shoved into a storm cellar, and then shot at blindly through the closed door. "Do you think I got 'em?" Kit asks Holly. "I dunno," says Holly. "Well, I ain't gonna bother looking," says Kit. Holly shrugs.

The Holly we hear on the soundtrack of Terrence Malick's blunt and beautiful first feature, "Badlands," employs the flat, expressionless tones that an uninterested schoolgirl might use when reciting Joyce Kilmer's "Trees." "Suddenly I was in a state of shock," Holly tells us with no urgency whatsoever. "Kit was the most trigger-happy person I'd ever met."

There are all sorts of fascinating displacements and distances in "Badlands," which last week closed the 11th New York Film Festival, making an otherwise so-so festival, which was no better or worse than many others, memorable indeed.

Eighteen films were featured in the festival, making it more easily comprehensible than most, though the general quality of the selections was not necessarily higher. There was the usual New York Festival emphasis on French films, five altogether, including François Truffaut's superb comedy, "Day for Night," one old film of historical interest (Fritz Lang's 1922 "Dr. Mabuse," shown here for the first time in all of its four hours or so), and odds and ends of films from West Germany, Italy, India (Satyajit Ray's fine "Distant Thunder"), Poland, Canada, England and Russia. The latter's entry was an apparently bastardized version of the 1967 epic, "Andrei Rublev," dealing with the physical and spiritual trials of the 15th-cenutry icon painter who shows up in the film from time to time, poetically framed in sun, rain, mist or dandelion fluff.

＊

There were three American films in this year's festival, which is about par for the course, and although they can't be said to have dominated the festival, they provided it with some of its most interesting moments. I didn't like James Frawley's heavily meaningful comic Western, "Kid Blue," but I liked the fact that the festival chose to give attention to this major company (20th Century-Fox) film that had had a few unsuccessful commercial dates before the festival latched onto it. This can be a valid function of the festival: to spotlight films that seem about to be overlooked in the hysteria of a hit-or-miss-oriented business.

In this case, I happen to believe that the festival's interest was misplaced, but there may be times in the future when it will be deserved. The two other American films most decidedly merited the festival's attention, Martin Scorsese's "Mean Streets," even though it had already been acquired for commercial distribution (it's now playing at the Cinema 1), and Malick's highly provocative "Badlands," which, I assume, will soon be discovered by a distributor and sent into release.

If there can be said to have been any discovery at the festival, it was this first directorial effort by Malick, a 29-year-old former Rhodes Scholar and philosophy instructor whose only other film credit is as author of the screenplay for last year's "Pocket Money," the gently nihilistic comedy about two American cowboys getting taken for everything they own in contemporary Mexico. There was an essential intelligence in that screenplay that is now realized through-

out the production of "Badlands," which Malick also wrote and produced.

The take-off point for the film is the story of Charlie Starkweather of Lincoln, Nebraska, who, in January of 1958, at age 19, went on a murder spree that eventually claimed 10 victims, including the mother, stepfather and half-sister of Caril Fugate, the 14-year-old girl who accompanied him. In separate trials, both Charlie and Caril were convicted of murder. Charlie later was executed in the electric chair and Caril was given life imprisonment.

The first question anyone asks when confronted by such a real-life story is why. Arthur Penn, the director, and Robert Benton and David Newman, the screenwriters, largely explained "Bonnie and Clyde" in terms of the times (the Great Depression) with a little help from Freud. Fritz Lang made a malignant society the villain in his classic "You Only Live Once" (1937). Malick offers no definitive answers in "Badlands," which, though specifically set in the late 1950s, as easily suggests the 1970s.

Instead he presents us with the spectacle—clear-eyed and mostly without any romantic notions (except for the ones that Kit and Holly have about themselves)—of two desensitized people moving through a world that could be an extension of either a television series or one of the stories Holly reads in True Romances. It's a place where there are no ultimate consequences, where even death may not be final.

At times there are veiled suggestions that Kit and Holly are, in their different ways, either simple-minded or psychotic. Holly tells us at one point that Kit has visions and complains of strange noises in his ears, but since we get this information from Holly, it must be taken with some caution, like her purple descriptions of herself and Kit. We can see what's going on. Holly has an uneasy relationship with her father (her mother died when she was born), but her father's discipline is hardly enough to explain the calm with which she accepts the sight of Kit pumping bullets into him.

Kit and Holly are out of touch with their feelings, and it's the scary suggestion of "Badlands" that this isn't an especially abnormal condition in this time and place. In almost the geographical center of this civilization, at the peak of its power and affluence, Kit and Holly have grown up to be not much different from the so-called wolf children that so fascinated Europeans in the 18th century—one of which was the subject of Truffaut's "L'Enfant Sauvage."

*

Although Kit and Holly know how to dress themselves, and have had plenty to eat and the society of other humans, and although they talk, they cannot communicate, within themselves or to each other. The language they use is made up of phrases learned by rote.

Three cameramen are credited with the photography, all of it beautifully and simply done, without excess gestures. Nor is there anything excessive about the performances of Martin Sheen and Sissy Spacek as the runaways. Miss Spacek manages the rather grand feat of being simultaneously transparent and mysterious, sweet and heedlessly cruel. Sheen, who does look like James Dean, whom Kit fancies, has what may be the role of his career. It allows him to recall the mannerisms of Dean-the-fallen-hero within the frame of a character who aspires to the kind of fame and power made romantic by films. It's like seeing a life-within-a-life, instead of a movie-within-a-movie. "Badlands" is hugely effective, a smash.

1973 O 21, II:1:1

SUMMER WISHES, WINTER DREAMS, directed by Gilbert Cates; screenplay by Stewart Stern; director of photography, Gerald Hirschfeld; editor, Sidney Katz; producer, Jack Brodsky; released by Columbia Pictures. At the Plaza Theater, 58th Street, east of Madison Avenue. Running time: 93 minutes. This film is classified as PG.

Rita Walden .... Joanne Woodward
Harry Walden .... Martin Balsam
Rita's Mother .... Sylvia Sidney
Anna .... Dori Brenner
Fred Goody .... Win Forman
Betty Goody .... Tresa Hughes
Joel .... Peter Marklin
Bobby Walden .... Ron Rickards

By NORA SAYRE

From time to time, there's a movie that makes you feel like a moderate heel. Although you respect the talents and the themes, it's not possible to respond emotionally, even though you might wish to. And that's the hitch with "Summer Wishes, Winter Dreams," which opened last night at the Plaza Theater.

Joanne Woodward plays a restive, well-tailored woman who has been married for 24 years to a devoted oculist (Martin Balsam). She has almost nothing to do but baby-sit for her daughter, lunch with her mother (Sylvia Sidney, bristling with fierce impatience: welcome back), redecorate her West End Avenue apartment, shop and fight with all her relatives.

The mother's sudden death hastens a probably inevitable crisis. All of Miss Woodward's regrets about the past and her fantasies about the future erupt: She mourns what she has missed, dreads dying, wrestles with earlier experiences that can't be altered or recaptured, agonizes over the things that she may never do before she dies.

This is a portrait of someone confronted by her own mortality, while watching the possibilities ahead diminish. Surely the subject is as valid as breathing. However, in the tradition of "Rachel, Rachel" and "Gamma Rays," Miss Woodward has been directed to win the sweepstakes. Misery floods the screen. Yet, it's very hard to believe that the kind of vigorous, sinewy character she evokes could feel so perpetually defeated.

Here, she plays much of her part at an unbroken level of irritation, slamming back at those around her with the gumption that's missing in our mayoral candidates. It's the same vitality that we saw in "The Three Faces of Eve," and we recall the range of feelings that has streamed through a number of her pictures. But since she acts as if she had been drinking Drano, the moments of vulnerability just aren't convincing.

Mr. Balsam, as the kindly, reassuring husband, is burdened with lines like, "Do you know that you are more beautiful than the day I met you?" and "You can't do better than your best." Again, we think wistfully of his brilliance in many other roles. But the alternate folksiness and banality of the script means that "Summer Wishes" is a forlorn waste of two fine character actors.

1973 O 22, 46:1

The Cast

SUMMERTIME KILLER, directed by Antonio Isasi; screenplay by R. Buckley and B. Degas; photographed by Juan Gelpi; produced by Mr. Isasi; presented by Avco Embassy. At the National Theater, Broadway and 44th Street, and other showcases. Running time: 100 minutes. (This film is rated PG.)

John Kiley .... Karl Malden
Ray Castter .... Christopher Mitchum
Tonia Alfredi .... Olivia Hussey
Lazaro Alfredi .... Raf Vallone
Michele Dobvien .... Claudine Auger

Splashes of background color—Manhattan streets, a bit of Rome, Lisbon's Estoril sector and the high-rise Madrid suburbs — erratically brighten a humdrum suspense melodrama titled "Summertime Killer," now playing around town.

The young killer, Christopher Mitchum (Bob's face, blond hippie hair), out to avenge his murdered father, picks off underworld kingpins, finally kidnaps a pretty girl, Olivia Hussey, and guess what happens.

Closing in, as love blooms, are the girl's father, Raf Vallone, and his hoodlums, and a dogged detective, Karl Malden, who must have taken a wrong turn from "The Streets of San Francisco," his television show. Compressed, the picture might have sufficed as a 40-minute segment (minus commercials).

Here, the punctuation and padding are obvious, as in the frenetic photography of Antonio Isasi, the director, and the prolonged resolution. For all the tense hopping around on all sides, it couldn't matter less.

HOWARD THOMPSON

1973 O 24, 38:3

The Cast

THE ALL-AMERICAN BOY, directed and written by Charles Eastman; director of photography, Philip Lathrop; edited by Christopher Holmes; produced by Joseph T. Naar and Saul J. Krugman; released by Warner Bros. At the Baronet Theater, 59th Street at Third Avenue. Running time: 118 minutes. This film is classified R.

Vic Bealer .... Jon Voight
Rodine .... Carlo Androsky
Drenna Valentine .... Anne Archer
Rockoff .... Gene Borkan
Larkin .... Ron Burns
Poppy .... Rosalind Cash
Nola Bealer .... Jeanne Cooper

By NORA SAYRE

Since old-style alienation is having a comeback, perhaps we'll soon get crinolines and quiz-show scandals as well. But the brand of mossy disaffection evoked in "The All-American Boy," which opened last night at the Baronet, has nothing to do with politics or generations or rebellion. Instead, it belongs to the old I-can't-connect school. We've seen that so often on the screen that the theme needs a fresh twist—which it doesn't get in this movie.

Jon Voight is cast as a weary, resentful mid-American who hates his small hometown and doesn't want to commit himself to anything or anyone. However, in spite of himself, he succeeds as a fledgling boxer and is promised a great career—until he suddenly refuses to participate in the next big fight.

He throws everything away—his fiancée as well as his future in boxing. But we never learn why. This picture flaunts such a stubborn disregard for characterization and motive that it could almost be billed as a mystery. For example, Voight is immediately established as a depressive. But there's no clue to whatever it is that keeps him staring broodily into space, rejecting intimacy or even contact with those around him. Charles Eastman, who wrote and directed the movie, absolutely refuses to explain what's biting his hero.

The film is especially frustrating because Voight is such an intelligent actor. Remembering the variety

Jon Voight

that he brought to his previous roles, we can sympathize with the dilemmas he must have had in working with dialogue like this: "What you thinkin'?" "I ain't thinkin' nothin'." "People are always thinkin' somethin'." And when one of his girlfriends says that he smells like a cantaloupe, it's merciful that we don't have to see his face in close-up.

But even in this picture, there are moments when Mr. Voight's quality comes through. He's very good at watching and listening, a skill that eludes many actors. He's also strong in showing his disgust at being treated like a slab of sirloin, when his boxer's body is displayed and examined by others.

Mr. Eastman also did Mr. Voight a particular disservice by having someone say in an early scene that he looks like Marlon Brando. Throughout, you suspect that the actor was resisting the director's efforts to make him imitate Brando. True, Mr. Voight's gloomy, downward gaze sometimes suggests a slight similarity, and this is certainly an inarticulate part. But Mr. Voight, who hasn't yet played the same role twice, doesn't deserve to be shoved toward someone else's style of performing.

1973 O 25, 56:1

The Program

JONATHAN LIVINGSTON SEAGULL, directed and produced by Hall Bartlett; adapted from Richard Bach's book by the author and Mr. Bartlett; photographed by Jack Couffer; music composed by Neil Diamond and Lee Holdridge; presented by Paramount Pictures. At the Sutton Theater, 57th Street at Third Avenue. Running time: 101 minutes. (This film is rated G.)

This "Jonathan Livingston Seagull," reportedly quite a book, is quite a bird in a beautiful and touching movie that falls short only toward the end when it perches instead of soaring.

How does one film a slim, cult-adored bestseller about an altruistic, rebel gull who sails and philosophizes through the seasons in search of self-fulfillment? Well, one starts with some perfectly magnificent photography by Jack Couffer.

This camera work is so stunning that it immediately establishes a sensitive texture for a simply story of a roaming nonconformist with wings and a human voice. Intelligently and tastefully, the director - producer, Hall Bartlett, and the author, Richard Bach, have integrated the bird's musings with arresting passages of silence and a surprisingly effective score sung by Neil Diamond, who composed it with Lee Holdridge.

To one viewer, who loved the first half, the only catch is the final footage, when our feathered hero comes home to convert his old flock with some gummy platitudes. This portion is a bit pat and even synthetic, for all the clever photographic simulations of massed bird chatter and anger. This aspect of the movie, its technical manipulation, is at times remarkable.

The picture also runs far too long. But the over-all flavor and impact remain striking, purposeful, sweet and at times heart-clutching. Jonathan, at least his human spokesman, generally says a mouthful. The comments are hardly new and too often humorless; nevertheless they fitted perfectly into this pictorial transformation from the printed page. Word and image made a combination that held this viewer.

Maureen, another gull, tells Jonathan, "you really are an exceptional flier." Amen, J. L.

HOWARD THOMPSON

1973 O 25, 59:1

MASSACRE IN ROME, directed by George Pan Cosmatos; screenplay by Robert Katz and Mr. Cosmatos, based on the book "Death in Rome" by Mr. Katz; director of photography, Marcello Gatti; editors, Francoise Bonnot and Robert Silvi; music, Ennio Morricone; produced by Carlo Ponti; released by National General Pictures. A Champion Film Flash Fiducial Films co-production in association with A. Seymour Cooper and Everett Hart. Running time: approximately 145 minutes. This film is classified PG. At the National, Murray Hill and 86th Street East Theaters.

Colonel Kappler .... Richard Burton
Father Pietro .... Marcello Mastroianni
General Maelzer .... Leo McKern
Colonel Dollmann .... John Steiner
Father Pancrazio .... Robert Harris
Elena .... Della Boccardo

By LAWRENCE VAN GELDER

Stars are generally an asset to a film. But in the case of "Massacre in Rome," which opened yesterday at the National, Murray Hill and 86th Street East Theaters, they constitute its chief flaw.

That is not to say that Marcello Mastroianni, as a principal priest and art restorer, and Richard Burton, as a German colonel in Rome as the Allies close in during World War II, give inept performances.

It is simply that their presence at the moral summit of this film unbalances its recounting of a controversial and bloody fragment of history that began with the destruction by partisans of a German SS detachment on the Via Rasella and ended with a reprisal that took more than 300 Italian lives.

•

The conflicts at the film's heart, the questions of where duty lies, of when the rules of war insult the souls of men beyond endurance, of when self-sacrifice becomes the ineluctable argument, become subsumed rather than illuminated by the interplay between two of the screen's more commanding presences.

And when they are not at the center of events, Leo McKern, as General Maelzer, Burton's superior, is so busy chewing scenery in a performance that seems to call for a leash if not a muzzle, that it becomes impossible to take matters seriously.

•

Directed by George Pan Cosmatos, "Massacre in Rome" is an opulent Carlo Ponti production with a warm eye for the spaciousness and beauty of the city's interiors and the panoply of its priesthood. The music, by Ennio Morricone, possesses all the subtlety of an elbow in the ribs.

In the end, for all its apparent concern for life and death, "Massacre in Rome" turns out to be a curiously bloodless film, a monument not to its victims but to its stars.

1973 O 25, 59:1

The Cast

FIVE ON THE BLACK SIDE, directed by Oscar Williams; screenplay by Charlie L. Russell, based on a play by Mr. Russell/ director of Photography, Gene Polito; film editor, Michael Economou; music, H. B. Barnum; produced by Brock Peters and Michael Tolan; released by United Artists Corporation. At the Cinerama Theater, Broadway at 47th Street and the 86th Street Twin 2 Theater, west of Lexington Avenue. Running time: 96 minutes. This film is classified PG.
Mrs. Brooks .... Clarice Taylor
Mr. Brooks .... Leonard Jackson
Ruby .... Virginia Capers
Gideon .... Glynn Turman
Booker T. .... D'Urville Martin
Gail .... Bonnie Banfield
Preston .... Richard Williams
Sweetmeat .... Sonny Jim
Stormy Monday .... Ja'Net Dubois
Marvin .... Carl Mikal Franklin

By A. H. WEILER

"Five on the Black Hand Side," which opened yesterday at the Cinerama and 86th Street Twin theaters, is amiable but realistic in attempting only to solve a few problems for a middle-class

---

black family. But by tickling the funny bone, Charlie L. Russell's adaptation of his Off Broadway play is a good deal more effective than most of the militant and violent so-called black films that are getting redundant.

In effect, the comedy is essentially the same as that staged by the American Place Theater in January of 1970, which delved into the harried home life of a barber who rules his wife, two sons and daughter as autocratically as Nero. His wife, of course, is more obedient servant than mate, and the communication between father and his grown, rebellious children is virtually nonexistent.

Naturally, this domestic despotism is disrupted when the barber's meek but loving spouse, now at the end of her patience and faced with anxieties about her daughter's imminent marriage, revolts in comic women's lib style by demanding and getting her long-deferred rights.

Mr. Russell's script may be a basically lightweight affair, but he writes with an affection and keen perception that make his people and the issues, couched either in jive talk or straight dialogue, three dimensional and pertinent. Credit for the giggles and truths is also due Oscar Williams, who directed with professional feeling for pace and comedy.

But "Five on the Black Hand Side" also rests on its varied principals and the rich incidents that make its slight theme real and enjoyable.

Leonard Jackson is properly outraged, pompous and funny as the barber who makes life with father a trial. Clarice Taylor, who is repeating her stage role as his wife, gives the once-timorous and now defiant Mrs. Brooks the finely underplayed indecision and dignity the part demands. She is entirely convincing when she wryly observes that the family loves her husband "but can't live with him."

Glynn Turman, D'Urville Martin and Bonnie Banfield are comically persuasive as the embattled offspring. And a large cast, including Virginia Capers and Ja'Net Dubois, as helpful neighbors; as well as Sonny Jim and Carl Mikal Franklin and even Godfrey Cambridge, in a minute role, adds small delights to a modest but meaningful entertainment.

1973 O 26, 51:1

The Cast

THE NEW LAND, directed, photographed and edited by Jan Troell; screenplay (Swedish with English subtitles) by Bengt Forslund and Mr. Troell, from a novel by Vilhelm Moberg; music, Bengt Ernryd and George Oddner; produced by Mr. Forslund; released by Warner Bros. At the Little Carnegie Theater, 57th Street, east

---

of Seventh Avenue. Running time: 161 minutes. This film is classified PG.
Karl Oskar .... Max von Sydow
Kristina .... Liv Ullmann
Robert .... Eddie Axberg
Ulrika .... Monica Zetterlund
Jonas Petter .... Hans Alfredson
Anders Mansson .... Halvar Bjork

By LAWRENCE VAN GELDER

With "The New Land," which opened yesterday at the Little Carnegie theater, Jan Troell, the Swedish director, brings to an end the arduous saga of 19th-century migration from his homeland to America, which he began in "The Emigrants."

What he has achieved seems no less than a masterly exercise in film-making, a rare union of carefully nuanced performances from a cast led by Max von Sydow and Liv Ullmann, a use of sight and sound that beggars, at least by its aspirations, the work of more easily satisfied men and a long but selective narrative as alert to the sins that taint national history as it is sensitive to the small dramas that ultimately seal the course and quality of lives.

•

The uniform excellence of "The New Land" (and "The Emigrants," which opened here little more than a year ago) is no accident.

Mr. Troell is credited with the direction, the editing and part of the screenplay and also with the photography, which could be mistaken as gratuitously lavish, were it not so sensitive to telling detail and were nature not so powerful a force in the rural lives these films depict.

Mr. Troell is a busy and flexible workman, as willing to use silence to make a point as he is to turn his soundtrack over to the song of unseen birds in the spring, to bees in the summer and to flies in the presence of death.

These are small touches, to be sure, but indicative of an intention to exploit the medium to its fullest, to construct impact cumulatively and to strike no false notes. Fingernails are dirty; tough hands pass an idle moment stroking a kitten's fur; age announces itself in broken capillaries.

The cast appears thoroughly responsive to Mr. Troell's commitments. Most deserving of praise are Mr. von Sydow and Miss Ullman as Karl Oskar, the farmer, and his wife Kristina; Monika Zetterlund as Ulrika, and Eddie Axberg as Karl Oskar's ill-fated brother, Robert.

Although for anyone who has seen "The Emigrants," this film will be enhanced by a pleasure akin to a reunion with old friends, "The New Land" is complete in itself. And it is a lovely and moving film.

1973 O 27, 17:7

From Matthau to Izzy Stone

By VINCENT CANBY

A FILM critic isn't supposed to like too many films. It gives him a bad reputation with his peers, with taxicab drivers (who don't go to movies but know they're all lousy anyway), even with movie producers, a lot of whom are compulsive gamblers: they need to fail. They figure there must be something wrong with the critic who likes their films. You give a producer a compliment and it's likely to worry him all night.

*

In spite of what you may have heard from taxicab drivers, sometimes known as hacks, the last couple of months have been rather abundant with good or interesting films: Truffaut's "Day for Night," Scorsese's "Mean Streets," Bakshi's "Heavy Traffic," Lucas's "American Graffiti," and Malick's "Badlands," which was presented at the New York Film Festival but hasn't yet been commercially released. The following is a rundown on seven more films that have opened recently, most of them within the last 10 days, and three of which merit your consideration:

"Charley Varrick" (Loew's State 2 and Orpheum Theaters). Here is a first-rate Don Siegel action film, unencumbered by the terrible philosophy that made last year's "Dirty Harry" so unpleasant, even though it was hugely successful at the box office. This time the philosophy is inoffensively romantic. Charley Varrick (Walter Matthau) is an ex-flying circus pilot who poses as a legitimate crop duster, but whose real calling is the robbing of small banks in the southwest for small payloads.

The movie ads describe him as "the last of the independents," as if he were a general store competing with A. & P., which, as it turns out, is what he is. The romance is in the way he attempts to humble the giant referred to in the film, with no mincing of words, as the Mafia.

When Charley and his associates knock off the little bank in Tres Cruces, New Mexico, they expect to get no more than $15,000 to $20,000. They wind up with over three-quarters of a million dollars. They've had the great bad luck to stumble onto a bank that is used as a way station by the Mafia sending "skimmed" Las

---

Vegas gambling money out of the country to be laundered, a term that needs not be defined, I assume, since the Watergate hearings.

The film has a good deal more violence than can easily be explained by its prim PG rating, but the violence is not especially disturbing in the make-believe context. "Charley Varrick" is essentially a tall tale told almost exclusively in terms of confrontation, escape, pursuit and fast thinking.

The opening sequence (the bank heist and escape) and the closing sequence (in which Charley, in the cockpit of an ancient biplane, faces down a Mafia hit-man in a high-powered automobile) are among the best things of this sort I've seen in any recent movie.

"I. F. Stone's Weekly" (First Avenue Screening Room). Jerry Bruck Jr., a Yale graduate (B.A. in History of the American South) in his twenties, and I. F. Stone, a college dropout in his sixties, were apparently made for each other.

Both are possessors of an amazing degree of persistence. Stone's has resulted in one of the most inspiring careers in American journalism, for the last 20-odd years as a Washington correspondent, the editor-publisher-mail boy of "I F. Stone's Weekly," which he folded in 1971 when he moved his reason, the spleen intact, to The New York Review of Books.

Bruck, who is as fascinated by Stone as Stone is by Washington, began his documentary three years ago and finished it a matter of hours before it opened last month in Washington. The result is a most engaging, moving and exhilarating film about a man who really is independent in the best sense.

Narration by Tom Wicker gives us what biographical information is needed, but most of the time Bruck just follows Izzy Stone around, allowing us to listen to him talk about journalism, government, civilization, and especially about the amazing idiocies of people in high places, which are there for us all to see if we'd just look with the piercing eye of Izzy.

Stone is such a great subject that it's easy to overlook the intelligence and art with which this 62-minute film was put together. Bruck effectively intercuts the Stone footage with interviews with Stone's associates, as well as with newsreel clips that help to make his and Stone's points. One stunning moment: a newsreel shot of the late President Johnson cutting a five-foot birthday cake to celebrate the anniversary of the U.S. Marines. One can justly say: Don't miss it.

*

"The Long Goodbye" (Trans-Lux East). Robert Altman's marvelously entertaining update of Raymond Chandler's 1953 novel, with Elliott Gould playing the legendary private eye, Philip Marlowe, opens today, so I'll reserve full comment until later. In the meantime, it is interesting to note that the film failed in its first three engagements early this year in Los Angeles, Philadelphia and Detroit, apparently because purists believed that the casting of Gould in a role so closely identified with Humphrey Bogart ("The Big Sleep") and Dick Powell ("Farewell, My Lovely") was some kind of sacrilege. That's nonsense. Altman's film acknowledges its origins but it's no slave to the past. It's an original, funny and sometimes somber film that works on a number of levels.

*

"The Paper Chase" (Columbia 1 Theater). This comedy about a first-year student at Harvard Law School starts off well enough and then slowly melts into warm ice cream. Timothy Bottoms and John Houseman are so good as, respectively, the student and the brilliant, vain professor of contract law whom the student idolizes, that you want the movie to take itself more seriously than it does. It's a would-be "Love Story," essentially frail though it has no blood disease.

*

"The Way We Were" (Loew's State 1 and Loew's Tower East). "Streisand/Redford/Together!" proclaim the ads. To which I answer: "Hammond, Indiana!"

I mean Robert Redford is a very good actor, who has given some excellent performances in various kinds of films, and Barbra Streisand, though no great shakes as an actress, is a superb vaudevillian with a great voice and stage presence. There's nothing wrong about putting them together (or should I say TOGETHER!), but it stirs about as much excitement in me as someone calling out the name of that city in Indiana that has a population of approximately 87,600 people, or did when my ancient atlas was published.

The screenplay is by Ar-

thur Laurents, who also wrote the same story more entertainingly as a novel, and the direction is by Sydney Pollack, whose good films include "They Shoot Horses, Don't They?" and "Scalphunters." It's about the love and marriage of an ugly duckling (Streisand), presented as a furiously committed college Communist in the 1930's, and an all-American WASP (Redford), who sells out his soul as a Hollywood writer during the red witch-hunts of the late 1940's. Unless you believe in its chemistry, which I find less interesting than H₂O, it makes no sense except as soft-focus exercise in Hollywood sentimentality.

*

"What?" (Coronet Theater). Roman Polanski is being a naughty boy in his new film, which is a series of not really surreal gags strung together with the help of a pretty American actress named Sydne Rome. She plays an indefatigable American girl, hitchhiking through Italy, who takes refuge in a beautiful but most peculiar seaside villa inhabited by a group of mad types, including a cheerful masochist (Marcello Matroianni) and a wealthy but dying art collector (Hugh Griffith) who now wants the object (Miss Rome) instead of its image. It goes nowhere in particular, but a lot of it is quite funny, like a good, unstructured, $2,000,000 dinner party.

*

"The Year of the Woman" (Fifth Avenue Cinema). Sandra Hochman, a recognized poet and novelist, describes this as her fantasy as a person oppressed, as a woman and an artist. "Oppressed people have fantasies," she said to me the only time I've ever met her (at this film's screening). "So do unoppressed people," I replied, by chance achieving the level of profundity of "The Year of the Woman."

Most of the film consists of interviews with women (Liz Renay, Florynce Kennedy, others) and men (Art Buchwald, Warren Beatty) about the feminist movement, photographed at the 1972 Democratic National Convention in Miami. The interviews and fantasy sequences feature a lot more of Miss Hochman than seems absolutely necessary for a film that is supposed to raise the consciousness to anything except an awareness of one woman's amazing talent to promote herself at the expense of others.

1973 O 28, II:1:1

THE LONG GOODBYE, directed by Robert Altman; screenplay by Leigh Brackett, based on Raymond Chandler's novel; produced by Jerry Bick; executive producer, Elliott Kastner; director of photography Vilmos Zsigmond; editor, Lou Lombardo; music, John Williams, distributed by United Artists. Running time: 112 minutes. (At the Trans-Lux East Theater, Third Avenue at 58th Street. (This film has been classified R.)

Philip Marlowe..........Elliott Gould
Eileen Wade..........Nina van Pallandt
Roger Wade..........Sterling Hayden
Marty Augustine..........Mark Rydell
Dr. Verringer..........Henry Gibson
Harry..........David Arkin
Terry Lennox..........Jim Bouton
Morgan..........Warren Berlinger
Jo Ann Eggenweiler..........Jo Ann Brody

By VINCENT CANBY

In "The Long Goodbye," Robert Altman, a brilliant director whose films sometimes seem like death wishes ("Brewster McCloud"), attempts the impossible and pulls it off.

Using a screenplay by Leigh Brackett, freely adapted from Raymond Chandler's 1953 novel, he has successfully transported Philip Marlowe, Chandler's private eye whose roots are in the depressed, black - and - white nineteen-thirties, to the over-privileged, full-color seventies in the person of Elliott Gould, who is nothing if not a child of our time.

The film, which opened yesterday at the Trans-Lux East, is Altman's most entertaining, most richly complex film since "M*A*S*H" and "McCabe and Mrs. Miller." It's so good that I don't know where to begin describing it. Perhaps at the beginning:

The nighttime view from a hillside high above Los Angeles is great, but inside the apartment you feel as if you're at the bottom of a well. It looks as if it had been furnished by San Quentin. There are smudges on the wall next to the bed where Philip Marlowe sleeps fully clothed and in desperate need of a shave.

A large, pushy yellow cat meows for something to eat, awakening Marlowe, who displays a cranky sort of affection for an animal that doesn't deserve it. When Marlowe tries to interest the cat in a plate of old cottage cheese, unconvincingly updated with a raw egg, the cat gives him a look that ought to have stuck at least four inches out of his back.

There is nothing for Marlowe to do but go to the supermarket to buy some canned cat food, even though it's 3 A.M. by the clock and in his soul.

It's the beginning of a crucial time for this particular Philip Marlowe, who, in spite of a lot of evidence to the contrary, persists in believing that not all relationships need be opportunistic or squalid.

When Marlowe returns from the supermarket, he meticulously pastes the label from a can of the cat's favorite brand over a substitute, but the cat is not fooled. It walks off, furious. A minute later Terry Lennox (Jim Bouton), an old friend of Marlowe's shows up and asks Marlowe to drive him to the Mexican border. Terry, a part-time hood and full-

Elliott Gould

time pretty boy, explains that someone has murdered his wife and the cops certainly won't accept his innocence. Marlowe does.

Almost immediately Marlowe is arrested by the police as an accessary to murder, roughed up by the associates of the syndicate boss (Mark Rydell) who suspects Marlowe of stealing $350,000, and invited to find the drunken novelist-husband (Sterling Hayden) of a tall, beautiful self-assured blonde (Nina van Pallandt), who looks like the promises made in a Coppertone ad.

Curiously enough, Gould's Marlowe, lonely, usually shabby, with a wit that is less often turned outward than inward onto himself, does not seem an anachronism in the world of contemporary freaks. That was the gnawing problem with Paul Newman, superman, tough in the screen adaptation of Ross MacDonald's "Harper," and the fatal flaw in "Marlowe," Paul Bogart's adaptation of Chandler's "The Little Sister," in which James Garner played it for laughs.

Gould's Marlowe is entirely different from Humphrey Bogart's ("The Big Sleep") and Dick Powell's ("Farewell, My Lovely" and the 1954 TV adaptation of "The Long Goodbye"). Gould's Marlowe is not especially tough. He's a bright, conscientious but rather solemn nut, a guy who hopes for the best but expects the worst, having experienced the social upheavals, the assassinations and the undeclared war of the sixties.

Altman, Miss Brackett (who collaborated with William Faulkner on the script for "The Big Sleep"), and Gould have had the courage to cre-

ate an original character and almost an original story that, by being original, does more to honor Chandler's skills than would any attempt to make a forties movie today.

There are lots of eloquent references to Chandler in Altman's method, which is to pack the screen with more bizarre visual and aural detail than can be easily taken in at one sitting. There are also references in the appreciation of California décor, luxurious as well as tacky, and in the throwaway lines and uniformly excellent characterizations, including two by actors who will surprise you, Nina van Pallandt and Jim Bouton.

Don't be misled by the ads. "The Long Goodbye" is not a put-on. It's great fun and it's funny, but it's a serious, unique work.

1973 O 29, 42:1

THE ICEMAN COMETH, by Eugene O'Neill; directed by John Frankenheimer; director of photography, Ralph Woolsey; editor, Harold Kress; producer, Ely A. Landau; presented by the American Film Theater. At selected theaters. Running time: 239 minutes, with two intermissions. This film has not been classified at this time.

Hickey..........Lee Marvin
Harry Hope..........Fredric March
Larry Slade..........Robert Ryan
Don Parritt..........Jeff Bridges
The Captain..........Martyn Green
The General..........George Voskovec
Joe Mott..........Moses Gunn
Rocky Pioggi..........Tom Pedi
Cora..........Evans Evans
Willie Oban..........Bradford Dillman
Hugo Kalmar..........Sorrell Booke
Jimmy Tomorrow..........John McLiam

By NORA SAYRE

Just at the moment when many have been stripped of their national illusions—concerning the purity of government—Eugene O'Neill's conviction that people cannot live without personal illusions comes through with a fresh tang of irony.

As a drama for any and every decade, "The Iceman Cometh," which opened yesterday at selected theaters, stresses that human dignity depends on dreams, even deceptions. Perhaps this is an especially American trait; many Europeans seem able to survive with fewer fantasies than we do.

●

Reeking with failure, the unbudgeable barflies in O'Neill's 1912 saloon still manage to shore up shards of self-respect with their own private myths. The former radical pretends to despise the Movement that disappointed him, and claims that he's merely a detached observer of life—which isn't true. The bar's proprietor, who hasn't been outdoors for the 20 years since his wife died, vows that one day he'll walk through his old neighborhood. We know he won't. The bartender who insists that he's not a pimp, just because he bosses prostitutes, and the women themselves, who say that they're only tarts, not whores, the musty anarchist who knows that life will be lovely after the

Fredric March, left, and Lee Marvin

Revolution, the boozehounds who are going to give up drinking, the unemployables who will surely recapture their lost jobs—all keep their rusty armor intact until they're manipulated by Hickey, the glib salesman who's determined to make them swallow the truth about themselves.

Nearly crazed by Hickey's challenge, they all fall apart. Some also turn against one another, suddenly pulling a gun or a knife or a broken bottle on the former companions of nickel whisky. Hickey's machinations even start the Boer War going again, between two furious wrecks who fought on opposite sides. Moreover, Hickey has the gift of making others suicidal. But finally, when the group learns that he purged himself of pipe dreams only by killing his wife, most return gratefully to the illusions that kept them going.

As Hickey, Lee Marvin has the salesman's slick authority, the talent for hustling his way across people's spiritual doorsills and invading their privacy. And we can believe in his ability to force their moods to change. As he lectures them about reality, Marvin achieves a maddening moral presence—both jovial and righteous at once. Later, he's powerful in the rage of self-hatred, also when he relives the decision to commit murder.

●

As one character says, Hickey has "the fixed idea of the insane," and Marvin does convey that. However, his Hickey seems deliberately charmless—although the play demands a maniac spellcaster. Marvin's performance is just too rationally earthbound for a part that needs the touch of a magician. Fredric March as the saloonkeeper has a fine, befuddled childlike air, Moses Gunn is superb as a ravaged black rebel, and George

Voskovec and Martyn Green fight splendidly together as the old warriors who share the rotgut. There's a moving glimpse of the late Robert Ryan as the exhausted ironist who waits for death; the stern pity he levels at others is tempered with an occasional youthful smile. And Tom Pedi, the pimping bartender, is deft at miming exaggerated patience.

Jeff Bridges, the child of the Movement who delivered his revolutionary mother to the cops, begins well but eventually overplays. So do Evans Evans (the key streetwalker), Bradford Dillman as the shattered law school graduate, and several of the others. Those who overact may have been directed to do so because the play has one lumpy problem: how do you convey drunkenness and fatigue without losing vitality? It can be done, as we've seen on other occasions, but the question tempts some performers to gnaw the scenery.

Infinite care and thought and respect have been poured into this production. But the play doesn't flourish in film form for one reason: even the simplest camerawork breaks the continuity. We're supposed to see these people as one huddled mass, imprisoned together in the room they rarely leave, perpetually affected by one another's words or presence. Inevitably, closeups destroy that.

We especially lose the impact of the ensemble during Hickey's last monologue. So we're denied the crowd's full recoil when he confesses to the killing, their collective efforts not to hear him, their agitation, their final relief in deciding that it's he who's crazy, not themselves. Admittedly, drunks don't make the world's best listeners. But here, the camera isolates them from the flow that O'Neill designed.

So this isn't the "Iceman" of your lifetime. And there

will be many who can't help recalling Jason Robards as Hickey; Robards is often regarded as the exclusive owner of that role. But the play is an inescapably great experience, and that fact isn't muffled by this film.

1973 O 30, 36:1

The Cast

TALES THAT WITNESS MADNESS, directed by Freddie Francis; screenplay by Jay Fairbank; produced by Norman Priggen; director of photography, Norman Warwick; music, Bernard Ebbinghouse; editor, Bernard Gribble; a World Film Services presentation, distributed by Paramount Pictures. Running time: 90 minutes. At neighborhood theaters. This film has been classified R.
Nicholas .... Jack Hawkins
Tremayne .... Donald Pleasence
Fay .... Georgia Brown
Sam .... Donald Houston
Paul .... Russell Lewis
Ann/Beatrice .... Suzy Kendall
Timothy .... Peter McEnery
Bella .... Joan Collins
Brian .... Michael Jayston
Auriol .... Kim Novak
Kimo .... Michael Petrovitch

By VINCENT CANBY

Considering the generally depressed state of horror films these days, it takes a special kind of optimism to continue seeing them, especially when they are made by Freddie Francis, the distinguished English cinematographer ("Saturday Night and Sunday Morning"), who turned director about 10 years ago. Like a small child who sends off a coupon for a valuable free gift, you keep expecting a treasure, then receive something made of cardboard.

"Tales That Witness Madness," which opened yesterday at neighborhood theaters, is Mr. Franci's glossiest, most absurd, almost-all-star horror film yet. Like his "Torture Garden" and "Tales From the Crypt," it is a collection of unrelated stories that, this time, have as their connecting link a mad doctor (Donald Pleasence) who theorizes to his friend (the late Jack Hawkins) that truth has physical substance that can be isolated, like hormones.

At least that is what I think his theory is, but the movie is less interested in theories than in grotesque effects, some of which are comic without being especially funny.

There is, for example, the episode in which Kim Novak, playing a London literary agent in her most inept Lylah Clare style, finds herself the hostess of a luau at which her teen-age daughter is served as a main course. In another episode, which recalls a much more interesting Ray Bradbury story in "The Martian Chronicles," a little boy's imaginary playmate, a tiger, devours his nasty parents.

The third tale is about a malevolent family portrait, and the fourth is about a shapely tree stump that comes between a not-so-young married couple played

by Joan Collins and Michael Jayston. Jayston falls in love with the tree stump, which he keeps in the living room although the jealous Miss Collins describes it as "ugly, sawn-off, upside-down and vile."

That's the best line in a film that otherwise depends on people saying such things as "Darling you're imagining things" and "I just can't believe all this has happened."

1973 N 1, 48:1

The Cast

TRIPLE ECHO, directed by Michael Apted; screenplay, Robin Chapman; from the novel by H. E. Bates; director of photography, John Coquillon; music, Marc Wilkinson; editor, Barrie Vince; producer, Graham Cottle; produced by Senat Productions; distributed by Altura Films International, Inc. At the Juliet I Theater, Third Avenue and 83d Street, and the Playboy Theater, 110 West 57th Street. Running time: 90 minutes. This film is classified R.
Alice .... Glenda Jackson
Sergeant .... Oliver Reed
Barton .... Brian Deacon
Subaltern .... Anthony May
Stan .... Gavin Richards
Christine .... Jenny Lee Wright
Shopkeeper .... Daphne Heard

"Triple Echo" is tenderly perceptive about such basics as loneliness, love and some aspects of sex, but as drama, the British import that arrived yesterday at the Playboy and Juliet I Theaters is disquietingly clouded. Although its sincerity and tragedy are obvious, the character and motivations of the principals in the World War II triangle involving an English farm woman, her soldier-lover and the rough sergeant who helps destroy their fragile idyll remain as indistinct as a distant echo.

One warms to the pastoral romance that develops between Glenda Jackson, as the self-sufficient farmer tending her lonely acres while her husband is a captive of the Japanese, and the errant, young private from a local base. A viewer accepts the eventual love and sex, her lover's decision to desert and her plan to dress him as her "sister" to avoid detection and gossip, among other things.

Miss Jackson's portrayal is, at first, poignant and convincing as she projects dignity and understandable desire for the love and companionship she has long missed.

●

But she is somewhat less than credible subsequently as the strong-willed, bickering woman who, for debatable reasons, creates problems and then suffers her somewhat childish lover's alienation because of them.

It is difficult to entertain the idea that Oliver Reed, as the brutish broth of a sergeant, would barge in on the household to make loutish advances, and invite the "sister" to an Army Christmas dance and not quickly discover the masquerade. And it seems improbable that

Brian Deacon, a newcomer from British TV in the role of the masquerader, would chance the dangers of near-rape as well as exposure as a deserter. He is youthfully handsome but emotionally shallow in a characterization that could benefit by further explanations.

Michael Apted, the director; Robin Chapman, the scenarist, and Graham Cottle, the producer, who are also making their movie debuts, fitfully capture nuances of speech and manners as lovely and real as the muted colors of the film's English countryside. But a larger helping of logic could have made their "Triple Echo" resound, rather than whisper.

A. H. WEILER

1973 N 1, 48:1

The Cast

THE ITALIAN CONNECTION, directed by Fernando Di Leo; written by Augusto Finocchi, Ingo Hermess and Mr. Di Leo; a German-Italian production, presented by American International. At the Penthouse Theater, Broadway and 47th Street; the 86th Street Twin 1, at Lexington Avenue, and the 59th Street Twin 1, east of Third Avenue. Running time: 92 minutes. This film is rated "R."
Luca .... Mario Adorf
Dave .... Henry Silva
Frank .... Woody Strode
Don Vito .... Adolfo Celi
Eva .... Luciana Paluzzi
Corso .... Cyril Cusack

Say this for "The Italian Connection." It ends in the right place, a Milanese junkyard, with the key figures slaughtering one another amidst piled, worn-out cars.

The film opened yesterday at the Penthouse, 86th Street Twin I and 59th Street Twin I theaters.

The picture itself is plain garbage, a German-Italian co-production with a splash or two of backstreet Milanese color and one good performance. The pointless plot has a quaking, small-time pimp (Mario Adorf) fleeing two American killers (Henry Silva and Woody Strode) and the local Mafia. The language (spoken and dubbed English) is as filthy as the action is dull, for all the bone-crunching and squealing.

Apparently, with such a title, the producers hoped somebody would mistake the picture for a sequel to "The French Connection" or even "The Chinese Connection." And isn't there "The Salzburg Connection" due around the bend? As the terrified dimwitted fugitive, Mario Adorf is credible, against formidable odds.

HOWARD THOMPSON

1973 N 1, 48:1

The Program

THE FILMS OF DANNY LYON, a program of three documentary films directed by Mr. Lyon: "Soc. Sci. 127," 21 minutes; "Llanito," 61 minutes; "El Chivo," six minutes. At the Film Forum, 88th Street, west of Broadway.

By VINCENT CANBY

"The Films of Danny Lyon," the new program at the Film Forum, is a collection of three documentary films by the 31-year-old Brooklyn-born still photographer turned film-maker. The two best films in the collection, "Llanito" (61 minutes) and "Soc. Sci. 127" (21 minutes) are defined less by a developed cinematic style than by compassion for the subjects.

"Llanito" is a sorrowful montage of scenes of Indian life in the tiny New Mexico town of that name. It is not an especially finished film, but perhaps Mr. Lyon does not mean it to be.

A couple of Indian men, half-kidding, dance around a beer can in a back alley. We listen to another man boast to the camera about his prowess as a hunter, while his mother mutters that the only thing he is good at is drinking.

Juxtaposed against these scenes are others set in a home for the retarded, where, among other things, we listen to a white teen-age boy, who speaks in a high falsetto voice, telling us about freedom, sin, the crucifixion of Christ and the creation of the world ("God made everything out of nothing").

Mr. Lyon's fondness for bizarre images is balanced by a kind of solemn respect for his subjects. This is particularly true in "Soc. Sci. 127," about an eccentric, hard-drinking tattoo artist named Bill Sanders, who, while he works, rambles on about Vietnam, lesbians and the art of what he advertises as "velvety tattoos."

The third film on the program, "El Chivot" (The Goat) is a series of free associations on the life of goat and Indian. It runs six long, pretentious minutes.

Mr. Lyon's skills as a photographer are evident throughout but I had the feeling in each of the films that he was still searching his images to find out what they might mean. This is not quite good enough.

1973 N 3, 15:1

The Program

SUNSEED, a documentary directed by Fredrick Cohn. At the Whitney Museum of American Art, 75th Street and Madison Avenue. Running time: 90 minutes.

By NORA SAYRE

Lavish hostility has been leveled against the new mysticism by those who feel that the upsurge of religious cults has siphoned off the political energies of the young. However, the charge doesn't seem to be historically valid—since many began dropping out of politics well before the latest wave of gurus arrived. Ranging from fatigue

to fears of Federal reprisal, fears of further Kent and Jackson States, ravaging fights among those on the same side, and the loss of confidence about being able to remake American society, the reasons for that massive recoil could (and no doubt will) make a book the length of "The Sotweed Factor."

Meanwhile, emotional malnutrition has been rampant in this country. Hence it seems rather inevitable that some—including people who tried and eventually rejected drugs — turned to various forms of religion.

"Sunseed," which opened yesterday at the Whitney Museum of American Art, offers a sympathetic introduction to the New Age. The director, Fredrick Cohn, partakes of that movement himself. But he doesn't preach or clutch at converts. The documentary, which tours India as well as America, is based on interviews with 10 spiritual leaders and shows some of them meditating with their followers.

From the Lama Anagarika Govinda in the Himalayan foothills to Ram Dass (formerly Dr. Richard Alpert) at a New Hampshire farm, or a Sufi meditation camp in Arizona, the stress is on both personal and world peace, receptivity to God (who is— and isn't—defined in a number of ways), a rejection of materialism, and the effort to dissolve the ego. There's also the suggestion that the new consciousness could free the enlightened from vulnerability. But we're also shown one young woman in tears because she feels guilty for not being able to embrace the faith.

There are beguiling glimpses of the late Murshid Samuel L. Lewis—who was known as Sufi Sam to his disciples and also described himself as "a roaring borealis"—separating egg yolks in his disarrayed kitchen and advising: "Be calm, cool, suave, diplomatic, and crazy." Even skeptics will note that his followers like almost everyone in this picture, do look amazingly happy.

Varieties of Buddhism and Hinduism overlap and alternate throughout "Sunseed," along with Yoga, and it's a bit difficult for outsiders to untangle them. But even if the contrasts were clear, it would be impossible for the unconverted to judge the contents of this sensitive and skillfully made film. However, it does show some of the impact of mysticism on young people in America, especially their sense of "skipping over a threshold" into experiences that they've never known before. And it's easy to savor the stunning camera work of Baird Bryant and Robert Frank, along with the singing of the Sufi Choir —even if you haven't blissed-out yourself.

1973 N 3, 15:1

The Cast

DON QUIXOTE, directed by Rudolf Nureyev and Robert Helpmann; photography, Geoffrey Unsworth; music, Ludwig Minkus; choreography, Mr. Nureyev after Petipa; production and costumes designed by Barry Kay; produced by John Hargreaves; presented by the Walter Reade Organization. At the Festival Theater, 57th Street at Fifth Avenue. Running time: 107 minutes. This film is classified G.

Don Quixote .... Robert Helpmann
Sancho Panza .... Ray Powell
Basilio .... Rudolf Nureyev
Lorenzo .... Francis Croese
Kitri .... Lucette Aldous
Gamache .... Colin Peasley
Dancers of the Australian Ballet

By ANNA KISSELGOFF

Rudolf Nureyev has done so well with "Don Quixote," his film version of a flawed 19th-century ballet, that he has actually made it more fun than the stage production. The result is a dance film for all audiences, an exciting, intelligently conceived spectacle.

It is a film that takes the dangerous risk of wedding cinematic realism with formal ballet conventions and triumphs as a genre of its own. The tone is so consistent that it is not jarring at all to see Sancho Panza hit on the head with a lobster in one scene and to watch a full corps de ballet in tutus in another.

Above all, "Don Quixote," starring Mr. Nureyev, Sir Robert Helpmann and Lucette Aldous with the Australian Ballet, is the work of top professionals who have a firm understanding of their material. The film opened yesterday at the Festival Theater.

In Geoffrey Unsworth, who photographed "Cabaret" and "2001: A Space Odyssey," there is a cameraman immune to the usual penchant for cutting off dancers' feet and focusing away from the choreographic climax. In the innovative use of an overhead diagonal view, Mr. Unsworth succeeds splendidly in showing the dancer's full body with no foreshortening.

This is as much a dramatic film as a ballet film. Not merely a photographed version of Mr. Nureyev's 1970 stage production of "Don Quixote" for the Australian Ballet, it now has crucial nondancing links. In Sir Robert, whose career has spanned ballet dancing and stage and film acting as well as directing, there is a co-director who (one suspects) is largely responsible for the coherence of the dance and nondance passages.

There is, finally, the other co-director, Mr. Nureyev. Probably no dancer onstage today has done more to bring the great 19th-century ballet classics alive and make them relevant to a modern audience. This "Don Quixote" is a tribute to his extraordinary understanding of the tradition behind those ballets.

Buy understanding the tradition, Mr. Nureyev can afford to depart from it occasionally. "Don Quixote" was not one of the masterpieces of Marius Petipa, the great French-Russian choreographer who is best known for "The Sleeping Beauty."

Created in 1869, revised by the Bolshoi choreographer Alexander Gorsky and others, the ballet is not even really about Don Quixote.

Mr. Nureyev has made an honest if conveniently spectacular statement about this ballet, by beginning the film in Barry Kay's vast street panorama of color and movement that focuses on the real hero and heroine — Basilio, the barber, and his love, Kitri —and not with the usual prologue of Don Quixote in his chamber.

The Kitri-Basilio romance is the crux of the story, and one of Mr. Nureyev's several new dances is a sexy duet in which Basilio persuades Kitri to go to bed with him.

When she danced the role of Kitri in New York in 1971, Miss Aldous—formerly of the Royal Ballet—was just a little too tough. Now she gives us a properly earthy village girl, dancing with

flourish and just right amount of comic upmanship to meet Mr. Nureyev on his own ground.

For this is a comic ballet full of sunlight, and Mr. Nureyev is its Sun King. Those who have never seen him onstage will find the full Nureyev myth here right down to the virtuosity of the smashing final grand pas de deux.

Only an actor who was also a premier danseur could handle the part of Don Quixote himself as excellently as Sir Robert. Detached but dignified, he turns the conventional 19th-century dream sequence away from a divertissement into a moment of dramatic truth.

There is an exceptional performance from Ray Powell as Sancho Panza, and the Australian Ballet does fine work in what is frankly a back-up position.

1973 N 3, 25:1

Time to Stop Playing It Safe

By STEPHEN FARBER

LOS ANGELES

AMERICAN movies have always been terrified of social and political ideas. Hollywood celebrates action and leaves the messages for Western Union. But ideas can be dramatically exciting; literate films don't have to be preachy. Our movies desperately need conversations and confrontations that reflect the concerns of intelligent adults; and that means some recognition of the social and political issues that are as much a part of life as gunfights, car chases and karate chops.

Although movies can no longer be considered a mass medium, the studios continue to aim most of their movies at a mass audience that no longer exists. Some of the sensational images may not be meant for children, but the ideas are still diluted for the 12-year-old mind.

Two new films with unusual possibilities ultimately disappoint because they insult the intelligence of the audience, and at crucial moments back away from the social and political ideas that they need to confront. James Bridges's "The Paper Chase," a chronicle of one pressure-ridden year at Harvard Law School, has some observant touches. It captures the day-to-day tensions in a class on contract law with a crusty old professor (brilliantly played by John Houseman), the petty rivalries within a study group, the panic of those long all-nighters spent cramming for exams. The details are amusing and convincing, but the film never cuts beneath the surface.

Vincent Canby is on vacation. He will return next Sunday. Stephen Farber is a critic and the author of "The Movie Rating Game."

One problem is that Harvard seems as insulated as one of those dream campuses in MGM musicals of the forties. The costumes are the only indication that the movie takes place in 1973 rather than in 1953. There is no mention of the social and political activity that touches the life of every university student today. Without this important social background, the central character is curiously indistinct. We never know why Hart (Timothy Bottoms) wants to be a lawyer. Perhaps the point is that *he* doesn't know either, but this doesn't ring true.

After four years of college, Hart seems as naive and bewildered as a freshman. But many of the law students I know have chosen law because they want to work for social reforms—protecting the rights of the poor, defending civil liberties and free speech, challenging the giant corporations that rule America or fighting discrimination against women and minority groups. This is not to say that all law students are idealistic, but not a single student shown in "The Paper Chase" seems even momentarily aware of any of those social issues.

The film takes on a safer, more general theme; it means to expose the virulence of competition in America. The girl played by Lindsay Wagner is the voice of "freedom" and irrationality; at regular intervals she gives little speeches to the hero attacking him for his grade-grubbing and mocking the regimented life that he accepts. In 1953, a film about student life that questioned the obsession with grades might have seemed startling. Today it seems like very old news.

The interesting dilemma is how a law student with a sense of social purpose holds to that purpose when forced to play by the cruel competitive rules of the university. Is it possible to do meaningful work within a corrupt system? How does one survive with ideals but no illusions? The facile conclusion to "The Paper Chase"—in which the hero tosses away his grades without reading them—evades all the pertinent questions. What the film shows isn't so much false as incomplete. "The Paper Chase" is innocuous enough, but so empty of ideas and so eager not to offend that it never catches fire.

"The Way We Were," adapted by Arthur Laurents from his own novel, is a good deal more substantial. Although it fails to resolve the social issues that bear on the story, it is an ambitious, consistently fascinating attempt. Spanning the period from the late thirties to the early fifties, "The Way We Were" centers on the marriage of Katie Morosky (Barbra Streisand), a passionately committed Jewish radical, and Hubbell Gardiner (Robert Redford), a charming but spineless WASP athlete.

Over the years, love stories have been among the dumbest of all American movies; in treating romance, filmmakers abdicate intelligence and drool about the sacred mystery of love. "The Way We Were" is almost a milestone because it's a thoughtful, believable love story for adults. For once, the characters are sharply defined, and their relationship develops and deepens persuasively.

To Katie, the Jewish outsider, Hubbell is the golden boy with the all-American smile; he offers her a connection with the normal, easygoing life that she secretly covets. And Hubbell, who knows his own limitations, loves Katie for her fire and her commitment, and because he is tantalized by what she sees in him, what she wants him to become. The differences that attract them will ultimately separate them; but there is real electricity between them, and when they argue, we're involved because we can see that neither of them is wholly right.

Some of the electricity comes from the two stars; their chemistry keeps the movie engaging. Streisand is still too shrill at moments; but this is the most forceful, controlled acting she's ever done. Redford is superb; in scenes where he has little to do except react, he fills in his character with extraordinarily subtle and evocative shadings. The stars play *together* beautifully, and for that, Sydney Pollack, a very intelligent, sensitive, tactful director, deserves a great deal of credit.

*

Unfortunately, there is more to "The Way We Were" than the love story. The political themes that should have balanced and strengthened the romantic drama are rushed over or simply ignored. Katie's character is the one that suffers most from these evasions. Dealing with a politically committed character is a challenge for American filmmakers; the makers of "The Way We Were" don't meet the challenge.

First, they soften and defuse Katie's radical ideas. Even at the very beginning, when she speaks at a campus rally about the Spanish Civil War, she makes such a bland plea for world peace that no one to the left of Hitler could disagree. Katie's ideas seem naive and primitive, and it would be easy to conclude that her political activism is no more than a symptom of sexual frustration; when she lands her man, she settles happily into the kitchen.

This condescension toward Katie undermined the early parts of Arthur Laurents's novel too, but in the concluding sections, Laurents showed his respect for the character's political involvement. Katie and Hubbell break up in Hollywood, against the background of the House Un-American Activities Committee investigations into Communism in the movie industry. The film had a chance to illuminate one of the most important chapters in recent American history—the tragedy of a generation that betrayed friendships, as Orson Welles once said, "in order to save its swimming pools."

But the nightmare of the blacklist is swept aside with a few abrupt, confusing references. The climax of Laurents's novel comes when Katie, named as a former Communist by a college classmate, must decide whether to cooperate with the Committee; if she refuses to give names of former left-wing colleagues, her husband's career will be damaged. So she is faced with a direct choice between her political convictions and her marriage, and she finally decides that she cannot compromise what she believes.

Incredibly, this episode is not in the film. (Pollack reports that the sequence was shot, but cut from the movie—along with several other scenes concerning the blacklist—after a sneak preview.) Without it, the movie has no dramatic climax. The marriage disintegrates between scenes. Worse, the political issues never develop an urgency because they never enter the characters' lives. Laurents's point was that no matter how hard people try to resist involvement, they are eventually implicated in the political controversies around them. In the movie this point is lost, and the depth of Katie's commitment is mocked. Because she never takes a truly courageous stand, the movie gives the impression that she is no more than a dilettante, a dabbler in radical movements, a political groupie.

*

Both "The Way We Were" and "The Paper Chase" are interesting because they reveal Hollywood's confusion about today's audience. The studios are taking a few risks, tackling offbeat subjects that they never would have touched 20 years ago. But they're still hedging their bets, trying to make provocative material as inoffensive as possible. Their timidity seems misguided. Even in its present form "The Way We Were" is far too subtle and intelligent for the fans of "Funny Girl" or "Hello, Dolly!" At the same time, it's too compromised for more serious moviegoers who are ready to see a sophisticated film about the McCarthy period and the blacklist.

Having taken as many chances as they did, couldn't these films have gone further? I don't believe they would have lost their audience if they had been bolder. When the lovers in "The Way We Were" debate politics, it's exhilarating to hear; but the debates just whet our appetite. We want more. American movies are begin-

ning to speak to our concerns, but they need to put more trust in the audience. Right now many movies seem schizoid, caught halfway between strong, serious art and old-fashioned glossy entertainment. They try to please everybody, and may end up satisfying nobody.

1973 N 4, II:1:6

SCREAMING TIGER, a kung fu melodrama starring Wang Yu, in Chinese with English subtitles; released by American International Pictures. At neighborhood theaters. Running time: 101 minutes. This film is classified R.

The "Screaming Tiger" that crashed into local theaters yesterday is proof that the Chinese movie makers are still doing their kung fu thing with bloody, stultifying regularity. Wang Yu, the only one identified in the meager credits of this latest exercise in puerile, perpetual motion, plays the clean-cut Chinese karate champ who has come to Japan to knock off droves of Sumo wrestlers and other grimacing types before dispatching the dastard who murdered his family.

Oh yes, he's an acupuncture expert, too. And acupuncture seems to be the only regimen that could possibly help this "Screaming Tiger." A. H. WEILER

1973 N 8, 58:6

The Cast

EXECUTIVE ACTION, directed by David Miller; screenplay by Dalton Trumbo, story by Donald Freed and Mark Lane; director of photography, Robert Steadman; film editor, George Grenville and Irving Lerner; music, Randy Edelman; producer, Edward Lewis; released by National General Pictures. At the Coronet Theater, Third Avenue at 59th Street. Running time 91 minutes. This film is classified PG.

Farrington	Burt Lancaster
Foster	Robert Ryan
Ferguson	Will Geer
Paulitz	Gilbert Green
Halliday	John Anderson
Gunman	Paul Carr
Tim	Colby Chester

By NORA SAYRE

If disbelief is one of our healthiest national reflexes, at least it has been well exercised in the years between the Warren Report and the latest protestations about the nonbeing of those Presidential tapes. The only danger is that fact itself can be a victim of disbelief: Ugly news that happens to be true becomes easier to ignore, and good news gets rejected with a cackle.

"Executive Action," which opened yesterday at the Coronet, offers a tactful, low-key blend of fact and invention. The film makers do not insist that they have solved John Kennedy's murder; instead, they simply evoke what might have happened, according to various researchers, including Mark Lane.

The result is a cool, skillful, occasionally confusing argument for conspiracy. Wealthy rightwingers (Burt Lancaster and Robert Ryan) wanted Kennedy removed because he was going to sign the test-ban treaty, "lead the black revolution" and probably pull out of Vietnam. The last two points may give you the hiccups, but that is what these characters say.

Like calm businessmen, they organize the event. While three talented marksmen rehearse by shooting at dummies in a car driven through the desert, the conspirators search for a nut to use as a patsy.

Throughout the stress is on technology — even Oswald's name comes out of a computer. The movie follows the "second Oswald" theory, and this part of the plot is deftly constructed, as is the disappearance of the three marksmen, also the calculations to "have the F.B.I. watching the C.I.A." and vice versa, while relying on the inefficiency of the Secret Service.

The conspirators are cleverly cloaked in the style of Camelot itself. Lancaster and Ryan appear as pensive, practical semi-academics, rationally planning an act as bloody as a small foreign invasion. (They admit that they sometimes "sound like gods," since they are also planning the world's future — "Well, somebody's got to do it.") Both have the confidence and the casual class that we recall in many Kennedy appointees. Lancaster, looking miraculously young, overdoes the "sincerity" at moments— an old habit of his. And there are too many shots of the conspirators smiling ironically at one another. But Ryan is wonderfully benign and wry, wisely underplaying where others might have gone all out for evil.

However, it is far more painful to think of Ryan's death — a few weeks after this movie was finished — than Kennedy's. And that is the problem lurking in this movie. Television footage is used to paw at the public's sentiments; we see Kennedy smiling and golfing and kissing his children, as well as making speeches. But "Executive Action" is emotionally disconnected from history to the degree that those with an affection for suspense can enjoy the build-up of the plotting — even though we know how the assassination turned out.

Despite the flags crawling down flagpoles and the drumbeats, a national trauma has become a competent thriller. And it is just as well. Reliving the shock of that killing would hardly benefit any kind of audience now.

So whether you chime with this interpretation, or, like a

few I know, decide to embrace all the conspiracy theories of the assassination, the movie is useful in rousing the questions once again. The film's sternest and strongest point is that only a crazed person acting on his own would have been acceptable to the American public— which, at that time, certainly did not want to believe in a conspiracy.

1973 N 8, 60:1

The Program

ROBIN HOOD, an animated feature produced and directed by Wolfgang Reitherman; story by Larry Clemmons; based on character and story conceptions by Ken Anderson; songs by Roger Miller, Floyd Huddleston, George Bruns and Johnny Mercer; released by Buena Vista Company, Inc., Walt Disney Productions. At the Radio City Music Hall, Avenue of the Americas and 50th Street. Running time: 83 minutes. This film is classified G.
With the voices of Roger Miller, Brian Bedford, Monica Evans, Phil Harris, Andy Devine, Carole Shelley, Peter Ustinov, Terry-Thomas and Pat Buttram.

By VINCENT CANBY

Once upon a time in Sherwood Forest there lived a fox named Robin Hood who, with his good friend, a sportive brown bear named Little John, stole from the rich to give to the poor.

Nearby Nottingham was occupied by elephants, rhinos, hippos and snakes, who were the escorts, advisers and chums of the evil Prince John, a scrawny lion whose crown was too big and who, in moments of national crisis, sucked his thumb and pulled his ear lobe. Nottingham Castle was run by incompetents. Guard duty was left largely to a dim-witted vulture who liked to yell "one o'clock and all's well" when it was often three o'clock and everything was terrible.

An all-animal/bird version of Robin Hood? Good grief! But then, why not?

The legend about the bandit of Sherwood Forest has survived more than a dozen screen adaptations, including "Son of Robin Hood" (1959), which was really about a daughter, and 165 half-hour television films.

Walt Disney's multigenus, animated film version, which opened yesterday at Radio City Music Hall, testifies to the legend's elasticity and durability. It should also be a good deal of fun for toddlers whose minds have not yet shriveled into orthodoxy.

The visual style is charmingly conventional, as gently reassuring as that of a Donald Duck cartoon, sometimes as romantically pretty as an old Silly Symphony. Roger Miller, the composer ("King of the Road") and humorist, provides the voice for Allan a Dale, the rooster who acts as the film's narrator, thus giving this "Robin Hood" a decidedly odd but not unpleasant country-and-Western flavor.

The other voices are supplied by Peter Ustinov (Prince John), Terry-Thomas

(Sir Hiss), Andy Devine (Friar Tuck), Phil Harris (Little John), Brian Bedford (Robin Hood) and Pat Buttram (the Sheriff of Nottingham), whose voice, like Ustinov's, is a very funny mixture of villainy and absolute fraud.

1973 N 9, 29:1

On the stage the Music Hall is presenting its annual Christmas show, including "The Nativity." It's not only that time flies, but also that the Music Hall helps rush it along.

The 'Iceman' Cometh Too Close

By VINCENT CANBY

FROM the opening frames of John Frankenheimer's film version of Eugene O'Neill's "The Iceman Cometh," you get the feeling that you're being taken on a guided tour of one of the greatest American plays ever written, instead of seeing a screen adaptation with a life of its own.

Look at the dusty lightbulbs, says the tour guide. Look at the texture of the walls. Look at the remarkable crevasses in the face of Larry Slade (the late Robert Ryan). Don't be shy. Come in close. Poke into his tired eyes.

Except for occasional long-shots that allow us to see all of the characters in a single frame, this version of "The Iceman Cometh" has been so Balkanized by close-ups and medium close-ups that it's sometimes difficult to remember who is sitting where in relation to whom, which is quite a trick when you realize that the play has only a single set: the interior of Harry Hope's grubby saloon, and the even grubbier room behind it, on New York's lower West Side in the summer of 1912.

Yet "The Iceman Cometh" is so monolithic in mood and intensity that not even this kind of cinematic fragmentation can destroy the play's impact. Just when you think you might have to leave the theater, or move to the back row to get away from the intimacy enforced by the camera, the play will suddenly reassert itself in some startling speech or confrontation or section of a performance.

It may be a bit of business by Fredric March who, as Harry Hope, has trouble getting his lips around his store-bought teeth so he can say with furiously forlorn resolve: "This dump is going to be run like other dumps!" Or it may be a terrible moment when Hugo Kalmar (Sorrell Booke), the anarchist, hears himself proclaiming: "I love only the proletariat! I will lead them! I will be like a god to them! They will be my slaves!"

These are small moments, not terribly important in themselves, but the art of "The Iceman Cometh," like the art of "Long Day's Journey Into Night," is the manner in which O'Neill allows these small moments to accumulate. The result is such a minutely detailed inventory of human emotions that "The Iceman Cometh" transcends both its bleakness and its something less than profound observations on the revivifying nature of pipedreams.

Like Theodore Dreiser, O'Neill is too often thought of as a primitive, as a man who just somehow managed to stumble onto the great works that came out of his typewriter.

It is one of the ironies of the Frankenheimer film version, which last week launched the highly touted American Film Theater subscription series here, that its fragmented cinematic form permits us to appreciate O'Neill's method, even though it doesn't do much for the play itself. Every time some character starts a long speech, the camera begins slowly to close in on him, as if spoken words created a kind of magnetic attraction the camera could not resist.

Most of the other characters are forgotten as the speakers and perhaps the heads of one or two other characters are isolated in the frame. The camera searches the faces of the actors for details that, in spite of the generally high level of all of the performances except one, simply do not match those of the extraordinary speeches O'Neill wrote.

O'Neill created the characters of "The Iceman Cometh" in such dramatic close-up—through their reveries, fights and philosophizing— that they manage almost to make a liar out of the close-up camera. The words have one reality and the images quite another.

Lots of good modern plays (Williams's "A Streetcar Named Desire" and Albee's ("Who's Afraid of Virginia

Woolf?") can be photographed in this intimate manner and work beautifully, perhaps because the plays have effective cinematic origins in being mostly one-to-one encounters. Yet "The Iceman Cometh," with its more than a dozen characters, most of whom are on the set much of the time, demands the audience remain at the kind of distance from its characters necessitated by a conventional stage proscenium.

We should be able to pick and choose where to look when Hickey launches into the climactic series of speeches in which he admits the inner peace he's been boasting of has been acquired through the murder of a beloved, forgiving wife whom he loathed. We should be able to check old Harry Hope, so marvelously played by March that we keep wanting to see more of him, to study his reactions.

If, while watching a stage version of "The Iceman Cometh," we come to the conclusion that the man playing Hickey isn't up to the role, we can attend to the other characters. In the sort of film that Frankenheimer has chosen to make, with, I'm sure, a lot of forethought, we are denied this freedom. We're locked into a seat with blinders at the sides.

Whatever happened to the more or less fixed camera and deep-focus photography with which William Wyler shot the film version of Lillian Hellman's "The Little Foxes"? If any theatrical work requires such screen treatment, it is certainly this O'Neill play, which, though not permanently damaged by a style more suitable to Stanley Kramer's "Oklahoma Crude," certainly is not enhanced by it.

Here let me register a note of self-doubt: while watching this version of "The Iceman Cometh" last week I kept remembering the Play of The Week television version some years ago that starred Jason Robards, Jr., as Hickey, the role Lee Marvin tries to scale in the new film. As I recall at this writing, I had no special reservations about the television show, no worries about close-ups, about the isolation of action and reaction within the small frame of the TV screen.

Yet I'm sure that Harry Hope's barroom could only have been visible on the small screen by the use of such a technique. Is it possible that what I remember as a most remarkable television show was made remarkable largely by the performance of Robards, and that what's lacking in Frankenheimer's film is a Hickey who is strong and dynamic enough to pull all those isolated shots together?

Marvin's Hickey actually is as clean-cut and properly groomed as Hickey mistakenly believes himself to be. There's no hint of mania either in his dress or his manner, no sense of desperation, no way of connecting him to these derelicts in some earlier period of his life.

There's nothing wrong with the other performers that would not be transformed were the film possessed by a more demonic Hickey. Several of the other performers are, indeed, superb. March, especially, as well as Bradford Dillman, Ryan, Tom Pedi and Moses Gunn as Joe Mott, the down-and-out gambling man, which may be one of the best roles for a black actor ever written by a white, 20th-century playwright.

The American Film Theater plan is to present a total of eight legitimate plays in screen adaptations that probably could not have been made except on this subscription plan, meaning on comparatively modest budgets with first-rate casts accepting less than their usual salaries.

Its production of "The Iceman Cometh" adds nothing to our film heritage, as did Sidney Lumet's verision of "Long Day's Journey Into Night" with those magnificent performances by Ralph Richardson, Katharine Hepburn and Jason Robards. Rather it is testimony to the stature of a play whose grandeur is apparent even in fleeting moments. It's like flying over the Grand Canyon on a cloudy day.

1973 N 11, II:1:7

This 'Spook' Has No Respect for Human Life

By MEYER KANTOR

DURING the darkest days of the sixties, those days when it seemed that the Vietnam war would never end and the war on poverty was grinding to a halt, those of us who were involved in the movements to change our country's policies from within the existing political system began to wonder if we weren't wasting our time, and—along with our time—

Meyer Kantor is a freelance writer.

the lives of all those people to whom we had pledged ourselves. It was during those lonely moments that frustration replaced hope, and we began to talk of revolution.

It was just an intellectual exercise; we realized how hopeless such a move would be, considering our small numbers. But the ideas of Marx and Mao filled the air like stale tobacco smoke, and we needed no marijuana or LSD to get high on as long as we could get comparable feelings with our idealism. So when it seemed that we could

cause no change with peaceful demonstrations and civil disobedience, we would sit around the college cafeteria tables and dream of seizing power.

Now Ivan Dixon has put a piece of our youthful dreams on the screen in his film, "The Spook Who Sat by the Door." And it seems that we were having nightmares. Dixon, the black actor turned director, keeps the action moving, and the screenplay by Sam Greenlee and Melvin Clay — based on Greenlee's best-selling novel — crackles with the wit and the heat of

men of anger. But it is just anger, and not reason, that comes through. In the end, it is the failure of Greenlee and Clay to present a clear indictment of white society's treatment of third world people that causes the film to drift from meaningful outrage to senseless, James Bond-like, violence.

*

Dan Freeman — portrayed with impressive fervor by Lawrence Cook — becomes the first black C.I.A. agent after an exhaustive effort by the agency to find a showcase "Negro." He goes through a training program designed to create killers, and that's exactly what he becomes. Then, after spending five years behind a reception desk as the black face to be pointed out to visiting Congressmen, he leaves the C.I.A. and goes home to the Chicago ghetto where he grew up.

Once there, Freeman begins to organize the black youth gangs into paramilitary forces. He trains them in the C.I.A. methods of killing and sends groups of young men out across the country to organize other gangs in other ghettos. In a series of daring raids on United States military installations and Chicago banks, the new army finances and arms itself. Then, when an addict is shot by the police, they strike back. The mayor's office is blown up, and the city's defenses deflate like a punctured life preserver.

The film ends when Freeman's old school buddy, a black civil rights activist turned cop, discovers that his friend is behind the present turmoil. They kill each other, and when word of Freeman's death spreads, violence erupts throughout the country. The President declares a state of national emergency, and the revolution we students used to conjecture about seems ready to begin.

The most obvious flaw in "The Spook Who Sat by the Door" is its lack of respect for the system, the enemy, and its ability to defend itself. Cops are portrayed as not only brutal but blindly stupid. Entire warehouses, filled with the most sophisticated weapons, are guarded by one lonely soldier who looks as if he is no more than 16 years old. He falls down before he is even hit. Small groups of revolutionaries take on entire regiments and win. It could only happen this way, as the cliché goes, in the movies.

Beyond this failing, there is a lack of respect in the film for human life that

makes the skin crawl. To kill a human being is the most awesomely frightening thing a man can do. No true revolutionary, past or present, would countenance the kind of cavalier slaughter that is presented in "The Spook Who Sat by the Door." It is devoid of reason; it is killing just to kill.

Excuses for the wholesale bloodshed are lamely made. Freedom, for instance. Freeman defines the word "freedom" so loosely that it becomes meaningless. Never before has such total disregard for such a splendid word been displayed on film. If we, the refugees of the various movements of the sixties, are guilty of encouraging this sort of thing, we must rethink everything we did.

*

It seems to me, however, that we were very certain about what we meant when we said "freedom." We knew that in order for people to be truly free, they must first have food, decent housing, proper medical care and self-respect—above all else, self-respect. We knew that without education and jobs, there can be no self-respect; so we decided that if we had the power, we would provide education and jobs. Either Freeman does not understand these principles or his creators have not seen fit to have him *say* that he does.

"The Spook Who Sat by the Door" has only one redeeming feature, but it is important enough to make the film worth seeing. For all its excesses, it sounds a warning to an over-stuffed goose of a society that it is swimming in a sea of human despair, with the tide rapidly rising. When the conditions of living become so unbearable that death is preferable to life, people can, and often do, choose to take their own lives. Occasionally such people may choose to strike out at the cause of their oppression and despair. Such attempts may be suicidal because the oppressor is so much more powerful than the oppressed, but dying can become an acceptable alternative to living under the lash.

So it is that revolutions come, kicking and screaming, into the world — like half-born children, fighting against the pangs of birth, hitting out blindly at everything within reach, suspended between new life and death. The innocent and the guilty become suitable targets, and what is new can often be worse than what is replaced.

Thus, "The Spook Who Sat by the Door" becomes not

Lawrence Cook, right, as an ex-C.I.A. agent, trains militants Clinton Malcome and Johnnie Johnson in "The Spook Who Sat by the Door," now at the DeMille.

just a film about black people, but a film about man's response to oppression. And, as such, it provides a valuable lesson: Should we fail to meet the legitimate demands of the millions of poor, ill-housed, hungry, sick and degraded Americans, we may, some day soon, find ourselves faced with a very real spook who sat by the door.

1973 N 11, II:11:1

The Cast

THE HOMECOMING, directed by Peter Hall; screenplay by Harold Pinter, based on his play; produced by Ely Landau; executive producer, Otto Plaschkes; director of photography, David Watkin; editor, Rex Pike; presented by the American Film Theater. At selected theaters. Running time: 116 minutes. This film has hot been classified at this time.

Sam	Cyril Cusack
Lenny	Ian Holm
Teddy	Michael Jayston
Ruth	Vivien Merchant
Joey	Terence Rigby
Max	Paul Rogers

By VINCENT CANBY

Harold Pinter's rabid comedy "The Homecoming," has been turned into a movie of astonishing dynamism by Peter Hall, who also directed the original London and Broadway productions, with six extraordinary English actors who, with one exception, appeared in the play on the stage. The film, the second offering in the American Film Theater series, opened yesterday at selected theaters.

"The Homecoming" is Pinter's most tumultuous full-length play, as menacing as "The Birthday Party," as mysterious as "Old Times," but so full of wild, essential life that questions about its meaning seem secondary if not superfluous.

•

One need not define life when one can point to it, which is what Pinter is doing in "The Homecoming," with marvelous control of exaggerated language and gesture that have the effect of a fluoroscope. Pinter keeps giving us glimpses of interior furies that most of us prefer not to acknowledge in the daytime.

For some peculiar reason, these glimpses are often hilariously funny. It may be that we laugh at the outrageous behavior of the members of the Cockney family in "The Homecoming" for the same reason that we laugh at the terrible things that happen to characters in slapstick comedy, because it's happening to them and not to us.

The film, as far as I can tell from a reading of the stage text, is a practically untouched adaptation of the play, though Hall's camera never seems to intrude on the life of the play. It never embarrasses the actors by exposing them to be what they are. Most of the action continues to take place in the barren parlor of the North London house ruled by foul-mouthed old Max (Paul Rogers), the patriarch of a clan now reduced to three, his sons Lenny (Ian Holm) and Joey (Terence Rigby) and his younger brother Sam (Cyril Cusack), a chauffeur for a private firm.

•

Max is losing his grip. He roams the house as purposely as a convict trying to hide the aimlessness of his confinement. Lenny, a small-time pimp and an dandy, ridicules him and calls him an old prat. Joey, somewhat simple-minded, doesn't understand him and thinks mostly of going to the top as a boxer, just as soon as he masters the arts of defense and attack.

The fastidious Sam, when he isn't busy washing dishes, which greatly irritates Max, suggests that he might once have had an affair with Max's late wife, Jesse. Max's moods wander, like a mind, often in mid-speech. He remembers Jesse fondly and then says: "She wasn't such a bad woman. Even though it made me sick just to look at her rotten stinking face, she wasn't a bad bitch,"

Into this totally male pride come Max's eldest son, Teddy (Michael Jayston), a professor of philosophy at an American university, and his wife Ruth (Vivien Merchant). While Teddy watches with apparent complacency, the members of his family transform Ruth into a whore, a role with which she is not entirely unfamaliar and which she is willing to accept, as long as she is given a written contract.

•

The film is so much of an entity, so beautifully integrated, that its spell is never broken, not even with one intermission. The mood begins with the bigger-than-life noises we hear behind the opening credits—someone rummaging through a drawer that seems to contain everything from silverware, and carpenter's tools to salvaged paperclips that no one will ever use—and does not let up until a final tableau that is both theatrical and cinematic.

Hall goes outside the house just once, when Ruth takes a late-night walk, but even the street we see her walk down is as sealed off from humanity as the interior of the house. It's not that we sense that other lives are not being lived elsewhere in Pinter's world, but rather that those lives are simply reflections and extentions of those Pinter has chosen to show us.

"The Homecoming," unlike the very literal production of "The Iceman Cometh," makes us take the American Film Theater seriously.

1973 N 13, 53:1

THE DON IS DEAD, directed by Richard Fleischer; screenplay by Marvin H. Albert, based on the novel by Mr. Albert; director of photography, Richard H. Kline; edited by Edward A. Biery; music by Jerry Goldsmith; produced by Hal B. Wallis; associate producer, Paul Nathan; released by Universal Pictures. Running time: 115 minutes. This film is classified R. At the Rivoli, 49th Street and Broadway, and other theaters.

Don Angelo	Anthony Quinn
Tony	Frederic Forrest
Frank	Robert Forster
Vince	Al Lettieri
Ruby	Angel Tompkins
Orlando	Charles Cioffi
Marie	Jo Anne Meredith
Don Bruno	J. Duke Russo
Mitch	Louis Zorich
Neila	Ina Balin

There is enough firepower in "The Don Is Dead," which crashed into the Rivoli and other theaters yesterday, to raise the dead. But the struggle for power between Anthony Quinn, other dons and the young gunmen in this Mafia-like gangland, is sound and fury that imitates but rarely flatters the big guns in the genre from the 1930 "Little Caesar" to "The Godfather."

Expertise, if not imagination, is evident in the explosive, action-oriented direction of Richard Fleischer as an aging Anthony Quinn battles the likes of Frederic Forrest, Robert Forster and others for control of the mob and its illicit enterprises. Naturally, these "families" are enmeshed in doublecrosses and misunderstandings that seem confusing only to the principals involved. A fairly attentive viewer can see it all coming before Quinn falls for Forster's girl, the pretty, altruistic chanteuse-songwriter, Angel Tompkins, and unwittingly sets off the fireworks.

Any red-blooded American boy should be delighted by the virtually incessant bullets and gore and a climactic bombing and shootout. But "The Don Is Dead" has the attributes of some lively, pithily accented performances that are adult and effectively natural. Among these are Forrest, as the brainly hood who attempts to escape the racket, but winds up a don; Al Lettieri, as his roughhewn, dependent, ill-fated brother, and Forster, as the rising, vengeful muscleman who is eventually cut down.

As the embattled don who is finally felled by a stroke, not a gun, Quinn is moodily menacing and as polished and relaxed as a professional long familiar with this sort of role. He is off the mark, however, when he observes, quality can be bought, talent can't." There's talent, if not quality, in "The Don Is Dead."

A. H. WEILER

1973 N 15, 58:3

THE FRENCH CONSPIRACY, (L'Attentat), directed by Yves Boisset; screenplay by Ben Barzman and Basilio Franchina; adaptation and dialogue (French With English subtitles) by Jorge Semprun; produced by Yvon Guezel; music, Ennio Morricone; director of photography, Ricardo Aronvich; a Two Worlds Films presentation; released by Cine Globe, Inc. Running time: 125 minutes. At the 68th Street Playhouse, at Third Avenue, and Eastside Cinema, Third Avenue at 55th Street..

Darien	Jean-Louis Trintignant
Kassar	Michel Piccoli
Sadiel	Gian Maria Volonte
Howard	Roy Scheider
Edith	Jean Seberg
Rouannet	Francois Perier
Garcin	Philippe Noiret
Lempereur	Michel Bouquet
Vigneau	Bruno Cremer

By VINCENT CANBY

"The French Conspiracy," which opened yesterday at the 68th Street Playhouse, is fiction based on the known facts surrounding the kidnapping of Mehdi Ben Barka, the Moroccan leftist opposition leader who, on Oct. 29, 1965, was arrested by two policemen on a Paris street corner and disappeared forever.

In the subsequent scandal, Moroccan Government officials and French gangsters were implicated, along with agents of the Service de Documentation Extérieure et de Contre-Espionage, the French counterpart to the Central Intelligence Agency. Reputations were ruined. Confidence was shattered and the S.D.E.C.E., which had been largely independent, was put under the jurisdiction of the French Defense Ministry.

•

The raw material is fascinating, but the only thing the film does is make one more appreciative of the skills of Costa-Gavras, whose slick, entertaining political melodramas, "Z" and "The Confession," if not his most recent film, "State of Siege," were apparently the models for Yves Boisset, the young Frenchman who directed "The French Conspiracy."

Boisset has courage (not even Costa-Gavras has yet gotten around to exposing political scandals in France), but his approach to filmmaking is a fatal mixture of reverence and foolishness. A stronger director, perhaps, could have disciplined his script writers, including Jorge Semprun, the man who wrote "Z" and "The Confession" and who is credited with having done the adaptation and dialogue for "The French Conspiracy."

Boisset and Semprun insist on overwhelming us with carefully detailed exposition at moments when we can't possibly be expected to make sense of it, and then they try to engage our more primitive interests with elaborate (but not very well staged) sequences of escape and pursuit, which are stuck into the movie like specialty numbers in a musical.

•

The actors, though all good people, often look ridiculous. Jean-Louis Trintignant, as the one-time journalist who becomes the political leader's Judas, spends a large part of the film running, which he does as if his shoe laces were untied. Gian Maria Volonte, who plays the exiled leftist from the never-named North African country, is called upon to speak some of the drippiest dialogue heard this year. If I remember correctly, he tells us that he dreams of home, and of "the faces of the workers learning to read at night."

Michel Piccoli, another ordinarily fine performer, plays the nasty Arab minister who has engineered Volonte's kidnapping. In what should be a stirring confrontation between the idealist and the opportunist, Piccoli turns on his enemy and says pettishly: "The people! You've been harping on that word ever since I've known you!"

Philippe Noiret and Michel Bouquet, as the two principal conspirators, tell us every now and then what is going on, but in lunch and dinner scenes that require them to talk a lot of the time with their mouths full.

The film's French title is "L'Attentat," which, I'm informed, has no direct English equivalent. It refers to a plot that leads to a political assassination.

1973 N 15, 58:4

HURRY UP, OR I'LL BE 30, directed and produced by Joseph Jacoby, who also wrote the original story; screenplay by David Wiltse and Mr. Jacoby; photographed by Burleigh Wartes; music by Stephen Lawrence, lyrics by Bruce Hart. Presented by Joseph E. Levine and released by Avco Embassy Pictures. Running time: 88 minutes. At the 34th Street East Theater, near Second Avenue, and the 86th Street Theater, between Second and Third Avenues. (This film is rated "R.")

George Trapani	John Lefkowitz
Jackie	Linda DeCoff
Flo	Maureen Byrnes
Petey	Danny Devito
Mr. Trapani	David Kirk
Mark Lossier	Frank Quinn
Vince Trapani	Ronald Anton
Mrs. Trapani	Selma Rogoff
Ken Harris	George Welbes

It would be hard to find a more likable—plain likable—movie around town than "Hurry Up, or I'll Be 30." You will leave this one amused and touched and with a sense of having shared the lonely life of a Brooklyn youth.

The picture, made on a modest budget, adroitly utilizes the New York scene, the photography of Burliegh Wartes and the music of Stephen Lawrence. The result is a wryly affectionate portrait of a younger "Marty," working his way out of the loneliness of an urban environment.

Everything in the picture works well without strain. The story flows evenly, the dialogue is unforced, the casually succinct characterizations ring true. All of this is a credit to Joseph Jacoby, who is co-writer, director and producer of the film, and, by the way, 31 years old.

The casting is virtually faultless, starting with John Lefkowitz as the wistful hero, a Brooklyn printer squirming under a paternal yoke and living a meaningless existence. My only quibble is the role of the heroine, an aspiring actress beautifully played by Linda DeCoff. Granted the opportunism of the theater, would a girl of such obvious character and feeling have led on an impressionable bumbler?

The supporting players are excellent, among them Maureen Byrnes, Danny Devito, David Kirk, Frank Quinn and Ronald Anton. David Wiltse was Mr. Jacoby's co-author.
HOWARD THOMPSON

1973 N 15, 58:5

SCALAWAG, directed by Kirk Douglas; story and screenplay by Albrt Maltz and Ben Barzman, based on a story by Robert Louis Stevenson; produced by Anne Douglas; director of photography, Jack Cardiff; music, John Cameron; editor, John Howard. An Inex-Oceania production, distributed by Paramount Pictures. Running time: 93 minutes. At the Forum Theater, Broadway at 47th Street, and other theaters. This film has been classified G.
Peg .... Kirk Douglas
Jamie .... Mark Lester
Brimstone/Mudhook .... Neville Brand
Don Aragon .... George Eastman
Velvet .... Don Stroud
Lucy-Ann .... Lesley Anne Down

"Scalawag" is of some historical interest on two counts: It is the first film to be directed by Kirk Douglas (who shows no great flair for the job), and it is a very loose adaptation of Robert Louis Stevenson's "Treasure Island," although it is set in Mexico and California and never puts to sea. I assume the property is in the public domain.

Douglas stars himself as the Long John Silver character, a one-legged, landlocked pirate here named Peg, who not only has a heart of gold but also a couple of chests full of doubloons, which have been stolen by a renegade associate. Mark Lester ("Oliver!") plays the Jim Hawkins character.

Douglas tries unsuccessfully to give the tale a nice, old-fashioned heartiness. He rides a horse that always rears up on its hind legs before charging off somewhere. There's a wisecracking parrot, and the pirates spend a great deal of time, when not doublecrossing one another, going ho-ho-ho, like the supers in "Naughty Marietta." The violence is constant but bloodless. The film, which was photographed in Yugoslavia, opened yesterday at the Forum Theater on Broadway and other houses.
VINCENT CANBY

1973 N 15, 58:7

SOME CALL IT LOVING, written and produced by James B. Harris; screenplay by Mr. Harris based on "Sleeping Beauty" by John Collier; photography, Mario Tosi; edited by Paul Jasiukonis; music composed and conducted by Richard Hazard. A Two Worlds Films presentation, released by Cine Globe, Inc. At the 59th St. Twin Theater, East of Third Avenue. Running time: 103 min. This film is classified R.
Robert Troy .... Zalman King
Scarlett .... Carol White
Jennifer .... Tisa Farrow
Jeff .... Richard Pryor
Angelica .... Veronica Anderson
Carnival Doctor .... Logan Ramsey
Cheerleader .... Brandy Herred

"I feel a need to be fulfilled," says one of the principals in "Some Call It Loving," which opened yesterday at the 59th Street Twin Theater. James B. Harris, the film's producer-director-writer, may have been fulfilled, but it is awfully difficult for even a willing viewer to appreciate the sadly diffuse fantasies of an erstwhile sideshow sleeping beauty, a rich, weird temptress and the bemused young man they both seem to adore.

Since this odd affair was inspired by John Collier's short story "Sleeping Beauty," it should be noted that the setting has been changed from Britain to a baronial mansion on the West Coast owned by Carol White, who not only goes for Zalman King, a jazz saxophonist, but also for Tisa Farrow, the resuscitated "beauty" he brings to that strange household. Miss White, by the way, also digs Veronica Anderson, the blonde maid, and loves to dress up as a nun.

Mr. King, who sports a wild mane of hair and a woebegone expression, cannot be faulted for appearing confused most of the time. Miss White, who is slightly imperious and sexy as the seductress, spouts such dialogue as "When a woman loves a man, there's no limit to her understanding." Tisa Farrow (Mia Farrow's younger sister) is pretty, but essentially juvenile, as the innocent, awakened beauty.

Mr. Harris, who produced Stanley Kubrick's "Paths of Glory," "Lolita" and "The Killing" and produced and directed "The Bedford Incident," has provided "Some Call It Loving" with sumptuous, rococo décor. But he has fashioned a rambling, contemporary fable that is merely pretentious.
A. H. WEILER

1973 N 17, 26:1

The Program

TO LIVE WITH HERDS and AVES, MAGNIFICENT FRIGATE BIRD, GREAT FLAMINGO, documentaries by David MacDougall and Nancy Graves, at the Film Forum, 256 West 88th Street. Total running time: 91 minutes. Screenings at 8, Friday through Sunday evenings.

The Film Forum, that small but enterprising showcase for experimental movies on West 88th Street, rings the bell solidly with its new double-documentary bill.

David MacDougall's "To Live With Herds" (68 minutes) is one of those rare documentaries that seem to have a life of their own. It records the life cycle of the Jie tribe of northeastern Uganda. Calmly and simply, with an occasional footnote from the director, the camera studies these people in some marvelously revealing interviews.

Mr. MacDougall's camera is quietly there, observing all, missing nothing in this moving, penetrating anthropological picture. No wonder it was cited at last year's Venice Film Festival.

●

With her color camera seeming to float high in space, Nancy Graves has evoked a kind of detachedly trenchant ballet of birds in flight in "Aves, Magnificent Frigate Bird, Great Flamingo." The natural sounds, the sense of suspension, the mass of winged creatures dotting the sky all merge in gradual, striking crescendo and impact. If the birds seem to know exactly what they're doing, so does Miss Graves.

The program will be repeated next weekend.
HOWARD THOMPSON

1973 N 17, 26:1

The Cast

THE MERCHANT OF FOUR SEASONS. Directed by Rainer Werner Fassbinder; executive producer, Ingrid Fassbinder; screenplay by Mr. Fassbinder; produced by Tango Films. At the Greenwich Theater, 97 Greenwich Avenue.
Irmgard .... Irm Hermann
Erna .... Hanna Schygulla
Hans .... Hans Hirschmuller

By NORA SAYRE

It gets harder and harder to believe in victims—in people who do not precipitate what happens to them. But Rainer Fassbinder's "The Merchant of Four Seasons," which opened this week at the Greenwich Theater, projects a kind of loserism that the main character seems powerless to control.

This German movie focuses on a stolid depressive (Hans Hirschmuller) whose middle-class family has always been ashamed of him, and its lack of enthusiasm appears to be the main cause of his breakdown and eventual suicide. They are also disgusted by his career of selling fruit in the streets, rather as though he were pimping.

●

Because of turgid directing and acting, most of the emotions in this picture ring false. When the hero's wife phones her lawyer for a divorce, her husband has the unlikeliest heart attack in movie history. And when he finally drinks himself to death in front of his relatives, they watch and gape like paralyzed puddings until his scene is played out—or like obedient actors who know that they must not interrupt the star.

Fassbinder's fiercest weakness is the way that his characters respond to one another. He also specializes in delayed reactions. Throughout, eyes lock in significant glances or in prolonged stunned stares. A man slaps a woman; she gasps and grabs her cheek, then both of them freeze. A wife learns that her husband is getting drunk in a bar, and she clutches the telephone receiver to her chest to show distress. Two long separated friends meet in a cafeteria:

One drops a tray of food (astonishment). And there is a maddening moment when the fruit vendor yells down the stairs for his wife, and then weeps—which is simply a crude crib from Brando in "Streetcar."

●

"The Merchant," which was shown at the New York Film Festival at Lincoln Center in 1972, is not so bad as Fassbinder's "The Bitter Fears of Petra Von Kant," one of the silliest movies I have seen in years. But here it looks as though the director was torn between chronicling a crack-up and making a film about how to run a small business. The problems of hiring a reliable staff and the proprieties of bookkeeping take up a good deal of footage, and that is boring. But this soggy picture allows the disintegration of a human being to be almost as dull as the way he earns his living—and that is appalling.

1973 N 17, 26:1

Swede's Shattering Film About Us

By STEPHEN FARBER

JAN TROELL'S "The Emigrants" was a fine film with some nagging flaws: the characters seemed too simple for the epic scope of the drama, and the movie as a whole did not supply the emotional impact that it promised. It was an extraordinarily impressive piece of filmmaking, but not entirely satisfying.

After seeing "The New Land," one realizes why. "The Emigrants" was only half a movie. "The Emigrants" and "The New Land" were filmed at the same time, and were meant to be seen together; "The New Land" is not an ordinary sequel, but the necessary conclusion to the story of the Swedish emigrants who arrived in Minnesota in 1850. Although Troell's prosaic characters still do not touch the imagination, the depth of his understanding of America accounts for this movie's power. Even in its slightly truncated American version, "The New Land" is a shattering film.

★

"The Emigrants" captured the arduousness but also the dramatic excitement of the journey from Sweden to America. Without sentimentalizing the odyssey, Troell swept us up in the adventure, and at the end, when Karl Oskar staked out his new homestead and sat down to rest by a beautiful Minnesota lake, we could share his exhilaration.

Some critics, however, attacked the film for that serene conclusion, and for what they interpreted as a sentimental affirmation of American myths. They could not have known where the second part would lead. The guarded optimism of "The Emigrants" is quickly displaced by the almost unrelieved bleakness of "The New Land." As the emigrants are transformed into Americans, the promised land proves to be built on broken promises.

Troell celebrates the fertility of the Minnesota soil, and he observes the emigrants' growing prosperity; but he also draws subtle parallels between their life in America and the barren life they left behind in Sweden, to suggest the futility of their search for paradise. Many of the emigrants fled Sweden to escape religious persecution, but "The New Land" makes it clear that they have brought their own prejudices with them to America; Karl Oskar and Kristina's neighbors urge them to break off relations with their friend Ulrika (the reformed prostitute from "The Emigrants") because she has married a Baptist.

One of the most resonant scenes in "The New Land" is the death of Robert, Karl Oskar's younger brother who went to hunt for gold in California and returned empty-handed and mortally ill; stripped of all illusions, he travels through a forest of golden autumn leaves and finally lies down to die by a tranquil stream deep in the woods. The scene makes us think back to our first glimpse of Robert in "The Emigrants" — sending his shoe down a stream in anticipation of his own escape from poverty.

Water has been used throughout both films to suggest freedom, most obviously during the long ocean voyage; and in "The New Land," Robert's journey to California begins on a steamboat down the Mississippi. But water represents death as well as freedom. Robert's friend Arvid dies after drinking poisoned water; and a stream similar to the one which first stirred Robert's

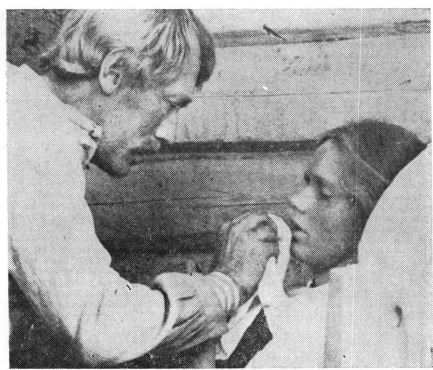

Max von Sydow nurses his wife, Liv Ullmann, in "The New Land," now at the Little Carnegie. Jan Troell's film concludes the story begun in last year's "The Emigrants."

imagination becomes his grave. He has traveled full circle, back to the point where he began. It is as if he had never left Sweden; everything has slipped through his fingers.

*

"The New Land" ends as a bitter repudiation of the legendary frontier sagas. Karl Oskar has done what he set out to do—he has secured a better future for his children; but after Kristina's early death, he grows embittered and, as an old man, he becomes hypnotized by the past, poring over a map of Sweden to recall the place where he was born. He is haunted by an inexplicable sense of loss. The emigrants have abandoned their homeland for a fraudulent pipe dream—as insubstantial as the wildcat money Robert brings back from California.

Some critics of "The Emigrants" complained that the soaring conclusion ignored the fact that the settlers' rich land was actually stolen from the Indians. "The New Land" confronts that fact, and its portrait of the Indians is one of the most interesting ever caught on film. The first image of hungry Indian women cautiously approaching Kristina is unforgettable; Troell understands that the Indians and the settlers are equally frightened of each other. The Indian faces, in this scene and in others, are exactly

Stephen Farber is a critic and the author of "The Movie Rating Game."

right — gaunt, weathered, suspicious, proud, homely, strange and individual faces.

A climactic sequence is boldly conceived: A group of starving Sioux attack a farm, and brutally kill a Swedish family for their food. (The most shocking image—of the wife's dead fetus nailed to their cabin wall—has unfortunately been eliminated from the American version, probably to satisfy the Rating Board's fastidious rules of "good taste.") The murders are disturbing, but shortly afterward, when Troell films the execution of 38 Sioux braves on a winter morning, he composes the scene as a poetic elegy for a ravaged culture. Troell can honor the nobility of the Indians without softening their desperate, barbaric acts; he is not interested in scoring easy points.

Taken together, "The Emigrants" and "The New Land" cover only about 20 years—from the early 1840's to 1862, with a brief epilogue going up to Karl Oskar's death in 1890. Yet the two films recount the primal American experience; the emigrants' flight from oppression, the triumph over the elements, and the growing disillusionment with their new Eden. I doubt that any American director could have brought the same distance and objectivity to a film about immigration. Troell's vision is finally deeply pessimistic, but we trust his conclusions because he is so completely open to the American experience. He

has no ax to grind, no fashionable thesis about American corruption to shove down our throats. The complexity in Troell's vision of America makes up for the complexity that we miss in the central characters.

And in dealing with the characters, Troell displays a sympathy and perception that free them from stereotype. He pays attention to the unexpected twists in the relationships — for example, the rivalry between the two brothers; Karl Oskar's angry belittling of Robert springs from his envy of Robert's more adventurous spirit. Troell gets marvelously telling moments from the actors: Liv Ullmann's embarrassed shrug as she stumbles over the word "flowers" while talking to an American shopkeeper; or the conflicting emotions on Max von Sydow's face when Kristina tells him that she wants to sleep with him again, despite the risks of another pregnancy. One might wish that Troell had selected more mysterious characters for his protagonists, but he never condescends to Karl Oskar or Kristina; he respects the intensity of their feelings.

The most remarkable thing about "The New Land" is the imagery. Troell, who directed, photographed, edited, and co-authored the screenplay, has a rare understanding of the sensuous possibilities of film. The images of nature linger in the memory: trees dripping maple syrup, golden fields of corn, a duck gliding through the

water at the beginning of spring, a crown of oak trees over a green hillside cemetery.

Although Troell's lyricism dazzles, the most indelible images in "The New Land" are those that crystallize the harshness of frontier life: Karl Oskar killing an ox and wrapping his son inside to warm him during a blizzard, a fatally wounded farmer trying to stop the bleeding in his neck with chicken feathers, the corpses of the executed Indians rocked by the winter wind.

Perhaps the most highly charged image is the very last one—a still photograph of Karl Oskar and his children and grandchildren taken shortly before his death. A letter to Karl Oskar's surviving sister in Sweden reports that his children no longer speak Swedish. They have settled in, and

have become Americans, as Karl Oskar wanted; they have forgotten their heritage. The photograph is the only reminder of their parents' epic struggle, the last link with the past; everything is compressed into that one frozen image.

Like Karl Oskar's children, we have lost touch with our origins, and we want to understand the bravery and determination that drove our grandparents to America. In this period of disillusionment, immigration is one chapter of American history that still has the capacity to inspire our wonder. It is a great subject, and in these two films Jan Troell has done justice to the subject. "The New Land" is a Swedish movie, but it is one of the few authentic American tragedies.

1973 N 18, 15:5

For 'The Long Good-bye,' A Warm Hello

By VINCENT CANBY

IF "The Long Goodbye," Robert Altman's updated film version of Raymond Chandler's 1953 novel, turns out to be a national box-office success following its hit engagement at the Trans-Lux East Theater here, those of us who are the film's partisans should be glad for Altman, its director, Leigh Brackett, who wrote the screenplay, and for Elliott Gould, its star who hasn't had a hit in some time.

Yet that success may well give New York City's film critics more clout than we necessarily deserve with producers and distributors. Like everyone else, we deal, much of the time anyway, in organized prejudices. It may also give movie ad men a distorted impression of their place in the creative process that occasionally results in a popular motion picture. I'm not saying this is true. I'm speculating.

"The Long Goodbye" takes a lot of liberties with the Chandler novel and especially with Philip Marlowe, Chandler's seedy private eye played earlier on the screen in various shades of thin-lipped tough-guy by Humphrey Bogart ("The Big Sleep"), Dick Powell ("Murder, My Sweet") and Robert Montgomery ("Lady in The Lake").

*

It's a thoroughly entertaining movie, very funny in spots but it's not as satire that the movie works, even

though it opens and closes with a nicely tinny arrangement of "Hooray for Hollywood," the sort of opening and closing credit music with which Andy Warhol and Paul Morrissey like to frame their improvisations.

More disturbing about the film is that at a story point when conventional private eye movies should be setting everything straight, in exposition that may not be comprehensible to anyone who isn't following the film with a score, "The Long Goodbye" erupts with violence and ends in a mood of moral confusion that sends you out of the theater wondering not what happened but why it did.

Actually, this is one of the most fascinating aspects of the film. Bogart and Powell would never have been allowed to do the sort of thing this Philip Marlowe does. And then you remember: Altman has had the nerve not only to update the Chandler novel, which, though published in the 1950's, has its true roots in the thirties and forties, but also to cast Elliott Gould as Philip Marlowe. It sounds as crazy as Barbra Streisand's playing Scarlett O'Hara.

I've no doubt that "The Long Goodbye" would still be a good film even if Gould were not in it, but Gould's idiosyncracies, his public personality as well as his talent, help give shape to this film as much as they made Bergman's "The Touch" seem even more ambiguous than need be.

Gould's Philip Marlowe is a child of the sixties and seventies. His toughness, which is questionable, is not born of attempts to survive the Depression, but of an attempt to control feelings, which well could have been ravaged by growing up alternately committed and disappointed by the events of the last 10 years. He's bright, hip, sardonic and, as someone says of him in the film, a born loser.

Women don't fall all over him. They tend to take advantage, not because they're rapacious but because he still wants to believe there's a bit of virtue left somewhere. Gould's Philip Marlowe is perpetually affable.

He lives in an eccentric, run-down eyrie, a curious multi-dwelling-unit habitat, a complex of outside walks and staircases on the side of a hill overlooking Los Angeles, in an apartment across a sort of footbridge from the apartment of a group of pretty, often nude sun-worshippers and pill-poppers. The girls do not hesitate to use him to buy their brownie mix at the supermarket at 3 A.M. His only companion is a large yellow cat, spoiled and perfidious, who abandons him halfway through the film without so much as a backward glance.

At this point you might suggest, correctly, that **this hardly sounds like Chandler's Philip Marlowe, at least the Philip Marlowe we have known on the screen, including the one played for laughs by James Garner in "Marlowe," an adaptation of Chandler's "The Little Sister."**

"The Long Goodbye" takes so many liberties that when it opened last spring in Los Angeles, Philadelphia and Chicago, the critics were generally appalled and the public, for reasons no one is certain of, stayed away by the theaterful.

United Artists, the distributors, withdrew the film from release and searched their souls as well as the advertising campaign (designed to sell the film as a straight Philip Marlowe private eye melodrama), Gould's reputation (has he been seen in too many flops?), and the running time (was it too long?).

When the panic subsided, it was decided not to cut the film but to release it in New York with a new ad campaign, designed by Mad Magazine artist Jack Davis, made up of cartoon figures that are supposed to stress the film's high hilarity. The film opened here several weeks ago to excellent notices and excellent business, but why?

Was it the new ad campaign? I hope not, for it is misleading in that it makes the movie seem almost a parody. The good reviews have obviously helped, but are New York critics any wiser than those elsewhere in the country? I'm not sure we are. Perhaps being aware of the sad reception given the film outside New York we wanted to like it, to be surprised at how good it really is. Did we over-react?

*

A second viewing of the film last week convinced me that we did not, and that, in fact, "The Long Goodbye" may be an even better movie than I first thought it was.

The story that Miss Brackett and Altman have freely rearranged from the novel has a few plot points that don't make a great deal of sense when you think about them later, but they are not fatal implausibilities. Much more interesting are the moral questions the film touches on without ever talking about. The entire movie rests upon Marlowe's feeling of responsibility toward a friend, a charming petty hood (Jim Bouton) who is accused of wife-murder and whom Gould persists in thinking the best of even though he's a courier for a local crime boss.

Gould's Marlowe is a born loser but he is the only decent, functioning individual in a world otherwise inhabited exclusively by sadists, double-crossers and failures, including a phony Hemingway sort of novelist (Sterling Hayden), the novelist's slightly beat-up but beautiful wife (Nina van Pallandt), a quack doctor (Henry Gibson), and a manic gangster (Mark Rydell) who, in the film's roughest scene, smashes a Coke bottle in the face of his mistress. "If I can do that to someone I love," he says to make his point to Marlowe, "think what I can do to someone I hate."

Altman's achievement has been to make a tough, funny, hugely entertaining movie that acknowledges its Chandler origins without ever turning into an anachronism, a forties movie made in the seventies. It's an original work, complex without being obscure, visually breathtaking without seeming to be inappropriately fancy. Vilmos Zsigmond, who was also Altman's cameraman on "McCabe and Mrs. Miller," does a lot of complicated things with reflections in glass, shots into the sun, or shots made with very little light at all, but they are very much part of the Southern California atmosphere of the film. They are the movie equivalents of the architecture of so many Los Angeles shopping centers, apartment houses, supper clubs and pubs. Often gaudy and vulgar and, sometimes, spectacularly beautiful. Sometimes the results are tactile. When Marlowe goes into his favorite neighborhood bar to pick up his telephone messages, you know immediately, without any special bit of business or line of dialogue, that the place is probably overly air-conditioned by as much as 10 degrees.

1973 N 18, II:1:1

BREEZY, directed by Clint Eastwood; written by Jo Heims; produced by Robert Daley and presented by Universal Pictures. At the Columbia II Theater, Second Avenue at 64th Street. Running time: 108 minutes. (This film is rated "R")

Frank Harmon	William Holden
Breezy	Kay Lenz
Bob Henderson	Roger C. Carmel
Betty	Marj Dusay
Nancy Henderson	Shelley Morrison
Paula	Joan Hotchkis

A cloyingly naive resolution mars "Breezy," which opened yesterday, an otherwise engrossing drama of an aging man's infatuation with a tender-hearted 17-year-old girl derelict.

Generally, the fine work of William Holden, who is perfectly cast as the dour, lonely hero, and the low-keyed direction by Clint Eastwood, good dialogue by Jo Heims and trim sideline performances by Marj Dusay, Roger C. Carmel and Shelly Morrison sustain the narrative flow and mood in this film.

Young Kay Lenz plays the girl appealingly. But it's hard to believe that a rather seasoned vagrant could exude such spiritual purity.

HOWARD THOMPSON

1973 N 19, 53:2

The Cast

ENGLAND MADE ME, directed by Peter Duffell; screenplay by Desmond Cory and Mr. Duffell, based on the novel by Graham Greene; produced by Jack Levin; director of photography, Ray Parslow; music, John Scott; editor, Malcolm Cooke; a Two World Film presentation, released by Cine Globe. Running time: 100 minutes. At the Paris Theater, 58th Street, west of Fifth Avenue. This film has been classified PG.

Erik Krogh	Peter Finch
Anthony Farrant	Michael York
Kate Farrant	Hildegard Neil
F. Minty	Michael Hordern
Haller	Joss Ackland
Liz Davidge	Tessa Wyatt

By VINCENT CANBY

"England Made Me," a screen adaptation of Graham Greene's ironic novel written in 1935, proves that a little hindsight can often be too much. In this case it's fatal.

Peter Duffell, the director of the film, which opened yesterday at the Paris, and co-author of the screenplay with Desmond Cory, has had the presumption to straighten out Graham Greene by transferring the story's locale from Sweden in the mid-nineteen-thirties to Nazi Germany, which is fast becoming a rather sick movie joke.

If, as some recent films would have us believe, the Nazis spent so much time at orgies, slurping up the old bubbly and snapping bra straps, it's a miracle they could ever stagger into the Rhineland, much less manage a coherent blitzkrieg.

•

The shift in place has had the effect of transforming Greene's novel, based loosely on the last days of Ivar Kreuger, Sweden's swindling match king, from a post-Depression story of ambition and fatigue into one of those heavily ominous, pre-holocaust dramas that see every event as an indication of Things To Come. It also allows for orgies, parades of storm troopers and other picturesque if irrelevant details.

Even though this is not Greene, "England Made Me" might have worked, were Mr. Duffell and Mr. Cory less superficial movie makers. They've retained a surprising amount of the Greene plot, even a lot of original dialogue, but the story is no longer comic and rueful, just wildly melodramatic. The prototypical Greene characters are evident, but they look out of place. The scenery is wrong. It throws everything out of focus.

•

This is most apparent in the performances of Peter Finch and Michael York. Mr. Finch plays the Kreuger character, now portrayed as a swindling German financier who has no love for the Nazis, but who doesn't hesitate to use Nazi strong-arm tactics. Mr. York is Tony Farrant, the twin brother of the financier's English mistress, Kate (Hildegard Neil), a supposedly charming scapegrace and liar whose English backbone finally stiffens when he is confronted with Mr. Finch's extraordinary amorality.

Unless you have read the novel, I doubt whether you'll have any idea of the relationships among the characters. Mr. Finch looks tired and glum, and Mr. York incapable of having the shabby past that is attributed to him. When he tells his sister "I'm not a sponge," you believe him, which is wrong. Similarly, I never did believe the passion that Miss Neil is meant to have for her brother. They all seem to be play-acting.

The only spot of pure Greene in the entire film is Michael Hordern as Minty, the scroungy, old-school Englishman who makes a living as a newspaperman in self-imposed exile. Poor old Minty, who once had a canary that sang too much and died, is a recurring theme in Greene's novels. When Minty is on screen, "England Made Me" suggests many levels of consciousness—of decisions made too late, of scruples wasted, of empire's end—that are nowhere else evident.

It's not that Mr. Duffell is an unread director. At one moment he lets the camera linger on a beaten-up copy of "The Waste Land" on the floor by Minty's unmade bed. He's just a very clumsy one.

1973 N 19, 53:1

BATTLE OF THE AMAZONS, directed by Al Bradley; screenplay, Mario Amendola and Bruno Corbucci; written by Fernando Izcaino Casas; director of photography, Fausto Rossi; music, Franco Micalizzi; produced by Riccardo Billi; released by American International Pictures. At the Penthouse Theater, Broadway and 47th Street and 86th Street Twin I Theater, west of Lexington Avenue. Running time 92 minutes. This film is classified R.

Zeno	Lincoln Tate
Eraglia	Lucretia Love
Ilio	Robert Vidmark
Sinade	Solvy Stubing
Valeria	Paola Tedesco
Melanippe	Mirta Miller
Erno	Benito Stefanelli

The Amazons lose the final "Battle of the Amazons" to meek villagers in the gory, Spanish-Italian-English dubbed fiction that landed with a dull thud yesterday at the Penthouse and 86th Street Twin I Theaters. For the record, also, the villagers, such as the pretty Lucretia Love and the tough outlaws led by Lincoln Tate, who help them to victory, are as nobly endowed as the queen-sized Amazons. But there is little else of stature in this action-accented, mythological mish-mash. On second thought, everyone, including a patient viewer, loses.

A. H. WEILER

1973 N 22, 51:2

The Cast

SAMBIZANGA, directed by Sarah Maldoror; screenplay (Portuguese with English subtitles) by Mario de Andrade, Maurice Pons and Sarah Maldoror, from the novel "La Vraie Vie de Domingos Xavier" by Luandino Vieira; photographed by Claude Agostini; released by New Yorker Films. At the New Yorker Theater, Broadway and 88th Street. Running time: 102 minutes. This film has not been classified.

Domingos	Domingos Oliviera
Maria	Elisa Andrade
Zito	Dino Abeiino
Petelo	Jean M'Vondo
Chico	Benoit Moutsila
Miguel	Talgongo
Bebiana	Henriette Meya

By NORA SAYRE

We've had all too little word of Angola since two black groups at Harvard and Radcliffe occupied a building in April of 1972, demanding that the university sell its shares of Gulf stock—in light of Gulf's relationship with the Portuguese colonial regime in Angola. Harvard kept its stock. And the issue of independence for black Angolans hasn't gained much attention in this country.

But now a very fine film, set in 1961, brings us a slab

of the recent Angolan past—and forces us to wonder if the present is any different. "Sambizanga," which opened Wednesday at the Fifth Avenue Cinema, was directed by Sarah Maldoror, who was the assistant to Gillo Pontecorvo for "The Battle of Algiers." One of her collaborators on the screenplay was her husband, Mario de Andrade, a leader in the Angolan resistance. Since the movie couldn't be made in Angola, it was filmed in the Congo.

"Sambizanga" focuses on a young black couple (splendidly played by Domingus Oliviera and Elisa Andrade), who bask in each other's presence until the husband, a tractor driver, is suddenly arrested as a political prisoner.

His wife, who knows nothing about his politics, walks with their baby on her back from village to village, between fields of tall grasses and huge hills, trying to locate him. Angry or desperate at moments, stoical at others, she struggles through a world that rarely explains anything to women. While she's sent from one police station to another, often repulsed or lied to, he's beaten by inquisitors who torture him in hopes of learning the names of others in the movement. He remains mute, but we almost wish that he would talk. And even his death is a relief.

The power of this picture lies in contrasts. The fact that the inquisitors are murderers as well as racists is highlighted by the calm continuity of the resistance—which includes whites as well as blacks. Despite the daily suffering, there's also a stress on friendship and affection, the ease of intimacy and some fond teasing among people who are close, plus the gaiety of dancing and music and feasting. Therefore, when we see prisoners walking slowly in a small circle inside the prison yard, we're all the more aware of the simple freedoms of those on the outside—who are at least able to stroll down a street or through a doorway.

When the prisoners delicately cleanse the bloodied face of the husband's corpse, singing to him rather as though they were trying to comfort the dead, we remember him laughing and joking with his wife. It's that range of possibilities—good or atrocious, life enhancing or death dealing—that makes "Sambizanga" a revolutionary picture. Both subtly and simply, we're shown how bad things are, how much better they could be. As Americans, we may feel helpless while we watch this film. Yet the determination for change is deeply contagious.

The movie doesn't put forth heroes or villains, and it offers a class analysis rather than a racial one. The emphasis is on the oppression of the poor by the rich—on the system that perpetuates a minority. Throughout, the plight of individuals helps to nail the political point. Meanwhile, let's hope that this impressive new director makes many sequels to her first feature film.

1973 N 22, 50:2

The Cast

ASH WEDNESDAY, directed by Larry Peerce; screenplay by Jean-Claude Tramont; produced by Dominick Duune; music, Maurice Jarre; director of photography, Ennio Guarnieri; editor, Marion Rothman; a Saggitarius production, distributed by Paramount Pictures. Running time: 99 minutes. At the Loews State 2 Theater, Broadway at 45th Street, and Loews Cine Theater, Third Avenue at 86th Street. This film has been classified R.

Barbara .... Elizabeth Taylor
Mark .... Henry Fonda
Erich .... Helmut Berger
David .... Keith Baxter
Doctor Lambert .... Maurice Teynac
Kate .... Margaret Blye

By VINCENT CANBY

Can Barbara Sawyer (Elizabeth Taylor), a woman in her fifties, rekindle the flame that once burned within the breast of her husband Mark (Henry Fonda) by getting, what is, in effect, a head-to-foot face lift?

Will Mark, after 30 years of marriage to Barbara, be put off by those funny little scars behind the ears, under the bosom and very high on the backs of the thighs? Should Barbara, after emerging from that fancy Swiss clinic looking a fabulous 41, have an affair with a much younger man whose stare contains a sexual message?

What should she say when Mark looks at her, his eyes filled with memories but empty of desire? Should she lie in the sun? Eat pastries? Hit Mark on the head with a shoe?

Every question save the last is proposed in "Ash Wednesday," and then answered at somewhat greater length than is absolutely necessary for anyone over the age of 2. The movie opened yesterday at Loews State 2 and Loews Cine Theaters.

"Ash Wednesday" was directed by Larry Peerce ("A Separate Peace," "Goodbye, Columbus," etc.) and written by Jean-Claude Tramont with all the fearlessness and perception demanded in the boiling of an egg.

It would have us believe that such pursuits of youth are doomed to failure, yet it treats the reconstructed Barbara (who is, after all, Elizabeth Taylor, one of the world's great beauties) less as a woman to be understood than as an artifact to be admired.

Barbara is miserable, of course, but miserable in some of the most magnificent settings (Cortina, the Dolomites) that money can buy.

●

"Ash Wednesday" has some shock effect in its early surgical scenes, showing us how the subcutaneous tissue is removed (what we really see is chicken fat) to firm up the skin under Barbara's eyes and other organs. Mostly the film is interested in what Barbara is going to wear next. This is not a male chauvinist's conception of a woman, but her hairdresser's, full of envy, awe and superficial compassion.

1973 N 22, 50:2

The Cast

WESTWORLD, directed and written by Michael Crichton; produced by Paul N. Lazarus 3d; music, Fred Karlin; director of photography, Gene Polito; editor, David Bretherton; distributed by Metro-Goldwyn-Mayer. Running time: 91 minutes. At the National Theater, Broadway at 44th Street, and other theaters. This film has been classified R.

Gunslinger .... Yul Brynner
Peter Martin .... Richard Benjamin
John Blane .... James Brolin
Medieval Knight ...... Norman Bartold
Chief Supervisor .... Alan Oppenheimer
Medieval Queen .... Victoria Shaw

Michael Crichton, the young medical doctor and author of more than a dozen popular novels, including "The Andromeda Strain," makes a creditable debut as a film director with "Westworld," a science-fiction melodrama about Doomsday in Disneyland. The film opened yesterday at the National and other theaters.

The setting is not really Disneyland but a complex of three resorts — Westworld, Romanworld and Medievalworld — that carry some of the Disneyland-Disney World concepts as far as they can go.

Guests at Westworld, for example, like the two Chicago businessmen played by Richard Benjamin and James Brolin, pay $1,000 a day each to realize their fantasies about living in the Old West.

In a perfect reproduction of a frontier town, they can spend two weeks having the times of their lives in barroom fights, robbing the bank, shooting the sheriff and sleeping with the local dancehall girls, who are, like all the other citizens of the town, life-sized, computerized robots.

Crichton the director seems to have had more fun with the film than Crichton the writer, whose screenplay can offer us no better explanation for the sudden, bloody robot rebellion than an epidemic of "central mechanism psychosis." This basic facetiousness is partly obscured by the vivid and sometimes amusing dimension of the film's anecdotes, which are mostly about the peril of the guests when make-believe gives way to reality.

In addition to Benjamin and Brolin, the cast includes Yul Brynner as the town sheriff, who has no more humanity or sense of justice than a multicycle washing machine.

VINCENT CANBY.

1973 N 22, 51:1

SHOWDOWN, directed and produced by George Seaton; screenplay, Theodore Taylor, story by Hank Fine; director of photography, Ernesto Laszlo; film editor, John W. Holmes; music, David Shire; released by Universal Pictures. At the Forum Theater, Broadway at 46th Street. Running time: 99 minutes. This film is classified PG.

Chuck .... Rock Hudson
Billy .... Dean Martin
Kate .... Susan Clark
Art Williams .... Donald Moffat
P. J. Wilson .... John McLiam
Martinez .... Charles Baca
Clem .... Jackson Kane

The Old West is merely an obvious Old West in "Showdown," which clattered into the Forum Theater yesterday raising a cloud of cliches. As a tale that attempts to focus on realistic, human qualities during an unwanted clash between two lifelong friends, this turn-of-the-century chase through picturesque Southwestern locales simply stresses phlegmatic performances in a plot as familiar as the Jesse James saga or the usual movie train holdup.

In this case, Dean Martin is largely lackadaisical as the errant cowhand who has been drawn into robbing a train and is hunted by an equally lethargic Rock Hudson, as the sheriff, his pal since boyhood and the husband of Susan Clark, the down-to-earth lady they both love.

●

Of course, there is a passel of bad guys such as Donald Moffat, the train robber who is also chasing Martin because he's turned himself and the loot over to Hudson, and John McLiam, the sneaky attorney who forces Martin to break out of jail and start all the shooting and galloping going again.

George Seaton, the producer-director, who is as professional as they come, has derived some action but little distinction from a script that is a good deal less than brilliant. One appreciates the many flashbacks used to delineate the principals' friendship from boyhood to manhood and their affection for the understanding Miss Clark. But they are, in effect, basically contrived, unexciting types.

A vintage clothes-washing machine, phonograph and train, as well as New Mexico's forests and mountains, give this Western authenticity and color. Unfortunately, the people and problems in "Showdown" are a letdown.

A. H. WEILER

1973 N 22, 51:1

The Program

DRY WOOD AND HOT PEPPER, a film in two parts directed, photographed and edited by Les Blank; sound and assistant editor, Maureen Gosling; produced and distributed by Flower Films. Running time: 91 minutes. At the Whitney Museum of American Art, Madison Avenue at 74th Street.

By VINCENT CANBY

Les Blank's "Dry Wood and Hot Pepper," which opened yesterday at the Whitney Museum of American Art, is a gentle, two-part documentary about the life and music of the French-speaking blacks in southwestern Louisiana's Cajun country.

The two parts, "Dry Wood," 37 minutes, and "Hot Pepper," 54 minutes, flow one into the other so easily that the only lines of demarcation between them are the closing credits of the first and the opening credits of the second.

Although the film was made within the last several years, it has the air of someone's remembering events of long ago. This is particularly true of "Dry Wood," and is due in part to the seemingly stable quality of lives being explored, as well as to Mr. Blank's manner, which is to pay almost as much attention to the landscapes, seasons and weather as to people.

This isn't necessarily the most interesting kind of film making. It has the effect of softening the focus so that we can barely define the sharp, rough edges of the lives he shows us. He prefers to record the happy times, the preparations for a rural Mardi Gras, the daily routines of farm life that are a continuing life cycle.

At one point a farm woman, who has borne 16 children and reared 14, recalls the good old days when people sat around and talked. Now, she says, the men drink and the children leave, one by one. She is, however, surrounded by members of her family, all at work preparing what looks to be a holiday feast.

Clifton Chenier, something of a local celebrity who plays an electric accordion and has a small band, is the star of "Hot Pepper," which devotes as much time to Chenier's music (a mixture of blues and Cajun) as it does to him and his friends. The music is full of soul and so exuberantly ironic that it cannot be especially sad, no matter what the lyrics say.

●

A bit of barroom dialogue in this sequence is worth preserving. Says one customer, solemnly: "People is people." To which his friend gravely assents: "Everywhere you go," prompting them both to laugh.

The people in "Hot Pepper" take themselves less pompously than the film maker does, which is my only reservation about Mr. Blank's work.

1973 N 23, 44:1

A Shabby Fiction About JFK

By VINCENT CANBY

DAVID MILLER'S "Executive Action," with a screenplay by Dalton Trumbo based on a story by Donald Freed and Mark Lane, suggests flatly (or better, perhaps, states equivocally) that President John F. Kennedy was assassinated not by a single crackpot, who also happened to be an extraordinarily lucky shot, but by three professional gunmen working with the kind of precision that was totally lacking at the Bay of Pigs.

These gunmen, according to the film, were in the pay of a group of political conspirators—wealthy, influential members of the military-industrial complex who feared that JFK was going to sign a test-ban treaty, pull out of Vietnam and lead a black revolution.

The movie gives these conspirators fictional names and they are played by actors of the stature of the late Robert Ryan, Burt Lancaster and Will Geer. The movie also embraces the "two Oswalds" theory: The real Oswald was a patsy who was set up by a man impersonating him on several conspicuous occasions, as when the fake Lee Harvey Oswald goes into a gun shop and asks to have his telescopic sight fixed in a hurry. "I may need it any day now," he announces as loudly as he announces his name.

The movie uses a lot of newsreel clips of JFK, before, during and after the assassination, and of Oswald distributing Fair Play for Cuba literature and at Dallas police headquarters, including his assassination by Jack Ruby. It also uses simulated newsreel footage and employs an actor to play Jack Ruby in those scenes needed to establish the movie's contention that Jack Ruby was linked to the conspiracy.

"Executive Action" doesn't say that this is really what happened. It says only that this is what could have happened, and that what is presented on the screen jibes with accepted facts.

*

However, even to people who are prepared to accept some sort of conspiracy theory, including myself, this manner of fiction simply isn't good enough. In spite of the rather pious, unexciting, low-keyed professionalism with which "Executive Action" has been put together, it is fiction of a gross and shabby order. Because it cannot say that this is true, the only point of the film is to raise the question of possibility. Having done that, which it does very quickly, it reduces one of the most turbulent events in American history to the dimensions of routine melodrama. This sort of thing seems very sad, if not reckless. We cut from a newsreel clip of JFK playing with his children, or giving a speech at the United Nations, to a meeting of the conspirators (the sort of men who drink bourbon and branch water), then to a rifle range in some lonely western reserve where the assassins are practicing on wax dummies that have been placed in an open limousine.

In an Introduction to the Dell paperback edition of the Freed-Lane novel, Professor Richard H. Popkin of the University of California at San Diego makes a rather fascinating presentation of the reasons why Americans don't want to accept conspiracy theories, why our political assassins are quickly labeled "nuts" and forgotten, although we are endlessly fascinated by big crime conspiracies and can hardly wait to read the latest in-depth study of some thrill killer. It is Prof. Popkin's theory that we don't want to be made uncomfortable by the awful thought that we might, after all, be living in the biggest banana republic of them all, unaware of the people in actual control of us.

He points out, correctly, I believe, that the Watergate revelations may have made many Americans receptive to the idea that conspiracies can and do exist at high levels of power and influence in the United States. But that is hardly justification for the bogus history offered by "Executive Action," the heavily-footnoted novel as well as the over-simplified film.

*

It's worse than the old You Are There television series. It is, instead, You Are There If It Ever Happened This Way. This is a waste of time considering all of the facts that are available still to be checked out, studied or collated, including a bit of information I'd never known before.

According to the professor, Aristotle Onassis's ex-butler reported that the Greek financier put a team of private detectives on the assassination case and in 19 months came up with the names of the "real" killers, information that now is locked in an Onassis safe in Greece. The publication of the information was, says the butler, squelched by an anonymous telephone caller who threatened Mrs. Onassis that publication would result in harm to her and her children.

It's one of the pitfalls of this kind of investigation that one gets so easily bogged down in peripheral details. When I read about the butler's story, my first thought had to do with the likelihood of Mrs. Onassis's ever taking anonymous phone calls, and if she didn't take this one, did she receive a discreet note from the butler, in writing or verbally?

*

As many non-essential as essential questions are raised by "Executive Action." It adds nothing of value to our knowledge about the assassination, and in some ways it distorts the time in which it occurred. Could JFK's public statement that he hoped to bring 1,000 men home from Vietnam by Christmas have triggered such a massive conspiracy? Somehow I doubt it.

Another fact-fiction film opened recently, the French-made "The French Conspiracy," and although it doesn't take the liberties that "Executive Action" does, it's no better as a movie.

"The French Conspiracy" is a botched attempt at the sort of movie that Costa-Gavras has made into his own art. As did Costa-Gavras in "Z," "The Confession" and "State of Siege," Yves Boisset, the director of "The French Conspiracy," has taken a public event, in this case it's the kidnapping and disappearance of Mehdi Ben Barka, the Moroccan leftist opposition leader, from Paris in 1965.

The subsequent investigation revealed that not only had members of the French police and one of the French intelligence agencies conspired with Moroccans in the abduction, but also members of the French underworld, who were on chummy terms with the intelligence people (they attended each other's weddings, among other things).

*

The material is fascinating, but Boisset and Jorge Semprun, who wrote "Z" and "The Confession" for Costa-Gavras, have turned it into hash that is sometimes unintentionally hilarious. It means to take its political points of view seriously, but the exposition is so complicated as to be virtually unintelligible.

One can't even get too excited rooting for the good guys against the bad guys (don't worry why they're good or bad, just trust the movie) when the film is so oddly staged that, in a moment of high drama, when Jean Seberg is telling her man that she loves him, she almost gets her nose caught in the closing of the door of a subway car.

1973 N 25, II:1:5

STEREO, produced, directed, written shot and edited by David Cronenberg; DANS LA VIE by Pierre Veilleux; LE BLEU PERDU by Paul Dreissen, running time: 79 minutes. At the Film Forum, 256 West 88th Street. Today and tomorrow and Dec. 7-9 at 8 P.M.

By NORA SAYRE

A helicopter silently descending, a figure in a long black cape: when an opening shot yields two references to Ingmar Bergman (from "Through a Glass Darkly" and "The Seventh Seal"), you immediately worry about the film maker's powers of invention. In "Stereo," the cape—worn by a young man with permanently arched eyebrows—appears to be the central character. The movie will be shown at the Film Forum, 256 West 88th Street, this weekend and next, along with "Dans la Vie" and "Le Bleu Perdu," two beguiling animated shorts from the National Film Board of Canada.

The theme of "Stereo" is the inhumanity of science: male and female guinea pigs at a Canadian Academy for Erotic Enquiry suffer through some fragmented experiments in telepathy and omnisexuality. The narration is shared by some academic voices that gargle about "human social cybernetics," the dependency of language on thought, "telepathic bonding," psychochemistry, the space continuum and so forth. The liveliest moment occurs when the cape-wearer eats a candy bar. Otherwise, doors that won't open, enigmatic card games, long empty corridors and sex on an examination table make it all quite old fashioned, and the images are as formless as scrambled eggs.

"Stereo" mainly proves that you can't successfully spoof psychology merely by making it dull.

1973 D 1, 41:1

Our Own Past Is in 'Graffiti'

By ALJEAN HARMETZ

"WHERE were you in '62?" ask the ads for "American Graffiti." In 1962, I was changing the diapers of my year-old son and watching my abdomen expand with the relentless growth of my second child.

In 1962, I was 10 years beyond the adolescent concerns of prey and preying that mark the restless night in which "American Graffiti" takes place. The incessant rock music that forms the backdrop of the picture was only noise to be turned off as soon as I became aware of it on the car radio.

I cannot even rummage through my memories to find some kinship with last year's senior class president (Ronny Howard) and this year's head cheerleader (Cindy Williams) as they lose their balance in the ebb and flow of high school love. Alone and aloof in a public high

Aljean Harmetz is a freelance writer based in Los Angeles.

school after six years as a boarder in a convent, I never went to a high school dance or had a hamburger and cherry Coke at the local rendezvous.

*

Why, then, does this extremely specific account of adolescents prowling the streets of a small California city from dusk to dawn on a Saturday night in the fall of 1962 move me to such sadness for my lost past? Most reviews of the film—many written by men and women who, like the director George Lucas, graduated from high school around 1962—stress the innocence of that moment in time compared to all the assassinations and polluted rivers and governmental invasions of privacy that have come after it. I suspect that they are confusing the innocence of a time period with their own innocence during that time period.

American innocence as an institution probably ended in October, 1929. The year before "American Graffiti's" sock hop in the high school gym had brought the Bay of Pigs invasion and a renewed intensification of the Cold War. If there was, on that autumn night, no hot war for the draft-bait 18-year-olds to be frightened of, there were already Russian missiles in Cuba. The end of the world was always potentially around the corner.

What makes "American Graffiti" so extraordinary a film is not that it recreates for us the world's innocence but that it recreates our own innocence. It evokes an unreachable time. The days and years which bar our passage back have reshaped us. What we were once is psychologically unreachable except in such dreams as "American Graffiti."

My mind constantly jumps from "American Graffiti" to the scene in Thornton Wilder's "Our Town" when Emily, —too early and untimely dead—begs to return to earth for one day. Warned not to try to relive an important day, she chooses her almost neutral 12th birthday but runs in terror back to her grave long before the day is over. The unendurable pain comes because of her foreknowledge of what is going to happen to *people*—who will grow old and who will die and who will lose without ever being aware of what he has lost.

My 12-year-old son, a movie connoisseur whose favorite films include "The Emigrants" and "Billy Jack," responded with guarded enthusiasm to "American Graffiti." It was, he said, "a good film, interesting," but it did not stir him. He has not yet approached that last moment of innocence when choices must be made and keys must be turned in the locks of the future. For him, everything is still possible. He can live a dozen lives in fantasy before choice becomes irrevocable.

*

For us—whatever our ages—for whom the choices were made long ago, "American Graffiti" is a metaphor for what we once had and lost. Drenched in life's ambiguities, we shiver to remember our boundaryless past and yet feel, also, a certain arrogance watching these children playing such important, meaningless games. Life has blooded us and will soon blood them.

In the end—despite its charm and gentle humor—"American Graffiti" is a melancholy film, pervaded with a sense that no choice can possibly be the right choice simply because choosing forecloses on the future. By morning, one of the protagonists has chosen to go away to college; another has chosen to stay at the comfortable junior college at home. Each wins. Each loses.

At the film's end, a note on the screen totals up the future, scattering the protagonists in the wind of life's capriciousness. This one is dead, that one an insurance agent in Modesto, California. It is the fact that the future is foreclosed for all of us that lends the film its melancholy universality.

Typing this, I wonder, rather wistfully, whatever happened to my quite rational decision, made at the age of 15, to spend my life searching for Atlantis?

1973 D 2, II:13:1

The Cast

SERPICO, directed by Sidney Lumet; screenplay by Waldo Salt and Norman Wexler, based on the book by Peter Maas; produced by Martin Bregman; editor, Dede Allen; director of photography, Arthur J. Ornitz; music, Mikis Theodorakis; a Dino De Laurentiis film, distributed by Paramount Pictures. Running time: 130 minutes. At the Baronet Theater, Third Avenue at 59th Street, and the Forum Theater, Broadway at 47th Street. This film has been classified R.

Serpico .... Al Pacino
Sidney Green .... John Randolph
Bob Blair .... Tony Roberts
Tom Keough .... Jack Kehoe
Inspector McClain .... Biff McGuire
Laurie .... Barbara Eda-Young
Leslie .... Cornelia Sharpe
Pasquale .... John Medici
D.A. Tauber .... Norman Ornellas

By VINCENT CANBY

Early in 1970, two New York City police officers, Detective Frank Serpico and Sgt. David Durk, put their careers and their lives on the line. After getting the runaround for months from their superiors, who preferred not to listen, they called on David Burnham, a reporter for The New York Times, to tell him their story of graft and corruption within the Police Department.

Detectives Serpico and Sergeant Durk had plates, dates and names, information that, when published, prompted Mayor Lindsay to appoint the Knapp Commission to investigate hte charges, leading eventually to the biggest shake-up in the Police Department's history.

In his book "Serpico," published this year, Peter Maas recalls this story exclusively from the point of view of Detective Serpico, the bearded, bead-wearing, so-called hippie cop who, in February, 1971, under circumstances that were puzzling, was shot in the face and critically wounded while attempting to make a narcotics arrest. When he recovered, Detective Serpico resigned from the department, exhausted and fearing for his life. Today he reportedly lives abroad, the bullet fragments still lodged a few centimeters below his brain.

●

Sidney Lumet's "Serpico," which opened yesterday at the Baronet and Forum Theaters, is a galvanizing and disquieting film adapted from the Maas book by Waldo Salt and Norman Wexler. It is galvanizing because of Al Pacino's splendid performance in the title role and because of the tremendous intensity that Mr. Lumet brings to this sort of subject. The method — sudden contrasts in tempo, lighting, sound level—seems almost crude, but it reflects the quality of Detective Serpico's outrage, which, in our society, comes to look like an obsession bordering on madness.

The film is limited only by its form, which carries the limitations of the Maas book one step further. Only Detective Serpico and Mr. Burnham are identified by real names. Everyone else has a fictitious name, in consideration, I suppose, of potential suits for libel and invasion of privacy. I assume the film makers may also have been hampered by other people's consideration of personal gain. Why should a man give a movie company the rights to his life if he's likely to wind up playing a supporting role in someone else's film?

The use of fictitious names is not in itself disquieting, only the suspicion that we are getting the truth—but sort of. One must suspect that Sergeant Durk played a much more important part in the Serpico story than is played by the character named Bob Blair (Tony Roberts) in the film.

The form also prevents Mr. Lumet and the screenwriters from much speculation about the motives that sustained Detective Serpico and made him the one officer in the precinct who refused even free meals, much less thousands of dollars in monthly payoffs from gamblers and numbers racketeers.

Detective Serpico is a driven character of Dostoyevskian proportions, an anti-cop cop. It's no accident, I suspect, that he has a great fondness for wild disguises, and that in his private life he adopts the look and manner of a flower child's vision of Christ.

Mr. Lumet and Mr. Pacino manage to suggest such a lot of things about Detective Serpico that one wishes they could have enjoyed even greater freedom in exploring the character of this unusal man who, like the worker priests in France, tried to change the system by working within it.

"Serpico" was photographed (by cameraman Arthur J. Ornitz) entirely in New York, a city that Mr. Lumet knows better than any other director working today. He also knows actors and has surrounded Mr. Pacino with a fine cast of supporting players of whom John Randolph, as an okay Bronx police captain, is the most prominent.

●

Aside from a couple of romantic interludes that threaten to bring things to a halt, the only major fault of the film is the absolutely terrible soundtrack score by Mikis Theodorakis. It is redundant and dumb, the way English subtitles might be.

If you can stop up your ears to this musical nonsense, which includes Neapolitan street airs whenever Detective Serpico's Italian immigrant parents threaten to appear, you should find the film most provocative, a remarkable record of one man's rebellion against the sort of sleaziness and second-rateness that has affected so much American life, from the ingredients of its hamburgers to the ethics of its civil servants and politicians.

1973 D 6, 61:1

The Cast

THE TESTAMENT OF DR. MABUSE, directed by Fritz Lang; screenplay (German with English subtitles) by Thea von Harbou; photography, Fritz Arno Wagner and Karl Vass; music, Hans Erdmann; produced by Seymour Nebenzal; released by Janus Films. At the New York Cultural Center. 120 minutes.

Dr. Mabuse .... Rudolph Klein-Rogge
Inspector Lohmann ...... Otto Wernicke
Kent .... Gustav Diessl
Dr. Baum .... Oscar Beregi
Lily .... Vera Liessem
Anna .... Camilla Spira
Monetary expert .... E. A. Licho
Hofmeister .... Karl Meixner
Dr. Kramm .... Theodor Loos
Jeweler .... Theo Lingen

By NORA SAYRE

Although we now live with melodrama on a weekly basis, it's still immensely refreshing on film. Fritz Lang's "Testament of Dr. Mabuse," the sequel to his "Doktor Mabuse" of 1922 (which was shown at this year's New York Film Festival), yields a sensational torrent of images that almost make the early nineteen-seventies seem tame.

The second "Mabuse," which can be seen at the New York Cultural Center tomorrow, was made in 1932 and had only a brief run in Germany until Goebbels banned it in 1933. (Evidently, the German original hasn't been shown in this country; only the French version has been exhibited.) Goebbels offered Lang the job of running the German film industry, and the director's response was to leave the country that day.

Goebbels at first tried to steer movies toward Brown

Fritz Lang

Shirt propaganda, but these did so poorly at the box office that he soon encouraged lush escapist films instead. Yet Goebbels also cherished the notion of a Nazi "Mrs. Miniver," which was attempted in Hamburg toward the end of the war. It wasn't completed, due to script trouble, actresses who failed to show up on the set because the German submarine fleet had landed, the vast British raid on Hamburg and a director who flipped his lid.

In Lang's 1932 classic, Mabuse, the master criminal and hypnotist who wanted to dominate the world, is now a lunatic in an asylum. The muscle-bound sensualist of the first film appears as a ravaged wraith in the second. But he continues to direct his gang of hoods: on his written orders, they kill and steal, set fire to chemical factories and plan to destroy crops and to poison water supplies.

Lang wrote in 1943 that he'd designed "an allegory to show Hitler's processes of terrorism. . . . I hoped to expose the masked Nazi theory of the necessity to deliberately destroy everything which is precious to people. . . . Then, when everything collapsed and they were thrown into utter despair, they would try to find 'help' in the new order."

●

Mabuse dies. But he has already hypnotized his psychiatrist, who continues to carry out the dead man's schemes. It's a fine case of mind poisoning and demonic possession, which also evokes the spell that Hitler cast on the German psyche. Pursued by the bulky, ebullient Inspector Lohmann (acted by Otto Wernicke, who played the same part and trailed Peter Lorre in "M"), the psychiatrist comes to look more and more like Mabuse, and finally goes as mad as his own mentor.

While this "Mabuse" lacks most of the surrealistic effects and the dazzling hallucinations that gave its predecessor such magic, it's rich in the images and the shocks at which Lang excelled. Mabuse's trained killers arrange a murder in a traffic jam: as the doomed man smiles at the rhythm of the cars' horns honking around him, and then presses his own horn to jibe with the same beat, we realize that he's unwittingly giving the signal for his own execution.

●

Mabuse's death is first announced by a close-up of still, bare feet: hands tie a name card to the stiff ankles. (But his supernatural powers have been stressed so often that it's hard to believe he's really dead.) A curtain — which used to reflect Mabuse's shadow while his voice gave orders—is parted to reveal a dark silhouette painted on a wall and a recording machine: the ruse merely makes him seem more ubiquitous than ever.

In "Mabuse," as in some of Lang's other movies, the director most brilliantly conveyed the sense of being trapped—the moment when death or lifelong consequences close in. Here, during a shootout with the police, the criminals panic and turn on one another, fighting savagely about whether to surrender or hold out. Meanwhile, a young couple locked in a basement with a ticking bomb decide to break a water pipe in hopes of diminishing the inevitable ex-

plosion; when the woman fears that they'll be drowned if they're not blown up, the man looks at her fondly and shrugs slowly.

For most of Lang's characters, there was rarely an escape-hatch. The climax of the first "Mabuse" showed the Doctor frantically trying to fight his way through bolted doors. Lang seemed to specialize in people who were desperate to escape: either from places where they might be killed or from situations that they found intolerable. The Mabuse films remind us again of what Lang himself escaped from—and of our own good fortune in being able to savor the body of work that he achieved after that escape.

1973 D 6, 61:1

DAVID HOLZMAN'S DIARY, written and directed by Jimmy McBride; screenplay by L. M. Kit Carson; production and cinematography, Michael Wadleigh; released by New Yorker Films. At the Whitney Museum of American Art, Madison Avenue and 75th Street, through Dec. 12. Running time: 74 minutes.
David Holzman ....L. M. Kit Carson
Penny Wohl .... Eileen Dietz
Pepe .... Lorenzo Mans

By NORA SAYRE

"Life as a work of art"—at least once a decade that ancient concept seduces some members of yet another generation, and inspires them to hash up their lives in the name of truth or beauty. Jim McBride's "David Holzman's Diary," a totally delightful satire on "the blubber about cinéma vérité," mocks those ghastly reels from the nineteen-sixties, when various film makers immortalized themselves or their friends by trying and failing to be spontaneous. "Diary," which derides directors who scorned imagination or invention while worshiping the camera, opened yesterday at the Whitney Museum of American Art.

Holzman, an earnest young Godard-hound, decides to film his life in order to understand it—and only succeeds in ruining it. As a voyeur, a gentle intruder into other people's lives, he can't understand that the filming makes his subjects feel self-conscious, or that "reality" is altered by the presence of his camera and his tape recorder and his lavalier mike, which he calls his "friends."

●

His girlfriend, who detests his movie-making, finally leaves him because of it. He's already told us in a dry, flat voice that he really loves her, though he can't resist pointing out that she's "dirty, sloppy." Forlornly, he adds, "I don't quite get her sense of privacy." After she's gone, he argues that masturbation is an improvement on the real thing because You can think of anything . . . pigs. Think of trains going in tunnels. Think of bagels. I mean, you're not

limited to women."

However, his obsession with freezing everything on celluloid rarely allows him any other fantasies. He gives manic attention to every detail of his New York neighborhood, from derelict sofas on the street to the installation of matchstick bamboo blinds in a nearby apartment, and finally gets slugged by a cop for filming people through their windows.

●

Soon, we realize that the camera is his analyst. He tells it everything, and then grows furious because it doesn't answer him with "the right things," and also makes him "do things" that he wouldn't ordinarily do. Accusingly, he asks it, "What do you want?" Then

he shouts at the lens that it hasn't helped him—just as a frustrated patient may denounce an all too silent psychiatrist.

"Diary" was made in 1967, and time has served it very well. We get a pungent flash on the past when a radio announces the numbers killed in the Newark riots, or refers to "the new Israel-Egyptian cease-fire," or quotes the Pentagon on the probable increase of American forces in Vietnam next year. But aside from politics, that period now seems a rather innocent one in retrospect, and the character of David Holzman (admirably played by L. M. Kit Carson) distills the eager naiveté that accompanied the zest for technology, deliberate inarticulation and

the mistrust of words, the vibes and the hoaxes and all the lighter put-ons of 1967.

At the end, Holzman is bitterly disappointed that his movie and his camera have taught him nothing — least of all how to control his life. The picture reminds me of the late A. J. Liebling's recollection of being 23 in Paris, when he felt that his life hinged on an impossible decision. Meanwhile, he was writing a novel about a 23-year-old in Paris whose future hung upon an insoluble choice. When the character caught up with the day of his own life that he was describing, he couldn't finish the book. Jim McBride's movie evokes the spirit of Liebling's enormous laughter when he remarked that few diaries yield conclusions or solutions.

1973 D 7, 34:1

Your Life Might Make A Good—or Bad—Movie

By VINCENT CANBY

THE fever began in Paris with Henri Langlois and his Cinémathèque Francaise where, in the 1950s, a generation of cineastes discovered that it was actually possible to survive 12 to 18 hours a day sitting in the dark watching old movies. No bends. No laughing or crying fits. No hallucinations uninvited. One might be a bit dizzy and inarticulate when one emerged, but the traumas were seldom fatal. In the 1960s the fever, not unlike a kind of medieval ecstasy, spread to America, where the effects were initially apparent on the postwar young. They were the most easily susceptible, but the older generations were also touched.

We learned to look at movies, especially commercial American movies, with a new respect, to recognize the art within Hollywood's assembly line product, as well as the contributions of the individual artists involved. This was all to the good. Then the fever turned into a kind of madness.

It was healthy to recognize the extraordinary heritage of films. It was one thing to appreciate this history, but it was quite another to start relating only to films, and to relate one film only to other films quite cut off from everything else in the world. It took just one more small step to recognize the camera as a holy instrument, as incapable of falsehood as The Redeemer.

"Cinema," said Jean-Luc Godard, "is truth 24 frames a second."

If you can swallow that without choking (and I'm not sure that Godard ever did), you can swallow anything, and you can make a good case for saying to hell with the formal study of literature, music, painting, philosophy, history, politics, and maybe even ceramics. If truth is there to be discovered by any Eclair camera, why fool around with all that other junk? Get a nice portable

16-millimeter camera, a tape recorder, and go to work. Which is, I'm afraid, one of the reasons why film courses are blooming on college campuses everywhere. Movies, given a certain basic technical skill, are not difficult to make, and if you study any series of moving pictures long enough, you can come up with some quite impressive truths to justify them.

*

The last word on this latter-day movie madness is Jim McBride's rambunctiously funny and wise first feature, "David Holzman's Diary," which was made in 1967 but is only now having its debut engagement in New York at the Whitney Museum of American Art. McBride made the movie in five days, for a cash outlay of $2,500, shortly after graduating from the New York University film school. It looks like a fact-film, heavily influenced by the cinéma verité work of Ricky Leacock, D. A. Pennebaker, the Maysles brothers, Andrew Noren and Andy Warhol, but it is fiction of extremely witty order, largely improvised but most carefully composed.

As the title says, it has the form of a diary photographed by a completely self-absorbed movie nut named David Holzman (L. M. Kit Carson) who, you have every reason to suspect, has probably just graduated from the NYU film school, owns a camera and a tape recorder and wants desperately to make a movie though he hasn't much in mind except himself.

*

One of the things that makes this movie remarkable is that McBride and his collaborators Carson (who, I assume, made up most of his own dialogue) and Michael Wadleigh (the cameraman, who was later to direct "Woodstock") had the perspective to see what was going on in the comparatively new cinéma verité form at that time. Two years later Milton Moses Ginzberg was still looking upon the camera as a magic instrument in "Coming Apart," a pretentious first feature about a mad psychiatrist (Rip Torn) who tries to fix truth by photographing his own life. "Diary" even predates Norman Mailer's haymaker of a pseudo-cinéma verité film, "Maidstone." There is nothing of interest in either of those two films that isn't done better by McBride, Carson and Wadleigh.

"Diary" covers eight days in the mixed-up life of David Holzman who, early on, tells us that "objects, people and events" seem to speak to him, that he's just lost his job, that he's been reclassified 1-A by the draft, and that he is attempting to get some grasp of his life by photographing it. He quotes Godard on truth and proceeds to examine himself as well as his friends, including Penny (Eileen Dietz), his girl, a pretty, rather grumpy model whom David introduces to us first with a still picture and the comment that she's a bit of a slob and has a dirty neck.

*

There's a lot of Antoine Doinel in David's preoccupation with self, with his inability to understand the feelings of others. When Penny gets fed up with David's stalking her around his upper West Side apartment with camera and tape recorder, when she slams out of his pad forever, all David can say is "I don't quite get her sense of privacy."

Another friend of David's, an artist named Pepe Lorenzo Mans), warns David that "some people's lives are good movies and some people's lives are bad movies." Pepe is especially upset by David's footage of Penny. "She's ridiculous," he says. "She's trite. She behaves melodramatically. She's just not credible."

Pepe becomes what I take to be a kind of devil's advocate on behalf of cinéma verité. He suggests that David's efforts to understand himself and his life through film are doomed to failure. David, he says, is too busy wondering about how he should frame himself, where he should put his hands. "Your decisions stop being moral decisions and they become esthetic de-

cisions," says Pepe. "Your whole life stops being your life and becomes a work of art—and a very bad work of art this time."

In a quote that is not included in "David Holzman's Diary," Godard once said that the best critique of one film is another film. In addition to being a very appealing portrait of a young man with an obsession, who trails girls in and out of subways with his camera, who interviews a woman in a Thunderbird who wants to take him to bed, who explores the architecture and faces of the upper West Side—"David Holzman's Diary" says more than any written review I've read about some cinéma verité movies I've liked ("Salesman," "Showman," "Primary") and some I haven't liked ("Gimme Shelter").

The films aren't mentioned by name, (some weren't even made then), but the arguments that Pepe raises, as well as the actions of David himself, highlight questions we all have about the quality of truth that can be captured by the cinéma verité camera.

These questions have not only to do with whether the presence of a camera distorts life, and with the awful possibilities for distortion through the process of selection that goes into editing a film, but with the way David's camera allows him to stand outside his own life, to be a disengaged spectator. Carried to an extreme, it becomes an escape from any commitment whatsoever. At the end of "David Holzman's Diary," David is totally bereft.

There is much that cinéma verité, which is also called direct cinema, can do, but it's a complete fiction to suppose that it can necessarily teach us to see and hear any more efficiently than a fiction film as intelligent as, say "Mean Streets," or "American Graffiti" or "David Holzman's Diary."

Historical note: McBride's second film, "My Girlfriend's Wedding," which played the Whitney last week and was made in 1969, is a fairly tedious cinéma verité portrait of a young English woman named Clarissa. His third film, "Glen and Randa," was released commercially in 1971. It's a post-Bomb story about two unlikely nature children wandering through the forests and the debris of cities on the Pacific coast, which, after the Bomb, has been altered to touch Boise, Idaho.

1973 D 9, II:3:6

The Cast

DON'T LOOK NOW, directed by Nicolas Roeg; screenplay by Alan Scott and Chris Bryant, based on a story by Daphne Du Maurier; produced by Peter Katz; executive producer, Anthony B. Unger; director of photography, Anthony Richmond; editor, Graeme Clifford; music, Pino Donnagio; an Anglo-Italian Co-production by Casey Productions (London) and Eldorado Films (Rome), distributed by Paramount Pictures. Running time: 110 minutes. At the Sutton Theater, 57th Street, east of Third Avenue. This film has been classified R.

Laura Baxter	Julie Christie
John Baxter	Donald Sutherland
Heather	Hilary Mason
Wendy	Clelia Matania
Bishop Barbarrigo	Massimo Serato
Inspector Longhi	Renato Scarpa

By VINCENT CANBY

Nicolas Roeg's "Don't Look Now," which opened yesterday at the Sutton Theater, is a fragile soap bubble of a horror film. It has a shiny surface that reflects all sorts of colors and moods, but after watching it for a while, you realize you're looking not into it, but through it and out the other side. The bubble doesn't burst, it slowly collapses, and you may feel, as I did, that you've been had.

Not only do you probably have better things to do, but so, I'm sure, do most of the people connected with the film. These include Julie Christie and Donald Sutherland, who play a haunted young English couple, and maybe even Mr. Roeg, the director, who has staged a number of individual sequences with a lot of dash and style, but not enough to disguise the emptiness of the screenplay.

This is credited to Alan Scott and Chris Bryant, who have taken a minor short story by Daphne Du Maurier and attempted, unsuccessfully, to elevate it into something on the order of "The Turn of the Screw."

It doesn't work. The film takes its supernatural phenomena seriously, but the suspense depends on a twist that comes not at the end but about halfway through. At which point, "Don't Look Now" stops being suspenseful and becomes an elegant travelogue that treats us to second-sightseeing in Venice.

For John Baxter, an art historian, (Mr. Sutherland) and his wife, Laura (Miss Christie) Venice is a city filling up with disasters as it sinks back into the sea. Unknown to John, though not to us, he is gifted with second sight. The film opens with an agonizing sequence in England when their five-year-old daughter drowns in a nearby pond, a fact that John senses without questioning why.

In Venice, where John is working on the restoration of an ancient church, the Baxters encounter a pair of mysterious English biddies, one of whom has the "power." They cheer up Laura enormously by telling her they've been in touch with her dead daughter. They also warn John that danger awaits him if he stays in town.

Actually this plays somewhat better than it tells. Mr. Roeg is able to maintain a sense of menace long after

the screenplay has any right to expect it, largely because of the sincerity of his actors and because of the presence of the sinking city itself.

Mr. Roeg, who was a cameraman before becoming a director with "Performance" (co-directed with Donald Cammell) and "Walkabout," gets a great performance from Venice, which is all wintery grays, blues and blacks, the color of the pigeons that are always underfoot.

The one bit of color that registers on John is that of a brilliant red parka worn by a child who, from the back, looks just like his dead daughter. The figure appears to him at night, at the end of dark alleys or fleeing from something on the other side of the canal. John also has some other hallucinations that I dare not describe without giving away the plot.

I *can* describe a beautifully photographed love scene between John and Laura, which is intercut — for essentially comic results—with post coital scenes of the couple getting dressed for dinner afterward. The point, I guess, is that if you can see into the future, it's often difficult to keep your mind on the present, no matter what you're doing.

One of the problems with "Don't Look Now" is that second sight does not easily translate as a terrifying talent for a film character to possess. It simply looks like a flash-forward, which, along with the flashback, the jump-cut and the fade, are standard story-telling devices in movies.

1973 D 10, 56:1

A DELICATE BALANCE, by Edward Albee; directed by Tony Richardson; screen adaptation, Mr. Albee; director of photography, David Watkin; editor, John Victor Smith; produced by Ely A. Landau; presented by the American Film Theater at selected theaters. Running time: 132 minutes. This film is classified PG.

Agnes	Katharine Hepburn
Tobias	Paul Scofield
Julia	Lee Remick
Claire	Kate Reid
Harry	Joseph Cotten
Edna	Betsy Blair

By NORA SAYRE

It would be nice if astral flights were possible in the movies. If only the cast of

magnificent actors appearing in Edward Albee's "A Delicate Balance" could be transported to another film before our eyes, we might see something marvelous—instead of suffering a sense of waste.

The movie, which opened yesterday at selected theaters, is an adaptation by Mr. Albee from his own stage play. "Balance" concerns a rich New England family seething with amorphous hate—these leisured persons have nothing to do but fight one another. Their best friends (an impeccable couple) move in on them unexpectedly, explaining that they were overwhelmed by an onslaught of nameless terror in their own home.

The hosts find their guests oppressive. Everyone bickers. A few explode. Eventually, the unwelcome visitors leave, having failed to enlighten or even infect the others with their particular plague. Some spectators have deduced that the theme is the disruption of privacy, but that doesn't wash, since the family was in a foul humor long before the guests arrived.

•

So "Balance" hangs on a crisis that's never defined. Still, Mr. Albee is faithful to his habit of evoking monstrous women and trodden men. Even the accessories make heavy points about the bonds of marriage: Paul Scofield wears a wide wedding ring; Katharine Hepburn's is even broader. But although Miss Hepburn has to call herself a "harridan," and the others treat her like an ogre, Mr. Albee hasn't given her the lines that would make her detestable. Actually, her only sin seems to be strength of character.

We never learn why these people loathe each other so deeply, though admittedly I wouldn't want any of them in my withdrawing room. The stunning insults that enhanced "Who's Afraid of Virginia Woolf?" are missing, and there's none of the passion that inflamed "The Death of Bessie Smith." (It's worth wishing that the American Film Theater had chosen that fine play instead.) Here, individuals turn on one another with little or no provocation, and the focus isn't fury but fatigue.

Katharine Hepburn and Paul Scofield

The relentless aridity of the script is shot with occasional profundities, such as "Time happens, I suppose, to people" and "They say we sleep to let the demons out." Tony Richardson has directed the actors as though they were wandering in and out of T. S. Eliot's "Cocktail Party" or almost anything by Christopher Fry or Enid Bagnold's "Chalk Garden"—without the wit. Often, the acutely mannered style means that the cast is poised to toss off epigrams that weren't provided.

At times, both Katharine Hepburn and Kate Reid, savage in sumptuous caftans, declaim too much. But Miss Reid, as an alcoholic, also has a harsh, sour resilience, an energy that seems to uncoil between hangovers.

Miss Hepburn drops some of her lines as though each word had a weight attached to it. And I suspect that Mr. Richardson had Dame Edith Evans in mind when he directed several of the Hepburn scenes. Yet the talents of both actresses burn through the lumpy wisecracks that encumber Miss Reid and the arias of leaden determination that were foisted on Miss Hepburn.

•

Paul Scofield endows a thankless, straight-man role with the complexities of ironic restraint. He's always interesting, although he mainly has to listen patiently to meaningless tirades. But he can even bring grace to a monologue about a cat that didn't like him. And what other great actor can laugh through his nose while his mouth is closed?

Betsy Blair, as an uninvited guest, mingles mystery with level propriety, Joseph Cotten has just the right urbanity as her husband, and Lee Remick plays the disgusted daughter of the house with a wry, flickering hostility that we've rarely seen from her before. In short, all of them rouse our memories of their past performances, and inspire an appetite to see them very soon again—elsewhere.

1973 D 11, 52:1

Karma of 'Bobby' Lovers Stirs India's Filmgoers

By BERNARD WEINRAUB
Special to The New York Times

NEW DELHI, Dec. 10 — He's a rich Hindu boy and she's a poor Christian girl. They fall in love, have a quarrel, are reconciled, stroll in fields of marigolds (hundreds of violins play tremulously) and meet stern objections from his father, an arrogant businessman, and her father, a lovable fisherman.

The heroine, Dimple Kapadia, doesn't quite die at the end of the movie as Ali McGraw does in "Love Story," but she tries. Dimple and her co-star, baby-faced Rishi Kapoor, attempt to jump off a cliff after a long chase and a short speech on the generation gap. The pair are saved by their fathers. Happy ending.

The month-old film, "Bobby", a sort of "Love Story" Indian-style, has emerged as the biggest movie success in years. The critics are surprised and even disgruntled about the film's success but "Bobby" has all the obvious elements: two new stars, musical numbers when the story lags, a touch of socialism, an obvious appeal to younger audiences, some sexy scenes, violence and three hours of extravagant escapism.

Beyond this, the Hindi film is one of the first to be dominated by youthful actors involved in a scenario, albeit lightweight, about adolescents and parents. The accent on youth is relatively new to Indian movies, whose performers are often older than the characters they portray.

"People wanted to see some new faces, especially a new girl, and Dimple's perfect," said Mohammad Shamim, film critic of The Times of India. "She's young, she's fresh, she's pretty in an Indian way, kind of thick around the waist."

"Of course it's a fairy tale," Mr. Shamim told a visitor. "These kind of characters don't really exist in India. Is there a boy anywhere who is so innocent about sex, so completely free of class consciousness, so good? It doesn't happen. It's all a dream."

"The film is an enormous success," he said. "It may be the biggest grosser we've had so far in India."

"Bobby" is now playing at a half-dozen theaters here, and is opening across the country to extraordinary ballyhoo.

Mr. Kapoor, who is 22 years old, is invariably besieged at airports, train stations and hotels by hundreds of girls wearing new shirts with the name Bobby printed on them. The actor's father, Raj, produced and directed the movie, and members of the Kapoor family themselves are known as the Redgraves of the Indian film world, with Rishi's uncles, Shashi and Shammi, major film performers.

Rishi's co-star, whom everyone calls only Dimple, is an ample, slightly awkward teenager who plays the title role, Bobby.

One critic wrote, "It is a male name . . . But never mind, our filmmakers were never sticklers for such minor details."

The plot leans heavily on surging background music and profound, silent glances between Dimple and Rishi. The story involves a rich youth who falls in love with his ayah's, or nanny's grand-daughter, whose father is a fisherman from Goa.

The pace rarely falters. There are ritzy parties in the hero's pseudo-Gothic family apartment, scenes in a garish discothèque, a tearful reconciliation in Kashmir, a masked ball and an elopement on a scooter. There is even a socialist touch: The youth, who has a picture of Nehru and Gandhi on the wall of his fancy bedroom, turn against his capitalist father and marries the fisherman's daughter.

"The film is a sad reminder that the old moth-eaten formula of dream merchandising still works wonders with the masses," said the critic for Shankar's Weekly of Bombay, said: "Of course any resemblance here and there to "Love Story" and "The Graduate" must be purely accidental! But even such resemblance does not lend substance to the hackneyed rich-boy-meets-poor-girl theme.'

1973 D 12, 58:1

HAPPY NEW YEAR (La Bonne Annee), directed and produced by Claude Lelouch; screenplay (French with English subtitles) by Mr. Lelouch; director of photography, Jean Collomb; music, Francis Lai; distributed by Avco Embassy Pictures. Running time; 112 minutes. At the Fine Arts Theater, 58th Street, west of Lexington Avenue. The film has been classified PG.

Simon....................Lino Ventura
Francoise....................Francoise Fabian
Charles....................Charles Gerard
The Jeweler....................Andre Falcon

By VINCENT CANBY

Claude Lelouch's "Happy New Year" ("La Bonne Année") is as much like any number of other Claude Lelouch films as one chicken egg is like another. It shouldn't be reviewed. It should be candled.

This one, which opened yesterday at the Fine Arts Theater, is a little old. It's about an off-season caper in Cannes, an attempt by Lino Ventura and Charles Gérard, two charming, naive, pragmatic, straight-laced, middle-aged con artists, to knock over the Van Cleef & Arpels shop down the Croisette from the Carlton Hotel. In the course of their preparations, Lino falls in love with Françoise Fabian, the beautiful, worldly, understanding, amusing, liberated, intelligent, witty, sensuous, compassionate, 30-ish owner of an antiques shop next to Van Cleef & Arpels.

Though Françoise rates five more adjectives than Lino, she, in turn, falls in love with him. The caper comes off, but not as planned. There's a lot of Francis Lai music on the soundtrack, a lot of footage devoted to transportation by car, truck and train, and a lot of Mr. Lelouch, including some scenes from "A Man and a Woman."

I find it difficult to understand how a director as intelligent as Mr. Lelouch, who has a feeling for comedy ("Money, Money, Money") and who hires such attractive performers, can make a film as totally vacuous as "Happy New Year." It bubbles occasionally, but like low-calorie club soda.

1973 D 13, 60:1

The Cast

HENRY VIII AND HIS SIX WIVES, directed by Waris Hussein; screenplay, Ian Thorne; photography, Peter Suschitzky; editor, John Bloom; music, David Munrow; produced by Roy Baird; distributed by Levitt Pickman Film Corporation. At the 86th Street East Theater, east of Third Avenue and neighborhood theaters. Running time: 125 minutes. This film is classified PG.

King Henry....................Keith Michell
Thomas Cromwell......Donald Pleasance
Anne Boleyn..........Charlotte Rampling
Catherine of Aragon ......Frances Cuka
Catherine Howard........Lynne Frederick
Anne of Cleves ....Jenny Bos
Catherine Parr........Barbara Leigh-Hunt

By NORA SAYRE

It's always intriguing to watch the development of an actor: Keith Michell has come a very long way since I heard him bellowing "If mew-HOO-sic be the food of *love* . . ." at Stratford, England, a good many years ago. It wasn't then foreseeable that he would become such a fine character actor, as is now clear in "Henry VIII and His Six Wives," which opened yesterday at the 86th Street East and is opening at neighborhood theaters. The movie production was shot afresh after the success of the British Broadcasting Corporation's television series, shown here on the Columbia Broadcasting System.

•

Mr. Michell vaults the decades with agility. After the boisterousness of his young Henry, he grows to look more and more like the Holbein portrait, and then as though that portrait itself had aged. Lurching from side to side on gouty limbs, waxing wider and bulkier with every scene, he excels at random rages and also in changes of mood—as he hurtles suddenly from fury to self-doubt. Tears are usually a test of talent, and his are touching when he weeps unwillingly at the death of one wife and the infidelity of another. He storms and lumbers through the period with gusto, hands laden with heavy rings land with a crash in a dish of succulent food, and it's pleasing to hear his scornful pronunciation of "imp't'nt" (impotent) and "*Papissst*". Throughout, the Tudor grunts are well orchestrated, whether inspired by feeding or love-making or dying.

Frances Cuka has a moving dignity as the rejected Catherine of Aragon, and Jane Asher manages to be both appealing and austere as Jane Seymour. However, Charlotte Rampling (Anne Boleyn) unleashes too many peals of carefree laughter, and Donald Pleasence overdoes his meaching rodent act as Thomas Cromwell: the twanging Northern accent that issues from his pleated lips seems more appropriate for Dickens or even Pinter.

•

This is a fairly sophisticated performance of a very simple-minded scenario — hence it's a bit hard to be certain whom this movie was designed for. Perhaps it should be ranked as healthy popular entertainment for those who enjoy the lusher style of English classical acting (I do), even when the script hardly threathens Shakespeare. For this "Henry," you need a soft spot for jousting, masques and mummeries, lutes and trumpets, pageantry rampant, hunting scenes and limpid evocations of the English countryside. Otherwise, the movie might make you yearn for urban grit and the most sarcastic jokes that our meanest streets can provide.

1973 D 14, 57:1

FILMS BY ED EMSHWILLER: LIFE-LINES, 7 minutes; THANATOPSIS, 5 minutes; GEORGE DUMPSON'S PLACE, 8 minutes; RELATIVITY, 38 minutes; FILM WITH THREE DANCERS, 20 minutes; SCAPE-MATES, 29 minutes; CHRYSALIS, 22 minutes. At the Film Forum, 256 West 88th Street, showings Dec. 13-16, 20-23.

Of the legion of avant-garde, experimental or, if you will, independent "underground" movie makers, Ed Emshwiller, who has been industriously filming since 1959, deserves the retrospective show that started last night at the Film Forum. If the collection of seven of his shorts, running a total of more than two hours, tends to be slightly repetitive and occasionally a strain on the eye and ear, it also forcefully illustrates the work of a creative professional who towers above many of his competitors.

Oddly enough, the sole new offering, the 22-minute "Chrysalis," made this year with the Alwin Nikolais modern-dance troupe, is only fitfully effective. In tracing and dissecting his choreography through simultaneous, split-screen, slow and accelerated motion, one often gets the impression of expert technique rather than drama or emotion.

And, his rarely seen 20-minute "Film With Three Dancers" (1970) is notable mostly for complex camera work that utilizes superimposed and double images (in addition to introspective dialogue) to stress the movement of its three principals.

•

List as the most striking and thoughtful, if not completely comprehensible, subjects in the lot, the 38-minute "Relativity" (1966) and last year's 29-minute "Scape-

Mates." In "Relativity," Mr. Emshwiller explores his personal concepts of man and his universe through complicated graphics, animations, several human figures and an electronic musical score. He conveys vaguely similar ideas through humans, animations and drawings in the five-minute "Thanatopsis" (1962).

"Scape-Mates," shown early this year on Channel 13, is a versatile videotape mix of computer-aided filming, the Moog synthesizer, animation and arms and legs and human forms to achieve swiftly moving, often arresting patterns from geometric shapes and lunarlike landscapes.

The earliest work, the 7-minute "Lifelines" (1960), seems to be merely experimental in its involvement with placental-like drawings and the nude woman seemingly evolving from them. And "George Dumpson's Place" (1964), is an 8-minute exercise concerned simply with affectionately examining dolls and other bric-a-brac strewn about an old black man's garden. The selection may be a special package for special tastes, but it vividly projects the talent and imagination of an artistic film maker.

A. H. WEILER

1973 D 14, 57:1

'Snapshots' Clicks as Film About a Film

Experimental films of a movie in production, with impromptu soul-baring by the contributors, are an avant-garde staple by now. Most of them are pretentious bores. But "Snapshots," which the Whitney Museum of American Art is presenting through Wednesday in its New American Filmmakers series, is an exception.

Produced by Kenneth E. Schwartz and directed by Mel Howard, the co-writers, the picture is apparently a truthful production diary involving on-camera embraces by some young Greenwich Villagers and off-camera bickering by one and all. This is not a movie for everybody. The sex is explicit and the language is fierce.

●

Yet the whole thing has a fresh, spontaneous flow and thoughtful texture. Mr. Howard's sideline use of his own family background is original and amusing, almost a movie in itself (with some haunting

camera shots of the Ellis Island shell). Wryly amusing, too, and revealing, is the bleak confusion after the director steps aside as leading man and hands over his heroine-mistress, Turid Aarsted, to his handsome photographer, Paul Goldsmith, the new hero.

Add to this some beautiful color photography, effective use of Mahler music and the pervading determination of Mr. Schwartz (heard but not seen) and his partner to get it all on camera, as something different. And it is—even touching, ultimately. The only catch is a redundant finale that suggests Hitchcock's "Psycho."

Let's ignore that candid postscript, with the two movie makers, who express their discouragement with the project. We need them around.

HOWARD THOMPSON

1973 D 14, 57:1

Serpico, the Saint Francis Of Copdom

By VINCENT CANBY

SIDNEY LUMET'S "Serpico," the first in what threatens to be an avalanche of movies about policemen, picks up the old cop film and brings it with lights flashing and sirens blaring into the middle of the Watergate era. It is Lumet's toughest, most provocative film in years, the story of the New York City detective, Frank Serpico, who in 1970 blew the whistle on graft and corruption within the New York Police Department, leading to the Knapp Commission hearings and the biggest shake-up in the department's history.

Serpico is not a new kind of hero. The man who attempts to buck the system has been a source of fascination ever since the first Greek playwrights questioned the wit and wisdom of some of their gods.

"Serpico," however, is a new kind of cop film and its title character, beautifully played by Al Pacino, is a new kind of hero to meet pounding a beat. He's obsessed in the way that Hollywood usually sees its painters, musicians and mad doctors obsessed. The difference is that Serpico is obsessed with such things as honesty and integrity and compassion for the underdog—to such an extent that when you leave the theater, your admiration for the man may be mixed with a certain amount of suspicion: he really is a driven figure, so neurotic that you begin to feel that his obsession has less to do with a sense of justice than with toilet training. This is not to knock the man but to credit the complexity of Lumet's movie and Pacino's performance, which are, after all, based on an authorized biography (written by Peter Maas), not always the most comprehensive source material.

*

Cop movies have come a long way from "G Men" (1935), in which James Cagney, though single-minded in his pursuit of gangsters, was a more or less conventional good guy, made distinctive only by Cagney's idiosyncratic talent as an actor. It may only be a coincidence, of course, but while J. Edgar Hoover was alive, few cop films were anywhere near as much fun as gangster films. Cops were nice, clean-cut, buttoned-down and essentially blah. The gangsters gots all the psychological ticks, the hang-ups and the good lines.

"The French Connection" tried to humanize cops by showing us that they had to be as cruel and ruthless as the people they were after, and recently we've been given films to demonstrate that good cops are hamstrung by the niceties of Constitutional freedoms, as in "Dirty Harry" and "Hit."

"Serpico" does something else. It presents its hero as a sort of St. Francis of Copdom, an Establishment dropout who talks to the street people and listens to Bach, a mystic who wears love beads and sandals, who studies Spanish and takes ballet lessons. "There are five positions," Serpico explains to an appalled cop in the Bureau of Criminal Intelligence. Says the cop to Serpico: "You're being short-changed."

The movie charts Serpico's growing disgust with police corruption without enjoying the freedom to analyze it. That's the form of authorized biography. At the beginning Serpico balks at accepting free lunches at the local restaurant simply because he doesn't like the leftovers the owner palms off on the free-loading cops. Serpico wants to eat first-class.

Serpico's awareness of the extent of corruption, everything from small bribes taken to forget a traffic violation to the acceptance of thousands of dollars a month from gambling and narcotics racketeers, eventually prompts him to go to his superiors, none

of whom, for various reasons, are particularly interested. The mayor, he is told, is hesitant to do anything to alienate the Police Department on the eve of what promises to be a long hot summer of possible civil unrest.

The deus ex machina of Serpico's drama is New York Times reporter David Burnham, who listened to the stories and evidence presented by Serpico and Sgt. David Durk (whose real-life role is downplayed in the film, which gives Durk the fictitious name of Bob Blair) and wrote the series of articles that led ultimately to the establishment of the Knapp Commission.

"Serpico" is essentially a thriller, one that has a number of smashing, bruising moments, as well as a few romantic ones that almost becalm the movie in midstream. These are not very interesting in themselves, al-

though his terrible relations with the girl he loves are necessarily dramatized in an attempt to explain the depth of his mania, his obsession with doing something about the second-rateness of the world around him.

Serpico's decision to blow the whistle on other cops and on his superiors is the sort that we accept rather more easily in drama (it is the right thing to do and heroes should do the right thing) than we do in life, particularly if it's our own. It is one of the achievements of Lumet's film that we get some idea of the mental cost of that decision to Serpico, which, in turn, makes us speculate about the kind of character who could survive the ostracism and threats that followed his disclosures.

"He must be a little nuts." That's what a friend of mine said about Dr. Daniel Ellsberg. Though the friend professed to admire what Ellsberg had done, he was also worried about Ellsberg's seeming to enjoy the publicity and notoriety that came when the case of the Pentagon Papers broke.

The American public is schizoid in such matters. We want heroes but we're also frightened of them. It's easier to feel comfortable with the kind of bunglers responsible for Watergate than it is with people whose moral codes are higher and more rigid than our own. We are reassured when the Rev. Davidson falls into bed with Sadie Thompson. There must be something wrong with anyone who professes piety.

"Serpico" is about our world, not simply its police corruption but its values, which have been so diluted that when we meet someone who acts on principle we know we're in the presence of a freak.

1973 D 16, II:3:1

The Cast

PAPILLON, directed by Franklin J. Schaffner; screenplay by Dalton Trumbo and Lorenzo Semple Jr., based on the book by Henri Charrière; produced by Robert Dorfman and Mr. Schaffner; executive producer, Ted Richmond; music, Jerry Goldsmith; director of photography, Fred Koenekamp; editor, Robert Swink; a Corona/General production, distributed by Allied Artists. Running time: 150 minutes. At Loews State I Theater, Broadway at 45th Street, Loews Cine Theater, Third Avenue at 86th Street, and Loews Tower East, Third Avenue near 72d Street. This film has been classified PG.

Papillon	Steve McQueen
Louis Dega	Dustin Hoffman
Indian Chief	Victor Jory
Julot	Don Gordon
Toussaint	Anthony Zerbe
Maturette	Robert Deman
Clusiot	Woodrow Parfrey
Lariot	Bill Mumy
Dr. Chatal	George Coulouris
Zoraima	Ratna Assan
Warden Barrot	William Smithers

By VINCENT CANBY

"Papillon," Franklin J. Schaffner's film version of the late Henri Charrière's book about his adventures in various penal colonies in French Guiana, is a big, brave, stouthearted, sometimes romantic, sometimes silly melodrama with the kind of visual sweep you don't often find in movies anymore.

Mr. Schaffner, the director of "Patton" and "Nicholas and Alexandra," looks to be the last of the big-time spenders. When he decides to show us a cargo ship steaming into a Caribbean port, that's what we see, in one magnificent long shot that includes the ship, the quay, the river, the jungles on the other side of the river and the sea in the distance.

●

"Papillon," which opened yesterday at Loews State I, the Cine and the Tower East Theaters, is full of such long shots, some of great beauty and all obvious expense. Though they aren't always necessary and though they give you the feeling the film was shot mostly from a Goodyear blimp, they recall an old-fashioned narrative style to which I'm partial, the kind that seeks to authenticate character and event by telling us a lot more about geography, climate weather, plant life and architecture than we absolutely need know.

The movie equivalent is the long shot. It fills the screen with information designed to convince us that, because the setting is real, so must be the people in it. "Papillon" desperately needs this sort of support because the Dalton Trumbo and Lorenzo Semple Jr. screenplay, like the book, defines its characters less in terms of what they feel or think than in terms of extravagant incidents and superhuman heroics.

"Papillon," the French word for butterfly, which was Charrière's nickname in the Paris underworld, is presented as an honorable safecracker dishonorably framed for the murder of a small-time pimp and thus sentenced to life in the penal colony in 1931. As played by Steve McQueen, Papillon is as all-American as a Rover Boy. He is manly, alert, self-reliant, deeply imbued with a sense of fair play. His love of freedom is so great that he must attempt the impossible, that is, to escape from Devil's Island.

His best friend is Louis Dega (Dustin Hoffman), convicted for counterfeiting government bonds, a fastidious, fussy man with bad eyesight and enough money to buy Papillon as his prison bodyguard. Hoffman is not especially convincing as a French counterfeiter, but he is fun to watch as an intelligent character as written.

There are dozens of other characters in the story, all more or less obligatory to a Devil's Island adventure—the cruel guard, the doomed prisoner (he prefers death to incarceration), the philosophical doctor, the perverted trustee (in other films he's sometimes presented as a male nurse). The horrors of prison life are graphically shown (including a decapitation that results in blood spurting onto the lens of the camera), cockroaches eaten to supplement the prison diet, storms at sea and a hand-to-hand encounter with a crocodile.

●

My tolerance for this kind of make-believe is fairly high. I like hairbreadth escapes and survivals against all odds, but I must admit that about three-quarters of the way through the two and a half hour of "Papillon" my tolerance was sorely tested.

It happened when Papillon is befriended by a tribe of Central American Indians resided over by Chief Victor jory. They inhabit what looks to be the West Indies' newest and most chic island resort and cabana colony and, to be hospitable, present

him with his very own Dorothy Lamour, a maiden named Zoraima who is played by Ratna Assan.

This finally establishes "Papillon" as the sort of movie Hollywood supposedly doesn't make any more. Though its native girls go topless and the production budget was huge, "Papillon" is the escapist movie we used to go see on Saturday night without even bothering to read the marquee.

1973 D 17, 59:1

---

best of Laurel and Hardy. It's the kind of film comedy that no one in Hollywood has done with style in many years, certainly not since Jerry Lewis began to take himself seriously.

●

"Sleeper" is a comic epic that recalls the breathless pace and dizzy logic of the old two-reelers. The setting is an American police state, ruled by a terrible dictator who has the genial manners of your favorite TV anchorman, where Miles is enlisted to aid the forces of the anti-government underground. Miles does his best to refuse. He is dirty-minded, mean-spirited, surreptitious and incurably literate and cowardly. As he points out: "I was once beaten up by Quakers."

The world in which Miles finds himself is truly alarming, a half-analyzed paranoiac's worst dream come true. Automobiles look like giant plastic turtles. Chickens are 12 feet tall and banana skins are as long as canoes. There are robot servants and robot dogs, and at the end of a dinner party a hostess comments: "I think we should have had sex but there weren't enough people."

How did America get this way? Was there a ghastly war? Someone seems to remember that a man named Albert Shanker once got hold of a nuclear warhead.

"Sleeper" is Mr. Allen's fourth film as star, director and writer (this time with Marshall Brickman) and it is, I'm sure, not only his most ambitious but also his best. The fine madness of "Take the Money and Run" and "Bananas," which were largely illustrated extensions of his nightclub routines, is now also apparent in the kind of slapstick comedy that can only be done in films.

When Woody wrestles with a butterscotch pudding mix that won't stop rising, when he runs afoul of an ill-fitting flying belt, or when he attempts to clone the entire body of the dead dictator from all that remains of the dictator (a nose), you realize that the stand-up comedian has at last made an unequivocal transition to the screen.

All of his original skills and humors remain intact. A fantasy in which Woody wins the Miss America contest, and another in which he plays Blanche Dubois to Diane Keaton's Stanley Kowalski, are vintage Allen.

As Woody continues to grow as a filmmaker, so does Diane Keaton (his co-star in "Play It Again, Sam")

---

continue to develop as an elegant comedienne along the lines of Paula Prentiss and the late Kay Kendall. In "Sleeper," Miss Keaton plays Luna, a beautiful, right-wing, absolutely awful poet whose metaphors are muddled by her inability to remember that caterpillars turn into butterflies, not the other way around. Through the love, aid, comfort and cowardice of a very small man, Luna is finally liberated.

There are some comparatively calm spots in the film, here and there, but they don't count. If anything, they allow you to catch your breath. "Sleeper" is terrific.

Woody Allen with oversized banana and celery stalk in a scene from the film "Sleeper"

SLEEPER, directed by Woody Allen; screenplay by Mr. Allen and Marshall Brickman; director of photography, David Walsh; editor, Ralph Rosenblum; produced by Jack Grossberg; executive producer, Charles H. Joffe; distributed by United Artists. Running time: 88 minutes. At the Coronet Theater, Third Avenue at 59th Street, and Little Carnegie Theater, 57th Street near Seventh Avenue. This film has been classified PG.

Miles Monroe	Woody Allen
Luna	Diane Keaton
Erno	John Beck
Dr. Nero	Marya Small
Dr. Orva	Bartlett Robinson
Dr. Melik	Mary Gregory

By VINCENT CANBY

Miles Monroe (Woody Allen), the part-owner of the Happy Carrot Health Food Restaurant in Greenwich Village, has a major problem. He had gone into St. Vincent's Hospital in 1973 for a minor ulcer operation, only to wake up 200 years later, defrosted, having been wrapped in aluminum foil and frozen as hard as a South African lobster tail when the minor ulcer operation went somehow wrong.

Thus begins "Sleeper," Woody's "2001" (actually, it's his "2173"), which confidently advances the Allen art into slapstick territory that I associate with the

1973 D 18, 52:1

The Cast

ALFREDO ALFREDO, directed by Pietro Germi; story and screenplay (Italian with English subtitles) by Leo Benvenuti, Piero de Bernardi, Tullio Pinelli and Mr. Germi; director of photography, Aiace Parolin; film editor, Sergio Montanari; music, Carlo Rustichelli; a co-production by RPA-Rizzoli Films-Francoriz Productions; released by Paramount Pictures. At the Plaza Theater, 58th Street, west of Fifth Avenue. Running time: 100 minutes. This film is classified R.

Alfredo	Dustin Hoffman
Mariarosa	Stefania Sandrelli
Carolina	Carla Gravina
Carolina's Mother	Clara Colosimo
Carolina's Father	Daniele Patella
Mariarosa's Mother	Danika La Loggia
Mariarosa's Father	Saro Urzi

By NORA SAYRE

Passive as a potato, timid as a fawn, Dustin Hoffman is cast as a victim once again in "Alfredo, Alfredo," which opened yesterday at the Plaza Theater. Here, he has almost returned to his role in "The Graduate": the innocent manchild overwhelmed by a devouring woman. As an Italian bank clerk who's pursued, married and mangled by a beautiful hysteric, (Stefania Sandrelli), Mr. Hoffman plays the kind of

---

character who can't even kick a stone in the road without injuring himself. Of course his marriage is a martyrdom, and divorce is as difficult as a Presidential impeachment.

●

The main problem with this picture is that Pietro Germi, the director, has made it (brilliantly) twice before. His "Divorce—Italian Style" and "Seduced and Abandoned" superbly satirized the cruelty of the Italian marital laws, before divorce became legal in that country. "Alfredo" is a rather diluted version of its predecessors: clearly, Mr. Germi has gone over the same material too often. The other problem is that Dustin Hoffman isn't Italian. Despite his efforts to tear into his food with a Latin gusto, or the slicked-down hair above the urban American face, he simply can't appear to be a native of a provincial Italian town—any more than Dwight

Eisenhower could have convinced us that he was a sleek Roman count.

However, there are beguiling details throughout. Mr. Hoffman's small, cautious smiles, the way his mouth and nostrils quiver when he smells his detested wife's perfume, and her scalp-chilling screams at the moment of orgasm—which alarm the neighbors and terrify the dog into fits of barking—all make for moments of fine farce. And it was a happy thought to have the couple's doctor prescribe sex two or three times a day, during the wife's most fertile hours; as Alfredo runs to and fro between his office and his home, he gets billows of guffaws from his colleagues. There's also a devastating scene when the wife's imaginary pregnancy is suddenly deflated.

•

Stefania Sandrelli has a gift for sulking. But she over-acts much of the time, and hence doesn't match her marvelous performances in Mr. Germi's earlier movies and in Bernard Bertolucci's "The Conformist." Also, "Alfredo" is weakened by some mossy male fantasies: the hero unfailingly inspires a tender sympathy in desirable women when they see him for the first time, and they always take the initiative in this picture. But that just isn't believable, since Mr. Hoffman is made to be too pathetic to rouse such attractions.

So "Alfredo" hasn't the wit or the bitterness of Mr. Germi's best films; for this director, savagery seems essential to comedy. If he's mellowed, it's our loss. But this isn't a bad movie — it's merely a disappointment because of the immense talent involved.

1973 D 18, 54:1

CINDERELLA LIBERTY, directed and produced by Mark Rydell; screenplay by Darryl Ponicsan, based on his novel; director of photography, Vilmos Zsigmond; supervising film editor, Donn Cambern; music editor, Patrick Kennedy, John Williams; a Sanford production; distributed by 20th Century-Fox. Running time: 117 minutes. At the Columbia I Theater, Second Avenue at 64th Street, and Embassy Theater, Broadway at 46th Street. This film has been classified R.

John Baggs Jr. ....James Caan
Maggie Paul..............Marcia Mason
Doug ....Kirk Calloway
Forshay ....Eli Wallach
Master-at-Arms ....Burt Young
Alcott ....Bruce Kirby Jr.
Miss Watkins........Allyn Ann McLerie

By VINCENT CANBY

Mark Rydell's "Cinderella Liberty" is a nicely acted but aggressively false and sentimental comedy about a middleaged sailor, a Seattle whore, and the whore's 11-year-old son who, being pre-pubescent, illegitimate and mulatto, has more problems going for him than anyone connected with the film seems to have recognized. The movie opened yesterday at the Columbia I and Embassy Theaters.

•

James Caan is fine as the dopey sailor who makes the right decision (to settle down) at the wrong time (with the whore). The role is well-written by Darryl Ponicsan, who adapted his novel for the screen. Mr. Ponicsan can write funny dialogue but he has no head for events. Almost everything that happens in the film is unbelievable, designed for short-term audience effect of easy laughter or tears.

Mr. Caan ("Brian's Song," "The Godfather") seems to be shaping up as the Paul Newman of the nineteen-seventies, an intelligent, versatile actor with a low-key but unmistakable public personality. Marcia Mason is also good as the wayward woman he marries, so good that you wish the script were equal to the complicated feelings that the actors every now and then manage to project.

Mr. Rydell, the director and himself a good actor ("The Long Goodbye"), photographed the movie entirely in Seattle with lots of contrasts between obvious prettiness and dismal squalor, the kind of thing usually fancied by budding film makers. Kirk Calloway underplays the little boy, which is okay, and Eli Wallach overplays Mr. Caan's cashiered sailor-pal as if he were doing an impersonation in someone's living room.

1973 D 19, 54:2

FANTASTIC PLANET, an animated feature directed by Rene Laloux; screenplay by Mr. Laloux and Roland Topor, based on the novel, "Oms En Serie" by Stefan Wul; original art work by Mr. Topor; graphic direction by Joseph Kabri and Joseph Vania; music by Alain Goraguer; a New World Picture presented by Roger Corman. At the 68th Street Playhouse, at Third Avenue. Running time: 72 minutes. (The rating is PG.)

Peace in outer space may be fine for Christmas but as a plot resolution it dampens and flattens "Fantastic Planet." Except for this curiously tame windup—when things should have been popping—this is highly engrossing science-fiction, a French-Czechoslovak co-production in animation.

•

The technique itself is fascinating. Instead of using the traditional method of drawing on acetate, the ingenious producers have sketched on cut-out and hinged paper. This comparative stiffness of movement, instead of the usual animated flash, gives a dignity and eerie depth to an adaptation by directors Rene Laloux and Roland Topor of Stefan Wul's novel, "Oms En Serie."

The story itself is a sci-fi honey, with tiny earthlings "from a destroyed planet" dominated as pets or outcasts by huge, robot-like rulers. This is somber, dead-earnest stuff. And when a Lilliputian revolution explodes, brilliantly evoked, the planet Ygam rocks.

The settings and deep panorama, while Daliesque in form, are colored in subdued pastels. Even the English titles, to spoken French, provide an outer-space flavor.

There is some inoffensive nudity and not one smidgen of humor, not even for Christmas. As for that ending, it simply seemed too tidy too soon. But for original, thoughtful, often strong (but tasteful) animation, I recommend "Fantastic Planet" for family viewing.

The Roger Corman presentation, for New World Pictures, is at the 68th Street Playhouse.

HOWARD THOMPSON

1973 D 19, 54:2

The Cast

THE DAY OF THE DOLPHIN, directed by Mike Nichols; screenplay by Buck Henry, based on the novel by Robert Merle; produced by Robert E. Relyea; executive producer, Joseph E. Levine; music, Georges Delerue; director of photography, William A. Fraker; editor, Sam O'Steen; distributed by Avco Embassy Pictures. Running time: 104 minutes. At the Ziegfeld Theater, 54th Street, near the Avenue of the Americas. This film has been classified PG.

Dr. Jake Terrell ...... George C. Scott
Maggie Terrell........Trish Van Devere
Mahoney ....Paul Sorvino
Harold DeMilo ....Fritz Weaver
David ....Jon Korkes
Mike ....Edward Herrmann
Maryanne ....Leslie Charleson
Larry ....John David Carson
Wallingford ....John Dehner
Schwinn ....Severn Darden
Dunhill ....William Roerick
Mrs. Rome ....Elizabeth Wilson

By VINCENT CANBY

In the superb opening shot of Mike Nichols's "The Day of the Dolphin," a large, sleek, blue dolphin suddenly leaps from the surface of the sea straight into the sky as if to break through all barriers of space, time and intelligence. The motion is slow. Drops of water change shape in airy suspension. The soundtrack heralds the event with the kind of aural splendor that accompanied the Dawn of Man sequence in Stanley Kubrick's "2001: A Space Odyssey."

Then you notice something oddly, purposely deflating: the dolphin has an orange ball in its mouth.

The leap that seemed to announce the dawn of the dolphin prompts, instead, memories of last winter's visit to Marineland. Performances every hour. Popcorn, peanuts, postcards and souvenirs.

•

"The Day of the Dolphin," which opened yesterday at the Ziegfeld Theater, is no dawn-of-a-new-era fiction, nor was the original Robert Merle novel, though it was inspired to a large extent by the research of American scientists, including Dr. John C. Lilly, who spent years trying to teach dolphins how to speak English.

Working (sometimes desperately) in several genres that are not their own, Mr. Nichols, one of America's most elegant directors of high comedy and low, and Buck Henry, his screenwriter, whose gift is for tumultuous satire ("Catch-22," "Is There Sex After Death?"), have made a Flipper film for adults, a "Day of the Jackal" for kids and a Lassie film for scuba divers of all ages.

There also are reminders of "Born Free," "Black Beauty," "Frankenstein," and at least one of the sequels to "Planet of the Apes." "The Day of the Dolphin" is not a movie with much personality of its own.

Unlike Dr. Lilly, who finally gave up his work on the grounds that it was cruel to take away the dolphins' freedom in the interests of research, the hero of "The Day of the Dolphin" pursues his experiments to their successful conclusion.

Dr. Jake Teller (George C. Scott), the head of a privately funded research center near Miami, scores his breakthrough when he separates his 4-year-old male dolphin, nicknamed Fa, from Fa's mate, Bi. Exhausted after an all-day tantrum, Fa finally pokes his bottle-nose out of his tank and says, through his spiracle, in a tiny, plaintive sort of midget voice: "Fa wants Bi."

Thereafter the film, which has quite charmingly followed the experiments with Fa and Bi, turns heavily to plot. Mysterious strangers appear at the research center to use Fa and Bi for their own evil purposes. The doctor ruminates about the meaning and morality of what he has wrought, while his wife, played by Trish Van Devere, tries to cheer him up.

Some of the cloak-and-dagger stuff that follows is so awkwardly staged that it's difficult to know whether the simplicity was designed for youngsters or as parody.

There are also times when the inter-species dialogues leave off being the dream of scientist and child come true and become the source of giggles. How can an actor like George C. Scott play a dramatic scene with a dolphin? No matter what he does, the dolphin is bound to uptank him.

•

Although the film is mostly played straight, in lovely, broad-horizoned seascapes, which, along with the dolphins, help reduce the actors to mere functions of the story, Mr. Nichols and Mr. Henry make their comic prances felt in a couple of key moments. One has to do with the film's climax and can't be reported.

The other features that fine actress Elizabeth Wilson, in what is little more than a walk-on, as one of those executive secretaries who sees herself as the keeper of the flame. "You must excuse us," she says to a visitor who has been kept waiting for five hours, "but today was just one of those days." Says the visitor: "Which one?"

1973 D 20, 57:1

The Cast

THE LAUGHING POLICEMAN, directed and produced by Stuart Rosenberg; screenplay, Thomas Rickman; based on the novel by Per Wahloo and Mai Sjowall; director of photography, David Walsh; film editor, Robert Wyman; music, Charles Fox, released by 20th Century-Fox Film Corporation. At the National Theater, 43d Street and Seventh Avenue and the Beekman Theater, 65th and Second Avenue. Running time: 112 minutes. This film is classified R.

Jake Martin .... Walter Matthau
Leo Larsen .... Bruce Dern
Larrimore .... Lou Gossett
Camerero .... Albert Paulsen
Lieutenant Steiner ...... Anthony Zerbe
Pappas .... Val Avery
Kay Butler .... Cathy Lee Crosby
Bobby Mow .... Mario Gallo

By A. H. WEILER

The continuing love affair between movie makers and a violent and photogenic San Francisco is exposed with fresh ardor by "The Laughing Policeman," which came to the National and Beekman Theaters yesterday.

Though an essentially familiar amalgam of murder, manhunt and dogged police work in that scenic city, this "Policeman" stands a good deal taller than the norm because of the expert guidance of Stuart Rosenberg, the producer-director. He is effectively aided by a fine script and a cast as convincing as a live cop or a dead gunman.

•

The plot tends to be convoluted from its lengthy opening sequence, in which all the passengers of a bus, including a detective, are massacred by a mysterious machine-gunner. A confusion of other corpses and a gory shootout help cloud the proceedings.

But Walter Matthau, as the veteran plainclothesman whose partner was slain; Bruce Dern, his new partner, and their teammates not only provide meticulous expertise in tracing the killer, but also reveal themselves and their views of rough jobs.

Credit much of the film's flavor and insights to Thomas Rickman's adaptation of the novel by the Swedish husband-and-wife team of Per Wahloo and Maj Sjowall. This script captures the character and the earthy, germane vernacular, four-letter and otherwise, of the police, street people, blacks, prostitutes and pimps of San Francisco that substitutes for the book's Stockholm.

Mr. Matthau gives an underplayed and forceful portrayal of the taciturn, gum-chewing sleuth frustrated by a lack of motives for the seemingly unrelated slayings, who turns to a previous, unsolved murder to unearth the killer. It is in keeping with his old-timer's dedication to a plodding and dangerous job that makes him a stranger to his wife and kids. Mr. Dern's delineation as his cynical sidekick, who occasionally

messes up procedures with hard-nosed tactics, is equally strong and natural.

•

The film juxtaposes police practices and points of view in varied vignettes, from Anthony Zerbe's characterization of the harassed lieutenant yelling for results to Lou Gossett's black detective who realy knows his black suspects and can handle them. And a number of bit performances, including actual police squads and a team of emergency-room doctors, lend vivid local color and authenticity to an engrossing and adult crime caper.

1973 D 21, 46:1

THE DEADLY TRACKERS, directed by Barry Shear; based on the story "Riata" by Samuel Fuller; director of photography, Gabriel Torres; film editors, Michael Economou and Carl Pingitore; music, Fred Steiner; produced by Fouad Said; released by Warner Brothers. At neighborhood theaters. Running time: 105 minutes. This film is classified PG.
Kilpatrick .... Richard Harris
Brand .... Rod Taylor
Gutirrez .... Al Lettieri
Choo Choo .... Neville Brand
Schoolboy .... William Smith
Jacob .... Paul Benjamin
Blacksmith .... Pedro Armendariz Jr.
Maria .... Isela Vega

Our sturdiest screen staple, the Western, is made to look viciously senile in "The Deadly Trackers," an unremittingly bloody search-and-destroy chase that pulled up lame yesterday at local theaters. The vengeance sought by a sheriff whose family has been slaughtered by an inept but bestial gang of bank robbers results simply in fireworks and gore and little more.

What the producers had in mind is difficult to discern from the foggy and arty, if explosive, action. Samuel Fuller, already adored by his own cult followers, reportedly began directing "The Deadly Trackers" from his story "Riata" and then was replaced by Barry Shear. But despite any credits or disclaimers, the sum total here appears to be, at best, a distressingly chaotic adventure.

Richard Harris, who gives the appearance of a Pilgrim ascetic with an unlikely rogue as the once peaceloving but now vengeful lawman, is given to musings, mumblings, gesturing and occasional ranting on his long trek down to Mexico to mow down the slayers of his wife and young son. Rod Taylor, as the outlaw chief, is vague and bland about the bloody business he's in, except for the climactic moments when he suddenly displays unexpected tenderness toward his illegitmate little daughter who is caught up in the final, fatal shootout in a Mexican convent.

Al Lettieri is mostly befuddled as the pudgy Mexican sheriff, also tracking the killers and occasionally tangling

Selected Short Subjects at the Whitney

The Whitney Museum of American Art has a generally good roundup of 14 short film subjects titled "Animation," a new program opening yesterday for two weeks. A couple of them are duds. Some of the better pictures are simply too short. Fittingly, the program closes with a dazzling tour de force, Philip Jones's "Secrets" (eight minutes).

This one, the best of all, hits you like a visual, mini-symphony, as Mr. Jones's animated shots of one image, a woman's face and its background, run a brilliantly effective gamut. Almost matching the impact is Eliot Noyes's "Sandman" (four minutes), a skillful, amusing delight, which manipulates blue and beige sand, of all things, like quicksilver.

Provocative exercises, such as Dan Bailey's "Gilgamish," John Haugse's "Encidmez-U," Lorraine Bubar's charming "Drawn in Blue" and Peter Virsis's "That's Life," are fragmentary and over too soon. So is George Griffin's sprightly "Trikfilm."

The one outright clinker is Scott Turner's "This Is No Movie," and he's not kidding, with this sputtering, coy "homage to Henri Matisse." Almost as coy, and stiffly animated, is a roundup of Pogo characters, credited to Walt Kelly, titled "We Have Met the Enemy and It is Us."

The computerized images of Lillian Schwartz's and Ken Knowlton's "Apotheosis" are aptly kaleidoscopic. But for pure, droll enjoyment, running just the right lengths, it would be hard to beat Charles Jepsen's and James Hoberman's "Rocky Raccoon" and Dan Bailey's "Squiggle."
HOWARD THOMPSON

1973 D 21, 45:1

The Cast

A KING IN NEW YORK, produced, written and directed by Charles Chaplin; a Classic Entertainment, Inc., release. At the Playboy Theater, 110 West 57th Street. Running time: 105 minutes. This film is classified G.
King Shadhov .... Charles Chaplin
Ann Kay .... Dawn Addams
Ambassador .... Oliver Johnston
Queen Irene .... Maxine Audley

By NORA SAYRE

He springs to his feet with an incredibly straight back, as though he had swallowed a telescope; in a noisy restaurant, he mimes his order to the waiter who can't hear him: a pop-eyed swimming fish for caviar, a scuttling turtle for turtle soup. Discussing dentistry at an elegant dinner party, he ties a napkin over a fat woman's bosom and fills her mouth with knives and sugar tongs. In an elevator, he thoughtfully slides his finger into the nozzle of a fire extinguisher, becomes wonderfully entangled in the loops of hose, runs off with yards of it trailing behind him and ends by soaking the judge who is investigating him as a Communist conspirator. The choicest moments pass very quickly, simply because Chaplin's best jokes were always sudden: it's the pratfall we don't foresee, or the lunge of improvisation, that reveal his genius.

•

"A King in New York," which opened yesterday at the Playboy Theater, was an effort to satirize McCarthyism. It was released in Europe in 1957, when Chaplin was 68. In 1952, when he was traveling abroad, the United States Attorney General stated that Chaplin (a British subject) would not be allowed to return to America without a hearing on charges of "moral turpitude and Communist sympathies." Chaplin stayed away, often repeating that he was not a Communist, but "an internationalist, a peacemonger." In 1956, he said that he wasn't interested in offering "A King in New York" for the American market. Now, we're able to see it for the first time.

Chaplin plays the ex-king of a nameless country, who lost his throne because he opposed nuclear weapons and planned to use atomic energy for peaceful purposes. Hurtling to Manhattan for sanctuary, he soon discovers that America is insane. Conventional shots of skyscrapers and jostling crowds inform us of our inhumanity. It's revealed that our movies are brutal, our commercials crass and that people have to do humiliating things for money. Clearly, Chaplin loved playing king. Here, as in some of his other pictures, he seems to be in awe of the rich and the class system, even though he has often derided both. But the camera ogles opulence. (As his autobiography shows, it was ironic that a man who loved money and property so deeply should have been accused of communism.) His king has little in common with the legendary tramp, except for the occasional wriggling shrug that accompanies the raised eyebrows and the nervous toothy grin. He tries to make this aristocrat seem angelic, almost saintly—which makes for some embarrassing moments.

The king has a brief skirmish with a young woman in advertising, played with relentless perkiness by Dawn Addams. He then gets involved with a child prodigy whose parents are former Communists; they're jailed for refusing to give names. The boy (acted by Chaplin's son Michael, then 11) has to appear as a tiny demagogue, spouting Marx while the indignant king attempts to argue or interrupt. Meanwhile, the rhetoric rises to a denunciation of all forms of government.

Chaplin crammed his own views between the boy's jaws—and deliberately made them sound foolish. The result is a failed farce. Caricaturing the child as a semi-monster hardly strikes a blow for liberalism. Actually, the result is oddly reactionary, since the anti-McCarthy mouthpiece is forced to be absurd. And some sticky spurts of pathos increase the political confusion. Finally, the boy turns informer in order to get his parents out of prison, and he becomes a shattered, weeping wreck. The king, like Chaplin, leaves America.

•

Despite Chaplin's denials, this is a very bitter film—and why should it be otherwise? We can applaud his anger, and it's easier than ever to sympathize with characters grown cautious about what they say over the phone, who worry that their rooms are bugged or sense that they're about to be subpenaed. However, the great man botched his own political arguments, and this movie sags below the rest of his work.

Yet, it's important to see "A King in New York": it brings back the bad old days. And the fact that even Chaplin couldn't make guilt by association funny is crucial to our past and present history.

1973 D 22, 11:1

The Program

JIMI HENDRIX, a documentary; a Joe Boyd, John Head, Gary Weis production; film editor, Peter Colbert; released by Warner Bros. At the Trans-Lux East Theater, Third Avenue and 58th Street, and the Trans-Lux West Theater, Broadway at 494th Street. Running time: 102 minutes. This film is classified R.

The producers of "Jimi Hendrix," which opened yesterday at the Trans-Lux East and West, have avoided the temptation to turn a hearse into a bandwagon. This documentary, about the rock star who died at 27 from an overdose of barbiturates, combines fragments of interviews with Mr. Hendrix's father, friends and acquaintances, with chunks of his performances at the Monterey Pop Festival, Woodstock, the Isle of Wight and others — without attempting a necrological high.

Mr. Hendrix's famous guitar-burning sequences—when he beckons the rising flames with encouraging fingers — are interspersed with the moments when he plucked the strings with his teeth or smashed the instrument, glimpses of him in flagrante delicto with an amplifier, the exhalation of "Sssock it to me" and his parody of the national anthem. Throughout, the reminiscences are fond, reflective, rather gentle. His father recalls him strumming a broom as if it were a guitar; Little Richard says, "At times he used to make my big toe shoot up in my boot," and several pronounce him shy. Early on, his admiration for Bob Dylan is underlined, and he sometimes appears like a black Mick Jagger. Later, he reminds you of no one.

Despite every success, he seems to have fallen between stools: An American who depended on England for his first major recognition, a black man who worried about his black friends' opinion of his music. We're told that black radio stations were at first reluctant to play his recordings, stating that his style did not "relate," while white stations thought it too rugged.

The conflicts mount steadily. Decked in the ruffled shirts and sequined boleros and jeweled headbands, he said that he didn't care what the public thought. But the friends stress that being conspicuous troubled him. Some think that he wanted to shed his spectacular act and "just get people to listen to the music."

•

While the ravages of promotion and the isolation of stardom are evoked, as well as "the load of leeches" that fed on him, one young woman says that Mr. Hendrix was no more self-destructive than a passenger on a plane that crashes. That image lingers. Yet it's difficult to weigh, since his black friends feel that he had "a fast fuse"—a sense shared with many black people that life wouldn't be long, that it was likely to burn out quickly. While this movie doesn't tell us quite enough about Jimi Hendrix the musician, it does convey some of the talent and the anguish and the exuberance that were there.
NORA SAYRE

1973 D 22, 11:1

with our hero, who is dispatched, along with Taylor, in that convent. The outlaws are simply simple-minded assassins who deserve their bloodbaths.

In bemoaning his wife's death, Richard Harris dolefully intones, "They've shot the roses from her cheeks." Unfortunately, neither script, direction nor its shot-up cast look very rosy in "The Deadly Trackers." A. H. WEILER

1973 D 22, 11:1

The Cast

THE SEVEN-UPS, directed and produced by Phil D'Antoni; screenplay by Albert Ruben and Alexander Jacobs, based on a story by Sonny Grosso, executive producers, Kenneth Hilt and Barry Weltz; director of photography, Urs Furrer; editor, Gerald Greenberg; distributed by 20th Century-Fox. Running time: 103 minutes. At the Rivoli Theater, Broadway at 49th Street, and other theaters. This film has been classified PG.

Buddy Manucci	Roy Scheider
Vito	Tony Lo Bianco
Max Kalish	Larry Haines
Barilli	Victor Arnold
Mingo	Jerry Leon
Ansel	Ken Kercheval
Moon	Richard Lynch
Bo	Bill Hickman

By VINCENT CANBY

"The Seven-Ups," which opened yesterday at the Rivoli and other theaters, is about a team of four New York City detectives assigned to trap hoods whose crimes are punishable by jail terms of seven years or more.

Off duty these four detectives are all-American boys. They take their kids to the dentist. They play basketball. They probably drink beer as they sit in front of their TV sets watching the Sunday afternoon games. On duty they are the kind of guys who beat up suspects with short lengths of hose. They break and enter without warrants. They torture a dying gangster in his hospital bed, and they shoot first, usually to kill, so there are no questions to ask afterward.

"The Seven-Ups," the first film to be directed by Phil D'Antoni, the man who produced "The French Connection," is a vicious, mechanical, clumsy thriller. It mindlessly uses the violence that in "The French Connection" could be seen as a manifestation of general urban rot. "The Seven-Ups" has no such thoughts in its head. It treats its vigilante cops with respect, not because of anything they might feel or believe in, but because of what they can do. The characters have even less individuality than performing bears.

The cast includes Roy Scheider, the co-star of "The French Connection," as the head of the Seven-Ups team, and Tony Lo Bianco, who was so good in "The Honeymoon Killers," as a young mortician whose funeral parlor is favored by the mob. The film was photographed entirely in and around New York, but it's just a lot of geography, even when it's flipping by in the obligatory chase sequence.

1973 D 22, 11:2

'Sleeper'— Woody's Best Yet

By VINCENT CANBY

THE arrival of Woody Allen's "Sleeper" last week at the Coronet and Little Carnegie Theaters brings to two the total number of first-class film comedies that have opened in New York this year. The other is Jacques Tati's "Playtime," which was made in 1967 and released here six years late.

Aside from their quality, and the conviction that the world is irretrievably mad, the two films have little in common. Tati is fascinated by the door fitted with an electric eye. Allen worries about meeting a monster who has the body of a crab and the head of a social worker.

Tati's comedy is serene, compassionate, composed in such a far distance that it seems as if he were looking at the world through the wrong end of a telescope. He is amused and benign, too tolerant, perhaps, for his own good, struck by the abstract beauty of the glass and steel city that is, at any given moment, making life progressively more unbearable. Language for Tati has no particular meaning. It is a chorus of noises that become life's soundtrack score.

Woody Allen's comedy is something else entirely. It uses the other end of the telescope. It is close-up, pushy, nervous, always bluffing despair. It is paranoid, fantastic, and as rude as a ride on a New York subway.

Language is immensely important in Allen's films, if not always as a means of communication. His characters don't talk as often as they trade clichés and the wispy ends of muddled ideas. When the character is Allen himself, he deals in free associations so sweeping that they would add 10 years to the treatment of any ordinarily neurotic analysand.

I suspect that it is this feeling of things seen in close-up in Allen's films, as well as their lunatic dialogue, which make his work seem so urgently funny today. All of us, but especially younger audiences, have been more or less conditioned by television. We want to *hear* comedy even if we can't see it very clearly. Thus a Tati movie, which makes almost all its demands upon our eyes, doesn't seem topical even though the setting is a city of awful, uncompromising up-to-dateness.

"Sleeper" follows "Take The Money and Run," "Bananas" and "Everything You Always Wanted to Know About Sex" as Allen's fourth film as star, director and writer (or as co-writer, in this case with Marshall Brickman), and it is the best of the lot.

It runs for something over 85 minutes but it seems shorter than most two-reelers, which it evokes not only in its title credits (plain white type spelling out the names on a black screen) but also in its high-handed way with plot, logic and character.

It's the nightmare story of Miles Monroe (Allen), the co-owner of the Happy Carrot Health Food Restaurant in Greenwich Village, who goes into St. Vincent's Hospital in 1973 for a minor ulcer operation and wakes up 200 years later in an American police state. When something went wrong during the operation, the hospital people had put

Miles into a deep-freeze capsule, from which he's defrosted in the year 2173, his feet neatly wrapped in aluminum foil.

"Sleeper" is Woody's "2001," in terms of budget and fancy futuristic effects— cars that resemble giant plastic turtles and houses that seem not to have been built, but dropped by huge cement cows. Although the production notes report that Woody shot the film in various parts of Colorado and northern California, most of the landscapes have that bland, dreamy look of barren Hollywood hills where people like Chaplin, Keaton and Laurel and Hardy shot their films in the 1920s.

I say dreamy because no matter how fast or how far Laurel and Hardy ran to escape some menace in one of their two-reelers, the scenery never changed much. There was always the suspicion that they had been running in place, standing still.

Miles was apparently frozen in St. Vincent's in New York, but he is thawed out in what seems to be California in the new society that evolved after the holocaust. (By way of explanation, someone reports that it's thought that a man named Albert Shanker had got hold of a nuclear warhead.) The country is ruled by a dictator called The Leader, who shows himself on TV screens in impressive profile shots and sounds like someone giving a sermonette.

All the men are impotent and the women are frigid, which necessitates the use of orgasm boxes. Looking like old-fashioned hot-water heaters, the boxes stand in the corners of the all-white living rooms of the well-to-do. When Luna (Diane Keaton), a beautiful but untalented right-wing poet, tells Miles that she earned her Ph.D. in oral sex, it's clear that she studied something as dead as ancient Greek.

Although the year is 2173,

Miles-Woody is obviously a hero for our time—when nothing remains sacred. He is sneaky, sex-obsessed, fearful, parsimonious, honorable in small ways ("I've never forced myself onto a blind person," he tells Luna), misinformed when necessary for comedy (he identifies a picture of Charles DeGaulle as "a famous French chef") and sometimes a wise-acre. He identifies Norman Mailer as "a great writer who left his ego to the Harvard Medical School."

He is also—in the tradition of great slapstick comedians — unable to cope with machinery and gadgets, which, in the new society, include flying belts and robot servants and robot dogs. It is a small but important point of the film that the members of the new society never are able to cope much better than Miles. When two impressively armed policemen finally corner Woody (who has been working against his will for the underground), they aim their guns and pull their triggers, only to blow themselves up.

Not so much in the tradition of the great slapstick comedians, he also wins the girl, who, as played by Miss Keaton, becomes very much worth winning—a funny, intense, reckless sort of woman who, by the end, gives every indication of being as full of idiosyncracies as Miles.

"Sleeper" is so good that as of this moment I vow to read no more material pretending to lament the fact that Woody Allen hasn't yet made the comedy of which he is capable. They also said that about Fields, and it's nonsense. Who knows who is capable of what?

It may also be about time to stop worrying about whether or not people 50 years from now will find Woody Allen funny. One betrays a rather alarming sense of insecurity to worry about generations yet unborn who might begrudge us our belly laughs today. "Sleeper" is an immensely funny film.

1973 D 23, II:3:7

'Don't Look Now' Will Scare You—Subtly

By STEPHEN FARBER

ENGLISH cinema seems to be enjoying a sudden burst of creativity. In the last few years, England has produced three extraordinarily talented filmmakers—John Boorman, Ken Russell and Nicolas Roeg. They have little in common except for their visual flair, their rejection of the literary conventions that still dominate most films, and their desire to experiment with a purely cinematic vocabulary.

Of these three directors, Nicolas Roeg's brilliant visual imagination would have been easiest to predict, for he began as a cameraman, and was recognized as one of the world's great cinematographers for his work on "Fahrenheit 451," "Far From the Madding Crowd" and "Petulia." In 1970, he co-directed "Performance" (with Donald Cammell),

the most provocative study of changing sexual mores on film, and in 1971, in Australia, he made "Walkabout," a dazzling romantic lament for nature and primitive life.

His new film, "Don't Look Now," confirms what the other two films had already indicated—that Roeg is a major contemporary artist. Like "Performance" and "Walkabout," "Don't Look Now" has been underrated by some critics who still do not know how to *look* at movies, but whether or not it is a commercial success, it will keep turning up in underground film programs and classic revival series. For this disturbing thriller about second sight is just possibly the most subtle and sophisticated horror film ever made, and a profoundly unsettling warning of the precariousness of everything we take for granted.

Roeg's three movies tackle very dif-

ferent subjects, but taken together, they express a remarkably coherent vision of experience. All three films focus on characters forced outside the orderly, well-regulated world that shelters them, disoriented and transformed by their ventures into the unfamiliar. Roeg wants to undermine our faith in the national, intellectual, skeptical tradition that is the cornerstone of Western culture — English culture, in particular; he sets out to discover the primitive, sensual, more mysterious sources of life that modern urban society has obliterated.

Over the last decade, a great many euphoric sages and plastic gurus have mindlessly celebrated the irrational or the supernatural, promising an easy salvation through Jesus or LSD. Roeg's mysticism is of a less comforting variety; he is a fierce visionary artist who unblinkingly contemplates all extremes —barbarism and madness, as well as ecstasy. And although his films are concerned with the irrational, they are notably hard-headed, thoughtfully conceived and rigorously controlled; the dream imagery has its own irrefutable logic.

"Don't Look Now" works within a well-worn genre; it uses elements that other horror films have used—ESP, premonitions and warnings from the dead,

a mad killer on the loose—not for cheap thrills, but to build a fabric of anxiety that calls all appearances into question. The plot itself, faithfully transcribed from a Daphne du Maurier story by screenwriters Allan Scott and Chris Bryant, is contrived; there are moments when the potboiler machinery still creaks a little.

For the most part, however, Roeg succeeds in transforming the pulp material into a richly evocative personal vision of possibilities of evil. And thanks to excellent performances by Donald Sutherland and Julie Christie, this film has a human center that most horror films lack.

The movie opens with the shocking accidental drowning of a little girl, and the most urgent question it raises is how people come to terms with death. After their daughter's death, John and Laura Baxter try to resume their normal lives, but they are still edgy, grief-stricken, and troubled by feelings of guilt and responsibility. In Venice, where John is restoring a 16th-century church, they come under the spell of two weird English sisters, one of whom is blind and psychic and claims to have had a vision of their dead daughter laughing. Laura collapses from the shock, but her tem-

Julie Christie, left, accompanied by Hilary Mason and Clelia Matania, rides in a funeral procession on the Grand Canal in "Don't Look Now"
"'Don't Look Now' confirms what 'Performance' and 'Walkabout' indicated—that director Nicolas Roeg is a major contemporary artist."

porary breakdown releases all her suppressed feelings; afterward, she feels relieved—she has finally received some of the consolation that she needs. That afternoon she lights a candle for her daughter in church, not as an affirmation of a new found religious belief, but simply to acknowledge an experience that her intellect cannot explain.

John, on the other hand, refuses to surrender his innate skepticism. "Our daughter is dead," he repeats doggedly, as if a hard-headed recital of the fact could somehow make sense of her death. His character is torn by contradictions: he has the gift of second sight, like the blind sister, but he ignores the warnings from the unconscious. Even his work restoring churches suggests his subliminal attraction to supernatural possibilities, though he performs his jobs with an icy, scholarly detachment.

Roeg is not advocating a return to religion or an immersion in the occult; his point is simply that reason is inadequate to deal with some essential questions—like the meaning of death. Although the search for a transcendent, supra-rational understanding is treacherous and possibly futile, it is still one of the deepest human impulses. In his stubborn skepticism, John denies part of what it means to be alive.

Challenging the authority of reason, Roeg uses all the resources of film to heighten the feeling of the indefinable menace in the everyday. He introduces recurring visual motifs — broken glass, death by water, the color red, headless statues and faceless mosaics in a church —with a painter's assurance.

In particular, Roeg gives a vivid sense of Venice in winter, a poisoned, over-ripe city of darkness. The juxtaposition of images — the crumbling palaces, a Coca-Cola sign, rats swimming in the canal and a child's doll abandoned at the water's edge, a hooded figure disappearing under a bridge, a corpse lifted from the slime—captures the city's engulfing, dread atmosphere. Searching the city, John retraces his steps through deserted squares and alleys, lost in a labyrinth without a pattern; the strange sounds—water lapping, a baby crying, snatches of laughter and pop tunes, the squealing of hungry cats, footsteps of people who never appear—intensify the mood of disorientation.

One of Roeg's unique talents, aside from his ability to evoke atmosphere, is his original approach to cinematic time. In some key scenes Roeg suspends time. When John puts Laura on a boat for the airport, the romantic shots of the boat caught in the early morning light seem to freeze the moment, conveying the emotional significance of this parting for John, the inexplicable sense of loss that he feels.

At other moments, Roeg uses cross-cutting to give us the sensation of being in two places—or two times—at once. Consider the already-celebrated love scene, which even in its slightly modified American version retains tremendous impact. Roeg enriches the sequence by intercutting the lovemaking with shots of John and Laura dressing for dinner.

This fragmentation of time suggests the way in which a satisfying sexual experience floods the memory, suffusing

casual moments afterward—Laura putting on make-up or John pouring a drink —with a lingering erotic charge.

At the same time, the intercutting adds a trace of the melancholy to the passionate lovemaking, foreshadowing John and Laura's imminent separation, and underscoring the evanescence of their moment of rapture. Roeg's complex, highly developed technique is far more expressive than straightforward linear storytelling.

It is because of this sustained artistry that the shock ending — which could have turned out to be nothing more than a gimmick — carries such force. John has resisted the subliminal reminders of his dead daughter that have haunted him throughout the film, but finally willing to face his own demons, he pursues a tiny figure in a red raincoat, helplessly drawn to this phantom from beyond the grave.

The nightmare chase along the canals, through doorways shrouded in fog, deeper into the maze, is one of the screen's classic scenes of terror — somewhat reminiscent of the great climax to Dickens's "Bleak House," which also involves the pursuit of a mysterious figure through the dark, wintry streets of London. Dickens transformed lurid melodrama into art of apocalyptic intensity; no artist has ever had a stronger sense of terror and evil. So it is high praise to say that the climax to "Don't Look Now" has a Dickensian power; it is a devastating look into the abyss.

Yet the very last image is curiously serene and darkly beautiful — a golden bird leading ebony-black boats in a magisterial funeral procession down the Grand Canal. This conclusion, touched with mythical associations, moves beyond horror to a kind of tragic understanding. To confront the unknown is terrifying, but there is at least a measure of comfort in knowing the truth. "Don't Look Now" does not aim to convert anyone to a belief in the occult; but by the end of the film, even the most skeptical may feel chilled, uneasy, shaken, unable to still the doubts and fears stirred in the dark, secret places of the imagination.

1973 D 23, II:15:1

'Hell Up in Harlem' Tracks Crime Czar

"Hell Up in Harlem" has the right title as a slaughter pile-up, with Fred Williamson as the super-duper "black Caesar of the underworld." He finally adds the most corrupt man in town, a fictional District Attorney of New York County, to his personal pyramid of corpses. The D. A. gets his, along with most of the other whites in the picture who dare to open their mouths.

There is a quietly vivid performance by Julius W. Harris, as a kind of unwilling Harlem godfather. Mr. Williamson himself, who also

The Cast

THAT MAN BOLT, directed by Henry Levin and David Lowell Rich; screenplay, Quentin Werty and Charles Johnson; story by Mr. Johnson; director of photography, Gerald Perry Finnerman; film editors, Carl Pingitore, Robert F. Shugrue; music, Charles Bernstein; produced by Bernard Schwartz; released by Universal Pictures. At the DeMille Theater, Broadway and 47th Street. Running time: 103 minutes. This film is classified R.
Jefferson Bolt .... Fred Williamson
Griffiths .... Byron Webster
Dominique Kuan ...... Mike Mayama
Samantha Nightingale .... Teresa Graves
Kumada .... Satoshi Nakamura
Carter .... John Orchard
Connie .... Jack Ging
Spider .... Ken Kazama

It hasn't been much of a year for Jim Brown. First O. J. Simpson bettered his National Football League rushing record. And now—judging by "That Man Bolt," which opened last week at the DeMille—Fred Williamson is expanding his inroads on Mr. Brown's hegemony over the black action genre that has become one of the gilt-edge Bonds of cinema in the seventies.

Already Mr. Williamson has surpassed Mr. Brown's statistics for emotional range (two: menacing and furious). He brings to his role as Bolt, the globe-trotting freelance courier charged with delivery of an unhealthy cash cargo of $1-million, a ready smile, an unforced display of charm and a redeeming glint of mockery of the time-honored incredible foolishness in which he is enmeshed.

And when it comes to muscle, Mr. Williamson appears every bit as ready as Mr. Brown to challenge Playboy's Little Annie Fanny for involvement in pectoral-baring episodes.

Lavishly set in Macao, Los Angeles, Las Vegas and Hong Kong, "That Man Bolt" offers enough local color to rival the side of an IRT No. 1 train, a display of martial arts sufficient, perhaps, to slake the tears of devotees of the late Bruce Lee, violence, unsullied by gore, sex on sight and a touch of humor.

It has all been said, done and seen before, and escapists will probably never tire of it.

LAWRENCE VAN GELDER

had another movie, "That Man Bolt, opening yesterday, certainly gets around New York in this one murderously trying to "make it a decent place to live for everybody." He must have meant every survivor. The line got a hearty laugh one morning last week at the midtown Cinerama Theater. The film is also showing at the R.K.O. 86th Street Twin 2, at Lexington Avenue.

HOWARD THOMPSON

1973 D 24, 21:1

THE STING, directed by George Roy Hill; screenplay by David S. Ward; produced by Tony Bill and Michael and Julia Phillips; director of photography, Robert Surtees; editor, William Reynolds; music, Marvin Hamlisch; a Richard D. Zanuck-David Brown presentation, distributed by Universal Pictures. Running time: 129 minutes. At Loew's State 2 Theater, Broadway at 45 Street, Loew's Cine Theater, Third Avenue near 86th Street, Murray Hill Theater, 34th Street at Third Avenue, and other theaters. This film has been classified PG.
Henry Gondoroff .... Paul Newman
Johnny Hooker .... Robert Redford
Doyle Lonnegan .... Robert Shaw
Lieut. William Snyder ... Charles Durning
J. J. Singleton .... Ray Walston
Billie .... Eileen Brennan
Kid Twist .... Harold Gould
Eddie Niles .... John Heffernan
F.B.I. Agent Polk .... Dana Elcar

By VINCENT CANBY

"The Sting," which opened yesterday at Loew's State 2 and other theaters, re-teams the director (George Roy Hill) and stars (Paul Newman and Robert Redford) of "Butch Cassidy and the Sundance Kid" in a comedy about a couple of exuberant confidence men operating in and around Chicago in 1936.

"The Sting" looks and sounds like a musical comedy from which the songs have been removed, leaving only a background score of old-fashioned, toe-tapping piano rags that as easily evoke the pre-World War I teens as the nineteen-thirties.

A lot of the other period details aren't too firmly anchored in time, but the film is so good-natured, so obviously aware of everything it's up to, even its own picturesque frauds, that I opt to go along with it. One forgives its unrelenting efforts to charm, if only because "The Sting" itself is a kind of con game, devoid of the poetic aspirations that weighed down "Butch Cassidy and the Sundance Kid."

Mr. Newman and Mr. Redford, dressed in best, fit-to-kill, snap-brim hat, thirties spendor, looking like a couple of guys in old Arrow shirt ads, are more or less reprising their roles in "Butch Cassidy."

Mr. Newman is Henry Gondoroff, the older con artist in charge of the instruction of Johnny Hooker (Mr. Redford), the bright, eager, younger man who yearns to make what the movie calls the Big Con (swindle), the

Paul Newman, as a con artist, playing poker in "The Sting."

way tap dancers in the movies about the twenties wanted to play the Palace.

Their quarry is a ruthless, vain, fastidious New York racketeer named Doyle Lonnegan, played by Robert Shaw in the broad manner in which the film was conceived by David S. Ward, who wrote the screenplay, and realized by Mr. Hill.

The director supplements the period sets and costumes with elaborate technical devices to move from one scene into another: wipes, iris-outs, images that turn like pages. Separating sequences are title cards that recall Norman Rockwell's Saturday Evening Post covers. It's all a little too much, but excess is an essential part of the film's style.

"The Sting" has a conventional narrative, with a conventional beginning, middle and end, but what one remembers are the set pieces of the sort that can make a slapped-together Broadway show so entertaining. These include a hilarious, thoroughly crooked poker game on the Twentieth Century Limited in which Henry blows his nose on his tie to the horror of Lonnegan, as well as a chase that lasts approximately two minutes, and the final swindle, the mechanics of which are still not one too clear to me.

The only woman with a substantial role in the film is Eileen Brennan, who plays a madam with a heart of gold and enough time off to be able to assist the stars in the

final con. "The Sting" is not the kind of film that takes its women very seriously, and the continuing popularity of these male-male co-starring teams should, I suppose, probably prompt some solemn analysis.

It is not, I suspect, a terrible perversion of the romantic movie-team concept idealized by William Powell and Myrna Loy, Clark Gable and Lana Turner but, rather, a variation on the old Dr. Gillespie-Dr. Kildare relationship, with a bit of Laurel and Hardy thrown in. It is also apparently very good box office.

1973 D 26, 60:1

The Cast

MAGNUM FORCE, directed by Ted Post; screenplay by John Milius and Michael Cimino; story by Mr. Milius, based on the character created by Harry Julian Fink and Rita M. Fink; director of photography, Frank Stanley; film editor, Ferris Webster; music, Lalo Schifrin; produced by Robert Daley; released by Warner Brothers. At the Criterion Theater, Broadway at 45th Street and the 86th Street East Theater at Third Avenue. Running time: 124 minutes. This film is classified R.
Harry Calahan...........Clint Eastwood
Lieutenant Briggs..........Hal Holbrook
McCoy ....Mitchell Ryan
Davis ....David Soul
Early Smith...............Felton Perry

By NORA SAYRE

Let's hear it for hypocrisy —or at least, for our old national tradition of hypocrisy refined. Before World War I, sexy scenes were fine onstage as long as they occurred in biblical shows; later, Cecil B. De Mille exploited the same formula in movies. Now, we can enjoy the lushest baths of violence on the screen in the name of law and order. Of course the principle is ancient. Yet it gains more sophistication with each decade.

Yesterday's Christmas package, "Magnum Force," which was unwrapped at the Criterion Theater and the 86th Street East, is a sequel to "Dirty Harry." Harry (Clint Eastwood) is the policeman who kills to protect the public from guns other than his own. The movie is a muddle of morality. "Somebody is trying to put the courts out of business" by rubbing out corrupt labor leaders, racketeers, and narcotics tycoons —the scum that flourishes in a liberal society where the courts fail to prosecute them. However, righteous policemen who kill "hoodlums" are "crucified by those young bastards at the D.A.'s office." Follow that verb.

Harry discovers that there's an execution squad within the police department. Hence it's his duty to bump off five policemen who are

equally keen on liquidating him. (After a red herring slightly larger than a sperm whale, and music that precedes each killing with all the subtlety of the Valkyries' entrance theme, no audience is going to swoon with astonishment.)

Throughout, there's a stress on dear old hubris: Harry earnestly repeats that "a man't got to know his limitations." Thus, it's reasoned that the killings he commits are justified — "There's nothing wrong with shooting, as long as the right people get shot" — but murderers do have to be discriminating.

Since the Supreme Court ruling on obscenity, we've seen a predictable acceleration of violence as a substitute for sex. There's little joy between the sheets in "Magnum Force." But bullets in bare breasts are still acceptable. Topless murderees in a swimming pool or nudes stoned at "$900 an ounce" reinforce the morality: people who take off their clothes may have been asking for it. There's also a gratuitous murder of a prostitute, climaxed with a shot of her killer's face grinning through her spread legs.

Young men who hold up a store have "hippy-looking hair" and some skyjackers resemble folk singers. The police lieutenant who warns against brutality (Hal Holbrook, behaving rather like a petulant professor of humanities), turns out to be the most demonic death-dealer of all. Still, the movie strains for some liberal seasoning: Harry's partner is black, and some young policemen suspected of oddness are defended for their talents: Harry says, "If the rest of you could shoot like them, I wouldn't care if the whole damn department was queer."

Mr. Eastwood's unshakable cool—as he dismantles a bomb or refuses a local anesthetic for seven stitches—makes me miss Richard Widmark's style in playing this kind of part. Mr. Widmark's eyes, which appeared to have been drilled into his head, often looked appalled—even frightened or frantic—in a desperate situation. But all that Mr. Eastwood can manage is a frown that suggests tension. The excitement is mainly in the camerawork, which is stunning—the sense of motion in space, as cars bowl over bridges or a helicopter rises, lends an exhilaration that's absent from the script.

You may pause before hastening your children off to this movie. But certainly policemen shouldn't see it. The picture merely thickens the soup of confusion about their role. However, "Magnum Force" might be interesting for caterers. Harry asserts

that San Francisco airport "has the greatest burgers in town" — and that's a mystery which is never fully unraveled.

1973 D 26, 60:1

The Cast

KEEP ON ROCKIN', a film by D. A. Pennebaker; photography, Barry Bergthorson, Jim Desmond, Randy Franklin, Richard Leacock, Richard Leiterman, Roger Murphy, Roger Neuwirth and D. A. Pennebaker; production, David McMullin, Peter Hansen, Mark Woodcock and Chris Darymple; distributed by Pennebaker, Inc. At the First Avenue Screening Room, at 60th Street. Running time: 95 minutes. This film has not been classified.
With Chuck Berry, Diddley Richard, Jerry Lee Lewis, Bo Diddley, introduction by Janis Joplin and Jimi Hendrix.

By NORA SAYRE

Surely, nostalgia is fattening. Mooning over what's bygone hardly stimulates the mental muscles—instead, it tends to stiffen the perceptions, to swell the spiritual flab. But time-traveling is very good exercise. When you're required to weave back and forth between the past and present, to study what has and hasn't changed, the consciousness can be limbered, clarified. D. A. Pennebaker's "Keep On Rockin'" affords us some excellent time-traveling, since it recreates the September, 1969, Toronto Rock and Roll Revival. At that festival, the music of the mid-nineteen-fifties captivated an Aquarian audience—just midway in time between Woodstock and Altamont.

This fine documentary— the first of the First Avenue Screening Room's program of pictures that haven't received adequate attention— will appear tomorrow and Saturday. The movie is prefaced by some footage of Janis Joplin and Jimi Hendrix: two ghostly guides to the musical past that preceded them. Then we're pitched into 1955 and 1956, with the swamp rhythms of Bo Diddley and the rockabilly of Jerry Lee Lewis, who tells his fans, "Ah love yew like a hawg loves slop." We're back in an era when the guitar was handled tenderly, rather than set afire, and it's a shock to see a short-haired violinist in a tie.

Chuck Berry's mournful, worn face splits with smiles as he lets loose with "Sweet Little Sixteen." Lights spring off Little Richard's mirrored tunic as he crows, screams and unleashes some falsetto whoops before he zeros in on "Tutti Frutti." His body glistens with sweat as he strips and hurls his garments to the crowd, holding up each garment like a teasing auctioneer.

Rock songs in praise of rock, lines about having fun tonight: The fact and the act of rockin' 'n' rollin' emerge as the prime theme of these lyrics. To an ear that was later formed by Bob Dylan, the Beatles and the Rolling Stones, most of the music is

far too repetitive to be exciting. But it's a pleasure to watch these seasoned professionals, whose energy equals their experience. Their songs show that they came from a time when people wanted extremely simple things. This is solid, reliable stuff—it seems unlikely that listeners could use it to summon any kind of high. Hence, it's intriguing that the very young (also very white) audience of 1969 was delighted by this blast from the past.

Mr. Pennebaker's film is an anthology of smiles: again and again, the camera closes in on beaming faces. (Sometimes, he begins with a dancing torso, or a pair of thighs and knees—we meet the head a few moments later.) We can't really tell if the film maker looked for innocence and stressed it, or if that was the over-all character of the crowd. But no one on screen looks druggy, most of the skin is fresh and clear, and there's even a flash of shaved armpits. Did the music of the fifties attract a rather sheltered audience in the late sixties? Or was this an early sign that some were eagerly retreating from the turbulence of that period?

Mr. Pennebaker, whose movies include "Monterey Pop" (1968) and "Don't Look Back" (Bob Dylan in 1965), both produced with Richard Leacock, is a specialist in observing changes. So we trust his instinct and his eye. And this film shows a sensitivity to individuals that some rock movies—such as "Woodstock" —lacked. Just when the press was awash with theories about death trips and the counter culture, Mr. Pennebaker witnessed something entirely different. And his work does tend toward prescience—to record what will be important before most of the public is aware of it.

1973 D 27, 49:1

THE EXORCIST, directed by William Friedkin; produced and written by William Peter Blatty, based on his novel; executive producer, Noel Marshall; director of photography, Owen Roizman (Iraq sequences, Billy Williams); supervising film editor, J. J. Leondopoulos; editors, Evan Lottman, Norman Gay; distributed by Warner Brothers. Running time: 121 minutes. At the Cinema I Theater, Third Avenue near 60th Street. This film has been classified R.
Chris MacNeil.............Ellen Burstyn
Father Merrin............Max von Sydow
Lt. Kinderman............Lee J. Cobb
Sharon ....Kitty Winn
Burke Dennings.........Jack MacGowran
Father Karras.............Jason Miller
Regan ....Linda Blair
Father Dyer......Rev. William O'Malley
President of University,
........................Rev. T. Bermingham

By VINCENT CANBY

The Georgetown dinner party being given by Chris MacNeil (Ellen Burstyn), a Hollywood movie actress making a film in Washington, is going beautifully, with diplomats, astronauts, Senators and show people carrying on in high style. A movie director gets drunk and tries to beat up the butler while a swinging Jesuit priest plays the piano for a sing-along.

Why Feel Sorry For These Hoods?

By FOSTER HIRSCH

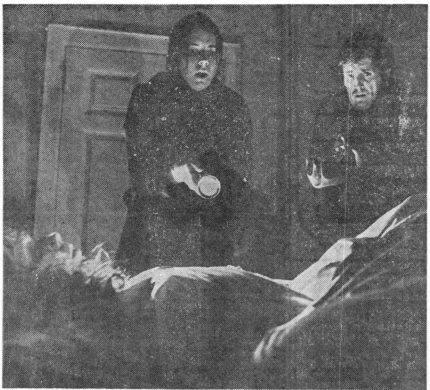

Linda Blair, lying in the foreground, Kitty Winn and Jason Miller

Everything is as it should be until Regan (Linda Blair), Chris's 12-year-old daughter, appears in the middle of the drawing room in her nightdress. As Chris watches appalled, Regan fixes her eyes on the astronaut, urinates on the floor and says:

"You're going to die up there."

That's more or less the first big scene in William Friedkin's film version of "The Exorcist," a chunk of elegant occultist claptrap that opened yesterday at the Cinema I. However, lots of other peculiar things have gone on before. A statue in the Catholic church down the street has been desecrated. Little Regan's bed has been bouncing around so antically she's been unable to sleep at night, and there have been unexplained noises in the attic of Chris's Georgetown mansion.

The devil, it seems, for all his supposed powers, can't break and enter without sounding like Laurel and Hardy trying to move a piano.

●

"The Exorcist," the story of the attempts to save the life of the demonically possessed Regan, is a practically impossible film to sit through, but not necessarily because it treats diabolism with the kind of dumb piety movie makers once lavished on the stories of saints.

It establishes a new low for grotesque special effects, all of which, I assume, have some sort of religious approval since two Jesuit priests, who are listed as among the film's technical advisers, also appear in the film as actors.

Among the sights to which the audience is treated are Regan, her face contorted and parched by the devil inside, vomiting what looks to be condensed split-pea soup onto an exorcising priest, and her paroxysms of fury as she jabs a crucifix into herself and shoves her mother's head down under her bloodied nightgown. In the context of this kind of spectacular nonsense, a carefully detailed sequence showing the child undergoing an encephalogram is almost therapeutic.

William Peter Blatty, who produced the film and adapted his best-selling novel for the screen, has succeeded in leaving out very few of the kind of ridiculous details that, I suspect, would have earned a less expensive, more skeptical film an X rating instead of the R rating that mysteriously has been achieved.

"The Exorcist" is not an unintelligently put-together film, which makes one all the more impatient with it.

●

The producer and the director have gone whole hog on (and over) their budget, which included the financing of a location trip to Iraq to shoot a lovely, eerie prefatory sequence at an archeological dig that is, as far as I can see, not especially essential to the business that comes after.

The cast is made up of some excellent actors: Ellen Burstyn (who is becoming America's answer to Glenda Jackson), Max von Sydow as the old Catholic priest who also functions as chief exor-

cist, the late Jack MacGowran as the director of the film within, Jason Miller as the priest who attains success through imitation of Jesus, and Lee J. Cobb as a kindly Jewish detective.

The care that Mr. Friedkin and Mr. Blatty have taken with the physical production, and with the rhythm of the narrative, which achieves a certain momentum through a lot of fancy, splintery crosscutting, is obviously intended to persuade us to suspend belief. But to what end? To marvel at the extent to which audiences will go to escape boredom by shock and insult.

According to trade reports, "The Exorcist" cost about $10-million. The money could have been better spent subsidizing a couple of beds at the Paine-Whitney Clinic.

1973 D 27, 46:1

EVER SINCE Peter Bogdanovich used a sad little rural movie house as the chief symbol of "The Last Picture Show," a number of young American directors have been drawing on their love for movies—and for moviegoing—as both subject and metaphor. In the Bogdanovich tradition, a new breed of young filmmakers, whose work clearly shows that they have been to the movies often and lovingly, are signing their pictures with the imprint of the buff.

In a few cases (John Milius' "Dillinger," James William Guercio's "Electra Glide in Blue," Brian De Palma's "Sisters"), the movies have been so indebted to other movies that they never succeed in finding a reel life of their own. Almost frame for frame, "Dillinger" was a re-play of "Bonnie and Clyde." In similarly incestuous fashion, "Electra Glide in Blue" confronted "Easy Rider," reversing the thematic thrust of Dennis Hopper's landmark road movie by making a good-guy cop the victim of trigger-happy freaks. "Sisters"—Hitchcock gone wild—offered baroque variations on "Psycho" and "Rear Window."

Movies that are really about other movies are not always so obvious, however; consider the case of the extravagantly overpraised "Mean Streets," Martin Scorsese's ode to the hoods of Little Italy. Big city ethnic naturalism set against crime thriller operatics, the movie ends up as a kind of "Marty Meets the Godfather." Fifties social realism, urban grittiness, the danger of life in the slums—the spirit of "On the Waterfront" hovers over the film. Scorsese's hyped-up actors perform in a manic style that crosses Actors Studio Method with home-movie improvisation: Kazan and Cassavetes are clearly two of the director's heroes.

Scorsese's movie-consciousness drenches the film. "Mean Streets" opens in the style of a home movie, the characters cavorting self-consciously in the streets and tenements that are the film's thematically important locations. When the characters get tense, when the pressure's on, or when they don't know what else to do, they go to the movies. It's almost a rule by now that buff filmmakers pay their respects to their favorite movies within the framework of their own pictures, and true to form, Scorsese shows us posters for "Point Blank," John Boorman's tough, stylish urban crime thriller, and for "Husbands," Cassavetes' improvised domestic drama of middle-aged crisis. This is a calculated homage that alerts us to Scorsese's own intentions of blending domestic naturalism with urban crime.

A moviegoer who grew up in Little Italy, Scorsese mixes nostalgia for the streets of his childhood with nostalgia

Foster Hirsch is a freelance writer.

for movies, and the result is a pot-pourri of quotations from other films, a flashy movie that earnestly seeks but never sustains an individual flavor. Reminiscences from other hours at the movies keep intruding.

Beneath its Mafia trappings, "Mean Streets" aims for a "true life" study of Italian life in the Big City. Much of the now easy, now tense banter among the buddies whose misfortunes are the movie's main concern is strictly Paddy Chayefsky "slice of life" territory. The memory of "Whaddya wanna do tonight, Marty?" "I dunno, whadda you wanna do, Angie?" hangs over the film. The small talk that goes nowhere, the meandering conversations, revive the old matter—thrashed out a dozen years ago when some critics were unhappy with "L'Avventura," of imitative form: how do you present characters who are bored or who have tedious lives without being boring and tedious yourself?

Scorsese certainly hasn't solved the problem: his hoods are an aimless, distracted bunch, and he has fallen back on the familiar device of shaping the rhythm of his movie to that of his characters. Like his bums, the movie goes in circles; the roundabout motion is supposed to be a hip, mod' way to present purposeless lives, and critics, forgetting the Continental Italians, have responded as if the director has discovered a new mode.

Scorsese is out to make a little people's crime movie, a mini-"Godfather," but hasn't Coppola's great epic movie almost used up the field? Can a director even choose a Mafia setting without courting the charge of imitation, cashing in on the big one? Scorsese's characters, at any rate, are ethnic stereotypes, stage Italians as predictable and as overstated in their flamboyant gestures and earthy speech as stage Irish or stage Jewish.

Robert De Niro, whose work as the most psychotic hood has been widely praised, is a particular victim of the movie's received notions of Italians and of slum kids. De Niro is a virtuoso actor, but, as Johnny Boy, he's not an original: the territory has already been staked out, classically, by Marlon Brando in "On the Waterfront." De Niro uses the same slum-drenched diction, the same restless, shifting movements, the same distracted sidelong glances. He's unquestionably found a rhythm for his character, he's obviously explored motivation, but his work, for all its terrific pace and energy, for all its bravura histrionics, is marked, indelibly, Brando-imitative. Like the movie in which it's the glittering centerpiece, the performance is too studied, too influenced by too many movies.

The ending of "Bonnie and Clyde" has had a pernicious influence on films; since Arthur Penn's powerhouse finale, which his protagonists are riddled with bullets, how many movies have died with a brutal slaying that elevates the victims to heroic and even legendary status? "Dillinger" and "Electra Glide in Blue" are two immediate examples and "Mean Streets," in which two buddies and the girl are shot down, slaughtered, by a vengeful rival, is for the same mythic heightening.

It's a powerfully staged scene, but it's manipulative, conferring heroic stature on characters who simply don't qualify.

Why are we asked to sympathize with these guys anyway? Johnny Boy is an idiot and his friend Charlie is only slightly deeper. Their prototype, Terry Malloy in "On the Waterfront," earns our admiration; capable of moral growth, he becomes a true rebel-hero. Johnny Boy and Charlie don't change, they don't have any perception about their crummy, crime-ridden lives, and yet we're asked to respond affirmatively to these blunted characters.

Enthusiastic critics have even taken the characters' amoral, valueless lives as an indication of modern times, a confirmation that heroism in Watergate America is an impossibility. Similarly, the film's corrupt environment, the pervasive rot that infects all these small-time hoods and their shabby, menacing streets, has been accepted as a potent metaphor for a benighted country.

But the hopelessness and the cynicism that the movie hits us with are facile, self-congratulatory in their would-be hip bleakness, and it may be that the country's present mood has prepared audiences for accepting the film as a revelation of a dark national consciousness. No heroes, no values, universal corruption—and a lot of people are buying this as a profound and original truth.

Following his mod instincts, Scorsese uses a flashy, elliptical style as a defense *against* content; he disguises his minimal story line and his defeated, uncomplicated characters by keeping us at a distance from both. The material is so plain, in fact, that it has little else to go on *except* its non-communicative delivery, its fractured, spliced, deliberately non-climactic narrative method which tosses us mere bits of characterizations and scraps of story.

Because he isn't out to make a conventional Mafia thriller, Scorsese withholds conventional narrative links and clues: the idea is to keep us guessing. That method may have been new with Pinter, or with Antonioni, or even with Richard Lester in "Petulia" (where fancy form disguised dangerously thin material), but the ploy is by now thoroughly tarnished.

Like George Lucas in "American Graffiti," the director is presenting, in a tone that wavers uncomfortably between proud documentary reconstruction and satiric distortion, a milieu that he grew up in. (Like "American Graffiti," "Mean Streets" is a memoir, only the settings have less universal appeal.) Here, the bars, the garbage-strewn streets, the dingy apartments, the church, and of course the local movie house correspond to Mel's Drive-In and to the small-town main drag with its cruising cars of "American Graffiti." In both movies, it's the settings that count, that supply the drama, the color, even the "explanation" for the characters. But like Lucas, Scorsese depends on the richly detailed background to compensate for the week narrative and the uncertain character development.

Going to the movies has given Scorsese a genuine movie sensibility. Like all the young directors currently enjoying praise that exceeds their accomplishments, Scorsese is talented; he has flair; he knows a lot about movie acting; he has a vivid feeling for place; dank and grimy, his film looks exactly right. Next time, or the time after that, he will be capable of distinguished work.

1973 D 30, II:11:1

Why Not Homage To the Movie Disasters of '73?

By VINCENT CANBY

MOVIES about male comradeship were very big this year. So were movies that looked fondly back to what are usually called simpler, more innocent times. Women got it in the neck, often from women, and all America suddenly didn't know it was waiting to see the screen version of "Jonathan Livingston Seagull." The huge billboard advertising the Hall Bartlett production had a longer run on Times Square than the film itself had at the Sutton.

Because it's still a little early to name the best films of the year, this week will be devoted to the commemoration of the year's disasters, as well as those men and women who made them all possible. Don't snicker. It isn't easy to fail on a grand scale. When you have a lot of money to spend, there's always the possibility you'll make a mistake and hire someone with talent.

The following awards were conceived with prejudice and are recorded in bad taste, in no particular order of malice or unimportance. To:

James Aubrey, The Movie Mogul of The Year Award, for putting M-G-M out of the film production-distribution business for all intents and purposes. It took four years, but he did it.

"Hitler: The Last Ten Days," The Single Most Arresting Line of Dialogue Award. Says an admiring Eva Braun to her intended, as Berlin is collapsing around their ears: "Adolf, you really *are* the most incredible person!"

"Ludwig," The Depravity Made to Look Prissy Award. Note: this award is sometimes worded so as to call attention to the film that has done most to make sex look dull, like the Nazi orgy in "England Made Me."

"Class of '44," The Old Songs, Old Cars, Old Haircuts Don't Make A Movie Award. Runner-up: "The Way We Were."

The United States Supreme Court (five of its nine members), The Anthony Comstock Award, for having come to grips with the obscenity question in decisions that prompted one southern state to find "Carnal Knowledge" "patently offensive" to its community standards.

Georgina Spelvin, the star of "The Devil in Miss Jones" and other porno films too numerous to mention, The Award to The Actress Who Most Tirelessly Demonstrates the Principles of Brotherhood Without Regard to Race, Creed, Sex, Origin, Orifice or Species.

"Executive Action," The How To Successfully Assassinate A Head of State Award. This was an obvious choice since the only competitors were "Day of The Jackal" and "The Day of The Dolphin," and they had to be disqualified.

Barbra Streisand, The Burt Lancaster Award that goes to the actor or actress whose performance most completely depends upon hair styling. This award is to be shared by Miss Streisand's hair dresser for "The Way We Were."

"Lost Horizon," The Most Vulnerable Film of The Year Award. Like "Love Story," this musical version of James Hilton's novel was one of those films that could have been adequately reviewed by simply reading the credit sheet, which begins with the name of the producer, Ross Hunter. A better film might have resulted by equipping the original "Lost Horizon" with Muzak.

*

"The Nelson Affair," The Stuffed Personage Under Glass Award, given to the year's worst historical film. Terence Rattigan wrote the lines that Peter Finch (Lord Nelson) and Glenda Jackson (Lady Hamilton) recited. Runners-up: "Lady Caroline Lamb" and "Ludwig."

"Paper Moon," The Life Can Be Beautiful Award, which goes to the film that most successfully ignores the reality of the things it's about. Runner-up: "Cinderella Liberty."

"A Warm December," The Death Can Be Beautiful (And Not necessarily Disfiguring) Award. Runner-up: "Love and Pain and The Whole Dammed Thing."

"Last Tango in Paris," The Least Talked About Movie in The Last Six Months Award. Is that the one with Brando?

"Papillon," "The Sting," "Scarecrow," "Emperor of The North Pole" and "Pat Garrett and Billy The Kid," The Women Aren't Terribly Interesting (Though Still Necessary for Certain Biological Functions) Award.

*

"Brother Sun, Sister Moon," The Award to The Film That Most Foolishly Exploits The Gospel According to St. Matthew. The only runner-up, "Godspell," was disqualified because of some good music and location photography around New York.

Dalton Trumbo, The Dalton Trumbo Award to the screenwriter who has most successfully confused quantity with quality. In recognition of "Papillon" and "Executive Action."

Dr. Aaron Stern, The Man on The Go Award, in recognition of Dr. Stern's rapid rise in the film industry from his humble origins as a Long Island psychiatrist, through his tenure as head of the Motion Picture Association of America's film rating system, to his recent employment by Columbia Pictures in an executive capacity.

"Year of The Woman," Sandra Hochman's self-celebrating moulage on behalf of Women's Lib. The Men Aren't Terribly Interesting (Though Still Necessary for Certain Biological Functions) Award. It also shares the Movie That No One Was Waiting For Citation with "Jonathan Livingston Seagull."

"40 Carats," The Broadway Is Dead Award, given annually to the film version of a Broadway play that best demonstrates that Broadway no longer has much to offer moviemakers. Moviemakers can create their own turkeys about women who are elderly (actually or simulated) and fall in love with younger men. Witness "Interval."

"Interval," The Award to The Worst Film With A Plot That Depends More Or Less On A Car's Breaking Down In A Strange Land. In "Interval," Merle Oberon's car has mechanical trouble in Mexico. Runner-up: "40 Carats," which begins when Liv Ullmann's car collapses in Greece.

*

"Papillon," The Marie Antoinette Severed Head Award, which goes to the film that most explicitly shows its audience a head being chopped off.

"The Exorcist," The Ken Russell Good Taste Award. William Friedkin's film version of William Peter Blatty's novel is also an early but leading candidate for The Most Expensive Claptrap of The Decade Award. The film should also be cited for special effects, including levitating beds, urine and devil's vomit, which looks like condensed split-pea soup.

1973 D 30, II:1:1

Charming Swan Song of Experimentalist

The Program

FILM PORTRAIT, a film by Jerome Hill, presented by Anthology Film Archive. Running time: 90 minutes. At the First Avenue Screening Room, at 61st Street. (Not submitted for rating.)

By HOWARD THOMPSON

Jerome Hill"s "Film Portrait," a 90-minute recapitulation of his early years and subsequent career as a movie maker, is an utterly charming swan song by the screen experimentalist who died in 1972 at the age of 67. The film, using old home movie footage, covers his childhood in a happy, wealthy Minnesota home and then shifts to his later avant-garde filming.

There is an endearing freshness to all this. A director, composer and painter, Mr. Hill outlines the course of his career in a simple, crystal-clear narrative. He loved the camera, we sense, as a wonderful toy of unlimited possibilities.

In spite of the acclaim his more conventional documentaries on Albert Schweitzer and Grandma Moses have received, this last work of his may turn out to be the most impressive of his efforts. Everything here flows steadily, skillfully and pointedly, starting with his evocative chapter on his early life in St. Paul, which imaginatively blends photographs, animated stills and color that has the quality of Tiffany glass.

Then as a wealthy young American roaming Europe in the nineteen-twenties, Mr. Hill slips behind the camera and remains there—a determined independent moviemaker, influenced by Dreyer, Melies and other pioneers. The Cocteau influence is obvious as we see in a runoff of his 1930 short, "Fortune Teller," in a flickering print.

Toward the end, the film dissolves kaleidoscopically within the image of a movieola as the spry, aging Mr. Hill demonstrates the vital role of editing ("alchemy") in his laboratory. These scenes were made shortly before his death.

"Every artist lends his own eyes to the audience,'" he muses, splicing a strip of negative. As an art form taking advantage of the machine, Mr. Hill tells us, "cinema was born just in time." He adds his credo: "A miracle is around every corner." Released by Anthology Film Archive, it was shown yesterday at the First Avenue Screening Room and will be repeated on Friday and Saturday.

1973 D 31, 25:1

The Ten Best Films of 1973

By VINCENT CANBY

SOMETHING quite peculiar happened in 1973: five of my best films of the year were made by American directors, as were six of the 10 runners-up. One way of reading this is to assume that more good films were made here in 1973 than in any recent year. Or one can be blunt and say simply that foreign films were worse, even though we usually receive the best of the lot.

The truth is a muddling mixture of a number of circumstances, including the fact that fewer films were being made abroad, and with the rising costs of distribution in this country, American distributors became more reluctant than ever to release even quality foreign films. Reason: A second-rate American film stands a far greater chance of making a profit in the domestic market than do most first-rate imports.

America didn't turn out more good films this year at all. Total production was down, which meant that the odds against producing something of value rose. There was what seemed to be a vast number of cop movies, the penalty we continue to pay for having made "The French Connection" a success two years ago. The cost-conscious studios generally held the line on movie budgets, though Columbia gambled a lot of loot on "Lost Horizon," and lost. The two other high-budget movies of the year, Allied Artists' "Papillon" and Warner Brothers' "The Exorcist," seem, at this writing, to be headed for commercial success, though probably not of the sort that will prompt the other companies to start the kind of spending sprees that almost sank Hollywood in the mid-sixties.

What does a Times critic have in common with Joan Crawford?

"THE LONG GOODBYE"—Elliott Gould was fine as a 70's Philip Marlowe in Robert Altman's brilliant film.

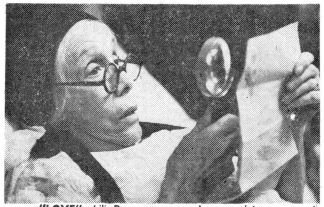

"LOVE"—Lili Darvas was superb as a dying woman in Karoly Makk's very precise and moving Hungarian film.

"SLEEPER"—Woody Allen's madness reached full flower in the far-out comedy, set in 2173. Diane Keaton was dandy.

"HEAVY TRAFFIC"—A Brooklyn boy has a ball with a barmaid in Ralph Bakshi's courageous, very funny film.

American movies are undoubtedly more violent than they've ever been. They're quicker on the trigger and more inclined to roll around in the catchup, but they're no more or less mediocre than they've ever been. What was encouraging in 1973 was the surfacing of a lot of new—or comparatively new—talent, like Don Taylor, the director of "Tom Sawyer," a good, completely conventional, spun-sugar sort of movie musical, and Howard Zeiff and W. D. Richter, the director and writer, respectively, of "Slither," a nutty, low-profile comedy that isn't good enough to make any 10-best lists but is too good to be ignored. The other names to be remembered this year are Ralph Bakshi, George Lucas, Martin Scorsese and, heavenly days, Woody Allen.

My choices for 1973, listed in alphabetical order, are:

AMERICAN GRAFFITI, directed by George Lucas; written by Mr. Lucas, Gloria Katz and Willard Huyck; produced by Francis Ford Coppola; released by Universal Pictures. About a last summer night on the town by three teen-age boys and their elderly (22-year-old) buddy who doesn't want to grow up. "American Graffiti" is a remarkably successful example of American movie-making of the sort that succeeds in telling its story entirely in terms of present action and character, with no recourse to canned exposition. The film is the second to be directed by 28-year-old George Lucas ("THX-1138" was his first), who here recalls his own teen years without sentimentality but with, instead, a great deal of toughness and high humor. The performances are all fine, but you're most likely to remember Charlie Martin Smith and Candy Clark, playing an epically clumsy young man and the magnificently dim-witted blonde he charms in spite of himself.

DAY FOR NIGHT (La Nuit Americaine), directed by Francois Truffaut; screenplay (French with English subtitles) by Mr. Truffaut, Jean-Louis Richard and Suzanne Schiffman; a production of Les Films du Carrosse (Paris)

"AMERICAN GRAFFITI" — Ronny Howard and Cindy Williams went steady in George Lucas's remarkable movie.

and P.I.C. (Rome); distributed by Warner Brothers. Forget "Such A Gorgeous Kid Like Me," which Truffaut gave us early in the year and remember "Day for Night," Truffaut's fondest, most compassionate film that is, not

"LAST TANGO IN PARIS"—Marlon Brando and Maria Schneider triumphed in Bernardo Bertolucci's movie about the ways of love.

"PLAYTIME"—Jacques Tati was magnificent in this gloriously funny French film.

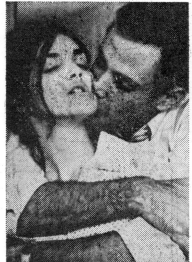

"MEMORIES OF UNDER-DEVELOPMENT"—Sergio Corrieri hugs Beatriz Ponchora in Tomas Gutierrez Alea's film.

"DAY FOR NIGHT"—Valentina Cortese and Jean-Pierre Aumont excelled in François Truffaut's witty movie.

"MEAN STREETS"—Robert De Niro, Amy Robinson and Harvey Keitel scored in Martin Scorsese's impressive work

accidentally, about the making of a movie at the Victorine Studios in Nice. The metaphor perfectly expresses Truffaut's bitter-sweet vision of life in which nothing is quite as simple as it seems, in which infatuation may be mistaken for love (and may be no less valuable), in which a lifetime of experience may be stuffed into no more than the seven weeks it takes to shoot a film. The movie has a lot about moviemaking in it, but it's not an inside movie. It's a witty, exhilarating story about the forms and fancies of love.

HEAVY TRAFFIC, an animated film written and directed by Ralph Bakshi; characters created by Mr. Bakshi; produced by Steve Krantz; released by American International Pictures. Ralph Bakshi was only warming up with his first animated feature, "Fritz The Cat." His second, "Heavy Traffic," is by far the most original, far-out, imaginative, courageous, outrageous movie of 1973, a blend of animation and live action that extends the frontiers of filmmaking techniques in a way that no one else has done in years. The story is about the decline and fall of a nice young Italian-American-Jewish boy from Brooklyn who refuses to acknowledge that life is a pinball machine forever proclaiming "TILT." Among the characters he meets on his downward path are Carole, a beautiful black bartender who hustles from time to time; Snowflake, a sad, shrivelled drag queen, and Shorty, a legless bouncer whose physical disadvantage has done little to improve his character. Very funny, very sad, very vigorous and full of life.

LAST TANGO IN PARIS, directed by Bernardo Bertolucci; screenplay in French (with English subtitles) and English by Mr. Bertolucci and Franco Arcalli; produced by Alberto Grimaldi; released by United Artists. The feelings of love, anguish and despair that erupt all over the place are so intense, so consuming, so self-absorbed, that Bernardo Bertolucci's "Last Tango in Paris" is occasionally very funny when it doesn't mean to be. The film is all about romantic love and its various expressions, the sometimes brave, sometimes foolish Laurentian gestures that are more easily written about than photographed for a movie. Marlon Brando gives one of his best performances as the middle-aged American living in Paris who makes the fatal mistake of trying to isolate himself through sexual love. Maria Schneider is funny and charming as the girl. In a few years I wouldn't be all surprised if the film is seen to be more of a satire than it is judged to be today. A clue exists in the lush physical production and camerawork. The movie has the "look" of a Henry Mancini album cover—lots of muted, fuzzy, golds, browns and mauves, the visual equivalents of a thousand violins.

THE LONG GOODBYE, directed by Robert Altman; screenplay by Leigh Brackett, based on Raymond Chandler's novel; produced by Jerry Bick; distributed by United Artists. Robert Altman updates Philip Marlowe, Raymond Chandler's private eye whose roots are in the depressed, black-and-white 'thirties, to the overprivileged, full-color

seventies with huge success, though "The Long Goodbye" is not for the purists. Elliott Gould is fine as Marlowe and Los Angeles looks just as bizarre today as Chandler found it 35 years ago, though it is quite, quite different. This is no anachronism—a forties movie made in the seventies. It is an original work by one of our most brilliant if erratic directors.

LOVE, directed by Karoly Makk; screenplay (Hungarian with English subtitles) by Tibor Dery; produced by Mafilm, Studio 1, Budapest. An Ajay Films release. Very precise, moving and fine-grained, this Hungarian import is virtually a two-character, one-set film that covers an extraordinary range of psychological, social and political feelings in terms of the relationship between a bed-ridden old lady (Lili Darvas) and her daughter-in-law (Mari Torocsik). The old lady believes her son (Ivan Darvas) to be in America making a film, a fiction originated by the daughter-in-law to cover the son's disappearance into a political prison. Karoly Makk directed the film and its three superb performances.

MEAN STREETS, directed by Martin Scorsese; screenplay by Mr. Scorsese and Mardik Martin; produced by Jonathan T. Taplin; distributed by Warner Brothers. "Mean Streets," Martin Scorsese's third feature film, is set in New York's Little Italy and deals, almost casually, with friendship, love, honor and ambition in the society-within-a-society. It is so good, so self-assured in its techniques, that it seems almost to be a debut performance rather than the more fully developed work of the same young man who made "Who's That Knocking At My Door?" and "Boxcar Bertha." Robert De Niro gives a spectacular performance as a simple-minded petty hood, but Harvey Keitel and Amy Robinson are equally good with less flamboyant material.

MEMORIES OF UNDERDEVELOPMENT (Memorias del Subdesarrollo), directed and written (Spanish with English subtitles) by Tomas Gutierrez Alea, based on the novel by Edmundo Desnoes; produced by the Instituto Cubano del Arte e Industria Cinematograficos; distributed by Tricontinental Film Center. "Memories of Underdevelopment," which was made five years ago in Castro's Cuba, may be the most remarkable movie yet to come out of a contemporary revolution. The film looks at the Cuban revolution through the eyes of Sergio (Sergio Corrieri), a middleclass intellectual in his late thirties whose critical faculties have rendered him incapable of any decisive action. "Everything happens to me too early or too late," he says at one point. Sergio can't stand the members of his middle-class family who have fled to Miami, but he also can't stand the revolution that is turning Havana into a provincial wreck of a city. The film manages the unusual feat of dramatizing alienation without ever slipping into the bored and boring attitudes its hero affects.

PLAYTIME, directed and produced by Jacques Tati; screenplay (English, French, German, Japanese) by Mr. Tati;

a Spectra Film production; distributed by Continental Films. Jacques Tati's most free-form comedy to date, "Playtime" is a gloriously funny movie about a Paris so modern it didn't even exist when Tati made the film in 1967, a Paris composed entirely of streets like the Avenue of The Americas, completely hemmed in by glass-and-steel towers in which, if we're quick about it, we can see reflected vestiges of the old Paris, the Eiffel Tower, the Arch of Triumph, Sacre Coeur. The magnificent comedy routines conclude with a hilarious Gotterdammerung in a terribly chic new nightclub of the sort only Tati could have imagined. Great.

SLEEPER, directed by Woody Allen; screenplay by Mr. Allen and Marshall Brickman; produced by Jack Grossberg; distributed by United Artists. The fine madness that Woody Allen fooled around with in "Take The Money and Run" and "Bananas" reaches full flower, comes to a head, blooms, overflows, and even climaxes in "Sleeper," a tale about a mild-mannered sneak named Miles Monroe (Allen) who goes to sleep in 1973 and wakes up 200 years later in an American police state. Woody-the-star is beautifully aided and abetted by Diane Keaton, who is not just a fine comedienne but also a pretty face.

*

The 10 runners-up, in no particular order of preference, are:

Charlie Chaplin's "A King in New York," not strictly a runner-up but in a class by itself. Time has neutralized bitterness. The comedy is constant and uproarious; "Blume in Love," Paul Mazursky's first solo effort as writer-producer-director, a California comedy set partially in Venice, about a man (George Segal) obsessed by his ex-wife; "Live and Let Die," the James Bond movie that introduces Roger Moore as Bond with no visible ill effects to the series, which is no less entertaining today simply because it has become an artifact of the long-lost 1960s; Satyajit Ray's "The Adversary," about a middle-class young man slowly dropping out of life in Calcutta; "Bang The Drum Slowly," America's first entertaining baseball movie, directed by John Hancock and written by Mark Harris, who adapted his own novel and its superb dialogue.

*

Also Jerry Bruck, Jr.'s "I.F. Stone's Weekly," a very funny, immensely touching documentary tribute to one of the great journalists of our day, the always incredulous watch-dog and writer known familiarly as Izzy Stone; "Charley Varrick," a thoroughly enjoyable Don Siegel yarn about a nice old bank-robber (Walter Matthau) and how he outwits the Mafia; "The Homecoming," the American Film Theater's screen version of the Harold Pinter play, directed by Peter Hall, proving that Pinter, even when he writes for the stage, is one of the best film writers around. All of the performances are fine, but Vivien Merchant and Ian Holm are outstanding; "David Holzman's Diary," Jim McBride's put-on of cinema verité, hugely witty and wise and nicely acted by Kit Carson as the solemn movie nut of the title; and "Serpico," the astounding

story of one of New York's most honest cops starring Al Pacino in what may be his best performance yet, under the direction of Sidney Lumet, with the artistic cooperation of the people who've made New York City the world's most photogenic sleazy set.

1974 Ja 6, II:1:2

FILM BY TRUFFAUT NAMED BEST OF '73

'Day for Night' Is Chosen by National Society of Critics

"Day for Night" ("La Nuit Americaine"), Françoise Truffaut's French romantic comedy-drama about the making of a movie, was voted the best film of 1973 in the seventh annual poll of the National Society of Film Critics.

The representatives of 21 magazines and newspapers also chose Mr. Truffaut as the year's top director and Valentina Cortese, who played a veteran performer, as the outstanding supporting actress, for their contributions to "Day for Night."

Marlon Brando's delineation of the anguished, sexually explicit hero of "Last Tango in Paris" was judged the year's outstanding starring portrayal. Liv Ullmann was named the year's best actress for her depiction of the Swedish emigrant heroine in the period drama "The New Land." The award for best supporting actor went to Robert De Niro for his characterization of the small-time underworld operative in the locally made drama, "Mean Streets."

The team of George Lucas, Gloria Katz and Willard Huyck won the critics' writing accolade for their screenplay for "American Graffiti," the nostalgic view of the nineteen-sixties scene. The top cinematography award was voted for Vilmos Zsigmond for his work on the Raymond Chandler private eye melodrama, "The Long Goodbye."

The organization's second annual Rosenthal Foundation Award of $2,000 for an artistic film not yet sufficiently attended by the public during the year was won by the Cuban director Tomas Gutierrez Alea for his Cuban drama "Memories of Underdevelopment." The other $2,000 Rosenthal prize for a movie maker who has not yet received public recognition went to Daryl Duke for his direction of "Payday," a drama about a country and western singer.

A special award was voted posthumously to Robert Ryan for his performance in the adaptation of Eugene O'Neill's "The Iceman Cometh."

The winners will be awarded citations at a reception at the

Algonquin Hotel next month.

The voting critics were: Hollis Alpert of Saturday Review/World Magazine, chairman of the group; Andrew Sarris, The Village Voice, who was elected chairman to succeed Mr. Alpert; Gary Arnold, The Washington Post; Vincent Canby, The New York Times; Charles Champlin, The Los Angeles Times; Jay Cocks and Richard Schickel, Time magazine; Judith Crist, New York magazine; David Denby,

Harpers; Bernard Drew, Gannett Newspapers; Roger Ebert, The Chicago Sun Times, Joseph Gelmis, Newsday; Penelope Gilliatt and Pauline Kael, The New Yorker; Roger Greenspun, Penthouse magazine; Molly Haskell, The Village Voice; Michael Korda, Glamour magazine; Paul Zimmerman, Newsweek, and Bruce Williamson, Playboy.

1974 Ja 7, 38:3

'Day for Night' Wins Film Critics' Award

By A. H. WEILER

"Day for Night" ("La Nuit Americaine"), the French romantic comedy-drama dealing with the filming of a movie, won three of seven prizes voted yesterday in the 39th annual poll of The New York Film Critics Circle. The import, released by Warner Bros., was judged the best film of 1973, and François Truffaut and Valentine Cortese were named the year's top director and supporting actress for their work in "Day for Night."

In closely contested voting that necessitated three ballots, Joanne Woodward emerged as the outstanding actress for her characteriza-

tion of the restless, middle-aged wife in the drama "Summer Wishes, Winter Dreams." She won by a vote of 28 to 26 over Glenda Jackson, who portrayed the mistress in "A Touch of Class."

Marlon Brando's delineation of the troubled American in the sexually explicit, French-made "Last Tango in Paris," won the best actor award by a vote of 38 to 33 over A. Pacino, who played the crusading New York police officer in "Serpico."

Robert De Niro, as the small-time hoodlum in "Mean Streets," edged out John Houseman's depiction of a teacher in "Paper Chase" for supporting-actor honors.

"American Graffiti," written by George Lucas (the director), Gloria Katz and Willard Huyck, easily won the accolade for screen writing.

"Day for Night" won the best film award over "Graffiti," a nostalgic view of California youth of the nineteen-sixties, as well as 13 other features. The French entry was named on the second ballot, with 40 votes to 30 for "Graffiti."

Two ballots also were needed before Mr. Truffaut received 41 votes to the 27 garnered by Costas-Gavras for the French-made political drama "State of Siege."

The 26 critics voted at the

Marlon Brando
Best actor

Joanne Woodward
Best actress

New York Newspaper Guild headquarters, 133 West 44th Street. They will present plaques to the winners at Sardi's Restaurant on Sunday, Jan. 27.

The voting critics were: Joseph Gelmis, chairman of the group, which earlier this year added "Circle" to its official designation; Judith Crist, New York magazine; Pauline Kael and Penelope Gilliatt, The New Yorker magazine; Kathleen Carroll and Ann Guarino, The Daily News; Archer Winsten and Frances Herridge, The New York Post, and Frances Taylor, The Long Island Press.

Also, Paul Zimmerman, Newsweek magazine; Jay Cocks and Richard Schickel, Time magazine; Robert Salmaggi, WINS Radio;

In "Day for Night," best film, François Truffaut, chosen best director for directing it, plays a director.

Bernard Drew, Gannett Newspapers; William Wolf, Cue magazine; Andrew Sarris and Molly Haskell, The Village Voice; Roger Greenspun, Penthouse magazine; Bruno Williamson, Playboy magazine; Hollis Alpert, Saturday Review/World magazine; James P.

Murray, The New York Amsterdam News; Joy Gould Boyem, The Wall Street Journal; Howard Kissel, Women's Wear Daily; Vincent Canby, Howard Thompson and A. H. Weiler, The New York Times.

1974 Ja 9, 24:1

Oscars for 'Sting,' Miss Jackson, Lemmon

By JON NORDHEIMER
Special to The New York Times

LOS ANGELES, April 2—A film about a pair of light-hearted con men, "The Sting," kept alive Hollywood's fascination with cops-and-robber movies by winning the best-picture award tonight in the annual Oscar parade.

Best-acting awards went to Jack Lemmon for "Save the Tiger" and to British actress Glenda Jackson for "A Touch of Class."

But a barefooted young man provided the Academy Awards audience and an estimated 76-million persons watching on television with the most dramatic moment of the evening when he jogged naked across the stage.

He appeared after David Niven gave an introduction toward the end of the evening, but the streaking event had not been entirely unexpected.

"That was almost bound to happen," the debonaire Mr. Niven, momentarily nonplussed, acknowledged.

But except for that brief interlude, the night belonged to "The Sting," winning the first best-picture award for Universal Studios, the biggest active studio in Hollywood, since "All Quiet on the Western Front," in 1930.

"The Sting," a prop-nostalgia story of two Depression-era bunko artists who swindle a big-time gangster, followed in the tradition of "The Godfather" and "The French Connection," the winners of the past two years, by capturing the top award and six other major accolades.

It completely overshadowed the most controversial film of the year, and Hollywood's biggest box-office smash, "The Exorcist," the graphic — some called it horrifying — study of the exorcism of demons from a young Boston girl.

The two films had been billed as the major contenders for the best-picture award, a struggle of sorts between the devil and the deep blue eyes of Paul Newman and Robert Redford, the stars of "The Sting," but "The Exorcist" only fetched only the best-screenplay award for William Peter Blatty, who adapted it from his book, and the best achievement in sound.

George Roy Hill took directing honors for "The Sting" and the film also took

the best original screenplay award for David S. Ward.

For a change of pace, Mr. Lemmon was around for his portrayal of a morally corrupted dressmaker in "Save the Tiger," he accepted it graciously.

"There has been a great deal of criticism about this award . . . [in recent years] . . . but justified or not, I think it's one hell of an honor and I'm thrilled," the actor said.

It was the second Oscar for Mr. Lemmon, who was named best supporting actor in 1955 for his ebullient interpretation of Ensign Pulver in "Mister Roberts.' It was the first time an actor had won Hayes was the only actress to accomplish the feat.

Ten-year-old Tatum O'Neal, the urchin-like girl who appeared in another Depression tale of fast-talking con men, "Paper Moon," became the youngest person ever to win an Oscar in any category, getting the best supporting actress award. She walked up to the stage wearing a tuexdo, beaming broadly as she walked off with the gold-plated statuette that appeared to be half her size.

The best supporting actor award went to John Houseman, a producer of 18 films, for his depiction of a stern Harvard law professor in "The Paper Chase."

Another award spree was achieved by Marvin Hamlisch, composer, who picked up three Oscars for the best song and dramatic score ("The Way We Were") and the best original song score ("The Sting").

"Day for Night," François Truffaut's comic drama about the making of a movie, and in fact Mr. Truffaut's unabashed tribute to Hollywood, was named the best foreign-language film. Mr. Truffaut, who produced, directed and starred in the film, received the award himself.

In one of the evening's spontaneous emotional tributes, Katharine Hepburn received a rousing standing ovation when she appeared as a surprise to give the Irving Thalberg Award to Lawrence Weingarten, the producer. Miss Hepburn, winner of three Oscars in the past, had never before made a personal appearance at the ceremonies.

Mr. Weingarten, former president of the Screen Producers Guild and onetime associate of Mr. Thalberg's,

Robert Redford, left, and Paul Newman in "The Sting," best picture

Jack Lemmon
Best actor

Glenda Jackson
Best actress

John Houseman
Best Supporting actor

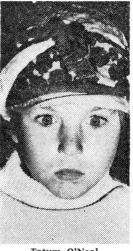

Tatum O'Neal
Best supporting actress

George Roy Hill
Best director

produced, among other films, "Adam's Rib," which starred Miss Hepburn, in 1949.

At the outset of the evening, Walter Mirisch, president of the Academy drew warm applause when he dedicated the evening "to the memory of that pioneer and master producer of so many great films" — Samuel Goldwyn, who died Jan. 31.

Groucho Marx accepted a special award from the academy in tribute to all the Marx Brothers. Appearing frail before a warmly applauding audience, Mr. Marx thanked the Academy members and said he wished his brothers had been there to share it with him.

An honorary award was presented to Henri Langlois, director of the Cinemathèque Français in Paris and renowned curator, collector and cataloguer of film.

The Jean Hersholt Humanitarian Award was presented by Alfred Hitchcock to Lew Wasserman, president and chief executive officer of MCA, Inc.

The Oscar awards ceremony, traditionally Hollywood's most extravagant celebration of itself, was broadcast live by the National Broadcasting Company from the Chandler Pavilion, a multi-column marble-and-glass edifice in the civic center.

The streaking episode starred a 33-year-old Los Angeles advertising agent, Robert Opel, who later told newsmen back stage, dressed in a blue jump suit, that he had ambitions to be a "comic." He revealed that he had gained entrance to the backstage area, despite rigorous sceurity, with the aid of a stolen press badge. He was questioned by security agents but released with no charges being pressed.

Elizabeth Taylor Unnerved

The only person inside the Los Angeles Music Center who appeared unnerved by the streaker was Elizabeth Taylor, the actress, who followed him to the stage.

"That's a pretty hard act to follow," Miss Taylor gulped. "I'm nervous—that really upset me. I think I'm jealous."

Other awards follow:

Short subjects, animated: "Frank Film," Frank Mouris, producer.

Short subjects, live action: "The Bolero," Allan Miller and William Fertik, producers.

Documentary features: "The Great American Cowboy," Keith Merrill, producer.

Documentary short subjects: "Princeton: A Search for Answers," Julian Krainin and DeWitt L. Sage, producers.

Sound: "The Exorcist," Robert Knudson and Chris Newman.

Editing: "The Sting," William Reynolds.

Art direction and set decoration: "The Sting," Henry Rumstead, direction, and James Payne, decoration.

Costume design: "The Sting," Edith Head.

Cinematography: "Cries and Whispers," Sven Nykvist.

1974 Ap 3, 36:1

The New York Times
Film Reviews
1974

Life of Wolf Pack Seen in 'Cry of the Wild'

By HOWARD THOMPSON

So few animal documentaries for family viewing are filmed these days that one called "Cry of the Wild" is doubly welcome. Even so, don't be misled by those television trailers, heralding a close-up study of snarling wolves in the wild.

While the footage has an atmospheric opening and closing in the Canadian Arctic, the wolf pack we see here in fascinating and remarkably intimate detail is roaming a carefully surveyed forest enclosure near Quebec. This middle portion of the picture, which was produced by the National Board of Canada and had a multitheater opening yesterday in the metropolitan area, is superb. At one Manhattan theater yesterday, the uptown Olympia, a capacity audience of children and parents drank it in raptly. No wonder.

The picture has a curious history. Made in 1972, running only 50 minutes and titled "Death of a Legend," it was widely shown nontheatrically (schools, clubs, etc.). This release is its first theatrical exposure, through an American company, with a new title and 40 more minutes of the original footage restored.

•

This footage is undoubtedly the prelude, which zeroes in scenically but rather meanderingly on the Canadian wilds, as the director-photographer, Bill Mason, and a narrator, generalize factually about the wolves, who snarl away in the distance.

It's another matter entirely back at the Mason enclosure, with the charming Mason family overseeing their semi-tame pack. The camera records the animals' life cycle, including tribal hierarchy, feeding rituals, courtship and birth. A candid, tastefully shown birth sequence of a litter, with the wolf as tenderly solicitous as a doe, is a touching, even beautiful sight.

1974 Ja 3, 45:1

Program of Shorts Is at Whitney Museum

By VINCENT CANBY

Outrage with the ways of the world is something that

The Program

OUTRAGEOUS FILMS, a program of eight short films: BITTER GRAPES by Dick Bartlett, 17 minutes; THE BEST OF MAY, 1968 by Jay Cassidy, 4 minutes; PRIMETIME by Standish Lawder, 4 minutes; FILET OF SOUL by Victor Faccinto, 16 minutes; CYBELE by Donald Richie, 21 minutes; YARD by Andrew Lugg and John Orentlicher, 8 minutes; PHYSIOGNOMY by Frederick Bailey, 6 minutes, and INTERVIEW by Gene Rosow, 10 minutes. At the Whitney Museum of American Art, Madison Avenue at 75th Street. Through Jan. 12.

must be carefully tended like a delicate mistrust. It must be protected; otherwise it erodes too soon and is forgotten. Outrage is healthy. It changes customs and topples governments. It is also much too fragile to be represented by a collection of short, mostly clumsy movies, titled "Outrageous Films," which opened yesterday at the Whitney Museum of American Art.

These eight films are meant to challenge sensibilities, but instead they simply exploit conventional reactions and humane biases. In Dick Bartlett's "Bitter Grapes," a sort of mini-"La Grande Bouffe," a nun captures a paunchy man and then stuffs him with food and drink until he vomits, at which point he returns to what I assume to be a more or less docile, postnatal state.

Jay Cassidy's "The Best of May, 1968," is a visually lyric montage of silent newsreel clips showing bombs bursting over Vietnamese villages and jungles. Victor Faccinto's "Filet of Soul," a 16-minute animated film, is the wanly comic epic of a man, Video Vic, attempting to survive in a universe ruled by a short-tempered god and some castrating assistants.

•

Castration also figures in "Cybèle," a 21-minute film made in Japan by Donald Richie, the novelist, film critic and historian. The movie is described as "a contemporary reconstructon of the 18th century ballet heroique," or "a pastoral ritual in five scenes." What we see are six thin, naked, terribly self-conscious Japanese youths rolling around a weedy garden with a nice, naked middle-class Japanese girl, who reminds me less of an earth goddess than of a waitress with very rude manners.

•

In other films, a young man makes faces at himself in a mirror, and another man grows a garden of small

flames, as if he were raising lima beans. Standish Lawder's "Primetime" wonders whether television is a cause or an effect of our rotten culture by showing us a man in a Nixon mask dialing a TV screen from banality to atrocity and back again.

Outrage is poorly served.

1974 Ja 4, 25:1

Ali-Frazier Bout Is Star of 'The Fighters'

THE FIGHTERS, produced and directed by William Greaves; editor, Mr. Greaves; associate editors, John Dandre and David Greaves; directors of photography, Joseph Consentino, Steven Larner, Terrence Macartney-Filgate, Jimmy Mannas and Roland Mitchell; a William Greaves Productions film, distributed by the Walter Reade Organization. Running time: 114 minutes. At the Apollo Theater, 253 West 125th Street. This film has not been classified. With: Muhammad Ali, Joe Frazier and others.

By VINCENT CANBY

William Greaves's "The Fighters," which opened yesterday at the Apollo Theater on 125th Street, is both a recollection and a coming attraction, being a documentary feature about the 1971 heavyweight title bout between Muhammad Ali and Joe Frazier, who meet again at Madison Square Garden on Jan. 28.

Although "The Fighters" is primarily a round-by-round record of the extraordinary 1971 fight, won by Frazier on a decision, this footage has been ably supplemented by other material designed to give the fight some of the same impact it had when it was being billed as "the fight of the century."

Interviews, training-camp sequences and even a brief glimpse into the complicated financial negotiations that made it all possible frame the footage of the 15-round bout that increased the stature—and the bank accounts —of both winner and loser. "The Fighters" is a first-rate film of its unprepossessing kind.

1974 Ja 5, 34:4

Experimental Works Vary in Quality

By NORA SAYRE

"I'm not very photogenic, visually or otherwise," a protesting middle-aged woman says as she shields herself from the camera. The scene is in "Ricky and Rocky," one

The Program

CHICAGOFILM: SILENT REVERSAL by Louis Hock; 12 minutes; ZIP TONE CAT TUNE by Bill Brand, 8 minutes; ALWAYS OPEN/NEVER CLOSED by Bill Brand, 12 minutes; FLY BITES by Bonnie Donohue, 7½ minutes; THE AUTOPSY by Royanne Rosenberg; 4½ minutes; FUNERAL by Lawrence Levy; 11½ minutes; MR. TRI-STATE, 12 minutes and RICKY AND ROCKY by Jeff Kreines and Tom Palazollo, 15 minutes. At the Film Forum, 256 West 88th Street. Through today and from Thursday through next Sunday, 8 P.M.

of the best of the "Chicago-films," a program of short experimental movies from the Middle West that is being shown at the Film Forum, 256 West 88th Street, through today and again from Thursday through next Sunday. This documentary by Jeff Kreines and Tom Palazollo depicts a surprise bridal shower in a sunny suburban backyard, where most of the subjects look pleased and a bit sheepish about being filmed. Garrulous guests praise the favors, wrappings, and decorations, while the young couple grows awkward when faced by the avalanche of gifts. They hold up a coffeepot, pots and pans, a very furry orange footrest, while their friends and relatives murmur "beautiful" in rather weary voices and repeat that the bride is darling.

•

The camera stresses pinched or pudgy faces, and there's a whiff of superiority to the middle Americans observed. However, if the subjects saw this film, they probably wouldn't know that they'd been shot for comedy—unless they heard the laughter of an audience. Still, this tribal ritual makes for a touching though joyless occasion, since the bride and bridegroom haven't yet acquired the materialism of the crowd surrounding them. They don't pant for presents—they almost recoil from them.

The same very talented pair of film makers is responsible for "Mr. Tri-State," a contest among amateur musclemen from Illinois; Wisconsin, and Indiana. Great lumpy torsos bulge and rip-

ple to scattered applause as "the 17 finest physiques of the Middle West" are inspected until a stunningly phallic trophy is bestowed on the grinning winner. "I eat a lotta bakery," he says—though he finally admits that he "stays away from starch." Again, the film subtly mocks the people who take certain rituals seriously. But it's also a fine piece of reporting.

All in all, this is an imaginative choice of structural films and personal documentaries, and the program reflects a variety of styles. Louis Hock's "Silent Reversal" resembles a cross-section of a sandwich: the screen is split twice horizontally to show trains sliding in and out of a station. This piece of 6-minute footage is projected both forward and backwards, and the result is a hypnotic study in motion. Bill Brand's "Zip Tone Cat Tune" employs multiple exposure techniques: glimpses of a cat prowling and washing and playing look as though they'd been filmed through a cheese grater.

•

"The Autopsy" by Royanne Rosenberg dwells on the instruments and the equipment used in that rite. There are a few meaty but hazy shots of the inner man, and sounds resembling the exhalation of breath suggest that the corpse has a memory. Lawrence Levy's "Funeral" alternates some abstract evocations of a family burial with street interviews of people being asked how they want to be disposed of. One woman rather jovially opts for cryonics—"freeze", wait, and reanimate" — but a younger one prefers a crypt: "My boyfriend told me all the bugs would get me if I was under ground." There's a successful grave's-eye-view in the final shot: lumps of dirt fall and shut out the light until you feel that you've been buried.

1974 Ja 6, 57:2

2d Animation Festival

By HOWARD THOMPSON

The second International Animation Film Festival will open today at 9:30 A.M. at New York University's Loeb Center Auditorium, 566 LaGuardia Place and Washington Square South. As with the first assembly held here in 1972, the public is invited to the four-day conclave of

distributors and makers of animated movies. In addition to special and retrospective screenings, the program will include a competition among 200 animated short-subjects from 20 countries.

•

The nonprofit festival is funded in part by a grant from the New York State Council on the Arts, with additional support from N.Y.U. It is one of three international events devoted exclusively to animation, with the other festivals being held in Annecy, France, and Zagreb, Yugoslavia.

At a press preview of the program, Fred Mintz, the festival's organizer, said that the program would stress the burgeoning activities and new trends of animation here and abroad.

"Animation is a thriving business both here and in Europe," said Mr. Mintz, who heads the Cinephile Company, a distribution agency in New York. "The main outlets now in the United States are, of course, television and the 16-mm., nontheatrical circuit of schools, clubs and libraries, which are buying more and more animated shorts as audio-visual aids in the graphic arts."

Mr. Mintz estimated that there was a total of 100 animation studios in Europe, most with government subsidies. There are, he said, about 200 studios here. Current trends are toward the mixing of computerization and animation and the production of more theatrical features, such as the French-Czechoslovak "Fantastic

Planet" and Ralph Bakshi's "Fritz the Cat" and "Heavy Traffic." (The Bakshi films will be given a double-feature screening at the festival.)

Other special events at the festival are screenings of animated works by Bruno Bozzetto (Italy), Yoji Kuri (Japan) and the late Jiri Trnka (Czechoslovakia), a showing of the United Nations Children's Fund movie, "The Selfless Giant," and a computer-animation conference.

"The wonderful thing about animation as a field," Mr. Mintz said, "is its built-in international language. With minimal, practical adjustments, animated pictures have an audience anywhere. Whereas the two European festivals stress the artistic products, we are also emphasizing new techniques in drawing and showing educational and industrial films and even the longer, made-for-TV specials, unlike Annecy and Zagreb."

●

A two-hour sampling of festival shorts, entered in competition, attested to the program's variety and quality.

The National Film Board of Canada's "The Family That Dwelt Apart" is a sprightly fable narrated by the author, E. B. White. "The Maggot" is a striking anti-drug cartoon set in Harlem but made in Britain by George Dunning (of "Yellow Submarine"). Francis Masse's "Evasion Express," from France, is a strong, brooding parable of train passengers, in contrast with a frisky college, "Mini-Mini," from Japan. The Italian-made "Opera" hilariously satirizes operatic performances in terms of social fantasy.

Other samplings were Wolfgang Urchs's "Neighbors," a sharp satire within a simple animated frame, and a radiant television commercial linking Eastern Airlines and the Walt Disney World. Two somber, artistic imports from Poland and Belgium, Richard Czekala's "The Son" and Raoul Servais's "Pagasus," were remarkably effective.

Festival tickets, excluding some special events, are $2 each, and $1 tickets, for students. They are available at the Loeb Center box office.

1974 Ja 9, 22:1

the Tupamaros may move next.

You need some background for these two movies, since the subtitles are often elusive. Both are roughly made and sometimes rambling. But

they afford a rare glimpse of varying kinds of resistance, and here are special thanks to the First Avenue Screening Room for making them available.

1974 Ja 11, 15:1

Why the Devil Dig 'The Exorcist'?

By VINCENT CANBY

IN addition to making millions of dollars for all concerned, William Friedkin's film version of William Peter Blatty's "The Exorcist" may help restore the reputation of The Prince of The Power of The Air, which went into a sharp decline after Benjamin Franklin invented the lightning rod. Old Scratch must be pleased this morning, though Franklin, wherever he is, most probably is suffering from acute shortness of breath.

A modest piece of metal, inscribed with nothing more magical than, perhaps, the name of a manufacturer, effectively neutralized the bolts of wrath with which His Satanic Majesty had for centuries been shivering, shaking and sometimes destroying chicken coops, silos, barns, houses and even great cathedrals. Like a number of other frauds, Beelzebub could not easily survive reason combined with a little pluck.

✳

There was, of course, some resistance to the lightning rod. The Reverend Thomas Prince, pastor of Boston's Old South Church, blamed the earthquake of 1775 on Franklin's iron points, which, he said, constituted a sacrilege: lightning rods interfere with God's plan, in which Satan, though he can never win, plays a formidable part.

For those of you who came in a couple of hundred years late, "The Exorcist," written and produced by Blatty and directed by Friedkin, is the story of the attempts of an actress (Ellen Burstyn), making a film in the Georgetown area of Washington, to save the life of her demonically possessed 12-year-old daughter (Linda Blair) through exorcism performed by two Roman Catholic priests, one of whom is young, guilt-ridden and a trained psychiatrist (Jason Miller), while the other is old, full of faith, experienced in matters of demonology and has a bad heart (Max von Sydow).

The film, playing locally at the Cinema I, is the biggest thing to hit the industry since Mary Pickford, popcorn, pornography and "The Godfather." When I dropped into the Cinema I the other weekday morning at the first showing of the day, it was apparent that here was a movie a lot of people wanted to see, including old ladies, single men with brief cases, loving couples and teen-age kids (seemingly with and without parents). The kids especially, several of whom lay in an orchestra aisle near my seat and smoked and talked about basketball during

---

Film: Latin-American Documentaries

'When People Awake' Deals With Chile

By NORA SAYRE

How do you cope with the fact that profound social change — whether it's progressive or reactionary — is often accompanied by violence? And can you untangle the concepts of "necessary" and "negative" violence, or determine the moment when resistance becomes aggression! Before having to answer in 25 words or less, students of these subjects should see and ponder "When the People Awake" and "Tupamaros!" at the First Avenue Screening Room today and tomorrow.

"When the People Awake," a documentary about Chile made by an anonymous group of Latin Americans between September, 1972, and May, 1973, echoes with pangs of tragic foresight—it practically prophesies the death of the Marxist President Salvador Allende Gossens in September, 1973. The picture explores the conditions that preceded his election, stressing that 4 per cent of the population controlled 80 per cent of the wealth.

●

While we're told about the landowners' response to the state's taking over their lands (destroying their own property), along with the workers' determination to share the land, the 1971 nationalization of the copper mines

and the opposition of the Chilean Congress to President Allende's programs (his Popular Unity party held only a third of the seats), we recall that he himself resisted the use of violence.

There are some bleak references to International Telephone and Telegraph's opposition to President Allende's election and this country's suspension of all credit to Chile. But the emphasis is on the gulfs between the economic classes in Chile herself, and the film offers interviews with those on both sides.

A supporter of President Allende says that he doubts that socialism can be achieved by "pacifist means" even after the election, a well-to-do woman is confident that Chile can be "saved" from her President through the democratic process. Later, she asserts that the professional army won't get involved in politics. An elderly peasant observes that the time is coming for a military coup, and that "we have to defend ourselves—because if we don't there will be a tremendous massacre." How right he was.

●

"We are the answer to an unjust system": thus, a member of the revolutionary Tupamaros, interviewed as a black silhouette against the flag of the National Liberation movement of Uruguay. Again, as in Chile, the theme is that power and profit re-

Uruguay's Tupamaros Subject of Second

side in the hands of a minority, while unemployment and prices rise but wages don't, and education and health deteriorate.

The Tupamaros state that the Government created violence and therefore created them. This documentary, made with their cooperation by the Swedish director Jan Lindqvist, aims to educate the public about the abuse of political power, the Government's use of torture and repression of all stripes.

There are interviews with officials whom the Tupamaros have kidnapped, including the then British Ambassador Geoffrey Jackson, and Pereira Reverbel, a presidential adviser. Both respectfully acknowledge the political and moral seriousness of the Tupamaros, and agree that the treatment of captives in the "Peoples' Prison" is acceptable. Both men sound sincere. Still, they were prisoners being interrogated by their jailers.

●

With regard to the execution of Dan Mitrione—as depicted in Costa-Gavras's "State of Siege"—the Tupamaros's logic gets creaky. They can't seem to realize that the act of murder will always be unacceptable to many. The film was finished in August, 1972. Uruguay is now under military rule, and one wonders where and how those sections of the film in which the tormented child on screen was not vomiting bile at the priests, masturbating with a crucifix, screaming obscenities about the young priest's dead mother, or, for fun, turning her head 180 degrees to the rear. At those moments the kids were spellbound, almost it seems in spite of themselves.

*

If "The Exorcist" weren't so popular, and if it didn't obviously fulfill the expectations of the audiences who are going to see it, it wouldn't be worth writing about.

True, it has a cast of good actors. Its settings, including those shown in a prefatory sequence shot at an archeological dig in Iraq, are handsome and give the production an impressively expensive look. It's been very fancily put together, with a good deal of canny crosscutting to build the mood of menace.

Yet "The Exorcist" is claptrap. It has hardly any narrative to speak of, and what it has contains more loose ends than the first draft of a 2,000-page novel. The entire Iraqi sequence is superfluous window-dressing. Unlike a lot of extremely dumb vampire movies, it's about nothing else but what it says, demonic possession and exorcism. Though I admit to being skeptical, even that would be defensible and possibly fun. I enjoy how-to movies about exotic occupations, whether the occupation is climbing Annapurna or saving rich, high-strung Lawrence Talbot (Lon Chaney, Jr.) from the lycanthrope that lurks within. All of us, skeptical or not, take a certain delight in suspecting the existence of unseen forces more powerful, mysterious and malignant than radio waves. We are delighted by the various systems of diagnosis, treatment, quarantine, etc. that legend and imaginative writers have imposed on such things as vampirism. What makes "The Exorcist" such an affront (and, I suspect, contributes to its huge popularity) is its cruelties and the big-budget piety with which they are presented.

While watching the film the first time at a press screening, I kept trying to figure out what the movie was really up to. Critics are like that. They keep trying to find hidden meanings in the most explicit, bald-face narratives. One friend later suggested it was actually about mothers and daughters, but that friend had just had a fight with her mother and was full of her own bile.

I thought it might actually be about film criticism: the possession of the child was imply a metaphor for the

young critic who finds himself possessed at various points in his career by consuming passions that have emanated from the brains of others.

I was even willing to accept "The Exorcist" as another, highly souped-up fictionalization of the battles of innate good versus innate evil, with the devil, as usual in such dramatizations, being able to cause a certain amount of fuss before necessarily coming off second best.

Not at all. "The Exorcist" is about demonic possession, which, presumably because the film has been made with the technical advice of three Roman Catholic priests (two of whom play roles in the film), allows the movie to exploit cruelties, and our fascination with them, in ways that would surely have had the police (and the church) down on a more skeptical film. The devil, says the movie, is almost (but not quite) indescribably foul. Thus, to do His Satanic Majesty justice, the movie can be allowed to pander to the silliest fantasies that a raging id (and the special effects men) can devise. It won't spoil the plot, I think, to tell you that God finally triumphs over the devil, but at a rather high price.

*

The solemnity with which all this is given to us would, I hope, prompt a few more giggles than I heard at the Cinema I the other day. It should also neatly classify the film as sensationalism of basically foolish mind. "It's like the doctor said," says the poor mum trying to soothe the daughter whom we already know to be in Scratch's clutches. "Nerves, that's all. You just take your pills and everything will be all right." That's a line you probably haven't heard since "The Werewolf of London." A little later, when all medical tests on the girl have been negative, a doctor says tentatively: "Of course, there is an outside chance for a cure. I think of it as a shock treatment . . ." Meaning formal exorcism approved by the bishop.

I suppose some people will try to argue that this is instructive, since, among other things, the story is based on a case of reported possession and exorcism that took place in Mount Rainier, Md., in 1949. They can present that argument, all right, but then they should monitor the behavior of the audiences at the Cinema I. Not five out of 100 people seem to give a hang about the instruction being received. They're getting their kicks out of seeing

a small girl being tortured and torn, quite literally. The audience watches as if attending a porno film, moving around in their seats, talking, smoking, staring at the ceiling, during the conventional exposition, and then paying attention only to the violence that has been sanctified.

Blatty somewhere suggests that the object of demonic possession is not necessarily to possess an individual but to sow doubt, confusion, suspicion and horror among

the onlookers. This the popularity of "The Exorcist" itself does to such an extent that I wonder if, perhaps, there aren't a large number of people who, deep-down, would like to outlaw the further use of Ben Franklin's iron points. We may be approaching that point in history.

1974 Ja 13, II:1:6

They Kill Animals And They Call It Art

More and more directors are using the deaths of innocent creatures to provide shocks their films might otherwise fail to deliver

By T. E. D. KLEIN

I'VE just returned from "The Holy Mountain." It was quite a trip. I saw an old man pluck out his glass eye and hand it to a little girl. I watched three men impale themselves over and over on bayonets. I passed a man whose face was covered with flies, and another whose body was covered with giant spiders. I met an armless psychopath, a quadruple amputee, a religious chimpanzee and a man whose excrement was turned into gold. I witnessed mother-son incest, transvestism in the church, several dozen executions, and one public castration.

Oddly enough, none of this bothered me. None of this was real. It was just a charade, courtesy of Alexandro Jodorowsky, the Chilean director whose "El Topo,"—a blood-drenched fairy tale shot in Mexico—became the first cult film of the seventies. His new film, now playing at midnight on Fridays and Saturdays at the Waverly, is entertaining enough at first, but it soon becomes filled with the sort of thing Stewart Brand has described in his "Whole Earth Catalog" as "dime store mysticism." It squanders a truly incredible amount of props, images, and money—all to little effect, for Jodorowsky tries so hard to be shocking that, in the end, he becomes merely monotonous. He reminds one of a Fellini without the feeling.

What did bother me, though, was Jodorowsky's use — or misuse — of animals. Their corpses fill the screen. A parade goes by carrying dozens of crosses on which the butchered bodies of sheep hang crucified. A tree stands decorated with hundreds of slaughtered chickens. During a "spiritual operation," the lump on a sinner's back is sliced open to reveal the inky body of an octopus.

*

T. E. D. Klein, a freelance writer, is now at work on a screenplay.

A dead pig is used as a vat for carrying plaster, a man sits within the carcass of a bull as if it were a bathtub, and the director himself, playing The Alchemist, reclines upon a throne made from the bodies of goats. When this same character offers to let his head be cut off by a disciple, the camera cuts away, then returns to find the decapitated body of a lamb, which spurts fountains of blood while Jodorowsky squats nearby, chuckling heartily at his joke.

He further offers us what looks to be a genuine dogfight, and in an early scene he dresses up a wagonload of frogs and horned toads to resemble Aztecs and Spanish conquistadors, then films the parched creatures as they die slowly in the noonday sun. Those left alive he destroys in a dynamite explosion.

This may hardly seem a major issue, of course, for frogs and the like die every day. They die in schoolrooms and they die in laboratories. Fishermen use them for bait, gourmets eat them, and small boys kill them for sport. These frogs, however, died so that Alexandro Jodorowsky could make "The Holy Mountain" and therein lies the difference. This is a new kind of violence, a kind apparently ignored by all but a few humane groups, bleeding hearts, and, I daresay, children. It points up a curious — and alarming—trend in filmmaking: what can only be called Death for Art's Sake.

As I've tried to suggest, Jodorowsky is one of its leading practitioners in Mexico. But when it comes to ego trips, Mexico has nothing on the U.S.A. Our own directors, too, enjoy playing God with the lives of their fellow creatures. Consider, for example, Dennis Hopper, who chopped off chicken heads in "Kid

Alix Jeffry

These sheep had their throats slit in a scene from Dennis Hopper's "The Last Movie"

one may also point to such recent European imports as "The Devil's Nightmare," in which the bloody body of a cat is riddled with steel spikes, and the German-language "Jonathan," in which the still-kicking bodies of slaughtered livestock add "color" (or at least one color) to the panorama of a massacre.

Billed as "the first adult vampire film," "Jonathan" also features close-ups of a mouse being slowly crushed to death beneath the heel of a boot. The intention? Simply to show that the prison guard in question is a cruel man — something we might have gathered already, since he's just finished whipping the hero bloody.

Yet for all his blood and crying, the hero's pain somehow failed to move me half so much as the mouse's. Maybe it's because the mouse's cries were authentic.

Authenticity is nice when you can get it, but when it comes to filmmaking I've always been perfectly content to look upon stuffed animals, or trained animals, or animals drugged or sleeping (e.g. the monkey in "The Andromeda Strain"), and to make believe they were dead. "The Godfather" employed an actual horse's head, for that horrifying bedroom scene, but the object came from a nearby slaughterhouse.

"Patton," on the other hand, actually killed the two donkeys that George C. Scott "shot" because they were blocking the advance of his troops. ("The two old donkeys were put to death when a doctor gave them painless lethal injections," explained the film's producer.) That may sound relatively humane, but I'd hate to think a filmmaker would actually destroy an animal just to make a scene look "real" or—as in "The Hellstrom Chronicle," when a mouse dies in convulsions from a bee sting—just to prove a point.

Of course, some people aren't bothered by all this. They merely smile, shrug, and point out that millions upon millions of animals die each year, killed by everything from bombs to mousetraps to speeding cars. Indeed, one can take a kind of gloomy solace in this fact, just as, to put things in perspective, one can profitably turn one's thoughts to the livestock regularly killed in our meatpacking plants—as Georges Franju pictured it years ago in "Le Sang des Bêtes." After all, amid carnage of this magnitude, what can a few more deaths possibly mean?

*

Certainly it's of no consequence to the buffalo and elk

Blue" and who went to Peru to film "The Last Movie"— another Personal Statement. In a 1970 article in The Times, entitled "A Gigantic Ego Trip for Dennis Hopper?," writer Alix Jeffry vividly described the making of "The Last Movie":

"For the sacrifice scene, seven sheep are lying on their sides, feet tied, waiting for their throats to be cut. Several hundred Indians have been engaged as extras for the day, for a little less than one American• dollar apiece . . . the blood-letting takes place matter-of-factly after a religious ceremony. An animal raises its head, blood streaming from its throat, and looks with glazed eyes at its executioner, and then its head slowly drops. Death is just another phase of life . . . violence breathes in and out of this film."

Violence — it's become something of a catchword. These days, of course, all right-thinking people have denounced "violence in the movies"—and, indeed, with good reason. But sometimes they get a little carried away, and act as if the violence on screen were *real:* as if, in "Dillinger," Warren Oates' victims bled real blood; as if, in "Charley Varrick," Walter Matthau's enemies died real deaths.

*

Whatever the eventual effects of such carnage upon our psyches and our society, it may be worth reminding ourselves that Hollywood's bullets are blank. But for animals, the bullets and the knives and the blood *are* real; and more and more directors are using the deaths of innocent creatures to provide shocks their films might otherwise fail to deliver.

As one might expect, horror movies are among the worst offenders. There are, for example, several Filipino imports—B-movie fare at its most primitive. One, "Mad Doctor of Blood Island" (seen on New York TV earlier this season, under a new title and, appropriately, butchered), features the usual hacked-off human limbs, glistening viscera and dangling eyeballs. But all this stuff is patently papier-mâché.

It's all good clean fun—until, halfway through, there's a scene in which a native tribe hacks to death a flock of sheep and pigs for some ritual sacrifice; and suddenly it's no longer very funny, for it's clear that real animals are being killed, and far from quickly.

Not that Asian horror films are the only such offenders;

killed in "Jeremiah Johnson" that they died for Art instead of for Sport; nor would it matter to a deer that it died for the Richard Burton film, "Bluebeard." Jean-Luc Godard had a pig's throat cut for "Weekend," Fernando Arrabal did the same for a steer in "Viva La Muerte," and a goose's head was chopped off amid the feasting of "The Grande Bouffe" —but these animals would hardly care that their butchered bodies appeared not on the dinner table but on the screen.

Unfortunately, I care.

And so does Harold Melniker, head of the American Humane Association's Hollywood office. "More and more, we hear of mistreatment of animals on overseas sets," Melniker wrote in a recent issue of Screen Actor magazine. "It would indeed be a giant step forward if an actor on a set in Spain or Italy, for instance, were to step forward and protest such action." He cites only one actor, Edd Byrnes, who's been willing to speak out.

Acting as a sort of unofficial adviser to the film industry (and, all too often, as its conscience), Melniker bemoans the current trend toward foreign production. Typically, Kirk Douglas had to go to Yugoslavia to shoot his new western, "Scalawag," which makes use of the notorious trip-wire to yank the legs from under horses; typically, too, the first TV movie to use trip-wires (and so far the *only* one) was ABC's "Hardcase," shot in Mexico.

Overseas productions are by no means the only culprits. In its monthly classification list, which rates films "acceptable" or "unacceptable" in their treatment of animals, the American Humane Association has recorded violations by every major American studio, from the cockfight in "The Legend of Nigger Charley" to the recent Burt Lancaster western, "Ulzana's Raid," filmed in Arizona, which—despite previous assurances to the contrary—went ahead and used trip-wires while an A.H.A. representative protested in vain to the local sheriff.

"When you want action," says Melniker bitterly, "tripping horses is a way to get it. It's easy and it's quick." Though John Wayne has always abided by A.H.A. guidelines, using only trained horses in his films, directors like Sam Peckinpah prefer to

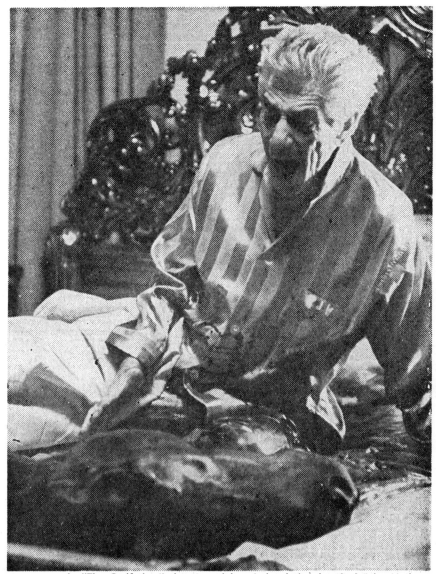

In "The Godfather," the severed horse's head that horrified John Marley came from a slaughterhouse. But two donkeys were actually shot for "Patton."

take the easy way out. Peckinpah's recent "Pat Garrett and Billy the Kid" got an "unacceptable" rating for both the trip-wiring of horses and the casual use of chickens, buried in the ground up to their necks, for target practice.

What has the Motion Picture Association of America been able to do about the abuse of animals in movies? As far back as 1939, it acted against "Jesse James," in which a horse was propelled over a cliff by means of a tipping plank, heavily greased. Until that time, the industry's production code had contained only vague references to the treatment of animals; a type of trip-wire called the "running W" was a common-

place in westerns, as were concealed pits, so that spills cost many a horse a broken leg—or even a broken neck.

The death of the horse in "Jesse James," however, resulted in such a public outcry that, in 1940, new stipulations were written into the code specifically outlawing the running W, and in 1956 it was further decreed that "in the production of motion pictures involving animals the producer shall consult with the authorized representative of The American Humane Association, and invite him to be present during the staging of such animal action."

*

Thanks to the provisions of the code, animals in Amer-

ican films were afforded decent and humane treatment under A.H.A. supervision — until, in 1966, the entire production code was discarded, and with it all mention of trip-wires and mistreatment during shooting. No longer was it required that an A.H.A. representative witness scenes involving animals; his presence on the set was left to the whim of the producer.

Since 1966, the abuses have grown, and the trip-wire has made a triumphant return. Where once Melniker's office received copies of virtually all American film scripts involving animals, so that the A.H.A. might act as consultant in the filming, Melniker says he now receives "very few," and spends far more time going over the 25 to 30 television scripts sent him each week.

*

"It seems as though we have, as a nation, entered into an era of permissiveness," he wrote in the National Humane Review. "In

all phases of life, individuals are making their own rules and anything goes! Regrettably, this attitude is reaching over into the handling of animals."

But perhaps there is still room for hope. Perhaps an Alexandro Jodorowsky, or a Dennis Hopper, or a Sam Peckinpah will one day go too far, and will unwittingly bring about a return to the 1956 provisions.

Or perhaps these artists will experience a change of heart similar to the one apparently experienced by actor-director Cornel Wilde. In the late 1960's, Wilde appeared on an odious ABC-TV show called "American Sportsman," in which the camera followed various celebrities as they tracked down and disposed of a wide variety of animals. Aided by a guide, a camera crew, and a high-powered rifle with a telescopic sight, Wilde was shown bringing down an Alaskan grizzly with two shots, chortling like a child over his kill. "Boy, oh boy, oh boy," he exulted. "We did it!"

However, by 1970, Wilde seems to have had second thoughts, as evidenced by "No Blade of Grass," his film depicting the effects of a worldwide agricultural famine. To be sure, Wilde stuffed his film with motorcycle gangs, graphic rape scenes, and lots of mashed-looking animal carcasses. It was, at best, enjoyable trash —hardly the responsible plea for environmental protection it pretended to be.

But, catching "No Blade of Grass" recently at a drive-in, I was unexpectedly gratified by the words that appeared on screen after "THE END" had replaced all the carnage. They said:

"No animal was killed or mistreated for the purpose of making this film."

How good it would be if those words could follow all films.

Sam Peckinpah's 'Pat Garrett and Billy the Kid' used chickens, buried in the ground up to their necks, for target practice

We Found Our Maturity, But Look What We Lost!

Elsa Lanchester was a bride created in the laboratory by mad doctor Colin Clive in the 1935 movie "Bride of Frankenstein"

Where are the films—good and bad—that do not aspire to art, films that are unashamedly not important? Whatever happened to intelligent fluff?

By ALLEN McKEE

I'VE been sitting around trying to think of the last time I saw a really good movie that had nothing to do with serious themes or cultural profundities, a movie that was made for no other reason than to give its audience a couple hours of fun. And the only thing I've been able to come up with is "Holiday," starring Gary Grant and Katharine Hepburn, which was made in 1938 and which I saw recently in San Francisco, along with "Vivacious Lady," an old Jimmy Stewart-Ginger Rogers movie that was also pretty good.

Movies are so solemn these days, so self-consciously aware of their status as art, that two minutes before the start of most major films an almost palpable sense of reverence can be felt in the audience, the same cautious reverence that hangs so heavily in foreign museums and funeral homes. Good films are good now because they are emotionally stimulating or artistically ambitious (like "Last Tango in Paris"), while bad films are bad because they're portentous or tricky, because they aspire to art without achieving it (like "Jesus Christ Superstar").

But where are the films—good *and* bad—that do not aspire to art, films which are unashamedly *not* important? Where are the contemporary equivalents of "His Girl Friday" and "It Happened One Night," "Bride of Frankenstein" and "The African Queen," "Sea Hawk," "The Thin Man," and "Destry Rides Again"? Whatever happened to intelligent

Allen McKee is a freelance writer.

fluff?

*

The answer, I think, may lie where all too many of our social ills reside: in the Tube. MGM's announcement some weeks ago that it was getting out of the movie business to concentrate its resources on television and other non-cinematic forms of entertainment released a small swamp into the basements of romance. There is so little excellence in contemporary life that even the myth of excellence—and MGM's greatness *was* partly myth—must be guarded against encroachment. Culturally, we are more and more a nation of pariahs, and the jackal that brought the Metro lion down was television.

Back when TV first kindled panic in the money-green souls of Hollywood moguls, the industry's greatest fear was that audiences would stop going to movies and spend their evenings in front of the box—a fear that proved justified. But television's impact was greater still than that. By forcing filmmakers to compete for an audience's attention, television in effect determined the ultimate direction of Hollywood, for movies were obliged to offer what the Tube could not: spectacle, sex, blood—and, most recently, art.

It was economically smart for movies to get serious, but the realization did not fully sink in until the sixties, when directors like Stanley Kubrick and Mike Nichols demonstrated that a serious American filmmaker could maintain his artistic integrity and still turn a profit. (It is ironic that

as American directors have become more sober, some of the European giants—whose early works were largely responsible for the artistic acceptance of film in the first place—have returned to simpler styles. Truffaut's recent films have been candy-like concoctions, while Fellini, Grand Master of synthetic chaos, sems to have revived singlehandedly the old De Mille ethic of extravagance for extravagance's sake—indeed, what else was "Roma" but a long parade, each sequence lumbering past like an outlandishly decorated float?)

Movies are mature now, and the best films of the last 10 years have been exciting in ways that Hollywood's old-timers could never have foreseen. But we've paid for that maturity. We've paid for it with the loss of fanciful, well-constructed, unpretentious diversions—movies made for the hell of it—the kind of movies on which Metro and the others built their empires. And we've paid for it also in the way people think about cinema, which is to say pompously.

*

There is so much sober consideration wasted on every aspect of film as an art that profundities sprout like weeds from the merest trifles: in his review of "Paper Moon," Rolling Stone's Jon Landau proclaimed, apparently in earnest, that a cigar box carried by 9-year-old Tatum O'Neal reflected the uncertainty of her sexual identity because it was a masculine object filled with her private feminine treasures. Which is just about the slickest bit of critical tap dancing that I have ever read.

Back when "The Godfather" seemed to slap some fleeting rosiness into the movie industry's pale old cheeks, we were told by various critics and people involved with the film that the whole thing was supposed to be a horrifying metaphor for the ruthlessness of American capitalism, which may have been the intention. But, if those critics and those filmmakers actually believe that that idea was what "The Godfather" communicated to its

Rosalind Russell, a hotshot reporter, calls in a big story in the 1940 film "His Girl Friday"

audience, they might as well sign up for the alchemists convention, because the message of Corleone and company—accidental, or otherwise—was that organized crime is the last true bastion of loyalty and blood oaths and feudal romanticism.

"The Godfather" was movie fluff on a sophisticated scale and the fact that the blood was more graphic than in "Scarface" or "Little Caesar" does not make it any less fanciful, no matter what we're told about metaphors and capitalism and Marlon Brando's politics.

And what are we to think when a good, hard-eyed critic like Pauline Kael rationalizes that Robert Altman's "The Long Goodbye" bombed in Los Angeles because it disturbed some primitive, subconscious fantasy life that lurks within our psy-

ches? Actually, I suspect the "The Long Goodbye's" initial failure might be blamed on the fact that, despite its intelligence and wit and sexy ripe texture, the movie is something of a muddle.

*

American films are not *pretending* to art; our directors, the good ones, can sustain an esthetic vision as well as any in the world. The problem is that there are almost no good movies which do not derive from such a vision, no movies done simply as ephemeral entertainment. Sometimes a hamburger tastes better than steak, which is why when Hollywood's Grand Old Men make good professional hamburgers — as Mankiewicz did with "Sleuth" and Zinnemann did with "The Day of the Jackal"—there is a freshness in their work that

other movies lack. It is the freshness of intelligent frivolity, of talented gentlemen enjoying themselves.

God knows you have to be careful when you speak out for more light entertainment; people are liable to assume you're talking about gooey little dollops of sorghum like "Jeremy," the kind of "modest" junk that gives fluff a bad name, and we certainly don't need any more of that. What we *do* need more of is fast, funny, unsentimental, craftsmanlike nonsense; Saturday afternoon movies, easily digestible, sleazy or chaste, small scale or large—it really doesn't matter.

Just as long as it's hamburger. Just as long as it's good.

1974 Ja 13, II:13:1

The Program

HOLLYWOOD'S NEW DIRECTORS: EARLY WORKS: WOTON'S WAKE by Brian de Palma (running time, 20 minutes); IT'S NOT JUST YOU MURRAY by Martin Scorsese (15 minutes); ELECTRONIC LABYRINTH by George Lucas (20 minutes); STICKY MY FINGERS FLEET MY FEET by John Hancock, (15 minutes); LANTON MILLS by Terrence Malick (18 minutes). At the Whitney Museum of American art, Madison Avenue at 75th Street, through Jan. 23.

By NORA SAYRE

Graceful as grizzlies, supple as mastodons, the middle-aged men who cherish their games of touch football in Central Park bruise their egos as well as their limbs in John Hancock's delightful short feature, "Sticky My Fingers Fleet My Feet," which is included in "Hollywood's New Directors: Early Works." The program opened Sunday at the Whitney Museum of American Art and will run through Jan. 23. The films are linked by the fact that these young directors developed out of film schools or with grants from the American Film Institute, rather than through years of work in Hollywood.

Mr. Hancock's film, with a script by himself and John Lahr, was adapted from a New Yorker short story by Gene Williams, who also plays the lead. It now appears as a dexterous warm-up for Mr. Hancock's "Bang the Drum Slowly." There's the same sensitivity to individuals and their obsessions —as revealed in the context of sports.

The happy amateur players of "Sticky My Fingers" are as vulnerable to aging as the doomed professional ball-player of "Bang the Drum" is to death. Although "When the goin' 'gets rough, the rough get goin' " is gleefully repeated, the amateurs are threatened from the start: They can't even protect their ball from a tiny child whose mother scornfully tells her to return their "toy." Then a teen-age boy joins their game and runs away with it. Stocky and pudgy bodies lurch and surge about, panting and stumbling and collapsing, but they can't catch the adolescent who politely calls them "sir." Equally funny and touching, this small film deserves a long life.

Martin Scorsese's "It's Not Just You Murray" focuses on the development of hoods, as does his "Mean Streets." But his early picture is a spoof, centered on an amiable fellow who begins by making

gin and ends up as a successful racketeer. What's pleasing throughout is the way that the narration contradicts what's taking place on the screen: A calm, cheerful voice accompanies the beatings and jailings and betrayals that appear as unavoidable hazards of the profession.

All of these early works partake of parody, with one exception: George Lucas's "Electronic Labyrinth." Unfortunately, it also seems like a parody—of many other films about the dehumanized future. Actually, it served as a dry run for Mr. Lucas's "THX1138," which concerned programed people with numbers stamped on their foreheads who were forbidden to love their "mates." Here, most of the film shows the man who rebelled against the system running through endless corridors—as though trying to flee from both the future and the past. A sense of panic is conveyed by the numbing whiteness of that labyrinth, but the actor's face can't manage to look frightened, and much of the film is just too clumsy to be chilling.

Terrence Malick, who later made "Badlands," is represented by "Lanton Mills." It's intended as a take-off on Westerns, but the acting is languid and stilted, and what comes through is a study in fatigue. Still, there are a couple of nice moments, as when two incompetent stick-up men warn a bankful of people not to "get upset"— and the unimpressed crowd isn't even ruffled—or when a dying robber chats casually with the repentant cop who shot him. But the movie makes one doubt if there's a market for slow satire.

Brian De Palma, whose films include "Greetings" and "Sisters," reveals a rather gentle affection for old-fashioned horror in "Woton's Wake," which parodies the styles of silent films. Woton grins and nods and squints like a number of your favorite monsters, as he chases his victims and sets them afire with a torch, or tries on wigs and fangs and noses with all the concentration of a beauty queen before the mirror. We could do without the shot of a mushroom cloud at the end, but otherwise this little pantomine of destruction works deftly and daftly.

1974 Ja 15, 28:5

DEMONS, directed by Toshio Matsumoto; screenplay (Japanese with English subtitles) by Mr. Matsumoto, based on a Kabuki play by Nanboku Tsuruya; director of photography, Tatsuo Suzuki; produced by Matsumoto Productions, distributed by Film Images. Running time: 135 minutes. At the First Avenue Screening Room, First Avenue at 61st Street. This film has not been classified.
Gengo .... Katsuo Nakamura
Koman .... Yasuko Sanjo
Sango .... Juro Kara
Hachiemon .... Masao Imafuku

By VINCENT CANBY

Because humor is in such short supply at the movies these days, one must be forgiven searching for it in the wrong places, as in a long, seriously intended Japanese samurai film.

Toshio Matsumoto's "Demons," based on a Kabuki play, is not, strictly speaking, a samurai film. It is violent but not especially robust. The film is about the revenge wreaked by a shabby, down-at-the-heels samurai warrior on a faithless courtesan and her husband after the couple swindle the warrior out of the 100 ryo with which he was planning to buy back his good name.

What makes it rather appealingly comic is not the English translation provided by vapid subtitles, though they *are* pretty funny, but the borrowed solemnity the director uses to decorate his movie, which looks like an expensive film-school exercise. It wears the furrowed brow of a 10-year-old boy struggling to recite "Thanatopsis" without having the vaguest idea what he's saying.

●

Everything takes place at night, which permits a lot of fancy lighting effects: stark contrasts between light and shadow—that sort of thing. There are occasional confusions between the real and the imagined. Actions are repeated, as if time had gotten stuck in the groove of a record. If a scene doesn't look interesting enough photographed head-on, the director shoots it in slow motion or from above, using the old fly-on-the-ceiling shot.

Nothing, however, succeeds in communicating the intensity of the passions of its poor hero. Told in this uninspired fashion, the tale of rage transformed to madness seems closer to farce than tragedy. Not helping much is a heavy emphasis on mistaken identities and curious coincidence. The style is soft, bogus, essentially frivolous, so that by the time a dying

husband clasps the severed head of his wife to him for one last kiss, I was ready to say "rats."

The film, which was shown at the First Avenue Screening Room Sunday, will be repeated there at noon and midnight today and tomorrow. Mr. Matsumoto, one of Japan's new young directors, was represented here last year by "Funeral Parade of Roses," an equally solemn though even sillier melodrama about Tokyo drug pushers and male prostitutes and their lives of noisy desperation.

1974 Ja 18, 22:1

FILMS BY VLATKO GILIC: IN CONTINUO, 10 minutes; ONE DAY MORE, 10 minutes; TO LOVE, 25 minutes and POWER, 34 minutes. At the Film Forum, 256 West 88th Street. Showings through Sunday and Jan. 24-27, 8 P.M.

By NORA SAYRE

Moisture makes dried blood flow again: there's a shock in that discovery as a hand scrubs the stained walls of a slaughterhouse, where men in white aprons prepare for the day's killing. "In Continuo" is one of four recent documentaries by the Yugoslav film maker Vlatko Gilic, who has won five prizes in his own country, several in Germany and deserves many more. His work can be seen at the Film Forum, at 256 West 88th Street, through Sunday and Jan. 24-27. Don't miss it.

Within the slaughterhouse, the preparations are quite ritualistic, as the men carefully wash the floor and sharpen knives that aren't intended for carving cooked meat—but for cutting into live flesh. Suspense builds up to the carnage that we know will come. The animals' slaughter isn't shown; instead, thick blood oozes and swirls toward the gutters, and the evocation is more powerful than seeing the act itself. The men's serious, intent faces imply that there are no jokes on this job. At first, they seem like soldiers getting ready for battle — later, as though they're in the middle of a war.

●

"One Day More" centers on a murky stream outside a small Yugoslav town, where the mudbaths are said to cure even deadly diseases. Old and young sink to their chins in the dark liquid, some rub parts of their bodies with jetty slime. Heads seem to float on the water, while mist rises in a shot that Fellini might envy. The atmosphere is dense with concentration and bleak hope. You feel that these people are terribly worried and fearful about their bodies. They wait as though for a miracle. Finally, they shower, cheer up and chat noisily—in contrast to the anguished hush that held while they were in the stream.

Deep concentration and preparation — while waiting for something to happen — are themes that recur in Mr. Gilic's work, whether his subjects are profoundly absorbed in butchery or in trying to regain lost health or—as in "To Love"—in one another. This film begins with a piece of machinery slowly moving in space: You can't tell what it is, but it's fascinating to watch it reach its destination. Again, there's suspense, which mounts to the satisfaction of seeing something accomplished. Eventually, we learn that two sides of a bridge are meeting in mid-air, and that we've been watching the key piece going into place. The mystery is solved in one shot, which also suggests the peril of working at great heights.

One of the construction workers climbs to the ground, where his wife waits with a picnic. All their feelings are conveyed through their expressions; there are almost no words. While waiting, she looks both eager and apprehensive: Clearly, she's anxious about his safety. She spreads a white cloth in the wilderness and sets forth a feast with as much care and deliberation as the men give to working on the bridge. Affection surges through brief gestures: She pats his knee, he pushes a strand of hair out of her eyes while she beams at him. Mainly, they gaze at each other and eat, and that simple act reveals an extraordinary sense of intimacy.

●

"Power" shows a hypnotist giving his disciples — six young men with ultra-white skin and dead black hair — a lesson in dominating the will of others. They follow the master's wordless instructions like zombies, repeating many of his actions. They also direct one another's behavior. He slides a giant black needle through both his cheeks without apparent pain; they do the same, but some can't help wincing. A hand moves in front of eyes that look momentarily terrified — as though watching something hideous that we

can't see. There's some groveling and hand-kissing and also some ecstasy afoot. The portrayal of the master's control of his followers is repellent — as it's obviously meant to be. But "Power" hasn't the same brilliance as the first three films, partly because the subjects seem self-conscious.

Mr. Gilic's films are called documentaries. But he's superb at finding the astonishing images that lurk

in the ordinary world. It's as if he'd nabbed some magic from the air and wedded it to facts. And it's a privilege to see through his eyes: Whatever interests him assumes a contagious excitement for us. It's evident that a major talent is already well developed, and since Mr. Gilic is in his mid-30's, we have a lot to look forward to.

1974 Ja 18, 25:1

Chaplin—Once a King, Always a 'King'

By VINCENT CANBY

CHARLIE CHAPLIN's "A King in New York" is like a letter written but unsent—until now—from a far-off time and place of great bitterness. It is quarrelsome, hardheaded, egomaniacal. Although it was produced in 1957, it looks very much like a movie made by a man who acted in his first films in 1913. When the camera moves, it has a way of making everything else seem static. It's a movie with absolutely no gift for small talk, the sort of tricks or narrative bridges that get the story from the climax of one sequence into the start of the next. People always seem to be walking across rooms, opening doors, letting other people in, and walking back again. Nothing seems to happen for great stretches. A lot of scenes look as if they'd been lifted from plays that were being acted before any scripts had been written.

Yet "A King in New York" is also, much of the time, hugely funny and healthily vulgar, and it is always extremely moving. It is a living work. It is one of a kind, a movie that cannot be compared to movies made today, or even to movies made in 1957. It is one part in what we can now see to be the completed body of films by a single artist whose genius forces us to pay as much attention to his failures as to his easily recognized successes.

I use the word failure very loosely. "A King in New York" is not a failure in the sense that dumb, vicious or empty-headed movies like "The Exorcist," "The Seven-Ups" or "Bone" are failures. It only fails because Chaplin's

long financial success allowed him to indulge himself in ways that he really wasn't up to. It fails because of his achievements.

*

Chaplin was angry when he made "A King in New York," and the entire experience, including the reception of the completed film, seems to have been so bitter that he not only withheld it from release here (he's a canny enough businessman to have known it would have probably failed at the box office), but he also didn't bother to discuss its production in his autobiography, published in 1964. The film is mentioned in some photo captions in the autobiography, and in the filmography at the end of the book, and always as "The King in New York," although it's being called "A King In New York" in its current release.

The film is so personal that to criticize it in any degree has a way of turning into a critique of the man. The story of the adventures in the United States of exiled King Shadhov (Chaplin) is very strange fiction. At the start of this film the King is deposed by the mobs for the curious reason that his ministers want to make atomic bombs when he wants to build atomic power plants for the greater good of all. At first Shadhov is humorously exploited in New York by ambitious hostesses and venal advertising interests. Then he runs afoul of some sort of Un-American Activities Committee because of his friendship for a 10-year-old anarchist (played by his son Michael), a character that manages to be less funny than

are not completely successful. I also suspect that this independence, backed by Chaplin's ability to survive, must nettle a lot of people.

Griffith and Keaton had gone through their fortunes by the time they died. Chaplin has kept his. At the same time his life became increasingly settled, serene and happy. Although great painters, novelists and musicians are allowed to grow old in affluence, moviemakers have a way of being resented unless they wind up on Skid Row or cadging free trips to second-rate film festivals.

Time has not made the politics of "A King in New York" any more profound, but it has softened the bitterness, so much so that at the end of the film, when the king goes sadly off to Europe after his encounter with the Un-American Activities Committee, all I could think of was Chaplin's triumphant return to America two years ago at the Lincoln Center gala. Fact and fiction get all muddled when watching the film, which is another way of saying that it plays on a lot of emotions that don't often get exercised in a movie theater. Time is partly responsible, but mostly Chaplin himself.

"A King in New York" is full of superb low comedy routines: A finger caught in the nozzle of a fire hose. A terrible face-lift that leaves the king with an upper lip so shortened that he can't say his m's and v's and, what's worse, he can't drink through a straw. A confron-

tation, presented as a nightclub act, between a man hanging wallpaper and a stuffy straight man who resents getting the wallpaper paste splattered all over him. Thrown away in prodigal fashion are pieces of sheer inspiration as when the king, defeated by the noise in a nightclub, tries pantomime to order first caviar and then turtle soup.

Chaplin's direction of his son Michael is a bit unnerving. The boy is so tense in several of his scenes that he can be seen silently reciting his father's lines as he waits for his cue. But all of the other supporting people are fine, including Dawn Addams who, at this late date, looks like a lacquered souvenir of the 1950s.

*

Especially appealing are Harry Green, who plays the king's lawyer when the king is subpoenaed by the Un-American Activities Committee ("Whatever you do," he says desperately, "don't give them contempt"); Sidney James, one of the "Carry On" regulars, who plays a pushy American ad man; Oliver Johnston, the king's faithful ambassador, and Maxine Audley, who plays the queen with a sweet, dated kind of unworldly graciousness that recalls Edna Purviance in her prime. She is part of the continuity of Chaplin's work that confers importance on even the minor self-indulgent moments of "A King in New York."

1974 Ja 20, II:1:1

grotesque.

When the boy is ultimately "broken" by the F.B.I. and persuaded to inform on his Communist parents, I had the odd feeling that I was watching a Walt Disney version of "Darkness at Noon."

I'm afraid that the idea of the kid's being turned into a political wreck at age 10 must also be regarded with the same jaundiced feelings that Chaplin calls forth when he first introduces the child parroting down-with-all-governments nonsense.

As my colleague Nora Sayre already has observed, Chaplin's method of satirizing the American political scene in the early 1950s seems peculiarly reactionary. It is worthy neither of the horrors of the era nor of the intensity of Chaplin's liberalism and courage.

*

Chaplin's casting himself as a virtuous, people-loving king in the last film in which he played the starring role (his "A Countess from Hong Kong," released in 1967,

starred Marlon Brando and Sophia Loren) is remarkably revealing about the man who survived longer at the top of his form than any other filmmaker I can think of.

As the king of comedy, actually the king of Hollywood, for so many years, he grew so powerful that he could explore a type of self-centeredness that less successful filmmakers must disguise. Chaplin didn't have to. This independence is so rare in films that I find the results fascinating even when they

When Boy Meets Boy

By ALJEAN HARMETZ

ELLIOTT GOULD and Donald Sutherland. Robert Redford and Paul Newman. Gene Hackman and Al Pacino. Dustin Hoffman and Steve McQueen. These are the new romantic teams of the 1970's—the replacements in our fantasies for Katharine Hepburn and Spencer Tracy, Mickey Rooney and Judy Garland, Ginger Rogers and Fred Astaire.

Starting with Elliott Gould and Donald Sutherland in "M*A*S*H" and Jon Voight and Dustin Hoffman in "Midnight Cowboy," recent movies have elaborated on that deep tradition in American

Aljean Harmetz is a freelance writer.

literature that portrays male friendship as a more encompassing and more satisfying emotional experience than love for a woman.

Though not overtly homosexual (and rarely latently so), these movies either ignore women or relegate them to the role of servicing men. They pour drinks, cook food, run errands, and warm beds. In "Scarecrow," Gene Hackman plunges on top of a gigantic lady for a few minutes of pleasure but saves both his money and his tears for Al Pacino. In "M*A*S*H" and the as-yet-unreleased "S*P*Y*S," Gould and Sutherland have so much fun with each other that a woman would be extraneous.

In "Butch Cassidy and the Sundance Kid," Katharine Ross could at least stand at the circumference of the Newman-Redford friendship. In "The Sting," the horse-faced women who attempt to muscle in on the golden Newman-Redford relationship are perennially ladling soup and opening bottles of beer. In "Mean Streets," Harvey Keitel allows himself to be destroyed because of his refusal to cut himself loose from his more than half-crazy friend, Robert De Niro. In "Bang the Drum Slowly," it is Michael Moriarty who protects his dying friend, De Niro.

*

In Elaine May's half-finished "Mikey and Nicky," John Cassavetes and Peter Falk are best friends, one of whom may or may not be given a Mafia "contract" on the other. Cassavetes' own "Husbands" was an examination of a trio of basketball-playing pals at the threshold of middle age (Cassavetes, Falk, and Ben Gazzara) who retreat from wives and children for a fling together in London. And the ads for "Papillon" show the sweat-stained faces of McQueen and Hoffman so close together that they almost merge.

Nearly half a dozen of these pictures glorifying male friendships make their

pair of protagonists police officers. One's partner is one's only pal, one's only defense against the world. In "Cops and Robbers," Cliff Gorman and Joseph Bologna trust each other enough to become criminals together. In "Super Cops," Ron Leibman and David Selby are modeled after two New York detectives who have actually been nicknamed "Batman" and "Robin." Vice-squad officers Elliott Gould and Robert Blake set out to break vice-king Allen Garfield in "Busting" — together defying city officials and their own sergeant; while Alan Arkin and James Caan are plainclothesmen who take on a numbers racketeer in "Freebie and the Bean."

There have always been a certain number of Hollywood films about male friendships. Necessarily. (There is, indeed, a male bond; and there are things men are unwilling to say to women.) What is unique about the current crop of films is that they do not fit into one of the two molds from which such films have been constructed in the past: 1) Older man teaching worshipful younger man. 2) Friendly enemies brawling over oil or coal or diamonds — and a woman.

*

There are no father figures in these films, no Dr. Gillespie teaching young Dr. Kildare about medicine and life. Nor is there any equivalent of Clark Gable and Spencer Tracy pushing each other into the mud in "Boom Town" before ending the film linked arm in arm. Rather than testing each other, the protagonists of these new films seem, from the beginning, to huddle together for emotional warmth, as Gene Hackman and Al Pacino huddle together for physical warmth against the wind and rain of the deserted highway in "Scarecrow." In the chill of the alienated present, such warmth may be necessary for sanity.

Though I am quick to take offense at the denigration of women — in film

Robert Redford and Paul Newman are partners in crime in "The Sting"
Women are for ladling soup and opening bottles of beer

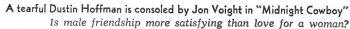

A tearful Dustin Hoffman is consoled by Jon Voight in "Midnight Cowboy"
Is male friendship more satisfying than love for a woman?

Gene Hackman and Al Pacino are close chums in "Scarecrow"
Hackman digs girls, but he saves his money and tears for Pacino

or in life — I seem to feel no anger at the exclusion of women from these male relationships. (I feel much less comfortable about the charlady chores women are required to perform in the films.) Our culture regards deep male friendships after adolescence with uneasiness. In my circle of acquaintances, it is the women who have emotionally penetrating relationships, while the men stay relentlessly on the surface with each other.

In that sense, the often adolescent and sometimes silly relationships between the protagonists of these films may be a psychological step up.

1974 Ja 20, II:1:4

The Cast

RHINOCEROS, directed by Tom O'Horgan; screenplay by Julian Berry, based on the play by Eugene Ionesco; produced by Ely Landau; executive producer, Edward Lewis; music, Galt MacDonald; director of photography Jim Crabe; editor, Bud Smith; presented by the American Film Theater. Running time: 101 minutes, plus two intermissions. At selected theaters. This film has been classified PG.

John ....Zero Mostel
Stanley ....Gene Wilder
Daisy ....Karen Black
Carl ....Robert Weil
Norman ....Joe Silver
Mrs. Bingham.............Marilyn Chris
Logician ....Robert Fields

By VINCENT CANBY

"People who try to hang onto their individuality always come to a bad end," says Stanley (Gene Wilder) in the last act of "Rhinoceros," the American Film Theater's screen version of the Eugene Ionesco play that opened at selected theaters here yesterday.

But do they always come to a bad end? Stanley, the hero of "Rhinoceros," is an unreliable mouthpiece in an unreliable metaphor so grossly overdirected by Tom O'Horgan that you might get the idea Mr. O'Horgan thought he was making a movie for an audience made up entirely of rhinoceroses instead of people.

•

Stanley, the mild-mannered, virtually identity-less office clerk, has admittedly had a terrifying time. He finds himself the only human being in a world where everyone else, for various reasons, is electing to turn into a rhinoceros.

His best friend John (Zero Mostel), a fastidious, prissy man who always carries a pocket mirror and an extra necktie, has transformed himself right in front of Stanley's eyes. At first it seemed only that John had a pesky virus. His voice sounded hoarse and he was irritable. Later there was no doubt what was happening when, between whimpers, John began to paw the floor, snort angrily and exclaim that he really didn't hate people, he was simply indifferent to them.

Daisy (Karen Black), Stanley's girl, tries to hold out but she too eventually gives in to the call of the wild: she can't resist the tremendous energy emanating from all the rhinoceroses now charging through the streets of the town that, in Julian Barry's adaptation of Ionesco, is situated not in France but in "Anywhere, U.S.A."

•

"Rhinoceros," which had a middling run on Broadway in 1961, is not ideal film material, being an example of the kind of theater of the absurd that should be played like old-time farce within a stylized, three-sided set or, perhaps, within no set at all. Even though the film never shows us any real rhinoceroses, the realism of the movie camera is undeniable. It reduces things absurd to the status of the merely silly.

Mr. O'Horgan's direction has the effect of exposing all of the play's weaknesses and none of its merits. It is clumsily inventive and obtrusive. The same was true of his only other film, "Futz," though it was probably responsible for his huge stage successes, "Hair" and "Jesus Christ Superstar."

•

Mr. Ionesco apparently wants us to see "Rhinoceros" as a parable about conformity and the contagion that could convert supposedly moral, rational people into the ecstatically mindless mobs that idolized Hitler as the last word in authority figures.

The lesson is both very small and very fuzzy. It is so determinedly out of focus that one begins to wonder whether the playwright had any ideas in mind at all and, if he did, whether they work out the way he intended. Stanley talks in clichés about "humanity" and "standards" and is, at heart, quite as ignorant as the rhinoceros he disdains. He also has a lot less fun than they do. All of which adds up to a philosophical so-what.

•

Mr. O'Horgan attempts to jazz up the film with music by Galt MacDermot ("Hair"), which is nice but superfluous, and with low comedy routines that he photographs in ways guaranteed to make them unfunny. The grace and continuity of a series of pratfalls are broken up into a lot of different, isolated shots. His feel for slapstick is as solemn as that of an archeologist photographing the individual bones of a dinosaur. For reasons best kept to himself the director also introduces into Ionesco a comparatively lyric dream sequence.

Considering the material, and considering the obstacles they had to act around, through and over, the performers come off very well. Mr. Mostel, comparatively subdued, is extremely funny, whether he is outlining the regime Stanley is to follow to become a cultivated man, or whether he is slipping unaware into the early stages of rhinoceritis, munching the leaves of a potted plant.

Mr. Wilder has an innate sweetness that neutralizes a lot of the dumbness of Stanley, a character called Berenger in the play but renamed in the movie, I suspect, to evoke unfairly the shade of the late great Stan Laurel. Miss Black, like Mr. Mostel, succesfully created a cartoon character out of pure flesh and blood, hers being a variation on Little Orphan Annie, though not so articulate.

"Rhinoceros" is the fourth in the American Film Theater's series of eight films based on stage plays. It may well be the least interesting.

1974 Ja 22, 30:3

RAZOR IN THE FLESH (A Navalha Na Carne), directed by Braz Chediak; screenplay (Portuguese with English subtitles) by Plinio Marcos, Fernando Ferreira and Emiliano Queiroz, based on the play by Mr. Marcos; director of photography, Hello Silva; editor, Rafael Valverde. Produced by Magnus Films, distributed by Ronin Film. Running time: 95 minutes. At the First Avenue Screening Room, near 61st Street. This film has not been classified.

Vado ....Jece Valadao
Neusa Suely ....Glauce Rocha
Veludo ....Emiliano Queiroz

"Razor in the Flesh" ("A Navalha Na Carne") is a very respectable Brazilian film, made in 1969, based on a rough but respectable Brazilian play that seems to have been inspired, at least partially, by the postwar American Theater of Humiliation, to which Tennessee Williams, William Inge and Edward Albee have all successfully contributed at one point or another.

The film was shown at the First Avenue Screening Room Sunday and will be repeated there Friday and Saturday, with showings at noon and midnight.

During the dialogueless first 10 minutes of the film that Braz Chediak, the director, takes to establish the characters (an aging prostitute, her young pimp and the homosexual who lives next door) and the setting (Rio de Janeiro's slums), I was impressed by the sleazy accuracy of the black-and-white photography, but I also feared the worst: that Mr. Chediak had opened up the play to such an extent that all real life had escaped.

When the film finally settles down in the room shared by the prostitute and her pimp (the beginning of the original play, I suspect), "Razor in the Flesh" becomes a fascinating exercise in the sort of bravura acting that usually doesn't work in movies. Glauce Rocha, who died in 1972, and was a look-alike for Jeanne Moreau, is superb as the prostitute who disintegrates, physically and emotionally, in the course of an hour or so of unequal combat with her lover, played by Jece Valadao.

There's a lot of Blanche Dubois-Stanley Kowalski here, as the pimp ridicules the woman, even forcing her to look at herself in the all-dreaded mirror. Miss Rocha's intensity is immense, but she controls it with a discipline that fuels the melodrama. It's been a long time since I've seen so much crawling around on the floor and heard so many self-conscious asides (She, after some new and entirely expected humiliation: "I wonder if I'm human"), without feeling sorry for the actors required to say such things.

•

Mr. Valadao behaves like a Brazilian Richard Burton (in "Look Back in Anger"), which isn't bad, though Emiliano Queiroz's blondined homosexual is so broad that it could have been patterned on the swishy character created by Dudley Moore in a sketch in Broadway's current hit, "Good Evening." The feather duster that Mr. Queiroz carries is a prop better used in farce than a film of the hoped-for seriousness of "Razor in the Flesh."

One major drawback: the white subtitles, which translate the Portuguese dialogue, are completely illegible when, much of the time, they are printed against the background of white sheets on a bed, which is a principal scene of action.

VINCENT CANBY.

1974 Ja 24, 44:2

WILLIE DYNAMITE, directed by Gilbert Moses; screenplay by Ron Cutler, based on a story by Joe Keyes Jr. and Mr. Cutler; produced by Richard D. Zanuck and David Brown; director of photography, Frank Stanley; editor, Aaaron Stell; music, J. J. Johnson; distributed by Universal Pictures. Running time: 102 minutes. At the DeMille Theater, Seventh Avenue at 47th Street. This film has been rated R.

Willie .... Roscoe Orman
Cora .... Diana Sands
Robert Daniels ...... Tholmus Rasulala
Pashen .... Joyce Walker
Bell .... Roger Robinson
Celli .... George Murdock
Pointer .... Albert Hall

By VINCENT CANBY

"Willie Dynamite," which opened yesterday at the Demille, is another rip-off on the black exploitation film for which, I suppose, all sorts of sociological rationales are possible, though, in this case, I don't feel like making them.

The movie, about the decline and fall of a black New York superpimp nicknamed Willie Dynamite, has a promising beginning. The costumes, language, melodrama, performances and even the soundtrack music are so outrageously broad it seems as if the film were putting itself on, parodying such earlier live-action black cartoons as "The Mack" and "Cleopatra Jones." Not at all. It wants a piece of the same action.

•

Willie Dynamite (Roscoe Orman), who dresses every morning as if he were going to a Mardi Gras ball before lunch, may not have happiness but he has everything else: a lavender-and-gold, supercharged Lincoln, a magnificent pad that looks like the Castro showroom on Duffy Square, a nice middle-class mother who lives in New Jersey and thinks he is some sort of artists' agent, and a stable of six superwomen who have free run of what could be the New York Hilton.

When the cops put the heat on whoring, Willie, idealistic loner that he is, refuses to join the city's other major pimps in a mutual-protection agency.

The proud Willie is punished not by the gods but by the Internal Revenue Service, by the other pimps, by the cops and mostly by a former prostitute, played wanly by the late Diana Sands in her last film appearance, a character who, having gone straight, describes herself as "a sort of Ralph Nader for hookers." The film is under the peculiar impression that Mr. Nader operates on behalf of the retailer rather than the consumer.

Before Willie meets his comeuppance, the movie indulges itself and us in a lot of dumb fantasies about how great it would be to be at the top of pimpdom, even if only for a little while. It talks pseudo hip, and it introduces (but never develops) an interesting character in the person of a black cop (played by Al Hall), who wears button-down shirts and Brooks Brothers suits and is, apparently, a Black Muslim.

•

The film spends a good deal of its time ogling Willie's women, who are black, white, oriental and beautiful, but its ménage is stupifying sentimental. The thing that convinces Willie to go straight is the death of his mink-stole-wearing mom, who has a heart attack when she learns where Willie's money really comes from. Says Willie through his tears: "I did it all for her," or some such baloney.

The movie was directed by Gilbert Moses, who has some good stage credits, including Melvin Van Peebles's "Ain't Supposed to Die a Natural

Death." As the beginning of the film shows, Mr. Moses may be a director with a true sense of comedy and parody, but one can't be sure. The screenplay, by Ron Cutler, is so awful.

1974 Ja 24, 45:1

WOMAN HOUSE by Johanna Demetrakas, 47 minutes; JANIE'S JANE by Geri Ashur and Peter Barton, 25 minutes; THE FEMINIST PARTY STREET-WALKS by Herstory Films, 6 minutes. At the Whitney Museum of American Art, 75th Street and Madison Avenue, through Wednesday.

By NORA SAYRE

Infinite stockings hang over a sinkful of suds, the walls and ceiling of a hot pink kitchen are plastered with fried-egg sculptures (many of them resembling breasts), a long satin bridal train pours down a flight of stars until it achieves a hilarious and burdensome length: the images of "Womanhouse" reflect "the longings, fears, and dreams that women have as they wash, cook, and iron their lives away."

In 1972, Judy Chicago, Miriam Schapiro, and a group of women artists from the California Institute of the Arts transformed an old, battered Hollywood house into an environmental anthology of women's experiences — especially in relation to the home. The result, filmed by Johanna Demetrakas, is one of three feminist films that are being shown at the Whitney Museum of American Art until next Wednesday.

•

The camera tours the rooms of the house along with the visiting public. There are metaphors of confinement: A nude mannequin trapped in a laundry cupboard, where the shelves bisect her body, and of the vulnerability of identity: a sand sculpture of a woman lying prone in a bathtub (the figure can be erased "with a simple swipe of a hand").

Although the stress is on the styles of suppression and the conflicts that so many women have known, there are abundant flashes of gaiety throughout this pensive satire, and it is clear that—for both the artists and the visitors—morale as well as consciousness were raised.

"The hardest thing is fightin' for what you never had": a welfare mother in Newark describes her dawning independence, along with her determination to raise her five children free from the passivity that society has encouraged in the poor. "Janie's Janie," a fine documentary by Geri Ashur and Peter Barton, unreels the self-discoveries of a woman who married at 15 to escape the constrictions of her own threadbare family. She later parted from the husband who used to hit her "when I got fresh with my mouth." (Pause.) "He should hear my mouth now."

There's sympathy for men —like her father and former husband — who were depressed by their dreary jobs and came home in a bad temper. But their frustrations merely diminished contact with the wife or children. Now, on her own, Janie acquires a confidence she never had, along with the chance to explore the world and "the right to be wrong," to make mistakes.

•

We see her hauling food out of the stove, or telling a small child to put on a sweater, as she talks about the job in the five-and-ten that didn't pay enough for the nine hours a day away from home, or the humiliations of welfare, and the problem-sharing with other women that broke down the mutual wariness. "There's less trust among poor people because you're afraid of what you might lose." Throughout, there's a ringing resolve for change — among working-class women who have been learning to fight the system.

"The Feminist Party Street-walks," made cooperatively by Herstory Films, shows a 1972 protest against the media's "whiteout" (limited coverage) of Representative Shirley Chisholm during her Presidential campaign. There are demonstrations outside The New York Times, N.B.C., C.B.S., A.B.C. and Time Inc.

Since the soundtrack is ragged, we are denied some of the eloquence of Florynce Kennedy, lawyer and founder of the Feminist party. However, the lines of one song come through plainly: "Give us Chisholm and McGovern/ Gotta get rid of Richard Nixon/Gotta get rid of corporate fixers/"We've had enough of them."

1974 Ja 26, 37:4

Film: Wildlife in Peril

Welcome—even thanks—to "Vanishing Wilderness," a fine new film for the entire family that opened here yesterday in a mass showcase booking. This nature documentary reportedly has been mopping up financially in previous showings across the country and Canada, and no wonder.

The feature is a documentary of wildlife, primarily in Alaska, the American Northwest and the Florida Everglades. Photographed in beautiful color, with a splendid sweep of seasonal settings, it closes in marvelously on a richly varied assortment of beasts and birds, many of them threatened with extinction.

The narration is easy, comfortable and interesting, rarely folksy and, wonder of wonders, the plea for wildlife protection is made pointedly but casually. The camera, manned by a German photographer, Heinz Seilmann, says it all, hovering intimately over an extraordinary, untamed cavalcade, large to tiny.

The picture swarms with wildlife—antelopes, mustangs, buffalo ("whose sad eyes tell their story"), geese, whooping cranes, pelicans, herons, alligators, caribou, big horn sheep, bears, water moose and many other species. The most beguiling scenes were those of a frisky little sea otter, beaver dambuilders and a spectacle of swarming fur-seals on the Pribilof Islands off Alaska, magnificently presented.

A charmingly informal prelude shows the family of Arthur Dubs, who co-produced with Mr. Seilmann, riding the rapids in a boat on the Rogue River in Oregon.

HOWARD THOMPSON

1974 Ja 24, 47:1

When Is a 'Rhinoceros' a Turkey?

By VINCENT CANBY

FOUR films seen. Four still to be released. With the two-day run here earlier this week of Tom O'Horgan's film version of Ionesco's "Rhinoceros," the American Film Theater has reached the halfway mark in its first subscription season designed to bring culture to the otherwise depressed, that is, the American moviegoer.

That isn't exactly the way the AFT is described by Henry T. Weinstein, the organization's vice president in charge of creative affairs. He says its aim is to bring "to audiences everywhere great works of the theater, performed by consummate artists, under the guidance of major directors, on film."

That definition is at my elbow in a press release I might not have read if, while scanning it, I hadn't gotten the impression it said that Mr. Weinstein, now planning the AFT's second season, was negotiating with Pirandello and Brecht. I'm aware that both playwrights have long since left us but I'm also aware that the AFT often thinks that it is thinking big. Actually the press release said that negotiations were going on with the *estates* of Pirandello and Brecht.

Because the AFT is apparently a financial success, despite early ticket problems when a computer system broke down, and because it is apparently going into a second season in the fall, it is fair, I think, to assess what has been accomplished so far. Unlike a couple of my more enthusiastic colleagues, I didn't review the entire first season series last September on the basis of several reels of excerpts from the eight productions.

Seen in New York so far have been O'Neill's "The Iceman Cometh," directed by John Frankenheimer, Pinter's "The Homecoming," directed by Peter Hall, Albee's "A Delicate Balance," directed by Tony Richardson and, most recently, "Rhinoceros." Upcoming are "Luther," "Butley," "Lost in the Stars" and "The Three Sisters."

With the exception of Peter Hall's fine production of "The Homecoming," which works so well as a film that you don't pay any attention to its theatrical seams, the AFT looks to be producing a new type of film—one that may not ultimately be in the greatest demand. The AFT is manufacturing the Coffee Table Movie, something that is supposed to establish one's intellectual credentials by physical association. Purchase tickets but give them to your friends.

I don't mean to sound furious about what the AFT is up to. These films won't harm anyone. They'll bore quite a few and perhaps make a lot of other people feel as if they've taken their culture vitamins for the year. The disappointing thing about the project to date is the *smallness* of the thinking, which, I'm afraid, accurately represents the extent of the so-called arts explosion in the

United States.

"The Iceman Cometh" is a tremendous, primal theatrical experience, but was it really necessary to film it again just so we could have the dubious pleasure of witnessing Lee Marvin fail in the key role as Hickey? It was nice seeing Robert Ryan and Fredric March in this version, but nothing can convince me that it was worth doing if, in the archives somewhere, there exists a print of that extraordinary

TV tape version directed by Sidney Lumet, produced by Worthington Miner and starring Jason Robards.

Why can't the AFT be truly adventuresome? If they insist on raiding O'Neill, why not do something tough and probably recalcitrant like "Strange Interlude" or "The Great God Brown"?

For that matter, why did they choose Edward Albee's "A Delicate Balance" if they wanted to give audiences everywhere great works of the theater performed by consummate artists under the guidance of major directors on film?

*

"A Delicate Balance" is an interesting idea for a play, but it is not a great work of theater. It starts off as a satire of the type of comedy on which Broadway thrived for decades: people meeting politely in three-sided drawing rooms, talking a great deal more than necessary about how they like their martinis mixed (in an era in which people swig vodka on the rocks, the comic shock of the five-to-one martini has been lost), but instead of worrying about who isn't sleeping with whom, the crisis with which they're faced is their own emptiness. It *sounds* like a good idea for a play, but Albee's grasp of satire is ambiguous. You can't be sure what he's up to. The play becomes as vacuous as the form it is satirizing, and boredom sets in with the limp epigrams.

Albee is a first-rate American dramatist, but why did the AFT elect to do his least interesting failure instead of—say—a double bill of "The Death of Bessie Smith" and "The American Dream"? The answer probably is that a double bill of short films wouldn't be as good box-office as something—in this case, anything — starring Katharine Hepburn, Paul Scofield, Lee Remick and Joseph Cotten. Those names, and the drawing room setting, I suspect, still mean something to those citizens of middle America for which the AFT was designed. It's all so highly cultivated—and so dead.

*

With the exception of "The Homecoming," none of the AFT productions has been quite the play it was written to be, or the film it is presented as being. None of the plays has been grossly "opened up," except for "Rhinoceros." They've pretty much stuck to their original theatrical locales, but they've been photographed in that dumb tennis-match style—the back-and-forth cutting from one medium close-up to another—that has about as much to do with the original theatrical experience as the intermissions with which the films are presented.

Intermissions are a theatrical heritage. They're also a necessity. They give live actors a chance to catch their breath, but they have the effect of anesthetizing any movie worth its salt, especially any movie less than two or three hours long.

The worst of the AFT ventures so far has been the O'Horgan version of "Rhinoceros," which is not great Ionesco, and not great Theater of The Absurd, to begin with. O'Horgan, perhaps in desperation, has taken this slight and fuzzy parable, about a civilization where people break their necks to turn into rhinoceroses, and has tried to straighten out the defects of the stage version, in which Zero Mostel was the riveting object of all attention even though he played a secondary role.

In spite of a lot of clumsy, badly choreographed slapstick, in spite of some nice music by Galt MacDermot and an extremely attractive performance by Gene Wilder, who plays the leading role, Zero Mostel still is the riveting object of attention in the film. The reasons are that Mostel is an audaciously surprising actor, even when you think you know his style, and that "Rhinoceros" is a far from interesting play. How much more provocative would have been screen versions (if possible) of Ionesco's "The Bald Soprano" and "The Chairs"?

Plays aren't films and films aren't plays, and three of the four AFT productions to date have landed in a no man's land between theater and film. With the exception of "The Homecoming," they do not record for posterity great theatrical performances, and they do not add anything to one's cinematic experience. Almost any five-minute segment of Robert Altman's "The Long Goodbye" is a greater artistic experience (pardon my language) than any 60-minute segment of the AFT's "Iceman," "A Delicate Balance" or "Rhinoceros."

*

For years I've wished that there were some organization that would have as its function the presevation on film of great theatrical occasions. I think of Laurette Taylor in "The Glass Menagerie," Tallulah Bankhead and Fredric March and Florence Eldridge in "The Skin of Our Teeth," Tallulah again in "The Little Foxes," Laurence Olivier and Vivien Leigh doing their back-to-back "Cleopatras," Ethel Merman shooting that stuffed seagull in "Annie Get Your Gun." I mean the simplest kind of preservation: the performance photographed, preferably from a fixed position, with no close-ups, no alternating two-shots, no cinematic junk.

Today, of course, there are fewer and fewer theatrical occasions worth saving. Those that are worth saving will probably be bought by Hollywood anyway.

The AFT seems bent on preserving, not really accurately, plays that either have already been better preserved by others, or plays that reflect not the vitality of the living theater but the poverty that is contributing to its decline. With its intermissions, its Playbill-like programs, its piety about great works of theater and consummate artists, the AFT is simply pumping stale air into the lungs of an audience that would be better revived by going out occasionally to see one of the works of a truly living cinema, be it "Memories of Underdevelopment," "Day for Night," "The Long Goodbye," "Sleeper," "Mean Streets," or "Heavy Traffic."

1974 Ja 27, II:1:7

'Black Belt Jones' Is Played by Jim Kelly

The Hollywood production team of Fred Weintraub and Paul Heller, who, with Robert

The Cast

BLACK BELT JONES, directed by Robert Clouse; screenplay by Oscar Williams, story by Alex Rose and Fred Weintraub; director of photography, Kent Wakeford; film editor, Michael Kahn; music, Luchi De Jesus; produced by Mr. Weintraub and Paul Heller. Released by Warner Brothers. At the Cinerama Theater, Broadway at 47th Street and the 86th Street Twin 2 Theater, west of Lexington Avenue. Running time: 87 minutes. This film is classified R.

Black Belt Jones..............Jim Kelly
Sydney ....Gloria Hendry
Pop ....Scatman Crothers
Toppy ....Alan Weeks
Quincy .... Eric Laneuville
Don Steffano ....Andre Phillipe
Big Tuna ....Vincent Barbi

Clouse, the director, gave us that Hong Kong-based kung fu bash, "Enter the Dragon," last summer, now have come up with the Hollywood-made "Black Belt Jones" to prove that travel isn't broadening.

This latest of the slew of kick-and-slash melodramas, which is playing at the Cinerama and 86th St. Twin 2 Theaters, is as basically silly as many of the previous, similarly action-packed adventures it imitates and is as obvious as a karate chop.

A minor change in the norm should be noted, however. In this case, "Black Belt Jones," played by the young, handsome, black, muscular martial arts devotee, Jim Kelly, one of the heroes of "Enter the Dragon," is ably assisted by Gloria Hendry, a photogenic soul sister who is just as roughly efficient as her tough, stoic partner in dispatching squads of white or black bad guys.

What they're fighting about is not really earth-shaking except to indicate that Mafia-like citizens, with the aid of black hoods they have strong-armed, are trying to take over a karate school building owned by Scatman Crothers, our hero's beloved mentor, and our heroine's father, in order to make a big realty killing.

Of course, the fearless team, assisted by the school's students and, unexpectedly, a covey of pretty trampoline experts, take the opposition in stride and also manage to make it romantically. But the succession of clashes and explicit street language tend to become repetitious and as unwittingly comic as the cast's largely mechanical performances. This "Black Belt Jones" is stale and overtrained despite all the chops, kicks and belts.

A. H. WEILER

1974 Ja 29, 21:1

MAN IS NOT A BIRD (Covek Nije Tijka), directed by Dusan Makavejev; screenplay (Serbo-Croatian with English subtitles) by Mr. Makavejev; director of photography, Aleksander Petkovic; music, Petar Bergamo; produced by Avala Film, for distribution by Grove Press. Running time: 80 minutes. At the First Avenue Screening Room, at 61st Street. This film has not been classified.

Hairdresser ....Milena Dravic
Rudinski ....Janez Urhovec
Barbulovitch ....Stojan Arandjelovic
His wife ....Eva Ras
Truck driver ....Boris Dvornik
Hypnotist ....Roko

By VINCENT CANBY

"Man Is Not a Bird," Dusan Makavejev's first film, was shown at the First Avenue Screening Room Sunday and will be repeated there tomorrow and Sunday with showings at noon and midnight. It was made in 1966, and it is by far the most original, intelligent, witty and important film I've seen so far this year, which is meant as high praise even admitting that January's movies hit something of a new low.

Mr. Makavejev is the brilliant, idiosyncratic Yugoslav filmmaker who was most recently represented here in 1971 by his anti-Stalinist "WR—Mysteries of the Organism," a collage of political and sexual satire, fantasy, porno film, musings on the life and teachings of Wilhelm Reich, interviews with Candy Darling (and others). It was a movie that I could either take or leave. The freedom of its form seemed dictated less by the artist's wide-roving imagination than by the footage he had on hand to edit into some kind of feature film.

•

Mr. Makavejev is a bristly sort of director. "Mysteries of the Organism" was never given full release in Yugoslavia, and a year ago he was drummed out of the Yugoslav Communist party, not because of the film but because of some remarks he made to a German newspaper allegedly insulting Yugoslav war veterans.

I mention all this to establish Mr. Makavejev's independence of spirit, which, in "Man Is Not a Bird," manages to be both profound and rollicking. The narrative seems to be about a moody, middle-aged, introspective factory engineer (Janez Urhovec) and the brief, unsatisfactory affair he has with a pretty, much younger woman, a barber (Milena Dravic) who seduces him out of boredom. The setting is a bleak Yugoslav industrial town that, though beautifully and realistically photographed, seems as mad and fantastical as something in a dream.

•

Mr. Makavejev is not particularly interested in photographing the real world, but in reproducing the feelings inspired by being in it, and since his is a socialized country, one can never escape an awareness of political systems and pressures. "Man Is Not a Bird" is less about the engineer and the bird-brained barber than it is a conception of life in Tito's eccentrically Communist state.

It's a world where the citizen-comrade dreams of the good life around the corner but makes do with considerably less, which, according to Mr. Makavejev, results in certain—well—emotional strains. At least half the people in the film seem teetering on the edge of hysteria or lunacy. A jolly scene is a workmen's nightclub, where an overfed stripper is performing mightily, erupts into a riot that leaves the stripper dead, off-screen.

A jealous wife has a knock-down, drag-out fight in the market place with her husband's mistress. The sadness is that the husband is a crazy old drunkard and both woman long past any primes.

•

While the engineer is inspecting the room he is to rent the soundtrack is full of unexplained screams from the street outside. Bits of a love scene between the engineer and the barber are cross-cut with scenes of a fight in a police station. At one point the camera pans up the nude body of the pretty barber, lying on her stomach on a bed, and lands in a close-up of her large, vacant eye.

Some of the film's ironies are heavy, but mostly they work. A worker at a smelting plant skylarks on top of a crane to amuse his buddies. "Man is not a bird," someone yells. That is, man cannot fly, but Mr. Makavejev is saying throughout the film that man can, at least, try.

Next to "Memories of Underdevelopment," "Man Is Not a Bird" is the most sophisticated and complex film from a Communist country that I've ever seen.

The freedom of style that was chaotic in "Mysteries of the Organism" is perfectly disciplined in this first film. It is so poetic and true and multi-leveled that it reminds me of the best prose. Not because it is literary but because it simply could not exist in any other form. It also makes me want to see two later Makavejev films that were released here earlier, "An Affair of the Heart," which is also known as "Switchboard Operator" (1967), and "Innocence Unprotected" (1971).

1974 F 1, 12:1

The Program

HOMAGE TO MARILYN MONROE: NORMA JEAN BAKER (1 minute) and **FAKE NEWSREEL** (5 minutes) by Robert Russett; **MARILYN TIMES FIVE** (13½ minutes) by Bruce Conner; **THE MARTYRDOM OF MARILYN MONROE** (30 minutes) by Alida Walsh; **MARILYN**—untitled (30 minutes) courtesy of Michael N. Dean. Total running time: 79½ minutes. At the Film Forum, 256 West 88th Street. Through Sunday and Feb. 7-10, 8 P.M.

By NORA SAYRE

How long can you dwell with self-parody? That special gift swims close to humiliation, and it's now more conspicuous than ever in the work of Marilyn Monroe. The hyperhappy smiles, the arched eyebrows, the body that she seemed unable to control, the playschool voice —all seemed to radiate increasing mockery as the years went by. Yet she didn't appear to be making fun of the audience, or of any target outside herself. Of course various directors channeled her tendency to caricature herself. But it's nowhere more apparent than when she sang "Happy Birthday" to John F. Kennedy in Madison Square Garden, where she spoofed her own style to a degree that was almost grotesque. There's also a bleak historical moment when Peter Lawford—gagging it up about her tardiness — introduces her as "the late Marilyn Monroe." This footage is part of "Homage to Marilyn Monroe," which is appearing at the Film Forum, 256 West 88th Street, through Sunday and from Feb. 7 through Feb. 10.

•

So many are possessive about Monroe: Some think that their own vision of her is the only one that's valid. Hence a virtue of this program is its variety. It's startling to see her screen test, which she performs so clumsily that it's a wonder that she ever got hired, and there are slices of newsreels and trailers that highlight the humor and the unwitting awkwardness. Robert Russett's two very short films, "Norma Jean Baker" and "Fake Newsreel," combine stills and TV images to build collages that convey dislocation — eventually, desperation and fright. In the latter, her recording of "Bye, Bye, Baby" is finally overwhelmed by chaotic noises on the soundtrack, and the result is an aural nightmare.

In contrast, "The Martyrdom of Marilyn Monroe" by Alida Walsh is both patronizing and sentimental. Among the images of autopsy and degradation and remorse, Nagaly Labau portrays the dead actress stripping and caressing herself before a cross on her own grave. There's a lot of symbol stomping throughout, such as the reappearance of infinite glass eyes to suggest a chilly audience. White paint crawls up naked limbs and saliva oozes from a reddened mouth—this corpse is camping. The film serves to evoke one of the persistent myths about Monroe: that someone who was so sexy and provocative and naughty must almost have invited death, or even deserved it.

In "Marilyn Times Five," Bruce Conner has reworked some old blue movie material. A nearly nude woman with an apple and a Coke rolls about in solitary ecstasy, while Monroe's voice sings "I'm Through With Love" over and over again. The repetition of the footage increases the sense of solitude, of an object alone with objects—another image that hovers over the memory of Monroe. The identity of the woman has been questioned. My guess is that it wasn't Monroe: there's a resemblance in some shots but not in others. However, the controversy might occupy students of skin for a while to come.

1974 F 1, 14:1

'Superdad' Is Typical Exercise by Disney

The latest Disney feature, "Superdad," is a typically scrubbed, bouncy exercise, in which an anxious, blundering father tries to separate his college-age daughter from her lively young cronies, only to have her mix with some weirdo hippies. Love—real family love and a faithful, home-town suitor—conquers all.

Some of this generation-gap exercise is quite funny, starting with the performance by Bob Crane as the father, although he tends to squeal and overact a bit. Kathleen Cody and Kurt Russell are so charming as the young sweethearts that one wonders why papa was determined to separate them. Barbara Rush does nicely as the mother, and Judith Lowry is briefly hilarious as a pool-playing, motorcycle-riding octogenarian.

The picture opened yesterday at the Radio City Music Hall.

HOWARD THOMPSON

1974 F 3, 46:1

The Cast

ROAD MOVIE, directed by Joseph Strick; screenplay by Judith Rascoe; produced by Mr. Strick; editor, Sylvia Sarner; director of photography, Don Lenzer; music, Stanley Meyers; distributed by Grove Press. Running time: 88 minutes. At the Plaza Theater, 58th Street near Madison Avenue. This film has not been classified.

Gil .... Robert Drivas
Janice .... Regina Baff
Hank .... Barry Bostwick
Harry .... David Bauer

By VINCENT CANBY

Independent truckers have problems. They have to pay off traffic managers to get loads. They have to pay off highway cops when their rigs are overweight. They have to pay off bank loans, and they consider themselves lucky just to be able to keep up the interest payments.

Gil (Robert Drivas) and Hank (Barry Bostwick), the independent truckers in Joseph Strick's "Road Movie," have all these problems in spades, but they are not destroyed by the big hauling firms, the banks, the unions or the cops. They are destroyed by a small, furious, frizzy-wigged, highway hooker named Janice (Regina Baff), because they are men.

"Road Movie," which opened yesterday at the Plaza, was directed by a man (Mr. Strick) and written by a woman (Judith Rascoe) and although their consciousnesses are raised, they're also terribly tangled. "Road Movie" seems to be two separate movies that have had an unprofitable collision. It starts as a neon-beautiful pseudo-documentary about the perils of independent trucking in America today, then slowly evolves into a self-conscious metaphor for the role of Woman in Our Society.

•

Janice, beautifully played by Miss Baff (who received great notices this season when she played in "Veronica's Room" on Broadway), is a first-rate character, a desperate, lonely, bitter woman who, in the course of the film, decides that she's degraded herself for the last time.

However, when she walks out on Gil and Hank, after they've rudely kicked *her* out, she just doesn't slam the door, she undoes the brake on their rig, with results that are so calamitous they have no relation to trucking or anything else. It has the effect of turning the first third of the movie into so much landscape reportage.

"Road Movie" is the first film that Mr. Strick has made in years not based on a work better left in its original medium ("Tropic of Cancer," "Ulysses," "The Balcony"), and he should be encouraged to pursue this original bent. He's good with actors, and even though he's inclined to beat us over the head with visions of America the Ugly, those visions are undeniably accurate.

•

The real subject of the film is Janice, which is, I suspect, the way the screenplay was written, though it's difficult to tell from all the early footage devoted to the independent trucker, highway life and America's roadside architecture. In her own gum-chewing way, Janice (who is the first woman I've ever seen to hide her money in her wig) is as much of a revolutionary as Nora Helmer. I'd have liked to know more about her than "Road Movie" ever tells us, although Miss Rascoe, a novelist and short story writer, gives her larger heaps of exposition to recite than can be conveniently handled on film.

Mr. Drivas and Mr. Bostwick are convincing as two different grades of male chauvinist pig, but the film belongs to Miss Baff's Janice who, in addition to Nora Helmer, also reminds me of an angry Minnie Mouse. It has something to do with the little skirts that Janice wears, the slightly knobby knees and the awareness that underneath the fury there was once, very long ago, a sweet, cheerful, bright-eyed drudge.

1974 F 4, 37:1

The Cast

LUTHER, directed by Guy Green; screenplay, Edward Anhalt; author, John Osborne, editor, Malcolm Cooke; music, John Addison; producer, Ely A. Landau for the American Film Theater, Henry T. Weinstein. At selected theaters. Running time: 112 minutes. This film is classified PG.

Martin Luther .... Stacy Keach
Hans .... Patrick Magee
Tetzel .... Hugh Griffith
Von Eck .... Robert Stephens
Cajetan .... Alan Badel
Katherine .... Judi Dench

By NORA SAYRE

Doubt and dogmatism coincide almost as often as ham and cheese: When conviction wavers, a remorseful skeptic can wax more righteous than ever. John Osborne's characterization of Martin Luther—as a masochist ravaged by uncertainty, who was also able to stand the 16th-century church on its spiritual ear—is a sympathetic portrait of an authoritarian. Luther's own self-hatred appears as fuel for his determination to reform the church, and to convince Christians that no one can be saved by "good works," but only through individual faith. Yet he wallowed in the suspicion that his own sins couldn't be forgiven.

•

At the same time, this Luther remains disconnected from events: When the peasants who backed him and his doctrines began to fight for the abolition of serfdom, he encouraged the lords and princes to kill them off. And he, who had been racked by infinite religious and personal guilts, seemed unmoved by the subsequent slaughter. Mr. Osborne's Luther resembles a motorist who precipitates casualties for others: While he drives undamaged, other cars pile up and crash behind him.

The American Film Theater's adaptation of the Osborne "Luther," which opened yesterday at selected theaters, does preserve most of the obsessions that blazed through the original. Understandably, the play was cut for the filmed version. However, some of the fiery Osborne language has been ironed out in Edward Alhalt's screenplay. Many strong metaphors and rhythms are lost, and part of the anal imagery has been purged. The Brechtian aspects of the play have been muted, and we're left with a conventional religious drama — hardly what the playwright wrought. Also, various key lines have vanished from certain scenes, only to pop up in others, and a minor character has been converted into a ponderous narrator. No doubt, clarity was intended. Cliché is the result.

When Stacy Keach's tonsure is bowed to the floor of a chapel or when he rolls up his eyeballs toward heaven, he doesn't persuade us of his devoutness. When the script demands reverence, his fixed eyes recall his catatonic performance in "End of the Road." But when he doesn't have to be worshipful, there's some fine acting afoot. He catches the focus of fanaticism, the hesitation and the doubt that permeate a defiant ego, the pleasure in pain. And he's gifted at sudden illness: when he bites his lip, we can sense the anguish in his gut. One of the best scenes is his confrontation with his father (Patrick Magee, who's very good—as are Alan Badel as Cajetan and Hugh Griffith as Tetzel). The mutual hostility and disappointment of father and son mingle with their concern for each other, their distress at getting on badly.

The sensitive camerawork by Freddie Young concentrates on individuals at the peak of their most personal emotions within the stony ecclesiastical set. Yet the problem of filming a play recurs as it has in most of the American Film Theater's productions. In "The Iceman Cometh" and "A Delicate Balance," it was absolutely right to keep the camera indoors, within the set. However, in "Luther," the off-screen yells and screams of embattled peasants fail to convey the rebellion that's taking place. A few shouts and one portable corpse don't suffice for the whole Reformation, and it's worth wishing that there had been a crowd scene or two. Without any evocation of the outside world, it's hard to believe—within the context of this movie—that Luther had much of an impact, or that Protestantism was more than a hiccup in the span of history.

1974 F 5, 30:1

THE FREE LIFE, directed by Ronnie Hersh, Russ Schwartz and Richard Searls; photography, Mr. Hersh; script, Mr. Schwartz and Snee; editing, Mr. Schwartz and Mr. Searls; produced by Trout Fishing in America Films. At the Whitney Museum of American Art, Madison Avenue and 75th Street. Running time: 63 minutes. This film has not been classified. Through Wednesday.

"The Free Life," like the balloon for which this documentary is named, is not free of faults. But it is buoyantly alive as a vivid portrait of a rare, undaunted trio (and their many willing aides) preparing to embark on an adventure they knew could possibly prove fatal.

As a record of this tragically unsuccessful attempt at a first trans-Atlantic crossing in 1970 in that 80-foot-high hot-air and helium balloon from East Hampton, L. I., to France, the film, which ends its brief run tomorrow at the Whitney Museum of American Arts, unfortunately skips over some of the illuminating facts supplied in newspaper and other accounts at the time. But the random vignettes of people, personalities and events captured by the cameras build to an eye-catching, fascinating combination of unusual, dramatic camaraderie and dedication in a joust between Man and Nature.

•

In effect, "The Free Life" concentrates on Malcolm Brighton, the handsome, blond, smiling British engineer and professional balloonist; Rod Anderson, the serious, cigar-smoking, 32-year-old commodities broker, and Pamela, his pretty 28-year-old wife, who took off in that 12-foot yellow gondola. But it also focuses on interested townspeople, such as Willem de Kooning, the painter, and Jean Stafford, the authof, and, more specifically, on local mechanics, storekeeper, farmer, fire chief and many others who supplied expertise, materials, muscle and gifts, such as food, to get the craft airborne from that pasture that fateful September day.

•

Of course, their doom is made obvious long before the takeoff and their last, crackling message sent from off Newfoundland 30 hours later. They were never heard from again.

But despite its episodic nature and its tragedy, "The Free Life" colorfully revives these beautiful dreamers and their final, broken dream.

A. H. WEILER

1974 F 5, 30:1

The Cast

MCQ, directed by John Sturges; written by Lawrence Roman; director of photography, Harry Stradling; film editor, William Ziegler; music, Elmer Bernstein; produced by Jules Levy and Arthur Gardner; released by Warner Bros. At the Criterion Theater, Broadway at 45th Street, and the 86th Street East Theater, east of Third Avenue. Running time: 114 minutes.

Kosterman	Eddie Albert
Lois	Diana Muldaur
Myra	Colleen Dewhurst
Toms	Clu Gulager
Pinky	David Huddleston
J.C.	Jim Watkins
Santiago	Al Lettieri

By NORA SAYRE

Reactionary movies about villainous cops have been as plentiful as children's nosebleeds throughout the last year. But "McQ," which opened yesterday at the Criterion Theater and the 86th Street East, is so much like "Magnum Force" that I'm awed by the nerve of Warner Brothers in releasing such similar pictures so close together.

Before the credit sequence is finished, two cops are shot dead — which establishes the political climate of this movie. The police captain (Eddie Albert) snarls, "With uniformed officers being gunned down in the streets, that smells like radicals to me." Young men with long hair spill out of a paddy wagon, shouting "Pig!", and a policeman identifies them as "garbage."

But Police Lieut. John Wayne discovers that some men in blue are involved in the narcotics trade. So he feels compelled to investigate the department itself. Meanwhile, his superiors are keen on curbing his feistiness — ever since he threw a man off a roof and that man's lawyers began "screaming about civil rights." Wayne replies, "Well, it kept him off the streets, didn't it?"

Like Clint Eastwood in "Magnum Force," Mr. Wayne gets some eager signals from a couple of women; he can resist or succumb to them with equal indifference. The sexy dialogue over the Scotch ranges from "Refill?" "Why not?" to his telling Coolleen Dewhurst, "You know something? You are attractive."

But Mr. Eastwood at his most languid isn't yet quite so wooden as Mr. Wayne. The latter's large, rosy face registers no more emotions than your grandmother's quilt. On learning that an old pal has been shot, his eyes widen slightly; his eyebrows droop a little when corruption in high places is unveiled; when Miss Dewhurst is killed, he manages to bang down the phone receiver and say "Damn." Still, he does convey some relish whenever he hits anyone.

In this wildly undramatic picture, music and gunshots have to provide the gumption that the acting lacks. Surely Mr. Wayne should stick to Westerns: he's simply too slow to play any kind of policeman. Horseless in the streets of Seattle, he looks as though he needs a shot of sand.

1974 F 7, 46:1

The Cast

PARTNER, directed by Bernardo Bertolucci; screenplay by Mr. Bertolucci and Gianni Amico, freely based on "The Double" by Dostoyevsky; produced by Giovanni Bertolucci for Red Film; released by New Yorker Films. At the Art Theater, Eighth Street at University Place. Running time: 105 minutes. This film has not been classified at this time.

Jacob	Pierre Clementi
Clara	Stefania Sandrelli
Saleswoman	Tina Aumont
Petruska	Sergio Tofano

"Partner," which opened yesterday at the Art Theater, was shown at the sixth New York Film Festival. The following is Vincent Canby's review, which appeared Sept. 24, 1968, in The New York Times.

"Partner," the third feature film by Bernardo Bertolucci, is an example of exuberant movie-making by a young (27) director who talks like an intellectual but makes movies like a poet. The Italian film stars Pierre Clémenti ("Belle de Jour") of France and is being shown in its Italian-language version.

Like Bertolucci's earlier movie, "Before the Revolution," which caused such excitement at the festival here four years ago, "Partner" is a difficult movie. It also is a beautiful and even funny one that uses sound, silence, music, color and an extremely literary frame of reference to create a two-hour sense impression of what it's like to be a romantic in today's world.

The screenplay, by Bertolucci and Gianni Amico, is very freely inspired by Dostoyevsky's short novel, "The Double," about an ineffectual young man who is taken over —and ultimately driven to madness—by his alter ego, who can do all the things he cannot.

In Bertolucci's movie, the young man (Clémenti) is a drama teacher and his alter ego (Clémenti again) is a sort of supernatural Julian Beck who proclaims repeatedly: "The only duty of a man of the theater is to make theater."

There is some irony in this because in spite of everything Bertolucci says (for publication) about the theater's being a metaphor for the world, whose spectacle must be world revolution, it's clearly the movies with which he is concerned, and world revolution is more or less a subsidiary inspiration.

If it isn't really a subsidiary inspiration, "Partner" must be one of the most romantic political tracts ever conceived. Clémenti, dark and impassioned, looks like a mod Lord Byron, and his adventures are all upside-down romances.

The girl for whom he longs (very funnily played by Stefania Sandrelli) can't keep from lovingly biting his fingers. Another rather mad girl arrives at his apartment selling detergents ("We live in a time of the decline of soap powders," she says) and offers herself to him. The young man's plan to stage a revolutionary spectacle in the streets fizzles when his performers fail to show up.

The specific meaning of many of the scenes is obscure, but the total effect is that of youthful explosion of movie talent.

1974 F 7, 46:1

The Cast

ZARDOZ, written, produced and directed by John Boorman; associate producer, Charles Orme; photographed by Geoffery Unsworth; edited by John Merritt; released by 20th Century-Fox. At the Trans-Lux East Theater, Third Avenue and 58th Street. Running time: 105 minutes. This film is classified R.

Zed	Sean Connery
Consuella	Charlotte Rampling
May	Sara Kestelman
Avalow	Sally Anne Newton
Friend	John Alderton
Arthur Frayn	Niall Buggy

As an exercise in futuristic abstractions, "Zardoz," which opened yesterday at the Trans-Lux East, is science-fiction that rarely succeeds in fulfilling its ambitious promises. John Boorman, who directed the exemplary "Deliverance," wrote, produced and directed this fantasy set in 2293 on Irish locations, merely proves that its major attributes are technical. His melodrama about a harried world order of the future is a good deal less effective than its special visual effects.

Mr. Boorman's diffuse script almost metaphysically unfolds the story of an eternally young group of super-intellectuals dominating aged lawbreakers and zombie-like Apathetics living in a verdant commune. It also discloses the saga of Zed, one of the slave-driver descendants of the 20th-century, working outside this Paradise governed by the god Zardoz, who, driven by a strange curiosity, arrives to overthrow the élitists and bring mankind back some 300 years.

•

Despite its pseudo-scientific gimcracks and a plethora of didactic dialogue, "Zardoz" (yes, there is a relationship to "The Wizad" of Oz") is more confusing than exciting even with a frenetic, shoot-em-up climax.

As Zed, Sean Connery, who scrambles around this ersatz Eden in little more than a red, breech clout, is moodily energetic but unimpressive as a muscleman-turned-thinker. And largely unreal as their far-out operations are Charlotte Rampling, as the decorative, if suspicious intellectual, who finally joins Zed as his loving mate, Sara Kestelman, who sees him as a research object, John Alderton, playing an effete, disenchanted type and Niall Buggy, the top manipulator of Zed and the other brutes.

Mr. Boorman's intentions are obviously noble but he and his cast make "Zardoz" a fiction that raises questions about man's fate but doesn't offer satisfying answers.

A. H. WEILER

1974 F 7, 46:1

THE LION HAS SEVEN HEADS, directed by Glauber Rocha; written by Mr. Rocha and Gianni Amico (French and Portuguese with English subtitles); made by Claude Antoine and Gianni Barcelloni for Polifilm. At the First Avenue Screening Room, 61st Street. Running time: 103 minutes.
WITH Rada Rassimov, Gabriele Tinti, Jean-Pierre Leaud, Giulio Brogi, Hugo Carvana and Rene Koldhoffer.

Glauber Rocha, the young, politically oriented Brazilian director, focuses on the exploitation and revolt of Africans against whites in "The Lion Has Seven Heads" with the dedication and stylization that were the hallmarks of his three previous films on injustice in his homeland. Unfortunately, his contemporary allegory, to be shown today and tomorrow at noon and midnight at the First Avenue Screening Room, is more theatrical than compelling, despite the sad truths it illustrates artistically.

Mr. Rocha was obviously not concerned with a simple, linear plot in shooting his feature in lovely color in the Congo three years ago. His "Lion" is composed of a succession of occasionally confusing vignettes, and set declamatory scenes steeped in religious and modern symbolism and African folklore. It depicts somewhat mystically the savagery and callousness of white colonialism over the centuries.

A viewer may have difficulty following the director's occasionally mystifying approach and unfamiliar characters, but his social stand and his intentions eventually become fairly clear.

The unbilled statuesque, blond, topless temptress, Rada Rassimov; Gabriel Tinti, her handsome lover, and Hugo Carvana and Rene Kohlhoffer, portraying evil exploiters, are in constant battle with Jean Pierre Leaud, as a Christlike soul; Giulio Brogi, as his militant, white aide, and with some unnamed revolutionary blacks, who finally succeed in striking down their oppressors.

These are largely strange, sometimes strident, larger-than-life figures spouting polemics on an exotic landscape. Mr. Rocha is justifiably arguing a case for decency and justice. But his convoluted pleading overpowers the pallid drama in "The Lion Has Seven Heads."

A. H. WEILER

1974 F 8, 17:1

THE CEREMONY (Gishiki), directed by Nagisa Oshima; screenplay (Japanese with English subtitles) by Tsutomu Tamura, Momoru Sasaki and Mr. Oshima; director of photography, Toichiro Narushima; editor, Keiichi Uraoka; music, Toru Takemitsu; produced by Sozosha/Art Theater Guild, for distribution by New Yorker Films. Running time: 122 minutes. At the First Avenue Screening Room, near 60th Street. This film has not been rated.

Masuo	Kenzo Kawarazaki
Ritsuko	Atsuko Kaku
Terumichi	Atsuo Nakamura
Setsuko	Aiko Koyama
Kazuomi	Kei Sato
Tadashi	Kiyoshi Tsuchiya

Although Nagisa Oshima, the 42-year-old Japanese director, has been making films since 1959, "The Ceremony," which opened yesterday at the First Avenue Screening Room, is only his second film to be commercially released in New York. The first, "Boy," was shown at the 1969 New York Film Festival and opened theatrically the following year.

"The Ceremony" is a handsome, elaborately choreographed film that seems far more Japanese than the work of the late Yasujiro Ozu, usually described as the most Japanese of Japanese directors. Ozu's films, though they used austere methods, are virtually documentaries of middle-class lives that have been lived with courage and purpose through the kind of crises comprehensible to even the densest occidental audiences.

Mr. Oshima's "The Ceremony" seems much more exotic because its concerns as well as its methods are so specifically Japanese. The film is a microcosm of Japanese political and social life from 1946 until the present as represented by a rich, powerful family presided over by a tyrannical grandfather whose authority remains undiminished.

•

I have an aversion to microcosms in general in everything exept political cartoons. In films they're especially hard to accept. You keep interrupting yourself to ask who so-and-so is meant to represent. Mr. Oshima mixes politics and Freud so thoroughly in his film, which takes place largely during various family ceremonies, that I am still not sure whether a nephew's seduction by his aunt is really a love scene or the collapse of trade unionism.

The family is loaded with archetypes: war-criminal soldiers, war-criminal industrialists, a Communist, an anarchist, a liberal and assorted innocent victims. There's also a good deal made of incest, illegitimacy and mysterious parentage.

●

The film comes to brilliant life in one sequence, a feast to celebrate a wedding to which the bride never came. The feast, in a hotel ballroom, goes on anyway, with a master of ceremonies who introduces the groom and the nonexistent bride, who is applauded politely as she doesn't walk among the guests showing off the robes she did not wear.

"The Ceremony" is beautifully photographed and set but to someone not familiar with the various currents in postwar Japanese political life, the rigid scheme of the melodrama remains impersonal and obscure.

VINCENT CANBY.

1974 F 8, 18:1

THE JAIL, by Michael Anderson, Paul Jacobs, Saul Landau and Bill Yahraus. At the Whitney Museum of American Art, Madison Avenue and 75th Street. Running time: 63 minutes. Until Wednesday.

"The Jail," which began its first theatrical, one-week engagement yesterday at the Whitney Museum of American Art, was shown on Channel 13/WNET in October, 1972. Television viewers also saw four hours of unedited footage from which this 80-minute feature was made. Filmed with official cooperation inside San Francisco County Jail in the spring of 1972 by Michael Anderson, Paul Jacobs, Saul Landau and Bill Yahraus, "The Jail" was termed by The New York Times as a realistic demonstration of the "structure of a jail society."

While the film makers do not take a position on that structure, they vividly illustrate the pursuits and points of view—often in street language—of prisoners, from homosexuals to a bitter poet, as well as the county sheriff and the jail's chief, captain, lieutenant, sergeants and deputies.

A. H. WEILER

1974 F 8, 20:3

BLAZING SADDLES, directed by Mel Brooks; screenplay by Mr. Brooks, Norman Steinberg, Andrew Bergman, Richard Pryor and Alan Uger, based on a story by Mr. Bergman; produced by Michael Hertzberg; director of photography, Joseph Biroc; editors, John C. Howard and Danford Greene; music composed and conducted by John Morris; a Crossbow production, distributed by Warner Brothers. Running time: 93 minutes. At the Sutton Theater, 57th Street, east of Third Avenue. This film has been rated R.

Bart ....Cleavon Little
Jim ....Gene Wilder
Gov. Lepetomane } ....Mel Brooks
Indian Chief }
Hedley Lamarr..........Harvey Korman
Lili von Shtupp ....Madeline Kahn
Taggart ....Slim Pickens
Olson Johnson..........David Huddleston
Rev. Mr. Johnson..............Liam Dunn
Mongo ....Alex Karras
Buddy Bizarre..............Dom DeLuise

By VINCENT CANBY

Some film comedies, like Jacques Tati's "Playtime" and Woody Allen's "Sleeper," stay with you after you've seen them. The humor, firmly rooted in the wilder contradictions of life, flourishes in the memory. Other comedies, like Mel Brooks's "Blazing Saddles," the best title of the year to date, are like Chinese food. A couple of hours later you wonder where it went. You wonder why you laughed as consistently as you did.

"Blazing Saddles," which opened yesterday at the Sutton Theater, is every Western you've ever seen turned upside down and inside out, braced with a lot of low burlesque, which is fine. In retrospect, however, one remembers along with the good gags the films desperate, bone-crushing efforts to be funny. One remembers exhaustion, perhaps because you kept wanting it to be funnier than it was. Much of the laughter Mr. Brooks inspires is hopeful, before-the-gag laughter, which can be terribly tiring.

●

In short takes Mr. Brooks's comedy has rewarding shock, especially when he's being insulting or rude or when he is going too far in areas usually thought to be in bad taste. Throughout the film, Madeline Kahn does a marvelously unkind take-off on Marlene Dietrich, playing a a dance-hall star named Lili von Shtupp who has a slight speech defect. When someone gives Lili a flower, she responds: "Oh, a wed wose! How womantic!" She also sings a song, "I'm Tired" (lyrics by Mr. Brooks), which lays waste for all time "Falling in Love Again."

The trouble is that "Blazing Saddles" has no real center of gravity. It has a story, something about a black sheriff (Cleavon Little) and his white sidekick (Gene Wilder) who save the town of Ridge Rock from land speculators, but as charming and funny as Mr. Little and Mr. Wilder are, the film's focus is split among the comic set pieces and the various eccentric supporting characters.

Some of these are very amusing in themselves: a bigoted preacher (Liam Dunn) who decries the fate of his town ("... our people scattered, our cattle raped...."; a lecherous, near-sighted governor (Mr. Brooks), and a huge, beagle-brained desperado (Alex Karras) who has a fist fight with a horse.

The result of the film's short attention span is to make the smaller roles more effective than the larger ones. Harvey Korman, a gifted comic actor who is so fine as Carol Burnett's television co-star, tries very hard to be funny as a crooked businessman and sometimes succeeds. But it's apparent that he's hard put to keep up with the movie's restless shifting from satire to parody to farce to blackout sketch.

●

Throughout "Blazing Saddles" I kept being reminded of 'Sleeper," both films being the work of men who had their first real successes as gag writers. Both worked for Sid Caesar, and both still appreciate the need for getting a joke to the audience fast and then moving on. However, "Sleeper" builds momentum through the continuing character played by Mr. Allen himself, and gives the impression of having been pared down to comic essentials.

"Blazing Saddles" has no dominant personality, and it looks as if it includes every gag thought up in every story conference. Whether good, bad or mild, nothing was thrown out.

Mr. Allen's comedy, though very much a product of our Age of Analysis, recalls the wonder and discipline of people like Keaton and Laurel and Hardy. Mr. Brooks's sights are lower. His brashness is rare, but his use of anachronism and anarchy recalls not the great film comedies of the past, but the middling ones like the Hope-Crosby "Road" pictures. With his talent he should do much better than that.

1974 F 8, 21:1

Film Depicts Violence in a Small Town

The Cast

WALKING TALL, directed by Phil Karlson; written and produced by Mort Briskin; executive producer, Charles A. Pratt; music, Walter Scharf; director of photography, Jack A. Marta; editor, Harry Gerstad; a BCP production, distributed by Cinerama Releasing Corporation. Running time: 125 minutes. At the New Embassy 46th Street Theater, Seventh Avenue at 46th Street, and other theaters. This film has been rated R.

Buford Pusser..............Joe Don Baker
Pauline Pusser........Elizabeth Hartman
Sheriff Al Thurman..........Gene Evans
Grandpa Pusser..............Noah Beery
Grandma Pusser............Lurene Tuttle
Luan Paxton................Brenda Benet
Prentiss Parley..............John Brascia
Grady Coker................Bruce Glover
Buel Jaggers..............Arch Johnson
Obra Eaker..................Felton Perry
Arno Purdy..........Richard X. Slattery
Callie Hacker..........Rosemary Murphy

By VINCENT CANBY

"Walking Tall," which opened yesterday at the New Embassy 46th Street and other theaters around town, comes to Manhattan as much a phenomenon to be analyzed as a film to be reviewed.

Like "Billy Jack," "Walking Tall" has already found a huge audience without a great deal of help from the critics. It's been in release for about a year (it played Staten Island last summer) and reportedly has earned profits to date in the neighborhood of $10-million.

Unlike "Billy Jack" the mind of "Walking Tall" is not befuddled by mysticism. Anything but. The film is a relentlessly violent, small-town American melodrama, smashingly directed by Phil Karlson, that cannily allows its audiences to have it both ways. They can identify with its hero, a southern sheriff who wants to be a man of peace, a sort of down-home Serpico with a Tennessee accent, while they enjoy the spectacle of deep-dish blood and guts he is the center of while fighting for the underprivileged

The film was written and produced by Mort Briskin, a veteran Hollywood producer, whose credits—"The Jackie Robinson Story" (1950) and "The Magic Face" (1951), among others—would seem to be markers in a career of absolutely no distinction.

With the apparent help of Mr. Karlson, who directed fine melodramas in the nineteen-fifties, including "The Phenix City Story," Mr. Briskin has at last come up with a winner. It's not a movie I like, but I can admire the manner in which it manipulates its audience through various notable clichés.

●

The screenplay is based on the true story of a young Tennesseean named Buford Pusser who set out, almost single-handedly, to bring law and order to McNairy County in the nineteen-sixties after he was rolled and almost killed in an illegal gambling joint.

As sheriff of McNairy County, Buford Pusser (Joe Don Baker) walks tall and carries a big stick with which he breaks a lot of vital bones, including skulls, though vice and corruption are not noticeably impeded until the end of the film, by which time Buford has begun to carry a gun.

"There's nothing wrong with a gun in the right hands," he says to his adolescent son early on, which is, I'm afraid, one of the sentiments that make "Walking Tall" so irresistable to the people who like it. Who is going to say that he himself isn't properly qualified?

●

The philosophy in "Walking Tall' is not all that hair-raising, however. We've accepted it in countless Westerns, including "High Noon," in which a single man sets out to be society's conscience. At its most benign, it teaches us that one good apple can save a barrel of rotten ones, which you may or may not want to believe.

●

I'm a skeptic, certainly about "Walking Tall." The film was shot entirely in Tennessee and in addition to being uncommonly well acted by Mr. Baker and the large cast, it looks and sounds most authentic. It's difficult to resist its suspense and its hero's almost monomanical sense of duty. It's also difficult not to be affected by the terrible price he eventually pays.

Some of its folksy scenes work, though the children, as they always are in films of this sort, are so fake they help restore one's sense of proportion about what's been going on.

●

I suppose we are all desperate for heroes, and the film's Buford Pusser is definitely that. The trouble comes in the way the film sets him up to triumph. At the end of the film, the society that has earlier cold-shouldered his do-gooding so mindlessly, just as mindlessly joins him in ravaging a McNairy County gambling den. One of the last images of the film, a bonfire of gambling equipment, suggests a nice K.K.K. bonfire or one on which you might want to burn some books.

1974 F 9, 18:1

THE LAST DETAIL, directed by Hal Ashby; screenplay by Robert Towne, based on the novel by Darryl Ponicsan; produced by Gerald Ayres; director of Photography, Michael Chapman; editor, Robert C. Jones; music, Johnny Mandel. An Acrobat film, distributed by Columbia Pictures. Running time: 105 minutes. At the National Theater, Broadway near 43d Street, and the Coronet Theater, Third Avenue at 59th Street. This film has been rated R.

Buddusky....................Jack Nicholson
Mulhall..........................Otis Young
Meadows......................Randy Quaid
M.A.A.........................Clifton James
Young whore....................Carol Kane
Marine O.D.................Michael Moriarty
Donna........................Luana Anders
Kathleen....................Kathleen Miller

By VINCENT CANBY

"The Last Detail" is one superbly funny, uproariously intelligent performance, plus two others that are very, very good, which are so effectively surrounded by profound bleakness that it seems to be a new kind of anti-comedy. It's a good movie but an unhomogenized one.

"New" is perhaps a poor word to use in connection with the film. Like the recent "Cinderella Liberty," which was also based on a novel by Darryl Ponicsan, "The Last Detail" considers the lives of career United States Navy sailors with a gravity that recalls the atmosphere of the late nineteen-forties and fifties, when World War II was still freshly won, Korea was being brought to a close, and Ike was going to throw the rascals out of Washington. In the years that preceded the political and social upheavals of the nineteen-sixties and seventies, ignorance still possessed some innocent charm.

●

It doesn't any more. It seems frivolous and a bit scary. So much so that I suspect that Hal Ashby who directed "The Last Detail," and Robert Towne, who wrote the screenplay, may have thought of their leading character, who is 20 years behind the times and only vaguely aware of the fact, as a lot more representative of many American lives today than the rest of us would care to think.

This character, remarkably played by Jack Nicholson, is Signalman First Class Buddusky, a 20-year Navy man of hilarious and often unwarranted self-assurance. Buddusky and Gunner's Mate First Class Mulhall (Otis Young) are assigned to escort from Norfolk, Va., to the naval prison in Portsmouth, N. H., an 18-year-old sailor sentenced to eight years in the brig for trying to steal $40 in polio contributions.

"The Last Detail" is the chronicle of this journey, which takes the better part of a week and dramatizes the increasing desperation of Buddusky as he tries to show the young prisoner his (Buddusky's) idea of a good time. There's a desolate beer party in a Washington hotel room, where Buddusky gets the kid drunk for the first time and tries to cheer him up. "Think of it this way," he says in effect, "you'll get two years off for good behavior."

In New York they crash a Nichiren Shoshu prayer meeting and wind up at a Village party where Buddusky tries to make out with a pretty, intensely serious young woman by talking about the romance of the sea, while she would prefer to talk about President Nixon or race relations.

In Boston, on their last day, Buddusky and Mulhall escort the young prisoner to a sleazy whorehouse where they introduce him to the wonderful world of sex by paying his tab. This experience, with a girl who manages simultaneously to be dimly sweet and a no-nonsense professional, is what finally unhinges the prisoner who, until then, has more or less accepted his fate.

●

Mr. Nicholson dominates the film with what amounts to an anthology of swaggers optimistic, knowing, angry, foolish and forlorn. It's by far the best thing he's ever done. If anything it's almost too good in that it disguises with charm the empty landscape of the life it represents.

Mr. Mulhall, by being black and playing a man who is as reflective and steadfast as Mr. Nicholson is errant, is the one person who gives the movie a contemporary look. In World War II, black sailors seldom got out of the galley.

Randy Quaid, who had a small role in "The Last Picture Show," is a marvelous foil for Nicholson as the ever-polite prisoner who, for a long while, refuses to share Buddusky's rage at the injustice of his sentence. Early on, he has admitted to Buddusky that he had had a scrape with the police before entering the Navy. Asks Buddusky professionally: "Was it in the nature of a felony or a misdemeanor?" Says the kid: "It was in the nature of shoplifting."

Mr. Ashby persists in making comedies ("The Landlord," "Harold and Maude") that are never as funny as the treatments he gives them would have you believe. "The Last Detail" is his most interesting and contradictory so far. You'll laugh at it, not through your tears but with a sense of creeping misery.

1974 F 11, 50:1

Production by Altman Illuminates an Era

By VINCENT CANBY

When Bowie, a 21-year-old country boy serving a life term for murder; Chicamaw, a surly, one-quarter Indian, and T-Dub, an aging bank robber with a game leg, escape from the Mississippi state prison farm, they simply amble away across a field to freedom. The time is the mid-nineteen-thirties and the local newspapers, ever alert to the possible appearance of a new Bonnie and Clyde or Barker gang, report the break in the most extravagant and flattering terms.

Throughout their short careers as bank robbers, Bowie, Chicamaw and T-Dub barely muddle through while the newspapers strain to create bigger-than-life myths. But Bowie, Chicamaw and T-Dub aren't very bright. Old T-Dub, who's supposed to be the most professional member of the trio, is so swept off his feet by his love for a frumpy beautician with burnt-blonde hair that he puts his real name on the license when he marries her.

●

Robert Altman's "Thieves Like Us," which opened yesterday at the 68th Street Playhouse, is such an engaging, sharply observed account of a long-lost time, and of some of the people who briefly inhabited it, that I hope it doesn't get confused with other films that seem, superficially anyway, to have covered the same territory.

I think of Arthur Penn's "Bonnie and Clyde" and Nicholas Ray's "They Live by Night" (1949), which, like "Thieves Like Us," was also based on Edward Anderson's 1937 novel. As fine as they were, this one is also an original work, limited only by the opportunities offered by the subject, and the style Mr. Altman has elected to work in.

There's nothing elegiacal about "Thieves Like Us." Its feelings are expressed tersely. It seems to have been stripped down like a stock car, as if excess verbiage were another form of chrome finish. Nor does one get any feeling of victims cornered by society, which was one of the marks of the Ray film and a carryover from those thirties movies that possessed social consciences.

The screenplay by Calder Willingham, Joan Tewkesbury and Mr. Altman closely follows the events and the tone of the Anderson novel, which was, of course, written in its own time, without being aware that it was, in effect, a historical novel.

Like the Anderson prose, the film is lean, uncluttered, even though Mr. Altman's method is full of irony and contrasts. The radio is constantly commenting on the action, whether it's a ripely acted love scene from "Romeo and Juliet," which we hear as Bowie and Keechie, his girlfriend, from the roadside filling station, are making their first awkward attempts to have sex, or a wildly inappropriate "Gang Busters" program we hear as the bank-robbing trio is carrying out one of its capers.

The Cast

THIEVES LIKE US, directed by Robert Altman; screenplay by Calder Willingham, Joan Tewkesbury and Mr. Altman, based on the novel by Edward Anderson; produced by Jerry Bick; executive producer, George Litto; director of photography, Jean Bouffety; editor, Lou Lombardo; distributed by United Artists. Running time: 123 minutes. At the 68th Street Playhouse, at Third Avenue. This film has been rated R.

Bowie	Keith Carradine
Keechie	Shelley Duvall
Chicamaw	John Schuck
T-Dub	Bert Remsen
Mattie	Louise Fletcher
Lula	Ann Latham
Dee Mobley	Tom Skerritt

Bowie and Keechie are beautifully played by Keith Carradine, another talented son of John Carradine, and Shelley Duvall, the wide-eyed Houston girl who was one of the few delights in Mr. Altman's "Brewster McCloud." I would have thought that young love, especially doomed young love, was virtually impossible to simulate in movies these days, but these two succeed with immense humor and the kind of tact that denies easy sentimentality.

All of the performances are quite special. Bert Remsen, who has been in other Altman films, though I must admit I don't remember him, is fine as T-Dub. John Schuck, as Chicamaw, is extraordinary in what I take to be the film's key scene when, near the end, after Bowie has improbably been able to spring him from prison, he turns on Bowie furiously for having succeeded in a plan that Chicamaw thinks Bowie is too dumb to have brought off.

●

Society doesn't destroy these men. The Depression may have given them a push into their chosen professions, but they are, at heart, so self-destructive that I'm not at all sure they wouldn't have wound up much the same had they been farmers.

"Thieves Like Us" is not so perverse and witty as "The Long Goodbye," nor is it so ambitious as "McCabe and Mrs. Miller," but it is a more perfectly integrated work. It is full of things to think about, that hang in the memory like the details of a banal crime story on page 32, which, though read quickly, won't go away. Somehow you know that this happened.

1974 F 12, 41:1

Oshima Work Brings Memory of Godard

Young Korean Rapist Survives Execution

By VINCENT CANBY

It begins as if it were going to be a solemn documentary about the horrors of capital punishment. We see the prison buildings in a long shot from the air. The narrator describes the death house as looking like any other ordinary house, situated on a small hill, and we cut to the interior of the execution building.

The narrator tells us that the walls are salmon pink (the film is in black and white) and notes that it has toilet facilities only for men. He invites us to watch a typical execution, which is when things go awry. Quite wildly. The heart of the victim, a young Korean convicted of two rape-murders, refuses to stop beating after the hanging. The execution team panics.

The prosecutor says that the man cannot be re-executed until he is restored to consciousness, but the doctor, who had intended only to verify death, is without his medical bag.

●

The Roman Catholic chaplain says it would be murder to hang the man again since the man's soul, which is responsible for the crimes, has left the body. Meanwhile the victim comes to and wonders where he is. The doctor is dumbfounded: He's never before heard of amnesia *after* an execution.

For about one-third of its running time Nagisa Oshima's Japanese film "Death by Hanging" is a surprisingly uproarious contemplation of the moral issues involved in capital punishment. The prison officials, prosecutors, chaplain and witnesses argue back and forth and pick at each other with a Lewis Carroll sort of purposeful, cross illogic. Everybody becomes nettled. Someone suggests that they call it a day. "This kind of work has its failures too," he says, but they all stay on to straighten things out, sort of.

"Death by Hanging," which was made by Mr. Oshima in 1968, was shown at the First Avenue Screening Room last Sunday, and will be repeated there again today and tomorrow at noon and midnight.

The Cast

DEATH BY HANGING (Koshikei), directed by Nagisa Oshima; screenplay (Japanese with English subtitles) by Tsutomu Tamura, Mamoru Sasaki, Michinori Fukao and Mr. Oshima; editor, Sucko Shiraishi; director of photography, Yasuhiro Yoshioka; music, Hikaru Hayashi; produced by Sozosha; distributed by Grove Press. Running time: 117 minutes. At the First Avenue Screening Room, First Avenue near 60th Street. This film has not been rated.

R	Yun-Do Yun
Execution Chief	Kei Sato
Education Officer	Fumio Watanabe
Chaplain	Toshiro Ishida
Security Officer	Masao Adachi
Doctor	Mutsuhro Toura
Girl	Akiko Koyama

●

It is the second Oshima film to open in New York in a week, and though it is less complex than "The Ceremony," which was made in 1972, it is no less schematic. It's the kind of didactic work that only Jean-Luc Godard has ever successfully transformed into film, not because Mr. Godard is such a brilliant political philosopher, which he isn't, but because his brilliance as a film maker is irrepressible.

On the basis of these two films, Mr. Oshima is certainly talented as well as hugely concerned and committed to the sort of cinema that plays an active role in its society. As long as "Death by Hanging" sticks to capital punishment, it is, in its absurd way, provocative and entertaining. But the film's interests keep widening, its methods become increasingly, arbitrarily Godardian (read Brechtian), until it reaches a point of total confusion.

●

In order to be able to execute the murderer again, the prison team decides it must convince the man who he is (his name is simply R). They act out charades designed to make R remember. Involved are his identity as a murderer, as well as his identity as a Korean, a people long oppressed by the Japanese. Kafka, Freud and some other weighty presences are evoked by Mr. Oshima as straight editorializing, through Godardian monologues. One of R's problems is that he loved his sister, which doesn't seem to have a great deal to do with legalized murder and capital punishment.

Some of it is funny. More of it is tedious, and a lot of it curiously old-fashioned, even though it reminds us of the great Godard films of the mid-nineteen-sixties. Extreme movie styles date more quickly than hemlines.

1974 F 15, 23:1

'American Moods' Examined in Five Short Films

Five short films running from 9 to 32 minutes each and collectively labeled "American Moods," which began a 10-day run yesterday at the Whitney Museum, are as American as apple pie, if not always a treat. The "moods" of these unheralded Americans may be unevenly documented, but they vividly sharpen often blurred visions of aspects of living that stir the mind and, occasionally, the conscience.

●

A viewer's emotions should be affected most by Bruce Davidson's 32-minute, aptly titled, "Living Off the Land." As a muted color study of a father and son who eke out a meager existence as scavengers of a New Jersey municipal dump, it states its

facts with unadorned realism while subtly implying the terrible imbalances that exist in our rich society. The grimy, laconic father; his oldest, teen-aged, equally inarticulate son; his wife and four other children emerge as a loving group and as proud citizens coping, without tears, with their dirty lot.

"Lambing," the 30-minute film by Bob Fiore and Barbara Jarvis, presents with similar dedication a bucolic view of David Hinman, a young New Hampshire shepherd and schoolteacher, and his wife, that personalizes their devotion to sheep and a way of life they love. The focus is on clinical views of births, but the total effect is a pastoral vignette as natural and picturesque as the film's snowy landscapes.

"Front and Back," a succession of postcards backed by narrations of vacationers' messages, made by Lynne Cohen and Andrew Lugg, is a clever idea that succumbs to redundancy. Another 9-minute subject, "Frank Film," a collage of biographical animations by Frank Mouris, has been shown here previously. And also seen here last year is Joseph Pipher's 25-minute "6344," a moving, yet amusing, record of a Fairfield, Ohio, family and the demolition of their ancestral home.

These "American Moods" may make a slightly flawed film package, but it does captivate the eye and ear and is a tribute to the talents of some sensitive and perceptive movie makers.

A. H. WEILER

1974 F 15, 23:1

Where Are Those Foreign Film Fans?

By VINCENT CANBY

TOMAS GUTIERREZ ALEA's "Memories of Underdevelopment" broke the house record when it was shown for one week last year at the First Avenue Screening Room here. The Cuban film received some of the most enthusiastic reviews to be given any foreign film in years, yet it died when it was moved over to continue its initial engagement at the posher Beekman Theater. Business improved when the movie played in Greenwich Village and it is currently being shown with good if not sensational results in several theaters in and around New York on a double-bill with Karoly Makk's small, fine Hungarian film, "Love."

So far, "Memories of Underdevelopment" has been seen in 12 American cities. It may eventually be seen in 10 or 15 more, and the distributors expect that non-theatrical organizations, mostly college film societies that rent 16 millimeter prints, will enlarge the market for the film. "Love" has had engagements in 18 cities and its distributor thinks it may play as many as 50 or 60 cities. With luck.

Two years ago Dan Talbot broke all records at the New Yorker Theater, which he then owned, with an extended engagement of the late Yasujiro Ozu's splendid "Tokyo Story." It subsequently played a couple of dozen more cities, doing nicely in Boston and failing almost everywhere else. "Tokyo Story" is played about 200 16mm engagements to date and Talbot thinks that it may earn $50,000 in two or three years. Fifty thousand dollars? That's less than most major companies spend just to advertise and promote the New

York opening engagement of an average American movie.

While "Tokyo Story" may ultimately earn $50,000 in the American market, Bernardo Bertolucci's "Last Tango in Paris" has earned $12,625,000 in less than a year.

Is the jackpot hit by "Last Tango in Paris" significant? Should the mind boggle? I'm afraid not.

The market for foreign-language films, which in the late 1950s and early 1960s, seemed so exciting to us and so financially rewarding to the entrepreneurs, has more or less collapsed in the midst of the so-called arts explosion.

"Last Tango in Paris" is not your average, run-of-the-mill foreign-language film. For one thing, less than half of it was shot in a foreign language. For another, it's a Marlon Brando spectacle. Although it was directed by Bertolucci, an Italian responsible for some terrific, bona fide foreign-language films ("The Conformist," "The Spider's Stratagem," "Before The Revolution") "Last Tango" is hardly more foreign than "On The Waterfront" or "The Godfather."

The unhappy truth of the matter is that American movie audiences today seem to be far less interested in good foreign films than they have been at any time since the immediate post-world War II

years, just before we first discovered the films of Roberto Rossellini and other directors of the Italian neorealist movement.

In the last 14 months there's been only one striking exception that has the effect of italicizing the rule: Ingmar

CRAZY JOE, directed by Carlo Lizzani; screenplay by Lewis John Carlino, based on a story by Nicholas Gage; executive producer, Nino E. Krisman; director of photography, Aldo Tonti; music, Gian Carlo Caramello; editor, Peter Zinner; a B-P Associates production, presented by Dino De Laurentiis; distributed by Columbia Pictures. Running time: 100 minutes. At Loew's State 2, Broadway at 45th Street, and Loew's Orpheum, 86th Street near Third Avenue. This film has been rated R.
Crazy Joe..................Peter Boyle
Anne...................Paula Prentiss
Willy..................Fred Williamson
Coletti..................Charles Cioffi
Richie.......................Rip Thorn
Falco....................Luther Adler
Frank.....................Fausto Tozzi
Nunzio..................Franco Lantieri
Don Vittorio..............Eli Wallach

By VINCENT CANBY

It's only fair, I suppose, that an Italian movie producer should be allowed to participate in the current Mafia boom. Although that nonexistent brotherhood only got going when it got going here, the Mafia does, after all, have its origins in Sicily.

Dino De Laurentiis, the man who gave us "The Valachi Papers," now gives us "Crazy Joe," a lumpy, violent, fictionalized biography of the late Joseph (Crazy Joe) Gallo, the flamboyant hood who was gunned down on April 7, 1972, at a clam house in Little Italy. The film opened yesterday at Loew's State 2 and other theaters in the city.

●

At the time of Gallo's murder, his sister is reported to have said that Joe had changed his image, which is why he was shot. The movie, though simple of mind, is a lot more complicated. Joe's movie enemies couldn't give a fig that he liked to hobnob with actors and writers. They don't even seem to mind that he attempts to stun his associates by dropping the names of Camus and Sartre, though the way the movie presents him, his intellectual pretensions do prompt a few giggles.

No. According to the screenplay by Lewis John Carlino, which utilizes facts of Joseph Gallo's life as put together in a story by Nicholas Gage, Crazy Joe was

rubbed out not because he was a party bore but because he was trying to take over a Mafia family run by his former protector. At least, I think that's the reason. The way the movie presents them, the ins and outs of Mafia family wars are as difficult to follow as pre-World War I Balkan politics, though not quite so fascinating.

Nothing in the production helps much. A re-creation of the 1971 Italian-American Day rally in Columbus Circle, where Joe Colombo was shot, is the film's one attempt at spectacle.

In life, Crazy Joe was supposed to possess a certain amount of charm, but Peter Boyle plays him as if he were a dim-witted numbers runner. He's such a slob that the casting of beautiful, intelligent Paula Prentiss as his girl becomes one of the minor mysteries of the movie year. Could she have wandered onto the wrong set?

Eli Wallach impersonates a Mafia don with as much conviction as is possible in a movie in which the aging process is represented by simply putting more blue into the actor's hair. Rip Torn, another good actor, is seen briefly as Joe's brother.

The film was directed by Carlo Lizzani, who seems to have done nothing to offset the weaknesses of the casting and the screenplay, which makes a ridiculous gesture toward black film audiences by inflating Crazy Joe's association with black hoods. Fred Williamson ("Hammer"), plays the black mob chief as if he thought the movie were really about civil rights.

As movies go these days, "Crazy Joe" is not very long (100 minutes), but after the first 15 I kept looking at my watch, wishing I could hurry things along to the clam house.

1974 F 16, 36:2

Bergman's "Cries and Whispers." The two Bergman films immediately preceding it, "The Passion of Anna" and "The Touch," had done so poorly at the box office that when "Cries and Whispers" came along no American distributors were especially interested. It was finally picked up for comparatively little money by a company called New World Pictures, run by Roger Corman ("The Wild Angels," "The Pit and The Pendulum"), and has so far earned $1,200,000 in 803 theaters around the country. A triumph for pictorial beauty and Bergman sensuality. The most an earlier Bergman film had earned in this country was in the neighborhood of $350,000.

★

It may not be entirely fair to say that American audiences are less interested in foreign films today than at any other time in the recent

past. It is probably more accurate to say that while the market for foreign films remains, it is being satisfied by more sophisticated American and English films. There is thus more competition for the attention of the audiences who used to attend foreign films with some regularity, and more competition for the theaters that once showed them exclusively.

A lot of it comes down to money.

The old World Theater on 49th Street, which introduced New Yorkers to Rossellini and many of the other great European filmmakers in the 1940s and 1950s, has found that it's much more profitable to show "Deep Throat" and other porn than to gamble on something as fine and esoteric as "Man Is Not A Bird," the extraordinary first film by Yugoslav filmmaker Dusan Makavejev, which had a limited engagement at the

Laura Antonelli, shown here in "Malizia," is the star of the year in Italy —but unknown thus far in America. *"Deep Throat" vs. Rossellini?*

First Avenue Screening Room two weeks ago, six years late.

The problem is cost. The cost of production abroad, of importing and preparing a film for American release, of running a theater. One exhibitor, who controls a number of theaters that used to be called "art houses" but now are devoted almost entirely to American films, told me last week that it simply isn't possible any longer to hold a film in one of his theaters if it isn't a fair-sized hit.

"It isn't only that costs have risen since we showed movies like 'Rocco and His Brothers' 10 or 12 years ago, they've risen since last year. Our heating bills this year are three times what they were in 1973."

Then, too, fewer American theaters are willing to accept subtitled prints of foreign-language films. If a foreign-language film wants to make it big in any way ("Z" earned $7,100,000), it has to be dubbed into English. These costs have risen, as have the costs of advertising. An executive at Columbia Pictures estimates that it costs his company an average of $180,000 to put a foreign-language film into release in this country. "Most of the time," he says, "it just isn't worth it."

Even though it won the Oscar as the best foreign-language film of 1970, Elio Petri's "Investigation of A Citizen Above Suspicion" earned only $324,000 in this country from 697 theaters out of a possible 10,000 to 12,000 theaters. Eric Rhomer's "Claire's Knee," also considered a hit, earned $410,000, and Francois Truf-

faut's "Bed and Board" $372,000 in 425 theaters. Truffaut's "Such A Gorgeous Kid Like Me" has so far played 97 dates and earned only $108,000. In comparison, "The Poseidon Adventure" earned $40,000,000 and "The Getaway" $17,500,000.

For the big distributing companies it is a poor gamble to spend $180,000 on the outside chance of earning $300,000 or $400,000. They'd prefer concentrating their attentions on getting back their multi-million dollar investments in films like "The Way We Were" or "Lost Horizon." Because of this, fewer and fewer foreign films are being imported into the American market, even by companies like Columbia that finance foreign films for local release abroad.

Complicating matters is the desperation (sometimes euphemistically called "unrealistic attitude") of European producers. When Jacques Demy ("The Umbrellas of Cherbourg," "The Young Girls of Rochefort," "Lola," etc.) finished his "Peau D'Ane" several years ago, the asking price for the American rights was $250,000, meaning that the film would have to gross close to $750,000 to break even, something that few films by directors as rare and special as Demy have ever done. Also, one hit film will throw the price structure out of balance. Until the hit of "Cries and Whispers," the American rights to a Bergman film

could be acquired for $75,000. Since the success of "Cries and Whispers," the asking price for the new Bergman has shot up to $250,000.

It should be remembered that the best foreign films— the films that still live on as major influences on the filmmakers who came after— have never at any point in movie history been the ones that have made the most money.

In Variety's list of all-time box office money-makers, there are only a handful of foreign-language films, and of these only one, Fellini's "La Dolce Vita" ($7,650,000), rates continuing serious attention.

The others in the list of films that have earned $4,000,000 or more in the American market include "A Man and A Woman" ($6,100,000) and "Dear John" ($4,250,000). Most of the foreign films that show up are on the order of Run Run Shaw's "Five Fingers of Death," a kung-fu joke.

You won't find Godard's "Breathless" listed, nor Truffaut's "Jules and Jim," Antonioni's "L'Avventura" or anything by Satyajit Ray, Akira Kurosawa or Kenji Mizoguchi.

A spokesman for Warner Brothers predicts that Truffaut's "Day for Night," which stands a good chance of winning the Oscar as the best foreign-language film this year, will play at least 1,000 theaters. Considering the 10,000-theater potential of a

hit American film, that's not terribly encouraging.

A lot of people have expressed hope that the 16mm outlets on college campuses throughout the country will eventually provide a continuing market for the kinds of foreign films that once had easy access to New York's eastside "art houses" and at least one or two theaters in all of the major cities in the country. That remains only a hope.

*

Says Dan Talbot, who has had a good deal of success in 16mm, the film societies do book films like "Tokyo Story" and Louis Malle's "Phantom India," but they're also just as inclined to want to book "A Thousand Clowns" or "The French Connection." The film society audience isn't necessarily a choosy one.

The situation is discouraging. The audiences for truly fine films have never been huge, but when the costs of distribution were lower, it was still possible for producers and distributors to survive on smaller returns. Today it's almost impossible.

Talbot suggests that part of what's happening is the result of conditioning by television. Young audiences today, he says, "don't like subtitles. They don't want to read. And they're absolutely hooked on color," except for ancient Bogart, Marx Brothers and Fields films, which they'll watch over and over again. However, if it's a new film from Yugoslavia or Senegal, interest declines when it's learned that the film was photographed in plain old black-and-white. It's apparently more fun to stay home and watch a football game in blazing green, blue and orange.

1974 F 17, 11:1:1

The Program

THE TRAITORS, written (Spanish with English subtitles), directed and acted by members of the Grupo Cine de la Base; produced by William Susman; distributed by Tricontinental Films. Running time: 114 minutes. At the First Avenue Screening Room, near 61st Street. This film has not been rated.

By VINCENT CANBY

As an example of film art "The Traitors," a new Argentine film, is about as riveting as a segment of "Marcus Welby, M.D." It tells the story of the 17-year rise and fall of a crooked union leader who has a wife, a mistress, a taste for the high life and absolutely no scruples. It is straightforward, conventional and competent. No nonsense here with Godard or Brecht.

However, the circumstances of the film's production, its subsequent suppression in Argentina, and the polarized political thinking it represents must fascinate anyone who has ever attempted to follow Argentine politics, especially the curious metamorphosis into left-wing saint of Juan D. Perón during his years in exile. The reputation, of course, has recently begun to tarnish.

•

"The Traitors" was financed by an American producer, William Susman, and made by a group of professional and amateur film people known only as the Grupo Cine de la Base, representing Argentina's new revolutionary left. The anonymity is understandable, since the film's chief targets are the right-wing Peronists who have taken control of the new Perón government.

"The Traitors" was shown at the First Avenue Screening Room last Sunday and will be repeated there today and tomorrow at noon and midnight. The film, made last year, anticipates what has apparently become an irrevocable split between the Peronist right and left, which, acting in concert, brought Mr. Perón back to the Argentine Presidency last year.

The Grupo Cine de la Base obviously couldn't care less about film art or about reaching the intellectuals. Except for the passion of its politics, it shares nothing with "La Hora de los Hornos," Fernando Ezequiel Solanas's extraordinary four-hour-plus Argentine political documentary that discovered Mr. Perón to be the first popular expression of Argentina's national consciousness. That film, which was also suppressed, was shown here in 1971, long before Mr. Perón's triumphant return to his homeland.

"The Traitors" is after the mass Argentine audience that won't put up with the sort of didacticism and distancing tricks that Mr. Solanas employed. It tells its melodramatic story straight.

•

The title refers to those members of the Argentine labor movement who, after Mr. Perón's ouster in 1955, continued to call themselves Peronists while secretly collaborating with the various regimes that were either military or backed by the military. It follows the career of one such fictional character, Roberto Barrera, from his first compromise with management to insure his election as union chief, until his assassination at the hands of urban guerrillas fed up with the subversion of labor's cause.

"The Traitors" carefully

avoids condemning President Perón himself but it is full of the kind of disillusionment that leads to despair and, finally, to the terrorist tactics that are rocking Argentina today. It supports violence matter of factly, without pretending to be about something else, as did Costa-Gavras's "State of Siege." It's not a movie I can praise or condemn. I accept it as a report from a new battlefront.

1974 F 22, 25:1

There's No Doubt—Jack Nicholson Is a Major Star

By VINCENT CANBY

HAL ASHBY'S new film, "The Last Detail," adapted by Robert Towne from Darryl Ponicsan's novel, is about the final, desperate spree that two aging career sailors force upon the 18-year-old apprentice seaman they're escorting from Norfolk, Va., to the naval prison in Portsmouth, N.H. The kid, a witless innocent whose only failing is his kleptomania, has been sentenced to eight years in the brig for attempting to steal $40 from the polio contribution box that was the favorite charity of the base commander's wife.

The trip takes almost a week and turns into a tumultuous movable beer party with stopovers in Richmond, Trenton, New York and Boston. There's a brawl with a bunch of Marines just for the exuberant hell of it, a Greenwich Village party at which the sailors are treated as oddities comparable to Confederate soldiers, and a visit to one of the few realistically seedy whore houses ever to be acknowledged in a film comedy, or what seems to be a comedy.

It ends in emotional hangover, with the awareness of consequences too soon come upon us, in the awful realization of important things blanked out, not from the night before but from an entire lifetime.

"The Last Detail," which is now at the Coronet and National Theaters, is a good if unhomogenized film, often terribly funny on its surface though underneath it is very bleak without being truly tragic. Its stature is small. It wants us to feel sorry for a narrow, Nixonian sort of out-of-touchness.

In its picture of male camaraderie, of friendships that are close without ever achieving intimacy, of laughter always on the edge of fury or hysteria, it reminds me a lot of John Cassavetes' "Husbands," though I suspect there was very little Cassavetes-style improvisation on the set of "The Last Detail." It has the sense of extraordinary life of the Cassavetes film without those great arid patches of actorish nonsense that crop up when Cassavetes allows his co-star-pals to show off for their own enjoyment.

The best thing about "The Last Detail" is the opportunity it provides Jack Nicholson to play the role of Signalman First Class Buddusky who, with Gunner's Mate First Class Muhall (Otis Young), is the well-meaning escort to the remarkably docile prisoner. Though the film is unnecessarily ambiguous in its feelings towards Buddusky (I think we're ultimately supposed to find him and his sort worthy of pathos, though I can't), there's no question about Nicholson's performance. It is big, intense, so full of gradations of mood that it becomes virtually a guide to a certain kind of muddled, well-meaning behavior.

In writing that last, I was about to say that Nicholson has come a long way since most of us were first aware of him in "Easy Rider" as the alcoholic, small-town lawyer who, as Nicholson played him, became a full-blooded, almost Faulknerian character in a southern landscape otherwise inhabited by cartoon figures. Nicholson has not come a long way. He's always been there: a fine, youngish (mid-thirties) American character actor who, with this performance, establishes himself at the head of a line that includes Al Pacino, Dustin Hoffman, James Caan and Robert Duvall.

To remember his career from "Easy Rider" onward is not to recall the development of a talent that began slowly, but to count up the bases the talent has touched. Not all of the films have been good by a long shot, but even when they weren't good, like "A Safe Place" and "The King of Marvin Gardens," the Nicholson performances provided little oases of reason in deserts of pretension.

When the films were good, like "Carnal Knowledge" and, to a lesser extent, "Five Easy Pieces," the virtues of the films tended to overshadow the contributions of the actor.

There's a deceptive lightness, almost a blandness about Nicholson's approach to acting that, even though it is self-assertive, defers to the role to such an extent that audiences remember the role as much as, if not more than, the actor who played it. Something of this sort, I suspect, has prevented a number of other very good actors from becoming major stars. Denholm Elliott is one. He was always too legitimate. He didn't have enough of what agents, producers and gossip columnists like to describe as "a personality."

The trouble with being a personality is that it has a way of limiting an actor's freedom of movement. Images have to be maintained. Salary demands kept up. Only certain roles can be accepted. It doesn't do to be seen in too inexpensive a production nor in a role that is not the obvious lead.

"The Last Detail" pushes Nicholson over the top. There's no doubt about it now. He's a major star as well as a personality. However, he's taken so much time to establish the personality that it promises to be flexible enough so that he needn't get concerned by the demands the image makes on him.

As Buddusky, the career sailor in "The Last Detail," a self-assured professional whose existence is measured by hash marks and whose vocabulary is made up almost exclusively of four-letter words (occasionally dressed up with a word like "misdemeanor"), Nicholson successfully creates a character quite unlike anything he's done before.

Buddusky's a rare, flamboyant bird and the fun of watching Nicholson bring him to life more than offsets the contradictory feelings inspired by the film itself. Good film acting—most of the time, anyway—should not be easily identifiable. Good film actors simply behave. They act natural. You can't see what they're up to. You can see what Nicholson is up to in "The Last Detail" but it's rather like hearing a musician in top form. You know there are mechanics involved and this awareness enhances the joy in the accomplishment.

1974 F 24, II:1:2

Oscar nominee Jack Nicholson, right, and Randy Quaid booze it up in "The Last Detail"

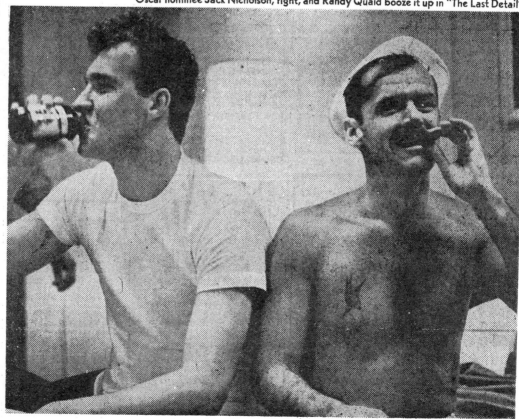

Isaac Singer Story Is a Delightful Short

By NORA SAYRE

How often writers wish that they might stroll into their own fictions, or be able to talk with their characters. I. B. Singer does exactly that in Bruce Davidson's delightful film, "Isaac Singer's Nightmare and Mrs. Puko's Beard," included in the program of "Biographical Cinema" playing at the Whitney Museum of American Art until March 6.

The narrative of one of Mr. Singer's superb short stories is intercut with questions from his friends and fans. From the documentary passages, we learn that he dreams in Yiddish, that his last visit to Israel was crazy "When I say crazy, I mean good"), that believing in reincarnation is helpful to him as a writer. And a glimpse of his gloriously cluttered desk will hearten other writers whose working surfaces seethe with a profusion of papers.

Meanwhile, he narrates his own story about a talented but unsuccessful writer named Puko, who grew rich from investments made late in life. Puko tended to use phrases like "the sky was loyal" and ragged English; "Psychology he pronounced pis-cology." Puko tries to bribe Mr. Singer to write about him, and is rejected. Later, the author is visited by Pupko's bearded wife, who reports that her husband is fatally ill because of that refusal. Fascinated by the beard, and eager to know why she doesn't shave if off, Mr. Singer discovers that. Puko fell in love with her because of it. Keen to unravel further human mysteries, he nonetheless savors her rebuke: "Nu, one mustn't know everything."

Afterward, when asked by a friend if — when inventing the story — he might have confused a beard with female pubic hair, Mr. Singer replies, "I am not so old that I should make a mistake like that."

Though we're long accustomed to fictionalized reporting in print and "produced reality" on the tube, two pictures at the Whitney offer something rather new in film: fictions built on a reportorial style. "No Lies" by Mitchell Block and "Merc" by Mark Obenhaus at first resemble slices of the old cinema verité. Until the actors' credits appear at the end, both movies might be mistakes for documentaries — as Jim McBride's "David Holzman's Diary" sometimes was.

In "No Lies," a man "interviews" a young woman who protests that the camera is making her self-conscious. Gradually, she reveals that she was recently raped by a man who pulled a knife while she was emptying the garbage. She talks offhandedly at first, trying to shrug off the experience. But pain

The Program

BIOGRAPHICAL CINEMA: LONDON SONGS by Nicholas Doob (25 minutes); NO LIES by Mitchell Block (17 minutes); ISAAC SINGER'S NIGHTMARE and MRS. PUPKO'S BEARD by Bruce Davidson (30 minutes); MERC by Mark Obenhaus (25 minutes). At the Whitney Museum of American Art, Madison Avenue and 75th Street, yesterday through March 6.

mounts as she relives the humiliating sessions with the cops and a prurient detective who became even more frightening than the rapist. Her listener begins to needle her: he says she's too resigned, that maybe it wasn't a rape at all. Soon she weeps with outrage at his obtuseness and angrily defines what rape is—speaking to the kind of male mind that seems utterly unequipped to understeand it.

In "Merc," a film maker follows a schizophrenic young man who spends his days standing against the walls of Grand Central Terminal; he sleeps on the window ledge of the Oyster Bar. Nearly speechless, he seems like a re-creation of Melville's "Bartleby," as well as one of our contemporary casualties — the strays whom New York swallows without leaving a footprint behind. As in "No Lies," although this is a fiction, we begin to resent the cameraman's impulse to manipulate the subject. And that's a tribute to the acting.

"London Songs" by Nicholas Boob follows a young street singer through different neighborhoods, as he alternates between sentimental tunes and rousing songs, ranging from "O Danny Boy" to "My Baby Does the Hanky Panky." He's tentative and quite withdrawn at moments, frenzied at others. His eyes bulge while he fiddles wildly, and even his features seem to change with the music — as though it gave him multiple personae.

All in all, one of the Whitney's best programs this winter.

1974 F 25, 18:3

BUSTING, directed and written by Peter Hyams; produced by Irwin Winkler and Robert Chartoff; music, Billy Goldenberg; director of photography, Earl Rath; editor, James Mitchell; distributed by United Artists. Running time: 92 minutes. At the Cinerama Theater, Broadway at 47th Street, and RKO 86th Street Twin 2, near Lexington Avenue. This film has been rated R.
Michael Keneely .... Elliott Gould
Patrick Farrel .... Robert Blake
Carl Rizzo .... Allen Garfield
Stephen .... Antonio Fargas
Marvin .... Michael Lerner
Sergeant Kenfick .... John Lawrence
Jackie .... Cornelia Sharp

By VINCENT CANBY

Peter Hyams's "Busting" is this week's new cop film and a good one for a change. It's not great but it's a cool, intelligent variation on a kind of movie that by this time can be most easily identified by the license numbers on the cars in its chase sequences. The film opened yesterday at the Cinerama and RKO 86th Street Twin 2 Theaters.

Elliott Gould, left, and Robert Blake

"Busting" is about a Mutt and Jeff team of Los Angeles vice-squad detectives. Keneely (Elliott Gould), the tall one, chews bubble gum, walks slightly stooped and talks in the manner of someone modeling himself on the hero of an Elliott Gould movie. Farrel (Robert Blake) walks like a man who wants to be tall and knows he never will be. It doesn't worry him but it makes him a little tougher than most other guys.

Keneely and Farrel live entirely in their work. They spend most of their time arresting people who are more of an emotional than a physical threat to society: call girls, massage-parlor employes and the clientele of homosexual bars. Keneely and Farrel feel no obsessive sense of mission. It's just what they do to keep traffic moving, like street cleaners.

It is one of the ironies of "Busting" that when the two detectives do get involved in their work, when they decide to go after the Mr. Big responsible for the large Los Angeles multi-million-dollar rackets as well as the petty ones, they get clobbered, both by the hoods and by their Police Department superiors who might, I suppose, represent the attitudes of the society whose servants they are.

Mr. Hyams, who wrote and directed "Busting," brings off something of a feat by making a contemporary cop film that is tough without exploiting the sort of right-wing cynicism that tells us all to go out and buy our own guns.

It is also comparatively humane. That is, it acknowledges that when cops and robbers are shooting it out in public places, the bystanders often get hurt. When Keneely and Farrel pursue some heroin pushers through a late-night market in a running gunfight, the movie communicates the terror of the onlookers as much as it does the suspense of the pursuit. It is this level of awareness that separates "Busting" from the kind of junk peddled by most of the other current cop movies.

"Busting" is the first theatrical film to be directed by Mr. Hyams, though he has directed films for television and wrote the screenplay for "T.R. Baskin," a movie that never stopped talking. The screenplay for "Busting" is a huge improvement, but it's Mr. Hyams's talent as a director that is most apparent in the visual emphases and in the performances.

I suspect that the personalities of Mr. Gould and Mr. Blake, rather than the screenplay, are responsible for the definition given the roles of Keneely and Farrel. They try a little too hard for eccentricity but they're successful at creating identifiable characters.

So, too, is Allen Garfield, who plays the Mr. Big as fat, edgy family man who simply can't keep up with the hip talk of the two cops who have set out to ridicule him to justice. Every verbal duel results in his losing a small bit of finger or the tip of an ear lobe. Nothing vital, but you know that more than anything else he resents his squareness.

"Busting" hardly overturns any film traditions, but it gives a little life to an exhausted genre.

1974 F 28, 33:1

The Cast

MAN ON A SWING, directed by Frank Perry; written by David Zelag Goodman; director of photography, Adam Holender; film editor, Sidney Katz; music, Lalo Shifrin; production design, Joel Schiller; produced by Howard B. Jaffe; released by Paramount Pictures. Running time: 109 minutes. At Loews State 2 Theater, Broadway at 45th Street, and Loew's Tower East, Third Avenue and 72d Street. This film has been rated PG.
Lee Tucker ....Cliff Robertson
Franklin Willis ....Joel Grey
Janet Tucker ....Dorothy Tristan
Dr. Nicholas Holnar ....George Voskovec
Dr. Anna Willson .....Elizabeth Wilson

By NORA SAYRE

Murderous mysteries can't and shouldn't conform to recipes. But the omission of certain staples may frustrate us. Suspects are rather like salt —you need enough to season the whole stew, to enliven the range of ingredients. Frank Perry's "Man on a

Swing," which opened yesterday at Loews State and Loews Tower East, lacks momentum because it's scant on potential killers. Out of sheer desperation, I even tried to suspect the righteous police chief (Cliff Robertson, nicely baffled)—an exercise that wasn't fair to either of us.

A young woman is killed, and the police are perplexed —to the extent of waxing sentimental about the murderer. The chief, who never met her, carries her picture in his wallet; there's lyrical music whenever she appears in a smiling flashback. It's stressed that she was "full of life" and fond of swimming, and she looks much prettier than most after strangulation.

Amid this bath of pathos, Joel Grey appears as a clairvoyant who's eager to help the police. He knows so much that he must be the killer. But maybe he isn't. And perhaps he's not a true seer. Still, as the plot disintegrates like an old shower curtain, it's a pleasure to watch Mr. Grey at work. That fragile ability, the savage changes of mood, the quietly ecstatic smile on the lemur's face, the thrashing body that relives the murder, his bright calm confidence in his gift—all yield a fine performance. Sinister and timid by turns, assertive or uncertain, he gives the movie an energy that isn't in the script.

George Voskovec is deftly shrewd as an expert on extrasensory perception and Elizabeth Wilson, as a psychiatrist, can convey more professional aplomb with an "Ah?" or a "Mmm" or the snap of her handbag than many of the garrulous movie-shrinks of the past. But Dorothy Tristan has a thankless role as the police chief's pregnant wife.

All in all, Frank Perry's cast is superior to his material. We're told that "Man on a Swing" was based on a real case. But that's not gripping, since this is a conventionally made picture. The soundtrack is overworked, to put it kindly: spurts of guttural music or throbbing tremolos insist that a key turning in a lock or a ringing phone or a knock on a door are important, (Often, they're not.) And the dud ending is rather insulting. Why be faithful to facts that we don't know, especially since all of the characters are disguised? Invention and distortion and imagination — bad reporting. if you like—could have made a better movie. A thriller, in fact.

1974 F 28, 33:1

Sifting Past for Space Visitors' Tracks

"Chariots of the Gods?" which landed yesterday at 122 theaters in the metropolitan area, is, as its title implies, questionable fare. This film version of the theories advanced by Erich Von Daniken, the 38-year-old former Swiss hotel employe, in three successful books on the possibilities of extra-terrestrial visitors to Earth eons ago, simply evolves as a placid, postcard picturesque but unconvincing travelogue that sometimes captivates the eye but rarely the mind.

The author, as well as the German producers who shot the film in 1971 (excerpts were shown on television more than a year ago), must be credited with moving about the remote areas of the globe to illustrate their clues to mysteries surrounding enigmas. The trip touches down at, among other points, Egypt's pyramids, Mayan temples, Incan cities, Baghdad, Japan and various Biblical sites, without really solving those enigmas.

●

Wasn't it possible, the narrators ask, that the 14th-century frescoes in a Yugoslavian monastery showing what seem to be astronauts and space ships suggest visits from super-intelligent beings from outer space long ago? And what about the possibilities of other-world visitors to our planet in the dim, unrecorded past who could have left the know-how to build the scientifically precise pyramids or formulate the Mayan calendar, construct Incan cities, carve colossal statues on faraway Easter Island and lay out what seem to be air-landing strips in remote Peruvian plains that pre-date history?

Unfortunately, until science verifies the author's and the film's assumptions and findings, "Chariots of the Gods?" merely rolls through a succession of pleasantly exotic places while posing a slew of unanswered questions.

A. H. WEILER

1974 F 28, 33:2

THE PEDESTRIAN, directed and produced by Maximillian Schell; screenplay (German with English subtitles) by Mr. Schell; directors of photography, Wolfgang Treu and Klaus Koenig; editor, Dagmar Hirtz; music, Manos Hadjidakis; an ALFA/MFG film co-produced by Zev Braun; distributed by Cinerama Releasing Corp. Running time: 97 minutes. At the Fine Arts Theater, 58th Street near Lexington Avenue. This film has not yet been rated.

Heinz Alfred Giese	Gustav Rudolf Sellner
Inge Maria	Ruth Hausmeister
Andreas	Maximilian Schell
Hubert	Manuel Sellner
Elsa	Elsa Wagner
Elke	Dagmar Hirtz
Michael	Michael Weinert
Rudolf Hartmann	Peter Hall
Karin	Gila von Weitershausen

By VINCENT CANBY

Maximilian Schell's "The Pedestrian," West Germany's Oscar nominee as the best foreign-language film of 1973, has what is usually described as a Big Theme, one that has already tested the talents of men such as Jean-Paul Sartre ("The Condemned of Altona") and Arthur Miller ("All My Sons").

The film is all about war crimes and responsibility, but it is only persuasive when it focuses on supposedly minor things, when it catches life unaware:

¶A little girl thoroughly snarls rush-hour traffic by pressing the walk button every time the traffic signal turns green. It gives her just enough time to cross the street and press the button on the other side.

¶Six grande dames in various stages of decay and expensive repair sit at a tea table talking at the top of their voices in a mixture of German, French and English. They trade muddled clichés about collective guilt and collective innocence and wonder whether Verdun was in World War I or II.

¶A rich, powerful old industrialist who has had his driver's license withdrawn sits on a bus, but he doesn't know how much to pay or where one pays it. The mysteries of public transport momentarily render him impotent.

●

"The Pedestrian," which opened yesterday at the Fine Arts Theater, is so good in its small details that its slow dissolution into banality comes with a kind of delayed shock.

The original screenplay, written by Mr. Schell, is about Heinz Alfred Giese (Gustav Rudolf Sellner), a respected German businessman who is exposed as having been responsible for the massacre of an entire Greek village during the Nazi occupation. Associations with My Lai and Lieut. William L. Calley Jr. are repeatedly made by the film in dialogue and images seen on a TV screen.

The revelations about his father's past have so affected the old man's son, Andreas (Mr. Schell), that Andreas has attempted to kill them both. One night while the father was driving them home from the office, Andreas grabbed the steering wheel to point the car at a truck, but succeeded only in killing himself. These pieces of information, and a lot more about the massacre, are presented to us in the dreamily photographed flashbacks that stuff the film like plums stuck into a pound cake.

Because the screenplay doesn't support the theme with grand insights, the complexity of the film's narrative structure and physical production comes to look like mere ornamentation, an attempt to disguise the empty truth. Much of this is quite beautiful — snowy German landscapes, serene Mediterranean seascapes, that sort of thing—but it is, after all, just scenery.

This is particularly disappointing because the characters, as written by Mr. Schell and acted by an unusual cast, keep teasing us with hints that they are interesting in ways the film doesn't develop.

The old man's relationship with his wife is brilliantly illuminated for a fraction of a second when she suggests, matter-of-factly, that perhaps he should go off with his pretty young mistress. A television panel discussion about the old man's crimes, with the old man himself participating, dramatizes the process by which almost anything can be made comprehensible and put at a safe distance.

Of the major performers, Mr. Schell gives himself the least to do as the son who is often seen dead, in the recurring flashback of the automobile accident. Mr. Sellner, a leading German theater director, is fine in his debut film performance as the father, as is Gila von Weitershausen, whose role as the mistress is small but vivid.

●

Peter Hall, the English stage and film director, appears in the movie as a German newspaper publisher, and the old women's tea party brings together, briefly, Peggy Ashcroft, Elisabeth Bergner and Françoise Rosay, as well as two stars of the original "The Cabinet of Dr. Caligari," Lil Dagover and Elsa Wagner.

There's a huge amount of talent in "The Pedestrian" but not in the right places.

1974 Mr 1, 16:1

Screen: Solas's 'Lucia'

By NORA SAYRE

At last we're privileged to see Humberto Solas's "Lucia," completed in 1969, when the director was 26; it opened at the First Avenue Screening Room on Tuesday. Spanning nearly 70 years of Cuban history, this extraordinary movie focuses on three generations of women whose lives reflect the society around them.

The first section of the movie is set in 1895, when the Cuban nationalists were warring against the Spanish rule. Lucia (Raquel Revuelta), an aristocrat with ruffles at her throat, has a brother in the rebel army. Since so many men are being killed off, she doubts that she'll ever marry. But she falls violently in love with a stranger who claims to be apolitical, and elopes with him even though he's married. As they ride toward the coffee plantation where the rebels are hidden, troops hired by the Spanish gallop out of the hills, her lover throws her off his horse, and she realizes that he was simply using her to discover the nationalist' secret headquarters. Many are killed, including her brother, and she later stabs her betrayer to death.

●

Some differ sharply in their responses to the three parts of "Lucia." I found this section lushly overacted — almost in the style of silent movies. The women have been directed to flutter and squeal until they appear like a parody of winsome maidenhood. Operatic music throbs whenever the lovers' eyes meet, and the enthusiastic battle scene seems straight out of one of our Westerns: It's odd that a Cuban film maker should have used such mossy capitalistic models. The men fight with a gleeful gusto that's almost amusing, and what comes through is the glory of war, not its tragedy — although that's probably not what Mr. Solas intended.

'Lucia, 1933" is far more successful. This Lucia, a delicate, discontented daughter of the middle class, flees her parents' world of canasta parties and posh country houses and takes off with Aldo, a young revolutionary, who's involved in the overthrow of the dictator Gerardo Machado. But the new régime is as rotten as the old one. Disgusted, Aldo tries to revive the revolution—and is shot dead.

The vulnerable young woman who dwells with loss and change is admirably played by Eslinda Nuñez, who can ring the changes from intense happiness to misery, and conveys fragility even when shouting at her mother or working, wan and pregnant, in a cigar factory. The street scenes, with everyone running and bleeding and weeping, distill all the confusion of urban warfare, the uncertainty of who did what to whom. The weaknesses are the images of corruption (an unconvincing orgy) and the fact that the revolutionary's character is inadequately developed. Since he lacks any dimension beyond his political beliefs, the impact of his death is lessened.

The final episode, "Lucia, 196 ," is absolutely splendid, and reveals Mr. Solas's vast talent for comedy. The third Lucia (Adela Legra) is a stunning young field worker—as robust as the last Lucia was frail. Newly wed to a beguiling hulk (Adolfo Llaurado), she revels in their long days of sexual clowning. (In "Lucia, 1895," sex was made to appear very threatening, and desire almost unbearable.) But the husband won't let Lucia return to work or even leave their house. As he nails up the windows so that other men won't see her, she complains that she's no longer allowed to look at her own mother.

●

Well-wishers warn the man that he's betraying the revolution through his machismo and his possessiveness; he replies that he's the revolution. Lucia is told that a wife is not a slave, that her husband must learn that times have changed. When he insists on total obedience, it's remarked that he's behaving as his father did, and according to his prerevolutionary upbringing.

Wretchedly divided, she leaves and goes back to the fields. There's a hilarious scene when he orders her home, chases her and is himself chased by her female coworkers, who surround and hold him while he and Lucia yell with fury. Daft about each other, they're unable to separate or to agree about her way of life, and as the movie ends they are still fighting between embraces. The whole picture stresses that—although many women haven't yet won the most ordinary kinds of freedom—the present is far superior to the past. I wish that "Lucia, 196 ." might be seen by all the sexes: it's the best discussion of equality (and inequality) I've seen on screen, and the clashes are clarified by comedy.

1974 Mr 1, 16:1

The Cast

ACE ELI AND RODGER OF THE SKIES, directed by Bill Sampson; screenplay by Chips Rosen, based on a story by Steven Spielberg; produced by Boris Wilson; director of photography, David M. Walsh; music, Jerry Goldsmith; editors, Louis Lombardo and Robert Belcher; produced and distributed by 20th Century-Fox. Running time: 92 minutes. At neighborhood theaters. This film has been rated PG.

Eli	Cliff Robertson
Rodger	Eric Shea
Shelby	Pamela Franklin
Hannah	Rosemary Murphy
Allison	Bernadette Peters
Sister Lite	Alice Ghostley
Rachel	Kelly Jean Peters

By VINCENT CANBY

The place is rural Kansas, and the time is midsummer in the early nineteen-twenties, not long after the Great War.

Eli (Cliff Robertson), a barn storming pilot who has the emotional make-up of an 11-year-old, and Rodger (Eric Shea), his 11-year-old son who possesses the wisdom of the ancients, set off to see the world, which means flying all the way to San Willow. To Eli, San Willow seems to be as fabled as Xanadu and quite as remote.

●

"Ace Eli and Rodger of the Skies," which opened yesterday at neighborhood theaters, is about the adventures of Rodger and Eli getting from nowhere to nowhere. Eli, a killer with the ladies at first, always leaves them unsatisfied. He seems to have a sex problem. Rodger spends a lot of his time getting his dad out of scrapes. He also drinks, smokes and goes to sleep at night crying for his mom, who was killed in a plane crash with Eli.

It's difficult to determine just what sort of movie the makers of "Ace Eli and Rodger of the Skies" had in mind when they began it. Americana? Comedy? Drama? A psychological study of the Oedipal relationship?

Little Rodger really does have a problem with his father, whose girlfriends he loves, whose whores he pays off and whom, at the very end, he comforts when a particularly bitchy woman has walked out on Eli saying that he was lousy in bed. "I love you," says Rodger, cradling his weeping dad.

•

The production appears to have been expensive. The aerial photography is lovely, and the performances are O.K., but the movie is such a mess of unexplored moods and loose ends that it makes the later, similar "Paper Moon" look like a masterpiece.

The film, which was made three years ago, is being shown here in a version that the original producers, writer and director so disapprove of that they took their names off it. The names included in the credit box above for those contributions appear on the screen and are fictitious. For the record, "Ace Eli" was actually produced by Robert Fryer and James Cresson, written by Claudia Ann Salter and directed by John Erman.

1974 Mr 2, 22:5

20-minute "The Climate of New York" (1949) and the 15-minute "Under the Brooklyn Bridge" (1955), the best of the lot in this observer's view.

"Climate," which takes its subtitles from the poetry of Mr. Burckhardt's friend, the poet and dance critic Edwin Denby, courses among empty lots and children and their elders enjoying a quiet Sunday in Astoria, through subways, to buildings at dusk in Manhattan, with perceptive, stark clarity that beautifully preserves the past. Just as sharp and memorable are the vignettes of the demolition of an ancient warehouse juxtaposed against scenes of nude boys swimming and diving from decayed piers in the blighted areas of "Under the Brooklyn Bridge."

Although it is out of step with the rest, the 1964 "Miracle on the B.M.T." (the Independent, really), provides a swift tour of subways and streets while it concentrates on a threadbare romantic comedy about a lonely boy and a girl, played by Red and Mimi Grooms.

However, "Eastside Summer" (1958) is a fond continuation of "Climate" in its unadorned portraiture of the tenements, shops and the largely Hispanic population of Avenues A, B and C. The past and present haven't changed much here or in the 1967 "Square Times" and its garish, sleezy Times Square night life.

"Rudy Burckhardt's New York" has not been previously shown theatrically, says the Film Forum management. But it is informative and fascinating visual history that deserves public recognition.

A. H. WEILER

1974 Mr 2, 22:5

Paris Critics Hail Malle's Chef-d'Oeuvre

By PIERRE SCHNEIDER
Special to The New York Times

PARIS, Feb. 27—Local film critics, who have seldom been tempted of late to apply the term of "masterpiece" to a French movie, are nearly unanimous in their description of "La combe, Lucien" as a chef-d'oeuvre. Louis Malle's new film tells the story of a more than ordinarily obtuse peasant boy in Nazi-occupied France. Because he is sick of his job in an old peoples' home, because his father is a war prisoner and his mother has taken up with the landlord, because he has a certain juvenile penchant for violence, because a Resistance member turns him down and he has a flat tire while bicycling back to town, Lacombe lands up in the Ger-

Arts Abroad

man police, swaggering, torturing, killing.

In the course of his sordid operations, he meets a Jew hiding in his provincial town with his mother and daughter. Come as one who exacts, Lacombe stays as one who wishes to be loved. And he is, in fact, loved—or at least wanted—by the daughter. Despite the horrors that he perpetrates, despite the father's surrender to the authorities in what amounts to suicide, the two young people, amidst the hysteric excesses provoked by the impending collapse of Hitler's armies, live a brief, improbable idyll. At the liberation, Lacombe Lucien is executed.

Unconsciously, one suspects, the critics must have reasoned thus: like life, masterpieces are ambiguous, "Lacombe, Lucien" is ambiguous, therefore it is a masterpiece.

Mr. Malle, whose previous films include "Les Amants" and "Le Souffle au Coeur," indeed proves himself superbly cool and skillful in recording the inextricable imbrications of good and evil, comedy and tragedy, as well as the chilling limitations of free will. Too skillful, perhaps: Everything and everybody is so perfectly "right" that one ends by feeling it is all wrong. In art as in life, the authentic likes to contradict itself: only copies are completely faithful. Still, Mr. Malle comes closer than ever before to converting the kind of glacial incapacity for involvement that has always marked his films into the dispassionate understanding required for rendering the terrifying indifference of fate.

1974 Mr 5, 28:2

'Montreal Main,' the Offbeat Life of 13-Year-Old Boy

"Montreal Main," the Canadian-made feature that opened yesterday at the Whitney Museum of American Art, is obviously the dedicated effort of a production crew and a cooperative cast who conceived and performed it all with a will. But despite a cinéma vérité-like approach, their delineations of the relationships between a young, bearded artist-photographer and a 13-year-old boy, the boy's parents who are disturbed by this strange friendship, and a covey of homosexuals and others, makes for dolefully sincere but vague and unconvincing drama.

Frank Vitale, who wrote the original story, directed and stars as the artist, has focused his color cameras on the sleazy, Bohemian areas of a Montreal far removed from a tourist's itinerary. And his disquieting, if not moving, slice of offbeat life is in keeping with its squalid, if authentic, surroundings.

•

The cast, reportedly nonprofessionals using their real names and improvising much of the dialogue, does not act so much as react to situations that often call for fuller explanations. There seems to be a good deal of confusion in Frank's sexual leanings.

He is in conflict both with girls and his apparently bisexual friend, Allan, who resents the attention he pays to John, the boy.

This odd couple eventually is forced apart by the youngster's parents, but the problems of the principals, the boy's family and the unloved and grimly gay types remain largely unresolved, even if they seem all too real.

The driven denizens of "Montreal Main" speak their minds, often in four-letter language, in a technically polished production that unfortunately doesn't generate much compassion for them.

A. H. WEILER

1974 Mr 8, 21:2

RUDY BURCKHARDT'S NEW YORK: Documentaries by Mr. Burckhardt including "Pursuit of Happiness," 7 minutes; "The Climate of New York," 20 minutes; "Under the Brooklyn Bridge," 15 minutes; "Miracle on the B.M.T.," 22 minutes; "Square Times," 7 minutes, and "Eastside Summer," 14 minutes. At the Film Forum, 256 West 88th Street. Through Sunday, and next Thursday through Sunday, at 8 P.M.

New York, which, in the case of the 59-year-old Swiss-born photographer and film maker Rudy Burckhardt, consists of only Manhattan and Queens, was a wonderful town. And it is nostalgically celebrated in the collection of six of his short subjects made from 1939 through 1967 that is being shown at the Film Forum, whose New York photographs have been lauded in one-man shows, now illustrates that he is equally artistic in his movie documentations of our town's people and places.

•

In the silent, 7-minute "Pursuit of Happiness," shots of hurrying mid-Manhattan crowds focus on not only now-quaint 1939 hair, dress and suit styles but also a variety of faces that ironically mock the film's title. And it sets the tone for subsequent subjects such as the

Film: Mekas's Very Personal Journey to Lithuania

"Reminiscences of a Journey to Lithuania" was shown at the 10th New York Film Festival. The following excerpt is from Vincent Canby's review, which appeared Oct. 5, 1972, in The New York Times. The film opened Sunday and will be shown again today and tomorrow at noon and midnight at the First Avenue Screening Room, at 61st Street.

In his open-ended, autobiographical film, "Diaries, Notebooks and Sketches," Jonas Mekas says at one point: "They tell me that I should always be searching, but I celebrate what I see." Although the photographed diaries are indeed a celebration—of friends, of enemies, of fine meals eaten, of beautiful weather enjoyed, of streets walked down—they also document a search for an unhackneyed use of the autobiographical motion-pic-

ture camera as an instrument of self-understanding.

Mr. Mekas's newest film, "Reminiscences of a Journey to Lithuania," is the 88-minute record of the trip he took last summer with his younger brother, Adolfas, and Adolfas's wife, Pola Chapelle, to the home in Lithuania the Mekases left during World War II, thinking they were going to the University of Vienna, although, instead, they landed in a slave-labor camp outside Hamburg.

It's successively moving, indulgent, beautiful, poetic, banal, repetitious and bravely, heedlessly personal. Although "Reminiscences" can stand by itself well enough, it is a continuation of the "Diaries" in style and mood.

•

The action is speeded up, as if to extract the essence of an event. There are parenthetical inserts referring to other places and times. And over all of it there is the

same feeling of passion, affection and wonder that marks Jonas Mekas as a film critic and a champion of underground film makers, even when he is being most rude and outrageous about the idiocies of nonbelievers.

"Reminiscences" is an especially appealing film, and a good deal more than a record of Jonas Mekas's summer vacation. It is a testament to all persons displaced, geographically, as the Mekas brothers were, and spiritually. Without sentimentality, Mr. Mekas recalls meetings in the early nineteen-fifties of displaced persons at Stony Brook, L. I., and "somewhere at the end of Atlantic Avenue." They were cheerful gatherings of people who seem sentenced forever to be out of touch.

There is something of this same feeling about his treatment of the family's reunion in Lithuania. The great familial love is still there. The joy of reconciliation is real. Yet

the years have created a gulf that no amount of touching and eating and drinking and singing together will ever quite bridge. "Reminiscences" is about growing away as well as up.

VINCENT CANBY.

1974 Mr 8, 21:1

MAME, directed by Gene Saks; screenplay by Paul Zindel, based on the Broadway musical by Jerome Lawrence, Robert E. Lee and Jerry Herman, which was, in turn, based on the Patrick Dennis novel and the stage play by Mr. Lawrence and Mr. Lee; produced by Robert Fryer and James Cresson; director of photography, Philip Lathrop; editor, Maury Winetrobe; music and lyrics, Jerry Herman; choreographer, Onna White; presented in association with the American Broadcasting Companies; distributed by Warner Bros. Running time: 131 minutes. At the Radio City Music Hall. This film has been rated PG.
Mame .... Lucille Ball
Vera .... Beatrice Arthur
Beauregard .... Robert Preston
Agnes Gooch .... Jane Connell
Older Patrick .... Bruce Davison
Young Patrick .... Kirby Furlong
Gloria Upson .... Doria Cook
Sally Cato .... Joyce Van Patten

By VINCENT CANBY

Some great characters of literature will not be still. They keep coming back. Dracula is one. Auntie Mame is another.

This determinedly eccentric Beekman Place hostess, who was first introduced to us by Patrick Dennis in his 1955 novel, appeared next as a 1956 Broadway comedy, "Auntie Mame," which was adopted into a 1958 film and then as a 1966 Broadway musical called "Mame," which has now reappeared as a 1974 movie musical.

It opened yesterday at the Radio City Music Hall, a little tired though certainly not out of breath.

The newest "Mame," with Lucille Ball in the title role wearing a different colored wig for every Administration from Hoover's through Truman's is as determined to please in its way as Mame is in hers.

The opening credits, which look like a Cubist collage in motion, are so good they could be a separate subject. The songs by Jerry Herman, when he isn't writing material ("Open a New Window") more fit for a lesser Walt Disney effort, are full of zest and sometimes wit. From time to time the dances by Onna White are allowed to take over the screen, a rare occurrence in most movie musicals these days.

It's all relentlessly good-natured but unless you've been packed in storage somewhere it's so familiar that it puts a tremendous burden on its star. Miss Ball is a great comedienne who has spent the last 20 years creating an in-home image as a lucky nut whose worst-laid plans always turn out successfully.

When the character of Lucy, an inspired slapstick performer, coincides with that of Auntie Mame, the Big-Town sophisticate, "Mame" is marvelous. I think of Lucy's turning a Georgia fox hunt into a gigantic shambles, or of her bringing the curtain down on a New Haven first-night when, as a budding actress, she falls off a huge cardboard moon. I even treasure her prying loose the fingers of a sloshed Beatrice Arthur who won't give up her martini glass.

•

Miss Ball has some great moments but she is not even a nonsinger who fakes singing very well, and as for the dances, well, she just more or less follows what the chorus people do with her, or she stands aside and sort of conducts them. What is worse is that she has been photographed in such soft focus that her face alternately looks beatific—all a religious glow—or like something sculptured from melting vanilla ice cream.

Gene Saks, the director, is so protected Miss Ball's appearance that when the comparatively rugged Robert Preston, who plays Mame's Georgia millionaire, comes into the same frame, he too, becomes suddenly fuzzy of contour, as if he'd walked into a Nylon tent.

Neither is the camera (or maybe its the customer) terribly kind to Beatrice Arthur, another fine comedienne who plays Mame's bitchy actress-friend. Miss Arthur ("Maude") has been dressed up to look like a football player in drag, which may be more in keeping with the kind of comedy "Mame" is than I remember from earlier incarnations.

So much of it is insult or put-down comedy that when Mame undertakes to save her nephew Patrick (Bruce Davison) from the clutches of bigoted suburban bores, the effect is less funny than smugly rude.

The movie does have two first-rate production numbers, one, early on, featuring Miss Ball and her 9-year-old nephew (Kirby Furlong), which becomes a salute to the nineteen-twenties. The other is the title song performed by the star and a chorus of what looks to be about 1,000 red-coated black-toppered fox hunters. Both numbers have a kind of plush, old-fashioned extravagance about them that takes us back not to the periods depicted in the film but to the innocent fifties when movie musicals hadn't yet thought of themselves as significant.

I have great reservations about "Mame," but I suspect a lot of people couldn't care less. All things being equal, Mame's next metamorphosis could be as a television series, by which time most of us may be too old to remember that her story wasn't handed down to us on tablets.

1974 Mr 8, 18:1

Will Duke Wayne Survive 'McQ'?

By VINCENT CANBY

'THERE'S nothing wrong with a gun in the hands of the right person," says the Tennessee sheriff in "Walking Tall." The San Francisco cop in "Magnum Force" puts it another way: "There's nothing wrong with shooting as long as the right people get shot." In "McQ," John Wayne plays a Seattle detective who looks as if he should be celebrating his diamond jubilee on the force. When the police captain scolds Wayne for playing fast and loose with the civil rights of a hood, specifically for throwing the hood off the roof of a building, Wayne draws himself up as tall as what seems to be his corset will allow, saying: "Well, it kept him off the streets, didn't it?"

Actually it sounds as if it spread the guy all over the sidewalks, but that's neither here nor there. Logic is not something that cop movies, with the exception of "Serpico," care much about. Thinking amounts to bad form. Even their nods to what is supposed to be a more enlightened society are distorted for the purpose of vigilante philosophy. In "Magnum Force," Clint Eastwood defends some young policemen: "If the rest o.' you could shoot like them, I wouldn't care if the whole damn department was queer."

For some time I'd been wondering what to think about these films. Should one try to interpret them as signs of the times? But of what times? Since it takes between 18 months and two years for any film to make it around the writer's blocks to the screen, these films must be reflecting 1972, probably the pre-Watergate 1972. Are they calls for right-wing revolution? Are they cries of frustration from citizens who feel helpless as they witness the erosion of cherished values? Should we be alarmed?

I'd been bothered by these questions for months and then, last week, I had the good fortune to see "McQ" in which John Wayne, now 67 and so thick of belly that even the most carefully draped suit can't hide the fact, writes the end of my cop-movie worries.

There are more cop movies coming up. "McQ," however should defuse them. When you see old Duke Wayne barrelling up and down the hills of Seattle in a snappy sports car, as ill at ease as Granny on a Honda, you suddenly realize what the cop movies are really all about.

Pure sensation.

Not that "McQ" is sensational. Because it tries very hard and because it packs the wallop of an angrily hurled feather, it exposes the limitations of the genre forever.

Of course, every movie, even every cop movie, is somewhat different, but when you see a movie fail so completely, as "McQ" does, it's possible to identify the formula.

What we are getting in films like "Magnum Force," "McQ" and "The Seven Ups" are urban Westerns.

For the time being the Western frontier for moviemakers has vanished. This has forced the loner-heroes, the men who stand for truth and justice defined in their own terms, to abandon the plains and emigrate to the big cities. It's not a coincidence that the most successful cop-movie star is Clint Eastwood, an actor who has also been hugely popular in Westerns. Indeed, Eastwood made one of the few entertaining cross-breeds between cop-film and Western in his "Coogan's Bluff," which was about the Western sheriff who sets New York's underworld straight.

Wayne's attempt to follow Eastwood's route to town was ill-advised. It isn't only that he's a bit old for the assignment, though that is a drawback. When the screenplay requires Wayne to run after a young punk who's just taken a pot-shot at him, you hold your breath until he reaches his destination. That kind of suspense we all can do without.

Unlike Eastwood, Wayne does not possess a physique that easily transplants to the city and the demands of urban melodrama. There's a scene in "McQ" in which Wayne is required to pick a lock and his massive hands are so gnarled from years on the range that you get the impression of a bear trying to tie a shoelace.

There's also a problem about his relations with women. In the legendary West where it's always 1870, every woman was either a virgin or a whore, which made life a lot easier for the usual John Wayne hero. They either did or they didn't. There were no subtleties to be expressed in dialogue. If, by some fluke, the screenplay allowed him to sleep with a woman, it was a whore, meaning that he could treat her much as he would treat his horse.

In "McQ," Wayne is given a chance to swing a bit in a sequence with Colleen Dewhurst. The total preliminaries to their bed-down consist of Wayne saying lethargically to Miss Dewhurst: "You're attractive," while the next morning he simply brings her a cup of coffee. Duke seems completely at sea.

John Sturges, who has directed some good action movies in the past ("The Magnificent Seven," "The Great Escape"), directed "McQ" as if receiving his tempo from Wayne. Instead of dashing from one sequence to the next, or from one spectacular location to another, it just sort of walks, meaningfully, the way Wayne would enter a saloon in Red River country.

Even the climactic chase in "McQ" recalls the Old West, though Wayne is at the wheel of one car that is being pursued along a Pacific Coast beach by hoods in two other cars. Wayne looks too big for the car, as if his feet might be hanging through the floor or his knees knocking against the dashboard.

It's still possible to go along with the deception until the shooting starts between the lead car and the two behind. The hoods would seem to have the advantage but throughout the running gunfight they never think to shoot out the tires of Duke's car. I doubt that they knew whether or not the tires were puncture-proof. It's almost as if they would have considered the gesture as unsportsmanlike as shooting down his horse.

"McQ" is a terrible movie, but it's also a reassuring one. The easy willingness with which it would suspend civil rights in the name of law-and-order, something it shares with most of the other cop films, may well be a true reflection of our times but it is also a philosophy inherited from one kind of narrative, the classic Western, which has been imposed on another kind, the gangster film of the thirties. We have survived all sorts of Westerns. I suspect we shall survive the cop movies. Wayne, however, may not.

1974 Mr 10, II:1:5

'Valerie'

The exquisite color of "Valerie and Her Week of Wonders" sustains this admirably conceived Czechoslovak film, directed and co-written by Jaromil Jires, now showing at the Elgin Theater, 171 Eighth Avenue.

As Mr. Jires depicts the tender, sensual and bizarre daydreaming of a 13-year-old girl, with the accompaniment of lyrical music and a flow of simple and surreal imagery, the picture evokes a pictorial music of its own. So do the expressions of the young heroine, Jaroslava Schallerova, looking like a beautiful young Rita Tushingham.

•

In content, the film is a weird exercise, striking out boldly in the paths of Bergman, Fellini and Buñuel with characters in something of a clutter who shift into evil incarnate or plain toothchomping vampires. One creepy sequence in a coffin-crammed lair is right out of "Dracula."

Mr. Jires finally brings his story back to reality in simple, neat fashion, but only after his Grand Guignol transformations have redundantly cluttered the action and landscape, like a milling horror-show road company. "What ails you, child?" the daydreaming girl is gently asked by her grandma, a part-time vampire.

The movie remains far more impressive when it blends the heroine's virginal wonderment with the sights and sounds of nature, minus the macabre symbolism tapped from other sources. A born director like Mr. Jires can be forgiven a lopsided beauty that still commands full attention.

HOWARD THOMPSON

1974 Mr 11, 34:2

Olivier's Stage Version of '3 Sisters' Shown

By VINCENT CANBY

"Three Sisters," which was shown twice yesterday at selected theaters and will be repeated twice today, is the American Film Theater's sixth presentation in its current subscription series, and by far its most rewarding to date.

It is not the film that Peter Hall's version of "The Homecoming," an earlier A.F.T. presentation, was. But then Anton Chekhov was not the scenarist that Harold Pinter is, even when Mr. Pinter is writing for the stage.

This "Three Sisters" succeeds because it re-creates a lot of the excitement of a special theatrical performance through methods that are primarily theatrical. When you watch it you have some idea why the live theater can be great and not just aridly high-minded, which you might have gathered from the A.F.T. productions of "A Delicate Balance" and "Rhinoceros."

•

In light of this praise it's probably unkind to point out that "Three Sisters" is the A.F.T.'s only presentation that was not produced with A.F.T. supervision. It is, in-

stead, Laurence Olivier's 1971 film version of a stage production done by Britain's National Theater Company when Lord Olivier was its director. With three major cast changes, it is the same production that the National Theater Company did four years ago in Los Angeles. The new cast members are Joan Plowright, who replaces Maggie Smith as Masha, Alan Bates as Vershinin in place of Robert Stephens, and Lord Olivier as the old doctor, Chebutkin, instead of Paul Curran.

Chekhov is not easily translated to the English-language screen, if you remember Sidney Lumet's cinematically souped-up, international-cast version of "The Seagull." The Chekhov rhythm is directly contradicted by most of the devices dear to filmmakers, including close-ups and cuts back and forth between two persons talking. Chekhov's characters exist so much in the society of others that directing Chekhov is more like choreographing a chorus than making a film.

Lord Olivier's awareness of this is apparent throughout his fine production, which never for a moment mistakes its stage origins, acknowledged in the lovely, not-quite-realistic settings by Josef Svoboda as well as in the easy grace of most of the camera movements.

There are only two moments when the movie goes rather badly awry. One is a quick sequence, looking almost like a stock shot, in which we see fire engines racing through the streets of the provincial Russian city inhabited by the three sisters. The other — and a major gaff it is — is a short, idiotic dream sequence showing us Irina and Masha in the Moscow they will never reach.

The film otherwise is a tribute to a kind of integrated stage performance we seldom see in this country, and to the play itself, which is Chekhov's most sorrowful, though bursting with optimistic intimations about the future, including the revolution that would erupt in Russia just 17 years after the play was written.

Lord Olivier takes no liberties with the text that I can tell, keeping intact those great chunks of exposition with which Chekhov introduces us to Olga, Masha and Irina, on the first anniversary of their father's death, longing to leave the provinces to return to the Moscow of their childhood. Once the exposition has been discreetly hurdled, the drama takes over: time passes, everyone ages, opportunities are lost piecemeal.

•

Miss Plowright is superb as the angry, love-torn middle sister who married a schoolmaster she thought to be the cleverest of men, only to find him the kindest. Mr.

Bates is marvelously self-deluding and foolish as her lover. They are the stars of the production, to the extent that there are any, but Jeanne Watts (Olga), Louise Purnell (Irina), Sheila Reid (Natasha) and Lord Olivier are equally fine.

The film's achievements are collective: the big, multi-character scenes of celebration avoided confrontation and resignation.

Movies, for all of their mobility and realism, have a way of oversimplifying drama, of reducing all conflicts to a one-to-one collision. In "Three Sisters" there are sometimes as many as eight major characters on stage at one time, talking around and through one another in a kind of genteel tangle of lives. The Olivier production allows us to respond to these people at our own speed and choice. This freedom, automatic in the theater, is so seldom granted in a film that "Three Sisters" becomes something quite rare.

1974 Mr 12, 34:4

Football Stars Cast as Gang Smashers

Good and evil characters aren't often so swiftly established as they are in "The Black Six," which opened yesterday at neighborhood theaters. From the first seraphic smile or demonic scowl, noble or foul natures expose themselves and their intentions—depriving us of any suspense whatsoever.

Six black stars of the National Football League—Gene Washington, Carl Eller, Lem Barney, Mercury Morris, Willie Lanier, and Joe Greene—are cast as a band of brotherly Vietnam veterans equipped with gleaming motorcycles. It's stressed that they don't want to live in cities, which are as dangerous for blacks as whites: "If I wanted to get mugged, I'd have stayed in Saigon." Encountering friendly whites as well as hostile ones, the veterans repeat that they want "peace," "no hassles," "no trouble" with anyone.

However, the younger brother of one has been murdered by a gang of white

bikers. The Black Six identify the killers, who plan to massacre them as well. The whole movie builds very, very slowly to a vast battle between the Six and more than a hundred white men. The camera bounces about so wildly that it robs the fight of almost any excitement. As flames rise from a ring of burning bikes, it's hard to tell who was or wasn't wiped out. But a final caption—"Hassle a brother and the Black Six will return"—hints at a sequel if not reincarnation.

Gene Washington and his fellow athletes have considerable charm, which comes through despite the arthritic dialogue. Even so, charm will never be a substitute for acting.

NORA SAYRE

1974 Mr 14, 42:1

By VINCENT CANBY

"Christo's Valley Curtain," directed by Albert and David Maysles and Ellen Giffard, is a 28-minute report on the hanging of a curtain in August, 1972. It was no ordinary curtain. It was made of nine tons of orange nylon polymide fabric, was a quarter of a mile long, was suspended from four steel cables as much as 365 feet above the floor of Rifle Gap, Colo., and cost $700,000. It lasted for less than 24 hours before it was torn to ribbons by the wind, but that didn't matter.

Christo, the Bulgarian-born New York artist who conceived the project, was not interested in hiding a garbage dump or a pot-bellied mountain. He's a compulsive "packager," and when he came to hang the valley curtain he'd already had experience as the man who wrapped one mile of Australian coastline and, Chicago's Museum of Contemporary Art. Separately, of course.

"Christo's Valley Curtain" was shown at the First Avenue Screening Room Sunday and will be repeated there today and tomorrow at noon and midnight. Technically, I suppose, you could say it supports the Screening Room's feature, "Confessor,"

an amateurish mishmash of poetic film making that you might want to break your neck to avoid.

If, at 73 minutes, "Confessor" is 72 minutes too long, "Christo's Valley Curtain" is not long enough. It makes no lugubrious attempt to explain Christo's art ("revelation through concealment," according to David Bourdin), which can be shown more easily than it can be explained.

Christo himself, a wiry, intense man wearing jeans and white hard-hat, talks about his esthetics as involving the entire process of packaging, or in this case, of curtain hanging. That is, the business of negotiating with engineers, architects, politicians and construction workers. It's like being a kid all over again, though here the play looks a bit dangerous.

•

The surprise of the film is the enthusiasm with which this project was greeted by the residents of the town of Rifle (pop. 2,150) and by the construction workers who risked limbs and lives on the stunt. Says one hard-hat: "It's not the erection of it [that's important], it's the thought."

The film is marvelous reportage of the sort the Maysles brothers do best, but it brought out every philistine feeling I've ever had. Seven hundred thousand dollars? Even though Christo raised the money from the sale of his own drawings and models, that seems the sort of staggering indulgence that once sent the mobs ransacking Versailles.

This much about "Confessor": It's a series of disconnected images, some surreal (a football player runs through a museum). Superman lies dead on a New York street) and all banal, describing urban alienation. It is less expensive to observe life in any midtown cafeteria on a weekday afternoon.

1974 Mr 15, 20:1

By NORA SAYRE

Three fiction films with a kinship to short stories make up the program of "Narrative Cinema—Part One," which opened Wednesday at the Whitney Museum of American Art and will run until Wednesday.

"Passing Quietly Through," by Denitia McCarthy, focuses on the reluctant ties between a middle-age nurse and her dying patient: a feisty, garrulous old man who's bedridden in a room that evokes a nightmare of solitude. He says he hates her cooking, she insists that he would be better off in a home—they bicker and take out their own anxieties on each other.

While she washes him, he talks about making love as though he still did so. He reminisces about his childhood, his disappointments; she tries to stay at an emotional distance from him. But finally, she tells him about her early loneliness in marriage and a miscarriage that she painfully relives as she describes it. Amid their rapid changes of mood, a rapport develops between the two—in a setting that conveys New York at its bleakest.

The film, which has its ragged moments, succeeds because both characters draw energy from mutual irritation—thereby avoiding pathos.

•

In "Hot Dogs for Gauguin," by Martin Brest, a hungry photographer deduces that the Hindenburg disaster of 1937—when a huge trans-Atlantic dirigible exploded just before landing—must have made a fortune for the photographer who snapped the picture. So he decides to arrange an equivalent windfall for himself by planting a charge in the nose of the Statue of Liberty. But his

camera topples over just as the head blows up, and he misses the shot. It's a beguiling idea, but the acting is too frantic and winsome to carry it off.

•

"Charlie Benson's Return to the Sea," by Victor Nunez, details a young man's rediscovery of his hometown on the Gulf Coast after having finished his Army service. He explores the seaside, ponders the decline of his father's crabbing business, drinks Pabst with his old acquaintances. Throughout, he appears to be very uncertain if he wants to rejoin what's familiar—even though it tugs at his sympathies.

Again, the theme has value. However, the film moves as slowly as rural life itself, and it lacks the narrative pull that could involve us.

1974 Mr 16, 16:2

THREE TOUGH GUYS, directed by Duccio Tessari; story and screenplay by Luciano Vincenzoni and Nicola Badalucco; produced by Dino De Laurentiis; music and lyrics, Isaac Hayes; director of photography, Aldo Tonti; editors, Mario Morra and Richard

Marks; released by Paramount Pictures. Running time: 92 minutes. At the DeMille Theater, Seventh Avenue at 47th Street. This film has been rated R.
Father Charlie ....Lino Ventura
Lee Stevens ....Isaac Hayes
Joe Snake ....Fred Williamson
Fay Collins ....Paula Kelly
Captain Ryan ....William Berger
Bishop ....Luciano Salce
Mike Petralia ....Vittorio Sanipoli

By VINCENT CANBY

"Three Tough Guys" is about a Roman Catholic priest (Lino Ventura) and a cashiered Chicago cop (Isaac Hayes) who joined forces to solve a bank robbery and murder involving an ambitious hood (Fred Williamson).

The exteriors were shot on location in Chicago and the interiors in Rome in what sometimes seem to be hand-me-down Fellini sets. The results are made even more disorienting by the post-synchronized English dialogue. Everyone sounds as if he were talking through an exhaust pipe.

The movie, which opened yesterday at the DeMille, is international junk of no interest, by far the worst film yet produced by Dino De Laurentiis since he left Rome to make movies in this country.

1974 Mr 16, 16:3

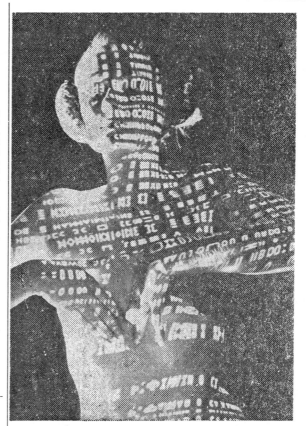

"ZARDOZ"—An eternal—and asexual—woman of the future dispenses computerized data in John Boorman's film, now at the Loew's Orpheum, Trans-Lux East and West and other houses. Sean Connery stars as a mortal but decidedly sexy brute.

Movies Are More Sci-Fi Than Ever

By VINCENT CANBY

IN John Boorman's "Zardoz," civilization in 2293 is in the control of an elitist caste known as Eternals, people who are so perfect they have forgotten what sexual desire is. The characters in Woody Allen's "Sleeper," set 200 years in the future, are neither perfect nor immortal but for a really satisfactory physical relationship they must repair to the orgasm box, which looks rather like an old-fashioned hot-water heater and is kept in the living room.

Michael Crichton's "Westworld" is all about a super Disneyland of the future, a resort community serviced by robots whose only function is to amuse the humans, which is fine until the computer breaks down and the robots suffer an epidemic of "central mechanism psychosis," meaning they start murdering the guests. A neurotic computer was responsible for much of the mayhem in Stanley Kubrick's "2001," which also hinted at the kind of dehumanized world that George Lucas foresaw in his "THX 1138," where love was outlawed.

According to "Silent Running" and "Soylent Green," the earth will soon be an overpopulated, overheated, arid desert. These two films do not predict the sort of cataclysm Woody Allen imagines in "Sleeper" (after a man named Albert Shanker gets his own nuclear warhead). Instead they see a world that is up to here in rubbish, like New York City after a five-week strike by sanitation workers.

For a society that spends so much time, money and effort pursuing pleasure as if it were happiness, we certainly are taking a gloomy view of the future in our science-fiction films. Cheer up, say these movies, everything

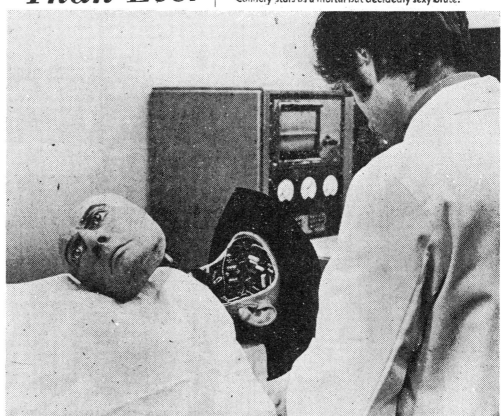

"WESTWORLD"—Robot Yul Brynner receives help in getting his head together in Michael Crichton's thriller set in a grotesque playground for grown-ups. The movie is such a hit that a sequel, "Futureworld," is in the works. Other futuristic films in our future include Crichton's "The Terminal Man," as well as "The Nine Lives of Fritz the Cat," which will bring us President Kissinger and secretary Rosemary Woodstock.

is going to get a lot worse. Ever since Georges Méliès' "Voyage to The Moon" (1902), sci-fi has been a standard brand of movie fiction, but never have our visions of the future been so essentially bleak as they seem to be now. It used to be that the spectacle of scientific achievement and the gadgetry involved were more or less enough to fascinate us, as in George Pal's "Destination Moon" (1950). Sci-fi was as optimistic as pessimistic. At its worst, the world of the future as shown in the old Buck Rogers serials was a place where Buck had to match his wits against those of Killer Kane. I can't remember that we worried whether or not Buck and Wilma ever made love, but if we did I'm sure it never occurred to us that they might not be capable of it *at all.* Buck and Wilma were red - blooded, all - American kids and in that day red-blooded, all-American kids didn't go all the way. Any society inhabited by them had to be pretty darn good, excepting for the few rotten apples that furnished the material for their adventures.

*

Sci-fi is clearly here to stay. Upcoming we're going to get a sequel to "Westworld" called "Futureworld." Michael Crichton's "The Terminal Man" has been completed, as has been "The Nine Lives of Fritz The Cat," which has an episode about a Martian journey and another about an American President named Kissinger who has a multi-armed secretary named Rosemary Woodstock. It will open here in late June. Saul Bass has one due called "Phase IV," about ants. Columbia is planning to make Isaac Asimov's "Caves of Steel," with Jack Nicholson playing a human policeman whose partner is a robot, while television is supplying the sci-fi demand with "The Six Million Dollar Man," "Star Lost" and an animated version of "Star Trek."

At their most simple-minded, these sci-fi films and TV shows are excuses for fancy effects and plots that employ magic under the somewhat more sober term: advanced technology. At their best, they are less often serious predictions of things to come than sharply observed and carefully recast satires of the world and the society for whom they were created, like Samuel Butler's "Erewon."

If, as Michael Crichton said in a recent interview, they are basically escapist entertainments, one wonders what, specifically, the audiences want to escape from, and why.

The awful guilt implied in sci-fi post-cataclysm films would suggest extremely ambiguous feelings toward the atom. We want all the industrial and economic benefits we can get from it, but then something in the old Protestant work ethic reminds us that things easily come by aren't worth having. If we go too far, we're going to find ourselves living in a world ruled by a chimpanzee named Cornelius.

Similarly the films reflect our love-hate feelings toward technology. The more we have, the more we want, and the less we enjoy it. We demand that our shirts be returned from the laundry in individual plastic bags and then become angry when the bags clog the garbage cans. We push ahead seemingly heedless of the dangers, though we know we're not. We depend on computers more and more even though there's not one of us who hasn't had his bank account totally fouled up by one.

*

The computers of today's sci-fi are the Frankenstein monsters of yesterday's gothic fiction. We are tampering with the Unknown. If God had meant telephone bills to be on pieces of cardboard that couldn't be folded, spindled or mutilated, that would have been the way they were at the beginning.

The most peculiar theme shared by so many of these films is the vision of a society in which love/sex is either unknown or forbidden —and this in an age of permissiveness! Do we hate it that much? It would seem to be a rather obvious dramatization of the old castration fears. And if the fears are so apparent, can the wishes be far behind? Perhaps the films are intended to short-circuit fates worse than death: by picturing the disaster, we render it impotent.

Of only one thing am I sure, and that's the test that sci-fi presents for the moviemaker. Sci-fi separates the men from the boys. Stanley Kubrick's superb "2001" and "A Clockwork Orange" gave him room in which he could fully exercise his talents. "Zardoz," on the other hand, exposes John Boorman, its producer - writer - director, as someone of considerably less wit, discipline and good sense than I would have thought of the man who made "Point Blank" and even "Deliverance."

*

"Zardoz" is Boorman's opportunity to create a world entirely from his imagination, which turns out to be amazingly banal and uninteresting. The film is very fancily photographed but it's been so over-costumed and over-gadgeted that it looks more like a charity ball than a movie. It presents no cohesive view of any society, ours or its, and toward the end, seems to have had no place to go.

Sean Connery, wearing fewer clothes than he should at his age, plays a kind of reverse messiah who brings the gift of death to an immortal society of the future. The screenplay seeks tone by quoting T. S. Eliot and by making some less than profound references to God's function. Ultimately it turns into a lugubrious chase movie with a lot of the extras wearing the kind of Greek tragedy masks that used to give style to college productions of Euripedes in the 1940s and 1950s.

"It's all just a joke," one character says toward the end. Boorman cannot get out from under a piece of junk that easily.

1974 Mr 17, II:1:1

"PHASE IV"—Life is no picnic when ants with a talent for hypnosis take over—as they do in Saul Bass's upcoming film. Another dark glimpse of the future will be offered in "Caves of Steel," with Jack Nicholson out to solve a murder. His partner? A robot.

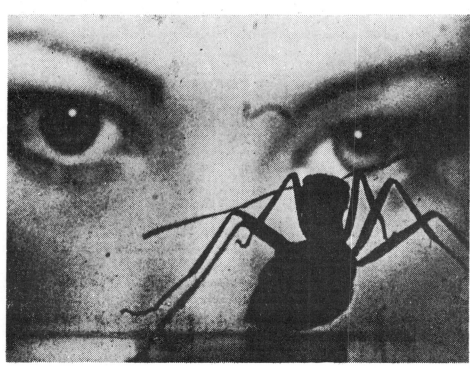

How the West Was Won by Mel

By PETER SCHJELDAHL

MEL BROOKS'S "Blazing Saddles" is an awesomely funny movie that some people are bound to despise; it wouldn't be for real if some people didn't despise it. Brooks is America's current patron saint of "going too far," a manic yok-artist in the checkered tradition of burlesque, the Marx Brothers and Mad magazine. A showbiz primitive, he specializes in the humor of affront—affront to civilized sensibilities, good taste and common sense—and makes us believe that he would do absolutely anything for a laugh.

For those who haven't heard, "Blazing Saddles" is a western about a black sheriff (Cleavon Little) hired to defend a small town against the minions of an evil, land-grabbing lawyer (Harvey Korman)—hired, that is, by the lawyer, who reckons the sheriff will be lynched by the townspeople. The lawyer's minions include a moronic lieutenant (Slim Pickens), a Marlene Dietrich-type singing prostitute with a lisp (Madeline Kahn) and a sub-human man-mountain named Mongo (Alex Karras). Backing the sheriff is an alcoholic fast-draw artist (Gene Wilder). Brooks himself plays two roles—a corrupt, cross-eyed governor and a Yiddish-speaking Indian chief.

The intricate and rambling plot—a pastiche of clichés from every western you've ever seen, with occasional bursts of lunacy from deep left field—is mostly just a pretext for jokes. Or, to put it another way, a film projector loaded with "Blazing Saddles" is a gag-firing machine gun. Some of the gags are priceless. My personal favorite involves Mongo, who is scolded by a citizen on horseback for illegally parking his Brahma bull. Mongo hulks over and knocks the horse out with one punch.

Other of the gags are pleasurable groaners, others are re-treaded chestnuts and still others may make one feel a little grim, but all of them, good and bad, come in a pell-mell torrent that leaves no time for reflecting on their quality. There is a kind of *horror vacuii* to Brooks' humor that can give a sense of desperation when things are fizzling. When a good joke is followed by a sensational one, however, it can also produce a feeling of helpless elation like nothing else in art or life.

One starts to laugh at "Blazing Saddles" long before the movie begins. The media ads for it and the delicious title song, in which

Peter Schjeldahl is a free-lance writer.

Frankie Laine obsequiously does to himself what many have longed to do to Frankie Laine, are a side-show all their own, an expert lampoon of total-hype "package" salesmanship that is also an expert example of the art. Once begun, the film remains a realistic western for about a minute. Then a bunch of black railroad workers, ordered to regale their overseers with a work song, break out suavely with "I get no kick from champagne," and we're off and running.

The promise of massive merriment embodied in these preliminaries, as it happens, is not completely fulfilled. It probably couldn't be. A film *that* funny would be a menace to public health. The proceedings are studded with television-type skits, some of them pretty icky, and the non-stop vulgarity—in a movie that milks the word "nigger" for one shocked laugh after another and features a symphony of flatulence from beans-eating cowhands—can make one yearn to come up for air. But the final effect of "Blazing Saddles" is devastating.

Coming out of "Blazing Saddles" with a funnybone battered black and blue, one may think only of the ache left by all that laughter. But the movie grows and becomes more fully satisfying in retrospect. The sheer wonder of its invention is really apparent only afterward, as one savors moments of delight that flashed by in the theater. In plot terms, these moments may have been entirely gratuitous—like a brief appearance in the middle of the desert by the Count Basie orchestra—but they come to seem more central to one's experience of the film than most of its story elements.

There are, moreover, some unexpected bite and substance to the story that also profit from hindsight. "Blazing Saddles" is a movie about movies and show business, on one level, but it is also a movie about racism and about human nastiness in general. And, despite a point of view that is studiously hip and uncommitted for the most part, its comic catalogue of meannesses and depravities has a cumulative, purging effect. Brooks seems to go with the medieval definition of man as the animal that laughs.

He is also evidently a man who lives to make people laugh. His main directorial talent consists in an ability to spread his laughter bug, by contagion, to everyone he works with—in this case, to our co-writers and several cast members with a flair for improvising. Mel Brooks with collaborators becomes a kind of mega-Mel Brooks, absorbing the talents of others into his own like a Martian amoeba.

Beyond that, he is only marginally better at film-making than he used to be. He is exasperatingly casual about production values. The visual tackiness of an obviously well-financed film like "Blazing Saddles" is inexcusable. For his next project, Brooks should hire a good, humorless cinematographer and let the guy earn his pay. It couldn't hurt.

It is hard to place a value on the genius of Mel Brooks, a genius that specializes in reducing all values to confetti. In terms of skill and emotional appeal, he is overshadowed among present comic moviemakers by Woody Allen, whose films are sturdy and beguiling. But in "The Producers" and now in "Blazing Saddles," Brooks has brought to the screen a brand of convulsive comedy so completely original that it seems to have dropped out of the sky. Whatever else he may be, Brooks is unique and irreplaceable; let us cherish him for that.

1974 Mr 17, II:15:5

Three Documentaries on Creative Men

ARTISTS AT WORK: FRANS ZWARTJES, FILMMAKER by Rene Coelho, 30 minutes; **COLOSSAL KEEPSAKE NO. 1 1969** by Peter Hentschel and William Richardson, 12 minutes, **SORT OF A COMMERCIAL FOR AN ICEBAG** by Michel Hugo, 24 minutes; **CHRISTO: WRAPPED COAST,** by Christian and Michael Blackwood, 28 minutes. At the Film Forum, 256 West 88th Street. Thursday through Sunday.

Artists, like their arts, obviously are widely varied, but "Artists at Work," the documentations on three disparate creative men, which opened at the Film Forum last week and will be shown again Thursday through Sunday, are only fitfully impressive. Color photography beautifully captures the implementation of their decidedly unusual art forms. The probings into the artists' inspirations and drives are a good deal less colorful or memorable.

The most successful is fusing elusive thought and action over two subjects on Claes Oldenburg's immense sculptures, "Sort of a Commercial for an Icebag" by Michel Hugo, and "Colossal Keepsake No. 1" by Peter Henschel and William Richardson. These dissections of the 18-by-11-foot mechanized icebag exhibited at the World's Fair in Japan and the giant steel carmine-tipped lipstick erected at Yale expose both the sculptor and his decidedly offbeat creations in honest and meaningful, if perhaps satiric, perspectives.

●

On the other hand, "Christo: Wrapped Coast," by Christian and Michael Blackwood, is visually impressive as it records Christo and a team of aides as they wrap an expanse of rocky Australian coastline in a million square feet of plastic sheeting and miles of rope—only to see it ripped by tides and roaring winds.

But "Wrapped Coast" cries for missing explanations. It would be helpful to learn the cost, the backers and the reasons for this project, and to know that Christo is a 38-year-old Bulgarian-born artist who has been involved in other monumental packaging commissions, all of which has been set down in newspapers and in the 1972 "Christo," by David Bourdon.

While "Frans Zwartjes," Rene Coelho's study of the Dutch avant-garde movie maker, is in its natural medium, it is a somewhat haphazard examination of his style as he films a pretty model, instructs students, composes and plays music for his film and intermittently philosophizes. The Dutch and English subtitles merely indicate his approach to creativity, but one line perhaps states it best when he observes, "you sense a mood and the mood is your picture."

The moods and some expertise, if not the whole men, are picturesquely projected in "Artists at Work."

A. H. WEILER

1974 Mr 18, 39:8

The Cast

LITTLE CIGARS, directed by Chris Christenberry; written by Louis Garfinkle and Frank Ray Perilli; director of photography, John Stephens; film editor, Eve Newman; produced by Albert Band; released by American International Pictures. At neighborhood theaters. Running time 92 minutes. This film is classified PG.

Cleo .... Angel Tompkins
Slick .... Billy Curtis
Cadillac .... Jerry Maren
Monty .... Frank Delfine
Rugo .... Emory Souza

If you're old enough to recall some of the off-color versions of Snow White and the Seven Dwarfs, then "Little Cigars," the mildly comic film adventures of a conniving well-stacked blonde who leads a carnival troupe of small-time, thieving midgets into big-time crime, might be your after-dinner pleasure. But like its likable midgets, the comedy-melodrama that opened at local theaters yesterday, unfortunately, rarely measures up to its king-sized intentions.

Angel Tompkins, as the double-dealing damsel on the lam from a mobster she has bilked, is, of course, not averse to latching onto Billy Curtis and the other midget "Little Cigars" in his troupe in order to avoid her pursuers. Thereafter, naturally, it's one caper after another until the big one and the ultimate double-cross.

It's not really a double-cross because, it turns out, Miss Tompkins loves Mr. Curtis as much as money —to the accompaniment throughout these hectic hold-ups of a series of one-liners in four-letter dialogue that are not terribly funny. As Mr. Curtis sardonically observes, "You get mixed up with midgets, there's no way you're gonna do anything big."

A. H. WEILER

1974 Mr 21, 52:4

Film Depicts Real-Life 'Batman' and 'Robin'

By VINCENT CANBY

"The Super Cops," this week's only new cop film, is based on the story of David Greenberg and Robert Hantz, the two New York City policemen who became known, not always fondly, as Batman and Robin because of their pow-bam-smash adventures fighting drug pushers in the streets of Bedford-Stuyvesant. It opened yesterday at the Criterion and other theaters.

The nicknames define the comic-book style of the film, which was written by Lorenzo Semple Jr., and directed by Gordon Parks, and is played, mostly super cute, by Ron Leibman (Greenberg) and David Selby (Hantz).

The movie is escapist sociology: rather silly but not boring. Its pace is set by the big beat of Jerry Fielding's soundtrack music, which scores the flights, pursuits and last-minute escapes, including one in which the two intrepid cops are rescued by a wrecking ball that is demolishing the building they're standing on.

The Cast

THE SUPER COPS, directed by Gordon Parks; screenplay by Lorenzo Semple Jr., based on the book by L. H. Whittemore; produced by William Belasco; music, Jerry Fielding; director of photography, Dick Kratina; editor, Harry Howard; an M-G-M film, released by United Artists. Running time: 93 minutes. At the Criterion Theater, Broadway near 45th Street, and other theaters. This film has been rated R.

Greenberg .... Ron Leibman
Hantz .... David Selby
Sara .... Sheila E. Frazier
Lieut. Novick .... Pat Hingle
Krasna .... Dan Frazer
Lieut. O'Shaughnessy .... Joseph Sirola
Judge Kellner .... Arny Freeman
D. A. Heller .... Bernard Kates
Carlos .... Alex Colon

As in "Serpico," the villains of the film are not really the hoods and drug pushers but the other cops, who are either corrupt or lazy.

In "The Super Cops" this corruption is hardly more than a plot device, something to impede what otherwise would be the immediate rise to success of the two ambitious policemen. The movie, however, is fuzzy on details and so inconsistent that, at the end, when Greenberg and Hantz are being promoted, I couldn't help wondering how they made it in the face of all the departmental opposition.

At one point in the film, the real Detectives Greenberg and Hantz show up playing crooked cops. Which makes me wonder even more. If one is a cop who isn't on the take, one can always sell his story to the movies. It has become one of the residuals of honesty.

1974 Mr 21, 51:1

IN THE NAME OF THE FATHER, directed by Marco Bellocchio; screenplay (Italian with English subtitles) by Mr. Bellocchio; photography, Franco di Giacomo; editor, Franco Artalli; music, Nicola Piovani; produced by Franco Cristaldi; released by New Yorker Films. At the Art Theater, Eighth Street at University Place. Running time: 107 minutes. This film has not been classified.

Angelo .... Yves Beneyton
Vice Rector .... Renato Scarpa
Franco .... Aldo Sassi
Franco's mother .... Laura Betti
Salvatore .... Lo uCastel

By NORA SAYRE

"Respect your father!": A furious man and his outraged son trade slaps in the corridors of a Jesuit school, and their mutual loathing establishes the climate of Marco Bellocchio's extraordinary film, "In the Name of the Father," which opened yesterday at the Art Theater. (Mr. Bellocchio also made "China Is Near.") In the savagely oppressive school, where adolescents are locked in their rooms at night, reminded that "You are merely death's plaything" and generally treated like bad animals, fear is used as a weapon for controlling others. So we initially sympathize with the students who spit on a marble bust that represents authority, or smoke defiantly in front of their teachers, whom they label "the fear of God specialists." But soon we realize that an ugly institution makes its creatures ugly. When the vice-rector (Renato Scarpa) tells the boys, "Your characters are formed here," their cruelty and stupidity prove him right.

●

Angelo, a cool young fanatic, manipulates his schoolmates into a rebellion against the school. He insists that they're protesting against poor teaching, which turns them into "cowards and idiots," that they want "less religion and more science," stricter discipline but no more foolish regulations. However, this clever terrorist is as devoted to power as the Jesuits, and he awakens a latent fascism in all the other students—until they become nearly as hateful as the school itself.

In Jean Vigo's "Zero for Conduct" and Lindsay Anderson's "If . . .", it was a pleasure to root for the rebels—which is impossible here. Mr. Bellocchio detects a taste for tyranny in every group or individual; with harsh conviction, he makes that point again and again. The brutalized students may overthrow their dictators. But their leadership will be just as destructive as their predecessors'

●

Mr. Bellocchio specializes in shocks. The dissenters put on a wild and blasphemous play designed to demoralize a devout audience; later, Angelo, wearing a dog's head, drags a corpse from its coffin and hurls it at the vice rector. Deliberately senseless or grotesque acts are employed to bewilder people, in order to make them more malleable. Meanwhile, a sense of mystery is maintained throughout the movie. A couple of passages may be fantasies, as when a student shoots his nagging mother, or when a bulldozer wrecks a school building—an image that confirms collapse, whether in the present or the future. Since the film is crammed with fascinating puzzles, it's unfortunate that the English subtitles are sometimes inadequate.

"In the Name of the Father" is also one of the few genuinely frightening movies I've seen—it makes "The Exorcist" seem rather like a lullaby. A sense of suppressed madness streams through Mr. Bellocchio's picture, along with the promise of violence that lurks in the characters. As the lunacies accumulate, you understand why most authorities cling to control at any cost—and that understanding generates a deeper chill, as it was meant to.

1974 Mr 21, 51:1

The Cast

CATCH MY SOUL, directed by Patrick McGoohan; screenplay by Jack Good, adapted from Shakespeare's "Othello"; producers, Richard Rosenbloom and Mr. Good; executive producer, Charles Fries; director of photography, Conrad Hall; editor, Richard Harris; background score by Tony Joe White; songs by Mr. White, Richie Havens, Leon Lumkins, Delaney Bramlett, Allene Lubin, Ray Pohlman, Emil Dean Zoghby, Family Lotus. Released by Cinerama. Running time: 95 minutes. At the Regency, Broadway at 67th Street, and other theaters. This film has been rated PG.
Othello .... Richie Havens
Iago .... Lance LeGault
Desdemona .... Season Hubley
Cassio .... Tony Joe White
Emilia .... Susan Tyrrell
With Delaney Bramlett, Bonnie Bramlett, Raleigh Gardenshire, Wayne (Eagle) Waterhouse, Family Lotus.

By VINCENT CANBY

Although George Bernard Shaw wasn't crazy about Shakespeare, he couldn't easily dismiss "Othello." Wrote Shaw: "Tested by the brain, it is ridiculous; tested by the ear, it is sublime." Tested by almost any organ you might want to mention, "Catch My Soul" is pricelessly funny though seldom meaning to be.

The film, which opened here yesterday, is the screen version of Jack Good's contemporary rock opera, based on "Othello" and odds and ends from the Old Testament, which was done on the stage in Los Angeles and London several years ago. The setting is the American Southwest, and the leading characters have been turned into a black evangelist, his flower-child wife and the ill-tempered leader of a hippie commune who thinks he's Satan and drives an old black school bus with blacked-out windows.

●

The music, a lot of it written by Tony Joe White, who plays Cassio ("a wino from Baton Rouge, Louisiana") is not at all bad, especially when it's being sung by Mr. White or Richie Havens, who is as creditable an Othello as it's possible to be under the nervy circumstances. It's the hybrid plot and dialogue that keep one in what is genteelly called stitches. I shall especially cherish for a very long time the scene in which Othello marries Desdemona (Season Hubley), a solemn girl in granny glasses who looks like the young George (Foghorn) Winslow.

Says Desdemona in plighting her troth: "Whither thou goest, I will go. Whither thou lodgeth, I will lodge." This sort of thing becomes intoxicating. It liberates the imagination. You wouldn't be at all surprised if she added: "In whatever car thou renteth, I will be beside thee, on the fronteth seat."

When Desdemona asks Cassio why Othello no longer favors him, the sodden Cassio pulls himself together just long enough to say: "Ah don' know. A mess a things. Ah ain't much of a talker."

"I like not that," says Iago, as Desdemona goes off to whisper into Cassio's ear. Says the distracted Othello: "Wha's dat?"

In something as wildly eclectic as this, it's impossible to know who did what. Jack Good, an English actor and producer, is credited as having thought up the original production and as being the movie's co-producer and screenplay author. Patrick McGoohan, a solid English actor, directed the film, which was photographed by Conrad Hall, a first-class cinematographer. According to the screen credits, the entire affair was "structured by Sid Levin," whatever that means.

Susan Tyrrell, who was so good in "Fat City," turns up as Emilia, a woman who talks like Mae West and who dresses as if she had access to the wardrobe of the Madwoman of Chaillot.

Forget the movie and get the soundtrack album.

1974 Mr 23, 20:1

The Program

PRINCETON: A SEARCH FOR ANSWERS, produced and directed by Julian Krainin and DeWitt Sage; photography, Mr. Krainin; editor, Sarah; music, Scott Joplin; released by Krainin/Sage Productions. Running time: 30 minutes.
CASUAL RELATIONS, produced, directed, written and edited by Mark Rappaport; camera, Mr. Rappaport and Alan Raymond. Running time: 30 minutes. At the First Avenue Screening Room, at 61st Street.

By NORA SAYRE

Impatience dwells a long way from outrage, and boredom never was a substitute for shock. Mark Rappaport's "Casual Relations," whose two-day run ends today at the First Avenue Screening Room, is supposed to be outrageous, but it's no more stimulating than one prolonged shot of a pitcher and a basin.

The movie yields a vague patchwork of preoccupations: a young woman dreams of monsters and wakes exhausted, a man suffers through a bad trip, another woman watches television all day long, a couple lunches one year after their separation, there's a very dull murder in a swamp, a chap who likes newsreels of catastrophes gets his knee fondled in a movie theater, a typist in an office recalls a threatening dream, and an amateur photographer admires one photograph in a gallery.

●

A woman who does nude modeling also performs in stag films and a vampire picture. Both are filmed with such enthusiasm that you suspect that these were the movies that the director really wanted to make. But his vampires—who move as slowly and stiffly as limbs in plaster casts—seem like forlorn traitors to their class.

A puff for Princeton on the same bill has been mysteriously nominated for an Oscar. But it seems more like a fund-raising kit than a documentary. "Princeton: A Search for Answers," by Julian Krainin and DeWitt Sage Jr., mocks the seriousness of teaching and learning when we're given only little scraps of lectures, ranging from "Man is an animal" equipped with "a mind which has a passionate lust to know" to "Nobody really knows what a galaxy is like." Scholars are poorly served when their work is presented as a slick collage.

Outside of one fine reading of "Measure for Measure" and a chorus rehearsal for Bach's B minor Mass, the professors and students appear desperately conscious of the camera. There's some further gargle about "the place of man"—ah, man—"in the scheme of things," plus praise for "the diversity of opinion" cherished at Princeton. Evocations of the arts and shots of Frisbees and a number of young blond persons fail to characterize the institution in any way that might distinguish it from any other leafy university.

1974 Mr 23, 20:1

The Program

NARRATIVE CINEMA-PART TWO: HONEYLAND ROAD by James Benning, 7 minutes; DISORDER by Barbara Noble, 24 minutes; MY WEAKNESS by David James, 6½ minutes; COLLUSION: CHAPTER 8 by Melina Jelinick, 24 minutes; INDUCTION by Ed Larstead, 10½ minutes; PILGRIMS by Peter Hoffman, 28 minutes. At the Whitney Museum of American Art, Madison Avenue and 75th Street, through Wednesday.

"Narrative Cinema, Part Two," the program of short, story films that opened at the Whitney Museum of American Art Thursday—the first series ended a week's stand there Wednesday—again illustrates the uneven, if sometimes commendable efforts of its varied but decidedly committed film-makers.

"Disorder," Barbara Noble's color study of a pretty, sensitive, obviously confused young woman searching for directions for living, is made up of kaleidoscopic shots of herself, her family, her boy friend and her beloved grandmother approaching senility. The visualizations are fleeting but nonetheless tender, touching and realistic.

●

Although Milena Jelinek's "Collusion: Chapter 8" is unrealistic in its approach to the perplexed and frightened middle-aged woman immersed in Kafkalike surroundings, it is, nevertheless, an artistically conceived work. The heroine's anxieties emerge with the stark sharpness of the black-and-white photography even if the fantasies she experiences in a strange house filled with strange people are not precisely defined.

There is no doubt that Peter Hoffman's "Pilgrims" does manage to develop the character of its two principals within the framework of a mere incident. It is the somewhat plaintive conversation in a roadside diner between a young, gentle, garrulous odd-ball who thinks his brain is loose in his skull, and a tired truck driver beset by problems who grudgingly accepts his insistent, unwanted dining companion. The dialogue artistically underlines loneliness, compassion and understanding.

●

The shorter films on the program seem a good deal more fragmentary than the others. "Induction," which explores with scientific documentation the implantation of electrodes in a rat's hypothalamus to induce enjoyment does not really make much of a point when a student asks, "How do we know if he's enjoying himself?" "Honeylane Road" seems disjointed as a series of images recalled by an anxiety-ridden young man.

As in the case of "My Weakness," an ineffectual off-screen lament about an unrequited love done to repetitious shots of a girl dancing on a lonely beach, the weaknesses of the briefer films outnumber their strengths.

A. H. WEILER

1974 Mr 23, 20:1

THE SLEEPING BEAUTY WAS A MAN

By CATHERINE HILLER

AMONG the most popular movies of the current season, one — "The Exorcist" — exploits a fundamental fear, while another—"The Way We Were" —explores a broadly-felt fantasy. This is perfectly natural.

For almost every successful movie works by either dramatizing our nightmares or by satisfying our daydreams. The psychotic killer, the sinking ship, the atomic accident—such universal terrors shape the films that move the millions. Similarly, the daring adventure, the piercing romance, the personal triumph—these universal longings make the movies that succeed.

Curiously, though, "The Way We Were" succeeds by depicting a fantasy that movies have previously neglected, a daydream that has barely been mined: hard-working girl gets beautiful guy. It is a dream that quietly reverses the sexual clichés—so quietly, indeed, that the critics seem not to have noticed that the film portrays the woman as propelled by sexual desire and the man as the passive creature of perfect beauty. How extraordinary— how revolutionary—that in a Hollywood movie with two glamorous leads, it is the male star who provides the erotic focus for the entire film.

This is evident from the very beginning. We first see Barbra Streisand as career girl Katie Morosky striding forcefully through a busy street scene. But our first glimpse of Robert Redford is carefully delayed by a slow camera pan down a row of people drinking at a fancy bar. Finally, the camera rests dramatically on the glorious Redford, sitting on a barstool, gracefully dozing, a veritable sleeping beauty. As Katie recognizes Hubbell Gardner,

Catherine Hiller, a freelance writer, is at work on a screenplay.

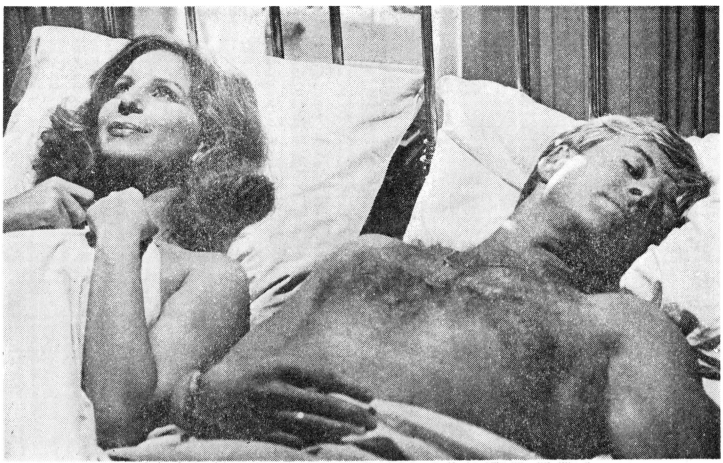

Barbra Streisand beams happily at finding herself with Robert Redford in "The Way We Were"
"If Barbra should win the best-actress Oscar, this scene will have cinched it"

her one-time college crush, she gives an incredulous gasp and the camera lovingly zooms in upon this male god, divinely drunk among the ordinary mortals jostling at El Morocco. Katie must touch his forehead lightly to see if he is real.

*

And, drifting into a reverie, she remembers college. She was an angry radical frump, he was a smiling society jock—whose type she despised, whose looks she adored, even as she noticed how purposefully he used them. For throughout the college sequence, handsome Hubbell is as conscious of his sexual power as any courtesan. Like any lovely woman, he plays on this power with his eyes, with his smile, with his touch. When he lightly fastens Katie's shoelace—in the manner that a woman might coyly adjust a man's tie—Katie, for all her misgivings, grows weak.

Now, years later, in much the same way that men have traditionally taken advantage of drunken women, Katie takes home the beautifully besotted man of her dreams. Breathlessly, she puts on the coffee and sets out the cups. But she turns around to find that Hubbell has already passed out in her bed.

And here we see Barbra Streisand at her most convincing. For if she is made to seem somewhat foolish as the political activist, she is absolutely marvelous as the modern woman poised between pride and desire. She wistfully hugs the military jacket he has dropped on the floor and charges it with more eroticism than a black lace brassiere. She gazes down uncertainly at the beautiful snoring man in her bed and creates more tension than a time bomb. At last, she shyly undresses and creeps in beside him: all aching vulnerability as she waits for his almost oblivious embrace, all bittersweet triumph as she finally receives it. If Barbra should win the best-actress Oscar on April 2, this scene will have cinched it.

But throughout the movie, how our hearts go out to Katie! From beginning to end, hers is the viewpoint we share, hers the drama that engulfs us. And this drama has little to do with politics, the overt subject of the movie. The McCarthy period is timidly presented, insufficiently dramatized, and ultimately blurred in the movie's sagging and strangely unmotivated second half. No, Katie's drama is the drama of all who have ever loved someone more beautiful than themselves, and of all who fear sexual rejection.

As the key speaker at her college rally, Katie can answer catcalls with aplomb —but she loses all composure when she sees the mocking sign "Any Peace But Katie's Piece."

Years later, when she begs Hubbell to spend one more night with her, she gives a poignant pledge: "I promise I won't touch you." This seems to do the trick: against his better judgment, Hubbell goes to her apartment. There, by the dawn's early light, he carefully explains why they must part. But Katie is convinced that the real reason he wants to break up with her has little to do with her social gaucherie. "It's because I'm not *attractive* enough," she sobs.

Now of course Barbra Streisand is attractive: her eyes are bright, her skin is smooth, her limbs are lithe. But every camera angle and costume choice seems to emphasize how the straight-nosed, straight-jawed Robert Redford outdazzles her. And this attraction-imbalance between the two stars is essential to the movie. It explains Katie's physical insecurity and why —when they are finally married—she is more upset by

his passing infidelity than by his perpetual political cowardice and the slow attenuation of his talent.

It also explains why during a chance encounter, after they have been divorced, Katie wistfully remarks upon the exquisite woman Hubbell is with before she even mentions her own child. And it explains why, as he leaves for the last time, she holds out her hand to his forehead in the same cherishing, wondering gesture she once made at El Morocco.

For the dream doesn't work, the fantasy fades. If movie nightmares generally end with a reassuring return to safety and sanity, modern movie daydreams tend to end on a note of despair. The loved one dies, the friend disappears, and Katie Morosky chokes back a sob as her golden hero deserts her forever. Reality asserts itself once more.

But it doesn't really matter. For the previous two hours, "The Way We Were" has fueled the fantasies of

'For once, the woman is propelled by sexual desire and the man is the passive beauty'

every woman in the audience. And it has done this very easily—by simply making the sexual object the man.

1974 Mr 24, II:13:1

The Cast
THE RAGMAN'S DAUGHTER, directed by Harold Becker; screenplay, Alan Sillitoe, based on an original story by Mr. Sillitoe; editor, Antony Gibbs; music, Kenny Clayton; camera, Michael Seresin; produced by Mr. Becker and Souter Harris. At the Festival Theater, 57th Street at Fifth Avenue. Running time: 94 minutes. This film has not been classified.

Tony Bradmore..........Simon Rouse
Doris Randall..........Victoria Tennant
Tony (at 35)..........Patrick O'Connell
Doris's father..........Leslie Sands
Doris's mother..........Rita Howard
Tony's mother..........Brenda Peters
Tony's father..........Brian Murphy
Older Tony's wife..........Jane Wood

By A. H. WEILER

The film version of "The Ragman's Daughter," adapted by Alan Sillitoe from his story published here 10 years ago, opened at the Festival yesterday. It again illustrates Mr. Sillitoe's keen perception of Britain's laboring poor and bourgeois, who were so pointedly projected in "Saturday Night and Sunday Morning" and "The Loneliness of the Long Distance Runner." But the British-made drama is befogged by unsympathetic, if believable, principals and thick Nottingham accents that dampen the youthful escapades and blasted romance it tenderly dramatizes.

The author, it must be stressed, is not angry, nor are his leading characters at odds with the wild world they make for themselves. They are simply young, adventurous and without real goals. The story of the antihero Tony and his excitements and love of Doris, the pretty, blond daughter of a well-to-do junk dealer, is candidly unfolded against flashbacks to Tony, the middle-aged worker but still hopeless family man.

If the idea that Tony and Doris would team from opposite sides of the track as thieves and lovers—he for money, she for kicks—appears somewhat illogical, it must be noted that it is logically played.

•

The robberies they commit are taut, occasionally comic, if basically aimless capers. And the romance and sex are treated with compassion, as is the depiction of the older Tony as a defeated but devoted husband and father, still nagged by stirring memories.

Harold Becker, the American director of short subjects and television commercials, is professionally polished in his feature film debut. His expertise is evident in a variety of mood-filled vignettes as well as in the development of touching, if not titanic, performances by a pair of newcomers: Victoria Tennant as the driven, loving and photogenic Doris, and Simon Rouse as her rootless, partner in love and crime. They are ably assisted by Patrick O'Connell's effectively low-key portral of the tough but philosophic older Tony.

There is a touch of soap opera in a denouement in which Tony, released from prison, learns that Doris has been quickly married off, has given birth to his son and has been accidentally killed by a car. Perhaps Mr. Sillitoe and Mr. Becker simply ran out of ideas at that point. But despite the soggy finish, the accents and a decidedly odd couple, a good deal of honesty and poignancy has been distilled from a bittersweet story.

1974 Mr 25, 39:1

The Cast

BADLANDS, produced, written and directed by Terrence Malick; directors of photography, Brian Probyn, Tak Fujimoto and Stevan Larner; editor, Robert Estrin; a Pressman-Williams presentation, distributed by Warner Brothers. Running time: 95 minutes. At the Beekman Theater, Second Avenue at 65th Street, and Embassy Theater, Seventh Avenue at 46th Street. This film has been rated PG.

Kit ....Martin Sheen
Holly ....Sissy Spacek
Holly's Father ....Warren Oates
Cato ....Ramon Bieri
Deputy ....Alan Vint

"Badlands," which opened yesterday at the Beekman and Embassy Theaters, was shown at the 11th New York Film Festival at Lincoln Center. The following is Vincent Canby's review, which appeared Oct. 15, 1973, in The New York Times.

The time is late summer at the end of the nineteen-fifties and the place a small, placid town in South Dakota. The streets are lined with oak and maple trees in full leaf. The lawns are so neat, so closed-cropped, they look crew - cut. Kit Carruthers (Martin Sheen) is 25, a garbage collector who fancies his cowboy boots and his faint resemblance to James Dean. Holly Sargis (Sissy Spacek) is 15. Until she meets Kit, she hasn't much interest in anything except her dog and her baton, which she practices twirling in her front yard.

In Terrence Malick's cool, sometimes brilliant, always ferociously American film, "Badlands," which marks Malick's debut as a director, Kit and Holly take an all-American joyride across the upper Middle West, at the end of which more than half a dozen people have been shot to death by Kit, usually at point-blank range.

"Badlands" is the first feature by Mr. Malick, a 29-year-old former Rhodes Scholar and philosophy student whose only other film credit is as the author of the screenplay for the nicely idiosyncratic "Pocket Money."

"Badlands" was inspired by the short, bloody saga of Charles Starkweather who, at age 19, in January, 1958, with the apparent cooperation of his 14-year-old girlfriend, Caril Fugate, went off on a murder spree that resulted in 10 victims. Starkweather was later executed in the electric chair and Miss Fugate given life imprisonment.

"Badlands" inevitably invites camparisons with three other important American films. Arthur Penn's "Bonnie and Clyde" and Fritz Lang's "Fury" and "You Only Live Once," but it has a very different vision of violence and death. Mr. Malick spends no great amount of time invoking Freud to explain the behavior of Kit and Holly, nor is there any Depression to be held ultimately responsible. Society is, if anything, benign.

This is the truth of "Badlands," something that places it very much in the seventies in spite of its carefully recreated period detail. Kit and Holly are directionless creatures, technically literate but uneducated in any real sense, so desensitized that Kit (in Malick's words at a news conference) can regard the gun with which he shoots people as a kind of magic wand that eliminates small nuisances. Kit and Holly are members of the television generation run amok.

They are not ill-housed, ill-clothed or ill-fed. If they are at all aware of their anger (and I'm not sure they are, since they see only boredom), it's because of the difference between the way life is and the way it is presented on the small screen, with commercial breaks instead of lasting consequences.

"Badlands" is narrated by Holly in the flat, nasal accents of the Middle West and in the syntax of a story in True Romances. "Little did I realize," she tells us at the beginning of the film, "that what began in the alleys and by-ways of this small town would end in the badlands of Montana." At the end after half a dozen murders she resolves never again to "tag around with the hellbent type."

Kit and Holly share with Clyde and Bonnie a fascination with their own press coverage, with their overnight fame ("The whole world was looking for us," says Holly, for who knew where Kit would strike next?"), but a lack of passion differentiates them from the gaudy desperados of the thirties. Toward the end of their joyride, the bored Holly tells us she passed the time, as she sat in the front seat beside Kit, spelling out complete sentences with her tongue on the roof of her mouth.

Mr. Malick tries not to romanticize his killers, and he is successful except for one sequence in which Kit and Holly hide out in a tree house as elaborate as anything the M-G-M art department ever designed for Tarzan and Jane. Mr. Sheen and Miss Spacek are splendid as the self-absorbed cruel, possibly psychotic children of our time, as are the members of the supporting cast, including Warren Oates as Holly's father.

One may legitimately debate the validity of Mr. Malick's vision, but not, I think his immense talent. "Badlands" is a most important and exciting film.

1974 Mr 25, 40:1

THE MOTHER AND THE WHORE (Le Maman et La Putain), directed by Jean Eustache; screenplay (French with English subtitles) by Mr. Eustache; photography, Pierre L'homme; editors, Mr. Eustache and Denise de Casablanca; executive producer, Pierre Cottrell; production companies; Elite Films, Cine Qua Non; Les Films du Losangeand Simar Film, V. M. Productions. At the Little Carnegie Theater, 57th Street east of Seventh Avenue. Released in the United States by New Yorker Films. Running time: 215 minutes.

Marie .... Bernadette Lafont
Alexandre .... Jean-Pierre Leaud
Veronike .... Francoise Lebrun
Gilberte .... Isabelle Weingarten

"The Mother and the Whore" was shown at the 11th New York Film Festival. The following excerpt is from Nora Sayre's review, which appeared Oct. 6, 1973, in The New York Times.

Time-traveling can be demoralizing — when you're going in reverse. Watching "The Mother and the Whore," you find that you're back in the movie-sludge of the nineteen-fifties, when a number of mediocre French films focused on sub-Sagan characters: numb, semi-paralyzed creatures who hardly had the calories to drag themselves through the day. Then, boredom was a hip disease — and it all comes rushing down the spout of memory when Jean-Pierre Léaud explains that he lives "in a world where people are old at 17," Jean Eustache's picture, which is running at the Little Carnegie Theater, is so reminiscent of those mossy productions that you start wondering if nothing has been learned about movies, about acting, about men and women. The discoveries of the last decade have been erased. Or else the sixties never happened: you were just hallucinating.

It's been claimed that the movie explores all the possible relationships between men and women — which seems like an invitation for a sack race to the nearest crematorium. Léaud has two girlfriends: Bernadette Lafont and Françoise Lebrun. He talks. They listen. It takes three and a half hours to state that women are unpredictable and that men are easily depressed. There's a bale of boastful talk about sex but not much of it. Finally, Miss Lebrun has hysterics, Léaud asks her to marry him, she says yes and throws up.

•

But this movie won the Grand Prix and also the International Critics Prize at Cannes. Before we all take sanity tests, let's examine the fantasies afoot. The director has said that we won't be able to distinguish between the mother and the whore. He's wrong about that. While both women are made to be incredibly passive, Bernadette Lafont is permitted a bit of gumption when she's jealous—an emotion that turns Léaud on. (He gets very jealous himself.)

When a woman is jealous, it must mean that she's possessive, therefore a mother: by definition a figure to be needled and punctually defied and, finally, left. A mother is someone to escape — when she's not changing spiritual diapers. "The whore" is simply a woman who has had a lot of sex. At first, she says she likes it; later she calls it sordid; ultimately, she has to repent.

Perhaps there's meant to be a whiff of grim maternity in her character: because she's a nurse who gives anesthetics. By implication, a nurse is supposed to cure everything, to heal all wounds. Françoise Lebrun is acutely severe, precise—thus evoking Léaud's childhood attraction to hospital nurses. He thought them alluring because they seemed cold and hard, impervious to pain. She asks if he's ever seen a pair of lungs, adding that they're pretty because they're pink.

•

All in all, it's tempting to mail the director a list of complaints as long as his movie. What possessed him to give us a tour of the inside of a refrigerator or lessons in putting records on turntables? And occasionally, when Eustache builds toward a scene that might be almost interesting—in which these weary people might have to cope with one another—he leaves it out.

The program notes report that he "now hates most films." So this picture may be his vengeance on the apes who like them.

1974 Mr 26, 34:4

The Cast

THE GREAT GATSBY, directed by Jack Clayton; screenplay by Francis Ford Coppola, based on the novel by F. Scott Fitzgerald; produced by David Merrick; director of photography, Douglas Slocombe; music, Nelson Riddle; editor, Tom Priestlz; distributed by Paramount Pictures. Running time: 146 minutes. At Loews State 1 and 2, Broadway at 45 Street, Orpheum Theater, 86th Street near Third Avenue. Tower East Theater, Third Avenue near 72d Street, and Paramount Theater, Broadway at 60th Street. This film has been rated PG.

Jay Gatsby .... Robert Redford
Daisy Buchanan .... Mia Farrow
Tom Buchanan .... Bruce Dern
Myrtle Wilson ....Karen Black
George Wilson .... Scott Wilson
Nick Carraway .... Sam Waterston
Jordan Baker .... Lois Chiles
Meyer Wolfsheim ...... Howard Da Silva
Mr. Gatz .... Roberts Blossom
Klipspringer .... Edward Herrmann

By VINCENT CANBY

The newest, biggest, most expensive and longest screen version of "The Great Gatsby," which had its premiere here last night, moves spaniel-like through F. Scott Fitzgerald's text, sniffing and staring at events and objects very close up with wide, mopey eyes, seeing almost everything and comprehending practically nothing. The film begins its regular engagement at four theaters today.

The language is right, even the chunks of exposition that have sometimes been turned into dialogue. The sets and costumes and most of the performances are exceptionally good, but the movie itself is as lifeless as a body that's been too long at the bottom of a swimming pool.

Francis Ford Coppola, who wrote the screenplay, and Jack Clayton, the director, have treated the book as if it were an illustrated encyclopedia of the manners and morals of the nineteen-twenties instead of a short, elegiacal romantic novel whose idiosyncratic beat demands something more perceptive from the moviemakers than mere fidelity to plot.

•

"The Great Gatsby" has been filmed twice before, first with Warner Baxter and Lois Wilson in 1926, the year after it was published. It was done again in 1949 with Alan Ladd playing the title role, the elegant young roughneck, Jay Gatsby, a part-time bootlegger and swindler whose smile according to Fitzgerald, possessed the quality of "eternal reassurance," and with Betty Field as Daisy Buchanan, the pretty, easily distracted rich girl who became for Gatsby, all there was to hope for in the American Dream.

Though I didn't see the first version and remember very little of the second, I can't imagine that either could have been conceived with the care that went into this production. Why, then, should this "Gatsby" be so lugubrious, threatening at times to turn into the longest movie ever made?

The answer I suspect, is the all-too-reverential attitude. It completely mistakes the essence of Fitzgerald's novel, which is not in its story but in its headline, elliptical literary style that dazzles us by the *manner* in which it evokes character and event, rather than with the characters and events themselves.

Nothing that Mr. Clayton does with the actors or with the camera comes close to catching the spirit of Fitz-

gerald's impatient brilliance. The film transforms "Gatsby" into a period love story that seems to take itself as solemnly as "Romeo and Juliet." The plot has been dismantled like an antique engine and photographed, piece by piece, preserved in lots of pretty, glistening images that bathe the film in nostalgia as thick as axle grease.

•

If reverence is one part of the problem, the other part is a stunning lack of cinematic imagination. The film's big set pieces—the wild parties at Gatsby's Long Island mansion—are almost embarrassingly awkward in their staging, the flappers and their beaux always caught doing their Charlestons at the same orgiastic pitch, like the figures on some complicated wind-up Bavarian toy.

Some of the movie's best moments are hardly more than recitations, as when the narrator, Nick Carraway (Sam Waterston), opens the film with a soundtrack exposition that sets the time, place and

characters. This includes the marvelous line in which Nick tells us how Daisy and Tom Buchanan, before moving to Long Island that fatal summer, had "drifted here and there unrestfully, wherever people played polo and were rich together."

Although Robert Redford is hardly an ideal choice to play Gatsby—he looks so Ivy League it's difficult to believe that he didn't prep at Choate—he's a good enough actor to carry the role without damaging the film. He'd make a much better Dick Diver in "Tender Is the Night.

Mia Farrow is lovely, eccentric and unfathomable as Daisy, which may be an impossible role, one that is much more easily accepted on the page than on the screen. I also liked Bruce Dern as her husband, a guy so securely rich and well-born he can be a slob, Mr. Waterston as Nick who, like Gatsby, remains an outsider in the society he inhabits, and Karen Black and Scott Wilson, as Myrtle and George Wilson, whose lives, like Gatsby's are so casually destroyed by the Buchanans.

As Fitzgerald wrote it, "The Great Gatsby" is a good deal more than an ill-fated love story about the cruelties of the idle rich. Though set in Long Island, it is very much about the Middle West. All of its major characters have moved east, from Minnesota (Gatsby), from Chicago (Nick and Tom), from Louisville (Daisy), literally reversing the direction of the migrations that established the American civilization, thus marking its doom. The movie can't see this through all its giant closeups of pretty knees and dancing feet. It's frivolous without being much fun.

1974 Mr 28, 32:1

CONRACK, directed by Martin Ritt; screenplay by Irving Ravetch and Harriet Frank Jr., based on the book "The Water Is Wide" by Pat Conroy; director of photography, John Alonzo; film editor, Frank Bracht; music, John Williams; produced by Mr. Ritt and Miss Frank; released by 20th Century-Fox Corporation. At the Trans-Lux East Theater, Third Avenue and 58th Street, and Loew's Cine, Third Avenue and 86th Street. Running time: 106 minutes. This film is classified PG.
Pat Conroy .... Jon Voight
Mad Billy .... Paul Winfield
Mrs. Scott .... Madge Sinclair
Mary .... Tina Andrews
Quickfellow .... Antonio Fargas
Edna .... Ruth Attaway
Little Man .... James O'Reare
Skeffington .... Hume Cronyn

By NORA SAYRE

Considering the number of rather reactionary movies we've had lately—cops rampant on a field of crimson, women portrayed as doormats or handy trulls, nostalgia as a device for perverting the past—Martin Ritt's "Conrack," which opened yesterday at the Trans-Lux East and Loews Ciné, is worth welcoming for its intentions. Set in 1969, based on Pat Conroy's "The Water Is Wide," the movie details the experiences of a young teacher (Jon Voight), who takes on the fifth

through eighth grades in a black school on an island off the coast of South Carolina. The picture revives the hopes and frustrations of the nineteen-sixties, including the idea that deprived people may be nourished by education—a notion that many prefer to neglect today.

Mr. Voight plays a liberal from the recent past—growing his hair until the war is over, sewing needlepoint and explaining to a child that "there's a whole new thing going on" (that men's roles are changing along with women's), battling through the web of suspicion that confronts a white outsider. At first, he's equally shocked by his students' ignorance—the four oldest in the class think that the Civil War was fought by the Germans and the Japanese—and by the grim black woman principal, who tells him, "Treat your babies stern, treat 'em tough. . . . Put your foot on 'em and keep it there" (Madge Sinclair, in an excellent performance.)

•

Soon he wins over the wary children and proceeds to teach them about the pyramids and Babe Ruth, the lotus position, their own genitals, the law of gravity, swimming, Brahms and Beethoven, while building their egos and their expectations of themselves. He also manages to charm the whole island, including a hostile bootlegger (Paul Winfield — one wishes that he'd had a heftier part). Predictably, the teacher is fired by a baleful school superintendent (Hume Cronyn), who labels the young man as "an outside agitator."

Many actors could have been too winsome or ingenuous in the part of such a professional good guy. But Jon Voight maintains his humor, gumption and versatility—although he occasionally overdoes the happy clown. His performance has a conviction that suggests that the theme of the movie matters a great deal to him. And he deserves special credit for acting with the 21 children selected from a local school — who could snatch a scene from many seasoned actors.

•

However, despite Mr. Voight's skill, the teacher's character never jells. He says that he was once a "bigoted" redneck: "I used to chuck watermelons at black kids . . . Then I did a 360-degree turn" —but we never learn why. Whatever it was that uprooted his racism isn't explained, and that omission is debilitating for the movie. Another weakness is the glaze of sentimentality that sugars much of the narrative. We know the flaws of liberalism well enough. Sentimentality doesn't have to be one of them. Since the best moments in "Conrack" generate a confidence in change, it isn't necessary to ask us to accept a miracle.

1974 Mr 28, 33:1

YOUR THREE MINUTES ARE UP, directed by Douglas N. Schwartz; written by James Dixon; film editor, Aaron Stell; director of photography, Stephen M. Katz; music by Perry Botkin, Jr.; produced by Jerry Gershwin and Mark C. Levy; released by Cinerama Releasing Corporation. Running time: 93 minutes. This film is classified R.
Charlie .... Beau Bridges
Mike .... Ron Leibman
Betty .... Janet Margolin
Mrs. Wilk .... Kathleen Freeman
Mr. Kellogg .... David Ketchum
Dr. Claymore .... Stu Nisbet
Eddie Abruzzi ....Read Morgan

and

THE PYX, directed by Harvey Hart; screenplay by Robert Schlitt; based on the novel "The Pyx" by John Buell; director of photography, Rene Verzier; film editor, Ron Wisman; music, Victor Feldbrill; produced by Julian Roffman; released by Cinerama Releasing Corporation. At neighborhood theaters. Running time: 111 minutes. This film has been classified R.
Elizabeth Lucy .... Karen Black
Jim Henderson ....Christopher Plummer
Pierre Paquette .... Donald Pilon
Keerson .... Jean-Louis Roux
Meg .... Yvette Brind'Amour
Superintendent .... Jacques Godin

What we have in the case of "Your Three Minutes Are Up," which opened yesterday at neighborhood theaters on a double bill with "The Pyx," is a 1968 movie with a 1974 ending. Far from the chucklesome comedy its advertising would encourage one to expect, it is, in the end, a finger-wagging morality lesson aimed at the sort of establishment-exploiting ripoffs, put-ons and put-downs that passed widely for radical expression half a dozen years ago.

For most of its length, it is, indeed, a 1968 movie, celebrating the easy ways of Mike (Ron Leibman), a dropout, as he attempts to pry his straight buddy, Charlie (Beau Bridges), away from the conventions of work and impending marriage to a sale-addicted fiancée played credibly by Janet Margolin. One suspects that back in 1968, this film would have ended with Charlie busting out to the glories of the free life. But that was before Watergate.

Now the flouting of convention, carried to excess, must lead to disaster.

It doesn't really matter that Bridges and Leibman are far too old for the adolescent hijinks of their automotive odyssey northward through California; this is a film begging for approbation, and the best lesson to take away from it is that pandering to an audience is as prevalent in 1974 as it was in 1968.

•

As for "The Pyx," neither devotees of murder mysteries nor devotees of the occult— the two principal elements of this gory policier set in Montreal — are likely to come away satisfied. Point the finger of guilt to a screenplay that tells less than enough about Christopher Plummer, the detective whose past is so essential to the denouement, and so much about Karen Black that it becomes too difficult to accept her metamorphosis into a junkie, a hooker and the victim of homicide at a black mass.

LAWRENCE VAN GELDER

1974 Mr 28, 34:1

Robert Redford and Mia Farrow

MEMORIES OF HELEN (Memoria de Helena), directed by David Neves; screenplay (Portuguese with English subtitles) by Mr. Neves; director of photography, David Drew Zingg; editor, Alvisio Vianna; a Mapa Films production, distributed by New Yorker Films. Running time: 81 minutes. At First Avenue Screening Room, at 61st Street. This film has not been rated.

Helen..................Rosa Maria Pena
Rosa..........................Adriana Prieto
Renato................Arudino Colasssanti
Andre............................Joel Barcelos

By VINCENT CANBY

"Memories of Helen" (Memoria De Helena) is an exceedingly uninteresting Brazilian film made in 1969 by David Neves, a Brazilian movie critic who has helped himself freely to the styles of such great directors as Godard, Bergman and Bresson, without having given much thought as to the function of those styles.

The movie, which was shown Sunday at the First Avenue Screening Room, will be repeated there today and tomorrow at noon and midnight.

The story is concerned with growing up wounded in middle-class Brazil where a woman is expected to be either a slave or a frivolous plaything. It's about a sensitive young woman named Helen whose sad experiences are told through her diaries and through home movies, which, though shot by Helen and her uncle, look exactly like the rest of the film.

On the soundtrack a woman narrator announces the themes of various sequences with a solemnity that never disguises the movie's banality. When Helen finally allows a rather nice but faithless young man to have his way with her, the voice prepares us by saying: "Helen's defloration. Occult." Later Helen writes in her diary: "Friendship always brings disillusion." She takes some pills and rolls into a lake to drown, sunk by her clothing and her insights.

1974 Mr 29, 25:1

The Cast

THE SUGARLAND EXPRESS, directed by Steven Spielberg; screenplay by Hal Barwood and Matthew Robbins; story by Mr. Spielberg and Mr. Barwood; photography, Vilmos Zsigmond; film editors, Edward M. Abroms and Verna Fields; music, John Williams; produced by Richard D. Zanuck and David Brown. At the Museum of Modern Art, 11 West 53d Street, tonight at 6 o'clock. Opens commercially tomorrow at the Cinema II Theater, third Avenue at 60th Street, and the National Theater, Broadway and 43d Street. Running time: 109 minutes. This film is classified PG.

Lou Jean...................Goldie Hawn
Captain Tanner.............Ben Johnson
Slide.....................Michael Sacks
Clovis...................William Atherton

By NORA SAYRE

Losers determined to win, nomads with a letch for roots, children hampered by adults' bodies: the young couple in "The Sugarland Express" is as American as pop-tops or the Grand Canyon. (The movie will be shown tonight in the New Directors series at the Museum of Modern Art and will open commercially tomorrow at Cine-

ma II and the National Theater.) Both wife and husband (Goldie Hawn and William Atherton) have done time in Texas for petty larceny; she bullies him into a jailbreak because their small son has been put up for adoption by the Child Welfare Board. Frantically resolved to retrieve the baby, they hijack a highway patrol car, and hold the patrolman as their hostage and chauffeur throughout several hundred miles.

A fleet of police cars hurtles after them across the Texas highways. Eventually, there are more than 200 vehicles in pursuit. Meanwhile, the naive outlaws bicker with their pleasant young captive and reject his warnings that the charges against them are formidable. Nonetheless, an offbeat bond of loyalty builds among them during the journey.

Thrilled crowds mass on the roadside to cheer and photograph them as they pass, while television crews scramble in their wake. (The movie is based on a real case in 1969, when many Texans were enthralled by a similar 300-mile chase.) The wife soars on their celebrity, queening it over the little kingdom of their car. But a police stake-out awaits them at their destination, and the husband is shot.

The movie has a casual craziness that seems especially native. From the drum majorettes who greet the fugitives to the press corps interviewing the gurgling baby, the narrative is studded with national lunacies, including the wife's passion for gold trading stamps. Above all, there's the familiar reek of overkill; the vast throngs of cars and cops and weapons that focus on one inefficient couple, and the fact that shooting the kidnappers is far more important to the authorities than preserving the hostage's life. The ending is a shock just because the movie isn't suspenseful —you don't expect these bunglers to draw the bullets reserved for Bonnie and Clyde.

Goldie Hawn has a manic concentration: No laws of any sort can girdle her, or prevent her from trying to regain her child. At moments, she's exasperation personified; at others, there's the sly, downward gaze we've seen before, plus the flaring sarcasm, the screams of pleasure. It's an extraordinary characterization of a defiant nature with an appetite for the conventions: Make-up and hairspray are crucial for public appearances; autographs are eagerly collected. William Atherton has to be as helpless as seaweed in relation to her. It's a hard part, and he appears strained now and then. Yet he's touching as the child-man who can't control anything around him. Michael Sacks is excellent as the hostage,

though Ben Johnson is somewhat ponderous as a fatherly police captain who seems just too noble to be true.

●

Steven Spielberg, the 26-year-old director, has built up Texas as a major character in his movie. As the herd of cars races and heaves and crashes through the landscape, the state's personality surfaces like a sperm whale. Mr. Spielberg has also made marvelous use of many Texans, some of whom haven't acted before. And he has choreographed his cars in a way that almost makes me want to learn to drive.

"Sugarland" is a modest picture, even limited, and the gypsy couple doesn't have the emotional range or depth of the young pair in Robert Altman's "Thieves Like Us." Here, the stress is on the story, on what happens to clumsy strays who lurch out of line and risk everything (including life) for their mistakes.

1974 Mr 30, 20:1

A Swiss Documentary About Capitalism

By VINCENT CANBY

Peter Ammann's "The Red Train" is a feature-length Swiss documentary that tries very hard to alert us to the dehumanizing effects of Swiss capitalism but succeeds mainly in making it seem safely dull. The film, which has English subtitles for its German, Italian and French dialogue, was shown yesterday at the Museum of Modern Art in the series "New Directors/New Films," being sponsored in association with the Film Society of Lincoln Center. It will be repeated at the museum tonight at 8:30.

The title is taken from the train that carries a group of mostly Communist migrant workers home from Zurich to Italy to vote in the national elections. As the point

The Program

THE RED TRAIN, directed, produced and written by Peter Ammann; director of photography, Jimmy Glasberg; editor, Jacques Morzier. Presented at the Museum of Modern Art by the museum and the Film Society of Lincoln Center in the series "New Directors/New Films." Running time: 90 minutes.

is made more than once, these workers, who can find work only in Switzerland, can vote only in their homeland.

It's a contradiction, perhaps, as the film's program notes state, but not one that blows the mind. Nor does the rest of the film: shots of workers at work in neat-as-a-pin capitalist factories, crosscut with scenes taken from three different variations on the William Tell legend, Schiller's play, Rossini's opera and a contemporary play by Alfonso Sastre.

The editing of the film is complex without being especially profound. It never adequately dramatizes what I take to be Mr. Ammann's sense of social outrage.

1974 Mr 30, 20:1

They've Turned 'Gatsby' to Goo

By VINCENT CANBY

"THEY were careless people, Tom and Daisy," says Nick Carraway, the narrator, near the end of F. Scott Fitzgerald's finest novel, "The Great Gatsby." "They smashed up things and creatures and then retreated back into their money or their vast carelessness, or whatever it was that kept them together, and let other people clean up the mess they had made. . . ."

In the latest screen version of "The Great Gatsby," in which Robert Redford plays the flamboyant bootlegger, ne James Gatz, from Minnesota and Mia Farrow is Daisy Buchanan, the well-born dream he held too long, Nick Carraway's casual reflection about the careless Buchanans has been transformed into part of the film's dialogue. Other reflections and pieces of exposition are utilized as voice-over narration on the soundtrack. A great deal of Fitzgerald's text has in this way been transferred to the screen, much more, I suspect, than survived the 1926 movie version, which I did not see, and the 1949 version, which I've mostly forgotten though I do remember the late Alan Ladd looking terribly dour and inscrutable as Gatsby.

Yet the substance of the novel has largely vanished. Remaining are the plot, some exceptionally good performances and an almost eye-bogging attention to the mid-nineteen-twenties Long Island settings (shot in Newport, R.I.), to the flapper costumes and to the private transportation employed. The automobiles are stunning.

To my knowledge, none of Fitzgerald's novels or stories, with one possible exception, has ever been successfully dramatized, which would seem

odd since Fitzgerald told tales that appear to have beginnings, middles and ends, the sort of things the popular narrative cinema is supposed to be all about.

Both "Babylon Revisited" (presented as a flashback encased in a concrete overcoat of a film called "The Last Time I Saw Paris") in 1954 and "Tender Is The Night" in 1962 failed to suggest any of the brilliance of the Fitzgerald works. Like this newest "Gatsby" they plodded — without a suggestion of wit or an awareness of feelings that wouldn't be familiar to a reader of confession literature.

The one possible exception that I can recall, though fuzzily, is a 1950's television adaptation of "Winter Dreams" in which Dana Wynter played Judy Jones, the beautiful, deceiving and ultimately foolish Fitzgerald heroine, of whom Daisy Buchanan is the richest example, and Bradford

Dillman played the not-quite-acceptable young man who loved her.

Because of one thing and another, including age, I never saw the 1922 silent film version of "The Beautiful and Damned," the so-sad story of Gloria and Anthony Patch, the young, golden New York couple who lived above their means in anticipation of an inheritance that was to come too late. According to an anonymous New York Times film critic, that film ended with the inheritance's finally arriving and Anthony's saying in a last title card:

"Gloria, darling, I'll try to be worthy of our good fortune and you."

*

Fitzgerald doesn't bring out the best in moviemakers, including Francis Ford Coppola, who wrote the screenplay for the new "Gatsby," and Jack Clayton ("Room at The Top," "The Innocents"), who directed it. But, up to a point, anyway, it may not be the moviemakers' fault.

The problem is that "Gatsby" really has a plot no bigger than a pea, which no one seems to notice until it's put on the screen. Reduced to mere story, it's about a mysterious tycoon (bootlegger? swindler? spy?) named Gatsby who spends one summer in a Long Island palace, giving parties and hoping to attract the attention across the bay of the first girl he ever loved, Daisy, now married to Tom Buchanan, a wealthy polo-playing, society slob who, on the side, is having an affair with a vulgar woman named Myrtle. That, essentially, is the story, but it isn't the reason that "The Great Gatsby" haunts us.

"Gatsby," which was published in 1925, is a historical novel that was written in its own time. Fitzgerald knew exactly what he was creating: an elegy for a present that was already a past, as represented by Gatsby's fierce devotion to the Daisy he'd known seven or eight years before and had loved ever since. But Gatsby is something more. Coming out of the West into the East, as do all the major characters in the novel, Gatsby, whom Nick Carraway describes as having "a romantic readiness" and "an extraordinary gift for hope," is the absolute end of the same American Dream that pushed the American frontier as far as the Pacific Ocean. Gatsby, the innocent, the pioneer, is ultimately destroyed by the failure of his dream, by its shallowness and lack of sense of consequence.

These are the echoes that we hear throughout the novel and that give it such poignancy. They also give serious dimension to Gatsby's quasi-hoodlum character, a man who, after all, is simply operating with a kind of frontier steadfastness and a lot of ingenuity.

The novel is so cleverly constructed that one doesn't become overly conscious of everything that's in it, nor of the things left out. Fitzgerald himself acknowledged "a BIG FAULT" of the book. In a letter to Edmund Wilson he wrote:

"I gave no account (and had no feeling about or knowledge of) the emotional relations between Gatsby and Daisy from the time of their reunion until the catastrophe."

This hole in the book is filled by exposition in which Nick tells us about Gatsby's early years and about his brief, intense affair with Daisy in Louisville when he was in the Army and about to go overseas. The movie, instead, treats us to shots of Gatsby and Daisy picnicking, holding hands, behaving like models in a soft-focus hair dye commercial.

Coppola's screenplay, faithful as it is, never succeeds in communicating any passion between Gatsby and his rediscovered Daisy, and since the film is playing so heavily on nostalgia from its opening credits, it has no further reserves of sentiment to draw upon when, in the center of the film, it flashes briefly back to Gatsby and Daisy in wartime Louisville. This should be the film's gut-clutching moment, but it just looks like more fuzzy, starry-eyed photography.

The pacing of the movie is ponderous, to be very kind about it. It's as if so much money and care had gone into researching the period costumes, sets and cars that the director and producer were damned if we weren't going to be impressed. This deliberate way in which each scene is set up and photographed, sometimes in emphasis-distorting closeups, adds the intolerable burden of portentousness to the film.

There are some attractive things to look at along the way. Mia Farrow is just odd enough to be right as Daisy, a woman who cannot conceive of the cruelties she so casually commits. Sam Waterston is splendid as Nick, the narrator, a role that might have looked like a tour guide's except for the fact that Waterston has the presence and weight as an actor to give it a kind of moral heft. Bruce Dern is appropriately boorish, without being a buffoon, as Tom, and Karen Black, as Myrtle, is as good as the camera allows. I'm referring to her major scene, when she tearfully describes her first meeting with Tom, which has been shot in such a tight close-up it almost destroys the actress with visual italics.

The smaller roles are also effective: Scott Wilson as the deranged garage man, and Roberts Blossom as Gatsby's father.

Redford, handsome, open-faced, all Ivy League in manner, is miscast as Gatsby but I can't see that he hurts a film that is otherwise so heavy-handed in design and execution. It would take a truly extraordinary actor, giving a truly extraordinary performance, to cut through the cinematic goo, most solemnly realized in Nelson Riddle's big-orchestra arrangements of the little-band songs of the time. That's more or less the style of the entire enterprise.

1974 Mr 31, II:1:1

ALL NUDITY SHALL BE PUNISHED (Todo Nudez Sera Castigada), directed by Arnaldo Jabor; screenplay (Portuguese with English subtitles) by Mr. Jabor, based on the play by Nelson Rodrigues; produced by Paulo Porto for R. F. Faria productions; director of photography, Lauro Escorel; editor, Rafael Justo Valverde. Running time: 102 minutes. Presented in the "New Directors/New Films" series by the Museum of Modern Art, in association with the Film Society of Lincoln Center, at the Museum of Modern Art, 53d Street west of Fifth Avenue. This film has not been rated.

Herculano ....Paulo Porto
Geni ....Darlene Gloria
Serginho ....Paulo Sacks
Patricio ....Paulo Pereiro

By VINCENT CANBY

Arnaldo Jabor's Brazilian film, "All Nudity Shall Be Punished" (Todo Nudez Sera Castigado), is an exuberant, sometimes slapstick social satire about a rich, self-absorbed, paunchy businessman named Herculano, whose wife has just died, leaving him so despondent he sits all day and night in his underwear, weeping over his fate.

This gives a great deal of worry to his ancient maiden aunts and especially to his brother. It interrupts their television viewing, besides which Herculano is their meal ticket. Herculano's 18-year-old son so identifies with his dead mother that, after considering a joint suicide pact with his father, he has sworn him to celibacy for the rest of his life. Clearly, here is a family with problems.

•

For much of the time "All Nudity Shall Be Punished" exaggerates and intensifies those problems for very funny and deadly serious effect, especially when Herculano falls madly in love with a whore who makes the one played by Melini Mercouri in "Never on Sunday" seem underfed and mean-spirited. Herculano simply must marry her, not only because she demands it but because he requires it. He has hangups.

"All Nudity Shall Be Punished" is a most curious and interesting film. Even when it pulls its punches, you are aware of the wit and the passion of the man who made it. The film was shown yesterday at the Museum of Modern Art in the "New Directors/New Films" series, sponsored in association with the Film Society of Lincoln Center. It will be shown again in the museum's auditorium today at 6 P.M.

Although the film wouldn't seem to have an obvious political purpose, it's difficult not to associate some of the butts of Mr. Jabor's satire with right-wing military regimes that have been all-powerful in Brazil.

It isn't just that the society that Herculano inhabits is inhibited by the past, but that his life and feelings are constantly bent in various directions to deny the truth around him. This is dangerous business, as is a dictatorship that denies a nation's needs. When Herculano finally does marry the whore, beautifully played by an actress named Darlene Gloria, the results are catastrophic.

•

Mr. Jabor's screenplay is based on a play by Nelson Rodrigues, but there is nothing in his direction of the film to suggest its theatrical origins.

It is a tumultuous movie, handsomely photographed and set in locations in and around Rio de Janeiro. They do almost as much as the screenplay and the acting to suggest that peculiar mixture of sensuality and repression that marks so much Brazilian life. Herculano's bedroom, where we first see him on his bed of tears and sweat, looks like the inside of an old mahagony armoire, which is no place to live.

1974 Ap 1, 42:1

BUT WHERE IS DANIEL VAX? written and directed by Avram Heffner; photographed by Amnon Salomon; edited by Jacques Erlich; produced by William L. Gross.
WITH: Lior Yaeni, Michael Lipkin, Esther Zevko, Yael Heffner, Zivit Abramson and others. Running time: 95 minutes.

Avram Heffner's "But Where Is Daniel Vax?" is a worthy entry in the current film series by new directors at the Museum of Modern Art. Set in modern Israel, the homeland of the writer-director, this is a charming, adult movie that wryly and serenely mirrors approaching middle age and life's casual ironies.

Most of the film is so quietly persuasive—Mr. Heffner's honest dialogue, his sure, unobtrusive direction, Amnon Salomon's lovely color photography and some good, steady acting—that an unappetizing protagonist can't spoil it. Mr. Heffner's hero, a successful popular-song minstrel, might have seemed less callow and dull had he not been portrayed in a blank-faced monotone by a tubby performer named Lior Yaeni. On the other hand, Michael Lipkin, Esther Zevko, Yael Heffner and an unidentifiable housewife are natural and appealing, like the rest of this modest, beautifully shaped and felt comedy, with its sweetly bleak wisdom and professional packaging.

Mr. Heffner's picture, shown last night, will be repeated tonight at 8:30 o'clock.

HOWARD THOMPSON

1974 Ap 1, 42:1

The Cast

DAYS OF 36 (MERES TOU 36), written and directed by Theo Angelopoulos; photographed by Georges Arvantitis; edited by V. Syropoulos; Greek with English subtitles; produced by George Papalios. Running time: 110 minutes. At the Museum of Modern Art on Friday at 8:30 P.M.

Deputy ....George Kiritsis
Convict ....Tharos Grammenos

By NORA SAYRE

When political trauma spreads like cholera, it's sometimes hard to root out causes and effects, or chains of consequence. "Days of 36," written and directed by Theo Angelopoulos, evokes, the atmosphere of terror and repression that preceded the dictatorship of General Metaxas in Greece in 1936. But the movie remains deliberately vague about the politics of the period and most of the individuals involved. (The film can be seen on Friday in the New Directors series at the Museum of Modern Art.) Mr. Angelopoulos has said that he was making a "montage" of events. Since his narrative has many parallels in Greece today, he keeps his political references oblique. The result is a very moving metaphor, rather than a clear slice of history.

•

A former pusher is jailed in connection with the murder of a trade-unionist. The prisoner has already served as an informer for the police—probably about political dissidents. Visited by a Conservative Member of the Greek Parliament whom he has known in the past, the captive suddenly pulls a gun and holds the politician hostage, demanding his own release and protesting that he's been framed. (There was such a case in the 1930's.)

While Parliament wrangles about the prisoner's ultimatum, and the stymied officials debate about how to kill him, the guards bring them baffling bulletins: that the prisoner has called for music, or that he and the hostage are laughing together. Finally, the prisoner is shot and the fainting politician is rescued.

The film is the most eloquent I've yet seen about life in prison. Humiliation and dignity mingle with helplessness until the three are inseparable. There's a brief, futile rebellion: some prisoners rush at the guards, free others from their cells, scale a wall and are immediately recaptured. Later, when they hear music from the prison courtyard, dozens stand silently in their cell windows, then beat violently on the bars, and subside only when the guards fire shots to remind them that they're potential targets. At the end, a few men about to be executed wait very patiently while they're tied to stakes before the firing squad.

•

Throughout, you feel the relationship of the characters to their own country — especially since the film-maker is highly sensitive to figures in a landscape: guards on horseback trotting through bleached grasses or chalky dust, prisoners tearing through a wheatfield. Mr. Angelopoulos also has a rich gift for the ludicrous or incongruous, as when the hostage's mother visits an elderly politician on her son's behalf and the two old acquaintances reminisce about the past and sing a song from their remote youth in wavery cracked voices. While you have to accept many mysterious moments in this movie, the call for freedom is as urgent as a nationwide alert. Meanwhile, let's hope that "Days of 36" will receive general distribution.

1974 Ap 3, 38:1

THE THREE MUSKETEERS, directed by Richard Lester; screenplay by George MacDonald Fraser, based on the novel by Alexander Dumas; produced by Alexander Salkind; music, Michel Legrand; director of photography, David Watkins; editor, John Victor Smith; distributed by 20th Century-Fox. Running time: 107 minutes. At the Columbia 1 Theater, Second Avenue at 64th Street, Guild Theater, 50th Street, west of Fifth Avenue, and other theaters. This film has been rated PG.

Athos .... Oliver Reed
Constance .... Raquel Welch
Aramis .... Richard Chamberlain
D'Artagnan .... Michael York
Porthos .... Frank Finlay
Rochefort .... Christopher Lee
Louis XIII .... Jean-Pierre Cassel
Anne of Austria ...... Geraldine Chaplin
Buckingham .... Simon Ward
Milady .... Faye Dunaway
Cardinal Richelieu ...... Charlton Heston
M. Bonancieux .... Spike Milligan

By VINCENT CANBY

Richard Lester, the man who gave us "A Hard Day's Night," "Help!," "Petulia" and "How I Won the War," now rips into "The Three Musketeers" with such high good spirits that I feel somehow lacking not to be able to respond with the same reckless enthusiasm.

The film, which opened yesterday at the Columbia 1, the Guild and other theaters, is, according to the records, the sixth to be based on the Alexander Dumas adventure novel. Here they are again: Athos, Porthos and Aramis, who, with the short-tempered D'Artagnan, loyally defend a muddle-headed Louis XIII

and, his adulterous Queen, Anne of Austria, against what I've always suspected was the perfectly reasonable, statesmanlike treachery of Cardinal Richelieu. Even as a boy I felt that way, which may be why the book was never my favorite.

Photographed in Spain, with lots of name-actors showing up in smallish roles (rather like an Oscar show), Mr. Lester's interpretation of "The Three Musketeers" looks like an evening in a bump-o-car arena, with magnificently costumed people in place of cars. The adventures are less swashbuckle than slapstick.

The narrative, mostly concerned with the efforts of the musketeers to retrieve the Queen's diamonds given to the Duke of Buckingham, moves forward through a series of physical collisions, man with man, man with woman, man with windmill, woman with inkwell.

D'Artagnan (Michael York) and Constance (Raquel Welch), the married seamstress he loves, are particularly accident-prone. When D'Artagnan swings on a rope to attack a man on horseback, he lands not on the man but in a puddle. For all his worthy spirit, D'Artagnan is a terrible judge of distances.

The three musketeers whom D'Artagnan aspires to join are played by Oliver Reed, Richard Chamberlin and Frank Finlay. Boisterously However, it took me almost the entire film to figure out which actor was playing which musketeer. I suppose such identification is not all that important, but the difficulty says something about the screenplay written by George MacDonald Fraser. It's extremely light on character.

Mr. Lester seems almost exclusively concerned with action, preferably comic, and one gets the impression after a while that he and his fencing masters labored too long

in choreographing the elaborate duels. They're interesting to watch, though they are without a great deal of spontaneity.

Another of the director's fascinations is period detail, which is sometimes more fun than the comic action sequences.

The movie is chock-full of research into the ways in which the upper crust of 17th-century France spent its leisure time (in tennis, gambling, falconry and jousting, among other things). Richelieu's dungeons are filled with prisoners enclosed in what look like decorative metal bird cages. While the King and Queen enjoy a country picnic, the court musicians stand apart from them, almost hidden by the high grass, sawing away at their instruments.

Some of the other prominent performers in the cast include Charlton Heston as Richelieu, Simon Ward as Buckingham, Jean-Pierre Cassel and Geraldine Chaplin as the King and Queen, and Faye Dunaway as Richelieu's beautiful English spy. Nobody plays it for laughs, which is as it should be.

If the story doesn't seem to go anywhere much, it may be because this film is, according to the trade press, just half of the film that was shot. Instead of releasing it as one three-hour movie, the producers decided instead to make it into two. The second part reportedly will be released at the end of the year.

1974 Ap 4, 52:1

THE CHRISTIAN LICORICE STORE, directed by James Frawley; screenplay, Floyd Mutrux; camera, David Butler; editor, Richard Harris; music, Lalo Schifrin; a Michael S. Laughlin-Floyd Mutrux production; a National General Pictures release; presented by Cinema Center Films. At the First Avenue Screening Room, at 61st Street. Running time: 90 minutes. This film is classified PG. Showings April 5 and 6 at noon and midnight.

Franklin Cane .... Beau Bridges
Cynthia Vicstrom .... Maud Adams

Jonathon Carruthers...... Gilbert Roland
Monroe................. Anne Arbus
Texas Girl............... Anne Randall
Joseph................. Monte Hellman
Mary................... Jaclyn Hellman

By NORA SAYRE

Every concept of box-office poison admits to exceptions; from "Gone With the Wind" to "M*A*S*H," supposedly toxic subjects have yielded hits. And with all respect to the exhibitor who once stated, "I don't want any more movies where people write with feathers," even the currently despised costume picture could have a comeback. But some in Hollywood suspect that sports movies (along with films about writers) rarely do well. "The Christian Licorice Store," which is playing today and tomorrow at the First Avenue Screening Room, offers some clues about potential sports flops.

The movie, which was made in 1971 by James Frawley, who later directed "Kid Blue," follows the fortunes of "the new golden boy of tennis," Beau Bridges, all floppy hair and ceaseless smiles. There's no excitement afoot while he smashes his way to victory, because we know we're watching actors and not a real game. So the grunts of effort fail to generate suspense. The camera does all the work; the players aren't athletes—it's the movie maker who decides who will lose or win.

Admittedly, "Licorice

Store" has other problems. The tennis star has a soupy sense of alienation and a beautiful, adoring girlfriend (Maud Adams) who was given no character whatsoever. Eventually, he's corrupted by lush offers for hairspray ads and movie roles. Decadence is his destiny—as established by a party scene where he strokes two young women (a timid imitation of "Blow Up") in a house with an unfilled swimming pool. Empty pools always mean that all's not well in Hollywood.

However, one vast, brief pleasure lurks within this picture: a visit with Jean Renoir. He talks about a book he's writing, and says that "it's going slowly—but I hope safely," adding that it's not an autobiography but "some souvenirs" from the present and the future, as well as from the past. That glimpse of the great man is worth the movie's oppressively lyrical soundtrack, and a script crammed with lines like "This is a damn good racket," or "I think the nicest things in life happen when you're naked." There's also one gallantry that wipes the eye of history: A young woman says, "I would have loved the thirties," and is told, "The thirties would have loved you."

1974 Ap 5, 27:4

Screen: Treat for Young

A genuinely delightful, hour-long program of short films for children is being shown through Monday at the Whitney Museum of American Art. Furthermore, youngsters under 12 years old are admitted free, with adults paying only $1 and $1.50 on weekends. The afternoon screenings start at noon.

The movies are bright, inventive and amusing, with no condescending cuteness or sugar-coating for small-fry viewers. "Frederick," Leo Lionni's and Giulio Gianini's yarn of an imaginative little field mouse, couldn't be more perkily charming and artistic. Derek Lamb's "Housemoving," with its speeded time-lapse techniques, is sprightly and funny. The children yesterday obviously loved Keith David's "The Other Barred," which

thoughtfully studies caged zoo animals and inquisitive humans. Lynn Smith's "Shout It Out Alphabet" posed a friskily diverting word game that the children yesterday pealed out with relish.

Another novelty is Suzan Pitt Kraning's "A City Trip," a collage animation of children's cut-outs.

There are two black-and-white entries, Eliot Noyes Jr.'s "Clay," a clever, speedy satire of the origin of species, and another hand-shaped effort, Caroline Lief's "Sand," which silhouettes the "Peter and the Wolf" story most ingeniously. There's also some grim but harmless cacophony as the wolf gobbles up Peter's pets. One adult viewer will still take the Disney color version and that cute little kerchiefed duck, Sonia.

HOWARD THOMPSON

1974 Ap 5, 27:5

From left: Frank Finlay, Oliver Reed, Michael York and Richard Chamberlain

The Cast

ORDINARY TENDERNESS (La Tendresse Ordinaire), directed by Jacques Leduc; screenplay by Robert Tremblay; produced by Paul Larose for the National Film Board of Canada; director of photography, Alain Dostie; editor, Pierre Bernier; distributed by Faroun Films and the National Film Board of Canada. Running time; 82 minutes. In the "New Directors/New Films" series, sponsored by the Museum of Modern Art and the Film Society of Lincoln Center, at the Museum of Modern Art, 53d Street, west of Fifth Avenue. This film has not been rated.

Esther Levesque............ Esther Auger
Jocelyn Levesque........... Jocelyn Berube
Bernadette .... Luce Guilbeault

By VINCENT CANBY

Jacques Leduc's "Ordinary Tenderness" (La Tendresse Ordinaire) is a French-Canadian film of complex sweetness, a truly poetic film that describes love entirely in terms of loneliness, friendship, boredom, the anticipation of reunion and the memory of moments of absolutely no apparent importance. The movie was shown yesterday at the Museum of Modern Art in the "New Directors/New Films," series and will be repeated there today at 11 P.M.

Unlike most filmmakers who mistake pretty or bizarre images for poetry, Mr. Leduc uses images of sometimes stunning banality to describe the contradictory emotions of Esther and Jocelyn Levesque, the young couple who, in the course of the film, are meeting after a separation of four months. Jocelyn, who has been working in northern Canada, is returning to his home in Quebec by train and car. The move cross-cuts between their separate present states and their memories.

•

The details of the film are as precise as good journalism, but the cumulative effect is as stunning and ambiguous as a nightmare. "Ordinary Tenderness" is, in fact, a film editor's dream, being composed of dozens of fragments that have one meaning alone and quite another in their various associations.

Mr. Leduc, who is in his early 30's and began his career as a cameraman, seldom traffics in scenery for its own sake. The movie is set mostly inside—in cramped kitchens, dining rooms, motel bedrooms and bars, in supermarkets and on trains. Like the early Andy Warhol, but less spectacularly so, Mr. Leduc is fascinated by the smallest, most common gestures, the drinking of a glass of beer or the maneuvering of a shopping cart through a supermarket. The gestures are not ends in themselves. They are the coded messages of lovers and friends. "Ordinary Tenderness" is quite unlike any movie I've ever seen. I'm not sure it sustains its feature length. Yet it is a courageous attempt to create a narrative of the emotions tied only loosely to events. Conventional narrative cinema works just the other way around.

1974 Ap 6, 16:1

The Cast

FOXY BROWN, directed and written by Jack Hill; director of photography, Brick Marquard; editor, Chuck Mc-Clelland; songs by Willie Hutch; produced by Buzz Feitshans; released by American International Pictures. At the Cinerama Theater, Broadway at 47th Street, and the 86th Twin 2 Theater, west of Lexington Avenue. Running time: 94 minutes. This film is classified R.
Foxy Brown...............Pam Grier
Link Brown............Antonio Fargas
Steve Elias.............Peter Brown
Michael Anderson........Terry Carter
Katherine Wall.........Kathryn Loder
Judge Fenton.......Harry Holcombe
Hays...................Sid Haig
Claudia...............Juanita Brown

Pam Grier, the well-endowed black beauty whose clothes, if not her good intentions, have been torn away in several bargain-basement epics such as last year's "Coffy," is in a rut—to judge by "Foxy Brown," which

crashed into the Cinerama and the 86th Street Twin theaters yesterday.

In "Coffy," it may be recalled, she played a nurse who destroyed legions of bad guys and gals, both black and white, in a good fight accentuated by a plethora of gutter dialogue, against hoods, drugs and pushers who hooked her kid sister and blasted her boyfriend.

Well, Jack Hill, the writer-director of "Coffy," has come up with no appreciable changes in doing the same for "Foxy Brown." This time, it's her kid brother, a pusher himself, and her man, an undercover narcotics agent, who are done in by those dope-dealing dastards. And, naturally, Miss Grier, who can handle a lover, a gun, a car, a plane, four-letter language and her enemies with ease, again emerges victorious over mobsters, a bigtime madam, pimps and rapists. Miss Grier is obviously durable but, unfortunately, is fast becoming a bore despite all the sex, brawls and gore in "Foxy Brown."

A. H. WEILER

1974 Ap 6, 16:2

THE GOLDEN VOYAGE OF SINBAD, directed by Gordon Hessler; screenplay by Brian Clemens, from a story by Mr. Clemens and Ray Harryhausen; director of photography, Ted Moore; film editor, Roy Watts; music, Miklos Rozsa; produced by Charles H. Schneer and Mr. Harryhausen; released by Columbia Pictures. At neighborhood theaters. Running time: 105 minutes. This film is classified G.
Sinbad..............John Phillip Law
Margiana...........Caroline Munro
Koura...................Tom Baker
Vizier.............Douglas Wilmer
Rachid................Martin Shaw
Hakim................Gregoire Aslan

"The Golden Voyage of Sinbad" is one of those hardy perennials of the movie business—the juvenile film that seems to sprout overnight in every imaginable neighborhood theater just in time for Easter, Passover and spring vacation.

For the record, the plot calls for Sinbad (played by John Philip Law) in the service of the Grand Vizier (Douglas Wilmer) to race against the evil prince Koura (Tom Baker), through perils impressively created by the co-producer and special effects artist, Ray Harryhausen, to the fountain of destiny, where youth, a shield of darkness and a crown of untold riches await.

•

Children who revel in clean-cut heroes, villains given to spells and incantations and the kind of special effects that breathe life into mandrake root, ships' figureheads, centaurs, griffins and statues of Kali (always a deity beloved of evil forces) will probably find it a happy concoction for passing a rainy afternoon.

Intellectually, "Sinbad" sails on shallow waters polluted with such nickel-wisdom as "He who walks on fire will burn his feet," "Trust in Allah but tie up your camel" and "He who is patient, obtains."

For older audiences, "The Golden Voyage" is not so much an excursion into the ancient past but into the modern past, when Raymond Massey was fomenting dissidence in northern India, Basil Rathbone was practicing condescension in Cartagena, and heroes, villains and bit-players spat pithy wisdom across clashing swords, like seeds at a watermelon-eating contest.

In the presence of such fare as "The Golden Voyage of Sinbad" one feels constrained to close with a warning from the sage Santayana: "Those who cannot remember the past are condemned to repeat it."

LAWRENCE VAN GELDER

1974 Ap 6, 16:4

Fascinated With Couples on the Lam

By VINCENT CANBY

TWO by two they ravage the landscape, drinking soda pop and chewing enough gum to stick a bull elephant to the sidewalk. Children-on-the-run, aliens in their own lands, bringing out the worst in the prose of the Sunday supplement writers and whipping up the imaginations of a restless citizenry. By some odd coincidence the three best American films to open in New York so far this year are about young couples who go beyond the law as easily and heedlessly as people embarking on summer vacations.

As if they were Hansel and Gretel wanting some day to find their way home, Kit and Holly, the outlaw-lovers in Terrence Malick's "Badlands," leave markers along the route they pursue in stolen cars across South Dakota toward Montana. Not bits and pieces of string but corpses, at least half a dozen, most of whom have been shot by Kit at point-blank range.

Bowie and Keechie, the doomed pair in Robert Altman's meditation upon the Great Depression, "Thieves Like Us," don't kill anyone themselves but because Bowie robs banks and tags along with men who do kill, they find themselves branded as desperadoes, their names, temporarily, household words, and their reputations as out-sized as government-issue clothing.

In Steven Spielberg's "The Sugarland Express," which opened last week at the National and Cinema II Theaters, Clovis, who has only four more months to serve on a petty larceny sentence, walks out of a prison rehabilitation center at the urging of his nut-brained wife, Lou Jean. Together they kidnap a highway patrolman and force him to drive them 300 miles across Texas in an absolutely fruitless attempt to retrieve their child, Baby Langston, who has been taken away from them by the court.

Followed by 200 county and state police cars, by a mobile television unit, and cheered on by roadside fans, high-school bands and drum majorettes, Clovis and Lou Jean ride joyously toward a disaster that is as inevitable as the "SPLAT!!!" made by any cartoon character who falls off a cloud.

"Badlands," "Thieves Like Us" and "The Sugarland

Express" have a number of superficial things in common, but they are essentially such different visions of American life I hope that the few things they share will not persuade you to think that if you've seen one, you've seen all three. You haven't. The form, it's now apparent, is as elastic as the Western that embraces everything from "Blazing Saddles" to "A Fistful of Dollars" and "My Darling Clementine."

The most interesting of the three films, as well as the toughest to sit through if you prefer movies to be cheerful and upbeat, is "Badlands," Malick's first directorial effort and a truly mesmerizing achievement. The story was inspired by the short, bloody career of Charlie Starkweather, who, at age 19, in January, 1958, with the seeming cooperation of his 14-year-old girlfriend, went on a murder spree that claimed 10 victims, including three members of his girlfriend's family.

Although Malick very carefully sets his film in the 1950's, its impact comes as a projection of American life today, not because it re-creates much more than the surface look of the placid fifties. Kit (Martin Sheen), a garbage man who fancies his resemblance to James Dean, and Holly (Sissy Spacek) take off on their joyride after Kit shoots Holly's father who, earlier, had punished Holly for seeing Kit by killing her dog. It's difficult to tell whether Malick means us to believe this first murder of Kit's to have been premeditated. Indeed, Malick may not know or particularly care.

"Badlands" makes no attempt to analyze the mind of the mass murderer who, more than likely, is psychotic. Malick, instead, presents Kit and Holly as models of our time, children of the television age run amok, overcommunicated, technically literate, but so completely desensitized they have very little connection with their own feelings and none whatsoever with those of others. Consequences to actions are beyond their comprehension.

The best that Kit can do is to see himself as the star in a James Dean movie: Cut. Print it. And everyone goes home in a sports car to a swimming pool. On the soundtrack Holly describes their flight from nowhere to nowhere as if she were living in the middle of a True Romance. "The whole world was looking for us," she says, as if reciting lines in a school play, "for who knew where Kit would strike next." Towards the end, when the pleasures of flight and pursuit have begun to pall, Holly tells us that she sat beside Kit on the front seat of the car, spelling complete sentences with her tongue on the roof of her mouth.

The performances by Sheen and Miss Spacek are superb, as clearly defined and precisely detailed as the flat Middle Western landscapes. They are designed, like the film itself, not to make mass murder comprehensible in a subjective way but to present us with the spectacle of what much of our life is like today. Not literally but spiritually. "Badlands" may well become an American classic.

Altman's "Thieves Like Us," based on Edward Anderson's thirties novel, is a less spectacular, more conventional film, but it too is a beautifully realized work. It's also one that makes me suspect that, without telling us, the director has embarked on a project to define in his films what might loftily be called the American Experience.

"M.A.S.H.," though supposedly about the Korean War, was an appalled though hugely funny reaction to the war in Vietnam, cast in the form of a gung-ho Hollywood war movie gone slightly but importantly askew. In "McCabe and Mrs. Miller" Altman examined the American frontier and saw in it something quite different from the pretty myth we'd all like to believe in.

I'm not quite sure where "Brewster McCloud" fits into this project, but "Thieves Like Us" certainly does. It's Altman's Depression movie, immensely enriched with the help of hindsight and, on the soundtrack, with old radio programs like "Gangbusters" and an awful, Lux-Radio-Theater-type of production of "Romeo and Juliet." At the center of it is the love story of Bowie (Keith Carradine) and Keechie (Shelley Duvall).

Unlike the couple in "Badlands," they both are aware of terrible consequences, prompting Bowie to make vague resolutions to reform. That he can't, or, at least, that he doesn't reform in time, seems a gesture towards the Depression gangster films on which "Thieves Like Us" is also a commentary. One of Altman's most important contributions is the disciplined sentiment, most evident in the affectingly self-conscious performance of Miss Duvall, and in the film's final sequence, which is devastating.

Like "Badlands," "The Sugarland Express" is a first directorial effort, though Spielberg has made two highly regarded features for television, "Something Evil" and "Duel," neither of which I've seen.

"The Sugarland Express" has neither the profound concerns of "Badlands" nor the complexity of "Thieves Like Us," but it is an exceptionally well-made film that gives Goldie Hawn what might be the role of her career as the foolish, self-absorbed, petty thief who decides, too late, that she really wants to be a mother to Baby Langston. The film has an almost cartoon-like gaity to it, which works well in describing the hoopla that is caused by the flight of Clovis and Lou Jean across Texas with a nice-natured cop as their hostage. But it also tends to make the characters into jokes who can't easily support the sentiment I think we're meant to feel for them at the end.

The film is at its best in portraying the American public's insatiable appetite for sentimental nonsense, which knows no bounds. Have you heard the current radio commercial hawking a paperback biography of Lucille Ball, who is described as having "survived her husband's indiscretions and her son's illegitimate baby" to become "one of Hollywood's richest women, and one of its loneliest. . . ."? When "The Sugarland Express" gives its attention to the dramatization of this sort of baloney, it is first-rate and very funny.

1974 Ap 7, II:1:6

THE PROMISED LAND (La Tierra Prometida), directed and written by Miguel Littin (Spanish with English subtitles); produced by Cinematografica Tercer Mondo and I.C.A.I.C.; photographed by Alfonso Beato; edited by Nelson Rodrigues; music, Luis Advis, Inti-Illimani Group; courtesy of Tricontinental Films. Running time: 120 minutes. At the Museum of Modern Art.

Jose Duran ....Nelson Villagra
Traje Cruzado ....Marcelo Gaete
Don Fernando ....Rafael Benavente
Virgin of Carmen ..Mireya Kulchewsky

Miguel Littin, writer-director of "The Promised Land," the Chilean entry in the New Directors series shown Saturday and last night at the Museum of Modern Art, states his case against Latin-American oppression with the fervor of an unvanquished revolutionary. But if his love of the land and its enfranchisement is as heartfelt as his impassioned rhetoric, his highly stylized drama is less than convincing in its treatment of the Establishment and foreign exploiters.

The 31-year-old movie maker, who completed his film last year when he was still head of the studio that was an official part of the overthrown, left-wing Allende Government, is obviously autobiographical in his treatment of a group of 1930, Depression-afflicted, homeless, wandering peasants who founded and cooperatively worked a village called Palmillo (the director's birthplace).

The sweep and the irony of "The Promised Land" are fitfully visualized against a colorful background of lush tropical and snow-draped, authentic backgrounds. Mr. Littin's hordes of peasants, led by Nelson Villagra, unsuccessfully attempt to rise against the entrenched capitalists in a neighboring town only to be cut down by the cavalry of another rightist government that has just come into power to thwart their desperate attempt at self-rule.

The tragedy of injustice is strikingly apparent, but its impact is lessened by a plethora of loving declamatory scenes and diffuse religious symbolism that tend to confuse, rather than impress, an uninitiated observer. It is easy to feel the irony and reality of the off-screen, narration of the aged peasant who survived doleful things past. The symbolism, however, is still distratcing, and a viewer can't help wonder of the estate owners, businessmen and the religious figures were as one-dimensional as they are depicted to be.

Mr. Littin, who is reported living in Mexico, is forthrightly biased, and his peasants and workers look truly confused and driven. But if this anguished outcry against exploitation is unbalanced, it is also a powerful illustration of the talents of a dedicated movie maker.

A. H. WEILER

1974 Ap 8, 43:1

The Cast

THE CONVERSATION, directed by Francis Ford Coppola; written by Mr. Coppola; director of photography, Bill Butler; editor, Richard Chew; music, David Shire; produced by Fred Ross; released by Paramount Pictures Corporation. At the Coronet Theater, Third Avenue at 59th Street. Running time: 113 minutes. This film is classified PG.

Harry Caul................Gene Hackman
Stan.........................John Cazale
Bernie Moran..............Allen Garfield
Mark....................Frederic Forrest
Ann.......................Cindy Williams

By NORA SAYRE

Early last summer, it was comforting when one authority on wiretapping referred to the equipment used to eavesdrop on the Democratic National Committee's headquarters as "sloppy" and "amateurish." And Dick Gregory's reflection on the White House tapes is worth preserving: "Imagine feelin' so lonely and insignificant that you'd bug your own phone!" But yuks about bugging recede swiftly while you watch Francis Ford Coppola's "The Conversation," which opened yesterday at the Coronet.

•

This extremely grim movie explores the character of a middle-aged surveillance wizard: a dedicated professional who prefers to "know nothing about human nature," or even about the people he's paid to spy on. Wedded to secrecy as a moral principle, he's the kind of man who lies down to neck with his shoes on—an acutely repressed solitary who repeats that he's not responsible for the outcome of his work.

He feels totally disconnected from the three murders that resulted from one of his assignments: "I just turned in the tapes." But he loathes even mild profanity, and when he confesses his sins to a priest, he includes failing to pay for some newspapers. It's an impressive portrayal by Gene Hackman: the inhibited laugh, the bland, bleak face with lips pressed flat together and chin drawn in, convey the ruthless stranger who knows our most intimate moments but won't react to them.

However, in the course of a routine job, he detects that a new murder's in the making. Against all resolve, he becomes involved—and desperately determined to forestall a possible killing. (His suspicions spring from what he's collected on tape—a powerful reminder of the photographer in Antonioni's "Blow Up." The movie's plot is twisted by a cleverly deceptive use of sentimentality; people who sound soupy later turn out to have sinister intentions.

Suddenly, those whose guilt he has spotted turn his own technology against him: he himself is bugged and spied on. So he becomes the hunter at bay—frantic because he knows that some equipment is unbeatable. In a futile effort to protect his privacy, he finally trashes his own apartment—even smashing a statuette of the Virgin Mary (and finding nothing)—and winds up a victim of his craft.

•

It's a brilliant idea for a movie, and much of it works. But some of the action drags—perhaps because the style is so muted, so deliberately dry and cool, that suspense is partially muffled. The scenes where two different women fawn on Mr. Hackman are unconvincing, since they have to behave as though this grubby, uptight man were irresistible. And I'm mildly mystified by the casting of Cindy Williams as an executive's roving wife, since she appears far too prim and conventional to stray over any kind of boundary. But Alan Garfield is splendid as a boastful wire-tapper, and there's a fine, nervy performance by John Cazale.

Mr. Coppola has certainly succeeded in making surveillance repulsive. While that's hardly a new notion, we can thank him for withering the last tendrils of romance: the dagger and the cloak have lost all dash—they're equally dangerous and dirty.

1974 Ap 8, 44:3

BUTLEY, directed by Harold Pinter; author and screen adapater, Simon Gray; executive producer, Otto Plaschkes; dierctor of photography, Gerry Fisher; editor, Malcolm Cooke; for the American Film Theater, Henry T. Weinstein; produced by Ely A. Landau. At selected theaters. Running time: 127 minutes. This film is classified R.

Ben Butley ....Alan Bates
Edna Shaft........ ....Jessica Tandy
Joey Keyston ....Richard O'Callaghan
Anne Butley...................Susan Engel
Reg Nuttall.................Michael Byrne

By NORA SAYRE

Are masochists more destructive than sadists? (Answers by Friday, 25 words or less.) It's easy to brush off sadists if you don't like them, and they're always terribly dependent on the cooperation of their victims. However, those who pursue pain or punishment are nearly always successful, and they tend to drag their friends or intimates along with them.

Of course, the most effective human time-bombs are larded with both ingredients. Alan Bates, in his superb performance in Simon Gray's victim and a helpless mugger "Butley," is both a dangerous — who forces others to abandon him. Few actors can embody that style of paradox. The American Film Theater's presentation of "Butley," directed by Harold Pinter, opened yesterday at selected theaters

The play, which rings with loud echoes of John Osborne's "Look Back in Anger" and "Inadmissible Evidence," also recalls the hero of Kingsley Amis's "Lucky Jim" — the teacher who recoils from teaching, plagued by irksome students who demand to be taught. But while Mr. Osborne and Mr. Amis used their protagonists as part-time social critics, Simon Gray is concerned only with the inner man.

"Butley" focuses on a sizzling depressive who gets "news of two divorces in the same day": Both his wife and the man he feels married to are leaving him for someone else. He doesn't seem to care at all about his marriage, and he has no apparent affection for the young man. But he can't stand rejection. "Butley" hasn't much emotional depth. However, there's plenty of verbal wit for Mr. Bates to mount and ride on, and the play's energy springs from one-liners, such as "I'm a one-woman man, and I've had mine, thank God," or "Toadying is the sincerest form of contempt."

Mr. Bates's performance has changed since I saw him on stage in London nearly three years ago. Then, he was all fury and disgust. Here, he has subtly toned himself down for the camera, and the characterization seems to be far more varied. As he sheds the layers of an excruciating hangover, he displaces more and more air — his bulky presence looms with the authority of rage, although he never quite has the total tantrum that we're expecting.

The mood keeps shifting, as he chants nursery rhymes, plays interrogator, strums on others' guilts, assumes an elegant upper-class voice to

Alan Bates

distill his exasperation and luxuriates in confrontation. Coughing hideously, bursting into song, he weaves complex webs of misunderstanding and revels in them.

Beaming with malice, he also runs through an anthology of smiles: faint smiles of pain or huge, dimpling flashes that contradict what he's just said; bland smiles to underline an insult; subdued, gleeful smirks as he closes in for the attack; grotesque, challenging grins. Butley is deft at self-mockery, as well as mimicking others. Meanwhile, whatever he feels is apt to be contagious for them. Gradually, he's converted from a giant, cackling gnome to a muted loser—bereft because he's driven everyone else away.

On stage, Butley's lengthy monologues were hard on other actors; you were aware of their efforts to keep responding while listening. But the camera can rest on his face to an advantage; many of his speeches seem just right for close-ups. On several occasions, Butley makes someone stay and hear him out who longs to escape his office; again, this works well in the movie, as it didn't in the theater.

Simon Gray has slightly altered his own text, and it flows smoothly onto film. And Jessica Tandy — crisp and direct, simmering against her will, stern but not grim — Richard O'Callaghan and Michael Byrne are all very fine as Butley's sparring partners. Along with "The Homecoming" and "The Three Sisters," this movie represents the American Film Theater's best work so far.

1974 Ap 9, 34:1

The Cast

OVER NIGHT (Uber Nacht), directed and produced by Karin Thome; screenplay (German with English subtitles) titles) by Miss Thome, based on an idea by Max Zihlmann; directors of photography, Martin Schaefer and Achim Lenz. Running time: 85 minutes. Presented in the "New Directors/New Films" series, sponsored by the Film Society of Lincoln Center and the Museum of Modern Art, at the Museum of Modern Art, 53d Street west of Fifth Avenue. This film has not been rated.
Fritz .... Werner Penzel
Laura .... Karin Thome
Panzer .... Rudolf Thome

By VINCENT CANBY

For reasons that totally escape me, the sponsors of the "New Directors/New Films" series at the Museum of Modern Art have chosen to close their mini-festival with a German film called "Over Night" (Uber Nacht), produced and directed by Karin Thome, who exhibits a certain awareness of cinema fads of the sixties and absolutely no talent as a film maker. The movie, shown last night, will be repeated at the museum tonight at 6 o'clock.

According to the program notes, "Over Night" was "a controversial hit" at the 1973 Berlin Festival and was exhibited "with varying degrees of success" at the festivals in Edinburgh, London and Melbourne, Australia.

I can't imagine how the film could possibly be called controversial. It's simply inept, a sloppily conceived ego trip starring Miss Thome as an alienated, thirtyish hippie who wanders carelessly around landscapes telling parables to anyone who'll listen. There's one about a wild bird that falls in love with a tame bird, one about a streetcar ticket, one about someone standing on a high place, which prompts the comment: "Fear enslaves."

Miss Thome ends her film with some sightseeing in North Africa, a sequence that looks suspiciously like her summer vacation.

The "New Directors/New Films" series is one of the worthier joint undertakings of the museum and the Film Society of Lincoln Center. In the past it has brought attention to such films as Alain Tanner's "La Salamandre" and Tomas Gutierrez Alea's "Memories of Underdevelopment." That a film as vacuous as "Over Night" could get into such a festival must be taken as a grim comment on the state of the new films being made by the new directors.

1974 Ap 9, 37:1

'Castle of Purity'

Arturo Ripstein's Mexican-made "The Castle of Purity," the story of a man who locked his family within urban walls for 18 years, had been hailed as extraordinary before its showings last week-

The Cast

LA VILLEGGIATURA (Black Holiday), subject and direction by Marco Leto; screenplay, Italian with English subtitles by Mr. Leto, Lino Del Fra, Cecilia Mangini, photographed by Voifango Alfi; edited by Giuseppe Giacobino; music, Egisto Macchi; released by New Yorker Films. Running time: 110 minutes. At the Museum of Modern Art, tonight at 8:30.
Professor Rossini ... Adalberto Maria Merli
Police Commissioner Rizzuto..Adolfo Celi
Scagnetti .... John Steiner
Mrs. Rossini .... Milena Vukotic
Mastrodonato .... Biagio Pelligra

"Black Holiday," the Italian feature directed by Marco Loto that was screened last night and will be repeated tonight as part of the New Directors series at the Museum of Modern Art, Iilluminates a somber past that, like old wounds, is real but has receded beyond pain. The 42-year-old director's concern with the moralities of fascism and antifascism is, in essence, an intellectual drama that disturbs but does not excite an intelligent observer.

He focuses basically on a young history professor who refused allegiance to Il Duce's regime in 1931, the carefully bureaucratic police commissioner and the others in the group of Communists, anarchists and apologetic liberals incarcerated under the commissioner's jurisdiction on a small island for their crimes against the fascist state. Their enforced "holiday" is relegated largely to an exposition of political credos that still stir the mind and heart, if not a viewer's pulse.

Adalberto Maria Merli is properly introspective as the pedantic professor confused by conflicting viewpoints until he is finally committed to action by unnecessary bloodshed. Adolfo Celi is bland and wily as the commissioner who befriends the professor and even allows him to teach and the added comforts of a villa, his wife, infant daughter and his books in order to stress his seemingly decent stewardship. And John Steiner is forcefully natural as the militant worker-leader of the prisoners who is murdered as a result of the commissioner's discreetly oblique orders.

"Black Holiday" has been photographed in black and white but its divided principals, their emotions and politics are neither black or white nor simple, as the English subtitles help make abundantly clear. The passage of time has dimmed a drama that is sometimes too talkative, but its ideas and people remain vivid and provocative.

A. H. WEILER

1974 Ap 9, 37:1

end at the Museum of Modern Art. It is indeed extraordinary and haunting.

Mr. Ripstein arranged his drama in a stately flow of lucid, exquisitely colored images that edge toward doom. The acting is so good that it is hardly noticeable as such. There is not one note of music, only the pelting rain, blending with Alex Phillips's photography and Manuel Fontanals's set design (a spacious but tottering house, not a chamber of horrors).

This bizarre, burrowing movie has been called an attack on Latin family tradition, a metaphor of Christian society and a suspense thriller. To one viewer, it is all three. With his small cast, headed by Claudio Brook and Rita Macedo, and his co-scenarist José Emilio Pacheco, the 34-year-old director has subtly shaped a remarkable film.

1974 Ap 9, 37:1

The Cast

OUR TIME, directed by Peter Hyams; screenplay by Jane C. Stanton; produced by Richard A. Roth; director of photography, Jules Brenner; editor, James Mitchell; music, Michel Legrand; distributed by Warner Brothers. Running time: 91 minutes. At the Sutton Theater, 57th Street, east of Third Avenue. This film has been classified PG.
Abby.................... Pamela Sue Martin
Muffy .... Betsy Slade
Michael.................... Parker Stevenson
Malcolm.............. George O'Hanlon Jr.
Laura .... Karen Balkin
Frank.................... Robert Walden

By VINCENT CANBY

"Our Time," which opened yesterday at the Sutton Theater, is a pre-pill romantic drama designed, perversely, for the prepubescent set. It combines the worst features of two kinds of ancient Broadway formula comedy with a gothic lack of sensibility all its own.

The time is 1955 and the place, most of the time, is Penfield Academy, a fancy Massachusetts boarding school for girls, including the elegantly boned Abby Reed (Pamela Sue Martin) and her roommate, the plain, sensitive Muffy Pratt (Betsy Slade).

Abby and Muffy are the literary descendants of Judy and Fuffy, the heroines of Sally Benson's New Yorker stories, which were later turned into a Broadway show by Chodorov and Fields. Abby and Muffy are what used to be called imps, meaning they do things on the order of talking during chapel. There is a difference, but, if you think about it, the difference is essentially one of degree, not kind.

Abby and Muffy are experiencing the sort of lusts that used to keep the curtain up for three acts in plays by F. Hugh Herbert, whose characters were generally older and married. In the jargon of Old Broadway, Abby and Muffy want to "do it." Abby does do it, quite successfully, with her friend Michael. Then poor Muffy tries just once,

and most unhappily, winds up instantaneously pregnant.

Although Peter Hyams, the director, is barely 30 years old, he has staged the film as if he had committed to memory all of the dumbest mannerisms of the pre-World War II Broadway theater. Characters talk to each other's backs. Nobody leaves the set without attempting some boff exit line or gesture. Some of these mannerisms may actually be in the screenplay by Jane C. Stanton. I have no idea. The program states, however, that Miss Stanton, 26, is the author of 42 one-act plays and three three-act plays, "none of them produced."

It is difficult to believe that Mr. Hyams was also the director of the recent "Busting," one of the better, more intelligent cop movies. Perhaps teen-age rich girls are not characters with whom he has much sympathy or understanding. It may be significant that the film's one episode that has any life features a muddle-headed young med-school student who, for contradictory reasons (money and sympathy), performs Muffy's abortion. As played by Robert Walden, there's a hint of a character here.

The abortion is a genuinely moving sequence in a film that is otherwise full of sentimental affectations, like the fussy camerawork and the orangy color, which, I suppose, is meant to evoke times past. Twenty years ago, the film says weepily, the wages of doing it was death.

1974 Ap 11, 31:1

The Cast

THOMASINE & BUSHROD, directed by Gordon Parks, Jr.; written by Max Julien; director of photography, Lucien Ballard; film editor, Frank C. Decot; music, Coleridge-Taylor Perkinson; produced by Harvey Bernhard and Mr. Julien. Released by Columbia Pictures. At The Penthouse Theater, Broadway and 47th Street and the 86th Street East Theater, at Third Avenue. Running time: 95 minutes. This film is classified: PG.
Bushrod .... Max Julien
Thomasine .... Vonetta McGee
Bogardie .... George Murdock
Jomo .... Glynn Turman

By NORA SAYRE

Two graceful bank robbers, an antique car jouncing through the landscape to larky music, outlaws who wonder what history will say about them—no, this isn't a carbon of "Bonnie and Clyde," although some parallels are powerful. "Thomasine and Bushrod," which opened yesterday at the Penthouse Theater and the 86th Street East, is a black Western of considerable freshness, directed by Gordon Parks Jr. It's dated between 1912 and 1915, when a number of black people dwelled throughout the West.

Bushrod, (Max Julien, who wrote and co-produced the picture) and Thomasine (Vonetta McGee) live on the lam in the wilderness. Between stickups tnd shootouts, they share many of their spoils with Indians, Mexicans and poor whites, for whom they become folk heroes. Pursued by a fabulously evil white sheriff (George Murdoch), who vows to kill them, Thomasine and Bushrod are both cowboys and Indians, the hunters and the hunted.

The movie is somewhat thin on plot, but the script gives some fresh twists to old formulas, especially the sex roles. Thomasine is an independent, feisty woman, who craves equal billing on their WANTED posters—and gets it. Bushrod, although lethal to his enemies, is a reluctant outlaw who yearns for another way of life, and he's characterized as a man who's not afraid to be gentle or sensitive. Meanwhile, these lovers fight with gusto. But they're definitely partners—in a way that's rare on screen, or among cow-persons.

There are some slow moments, but the picture is carried by the talents of the two performers. Their style is utterly contemporary—not that it really matters. Miss McGee — laughing or raging, reveling in risks — alternates a luxurious cool sass with a rebel's defiance, and Mr. Julien's beguiling humor and flexibility make him all the more formidable when he's behind a gun.

1974 Ap 11, 31:1

ATTICA, directed and produced by Cinda Firestone; edited by Cinda Firestone and Tucker Ashworth; camermen, Roland Barnes, Jay Lamarch, Mary Lampson, Jesse Goodman, Carol Stein and Kevin Keating; distributed by Attica Films, Inc. Running time: 80 minutes. At the First Avenue Screening Room, First Avenue at 61st Street. This film has not been rated.

By VINCENT CANBY

The place is the Attica, N.Y., prison on a September day in 1971. The prisoners mill around the yard, improvising tents, sleeping, looking uneasily at cameras, which, equipped with telescopic lenses, can see them far more clearly than they can see the cameras.

The prisoners at Attica are in the middle of rebellion. They've issued a manifesto demanding reforms dealing ,.ɔn treatment of blacks and Puerto Ricans, with food, medical care, education. Says one prisoner: "They [the prison authorities] think we're just shucking and jiving." Says another: "We're not advocating violence. We're advocating communication and understanding."

Four days after the rebellion began, troopers armed with shotguns and rifles, some using dum-dum bullets, stormed the walk to secure what is genteelly called the correctional facility, leaving 32 inmates and 11 of their hostages dead, most from shots fired by the state police.

"Attica," produced and directed by Cinda Firestone, who also edited the film with Tucker Ashworth, is an exceptionally moving, outraged recollection of that terrible event. It's a documentary record of the event itself, the conditions that helped prompt it, and some of the things that have (and haven't) happened since. Though it asks questions that go unanswered, it is surprisingly temperate in tone.

"Attica" opened yesterday at the First Avenue Screening Room and it is, like "I. F. Stone's Weekly," a superior example of committed film making.

The thing that made Attica such a consciousness-raising event is preserved on film in the voices of the prisoners, both during and after the event, in interviews with the hostages, and in coverage of the official inquiries that followed it. We see it in the unity of the prisoners, in the discipline they maintained during the fruitless negotiations with correctional officials, in the faces of civilians who served on the unofficial "observers' committee," as well as in the faces of the men who made the decision to retake the prison by force.

●

Does a commitment to a desperate cause make a man lean and strong? Does representing an established system make another man look sort of swollen, overfed, the way the sheriff of Nottingham is always portrayed? I was beginning to think so while watching "Attica" until we are presented an interview with one especially articulate, passionately angry black prisoner who is in fact, almost plump. Stereotypes do not hold in "Attica."

Nor is its anger self-defeating. One of the most moving sequences in the film is composed of interviews with the members of the family of one black prisoner who, post-rebellion, has apparently embarked on a self-improvement binge. "You wouldn't be able to walk into my cell, for all the books I got," he has written his sister.

Eloquence keeps turning up in the midst of jargon, and there is nothing so eloquent as the last line of the film, spoken on the soundtrack by an ex-inmate who would shake the public out of its historic disinterest in penal reform. "Wake up," he says, "because nothing comes to a sleeper but a dream."

1974 Ap 12, 18:1

Comment on Stills

Jean-Luc Godard's "Letter to Jane," which served here a couple of years ago as a curtain raiser to his revolutionary film "Tout Va Bien," is now the afterpiece to Nagisa Oshima's "Diary of a Yunbogi Boy" which opened yesterday at the Film Forum —and probably the better for it.

Vexing, didactic, droning, occasionally ridiculous, this study of a single photograph of Jane Fonda in North Viet-

The Program

LETTER TO JANE by Jean-Luc Godard and Jean-Pierre Gorin, 55 minutes; DIARY OF A YUNBOGI BOY by Nagisa Oshima, 24 minutes; released by New Yorker Films. At the Film Forum, 256 West 88th Street, at 8 P.M. tonight, tomorrow and Sunday, and then, next Thursday through Sunday.

nam as printed in the French magazine L'Express becomes almost winning in the presence of Oshima's short film.

●

In technique, the two are strikingly similar—commentaries on a series of stills—essentially hortary in the case of "Diary of a Yunbogi Boy," soberly instructive in the case of "Letter to Jane." And while the remarks of Godard and his political mentor, Jean-Pierre Gorin, range from outright foolishness to undeniably illuminating, especially where they deal with the photograph as a photograph, the voice-over commentary on "Yunbogi Boy" smacks of an inept pastiche of the late Jimmy Cannon.

"Letter to Jane" strives to raise consciousness through its analysis of the question, "What role should intellectuals play in revolution?" "Diary of a Yunbogi Boy" seeks to stroke the fires of rebellion with the lump in the throat that presumably arises in the presence of what is intended to be a touching study of an improverish Koran boy.

With all its drawbacks, looking at "Letter to Jane" after watching "Diary of a Yunbogi Boy" is almost like standing in the presence of a Rembrandt after being exposed to a one of those hollow-eyed Keane paintings.

LAWRENCE VAN GELDER

1974 Ap 12, 18:3

'Jackal ot ɪvahueltoro,' Strong Chilean Film

EL CHACAL DE NAHUELTORO (The Jackal of Nahueltoro), directed by Miguel Littin; Spanish with English subtitles; camera and photography, Hector Rios; music by Sergio Ortega. In the First Avenue Screening Room, at 61st Street, today at noon and midnight. Running time: 95 minutes. WITH Nelson Villagra, Shenda Roman, Marcelo Romo, Hector Noguera and Luis Alarcon.

When a murderer seems as vulnerable as his victims, that's proof of the film maker's talent. "The Jackal of Nahueltoro," written and directed by Miguel Littin of Chile, is a remarkable picture, based on a real case. It was made before the election of Salvador Allende Gossens; while he was president, Mr. Littin was the head of the state-owned film company. The movie, which was a vast success in Chile, is playing at the First Avenue Screening Room today.

●

The picture's strength springs from the extreme simplicity of the narrative, which was clearly designed for an audience of all classes. The acting style is plain, some of it close to pantomime; the plot, rather than the actors, is the star. A burly peasant kills a farm woman and her five children for no apparent reason. The one clue is the grinding poverty that both had always known—which serves as a reminder that the poor can turn on one another.

In jail, the illiterate murderer is educated, converted to Catholicism, taught to value life as he never did before—and then executed. It's the agonizing buildup to his death that gives this film its emotional and political depth. The director condemns institutions (the church and the state) rather than individuals, and the system that perpetuates poverty and ignorance is cited as the true killer. Throughout, a benevolent prison system appears just as cruel as its most brutal counterparts.

NORA SAYRE

1974 Ap 13, 18:1

Rebellious inmates in the prison yard at Attica, N.Y.

A Great Deal of Fun—But Is It Worth Doing?

By ALLEN McKEE

IF ONE were to arbitrarily smack a label on the sixties, the Age of Camp might not be appropriate from a cultural standpoint, for it was, after all, the sixties that brought us James Bond, Twiggy, Andy Warhol, and the war in Vietnam—each in its own way a kind of put-on, dreadful or sublime. By the end of the decade, movies at least seemed to have developed beyond Camp's cynical reign, an advisable progression since the artistic potential of the tease would appear to be rather small. Recently, however, anchored in the mire of the somber seventies, one has begun to notice a possible resurfacing of the old sixties put-on and nowhere is that resurfacing more evident than in the current movie version of "The Three Musketeers."

Director Richard Lester, whose films are like intricate toys, and screenwriter George MacDonald Fraser, who wrote the Flashman adventure books, have assembled one of the most peculiar casts in recent film history to recreate Alexandre Dumas' antiquated novel and the result is an extravagant kinetic marvel,

from the palace chandelier; it was film refined to a conceptual level—pure speed and motion, like a fabulous dance. (Indeed D'Artagnan in the 1948 "Musketeers" was none other than Gene Kelly.)

Lester's movie uses that tradition within a sophisticated context. The combat here is not clean and balletic. The swordsmen sweat and bleed and kick each other in the groin; and when this sort of realism is mixed with crude slapstick we can only respond to it as a tease: the absurdity eliminates our compassion for the victims but the blood is too authentic to allow us to laugh.

Lester has experimented with this kind of frivolous cruelty before but never so successfully as in "The Three Musketeers." It is a style which, like all Camp, deadens emotion and appeals directly to the intellect. One admires it for its cleverness—as in that delicious moment when Geraldine Chaplin's china-doll Queen rides a merry-go-round propelled by servants and cries out gaily, "Oh make them go faster! Whip them or something!"

The cast, as previously mentioned, is bizarrely varied, and that, I think, provides the key to Richard Lester's approach. In addition to Miss Chaplin there are four young actors, Oliver Reed as Athos, Richard Chamberlain as Aramis, Michael York as D'Artagnan, and Simon Ward as the Duke of Buckingham; character actor Frank Finlay as Porthos; spectacle veteran Charlton Heston as Cardinal Richelieu; American belle Faye Dunaway as Milady De Winter; British "goon" comic Spike Milligan as the Innkeeper; horror film specialist Christopher Lee as Rochefort; and that perpetual starlet Raquel Welch as the Queen's confidant. The various styles of acting (and non-acting) represented by this irregular bunch would be sufficient to reduce an average film to chaos, but Lester's trick is to neutralize them all by turning them into cartoon characters.

Action here is everything, and the performers are scarcely called upon to give of their talents; Lester needs only their bodies. Between duels, everyone stands around with arched eyebrows looking confident and casual, and that is quite sufficient. When Raquel Welch's

name appeared in the opening credits, the San Francisco audience with which I saw the film began to hiss, but by her climactic battle with Faye Dunaway for the Queen's diamond studs, she was being cheered—an indication perhaps of Lester's success in divesting his performers of virtually everything but their physical presence.

If "The Three Musketeers" succeeds on its own terms as self-satirizing Camp, one must nonetheless raise the question as to whether or not it is worth doing at all. Do we really want to see a filmmaker of Richard Lester's stature remain artistically embalmed by a style that developed in response to the lies and lunacy of the late sixties and that now seems almost as smug and outdated as the hypocrisies which made it necessary?

The nature of Camp is such that it is esthetically unassailable, for to criticize it at all one must take it more seriously than the people who created it. And that is precisely why I think Richard Lester should now move on to more fruitful forms of expression. It is time for him to take a chance on his talent and make himself vulnerable again. Ever

Faces from Richard Lester's new version of "The Three Musketeers": Richard Chamberlain, Raquel Welch, Michael York, Oliver Reed and Frank Finlay. "Let us hope

Lester's most intricate toy yet. With usual brutality and a self-indulgent reliance on Keystone Kops slapstick, this y, mannered movie—a certain disaster from the outset—somehow manages to come off. Just as one is about to dismiss as an unfortunate mistake, the whole ch mess shudders to life and, soulless it is, begins to charm us.

Movies are essentially a cannibal medium, consuming tradition at a mercis rate; and the fodder devoured by the Three Musketeers" is the swashckling adventure film of the thirties d forties. There was something marously virginal about those old vies: Errol Flynn racing sword-ind through an enemy castle, pursued countless villains, pausing briefly to l on the stairs, swinging to safety

llen McKee is a freelance writer.

since "A Funny Thing Happened on the Way to the Forum," Lester has armored his sensitivity in self-deprecating cynicism—like a cinematic Gore Vidal. And like Vidal, his talent and his intelligence have often been at odds, as if he feared too great an expression of feeling might compromise his sophistication. Lester has proven (in "A Hard Day's Night," "The Knack," and parts of "Petulia") that he can handle real characters with genuine emotions, and he has demonstrated in the rest of his films an uncommon talent for movie pyrotechnics. One hopes that in some future work the two gifts will be combined, for the result could be a masterpiece.

Finally, it must be said that "The Three Musketeers" is a great deal of fun (and one of the new recent films that children might also enjoy). When one has been wrestled to the ground and sat upon by movies like "Papillon" and "The Exorcist," it is pleasant to encounter something so splendidly inconsequential. Those flashing swords and daggers scorch the sludge out of our veins—one emerges from the theater with a fierce desire to scale the nearest parapet.

But it is still just a put-on, and there are too few directors of Richard Lester's caliber around to justify this kind of artistic slumming. Let us hope that "The Three Musketeers" is Lester's raucous farewell to Camp.

1974 Ap 14, II:13:1

Texas Farm Woman Not True to Type

By VINCENT CANBY

"Molly always stood where you left her, as long as she could see you," says Gid, one of the three narrators of "Lovin' Molly," which opened yesterday at the 68th Street Theater. That's the sort of thing you or I might say about a well-trained, apartment-bound Labrador retriever, one that wags its tail at the sight of a leash and stays the proper distance when told to heel.

But Gid is not talking about a brain-washed dog. He's talking about Molly Taylor (Blythe Danner), the independent, headstrong Texas farm woman who, in the course of the 40 years covered by "Lovin' Molly," is so overflowing with love she can give herself equally to Gid (Anthony Perkins), an uptight farmer, and Gid's best friend Johnny (Beau Bridges), a footloose cowboy, without anyone feeling even a mite peeved or jealous.

Molly is one of those great, life-affirming fictional characters that you may or may not be able to believe. I can't, any more than I can believe most of this movie. I'm not sure whether it's because of the performances, the direction by Sidney Lumet, a born-and-bred city fellow, or some of the nonsense the characters have

The Cast

LOVIN' MOLLY, directed by Sidney Lumet; screenplay by Stephen Friedman, based on the novel, "Leaving Cheyenne," by Larry McMurtry; produced by Mr. Friedman; director of photography, Edward Brown; editor, Joanne Burke; music, Fred Hellerman; distributed by Columbia Pictures. Running time: 98 minutes. At the 68th Street Playhouse, at Third Avenue. This film has been rated R.
Gid	Anthony Perkins
Johnny	Beau Bridges
Molly	Blythe Danner
Mr. Fry	Edward Binns
Sarah	Susan Sarandon
Eddie	Conrad Fowkes
Mr. Taylor	Claude Traverse
Mr. Grinsom	John Henry Faulk

been given to say in Stephen Friedman's screenplay, adapted from Larry McMurtry's novel "Leaving Cheyenne."

Much, I suspect, has to do with the screenplay, which comes across just as rural phony as the apostrophe in the new title. Molly, sitting on her porch at evening, is likely to reminisce about her various lovers: "My menfolk began rising with the moon."

This is definitely not meant to be funny. A kind of patronizing poetry has been imposed upon her. In an earlier scene she has been so overwhelmed by the miracle of birth that she has kissed a new-born calf, afterbirth and all—exactly the sort of gesture that would make any real-life, no-nonsense farm woman roar with unkind laughter.

There also seems to be a real problem in the film's continuity. Important motivations have either been left on the cutting room floor or perhaps they were never shot. This puts a further burden on the credibility of the

three leading performers, who also must overcome some of the worst make-up ever seen in a first-class movie.

As Beau Bridges gets older, his eyebrows simply become thicker until, as an old man, they look like Groucho Marx's. As Blythe Danner ages, she turns increasingly pale and appears to chop off her gray hair with sheep shears. Anthony Perkins, who doesn't look like the young man in his early 20's he is supposed to be at the beginning, returns to his "Friendly Persuasion" mannerisms. He acts mostly with his jawbone as the young Gid, then ages in the stiff-faced manner of a person who's had too many facelifts.

Undermining the film, however, is a more important fault of San Andreas dimensions: Who loves whom and why? Ménages à trois are difficult propositions, in fiction as well as life, unless you can believe in the heightened sensitivities of the participants. Truffaut managed it successfully in "Jules and Jim" through a soaring lyricism of style and by having the extraordinary Jeanne Moreau at the mysterious center.

•

Miss Danner is attractive in short takes but lacks the dynamism that could have given the film a focal point. It is so literally staged and acted that one begins to question the true psychological relationship between the two men. Is Molly important to each of them as herself or, as a kind of sexual surrogate, for the other? The Molly of the novel possesses a splendid self-assurance and a will to self-determination that the movie talks about but never successfully demonstrates.

The backgrounds of "Lovin' Molly," which was filmed entirely in Texas, look right. In the foreground, however, are all those city-folk-actors playing make-believe.

1974 Ap 15, 41:1

The Cast

LOVE AND ANARCHY; written and directed by Lina Wertmuller; Italian with English subtitles; photographed by Giuseppe Rotunno; edited by Franco Fraticelli; music by Nino Rota; a Herbert R. Steinmann-Billy Baxter presentation distributed by Peppercorn-Wormser Film Enterprises, Inc. Running time: 108 minutes. At the Little Carnegie Theater, 146 West 57th Street. This film has been classified R.
Tunin	Giancarlo Giannini
Salome	Mariangela Melato
Tripolina	Lina Polito
Spatoletti	Eros Pagni
Mme. Aida	Pina Cei
Donna Carmela	Elena Fiore

Despite her Germanic name, Lina Wertmuller is one of Italy's rare distaff directorwriters, a biological distinction that has no bearing on the fact that "Love and Anarchy" is a solidly professional work. Her anti-Fascist drama about an abortive attempt on Mussolini's life in the nineteen-thirties, which opened at the Little Carnegie yesterday, is a mite

closer to love and lust than to anarchy. However, it is passionate and stirring in its hatred of oppression and its love of the indomitable battlers against tyranny.

Miss Wertmuller obviously is stressing that some of the anonymous masses did a good deal of the fighting and dying against dictatorship by concentrating on such disparate principal plotters as a confused, timorous country bumpkin and a pair of prostitutes in one of Rome's poshest bagnios.

But her vignettes grow in tension and meaning as she develops an awareness of the time, the place and her driven people in a succession of vigorous, coarse and violent scenes. Tunin, her callow hero, is simply a freckled, bearded young farmer, who has come to this bordello on vague instructions from an anarchist friend who has been murdered by Fascists. Salome, the blonde, outspoken queen of the establishment and his mentor, is—it turns out—a dedicated revolutionary who joined the oldest profession after her anarchist lover was slain.

Of course, there are complications. Our hero and Tripolina, another of Madame Aida's girls, fall in love. And, Spatoletti, one of Mussolini's rough enforcers who bears a surprising resemblance to Il Duce and is a regular patron of the "maison," also is on hand to mess up the plan. However, Miss Wertmuller and Giuseppe Rotunno, her cinematographer, manage to give these bare outlines substance and color that underline the irony and tragedy of unrequited sacrifice.

Perhaps there is more here for the voyeur than the historian. But the scenes inside the bordello that are reminiscent of Toulouse-Lautrec, as well as having explicit, four-letter dialogue, are vividly multidimensional. The physical aspects of Rome, its streets, squares, monuments and the green countryside also evoke the period and the the effects of the dictatorship.

As Salome, Mariangela Melato wears her blond, Jean Harlow coiffure to the manner born. But above all, she is an inflexible patriot who projects idealism as grossly and fervently as she purveys her charms. Giancarlo Giannini's portrayal of Tunin is a shaded stint ranging from the shy peasant—a tender, love-smitten swain—to the man driven to a fatally violent act in a cause he has failed. Lina Polito is pitiably real as the pretty, anguished, brunette Tripolina, whose unwittingly selfish love helps push him toward self-destruction. And, Eros Pagni is properly vicious as the bullying Spatoletti.

"Love and Anarchy" may be slightly biased in its view of Fascist Italy, but Miss Wertmuller has illustrated it

with enough power and style to make it memorable and often moving.

A. H. WEILER

1974 Ap 15, 41:1

ZATOICHI'S CONSPIRACY, directed by Kimiyoshi Yasuda; story (Japanese with English subtitles) by Kan Shimozawa; photography, Shozo Honda; music, Akira Ifukube; produced by Shintaro Katsu and Nishioica Kozen; released by Toho International. At the Regency Theater, Broadway between 67th and 68th Streets. Running time: 90 minutes. This film has not been classified at this time.
Zatoichi	Shintaro Katsu
Shinbei	Eiji Okada
Bailiff	Kei Sato
Sakubel	Takashi Shimura
Omiyo	Yukie Toake

The Japanese film festival, having promised good things old and new, got off with a combination of both yesterday with "Zatoichi's Conspiracy" at the Regency Theater. The program notes that this period adventure feature is the latest (1973) of more than a score starring the titular blind swordsman. And, if his newest exploits are strongly reminiscent of a few others seen here, such as "Zatoichi's Sword Cane" (1971), they are never short on action or goodwill.

It would be virtually unlawful to criticize the stocky, unkempt, crew-cut itinerant do-gooder. As a period oriental Galahad, who masquerades as a masseur, he has his heart and blade in the right place at the right time and always in a good cause.

This time he has wandered back to his home town after a long absence only to run into a boyhood friend, who has turned into a racketeer and is about to take the peasants' rice and their stone quarry.

Ichi, as he is known to his intimates, may be sightless but he is far from powerless. He takes on the villainous magistrate, his larcenous friend, gamblers and their pug-uglies with the amazing ease of a man endowed with superhuman hearing and the ability to singlehandedly dispatch dozens of adversaries in the bloody, climactic fight to the death.

Zatoichi, as portrayed by Shintaro Katsu—who has played the role previously and who also happens to be co-producer of this freeswinging saga—is an amiable, tough but compassionate type who also adores Yukie Taoke, the pretty peasant maid, and saves her from a fate worse than death at the hands of Eiji Okada, his dastardly boyhood pal.

"Zatoichi's Conspiracy" follows what obviously is a successful pattern. Our hero is a gentle, if powerfully endowed, man who deserves to win, and does, against obvious villains. As usual, he wanders into the sunset at the film's finish, indicating there might be another Zatoichi adventure coming up that could be as unbelievable and as fairly diverting as this one. A. H. WEILER.

1974 Ap 16, 44:1

Film: 'Blues Like Showers of Rain'

30-Minute Movie Is on Program at Whitney

A marvelously indigenous short movie combining photographs of underprivileged Negro life in the Depression-era Deep South, reminiscences by blues singers and blues songs is the highlight of the new program at the Whitney Museum of American Art.

The simple power and heartbreaking authenticity of this 30-minute film make it tower as the centerpiece of the museum program, which opened yesterday and continues through April 24. Titled "Blues Like Showers of Rain," the film was assembled by John Jeremy from field recordings and photographs collected and made by Paul Oliver in 1960. Musically and sociologically, the result is truly memorable.

The other film segments are more loosely and superficially evocative of the program's title, "The South."

The candid, cheerful "A Tour Through the Brooks Home," a spacious old-age haven, happens to be set in the Southwest—in Sun City, Arizona. Rhody Streeter and Tony Ganz directed. The homespun musings and vigorous fiddling of North Carolina natives in "Red, White and Bluegrass," directed by Elliott Erwitt, look and sound refreshingly real, in remote contrast to the million-dollar "country music" bonanza emanating from Nashville.

Southern Theme Also Marks Other Works

Richard Leacock's "Queen of Apollo" entertainingly eavesdrops on home preparations for a Mardi Gras ball in New Orleans. John Preble's "Cotton Rise," reprising an unlabeled old "educational" documentary made by a vehement racist, is almost laughable — almost. "Panola," by Ed Pincus and David Neuman, is a cinéma-vérité study of a deranged black handyman in Natchez that is often unintelligible, more often disturbing.

HOWARD THOMPSON

1974 Ap 16, 44:1

A Haunting 'Conversation'

By VINCENT CANBY

HAVE you considered the possibility that everything that's ever been said in this world might still be echoing somewhere, maybe rattling around within the interior of a stone, a tree trunk or at the bottom of the sea? Though becoming increasingly faint, the sounds shall never disappear entirely and one day, perhaps, there will be equipment sensitive enough to retrieve and record mankind's oral history. In 24 abridged volumes it would make a perfect introductory offer to a book club. Or even a book club all of its own.

In the meantime our technicians have developed eavesdropping equipment of almost staggering complexity and efficiency, to be used not for historical purposes (as we all now know, only the cheap stuff is used for that) or even to satisfy curiosity about human nature. Rather it's more often used for personal and corporate gain, which sometimes means murder.

That's the idea behind Francis Ford Coppola's haunting and bothersome new film, "The Conversation," now at the Coronet. One of the lessons implicit in "The Conversation" is that private enterprise, as always, leads the way. Government breakthroughs, like break-ins, are usually a mistake.

*

The film is haunting because its suggestion that technology has gotten out of hand, though not exactly new, is so convincingly and fastidiously detailed. It's bothersome because Mr. Coppola, the writer as well as the director, has nearly succeeded in making a great film but has, instead, made one that is merely very good. Among its virtues is a superb performance by Gene Hackman in a role that comes very close to being the uptight Watergate era's equivalent of the mad doctors in old-fashioned Vincent Price films.

Harry Caul (Hackman) is pre-eminent in his field. His trade magazine is called "Security World" and sound is his universe. Harry Caul is an expert professional eavesdropper. He once placed a bug in a parakeet. When he is not planning and executing elaborate taps, mostly without wires, he returns to his bleak, furnished San Francisco apartment, which is protected by four locks on the front door as well as by a burglar alarm system, to relax by playing riffs on his saxophone to the accompaniment of records. Harry is a queer fish indeed. He is suspicious of everybody and everything. Rain or shine he always wears one of those transparent plastic raincoats, as if for prophylactic protection against society.

Harry is unmarried and probably incapable of marriage, though not of desperate, anonymous sex. He keeps a sweet, none-too-bright girl in a small apartment that he visits when he can, turning the key in the lock slowly then pushing the door suddenly open, to mash anyone who might possibly be hiding behind it. A birthday present from his landlady, which she has somehow managed to put into his apartment without his knowledge, prompts a near-paranoid fit. If you're in the business of spying on other people, it's difficult to believe that other people are not spying on you. If you're in the business, it may also mean that the forbidden and the clandestine have an immense fascination for you.

This, however, Harry vehemently denies. He tells an associate, a young man who admits that Internal Revenue assignments always send him to sleep with boredom, that he isn't interested in human nature, nor does he have any curiosity about the people whose conversations he bugs. It's just a business, says Harry, yet Harry is riddled with guilts. When he goes to confession, he asks forgiveness for having swiped several newspapers from a blind dealer and for having taken the Lord's name in vain and pleasure in impure thoughts. He's also bothered by the suspicion that the current job he's working on may well be endangering the lives of the two young people whose conversations he has recorded during their lunchtime tryst in a busy San Francisco park. More of the story I cannot reveal.

Mr. Hackman is fascinating as this eccentric loner, and the character itself is thoroughly realized up to a point, when he becomes, if possible, *overly* realized. Harry isn't simply neurotic. He gives every indication of being psychotic, which lessens the impact of the story Mr. Coppola has written for him. Psychotics make unreliable heroes. No rules need apply to them. Then there are times when Mr. Coppola seems to have forgotten the sort of character he has created.

At a crucial point in the film he allows Harry, who is constantly on his guard with strangers, to invite a group of drunk, newly made friends back to his loft, where he keeps all of his extraordinary equipment and tapes. Because it's about the last thing in the world Harry would ever do, you begin to hear plot-devices bumping around just off-screen.

It could be that Mr. Coppola really wasn't aware how good a movie he was on the verge of making in "The Conversation." Perhaps he only wanted to make a better-than-average melodrama, which might explain some beautifully photographed but basically foolish dream sequences and hallucinations. Such devices, even in Hitchcock, are usually cop-outs of one sort or another, or such overly simplified Freud that they hardly bare scrutiny except as comic-strip psychiatry.

Everything about "The Conversation" prompts you to demand better than that. The nightmare situation that Harry finds himself in is both funny and compelling, and although I'm not much taken by the sort of "Blow-Up" ambiguity that Mr. Coppola eventually has recourse to, the movie leaves you wanting more, which is a nice change from all the other movies that send you groggily from the theater feeling as if you'd been force-fed on jelly beans.

The members of the supporting cast are almost as good as Mr. Hackman, particularly Allen Garfield as a surveillance expert from Detroit who bugged his first phone at the age of 12 and then went on to become famous in the trade as the man who told Chrysler that Cadillac was getting rid of its fins. America, America.

1974 Ap 21, II:11:1

'House on Chelouche Street,' From Israel

"The House on Chelouche Street," Israel's nominee for this year's Oscar as best foreign-language film, is a mostly gentle, sweet-natured movie about growing up poor but good in Tel Aviv in the summer just before the 1948 War of Independence. The film, which is classified PG, opened yesterday at the Columbia 2 Theater.

The movie's virtues are a kind of steadfast modesty, even in its melodramatic moments, and the precisely detailed performances, especially by Gila Almagor as a pretty, youngish widow and Ophir Shalhin as her 15-year-old son, who is the film's focal point.

Moshe Mizrahi, who was responsible for last year's "I Love You, Rosa," wrote and directed the film, which is in Hebrew with English subtitles. VINCENT CANBY.

1974 Ap 18, 51:1

ONCE AGAIN, THE WHITE LIBERAL TO THE RESCUE

By EUGENIA COLLIER

UNDOUBTEDLY "Conrack" is a cut above the black exploitation films that have recently befouled the screen and enriched the movie-makers. It is a serious attempt to deal with human relationships. It portrays genuine love between a fifth-grade class of black youngsters on Daufuskie Island, one of the Sea Islands off the South Carolina coast, and their young white Southern teacher — a teacher who shows his love by his untiring efforts to educate his

Eugenia Collier teaches black literature at the Community College of Baltimore.

'Conrack,' starring Jon Voight as a white liberal teacher, is a step up from the trash of 'Super Fly,' but ...

charges in life as well as in letters and eventually by sacrificing his job.

The pity of it all is that in spite of certain decided advantages — effective acting, excellent photography, and a bunch of appealing kids—the film nevertheless manages to be mediocre. Based on a true experience as described by Pat Conroy in his book, "The Water Is Wide," the film shows Conroy (the islanders call him "Conrack"), played by Jon Voight, bringing the light of Western culture through unorthodox teaching methods and mainly through the force of his own personality.

And herein, for me, lies the difficulty. Martin Ritt's film is not really about the Sea Islanders — it is about the young white liberal. We view the setting and the people only through his perspective, and in terms of what is omitted it is a narrow perspective indeed. And it is *his* humanity that we cheer, his magnanimity in giving of himself unto the lowly.

For once again, blacks are depicted as the Culturally Deprived, the helpless and hopeless, awaiting the beneficence of the enlightened and liberal white to lift them from their state of abysmal ignorance. This image is projected by the total absence of any hint of indigenous Sea Island culture. Actually, the Sea Islands have a very rich folk culture, fascinating to folklorists and to laymen who take the trouble to look.

But the young teacher apparently puts no value on this culture, and the film never shows it, not any of it. All we see is this beautiful blond teacher filling an apparent void with the symbols of white America. He teaches the children football, but we never see any of their own native games. He teaches them the names of wildflowers from their own environment — but didn't they have their own names for these familiar flowers? He teaches them classical music, but there is no

hint of any native music. He hangs a Picasso in the classroom, but there is never evidence of Sea Island folk art. In fact, there is no sign anywhere of any creativity among the Sea Island folk.

Or any efficiency among its educators. Five years of schooling have taught the children nothing, not even how to count. The principal, Mrs. Scott, played by Madge Sinclair, is an overbearing black woman, gratuitously harsh to the point of sadism, who calls the pupils "babies" and insists that they must be beaten into learning because that is the way "colored people" must be treated. Aunt Tom with Simon Legree's whip!

*

Nowhere is there a glimpse of the wisdom and strength which have enabled these blacks to survive. Nowhere is there any real humor — humor which is also a survival tool. Never does Conrack seek to understand *their* culture. He is there to "educate" them, to shed light on their darkness. He has taken on the White Man's Burden of bringing civilization to the uncivilized. The ending symbolizes the triumph of Western technology: The children gather at the pier to bid a last farewell to Conrack. Apparently lacking any way of their own to express deep emotion, they produce a record player and record, and Conrack exits to the strains of Beethoven's Fifth Symphony.

Somehow the image of blacks is distorted, is not quite real, and this lack of reality persists in the development of the characters. There are other glaring omissions which cost the film a great deal in believability. What has motivated this white Southerner—a confessed ex-bigot — to become so intensely devoted to his black charges? What accounts for Mrs. Scott's peculiarities? What forces have created the hermit Mad Billy, played by Paul Winfield, and why does he suddenly become Conrack's docile fishing buddy?

In these characters "Conrack" has a fine opportunity to reveal the complexities of human existence, to show what it is like to grow up in an isolated area, to exploit the conflicts and spiritual groping which would lead a person from bigotry to a more complete humanity. But the opportunity is flubbed, and instead of deep involvement with characters and, through them, a meaningful confrontation with ourselves, we are left with only an entertaining glance.

It is entirely possible that this is the way these people were perceived by the real Pat Conroy. But art is not history, and film is— or ought to be—art. The screenwriter is obligated to probe deeper than the surface reality, to answer questions (or at last raise them) about the human condition, to reveal the various dimensions of experience. In this respect, "Conrack" is lacking.

Because of this lack, the film misses an opportunity to make an important statement. Somehow, this film, like too many others, seems preoccupied with the amazing discovery that blacks are, in certain vital respects, human—a discovery which may excite white audiences, who may have had their doubts, but which is irritating to us blacks who have known all along that we were people. I had expected a powerful film, one which not only *recorded* a significant experience but which also (and more important) *interpreted* this experience in terms of deeply rooted human relationships. Instead, I found a mildly entertaining picture in which blacks are harmless and not angry, the white hero a savior, and our world not seriously disarranged.

Nevertheless, "Conrack" is, as I have said, a step up from the trash of the "Super Fly" and "Sweet Sweetback" ilk. Perhaps there is yet hope that someday audiences will demand not comfortable portrayals that reinforce ingrained prejudices but portrayals which show us reality and thus enable us to cope. "Conrack" is a step in that direction.

But a long and rocky road stretches ahead.

1974 Ap 21, II:1:1

CLAUDINE, directed by John Berry; screenplay by Lester and Tina Pine; produced by Hannah Weinstein; executive producer, J. Lloyd Grant; music, Curtis Mayfield; director of photography, Gayne Rescher; editor, Luis San Andres; a Third World Cinema production, in association with Joyce Selznick and Tina Pine, distributed by 20th Century-Fox. Running time: 94 minutes. At the De Mille Theater, Seventh Avenue at 47th Street, and the Fine Arts Theater, 58th Street near Lexington Avenue. This film has been rated PG.

Claudine	Diahann Carroll
Roop	James Earl Jones
Charles	Lawrence Hinton-Jacobs
Charlene	Tamu
Paul	David Kruger
Patrice	Yvette Curtis
Francis	Eric Jones
Lurlene	Socorro Stephens
Owen	Adam Wade
Miss Kabak	Elisa Loti

By VINCENT CANBY

Claudine (Diahann Carroll) has a number of problems, including a small Harlem apartment and six children, who are all that remain of two marriages and what the Welfare Department describes as two "consensual unions." Although she is on welfare, Claudine works clandestinely as a maid in the Riverdale section of the Bronx to give her kids something more than the bare necessities.

When Claudine falls in love with an exuberant, twice-married garbageman named Roop (James Earl Jones), matters become more complicated. Roop sees welfare as the ultimate indignity. Nothing short of castration. If he moves in with her, she can remain on welfare, but she must deduct everything he gives her. However, if he loses his job, he too must go on welfare whether he wants to or not. To top everything off, Roop is sued for the nonsupport of his own children and his salary is garnisheed.

•

"Claudine," the comedy that opened yesterday at the De Mille and Fine Arts Theaters, has its own problems, including a tendency toward cuteness and a form that recalls television's worst situation comedies. You know the ones — about resourceful moms, dumb dads and smart-talking kids who can burp on cue. The good news this morning is that "Claudine" manages to be very funny, in a couple of instances, triumphantly so.

The screenplay was writ-en by Tina and Lester Pine, who also wrote "Popi," which was quite awful except for Alan Arkin and some isolated wisecracks. Unlike "Popi," however, "Claudine" succeeds in being comic without denying the realities of ghetto life.

It softens them a bit, perhaps. Not through fraud, but through the presence of the two larger-than-life characters played marvelously by Miss Carroll and Mr. Jones. Claudine and Roop are comic romantics of the most honorable, appealing sort, people who have a firm grasp on everything but themselves.

Miss Carroll is an exceptionally beautiful woman, but the beauty of this performance is in the force of her toughness and wit. It's in the furies she directs at the idiocies of her children, at the 16-year-old daughter who becomes pregnant by Abdullah (né Timmy) and at the 18-year-old son who arranges his own vasectomy to make sure he won't pollute the country with babies.

Mr. Jones turns Roop into a gargantuan clown, which is not to be confused with buffoon. Roop thinks he means it when he explains his job on the garbage truck by saying that he has consciously avoided success because losers are more popular. He's a huge tangle of contradictions, wise, foolish, self-pitying, thoughtful. It's by far the best thing Mr. Jones has ever done in films.

Part of the reason for this success, I suspect, is the director, John Berry, who made films in Hollywood ("He Ran All the Way") before going to France in the nineteen-fifties, in the dark days of the Hollywood red scare. More recently, he has been directing Off Broadway, including "Boesman and Lena" with Mr. Jones. Though I would never mistake "Claudine" as anything but a film, it displays an attention to dramatic rhythm and to dialogue that is essentially theatrical.

Even the children are exceptionally good, especially a new actress named Tamu, playing the daughter who goes out one evening to learn how to meet people and hold her liquor and winds up first sick and, eventually, pregnant. Tamu has the kind of intensity touched with humor that one associates with the late Diana Sands.

"Claudine" is more than the sum of its performances, however. Two sequences are standouts. One, set in a welfare office, is simultaneously satiric and moving, because it is the first time that Claudine and Roop see themselves aligned against a common enemy, sinking into a marsh of red tape. I won't describe the last sequence in the film beyond noting that it achieves—and holds for not one second longer than it can be sustained—the level of true farce.

There are times when "Claudine" threatens to go as soft as a "Doris Day Show" rerun, when you are aware that some of its middle-class sensibilities don't quite fit. They seem borrowed from the white media. Then it recoups with the sort of line or gesture that makes this one of the few recent black films to reach beyond the black audience without, as far as I can tell, insulting it.

A word about the production auspices: "Claudine" is the first film to be made by a company called Third World Cinema, designed by its founders—Miss Sands, Ossie Davis, Mr. Jones, Rita Moreno and Hannah Weinstein, the producer—to make films, that not only give blacks, Puerto Ricans and other minorities substantial film-making roles but also improve the quality of the films thtmselves. "Claudine is a very happy debut performance.

1974 Ap 23, 34:3

30-Year-Late B Movie From M-G-M Opens

By VINCENT CANBY

"The Outfit," one of the last films to be produced during James Aubrey's administration at M-G-M, stands as an explanation of what happened to drive that once-great company from the ranks of the major studios.

"The Outfit" is not really a bad movie. It doesn't fail in an attempt to do something beyond its means. It doesn't attempt to do anything except pass the time, which simply isn't good enough when most of us have access to television. It's a B movie, made approximately 30 years too late for the market, about a nice, honorable, revenge-driven bank robber (Robert Duvall) who sets out to destroy the syndicate that murdered his brother.

Because the movie is about the ways and means by which that revenge is carried out, it contains a good deal of action in terms of gunfights and holdups, that sort of thing, and hardly anything to think about except, possibly, the members of the cast.

John Flynn, a director who has yet to distinguish himself, has reinforced the film's B-picture image by casting it with lots of players one associates with a more innocent time, if not directly with B pictures. Richard Jaeckel, Marie Windsor, Anita O'Day, Jane Greer and Elisha Cook, among others, turn up in roles so small you might miss them without a scorecard.

They're all good performers, as are the stars, Mr. Duvall, Joe Don Baker and the late Robert Ryan (in one of his last roles), but the film doesn't appreciate them by giving them anything to do.

"The Outfit" opened yesterday at the Trans-Lux West and other theaters. With its profanity bleeped out, it could be television fare tonight.

1974 Ap 25, 48:2

The Cast

THE OUTFIT, directed by John Flynn; screenplay by Mr. Flynn, based on a novel by Richard Stark; produced by Carter De Haven; music, Jerry Fielding; director of photography, Bruce Surtees; editor, Ralph E. Winters; an M-G-M film, distributed by United Artists. Running time: 103 minutes. At the Trans-Lux West Theater, Broadway at 49th Street, and other theaters. This film has been rated PG.

Macklin	Robert Duvall
Bett Harrow	Karen Black
Cody	Joe Don Baker
Mailer	Robert Ryan
Menner	Timothy Carey
Chemey	Richard Jaeckel
Buck's wife	Sheree North
Frank	Felice Orlandi
Madge Coyle	Marie Windsor

DREAMS AND NIGHTMARES, a documentary written and directed by Abe Osheroff; produced and edited by Larry Klingman; distributed by New Yorker Films. Running time: 60 minutes.

GREECE OF THE CHRISTIAN GREEKS, a documentary by Kostas Chronopoulos, Simon Louvish and Jorge Tsoucarossa; music by Mikis Theodorakis; a Contemporary Films production, distributed by Monument Film Corporation. Running time: 43 minutes. At the First Avenue Screening Room, near 61st Street. These films have not been rated.

By VINCENT CANBY

The latest in the First Avenue Screening Room's weekend programs of special films is a bill of two documentaries that are all content without luminating style. The films, which were shown Sunday, will be repeated today and tomorrow at noon and midnight.

Both films demand an appreciation of commitment, if not bias. "Dreams and Nightmares," the more moving of the two, is a 60-minute recollection of the Spanish Civil War by Abe Osheroff, a New York carpenter who, 36 years ago, served in the Lincoln Brigade. Last year Mr. Osheroff returned to Spain with a camera to see whether the sacrifices of his colleagues had been in vain.

•

"Dreams and Nightmares" is a montage of newsreel footage of Depression America and the Civil War itself, intercut with material shot by Mr. Osheroff in contemporary Spain. He is both sad that Francisco Franco managed to survive the World War defeat of his fascist allies in Germany and Italy, and alarmed at the role that America has played in that survival. The film is less interesting as a documentary than as a personal document by a very rare breed of man, a youthful idealist who managed to keep his ideals intact into age.

"Greece of Christian Greeks" is a 43-minute indictment of the continued exploitation of the Greek people by state, church, and foreign governments. The film is never much more than an inventory of injustices. The subject deserves better.

1974 Ap 26, 30:1

Something Sour

By STEPHEN FARBER

HOPING to cultivate an American New Wave, critics have recently given considerable attention to several young directors, including George Lucas ("American Graffiti"), Martin Scorsese ("Mean Streets"), Ralph Bakshi ("Heavy Traffic") and John Hancock ("Bang the Drum Slowly"). Two more names can now be added to the list of contenders: Steven Spielberg, the 26-year-old director of "The Sugarland Express," and Terrence Malick, the 29-year-old director of "Badlands." A comparison is tempting because both movies are drawn from true crime stories about young lovers on the lam; but they represent opposite approaches to filmmaking.

*

"The Sugarland Express" is a prime example of the new-style factory movie: slick, cynical, mechanical, empty. Spielberg and his young writers, Hal Barwood and Matthew Robbins, have been weaned on old Hollywood movies, and they want to recreate the schlock that once mesmerized the masses. They have good memories, and a shrewd commercial instinct that the industry often confuses with talent.

Although "The Sugarland Express" is based on a real incident that happened in Texas in 1969, it seems perfectly synthetic — pure Hollywood —from first frame to last. At the beginning Lou Jean Poplin (Goldie Hawn) persuades her husband to break out of prison so that they can retrieve their baby from a foster home. They take a young patrolman hostage, and most of the Texas police force pursues them on their drive across the state, while ordinary folks line the roads to cheer them on; Lou Jean and Clovis (William Atherton) become miniature folk heroes before they meet their predictably tragic end.

It isn't hard to pick out the tattered pieces of "Bonnie and Clyde," "The Getaway," "Roxie Hart," "Ace in the Hole," and the larger chunks of a little-seen 1971 film, "Vanishing Point."

However, the derivative nature of the script is less offensive than the filmmakers' manipulative technique. Everything is underlined; Spielberg sacrifices narrative logic and character consistency for quick thrills and easy laughs. He has a very crude sense of humor, indicated by his obsession with toilet jokes, and an irrepressible maudlin streak. Early on Spielberg lingers over a shot of the couple's baby playing with a dog, and after the final tragedy, he moves in for a close-up as a police car drives over a discarded teddy bear. It's depressing to see a

Stephen Farber is a freelance writer.

William Atherton and Goldie Hawn hold Michael Sacks hostage in "Sugarland Express"
"The new-style factory movie: slick, cynical and empty"

young director who is already so shameless.

This kind of movie is like a shifty campaign speech designed to please every segment of the public. Young moviegoers can weep for Lou Jean and Clovis as rebels against the system, cut down by the authorities because they love their baby. At the same time, Spielberg cunningly softens his portrait of the police so as not to alienate the Law and Order crowd. The police captain played by Ben Johnson is presented as a wise, decent, humane man; in one of the most implausible scenes, he angrily wrecks the car of some rightwing vigilantes who have joined the manhunt. "The Sugarland Express" is a "social statement" whose only commitment is to the box office.

Interestingly, the real villain of the story is Lou Jean. In Hollywood mythology the woman usually is the source of evil. Lou Jean is directly responsible for her husband's death—at the climax she forces him out of the car into a police ambush. But she survives, and an "ironic" end title tells us that she got her baby back after serving only 15 months in prison. Maybe that is what really happened, but the filmmakers take unnatural pleasure in demeaning Lou Jean. The cheapest laughs are always at her expense: she clutches her gold stamps even during a shootout, takes time to put curlers in her hair, and has to order a portable toilet because she can't control her bladder.

Toward the end the movie turns into another tired celebration of male camaraderie. Clovis and patrolman Slide (Michael Sacks) are striking up a beautiful friendship that the dumb bitch-wife de-

stroys. In its misogyny "The Sugarland Express" echoes a whole series of popular American movies, but this is one element in the film that may not have been consciously calculated to sell. The amusing thing is that even these filmmakers' unconscious prejudices are not their own; their souls belong to Hollywood.

Spielberg is admittedly a skillful (if vulgar) technician, and he understands how to engineer car chases and crashes; but he doesn't have an original idea or the slightest feeling for people. A good way to test a young director is to look at his handling of actors; Spielberg fails that test miserably. Under his direction even the nonprofessionals act like Hollywood hams, and Goldie Hawn pulls all the stops out in some hysterical screaming scenes that are embarrassingly amateurish.

*

Could this be the movie that Pauline Kael called "one of the most phenomenal debut films in the history of movies"? Kael and some other gullible critics have probably been intimidated by Spielberg's youth, and by his technical facility. Don't they know that hundreds of student filmmakers all over the country could turn out an equally proficient hack job? These young film freaks have often been handling cameras since the age of three, and they know everything there is to know about lenses, filters, color stock, and solarization. Unfortunately, they are ignorant of everything else. They haven't had time to read a book; they are technical wizards with pea-sized brains. Maybe Spielberg will

develop and do better work; it is possible that he was constrained by the producers or the studio. But so far there is no evidence of a talent struggling to break free.

Among young directors technical facility can almost be taken for granted; the astonishing thing is to find the intelligence and originality of Terrence Malick's riveting first feature, "Badlands." Some critics have attacked Malick for his coldness, and it is true that, unlike Spielberg, he doesn't pander to the audience by giving his hick characters cute, "human" touches that will make them lovable. A fictionalized account of the killing spree of Charles Starkweather and Caril Ann Fugate in the late fifties, "Badlands" is a harshly sardonic film; Malick wants to expose the emotional numbness of his young outlaw lovers, and the influence of the media on their stunted lives. Although set in the past, "Badlands" says a great deal about the passivity of Americans in the seventies, the enervation of a movie-gorged generation that can only experience life secondhand.

Kit, who looks like James Dean, and Holly, his baton-twirling nymphet, daydream in the images marketed by trashy movies and pop ballads; Holly even narrates the film in the gaudy, swollen style of True Confessions or Modern Screen. They are so completely immersed in an imaginary kingdom that reality no longer touches them. Even murder has no impact; the blood looks too much like catsup. Malick observes the terrifying effects of their kitsch fan-

tasies, but he is not simply contemptuous of his young zombie lovers. A closer look at the film reveals a complexity in his attitude, a trace of affection for the twisted Hollywood dreams that impel Holly and Kit. Pulp romance offers them their only hint of extraordinary possibilities. In chronicling their crazy macabre courtship, Malick enriches the film with flashes of lyricism —when Kit sends up a giant red balloon with a testament to their undying love, or when they stop their car in the wilderness and get out to dance to Nat King Cole's "A Blossom Fell" in the glare of the headlights. These beautiful, ridiculously extravagant gestures represent the characters' futile, desperate search for an alternative to the drabness of American smalltown life.

A feeling of melancholy suffuses the film. Holly will never again have the luxury to imagine an exotic, mysterious future for herself. Driving toward Montana, she sees the lights of Cheyenne in the distance, and longs to return to the safe anonymity of the herd. Although her romantic illusions are banal, we cannot help feeling a poi-

gnant sense of loss when she decides to settle down to a perfectly regimented domestic nightmare; we know that her life is over.

"Badlands" contains a subtle mixture of moods, from horror to black comedy to elegiac sadness. Malick will be an even better director when he can be more open to surprises of character that might complicate his theories of human behavior. But he already has the intellectual discipline that most American directors could use. He also has a remarkable gift for dialogue, a striking eye for composition, and a fine control of actors; Martin Sheen and Sissy Spacek give beautifully detailed performances. Most important, he has an intense personal vision that gives his work direction and purpose.

Malick, like Spielberg, obviously grew up under the influence of pop culture. The difference is that Malick is trying to break the spell of those B-movie dreams; "Badlands" is a bitter ironic commentary on Hollywood myths, while "The Sugarland Express" only perpetuates the old lies.

1974 Ap 28, II:11:1

Kurosawa's '43 'Sanshiro Sugata' Opens

Glimpses of his subsequent greatness are plain to see in Akira Kurosawa's 1943 movie, "Sanshiro Sugata," his first directorial stint.

In its American premiere, the import opened yesterday and runs through tomorrow in the Japanese "Cinema East" festival at the Regency Theater. The picture has the bold freshness of imagery and cinematic flow that led to Mr. Kurosawa's "Rashomon," the 1952 work that did so much to put him and the Japanese film industry on the international movie map.

●

A festival foreword to this carefully edited version states that part of the negative (about 20 minutes) of the original underwent a state ordered wartime scrapping. Deletions are obvious especially toward the end. But genius — Mr. Kurosawa's— will out, and the film we see remains fascinating.

The 80-minute drama, adapted by the director from Tsuneo Tomita's popular novel and set in the eighteen-

eighties, traces a youth's development into manhood and mastery of judo during a competitive transition of the country's traditional martial art from jujitsu. The exact technical difference is never pinpointed, even with the two fiercely rival factions matching their champions in exciting, highly ritualistic bouts, staged with full pomp and ceremony.

By the time the stalwart young hero, Susumu Fujita, is forced to combat the brave old father of the girl he loves, Mr. Kurosawa's drama has taken on strong, human overtones. And this is topped by a stunning graphic fight in a field, to whistling wind and scudding, shadowy clouds overhead. Here the inimitable Mr. Kurosawa really goes to town.

His players are excellent, starting with the open-faced Mr. Fujita, and with Denjiro Okochi, Yoshio Kosugi and the piquant Yukiko Todoroki.
HOWARD THOMPSON

1974 Ap 29, 49:1

Short-Subject Colors Spark Forum Show

The idea that artists and creativity are synonomous is only partly illustrated by "Films by Artists," the collection of six short subjects that opened last week at the

Film Forum. The five artists involved are obviously sincere in attempting to fuse avant-garde visions with the movie medium but only two appear to have succeeded with ideas that are visually arresting.

The most striking of the entries are Charles Ross's 25-minute "Sunlight Dispersion"

The Program

FILMS BY ARTISTS: HAND CATCHING LEAD by Richard Serra, 4 minutes; WISCONSIN by Robert Morris, 15 minutes; SONG DELAY by Joan Jonas, 18 minutes; ART MAKEUP: BLACK by Bruce Nauman, 11 minutes; SUNLIGHT DISPERSION, 25 minutes and ECLIPSE, 8 minutes by Charles Ross. At the Film Forum, 256 West 88th Street. Thursday to May 5, 8 P.M.

and the 8-minute "Eclipse." He has combined scientific filming technology with a truly artistic appreciation of colors in "Sunlight Dispersion" in a professional, sensitive recording of nature's own, prismatic changes of hues on such homely objects as a cup, a chair, a room and a hand. On the other hand, "Eclipse" is, quite naturally, what its title implies: a moment in time that is also an extraordinary happening.

Robert Morris's "Wisconsin" melds groups of people in various geometric patterns, moving about, running or emerging from clouds of vapor against an autumnal country background that also makes for imaginative, pictorial, black-and-white effects.

Joan Jones's "Song Delay," filmed by Robert Fiore, is over-ambitious in offering a profusion of such disparate scenes as stylized dancers, a steamer passing by in the background, people talking at random and snippets of songs seemingly unrelated to these varied actions.

There is a vague impression of sculpture in the making in Bruce Nauman's "Art Makeup: Black" as the camera focuses solely on the artist transforming his white torso into a bronzelike figure. But this, like Richard Serra's "Hand Catching Lead," which is simply a succession of literal shots of an arm and hand snatching at dropped objects, are largely repetitious exercises that project little that is memorable.

If most of the artists here do not succeed as polished film makers they all prove, if only experimentally, their appreciation of filming as an expressive art form.

A. H. WEILER

1974 Ap 29, 49:1

The Cast

THE SPIKES GANG, directed by Richard Fleischer; screenplay by Irving Ravetch and Harriet Frank Jr., based on a novel by Giles Tippette; produced by Walter Mirisch; music, Fred Karlin, film editors, Ralph Winters and Frank J. Urioste; director of photography, Brian West; a Mirisch Corporation production distributed by United Artists. Running time: 96 minutes. At the Trans-Lux West Theater, Broadway at 49th Street, and other theaters. This film has been rated PG.

Harry Spikes....Lee Marvin
Will Young....Gary Grimes
Les Richter....Ron Howard
Tod Mayhew....Charlie Martin Smith
Kid White....Arthur Hunnicutt
Jack Basset....Noah Beery

By VINCENT CANBY

"The Spikes Gang," which opened yesterday at the Trans-Lux West and other theaters, is a Western about an elderly desperado and the three young farm boys he tries, unsuccessfully, to turn into bank robbers.

It's a movie without a center, with no coherent tone, directed by Richard Fleischer, fresh from such triumphs as "The Don Is Dead" and "Soylent Green." Mr. Fleischer is incapable of sustaining even minimal audience interest in the material. During something as basic as a chase one's mind is likely to notice the cloud coverings.

The screenplay by Irving Ravetch and Harriet Frank Jr. is no help. It's nominally based on a novel by thors don't hesitate to lift a thors don't hestitate to lift a line ("Money is like manure. . . .") most recently used in "Hello, Dolly."

The film stars Lee Marvin, as the old desperado, and Gary Grimes, Ron Howard and Charlie Martin Smith, as the boys, but none are of particular help, either. The entire enterprise is as convincing as the Spanish landscapes, which are meant to suggest the American Southwest but don't.

1974 My 2, 61:4

The Cast

THE LORDS OF FLATBUSH, directed by Stephen F. Verona and Martin Davidson; screenplay by Mr. Verona and Gayle Gleckler; photographed by Joseph Mangine; edited by Stan Siegel and Muffie Meyer; music, Joe Brooks; produced by Mr. Verona; released by Columbia Pictures. At the Baronet Theater, 59th Street at Third Avenue and Kenmore Theater, Brooklyn. Running time: 88 minutes. This film is classified PG.

Chico Tyrell....Perry King
Stanley Rosiello....Sylvester Stallone
Butchey Weinstein....Henry Winkler
Wimpy Murgalo....Paul Mace
Jane Bradshaw....Susie Blakely
Frannie Malincanico....Maria Smith
Annie Yuckamenelli....Renee Paris
Crazy Cohen....Paul Jabara

"Grow up, you're so immature," the tearful truth flung by an anguished, pretty teen-ager at the class Adonis on the make, seems fitting for "The Lords of Flatbush," which arrived yesterday at the Baronet and Brooklyn's Kenmore theaters. Like first love, this study of the growing pains of the leather jacket-bobby soxer Brooklyn high school set of 1957 is, by turns, cheerful, confused, juvenile and never fully realized.

Reportedly the first effort of its directors, Stephen F. Verona and Martin Davidson, who filmed on Brooklyn locations, this largely lighthearted remembrance of the past concentrates more on incidents than fuller explanations. If the incidents project some bittersweet emotions, the character and goals of its carefree, fumbling principals remain, for the most part, dated and indistinct.

As the rough but happy-go-lucky quartet, the "Lords" make school a blackboard jungle and spend most of their time on sex drives, a casual car heist, a quick rumble, in pool rooms or in goofing off in a local candy store gulping egg creams.

Handsome Chico, a proud owner of a motorcycle, is, for example, frustrated by an unrequited affair with Jane, the blond daughter of an Army colonel who finds his passionate advances immature. On the other hand, Stanley, the muscular, inarticulate pigeon fancier, is partly conned into marriage by the anxious Frannie, whom he has bedded down more than once on a local beach. And Butchey and Wimpy are content to go along, somewhat aimlessly, with the club's "social and athletic" activities.

•

Perry King, Sylvester Stallone, Henry Winkler, Paul Mace, Susie Blakely, Maria Smith and Renée Paris (as Frannie's scheming friend) are fairly believable in the leading roles even though they seem to be out of place in the clean, tree-lined streets and comfortable homes of Flatbush.

Individual scenes and indigenous humor touch the heart and tickle the funny bone in this obviously tender reminiscence. But in the end, "The Lords of Flatbush" fades from memory like the summer of 1957. A. H. WEILER

1974 My 2, 61:5

BADDEST DADDY IN THE WHOLE WORLD, a documentary by Fred Haines, 52 minutes; CHISHOLM: PURSUING THE DREAM, a documentary by Robert Denby and Tom Werner, 52 minutes. At the Whitney Museum of American Art, Madison Avenue and 75th Street, through Wednesday.

Pugilistically, Muhammad Ali and Shirley Chisholm constitute a mismatch. But on film at least, the contender for the heavyweight boxing championship of the world and the contender for the Presidency of the United States in 1972 make anything but an odd couple.

Intriguing is the word for their pairing in the documentary double bill—"The Baddest Daddy in the Whole World" by Fred Haines and "Chisholm: Pursuing the Dream" by Robert Denby and Tom Werner—that opened yesterday in the New American Filmmakers Series at the Whitney Museum of American Art.

•

Stylistically, neither film breaks new ground. What fascinates ultimately is the recognition of unsuspected similarities in the two campaigners and the question of the extent to which each might have turned the presence of the camera to his own ends.

At the outset of "The Baddest Daddy," constructed around Ali's seven-round knockout of Jürgen Blin of Germany in Zurich, Switzerland, on the day after Christmas, 1971, a voice emerging from a crush of press at the airport asks, "Why did you come to Switzerland?" And Ali replies, "To box."

At the end, as he and his entourage speed out of town, there is no reason to think otherwise. Save for one warm scene of Ali and his daughter at breakfast, there is no reason to suppose that the answer might have been "To reveal myself fully to this camera."

While Ali likes to give the impression of being unaware of the camera, a pretense in which the film maker serves as willing accomplice, Mrs. Chisholm is allowed to relate directly to it as it covers her Presidential campaign. The difference, insofar as it succeeds in persuading that either of these two immensely fascinating and complex individuals has been lulled into surrendering the core of his truth to its eye, is negligible.

•

What remains are the similarities of their lives—the pride, the goals, the hardships, the disappointments, the unpopularity, the lingering pain of defeat, the fatigue, the demands, the necessity to cultivate the masses of people, the understanding that it rests with children to realize much of what they and other blacks hope for.

"In order to bring about change, what one doesn't have to go through."

Mrs. Chisholm says it. The accomplishment of these films lies in the realization that Ali might have said it, too.

LAWRENCE VAN GELDER

1974 My 3, 47:1

'Trail of Blood'

Yoshiro Harada's strong, brooding performance as a reformed derelict in Old Japan who is goaded into his murderous, sword-swinging specialty gives strength to "Trail of Blood," part one, which opened yesterday and plays through Saturday (with Kurosawa's "Sanjuro") in the Regency Theater's Cinema East festival of Japanese films. Part two will follow late this month.

As an action melodrama, with a feasible story line and the sensitive force of Mr. Harada's acting, the film is a well-made one. Its director, listed in the credits only as Ikehiro, uses color effectively, paces his story intelligently and opens up periodically with some vivid massacre sequences. This is one of those chop-chop exercises of flying kimonos, whistling blades and perpetual skewering. Bodies fall likes leaves. Oozing gore, the film is perfectly titled.

•

The film's most curious aspect for a story set in medieval times, is its ripely Occidental musical score. Ranging from ominous to plain jivey, it suggests the soundtrack of one of those Italian westerns that produced Clint Eastwood. Updated and with guns substituted for swords, the picture indeed could be a western from anywhere.

It also, again, happens to be well done, thanks principally to its director and to the acting of Mr. Harada. Part two will be welcome.

HOWARD THOMPSON

1974 My 3, 47:1

LE PETIT THEATRE DE JEAN RENOIR (The Little Theater of Jean Renoir), produced, directed and narrated by Jean Renoir; screenplay (French with English subtitles) by Renoir; editor, Genevieve Winding; director of photography, Georges Leclerc; produced for French television by Son et Lumiere and the Jean Renoir Company; distributed by Phoenix Films. Running time: 100 minutes. At the First Avenue Screening Room, near 61st Street. This film has not been rated.

The Last Christmas Dinner

Le Clochard....Nino Formicola
La Clochard....Milly
Gontran....Roland Bertin
Le Gerant....Andre Dumas

The Electric Waxer

Emilie....Marguerite Cassan
Gustave....Pierre Olaf
Jules....Jacques Dynam

La Belle Epoque

Singer....Jeanne Moreau

Le Roi d'Yvetot

Duvallier....Fernand Sardou
Isabelle....Francoise Arnoul
Ferand....Jean Carmet
Blanc....Andrex
Paulette....Dominique Labourier

By VINCENT CANBY

It has taken almost five years for Jean Renoir's marvelous "Le Petit Théâtre de Jean Renoir" ("The Little Theater of Jean Renoir") to obtain a commercial release in New York, and now that it is here, I trust it will be around for a long, long time. It will be shown at the First Avenue Screening Room today and tomorrow at noon and midnight and then open a regular engagement there next Thursday.

"Le Petit Théâtre" is as much a cause for celebration as an act of it, by one of the greatest of all film directors, who will mark his 80th birthday this September. It is precise, witty, and luminous, and it stands just a little apart from time in the way of a work by an artist whose career spans the better part of a century.

•

"Le Petit Théâtre" was originally commissioned for French television. It is composed of three short comedies plus an outrageously funny, between-the-acts performance by Jeanne Moreau as a beautiful, dead-pan, turn-of-the-century Parisian music-hall singer who, like Zola's Nana, takes her talent a lot more seriously than her audiences may be able to.

The director himself, the Octave in "Rules of the Game," now older and in his own character as master of illusion, introduces the acts on screen, standing over one of those miniature theaters that any child would give up a month of Saturdays to own.

Marguerite Cassan as the widow in "The Electric Waxer," one of the three short comedies that make up "Le Petit Théâtre de Jean Renoir."

As Renoir gives credit to his "collaborator" on the first sketch (Hans Christian Andersen), the camera moves away from him over the tiny footlights into the "real" world of the theater. Back and forth we go until, at last, in the concluding sequence, the players, at a critical moment, release us from our commitments to them by turning toward the camera to bow from the apron of Jean Renoir's little theater.

The moment is both playful and exceptionally moving because, like so many other moments within the film, it recalls Renoir's blessed preoccupation with performance, with theater, as a means of getting a fix on life, if only for a little while.

The opening sequence, "The Last Christmas Dinner," is another adaptation —or variation really—of the Andersen story from which Renoir made "La Petite Marchande d'Allumettes" in 1928. It's about two ancient panhandlers, an old man and an old woman (in place of the match girl), and their last Christmas eve on the bank of the Seine, being covered by snow that doesn't melt, warding off the cold that doesn't penetrate. Renoir deliberately exploits the artificiality of sets and circumstances to upstage any sentimentality that would interfere with true sentiment.

The second sequence is a comically mad opera, complete with singing choruses, arias and sudden deaths, called "The Electric Waxer," about a woman fatally obsessed with the shine on her parquet floor. It is played with hilarious self-absorption by Marguerite Cassan, who has the superb nuttiness of the late Florence Lake, and by Pierre Olaf, as her unfortunate husband.

The last sequence, "Le Roi d'Yvetot," is set in the Midi of so many of Renoir's earlier films and concerns the "revolution" effected by an elderly landowner (Fernand Sardou), his pretty young wife (Françoise Arnoul) and her young lover (Jean Carmet) when they find themselves quite happy in spite of conventions.

This sequence in particular has the cheerful, sunny look that distracted a lot of critics in the nineteen-thirties from seeing the tougher side of Renoir's comedies. The compromises effected by his characters are amusing but there's always the realization that they've never been lightly made.

Something of this same awareness is apparent in many of the comedies of Francois Truffaut (who has described himself as one of Renoir's children), especially in "Stolen Kisses" and "Bed and Board," films that, like a number of Renoir's, have on occasion been incorrectly labeled lightweight.

"Le Petit Théâtre" gives this mostly empty season a big boost. It looks like a work in miniature, but because the scale is perfect one never thinks about physical size. The movie is as big or small as our minds and emotions make it.

1974 My 3, 46:1

What the Devil Happened to 'The Exorcist's' Oscar?

By FOSTER HIRSCH

"THE EXORCIST" was cheated. It ought to have won the Oscar that went to "The Sting." In conspicuously bypassing William Friedkin's thriller, did the Academy choose safe entertainment, wholesome fun over wicked horror-show titillation? Or did "The Exorcist's" defeat indicate the Academy's displeasure with the tawdry publicity surrounding the film, the furor over who in fact dubbed what dialogue for whom, played what agonizing scenes for whom?

Publicity and awards aside, Friedkin's version of William Peter Blatty's best seller remains a riveting, compelling performance: the director's grip on his audience is merciless. Mesmerized by the film's palpably rendered vision of evil, we respond exactly the way Friedkin wants us to, with a series of escalating shudders, moans, gasps, and shrieks. His pacing is expert: when Friedkin lets up for a minute or two, we relax with great explosive

Foster Hirsch is a freelance writer who is currently at work on a book on Edward G. Robinson and his films.

sighs.

Audiences probably haven't responded so animatedly to a movie since Hitchcock went to work on our nerves in "Psycho." Like the Master, Friedkin knows just how to prime us for his shock effects. With graphic precision, and step by gruesome step, he shows us the devil's possession of a twelve-year-old girl. A head that revolves 360 degrees; a tongue that has the speed and the texture of a lizard's; devil's vomit, the ultimate in defensive weaponry — the details are hideous, and Friedkin has the audience cowering gleefully in anticipation of more. Shock us, scare us, disgust us, take us out of ourselves, the keyed-up audiences seem to be asking: "The Exorcist" is a flagellant's delight, a masochist's field-day.

It surely tells us something about the level of excitement in our own lives if we revel in Friedkin's blunt shock tactics, if we use the movie, as audiences are doing, as a kick, a pick-me-up, a catharsis through somebody else's schlock nightmare. Here's a film that treats its audience with profound disrepect; ultimately, it's we who are at the receiving end of the devil's green vomit, and yet "The Exorcist" is the audience-pleaser of the season, a critic-proof thriller that people are talking excitedly about. The "trip" movie of the year, it's a grand guignol floor show that's guaranteed to blow your mind.

Watching a very young actress mouth the devil's profusion of obscenities, stab her sexual organs with a crucifix and smear her mother's face in the blood, is much more startling (and of much less socially redeeming value) than anything Brando did to Maria Schneider in "Last Tango in Paris." But it is beside the point to comment on "The Exorcist's" spectacular and gratuitous bad taste (what the London critics wrote about Ibsen's "Ghosts" in 1891 might more aptly apply to Friedkin's horror show: "An open drain; a dirty act done publicly; gross, almost putrid indecorum; nastiness and malodorousness laid on thickly as with a trowel"). The film's prodigal ghoulishness is exactly what the delighted, tittering, applauding, semi-hysterical audiences want.

It's possible to appreciate Friedkin's manipulative skills and at the same time to note that "The Exorcist" is not a serious, self-respecting film of its genre; it is simply a sequence of creepy gags and cheap thrills. Contentless hokum. The worthy films of the supernatural — Don Siegel's "Invasion of the Body Snatchers," for instance, and George

Romero's "The Night of the Living Dead"—are charged with psychological and metaphysical resonances. A story of supernatural possession that's legit contains Freudian and Jungian overtones; it explores the dark side of our personalities, showing us our nightmare selves. It plays on submerged fears, it dips into the unconscious.

Satan makes a wonderful anti-hero; there's good reason why he has captivated our imaginations for so long. In a devil story with substance, a bout with Satan can be therapeutic, can reveal or exorcise our paranoia, our concealed, undealt-with anxieties. A solid supernatural tale, then, must create a context for its devils: the evil must be called into action for some reason deeper than that of simply scaring the hell out of us.

The devil in "The Exorcist" is a creature of spontaneous combustion, and as such, for all his animosity and his proudly displayed dark powers, he is a shabby being, almost innocent of symbolic thrust or psychic energy. The possession of 12-year-old Regan, unlike Siegel's nightmare vision in which citizens of an archetypal American community are taken over by giant pods, is an isolated phenomenon; it tells us nothing about the state of the nation and it offers little insight into the dark possibilities of human psychology.

Presented with a story of a girl who is possessed, we have a right to ask why. The movie provides few clues. The girl has no real personality; no bad seed, she's simply a conventional movie brat. Her punishment not only far exceeds any crime of which she may be capable, it also has nothing whatever to do with her character or her world as the film's opening blandly presents them.

Perhaps, then, Regan is "taken" as a lesson to her family, a punishment for her negligent father and her movie star mother? These speculations are also profitless; we never see the father, we have no reason to care about him. And the mother, despite her movie star status, seems a concerned parent; Regan isn't possessed, or doesn't will herself into possession, in order to attract the interest of an inattentive mama. (Nor is the diabolic pestilence a comment on the mother's movieland, cocktail party world—this isn't one of those bitter Hollywood on Hollywood jobs. The movie crew background isn't really used at all, in fact.)

The girl's predicament has a deep and unconventional impact only on the priest who saves her. Father Karras

Ellen Burstyn struggles with the demon-driven Linda Blair in "The Exorcist"
"The film is a flagellant's delight, a masochist's field-day"

is the true exorcist, but why has he been "chosen"? Is it, as the film suggests, to expiate his feelings of guilt about the death of his mother? The conceit doesn't work because his mother, a nagging crone who works overtime at making her son feel guilty, is more sinning than sinned against. And with his deep dark eyes that express such earnest concern and pain, Jason Miller plays Father Karras so soulfully that the character is saintlike from the beginning; he doesn't need to atone for anything, and so, like so much else in the film, his Christ-like self-sacrifice seems purely arbitrary.

The film is cluttered with red herrings and unfinished business. At its cheapest, it even intimates that the German butler really did it. The character of a detective is extraneous—he never finds out any more than we do. And at the end, the girl, presumably cleansed, her memory a blank, kisses a friend of her savior's on the neck: it's an ominous moment, but it's unresolved. Has evil triumphed, as in "Rosemary's Baby?" Is Regan unknowingly spreading the devil's cancer, or is Friedkin only trying, clumsily, to send us home happy?

The movie opens with a portentous, beautifully filmed prologue. In Iraq, the nominal exorcist (Max von Sydow, in old man make-up) discovers an ancient icon, the source, presumably, of a prehistoric evil, and the token of universal evil. At the end of the prologue, the shaman confronts the statue (which reappears, inexplicably, at the

climax of Regan's exorcism). These emblems of evil forces are introduced with all the weight and solemnity of the giant slab in "2001." But they are successful neither as artifact nor symbol. Their supposedly magical properties aren't connected to the prosperous Georgetown in which the hapless girl's possession and exorcism take place.

Friedkin has splendidly managed the spooky embellishments, the noises in the attic, the levitating beds, the sudden bursts of harrowing violence. But the showy gothic paraphernalia are merely chic and empty adornments. "The Exorcist" is a powerful, meaningless movie.

1974 My 5, II:11:3

Cheers for 'Claudine'

By VINCENT CANBY

THERE are a number of unusual things about "Claudine," the sometimes triumphantly funny new film at the De Mille and Fine Arts Theaters. It's about being black, about being poor, about being on welfare, and about trying to make economic and emotional ends meet without being forced by the system to cheat. The most unusual thing about "Claudine" is that it seems to take family life seriously, something done by very few films these days, perhaps because the situation comedies on television have given family life such a bad name. I can imagine some exceptionally impressionable child of the television generation growing up to think he had been deprived because his house had never rocked with canned laughter.

"Claudine" is not very far removed from a typical TV sitcom, at least stylistically. It's a very pretty *looking* movie. The colors, even of refuse-strewn Harlem streets, are as bright and cheerful as any you'd find in a Caribbean travel brochure. The title character is played by Diahann Carroll, a woman of unique beauty and the sort of chic that couldn't easily be disguised with flour sacks. Her six children, the results of two marriages and two "consensual unions," are never at a loss for words, which are occasionally blunt but quite often explosively funny in the way that real children would like to be but seldom are, being, instead, loudmouthed brats.

All of this is true. Yet "Claudine" is a first-rate American comedy that gives stature to a popular form. The difference between it and dozens of television come-

dies is the difference between interests, to say nothing of talents. It is also the first major film about contemporary black life to consider the hopes, struggles, defeats and frustrations of blacks who aren't either supercops, supermusicians, superstuds, superpimps or superpushers. But don't misunderstand. "Claudine" doesn't succeed because it's pious and especially clean. It isn't.

It couldn't accurately be described as a family film, if you mean a movie that is guaranteed not to disturb anyone's dreams and that doesn't talk dirty. In its footloose, unselfconscious way, it also says a lot more about black identity than the solemn "Sounder" and a lot more about certain aspects of the American system than last year's Jack Lemmon weeper, "Save The Tiger."

Claudine (Miss Carroll) is as cornered in her way as was the Lemmon character in "Save The Tiger." With six children and no husband she must go on welfare, but to give the family a life that is above subsistence level, she must also work as a maid, which is, of course, against the rules. The system invites cheating. Cheating is more or less built-in. It also provides the film with a couple of uproarious comic setpieces: the frantic activity that takes place within Claudine's Harlem apartment—hiding toasters, steam irons, rugs and what-have-you — whenever the welfare worker comes to call.

*

There is concern behind the comedy, however. When Claudine falls in love with Roop (James Earl Jones), a proud, big-talking garbage man who has himself run through two marriages, she and Roop are told that he can live with her, with the Welfare Department's blessing, as long as she deducts the monetary value of everything he gives the family, and as long as he goes on welfare if he by chance should lose his job.

That is pretty much the crux of the comedy about two immensely independent, resourceful people who are due to be damned no matter what course they take. "Claudine," which was written by Tina and Lester Pine and directed by John Berry, observes this situation with a sophistication that might well offend some audiences. It may be taken as ammunition by people who are out to shoot down all welfare programs as corruptors of self-respect and ambition. But the film's portrayal of the practical application of welfare may as easily be interpreted as a call for a more responsive system.

Though it is a quite pretty, romantic looking physical world in which Claudine and Roop carry on their hectic affair and courtship, the problems they face are undeniably real ones. Claudine's oldest son teeters on

the edge of militancy. Her oldest daughter, age 15, becomes pregnant and seems to be starting the cycle that landed her mother with six children and no husband by the time she was 36. One of the younger children is so traumatized he refuses to speak, preferring instead to communicate with the world by cryptic notes written on a sketch pad. How, then, can "Claudine" be simultaneously so good-natured and so moving?

Miss Carroll and Mr. Jones have a great deal to do with it. Even when the dialogue gets cute, as it does from time to time, their characterizations retain an intensity that gives the movie a basic, no-nonsense toughness. John Berry, who has directed Mr. Jones Off Broadway ("Boesman and Lena") and made films in Hollywood years ago ("He Ran All The Way") before going to Europe in the Joe McCarthy era, creates a sense of epic comedy at times, largely through Mr. Jones who plays Roop so broadly that he passes beyond buffoon to become a kind of classic clown, a man in whom everything is exaggerated, including love, loyalty, self-pity, self-indulgence. It's a hugely appealing performance, one that makes the love story not only understandable but important. A standout member of the supporting cast is Tamu, an actress new to films, who plays the pregnant daughter. She's a lean wiry girl who possesses an extraordinary fierceness that is effective in the comic as well as the dramatic sequences, whether screaming derisively at her younger brothers and sisters (who root for Tarzan on TV instead of for the blacks) or sobbing a confession about her delicate condition.

"Claudine" is the first film to be produced by Third World Cinema, a company set up five years ago by the late Diana Sands, Ossie Davis and Hannah Weinstein, the producer, among others, to provide training facilities for blacks and Puerto Ricans who wanted to make films, and to produce films that would more accurately reflect the minority experience in America.

In 1969, there were 13 blacks and six Puerto Ricans among the 6,000 members of New York City's various film unions. Today there are more than 40. That may not look like a great leap forward but it's more than a beginning, as is "Claudine," which is a buoyant American comedy about things that don't often get mentioned in what is sometimes called the popular cinema.

1974 My 5, II:1:7

The Cast

LOST IN THE STARS, directed by Daniel Mann; screenplay by Alfred Hayes, based on Maxwell Anderson's musical play adapted from Alan Patón's novel "Cry the Beloved Country;" music by Kurt Weill; producer, Ely Landau; musical supervisor, Alex North; director of photography, Robert Hauser; editor, Walt Hannemann; an American Film Theater presentation. At selected theaters. Running time: 114 minutes. This film is rated G.

Stephen Kumalo .... Brock Peters
Irina .... Melba Moore
John Kumalo ...... Raymond St. Jacques
Absalom .... Clifton Davis
James Jarvis .... Paul Rogers
Grace .... Pauline Myers
Rose .... Paula Kelly

By VINCENT CANBY

Except for Kurt Weill's score, which remains one of his loveliest, everything about the Maxwell Anderson-Weill musical play, "Lost in the Stars," seems to have aged badly in the screen adaptation that opened here yesterday at selected theaters.

The film is the eighth and last presentation in the American Film Theater's first subscription series. It's also by far the worst, but since the A.F.T. offerings included one fine film, "The Homecoming," one recording of a fine production, "Three Sisters," and a number of superlative performances, including that of Alan Bates in "Butley," the A.F.T.'s initial season shouldn't be judged to have been as much of a failure as were some of its parts.

●

"Lost in the Stars," based on Alan Paton's 1948 novel, "Cry the Beloved Country" (which was filmed in 1952), was first done on Broadway in 1949 and then revived in 1972. From the way that Daniel Mann has directed this film version, it seems to be a work completely dependent upon the conventions of the stage.

In the theater we accept illiterate characters who sing Broadway-type lyrics and we pretend that the lyrics are poetry. We also accept startling narrative coincidences because, after all, the stage is so small that the most unlikely people might well bump into one another—and often do when dancing.

Mr. Mann has apparently had no idea how to create an equivalent reality in a film that appears to have been shot mostly on exterior locations meant to simulate those in South Africa, where the story is set. One result is a kind of aimlessness that pervades the film. The camera doesn't seem to know quite what to do when a character bursts into song over a real washtub in a real backyard. It seems almost embarrassed, as you might be if the person next to you in the subway suddenly launched into a full-throttle "Some Enchanted Evening."

Thus the music and the lyrics that are supposed to be in the service of the drama are constantly upsetting it, making it look fabricated and false. This is too bad, since I suspect there is still a lot of power to be gotten from Mr. Paton's story of the old black country preacher, a man of orderly faith, and his search through the Johannesburg slums for the son who has become a murderer.

For reasons best known to the film makers, they've pretty much dropped the original idea of the reconciliation between the black preacher and the wealthy old white bigot whose son was the victim of the murder. Even if that optimistic conclusion was dropped as smacking too much of 1949 liberalism, it still is dramatically more effective than the nothing ending that "Lost in the Stars" now has.

The performers do much better as singers than as actors, and because Brock Peters, who plays the old preacher, has given good performances in the past, I assume his uneasiness here must stem from the aimlessness of the production as a whole.

●

None of the actors come off well, and that includes Melba Moore as the poor ghetto girl, Clifton Davis as the black boy who goes wrong and Paul Rogers (so fine in "The Homecoming") as the bigoted white landowner.

"Lost in the Stars" is a very bad movie but it does contain the Weill score. The music almost compensates for the foolishness of the images, the lyrics, the drama and the point-of-view, which, in spite of the ending, recalls the "ain't-black-folks-noble?" philosophy evident in so much well-meaning theater of 40 to 50 years ago. Tote dat barge. Lift dat bale. A card at the beginning of the movie identifies the time of the story as "The Recent Past." That isn't enough to get the movie off the hook.

1974 My 7, 54:1

FACE OF ANOTHER, directed by Hiroshi Teshigahara; screenplay (Japanese with English subtitles) and original story by Kobo Abe; director of photography, Heroshi Segewa; a Toho film produced by Teshigahara Productions and Tokyo Eiga, distributed by Rising Sun Enterprises. Running time: 124 minutes. At the Regency Theater, Broadway at 67th Street. This film has not been rated.

Okuyama .... Tatsuya Nakadai
Doctor .... Mikijiro Hira
Nurse .... Kyoko Kishida
Mrs. Okuyama .... Machiko Kyo
Director .... Eiji Okada
Girl .... Miki Irie

By VINCENT CANBY

A youngish engineer named Okuyama has had his facial features almost completely obliterated in an accident. Once out of the hospital he lays about the house all day and broods. He wears the kind of white bandages and dark glasses that the Invisible Man used to wear so people wouldn't look through him. Okuyama is nasty to his wife, curses fate and is numbingly philosophical. "A faceless man can feel free only in the dark," he may say. Or: "The face is the door to the mind. Without it, the mind is shut off."

In view of all the talking Okuyama does, the latter statement doesn't make much sense, but that's the sort of movie Hiroshi Teshigahara's "Face of Another" is. It talks too much and too foolishly for its own good, like someone who can only be reassured by the sound of his own voice.

The film was shown yesterday at the Regency Theater as part of its current festival of Japanese films. It will be seen again May 29-30 at Japan House as part of another festival of Japanese films sponsored by the Film Society of Lincoln Center and the Japan Society.

"Face of Another," which was made in 1966, shares with an earlier, better Teshigahara film, "Woman of the Dunes," a preoccupation with modes of identity. When Okuyama receives what is, in effect, a facial transplant, the new face takes over the old personality for eventually fatal results. As fiction it's too fanciful to be seriously compelling and too glib to be especially thought-provoking.

1974 My 8, 36:3

'Kazablan' From Israel Is a Musical Delight

Considering the bleak news from overseas, it might be welcome to have a sunny, sparkling Israeli-made musical, foaming with melody and dancing and with a sweet underlying spirit of brotherhood. And this is exactly what happened yesterday with the arrival of "Kazablan" at the Festival and other showcases. The picture is delightful.

The tonic effect of this English - language import, which recounts neighborhood troubles in a picturesque, rundown sector of Tel Aviv, is so tunefully exhilarating that the picture should certainly play on here into the hot months ahead. Based on an Israeli stage musical and beautifully photographed in color, the film spills out elastically across striking settings, under the direction of Menahem Golan, who also produced. In between the musical numbers, the dramatic vignettes are quietly effective.

The film also has some fine performances, especially by Yehoram Gaon, displaying an excellent tenor in the title role and by the lovely Efrat Lavie, Yehudah Efroni and Arie Elias. But what you'll remember are those lilting songs, which pour out thick and fast, the colorful backgrounds and the spirit of simple, sensible joy and contentment. Dov Seltzer wrote the music and Yigel Mossinson and Yoel Silberg the stage musical, and one viewer wishes he would see that, too. HOWARD THOMPSON

1974 My 9, 54:1

The Program

EROTIC CINEMA, a program of seven short films: NORIEN TEN, by John Knoop, running time, 10 minutes; EURYNOME, by John Straitton, 8 minutes; KISS, by Ross Albert, 3 minutes; JANUARY, by James Herbert, 15 minutes; LOVEMAKING by Scott Bartlett and distributed by Grove Press, 13 minutes; BLUE STREAK, by Mark Rappaport, 16 minutes; HOLDING, by Connie Benson, 13 minutes. At the Whitney Museum of American Art, Madison Avenue at 74th Street.

By VINCENT CANBY

If you can clearly see who's doing what to whom, it's a dirty movie. If it's out of focus or photographed in such tight close-ups that hairs look like African marsh grass and an expanse of human skin looks like the floor of the Gobi Desert, then it can be called erotic cinema, even though it's not terribly erotic.

That seems to be the point of the program titled "Erotic Cinema" that opened a two-week run yesterday at the Whitney Museum of American Art.

At least four of the seven films in the program depend to a greater or lesser extent on precious visual confusion to create something on the order of suspense. Is that an elbow or a kneecap I see before me, a buttock or a breast, a he or a she? Sometimes you never find out.

Patrons at porn houses would demand their money back. At the Whitney, I suspect, everyone will mind his manners in the higher, more boring cause of Art.

Both John Knoop's "Norien Ten" and Scott Bartlett's "Lovemaking" show us a couple making love, though you can't be quite sure until the final moments. The emphasis in both films is on pretty, fuzzy images, plus, in "Norien Ten," some rather fancy laboratory effects, the sort used by Stanley Kubrick in "2001" when the spaceship was passing through the rings of Jupiter. Erotic? Not really.

In Connie Beeson's "Holding," two pretty young women romp nakedly through landscapes in double images of the kind you see through a camera's rangefinder before getting the distance right. Later they settle down to make love, one image per person. James Herbert's "January" is a contemplative, quite beautiful but unerotic film that focuses on a naked young man and woman who wander through a farm house on a cold winter day being photographed in stop-motion, in still pictures and in conventional motion.

●

John Straitton's "Eurynome" shows animated clay figures acting out the Greek myth about the woman who mated with a snake to give birth to "the universal egg." It ends with a newsreel clip of an A-bomb explosion, the favorite conclusion of so many awful avant-garde films in the nineteen-fifties.

Two of the films are funny and mean to be: Ross Albert's "Kiss," in which a couple, seen in close profile, kiss for three minutes, making noises that sound like a Con Ed crew tearing up a street, and Mark Rappaport's "Blue Streak," a very comic, deadpan commentary on naughty words and pornographic literature. Even though they, too, are not erotic, they are entertaining and intelligent.

1974 My 10, 24:3

The Program

SPRING POTPOURRI: GREED by John Canemaker, 1 minute; CHOW FUN by Sally Cruikshank, 4½ minutes; THE PRODIGAL WIENER by Robert Hutchinson, 2½ minutes; LA-DEE-DA by Charles Wright, 4½ minutes; GULLS AND BUOYS by Robert Breer, 7 minutes; THE VANGUARD STORY by Jay Cassidy and Fred LaBour, 17 minutes; HIGH KUKUS by James Broughton, 3 minutes; THE MATING HABITS OF THE NORTHERN PACIFIC KELP by Mr. Hutchinson, 2½ minutes; MUSA PARADISIACA SAPIENTUM by Steve Klocksiem, 5 minutes; RAIN by Louva Irvine, 5 minutes; WOMEN by Connie Beeson, 11½ minutes; BOGGY DEPOT by Curt McDowell and Mark Ellinger, 17 minutes; RUSSIAN ROOSTER by Steve Segal, 3 minutes. At the Film forum, 256 West 88th Street, through Sunday and May 16-19, 8 P.M.

Lighthearted is the word for "Spring Potpourri," the collection of 13 short subjects that arrived yesterday at the Film Forum. And true to the label, the wares of these avant-garde film makers are varied, even though they are not preponderantly effective in executing their largely humorous or satiric themes.

In an almost equally divided package of live action and animated films, Jay Cassidy's and Fred LaBour's "The Vanguard Story," is an outstanding, biased but ironic reminder of the attitudes of some of our confused and/or angry national leaders following the launching of Russia's sputnik. Their carefully edited nineteen-fifties newsreel footage is hindsight, of course, but it is a clear, close, sometimes comic focus on such harried figures as President Dwight D. Eisenhower, Lyndon B. Johnson, Richard

M. Nixon and Nelson A. Rockefeller.

Arresting expertise also is evident in Connie Beeson's live-action look at "Women," which illustrates through nudes, sharply etched vignettes and cutting definitions, the silliness of sexual stereotyping. And, in "Boggy Depot," Curt McDowell and Mark Ellinger, aided by lampooned ballads and broad, properly hammy acting, mercilessly rib the romantic musical genre.

Robert Breer's "Gulls and Buoys" is the most striking of the animated films in its imaginative use of line drawings to project live-action effects in varying beach scenes and seascapes. "Rus-

sian Rooster" also infuses whimsy into uncluttered shots of the rooster and its hunters with charming results. But the other animated entries including "Greed," "Chow Fun," "The Prodigal Wiener" and "La-Dee-Da" are predominantly technical exercises in patterns, forms and colors.

●

There are momentary flashes of inspiration in the wacky antics of kelp and bananas in "The Mating Habits of the Northern Pacific Kelp" and "Musa Paradisiaca Sapientum." But like James Broughton's static "High Kukus" and Louva Irvine's frenetic "Rain" they are redundant, rather than

revealing, in their approaches to simple subjects. In essence, "Spring Potpourri" is a cheerful collage even if only some of its parts are memorable.   A. H. WEILFR

1974 My 10, 24:5

Out of materials as timeless as mysticism, faith and the profound burdens of the human condition, the Brazilian director Ruy Guerra constructed a film as unsparing as its initial image—the sun that parches the earth where his characters play out their wretched lives.

The film, "Os Fuzis" ("The Guns") was made 11 years ago and is being shown today and tomorrow at noon and midnight at the First Avenue Screening Room.

Set in drought-stricken northeastern Brazil, where misery and religion, intensified by the remorselessness of nature, border starvation and fantasy, the film employs a relatively small canvas to make broad statements. Embraced within the canvas are a single town, a handful of soldiers sent to guard from the passive, hungry populace a food shipment owned by one man; a nubile girl, a lone truck driver and a swelling legion of impoverished migrants in the train

of a mystic with a sacred ox embodying the promise of the miracle of rain.

Building slowly and at times in a manner difficult to comprehend until the cohesion of Mr. Guerra's design establishes itself, the director moves through his introductions and the surface of things—glare, enervating heat, shaded and squinting eyes, dust and sweat—into his characters as individuals and then beyond them to comment on and question the nature of mankind.

His vision of life is sharp, saddened, suffused with awareness of futility and failure—of men, governments and faiths. It is no accident that the voice of the mystic resounds through this film with hoarse agony.

LAWRENCE VAN GELDER

1974 My 10, 24:3

The Riches Of Jean Renoir

By VINCENT CANBY

ON Sept. 15 Jean Renoir will be 80 years old. It is thus unlikely that this giant among directors will work on any more films. This makes all the more special the appearance here this week (at the First Avenue Screening Room) of his most recent production, the limpid, lovely, rollicking, four-part movie titled "Le Petit Théâtre de Jean Renoir," commissioned five years ago for French television but just now having its commercial debut in Manhattan.

From the opening sequence in which Renoir, in his first appearance on screen as himself, greets us, the audience, as he stands beside his miniature theater where the stories will unfold, and from the very first scene in the first story ("The Last Christmas Dinner"), in which two cranky Santa Clauses fight for territory outside a posh restaurant, until the bow of the actors that concludes the program, "Le Petit Théâtre de Jean Renoir" unfolds with the kind of breathtaking effect that I associate with Hitchcock's "Frenzy" and with Buñuel's "Tristana" and "The Discreet Charm of The Bourgeoisie."

These films have nothing in common except that they are the works of superlative artists working in modes that they have been mastering for more than five decades. I'm perfectly aware that age doesn't automatically enrich a talent. It has a way of eroding all but the most profound talents, especially those of filmmakers who always are under particular stress to be responsive to the mass audience that, ultimately, allows the filmmaker to continue working. It's a terrible business, really. Compromises must be effected. So many that finally it becomes a triumph of sorts just to secure the necessary financing, to get a movie into production and, eventually, into a theater. After all that

wear and tear, who can have the discipline of purpose to remember the film itself?

Fine old moviemakers are very rare, largely, I suspect, because we — you and I — have a way of looking at each new film much in the manner that we peruse the front page of a daily newspaper. If it doesn't report some ghastly disaster, some startling development in science, some scandal, we're inclined to throw it aside. We've seen it before.

Impatient critics and moviegoers in 1967 dismissed Charlie Chaplin's charming, 1930-esque comedy, "A Countess from Hong Kong," with Marlon Brando and Sophia Loren playing extensions of Chaplin, because it didn't measure up to what they wanted that year (which included "Elvira Madigan" and "In Cold Blood," to name just two of 1967's major hits).

If the filmmaker lasts into old age, the results can sometimes be as remarkable as "Bonaparte and The Revolution," Abel Gance's extraordinary reworking of his 1927 silent epic, "Abel Gance's Napoleon," which was shown at the New York Film Festival several years ago. At the age of 82 Gance re-edited "Napoleon," added sound to those sequences that were still without it, and shot additional material, to make a new epic film as well as an epic commentary on the evolution of films. (I understand that both "Abel Gance's Napoleon" and "Bonaparte and The Revolution" may soon be available for commercial distribution in this country, which is, to put it calmly, about time.)

The pressure on theatrical film directors is the sort that can reduce strong men to jellies composed of flabby flesh, fear and avarice. Roberto Rossellini, who will be 68 this year, has survived and grown only by turning his back on theatrical films entirely, working instead on a series of educational films, financed

by TV interests, that allow him to be as idiosyncratic as he wants. Had Rossellini cared that much for the high life, he'd probably be directing Mafia movies today for Dino De Laurentiis, or for some lesser equivalent.

All of which makes the longevity and the richness of the careers of Hitchcock, Buñuel and Renoir so rare. Attention must be paid, particularly at this moment to Jean Renoir.

By some poetic chance, "Le Petit Théâtre" is both a cause for celebration and an act of it. It is nothing so grand as a retrospective of the entire career of the man who made, among other masterpieces, "Rules of The Game," "Grand Illusion," "Picnic on The Grass," "The Southerner," "The Diary of A Chambermaid," "The River," "The Golden Coach" and "French Can-Can."

It is a small film composed of three separate comedies plus a between-acts song sung by Jeanne Moreau, playing a solemnly untalented Parisian music hall performer, circa 1900. Yet the whole thing is so effortlessly composed, so wise and so full of the concerns that make each Renoir film memorable, it vividly evokes the spirit of the remarkable man we can still honor in his lifetime.

The form of the film, a familiar sort of television device, has a special aptness for Renoir's career. Renoir, the host, introduces each story with a few words, at which point the camera moves from the director and crosses the tiny footlights of his miniature stage, where the stories are played. Life changes to theater which changes to life which changes to theater, until, at last, the people in Renoir's last little comedy have to walk to the apron of the stage and bow to us to return us to our own world.

This Renoir fondness for theater is, I propose, less the philosophical expression that

some critics would have you believe than it is a kind of polite recognition of life's most awesome, most banal riddles. What is real? Is everything a hopeless mess directed by someone with absolutely no interest in us? Renoir, I'm sure, doesn't know, nor if he thought he did, would he presume to say.

None of the three little comedies is quite as simple as it might seem. "The Last Christmas Dinner," about two Parisian clochards, an old man and an old lady whose make-up as derelicts is as artificial as the sets they inhabit, is the sort of fairy tale in which a character can say that "Christmas is our most successful cliché" and then the sketch goes on to prove it.

"The Electric Waxer" is a modern "opera" about a furiously foolish housewife who loves her parquet floors more than she loves her husband or, as she says: "Trust my floors to a maid? I'd rather die!" Which, eventually, she does. The marvel is that Renoir manages to cover much of the same ground about the "new Paris" covered by Godard in "Two or Three Things I Know About Her," without once slipping into the attitude of the shocked polemicist.

He's hugely amused without being cruel or bitter, or, for that matter, unconcerned.

*

The final sketch is Renoir returning to Marcel Pagnol country, the sun-filled, verdant Midi where a wealthy old landowner must come to terms (which he does) with the wife he loves and her young lover, who's his best friend. Renoir's love of nature is bursting out all over this sequence, but it has less to do with foliage than with people, with the troubled but flexible old man (Fernand

Sardou), his beautiful, all-too-desirable bride (Françoise Arnoul), the conscience-stricken lover (Jean Carmet), and the nice, clumsy young maid (Dominique Labourier), who doesn't care who knows that she eavesdrops and who dreams of being a courtesan on the order of Messalina. She is, of course, the least likely Messalina anyone

might imagine, but Renoir, and the rest of us with him, have a special fondness for the enormity of the dream.

That, I think, is one of the enduring qualities that illuminate Renoir's little theater, his world. Nothing in it is ever inconsequential.

1974 My 12, II:1:7

A Nightmare World With No Secrets

By STEPHEN FARBER

UNION SQUARE, SAN FRANCISCO: An attractive young couple —clandestine lovers—weave in and out of the crowd, having what seems to be an innocent, banal conversation about Christmas presents. A man with a hearing aid and a shopping bag trails after them. High above the square, another man watches them through an exotic telescope. Finally, a third man enters a large van where tape recorders are playing fragments of the couple's conversation.

From these first moments, Francis Ford Coppola's "The Conversation" seizes our attention with unsettling images of omnipresent snoops in control of the most devious and elaborate technology for surveillance. The film

Stephen Farber is a critic and author of "The Movie Rating Game."

immediately touches the peculiar anxiety of the Watergate era; the central character, Harry Caul, "the best bugger on the West Coast," might be a cousin to James McCord or Tony Ulasewicz. After months of irrelevant movies, "The Conversation" hits with the explosiveness of the morning headlines. Fortunately, it has a good deal more substance. Like the taped conversation that Harry compulsively replays, the film as a whole has more mysterious and profound implications than first impressions suggest.

The movie succeeds on a number of levels—most obviously, as a penetrating psychological study of a professional wiretapper, played with great intensity and compassion by Gene Hackman. Living in an impersonally furnished apartment, working in an abandoned warehouse, visiting a mistress who knows nothing about him but his name, Harry Caul is the modern invisible man: he

craves anonymity.

Because of his skill at spying on other people, Harry is obsessed with guarding his own privacy. He cuts himself off from all human contact because he is so terrified of being exposed or betrayed. Paranoia may be the wiretapper's congenital malady, but his fears are not simply fantasies. Considering the sophisticated technological universe that Harry has helped to create, everyone is vulnerable; the concept of privacy has become virtually meaningless. The film deals with a uniquely 20th-century nightmare—the erosion of any sense of personal identity in a world without secrets, a world where nothing is inviolate.

At the same time, "The Conversation" examines the question of responsibility, and it exposes the moral bankruptcy of the professionals who do their jobs without considering the consequences. Harry does not know or care how his tapes will be used. He is fascinated by the technical challenges of his work, and proud of his imaginative methods of eavesdropping; when he talks about solving a particularly difficult engineering problem, his voice quivers with excitement. Harry resembles the Rand Corporation strategists who devise ingenious war games but refuse to think about the real battlefields where the "games" will be played.

Dramatically, "The Conversation" centers on Harry's gradual breakdown when he becomes emotionally involved in an assignment for the first time in his life. In the opening scene, when his assistant asks a question about the lovers' conversation, Harry replies simply, "I don't care what they're talking about. All I want is a nice fat re-

cording."

But as he plays the recording over and over again, he becomes haunted by the strange, ominous undertones that he hears in apparently trivial words and phrases. Harry Caul, the electronics expert, can record any conversation, but he cannot interpret the recordings; he cannot read the inflections. As Harry confronts the ambiguity of language, the unexpected gulf between words and meaning, he begins to lose his bearings.

His growing sense of guilt intensifies this disorientation. Once before, one of Harry's bugging assignments led to the deaths of three people, and although he disclaims responsibility — "I just turned in the tapes"—he cannot forget the case. Now he becomes convinced that the young lovers he is surveying may be in danger from the woman's husband, and he fears that if he turns in the tapes, he will be responsible for another murder. But he does not know how to act to prevent the murder. His characteristic professional detachment has paralyzed him, and he can only sit on the sidelines and watch, overwhelmed by morbid fantasies that he cannot exorcise.

Until this point, the film is still relatively straightforward — a devastating study of the moral and psychological consequences of cold-blooded professionalism. The surprise ending, however, turns everything upside down. The murder plot Harry is attempting to uncover is much more diabolical than he imagines; we suddenly realize how utterly helpless he is. Coppola indicts Harry for his passivity, but he also suggests the futility of positive moral action in a bewildering, deceptive, finally un-

Gene Hackman, a surveillance expert, scrutinizes unsuspecting girls through a one-way mirror in 'The Conversation.' Does his responsibility end with turning in the tapes?

intelligible and irredeemably corrupt universe.

The ending makes this point explicit, but Coppola absorbs us in a disjointed world of misleading appearances and unspoken menace from the very first frames: In Union Square, a mime follows Harry with discomforting persistence; what looks like the scope of a rifle turns out to be an elaborate instrument of surveillance; a Christmas present conceals a microphone. Nothing is quite what it seems, and no one can be trusted.

During the course of the film Harry's assistant deserts him and goes to work for a rival; Harry's most intimate confession—to a sympathetic call girl—is recorded and broadcast as part of a practical joke; and the call girl herself is merely manipulating Harry to get hold of his tapes.

As the plot unravels, Coppola discloses an ever-deepening whirlpool of treachery and deceit. He obviously intends a comment on the amorality that has permeated all segments of American society, but the film goes beyond social criticism. It is a murder mystery, a horror film in a fundamental sense—a consideration of the most terrifying human potentialities, the capacity for ruthlessness, duplicity, evil. Harry Caul, like most of us, has relied on familiar routines to give his life a sense of order. But the facade begins to crack, and he sees that he is surrounded by chaos and absurdity, an isolated figure in a labyrinth he can never penetrate or decipher.

The film concludes on an unforgettable image of decay. The hunter has become the hunted. Convinced that he is being watched, Harry searches his apartment for a hidden microphone or camera; as he grows more frantic, he wrecks the whole place, removing the wallpaper and tearing up the floorboards. Finally he sits alone in the completely demolished flat, playing his saxophone in a last pathetic attempt to recover the stability that he has lost forever.

At the beginning of "The Conversation," one may feel comfortably superior to Harry Caul, but by the end we have been too deeply implicated to condescend to him. His deterioration illuminates *our* vulnerability, the precariousness of our own attempts to create order out of chaos.

There are some minor flaws in the film—a clumsy, predictable scene with Harry's mistress, a superfluous, visually banal dream sequence, a heavy-handed bit of symbolism involving a figurine of the Virgin Mary—but they hardly matter. It is exhilarating to find a movie as ambitious and provocative, as rich in ideas as "The Conversation." This is not the kind of film one expected Coppola to do after "The Godfather," though it has the same technical assurance, the same narrative grace, and equally fine performances. (In addition to Hackman, Allen Garfield's dazzling comic portrait of a rival wiretapper deserves special mention.)

But "The Conversation" reveals a much more complex sensibility than "The Godfather" suggested; it fulfills the promise of Coppola's underrated early film, "The Rain People." What is more startling about "The Conversation" is the genuine anguish that comes through—not the fashionable cynicism of so many Hollywood directors, but a tormented, profoundly despairing personal vision of a wholly faithless world.

"The Conversation" may not give "The Godfather" much competition in Variety's list of top grossers, but it is Coppola's best movie, a landmark film of the seventies and a stunning piece of original American fiction. Literary critics who still look down on American movies should be required to see this film. I doubt that any American novel published this year will have the imagination and immediacy, the sheer dramatic power of "The Conversation." Coppola has caught what it *feels* like to be living through this period of disillusionment and full-scale social disintegration.

There is little consolation to be drawn from "The Conversation," one of the darkest and most disturbing films ever made in this country. The pleasure comes from watching an artist working at the height of his powers.

1974 My 12, II:13:1

PALE FLOWER, directed by Masahiro Shinoda; written by Ataru Baba and Mr. Shinoda (Japanese, with English subtitles), based on an original novel by Shintaro Ishihara; photography, Masao Kosugi; music, Toru Takemitsu; a Shoiku Release. Running time: 96 minutes. At the Regency Theater, Broadway between 67th and 68th Streets, through tomorrow.

Muraki .... Ryo Ikebe
Saeko .... Mariko Kaga

To see one of Masahiro Shinoda's films, it seems, is to bear witness to a triumph of style over substance. Whether it is one of the director's samurai films, such as "the Assassin" or "Sasuke Against the Wind," which played here last year, or one of the yakuza — gangster films—such as "Pale Flower," which opened yesterday at the Regency Theater, the result is the same.

One comes away with the memory of a well-defined pictorial style, moody, black and white, given to depicting people in the shadowy perimeters around cores of light.

The stories are another matter. And "Pale Flower," a 1964 film being shown here for the first time, shares with some of Mr. Shinoda's other works some vexing characters, some unintentional vagueness and a set of subtitles that probably could have been more illuminating.

"Pale Flower" is an existential work, chiefly occupied with the rather remote relationship between a gangster (Ryo Ikebe) released from prison after serving time for murder and a mysterious young woman (Mariko Kaga), who lives for such kicks as high-stakes gambling, fast driving, drugs and witnessing the murder that sends the gangster back to jail again.

"Pale Flower" is a film that has been likened to Jean-Luc Godard's memorable "Breathless." At least, it is no more than a pale imitation.

LAWRENCE VAN GELDER

1974 My 13, 36:8

Blier Directs Tale of Two Errant Youths

By VINCENT CANBY

"Going Places," the new French film by Bertrand Blier, the 35-year-old son of the actor Bernard Blier, is about two muscular young men on the road, going no place though they never stop moving. Jean-Claude (Gerard Depardieu) is the more aggressive of the two. Pierrot (Patrick Dewaere) seems the more resourceful, though he apparently enjoys being told what to do by his buddy. They share everything — stolen loot, hypochondria, boredom, women and, when there are no women, each other.

At the beginning of the film, which opened yesterday at the Cinema 2, Jean-Claude and Pierrot rough up a middle-aged woman of faint heart and large pocketbook. They scare hell out of her but don't get around to rape. They later steal a car and kidnap a dim-witted blonde who doesn't mind being kidnapped at all, though she doesn't like getting shot at and beaten up, which the boys do, not so much out of viciousness as out of impatience.

•

By the end of the film, after some funny, horrendous adventures that take them aimlessly from one end of France to the other, Jean-Claude and Pierrot have clearly become the victims. They are the pursued, doomed like that mythical bird Tennessee Williams sometimes writes about, the one that must spend its entire life flying, since evolution has denied it landing gear.

"Going Places" is handsome, mock-tough and thoroughly empty-headed, like Jean-Claude and Pierrot. It's a movie whose good performances and technical expertise can never disguise the vacuity of its assumed nihilism, which bears about as much relation to the real thing as fashion photography does to the work of Cartier-Bresson.

Mr. Depardieu and Mr. Dewaere have a high old time in characterizations that seem composed less of attitudes taken from life than from old movies, early Belmondo, James Dean and any number of early Godard characters. Miou-Miou is also extremely attractive as the blonde who tags along with them, because there really isn't anything better to do. She later gives the pair her overwhelming gratitude when by chance, they set up the circumstances that result in her achieving her first orgasm. Such is the nature of much of the film's sense of humor.

Jeanne Moreau, looking tired, wise and very beautiful, comes on screen in the middle of the movie as a woman who's just completed a 10-year stretch behind bars. She gives it, briefly, the weight and direction the film otherwise lacks, much in the manner that Jack Nicholson's appearance showed up the superficial attitudes of the rest of "Easy Rider." You may want to be forewarned, however, that the sequence concludes with what appears to be a suicide in a manner that more or less sums up the film's feelings about women. The suicide makes no sense on any level I can think of.

•

The French are a funny race. The film's ads quote one Parisian critic who found "Going Places" to be "a hymn to life" of the sort that makes one glad to be alive. I must say that though I thought parts of it funny, and Miss Moreau riveting, the net effect was one of irritation and gloom. It's not very invigorating to see so much talent squandered on such foolish mixed-up romanticism.

The Cast

GOING PLACES, directed by Bertrand Blier; screenplay (French with English subtitles) by Mr. Blier and Philippe Dumarcay, based on Mr. Blier's novel "Les Valseuses;" produced by Paul Claudon; director of photography, Bruno Nuyten; editor, Kenout Peltier; music, Stephane Grappelli; a C.A.P.C.-U.P.E.-SN production, distributed by Cinema 5. Running time: 117 minutes. At the Cinema 2 Theater, Third Avenue near 60th Street. This film has not been rated.

Jean-Claude .... Gerard Depardieu
Pierrot .... Patrick Dewaere
Marie-Ange .... Miou-Miou
Jean Piroles .... Jeanne Moreau
Jacques .... Jacques Chailieux
The surgeon .... Michel Peurilon
Young mother .... Brigitte Fossey
Jacqueline .... Isabelle Huppert

1974 My 14, 31:1

The Cast

ANDY WARHOL'S FRANKENSTEIN, written and directed by Paul Morrissey; photography, Luigi Kueveillier; editing, Jed Johnson; music, Claudio Gizzi; a Carlo Ponti/Andrew Braunsberg/Jean-Pierre Rassam Production; a Bryanston Pictures Release; filmed in 3-D. At the Trans-Lux West Theater, Broadway at 49th Street and the Trans-Lux East Theater, Third Avenue and 58th Street. Running time: 95 minutes. This film has been classified X.

Field Hand .... Joe Dallesandro
Baron's Wife .... Monique Van Vooren
The Baron .... Udo Kier
The Farmer .... Srdjan Zelenovic
Girl Zombie .... Dalila Di Lazzaro
Baron's Assistant .... Arno Juerging

By NORA SAYRE

Nowadays, flashing your hash can be a tribute to the film maker—just as belching was said to compliment the hosts of ancient China. While one suspects that the tales about upchuck at "The Exorcist" were eagerly exaggerated, "Andy Warhol's Frankenstein," written and directed by Paul Morrisey, almost begs the gorge to rise. Hence those with iron guts may rank as philistines — unable to respond to the call of art. The movie opened yesterday at the Trans-Lux East and West.

A fascistic baron (Udo Kier), who plans to create and control a new master race, assembles beautiful rigid zombies out of freshly killed spare parts. As his hands caress kidneys, spleens and gall bladders, his unfinished creatures appear like mutilated corpses, and disembowelment becomes a substitute for sex. (Some of the innards resemble lobster salad, an evocation that stresses the obvious expense of this production.) Throughout, the accents of the wicked are as thick as minestrone—"Let's get rrrid of ziss useless trrrunk" — and the blood splashes as noisily as an open fire hydrant.

3-D effects (summoning wistful memories of "House of Wax") are used to project the butchery: Dripping giblets on forceps are thrust into the audience, while the performers — including Joe Dallesandro as a sulky stud and Monique Van Vooren as the baron's huffy wife and sister — practically leap into your lap. Since much of the action is slow, these diversions are welcome, although hanging onto the 3-D glasses can be rough if you're a near-sighted, note-taking smoker.

In a muddy way, the movie attempts to instruct us about the universal insensitivity, living-deadness and the inabilty to be turned on by anythng short of the grotesque. However, this "Frankenstein" drags as much as it camps; despite a few amusing moments, it fails as a spoof, and the result is only a coy binge in degradation.

1974 My 16, 52:1

The Cast

THE BLACK WINDMILL, produced and directed by Don Siegel; screenplay by Leigh Vance, from "Seven Days to A Killing" by Clive Egleton; photography, Outsama Rawi; film editor, Antony Gibbs; music, Roy Budd; released by Universal Studios. At Radio City Music Hall, Avenue of the Americas and 50th Street. Running time: 106 minutes. (This film has been classified PG.)
Maj. John Tarrant ....Michael Caine
Sir Edward Julyan ....Joseph O'Conor
Cedric Harper ....Donald Pleasence
McKee ....John Vernon
Alex Tarrant ....Janet Suzman
Ceil Burrows ....Delphine Seyrig
Chief Superintendent Wray ..Joss Ackland

By NORA SAYRE

How welcome a spy who stumbles, worries or even pauses to reflect would be if he or she were appearing on a double bill with "The Black Windmill," in which Michael Caine's exasperating cool robs this very well-made movie of some of its potential excitement. The Don Siegel picture opened Thursday at Radio City Music Hall.

●

Mr. Caine, an agent whose small son has been kidnapped by an international arms syndicate, is also suspected by his British colleagues of having arranged the snatch—partly because of his uncrackable composure. The actor makes an unlikely father (also husband). Much of the time, he appears as a tin man, with tiny wheels whirring punctually inside him. Although he manages to smoke one cigarette with a certain intensity and to achieve a little hard (if shallow) breathing when his son's life is at stake, he seems to lack a central nervous system, and that deficiency deprives the audience of sympathetic thrills.

Still, the flatness of the Caine persona is balanced by Donald Pleasence in his best form, as the phobic but stony head of the Department of Subversive Warfare—a type who even shreds his own Kleenex. With his lower lip sucked in, fingers twisting bits of his mustache, alternating a gutteral with a nasal voice, revulsion hardening in his boiled gooseberry eyes, he projects the kind of character who could burst with frustration if he ever allowed himself to unbutton at all. And surely few actors can deliver such a line as "Kindly have the goodness not to smoke in here" with such sensitive hostility. However, Delphine Seyrig, as one of the kidnappers, makes not one uncalculated gesture; "performing" with every tendon, she does the silken stunt that we've often seen from her before.

●

I feel some pangs about this picture: It's an admirably professional job, and distinctly entertaining. But the plot scatters into a flurry of devices for chases and escapes, and there are no lunges of astonishment, despite all the athletics. (Remember the shock of suddenly seeing a red London bus in "The Ipcress File"—when the Michael Caine character didn't know he was in England. That's the kind of invention that's missing here.) Really, "The Black Windmill" is an action movie, rather than a suspense thriller. And, in the age of Watergate, we need nimbler or more fantastic material to engage us—to grab our attention from wondering what may be on the news tonight.

1974 My 18, 18:4

The Cast

BLACK EYE, directed by Jack Arnold; screenplay by Mark Haggard and Jim Martin, from Jeff Jacks's novel "Murder on the Wild Side"; director of photography, Ralph Woolsey; film editor, Gene Ruggiero; music, Mort Garson; produced by Pat Rooney; released by Warner Bros. At the Criterion Theater, Broadway at 45th Street and 86th Street East Theater, at Third Avenue. Running time: 98 minutes. This film is classified PG.
Stone ....Fred Williamson
Miss Francis.........Rosemary Forsyth
Cythia ....Teresa Graves

"Black Eye" begins with such swift promise — footage from an old silent film, a rapid transition to the funeral of its caddish star and the mysterious theft of his silver-headed cane from the coffin lid by a prostitute soon murdered—that its subsequent decline into hack work leaves a sense of extraordinary disappointment.

What could have been an almost savage commentary, juxtaposing the traditional private eye to a modern California background of Jesus freaks pornographic film makers, the narcotics trade and transitional sexual styles, stutters over its script and its performances.

●

The hero of this film, which opened yesterday at the Criterion and 86th Street East Theaters, is Shep Stone, a private investigator played by Fred Williamson, who in the past has at least brought panache, charm and intelligence to his roles.

Here, in the presence of a script that creakily explains his past and tries but fails to establish in Shep Stone a character of the highly idiosyncratic morality that motivated Sam Spade, he commits the unforgivable sin of communicating the impression that he knows how everything is going to turn out. And since everything turns out all right, what we have in place of essential tension and doubt is a mood of smug, slothful assurance.

Some smooth character portrayals are contributed by Bret Morrison as the sinister pornographer, Richard Anderson as a man ostensibly seeking his runaway daughter, Richard X. Slattery as a cop, Larry Mann as the head of a flock of Jesus freaks and Cyril Delevanti as another of the movie's contingent of villains. Teresa Graves seems alive and honest as Stone's bisexual girl friend, but Rosemary Forsyth as Stone's rival in love seems contrived.

With its evocation of the movies' past, with its resurrection of the private eye, with its obligatory car chase over terrain figuratively and literally familiar, "Black Eye" could prompt a kindly soul to accept it as a homage to Hollywood. Actually, with its disappointments and shortcomings, it is more of an obeisance to television. And when it turns up there, it will have achieved its proper setting.

LAWRENCE VAN GELDER

1974 My 18, 18:4

Why Are They Being So Mean to 'Gatsby'?

By FOSTER HIRSCH

VICTIM of its own publicity overkill, "The Great Gatsby" has become the movie to hate. Slaughtered by the critics, the film is also being insulted in the subways: "this movie stinks," and less flattering evaluations, are scribbled on many of the ads. The picture has been dismissed as a desecration of a great American novel; it's been damned as insensitive, numbingly reverential, ludicrously miscast, stultifyingly dull.

Some critics have even speculated that the project was doomed from the start. Fitzgerald's novel, they claim, is unfilmable, and besides, since no movie could ever be as full and as satisfying as the original, why bother? Even if the material were made to work as a movie, the scoffers insist, it would inevitably be a short-cut for those who don't want to read and a bargain basement version of the story for those who do.

The truth of the matter is that "The Great Gatsby," with its strong melodramatic narrative, its lavish backdrops, and its solid evocation of time and place, is eminently congenial to the kind of world that movies can create. Further, for all its rich verbal texture, Fitzgerald's book is not a high-toned "classic," of use only to scholars and graduate students. It is wonderfully accessible. An "important" and "serious" novel with broad popular appeal, "Gatsby," in short, is best-seller material of distinction, just the sort of prop-

Foster Hirsch is a freelance writer.

erty that movies are equipped to handle.

*

Jack Clayton's film does not accomplish the (probably) impossible; it is not as rounded, as finely etched, as unfailingly trenchant, as its source, but it is nonetheless a rich and elegant piece of work, and it is obedient without being obsequious to the spirit of its legendary author. As in the book, it's atmosphere, tone, and sensibility that count most.

The drapes billow gracefully in the afternoon breeze. Two women in white recline languidly on white couches. "Nick, is it you?" one of the women asks lazily, in a high, nasal, flute-like voice, as a bumbling young man enters the bewitching living room. "Oh, Nick," the hostess coos archly, "I'm paralyzed with happiness!" This is our introduction, early in the film, to the high society world that Fitzgerald had a life-long crush on,. and the scene has just the right high-strung pitch as it eases us into a long-ago golden New York summer among hot and temperamental people who are very rich and very careless. Like so much of the rest of the movie, the atmosphere of this early scene is thick with money and heat.

The film is filled with images of rich people idling away an overripe summer. There are teas on the polo grounds and in a summer garden, to the accompaniment of the buzz of flies and the hum of birds. There are, of course, Gatsby's big foolish parties at which the guests cavort in a madcap frenzy that yet has elegiac underpinnings. Best of all, there is an afternoon at the Plaza, on a day in high summer when the town is

empty and the air vibrates with tension among the sorry characters.

The palatial rooms of East Egg and West Egg, the brilliant tea service, the long cool drinks served in cut-glass crystal, the natty suits and colorful dresses, the sporty cars, the silks and linens—these tokens of Fitzgerald's attraction to wealth are all generously re-created. And yet the movie is not mindlessly sumptuous—the filmmakers haven't lost sight of the fact that what matters in "Gatsby" are the characters' *attitudes* to wealth and class.

Fitzgerald thought that the very rich were different from the rest of us, and "Gatsby" acknowledges some unpopular truths. Faithful to its source, the movie suggests that we are a class-divided and class-conscious society; that great wealth is not the same as pedigree; that social position often defines social conduct. Indisputably well-born, Daisy and Tom play with other people's lives; almost without flinching, they destroy the garage mechanic George Wilson and his unfaithful wife, Myrtle, and they are ultimately responsible for Gatsby's death. They know the rules, just how far they can go and what they can get away with; Gatsby and the working-class Wilsons do not.

Fitzgerald's snobbishness is softened by his wry, likable narrator, Nick Carraway, who serves as our moral anchor among the untouchable Long Island set. Nick knows how to respond to people regardless of dollar signs. Beneath the masquerade, he sees Gatsby's real worth, he understands the nagging sense of inadequacy that motivates

Gatsby and that underlies the character's diseased conception of the American Dream. And beneath their charm, beneath their seductive trappings, Nick also sees the hollowness of his beautiful cousin Daisy and her polo-playing husband, their capacity for casual cruelty.

The movie keeps the novel's sensible perspective on the very rich; we're not asked to gawk at the parade of wealth but to see, through Nick's eyes, the pomp, the frenzied partying, and the soul-denying class conventions for what they really are. Nick is beautifully played by Sam Waterston, who has just the correct mixture of compassion and detachment. He's a severe yet humane judge of human follies. And he reads Fitzgerald's cadenced sentences with becoming naturalness. As if they hadn't been forewarned that the movie is a dud, audiences are responding warmly to Waterston's kindly, wide-eyed hero. Confounding the skeptics, Waterston makes it all work.

Fittingly, since we see them from a distance, filtered through Nick's consciousness, most of the other actors perform in a quietly stylized manner. Consider Mia Farrow as Daisy. She's received some most uncharitable reviews and yet hers is immense, courageous work. She's not afraid to make Daisy unlikable. Pampered, useless, bored, a neurotic privileged plaything, her Daisy yet has feeling and dignity. Farrow plays a rich woman not from the outside, as a comedy of manners caricature, but from the character's own point of view.

As Tom, Bruce Dern is not ideally cast (perhaps he and Robert Redford should have switched roles), but Dern is a good solid actor, and he makes the character work despite the odds. Unlike Farrow, whose voice drips money, Dern does not convince us that he is to the manner born. His bearing does not immediately connote class; his diction, and his chunkiness around the middle, violate upper crust decorum. But, by sheer strength of personality, the actor gets Tom's condescension, his cruelty, his sense of privilege, his pride of ownership.

As in the book, Gatsby himself remains an enigmatic and peripheral figure. As Gatsby, Robert Redford is too poised, too obviously "acceptable." Had they the nerve, the filmmakers ought to have cast the part with an unknown, a dark, brooding actor, his ethnic features a little lopsided, his voice edged with coarseness, his stance as a gentleman too eagerly insisted on to be entirely convincing. Gatsby is a man who creates himself according to his image of what an American millionaire should live like and look like. Underneath the cosmetic dazzle, of course, he is an amateur: Gatsby is one of the great losers in American literature. Does Redford, with his male model looks, answer such a description? Redford wears his pink summer suit much too well; he looks and sounds as if he belongs right at the center of his extravagant, dopey parties.

Redford tries, though. In searching for a rhythm for his character, he gives his lines a clipped, edgy reading. He uses his toothpaste-ad smile, but this isn't one of his walk-through performances. As he offers glimpses of his character's hidden life, Redford works conscientiously against his leading man image. It's thoughtful work that's never quite right but that's never simply a star turn either.

Jack Clayton's direction of "The Innocents" (based on Henry James's "The Turn of the Screw") was the finest film adaptation of great literature I've ever seen. "Gatsby" doesn't have the authority that distinguished the earlier film. It isn't Clayton's collaboration with a master, the way "The Innocents" was, but it is by no means the crude Hollywood hustle or the blatant bore that its reputation suggests. "The Great Gatsby" is a graceful and intelligent complement to the novel rather than a dimwitted bludgeoning of it. It is eminently worth savoring.

1974 My 19, II:13:1

Robert Redford and Mia Farrow, as the trysting Jay and Daisy, in "The Great Gatsby"
"It is by no means the crude Hollywood hustle or the blatant bore that its reputation suggests"

Liv Ullmann, Hackman in 'Zandy's Bride'

By HOWARD THOMPSON

What promises to be an engrossing character study of a lovely, lonely mail-order wife and her adaptation to a crude, pioneer huband tapers off episodically and disappointingly in "Zandy's Bride."

It does so despite an intelligent performance by Liv Ullmann, whose luminous eyes light up the screen every minute, and the steady, watchful direction of Jan Troell, who has impressively rooted his first California film in a wild sweep of the Big Sur area. But for simple, sustained impact and depth, the new picture can't touch Mr. Troell's two superb pioneer dramas, "The Emigrants" and "The New Land," filmed in his and Miss Ullmann's native Scandinavia.

The Warner Bros. release that opened yesterday at the Sutton has two snags in character and drama. The first is the role—not the performance —of Gene Hackman, that of a selfish, thick-skulled hero, who savagely assaults his new bride and actually expects her to accept and love him. And indeed she does, though our acceptance is something else. An actress less skillful than Miss Ullmann might have run him through, for his persistent brutality, with a pitchfork, script or no script.

Furthermore, the emotional tug-of-war is scuttled toward the end of the picture by isolating Mr. Hackman with some cattle thieves and then scooting him farther away to San Francisco for some brief soul-searching. This is the fault of Marc Norman's screenplay, adapted from Lillian Bos Ross's novel, "The Stranger." By shedding the wife's viewpoint, it breaks the real narrative. The story-line and Mr. Hackman have nothing to do but ramble back home, where, of course, the mountain grass is greener.

•

Of the supporting cast, Eileen Heckart wisely underplays a burdened pioneer mother. Maria Cordova is especially good as a warm-hearted but wanton woman. Eventually, though, the restless viewer begins peering more and more beyond the people to the awesome reality of Big Sur, where at least Miss Ullmann, her director and his photographer, Jordan Cronenweth, find and hold firm footing.

1974 My 20, 39:1

By A. H. WEILER

As the most ambitious of the Japanese yakuza (gangster) features in the current series at the Regency Theater, "Theater of Life," which opened a two-day stand here yesterday, is essentially familiar both as life and theater, despite its exotic trappings. Life in this case is a convoluted, bloody, theatrically love-filled affair that is as close to soap opera as to ritualistic melodrama.

The tattooed, sword-swinging, gun-toting yakuza involved here in the 10 years starting in 1916 are devoted, as usual, to their fighting clans and are also caught up in complex, confusing struggles with changing life-styles and lachrymose romances.

The Cast

THEATER OF LIFE; screenplay by Yoshitaro Nomura, Haruhiko Mimura and Tai Kato; from an original story by Shiro Ozaki; directed by Tai Kato; produced by Yoshiji Mishima and Mr. Nomura; photographed by Keiji Maruyama; edited by Shizu Ohsawa; released by Shochiku Films. At the Regency Theater, Broadway and 67th Street. Running time: 166 minutes. This film has not been rated.

Hyokichi Aonari	Muga Takewaki
Kira Tsune	Jiro Tamiya
Hishakaku	Hideki Takahashi
Miyagawa	Tetsuya Watari
Hyotaro Aonari	Hisaya Morishige
Omina	Keiko Tsushima
Osode	Yoshiko Kayama
Otoyo	Mitsuko Baisho

Will the son of an upstanding yakuza chief who, defeated by change, has committed suicide, follow in family tradition in spite of his desire to break with his past and become a writer? Will his father's devoted servant succeed in bringing the son back to the fold? Will the rough opposition be cut down? And will the loving, if ill-used women in their lives find true happiness?

Tai Kato, the director—reportedly an expert with some 35 films in this genre to his credit—is not the man to give us quick answers. He dotes on a succession of battles between rival yakuza clans that are as gory as any Western shootout and a plethora of affairs in which true love is finally and expectedly triumphant.

In a legend that slowly wends its way from Tokyo and the hinterlands to Shanghai and back, Mr. Kato has gotten some effective, if necessarily stylized, performances from Jiro Tamiya, as the father's ill-fated, dedicated henchman; Muga Takewaki, as the son torn between writing and filial love; Hideka Takahashi, as a loyal, love-smitten, jealous yakuza, and other principals in a large, energetic cast.

They are aided by eye-catching color vignettes and English subtitles that eventually make the complicated proceedings fairly clear to a Western viewer. However, one is left with the gnawing feeling that their troubles could have been resolved in less than the 166 minutes it takes to spin their moody saga.

1974 My 21, 51:1

Jackie Mason Portrays Character on the Run

"The Stoolie," which opened yesterday at the 68th Street Playhouse, is a sentimental little fairy tale that tries to nuzzle its way into your affections like a mongrel dog that is long on heart and a little short on brains.

It is a film with a nice eye for seamy locales, a firm grip on the stuff of which losers are made, a couple of laughs, an interesting cast and one of those fatal lapses in logic that leave audiences squirming because the characters are doing a lot of running around for nothing.

•

The title role is played by Jackie Mason, best known as a comedian, who is also credited here as the movie's executive producer. As Roger Pittman, he is the Ratso Rizzo of Weehawken, a pallid, rheumy-eyed small-time hustler whose principal income is derived from setting up his friends for arrest by a seedy detective named Alex Brogan (Dan Frazer.)

One day, Roger takes off for Miami with $7,500 in Police Department cash entrusted to him by Brogan. Down South, he checks into a luxury hotel, rids himself of his constant stubble, discards his peg pants and grubby jacket for a new wardrobe and goes looking, without much success, for women. And then he runs into Sheila Morrison (Marcia Jean Kurtz), a legal secretary from Hempstead, L. I., all freckles and frizzy hair, looking for all the world like an apprentice Barbra Streisand.

The Cast

THE STOOLIE, directed by John G. Avidsen; written by Eugene Price, Larry Alexander and Marc B. Ray; director of photography, Ralf Bode; edited by Gerald Greenberg and Stanley Bochner; music, William Goldstein; produced by Chase Mellen 3d; executive producer, Jackie Mason; released by Continental Distributing, Motion Picture Division of the Walter Reade Organization, Inc. At the 68th Street Playhouse, at Third Avenue. Running time: 90 minutes. This films is classified PG.

Roger Pittman .... Jackie Mason
1st Hijacker .... Josip Elic
2d Hijacker .... Reid Cruikshank
Alex Brogan .... Dan Frazer
Maxie .... Leonard York
Sheila Morrison ...... Marcia Jean Kurtz
Marco Ruiz .... Richard Casballo
Sylvia .... Babette New

Roger and Sheila fall truly in love just as Brogan, like a Keystone Fury, descends on them, demanding restitution of the $7,500. The rest of the film is devoted to Roger's effort to escape jail and remain with Sheila by coming up with the money and Brogan's effort to escape the loss of his job by restoring the funds to department coffers.

•

And there, through it all, as they run around is Sheila, cooking a little, nagging a little. But it never seems to have occurred to her companions or the scriptwriters that the legal secretary could have spared everyone a lot of trouble by helping Roger obtain the loan he tries for in vain.

"The Stoolie," like its characters, is a loser. But not for lack of effort.

LAWRENCE VAN GELDER

1974 My 22, 36:2

DAISY MILLER, directed and produced by Peter Bogdanovich; screenplay by Frederic Raphael, based on a story by Henry James; director of photography, Alberto Spagnoli; edited by Verna Fields; music, Bach, Mozart, Strauss, Boccherini, Haydn, Schubert and Verdi; released by Paramount Pictures. At the Baronet Theater, Third Avenue at 59th Street. Running time: 91 minutes. (This film is classified G).

Annie P. (Daisy) Miller..Cybill Shepherd
Frederick Winterbourne.....Barry Brown
Mrs. Ezra B. Miller.....Cloris Leachman
Mrs. Costello ....Mildred Natwick
Mrs. Walker ....Eileen Brennan
Mr. Giovanelli...........Duilio Del Prete

By NORA SAYRE

Often, filming a classic appears almost as perilous as tangling with your local terrorist group. Translating Henry James's "Daisy Miller" for the screen seemed like an absolutely hopeless project—but Peter Bogdanovich has made a movie that works amazingly well. The picture opened yesterday at the Baronet.

James's tale of a naive, headlong young American tourist who scandalizes her snobbish compatriots has been directed with freshness and intelligence—and none of the ghastly reverence that crippled "The Great Gatsby." The world of lost Americans abroad—some weakened by too much alien culture, others penalized for their ignorance — is skillfully re-created Meanwhile, as Leon Edel observed, the defunct issue of propriety has been replaced by contemporary questions of "permissiveness"; since Daisy and her young brother rule their mother quite tyranically, "Daisy Miller" is relevant to the latest debates about growing up in America.

•

At moments, Cybill Shepherd overdoes the breathless chatter and the parasol-twirling. But much of the time, she catches the gaiety and the directness of Daisy, the spontaneity of a spoiled but very likable person. She also manages to be thoughtless without playing dumb or dizzy, and to convey that mixture of recklessness and innocence that bewildered the other Jamesian characters—those who discovered that "the unexpected in her behavior was the only thing to expect."

Barry Brown as Winterbourne, the inhibited, over-refined young man who's cautiously attracted to Daisy; Mildred Natwick as an impeccably authoritarian aunt, Cloris Leachman as Daisy's flustered mother, Eileen Brennan as a hostess who personifies social cruelty, and Duilio Del Prete as Daisy's sleek Italian playmate are all very good indeed. (The only blemish on the cast is a small boy who's been directed to exceed all bounds of brathood.)

Admittedly, there are a couple of literary problems. The novella was told from Winterbourne's point of view. In the movie, close-ups of his gaze resting wistfully on Daisy yield a rather clumsy substitute for James's narration, and there are too many reaction shots. (We don't need to see the character "thinking" quite so often.) Moreover, James's own "Daisy" is a one-dimensional work—it hasn't the emotional depth of his best inventions, and the film mirrors the flaws of the charming but fairly bloodless original. People reproach Daisy for her casual flirtations, and she simply can't believe that they are shocked—there's not much dramatic content here, and the actors have little chance to vary their performances.

But even though "Daisy" wasn't one of the master's meatiest scenarios, Peter Bogdanovich has provided a sensitive glimpse of the hypocrisies and contradictions of the past—without one whiff of nostalgia. (In fact, the movie says far more about the American condition than "American Graffiti.") And another virtue of "Daisy" is that it makes you appreciate the present.

1974 My 23, 52:1

The Cast

WEDDING IN BLOOD, directed by Claude Chabrol; script and dialogue by Mr. Chabrol (French with English subtitles); photography, Jean Rabier; music, Pierre Jansen; a Franco-Italian Co-production: Les Films la Boetie (Paris), Canaria Films (Rome); released by New Line Cinema. At the Playboy Theater, 110 West 57th Street. Running time: 98 minutes. (This film is classified R).

Lucienne .... Stephane Audran
Pierre .... Michel Piccoli
Paul .... Claude Pieplu
Clothilde .... Clothilde Joano
Helene .... Eliana de Santis

By LAWRENCE VAN GELDER

The opening words of "Wedding in Blood" ("Les Noces Rouges"), the new Claude Chabrol film that opened yesterday at the Playboy Theater, are spoken by a wife to her husband: "Don't touch me." Its final image is the intertwined hands of its lovers.

What lies between is a memorable exploration of extramarital passion ignited in the presence of physical estrangement, and dual murder undertaken in the name of freedom and with shocking respect for appearances —the discreet harm of the bourgeoisie.

It is a film of relentless irony, masked anger and the sort of mature artistic control that is characterized by a graceful economy in the presentation of telling detail, to create characters that first arrest us by their individuality and then astonish us with the realization of their capacity for universality.

•

Although "Wedding in Blood" appears to focus only on its five central characters, it is the town they inhabit and the townspeople (the film was shot in Valençay in central France) that infuse everything with an inescapable moral gravity.

Sketched in a deceptively offhand manner, it is a place where life seems, on the surface, pleasant and uncomplicated. But behind closed doors, the sickly, devitalized Clothilde Maury (Clothilde Joano) tells her husband, Pierre (Michel Piccoli), the town's vice mayor, "Don't touch me."

In a larger, more opulent home, Paul Delamare (Claude Pieplu), the town's leading official, sleeps alone. His beautiful wife, Lucienne (Stéphane Audran) and her illegitimate daughter, Hélène Chevalier (Eliana de Santis) peer into his bedroom and laugh. With no passion for his wife, he cares solely for vote-getting and a secret, corrupt land deal that draws him to and from Paris and threatens the town with upheaval.

Little wonder, then, at the intensity of the affair between Lucienne, whose husband commands her presence on the hearth but not in his bed, and Pierre, whose wife offers him cold chicken and soup he embodies with wine. These are lovers who cannot keep their hands and mouths from each other. Literally and figuratively, they devour each other. He comes at her with uproarious animal cries. They seek each other open-mouthed, and in the film's most striking image, their lips are bridged by a web of spittle against a background of flame and death.

We have progressed from watching the lovers evade the town's knowledge of their affair, through listening to Pierre explain away to Lucienne the murder of his wife ("She didn't care about anything"), to seeing Paul seal his doom by reducing his wife to hysteria with a reaction to her infidelity she can only construe as unspeakably immoral.

And so, toward the end, we are left with a widow and a widower, both killers, both preoccupied not with guilt but with satisfying their society's hunger for maintenance of the niceties, including the passage of a decent interval of time before they can live happily ever after. They have inhabited a world where murder has become more reasonable than its alternatives.

The performances are superb. Claude Chabrol's "Wedding in Blood" is a film of exceptional merit.

1974 My 23, 52:1

Invasion by Bats in 'Chosen Survivors'

Movie science-fiction, which has threatened mankind with all kinds of berserk fauna from ants to dinosaurs, now is transmitting future shock with bats in "Chosen Survivors," which landed at Loews State and other theaters yesterday. If the chills are intermittent, the combination of the voracious vampires and fumbling scientists as unwitting partners in disaster gives some novelty and a sardonic twist to this latest manufactured view of a possible doomsday.

The 11 survivors here have been selected by computer to live in a seemingly safe, luxurious, gadget-filled environment miles below the earth's surface, presumably to save mankind after a wholly destructive thermonuclear war.

Naturally, this American élite includes young, handsome male and female scientists, a tycoon, a writer, a Congresswoman and a black Olympic gold medal winner, who cautiously accept their fate until those screeching bats invade their haven. And the behaviorial expert among them soon drives them up the stainless steel walls by confessing that there is no nuclear holocaust and that they're actually guinea pigs in a controlled experiment.

Who survives is not important here. Sutton Roley, a television director, maintains a fair level of suspense aided largely by scientific gimmickry, technical effects and action sequences that accentuate the inmates' terror. The script by H. B. Cross and Joe Reb Moffly, newcomers to this observer, offers them some dialogue that realistically reflects on man's inhumanity to man.

Properly taut, if not memorable, performances are contributed by the principals, among them Jackie Cooper as the self-centered tycoon; Lincoln Kilpatrick as the proud Olympian; Barbara Babcock as the pretty and proficient doctor; Bradford Dillman as the behavorial observer hoist by his own experiment, and Richard Jaeckel as the beleaguered electronics overseer.

A. H. WEILER

1974 My 23, 52:1

THAT'S ENTERTAINMENT!, scenes from movie musicals by M-G-M from 1929 to 1958; written, produced and directed by Jack Haley Jr.; executive producer, Daniel Melnick; additional music adapted by Henry Mancini; released by United Artists Corporation. At the Ziegfeld Theater, Avenue of the Americas and 54th Street. Running time: 120 minutes. (This film is classified G).

By NORA SAYRE

When Graham Greene was a movie critic in the nineteen-thirties, he detested close-ups of the open mouths of singers; his reviews complained steadily of teeth and tonsils. He would be miserable at "That's Entertainment!," a tour of M-G-M musicals from 1929 to 1958 —but those who don't share his phobia will hugely enjoy this movie. Written, produced and directed by Jack Haley Jr., it opened yesterday at the Ziegfeld.

The pleasures are abundant: Gene Kelly squelching sublimely through puddles in "Singin' in the Rain"; Judy Garland singing "Get Happy" over a series of clips of her faces at all ages—the result is a joyful obituary; Donald O'Connor dancing on his knees; Fred Astaire and Eleanor Powell in a breath-stopping duet from "Broadway Melody of 1940." Glimpses of Mr. Kelly, springing about

"That's Entertainment!" includes scenes of Nelson Eddy and Jeanette MacDonald in "Rose Marie," left, a 1936 musical, and Ginger Rogers and Fred Astaire in "The Barkleys of Broadway" (1949).

on the scaffolding of a half-constructed building, and Mr. Astaire, dancing with a hat rack, distill the contrasting styles of both great hoofers.

•

Mr. Kelly's acrobatic talents make you aware of the exertion as much as the dexterity: what he does is triumphantly difficult, and we know that almost no one else could leap so smartly from one spot to another. But, as many have noted, Mr. Astaire makes every step look easy: as he soars and swoops and glides, infinite spectators feel that they could do exactly the same.

•

Some of the musicals of the early thirties were creaky because dramatic actors were suddenly pushed into a medium that didn't suit them. In "Idiot's Delight," Clark Gable dances and sings abominably, and Joan Crawford—one rigid finger laid against her cheek — prances like a lumberjack. The movie's funniest moment may be the apotheosis of Esther Williams in the early fifties: climactic scenes of that brawny Venus sinking into or rising from the water appear to mock the imagery of the Aquarian age. Incidentally, the big ballet from "American in Paris" seems soupier than ever.

Ars Gratia Artis indeed . . . Today, there's a pang in watching that lion roar above M-G-M's motto, to see the ravaged sets of the studio whose existence was imperiled for a while (although movie production has resumed). Elizabeth Taylor, James Stewart, Mickey Rooney and the other stars who narrate this picture are sentimental about the past—but why shouldn't they be? Meanwhile, most of the numbers—from Jimmy Durante coaching the young Frank Sinatra in "It Happened in Brooklyn" to Leslie Caron drifting in and out of Mr. Kelly's grasp — run long enough so that you can re-experience the original. Hence this isn't nostalgia, it's history.

1974 My 24, 22:1

Screen: Poignant Glimpses of History

Whitney Offers a Bill of 5 Short Subjects

Facets of the turbulent history of the last 40 years are engrossingly captured in "Looking Forward, Looking Back," the collection of five short subjects that opened yesterday at the Whitney Museum of American Art. If some of them are not new and the focus on the future is only minimal, the past is vividly spotlighted by these reminders of events that are being dimmed by the passage of time.

A case in point is the rarely seen 30-minute Republican party-sponsored television address made by President Nixon in 1952 as the Vice President candidate defending himself against allegations of having accepted funds from California Republicans. As a verbatim record, the "Checkers Speech," makes the past and present startlingly meaningful.

•

The Cast

THUNDERBOLT AND LIGHTFOOT, written and directed by Michael Cimino; produced by Robert Daley for the Malpaso Company; photographed by Frank Stanley; released by United Artists. At the Cinerama Theater, Broadway and 47th Street, and other showcases. Running time: 115 minutes. (This film is rated R.)
Thunderbolt...............Clint Eastwood
Lightfoot...................Jeff Bridges
Leary.....................George Kennedy
Goody.....................Geoffrey Lewis

Of the current movies on vagrant banditry, a theme that is being run into the ground, the most engaging is "Thunderbolt and Lightfoot," a funny, tough-fibered crime comedy with an unobtrusive edge of drama. With Clint Eastwood as an older, wise thief and Jeff Bridges as his grinning apprentice, the picture is consistently entertaining and interesting.

Mr. Eastwood is a smart fellow. For his Malpaso Company unit, he engaged a bright new young director, Michael Cimino, who also wrote an original script that is freshly turned in characterization and plot, amusingly ribald and neatly paced.

The Program

LOOKING FORWARD, LOOKING BACK: THE THIRTIES by Richard King, 18 minutes; HIROSHIMA/NAGASAKI, AUGUST 1945 by Paul Ronder, 16 minutes; CHECKERS SPEECH, 30 minutes; ASSASSINATION RAGA by Lawrence Ferlinghetti and Max Crosley, 13 minutes; MARS, THE SEARCH BEGINS by NASA, 28 minutes. At the Whitney Museum of American Art, Madison Avenue and 75th Street. Through June 2.

The 16-minute selection from the footage of nine Japanese cameramen who shot "Hiroshima/Nagasaki" right after the first atom bombs were dropped in 1945 is a largely placid but stark accentuation of the horrors of nuclear war. And the fact-filled English narration powerfully underscores these vignettes, which deserve this first public showing.

As the most recent point in history, the 28-minute "Mars, the Search Begins" evolves as a spellbinding and educational document culled from thousands of color photographs made by Mariner 9 for the National Aeronautics and Space Administration in 1972. The brilliant blow-ups and three-dimensional re-

The pattern is essentially familiar—crime still doesn't pay and the big climactic heist misfires—but Mr. Cimino's expert piloting scoots the action forward colorfully. The playing is entirely disarming, with Mr. Eastwood's wry restraint meshing perfectly with Mr. Bridges's impish exuberance, and Geoffrey Lewis and George Kennedy lending sturdy support.

As Frank Stanley's beautiful photography evokes the sweep of Montana's Big Sky country, the picture mercifully avoids footnotes on social significance except for one subtle, succinct touch in a climactic, schoolhouse scene, a thoughtful twist. The Eastwood team has pulled off a modest enjoyable winner.

HOWARD THOMPSON

1974 My 24, 23:3

productions of the dusty, mountainous Martian terrain, coupled with exemplary explanations by three eminent scientists, who speculate only briefly about life on Mars and future applications of the discoveries, make a complex subject lucid and relevant.

"The Thirties," a collage of newsreels set against a musical background of now campy jazz bands, is a poignant and pointed remembrance of the Depression era and its strikes, its unemployed and a fearless, young President Franklin D. Roosevelt resolutely taking over the reins of government.

"Assassination Raga," which has been shown previously, is a mite too arty in its montages and in Lawrence Ferlinghetti's poetic laments for the slayings of the Kennedys, the Rev. Dr. Martin Luther King Jr. and others. But it serves, like the other entries, to make fading history come fascinatingly alive.
A. H. WEILER

1974 My 24, 23:2

HUCKLEBERRY FINN, directed by J. Lee Thompson; screenplay, Robert B. Sherman and Richard M. Sherman; director of photography, Laszlo Kovacs; film editor, Michael F. Anderson; music, Richard M. Sherman and Robert B. Sherman; produced by Arthur P. Jacobs; released by United Artists Corporation. At the Guild Theater, 50th Street and Rockefeller Center, 86th Street East, east of Third Avenue, and the Eastside Cinema, Third Avenue at 55th Street. Running time: 118 minutes. (This film is classified G.)
Huckleberry Finn...............Jeff East
Jim........................Paul Winfield
The King..................Harvey Korman
The Duke...................David Wayne
Colonel Grangerford.....Arthur O'Connell
Pap.......................Gary Merrill
Mrs. Loftus..............Natalie Trundy

By LAWRENCE VAN GELDER

After about an hour, just when "Huckleberry Finn" is about to drowin in its own treacle, up bob Harvey Korman as the King and David Wayne as the Duke, and for half an hour or so, life on the Mississippi seems well worth living.

But all too soon, Messrs. Korman and Wayne, as irresistible a pair of rogues to enliven a music film since Honest John the fox and his sidekick, Gideon, did the trick in "Pinocchio," disappear behind the bars of the Jackson's Landing jail.

And "Huckleberry Finn," all sunsets, leafiness and thin riparian righteousness, drags its way to a finish.

Goodness, there are parents all over the country eager for a movie to take their children to; and there are, doubtless, a few million children who would be delighted to find one they're allowed to see.

But aside from the all-too-few minutes when Mr. Korman and Mr. Wayne are on the screen — fleecing yokels and orphans, putting on airs, putting down lynch mobs and putting up with all the dullards around them—"Huckleberry Finn," which opened yesterday at neighborhood theaters, is a lavish bore.

The setting is Disneyland South; Jeff East as Huck gives one of those performances that afflict child actors with a bad name; J. Lee Thompson directs as though excitement hadn't been invented yet; and with the exception of one tune—"Royalty," rendered by Messrs. Korman and Wayne — the songs by Richard M. and Robert B. Sherman are memorable chiefly for their forgettableness.

Paul Winfield merits praise for a strong, dignified performance as Jim. What honors there are belong to him, Mr. Korman and Mr. Wayne.

1974 My 25, 16:1

'The Divine Mr. J.'

A dull, dirty-mouthed and utterly infantile "religious satire" movie titled "The Divine Mr. J." is a piece of amateur camp claptrap. It opened like a garbage-can lid, yesterday at the Festival Theater. Directed and produced by Peter Alexander, it displays some of the world's worst actors self-consciously mincing around various lawns—with some wedged-in footage from other sources — and mocking the story of Jesus.

The picture also "stars" Bette Midler, according to the ads and opening credits, who appears as the "Virgin Mary," for about 10 minutes, singing a bar or two, and gushes as coyly and tastelessly as the others. A wan mumbler named John Bassberger portrays Jesus.

A battery of Midler fans were in front of the theater yesterday handing out "a personal statement" from their idol explaining that her "sequences were shot several years ago in the very early stages of my career." The statement protestd exploitation of "my current professional status." It adds: "However, I did it and there's nothing I can do about it." She atones, partly, by adding: "In my opinion, the movie is dreadful." Further, she sued in State Supreme Court yesterday to have the film billed as her movie debut. Bingo, Bette.

HOWARD THOMPSON

1974 My 25, 16:2

U.S. Film Wins Top Cannes Prize

By VINCENT CANBY
Special to The New York Times

CANNES, France, May 24—American films and film makers won three of the five top prizes awarded at the close of the 27th Cannes International Film Festival tonight.

"The Conversation," written and directed by Francis Ford Coppola, was named the grand prize winner as the best film. Jack Nicholson was named best actor for his performance as the tough-talking, beer-drinking shore patrolman in "The Last Detail," and the best screenplay award went to "Sugarland Express," written by Hal Barwood and Matthew Robbins.

The special jury prize was given to Pier Paolo Pasolini's visually spectacular "A Thousand and One Nights," an Italian entry. This is, in effect, the second prize in the best film category. Marie José Nat was cited as best actress for her performance in "Les Violons du Bal," the autobiographical French film written and directed by Michel Drach (Miss Nat's husband) about the early days of the Nazi occupation.

Charles Boyer, the veteran French actor who was a romantic star in Hollywood for many years, was voted an "hommage" by the jury for his role as a philosophical aristocrat in Alain Resnais's film "Stavisky" about the notorious swindler.

Carlos Saura, director of Spain's "La Prima Angelica" (Cousin Angelica), won this

'Conversation' Cited At 27th Festival— Nicholson Named

year's jury prize in recognition of his new film as well as his entire body of work. Mr. Saura's film managed the difficult task of being both comic and bitter about Spanish life without offending the Government.

Awarded at Ceremonies

The prizes, which were announced in the afternoon, are awarded to the winners in formal ceremonies at the Festival Palace tonight.

Robert Bresson, whose new film, "Launcelot du Lac," was not invited to the festival but was shown out of competition here last night, created some excitement this morning when he refused to accept the award (a scroll) of the International Federation of Film Critics. The critics had voted to cite jointly Mr. Bresson's film and the West German film by Rainer Werner Fassbinder "All the Others Are Called Ali."

When informed of the award during a news conference, Mr. Bresson said that he did not want to share any awards. He said also that he hadn't journeyed to Cannes "for prestige" but for money. Grand prize winners mean a great deal at the box office in France and in the rest of Europe, but critics' prizes do not sell tickets.

Mr. Bressons's producer, Jean-Pierre Rassam, took the opportunity of the news conference to criticize the men who run the Cannes festival for not having invited "Launcelot" to be a part of the main competition.

American films dominated the festival in number and quality. Six of the 27 films in competition were American and all, with one exception, were well received. The surprise here tonight was that the jury made no attempt, as juries in the past have done, to apportion the prizes evenly among the competing nations. Said a French journalist: "It's a revolution, a small one, but a revolution just the same."

1974 My 25, 16:1

Cannes You Believe What's at Cannes?

By VINCENT CANBY

CANNES.

FILM festivals are probably the worst places in the world for assessing individual films. They come at one in such number, in such a short space of time, that one is apt to lose one's bearings. The professional critic finds himself feeling a little like the wine taster who gets suddenly drunk. It's not fatal. It's not always incapacitating, but it tends to blunt judgment.

Several years ago, Dusan Makavejev's "W. R.: Mysteries of the Organism" became the rage at the Cannes Festival. A little later, in the comparative serenity of New York, it looked like a mess, even if an intelligent one. Can you remember the name of the Grand Prize winner at the 1961 Festival? For the record, it was Henri Colpi's "After Such a Long Absence." After a rather short time, it's been forgotten.

Nevertheless, one thing did become quickly apparent here during the first week of the 27th annual Cannes Festival: the old, seemingly conventional narrative forms are still the most satisfactory. Which may be one reason that the American films in competition here this year, particularly Robert Altman's "Thieves Like Us," Hal Ashby's "The Last Detail" and Steven Spielberg's "Sugarland Express," look so good in this Cote d'Azur context. The American films have a directness and vitality that seem to escape the work of European directors who, for the most part, enjoy much greater artistic freedom than American directors.

It is, I'm sure, some measure of the way that Europeans look at films that Terrence Malick's "Badlands," a stunningly original work conceived within a conventional form, was not even invited to Cannes this year, while Martin Scorsese's fine "Mean Streets" is here but out of competition, as part of the festival-within-the-festival called the Director's Fortnight, sponsored by an association of film directors.

Demonstrating the differences between American and European filmmakers these days are three films shown in the festival's first week, Federico Fellini's "Amarcord," Dusan Makavejev's "Sweet Movie" and Alain Resnais's "Stavisky." In "Amarcord," which was shown out of competition at the festival's opening gala, Fellini continues with the autobiographical form of "The Clowns" and "Roma," something that I'd rather see him do than almost any director I can think of. Fellini is so full of exuberance and stylistic bravado that nothing he does is uninteresting, yet by employing this form he seems to be asking us not to expect the discipline that is apparent in his greatest achievements, "Nights of Cabiria" and "8½."

"Amarcord" looks as if Fellini were spending his time extravagantly doodling while awaiting an idea for his next real movie. Which poses a question I'm not prepared to answer: Why should reminiscences and childhood fancies, restaged as film fiction, be somehow less acceptable to us than written memoires? It may be, of course, that we shall see these films as landmarks in personal cinema of a sort for which we're unprepared now. It's always possible that it's the imagination of the audience that has shrunk, not Fellini's. Time will tell.

Time, I'm sure, will not tell us anything we don't already know about Makavejev's "Sweet Movie," presented here as part of the Director's Fortnight. "Sweet Movie" is personal cinema carried deep into the swamps of self-indulgence. Makavejev, you may remember, got into all sorts of trouble with the Yugoslav Government over "W. R.: Mysteries of the Organism." The authorities suspected that he was making fun of Communism through Stalinism, which he was.

In "Sweet Movie," a Canadian-French co-production, Makavejev continues to explore a film form that I'm not sure exists outside his own imagination. Like "Mysteries of the Organism," it is, I think, supposed to be an erotic political comedy, which may be a contradiction in terms. It's the sort of film that makes one think longingly of movies with ordinary beginnings, middles and ends, and of movies that demonstrate ideas rather than pronounce them. It also makes me think most fondly of his first film, "Man is Not a Bird," which said within the highly disciplined narrative form much more about sex, politics and human relations than does "Sweet Movie."

Although highly schematic and bursting with intellectual references, "Sweet Movie" asks us simply to look and feel and not to think, as if thinking were something to be given up, like chewing one's fingernails. Thinking is also one of the ways we realize that the emperor is naked as a jaybird, like Makavejev's newest film.

For the record, I should report that "Sweet Movie" has two main "story" lines. One concerns a character named Mr. Kapital (John Vernon), a psychotic capitalist, who marries Miss World of 1984, the winner of a television contest sponsored by the Chastity Belt Foundation.

The other story line is an elaborate metaphor: The canals of an unidentified city (actually Amsterdam) are plied by a huge, extravagantly decorated barge named the Survival. The prow of the barge is a papier maché head of Karl Marx and the skipper is a siren named Anna Planeta who lures innocent young idealists aboard for sex and then murders them. "Leave now," Anna says at one point to a sailor from the Potemkin (Pierre Clementi), "this boat is full of corpses."

In an extended sequence made with the members of the Therapie-Komune of Vienna, the film watches people gorge themselves on food, then vomit, and people defecate. The film has been drawing capacity audiences at its various screenings by people who tell you they want to see it to see if it's as bad as they'd heard. The usual discovery is that it is.

Alain Resnais's "Stavisky," one of the most interesting films in the festival's competition and the director's first film in six years, is more conventional than almost anything he's ever done, but the director of "Hiroshima, Mon Amour" and "Last Year in Marienbad" is still fooling around with time in ways that are not especially interesting.

The movie, with Jean-Paul Belmondo in the title role, is about the charming swindler, a French Jew of Russian descent, whose unmasking and subsequent suicide in 1933 caused such a scandal that it almost toppled the Government. Resnais and Jorge Semprun, who also wrote the screenplay of Resnais's superb "La Guerre est Finie" and Costa-Gavras's "Z," cross-cut between the story of Stavisky's last days and the last days of Trotsky's exile in France, making an analogy so loose that it's subject to any interpretation you might want to give it.

"Stavisky" jumps from present to past to future and back in a fashion that seems less in service of some narrative truth than for the purpose of fancy cinematic effects. The cuts are chrome fins on an old Cadillac, sometimes quite spectacular but without a function that wouldn't be more modestly performed by conventional ellipses.

The city of Cannes, which helps sponsor the festival, couldn't care less about such considerations. Late word has it that this festival has brought in approximately 25,000 people who, one assumes, wouldn't have come to Cannes otherwise.

Including the films that are being screened for buyers outside the festival, an estimated 366 movies are available for viewing during this two-week tournament. Among those I've missed is one from Finland, whose Finnish title has been translated into English as "Earth Is Our Sinful Song." Yesterday I heard someone describe it, quite seriously, as "a sort of 'Peyton Place,' only set in Lapland."

1974 My 26, II:1:1

Harold's Back and Maude's Got Him

By ALJEAN HARMETZ

LOS ANGELES

IT was Dec. 22, 1971, and Paramount was sure it had a winner. "Harold and Maude" opened for Academy Award consideration during the strongest box-office week of the year, with an expensive advertising campaign featuring 75-year-old Ruth Gordon and 21-year-old Bud Cort—two wildly incongruous lovers—on a stolen police motorcycle.

Neither the Academy nor the public considered "Harold and Maude" for very long. The lively Los Angeles box office that week brought exhibitors $210,000 for the reissue of Disney's "Lady and the Tramp," $75,000 for "Fiddler on the Roof," a "sizzling" $40,000 for "Dirty Harry," and a "dismal" $8,500 for "Harold and Maude." In city after city the ill-matched lovers were box-office poison, a wrong guess on the part of the Paramount establishment, a $1.5-million mistake.

But not quite *everywhere*.

"Harold and Maude" returns to New York today. The advertising copy for the open-ended engagement at the Thalia Theater reads, "What Do They Know in the Midwest That We Don't Know in New York?" and "Minneapolis Is Three Years Ahead of New York," and "We've Heard of Word of Mouth, But This Is Ridiculous."

On March 20, 1972, "Harold and Maude" opened at the Westgate Theater in suburban Minneapolis. On March 20, 1974, it started its 105th week there. (The previous Minneapolis record was 93 consecutive weeks for "The Sound of Music.") Paramount's celebration at the theater was picketed by neighbors insisting that any change of program "other than hard-core pornography" would be gratefully appreciated. They carried signs insisting that "two years is too much" and "why must the show go on . . . and on . . . and on?"

In its 112 weeks at the Westgate Theater, the film has grossed nearly $500,000. According to theater manager Ralph Watschke, on any given night at least half the audience has seen the film before. And one 22-year-old patron of the Westgate claims to have seen it 138 times.

Minneapolis, alone, could be dismissed—an accident, an aberration. But this failure at a hundred box offices, this comedy about a 19-year-old depressive who drives a hearse and has faked suicide 15 times and the woman with whom he falls in love—an 80-year-old eccentric optimist who shares her licorice with him at a funeral—also played 112 weeks in Montreal, 72 weeks in Detroit, and two years in Paris. For the past seven months Madeleine Renaud has been starring on the stage as Maude, in the theater her husband, Jean-Louis Barrault, recently built in Paris. By fall, productions of the play Colin Higgins wrote from his screenplay are scheduled for Berlin (Elisabeth Bergner), Rome, Madrid, Copenhagen and London (Gloria Swanson or Ruth Gordon).

"I can walk down the streets of any city," says Ruth Gordon, "including Edgartown on Martha's Vineyard, and people hand me oat straw tea. (A symbol in the movie.) Boxes of chocolates. Photographs of their city. And daisies, daisies, daisies.

Aljean Harmetz is a freelance writer.

Two men and two girls brought a floral set-piece of 12 dozen daisies to my hotel in Dayton, Ohio, to show me what it meant to have 'Harold and Maude' in Dayton. At 7:30 A.M., a middle-aged man stopped me to say that he had especially admired 'Harold and Maude.' He was a vice president of National Cash Register. At lunchtime, the waitress said, 'Your check has been paid. That gentleman said to tell you he saw "Harold and Maude." ' "

Very few people have seen "Harold and Maude," but most of those who have seen it have seen it more than once. West Los Angeles friends of mine —a 37-year-old lawyer and his wife—describe their collision with the film in this way: " 'Harold and Maude' was an 'it' that was the bottom half of a double bill. We were going to see some classic we had been looking forward to, but 'Harold and Maude' came on first. When it was over, we left the theater without staying for the film we had come to see. 'Harold and Maude' was a gem. Deliciously funny. Stretching our limits of acceptance. We couldn't let anything else touch it, spoil it. We never see a picture twice. We barely get there the first time. But, one month later, we dragged a couple of friends, kicking and screaming, to where it was playing as the bottom half of another double bill. We telephoned everybody we knew, forced all of our friends to go see it."

The fanatics who have seen "Harold and Maude" three, six, nine times speak of it as "a regenerative thing" or "like getting your battery recharged." It is not the comedy but the philosophy that sends people plunging back into the darkness of the theater again and again.

"What do you do for fun, for that special feeling of satisfaction?" asks Harold's psychiatrist. "I go to funerals," he answers. For Maude, "burials and births" are "all leading to one another—the great circle of life." Things "grow and bloom and fade and die and change into something else." She, herself, "would like to change into a sunflower most of all."

On a conscious level, the film is a conquest of death, with Maude leading Harold out of his depressed fascination with dying until in the end he abandons the Jaguar he has turned into a hearse, symbolically sending it over a cliff. "Reach out," she says. "Take a chance. Get hurt even. Go, go . . . live. Otherwise, you've got nothing to talk about in the locker room."

On an unconscious level, it is much more. Los Angeles psychiatrist Larry Ruzumna—who thinks that the incest theme in "Harold and Maude" is even more apparent than it was in Louis Malle's explicit story of a mother-son relationship, "Murmur of the Heart"—sees Maude as "immortal, a timeless figure, an eternal earth mother, an idealized mother figure who leads her son out of his depression, makes him fall in love with life. Once she fulfills that role, she disappears. She is an all-accepting mother who transcends morality."

Harold stages mock suicides as a psychic attack on his real, castrating mother. Maude actually commits suicide on her 80th birthday because more time is unnecessary. Ruth Gordon, like psychiatrist Ruzumna, doesn't think "that Maude is dead, at all." Despite the concreteness of pills, ambulance, emergency hospital, the film is ambiguous. We never see Maude dead.

A few days earlier, Harold has given Maude a pressed metal disk that reads, "Harold Loves Maude." "And Maude Loves Harold," she responds. "The nicest gift I've received in years." With the words, she flings the gift away. "Now we'll always know where it is." If, as Ruzumna thinks, "the anxiety-provoking quality of the incest theme" kept the film from being a commercial success, the fairy-tale, wish-fulfilling quality of the death scene conquered by reverse has made it a cult success. (On a more mundane level, however, some people feel that Maude's death killed the movie's chances at the box office.)

The original commercial failure of the film, however, puzzled everyone connected with it. In an industry where nothing gets accomplished without acid indigestion and months of agonized waiting "Harold and Maude" never caused a single person involved—with the possible exception of Ruth Gordon—to reach for Maalox.

*

The script was written in 1970 by then 28-year-old U.C.L.A. film student Colin Higgins (who is now writing a 20th Century Fox-U.S.S.R. co-production of Maeterlinck's "Blue Bird"). In return for free lodging on the Bel Air estate of producer Edward Lewis ("Spartacus," "Grand Prix"), Higgins swept the tennis court, cleaned the swimming pool and drove Lewis's 10-year-old daughter to school. He wrote "Harold and Maude" as the basis for the 20-minute film he would have to make for his Master's Thesis and gave it to Lewis's wife, Mildred, to criticize.

Mildred Lewis (who became executive producer of "Harold and Maude") told Higgins he was "crazy to blow this great idea on a 20-minute job." Higgins rewrote the script as a full length movie and handed it back to his employer's wife. Before the script took third place in the 1970 Samuel Goldwyn Creative Writing Awards at U.C.L.A., Edward Lewis had already sold it to Paramount.

"Paramount was the first and only studio I gave the script," says Lewis. "I knew Peter Bart (assistant head of production at Paramount) well, and I figured Bart would dig it. I also felt the script was very commercial. So did Paramount. We could have sold out our share for a lot of money before the picture was released."

*

Paramount offered the script to Academy Award winning cinematographer Hal Ashby ("In the Heat of the Night"), whose one previous directing job, "The Landlord," had dealt with an equally passive though less neurotic rich boy trying to cope with a world beyond his emotional capabilities. Ashby was the only person connected with the film who didn't expect a smashing success. Pausing in the midst of directing Warren Beatty in "Shampoo," Ashby forces his thoughts back to "Harold and Maude" and says softly that his doubts were more "my natural tendency to pessimism" than any reflection on the picture.

For months, Ashby pondered the casting. "Casting decisions are always the most difficult thing for me," says Ashby. "Once you say, 'Let's go this way,' you're set, locked in."

Paramount's head of production, Bob Evans, had already given the script to Ruth Gordon, with the comment, "I've got the greatest part in the world for you." However, when Miss Gordon met Ashby in his New York hotel room, Ashby was non-committal. "Everyone always wants Ruth Gordon," he told her, "but . . . ." He was, he said, on his way to Europe to talk to Dame Edith Evans, Gladys Cooper, Mildred Natwick, Wendy Hiller. "The hell with him," Ruth Gordon thought.

*

Once in Europe, Ashby "kept drawing myself back to the feeling the role should be played by an American." He called and asked Ruth Gordon for a second meeting, this time in her Hollywood home.

"Now I was sure the part was mine," says Ruth Gordon. After half an hour of polite conversation, Ashby left without making any commitment. "The hell with him in spades," she thought.

In his cautious way, Ashby eventually decided that "Ruth Gordon would be the best Maude. The character was there in her optimism, her energy."

Harold was easier. Ashby "looked at a lot of young actors," but after interviewing Bud Cort and seeing Robert Altman's partially completed "Brewster McCloud" in which Cort starred, he asked Paramount if he could sign Cort without doing a screen test. "It never hurts to test," was the response. Ruth Gordon tested with Cort and with five other unknown actors (John Rubinstein, Bob Balaban, John Nielson, Todd Sussman, Dan Fortas.) After the tests, Ashby's original decision stood.

"While we were making the film," says Ruth Gordon,

Ruth Gordon and Bud Cort are lovers in "Harold and Maude," the 1971 film which begins a return engagement today at the Thalia
So what's wrong with an 80-year-old woman falling in love with a 19-year-old boy?

"none of us doubted its success." But at some point during the filming she began to worry about "marrying the film to the public," her phrase for the difficulties of tastefully publicizing the film. "It will be a woman 80 years old making love to a boy of 19 and it'll go in 42d Street porny theaters," she thought.

"So I looked about for someone to talk to, an innovator. I took the script to Thornton Wilder. I rarely use Thornton. He's too precious. But I asked if he would read the script. When 'Our Town' opened in Princeton and there was no scenery, the audience walked out. 'We'll wait until the scenery comes,' they said. They'd never seen a play that didn't have scenery before. Thornton felt that 'Harold and Maude' was like the Greek myth of Endymion in love with the moon. In a sense, he said, that's Harold with Maude. Harold's in love with the impossible, and somehow the impossible works out for him."

＊

With hindsight, most people connected with "Harold and Maude" feel that the crucial error was not the advertising campaign but the timing. The picture was buried by the avalanche of major films launched during the 1970 Christmas season. "Dirty Harry" and "Diamonds Are Forever" and "Fiddler on the Roof" and "Sunday Bloody Sunday" overshadowed "Harold and Maude." The picture needed time to grow. It didn't get it. And, says a Los Angeles exhibitor, "once a film has a bad start, it very seldom manages to reverse the trend."

＊

The decision to reopen "Harold and Maude" was not sudden. Says Charles O. Glenn, Paramount vice president in charge of marketing, "For years, in cars going to and from airports, we've said to each other, 'Harold and Maude' was a good film.'"
It will play in New York "as long as people come to see it." The Thalia was

chosen because of its proximity to Columbia University and because of the theater's reputation for having "an audience of film buffs who appreciate American classic films as well as foreign ones."

Glenn cannot remember "ever before bringing back a film that was a failure in its initial run." New York is a test. If the film is successful here, it will be reopened in other cities.

"Maude," said my 13-year-old son after seeing the film for the second time, "replanted Harold like she did the tree that the smog was killing."

And now Paramount is replanting "Harold and Maude" at the Thalia.

1974 My 26, II:1:4

Why Does 'Going Places' Infuriate So Many of Its Critics?

By PETER SCHJELDAHL

IF I hadn't already read and heard the appalled reactions of many critics to Bertrand Blier's "Going Places," I might have been disturbed myself by some of that film's calculated crudities. Reviewers had found the movie "sordid," "disgusting," and "a grotesque exercise in sadism"; one had even said he felt "molested" by it. Well, I emerged from the theater full of admiration for what I'd just seen and amazed that it could have caused such a fuss. At its worst, "Going Places" is simply not that bad. And at its frequent best, it has to be one of the most mordant satires ever made about rebellious youth.

Peter Schjeldahl is a freelance writer.

This careening picaresque French film relates the adventures of two loutish young anti-heroes knocking around present-day France. What do they do that's so horrible? They bully people, they steal cars and money and, when not seized by an occasional kindly impulse, show a gift for all kinds of raunchy and infantile behavior. Their one really chilling act, performed in a tantrum of vengefulness, is the potentially lethal booby-trapping of a car belonging to a man who has shot and wounded one of them. But even this seems pretty mild compared to the hijinks in your average American film about off-kilter young people, from "Bonnie and Clyde" to the present.

It would not seem to be what these characters do that has inspired the negative responses to "Going Places" so much as what they are and represent, some deep, disquieting chord they strike. To be fair, it may also have something to do with the coincidental timing of the film's release. Probably at no time in the past 15 years has the public stock of free-spirited youth been lower than it is today, in the *Walpurgisnacht* of Patty Hearst and the SLA. There is a sequence toward the end of "Going Places" when a teen-age girl, encountered by chance, abandons her parents to take up with the fugitives—that hits just close enough to the Hearst affair to give one fortuitious tremors of revulsion.

But to dwell on such reactions is only to confuse the moral attitudes acted out in the film with the moral vision of the film itself, a satirical vision that is harrowing and profound. Unlike "road movies" of the "Easy Rider" genre, this is not a work pitched to the sentimental, self-enchanted level of its protagonists. Blier's ruffians, Jean-Claude and Pierrot, are no more liberated than rats in

a maze, mindlessly pursuing happiness in a social landscape from which the possibility of human fulfillment has been methodically factored out.

Jean-Claude and Pierrot—played with star-quality presence by Gerard Depardieu and Patrick Dewaere—are lower-class lads in the suburbs, age 25 and 23, apparently jobless and homeless, obsessed with sex and danger and courting both with manic machismo. Viewed one way, they belong to a class of fantasy-driven young heroes that is a virtual staple of post-1950s French cinema; but they are more keenly observed, more joltingly real, than their predecessors in the films of Godard and Truffaut. Their one unreal feature is their almost supernatural good luck, notably in evading the law.

For whatever pickles their lust, greed, bravado and stupidity land them in, a smiling fortune is invariably there to extricate them. And this absence of just desserts, of the bullet that usually awaits the protagonist at the end of the conventional criminal-youth picture, may be part of what infuriates some viewers. But reality, after all, is itself unconventional, and Blier's decision to spare his heroes the normal consequences of their actions bespeaks the wry intelligence of a classical satirist.

'A view of society that ought to be seen by anyone who cares where we're going'

If the world Blier depicts resembles that of any other director, it might be Jacques Tati's. Like Tati's cityscapes, Blier's suburbs and towns are big and

empty, devoid of habitable-looking architecture, and inhabited by people who look either mechanized or furtive. The main difference is that Blier's comic innocents are demonic rather than shy, deliberately smashing into things instead of, like Hulot, being disruptive through a simple failure to grasp what is expected of them.

In this depersonalized world, ambivalence reigns. Even the most absurd or ugly human emotion has a positive aspect just in being *human*, in being a momentary relief from deadness. In this limited sense, Jean-Claude and Pierrot are almost benefactors, bringing at least excitement into the lives of persons whose paths they cross and leaving few of them—except perhaps a driver of the booby-trapped car—terribly worse-off for the experience. But this can only be the case because everyone, whether he knows it or not, is about as bad-off as can be, and nearly every comic or perilous episode ends in boredom and frustration or with a whiff of dread.

Even the best luck in the world can't outwit death, and the movie's most memorable sequences bring the heroes together with two personages whom death has already claimed for its own. These are a mother and her son, played stunningly by Jeanne Moreau and with quirky charm by Jacques Cailieux, who at different times emerge from prison to become pet reclamation projects for Jean-Claude and Pierrot. Separately, they are lavished with sex, food and affection by the two friends, who study with interest the effects of their ministrations.

Benumbed and suspicious at first, each gradually thaws out. Moreau blossoms like a dark, twisted flower. The son swells with a mysterious potency, in-

cidentally succeeding in giving the boys' communal girlfriend (Miou-Miou) the first orgasm of her considerable sexual career. Then each in turn, as if suddenly conscious of a long-buried priority, hatches an act of grisly and catastrophic violence, a suicide and a murder from which the heroes recoil with dumb terror, like animals from fire.

Jean-Claude and Pierrot are, in fact, like monkey wrenches tossed by chance into the works of a self-oppressed society, runaway mechanisms full of coarse energy and the illusion of free-will. "Going Places" is replete with images of determinism, of roads—like France's tree-lined "grand routes," which resemble barred corridors — that lead only from one treacherous nowhere to another in a kingdom of vain hopes and poisoned fantasies.

The psychological object of the heroes' quest, meanwhile, is hinted at in another set of images, notably of tunnels and the sea, as well as in the action. Feeling dimly that, via sex and love, they are fleeing death, they are actually rushing hell-for-leather back to the womb, which is death's other door. This irony is the ultimate content of "Going Places," a vast, sad cackle that echoes louder in one's mind the more one reflects on the film.

"Going Places," for all its moments of bizarre fun, is not an agreeable movie, but it might be a great one. In any case, it is an important one, both artistically and as a view of modern society that ought to be attended to by anyone interested in the way our century is going. In accents startlingly new and pungent, Bertrand Blier seems to be telling us that our century is not going very well, though it is certainly going very fast.

1974 Je 2, II:11:5

"For all its moments of bizarre fun, 'Going Places' is not an agreeable movie, but it might be a great one," argues this critic. Patrick Dewaere and Gerard Depardieu play a pair of ruffians with "star-quality presence."

Sex Dominates Malice in Comic 'Malizia'

By VINCENT CANBY

"Malizia," the title of Salvatore Samperi's new Italian comedy, is translated as "malice" but the real subject is lust. It's lust in the various comic disguises that Italian film makers seem to associate particularly with Sicily where Marcello Mastroianni once sought desperately—and hilariously—to murder his wife in "Divorce, Italian-Style."

"Malizia," which opened yesterday at the Little Carnegie, is a softer, less satiric comedy, but its preoccupation with sex is often very funny. It's also reassuring: There's at least one place on earth today where, because of societal taboos, the pursuit of sex can still be a satisfactory, full-time avocation.

•

The object of all the plotting and counterplotting in "Malizia" is Angela (Laura Antonelli), an extraordinarily gifted housekeeper who is not only pretty, young, gentle, wise and pliant (up to a limit) but also a first-rate cook, sewer and washer-up.

Angela is almost too good to be true. She represents the sacred, the profane and the practical, especially to the head of the family, Don Ignazio (Turi Ferro), newly widowed and not at all sure he wants his dead wife's beneficent spirit hanging around the house, as the priest has promised. The spirit gets in the way of his pursuit of Angela. Antonio, the 18-year-old son, makes passes at Angela, and 9-year-old Enzino accepts her as a huge improvement over the mother he lost without visible unhappiness.

The most deeply smitten is 14-year-old Nino (Alessandro Momo), who begins by presenting Angela with an anonymous rose every day. When his father announces his intentions of marrying Angela, Nino's courtship evolves into a curious cat-and-mouse game, though the roles of cat and mouse are reversed in midgame.

The Cast

MALIZIA (Malice), directed by Salvatore Samperi; screenplay (Italian with English subtitles) by Ottavio Jemma, Mr. Samperi and Alessandro Parenzo, Based on a story by Mr. Samperi; produced by Silvio Clementelli; director of photography, Vittorio Storaro; editor Sergio Montanari; a Dine De Laurentiis presentation, distributed by Paramount Pictures. Running time: 98 minutes. At the Little Carnegie Theater, 57th Street, east of Seventh Avenue. This film has been rated R.

Angela .... Laura Antonelli
Don Ignazio .... Turi Ferro
Nino .... Alessandro Momo
Luciana .... Tina Aumont
Grandmother .... Lila Brignone
Don Cirillo .... Pino Caruso
Widow Corallo .... Angela Luce
Antonio .... Gianluigi Chirizzi
Enzino .... Massimiliano Filoni

Nino effectively plays on Angela's good heart to grab a quick feel or two, then uses these indiscretions to blackmail her into going about her housework fully clothed but without her bra. Underwear and its removal play a big part in Nino's fantasies, which somehow don't extend to consummated sex.

There's a good deal of malice on Nino's part. This adds a dimension of cruelty to the comedy that expresses the intensity of the boy's frustrations, though it doesn't quite match the tone of the rest of the comedy. "Malizia" is at its best when it's examining the rituals of middle-class Sicilian life (a funeral where everything goes wrong and the corpse is almost burned up) and when it is leering at its sexually driven characters.

Because Mr. Samperi has shot the film so close up, both literally and metaphorically, I suspect he's less interested in society than in psyches. "Malizia" is fairly murky in this department though the performers are true and precise.

Miss Antonelli is angelic enough to be properly shocking when she begins to supply Nino with fetishes, and Turi Ferro is fine as the lustful but ever practical father. It's a role that became a principal resource for Italian comedy of this sort, which reached its peak in the nineteen-fifties and sixties, but is still nice to have around.

1974 Je 6, 49:7

The Casts

DIRTY O'NEIL, directed by Howard Freen and Lewis Teague; written by Mr. Freen; music, Raoul Kraushaar; produced by John C. Broderick; executive producer, Leonidas Capetanos; a United Producers Release, through American International Pictures. At neighborhood theaters. Running time: 89 minutes. This film is classified R.

Jimmy O'Neil .... Morgan Paull
Lassiter .... Art Metrano
Lisa .... Pat Anderson
Ruby .... Jean Manson
Vera .... Katie Saylor

and

THEY CALL HER ONE EYE, directed by Alex Fridolinski; screenplay by Mr. Fridolinski and Bo A. Vibenius; produced by Mr. Vibenius; a United Producers Release, through American International Pictures. At neighborhood theaters. Running time: 89 minutes. This film is classified R.

Frigga .... Christina Lindberg
Tony .... Heinz Hopf

"Dirty O'Neil" and "They Call Her One Eye" arrived at local theaters yesterady to illustrate once again that a shallow, unappetizing double dish of crime, violence, ersatz sex and ersatz cops is certainly no better than one helping. For the record, "Dirty O'Neil" is American-made and "One Eye" is a Scandinavian, English-dubbed entry but neither does much for either girl-watching or crime-watching.

•

Credit "Dirty O'Neil" with a rudimentary sense of humor about sex and cops, if not crime. Morgan Paull, as its titular, young, small-town police officer in California may be bored by his job but admits liking what he does, which is largely a dizzying series of quick dalliances with well-endowed local chicks. He may turn serious momentarily by knocking off three killers who have raped one of his willing girlfriends but in the end he is happily ready to return to the carefree amorous life.

On the other hand, Christina Lindberg, has every reason to be grim as the ill-used, brunette beauty known as "One Eye." She's been rendered mute after having been raped as a child and things don't improve after she naively falls into the clutches of a notorious pimp (Heinz Hopf), who turns her into a dope addict and viciously blinds her to keep her in line.

•

Naturally, Miss Lindberg can't be faulted for hating her "clients" and the malevolent boss and for becoming expert in karate and other handy talents, which she uses to destroy them systematically.

Of course, Miss Lindberg, who is easy to look at, is constantly doleful since most of what occurs in "One Eye" is dreary. However, she brings one unique, cheerful fashion note to this rough, somber tale by wearing eye patches to match the color of each of the ensembles she appears in. It could start a trend.

A. H. WEILER

1974 Je 6, 49:7

HERBIE RIDES AGAIN, directed by Robert Stevenson; screenplay by Bill Walsh, based on a story by Gordon Buford; produced by Mr. Walsh; director of photography, Frank Phillips; music, George Bruns; editor, Cotton Warburton; a Walt Disney Productions presentation, distributed by Buena Vista. Running time: 88 minutes. At the Radio City Music Hall, Avenue of the Americas at 50th Street. This film has been rated G.

Mrs. Steinmetz .... Helen Hayes
Willoughby Whitfield .... Ken Berry
Nicole .... Stefanie Powers
Mr. Judson .... John McIntire
Alonzo Hawk .... Keenan Wynn

By VINCENT CANBY

Walt Disney Productions' "Herbie Rides Again," which opened yesterday at the Radio City Music Hall, is a movie that takes a firm stand for the defense of architectural landmarks and against real estate developers like mean, greedy Alonzo Hawk (Keenan Wynn), the sort of man who, when he sees Rome's Colosseum, dreams of replacing it with a shopping center.

The problem with comedies as witless as this is that the villains are much more appealing than the good guys. One winds up rooting for the fellows who would tear down the Plaza to put up a 100-story, glass-and-brass breadstick.

•

"Herbie Rides Again" is set in San Francisco and in that never-never land suggested by bad trick photography, when foreground objects have no visible relation to backgrounds. The film brings back the leading character of that earlier Disney box-office smash, "The Love Bug." Herbie, a 1963 Volkswagen sedan, is as bright and stanch as Lassie and 20 times as fast.

In the course of the movie he has a major part in the successful campaign of a Nice Little Old Lady, to ward off Alonzo Hawk's wreckers to save her home, an old firehouse on top of a San Francisco hill.

As played by Helen Hayes, the Nice Little Old Lady seems to be ineligible for sainthood only because of a minor technicality: she's still alive. She won't hear ill of anyone, she sees good in almost everything and she is able to converse with inanimate objects that, in addition to Herbie, include a retired San Francisco cable car and an ancient, upright music box.

The film was directed by Robert Stevenson and written by Bill Walsh, who also collaborated on "Mary Poppins" and "The Love Bug." There's nothing harmful about "Herbie Rides Again"; it's simply not very good. All the technical and economic resources of the Disney empire cannot bring sincerity to a machine-made paean in praise of little-guy pluck.

Of course, I felt the same way about "The Love Bug" and it earned $21-million in the United States alone. "Herbie Rides Again" may make only $15-million.

1974 Je 7, 23:1

LA FEMME DU GANGE ("Woman of the Ganges"), written and directed by Marguerite Duras (French with English subtitles); produced by O.R.T.F., at the First Avenue Screening Room, at 61st Street. Running time: 90 minutes. This film has not been classified.
WITH Catherine Sellers, Dionys Mascolo and Nicole Hiss.

By NORA SAYRE

Stiff as uncooked asparagus, the figures who stalk through Marguerite Duras's "Woman of the Ganges" don't have to act, since the movie is narrated in English by two invisible women with lush French accents. "Soch loff, soch dee-sire!" they repeat, as they warble away about a middle-aged man who's returned to a seaside town to kill himself; there, he encounters a woman he loved long ago. The picture is playing at the First Avenue Screening Room today and tomorrow.

Above a wintry beach, gulls wail obligingly, while the disembodied voices whimper as they evoke lost loves — "Izzat rrreally her by ze edge of ze sea?" — and it becomes quite difficult to tell who's alive or dead in this movie. (All of the performers behave like zombies, but some are probably supposed to be ghosts.) It's also very hard to know who did what to whom in the past.

•

Amid all the pacing through corridors, there's little spoken dialogue and barely any action. So it's an event when two characters bid each other good evening, when sand dribbles between someone's fingers, or when a muslin curtain stirs in the wind. There's some pretension to significant imagery here, but the result makes you want to yell or weep with boredom.

Meanwhile, the narrators sluggishly state their passion for one another — "You're so yonk, and I loff you ssso moch" — and some of the others say that they've lost their memories. Since Marguerite Duras neglected to give them any perceptible emotions, the response seems healthy.

1974 Je 7, 23:1

Tale of Youngsters in Appalachia Opens

By HOWARD THOMPSON

An endearingly simple, honest and moving film like "Where the Lilies Bloom" would be welcome any time. Arriving now on a screen splattered with violence and sex, this beautiful little movie is like a cool, clear dip of mountain spring water.

Without one false, hayseed note or drop of sugar, it depicts the struggle of a brave, stubbon Appalachian teenager to hold together her orphaned family. The story is comfortably alive, in its regional characterizations and in the astonishingly effective use of many nonprofessional players and in the natural grandeur of its North Carolina setting.

•

Robert Radnitz, the unswervable producer of "Sounder" and all those excellent predecessors for family viewing, has done it again, with typical, sterling help. Much of the film's texture and tone should certainly be credited to the young director, William A. Graham, and to Earl Hamner Jr., the Appalachian writer who created "The Walton's" on television and has now transcribed the prize-winning novel for young readers by Vera and Bill Cleaver. And surely, Mr. and Mrs. Cleaver would feel reinspired by Urs Furrer's evocative photography alone, framing the encompassing sweep of the misty ridges, a ramshackle cabin, a house or two, a store and a bustling grammar school.

But the people come first here. And these are real, starting with the remarkably convincing performance of Julie Gholson, an inexperienced native of Birmingham, as the gritty, 15-year-old heroine, determined to keep her orphaned siblings out of an institution, staving off her older sister's inquisitive suitor and finally shedding flint sparks, like a baby Scarlett O'Hara.

The Cast

WHERE THE LILIES BLOOM, directed by William A. Graham; screenplay by Earl Hammer Jr., based on the book by Vera and Bill Cleaver; photographed by Urs Furrer; music by the Earl Scruggs Revue; produced by Robert B. Radnitz; presented by United Artists. At the Forum, Broadway and 45th Street, Cinema Studio, Broadway and 66th Street, Trans-Lux 85th Street, on Madison Avenue, Eastside Cinema, Third Avenue and 55th Street, and neighborhood theaters. Running time: 97 minutes. This film is rated G.

Mary Call .... Julie Gholson
Devola .... Jan Smithers
Romney .... Matthew Burrill
Ima Dean .... Helen Harmon
Kiser Pease .... Harry Dean Stanton
Miss Fleetie .... Sudie Bond
Roy Luther .... Rance Howard
Mr. ~Connell .... Tom Spratley
Mrs. Connell .... Helen Bragdon
Goldie Pease .... Alice Beardsley

•

Nor could Matthew Burrill, Jan Smithers and cherubic little Helen Harmon be more appealing as her brother and sisters. Careful casting of adult roles, mixing professionals and nonprofessionals, also scores, with Harry Dean Stanton as an understanding farmer-suitor and a touching schoolteacher bit by Sudie Bond. Tom Spratley, Helen Bragdon, Rance Howard and Alice Beardsley and an unidentified Carolina couple do well in other parts. Original music by Earl Scruggs lends good, regional flavoring.

Whether the four plucky mountain youngsters are "wildcrafting" for survival (a fascinating sequence about medicinal herbs) or squinting toward life beyond a rhododendhron ridge, they share with us something called the human spirit. For young and old, "Where the Lilies Bloom" is a refreshing reminder.

1974 Je 8, 18:4

Soviet 'Golden Calf' Offers Some Smiles

By NORA SAYRE

Deception had better be charming—at least, in the movies. When you want a quick breather from the bulkier questions of political deceit, pictures like "The Sting" or "The Golden Calf" (from Russia) can be refreshing. In these scenarios, the victims have committed larger crimes than those who prey on them, and the con men are harmless clowns. Meanwhile, Mikhail Shveitser, who made "The Golden Calf," seems to savor the fantasy of charming crooks almost as much as we do. The movie is playing at the First Avenue Screening Room today and tomorrow.

The Cast

THE GOLDEN CALF (If I Had One Million Rubles). Written, produced and directed by Mikhail Shveitser; English version by Zeon Prochnik; photography, Sergei Poluyanov; music, Georgy Firtich; art director, Abram Freidin; based on "The Golden Calf" by Ilf and Petrov; a Mosfilm Sorexport Film Production; an EYR Program Presentation. At the First Avenue Screening Room, at 61st Street. Running time: 95 minutes.
The Cast Bender .... Sergei Yursky
Panitovsky .... Zinovi Gerdt
Shura .... Leonid Kuralev
Koreiko .... Yevgeny Yevstigneev
Adam .... Nikolai Boyorsky
Zosya .... Svetlana Starikova

Set in 1927, the picture follows three beguiling charlatans' search for a millionaire to milk. Their goal is Rio, which will surely be awash with beautiful women, white linen suits, gold dentures and Japanese houseboys. Eventually, the most determined of the band blackmails a timid, underpaid clerk who has embezzled a fortune. But the con man discovers that a million rubles is difficult to spend, that it hashes up his relationships with others, that he sleeps badly.

The abrupt recoil from wicked capitalism is too slick; also, the young blackmailer is overly ruthless at moments. And, as in some other Russian movies, the director seems to rely on a fairly pure-minded audience. But there are many pleasing scenes throughout this movie —such as a poison gas drill, where healthy citizens must pretend to be casualties—and I'll long remember the chagrin of two thieves who saw away at some heavy dumbbells until they find no gold within.

1974 Je 14, 19:1

THE MIDNIGHT MAN, directed and produced jointly by Roland Kibbee and Burt Lancaster; screenplay by Mr. Kibbee and Mr. Lancaster, based on David Anthony's novel "The Midnight Lady and The Mourning Man"; director of photography, Jack Priestley; editor, Frank Morriss; music, Dave Grusin; distributed by Universal Pictures. Running time: 117 minutes. At the Lyric Theater, 42d Street, west of Seventh Avenue, and other theaters. This film has been rated R.
Jim Slade .... Burt Lancaster
Linda .... Susan Clark
Quartz .... Cameron Mitchell
Clayborne .... Morgan Woodward
Casey .... Harris Yulin
Dr. Pritchett .... Robert Quarry
Judy .... Joan Lorring

By VINCENT CANBY

Superlatives are dangerous, so it may only be safe to say that "The Midnight Man," jointly produced, written and directed by Roland Kibbee and Burt Lancaster, is the second worst film of 1974.

It's a murder mystery, photographed entirely in South Carolina (not very well) about a college night watchman who solves a series of killings so confused that not even the movie has time to explain them adequately.

•

The cast includes a lot of local actors plus Mr. Lancaster as the night watchman, who also happens to be an ex-Chicago cop as well as an ex-con (he once shot his wife's lover, though that has absolutely nothing to do with the story). Among the professionals in the film are Cameron Mitchell, Susan Clark and Joan Lorring.

Mr. Lancaster is an intelligent actor. He thinks about his characterizations. He makes choices. He moves through "The Midnight Man" with studied humility, saying "yes, sir," and "no, sir," more often than is always necessary, listening attentively when spoken to. The mannerisms don't suggest a middle-aged parolee, uncertain of his future, as often as they suggest a reformed alcoholic trying desperately to succeed as a liveried chauffeur.

"The Midnight Man" opened yesterday at the Lyric and other theaters in the city.

1974 Je 15, 26:1

'Daisy' Is an Unexpected Triumph

By VINCENT CANBY

DAISY MILLER, née Annie P. Miller back in Schenectady, goes on and on, non-stop, in a voice trained to a register a little too high to sound completely natural. She chatters literally — the effect is that of a venetian blind rattling in the wind— about her mother's dyspepsia, about an English lady named Featherstone once met in a railway carriage, about European hotels, about New York society, about her dreadful little brother Randolph who doesn't much care about old castles like the Chateau de Chillon.

Her pretty face framed by a white parasol, her fine figure set off by the freshly starched flounces on her white dress, Daisy Miller seems almost as harmless and innocent and desirable as she sounds, but something spoils the effect. It's the chin. There's just a bit too much of it. No wonder it's always stuck out — there's no way to keep it tucked in. It challenges fate in the form of European manners, though it hardly invites the disaster that eventually befalls Daisy in Rome, circa 1870.

This is Henry James's Daisy Miller as played by Cybill Shepherd in Peter Bogdanovich's handsome film version of the classic novella. "Daisy Miller," currently at the Baronet, is something of a triumph for everyone concerned and very much an unexpected one, considering the lifeless results of another recent attempt to film holy literary writ. Fitzgerald's "The Great Gatsby" is, however, a very different proposition from James's work. Among other things, it's better. At least, "Gatsby" is more complex, less conventionally structured, more ambiguous, less consistent in tone. "Gatsby" is also full of narrative ellipses that can't be tolerated in big-budget, commercial filmmaking.

James, on the other hand, tells us all that we need know about Daisy Miller and since, at the time he wrote about her, James had not yet begun to create universes that exist as much in the complexity of his syntax as in the psychology of his characters, "Daisy Miller" transfers to the screen simply and elegantly. Very little is lost that isn't regained through the always unpredictable conjunction of performers with material.

"Daisy Miller" says as much about pioneering in its way as do Jan Troell's "The Emigrants" and "The New Land," though, of course, the direction is reversed. James's novella is about the first great push of vulgar, newly rich, post-Civil War Americans into Europe in search of culture, society and titled husbands. The subject fascinated James

Cybill Shepherd triumphs as the high-spirited heroine of Peter Bogdanovich's film of "Daisy Miller."

throughout his life. Mark Twain also had a high old time with it in "The Innocents Abroad." The succeeding waves of eastward migrants preoccupied American writers of every stripe, from Bromfield to Loos, Hemingway and Fitzgerald, though in the 1920s and 1930s there was the feeling that America had begun to sink. Some of the authors and their characters saw themselves as having abandoned ship.

Not so Henry James who, having set up shop in England where he was to live until his death in 1916, proceeded to write about the collision of Americans and Europeans with amazement, wit, compassion and peculiar regard for the vitality of the

land he had chosen not to live in. Although the narrative line of "Daisy Miller" is straight and to the point, the conflict is so rare, being one of taste and manners, that it seems hardly to exist. It is to the tremendous credit of Bogdanovich and his screenwriter, Frederic Raphael, that they have succeeded in preserving so much of the spirit and the text of the novella and made it seem so important.

Neither in the novella nor in the film is Daisy Miller made out to be a tragic heroine in spite of her rather premature demise. Daisy, so forthrightly played by Miss Shepherd, is a figure of high comedy as she plows chin-first through Switzerland, where we meet her flirting beside the lake at Vevey, to Rome where, because she likes the company of gentlemen and refuses to be rude, she allows herself to be the target for "the regular Roman fortune hunters of an inferior sort."

Daisy, the brash American girl, spoiled by her parents and used to personal freedom that in Europe is afforded only married women and widows, is destroyed first by transplanted Americans, who slavishly follow European etiquette, and then by her own wilfullness, which serves her well until she gets bitten by a Roman mosquito.

*

In this connection I must say that James's use of the mosquito is one of his most brilliant plot devices, insuring, as it does, the essentially comic nature of the story.

Bogdanovich's film may be read as a cautionary footnote to our permissive age, and thus relevant, though I think that's freighting the movie with a reason for being that it doesn't need. I suspect James himself would have shied away from such attempts to apply contemporary meaning to it. In "Pandora," a later novella, he didn't hesitate to have a totally humorless German diplomat, Count Otto Vogelstein, methodically study the pages of "Daisy Miller" for some clue to the behavior of an American girl who bears absolutely no relation to Daisy. It is similarly possible to over-read the film.

*

Bogdanovich's casting is, as always, nearly flawless. Barry Brown, the actor who was so good in Robert Benton's "Bad Company," as the young American who has lived too long in foreign parts and who would, were he less innocent or less worldly, have become Daisy's suitor; Mildred Natwick, as his snobbish, vitriolic aunt ("Whether or no being helplessly vulgar is being 'bad' is a question for metaphysicians"); Cloris Leachman, as Daisy's perpetually disoriented mother, and Duilio Del Prete, as Daisy's Italian admirer, a "little barber block" of a man.

"Daisy Miller" is Bogdanovich's fifth feature, (his most recent: "Paper Moon"), continuing a career that resolutely refuses to be typed in genre or style, thus carrying on the tradition of the old-time Hollywood directors he so admires. It is also, I think, his best, most original film, a romantic comedy that would, I'm certain, have totally baffled the old-timers. Can you imagine what Harry Cohn, Darryl Zanuck or Jack L. Warner woud have said if some wet-eared kid had suggested he wanted to make a love story in which the lovers don't even kiss?

Send him back to Republic.

1974 Je 16, II:1:5

The Cast

UPTOWN SATURDAY NIGHT, directed by Sidney Poitier; screenplay by Richard Wesley; produced by Melville Tucker; director of photography; Fred J. Koenekamp; editor, Pembroke J. Herring; music, Tom Scott; a First Artists production, distributed by Warner Brothers. Running time; 104 minutes. At the Criterion Theater, Broadway at 44th Street, and the 86th Street East Theater, 86th Street east of Third Avenue. This film has been rated PG.
Steve Jackson.................Sidney Poitier
Wardell Franklin...............Bill Cosby
Geechie Dan Beauford...Harry Belafonte
The Reverend................Flip Wilson
Silky Slim.............Calvin Lockhart
Sharp Eye Washington...Richard Pryor
Sarah Jackson............Rosalind Cash
Congressman Lincoln..Roscoe Lee Browne
Leggy Peggy.................Paula Kelly

By VINCENT CANBY

"Uptown Saturday Night" is the sort of film in which Harry Belafonte shows up as an all-powerful but somewhat befuddled black gang boss named Geechie Dan Beauford. Geechie Dan looks eerily familiar though nothing like Mr. Belafonte. With those extraordinary, cotton-filled jowls, the pencil mustache and a manner of talking as if through a voice box lodged in his stomach, he is Marlon Brando's Godfather in burnt cork.

Screen: 'Gravy Train,' American Style—Almost

By NORA SAYRE

This continues to be the year for romance between heterosexual males. "The Gravy Train," which opened yesterday at the Beekman and Forum Theaters, focuses on a pair of brothers who are so devoted to each other that there has to be a scene in a massage parlor to show that they have any use for women

Two West Virginia coal miners (Stacy Keach and Frederic Forrest) quit the jobs they loathe to make their fortunes through armed robbery. (Since they hate their factory as well as the work itself, it would have been interesting if their mu-

tinous feelings had been further developed.) They're soon betrayed by their fellow hoods, and the battles within the small gang become the bulk of the picture.

There are some substantial intentions here — above all, the effort to make a very American movie, to reflect the native condition. These rebellious workingmen also detest cops, though they're hardly liberal, and the film is sprinkled with racial hatreds.

Throughout, there's too much moralizing about materialism: It's obvious that the greedy brothers are going to be punished for pursuing that gravy train, and much of the script seems like a recipe

for retribution. The chase scenes and shootouts aren't exciting, despite several falling bodies — whenever the plot sags, one of the supporting actors is deprived of all support, and he falls screaming from great heights. And, although this isn't the bloodiest movie of the month, it's exceptionally brutal — to a degree that numbs your response, makes you feel detached.

Mr. Forrest, as a callow sadist who cackles whenever the bullets fly, and Mr. Keach, as a man of manic authority — whose yells of rage or pain evoke Marlon Brando howling "Stella!" — are both fine, even though their parts don't

give them much range.

All in all, it's impossible to tell whom this movie was meant for. At moments, it seems to be aimed at mid-America. Yet that audience is sneered at when the brothers are caricatured as hicks in a swank city restaurant: It's supposed to be hilarious when they can't pronounce filet mignon or don't know what scampi are.

Meanwhile, the preachiness of the script won't beguile those who, like money or possessions; although this is meant to be an action movie, it comes off as an Awful Warning to the young men of America.

1974 Je 17, 25:5

Bill Cosby, left, and Sidney Poitier

Like the Belafonte performance, "Uptown Saturday Night" is essentially a put-on, but it's so full of good humor and, when the humor goes flat, of such high spirits that it reduces movie criticism to the status of a most nonessential craft.

•

The star as well as director of "Uptown Saturday Night" is Sidney Poitier, a man whose way with comedy is reminiscent of Stanley Kramer's in "It's a Mad, Mad, Mad, Mad World." It's less instinctive than acquisitive. He himself can't make anyone laugh but he knows people who can. Mr. Poitier has had the good sense to hire a lot of exceptionally talented and funny people, including Richard Wesley, who wrote the screenplay for "Uptown Saturday Night."

The film combines blunt, rollicking observations on life —the kind favored by black comedians—with the sort of fabulous narrative that has always been a staple of American comedy, from today's Woody Allen back through silent comedy to frontier literature.

Until recently true black comedy (not to be confused with black humor) has been something of an unknown frontier for most Americans who didn't have access to Harlem's Apollo Theater, Moms Mabley, Redd Foxx and the other headliners. Today, of course, Moms, Redd and the others are tele-

vision headliners, and it's now apparent that a lot of the comedy of Freeman Gosden and Charles Correll (Amos and Andy) was a good deal more witty and accurate than it was fashionable to admit in the nineteen-fifties and sixties.

"Uptown Saturday Night" is an exuberant black joke that utilizes many of the stereotypical attitudes that only black writers, directors and actors can decently get away with. You've never seen so much eye-popping fear and unwarranted braggadocio used in the service of laughs. Yet the result is not a put-down comedy but a cheerful jape that has the effect of liberating all of us from our hangups.

•

"Uptown Saturday Night," once it gets started (and that takes a bit of time), is about a pair of stupendously ill-equipped innocents, Steve Jackson (Poitier), a factory worker, and Wardell Franklin (Bill Cosby), a taxi driver, who set out to recover a winning lottery ticket contained in a wallet stolen during the pair's one and only visit to a fancy black after-hours club.

The course of their search takes them through a gallery of rogues, dead-beats and affable con-artists: Sharp Eye Washington (Richard Pryor), a down-at-the-heels, double-crossing private detective who takes their money and

runs; Congressman Lincoln (Roscoe Lee Browne), the sort of phony, black-is-beautiful politician who wears Brooks Brothers suits in the privacy of his home; Silky Slim (Calvin Lockhart), a gang boss whose mythic nonchalance is matched only by his greed; The Reverend (Flip Wilson), a rousing orator who almost stops the film with a sermon about loose lips that not only can sink ships but also can get husbands into a peck of troubles.

•

All of these performances are marvelously funny in their short takes, while Mr. Cosby is particularly good as the more skeptical of the two amateur sleuths. Mr. Poitier's intelligence and taste are most noticeable in the film's casting, in the leeway he gives his actors, and in his ability at times to make himself seem physically small and downright intimidated. For a man of his stature, that cannot be easy.

The title of the film refers to neither a time nor a place (the setting seems to be Los Angeles where, as far as I know, there is no uptown). It defines, instead, a film fantasy in which fun needn't have boring consequences, in which gangsters shoot it out without anyone's getting bloodied up, and in which it's possible to have a high old time without fear of a hangover.

1974 Je 17, 25:1

A FREE WOMAN, directed by Volker Schlondorff; screenplay by Margarethe von Trotta and Mr. Schlondorff; photographed by Sven Nykvist; music by Stanley Myers; produced by Hallelujah Film and released by New Yorker Films. At the Paris Theater, 58th Street, east of Fifth Avenue. Running time: 100 minutes. (This film has not been classified.)
Elisabeth.............Margarethe von Trotta
Hans-Helmut...........Friedhelm Ptok
Oskar.................Martin Lüttge
Schmollinger............Georg Marischka

At the Paris Theater, an uncommonly engrossing and wise new German movie, "A Free Woman," records the losing battle a divorced woman in her thirties fights in

Munich to attain belated self-fulfillment. The die is cast in a briskly impersonal society geared to male dominance and early training for career women. This attractive, capable young woman, needing love and encouragement, determinedly sidesteps her former slot of housewife, studies voice and dance, takes on subordinate jobs and painfully maneuvers with her former husband (a cold fish who shrewdly remarries) for child custody.

All this is quietly and beautifully projected by an unobtrusive camera and stunningly personified by the feeling, low-key performance of Margarethe von Trotta in the central role. The blond star also happens to be the wife of the gifted director, Volker Schlondorff, as well as his co-screen writer.

They and the other performers and contributors have forged a fine, thoughtful and stimulating film that observantly mirrors a human condition, the traditional subordination of women with truthful, biting irony. It would be hard to find a more persuasive and appealing proponent of feminism than Mrs. Schlondorff.

HOWARD THOMPSON

1974 Je 18, 31:1

THE SEDUCTION OF MIMI (Mimi Metallursico ferito nell'onore), directed by Lina Wertmuller; story and screenplay (Italian with English subtitles) by Miss Wertmuller; editor, Franco Fraticelli; cameraman, Blasco Giurato; music, Piero Piccioni; produced by Daniele Senatore and Romano Cardarelli; released by Euro International Films and New Line Cinema. At the 68th Street Playhouse, at Third Avenue. Running time: 89 minutes. (This film has not been classified.)
Mimi..................Giancarlo Giannini
Fiore................Mariangela Melato
Rosalia..............Agostina Belli
Signora Finocchiaro.........Elena Fiore

By NORA SAYRE

Sexual hypocrisies and political dilemmas rarely flow smoothly onto the screen. But Lina Wertmuller excels in conveying both, in "The Seduction of Mimi," which was made before her "Love and Anarchy." Her films are deeply political, and her characters dwell in realms where politics cannot be escaped — whether in Mussolini's Italy or modern Sicily. "Mimi," a furious farce that won her the best-director award at Cannes in 1972, concerns a young laborer who lurches between the local Mafia and the Communists — when all he really wants is a personal life. The movie opened yesterday at the 68th Street Playhouse.

Mimi refuses to vote for the Mafia's candidate in his town's elections, hence he loses his job. He believes in the rights of working people, yet he makes a half-baked Communist because he's eager to earn well, to provide for his child. Meanwhile, he shuns the wife who displeases him in bed and falls violently in love elsewhere. He thinks of himself as "a civilized man." But when his neglected wife cuckolds him, all his energies surge into plotting vengeance against her lover — an obsession that has horrendous consequences for Mimi and puts him again at the mercy of the Mafia.

In Mimi, Miss Wertmuller has created a sympathetic character who's also capable of barbarity, a likable person who can (and does) behave like a monster. It's her talent to be honest about cruelty; she also specializes in vulnerable people. Of course, the double standards of Sicily are stressed: a man is admired for having a mistress, yet he goes berserk when his wife hits the hay with another man; at the same time, none of his male friends would marry a divorced woman. Throughout, the bitterness is shot with comedy, while the macho code of revenge appears as a disease, and lunacies are committed in the name of "honor."

Although Miss Wertmuller emphasizes that women are steadily humiliated in Sicilian society — while showing that men are also victims of their country's traditions — her own feminism seems inconsistent at moments. Some of her scenes and characters embody strictly male fantasies — such as the titillating fight between two prostitutes in "Love and Anarchy," or the transformation of Mimi's girlfriend from a gutsy, independent person into an ideally patient, faithful, adoring handmaiden. And there's a passage of searing brutality when Mimi seduces the fat, aging wife of his own wife's lover. His disgust at the grotesque body — which is filmed from angles that make it all the uglier — makes you wonder if the director occasionally relishes the degradation of other women.

But whatever Miss Wertmuller's commitments, "Mimi" is one of the best films of this season. And it's far more substantial than "Love and Anarchy" — a movie that did absorb and touch me, even though I hardly believed a moment of it. (There, the insistence on love at first sight and the oozing innocence of

the lovers seemed too artificial to swallow.. Yet the absurd romanticism was enjoyable as well.) sistence on love at first sight

In both of the Wertmuller movies, the film maker's harsh judgments of people emerge in a style that's visually delectable. As Mimi, Giancarlo Giannini runs a range of moods from misery to delight or defiance and surpasses his performance in the other picture; a number of the same actresses (especially Elena Fiore and Mariangela Melato) are splendid. "Love and Anarchy" appears as the more commercial work: the splashy sex scenes sometimes seem like an apology for the political discussion. But in "Mimi," politics and sex are so well balanced that all the raw emotions and the devastating jokes ring true.

1974 Je 19, 40:3

THE PARALLAX VIEW, directed and produced by Alan J. Pakula; screenplay by David Giler and Lorenzo Semple Jr., based on the novel by Loren Singer; executive producer, Gabriel Katzka; director of photography, Gordon Willis; music scored by Michael Small; editor, Jack Wheeler; distributed by Paramount Pictures. Running time: 102 minutes. At the Cinema 1 Theater, Third Avenue near 60th Street. This film has been rated R.

Frady	Warren Beatty
Lee Carter	Paula Prentiss
Austin	William Daniels
Jack	Walter McGinn
Rintels	Hume Cronyn
L.D.	Kelly Thordsen
Assassin	Chuck Waters
Red	Earl Hundman

By VINCENT CANBY

It's difficult not to feel a certain amount of suspense when you see a man standing below a huge hydroelectric dam, as blandly unaware of danger as a nearsighted pigeon walking across the Belt Parkway. The man doesn't know that at any minute several hundred thousand tons of water are going to come roaring out of the spillway, most likely onto his head.

Since the man is Warren Beatty, the star of "The Parallax View," and since the film is more or less just beginning, you know he can't be fatally clobbered. The suspense comes from wondering how he's going to escape, as in old-time movie serials.

A little later Mr. Beatty, who plays a reporter investigating a political assassination conspiracy, is lured aboard a commercial airliner that is ostensibly headed for Denver, though we know that his appointment could be in Samarra: The villains have stashed a time-bomb aboard the plane. Will he get back to earth safely? Check your watch.

"The Parallax View," which opened yesterday at the Cinema 1, is the sort of suspense melodrama that travels a horizontal course from beginning to end. The thrills don't mount as the film goes on. They don't even accumulate. Once they are

experienced, they dissolve so thoroughly that by the end you're likely to feel as cheated as I did.

The movie, which was directed by Alan J. Pakula, never rewards the attention we give it with anything more substantial than a few minor shocks.

●

Neither Mr. Pakula nor his screenwriters, David Giler and Lorenzo Semple Jr., display the wit that Alfred Hitchcock might have used to give the tale importance transcending immediate plausibility. The moviemakers have, instead, treated their central idea so soberly that they sabotage credulity.

Without giving away the plot, the idea, simply stated, is that there is somewhere in this country a giant corporation dedicated to training and putting out for hire misfits and malcontents who have been elevated to professional assassins.

According to this film, the Parallax Corporation has a recruiting program as thorough as that of General Motors, and much more paternal. Parallax seems to be vaguely right-wing, but the movie is fuzzy on this. It's also fuzzy on logistics. If, as is shown, Parallax insists on eliminating not only contracted targets but also all possible witnesses, as well as witnesses of witnesses, it would seem the population could, theoretically, be reduced by half in 18 months.

This may be taking the movie more seriously than is intended, but to treat a political assassination conspiracy merely as a subject for fun is frivolous.

In addition to Mr. Beatty, the cast includes Paula Prentiss as a TV news reporter, Hume Cronyn as a harassed city editor and a number of other good actors. "The Parallax View" is not the kind of movie that depends on unusual performances, or even asks for them.

1974 Je 20, 47:1

The Cast

HOODLUM SOLDIER (Heitai Yakuza), directed by Yasuzo Masumura; screenplay by Ryuzo Kikushima, original story by Yoriyoshi Arima; photography, Setsuo Kobayashi; produced by Masaichi Nagata; Daiei Motion Picture Company Production; an Altura Films Release. At the Cinema Studio, Broadway and 66th Street. Running time: 103 minutes.

Kisaburo Omiya	Shintaro Katsu
Sup-Pvt. Arita	Takahiro Tamura
Otomaru	Keiko Awaji
Midori	Eiko Taki
MP	Kikio Narita

The idea that the army and war are hellish and not singularly an American concept is starkly illustrated in "Hoodlum Soldier," the final, new offering in the Japanese film series that opened yesterday at the Cinema Studio. Yasuzo Masumura, the director, has projected a cynically realistic view of the Japanese World War II conscript even though the friend-

ship between two mismatched soldiers is evoked in constant, violent and bloody action.

●

This appears to be the norm for Mr. Masumura, who is known for "The Red Angel," a 1963 feature released here in 1971, which, with equal force, depicted the reactions of an ill-used purse to the 1939 Japanese-Chinese conflict. "Hoodlum Soldier" unfolds on the Manchurian-Russian border in 1943 as a rough, tough former Tokyo gangster becomes the pupil of a sensitive, college-trained non-com.

Muscle is the order of the day as the "Hoodlum Soldier" takes on all comers who try to slap him around. And, his sidekick, ever ready to protect his charge even on an inhuman, grueling 170-mile march, is, in turn, protected by his indestructible mate.

The fact is, the performances of these principals are more of an asset than the profusion of English subtitles. Both men obviously hate the bestialities, class distinctions and protocol of army life but with valid reasons. As a simple, contrite man, the titular hero is willing to take the hard knocks but is driven to break out so he could support the family of a man he killed in a Tokyo brawl. On the other hand, his pal is shaken from devotion to duty when he learns he is to be sent to the front, even though his enlistment is up, because Japan is losing the war.

●

Shintaro Katsu, as the blind swordsman, Zatoichi, in several of the period adventures in the series, gives a strong, if broad, portrayal of the "Hoodlum Soldier," a seemingly dim-witted, loutish brute, who, however, instinctively responds tenderly to the affection shown him by Eiko Takim as a pitiable, loving prostitute, and, of course his mentor. And Takahiro Tamura, whom he finally leads to liberty, is impressive as his intellectual, understanding buddy.

"The war is stupid and I don't want officers to tell me to die," he says in final rebellion. And this black-and-white movie made in 1965 states its case in similarly simple but harsh and compelling melodramatic terms.

A. H. WEILER

1974 Je 20, 47:1

The Cast

THE TERMINAL MAN, directed by Mike Hodges; screenplay by Mr. Hodges, based on a novel by Michael Crichton; director of photography, Richard H. Kline; film editor, Robert Wolfe; music, J. S. Bach; produced by Mr. Hodges; released by Warner Bros. At Loew's State 2, Broadway and 45th Street and Loew's Tower East, Third Avenue and 72d Street. Running time: 104 minutes. (This film is classified PG).

Harry Benson	George Segal
Dr. Janet Ross	Joan Hackett
Dr. John Ellis	Richard A. Dysart
Angela Black	Jill Clayburgh
Dr. Arthur McPherson	Donald Moffat

By NORA SAYRE

The oops-sorry school of medicine is featured in "The Terminal Man," where the psychosurgery intended to make brain-damaged George Segal less violent only serves to make him more so. With a headful of wires and a tiny computer planted in his neck, he runs amok on the conviction that machines are taking over the world. But since the surgeon who operated on his brain is the kind of person whom you wouldn't allow to trim your nails, let alone cut your hair, Mr. Segal's mistrust of science seems quite rational. Based on Michael Crichton's novel, the movie was written, directed, and produced by Mike Hodges; it opened yesterday at Loews State and Tower East.

The picture moves as slowly as a glacier—an image that's reinforced by the repetitive shots of long, white hospital corridors, white bathrooms and home décor—in fact, it's a white-on-white movie. There's no suspense; the only frightening moments occur when you fear it may last forever, especially during the seemingly endless operation and an interminable manhunt. It's also a bit corrupting for the viewer, since the acting style is so muted that you start longing for a dash of violence—though when it comes, the camera slights the victim, and Mr. Segal mainly succeeds in ruining a perfectly good waterbed.

George Segal's resilience, humor, and versatility have redeemed quite a few bad scripts. But this role gives him little chance to act, beyond making like a zombie and rolling his eyeballs back (there's that touch of white again). Still, it's rather refreshing when his bandaged head is covered by a blond wig that pays distinct homage to Harpo Marx.

While this movie seems unsalvageable, it might have had some punch if we'd been told more about the Segal character's past, before his operation. Meanwhile, Joan Hackett's talents are wasted as a doctor who's merely required to look patient or perturbed—although she is permitted an occasional worried smile. And a clumsy attempt to cash in on the shower scene in "Psycho" stresses the poverty of invention that withers this whole nonthriller.

1974 Je 20, 47:2

Buckminster Fuller Is Studied in Depth

By PAUL GOLDBERGER

With the exception of a single student's question that somehow slipped by, Buckminster Fuller's voice is the only one heard during the entire 90 minutes of Robert Snyder's new film on the visionary architect and engineer, "The World of Buckminster Fuller."

That is a lot of Buckminster Fuller for anybody, since Mr. Fuller tends to repeat himself frequently and to offer up lessons out of freshman physics as if he'd just invented them himself.

●

He remains, of course, a remarkably compelling figure, if a bit wordy, and Mr. Snyder has captured him well —indeed, careful editing has made this film a lot more coherent than most of Mr. Fuller's lectures. We see him in a variety of settings around the world, rambling and philosophizing about energy (he was, as he does not hesitate to remind us, way ahead of the bandwagon on that question), television, architecture, democracy, mathematics, and social problems.

There is some gibberish, like Mr. Fuller's suggestion that housing problems could be solved by finding something else for the middle-class to do and then moving the poor into skyscraper office buildings, and much that makes great sense, like his explanation of his work as "not trying to imitate nature, just trying to find the principles she's using."

●

The most fascinating sections of the film are those that relate to Mr. Fuller's actual built work — his famous geodesic domes, his "Dymaxion" house and car of the nineteen-twenties, indications that he was far more serious about the implications of technology than the early modern architects of the period who talked about a machine-age architecture, but built essentially traditional buildings.

The film will be shown at noon and midnight tomorrow and Saturday, and at 10 o'clock Sunday mornings for an indefinite period at the First Avenue Screening Room at 61st Street.

1974 Je 20, 49:1

Polanski's 'Chinatown' Views Crime of '30s

By VINCENT CANBY

Pin-stripe suits, men's hair parted slightly off-center like Richard Arlen's, four-door convertible touring cars (not yet declared unsafe), official portraits of Franklin D. Roosevelt in public buildings, women with marceled hair and elegant slouches.

These are just some of the nineteen-thirties' artifacts that decorate Roman Polanski's "Chinatown," a new private-eye melodrama that celebrates not only a time and a place (Los Angeles) but also a kind of criminality that to us jaded souls today appears to be nothing worse than an eccentric form of

legitimate private enterprise.

●

There's nothing wanton, mindless or (with one exception) especially vicious about the murders and assaults that J. J. Gittes (Jack Nicholson), a private detective who has heretofore specialized in matrimonial disputes, sets out to solve in "Chinatown." No senseless massacres, no rapes, no fire-bombings of innocents.

In that far-off time—midway between the repeal of Prohibition and the inauguration of lend-lease—murderers, swindlers and blackmailers acted according to carefully premeditated plans. These plans, in turn, were always there for the uncovering by a Sam Spade or a Philip Marlowe or, in this case, a J. J. Gittes, a man whose name is repeatedly mispronounced as Gibbs, which is one of the burdens he learns to live with, along with a vulnerable nose.

CHINATOWN, directed by Roman Polanski; screenplay by Robert Towne; produced by Robert Evans; director of photography, John A. Alonzo; music, Jerry Goldsmith; editor, Sam O'Steen; distributed by Paramount Pictures. Running time 130 minutes. At the Loews State 1 Theater, Broadway near 45th Street, and Coronet Theater, Third Avenue near 59th Street. This film has been rated R.
J. J. Gittes .... Jack Nicholson
Evelyn Mulwray .... Faye Dunaway
Noah Cross .... John Huston
Escobar .... Perry Lopez
Yelburton .... John Hillerman
Hollis Mulwray .... Darrell Zwerling
Ida Sessions .... Diane Ladd
Mulvihill .... Roy Jenson
Man with knife .... Roman Polanski

This fixed order of things, of a cause for every effect, explains the enduring appeal of fiction like "Chinatown," but it also is something of a test for the writer who comes after Dashiell Hammett and Raymond Chandler and who doesn't hesitate to evoke their memories and thus to invite comparisons.

Robert Towne, who adapted "The Last Detail" and wrote the original screenplay for "Chinatown," is good but I'm not sure he's good enough to compete with

the big boys. When Robert Altman set out to make Chandler's "The Long Goodbye," he had the good sense to turn it into a contemporary film that was as much a comment on the form as an evocation of it.

●

Mr. Polanski and Mr. Towne have attempted nothing so witty and entertaining, being content instead to make a competently stylish, moore or less thirtyish movie that continually made me wish I were back seeing "The Maltese Falcon" or "The Big Sleep." Others may not be as finicky.

Among the good things in "Chinatown" are the performances by Mr. Nicholson, who wears an air of comic, lazy, very vulnerable sophistication that is this film's major contribution to the genre; Faye Dunaway, as the widow of the film's first murder victim, a woman too beautiful to be either good or

true, and John Huston, who plays a wealthy old tycoon whose down-home, sod-kicking manner can't quite disguise the sort of fanaticism displayed by Sidney Greenstreet in Mr. Huston's "Maltese Falcon."

The plot is a labyrinth of successive revelations having to do with Los Angeles water reserves, land rights, fraud and intra-family hanky-panky, climaxing in Los Angeles's Chinatown on a street that seems no more mysterious than Flatbush Avenue.

Mr. Polanski himself turns up in the film's most vicious scene, playing the half-pint hood who neatly slices one of J. J. Gittes's nostrils, thus requiring the detective to go through the rest of the picture with stitches that look like blood-encrusted cat's whiskers sticking out of his nose.

1974 Je 21, 26:1

That Rarest of Birds, a Successful Political Movie

By HANS KONING

"LOVE and Anarchy," the current Italian movie about a young farmer-anarchist who sets out to assassinate Mussolini, was generally well received, but I want to write about one scarcely mentioned aspect only: the film's politics. I want to single out this movie as one of the very few totally successful radical political films. If I weren't afraid of unqualified statements, I would write: the very first one.

I come to this high opinion of the film as someone who has been trying for years in books and films to be artistic and yet political, and who doubts that he will ever make it. (The word "artistic" here should not be understood as self-praise, but merely as a description of the normal, professional approach to art.) It is a staggering job, to be radical in the same implied, almost unconscious way that 95 per cent of our films (and novels) are free enterprise-dog-eat-dog political. That is to say, seemingly unpolitical, as they take the present facts of economic life for granted.

The hidden way is the only way to get away with a political message for a Western film audience, for the generalizations of ideology bore us as much as or even more than the generalizations of commercialism. This is especially true for an American audience, which will not be preached or lectured at in a movie house, and which finds itself at the tail-end of half a century of anti-radical conditioning. During the last 50 years, our movie Reds, from social democrats to anarchists, have been either scoundrels with foreign accents or do-gooders duped by guys with

Hans Koning, who also writes under the name Koningsberger, is a journalist and novelist.

foreign accents. The last category was dominant in Hollywood's golden biography days which produced such inanities as a Hubert Humphrey-like Emiliano Zapata.

Another category, come and gone, included films aimed at the allegedly radicalized youth audience at the turn of the sixties. But these often showed "uneasy" rather than radical people and ideas, and were almost invariably designed to turn a buck. Even those that were serious (and I include in that group my own "The Revolutionary") didn't quite come off. Trying to describe why they failed and why "Love and Anarchy" succeeds, I find my clue in the basic qualities of our audience.

Our audience is, first, less political than any European audience. (I am thinking of political theory, not of politicians' antics.) It lives in a country without serious radical politics, and where the Cold War was waged right down to our last brain cells. The first audience condition combines with the second, our aversion to being the object of "messages." Now it is clearly the combination of these qualities that makes the going for socialist or anarchist realism so rough. The first condition makes it necessary to start from below scratch, to set the stage, to explain, to redefine all those poisoned political terms. Condition two forbids you to do that, on pain of speaking to an empty hall.

I find it well-nigh miraculous that Lina Wertmuller, the Italian writer-director of "Love and Anarchy," has coped so triumphantly with those handicaps. What she has done, first of all, is to set her film in a brothel, where the anarchist-hero hides out during his last few days before the assassination at-

tempt. This detail may have helped the movie find a distributor here and it also enabled the distributor to place idiotic ads in the newspapers, but it was not a gimmick. For the brothel was precisely the one genuinely anti-establishment establishment to be found in the Fascist Rome of the 1930s, the one non-drug, non-hippie, commercial, yet violently anti-bourgeois, set-up.

And it is shown as such in "Love and Anarchy" to the last moment when the whores try to stop the police from arresting and beating the anarchist, while the "nice" passers-by just stand and gape. It is true to life, too. Prostitutes were and are a reliable support for European radicals. Italy, which — along with Spain — is the only place in Europe where anarchism is an important political theory and force, has a solid tradition along those lines.

Thus, far from being a device for introducing gratuitous sex, or—as one reviewer had it—a way of showing that passion and politics don't mix, the brothel is a setting of genius for a radical film. It defines the anarchist both by the setting and by his relationships: explanations are suddenly no longer needed. The introduction of the brothel girls makes it easy and natural to reveal a second essential element of truth about real radicals. They are not gun-toting toughs; they are, by definition, of the people. They are romantic and they are "good."

The farmer in "Love and Anarchy" is such a man. His falling in love with his whore is not a freak hindrance to his task; it is an unavoidable happening, a choice he makes. He wants to be in love, because he has only two more days to live, and this reaching out for love will, by necessity, impede or wreck his reaching out for violence. The true radical is an anti-hero hero, forever caught in the terrible dilemma of having to commit private violence to end the violence of the state. Since, being different from his opponents, he cannot ever be Machiavellian enough to put his principles aside, he loses, again and again through history.

＊

The terrible death of the farmer-anarchist in this film is not a chance ending, one that could have been avoided *if only* this or that had gone differently. After all, through 20 long years of tyranny, Mussolini was not assassinated. The death of the anarch-

ist in "Love and Anarchy" is a fate he shares with almost every real-life anarchist who ever appeared on the world stage.

The anarchist has the courage to be afraid and to be alone, and yet to go on. This is a higher human morality (or so it seems to me) than the "sleep-walking courage" of men conditioned to march to the tune their government plays for them. It is the same kind of courage that possessed the director of this film when she avoided that long list of readily available clichés of human behavior; her refusal to stack the cards.

Thus, even those who have never con-

'The hidden way is the only way to get away with a political message'

sciously identified with an oppressive class, those who have never felt tempted to take up arms for justice's sake, those who have been lucky enough never to see themselves as "by-standers" looking the other way while men and women die for their sake, may feel compelled to say, "Yes, this is how man behaves toward man."

That, to me, is as nice a description of social realism as any. And while "Love and Anarchy" is a film depicting anarchism and fascism as the opposite poles of political life, audiences may not even think of the film as political, let alone radical. Which is perhaps the highest praise for a political movie.

1974 Je 23, II:13:1

"The brothel is a setting of genius for a radical film," says this critic. In "Love and Anarchy," above, would-be-assassin Giancarlo Giannini is restrained by two prostitutes.

King of Porn, ah—Corn

By VINCENT CANBY

THE sharp, cheerlessly reassuring smell of disinfectant seeped through the balcony of the World the other afternoon. A half-dozen men, smokers all, sat there singly, trying to ignore both the smell, as depressing to the erotic instinct as a stop watch, and the loud conversation from the theater lobby. Several employes were bent on discussing coffee breaks or some other subject of equal importance, which made the screen dialogue difficult to understand. I very much wanted to hear. Not only had I paid five dollars to pass through a turnstile to get in, but I was anxious to see "Memories Within Miss Aggie," a movie that one critic has described as being "rich with intimations of 'Psycho,' and 'Images' and Faulkner," and whose director, Gerard Damiano, a former hairdresser and X-ray technician, has been called the Ingmar Bergman of porn.

That last must have been a typo. Corn is more like it.

On the screen a small, intensely yellow-haired young woman and a young man of no evident passions frolic through the show in a wildly unconvincing mime of rural innocence. The woman's pencil-thin eyebrows suggest an easier access to tweezers and urban fashion than provided for in the screenplay, but that could be dramatic license. The couple giggle, roll about in the drifts and toss snowballs at each other, though neither is very good. Each throws in the cautious underhand manner of the rookie pitcher on a team of Brownies. Finally the young man and the young woman fall into each other's arms, exhausted, prompting the following bit of Ingmar Bergman dialogue, spoken in ersatz Ethan Frome accents:

> She: "I feel funny."
> He: "I do too."
> She: "I wonder why."
> He: "Being close, mebbee."
> She: "I feel funny."

Which, perhaps because it's where they began, leads them to an empty house where they take off their clothes and, in the words of still another critic, perform sex "with feeling."

As a matter of fact, feeling is one of the things that is conspicuously absent in the porn parts of "Memories Within Miss Aggie."

The actors work earnestly enough, but they don't seem to be interested. Even Harry Reems, the supporting star of Damiano's "Deep Throat" and "The Devil in Miss Jones," seems to be tiring. This may be why he doubled as production manager on this new film and is listed as Herb Streicher in the credits, which may or may not be his real name. His fatigue may also have prompted him to wear the fake moustache he does in "Memories Within Miss Aggie," as if he didn't want to be recognized. However, pasting a moustache on Harry Reems is like trying to disguise a camel by making him wear galoshes.

"Memories," in one of its earlier weeks at the World Theater, was reported by Variety to be the second highest grossing picture in New York, topped only by "Mame" at Radio City Music Hall. This is depressing news for anyone seriously interested in the fate of movies, or even seriously interested in the liberation of pornography.

"Memories Within Miss Aggie" is an overcooked, guilt-stuffed cabbage of a movie, which, like "The Devil in Miss Jones," pretends to seriousness through its synthetically solemn framing device.

Miss Aggie (Deborah Ashira), a tall gaunt woman whose makeup isn't quite good enough to convince me she's the old lady she's supposed to be, wanders around her farmhouse in what I take to be upstate New York. The snowy landscape outside is photographed adequately by Harry Flecks, and I suspect it's the existence of the snow, not any Nykvist-like talent on the part of the cameraman that makes people compare Damiano to Bergman.

Aggie has lived alone too long, as she tells us several more times than is necessary if we're over the age of 21 or even 6. She moves about the house grumpily, talking to a portly New York actor (Patrick Farrelly), who's presented as being a handyman

It may look like a scene from a Bergman movie, but it's really Deborah Ashira in "Memories Within Miss Aggie," a porno flick

but who just sits by the stove all day.

Aggie has troubled memories of having done something "bad" when she was younger. When she thinks about it hard enough we, the audience, are treated to her fantasies, three in all, each with a different New York porn queen masquerading as Aggie's vision of herself.

In the first one, in which the very worldly, very yellow-haired Aggie is supposedly deflowered, Aggie is played by Kim Pope. In the second fantasy, Aggie is played by an actress who looks so butch that only wide-angle close-ups can testify to the fact that she's not really Holly Woodlawn. In the third fantasy, and the only one that has a suspicion of humor or erotic style, Aggie (Darby Lloyd Rains) sees herself in an old-fashioned, turn-of-the-century bordello.

When Aggie has gotten through her three fantasies, which are probably all that the budget would allow, Damiano lets us in on a secret that we could have been let in on at any earlier point in the film. That is—are you ready?—that none of these things really happened, and that Miss Aggie, as crazy as a bedbug, put a carving knife through the skull of the man whose body she still keeps by the kitchen stove.

Damiano, I'm afraid, is no Hitchcock, no Polanski, no Faulkner. He's just your ordinary, run-of-the-mill moviegoer and sometime reader who doesn't hesitate to lift the cast-offs, the remnants, of other people's ideas, which are evidently all he is capable of lifting.

It is significant that the only scene in the film that has any impact is the murder scene, not because it's well

done but because the violence seems cruel to a much greater degree than any of the sex scenes have seemed erotic.

Damiano's approach to sex is, if anything, anti-erotic, from Linda Lovelace's grotesque, nose-drooling accomplishments in "Deep Throat," to the emphasis on guilt and repression in both "Miss Jones" and "Aggie."

Although I hope I've an open mind on the subject, I think it's quite likely that there is no such thing as good pornography. If it's good, then it's not pornographic. Which is not quite the same thing as saying there isn't high class pornography. Some of the films made by the Mitchell Brothers in San Francisco, including "Behind The Green Door," have a kind of slickness about them—good looking people and a lot of smooth, swoopy camera movements. However, these things are to serious movies what Andre Kostelanetz's arrangements are to serious music. In Damiano's case let's not get carried away and so confused by drabness that we start calling his ugly little movies art.

If the man seems to have hit on a successful thing, it may well be because many people in his audience feel freer to enjoy the pure porn interludes if they're wrapped in a dreary moral fable with all of the psychological depth of a True Romance story.

To a greater or lesser extent, most Americans are puritans, and from the evidence of his three most successful films, Damiano is one of the fiercest. Sex is bad. Sex is dirty. It is something to be disinfected, one way and another. If Damiano had written "The Scarlet Letter,"

you can bet that Hester Prynne would have gone just as looney as poor old Rev. Dimmesdale—and died an even worse death, I hesitate to imagine how.

1974 Je 23, II:1:1

THE GROOVE TUBE, directed and produced by Ken Shapiro; written by Lane Sarasohn and Mr. Shapiro; a K-S Production and Syn-Frank Enterprise presentation, distributed by Levitt-Pickman Film Corporation. At the Eastside Cinema, Third Avenue at 55th Street, and other houses. Running time: 75 minutes. (This film is rated R.)

By HOWARD THOMPSON

"The Groove Tube," a 75-minute, running satire of stultifyingly familiar television staples — from kiddie shows to newscasts to serials to commercials—has arrived here, on the heels of out-of-town acclaim and an ad hailing "1974's most hilarious, wildest movie." It is indeed wild, and often hilarious. But much of it is blandly dull.

The movie that opened here yesterday at the Eastside Cinema is an outgrowth of a local theater "happening" five years ago. Audiences and reviewers acclaimed a package of videotaped satirical skits devised by two bright young men, Ken Shapiro and Lane Sarasohn that was beamed by several monitors in a small showcase.

But "The Groove Tube" must have been infinitely funnier and certainly fresher in its original proportion, beamed from a home-screen exactly the size of its target. Now, bowdlerized and stretched out on a large, movie-house screen, the joke wears thin.

Some of it is funny indeed, such as a kiddie show with a host-clown reading from "Fanny Hill." A methodical warning against venereal disease is outrageously funny. And so is a punctiliously scathing wrap-up of a typical, network... scast.

But the torrent of "commercials" gets tiresome, especially one product extolling — and showing — human excrement. A "hitchhiker" prologue is flat, so are a "sex olympics" bit and several others.

Mr. Shapiro, most prominently, and Mr. Sarasohn are also in the cast that includes Richard Belzer, Chevy Chase, Mary Mendham, Bill Kemmill and others.

It's too bad "The Groove Tube" had to go Hollywood, or at least Wagnerian. Besides, is TV really as awful as this, when you can get the Marx Brothers night after night—free?

1974 Je 24, 25:1

The Cast

FOR PETE'S SAKE, directed by Peter Yates; screenplay by Stanley Shapiro and Maurice Richlin; produced by Martin Erlichman and Mr. Shapiro; executive producer, Phil Feldman; director of photography, Laszlo Kovacs; editor, Frank Keller; a Rastar production, distributed by Columbia Pictures. Running time: 90 minutes. At the Loews Astor Plaza Theater, 44th Street west of Broadway; Loews Orpheum Theater, 86th Street at Third Avenue, and the Columbia 2 Theater, Second Avenue at 64th Street. This film has been rated PG.
Henry .... Barbra Streisand
Pete .... Michael Sarrazin
Helen .... Estelle Parsons
Fred .... William Redfield
Mrs. Cherry .... Molly Picon
Nick .... Louis Zorich
Loretta .... Vivian Bonnell
Bernie .... Richard Ward
Judge Hiller .... Heywood Hale Broun
Mr. Coates .... Joe Maher

By VINCENT CANBY

Some of the Brooklyn locations in 'For Pete's Sake" are recognizably Borough Hall, Fourth Avenue, Grand Army Plaza and Prospect Park, while some are recognizably mock-ups built on a Hollywood backlot. It doesn't make any difference, however.

"For Pete's Sake," a movie put together to honor its star, Barbra Streisand, is an often boisterously funny old-time farce. Its interest is not the truth that is a reflection of reality but an arm-twisting, gag-stuffed exaggeration of it. Or sometimes the method is diminution. When a bomb explodes to demolish an entire building, it's the equivalent of a hot foot in our dreary world.

The movie opened yesterday at the new Astor Plaza, Orpheum and Columbia 2 Theaters.

The story is about a young Brooklyn taxi driver named Pete (Michael Sarrazin) and mostly about his wife, Henrietta (Miss Streisand), nicknamed Henry, a smart-mouthed, brassy girl whose confidence in herself is always unwarranted. When Pete decides he wants to go back to college to get his degree, Henry borrows $3,000 from a Mafia loan shark to invest in pork-belly futures, thus to finance their future.

From the Mafia, Henry's downward path leads her to a more or less enforced membership in a call-girl operation, which proves short-lived when she accidentally breaks the nose of her first

client, and finally to fronting for a gang of contemporary cattle rustlers. The latter provides the opportunity for one of the picture's most spectacular gags, the sort that is funny because of its predictability, not in spite of it.

Without apology, Stanley Shapiro and Maurice Richlin, who wrote the screenplay, and Peter Yates, who directed it, make use of the most ancient devices of farce: outlandish disguises, sudden reversals in fortune, pratfalls, wisecracks. Some of their material is fondly familiar; some is in raucously bad taste.

How long has it been since you've seen a movie in which a man has to hide in a closet when a husband comes home early, or in which there's a lazy, ill-tempered maid? That is, one who is black? "For Pete's Sake" courts disaster, but most of the time manages to sidestep it.

Mr. Shapiro and Mr. Richlin, who wrote some very successful nonsex comedies in the late nineteen-fifties and early sixties ("Pillow Talk," "Lover, Come Back"), have the good, glib form of the best of television's situation-comedy writers. The movie may not hold together as any kind of larger comic statement, but the laughs are self-sustaining throughout.

●

The picture is also beautifully cast in its supporting roles, with Heywood Hale Broun as a libidinuos Brooklyn judge, with Estelle Parsons as Henry's hilariously greedy, self-satisfied sister-in-law and, particularly, with Molly Picon as a motherly Brooklyn madam named Mrs. Cherry, who congratulates Henry on coming to realize that sex is, after all, a business not a pleasure.

Mr. Sarrazin, like most of Miss Streisand's leading men, isn't called upon to do much more than to be present, which he does well enough. The star herself barges through the movie with a self-assurance that is very funny, because it seems always on the edge of collapse, as when she finds herself pursued by a police dog that is able to read subway signs.

Miss Streisand's comedy range is narrow, like a cartoon character's, but "For Pete's Sake" operates almost entirely within that range. She's at her best in this kind of farce. It manages to make her aggressiveness, undisguised in films such as "The Way We Were," seem more like pluck.

1974 Je 27, 54:2

The Cast

TRUCK TURNER, directed by Jonathan Kaplan; screenplay by Oscar Williams and Michael Allin, story by Jerry Wilkes; director of photography, Charles F. Wheeler; film editor, Michael Kahn; music by Isaac Hayes; produced by Fred Weintraub and Paul Heller; presented by Samuel Z. Arkoff and released by American International Pictures. At the Cinerama Theater, Broadway at 47th Street, and the 86th

Street Twin 2, west of Lexington Avenue. Running time: 91 minutes. (This film has been classified R.)

Truck Turner	Isaac Hayes
Harvard Blue	Yaphet Kotto
Jerry	Alan Weeks
Annie	Annazette Chase
Dorinda	Nichelle Nichols
Nate	Sam Laws
Gator	Paul Harris

As the latest addition to the manufactured movie annals of black machismo, "Truck Turner," which crashed into the Cinerama and 86th Street Twin 2 Theaters yesterday, is proof that imitation of the likes of "Shaft" or "Superfly" is not especially flattering. And, as the saga of an indestructible strong-arm sleuth for a bail bondsman, its constant barrage of chases, bloody fights and shootouts is as unusual as a local Fourth of July fireworks display.

Credit the writers with providing the cast with an inner-city patois that is authentic, if largely four-letter, and funnier and pithier than the obvious plot. Let's say there's no doubt from the outset that our hero, the bald, bearded composer ("Shaft," etc.) Isaac Hayes, eventually will mow down the hordes of pimps headed by Yaphet Kotto and Michelle Nichols, who are running scared because he's put a crimp in their racket for killing his sidekick and maiming his bail-bondsman boss.

As an actor, Mr. Hayes indicates that much of his soul is still in his music. Mr. Kotto, Alan Weeks, as Mr. Hayes's unfortunate partner, and Annazette Chase, as his ever-loving girl, are, like the other principals, largely physical throughout the frenetic action. "Sometimes I think we ought to give it up," Mr. Hayes's pal says disconsolately at one point. It's a fine suggestion for all concerned.

A. H. WEILER

1974 Je 27, 54:4

The Cast

ANAIS NIN OBSERVED, a film portrait of a woman as artist by Robert Snyder; director of photography, Baylis Glascock; editors, R. A. Fitzgerald Jr. and Tom Schiller. Distributed by Grove Press. At the First Avenue Screening Room, at 61st Street. Running time: 70 minutes.

By NORA SAYRE

As preparation for the first volume of Anaïs Nin's Journal, I read three of her early novels, and discovered that heroines named Sabina, Djuana or Zora tested many lovers, including primitive men christened Rango ("like Heathcliff") or Mambo, while seeking "a joyous, joyous joyous, joyous impaling of woman on man's sensual mast." The result was a dissatisfaction with "the flaming eucalyptus of the flesh." Hurtling between "ancient holocausts," "abysms," "miasmas" and "charivaris of freedom," these women don't drink,

travel or make guesses: Instead, they imbibe, peregrinate and divine. Yet men are very grateful to know them: "By touching her naked foot he had felt a unity resembling the first unity of the world. . . ."

•

The legendary Journal, which Henry Miller compared to "the revelations of St. Augustine, Petronius, Abélard, Rousseau and Proust," mainly stated that realism is ugly, symbols are good, surrealism is beautiful, men are children and artists are unique. It's stressed that Miss Nin's friends recognized her as "the mother and muse and servant and inspiration" of artists. "I was an archangel. They all want to sanctify me. . . . They want to idealize me and pray to me. . . ." Throughout, the text is crammed with critical judgments: "One admires the French writers. They are like Bach. . . ."

So I couldn't make it with Anaïs Nin's writing, rather to my regret. Her work does mean a great deal to readers of several generations, and she insisted on her personal freedoms long before many other women did. Meanwhile, Robert Snyder's good documentary, "Anaïs Nin Observed" (1973), reveals a sympathetic person of quite remarkable serenity. The movie is playing at the First Avenue Screening Room today and tomorrow.

•

On screen, Miss Nin muses on her experiences as a writer, psychoanalysis with Otto Rank, dreams as blueprints for literature, her methods of editing the Journal and an experiment with LSD, (which made her feel that she was turning into gold). There are fond words for rebellion and independence. When she recalls her friends and mentors from the nineteen-thirties and forties, there are glimpses of Henry Miller (who tells her, "Your listening was always eloquent"), Isamu Noguchi, Frances Steloff of the Gotham Book Mart, the youthful Martha Graham, Caresse Crosby and others. Young writers from the University of California at Los Angeles visit Miss Nin in her Frank Lloyd Wright house outside that city and one young woman tells her that she's a heroine for other women.

Appearing equally delicate and robust, Miss Nin is impressive as a survivor — also as a flexible, generous person who has spanned such a range of decades. She still makes me nervous when she talks about the vision of the artist. But all of her fans should be sure to see this movie.

1974 Je 28, 20:1

Screen: A Fatal Flavor

"Three the Hard Way," which opened yesterday at the DeMille and Loews Cine Theaters, is a hideously inane black exploitation movie that glories in reverse racism. It's about a plan to kill off all of America's blacks by tainting the water supply with a liquid that looks very much like strawberry syrup.

"It works like sickle-cell anemia," says the mad doctor, "only quicker." "Good," says his rich white employer. "It took God seven days to create the world. We'll cleanse it in three."

Jim Brown, Fred Williamson and Fred Kelly, three of the more popular black actors of the day, play the amateur agents who thwart the plans. They all swagger too much and don't know what to do with their hands when they aren't massacring the enemy. Sometimes they play chess.

The most startling thing about the film is that it was directed by Gordon Parks Jr., who seemed to know what he was doing when he made "Super Fly" and "Thomasine and Bushrod." "Three the Hard Way" is badly written, staged and edited. It is also terribly acted by the stars as well as by Jay Robinson, who plays the rich white fanatic with all the force of a man who should wear paperweights in his shoes.

VINCENT CANBY

1974 Je 27, 55:1

THE NINE LIVES OF FRITZ THE CAT, an animated feature directed by Robert Taylor; written by Mr. Taylor and Fred Halliday; cinematography, Ted C. Bemiller and Greg Heschong; film editor, Marshall M. Bordon; music, Tom Scott and the L.A. Express; produced by Steve Krantz; presented by Samuel Z. Arkoff. At the Penthouse, Broadway and 47th Street; the 59th Street Twin, east of Third Avenue, and the 86th Street Twin. Running time: 76 minutes. (This film has been classified R).

If you liked Ralph Bakshi's "Fritz the Cat" (based on the R. Crumb character) or his "Heavy Traffic," don't go to "The Nine Lives Of Fritz the Cat"—and you should also stay away if you didn't enjoy the Bakshi animations. The new "Fritz" has the same producer (Steve Krantz), but Mr. Bakshi had nothing to do with it, and his imitators have neither his talent for graphics nor an ounce of his brutal humor. The movie opened Wednesday at the Penthouse and neighborhood theaters.

•

While Fritz's despised wife berates him for being jobless, his stoned spirit departs from his body, and he travels through fantasies about hanging out with Hitler, being "a sharp dude" during the Depression—while he struts in top hat and tails, flickering background shots of breadlines suggest that unemployment was a groove—blasts off in a rocket to Mars, runs errands for President Kissinger (a slippery rodent), and is sentenced to death by the black crows who govern New Jersey—which has been given to blacks as a way of getting rid of them.

Of course this whole cartoon is meant to be offensive —though it probably wasn't supposed to be dull as well. But it's also racially and sexually repulsive: a real loathing of women comes through, and much of the action plays on white people's fears of black people. The black world itself is made to be as ugly and threatening as possible, and naturally, the blacks detest whites.

•

There's a fashionable fallacy afoot here: that a hip style can make racism or sexism beguiling, that what's jazzy can't be reactionary. But amid all the hee-haws and the repeated shots of toilet bowls, this "Fritz" makes the John Birchers seem downright liberal. Though I'm no friend to censorship, it's disturbing to think of this movie's being widely distributed throughout the country, because it has a built-in audience—among teen-agers. If they respond to this little binge of hatred as a gas, there will be further material for all those articles about the pornography of violence and the expanding national numbness.

NORA SAYRE

1974 Je 28, 21:1

The Cast

A VERY NATURAL THING, directed by Christopher Larkin; original story and screenplay by Mr. Larkin; director of photography, C. H. Douglass; film editor, Terry Manning; music by Bert Lucarelli, Gordon Gottlieb and The Musemorphoses; produced by Mr. Larkin and Montage Creations; released by New Line Cinema. At the Cine Malibu, 59th Street, between Second and Third Avenues, and Cinema Village, 12th Street east of Fifth Avenue. Running time: 85 minutes. (This film has been classified R.)

David	Robert Joel
Mark	Curt Gareth
Jason	Bo White
Alan	Jay Pierce
Hughey	Barnaby Rudge
Valerie	Marilyn Meyers

"Being gay is a very natural thing," a young Lesbian gently says in a keynote observation in "A Very Natural Thing," which opened Wednesday at the Cine Malibu and Cinema Village. Natural or not, this dramatization of the trials and joys of male homosexuality is, like "The Boys in the Band" or "Sticks and Stones," pervasively heartfelt in its special pleading but somewhat less than overwhelming in dramatic impact.

In making his feature-film debut, Christopher Larkin, the co-author-director-producer, who reportedly once led a monastic life and was a teacher, appears to have drawn his theme from life in focusing on the affairs of a young, homosexual, local high-school master.

Sincerity underlines his romance with an aggressive but restless, handsome executive type. And it is equally obvious when this liaison turns stormy and breaks up and our harried hero enters into another relationship, but this time as a wary lover not entirely committed to his affectionate partner.

Unlike the strictly pornographic exercises on view hereabouts, "A Very Natural Thing" is sensitive and realistic in its approach, even though the homosexual bars, the local and Fire Island beach soirées and artistic couplings are not in short supply. And its Manhattan, Fire Island and Cape Cod vignettes have been captured in pastel colors that are strikingly lovely and lend a documentary effect.

Robert Joel, as the sorely tried teacher who has not yet emerged from the closet for fear that it will affect his job; Curt Gareth, as his eventually disenchanted lover, and Bo White, as the new light of his life are, to borrow from the title, impressively natural in roles that easily could have become caricatures.

But aside from several scenes, especially one in which Mr. White awkwardly but poignantly meets with his estranged wife and their little daughter, "A Very Natural Thing" is not especially moving. The succession of ecstasies, tiffs, quarrels and searchings for meanings are, despite the essential honesty, the stuff of standard, not unusual, drama.

A. H. WEILER

1974 Je 28, 22:1

Shock Treatment

By VINCENT CANBY

ONE way and another, popular film comedy seems to be going to pieces. Sometimes literally. In "Andy Warhol's Frankenstein," directed by Paul Morrissey, the mad doctor and his faithful assistant Otto seek a head to attach to the otherwise-finished, "perfect specimen of Serbian youth" they are stitching together in the lab. When they find the right man, they decapitate him on-screen with a pair of shears that look like King Kong's toenail scissors.

The afternoon I saw the film at the Trans-Lux West, the packed audience roared with laughter at this sight and others like it—which is Grand Guignol of a more or less competent order. Much fake blood and lots of wax appendages, including the head. The audience also found it hilarious when, late in the film, the doctor gets his own hand chopped off and staggers around the lab, spouting blood and words. "All I had was a labwatowy and a dweam," says the dying doctor, who lisps.

The Warhol-Morrissey production team ("Trash," "Women in Revolt," "Heat") has left sex to the serious pornographers to explore other frontiers of movie comedy: decapitation, disembowelment, necrophilia, and related matters. It's Morrissey's conceit in his "Frankenstein" that the mad doctor is the sort of fellow who would like to fondle a girl from the inside, that is, through an incision in her stomach that allows him to stroke her gall bladder.

The movie is making a lot of people gasp and chuckle with what appears to be delight. So too is Mel Brooks' satiric Western, "Blazing Saddles," which gets some of its biggest laughs by the use of a four-letter word as what Tom Swift would have called a rejoinder. It may not be especially witty but it's some-

The notion that "insult and assault have always been fixtures in popular American comedy was made apparent by the return of the Marx Brothers' 'Animal Crackers.'"

times funny in the way that a rude burp in church can be.

That insult and assault have always been fixtures in certain kinds of popular American comedy was made especially apparent this week by the return of "Animal Crackers," the 1930 Marx Brothers film (only their second) that is now at the Sutton Theater after having been out of circulation for years.

*

"Animal Crackers" may not be the absolute, pluperfect Marx Brothers picture but perhaps none of their pictures really is. Marx Brothers movies form a kind of continuum, segments of which have been given individual titles that are hardly any help at all in distinguishing one from another.

"Animal Crackers" is NOT the film in which everyone gets crammed into a tiny stateroom. That scene is in "A Night at The Opera." Nor is it the one in which Thelma Todd takes Groucho for a ride in a canoe and, while paddling, remarks that Groucho is full of whimsy. "Can you notice it from there?" asks Groucho. "I always get that way when I eat radishes." That was in "Horsefeathers."

"Animal Crackers" is the movie in which Groucho plays Capt. Jeffrey T. Spaulding, the African explorer, in which Harpo goes berserk with a gun at Mrs. Rittenhouse's houseparty and starts shooting canaries and vari-

Srdjan Zelenovic is keeping audiences in stitches as the mad monster in "Andy Warhol's Frankenstein."

ous other moving targets, and in which Groucho introduces Chico at the piano by saying that "Mr. Ravelli will now play 'Somewhere My Love Lies Sleeping' with the male chorus." The chief victim of Groucho's insults and Harpo's assaults is, as always, the sublimely unflappable Margaret Dumont, the sort of woman who thinks nothing odd about having a fist fight with Harpo one minute and then sitting down for a hand of bridge with him the next.

The insults and assaults and the anarchy that became art in the Marx Brothers movies look more like desperate measures when carried to the extremes they are in so many of today's comedies. The madnesses that Mel Brooks exalts in "Blazing Saddles" have a sort of "Hellzapoppin" vigor to them but they don't add up to much. The targets of Brooks's humor are too many and too easy. One laughs more often at the energy than at the resulting jokes.

That we are prepared to laugh so easily is, I suspect, less a compliment to Brooks's wit than it is a comment on the blandness of mass entertainment comedy, that is, comedy on television where there still are taboos that must be respected. Without taboos, however, a comedy comes apart. It loses form.

*

As Woody Allen continually demonstrates, it's possible to be witty today, to be disciplined and comically coherent. But Allen is an artist; less talented men become confused.

The blandness of most television fare, especially the hypocrisy of the ever-intrusive commercials, invites the kind of outrageous overreaction to so-called middle-class values exhibited in "Blazing Saddles" and "Frankenstein."

The outrage and cynicism expressed in so much com-

edy today has been a longtime in coming. It pre-dates the Watergate revelations, which simply confirmed suspicions that there was in Washington, as elsewhere, a rather large gap between word and deed. After reading the White House transcripts one remembers President Nixon's pained comments on one of his favorite movies, "Love Story," to the effect it would have been practically perfect. If Ali MacGraw hadn't been required to say that filthy word all the time.

In the nineteen-sixties that filthy word, and another one of the same length, became weapons in anti-Vietnam demonstrations. They were painted on placards, which, when pointed at the cops, infuriated the cops into skull-busting reprisals, or when glimpsed on TV, convinced the stay-at-homes that the country was, indeed, coming apart.

Naughty words had power in the sixties, and apparently still do in the comparatively conservative commercial cinema.

The underground cinema, however, is pointing the way to another plateau of shock. Not sex. Not disembowelment or decapitation. The message, demonstrated on screen in a number of avant-garde and underground films,

is excrement. That's what the system, our life, the world adds up to. In "Pink Flamingos," being shown at midnight on weekends at the New Yorker Theater, the ultimate jest is a dog's bowel movement, which fascinates the film's heroine played by a 200-pound transvestite who calls himself Devine, perhaps in homage to Genet.

Shock is still the operating factor, in drama as well as comedy. Back when Bob Downey was making "Chafed Elbows" and "Putney Swope," we were shocked into laughter when Downey's nuns, old ladies and children used obscene language. Some of the success of "The Exorcist" depends on this same sort of shock. It goes beyond the bounds of good taste, which, as everyone knows, exist only to be gone beyond.

The number of things that can still shock us or make us uncomfortable is dwindling all the time. If, as now seems possible, our increasing sophistication leaves us only bodily functions as a subject to contravene the acceptable in art, we shall have taken a giant leap forward only to land back in the bathroom, one year old and once again preoccupied by a process that none of us can safely deny.

1974 Je 30, II:1:5

A Sexual Battle

By MICHAEL SRAGOW

YOU can almost judge a film director by the magazine that puts him on its cover. The track record is too good for mere coincidence: Frank Capra, Hollywood's favorite Depression Pollyanna populist, earned a Time portrait in the 1930's. (Orson Welles and John Huston couldn't cut Mr. Luce's mustard later on.) Stanley Kubrick made the cover of Saturday Review just at the time his work turned from supple satire to sour pseudo-philosophies.

And a few weeks ago, Peter Bogdanovich, the tyro director of "The Last Picture Show" and "Paper Moon" and currently "Daisy Miller," was emblazoned on People, along with starlet sidekick Cybill Shepherd. The only question now is what new media worlds are left for Hollywood's latest glory boy to conquer.

A Second Opinion

On June 16, Vincent Canby described "Daisy Miller" in these pages as "something of a triumph for everyone concerned." It was, he continued, the "best" and "most original" of Peter Bogdanovich's five films. Herewith, a contrary view.

Bogdanovich may be the most shameless Hollywood celebrity since exhibitionism became a national life-style. Every piece he writes as a "film critic" is peppered with forced buddy-buddy anecdotes and reverential references about film buff favorites like John Ford and Howard Hawks. His own interviews carry ceaseless self-endorsements of his obsessive moviegoing, simpleminded art-for-art's-sake stance, and grand enduring passion for Miss Shepherd.

Of course, the man's films are the most damaging evidence against him as an artist: they display nothing but his overpowering ambition to make old-fashioned movies. "Targets," financed on a shoestring, struck most viewers as a worthy fledgling's first try; though the drama was contrived, and its mass murder thrills cheap, the film's faults could be chalked up to its modest budget and hurried production schedule. "The Last Picture Show" had such an affecting story, and came when so few good ones were being filmed, that John Simon was virtually the only critic to complain about the self-consciousness and artificiality that encroached around the movie's core.

But as early as "What's Up, Doc?", a desperate attempt to revive screwball comedy, chinks emerged in Bogdanovich's armory of raves, as his talent's hollowness and pointlessness — his reduction of all characters to types and of human drama to movie clichés — began to appear. And "Paper Moon," his recent updating of con-man tricks (a matching paperweight to George Roy Hill's "The Sting"), proved to many remaining doubters what they only suspected before: that Bogdanovich is a good director for actors and no one else.

"Daisy Miller" is Bogdanovich's latest and most ambitious attempt to break into the cultural big leagues. The director laid the framework for his assault with arrogant self-serving remarks, like "Henry James wrote his book for Cybill Shepherd." He hired Frederic Raphael, a suitable British novelist, to write his screenplay, and got Bertolucci's fancy

Michael Sragow was film critic for the Harvard Crimson until his college graduation in 1973. He is now a freelance writer living in Boston.

photographer, Vittorio Storaro, to mind his lights and colors.

On completion, he even had the film premiered in real Henry James/Bogdanovich country: the Orson Welles Cinema in Cambridge, Mass. James fans in attendance were too entranced by the Master's voice to scurry out aghast at its vulgarization; film people were too excited from catching sight of a preview print to admit their boredom. When Bogdanovich fielded questions afterward, the audience laughed at his compulsive telling of Orson Welles stories, and at his put-down of John Simon (he called the critic "a poop"). But when he mentioned that he felt Larry McMurtry's "All My Friends Are Going to Be Strangers" was too good a novel to be filmed, someone (thankfully) called out "What about James' 'Daisy Miller'?"

The film has been in general release for about a month and a few critics have bought Bogdanovich's slick movie package. Some have contrasted "Daisy Miller" with Jack Clayton's reverential filming of Fitzgerald's "The Great Gatsby" and say that Bogdanovich's treatment of James is refreshingly daring. Others contend that the film contains the crystallization of some essential traits of the American character.

Let us put both these rumors to rest. Bogdanovich reconstructs James's plot quite literally and neglects to dramatize it effectively for the screen. Its pace is deadly. And Bogdanovich fails to fill out any of James's situations with film details that could give them vitality. Bogdanovich's one inventive scene features Daisy singing soppy 1870's pop music, and her Italian boyfriend winging his tenor through "Pop Goes the Weasel." (This actually seems more fit for "What's Up, Doc?" than for "Daisy Miller.")

The director also adds quite extraneous touches like a man playing mood music on a harmonica as Daisy rustles through a castle; the same guy must have played "Battle Hymn of the Republic" before Ford and Hawks battle scenes. The extent of the film's "intellectual" statement is that 19th-century Europe had a rigid, psychologically repressive high society, that old-fashioned, homespun Americans were vital and giving, and expatriate Americans were hopelessly pretentious and confused.

All this, of course, is far from James. In fact, Bogdanovich recently admitted in an interview in a British film magazine, "What James meant to say with the story doesn't really concern me . . . I think all that (social-cultural) stuff is based on some other kind of repression anyway." Bogdanovich might not even realize how much he has reduced James's classic. While "Daisy Miller" is actually not one of James's major works, it does contain his major themes, and, more important, his divided point-of-view.

James's Daisy is a spoiled child unequal to the refinements of the highly developed cultures she samples in Switzerland and Rome; she is curious and lively, but she is also slightly obtuse, and not a wholly committed quester after a sense of self in history. She is partly a flirt, both in feeling and thought, and her lack of seriousness is

"'Daisy Miller' is Peter Bogdanovich's most ambitious attempt to break into the cultural big leagues," says this critic. But it is only a slick distortion of a fine novella. Below, Bogdanovich and his protegee Cybill Shepherd.

Jack Mitchell

a form of self-protection.

Her would-be lover Frederic Winterbourne is a much more intelligent expatriate, but his appreciation of European history and politesse has become estheticized; he recognizes their grace, but not the human needs they account for. He is genuinely conflicted by his attraction to Daisy; he desires the forthright American girl, but cannot break his broader allegiances. When Daisy dotes on the company of a buffoonish, well-oiled Italian, Winterbourne only half-heartedly tries to save her from her foolishness, and from ostracism by Europeanized Americans. The novel's comedy comes from these characters' disjunctions; its sadness from our knowledge that, together, these two people might have grown whole.

Bogdanovich's film reduces James's complex love story to a simple flirtatious sexual battle. His Winterbourne is simply a tentative twerp, weakly acquiescing before alien standards, and his Daisy Miller is coquettish where she should be dangerous. All the other characters are snots, bumpkins, hangers-on and harridans. Actor Barry Brown is so restricted as Bogdanovich's Winterbourne that his own native charm (used to good purpose in his previous film, the otherwise unfortunate "Bad Company") is obliterated. Bogdanovich even afflicts him with affectations — a habit of mustache-twirling, and a genteel lockstep of a walk — that grates on us rather than amuses.

Brown's screen presence is also stunted here by the non-acting of his superficially lovely co-star Cybill Shepherd. Her classic body cannot save her performance: Daisy's high-collared Victorian outfit, complete with bustle, hides Miss Shepherd's best features. Days after, all you can recall of her performance is a rapid, flat sing-song delivery.

She never flickers with true emotion. Daisy is a shallow character but she does flaunt herself with sparks of passion. (One questioner at Harvard asked Miss Shepherd: "Do you ever smile for real?")

Moreover the film is boring. The director has no appreciation of Europe at all, and his camera has grown as static as his inspiration. The settings are pretty but inexpressive, and the scenes stagey. The sliding, conflicting emotions of James are reduced to simple-minded confrontations. At his film's very beginning, Bogdanovich betrays his narrative ineptitude. When he wants to impress us with the contest between Old Europe and Young America, he makes us suffer through stodgy glimpses of a palatial Swiss hotel and then plants obvious (and non-Jamesian) sight gags— Daisy's little brother shuffles the shoes that stand outside the other guests' bedrooms and then slides down the hotel bannister.

In James' novella, Mrs Walker, the main spokesman for Rome's high-living Americans, cuts Daisy off from Roman society because she outrages etiquette. Bogdanovich, on the other hand, says, "I found her [Mrs. Walker] difficult to accept because she seemed rather unmotivated, except for her social reasons . . . . I thought there should be more beneath that. In the way I've cast it and in the way she's played, she's rather heavily motivated sexually."

Because of this choice, "Daisy Miller" audiences might well feel that they have left the land of the Colosseum and landed in Peyton Place.

1974 Je 30, II:5:1

FIRST CHARGE OF THE MACHETE (La Primera Carga al Machete), directed by Manuel Octavio Gomez; produced by Miguel Mendoza; screenplay (Spanish with English subtitles) by Julio Garcia Espinosa, Alfredo De Cueto, Jorge Herrera and Mr. Octavio Gomez; director of photography, Mr. Herrera; editor, Nelson Rodriguez; music, Leo Brower and Pablo Milanes; a production of the Instituto Cubano del Arte e Industria Cinematograficos, distributed by the Tricontinental Film Center. Running time: 84 minutes. At the First Avenue Screening Room, First Avenue at 61st Street. This film has not been rated.
With Rigoberto Aguila, Idalia Andreus, Miguel Benavides, Carlos Bermudez, Luis Carreres and others.

By VINCENT CANBY

"First Charge of the Machete" is an overly fancy Cuban variation on American television's old "You Are There" series, those re-creations of great moments in history as they might have been recorded by reporters equipped with hand-held cameras and 20-20 foresight.

The time is October, 1868, when Cuban nationalists in Oriente province rebelled against the Spanish colonial regime, captured the city of Bayamo and, later, decimated the Spanish troops sent in to put down the rebellion. The principal instrument of the Cubans was the machete, the lowly farm tool that was elevated to the status of lethal weapon in a time of crisis.

The film, which was made in 1969, was shown at the First Avenue Screening Room Sunday and will be repeated there at noon and midnight today and tomorrow.

No matter how cleverly planned and ingeniously executed, there is always something bogus about these attempts to pretend that history happened yesterday, when sound cameras were on hand to record the events. The more clever and ingenious, in fact, the more bogus.

It is the conceit of Manuel Octavio Gomez, who directed this film, that motion-picture photography of 1868 would look like very crude Mathew Brady, even though the sound-recording equipment is on a par with today's. "First Charge of the Machete" is almost impossible to look at—the images being all black or white with no intermediate shades. It not only is a terrible strain on the eyes, but it also makes the white subtitles invisible at least half the time.

Mr. Octavio Gomez's attempt to give contemporary purpose and passion to events first obscures and then ultimately overwhelms them: we're too busy noticing the elaborately designed cinema to give much heed to the vérité behind it.

He also apparently thinks that 19th-century newsreel cameramen would have been absolutely committed to close-ups and to movement. If the subject of an interview is not moving around, then the camera moves around him. Nothing is allowed to be static. At one point this incessant movement gave me the impression that the director somehow resented buildings and trees for not being able to walk.

1974 Jl 5, 11:1

Ray 'Charulata' Opens Commercial Run

CHARULATA, based on a short story by Rabindranath Tazore; directed and written by Satyajit Ray; music, Mr. Ray; photography, Subrata Mitra; produced by R. D. Bansal. Running time: 112 minutes.
Charulata .... Madhabi Mukherjee
Bahupati .... Sailen Mukherjee
Amal .... Soumitra Chatterjee

"Charulata," which opened commercially yesterday at the First Avenue Screening Room, was shown in the third New York Film Festival at Lincoln Center. Following are excerpts from Howard Thompson's review in The New York Times, Sept. 11, 1965.

Nobody but Satyajit Ray could have made "Charulata." This time the Indian film maker responsible for the memorable "Apu" trilogy is delineating an emotional marital triangle that develops in a comfortable Bengali household.

What happens on the screen? Actually, very little. Husband, a liberal newspaper publisher, neglects pretty young wife. Wife is attracted to husband's young cousin, a dashing derelict. He nobly departs just in time, and the couple begin again—yes, older and wiser. As do all Ray films, it moves like a majestic snail.

The picture is an artistic masterpiece, impeccably performed (by Madhabi Mukherjee, Sailen Mukherjee and Soumitra Chatterjee), but diluted in impact and power by the stately, inchworn pace and a plot basically as old and familiar as the hills. Arranging every single camera frame to convey nuance, mood or tension, Mr. Ray has photographically embroidered a steady flow of quiet images with precise, striking acuity.

"Charulata" is not topnotch Ray. But, again, nobody else could have made it.

1974 Jl 5, 17:1

Whatever Happened To Movie Musicals?

By VINCENT CANBY

HIGHLIGHT: Gene Kelly, full of the kind of high spirits available only to lovers, children and small domestic animals, dances down a rain-drenched, Hollywood soundstage street, missing not one important puddle in his demonstration of what feeling absolutely super should look like. ("Singin' in The Rain," 1952.)

Highlight: Fred Astaire and Jack Buchanan, wearing the white ties, the tails and the top hats that are the badges of a sophistication none of us will ever know, move against a plain stage backdrop as they sing and dance "I Guess I'll Have to Change My Plan," the manner rueful but not defeated, as it should be at the end of a long, exhausting and thoroughly satisfying evening, or the end of a short, tumultuous, too-good-to-be-true affair. ("The Band Wagon," 1953.)

Highlight: Her vitality harnessed for a few vivid minutes, Judy Garland, wearing a black slouch hat, form-fitting jacket, black net stockings and high heels, sings and dances a version of "Get Happy" that was to become one of the triumphs of her career, as well the last musical number she would ever film at M-G-M. ("Summer Stock," 1950.)

Highlight: A very young Joan Crawford, her alleged twinkletoes having been dipped in lead, her lipstick put on in the kidney shape of a desperate smile, goes one-two-three-thump, to the left, one-two-three-thump, to the right, while her partner, Fred Astaire, dances around her with such grace, good will and concern that it seems almost a metaphor for love's blindness. ("Dancing Lady," 1933.)

These are only four of the dozens of marvelous sequences in "That's Entertainment," a collection of many memorable and some not-so-memorable musical numbers from M-G-M films from 1929, when sound became generally available, through 1958, when the company produced its last great musical. "Gigi," with book and lyrics by Alan Jay Lerner and Frederick Loewe.

"That's Entertainment," produced, written and directed by Jack Haley, Jr., is a documentary at heart, the sort of compilation feature that depends largely on the genius of others a movie made by ravaging earlier movies, and, as such, a movie that one probably shouldn't feel too kindly towards. Theoretically, anyway.

Actually, however, "That's Entertainment" is a consciousness-raising delight, an immediate high, a revue that doesn't only evoke the past but, in addition, lays the past out there to compete with the present on its own terms.

And, as any ponderous, sober-sided documentary should, it asks a question: what the hell ever happened to the American movie musical?

Fred Astaire and Gene Kelly in "Ziegfeld Follies of 1946" — a highlight of "That's Entertainment."

The joy in our musical films, exemplified by Gene Kelly dancing down that watery street, has gone. It's an awareness of this loss that transforms "That's Entertainment" into something on the order of a profound experience when we watch Jimmy Durante teaching Frank Sinatra how to sell a lyric (in "It Happened in Brooklyn" in 1947) or wonder at the possible philosophical interpretations of Busby Berkeley's outrageously abundant use of fire, water, earth, air and colored smoke as background elements against which to present Esther Williams in "Million Dollar Mermaid" in 1952. What could Busby have really meant?

The fun and the nuttiness have disappeared — for any combination of a dozen good reasons, I suspect.

More than any other kind of movie, the musical has been tied to Broadway, and as the Broadway musical became bigger, more expensive and more solemn, so have the movies made from them at such huge expense, including the cost of the film rights, which soared as the gap between Broadway hits and flops grew wider and wider in the fifties and sixties.

"Nice little musicals" couldn't last on Broadway any longer, and the ones that did last became so distinguished by the amount of profits they represented that they were virtually public institutions by the time they became movies.

This, I'm sure, explains a good deal of the solemnity of such films as "Fiddler on The Roof" and "West Side Story." If not solemn, the film versions were awe-struck ("Funny Girl"), well-meaning but flat-footed ("Sweet Charity") over-sanctified ("Sound of Music"), over-produced ("Jesus Christ Superstar"), or totally out of control ("Hello, Dolly"). Several exceptions: "My Fair Lady," "Cabaret" and perhaps "Godspell."

It seems curious to acknowledge at this late date but the only two original musicals of real class to be produced by Hollywood in the last 10 years are, of all things, "Mary Poppins" and "Tom Sawyer," both with music and lyrics by Richard M. and Robert Sherman.

"That's Entertainment" draws on the output of only one studio and thus can't be described as a definitive history of the Hollywood musical, or even of M-G-M's output. For one reason and another (perhaps because a sequel already is in the works) a lot of M-G-M films are not represented, including "Love Me Or Leave Me," "Les

"'That's Entertainment' is an immediate high," says Vincent Canby. Judy Garland and Mickey Rooney in a scene from "Babes on Broadway," above, provide some of the film's fun.

Girls," "Kiss Me Kate" and "Silk Stockings," all of which were made before 1958.

However, it includes enough material to make the mind boggle at all the behind-the-screen talent represented: Cole Porter, Frank Loesser, Betty Comden and Adolph Green, Leonard Bernstein, Oscar Hammerstein II, Hugh Martin and Ralph Blane, Jerome Kern, Michael Kidd (who also appears on screen), Johnny Mercer, Arthur Freed, Nacio Herb Brown, Stanley Donen, Sammy Cahn, Jule Styne, Gus Edwards, Hermes Pan, Harry Gordon, Leo Robin, Clifford Grey, Irving Caesar, Mack Gordon, Harry Warren, and, or course, Arthur Schwartz and Howard Dietz, who wrote the music and lyrics not only for "i Guess I'll Have to Change My Plan" and "By Myself" but also for the great title song, which never slops over into the well-intentioned sentimentality of Irving Berlin's "There's No Business Like Show Business."

It's possible to find minor irritations in the film. We are given only fitful flashes of production numbers we'd like to see all of ("A Couple of Swells," "Be A Clown") and occasionally a soundtrack narrator will insist on passing on some information we could do without when we'd like to hear the image on the screen. In this fashion Fred Astaire's "By Myself" is made almost completely visual, and Astaire, like Gene Kelly, is as stylish as a singer as he is a dancer.

I would also question some of the facts. I doubt that Louis B. Mayer had hopes of turning Clark Gable into a musical star by casting him in Robert E. Sherwood's "Idiot's Delight," which was, after all, about a second-rate hoofer, or that "Reckless" was meant to do the same for Jean Harlow. The film was a thinly disguised fiction based on Libby Holman's well-publicized troubles, a melodrama with musical interludes, no more.

But these are reservations of no importance whatsoever. When you go to "That's Entertainment," you'll see how the American musical film grew out of its innocence to peak in wit and sophistication in the fifties, only to slide back into the pious, lugubrious, pseudo-innocence of recent years. The genre has just about disappeared except for rock musical documentaries, but rock musical documentaries are essentially found objects.

1974 Jl 7, II:1:6

Is 'A Free Woman' The Woman We've Been Waiting For?

By MARJORIE ROSEN

"A FREE WOMAN," by the German director Volker Schlondorff, is not only the first film from any country dealing intelligently and sensitively with a modern woman influenced by the feminist movement, but it is also such a tender and a personal movie that musing in public as to why it doesn't totally work makes me feel something like Benedict Arnold. After all, having been denied for so long a screen portrayal of a real woman, a heroic and sympathetic woman, why complain on finally getting one? And, indeed, Elisabeth, the heroine of "A Free Woman," is such a figure.

We meet Elisabeth on the morning her divorce is granted and follow her as she hassles over the custody of her small son, Nikki, and as she vainly attempts to find meaningful employment and pursue the singing and tap dancing

Marjorie Rosen, the author of "Popcorn Venus: Women, Movies and The American Dream," is currently at work on a screenplay.

A Second Opinion

On June 18, Howard Thompson referred to "A Free Woman"—a film which has received generally favorable reviews — as an "uncommonly engrossing and wise new German movie." The Times reviewer went on to say, "It would be hard to find a more persuasive and appealing proponent of feminism" than Margarethe von Trotta, the star and co-author of the film. Herewith, a woman critic's view.

lessons she once would have liked. Elisabeth, as portrayed by Margarethe von Trotta, has the gentle tentativeness of a particular kind of loving and bright female who has been drained of life by a brow-beating perfectionist partner.

Even in her brief freedom she can't completely lose this doleful definition—not when chirping "Let's Call the Whole Thing Off" in a deliciously accented English, not when making love with a new man who matters or, dressed in a silly costume, guiding Japanese tourists around an industrial exposition, one of

a string of tacky jobs she just barely secures. Her seemingly simple decision to break away from a man who shows all the warmth of a storm trooper is heroic enough, but the plaintive stabs Elisabeth makes at independence, and her inevitable compromise, speak to women in an intimate, pertinent way that few films have since the "women's pictures" of the forties.

"A Free Woman," made in 1972, was written by von Trotta herself and Schlondorff, her real-life husband, and is based on her own experience, which may account for the splendid nuance with which she acts the role of Elisabeth. However, translating autobiography to the screen is tricky, and the fictional reality that the two come up with boggles under a spate of rhetoric that is more than awkward; it's five years behind the times, at least here in America.

Not since Mai Zetterling's "The Girls" (1968) have characters wandered through a picture delivering such clumsy consciousness-raising speeches to their audience. A tour through an art museum evolves into a deliberate history of the oppression of females as demonstrated by the painter's positioning and attitude toward his subjects. Elisabeth's singing teacher comments that one musical piece is "a dignified expression of love. It doesn't treat women like babies," and later she remarks of a work of sacred music, "Women were not allowed to sing in church." When Elisabeth's roommate chuckles over a news item about a woman robbing a bank in drag, Elisabeth mourns, "Even at a holdup, to be taken seriously you have to be a man."

From the other side of the fence, pronouncements thunder from piggie males like her boss in the art gallery: "A woman has just one aim—to fascinate a man." Or from her ex-husband: "Every woman is replaceable."

The frequency, intensity, and dichotomy of these male and female voices reduce to polemic a drama which would have moved us more had it been genuinely dramatized; this overstatement also disrupts the flow toward which von Trotta's extraordinary performance strives. In Germany, where the women's movement is just breaking ground, this crisply drawn manifesto of grievances may be necessary, but here it's alienating and annoying, as if the writer and director trust neither the strength of their material nor the perceptiveness of their audience. I also suspect that the rhetorical thrust of the film stems in part from the couple's own personal passion and anger. Although empathizing with it, I suspect that its graceless distillation is an almost inevitable result of making a fictional account of a personal, wounding experience.

Another flaw of "A Free Woman" is its superficial handling of the male characters. Elisabeth's naturalness, her fullness as a "real" individual, underscores the oversimplified manner in which the men are drawn, Hans-Helmut (Friedhelm Ptok), her husband, spews forth a petulance so deadly that he becomes a buffoon in his own way, and save for one brief scene where he inexplicably acts human, his grating infantilism shields an underdeveloped persona. Schmollinger (Georg Marischka), her art gallery boss, is another clown, a corpu-

When a marriage busts, who gets the books? Margarethe von Trotta and Friedhelm Ptok, a bitterly divorced couple, do a bit of bickering in the library in "A Free Woman."

lent, slobbering lech who makes a pass between meals, then spitefully punishes Elisabeth for spurning him.

Even Oskar (Martin Luttge), the man she ultimately marries in order to gain custody of Nikki, is simply too ready and willing to be believed. Immediately after meeting her, he's willing to pay her rent. Upon receiving a phone call from her he obediently flies from Frankfurt to Milan. Then, hearing of her distress, he promptly proposes marriage and security. If such a compliant man exists, I'd like to know him.

The shallowness of these portraits clashes with and devitalizes Elisabeth's carefully-etched heroine. Once, and crucially, however, von Trotta and Schlondorff even set Elisabeth up in a situation which rings dangerously false. This woman who is so compassionate that she at first refuses to take her son away from her husband because "I didn't want to take everything away from you at once," later toys with the idea of claiming — deceptively — that another man fathered her child. Then, in the end, she flatly refuses to make a strong, legitimate case by asking mutual friends to testify in court about her husband's verbal abuse to her in front of the boy. Consequently, by marrying again she makes a peculiar trade—surrendering her independence, her most precious freedom, out of a disproportionate concern for friends' momentary discomfort. This suggests that her passivity is simply due to ambivalence, or that at bottom she never wanted the burden of freedom in the first place.

Such inconsistencies, rhetoric, and glib portraits flaw "A Free Woman" and pos-

sibly distance rather than encompass those of us in the audience needing enlightenment. Yet the film contains moments of sublime insight and gorgeous attention to detail. How nice, yes nice, to see a woman desperately squeezing a blackhead to make herself more attractive to a new suitor. How nice to see her daubing off eye cream or buying a wig which looks lousy, then walking off with a jaunty new attitude. This process of female demystification, through scrupulous attention to detail, is one usually reserved on the screen for men, and here it's more than a pleasure; it gives us a deepening, a mellowing of our knowledge and feeling for this woman's struggle.

Margarethe von Trotta's Elisabeth is uncomfortably, excruciatingly real, and her world is reflected in Sven Nykvist's careful, contained camera work. The Schlondorff vision looks so different from the Ingmar Bergman films Nykvist often shoots: it's a cluttered, confined world—a "real" world of windows, doors, of panelled wood and suffocating warmth, of books and of mirrors which don't lie. It's a world which precisely defines the limitations of Elisabeth's life without losing us in an affectation of romance, one which underscores how many miles there are to travel before freedom.

No, this isn't a picture about a free woman, but rather about a real woman. Many feminists have been arguing for an honest, accurate portrait such as this, but now that it's here, is it really enough?

I don't think so. We may be starved for identification with "real" screen women, but desperation shouldn't compromise us into settling for something less than an overwhelming, deeply moving experience in our moviegoing. Unfortunately in this case, the exquisite tension and nurturing of characters through their special reality that might have produced such satisfaction gets lost in the mire of Elisabeth's sometimes banal battle.

Still, with all its imperfections, "A Free Woman"—for those who care—is all we've got right now. She's a promising beginning for women's pictures, and we'd best treasure her while she's here.

1974 Jl 7, II:11:1

The Power and the Gory

By STEPHEN FARBER

THE books on the history of film describe the stunning effect on audiences of the earliest two-reelers: At the sight of a moving train on screen, some people actually fled the theaters, screaming in horror. Others were struck with awe and delight. Movies were a form of circus spectacle before they began to tell stories—and long before they were considered an art. Since then, narrative and cinematic techniques have been refined, and the new medium has finally achieved intellectual respectability.

In recent times, however, moviemakers have been forced to compete with lucrative, high-powered rock concerts as

Stephen Farber, a freelance critic, is the author of "The Movie Rating Game."

well as with television, and they've had to search for an added charge—bigger, splashier gimmicks that will enthrall audiences just as that locomotive once did. With fewer and fewer movies being produced by the major studios, almost every one must be an event, a blockbuster. Colossal budgets are back in fashion, and the studios are marketing a new brand of sensationalism, gaudier and more lurid than at any time in movie history.

"The Exorcist," already one of the top-grossing films of all time, is the major influence on the new cinema of cruelty. Although the film may not have many direct imitators, it has established a unique approach to entertainment; movies are now conceived as kinky, gory, decadent circus spectacle. As most critics have pointed out, "The Exorcist" is incoherent as a piece of

storytelling; the plot is so full of holes that it is often impossible to make any sense of the bizarre events. Screenwriter William Peter Blatty has even talked of tacking on a new ending because so many people have misinterpreted the original conclusion.

But most viewers don't care that "The Exorcist" is riddled with red herrings, pointless scenes, irrelevant characters, and unanswered questions. They may actually prefer an illogical narrative because they don't have to concentrate in between the seven or eight shock scenes.

Director William Friedkin has revolutionized the movie business by going further than anyone else had dared; he found the perfect mixture of blood, excrement, perverse sexuality, and religious symbolism to drive audiences wild. (Actually, the same elements were present in an underground hit of a few

years ago—Jodorowsky's "El Topo"—but Friedkin has reworked the formula for a mass audience.) "The Exorcist" is a new kind of sex-horror circus, and one can almost imagine carnival barkers outside the theaters, promising dirty treats in the dark: "This is the big one, folks! Step right up! See the famous crucifix scene! See little Regan urinate and vomit—in glorious Technicolor!"

When the public is in the market for carnival thrills, criticism is virtually irrelevant. Bad reviews couldn't keep people away from "The Exorcist," or from "Papillon," with its scenes of prison torture, the ravages of leprosy, decapitation, and throat-slitting. At the same time, critics have not been able to persuade people to see subtler, quieter films like "Badlands," "Thieves Like Us," or "The Conversation."

One of the few recent movies to score at the box office is the Warhol-Morris-

"The Exorcist" started the movies-for-shock trend by finding the perfect mixture of blood, excrement, perverse sexuality and religious symbolism to drive viewers wild. Kitty Winn and Jason Miller, above, discover a startling message scrawled on Linda Blair's stomach.

Los Angeles will be jolted by giant tremors in "Earthquake," and so will moviegoers, thanks to an apparatus approximating the sensations of an actual quake. Later, customers will have their legs tickled at the cockroach movie, "The Hephaestus Plague."

sey 3-D version of "Frankenstein," featuring necrophilia, dismemberments, and disembowelments, with human entrails oozing right off the screen into the auditorium. Unlike "The Exorcist," "Frankenstein" is so exaggerated that it turns out to be comic rather than horrifying, and the 3-D compositions are witty and inventive; but it is discouraging that this bloody camp extravaganza drew a much larger audience than "Badlands" or "The Conversation."

Even the most successful comedy of recent months, Mel Brooks's "Blazing Saddles," is in the carnival style of filmmaking. It has no plot, no satiric point, no logic or coherence; it's a collection of outrageous gimmicks and set-pieces—a burlesque show not quite at home on the range. The humor depends on shock—often the cheap shock of hearing respectable churchmen or dowagers utter four-letter words. Just as people go to "The Exorcist" to see the

masturbation and vomiting scenes, they go to "Blazing Saddles" to see the highly-publicized campfire scene, with cowboys passing wind after a dinner of baked beans.

But these films represent only the beginning in this new wave of sensationalism. Along with the predictable "Exorcist" ripoffs, some of the films in preparation include "Jaws," a movie about a killer shark that the director promises will "tear your guts out"; "The Fan Club," concerning a group of men who kidnap a Hollywood sex goddess in order to act out all their forbidden fantasies; and a batch of multimillion-dollar disaster movies starring towering infernos, earthquakes, jumbo jets in jeopardy, and an army of giant cockroaches.

Some of these movies hope to intensify the horror with the aid of new technical equipment in theaters: A sophisticated sound system will approximate the sensations of an actual earth-

quake, and wires attached to the seats will tickle customers' legs while they are watching the cockroach movie, "The Hephaestus Plague."

Hollywood only reflects what it thinks the public wants, and the most disturbing question is not why the studios are cashing in on a profitable trend, but why sensationalism delights such a huge audience. Of course there are a few other popular formulas. Nostalgia still draws, as the success of "The Sting" and "That's Entertainment" demonstrates. But sensationalism seems more dependable. Television—with its commercial breaks—probably helped to destroy people's ability to concentrate for more than 15 minutes at a time; now movies have to have regular doses of violence in order to hold the interest of an impatient public.

Rock concerts of the last few years, with their emphasis on spectacle and sensationalism, have also affected the expectations of young moviegoers. How can an ordinary movie rival a glitter rock concert that boasts mixed media effects, fireworks explosions, snake-charming acts, simulated hangings, and sound amplified to the level of a jet roar? But "The Exorcist" has the electric shock appeal of a David Bowie or Alice Cooper concert, and that may be why kids go back to see it again and again; they're addicted to its overpowering images of defilement.

Yet those explanations do not really account for the masochism and passiv-

ity of audiences at the new cinema of cruelty. They resemble packs of zombies twitching to life when the electricity is turned on. Are their feelings so deadened that they need shock treatment to make them respond? Maybe this inertia is the end result of all the national traumas of the last decade; by now Americans feel helpless to control their lives, powerless even to discover the truth about what is going on. In this mood of weariness and cynicism, audiences no longer expect a film to provide a meaningful experience; they just want their kicks, and any freak show satisfies them.

I can only guess at the underlying reasons for the new wave of sensationalism, but these movies are signs of a profoundly disturbed society. Torture is entertainment, and only disaster seems real. Since the Supreme Court has discouraged honest sexual films, sadomasochism—violence with an erotic charge—is at a premium. Our priorities are outrageously distorted.

If this brand of sensationalism continues to draw crowds, it spells the end of movies as art or even as intelligent, stylish entertainment. When movies become more and more like carnivals, the only things people will go to see are sensational attractions they haven't seen before—a child masturbating with a crucifix, disembowelments in 3-D, simulated earth tremors in the theater. What is left to show? Rape is already passe;

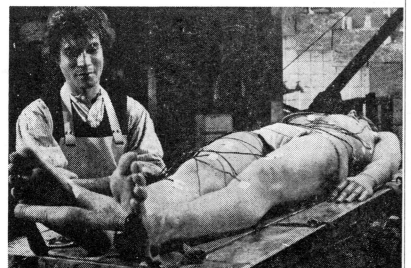

Arno Juerging plays sado-scientific footsie in "Andy Warhol's Frankenstein," a kinky flick in 3-D which also features necrophilia, dismemberments and disembowelments, with entrails seeming to ooze right off the screen.

castrations and sexual mutilations may be next, along with holocausts of unimaginable ferocity.

If "Earthquake"—with its artificial tremors—catches on, the spectacle in the theaters will begin to surpass the action on screen. For the premiere of "The Towering Inferno" perhaps some shrewd publicity man can arrange to set the theater on fire. One of these days an ambitious producer may come up with the idea of running a real train through a movie theater to add suspense to a chase scene. That will bring the history of movies full circle: Films began as three-ring circus, and that's the backward direction they seem to be taking in the seventies.

1974 Jl 7, II:11:1

DIRTY MARY CRAZY LARRY, directed by John Hough; screenplay by Leigh Chapman and Antonio Santean, based on the novel, "The Chase," by Richard Unekis; produced by Norman T. Herman; music, Jimmy Haskell; editor, Chris Holmes; director of photography, Mike Margulies; an Academy Pictures production, distributed by 20th Century-Fox. Running time: 93 minutes. At the Forum Theater, Broadway at 47th Street, and other theaters. This film has been rated PG.

Larry	Peter Fonda
Mary	Susan George
Deke	Adam Roarke
Franklin	Vic Morrow
Hank	Fred Daniels
Stanton	Roddy McDowell

By VINCENT CANBY

"Dirty Mary Crazy Larry," which opened at the Forum and other theaters yesterday, is about a couple of young, down-on-their-luck racing car drivers named Larry (Peter Fonda) and Deke (Adam Roarke) who extort a lot of money from a supermarket at the beginning of the movie and spend the rest of the time, less than a day, attempting to outwit the county police. They are accompanied on the ride by Larry's girl, a parolee named Mary (Susan George), who has a good figure, a pretty face and even fewer brains than Larry or Deke.

Although it's one long chase (from where to where is never known), "Dirty Mary Crazy Larry" is as aimless as its dimly seen characters, who talk a lot of dreadful, cute-tough dialogue but are never recognizable except as the actors who play them.

Even that factor isn't much help in enjoying the film. At least half of it is devoted to semi-spectacular examples of trick driving and multi-vehicle smash-ups, at which point you are perfectly aware that the actors have been replaced by stuntmen. The film is so bereft of emotion and so full of physical movement that it's possible this is a point that John Hough, the director, and the screenwriters wanted to make. It's a very small point to be made by such a noisy picture.

1974 Jl 11, 27:1

Treatment of Israel Is at Screening Room

By NORA SAYRE

Susan Sontag's film about Israel, "Promised Lands," which was made in October and November of 1973, isn't intended to be a documentary. However, that country's situation is just too factually complex to be treated as a tone poem. In an effort to eschew talking heads, there's a lot of voice-over narration, as people walk through the streets, but sometimes we don't know who's talking. There's some handsome photography — especially of figures in landscapes — although what's seen and what is said often don't go together, and many shots seem irrelevant. The movie opened yesterday at the First Avenue Screening Room.

One's ready to be moved

The Program

PROMISED LANDS, a documentary directed by Susan Sontag; camera, Jeri Sopanen; editing, Annie Chevalley and Florence Bocquet; produced by Nicole Stephane; released by New Yorker Films. Running time: 87 minutes. This film has not been classified. At the First Avenue Screening Room, at 61st Street.

by the subject. But the viewer almost has to function as an editor, since the selection of the footage is so haphazard. Hence the emotions of or about Israel don't come through, even though glimpses of graveyards and corpses and the consciousness of Auschwitz, the lingering shock of the October attack and the awareness that the struggle between Arabs and Jews may be insoluble — as one man says, "There's no solution to a tragedy" — run through the marrow of the picture. Throughout, the ideas and the people and the machines of war are examined from a distance, as though everything had been observed through some kind of mental gauze.

The Israelis — particularly those in robes — are filmed as if they were extremely foreign or exotic. Also, Israel

seems like a nearly all-male country, since few women appear and none have been interviewed. There are a few sympathetic words for the Arabs, but their existence seems shadowy and abstract — almost as bloodless as the statues in a wax museum devoted to Israeli history.

•

Two scenes are particularly disturbing. At a mass burial, the camera rushes in on a weeping profile in a way that's intrusive — because we've been given so little sense of the dead or even of the war. Later, in a hospital, a shell-shocked soldier relives his battlefield experiences under drugs, while a psychiatrist and the hospital staff recreate the noises of shooting and bombing. (This is said to be therapeutic for the patient. The staff looks as though it rather enjoys the task.) It should be devastating to watch this man burrow into the pillow, shudder, dive beneath the bed. But these moments have been filmed with such confusion that we can't respond to his suffering — indeed, suffering's hardly conveyed in "Promised Lands." Because the movie is dull and badly organized, the war is made to seem unreal.

Unlike Claude Lanzmann's very fine documentary, "Israel Why," which was shown at the 1973 New York Film Festival, the Sontag film won't increase your understanding of Israel. Perhaps the latter should have been a book instead of a film.

1974 Jl 12, 41:1

THE PLASTIC DOME OF NORMA JEAN, directed by and screenplay by Juleen Compton; camera, Roger Barlow; music, Michel Legrand; produced by Juleen Compton and Stuart Murphy. At the First Avenue Screening Room, at 61st Street. Running time: 90 minutes. (This film has not been classified.)

Vance	Robert Gentry
Norma Jean	Sharon Henesy
Bobo	Marco St. John
Andy	Sam Waterston
Francis	Skip Hinnant

You know that you're in for a festival of innocence—which will almost certainly be betrayed—in almost any movie that opens with a shot of sunlight dropping through leafy trees while music soars and a young couple scampers through the woods. (Well before "Jules and Jim," people running outdoors meant happiness on the screen, as long as the weather was good.) It helps if the couple is blond, if they have an affinity for a pure white rabbit and if the landscape contains crickets to provide some blameless sounds. Then all that's needed are some forces of corruption — which will be sure to stone the rabbit.

Juleen Compton's "The Plastic Dome of Norma Jean," which is playing at the First Avenue Screening Room today and tomorrow, is an infantile ripoff of the Marilyn Monroe legend. In case the title fails to zap your reflexes, there are some early shots inside a truck

that refer directly to Clark Gable and Monroe in "The Misfits."

This Norma Jean is a clairvoyant whose talents are exploited by cruel materialists until she nearly goes bats and is finally wiped out. Sharon Henesy has been directed to speak in a quavery little voice laced with aspirates, to heave with distress and clutch her stomach while others grin or chortle wickedly, and to use regression to suggest suffering. She seems about 16 when the movie begins, but soon appears to be 12 and then rapidly retreats to 6.

The film was made in 1967, but it seems more antique than that, because of the elderly rock music as well as the insistence on the purity of youth. (Several New York actors — Robert Gentry, Marco St. John, and Skip Hinnant — are on hand, along with Sam Waterston, who seems to be avoiding the camera.) Throughout, the strained and artificial vision of doomed innocence serves as a reminder that it's fatal to fool with a myth if you can't deliver the comedy that enhanced it. For all the whimsy, "Norma Jean" is a harmless picture. And yet it's discomforting to be embarrassed in the name of a dead person — whose death has been worked over so often.

NORA SAYRE

1974 Jl 12, 44:1

The Cast

THE TAMARIND SEED, directed by Blake Edwards; screenplay by Mr. Edwards, based on the novel by Evelyn Anthony; produced by Ken Wales; music, John Barry; director of photography, Freddie Young; editor, Ernest Walter; an I.T.C. presentation, distributed by Avco Embassy Pictures. Running time: 123 minutes. At Radio City Music Hall, Avenue of the Americas at 50th Street. This film has been rated PG.

Judith Farrow	Julie Andrews
Feodor Sverdlov	Omar Sharif
Jack Loder	Anthony Quayle
Fergus Stephenson	Daniel O'Herlihy
Margaret Stephenson	Sylvia Sims
General Golitsyn	Oscar Homolka
George MacLeod	Bryan Marshall
Richard Paterson	David Baron
Rachel Paterson	Celia Bannerman

By VINCENT CANBY

Blake Edwards, a very talented director of comedy ("The Pink Panther," "What Did You Do in the War, Daddy?" and others), has disappeared. Absorbed, perhaps, into the first image we see in his new film, "The Tamarind Seed," which opened yesterday at the Radio City Music Hall.

That image is an eyeball but it's no ordinary eyeball. It's an eyeball so huge, so clear, so pure, so all-seeing and so fiercely knowing that it could be the mind of God. When the camera pulls back we see the eyeball to be one of a pair belonging to Julie Andrews (Mrs. Edwards), who has been the star and, I assume, the inspiration of two of Mr. Edwards's more recent films. The first was "Darling Lili," a charming comedy with music in which

Miss Andrews played a World War I spy working stanchly if wrong-headedly for the Kaiser's victory. The second is "The Tamarind Seed," a film of the sort of staggering sober-sided romantic foolishness one seldom encounters outside the pages of first-person-narrated gothic fiction written by Victoria Holt and her sisters of the virgin quill.

•

"The Tamarind Seed" is not gothic fiction, technically speaking. It has the form of a contemporary love story set against a background of cold war intrigue stretching from London and Paris to Barbados and Canada. But don't be fooled by the time and places. The game is given away by the film's total absorption in the chastity of its heroine, a woman who considers a goodnight kiss as the first, irrevocable step toward total degradation.

Mr. Edwards's screenplay, though it changes some geographical details, is an unfortunately faithful adaptation of the book by Evelyn Anthony, a novelist who attempts to avoid bad writing by more or less standing on its back: "Looking up, Judith found every cliché speeding through her mind. The moon was like a pearl, the stars were like diamonds, the palm trees waved and the crickets sang. It was all so corny and impossible until one saw the reality."

"The Tamarind Seed" is about Judith Farrow (Miss Andrews), a plucky widow and the veteran of a recently ended six-month affair with a married man, a fellow who is shown by the film to be of such clottishness that it does permanent damage to any sympathy we might have for poor Judith. On a holiday in Barbados, where she has gone to find herself, Judith meets Feodor Sverdlov (Omar Sharif), a tall, dark, handsome man to whom Judith feels—how should I say it?—strangely drawn.

There is, however, a problem. Judith is the assistant to a Very Important Person in the British Home Office in London and Feodor is the Soviet air attaché in Paris. Did they meet just by chance? Is he trying to recruit her for spy work by seducing her? The British Intelligence officer (Anthony Quayle) attached to the Paris embassy thinks so. And this is what Feodor tells his boss, craggy old General Golitsyn (Oscar Homolka).

What in heaven's name is a plucky girl to think? Or, as Judith says: "This whole thing has gotten out of proportion."

The movie hops back and forth between embassies in London and Paris. Thoroughly mixed into the love story are subsidiary plots about a Russian spy highly placed in Allied diplomatic circles and the attempts to defect of a Soviet agent.

The supporting performances are not at all bad,

especially those of Mr. Homolka, Mr. Quayle, Dan O'Herlihy (as the British minister in Paris) and Sylvia Sims (as his unhappy wife). Mr. Sharif is animated and gallant as he gives Miss Andrews her line cues, which is his principal function.

●

Miss Andrews, who can be a marvelous comedienne, is allowed to be funny here. However, instead of appearing vulnerable, she seems totally removed and above everything, as if she were a ballroom chandelier. There's no time for a performance when the camera insists on examining her with such love and admiration.

1974 Jl 12, 41:1

Those Films Which Refuse to Fade Away

By VINCENT CANBY

LIKE unused skis, a second tennis racquet or an out-of-date bankbook, movies occasionally get "lost." They disappear physically. The negative is thrown out. The cans of film are misplaced. No one remembers where they were stored. However, movies also are sometimes "found." Movies like "Walking Tall" and "Billy Jack" belong to one type of "found" movie: the movies that more or less ignores New York with the same kind of persistence as a bad but popular Broadway show that stays on the tryout road making nothing but money. "Walking Tall" and "Billy Jack" were found in the provinces. People out there loved them and, in the case of "Walking Tall," they made it a giant hit long before it was seen in Manhattan. The New York critics had nothing to do with it. They had been ignored.

So have they been ignored in the certain if limited box-office successes of such underground films as "El Topo" and "Pink Flamingos," whose distributors wisely presented them initially at midnight screenings where critics seldom venture. By the time the critics did demolish them, the films had become invulnerable to criticism.

It's now apparent that there is a third kind of "found" movie. These are movies that have had perfectly conventional New York openings, that have received reviews (usually mixed), and then gone into national distribution, heading eventually for that special limbo of television where films may be seen for eternity, but never mentioned by anyone again. For one reason or another there is, every now and then, a film that escapes this sort of un-death. Even though it goes through regular exhibition channels and then is sold to TV, it never loses its theatrical life.

I'm not talking about the standard classics, movies on the order of "Citizen Kane," "King Kong," "The Maltese Falcon," "Casablanca" and the comedies of the Marx Brothers and W. C. Fields. I'm talking about Hal Ashby's

Why have 'King of Hearts' and 'A Thousand Clowns'—box-office flops in the sixties—become cult films in the seventies?

"Harold and Maude," which played for two years in Minneapolis and has now returned to New York for an extended run at the Thalia Theater. I'm also talking about Fred Coe's "A Thousand Clowns," the 1965 film version of Herb Gardner's play, a movie that, I'm told, remains one of the steadiest moneymakers in a number of suburban shopping center theaters. About a year and a half ago, one Long Island theater manager told me: "Whenever business gets bad, I just bring back 'A Thousand Clowns' for a while."

Other theater managers have had the same luck with Philippe De Broca's "King of Hearts," the 1967 French comedy that starred Alan Bates.

The reasons behind the seemingly inexhaustible popularity of "Harold and Maude," "A Thousand Clowns" and "King of Hearts" are difficult to understand, even after the fact.

The other afternoon in a paperback book store on Broadway, I overheard one young clerk telling another solemnly: "I'm going to see it again tonight. It's really great. It's about this guy 20 years old who falls in love with this lady 80 years old. The thing is that it's funny. It's not sick, and the photography is great."

This was the voice of the great American public, of course, and it was describing "Harold and Maude," a movie whose photography made no special impression on me when I reviewed it and found the film only mildly amusing three years ago.

"A Thousand Clowns," in which Jason Robards stars as a former television writer who doesn't believe in work, and "King of Hearts," about a World War I soldier who elects to live in a community of lunatics rather than face the sane world, share a kind of respectable iconoclasm. The former takes pot shots at commercial television. The latter says that war is ridiculous and that the sane people who wage it must be the real loonies. No argument there, not even, obviously, in middle America. "Harold and Maude," which turns sexual myths inside out, is not much tougher but it is somewhat more grotesque.

A newcomer to this list of "found" movies is "The Harder They Come," the first Jamaican feature ever made and the only film on the list that qualifies as a true original, a movie so good that it deserves somewhat more than the limited cult attention it is now receiving when it is shown Thursday midnights only at the First Avenue Screening Room.

When it first opened here at the Embassy Theater in February of last year, "The Harder They Come" received mostly good notices and only one or two unqualified raves. The business was okay but not great. In Boston, however, it played for 26 weeks last year at the Orson Welles Cinema, and reopened there again on April 10, this year, and is still playing. I think I can understand why, now that I've seen it at the Screening Room.

Although it's a sometimes technically ragged movie, "The Harder They Come" has more guts, wit, humor and sheer exuberance than most movies you'll see in any one year of movie-going. A lot of this—though not all—has to do with the superb music, Jamaican reggae (rhymes with leggay), strictly local, highly syncopated rhythm and blues with associations to rock and calypso.

The film was produced, co-written and directed by Perry Henzel, a white Jamaican with experience at the B.B.C. and in industrial and documentary films, and it stars Jimmy Cliff, the black Jamaican reggae star whose life story provides the raw material for a film that simultaneously explores a fantasy and satirizes it.

Like Ivan, the character he plays in the film, Jimmy Cliff came out of the Jamaican hills to make his career as a Kingston recording artist. Unlike Cliff, who went on to become successful as a hugely independent artist, Ivan, once swindled in his initial show biz contacts, seeks his fortune as a ganja (marijuana) courier, only to be swindled again by the local mob. For the brief period he is being hunted by both the mob (for questioning its hierarchy) and the police (for murdering a cop), Ivan enjoys the fame he has wanted all along. His record hits the top of the Kingston charts. He becomes a comic Robin Hood whose autograph is sought for such insolence as writing on walls (sample grafitti: "I am everywhere").

The newspapers give space to him. The police are so infuriated by his boldness they threaten to shut down the carefully monitored ganja trade, which, in turn, infuriates the mob. At the end, Ivan is overwhelmed, but for a few short weeks he has been eating the pie that for everyone else remains in the sky. For a film that ends so tragically, one comes out of the theater feeling remarkably invigorated.

This, I think, has to do with the sheer velocity of Jimmy Cliff's performance, the beat of the music and the uncompromised simplicity of the melodrama itself, which takes place in a milieu of shanty towns, garbage dumps, ganja halls, pool rooms and dance halls that are enough to propel any heroic character into mad attempts at upward mobility. The film, which uses its music beautifully, is also about music and about the Jamaican music industry that, though crooked, offers the only route by which an ambitious boy from the hills can strike it big in a hurry. It's also about the making of the music itself, a pop form that is part soul, part social protest, part high spirits, part insolence. This is not a movie to lift the hearts of the members of the Jamaican Tourist Board. Its sympathy is with "the rudies," the jobless young men who hang around Kingston street corners making rude remarks to people who could be tourists.

Although "The Harder They Come" takes place almost entirely in the Jamaican's Jamaica (there is only one short scene involving a resort hotel), and although it is very careful not to portray whites as the oppressors (we see only blacks ripping off blacks), it is a more revolutionary black film than any number of American efforts, including "Sweet Sweetback's Baadasssss Song." Its anger is less facile, more profoundly moving. Never for a minute is it confused with self-pity, which, more than any other factor perhaps, gives the film its power as well as the continuing appeal that won't let it get "lost."

1974 Jl 14, II:1:7

Films like "King of Hearts," with Alan Bates, have a cult following.

Creepy Gothic

By PAUL GARDNER

"WE'RE interested in making nice clean comedies," says Andy Warhol, munching on a cookie and sipping peppermint tea at The Factory, his art decostyled office near Union Square. "But violence is what people want, so we're giving it to them. That's the secret of my success—just give the people what they want."

When others carried the sex movie to new extremes in explicitness, Andy Warhol moved on to the macabre.

Jack Mitchell

"Yes 'Frankenstein' is deliberately excessive," says Paul Morrissey, who directed the Warhol hit.

Henri Dauman

Udo Kier is about to sink his teeth into the neck of Maxine McKendry in "Andy Warhol's Dracula."

The statement, coming from an Andy Warhol with streaked gray hair, granddaddy spectacles and a younger Carl Sandburg look, sounds exactly like a mischievous put-on from the silver-and-vinyl Warhol of the mid-sixties. But, as usual, Warhol is serious even when his tongue seems firmly in cheek.

Evidently people *do* want "Andy Warhol's Frankenstein," with its vivid scenes of severed heads and hands, its impalements, and wriggly purple scar tissues disfiguring naked torsos — all captured in blood-red 3-D. After playing two months at theaters in New York, Chicago, Los Angeles, Boston and four other cities, the X-rated "Frankenstein" has pulled in a ripping $1,003,932 at the box office, despite generally disastrous reviews. The distributors have reportedly booked the film into 150 additional theaters, and the general prediction is that "Frankenstein" will eventually earn $10-million in rentals.

Not bad for mini-mogul producer Warhol — and director Paul Morrissey — whose low-budget movies, "Trash" and "Heat," did respectable but decidedly unsensational business. What does it all mean? Probably that today's moviegoers, who can see all the hardcore fare they want at the so-called skin flicks, prefer their sex spiked with horror, and with humor. Audiences are laughing at Frankenstein, his sexually repressed, bug-eyed assistant and the doctor's sister-wife, who makes the fatal mistake of seducing a zombie. They even giggle when one victim's stitches pop open, spilling something that looks like beet soup-and-knishes across the screen.

Some people might call "Andy Warhol's Frankenstein" a sick movie. "Naw, I don't think it's sick," said a Columbia University student recently after leaving his seat in the middle of a talky sequence to buy a soft drink in the lobby. "Some of it is funny, some of it is boring—like the other Warhol films.

The 44-year-old Warhol, who has been called everything from Saint Andrew to the Peter Pan of Pop to the apostle of tasteless trivia to the Cecil B. deSade of the screen, began turning out his cinema-verité movies back in the sixties when he lost his zest for painting Campbell's soup cans and Brillo boxes. In 1965, he teamed up with Paul Morrissey, who had been showing his own 16mm. movies in a storefront near the Bowery. Since then, Morrissey has been the chief director for the Warhol factory.

When asked what *he* does, since Morrissey receives credit as writer-director on their films, Warhol says, "I go to the parties." But then—getting serious—he adds, "All of us at The Factory contribute ideas."

Morrissey's major contribution to the factory output has been that of structure. Warhol's early films had almost no movement and no story; instead, they literally focused for hours on such varied subjects as the Empire State Building, a sleeping man, or off-beat couples talking, talking, talking. Morrissey added plot and subtracted some of the verbiage from the improvising "actors" who never seemed able to stop chattering. Not only did he edit his footage, but he also dared to move his camera around in order to achieve a variety of set-ups.

Passionate advocates of the old Warholian stationary-camera technique have complained that Morrissey, in his

Paul Gardner is a freelance writer living in New York City.

effort to be commercial, stained the "purity" of Warhol's art. "I didn't move the camera because it cost too much," explains Warhol, stroking his dachshund Archy.

"As if Andy could be corrupted," says the 36-year-old Morrissey, who has stopped by for cookies and tea at The Factory. "When Andy started making movies, he went all the way back to Edison. The only thing he could do was move forward."

To some critics, the move forward seemed more like a slippery leap. Back in the mid-sixties, after watching an early Warhol film with its scenes of "perversion and degradation," Bosley Crowther, then the movie critic of The Times, issued a stern warning. "It has come time to point a wagging finger at Andy Warhol and tell him he is going too far."

New York City's police force shared Crowther's concern. In 1969, they seized a print of Warhol's "Blue Movie" because it showed Viva, The Factory's reigning superstar, doing some fancy sexual acrobatics with actor Louis Waldron. The critic from Cue magazine took one look at "Blue Movie" and predicted, "One day stag films will surely be playing freely in commercial theaters." Two years later Cue was proved right.

Warhol, whom one admiring associate calls "a prophetic mirror" with a genius for anticipating changes in public taste, is undoubtedly a canny showman. When others carried the sex movie to new extremes in explicitness with films such as "Deep Throat" and "Boys in the Sand," and the arty "Last Tango in Paris," he realized that sex, as a cinematic commodity, was out for him. What was in for him was gruesome gothic; the hour had come to move on—from private parts to cold cuts.

Violence is a brand new ingredient in Warhol's films. Generally, the ambiance has been one of kinky permissiveness. "Trash," starring transvestite Holly Woodlawn and Joe Dallesandro, the factory's prime piece of beefcake, teasingly showed the social problems of an ingenuous dope addict; "Heat" offered Sylvia Miles as a fading movie star who lured Dallesandro, as a former child actor, to her pool on Sunset Boulevard. The beach bums and rouged vagabonds in these films were raunchily amoral, but never dangerous.

"Frankenstein" is a departure in other respects, too. It is the first Warhol film to be shot in 35 mm., it has a mostly German cast and it was filmed back-to-back in Rome with its sequel, "Dracula." And there isn't an American nickel in either production. Andrew Braunsberg, the London producer who set up the two-picture package, raised the necessary $700,000 from Carlo Ponti in Italy, Cinerama in Germany and Jean Pierre Rassam in France. Bryanston Pictures picked up the American and Canadian rights to both "Frankenstein" and "Dracula."

What does Warhol say to those critics who accuse "Frankenstein" of excessive gore? "We're *mocking* those expensive Hollywood films," replies Warhol, quietly sipping his tea, "with their realistic stabbings and shootings and death scenes in pasteled slow-motion. But *they* don't get X-ratings."

"If you want to satiate an audience's appetite for violence," insists Morrissey, "you must reduce that violence to absurdity. Yes, 'Frankenstein' is deliberately excessive."

For Morrissey, "Frankenstein" is more than just a parody of Hollywood chillers that mysteriously surface with respectable family ratings. It is an attempt to exorcise—cinematically—the recurring nightmare of genuine horror in Warhol's life. Six summers ago, Warhol was shot by a mentally disturbed woman, a bit-player who wanted to be a superstar in Warhol's instant-celebrity world. In his work, Warhol had always remained a voyeuristic, passive observer. Suddenly, he became a participant in a tabloid drama. After five-and-a-half hours on the operating table, he returned to life "glued together."

Warhol doesn't talk about the incident today. The memory still frightens him. But two months after the shooting, he told Leticia Kent of The Village Voice, "When you hurt another person, you never know how much it pains. I'm afraid to take a shower. It's sort of awful, looking in the mirror and seeing all the scars. It's scary. I close my eyes. I wasn't afraid before. But I am afraid now."

Morrissey, however, who usually acts as the executive spokesman for Andy Warhol Films Inc., offers some insight into Warhol and "Frankenstein." Running a hand through his shaggy red-hair, the freckled director says, "Andy once told me that he felt as if he would pop open someday. When I filmed 'Frankenstein,' I thought it might be a kind of exorcism for Andy and all the people who are crippled and haunted by some nut-case. And then I added laughter, because that's the only way we survive."

1974 Jl 14, II:11:1

The Cast

THE APPRENTICESHIP OF DUDDY KRAVITZ, directed by Ted Kotcheff; screenplay by Mordecai Richler, based on his novel; adaptation by Lionel Chetwynd; produced by John Kemeny; executive producer, Gerald Schneider; director of photography, Brian West; editor, Thom Noble; distributed by Paramount Pictures. Running time: 121 minutes. At the Baronet Theater, Third Avenue near 59th Street, and Forum Theater, Broadway at 47th Street. This film has been rated R.

Duddy	Richard Dreyfuss
Yvette	Micheline Lanctot
Max	Jack Warden
Virgil	Randy Quaid
Uncle Benjy	Joseph Wiseman
Friar	Denholm Elliott
Dingleman	Henry Ramer
Farber	Joe Silver
Grandfather	Zvee Scooler
Calder	Robert Goodier
Lennie	Allen Rosenthal

By VINCENT CANBY

Duddy Kravitz (Richard Dreyfuss) is an 18-year-old Canadian Jewish boy with the face of an angelic WASP. Bute he has his problems. He's not only Jewish, he's very poor. Also, the time is the mid-nineteen-forties, when the other comers who came before Duddy had already invented the light bulb, the radio, the Toni Home Permanent and Kleenex.

"The Apprenticeship of Duddy Kravitz," which opened yesterday at the Baronet and Forum Theaters, is the funny, fantastic and often moving story of Duddy's adventures as he desperately tries to establish himself as a comer. By hook and by crook and by studying books like Willard Funk's "It Pays to Increase Your Word Power."

Duddy waits on tables, drives a taxi, smuggles dope, becomes a film producer (for his own Dudley Kane Enterprises), rents out pinball machines and dabbles in odds and ends of other occupations, including forgery.

"The Apprenticeship of Duddy Kravitz" is a Canadian production that was filmed mostly in and around Montreal. It was written by Mordecai Richler, the Canadian author who wrote the original novel, and directed by Ted Kotcheff, the Canadian film director, none of whose earlier films ("Outback," "Life at the Top") are anywhere near as good as this.

Perhaps because of the close collaboration between Mr. Richler and Mr. Kotcheff, and because of the obviously high regard the director has for the author and his work, the film looks very much like a novelist's movie. Such an abundance of visual and narrative detail is essentially literary.

This could mean disaster for a movie but not this time. It's true that the frantic pace and the cramming of so many incidents into the film results in certain problems: the continuity is often sketchy and some characters seem less like people than vivid apparitions.

Yet the manic, fragmented structure of the film is an almost perfect reflection of Duddy's state of mind as he goes barging from one get-rich-quick scheme to the next, never quite sure where he's headed nor how he's gotten as far as he has without being arrested.

When Duddy latches on to Mr. Friar (Denholm Elliott), a perpetually sloshed, black-listed film director of dubious achievements, and sets up a company to film weddings and bar-mitzvahs, the movie takes on the air of a slightly lunatic fairy tale. Their first production, "Happy Bar-Mitzvah, Bernie!", which we are allowed to see, is a riotously abrasive home-movie that cross-cuts between shots of Bernie's nice, middle-class bar-mitzvah and shots of Zulu rites, Hitler, a circumcision ceremony, storm troops marching, the bar-mitzvah feast and a man eating razor blades.

It is superbly loony, a bit frightening and riveting, which is, I suspect, how we're supposed to feel about Duddy who, as played by Mr. Dreyfuss (the intellectual schoolboy in "American Graffiti"), is part cblean-cut con-man, part corrupted prophet.

"It's little money-grubbers like Kravitz that cause anti-Semitism," says a Jewish friend. His rich Uncle Benjy (Joseph Wiseman), who has a portrait of Trotsky on the wall, describes himself as a socialist and owns a blouse factory, calls Duddy "a pushy Jew boy" and says, "People like you make me sick." But then a wealthy Jewish scrap-metal dealer who has befriended Duddy reminds him: "It's war. It's war and the white man has all the guns."

The film's attempt to cover so much ground reinforces the feeling that we're watching a kind of urban fable. I have no idea how much time passes in the course of the picture. Duddy's successes and disasters follow upon each other as quickly as those of Dick Whittington. They seem almost magical.

This is responsible, I think, for the special appeal of "The Apprenticeship of Duddy Kravitz" and differentiates it from the usual literature about unscrupulous ambition, most of which is pious and dull and goes without saying.

There's not a bad performance in the film. In addition to the actors already mentioned, one should also cite Jack Warden who, as Duddy's father, has an especially funny Richlerian monologue at the beginning of the film, Micheline Lanctôt, as the French-Canadian girl whom Duddy uses so meanly, and Randy Quaid (the prisoner in "The last Detail") as Virgil, an American gentile and epileptic who becomes one of Duddy's most willing victims.

•

It's Virgil's fondest dream to unite the world's epileptics into an organization that would be rather like the B'nai Brith, the National Association for the Advancement of Colored People, and the Mattachine Society.

"The Apprenticeship of Duddy Kravitz" is an alternately sad and hilarious movie of dreams rampant.

1974 Jl 15, 31:4

The Cast

MY NAME IS NOBODY, directed by Tonino Valerii; screenplay by Ernesto Gastaldi, based on a story by Fulvio Morsella and Mr. Gastaldi, from an idea by Sergeo Leone; produced by Claudio Mancini; executive producer, Mr. Morsella; directors of photography, Giuseppe Ruzzolini and Armando Mannuzzi; music, Ennio Morricone; editor, Nino Baragli; an Italian-French-German co-production, presented by Mr. Leone; distributed by Universal Pictures. Running time: 115 minutes. At the Loew's State 2, Broadway at 45th Street; Loew's Orpheum, 86th Street near Third Avenue and Murray Hill Theater, 34th Street at Third Avenue. This film has been rated PG.

Nobody	Terence Hill
Jack Beauregard	Henry Fonda
Sullivan	Jean Martin
Sheriff	Piero Lulli
Red	Leo Gordon
Honest John	R. G. Armstrong
Westerner	Neil Summers

By VINCENT CANBY

Sergio Leone's "My Name Is Nobody" is the kind of Western that only an immensely appreciative and witty Italian film maker could make. It stars Henry Fonda, one of Hollywood's most noble performers, as the greatest of the old West's gunslingers, and Terence Hill, one of Italy's newest young actors with an anglicized name, as the blond, intensely blue-eyed Nobody who goads, pushes and finally shepherds the older man safely into history.

The film, an Italian-French-German co-production that was photographed in New Mexico, Colorado and Spain, opened yesterday at the Loew's State 2, Orpheum and Murray Hill Theaters.

Mr. Leone did not actually direct the movie, a job that was handled by Tonino Valerii, a former assistant to Mr. Leone ("A Fistful of Dollars," "Once Upon a Time in the West," etc.), the man who gave the so-called spaghetti Westerns class.

Yet it very much looks like a Leone film and, I suspect, it is. It's called "a Sergio Leone presentation," and it's based on his idea. In addition, it's filled with Leone observations about a West he originally encountered in old Hollywood movies.

The time is 1899, midnight for the 19th century, when Jack Beauregard (Fonda), the fastest gun still alive, is making his way toward New Orleans and a one-way passage to Europe, where, he assumes, no one will try to pick a fight with him in bars along the Via Veneto. En route to New Orleans, he meets a mysterious young man who says he is Nobody (Hill) whose skills with a gun match his own and who doesn't want to see the great Jack Beauregard fade quietly into anonymity.

At times Nobody seems to be a malignant clown who wants nothing more than to ridicule the older man. At still other times he talks half-seriously to Beauregard about ways in which the older man can realize his potential as a legend. Nobody thinks it would be nice if Beauregard single-handedly took on the 150 members of the fabled Wild Bunch (not yet gone to seed as shown in the Sam Peckinpah film), and so arranges this spectacular battle.

The plot of "My Name Is Nobody" makes less sense as narrative than as a device on which to hang a series of incidents that are variations on the theme. In this fabled West, life is a continuing series of contests, in barrooms, on main streets and on vast plains where two opposing forces miles apart, come together so inevitably and so perfectly it seems they must be equipped with batradar.

Though it may be too schematic for the taste of many Americans, "My Name Is Nobody" is filled with tumultuous beautifully choreographed action sequences that are so bloodless (a change from the early Leone films) they seem to be slapstick. The style of exaggeration is evident even in the extraordinary clarity of the images and of the sound, so that when we hear the rasping of a straight razor going over a week-old beard, it's as if we were being made aware of each whisker's fate.

Mr. Hill is surprisingly effective and sometimes very funny, in a rôle that is an impossible mixture of Puck, the stage manager in "Our Town," Shane and conventional Ryan O'Neal. Mr. Fonda, as always, is firmly down-to-earth, creating a specific character of the sort that has little truck with the Leonelike introspection. He's a man of action at the end of his career.

"My Name Is Nobody" is terribly knowing. It has the manner of a buff who knows absolutely everything about a subject most other people haven't time for, but it's also very entertaining.

1974 Jl 18, 30:1

Louis De Funes's Gifts Carry French Farce

Louis De Funes, reportedly the biggest thing to hit French films since Brigitte Bardot, is a tiny middle-aged man, bald and usually frowning. He looks a little bit like Leon Errol, but he acts a lot more like a souped-up version of Edgar Kennedy.

In the time the late Mr. Kennedy would have used to go through one slow burn, Mr. De Funes can experience three completely disconnected rages, register a couple of alarmed double takes and survive one or two near-fatal prat falls. He's a two-reel comedian for the jet age, when, of course, no one is making two-reel comedies any more.

This means that a feature film like "The Mad Adventures of 'Rabbi' Jacob" uses up an awful lot of Mr. De Funes very quickly. It's a credit to Gerard Oury, the director and co-author of the screenplay, and to the rollicking bad temper and bigotry of the star that so much of "The Mad Adventures of 'Rabbi' Jacob" is so funny so much of the time.

The Cast

THE MAD ADVENTURES OF "RABBI" JACOB, directed by Garard Oury; screenplay (French with English subtitles) by Mr. Oury and Danielle Thompson⅛ produced by Bertrand Javal; music, Vladimir Cosma; director of photography, Henri Decae; distributed by 20th Century-Fox. Running time:, 96 minutes. At the Trans-Lux East Theater, Third Avenue at 58th Street, and the Beacon Theater, Broadway at 74th Street. This film has been rated G.

Victor Pivert	Louis De Funes
Germaine Pivert	Suzy Delair
Rabbi Jacob	Marcel Dalio
Slimane	Claude Giraud
Andreani	Claude Pieplu
Fares	Renzo Montagnani

•

The movie, in French with English subtitles, opened yesterday at the Trans-Lux East and Beacon Theaters.

In "The Mad Adventure of 'Rabbi' Jacob," Mr. De Funes plays a furiously prejudiced bourgeois businessman for whom life is almost insupportable because the world isn't inhabited exclusively by white French Catholics. As a result of a series of terrible coincidences he finds himself (1) sought by the police as a political assassin, (2) up to his chin in a vat of green bubble gum, (3) chased by a group of Arab terrorists, (4) the hostage of an Arab nationalist hero and (5) disguised as an American rabbi making his first visit in 50 years to his Parisian birthplace.

Supporting the star who works tirelessly—and mostly with success—for laughs, are a number of fine sight gags and some very good supporting actors, including Suzy Delair, who plays Mr. De Funes's wife, a bossy woman with a passion for dentistry.

VINCENT CANBY.

1974 Jl 18, 32:1

"The Education of Sonny Carson," which opened yesterday at the Penthouse and 86th Street East theaters, is a howling brute of a film. Riddled with flaws, inexpressive as art, it shakes off its shortcomings with a primal energy that imbues it with terrifying eloquence.

Based on the autobiographical account of the early years of Robert C. (Sonny) Carson, a black activist now under indictment for murder, filmed on location in the black slums of Brooklyn with a cast recruited in part from the streets, it is a work easy to fault.

Episodic to the verge of incoherence, directed by Michael Campus with an eclecticism that bespeaks craftsmanship but not control, saddled with interludes of song that disrupt pacing and fail as explication, burdened with uneven portrayals and a star (Rony Clanton) whose ability to react far surpasses his ability to act, starved and simplistic in its motivations, it would seem a film beyond redemption.

•

Certainly it fails as biography. To the very end, Sonny Carson—who goes from prize-winning schoolboy essayist (Tommy Hicks portrays the young Sonny), to juvenile burglar, to war lord of a street gang, to hold-up man, to prisoner and out again—remains an enigma.

Yet this film possesses very real beauty and power. It is rich with the language of the streets, lyrical in a scene that captures the glowering twilight sky above the desolate landscape of tenements, pulsating in its documentation of the tribal rhythms of the gangs, hideous in its depiction of police and prison brutality, chilling in its revelation of the devastation wreaked by heroin.

Some people will find its bloodiest scene beyond endurance.

"The Education of Sonny Carson" is by no means the perfect film. Beyond question it beggars every one of the black exploitation films of a year or two ago. That was one of the goals of Irwin Yablans, its producer.

He wanted a film about the black experience. What he achieved derives its awesome force from what it insists on saying about the American experience.

LAWRENCE VAN GELDER

1974 Jl 18, 32:1

The Cast

THE EDUCATION OF SONNY CARSON, directed by Michael Campus; screenplay by Fred Hudson and Mr. Campus, based on the book by Sonny Carson; director of photography, Ed Brown; music by Coleridge-Taylor Perkinson; film editors, Edward Warschilka and Harry Howard; produced by Irwin Yablans; released by Paramount Pictures. At the Penthouse Theater, Broadway and 47th Street and the 86th Street East Theater, at Third Avenue. Running time: 104 minutes. This film has been classifed R.

Sonny Carson	Rony Clanton
Pigliani	Don Gordon
Virginia	Joyce Walker
Pops	Paul Benjamin
Young Sonny	Thomas Hicks
Moms	Mary Alice

The Cast

GOLDEN NEEDLES, directed by Robert Clouse; written by S. Lee Pogostin and Sylvia Schneble; director of photography, Gilbert Hubbs; music, Lalo Schifrin; film editor, Michael Kahn; produced by Fred Weintraub and Paul Heller; released by American International Pictures. At the Cinerama Theater, Broadway at 47th Street, 86th Street Twin 2, west of Lexington Avenue, and 59th Street Twin, east of Third Avenue. Running time: 96 minutes. (This film has been classified PG).

Dan	Joe Don Baker
Felicity	Elizabeth Ashley
Finzie	Ann Sothern
Winters	Burgess Meredith
Jeff	Jim Kelly
Lin Toa	Roy Chiao

If acupuncture hasn't been a major point in theatrical movies heretofore, its value is still debatable to judge by "Golden Needles," which surfaced yesterday at the Cinerama, 59th and 86th Street Twin Theaters. The clutch of good and bad guys and dolls fighting over an alleged Sung Dynasty gold statuette bristling with those needles that promise either endless virility or death, is neither Sung, 20th century, medical nor movie art.

"Golden Needles" is, to put it simply, the latest variant of the karate school of adventure in which continuous, muscular, gory action substitutes for logic. Involved in the frantic chase are the indestructible Joe Don Baker and Elizabeth Ashley (wearing a wide-brimmed tea-planter's hat), as American fortune hunters trying to grab that legendary bauble from assorted oriental villains in Hong Kong for Burgess Meredith, who plays with the relish of Fu Manchu a weird California millionaire.

Naturally, they discover that the $300,000 he's offered isn't worth all the wear and tear, especially since they feel the Chinese Government is the rightful owner and that money isn't as important as true love. In any event, Mr. Baker, as big and rough as a linebacker; the elegant Miss Ashley; Ann Sothern, as a corpulent American expatriate presiding over a sleazy mah-jong dive, and Jim Kelly, as Mr. Baker's tough, black sidekick, are not nearly as picturesque or credible as the authentic, teeming alleys and waterways of Hong Kong.

Miss Ashley should be credited with the film's most convincing line when she exclaims, "My employer won't believe a word of this!"

A. H. WEILER

1974 Jl 18, 32:1

The Cast

MR. MAJESTYK, directed by Richard Fleischer; written by Elmore Leonard; produced by Walter Mirisch; presented by United Artists. At the Rivoli Theater, Broadway and 49th Street, and other theaters. Running time: 119 minutes. (This film is rated PG.)

Vince Majestyk	Charles Bronson
Frank Renda	Al Lettieri
Nancy Chavez	Linda Cristal
Detective McAllen	Frank Maxwell
Gene Lundy	Taylor Lacher
Larry Mendoza	Alejandro Rey
Wiley	Lee Purcell

"Mr. Majestyk" is a competently standard showcase for Charles Bronson's superhero cool. This time, as a Colorado melon farmer, he jostles an obsessive killer with syndicate backing. Guess who wins.

Basically the picture, which opened yesterday at the Rivoli and other theaters, is as obvious and old-fashioned as any good-guy-vs.-bad-guy film dating back to Hoot Gibson. A couple of things render it harmless.

Except for some dutiful splattering of gore, it ticks along rather steadily, under Richard Fleischer's unruffled direction. There is a take-it-or-leave-it air that snugly suits the star's performance, or vice versa. This includes such players as Al Lettieri, Linda Cristal and several others.

The picture might have amounted to more, originally, with sharper use of its migrant-worker background, instead of sloping off to the usual showdown. Bronson addicts, here he is, at it again.

HOWARD THOMPSON

1974 Jl 18, 32:1

NAYAK—THE HERO, direction, story and script by Satyajit Ray; photography, Subrata Mitra; edited by Dulal Dutta; produced by R. D. Bansal; distributed by Trans-World Films (Chicago). Bengali, with English subtitles. Running time: 120 minutes. At the First Avenue Screening Room, at 61st Street. Showings today and tomorrow, noon and midnight. The film will be shown, beginning Monday, on a regular daily schedule through at least July 28.

Arindam	Uttam Kumar
Aditi	Sharmila Tagoro
Haren Bose	Ranjit Sen

. On a train speeding through the Indian countryside, place one movie star beset with self-doubt, a liberated woman journalist, a wealthy businessman and his family, an ambitious advertising man willing to commit his pretty wife to his campaign to make the businessman a client and a host of well-realized minor figures.

•

This is what Satyajit Ray has done in "Nayak" (The Hero), a 1966 film in Bengali with English subtitles playing today and tomorrow at noon and midnight and on a regular schedule beginning Monday at the First Avenue Screening Room. And as we know from countless novels set on trains or ships or in hotels, there is nothing like being cooped up with a fascinating set of characters to grip one's attention.

Mr. Ray does precisely that. The problems arise from what happens afterward, which it not very much at all.

The focus of everything is the movie star, Arindam, played with great ability by Uttam Kumar. In the course of the journey to Delhi, where he is to receive an award, he reveals a good deal about himself.

•

People who revel in tales wherein film idols suffer from insecurity, are shaken by nightmares, fail in their relationships with mentors, old friends and the opposite sex and take refuge in pills and liquor will find him every bit as entertaining as his familiar counterparts. Everybody else aboard the train, including the woman journalist, given admirable characterization by Sharmila Tagoro, seems rather peripheral.

At journey's end, nothing has really changed, which will surely disappoint those who look to art for liveli-

ness, not life. Mr. Ray, best known for his "Apu" trilogy, handles the proceedings with formidable deftness marked by a penetrating vision of performers and film-making. The trouble with "Nayak" is that it is less a statement than an exercise.

LAWRENCE VAN GELDER

1974 Jl 19, 24:1

Female Stars: Are Men the Sex Objects?

By VINCENT CANBY

IN "For Pete's Sake," Barbra Streisand plays a Brooklyn taxi driver's nutty wife who gets hopelessly involved, in succession, with the Mafia, with a call girl operation and with a gang of urban cattle rustlers as she desperately tries to raise enough money to send her husband (Michael Sarrazin) back to college. It's true that it's ultimately Sarrazin who has to bail Barbra out of jail but until that moment, it's been her picture all the way.

She's been the driving force behind it and behind the comedy. It's Barbra who gets all the laughs, who initiates the intricacies of the plot and who, ultimately, is responsible for the happy ending. Sarrazin is little more than a function of the story.

In Blake Edwards's latest film, "The Tamarind Seed," Julie Andrews (Mrs. Edwards) is cast as a young widow, dimly unhappy after a six-month affair with a married man, who falls in love with the Soviet air attaché (Omar Sharif), a known intelligence agent, assigned to the Russian embassy in Paris.

Because Julie works for a Very Important Person in the British Home Office in London, there's some question in her mind whether Omar is romancing her for her carbon copies or for herself. The picture is three-quarters over before Julie allows Omar to take his first, tentative liberty with her. Up until that moment Julie has maintained her starchy calm while poor Omar, who may or may not be a cad but who is, after all, a man, has had to go for sudden swims to bank the fires of his heart.

"The Tamarind Seed" has the form of a suspense melodrama, but its obsession with its heroine's chastity—as much a weapon as it is a prize—reminds one of dopey gothic fiction about virginal nannies facing unspeakable fates a long way from home. In an apparent attempt to correct this, Mr. Edwards (who wrote as well as directed the film) at one point introduces the following bit of dialogue:

She: "Has it ever occurred to you that I might be slightly frustrated myself?"

He: "Then come to bed with me."

She doesn't so they don't. The movie rolls on and on until, largely through the efforts of its spunky heroine, some kind of optimistic resolution is reached.

At a casual glance these two films would seem to have little in common. "For Pete's Sake" is fairly ramshackle

In "For Pete's Sake," it is Barbra Streisand who "gets all the laughs and is the driving force behind the comedy."

comedy highlighted by a number of hugely funny, old-fashioned, farcical sequences that display Barbra's limited comic talents to their best advantage. As a misguided Miss Fixit she is as appealing as she'll ever be, whether wrestling in bed with her first "john," whose nose she accidently breaks, or riding on the back of a steer through downtown Brooklyn. The movie allows its heroine to have sexual feelings and to respond to them with an intensity that, one suspects, somewhat outdistances her husband's.

"The Tamarind Seed" is a much more intelligently conceived film, and much more fancily made, though the total effect is that of a very frigid Cold War romance, a movie not about people or ideas or even events. It's a movie constructed as a kind of tribute to its star. So is "For Pete's Sake." In both films the men get second billing in every way possible. They are denatured by the status of their co-stars and by the requirements of female superstardom. The men are vibrators needed to keep the plots going.

A lot has been written about the place of women in the vast majority of the films being made today for the mass market. That is to say that women are nowhere.

Steve McQueen has Dustin Hoffman as his co-star in "Papillon." Paul Newman has Robert Redford in "The Sting" and Clint Eastwood has Jeff Bridges in "Thunderbolt and Lightfoot." There was a woman in John Wayne's "McQ," but she was disposable, and in "Serpico" Al Pacino was more often turned on by the subject of police corruption than by either of the two women with whom he was shown consorting.

Could it possibly be that "For Pete's Sake" and "The Tamarind Seed" were designed to balance the books by transforming men into witless sex objects? Though the idea sounds attractive, I doubt it.

What's happening has more to do with movie economics than it does with sexism. There's no guaranteed market today for any one kind of film, though the action-adventure picture is probably more often successful than any other kind. Since males are usually the dominant personalities in such films—there have never been many women swindlers or private detectives — it's not particularly mysterious that actors rather than actresses are more visible. This is not a time likely to produce many female superstars. There isn't the opportunity today for actresses to develop the clout of a Streisand or, to a much lesser extent, of an Andrews. Miss Streisand's clout is, in fact, unique, and as much a result of her recording and television careers as of her films, several of which have been financial disasters. Miss Andrews had the great good fortune to be the star of two fantastically successful films in a row, "Mary Poppins" and "The Sound of Music," both of which depended to a greater rather than lesser degree on the precise, essentially sexless purity of her talents as singer, actress and comedienne.

Whether or not they wanted to, both actresses have become such formidable screen personalities that it's practically impossible now to cast them in films in-which they don't defuse the men around them. Blake Edwards, who fails with "The Tamarind Seed," was much more successful with Miss Andrews 'in "Darling Lili," in which he cast his wife against type as a fresh-faced, sweet-tempered Mata Hari collecting Allied military secrets for the Kaiser during World War One. The adoration with which the director regarded his star had the effect of charmingly reinforcing the upside down comedy.

Miss Streisand, a powerhouse of a stage and concert personality, is too big and aggressive for most of the films she appears in—and for most of the

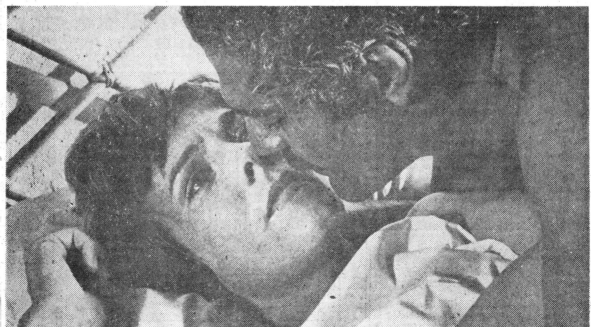

"The Tamarind Seed" is "a movie constructed as a kind of tribute to its star"—not Omar Sharif, who gets second billing, but Julie Andrews, above, who dominates with "starchy calm."

men who play opposite her. The actors who have come off best — Walter Matthau in "Hello, Dolly," Ryan O'Neal in "What's Up, Doc," and George Segal in "The Owl and The Pussycat"—have succeeded only by displaying a sort of furtive disinterest (Matthau) or a self-absorption that equals Miss Streisand's (O'Neal and Segal).

This business of powerhouse female stars is not new, of course. Very few men who acted opposite Greta Garbo, Joan Crawford, Bette Davis or Barbara Stanwyck seemed terribly important at the time. Good actors and bad, whatever their names were, they were all George Brent.

One is made conscious of the situation now because there are so few women stars, and because of the comparatively new practice of pyramiding male stars on top of one another in individual films. It's either all one thing or all another.

In this connection I find it interesting that the only recent film that has presented a satisfactory love story between an evenly matched man and woman—people who are equal but separate, much like Tracy and Hepburn and Powell and Loy were—is a black film. I mean "Claudine."

Among the many good things in that movie is the casting of Diahann Carroll and James Earl Jones as the beleaguered lovers. Never for a moment is the outcome of the hectic affair in doubt, but, also, never for a moment does it look as if one party is about to become a kind of appendage or annex to the other. There are no super-stars to confuse the issue.

1974 Jl 21, II:1:1

Three Whalers Saved by Eskimo Tribe

By VINCENT CANBY

"The White Dawn," an adaptation of James Houston's novel, is reportedly based on a true story about three New England whaling seamen who, in the spring of 1896, became separated from their ship while on an Arctic hunt and whose lives were subsequently saved by a small tribe of Eskimos living on Baffin Island, below the North Pole.

The movie, which opened yesterday at Loew's Tower East, is earnest, cold and apparently authentic. It was filmed on Baffin Island, under the direction of Philip Kaufman ("The Great Northfield, Minnesota Raid"), with Warren Oates, Timothy Bottoms and Lou Gossett playing the marooned sailors and with Eskimos playing Eskimos.

As an Arctic travelogue it is sometimes so striking that I spent much of the time wondering how certain scenes were photographed: long shots of men walking across ice-flows, the killing of a polar bear, a walrus hunt, the capsizing of a boat that sends the actors into icy water.

Because such things are difficult to stage, one's mind is likely to be on the production problems as often as on the film itself, which, as drama, is almost as bland as the Eskimos appear to be to the three sailors.

I would think, too, that the difficulties of filming in such a location, with a mostly amateur cast, had as much to do with the style of the finished film as did the initial intention of the director and the writers.

Mr. Houston's novel is told in the first person by an Eskimo narrator, which allows the author to provide all sorts of documentary details as well as idiosyncratic portraits of the individual Eskimos. The book is a simple, moving account of a little-known people and of the inevitable confrontation between two civilizations.

Aside from the exotic beauty of its landscapes, the film offers no comparable pleasures and not even much information. It's the story of how the three sailors have the bad judgment to be so rude and boorish to their hosts that they invite a fate they would never understand. The movie is more a story of poor luck than of characters experiencing culture shock.

●

Warren Oates plays the mean-tempered sailor, Lou Gossett the gentle one and Timothy Bottoms the philosophical one. They are fine.

Some of the hunting scenes (polar bear, seal, walrus) are probably too bloody for small children but I suspect that the film received its R rating because of a couple of shots of bare female breasts and because the movie suggests that the sailors slept with Eskimo women. This rating is absurd and a waste.

"The White Dawn" could have been the sort of movie that a child could go to, with or without parent or adult guardian.

1974 Jl 22, 41:1

Story of Gunman Takes Dim View of City

By VINCENT CANBY

"Death Wish," which opened yesterday at Loew's Astor Plaza and Cine Theaters, is a movie that takes a very dim view of New York City, particularly of its muggers who, according to this film, could be easily eliminated if every upright, middle-class, middle-aged citizen got himself a gun and used it at least three times a week.

This is pretty much the plot of "Death Wish," a bird-brained movie to cheer the hearts of the far-right wing, as well as the hearts of those who don't think much about politics but just like to see people get zapped, without regard to color or creed.

The movie, directed by Michael Winner and written by Wendell Mayes, seems to have been made for no reason except to exploit its audience's urban paranoia and vestigial fascination with violence for its own sake. I have no doubt that muggers, especially, will find it a great deal of fun.

The story is about a well-to-do New York businessman, played by Charles Bronson, a man improbably described early on as a bleeding-heart liberal, who becomes a one-man vigilante force after his wife dies and his daughter is turned into a catatonic mute as a result of an attack by muggers.

The Cast

DEATH WISH, directed by Michael Winner; screenplay by Wendell Mayes, based on the novel by Brian Garfield; produced by Hal Landers and Bobby Roberts; co-producer, Mr. Winner; director of photography, Arthur J. Ornitz; music, Herbie Hancock; editor, Bernard Gribble; a Dino De Laurentiis presentation, distributed by Paramount Pictures. Running time: 93 minutes. At the Astor Plaza Theater, 44th Street west of Broadway, and Loew's Cine, Third Avenue near 86th Street. This film has been rated R.

Paul Kersey	Charles Bronson
Joanna Kersey	Hope Lange
Frank Ochoa	Vincent Gardenia
Jack Toby	Steve Keats
Sam Kreutzer	William Redfield
Ames	Stuart Margolin
Commissioner	Stephen Elliot
Carol Toby	Kathleen Tolan

Thereafter Charlie roams the nighttime streets of New York, which, according to the film, are so filled with vandals, would-be muggers, rapists and the like that Charlie never goes home without scoring. On streets, in parks, on subway platforms, in subway cars, It's like shooting ducks in a bird sanctuary.

Does Charlie enjoy his hobby? Has he himself gone off the deep end? It's difficult to tell from Mr. Bronson's performance, which, for impassivity, is a challenge to Stone Mountain. However, the other good citizens are immensely pleased. The mysterious vigilante becomes such a folk hero he gets cover treatment by Time and New York magazine and, what's more important, the rate of muggings decreases dramatically.

The movie is chock full of peculiar cross-references. The man who first gives Charlie a gun, saying that "a gun is just a tool," is a gun-club enthusiast of a highly virtuous sort. We know this because he insists that the housing project he is building be constructed with the kind of living area that modern architects call waste space. He's a man who hangs on to the old values.

At the same time the film equates kids who carry spray-paint cans with muggers and murderers. Of course, to make its pro-gun message more persuasive, the movie portrays most of the muggers as guys who favor knives.

●

The movie seems to assume that the city's young hoods would be too poor to buy arms if the gun laws were made more liberal. Surprisingly (since the movie is very mixed up), it doesn't consider the possibility that, in such an event, some bleeding-heart social worker would advocate the issuance of guns by the Welfare Department.

"Death Wish" is so cannily fabricated that it sometimes succeeds in arousing the most primitive kind of anger. Yet it's a despicable movie, one that raises complex questions in order to offer bigoted, frivolous, oversimplified answers.

1974 Jl 25, 27:1

TOUGH, produced, written and directed by Horace Jackson; music, courtesy of Sussex Records; executive producer, Wendell Franklin; distributed by Dimension Pictures, Inc. A Jina Films Production. At neighborhood theaters. Running time: 87 minutes. (This film is classified G.)

Johnny Banes	Dion Gossett
Phil Banes	Renny Roker
Denise Banes	Sandy Reed
Mr. Bishop	Rich Holmes
Chris	Christopher Townes
Bonnie	Detra Piernas
David	Phillip Hadler
Joseph	David Shafer

The generation gap, which is as old as time itself and, of course, isn't restricted to race, creed or color, is given sincere but simplistic treatment in "Tough," which arrived at local theaters yesterday. As a dramatization of a rebellious black youngster's need for love and understanding from his bickering, middle-class parents, his schoolmates and his white teacher, it states its case honestly but superficially. The emotion generated is rarely equal to the drama's good intentions.

●

Horace Jackson, the writer-producer-director, is far removed from the likes of, say, "Superfly," in his view of the black experience. "Tough," which was filmed in pleasing color in Los Angeles, presents us with tree-shaded homes with immaculate lawns and an equally immaculate, integrated school. But the lives of Johnny Banes, his insurance-salesman stepfather, and his restless' young mother with vague visions of a glamorous acting career, are hardly well ordered.

The Afro-haired stalwart and basically lovable boy, it evolves, is being driven to petty thievery, lying and truancy because his parents are constantly squabbling and, more importantly, ignoring his need for affection. And the climactic theft that involves the family and the police, as well as Johnny's desperate flight from detention, merely underscores the film's straightforward but generally ill-defined and unresolved statements.

Mr. Jackson, who wrote and produced a well-received (1971) racial drama, "The Bus Is Coming," has elicited energetic but surface portrayals from his adult cast. Although the problems of Renny Roker and Sandy Reed, as the confused, battling parents, and Rich Holmes, as the harried teacher, are exposed realistically in clean dialogue, they appear to be performing, not feeling, their shocks and anguish.

●

On the other hand, the youngsters, including Christopher Townes and Detra Piernas, but especially Dion Gossett, as the sullen, rebellious but sensitive Johnny, are natural and convincing. His reactions to misunderstanding and occasional parental tenderness are genuine and touching. But "Tough," despite its sad truths, only occasionally touches the heart.

A. H. WEILER

1974 Jl 25, 27:1

Dillies and Duds

By VINCENT CANBY

IT'S midsummer, that time of year when it's difficult to keep up with everything in what even taxicab drivers now refer to glibly as "the media." Slick magazines become sticky in hot hands, the color comes off on the fingers. Newspapers blow inside out if you're on a beach and, if you're not, they pile up at an alarming rate beside favorite chairs or atop night tables, unread. Even television, the instrument for people who take their information intravenously, can be too much at July's end. If you have an ancient set like mine, it gives off more heat than light.

The following is a quick midsummer guide to 12 current films, some of which you may want to see and some of which you may want to break your neck avoiding. It could be, of course, that you never go to the movies anyway. In that case the guide is designed to provide you with a few basic facts that could save you minor social embarrassments. "Chinatown," for example, has nothing to do with Fu Manchu, tong wars, or Charlie Chan. It's about water rights, and that's as much of the plot as you'll learn here. The films are listed alphabetically.

"The Apprenticeship of Duddy Kravitz." Mordecai Richler's fine novel about a poor young Jewish boy on the make in Montreal in the late nineteen-forties has been turned into a manic, moving film by Richler, who wrote the screenplay, and Ted Kotcheff, the director. The movie tries to cover more narrative ground than is good for it, resulting in some confusion in the continuity, but this abundance also gives the film the feeling of a marvelous fable. "Once upon a time," the movie seems to say, "there was this nervy Jewish kid named Duddy and he was a stinker, but . . ." It's all the "buts" that make "Duddy Kravitz" so complex and appealing. Also the superb performances by Richard Dreyfuss (Duddy), Jack Warden, Micheline Lanctôt, Joseph Wiseman, Randy Quaid and especially Denholm Elliott, as the seedy, black-listed Hollywood director with whom Duddy joins forces to make films of weddings and bar-mitzvahs. Like "Goodbye, Columbus," "The

"The Apprenticeship of Duddy Kravitz," with Richard Dreyfuss, is perhaps the best of a dozen new films.

Apprenticeship of Duddy Kravitz" is going to be called anti-Semitic because of its sometimes satiric, irreverent attitudes, but that's to ignore the large amount of love and affection the film otherwise demonstrates.

"Chinatown." Written with a good deal of humor by Robert Towne, directed with uncustomary restraint and discipline by Roman Polanski and acted with immense style by Jack Nicholson, Faye Dunaway and John Huston, "Chinatown" is a well-made period (nineteen-thirties) whodunit that a lot of critics have badly served by describing it as if it were "Citizen Kane" or "The Big

Sleep." It's not by a long shot, but if you go with tempered expectations you should have a good deal of fun. By the way, the story (though not the murders that punctuate it) is based on Los Angeles history and helps to explain modestly how the city got spread out over the map the way it is. You may or may not have had this on your mind, along with Cyprus, Watergate and the price of Maine lobsters.

"Dirty Mary Crazy Larry." Movies as dumbfoundingly pointless as this one sometimes get taken seriously, if only because no one can believe that adults could occupy themselves making such junk

unless there really was a point. There isn't. "Dirty Mary Crazy Larry" is one long chase, from nowhere to nowhere in less than a day, about two guys who've extorted a small fortune from a supermarket in order to buy a super racing car. The two guys (and a girl) are in one car. The county police are in dozens of others in pursuit. Lots of tricky driving and noise but, in spite of all the simulated speed, a sense of standing still. With Peter Fonda and Susan George, among others not worth mentioning.

"For Pete's Sake." This season's Barbra Streisand film, a truly funny one for a change, has the added attraction of supporting actors of the caliber of Estelle Parsons, Heywood Hale Broun, William Redfield and, best of all, Molly Picon, playing another dimension of matchmaker. She turns up this time as a sweetly efficient Brooklyn madam who wears little white gloves and hats and who, in a pinch, can be relied upon to make chicken soup or provide the means for disposing of a suddenly dead client.

"The Mad Adventures of 'Rabbi' Jacob." Louis de Funes, France's most popular comedian at the moment, looks the way Leon Errol might have looked after getting a nose full of red pepper. His furies are very funny most of the time, though the movie runs on just a bit too long to be as entertaining as its best moments are. These moments include one particularly riotous sequence in which de Funes, trying to es-

cape a band of Arab terrorists, finds himself up to his neck in lime green bubble gum and another in which, disguised as a rabbi, he must officiate at a bar-mitzvah. Gerard Oury directed. In French with English subtitles.

"My Name Is Nobody." This is called "a Sergio Leone presentation" and though it was directed by Tonino Valerii, a former Leone assistant, it's very much a Sergio Leone film, a rather brainy meditation upon the kind of Hollywood Westerns that prompted Leone to make his Italian variations: "For A Fistful of Dollars," "For A Few Dollars More," "Once Upon A Time in The West," etc. Henry Fonda plays the fastest gun in the West, an aging gunslinger who wants to retire peacefully, and Terence Hill, a young Italian actor, plays a mysterious young man called Nobody who nudges the older man into the history books. There's lots of talk about legend, myth, fate, and an almost non-stop series of good guy-bad guy confrontations to illustrate the ideas if you've been listening. However, you don't have to listen. The film manages to be very entertaining on just its action level. Unlike Leone's earlier films, "My Name Is Nobody" goes very light on the catsup that is so thick in other spaghetti Westerns.

"The Parallax View." In the course of this film, directed by Alan Pakula, two United States Senators are assassinated on screen, along with some other people of lesser rank. Because the movie is about the possibility of a secret organization devoted to political assassination and murder-by-contract, the blood and guts are supposedly justified. They aren't. The movie is essentially cheap melodrama, sometimes well staged and well acted (by Warren Beatty, Paula Prentiss, Hume Cronyn and others), which exploits serious questions by offering foolish answers.

"The Tamarind Seed." Her head tells Julie Andrews, who has an important job at the British Home Office, that she shouldn't fall in love with Omar Sharif, the Soviet air attaché in Paris, but her heart tells her something else. Do you want to hear more? Blake Edwards directed the film in London, Paris and Barbados. The movie is enough to put you off intrigue and romance for at least a week.

"That's Entertainment." Production-number highlights from dozens of M-G-M musicals made between 1929 and 1958, including "Singin' in

The Screen

"Man Who Had His Hair Cut Short" was shown at the fourth New York Film Festival under the title "The Man With the Shaven Head." The following excerpt is from A. H. Weiler's review, which appeared Sept. 21, 1966, in The New York Times. The film opened Sunday and will be shown again today and tomorrow at noon and midnight at the First Avenue Screening Room, at 61st Street.

The Belgian-made feature, the first work of André Delvaux, a director new to American audiences, is "a moody, often garrulous, disjointed evocation of a married teacher and, later, a law clerk whose secret love for one of his pupils ends in disaster." The drama's "Flemish dialogue and English subtitles make it plain that Mr. Delvaux and Senne Rouffaer, as the anguished lover, and the Polish actress Beata Tyszkiewicz, whom he adores from afar, harp too much on their romantic pains and tribulations. A viewer is befogged by philosophical and mystical allusions long before Mr. Delvaux arrives at a somewhat amorphous ending to his psychological and occasionally melodramatic story."

1974 Jl 26, 25:2

The Rain," "The Band Wagon," "Gigi," "Million Dollar Mermaid" and some others you probably never saw or even wanted to. In spite of the awkward, TV-like format, in which "hosts" like Frank Sinatra and Liza Minnelli introduce the numbers, the film vividly recalls an art that today seems as precise, witty and long-gone as cave painting.

"Three The Hard Way." Jim Brown, Fred Williamson and Jim Kelly save America's blacks from instant death at the hands of a rich white supremacist who plans to poison the water supply. The actors move around with energy in fancy clothes, but they always look quite shy, as if they understood they were being paid too much for making a faulty bilge pump.

"Uptown Saturday Night." A very ragged but funny black comedy directed by Sidney Poitier, who also stars in the film with Bill Cosby, Harry Belafonte, Flip Wilson, Roscoe Lee Brown, Calvin Lockhart and a number of other fine performers, to each of whom Poitier defers with great good humor.

"The White Dawn." Near the turn of the century three New Bedford seamen, on a whaling expedition to the Arctic, became separated from the mother ship when their small boat was hauled into fog-bound ice by a harpooned whale. They were never seen alive again, at least by white men. "The White Dawn" is novelist James Houston's suggestion of what happened, based on tales he heard on Baffin Island. It has to do with Eskimo innocence and the inability of the three sailors, played by Warren Oates, Timothy Bottoms and Lou Gossett, to understand the subtleties of the society they'd crashed. The melodrama is tepid but the travelogue, shot on Baffin Island with a lot of difficulty, I'd imagine, is beautiful.

1974 Jl 28, II:1:1

FLESH GORDON, directed by Michael Benveniste and Howard Ziehm; screenplay by Mr. Benveniste; produced by Mr. Ziehm and William Osco; director of photography, Mr. Ziehm; editor, Abbas Amin; music Ralph Ferraro; a Graffiti Productions film, distributed by Mammouth Films. Running time: 82 minutes. At the Plaza Theater, 58th Street east of Madison Avenue. This film has been rated X.
Flesh Gordon.............Jason Williams
Dale Ardor..............Suzanne Fields

By VINCENT CANBY

"Flesh Gordon," now playing at the Plaza Theater, is an X-rated though not pornographic parody of old-time movie serials, specifically of "Flash Gordon's Trip to Mars" (1938) in which Flash, his girlfriend Dale and the good Dr. Zarkov zoomed to Mars to save earth from a mysterious ray.

"Flesh Gordon" uses much the same story but all of the character names have been slightly changed to titillate the innocent. Though Flesh and Dale spend a great deal of the time attempting to protect their honor, often unsuccessfully, the movie is much too pushy and aware to be funny as the original, which was blessed with a truly dead pan.

What wit the film possesses has gone into the physical production in the re-creation of the kind of badly proportioned miniatures used in the original serial, in the snappy plywood sets, and in the barren exterior locations (when I was a boy I wondered why Mars always looked so much like southern California).

The dirty, intentionally bad jokes and puns never attain the high quality of imaginative awfulness of these sets and props. The acting is broad, which may be as it should be, although it quickly becomes monotonous unless you have a high tolerance for contemporary camp.

1974 Jl 31, 20:1

BANK SHOT, directed by Gower Champion; screenplay by Wendell Mayes; based on the novel by Donald E. Westlake; produced by Hal Landers and Bobby Roberts; director of photography, Harry Stradling Jr.; music, John Morris; editor, David Bretherton; distributed by United Artists. Running time: 83 minutes. At the Rivoli Theater,

Broadway at 49th Street; the Eastside Cinema, Third Avenue at 55th Street, and the UA East Theater, First Avenue at 85th Street. This film has been rated PG.
Walter Ballantine .... George C. Scott
El .... Joanna Cassidy
Al G. Karp .... Sorrell Booke
F.B.I. Agent Constable .... G. Wood
Frank "Buldog" Streiger .. Clifton James
Victor Karp .... Robert Balaban
Mums .... Bibi Osterwald
Herman X. .... Frank McRae
Stosh Gornik .... Don Calfa

By VINCENT CANBY

Though at this point in history caper movies are less easily remembered than individual blades of grass, Gower Champion's "Bank Shot" is a disarming exception. It's not a great movie. It's not worth taking a taxi to see. Yet there are many less invigorating ways to waste one's time.

"Bank Shot," which opened yesterday at the Rivoli, Eastside Cinema and UA East Theater, is a rather ordinary pound-cake of a movie that's been stuffed with unexpected prizes. This includes the explanation by a girl who has unfortunately bought water paint to camouflage the exterior of a house trailer. When the paint comes off at a crucial moment, the girl wrings her hands. "It said 'washable'" she says. "I thought it sounded clean."

The thing about "Bank Shot" is that all its would-be crooks are not only clean, they also are proper, thoughtful, optimistic and filled with the kind of gung-ho spirit that would do service to a Save-Our-Parks committee. The film has something of the verve of last year's "Cops and Robbers," probably because it's also based on a novel by Donald E. Westlake, who sounds as if he were a funny man.

Wendell Mayes's screenplay is about a brilliant bank robber named Walter Ballantine (George C. Scott) who is always in a bad temper, probably because his best-laid plans have a way of going nuttily wrong. His latest caper involves a branch of the Los Angeles Mission Bell Bank, which is temporarily located in a house trailer.

After he cases the job, Ballantine turns down the idea of a simple robbery because of the bank's location in the middle of a parking lot at a shopping center. Says Ballantine: "It's a flee-on-foot bank." He proposes an alternate plan to put wheels under the trailer and carry off the entire bank.

The intensity of Scott's performance is highly comic. His Walter Ballantine has the discipline, self-assurance and narrow vision of the true fanatic. So, too, do most of the other characters in the film, including the eccentric prison warden played by Clifton James, who, as the red-neck sheriff, was one of the highlights in "Diamonds

Are Forever." Also remarkably funny are Sorrell Booke, as a bank robber with absolutely no gift for the disguises he likes to wear, and Robert Balaban, as his nephew, a cashiered F.B.I. man with a sincere ambition to go wrong.

Gower Champion, who has had more success as a Broadway director ("Hello, Dolly") than as a maker of films ("My Six Loves"), seems to have had a great deal of fun with first-rate actors doing a nonsense story. "Bank Shot" has the effortless grace of a work by someone who knows exactly what he's doing.

1974 Ag 1, 18:6

A Priest Takes a Look at the Devil and William Blatty

By EUGENE C. KENNEDY

"THE EXORCIST" may be the greatest thing since Bobby Riggs started playing against girls in getting otherwise sensible people to involve themselves in things they would ordinarily have the good sense to avoid. The movie has now reached the suburban rim of American life, having just cashed in on an elaborate and highly lucrative arrangement with exhibitors that made it something like the circus coming to town. . . .

"Right this way to see the little girl spew pea soup over the good father! Don't miss the scene with the bloody crucifix!"

In truth, "The Exorcist" rates high on the list of phenomena not to be taken seriously; it should be filed under "Midwinter Madness" and forgotten as soon as possible by all literate and mature people. Discussing the movie seriously gives it an importance that, of itself, it does not deserve. And making analytic statements about it is as silly as the famous one made by a social scientist about "The Godfather"; he said, you may recall, that the movie was a hit because people liked the example it provided of family solidarity. The family that slays together stays together.

The best thing about "The Exorcist" was its timing, arriving as it did in a winter of discontent when people were aching to find somebody to blame for our national frustrations, and the devil has served admirably as a scapegoat throughout history. But the popularity of the film and the tortured analyses with which it was greeted must have surprised even its makers. In the beginning, director William Friedkin claimed that he had only made a horror movie to thrill people; he did not get profound until later on.

Author William Peter Blatty, of course, has tried to sound like a savant all along, but he has just given savants a bad name in the process. He has also given a bad name to religion, priests, and believers in general. However, as William James once noted, "We believe anything we can and would believe everything if only we could."

"The Exorcist" is not a statement about good and evil or about religious belief; it is a formula horror movie like the ones turned out by Monogram and Republic studios during the thirties to fill the bottom half of double-bills. Hor-

Eugene C. Kennedy, a Maryknoll priest, is a professor of psychology at Loyola University of Chicago and the author of "Believing."

ror films are a durable genre; they are only one reflection of our human fascination with being shocked or having the wits scared out of us. That is why we have roller coasters, parachute rides and tourist rafts on the white water of our most dangerous rivers. Science tells us, in the law of parsimony, always to take the simplest explanation for the observed data. The simple truth about "The Exorcist" is that it is an old fashioned scare movie and nothing more.

Consider for a moment the simple story: a golden autumn neighborhood a few blocks from the religious institution (it was the parish church in Transylvanian films) whose calm is suddenly shattered by the sounds of a beast in an otherwise beautiful house. Why, there is even a suspicious butler and a bumbling, mustache-pulling detective.

Perhaps the most obvious figure in the film is the doomed Father Karras, the famous priest-psychiatrist who is reluctantly drawn into the exorcism. B movies were always filled with doomed good guys. You could tell early by the look on their faces that their destiny was star-crossed and they would be killed in the end. Sincere persons with knitted brows either lost the girl or were tragically killed a thousand times in the Hollywood legend. Karras belongs to that order rather than to that of Melchisedech. His story is not one of a troubled cleric anguishing over conflicts of faith; it is the story of the rather attractive character whipped up in the Hollywood Dream Factory long ago—he suffers from terminal goodness. And, as a footnote to a film that has been hailed for its technical excellence, Father Karras does not even know how to say Mass correctly. (He mistakenly breaks the bread while reciting the words of consecration.)

"The Exorcist" also owes a debt to the shade of Cecil B. DeMille, who was such a master of mixing mock religiosity with sexiness. Hollywood has never been very good with religion. In this film it shows that it is not very good with psychiatry either. The movie, to be understood, must be interpreted in terms of old movies rather than theological or scientific truths or practice. It is a quintessential product of the Hollywood myth and is filled with staple stock characters and effects that have demonstrated their box-office appeal over the years. You can hardly beat vomit, blood and violence. In a picture supposedly about good and evil, what's good for the box office, the money men say, is good for the American soul.

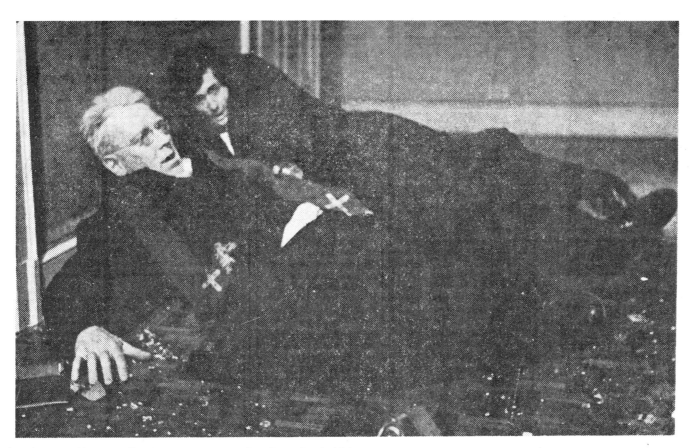

What of audience reactions to a film so devoid of genuinely human or religious content? The law of parsimony leads us again to the simplest explanation and the lore of Hollywood leads us to the most obvious. As to the celebrated passing out and throwing up that occurred during the picture's well-advertised horrors, a group of college students laughingly told me, "If you had to wait in line for two hours in a lobby where everybody was smoking grass you'd get sick and pass out too." And it is well known that you can catch things from the movies. It has happened for years, not because of the skill of the filmmakers, but because of the human need for identification with fictional characters. Thus, a great many people caught the symptoms of leukemia from watching "Love Story." It is not surprising that some people would catch some of the symptoms of demonic possession from "The Exorcist."

It is also clear that the author, who has woefully distorted the facts of the real-life case on which the movie was supposedly based, tells us more about his own psychic life than anything else. It is small wonder that Blatty has been stamping his feet in irritation at those who do not take the picture as seriously as he would like. He has clearly admitted, for example, that he is writing about his own relationship with his mother in telling the story of Father Karras and *his* mother. This is symbolized in the dream sequence, in which the soulful mother disappears before the panicked priest can reach her. He recently told reporter Fred Robbins, "It is my mother . . . the dream sequence in 'The Exorcist' is identical to my dreams that I recount concerning my mother. . . ."

The fact that Blatty has not resolved

his relationship with his mother is his own business, but that is what he is *really* writing about. He also used the book and the movie, according to many observers, to even an old score with British director J. Lee Thompson who once ordered him off the set of "John Goldfarb Please Come Home," for which Blatty wrote the screenplay. Well, Blatty has achieved a double revenge by first dramatizing the director's alleged edgy temperament and then murdering him off. That is the kind of game writers can play, of course, but the possibility that Blatty has done it in "The Exorcist" tends to deflate some of the pretentions that have accumulated around the movie. (It may be helpful to remember that the things about some people which drive us crazy are the very things which keep *them* sane.)

The saddest fact about the film is that people who have not seen it tend to take it seriously because they have heard so much seemingly solemn talk about it. The best solution—and one that would delight the moviemakers—is to get these people to see it. It is drastic, but it is the only known antidote. Once sensible people see it, the spell of "The Exorcist" is broken and they never take it seriously again.

"The Exorcist" is the kind of movie you get when you leave religion to screenwriters and businessmen. It is the same kind of thing we got in Watergate as a result of leaving government to advertising men. Such entrepreneurs strive ultimately for effects rather than for substance because that is the game they know best. The melancholy truth is that both enterprises trivialize some of the most important aspects of our experience — truth, belief, and human relationships.

Jill Krements

In "The Exorcist," William Peter Blatty, above, "gives a bad name to religion, priests, and believers in general," says a priest and critic. At left two priests—Max Von Sydow and Jason Miller—shrink from the devil.

There was some residual common sense in the award of the Best Picture Oscar to "The Sting" rather than to the heavily favored "Exorcist." It was a kind of health breaking through, a wise and winking judgment that, in the long run, we would rather be taken by a trifle about admitted con men than be mesmerized by a trifle that doesn't even know how trifling it is.

The persistent danger, of course, is that people will continue to try to find theological and human truths in "The Exorcist" which it simply cannot deliver.

There is indeed less there than meets the eye. In a way, however, the film does fit into American pop culture. In a country that can find a spiritual message in "Jonathan Livingston Seagull," that thinks Rod McKuen is deep, sees another Harry Truman in Gerry Ford, and has suddenly made Barry Goldwater into an elder statesman, the success of "The Exorcist" may not be so surprising after all.

1974 Ag 4, II:11:1

'Death Wish' Exploits Fear Irresponsibly

By VINCENT CANBY

NEW YORK CITY, like all major American cities, has its problems: bad bookkeeping, polluted air, rising costs, reduced services, high crime rates, a fleeing middle class. Now you might want to add a movie to the list, Michael Winner's "Death Wish." It's a tackily made melodrama but it so cannily orchestrates the audience's responses that it can appeal to law-and-order fanatics, sadists, muggers, club women, fathers, older sisters, masochists, policemen, politicians, and, it seems, a number of film critics. Impartially. Its message, simply put, is: KILL. TRY IT. YOU'LL LIKE IT.

The New York City shown in "Death Wish" looks to be about three years from now but still about three years short of the urban shambles in which Jules Feiffer set his nightmare comedy, "Little Murders." The hero, Paul Kersey (Charles Bronson), a well-to-do New York architect, is identified as a bleeding-heart liberal because he once apparently expressed some concern for the welfare of the Lower Orders, that is, those people who don't have quite as much money as he does. Paul's credentials as a social activist are questionable to say the least, but we accept them in the interests of art.

Suddenly, after his wife is killed and his daughter is turned into a psychotic vegetable as a result of a mugging, Paul changes. He redecorates his roomy Riverside Drive apartment in a period that might be called Middle Walter Reade Theaters. It's so gaudy you're surprised not to see a popcorn stand in the living room. Paul also takes to playing his stereo very loud, which may have something to do with the release of his pent-up emotions.

Most important, Paul has become a one-man vigilante force who, comes nightfall, packs his .32 pistol into his coat pocket and roams the city looking for would-be muggers. He never has to look very far. Muggers are everywhere, stopping traffic the way garbage trucks do today. Without visible emotion Paul executes them, often at point blank range. Blacks, whites, Puerto Ricans. Paul is no racist.

Nor, for that matter, is the film. After showing us mugging teams that are ei-

The message of this Charles Bronson movie, according to Vincent Canby, is "Kill. Try it. You'll like it."

ther all one color or all another, the film presents us with an integrated mugging team in its climactic sequence. In a movie as mixed up as "Death Wish" is, I think this can be interpreted as progress.

From the early reports, "Death Wish" is on its way to becoming one of the big dumb hits of the summer season, which is depressing news but not terribly hard to understand. Its powers to arouse—through demonstrations of action—are not unlike those of a pornographic movie.

It cuts through all sorts of inhibitions, first by making us witnesses to the murder and rape of Paul's wife and daughter, graphically and agonizingly, shown, thus to certify Paul's (and our) right for vengeance, then by allowing us to share Paul's immense feeling of power as unsuspecting punks, one after another, attempt to mug him, only to be met by a blast in the face (chest, back, stomach) from his trusty .32. If you allow your wits to take flight, it's difficult not to respond with the kind of lunatic cheers that rocked the Loew's Astor Plaza when I

was there the other evening. At one point a man behind me shouted with delight: "That'll teach the mothers!"

According to the peculiar politics of "Death Wish," it does. Paul's one-man crusade is said to be responsible for a decrease in the weekly mugging rate from 950 to 470, though the film does have the cleverness, if not the wit, to cover its tracks by suggesting that as a result of the vigilante's activities, the city's muggers have begun to concentrate exclusively on old ladies.

For all of its cold, macabre comedy, "Little Murders" was a movie obviously made by people not only concerned by the quality of urban life but also aware of the complex problems that contribute to the daily frustrations and horrors. "Death Wish" is a movie produced by tourists, which is a point I'd make even if its director were not an Englishman, its executive producer (Dino De Laurentiis) an Italian and its writer (Wendell Mayes) a resident of Los Angeles. For short-term fun it exploits very real fears and social problems and suggests simple-minded remedies by waving the American flag much in the fashion that former Vice President Agnew used to do.

Paul Kersey describes his actions in the film as "the good old American custom of self-defense" (as once practiced against the Indians?) and the movie clearly agrees. In other words, there's nothing wrong with this country today that giving guns to all the right people wouldn't cure. Who are the right people? White middle-class maniacs. For anyone with two brain cells to rub together that might be a tough question, but not for "Death Wish."

It's the demonstrated premise of this picture that muggers, vandals and kids who carry spray-paint cans (they should be eliminated too) prefer knives most of the time and thus wouldn't be able to shoot first or back. Occasionally some upstart punk might have a gun, but that would be the exception to the rule.

What ideas the movie has are so muddled that at times they give the game away. In a sequence early in the film, Paul travels to Arizona to work on a fancy housing project being financed by an eccentric millionaire who is also a gun club enthusiast and a man who hangs onto good old American values. He urges Paul to include a lot of so-called waste space in his plans for the housing project and he ridicules people who have a fear of guns. "A gun is just a tool," he says reason-

ably and he points out that there are no muggers out here because "muggers operating out here just plain get their tails blown off."

Paul, whose capacity to think is not enormous, doesn't bother to point out that there probably aren't many muggers in the desert anyway, nor does he find any contradiction in his employer's loudly proclaimed allegiance to good old American values and his desire to pollute a beautiful, unspoiled desert landscape with high-rise apartment units, no matter how much lovely waste space each might contain.

I suppose "Death Wish" shouldn't be taken too seriously. It is, after all, not much different from the cheap melodramas about killer-heroes that Winner and Bronson have made in the past, sometimes separately and sometimes together ("The Mechanic"). The only difference is that this time the killer is presented as nothing less than the redeemer.

It is to Winner's credit that "Death Wish" manages to be as effective as it is even though the production is of a sloppiness that would destroy a movie of fewer visceral responses. At times throughout the film the policemen have to be ludicrously slow-witted in order not to catch the mysterious vigilante. There also seems to be no way to justify a movie in which a man enters his apartment building at night, goes up the elevator and looks out the living room window to see broad daylight, although it's night again when he looks out the kitchen window.

It was, however, a stroke of genius to cast Charles Bronson in the unlikely role of an upper middle-class New York liberal who sees the light. Almost any other actor I can think of would probably look very sheepish under the circumstances. Not Bronson, who seems no more capable of intellectual activity than a very old, very tired circus bear. It's enough that he is able to walk around on his hind legs and occasionally shoot a gun.

1974 Ag 4, II:1:6

.

ESCAPE TO NOWHERE, directed by Claude Pinoteau; produced by Alain Poiré for Gaumont International/Medusa; distributed by Peppercorn-Wormser. At the Cinema II Theater, Third Avenue and 60th Street (in French with English subtitles); and at the Victoria Theater, Broadway and 46th Street (in English). Running time, 118 minutes. (This film is classified PG.)

By NORA SAYRE

Everyone seems to be watching him: even an elderly woman feeding pigeons, any stranger on a sunny street. Every chance encounter seems threatening, and the taxi meter ticks as if it were measuring the moments of his life.

But this small, respectable stoic is no frothing paranoid. He's a French physicist, kidnapped twice in 16 years—once by the Russians, once by the British—and the Russians are going to kill him unless he can arrange to be traded for a Russian spy. His plight is a harsher condemnation of the Secret Service than anything by John Le Carré. But this conventional middle-aged man is incredibly hard to kill, and "Escape to Nowhere," which opened yesterday at Cinema II and the Victoria Theater, is a celebration of magically swift wits.

The movie, which makes an impressive debut for the director, Claude Pinoteau, is no ordinary thriller, due to the depth of the characterization of the physicist and the superb performance of Lino Ventura. The fugitive has only one chance for survival, but very little hope. Like Graham Greene's confidential agent, he carries the infection of danger: anyone who merely contacts him may be wiped out. Hurtling between desperate situations, he makes his very reserve a mark of defiance, of his determination to stay alive; the lips pressed flat, the hands clasped behind his back, and the exhausted patience convey the concentration on survival.

In contrast to the terribly dull cool maintained by the heroes of some recent action pictures, Lino Ventura gives us response that we can share. Smoothing his hair or straightening his tie — even when his life's at stake—he sometimes catches his breath at a ravaging shock of the relief of a miraculous escape. And sudden sweat on the face occasionally betrays the anguish of the hunted. Also like a Greene character, this dignified scholar lives as he was never meant to—scrambling over rooftops, keeping a gun on the bedside table, hiding in laundries, stealing a nun's microbus.

Throughout, the suspense is devastating, not only because of the fine acting but thanks to the soundtrack: soft, reasonable public voices, — announcing flights at airports or programs on the radio — only serve to make you more nervous. And there's a brilliant use of music, especially when a conductor who's also a spy nears the conclusion of a Bach concerto. Many noises sound like gunshots—a train banging along the tracks, a typewriter pounding out a victim's dossier. And even the car chases will excite an audience already jaded by that tradition.

Leo Genn, as a silky British top agent who's showing off his French, flicking ash from his cigar to punctuate his meaning, Lea Massari, and all the others are sensitively cast, and there's a loving use of locations, particu-

larly of the French countryside—seen through the eyes of an exile. Claude Pinoteau has worked with Max Ophuls, René Clément, Claude Lelouch and Jean-Pierre Melville, among others. But the emotional punch of this movie is all his own, and it makes one eager to see what he'll do next.

1974 Ag 5, 30:1

CALIFORNIA SPLIT, directed by Robert Altman; screenplay by Joseph Walsh; produced by Mr. Altman and Mr. Walsh; executive producers, Aaron Spelling and Leonard Goldberg; director of photography, Paul Lohmann; editor, Lou Lombardo; distributed by Columbia Pictures. Running time: 111 minutes. At the Cinema I Theater, Third Avenue near 60th Street. This film has been rated R.

Bill Denny .... George Segal
Charlie Waters .... Elliott Gould
Barbara Miller .... Ann Prentiss
Susan Peters .... Gwen Welles
Lew .... Edward Walsh
Sparkle .... Joseph Walsh
Helen Brown .... Bert Remsen

By VINCENT CANBY

Robert Altman's "California Split," which opened yesterday at the Cinema I, is a fascinating, vivid movie, not quite comparable to any other movie that I can immediately think of. Nor is it easily categorized.

It's the story of several weeks in the lives of two compulsive gamblers who meet in a Los Angeles poker parlor and become fast friends, more or less as a result of being jointly mugged in a parking lot.

Charlie Waters (Elliott Gould) is your classic little league bettor, debonaire and incurably sloppy, existing happily on the brink of small-scale financial disaster. More to have company than because of emotional involvement, he sleeps in the apartment of two sweet, pretty Los Angeles girls who probably would be serious hookers if they had any ambition.

Bill Denny (George Segal) is another kind of gambler. He's an upper middle-class fellow (a magazine editor) whose compulsion appears to be well on the way to wrecking his life. He's separated

from his wife, in debt to his bookie and, in the course of the film, ready to sell everything he has—camera, tape-recorder, car and real estate —in order to get the stake he needs to play poker with the big boys at the casino in Reno.

Like Charlie Waters and Bill Denny, "California Split" spends a great deal of its time in poker parlors, at race tracks, in casinos and barrooms, mostly seedy places, smoky, overcrowded, either much too bright or dark as tombs. The sounds of these places — the voices of the croupiers, gamblers and hangers-on, and the songs of Phyllis Shotwell who belts out boozy ballads at a piano bar—are never long from the soundtrack. Even when Charlie and Bill go into the straight world, these sounds follow them.

●

Mr. Altman has been quoted as saying that "California Split" is "a celebration of gambling," which is, I think, to underrate it, at least so it seems to someone who is not a gambling nut. The director, his screenwriter Joseph Walsh and the actors have created a movie of so many associations that it's impossible not to see "California Split" as something much more complex and disturbing.

Most of the gambling here doesn't really look like much fun. It's as desperate as the woman at the track who furiously throws her pocketbook and several oranges at Elliott Gould because he's touted her off a winner.

"California Split" is sometimes very funny, but the world it depicts is as bleak as a landscape composed entirely of used-car lots. The present tense for everyone in the film is grim. The clocks are out of sync. A character has Fruit Loops and beer for breakfast. Someone says of a poker game: "It just got started yesterday."

All hopes are pinned on tomorrow. Even those of the two would-be hookers (mar-

velously well played by Ann Prentiss and Gwen Welles), who have been promised a trip to Hawaii by a couple of otherwise unpromising johns. For the two gamblers, tomorrow is another visit to the track, another game. In the meantime one bets the other that he can't name all seven dwarfs.

Like all Altman films, "California Split" is dense with fine, idiosyncratic detail, a lot of which is supplied by Mr. Gould and Mr. Segal as well as by members of the excellent supporting cast. Bert Remsen, who was the aging bank robber in "Thieves Like Us," appears briefly and hilariously as a fearful old transvestite much like Scobie, the ex-seaman who became a Muslim saint in Lawrence Durrell's "Justine" novels.

●

Up to a certain point, "California Split" is, I suppose, a celebration of gambling. It's a movie that avoids as much as possible any simplified Freudian explanations. I say up to a point, because the ending has the effect of making us think back over everything we've seen earlier. To win at poker or anything else can sometimes be as devastating as losing.

The compulsive gambler will put up with any loss or indignity in the hope of recouping later, thus placing a terrible burden on the future. For once he does win, everything is over.

1974 Ag 8, 28:1

The Cast

OPHELIA, directed by Claude Chabrol; screenplay (French with English subtitles) by Mr. Chabrol and Martial Matthieu; photography, Jean Rabier; editor, Jacques Gaillard; music, Pierre Jansen; production manager, Jean Lavie; released by New Line Cinema. Running time: 100 minutes. At the Playboy Theater, 110 West 57th Street. This film has not been classified.
Claudia .... Alida Valli
Yvan Lesurf .... Andre Jocelyn
Lucie .... Juliette Mayniel
Adrien Lesurf .... Claude Cerval

By NORA SAYRE

When it takes 12 years for a renowned director's movie to reach our screens, the product is apt to be a jewel or a dog. Claude Chabrol's "Ophelia," made in 1962, has just emerged from the kennel, and although the picture has a bit of historical interest, much of it strays far from the film maker's own talents. "Ophelia" opened yesterday at the Playboy Theater.

A wealthy young provincial suspects his mother (Alida Valli, a study in bitter restraint) and his uncle of having killed his father in order to marry each other. Clutching some clues from "Hamlet," he tries to expose them by shouting accusations at meals, pretending to be crazy, and by making a short movie about an incestuous crime. Obsessed with seeming and being, denouncing humanity at large, he trots about in the woods in a business suit and tie, hugging his divine discontent.

Meanwhile, he attempts to force a young woman (Juliette Mayniel) into the role of his Ophelia. Their relationship mainly consists of his murmuring claptrap about the beauties of nature into her ear, while she laughs skittishly and favors him with somber or demure smiles. Eventually, her father — who is of course labeled Polonius — dies in a tree after one of the funniest heart attacks I've seen in years. The quasi-Hamlet remarks that trees bear strange fruit these days.

The movie is equally boring and pretentious, because of the characterization of the tormented hero. Played by André Jocelyn, he comes across as a huffy bundle of affectations, and between the bouts of hollering, his style is stiff and vapid.

However, there are moments that will reward some students of Chabrol, such as the theme of individuals feeling guilty when they're innocent. The elegant camerawork lifts the woodland episodes above the general banality, and the formal meal scenes contain some of Mr. Chabrol's choicer observations of people chewing and swallowing while their pleasure in food is spoiled by the anger in the air. And there are a couple of nice thugs. But "Ophelia" hardly evokes Mr. Chabrol's best films, such as "La Femme Infidèle"; instead, it recalls his creakiest earlier work, like "Les Cousins" and "Landru."

1974 Ag 8, 30:1

RETURN OF THE DRAGON, directed by Bruce Lee; screenplay by Mr. Lee; cinematographer, Ho Lang Shang; music, Ku Chia Hui; film editor, Chang Yao Chang; produced by Kuam Chih Chung and Chang-ying Peng; released by Bryanston Pictures. At neighborhood theaters. Running time: 91 minutes. This film is classified R.
Tang Lung .... Bruce Lee
Chen Ching Hua .... Nora Miao
Kuda .... Chuck Norris

George Segal, right, and Elliott Gould, beside him, watching a race

Kicking an enemy into oblivion with his flying feet, grunting and screaming triumphantly, achieving suspenseful pauses between blows, the late Bruce Lee is a pleasure to watch in his last kung fu picture, "Return of the Dragon," which opened Wednesday at neighborhood theaters. Lee's small compact face reveals a flurry of responses as he sends his opponents' torsos hurtling through the air, and he specializes in unpredictable movements.

The picture concerns a Chinese restaurant in Rome which is menaced by gangsters who want to buy the property. On behalf of the owners, Mr. Lee has a duel with a vast American karate champion in the Roman forum. Unlike its predecessor, "Enter the Dragon," which was praised as a well-made movie, this picture is dreadfully slow and feeble whenever the cast isn't fighting. So you yearn for each battle, just as you wait impatiently for the songs or dances in a tedious musical. Mr. Lee scripted and directed this picture, and his dialogue — "Make some tea." "Sure, right away"— wasn't up to his choreography.

•

There's little bloodshed beyond a couple of discreet nosebleeds, and this brand of meticulous hand-to-hand combat seems rather refreshing, compared to our splashiest gun-flicks, such as "Magnum Force." Here, the audience cheers for quick wits instead of weapons, and skill defeats sadism. And it's regrettable that Mr. Lee didn't appear in some more substantial movies, since he did perform so nicely as a furniture-smashing villian in "Marlowe" in 1969.

NORA SAYRE

1974 Ag 8, 30:1

The Cast

TOGETHER BROTHERS, directed by William A. Graham; screenplay by Jack DeWitt and Joe Greene; story by Mr. DeWitt; directors of photography, Philip Lanthrop and Charles Rosher; music by Barry White; film editor, Stanley E. Johnson; produced by Robert L. Rosen; released by 20th Century-Fox Film Corporation. At the National Theater, Seventh Avenue between 43d and 44th Streets and neighborhood theatres. Running time: 96 minutes. This film has been classified PG.
H.J. .... Ahmad Nurradin
Tommy .... Anthony Wilson
A.P. .... Nelson Sims
Mau Mau .... Kenneth Bell
Monk .... Owen Pace
Gri' Gri' .... Kim Dorsey
Mr. Kool .... Ed Bernard

Carbon-dating may well be the only way of determining precisely when it was that the basic story of "Together Brothers" first saw the light of a projector.

Certainly anyone whose moviegoing experience extends into the pretelevision era or whose television watching spans only the last couple of years would be hard pressed to find any grounds for applying the adjective "original" to the plot of this modest and generally well-intentioned film.

"Together Brothers," which opened yesterday at the National and neighborhood theaters, is, after all, the tale of how a small band of youngsters goes about solving a crime, in this instance, the murder of a kindly policeman.

What jerks the film out of the past, implants it firmly in the present and lends it at least a suggestion of novelty is that the policeman and the youngsters are blacks; the setting is not some neat little town but the rotting slums of Galveston, Tex; black-Chicano animosity is explored; and among the characters are whores, gangsters, pimps, transvestites and psychopaths.

Insofar as he captures the present, William A. Graham, the director, has refreshed a tired story; but the performances tend toward unevenness, and one yearns for a more gifted directorial hand when the killer stalks the sole witness to the crime, a little boy struck mute by what he has seen.

Preaching cooperation, brotherhood and a sense of obligation while stopping short of advocating vigilante justice, "Together Brothers" has its heart in the right place. Street-wise older children might find it to their taste; but all the new trappings cannot disguise the fact that "Together Brothers" is an old story, being retold perhaps wisely, but not exceptionally well.

LAWRENCE VAN GELDER

1974 Ag 8, 30:1

WORKER'S DIARY, directed by Risto Jarva; screenplay (Finnish with English subtitles) by Mr. Jarva and Jaakko Pakkasvirta; presented by Cinema Dimensions, Inc.; a Filminor Production. Running time: 90 minutes. At the First Avenue Screening Room, at 61st Street, today and tomorrow at noon and midnight. This film has not been classified.
With: Elina Salo and Paul Osipow

Taking as its subject matter a tissue-thin slice of life infected by bleakness, monotony and the sort of problems that do not so much shatter characters as nag them to death, "Worker's Diary" is a film that flirts with disaster.

So it is a tribute to the skill of its director, Risto Jarva, that this Finnish film playing tonight and tomorrow at noon and midnight at the First Avenue Screening Room manages eventually to avoid the fate that usually awaits works that deal with dreariness—boring the audience, too.

But it is a narrow escape, and the less patient may weary of its two focal characters — the newlyweds, Ritva, a secretary in a state office, and Juhani, a welder —long, before the introductions are over and their problems — his job, moving, her relatives, his memories, her pregnancy, his affair — crystallize.

•

Set in a society not usually depicted in films seen here, "Worker's Diary" begins by making us conscious of what is foreign and ends by immersing us in the familiar. And the familiar smacks a little of soap opera, with an ending so coated with sugar that even Mr. Jarva seems impelled in the final frames to set his work in its proper place in the cosmos.

It is a place, it would seem, just adequate for a craftsman's miniature.

LAWRENCE VAN GELDER

1974 Ag 9, 22:4

The Signals Movie Actors Give

By URJO KAREDA

ACTING used to be something that people did. Regardless of whether it was done well or done poorly, the activity resulted from the preoccupation of actors with solving the problems of expressing emotion. By what means, people used to ask, did an actor portray anger or joy or despair? What combination of facial attitude, body tension, or vocal edge would most emphatically indicate the feeling required? Both talented and untalented performers pursued the challenge, and their solutions formed the activity, the labor, or, if you were lucky, the art of acting.

Because acting involved both a problem and a solution, because it resulted from more or less successful manipulation of certain accredited techniques, it could be observed and judged in itself. You couldn't miss it. People might have argued about whether Barbara Stanwyck was a good actress or a bad one, but nobody could say that she didn't act at all. Whether you liked or disliked the results, the performer wasn't playing hooky.

Now, that equanimity of judgment no longer exists. I felt this very strongly when I came out from seeing Peter Bogdanovich's film "Daisy Miller." I knew that I'd been moved by the film, disarmed by its surprising wit and, particularly, that I'd admired Cybill Shepherd's Daisy. But for all that, I could not honestly tell whether or not Cybill Shepherd could act. What she had done in the film to embody Daisy's ingenuousness and enthusiasm had seemed so unconscious, even accidental, that I could with no confidence decide whether I had been responding to Cybill Shepherd's characterization of Daisy's gaucheness or simply to Cybill Shepherd's own gaucheness as an actress.

Urjo Kareda is drama critic for The Toronto Star.

Was Miss Shepherd a thoughtful performer or merely a shrewdly-selected actress caught, held and defined by a director's camera - eye? A reference to her previous work was no help, since I've had the same reaction to Miss Shepherd's appearances in "The Last Picture Show" and "The Heartbreak Kid." To be sure, there are plenty of screen performances which produce breathtaking realism with all-but-invisible technique — Liv Ullmann's appearances in Jan Troell's "The Emigrants" and "The New Land," for instance — but they left me satisfied, without that sense of discomfort which Cybill Shepherd's Daisy aroused. Moreover, the old blabber about total identification with a role ("She didn't play Camille, she was Camille!") seemed misapplied here, because I couldn't tell whether Cybill Shepherd was Daisy, or whether Cybill Shepherd was just Cybill Shepherd. That pause for doubt about her as an actress, my inability to determine whether she acted Daisy Miller or happened upon Daisy Miller almost inevitably robbed me of a comfortable, secure response. It made my reactions jittery, and I don't think I am alone in this, since critical opinion about the performance has been so sharply divided.

Perhaps the matter can be illuminated by considering the business of signals. Many performers will transmit hidden beeps to the audience as an indication that they are in full command of the effects they are producing and of the manner in which those effects work on us. This signalling needn't be a distressing come-on of technique blatantly sloshed over us, although in some cases it is. We require only a delicate signal of assurance that someone is in control. Furthermore, the beep doesn't necessarily coincide with the biggest dramatic moment.

Both good and bad actors send out signals. A good film actress like Bette Davis lets an audience share the excitement in her own sense of authority, her instinct for definition. Surely part of the joy of Davis performances is our collaboration with the actress in the recognition and enjoyment of her prowess. In "All About Eve," for instance, there is the restaurant scene late in the film, in which Miss Davis, Gary Merrill and their friends watch Anne Baxter's arrival after another stage success. For Miss Davis's character, calm has been restored; she radiates a confidence and assurance which reveal that the woman she is playing has found emotional security. Miss Davis moves from this poise to an incredible moment in which she suddenly picks up a green scallion from the table at which she is seated, raises it in toast to Anne Baxter, and with guillotine-like teeth, bites into it. For me, Bette Davis in that moment signalled the defiance with which she transforms incongruous effects into inevitable behavior in such a way as to reveal the personality of the actress herself.

In "All About Eve," this was Bette Davis's possessive beep to me. I can't expect that the same signal will work for all people; others will find different examples. I don't claim, either, that Miss Davis was at all conscious of her signal at that moment. I can't even know whether this specific gesture was her idea or that of Joseph Mankiewicz, the director. But I know that whenever I see the film, or think about it, that this was the instant in which Bette Davis sought out and obtained my cooperation in accepting her performance wholeheartedly. It was like a secret treaty.

A bad film actress like Natalie Wood, on the other hand, is also likely to send out signals, but something will be amiss. Either she will beep out promises of more drama than she can deliver, or more acting than we want. She can also signal a staggering into the borderlands where self-awareness becomes self-consciousness. Miss Wood's signalling — and hers was always a busy signal — tended to be a frown, an intense knitting of the forehead which always anticipated but never quite delivered some unburdening of psychic truths.

I don't want to suggest that the presence of a signalling mechanism precludes the possibility of random, unexpected effects, or what used to be called inspiration. Most memorable performances are filled with spontaneity and surprise, both of which work best after an initial bond has been established between the actor and ourselves, a bond for which we need a signal. When this is done we are willing to stick with the actor in the pursuit of the unexpected.

Nor is signalling, to good or bad effect, one of the lost arts. Barbra Streisand is now Hollywood's supreme signaller. When she is in full force, as in "The Way We Were" and parts of "For Pete's Sake," we certainly know what she wants us to respond to. We can almost intuit the passages which she has underlined in the script for special communication, and the scenes which she has rehearsed in front of a mirror. As she has become more and more a celluloid diva, Miss Streisand's beeps have become all-pervasive. What once seemed so raw and urgent has now become a process whereby her performances gild themselves even as they're being acted.

Signalling may also become an unbreakable habit: an actress like Elizabeth Taylor is such an experienced signaller, her every breath a considered public appearance, that now she cannot even read her part of the narration in "That's Entertainment" without making it seem like a previously undiscovered Tennessee Williams manuscript, all bittersweet recollection and shy innuendo. It becomes absurd because the signals have nothing to do with the nature of the material.

Signalling is usually considered a symptom of more theatrical performances, ones in which the effects are riper, more overt, associated with a style of film-acting no longer much in fashion. In the forties and fifties even a mediocre actress like Lana Turner went through the vehement motions of acting, no matter how undistinguished the results proved to be. But now, in this day of less ostentatious dramatic behavior, even the second rate actors are using much less technique than the Turners of two or three decades ago. Now that the whole scale of performing has been tuned to a lower key, you have to strain harder to find the signals — if they are there. But even in the context of a more subdued acting technique, the most naturalistically - based performance can, and really must, send out signals of planning and reassurance.

Take Liv Ullmann. The effect of her acting is to isolate each member of the audience into thinking that only he alone is able to read the message hidden in her features. Her muted, almost subliminal effects are still united to the bond of trust she requires from us. Our willingness, won by signal, gives her the freedom to proceed with her art of minimal apparent effort. We are warned by the signal that we'd better watch closely, or we'll miss her magic. Naturalism of this order is precarious and it could not succeed as Miss Ullmann's does without the signal being sent and received between performer and perceiver.

In "The New Land," for instance, she usually chose to diminish rather than to intensify her expressive responses in times of crisis. In the scenes in which the unhappy woman responds to disaster — the death of her child, for example— Miss Ullmann would make her character

withdraw into almost numbed behavior. The audience, caught by the unexpected, senses that a signal has been given to them. Our expectations had been for a scene of agitation and violent feeling, but Miss Ullmann pushes us off guard. Her signal, which is that she won't give us what we wanted, catches us in the awareness that the actress has made a choice, one which we scarcely expected. The timing of these scenes is almost unchartable, but in making us realize that we are off guard, the actress also puts us on guard for future signals. The signals in Liv Ullmann's exciting performances make us aware that her choices will be unconventional. In her reaction to the death of her child in "The New Land," our rush of ready emotion fills up the vacuum which her numbness has created, and the scene works so memorably because Miss Ullmann makes us participate in it. (I am thinking here only of her Swedish films; in her English-language films, she does not seem at home and signals her distress.)

I've been using actresses for my examples, but I don't mean to suggest that men are deficient in signalling techniques. Indeed, two of the more congenial male performances this summer — Jack Nicholson in "Chinatown" and Warren Beatty in "The Parallax View" — build their effects directly and solely from the signals they offer. They seem to be telling us that they know there isn't much to be made from the muddle around them but that they have things under control, that we should not worry, and that if we stick with them we won't be disappointed.

Nicholson's signals create their loose, relaxed charm best in those films in which he has the least material to work with. His refusal to be panicked by

weak scripts, his sly gallantry in carrying on, works with greater potency when he isn't stuck with some literary, over-written concept as in "Five Easy Pieces" and "King of Marvin Gardens". Film-makers seem to have caught on to the fact that Nicholson is at his best when working in the shallows, and nowadays screenwriters no longer feel they need to provide him with even a characterization; in "Chinatown," they've written him a wardrobe instead. They know that a vacuum will more effectively release the insinuating signals from which he builds his humor. Much of the tension in "Chinatown" collects in the contrasts between Nicholson's calmly signalling insouciance and cool, and Faye Dunaway's furious, hyper-kinetic signalling of the most intensely Joan Crawford dimensions — frozen, mannered acting, only barely disguised as neurotic characterization.

What happens, then, with Cybill Shepherd's refusal, or inability, to signal? That, finally, is what goes wrong with her Daisy Miller. We are left not knowing whether she is in control of her performance, whether she knows what she is doing. When her Daisy, warned that American society in Rome will reject her unless she stops her indecorous behavior, looks out at us so directly and says that she cannot believe they would be so cruel, the moment is both dazzling and perplexing. Is the absolute simplicity of her delivery of the line a choice Miss Shepherd has made or was it just the best that she could manage? Do the eyes staring directly at us try to indicate Daisy's wasted frankness, or is the actress dutifully and numbly answering a director's command? There is nothing in the way Miss Shepherd plays the moment to indicate that it represents a choice, and we don't know whether she engineered the moment or just happened to get away with it.

From our position of unease, we project a center of nervousness upon her as well; perhaps she, too, is uncertain whether she can handle the role. The performance hovers at the edge of amateurishness, but, then again, it might just be Miss Shepherd's perception into Daisy's amateurishness as a human being.

A greater loss in the absence of signals is that the actress must forfeit our attachment to the character. It seems a surprising aspect of audience sophistication that we still need to like the characters in a film, to link up with them in some way, whether or not the roles are sympathetic. Yet the fact is there has to be some connection with our feelings. A signal is required to set that relationship in motion.

There are endless lists of perfectly disreputable film characters to whom audiences respond with a positive instinct; in most cases, the actor within the character has sent out a reassuring signal which has established an emotional cohesion between the character, the actor and the audience. As long as the signals are clear — as are John Huston's in "Chinatown," for example — we can accept monstrous corruption with something strangely like geniality.

Because Cybill Shepherd's Daisy Mil-

"While I was watching them, I thought Cybill Shepherd's Daisy Miller and Mia Farrow's Daisy Buchanan were among the most beautiful performances I'd seen this year," says the critic. Yet it's hard to know if they can really act.

ler doesn't beep, however, audiences are left with their sympathy in a limbo. The ambivalence of the film's heroine isn't all Henry James'; part of it is an audience's reaction to a performance which doesn't beckon. Audiences need an outlet for the empathy they bring along, and if an actor doesn't signal that he wants a share of it, what are they to do? Oddly, audiences usually then transfer their empathy to the character itself, isolating the actor's coolness as a flaw in interpretation. Unsignalled performances turn audiences off the performer.

*

The other current example is another Daisy, Mia Farrow's performance in "The Great Gatsby." Miss Farrow, too, offers no signals and what has happened is that audiences (and some critics) have come to sentimentalize the role while rejecting the performance. Miss Farrow's Daisy Buchanan has been called an extraordinarily shallow portrayal, whereas instead, in my opinion, it is an extraordinarily clever portrayal of a morally shallow character. An even more notorious example was Elliott Gould's performance in Ingmar Bergman's "The Touch" a few years ago. Gould, perhaps intimidated by the circumstances of being Bergman's first non-Scandinavian star, got through no signals at all, with

the result that his very interesting performance of an awful man was misread. People wanted the character to be nice so that they could dismiss Gould as a self-indulgent, boorish actor. I don't think "The Touch" made sense unless the character Gould played was meant to be unpleasant, but because Gould could not transmit that (or perhaps didn't grasp it), the audience transferred their disenchantment to the actor.

These good but unsignalled performances must pay the penalties of indifference, misunderstanding, bewilderment, harsh judgement and finally disappearance from memory. While I was watching them, I know I thought that Cybill Shepherd's Daisy Miller and Mia Farrow's Daisy Buchanan were among the most beautiful performances I'd seen in films this year. Now, the shape of their acting seems less distinct, and I find I remember inferior performances better. I don't know how much I'll remember a year from now. It seems a mutual separation. Acting needs partners on the receiving end. If I find that in time I don't remember Miss Shepherd's and Miss Farrow's roles, it may be because I wasn't asked to be a part of them.

1974 Ag 11, II:1:1

said that people found these theories comforting because they provided a rational explanation for a bewildering national trauma. If the assassination was actually executed by one deranged individual acting on his own, then the course of history had been changed by a freak accident. That in turn raised the possibility that life might be fundamentally senseless, chaotic, purposeless — and such a possibility was too disturbing for many Americans to contemplate. They preferred believing all the ingenious scenarios that gave the assassination the same logic as one of Perry Mason's cases.

"The Parallax View" draws plot details from both Kennedy assassinations, and manipulates these associations to titillate the audience. In making a fictional movie about the assassinations of the sixties there are many possible approaches, but any filmmaker who reopens these still-painful wounds has a responsibility to illuminate the issues. Whether the movie speculates on a possible conspiracy, or explores the psychology of a single assassin, or merely tries to probe the climate of violence that fostered the assassinations, the least we should demand is a measure of fresh insight. "The Parallax View" exploits real anguish for the sake of juicy chills and spills.

*

Director Pakula evades all the pertinent questions by refusing to identify any of the political factions involved in the labyrinthine conspiracy. Like last year's "Executive Action"—a semidocumentary consideration of the

assassination of President Kennedy— "The Parallax View" is too cowardly to make direct accusations. We don't even know which party the murdered politicians belong to, or what philosophies they espouse, and as a result, we can't begin to guess why anyone would want them killed.

In keeping the conspirators and the candidates so shadowy, Pakula may have hoped to broaden the movie's appeal by allowing every member of the audience to nominate his own favorite demon as the evil genius behind the assassinations. If you fear the American Nazi Party or the American Communist Party, the oil industry or the C.I.A., Henry Kissinger or Ralph Nader, any or all of them might be involved in the mysterious Parallax Corporation. This film exemplifies the emptyheaded, fence-straddling approach to controversial issues that has made Hollywood's political movies such a joke.

In place of any sustained political or psychological analysis, "The Parallax View" ends by suggesting that the wave of American assassinations could have been masterminded by a giant corporation without any political ideology, an organization that hires out assassins to anyone who pays and so ends up murdering both left-wing and right-wing politicians. There is a germ of a satiric idea here—the notion that America is so completely capitalistic that even assassination becomes a business proposition; maybe this solemn, ponderous movie would have worked better as a wicked black comedy.

A murdered Senator's blood streaks a window as witnesses look on in horror in "The Parallax View," which draws details from the assassination of Robert Kennedy, above. The film may be "the most mindless and irresponsible" of the new "conspiracy" films, says the critic.

'Conspiracy' Movies

By STEPHEN FARBER

SINCE the Watergate disclosures, stories about conspiracy have captured the popular imagination. Therefore, it is not surprising that a number of recent movies— including "The Parallax View," "The Conversation," "Chinatown," "The Tamarind Seed," "SPYS"—have dealt explicitly with political intrigue and conspiracies of varying magnitude. These films range from incisive to inane, but as a group they illustrate an intriguing national obsession.

Alan J. Pakula's "The Parallax View" is probably the most mindless and irresponsible of the lot. The film is a political thriller in the tradition of "The Manchurian Candidate," about a reporter (played by Warren Beatty) who tries to track down the cabal responsible for the assassination of a rising young senator. Movie audiences used to be able to count on the triumph of the hero, but at the end of "The Parallax View," the conspirators kill the crusading reporter and cunningly camouflage the truth so that no one can penetrate the secret Parallax Corporation.

"The Manchurian Candidate," a uniquely prophetic movie made shortly before the assassination of President Kennedy, ended with the discovery and eradication of the conspiracy to kill a Presidential candidate; the more pessimistic conclusion of "The Parallax View" suggests how radically American

attitudes have changed in the last 10 years. The plot of "The Parallax View" is full of holes, and its cynicism is glib, but the interesting point is that a large public is willing to buy such a bleak paranoid vision. Today's mass audience wants to believe in omnipotent, omniscient, indestructible conspiracies.

In analyzing the persistence of conspiracy theories of the Kennedy assassination, Henry Steele Commager once

Stephen Farber is a freelance critic and the author of "The Movie Rating Game."

Los Angeles Times

Although "The Parallax View" owes a great deal to "The Manchurian Candidate," it overlooks the one quality that made "The Manchurian Candidate" so abrasive—its mixture of horror and comedy. John Frankenheimer's unpredictable, electrifying thriller expressed an important paradox of contemporary political life—the fact that conspirators might be clowns or buffoons and, *at the same time*, dangerous madmen.

Irvin Kershner's "SPYS" takes this double-edged vision into the Watergate era. One thing we should have learned from Watergate is that while conspiracies do indeed affect the lives of all Americans, they are not quite so efficient or omnipotent as even the conspirators themselves would like to believe. The bizarre fantasies of Gordon Liddy and Howard Hunt seem to have been inspired by James Bond movies, but the plumbers performed their roles like Woody Allen rather than Sean Connery.

"SPYS" perceives this surreal comedy, while the "The Parallax View," with its sinister, fiendishly brilliant conspirators, seems oddly dated; the latter recalls the apocalyptic speeches given by Mark Lane or Jim Garrison in the late sixties. "SPYS" has the sensibility of the seventies; it captures the childishness of spies and C.I.A. conspirators, and the huge disparity between their glamorous fantasies and their actual bungling performance.

Donald Sutherland and Elliott Gould play two C.I.A. operatives marked for murder by their own agency; they find themselves pursued by the Americans, the Russians and the Chinese, as well as by a youthful terrorist gang that wants to destroy the C.I.A. Chronicling their misadventures, "SPYS" blends satire, farce and violence into an original, macabre vision of Cold War politics. Memorable black comic scenes freeze the insanity: During the defection of a Russian gymnast, one of the spies posing as a TV newsman fires the gun concealed in his camera, and an innocent athlete gets in the way of the bullet; as the C.I.A. men put electrical wires under Sutherland's finger-nails, he sings repeated choruses of "Old MacDonald" to keep from cracking; a baby-faced anarchist who is more concerned about his father's new car than about the revolution nevertheless succeeds in bombing a building. The conspirators in this movie have crazy human quirks which only make them more dangerous. People die while the loony spies and anarchists act out their comic book fantasies: that is the true post-Watergate nightmare.

"SPYS" is lightweight and unpretentious, directed with great energy by Kershner, and played in a relaxed screwball style by the entire cast. But I think its absurdist vision of a disintegrating world where the screwballs fire real bullets and draw real blood is a lot more meaningful and provocative than the grim deterministic approach of "The Parallax View," where everything happens according to a preordained diabolical plan.

The single-minded paranoid vision of "The Parallax View" appears with only a few variations in "Chinatown" (written by Robert Towne, directed by Roman Polanski), a pretentious detective story set in the thirties. Although less overtly political than the other two films, "Chinatown" does concern a conspiracy between big business and government that has unmistakable parallels to contemporary events. Based on a real scandal from Los Angeles history, the movie indicts official corruption. In the course of investigating the murder of a Los Angeles engineer, detective Jack Nicholson unravels a plot by a group of leading citizens to divert the city's water supply to their own land holdings in the uncultivated San Fernando Valley; they are using taxpayers' money to secure a private fortune.

"Chinatown" has been praised as a hard-hitting movie because it confirms prevailing liberal prejudices. The conspirators in the film are a band of rich, decadent fascists who control the police as well as the city's water supply. Their leader—played by John Huston—is such a leering, gloating caricature of the greedy capitalist that he might have stepped out of Victorian melodrama; all that's missing is a twirlable mustache. He doesn't even have the charm that makes powerful men insidious and seductive.

*

Even melodrama needs a measure of complexity. "Chinatown" allows us to remain smugly superior to its cardboard villains; we are never surprised or implicated by its expose of political corruption. Like "The Parallax View," "Chinatown" draws overly neat distinctions between good and evil, simplifying the truth in order to comfort the ignorant.

In both these movies the evil conspiracies survive, and the audience seems relieved to learn that heroism is futile and irrelevant; anyone who tries to unlock the truth—the reporter in "The Parallax View" or the detective in "Chinatown"—will be punished for his initiative. These films may have been meant to awaken concern, but they only succeed in reinforcing the passivity of a jaded public. If life is governed by evil forces too devious to understand and too powerful to defeat, then we are all completely helpless, and there is no point in getting involved in the fight for social change. Hollywood's new conspiratorial fantasies promote cynicism, self-righteousness, and complacency—an unhealthy combination.

1974 Ag 11, II:11:1

The Cast

HARRY AND TONTO, directed by Paul Mazursky; screenplay by Mr. Mazursky and Josh Greenfeld; director of photography, Michael Butler; film director, Richard Halsey; produced by Mr. Mazursky; released by 20th Century-Fox Film Corporation. At the Paris Theater, 58th Street West of Fifth Avenue. Running time: 116 minutes. This film is classified R.

Harry....................Art Carney
Shirley....................Ellen Burstyn
Old Indian....................Chief Dan George
Jessie....................Geraldine Fitzgerald
Eddie....................Larry Hagman
Wade....................Arthur Hunnicutt

By NORA SAYRE

At the Wedding of the Generations in 1972—when Allen Ginsberg and others decided that it was time to end "youth chauvinism" and performed a symbolic marriage between all the young and all the old in Miami Beach—it was pleasing to hear the poet chanting "the generation war is at an end" while people of all ages danced and sang around his stepladder by the sea. There were quite a few conversations that focused on what the old and the very young have in common—in a society that deeply distrusts both.

•

Some of the same spirit pervades "Harry and Tonto," which opened yesterday at the Plaza Theater. Harry (Art Carney) is an independent 72-year-old who demands freedom and privacy and welcomes almost any chance to expand his experiences. Evicted from his building on the Upper West Side, he feels a kinship with King Lear: "He gave up his real estate, too." The police finally have to carry him out in a chair. Then, this devout New Yorker recoils from a dreary suburban existence with his son's family, and strikes out on a voyage across the country.

Paul Mazursky, director and co-author of "Bob & Carol and Ted & Alice," and author and director of "Blume in Love," directed "Harry" from the novel he wrote with Josh Greenfeld. The result is an anecdotal chronicle of Harry's encounters with various individuals, including his now semisenile first love—played with batty precision by Geraldine Fitzgerald—and an Indian chief whom he meets in jail. Mr. Carney maintains a gentle dignity and resilience throughout, though he has to address too many of his lines to a cat named Tonto. His scenes with two benign young performers (Melanie Mayron and Joshua Mostel) nicely emphasize his agelessness.

The narrative of this sympathetic movie wobbles on the edge of sentimentality, though there are only a few sticky moments. But—unlike the novel, which moved swiftly—it has been directed at far too slow a pace, which means that the comic possibilities and the social comment have been diminished. The muted style robs the picture of the liberating point it's meant to make: that imaginative energy transcends the generations.

1974 Ag 13, 24:2

Small Fry and Parents Enjoy Disney Tale

The Cast

THE CASTAWAY COWBOY. Directed by Vincent McEveety; screenplay by Don Tait; produced by Ron Miller and Winston Hibler for Walt Disney Productions and presented by Buena Vista. At neighborhood showcases. Running time: 90 minutes. (This film is rated G.)

Costain....................James Garner
Henrietta MacAvoy....................Vera Miles
Booton MacAvoy....................Eric Shea
Bryson....................Robert Culp
Kimo....................Manu Tupou
Liliha....................Elizabeth Smith

Thank heaven for a new Disney live-action movie that won't, for a change, make parents wince. Such is "The Castaway Cowboy," a cheerfully agreeable and picturesque little Western, set in, of all places, Hawaii. This is a homey, comfortably amusing and niceiy colorful package about a Texas castaway who helps a pretty widow and her small son pioneer a Pacific isle cattle ranch. Yesterday the children—flanked by smiling parents—took to it like popcorn, at the midtown Festival Theater, one of the metropolitan showcases double-billing the new picture with a vintage Disney feature. The film's rudder is James Garner, whose leathery, laconic expertise (minus that pat blandness) winningly sets the tone and flavor. Vera Miles and young Eric Shea are appealing, likewise a gallery of grinning, native islanders who play Mr. Garner's "pineapple cowboys." Robert Culp is the smooth villain of the uncomplicated little plot, steadily unwinding under Vincent McEveety's direction.

•

The picture has genuine charm and sturdiness in the scenes of the natives becoming cowboys, learning to lasso and punch wild steers. For stand-bys, there are several crunching fights and a good old cattle stampede. The Hawaiian locale (the island of Lauai) makes an exotic, often luscious backdrop. It's hard to resist the sight of Tex Garner, Master Shea and those happy island buckaroos singing "Come-a-Ki-Yi-Yippy" as they hit the Hawaii trail.

HOWARD THOMPSON

1974 Ag 15, 25:1

The Cast

BLACK SAMSON, directed by Charles Bail; screenplay by Warren Hamilton Jr.; story by Daniel B. Cady; director of photography, Henning Schellerup; film editor, Duane Hartzell; music, Allen Toussaint; produced by Mr. Cady; released by Warner Bros. At the Forum Theater, Broadway at 46th Street and the Roosevelt Theater, Seventh Avenue and 145th Street. Running time: 88 minutes. This film is classified R.

Samson....................Rockne Tarkington
Johnny Nappa....................William Smith
Tina....................Connie Strickland
Leslie....................Carol Speed
Arthur....................Michael Payne
Harry....................Joe Tornatore

Out of the netherworld of cinema make-believe, where lone urban heroes, kung-fu experts and other assorted cool types have been defying credibility in recent years, has emerged a motion picture called "Black Samson." The film opened yesterday at the Forum and Roosevelt Theaters.

Its hero, as the title indicates, is a black man named Samson, a towering barkeep who carries an even taller staff and employs it and his fists to belabor anyone—but particularly Mafia types—who would sully his street and his people, especially with narcotics.

"Black Samson" is a cinematic masquerade. In the guise of presenting a story of courage against odds, it is, in truth, an ugly and brutal film, reveling in cruelty and the bloody abuse of women.

The most admirable character in it is an old gangland boss who counsels wisdom and gentleness; but there is no reason to believe that the people who made "Black Samson" would recognize a real hero if they saw one.

LAWRENCE VAN GELDER

1974 Ag 15, 25:1

The Program

THE RA EXPEDITIONS, an adventure film of Thor Heyerdahl's RA Expeditions Across the Atlantic Ocean in a Papyrus Boat; photographed by Carlo Mauri and Kei Ohara; editing, Bengt Gunnar Eriksson; music, Ed Norton; executive producer, Lennart Ehrenborg; narration, Roscoe Lee Browne and Mr. Heyerdahl; a Norwegian-Swedish Production, Thor Heyerdahl Swedish Broadcasting Corporation TVI; released by Universal Pictures. At neighborhood theaters. Running time: 93 minutes. This film is classified G.

EXPEDITION MEMBERS: Thor Heyerdahl of Norway; Norman Baker of the United States; Santiago Genovés of Mexico; Carlo Mauri of Italy; Yuri Senkevitch of the Soviet Union; Georges Sourial of Egypt; Kei Ohara of Japan; Madani Ait Ouhanni of Morocco; and Abdullah Djibrine of Chad.

Some of us are allergic to almost any kind of boat life: the equipment or the weather nearly always goes awry, and persons who are pleasant ashore can become raging authoritarians at sea. But you don't have to love boats in order to relish "The RA Expeditions," a fascinating documentary record of the two long ocean voyages made by anthropologist Thor Heyerdahl in a small papyrus boat. The film opened yesterday at neighborhood theaters.

Mr. Heyerdahl, who sailed the wooden raft Kon-Tiki across the Pacific in 1947, was intrigued by the similarity between both reed boats and certain pyramids in Egypt and Latin America. To determine whethers pre-Columbian people might have been able to cross the Atlantic, he commissioned the construction of a buoyant paper boat, identical to those of the past. A small crew of international experts sailed it from Morocco toward Barbados. The 1969 expedition didn't quite make it, but success came in 1970.

As the voyagers contend with hurricanes, sharks, broken steering oars and sinking sterns — while discovering that the whole Atlantic is polluted with lumps of oil — we absorb a lot of historical information, along with the conatgious excitement of their journey. The film (impeccably narrated by Roscoe Lee Brown, with some comment by Mr Heyerdahl) yields an engrossing piece of scholarship as well as an adventurous summer cooler.

NORA SAYRE

1974 Ag 15, 25:1

BRING ME THE HEAD OF ALFREDO GARCIA, directed by Sam Peckinpah; screenplay by Gordon Dawson and Mr. Peckinpah; story by Frank Kowalski and Mr. Peckinpah; director of photography, Alex Phillips Jr.; editors, Robbe Roberts, Sergio Ortega and Dennis E. Dolan; music by Jerry Fielding; produced by Martin Baum; released by United Artists Corporation. At the Cinerama Theater, Broadway at 47th Street; 59th Twin 2, east of Third Avenue; 86th Twin 2, west of Lexington Avenue. Running time: 112 minutes. This film is classified R.
Bennie....................Warren Oates
Elita....................Isela Vega
Quill:...................Gig Young
Sappensly................Robert Webber
Max......................Helmut Dantine

By NORA SAYRE

From the deceptive tranquility of the first shot— when ducks and swans glide past a very young pregnant woman who sits humming at the water's edge in a white dress—to the frenzy which erupts when her outraged father (a Mexican aristocrat) offers a million dollars for the head of the man who impregnated her, Sam Peckinpah's "Bring Me the Head of Alfredo Garcia" begins brilliantly, especially because of

the pacing. Knowing just when to speed the action up or slow it down, Mr. Peckinpah grabs our total attention. Then the movie disintegrates rapidly. "Garcia" opened yesterday at Cinerama, and the East 59th Street Twin 2 and the RKO 86th Street Twin 2 theaters.

Warren Oates

Initially, you fear for the hunted man—above all because this is a Peckinpah picture. But it's quickly explained that Garcia is already dead—of drunken driving, which seems about as dramatic as dying of vichyssoise. Without Garcia as a victim, the plot has almost nowhere to go. Therefore, random episodes are slung into the narrative, including one of the silliest near-rape scenes I've ever seen. The woman is supposed to welcome rape, and the acting oozes with a phony lyricism: the assailant focus with her hair, which inspires her to kiss him. But even this gratuitous garbage can't prevent the movie from dragging.

•

"Garcia" focuses on Bennie, (Warren Oates), an American obsessed with locating Garcia's corpse and pocketing the loot. He lurches through Mexico with a testy though super-submissive girlfriend (Isela Vega, a study in wood), who dissolves into sodden, doggy gratitude when he says he loves her.

Bennie guns down anyone who gets in the way; often, he seems to kill out of sheer bad temper. Among the repetitive shoot-outs, there's one fine moment which recalls Mr. Peckinpah's best work: after a large family has been wiped out at a roadside, one old man survives, his hands meekly raised while the murderers turn on one another and ignore the patient figure that's waiting to live—or die.

Corpses are roughly treated throughout this movie: Bennie fires a couple of shots into a fresh stiff "because it feels so goddam good!" Meanwhile, decapitation seems like a spoof on castration.

After Garcia's grave is robbed, his severed head becomes the leading character in the picture. Bennie chats to it, pours booze on it, and it even gets a shower. When the thing is eventually brought to the christening of Garcia's newborn child, the camera dwells on the baby's head: a close-up that's repeated just in case you missed the point.

The movie isn't as bloody as some of Mr. Peckinpah's others. Instead, it's profoundly pessimistic — because of the emphasis on obscene acts committed merely for money. Bennie is momentarily made to rebel against the many deaths. But we can't believe him, since he had to kill all those people simply to flesh out this movie.

Warren Oates is blustery, sometimes frantic, and Isela Vega gives the most awkward performance by an actress since Kerima played the primitive in "An Outcast of the Islands." Gig Young, Kris Kristofferson and Helmut Dantine are wasted in roles that give them little chance to act. But the movie's main problem is that the protagonist — the dead head — is a bore.

1974 Ag 15, 28:1

'Confessions,' Film Study Of Bribery and Immunity

By NORA SAYRE

A corrupt Public Prosecutor—whose guilt has just been discovered by his former disciple, a young District Attorney—asks the latter, "Is anything wrong?", and the line has almost as much dramatic impact as if it had been uttered by Richard M. Nixon to James D. St. Clair. "Confessions of a Police Captain", directed by Damiano Damiani, was made in Italy in 1971, but it's nicely up to date on the questions of political cover-ups, bribery and immunity. The movie is playing today and tomorrow at the First Avenue Screening Room.

Martin Balsam has a brash, brisk authority as a police captain obsessed with nailing criminals who have stayed above the law, thanks to the aid of local politicians. He and Franco Nero, as the elegant District Attorney, both initially suspect each other of shielding the Mafia, which controls the construction trade. Meanwhile, official corruption flourishes,

The Cast

CONFESSIONS OF A POLICE CAPTAIN, directed by Damiano Damiani; screenplay by Mr. Damiani and Salvatore Laurani; director of photography, Claudio Ragona; editor, Antonio Siciliano; cameraman, Giuseppe Di Blase; produced by Bruno Turchetto and Mario Montanari; a Euro International Films Explorer Film '58 Production; an Avco Embassy Release. At the First Avenue Screening Room, at 61st Street, today and tomorrow at noon and midnight. Running time: 92 minutes.
Bonavia...............Martin Balsam
Traini................Franco Nero
Serena LiPuma.........Marilu Tolo
Attorney General Malta...Claudio Gora

and uncooperative witnesses tend to wind up in cement.

The elaborate plot is occasionally confusing. But this thoughtful, modest movie about the perversion of justice is worth seeing—especially for Mr. Balsam's performance as a man accused of fanaticism. This actor is always good at losing his temper, and he brings subtlety to a complex character who has come to feel that the police are the instruments of the gangsters and who breaks the law because he has lost all faith in the courts.

1974 Ag 16, 18:2

Is There Any Future For Bad Taste?

By URJO KAREDA

EVERY society has its unspoken taboos. They linger in the twilight of public consciousness until something called bad taste brings them into the open. Bad taste triggers a kind of shock by the very fact that the unspeakable has been spoken, and the unpresentable presented. The effect may be to stimulate a reconsideration of those taboos which have been violated. Bad taste—well employed by a comedian such as Lenny Bruce, a novelist like Philip Roth or a playwright such as Joe Orton—can become a force of liberation. In other cases, where lesser artists are playing with this kind of social dynamite, the result may be that the taboos become reinforced.

Elements of deliberate bad taste have steadily been working their way into films over the past decade. I do not mean the sort of esthetic tastelessness which, in the 1950's, produced those Esther Williams aqua spectacles which are now wiping out a whole new generation of audiences in "That's Entertainment." I mean calculated bad taste, a considered preoccupation with grossness.

For a long time, the American underground led the noxious way. An oddity like "Pink Flamingos" (from Saliva Films), with its zeppelin-shaped transvestites and obsession with excrement, became a cult film. The European cinema, too, has offered many varieties

of cultivated bad taste, ranging from the caustic satirical fantasies of Luis Buñuel such as "The Discreet Charm of the Bourgeoisie" in which meticulously planned dinner parties are given precedence over wars, revolutions and death itself, to the monstrous farce of "The Grande Bouffe," in which four men commit suicide by literally eating themselves to death.

In American above-ground films, the pioneers have been comedian-directors like Woody Allen, with his skits about bestiality, transvestism and rabbis with pork fixations in "Everything You Always Wanted to Know About Sex," and Mel Brooks, with his "Springtime for Hitler" musical numbers in "The Producers."

Interestingly, the bad taste movement in commercial movies peaked quickly and appears to be waning. Now, a film like Sidney Poitier's "Uptown Saturday Night," which could certainly use a little ingenious bad taste to authenticate its street-world atmosphere, is prim, clean and well-behaved. Even those films which do contain precarious elements, scenes which were designed to offend, seem to lack the desired impact. Has bad taste gone too far for us? Or have we gone too far for bad taste?

Roman Polanski's "Chinatown," for instance, seems almost desperate in its

Urjo Kareda is drama critic for The Toronto Star, and an avid moviegoer besides.

eagerness to discover a taboo which might still startle us. The view of 1930's California is so overgrown with corruption and decay that the film's structure needs that final de luxe frisson. What screenwriter Robert Towne finally comes up with is incest, presumably thinking it one of the few remaining sexual taboos with the power to alarm us. However, since incest in drama is usually recollected rather than enacted, it has no immediate shock effect; even if it were enacted in "Chinatown," it probably wouldn't rock us, unless the actors playing the secret lovers happened to be related in real life. (The melodramatic revelation of the incestuous relationship between John Huston and Faye Dunaway strikes us as an affectation, but what if Henry Fonda and Jane Fonda had played the father and daughter roles?)

The way that incest makes its show-stopping appearance in "Chinatown" doesn't quite work, because it smacks too much of a little boy's final shock held in reserve. What an appalling commentary it is, too, that the film's creators assume—rightly, I think—that an audience wouldn't be much troubled by "Chinatown's" revelations of murder, land-grabbing, graft, corruption and political duplicity, but needed some bigger thrill to make the story sufficiently harrowing. Incest, in "Chinatown," is what finally uncovers the rottenness of California's history, but that transgression seems puny in relation to all the rest.

"The Apprenticeship of Duddy Kravitz" has not yet become the center of a storm of charges against bad taste, but it wouldn't surprise me if it did, and it certainly wouldn't surprise the film's author, Mordecai Richler, who has spent a lot of time throughout his career fighting off accusations of anti-Semitism in his writing. The feeling seems to be that the depiction of Duddy Kravitz as a pushy, ambitious, tough and conniving young man is an unflattering and distorted presentation of a Jewish stereotype, much as the character played by Jeannie Berlin in "The Heartbreak Kid" was considered by many to be an unpleasant cliché about young Jewish brides. In both Richler's novel and his film, Duddy's own Uncle Benjy sums up the protest when he tells Duddy, "You're a *pusherke*, a little Jew-boy on the make. Guys like you make me sick and ashamed."

Racial humor has certainly worked

itself around. Although it still comes as quite a jolt to see Mickey Rooney and Judy Garland prancing about in blackface in "That's Entertainment," there is an innocence about them which tends to neutralize the effect. The new methods of neutralization, however, draw on members of the race itself in the presentation of racial mockery—a conscious send-up of bigotry.

On its limpest level, this new approach is exemplified by the black cleaning woman in "For Pete's Sake." The character sarcastically announces her arrival with the statement, "It's the colored woman," works through the clichés of shiftlessness by demonstrating an unwillingness to do anything much besides eating lunch, and then informs Barbra Streisand that she herself couldn't afford a white cleaning lady but has hired a Puerto Rican.

On a more sustained level, however, it is the kind of thing which Richler does in "The Apprenticeship of Duddy Kravitz." The question of anti-Semitism is slightly defused—though I grant that, for some, it may be only further aggravated—by having some of the mockery work its way out from the inside of the film. If there is any anti-Semitic sentiment in Duddy Kravitz, it comes from characters within the film itself, in most cases from Jews themselves; it becomes a part of the film's debate about honor and behavior. If the film is able to disassociate itself from charges of racial offensiveness, it is because Richler, himself a Jew, and the director Ted Kotcheff, a gentile, have been careful to use Jewishness not as a method of generalizing the story, making it universal, but, instead, to do just the opposite; they have used Jewishness to make the story specific—of a time, a place, a group of people, a situation. Jewishness isn't employed here to transform Duddy Kravitz into a cartoon or caricature, but to make his story realistic.

In "Blazing Saddles," however, director Mel Brooks seems to be striving for complete, rather than partial, offensiveness. The film studiously insults almost every special-interest group; it hits out at black men, white women, Indians, Jews, and it even takes a few extra minutes at the end to ridicule homosexuals and—if I am not mistaken—Esther Williams. It invites us to laugh both at the unspoken social taboos—as in the "Hallelujah" chorus scene, where a band of men break wind after a

bean dinner around the campfire—and at people who have the misfortune of being aged or unattractive or physically handicapped.

Among the movie's devices for milking laughs are old jokes and clichés turned round and round so many times that a viewer can only guess what the original intention might have been. Brooks' method seems designed to eliminate any possibility of audience resistance, scattering and then mixing so many taboos and private prejudices together that something, sooner or later, must reach us. This is insult used as buckshot, a frantic attempt to keep us jumping and responding. Bad taste often has the effect of dividing an audience, separating the complacent from the inquisitive, forcing at least some of the people to re-examine old taboos. But Brooks tries to use it to unite his audiences, as if the sheer proliferation of crudities might melt individual hesitation into whole-hearted yielding. He doesn't want to knock down our reactions in order to construct something new out of them—as would Bruce or Roth or Orton. He just wants to floor us.

The offensiveness in "Blazing Saddles" has obviously been catered to mass audience appeal. The popularity of the film suggests that for a large portion of the public bad taste is no longer a

controversial issue. And this mass consumption of bad taste hints at a society with far fewer taboos than ever before, hence a society one might have thought more liberated and healthy.

But is that in fact the case? Or is it that in the context of a post-Vietnam, post-Watergate America, any consideration of good as opposed to bad taste seems cruelly irrelevant? What is left to qualify as good taste? The little joke about the President who criticized "Love Story" for its foul language and who was subsequently exposed, as an unlikely model for decorous expression himself has gone far past the easy guffaw. And without some unanimity of opinion about good taste, what will happen to its opposite? What will have the power to shock the country in the future?

If we could imagine a restoration of the codes of good and bad taste, of graded taboos, it needn't be a regression but perhaps a route to a saner, more balanced national health. In that event, the selective use of bad taste might regain its potential for reform. But bad taste spattered around as glibly and carelessly as Mel Brooks spatters it around in "Blazing Saddles" is evidence of a mechanism being used without the shrewdest understanding of its powers.

1974 Ag 18, II:1:1

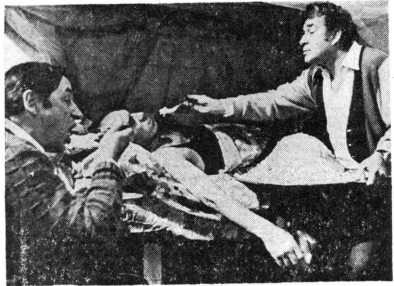

"Deliberate bad taste has been working its way into films over the past decade," says the critic. In "The Grande Bouffe," above, Philippe Noiret and Ugo Tognazzi help Michel Piccoli eat himself to death.

The Program

PINK FLOYD, a cinema concert starring the avant-garde rock band of the same name; directed by Adrian Maben; distributed by April Fools Films. At the Rivoli Theater, Broadway and 49th Street; the UA Eastside Cinema, Third Avenue and 55th Street, and neighborhood Theaters. Running time: 85 minutes. This film is classified G.

"Pink Floyd," which opened yesterday at the Rivoli Theater, Eastside Cinema and other theaters, is an 85-minute commercial for an English rock group called Pink Floyd.

It is a fan-magazine article dressed up as a movie, with lots of close-ups of its heroes and an off-screen interviewer who occasionally drops in a question or a comment—

about their equipment or their compatibility—and is satisfied with whatever he is told.

With an ancient amphitheater and a recording studio as settings for the group's music and an eatery of some sort as the setting for the musicians' uncomfortable efforts at banter, "Pink Floyd" has recourse to an assortment of effects—split screens, montages, rapid cuts, clips of flowing lava and masks—in an effort to rescue itself from visual boredom. The pictorial result ranges in quality from picture postcard to album cover.

Since its principals possess neither interesting personalities nor captivating philosophies, it is fortunate that the bulk of the film is given over to their music. It is unfortunate that their music, which ranges from traditional rock to sci-fi, fails the test one of the group sets for it—moving the listener—despite the array of electronic equipment marshaled in its behalf.

"Pink Floyd" may be for Pink Floyd fans. It may be for rock fans. But it's not for movie fans.

LAWRENCE VAN GELDER

1974 Ag 22, 27:2

Film Turns on Violence and Humiliation

By NORA SAYRE

Perhaps we'll get a substantial movie about contemporary prisons and prisoners one of these days—a picture that can actually tell us what it means to be a captive. Meanwhile, we're stuck with splashy fabrications, such as Robert Aldrich's "The Longest Yard," which opened yesterday at Loews State 1 and Loews Orpheum. While we know that prisons throng with sadistic guards, the ones in this movie behave

like leering sci-fi monsters—which makes it easy to forget that atrocities occur off screen as well as on.

The picture dwells on the preparations for a ferocious football game between prisoners and guards. Both sides look forward eagerly to mangling one another. Burt Reynolds, as an imprisoned former football star who coaches the convicts' team, contends with Warden Eddie Albert, who's determined that the guards must win and that the prisoners must be humiliated.

I suspect that Mr. Reynolds

The Cast

THE LONGEST YARD, directed by Robert Aldrich; screenplay by Tracy Keenan Wynn; based on the story by Albert S. Ruddy; director of photography, Joseph Biroc; music, Frank DeVol; film editor, Michael Luciano; produced by Mr. Ruddy; released by Paramount Pictures. At Loews State 1, Broadway and 45th Street, and Loews Orpheum, 86th Street at Third Avenue. Running time: 123 minutes. This film is classified R.
Paul Crewe .... Burt Reynolds
Warden Hazen .... Eddie Albert
Captain Knauer .... Ed Lauter
Nate Scarboro .... Michael Conrad
Caretaker .... Jim Hampton

may have watched "On the Waterfront" at least a dozen times just before this movie was shot, since he apes Marlon Brando's performance all through "The Yard." Pursing or smacking his lips, chewing gum or smirking or wrinkling his nose, he surpasses flattery with his lumbering imitation. Mr. Reynolds departs from mimicry only in his style of wearing clothes: he manages to make even the prison chains look like fashionable men's wear, as though he were modeling the latest in metal accessories.

The discomfort of watching Mr. Reynolds is alleviated by Eddie Albert's sly, silky characterization of the sinister warden. He comes on like a restrained but toothy college dean who's welcoming the freshmen—"It's nice to have you here"—smiles especially when he's angry, and recoils with an academic's sternness when he doesn't like what he hears.

•

Though "The Yard" is a terrible picture, I'll admit to having unwillingly enjoyed some of the football practice and parts of the final game —even though it's much too long. There's no thrill in the sport, since it's the movie director who decides who wins or loses. But the plot does yield some dramatic tension—because of what winning or losing represents. The prisoners are playing for their dignity, and even the most reluctant spectator is forced to respond to that theme.

Some may want to ponder Mr. Aldrich's appeals to the baser instincts—with references to his "The Dirty Dozen." But that seems like an unnecessary exercise, since the issue itself can be better discussed in light of other recent movies. Still, this picture will enlarge the director's dossier of nasty build-ups to violence: a man we know will become a human torch delays that torching by pausing to comb his hair before the inevitable explosion, and it's one of the cheaper tricks to grace our screens of late.

1974 Ag 22, 28:1

NEWMAN'S LAW, directed by Richard Heffron; written by Anthony Wilson; director of photography, Vilis Lapenieks; film editor, John Dumas; music, Robert Prince; produced by Richard Irving; released by Universal Pictures. At neighborhood theaters. Running time: 98 minutes. This film is classified PG.
Vince Newman........... George Peppard
Garry................... Roger Robinson
Reardon................ Eugene Roche
Eastman................. Gordon Pinsent
Falcone................. Louis Zorich

August is the month for very dumb action pictures aimed at the drive-in trade. Some are the too-familiar urban Westerns — where the city cop stands in for the local sheriff, while the Indians are replaced by drug dealers — and they tend to be pitifully poor of plot, with almost no suspense to link the shoot-outs or chases. In fact, I'd love to learn why many action movies have to be so dull.

•

"Newman's Law," which opened yesterday at neighborhood theaters, trots out the mossy formula that should be given at least one month's rest: an incorruptible detective is accused of being on the take and is therefore suspended. Hence the outraged law-lover continues to investigate the case on his own. There's hardly an episode in this picture that you haven't seen before, from the man with a gun on top of a vast tank (a bumbling reference to James Cagney's great moment in Raoul Walsh's "White Heat") to a stabbed waterbed ("The Terminal Man"), and much of it resembles "McQ," John Wayne's dud of last winter. Still, there is one original detail: a man who's been beaten by thugs falls bleading onto a pile of giant toy pandas.

•

It's disheartening to see George Peppard playing the quasi-Serpico. I've always had a soft spot for this actor, partly because he often makes one feel that he's more intelligent or sensitive than the characters he personifies. But in recent years, he's shown a gift for picking dreary scripts. Here, he hardly bothers to act. Below the blazing blue eyes, he grits his teeth, clenches his jaw, wipes his mouth with the back of his wrist (a gesture that means tension), or flares his nostrils — all in all, he seems to be auditioning for a parody of the warmhearted hard head. Meanwhile, several good black actors—Roger Robinson, for example — are wasted in this movie, which is also far too gloomy to pass for entertainment.

NORA SAYRE

1974 Ag 22, 28:1

The Cast

BUSTER AND BILLIE, directed by Daniel Petrie; screenplay by Ron Turbeville; story by Mr. Turbeville and Ron Barton; director of photography, Mario Tosi; music, Al DeLory; film editor, Michael Kahn; produced by Ron Silverman; released by Columbia Pictures. At the Columbia II Theater, 64th Street and Second Avenue, and neighborhood theaters. Running time: 100 minutes. This film is classified R.
Buster Lane.........Jan-Michael Vincent
Billie...................Joan Goodfellow
Margie Hooks.......Pamela Sue Martin
Jake..................Clifton James
Whitey..................Robert Englund
Mrs. Lane.............Jessie Lee Fulton

The time machine that transported audiences of a year or two ago back to the summer of '42 and the class

of '44 is open for business again. And in this summer of '74, a trip to the spring—and the class—of '48 in rural Georgia is being offered in the form of a film called "Buster and Billie," which opened yesterday at the Columbia II and neighborhood theaters.

"Buster and Billie" is at once an alluring and fiercely disappointing movie that leaves one full of regret for what might have been. Chief among its virtues, at a time when so many film makers, either through sloth or contempt, treat originality with disdain, is the focus of its story.

Billie (Joan Goodfellow) is an unusual heroine. Bovine in her submissiveness, she is the silent and undemanding dispenser of ultimate sexual favors for the coterie of her teen-age high-schoolmates who surround Buster (Jan-Michael Vincent).

Unlike his fellow members of Tomorrow's Farmers of America, Buster, an otherwise unexceptional youth, does not seek out Billie—at least at first. He is faithful to, if not content with, his fiancée, Margie (Pamela Sue Martin), who allows him frustrating liberties but busily preserves her virginity during their contortions at night in the front of his little truck.

And then, one day, Buster decides to seek out Billie, at first furtively and for the same reason as his classmates; later he dates her openly, to the disapproving astonishment of his townsfolk and because he has come to cherish her as a person. Billie has changed, but the townspeople, especially Buster's classmates, remain the same, with disastrous consequences.

But if art resides in the quality of revelation, "Buster and Billie" is a failure. For all that the movie suggests, Billie's past is a side effect of impoverished and laconic parents in a community no table neither for its riches nor the garrulousness of its inhabitants.

In dealing with Buster and Billie and their schoolmates, Daniel Petrie, the director, and Ron Turbeville, the screen writer, have contended themselves with types, observed keenly but unexplained, remote rather than real, remembered but not revealed. The film suffers, too, from a monotony of judgment that assigns each scene an equal value, whether it is a trimmable segment involving a softball game or a fatal encounter.

It's too bad. One wishes this film were less like the early Billie—to be visited because it's available — and more like the later—to be cherished because it's special.

LAWRENCE VAN GELDER

1974 Ag 22, 28:1

Goldie Hawn and Hal Holbrook

THE GIRL FROM PETROVKA, directed by Robert Ellis Miller; screenplay by Allan Scott and Chris Bryant, based on the book by George Feifer; director of photography, Vilmos Zsigmond; film editor, John F. Burnett; music, Henry Mancini; produced by Richard D. Zanuck and David Brown; released by Universal Pictures. At Radio City Music Hall, Avenue of the Americas and 50th Street. Running time: 104 minutes. This film is classified PG.
Oktyabrina .... Goldie Hawn
Joe .... Hal Holbrook
Kostya .... Anthony Hopkins
Minister .... Gregoire Aslan
Ignatievitch .... Anton Dolin
Leonid .... Zoran Andric

By NORA SAYRE

How ever Moscow may judge us this week, "The Girl From Petrovka" isn't going to be good for détente. According to this movie—which concerns a gluey romance between a young Russian (Goldie Hawn) and an American newsman (Hal Holbrook)—the Soviet Union is deeply dismal country where people declare their love in graveyards, and sheets of rain or heavy snow descend when they're depressed. The Russians themselves are children who lie a lot. Yet they're also lovable—as greedy little materialists who clamor for the spoils of capitalism. In fact, they haven't changed much since "Ninotchka" was made in 1939. "The Girl," directed by Robert Ellis Miller, opened yesterday at Radio City Music Hall.

•

Meanwhile, here's a plea to American performers to stay at home. Goldie Hawn can't play a Russian, any more than Dustin Hoffman was able to seem Italian in "Alfredo, Alfredo." Like all the Russians in this picture, she talks English with a lush accent, landing hard on the d's and r's, while swallowing the l's: "Ow, my pour doorllink." Admittedly she has a difficult part, since sexual teasing is supposed to be cute —a slightly staggering notion for the nineteen-seventies.

We know that Miss Hawn can act. But her abundant energies — which were so well channeled in "The Sugarland Express" — have been made to seem merely windsome here. As a throbbing waif, she's been directed to frisk and dither, to run about in tiny steps while waving her arms. Twice, the camera dwells on on her sleeping face in close-up — as though to prove that she can manage to hold still. When she's unhappy, she has to do a tragic Pekingese stunt — snuffling and drizzling—and let's hope that she never repeats it.

Hal Holbrook, who's bewitched by this sprightly depressive, has little to do beyond shaking his head when he thinks of her or smiling indulgently when he looks at her. Still, he's permitted some moments of exasperation and frustration —which seem to be the basis for the attraction. As a reporter must, he wears a belted trench coat—which also seems like a symbol of the constriction of his role.

•

Certainly, neither performer has been aided by the script. The dialogue heaves along on the level of "I took a master's at Harvard and a mistress at Radcliffe," and, "What's the transitional period from Socialism to Communism?" Answer: "Alcoholism." There's even a prehistoric joke about a bidet's being mistaken for a footbath. Henry Mancini's music is as maudlin as the action. All in all, it's hard to imagine what audience this movie was made for. Perhaps it might amuse the Chinese. Or reassure them?

1974 Ag 23, 16:1

THE GOAT'S HORN, directed by Methodi Andonov; screenplay (Bulgarian with English subtitles) by Nikolai Haitov; photography, Dimo Kolarov; music, Simeon Pironkov; distributed by Film-bulgaria. At the First Avenue Screening Room, at 61st Street. Running time: 100 minutes. This film has not been classified at this time. Playing Friday and Saturday at noon and midnight.
Maria .... Katia Paskaleva
Kara Ivan .... Anton Gortchev
The Shepherd .... Milene Penev

A movie of extraordinary beauty, so replete with accomplishment on every level — visually, aurally, in its story, its acting and its direction—that it seems almost effortless, is playing at the First Avenue Screening Room today and tomorrow at noon and midnight.

Its title is "The Goat's Horn"—the object, used as a dagger, that is the most singular weapon employed in this engrossing tale of the perversion of love. "The Goat's Horn" is a Bulgarian film, made two years ago in black and white with English subtitles by Methodi Andonov, one of those increasingly rare film makers, capable of telling a story by pictures alone. "The Goat's Horn" is an eloquent film with little dialogue. Set in 17th-century Bulgaria, it begins with the rape of a young mother by a band of Turks as her little daughter watches in horror.

Determined to spare his child her mother's fate, her father, a burly goatherd, takes her to live high in the hills. Telling her there is no place for woman in their world, he shears her hair and raises her as a man—skilled in the deadly uses of the staff, the dagger, the blunderbuss. Together, they extract vengeance from the Turks. And then, into her unchanging life, comes a young shepherd and a love that shatters everything.

The performances, especially by Katia Paskaleva as the girl and by Anton Gortchev as her unsparing father, are brilliantly expressive.
LAWRENCE VAN GELDER

1974 Ag 23, 16:4

Science Fiction Movies Are Catching on

By ARTHUR HERZOG

NO LESS a citadel of science than the Hayden Planetarium recently presented a series of science fiction films in its great dome. That is, of course, a surprising fact because the Planetarium is normally thought to be reserved for serious galactic affairs.

Indeed, this presentation was more than just a straw in the solar wind. It suggests a new standing for the genre.

"I hate to say that science fiction has finally come out of the closet," says Dr. Mark Chartrand, chairman of the Planetarium and organizer of the film program, "but there is no question that it has come to be regarded as respectable."

It has also become quite profitable, judging by Hollywood's box-office receipts. Starting in 1968 with the first of the "Planet of the Apes" series, accelerating in 1970 with Stanley Kubrick's landmark film "2001: A Space Odyssey," and continuing with such noteworthy entries as "THX-1138," "The Omega Man," "The Andromeda Strain,"

Arthur Herzog is the author of "The Swarm," a new science fiction novel which Irwin Allen will make into a movie this fall for 20th Century-Fox.

"Slaughterhouse-Five" and "Silent Running," outer space has more than rivaled the wild wild west as the place where the movie action is.

*

In the near future, sci fi buffs can look forward to seeing "Phase IV" (aggressive giant ants), "The Hephaestus Plague" (relentless cockroaches), "Whiffs" (Elliott Gould at the mercy of computers), "Star Wars" (bloodshed up above), "Cages of Steel" (a detective and his robot sidekick), "Rollerball" (James Caan playing lethal Olympic games in the 21st century) and "Futureworld" (sequel to the popular "Westworld"). Not to mention the reissue of "2001"—a huge success in its recent Los Angeles revival—and the upcoming TV spinoff of "Planet of the Apes."

What accounts for the popularity—the coming out of the closet—of sci fi? According to Ben Bova, editor of Analog, fascination with the unknown is as old as man himself. "People have always been turned on by stories telling them that they can become immortal, fly to the stars, do superhuman things, that life is not restricted to the here and now. Science fiction tries to put that yearning to transcend the present into an accurate scientific context. It offers possible solutions to the problems the rest of literature only asks.

"I picture history," he goes on to say, "as a vast migration of billions of human beings across a titanic landscape over millions of years. The creators of science fiction are like scouts going out ahead of the other people, taking a look at the terrain...the pasture land, the lakes, the forests, the mountains... and coming back with a report of all the possible paths we might follow, in the hope that we will pick out the decent ones and avoid the evil ones. As Isaac Asimov says, 'Science fiction is an escape into reality. It deals with today, and—more important—tomorrow.'"

The question remains: what accounts for the popularity of sci fi *now*? More than one observer is willing to bet that this accent on escapism has quite a bit to do with the quality of the here and now. Bombarded by daily reports about inflation, pollution and corruption in high places, is it any wonder that Americans want to take flight to another time and another place? On the other hand, it could be a simple case of monkey see, monkey do; perhaps box-office minded producers are just aping "The Planet of the Apes."

Of course, many who take sci fi as seriously as do Messrs. Bova and Asimov may not be pleased by the current sci fi deluge. For rarely has there been an art form with such a vast potential for making a fool of itself; the more sci fi that is turned out, the more foolishness there will certainly be. The unique characteristic of sci fi (the heavies object to this abbreviation, but let them) is that it deals in futures and must therefore make convincing that for which there may be little or no basis in existing reality.

Even when sci fi succeeds, it frequently does so at the expense of the usual elements of fiction and drama—plot, characterization and plausible dialogue. In films, the problem is magnified because producers often demand strong visual effects—flashy gadgets and gimmicks which invariably dominate the worst sci fi, carrying with them a credibility gap big enough to float a space ship through.

In spite of its inherent pitfalls, however, sci fi still has a window all its own. No other art form is as well equipped to focus upon the destiny which lies out there on the edges of science and society. There are those, in fact, who see sci fi as a kind of dress rehearsal for things to come, and it would be quite possible to construct a history of recent cultural moods as revealed by sci fi films: Optimism giving way to pessimism, predictions of war and dictatorship, fears of tech-

Culver Pictures

"Trip to the Moon" (1902)

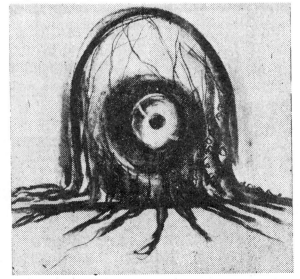

"It Came From Outer Space" (1953)

"2001: A Space Odyssey,"

nology, awe of space—all are nakedly shown.

Sci fi aficianados insist on making a distinction between science fiction and fantasy, their stubborn assertion being that sci fi creators are free to invent anything, so long as it cannot be proven wrong. That which is not scientifically plausible—a monster like Godzilla or Mithra or any of the other denizens of those campy Japanese potboilers—is deemed fantasy and automatically relegated to a lower order.

This attitude is not merely snobbish—it misses the space ship. Much of the charm and power of such sci fi movies as "2001" and the wonderful "Fantastic Planet" have derived precisely from fantasy. Indeed, it was chiefly the fantastic element which made some of the films in the Hayden Planetarium's program worth resurrecting.

"Trip to the Moon" (1902), the first film in the series, was the creation of Georges Méliès, a Parisian who owned a theater in which he produced magic shows as well as vaudeville, both of which figure prominently in this, the father of all science fiction movies. A sorcerer convinces a court that a moon voyage is possible, whereupon chorus girls shove a projectile into a cannon. As the ship ascends into space, the face of The Man in the Moon appears, only to grimace as the cannister smashes into his eye. A vigorous Moon Men-Earth Men battle ensues (nobody has the slightest need for breathing equipment) and the Earth Men manage to escape by merely jumping off the edge of the Moon. Back on Earth, they are joyously received by the chorus line.

Not only is Méliès's lunar excursion great fun, but it also gives us the chance to witness the birth of such visual techniques as the freeze-frame, superimposition of images, dissolves and model animation techniques which are used to this day in virtually every fantasy and science fiction film. All that, and magic and vaudeville, too.

Because the now-concluded Hayden Planetarium series offered the viewer a veritable laboratory of cinematic techniques and a catalog of sci fi triumphs and failures, as well as a superb opportunity to see this much maligned genre in its proper historical perspective, let me continue to describe the films it

offered. (Many of these films, by the way, crop up from time to time on television.) The second in the Planetarium series, in chronological order, was "Metropolis" (1926), directed by Fritz Lang. Costing $4-million, it was the most expensive movie produced in Europe—and perhaps America too—up to that time. Though considerably shortened from the original, "Metropolis" is still splendid on almost every count. For one thing, it shows what could be done with special effects even in the days of silent movies. A hulking 21st century city, modeled on New York, looms with aerial highways, airplanes flitting between the high towers, television, joyous crowds.

But wait: all is not well in Metropolis, a city socially and physically divided into two classes—the upper, living gaily above the ground, and the lower, toiling grimly beneath it. When the workers finally rebel, a robot is fashioned by the rulers to mislead and defeat them. This scheme fails, however, and the workers triumph—as the Ruler of the Metropolis comes to realize, too late, that no society, however efficient, can survive without love.

"Metropolis" reflects a fear that is

still strong today, a fear that human society, for all its technological accomplishments, lacks the ability to bring personal happiness and social order simultaneously. It is a strange, brooding movie, one which vividly demonstrates just how good science fiction can be at social prophecy.

Many people assume that science fiction was born out of a marriage between science and fiction, but there is a third party to be considered: utopian literature. Since the time of ancient Greece, seers of every stripe have taken their turns at imagining future societies that would banish the inequities of present ones. The mood of these Utopians was optimistic: they felt that even if their imaginary world never materialized, they were at least providing signposts for a better way of life. Around the turn of the 19th century, however, the mood began to change, and what emerged was not U (the good) topia, but *Kaka*topia, the bad one. "Metropolis" is a mingling of these two moods. Even more so is "Things to come" (1936), adapted by H. G. Wells from his book "The Shape of Things to Come: The Ultimate Revolution."

"If we don't end war," the protagonist, a thirties scientist, preaches stiffly, "war will end us," and it almost does. The film depicts a ghastly world war, beginning in 1940 and lasting for a quarter of a century—by which time the Dark Ages have returned. Ultimately humanity is saved by a group of technocrats who succeed in restoring order and paving the way for progress. By the 21st century, the world is a technical paradise—but there is trouble in this paradise. The trashy, ever-romantic populace craves excitement, having found progress incompatible with happiness. In the end, the first moon shot is carried out as a means of reminding mankind that its real task is not flabby self-satisfaction, but rather the disciplined conquest of the unknown.

There were remarkably few sci fi films during the 40's and what emerged next in the planetarium's series was "Destination Moon," a 1950 film glorifying space technology. "The Moon? Impossible!" someone remarks in the movie. But a group of businessmen decide that a moon shot is not only possible but necessary for America's survival—if we don't accomplish it, the Russians will, and it is feared that the moon would be used by them as a launching pad for rockets.

The U.S. government is portrayed in "Destination Moon" as being not only incapable of organizing a space flight but as being an active bureaucratic enemy of the people: the flight is finally launched on less than a day's notice in order to avoid red tape. That's not the way they later did it at Cape Canaveral, but the movie does offer realistic depictions of a space walk and a lunar landing. In fact, the film is credited with having convinced many people that a moon flight was indeed possible and desirable.

Some of the obvious mistakes in "Destination Moon" can be excused on the grounds of technological infantilism —one has to see the film to realize how greatly increased has popular technical sophistication become. This is not the case, however, in "The Day The Earth Stood Still" (1951). By then, sci fi was entering a generally naive period,

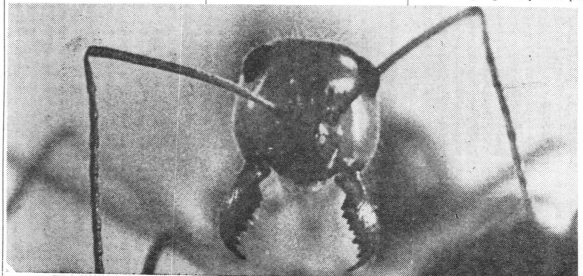

This giant ant will have mere humans crying uncle in "Phase IV," due this fall. Fans can also look forward to fire-belching cockroaches in "The Hephaestus Plague."

one in which it was used as a launching pad for moralistic and mawkish ideas. It was a time when xenophobia—the dislike of that which is different—flourished.

I don't know how you'd react, but if a flying saucer came to rest in *my* proximity, and the door opened, I'd be inclined to be as suspicious as the soldier in "The Day The Earth Stood Still" who wounds the gentle spaceman in the arm. But, as it turns out, this emissary from outer space has a message of importance for the unsympathetically drawn soldier. So long as earthmen confine their warlike ways to their own planet, it's fine. But if we pose a threat to other, more sophisticated civilizations, we will be forced to either accept being supervised by robots from outer space or to face certain obliteration. Proof that the emissary means business is the fact that an omnipotent robot, equipped with a laser beam, stands at his side.

"The Day the Earth Stood Still" is nicely restrained but, all the same, it contains the sort of errors of omission which are all too common to the breed. Poor old humanity simply must stop fighting wars and hating strangers, it says, without once admitting that the superior space people actually threaten total war if their demand is not met. (And who, we might have asked, would control the robot?) Moreover, the space man, who has the power not only to cross intergalactic reaches but is also able to shut off all electricity on our planet for half-an-hour as a simple demonstration of his skill, spends much of his time risking his hide while trying to find a forum from which to deliver his words. Couldn't he simply have used his radio? Loose ends like this help us to recognize bad sci fi.

Another film which can be described as a masterpiece in sci fi terms only is "It Came From Outer Space" (1953). This time, some small-town Arizonians are portrayed as unpleasant xenophobes because they won't accept the idea that spacemen who have landed and taken hostages into their space ship are really peaceful—as the earth-man protagonist keeps insisting they are. The sheriff, typically, wants to storm the citadel—not a very good idea, since whatever it is that the outer-spacers are up to, they must have more than mere guns with which to defend themselves. Nobody thinks for a second of getting outside help. The aliens, it turns out, had actually landed here for emergency repairs and, in the end, they depart peacefully, not carrying out a twittily tearful threat to blow themselves up if the nasty earthlings won't leave them alone. "They will return," the human hero announces reverentially into the sunset.

They will return, that is, when we're ready for creatures that look like walking eyeballs—sci fi monsters which are inadequately conceived and depicted.

In "Forbidden Planet" (1956), sci fi surmounts the jingoism, naivete, bad dialogue, loose ends and the other ills to which it is prone, perhaps because the movie is vaguely modeled on Shakespeare's "The Tempest." At any rate, it is nearly unique among sci fi movies in that it develops a convincing central character, thereby securing a tight focus for its effects.

Dr. Morbius (Walter Pidgeon) uncovers the secrets of the planet on which he has been marooned with his young daughter for almost 20 years. A previous civilization, he learns, had developed unlimited sources of energy but then perished when the tribes transformed themselves from flesh to pure spirit. When a space patrol arrives from earth to rescue Dr. Morbius, he resists, the reason being that he is subconsciously in love with his teen-age daughter (Anne Francis). Going into a trance, Dr. Morbius summons the planet's energy reserves and converts himself into a remarkably convincing monster. With "Forbidden Planet," sci fi entered a period of new technical expertise, the fruits of which have cropped up in TV series like "Star Trek" ever since. The movie proved once again that with sufficient care and budget, sci fi could be both provocative and entertaining.

Skipping the 1960's, the Hayden series arrived at its final destination, "Silent Running" (1972)—an almost perfect choice with which to conclude, since the movie shows how far sci fi has traveled since the days of Méliès. A fleet of huge American Airlines space freighters are seen plowing through the empyrean, and —with the exception of "2001"—no other movie has ever offered such spectacular visual effects. Four young spacemen-foresters have been given the task of growing plant life in outer space— now that it can no longer survive on earth. Then, one day, the order comes: destroy the forests, for the ship must return to commercial service. Since the plants will surely die without the aid of the spacemen, the hero won't comply, and to save the greenhouse, he murders his companions and heads his ship beyond Saturn, where he is eventually found. He leaves the forest in charge of a robot attendant, and destroys himself and the spaceship. Songs by Joan Baez.

Anyone who fails to be excited by the space scenes—especially the one in which the freighter is buffeted by a solar storm in much the same manner real ships are tossed about on terrestial waters — is beyond science fiction's reach. The fantasy that animates such sequences is in the best tradition of sci fi.

Still, the film caters to a trendy kind of ecological mixture of pessimism and hope. Could the earth really survive with a mean temperature in the 70's and little vegetation? How long will the forest make it in outer space? What accounted for the spaceman's individualism? (Incidentally, sooner or later the sci fi films will have to explain exactly what sort of person would spend years at a stretch in space without sex). The space foresters can't understand why the forest turns brown, but the answer should have been obvious to a 6-year-old. Out in space the plants don't receive enough sunlight! This detail, which all but unhinges the movie's credibility, suggests what can happen when characterization and plot are neglected in science fiction.

The Hayden series, which included a question-and-answer period after the screenings, was a sell-out, even at $25 a subscription. So delighted are its sponsors—the planetarium, Analog magazine and the New York Science Fiction Film Society—that they plan to hold *two* sci fi film series next year.

1974 Ag 25, II:1:1

Why Did They Turn 'Duddy Kravitz' Into a Charmer?

By URJO KAREDA

TORONTO

To describe "The Apprenticeship of Duddy Kravitz" as the most successful Canadian movie ever made is a nation's private joke. It is the truth, but the truth doesn't tell you quite enough. There hasn't been all that much competition for the crown, and the Canadian film industry remains in so limited a stage of development—like, I suspect, the black cinema in the United States—that each new film of any merit gets its turn. With only a handful of films jostling for the crown, a newcomer can be worked through the competition quite quickly.

A few qualifications may help in explaining "Duddy's" right to the crown. First of all, it must be made clear—as it must be in discussions of any aspects of Canadian culture, whether it be films or theater or literature—that what is under discussion is *English*-Canadian achievement. French-Canada, in Quebec, is another country, with its own history to render, its own successful films to record, one of which—Claude Jutra's "Mon Oncle Antoine"—is probably the most artistically unified film made in this country.

One justification for "Duddy's" crown is that it has been acclaimed both by audiences and by critics. Some Canadian films, like Donald Shebib's "Between Friends," were better treated by critics than by audiences; others, like Peter Pearson's "Paperback Hero" or Peter Carter's "The Rowdyman," drew crowds but scant critical acclaim.

Urjo Kareda is drama critic for the Toronto Star.

Some, like Shebib's "Goin' Down the Road," even drew both, but never enjoyed the kind of runaway success which has greeted "The Apprenticeship of Duddy Kravitz." "Duddy" is also the first Canadian film, English or French, to attract sizable American audiences.

The most successful Canadian movie ever made? Sure, then, why not? It has earned the crown, as well, through the passion and confidence with which it has been assembled. The energy spent in its making has been recorded and preserved in the finished product. It is a movie about the compulsions of making it, and those compulsions propel not just the title character, but also the project of making this film about him.

It is one of the few Canadian films which has turned to a major work in our national literature as its source. Since its publication in 1959, Mordecai Richler's "The Apprenticeship of Duddy Kravitz" has become one of the signal novels of Canadian writing, a work so revealing of a part of the national experience that it has now undergone the dubious apotheosis of becoming a high school textbook.

For a long time, Richler, who wrote the novel at one point during his nearly two decades of expatriate life in London, had tried to get the work filmed. When grants from the government's Canadian Film Development Corporation finally came through, Richler had become so removed from his original involvement with the project that he initially declined to write the screenplay himself. Eventually, though, he surrendered to the pleading of the director, an old friend, Ted Kotcheff (also an

'Is this the most successful Canadian film ever made? Sure, why not?'

expatriate in London).

The film could not have come at a better time. It landed in Canadian theaters at that precise point when audiences felt worn out by cinematic examinations of the Canadian tendency to celebrate losers. This phenomenon has been codified in Margaret Atwood's influential book "Survival," which examines our literature as a recurring pattern of victimization; if a Canadian had written "Moby Dick," she explains, the story would have been told from the whale's point of view.

Film after film seemed to fall into this slot of glorifying the loser. It wasn't the most pleasant kind of revelation to live with, although it yielded its returns. If Canadian culture has been preoccupied with losers, they have at least been losers who acquired consolations, an almost perverse enoblement attained through their numbed acceptance of reality. "Duddy Karvitz," however, is about a winner, an ambitious young man who shoves until he gets what he wants; the irony, of course, and for once a not uniquely Canadian irony, is that he loses part of himself by becoming that winner, having destroyed his relationship with the very people on whose behalf he thought he was shoving.

Still, the exhilaration and energy which drive Duddy to win seized hold of our imagination. Energy isn't really a neutral force, though it can of course be directed toward both positive and negative achievements; it projects a vitality which is hard to resist. By exploring the pathology of winning so acutely, Richler and Kotcheff have finally created the Canadian film which brings their audiences closer to an image they might like to project of themselves.

Like Duddy himself, however, the film may lose something in the winning. Richler, a skillful manipulator of public controversy, anticipated this objection early in the game. He has written, "If the film succeeds in New York, it will be disowned by Canadian critics as a venture cunningly contrived to appeal to international audiences. If it fails, the same critics will hail it as an unrecognized Canadian classic."

Well, it has succeeded in New York, and I am a Canadian, and loath as I am to be eased so smoothly into Richler's cover-all-bases stereotypes, I do believe that there has been a shift in our perception of Duddy between the original and the cinematic adaptation. Although I essentially respect the film's gusto and momentum, I miss the Duddy Kravitz whom Richler created before he sought to make him palatable for mass-media marketing.

"The Apprenticeship of Duddy Kravitz," novel and film, is about a young man, a product of the Jewish ghetto in Montreal, who connives, cheats and pushes his way to the top. That victory is seen both as a means of cancelling a childhood of poverty and humiliation —the time is the late 1940's—and as the whooping articulation for the inexpressible drive within himself.

His push is for property. Early in his life (at the age of 7 in the novel; in his late teens in the film), he is told by his grandfather that "a man without land is nobody." The particular land he covets is a Laurentian lakeside discovered during a summer of work in a resort hotel. In the novel, the property is immediately decorated in his fantasy ("I'm going to build a children's camp and a hotel here. I want to make a town"), while the film leaves the practical dimensions of his ambition unspoken until near the end. To earn the money, Duddy starts a film business (Dudley Kane Enterprises, specializing in bar mitzvah documentaries), runs dope across the border to New York, drives his father's taxi at night, distributes pinball machines around the province, and—in a moment of desperation— forges a friend's check.

And, in the end, he has his lake. In getting it, he has alienated his long-suffering French-Canadian girlfriend Yvette and betrayed Virgil, a crippled epileptic friend. He has quarreled with his dying Uncle Benjy ("You lousy, intelligent people" he shouts at the man on his deathbed), and he has even cracked the illusions of his beloved grandfather. "You see, you see" he says, grinning at his father, showing him the lake for the first time. And Duddy is too excited and defiant and dumb to see himself what has passed out of his hands.

Both the book and the film are precise and unsentimental about the hunger to move forward, which results from a need to resconstruct the past and in-

sure the future. An older businessman advises Duddy on the making of shady business deals, saying that at least his own son will never have to cheat, but then, he adds, his son didn't arrive in Canada with three words of English and 50 cents in his pocket.

Richler's novel presents the paradox of Duddy, his lust for making it, as well as his destructiveness, with considerable complexity. It is just this intriguing duality, this spikiness, which gets diluted in the film. For all its steamrolling verve and comic vitality, "The Apprenticeship of Duddy Kravitz," as a film, is dangerously ingratiating. Most of the young directors making Canadian films are as hungry to make it as Duddy was, and the edge sometimes shows through. But Richler and Kotcheff, both successful and respected in their fields, look back to their own Duddy days with mellowness, a feeling of generosity obtained through hindsight.

Part of the difficulty is the relationship between Kotcheff's direction and Richler's own screenplay, which offers a fairly faithful reproduction of the novel's big scenes. Some important connecting scenes have been omitted, however, making certain developments, like Duddy's inheriting his uncle's house, incomprehensible to those who have not read the book.

It is possible that both Richler and Kotcheff loved the material so that they were unwilling or unable to judge the weight of individual scenes. Kotcheff directs all of the scenes with such flourish and feeling that they tend to even out, so that it is difficult for a viewer to know which sequence is important and which is not. For instance, the scenes of Duddy's bar mitzvah filmmaking are as developed and detailed as the sequence involving Virgil's accident and paralysis, though the first merely adds color while the second is structurally crucial. Kotcheff's equal treatment of Richler's parade of scenes gives the film a picaresque quality, full

of tumult and adventure but not leading anywhere in particular.

A more nagging flaw reveals itself in the casting. Many of the secondary roles are superlatively done—Randy Quaid's Virgil, Denholm Elliott's alcoholic film director and Joe Silver's unscrupulous businessman. But in the novel, it is the girlfriend, Yvette, who provides the most solid moral counterpoint to Duddy's unethical behavior and who functions as our touchstone in the judgment of his progress. In the film, Yvette is played by Micheline Lanctôt, whom the 1940's hairstyles and make-up conspire to display as twice Duddy's age. She is a low-energy actress, so that instead of serving as an active counterweight, she responds with cowlike placidity. Thus a strong thematic balance is lost in general blandness.

Diminished also is the figure of Duddy's Uncle Benjy (Joseph Wiseman), who is reduced in the film to a sentimental figure, loving Duddy and his brother as sons because of his own impotence, quite the opposite from the complex figure in the book.

These miscalculations, heightening Duddy's flamboyance by washing out those around him, are intensified, I feel, by the casting of Richard Dreyfuss as Duddy Kravitz. For all his drive, for all the panache he brings to Richler's funny dialogue, Dreyfuss doesn't exactly ring true. He looks too well-fed and healthy for a war-time ghetto product. "Where Duddy Kravitz sprung from the boys grew up dirty and sad, spiky also, like grass beside the railroad tracks," is Richler's description in the book, but Dreyfuss's Duddy, rather like Cybill Shepherd's Daisy Miller, looks like the triumphant result of tons of homogenized milk consumed during the formative years.

Dreyfuss simply is not hungry enough. He seems too middle-class to be a street fighter, although admittedly the film, unlike the novel,

shows Duddy on the streets only for a few moments at the beginning and then again in the very last shot. The two recurring details Dreyfuss provides for Duddy—the woodpecker laugh and the itch which no scratching will sooth—are intelligent choices but also too transparently the products of an actor's calculation.

The thing which most undermines Dreyfuss's performance is also the thing he can least help: his innate charm. This is such an exceptionally engaging young actor, so high on the excitement of a marvelous role, that it seems perverse to ask him to rein in the exuberant appeal which probably won him the role in the first place. But Dreyfuss's charm, though presumably near the top of the list of factors which make the film a success with audiences, does alter Duddy's character. It serves to divert our attention from the fact that Duddy is also often a fool: Dreyfuss sustains the role at such a pitch that aberrations stemming from Duddy's moral failures seem only momentary delay in a generally inspired improvisation.

Dreyfuss's charm tends to soften the occasional ugliness of Duddy's behavior. His plotting merely appears to be the unstoppable manifestation of a temperament in which moral values are secondary to invention. From Richler and Kotcheff, Dreyfuss picks up the cue of energy and he mixes it with quick, ingratiating buoyancy, so that we don't have time to ask the questions which could present a satisfying perspective on Duddy's behavior.

That, finally, is how the film oversimplifies and weakens the original material. Richler, in the novel omits any direct explanation of why we should stick with Duddy during his apprenticeship. He provides no overt indication of why this rough, mean, loving, contradictory boy should be allowed to work us over. We are left to make that decision for ourselves, until we discover some aspect of Duddy which is uncomfortably similar to a more common hunger which we, too, may share. From our own experience, we must fill in the reasons for the Duddys of the world, and perhaps give them their due.

The film of "The Apprenticeship of Duddy Kravitz" fills in that missing blank of the character with Richard Dreyfuss's charm; in doing so, it provides a joyous popular entertainment. But it fails to provide the challenge

"I miss the Duddy Kravitz whom Mordecai Richler created before he sought to make him palatable for mass-media marketing," says the critic. Richard Dreyfuss and Jack Warden play Duddy and his dad.

to an audience's introspection, which in the novel made our examination of Duddy a self-examination, a part of our own apprenticeships.

1974 Ag 25, II:11:1

THE TESTAMENT OF DR. MABUSE, directed by Fritz Lang; screenplay (German with English subtitles) by Thea von Harbou; photography, Fritz Arno Wagner and Karl Vass; music, Hans Erdmann; produced by Seymour Nebenzal; released by Janus Films. Running time: 120 minutes.

Dr. Mabuse .... Rudolph Klein Rogge
Inspector Lohmann ....Otto Wernicke
Kent .... Gustav Diessl
Dr. Baum .... Oscar Beregi

"The Testament of Dr. Mabuse" was shown at the New York Cultural Center. The following excerpt is from Nora Sayre's review, which appeared Dec. 6, 1973, in The New York Times. The film will be shown today and tomorrow at the Cinema Studio, Broadway and 66th Street.

By NORA SAYRE

Although we now live with melodrama on a weekly basis, it's still immensely refreshing on film. Fritz Lang's "Testament of Dr. Mabuse," the sequel to his "Doktor Mabuse" of 1922, yields a sensational torrent of images that almost make the early nineteen-seventies seem tame.

The second "Mabuse" was made in 1932 and had only a brief run in Germany until Goebbels banned it in 1933. Goebbels offered Lang the job of running the German film industry, and the director's reponse was to leave the country that day.

In Lang's 1932 classic, Mabuse, the master criminal and hypnotist who wanted to dominate the world, is now a lunatic in an asylum. The muscle-bound sensualist of the first firm appears as a ravaged wraith in the second.

Lang wrote in 1943 that he'd designed "an allegory to show Hitler's processes of terrorism. . . . I hoped to expose the masked Nazi theory of the necessity to deliberately destroy everthing which is precious to people. . . .Then when everything collapsed and they were thrown into utter despair, they would try to find 'help' in the new order."

Mabuse dies. But he has already hypnotized his psychiatrist, who continues to carry out the dead man's schemes. It's a fine case of mind poisoning and demonic possession, which also evokes the spell that Hitler cast on the German psyche.

The climax of the first "Mabuse" showed the Doctor frantically trying to fight his way through bolted doors. Lang seemed to specialize in people who were desperate to escape: either from places where they might be killed or from situations that they found intolerable. The Mabuse films remind us again of what Lang himself escaped from — and of our own good fortune in being able to savor the body of work that he achieved after that escape.

1974 Ag 27, 25:4

Buster Keaton Shines in 1920 Feature

By NORA SAYRE

Waiting for someone who will never come: it makes an easy poignancy on screen—a solitary, expectant figure who grows mutely more forlorn can milk almost any spectator's fears of rejection. The image recalls Charlie Chaplin in "The Gold Rush" (1925), as he waits for the girl who won't be coming to dinner. The Chaplin scene is sheer pathos. But Buster Keaton in the same situation is far funnier, thanks to the kind of mistake that's so easy to make: the beloved's train arrives at Grand Central, while he stands with his armful of flowers at Penn Station. It's one of the passages worth cherishing in "The Saphead," which is playing today to Saturday at the Elgin Cinema.

•

The movie was made in 1920, and—due to a snarl of legal problems — it hasn't been shown for almost 50 years. It was Keaton's first feature-length film, and was adapted from a Broadway play of 1913 that was based on a play of 1887. The print is marvelously clear.

"The Saphead" is a fairly straight melodrama that drags occasionally, but there are some choice glimpses of Keaton. He plays a rich young drone who's convinced that the woman he loves will spurn him unless he's a wild sport. He studies a manual on "How to Win the Modern Girl," which advises that women prefer daredevils. Striving for decadence in his oriental morning costume, trying and failing to get arrested in a gambling palace, lighting a huge cigar that he can't manage, he makes a most unlikely rake. Now and then, he seems like a forebear of Dustin Hoffman in "The Graduate."

Even though Keaton was only 25 years old when "The Saphead" was made, his genius for impassivity was already flourishing—there's no response when the love-object embraces him, not even when she has twins. The sublime somersaults and the stoicism enhance a hazing scene where men knock one another's hats off on the floor of the Stock Exchange—a refreshing view of that institution.

•

The theme of Keaton's role is solitude — of being alone when someone else should be with him. When his marriage is briefly foiled, he's doused with rice though he's still brideless, and the grains remain on his hair and shoulders as he sits down to eat his wedding feast alone. But where others might have played for pity, Keaton maintains what James Agee called his "mulish imperturbability."

Also on the program are two fine shorts: "Convict 13" (1920) and "The Bellboy" (directed by Roscoe Fatty Arbuckle in 1918). The latter evokes a world of disasters where elevator cables snap, cars and trolleys run through buildings, and a bystander can be hurled into the air and find himself seated on a giant stuffed moosehead upon a hotel wall.

1974 Ag 28, 16:1

The Cast

THE SAPHEAD, directed by Herbert Blache; written and produced by Winchell Smith; based on the play "The New Henrietta" by Mr. Smith and Victor Mapes; produced on Broadway by John Golden; distributed by Raymond Rohauer. At the Elgin Cinema, 171 Eighth Avenue. Running time 68 minutes.

With Buster Keaton, Beula Booker, William H. Crane, Irving Cummings, Edward Alexander.

SAVAGE SISTERS, directed by Eddie Romero; screenplay by H. Franco Moon and Harry Corner; director of cinematography, Justo Paulino; film editor, Isagani V. Pastor; music composed and conducted by Bax; produced by John Ashley and Mr. Romero; released by American International; presented by Cinema Projects International. At the Penthouse Theater, Broadway and 47th Street, and the RKO 86th Street Twin I Theater. Running time: 89 minutes. (This film has been classified R.)

Lynn Jackson ....Gloria Hendry
Jo Turner.....................Cheri Caffaro
Mei Ling ....Rosanna Ortiz
W. P. Billingsley............John Ashley

By NORA SAYRE

It was a bit rum to see "Savage Sisters" on the 54th anniversary of the ratification of the 19th Amendment, which gave women the right to vote. The movie, which is more concerned with the right to fight, opened yesterday at the Penthouse and RKO 86th Street Twin I theaters.

Entangled in a plot of staggering complexity, three women "subversives" — including an American dropout from the Social Register — wage the revolution on a nameless leafy island. The inhabitants of this mango republic appear to be the result of an awesome genetic breakthrough: some seem Oriental, some Latin-American, and others suggest Arabs. Reeling in pursuit of a million dollars that no one wants to share is John Ashley, the coproducer as well as a member of the movie cast. His voice rises frequently to a squawk, and that desperate note sounds like an anticipation of the rushes.

Jail is the place for sexual games, and no woman can wield a rifle unless her shirt's unbuttoned. But the movie's just too silly to be offensive. If forgiveness is the national mood of August, 1974, we might as well extend some to "Savage Sisters."

1974 Ag 29, 23:4

Czech Production Is a Medieval Hodgepodge

Ever wonder who is responsible for the sorry state of the world? Well, the answer is: the Kosliks.

At least, that is, according to "Marketa Lazarova," a Czechoslovak film of epic grasp and butter fingers playing today and tomorrow at noon and midnight at the First Avenue Screening Room.

"Marketa Lazarova" is a colossal—and very nearly interminable—hodgepodge of medieval mayhem and myth, leaden symbolism and bloated piety directed by Frantisek Vlacil and photographed by Bedrich Batka as though they had taken vows to supersede the dictionary as the ultimate source of definition for the word "excess."

•

As for the Kosliks, and the pageant of brutish half-wits who people their retinue, they are a 13th-century Bohemian clan of such unmitigated savagery that next to them the Visigoths would resemble a Red Cross mercy mission.

For a Koslik, nothing is too bad. Robbery, murder, kidnapping, rape and incest are to the list of Koslik baseness what two handkerchiefs, a couple of undershirts and a pair of socks are to a Sears, Roebuck catalogue.

The business of "Marketa Lazarova" originates from the kidnapping of a young German traveler named Christian, who is destined to become a bishop—if the Kosliks do not gut him first. This leads in turn to the kidnapping and rape of the daughter of the Kosliks' smarmy neighbor, Lazar. The daughter, Marketa, as pious as she is beauteous, is headed for the nun's life, until carried off and ravished by one of the Koslik boys, Nikolas, while Christian yields up his virtue to one of the Koslik girls, Alexandra.

The Cast

MARKETA LAZAROVA, directed by Frantisek Vlacil; script by Frantisek Povlicov and Mr. Vlacil; based on the novel by Vladislav Vancura; photography by Bedrich Batka; music by Zdenek Liska; presented by Arnold Jacobs. At the First Avenue Screening Room at 61st Street. Running time: 100 minutes.

Marketa: ....Magda Vasaryova
Kozik ....Josef Kemr
Nikolds..................Frantisk Vickery
Adam ....Ladislaw Povozay
Alexandra.................Pavla Polaskova
Lazar......................Michal Kozuch

•

All this ruttishness to the neglect of fouler deeds so enrages old man Koslik that he forces its addicts to sleep chained on the ground outside his redoubt during the melty season.

The melty season is one of the two seasons during which the action of "Marketa Lazarova" takes place. The other season is the snowy season, and sometimes the seasons change every five minutes.

During the snowy season the camera never misses a chance to show stark figures against the white landscape or the shadow of a horse against the snow. During the melty season, the sun slants through bare branches onto the forest floor. Sometimes it snows during the melty season, mainly when snow will look good on someone's face or hair.

During both seasons, the camera likes to peep at everyone through slats or closing doors, and occasionally it wanders down a corridor in search of a good-looking shadow. Sometimes it goes looking for a symbol. Snakes, hawks and stags are favorites.

Busy though it is, the camera finds time for other things. The High Sheriff mounts a campaign against the Kosliks; nuns sing; a holy man wanders over the landscape accompanied by a lamb until the lamb encounters the Kosliks and is served for dinner. The holy man then acquires a goat, which wanders off while he is attempting to induce Marketa to wander the world with him.

•

Marketa, by this time, is a pregnant widow, her lover having been skewered while attempting to free old man Koslik from prison. With the old man in attendance, the High Sheriff marries Marketa to Nikolas who thereupon keeps a long overdue date with the local headsman. Christian's love, Alexandra, is also pregnant. Christian is also dead, having been rewarded for searching for Alexandra after her father's capture by having her dash his brains out with a handy rock.

A postscript to all this tells us that the children of Marketa and Alexandra were boys, and in them — and in the generations of mankind that followed them—were mixed both love and cruelty.

"Marketa Lazarova" is a lesson to us all.

LAWRENCE VAN GELDER

1974 Ag 30, 19:1

99 AND 44/100% DEAD, directed by John Frankenheimer; produced by Joe Wizan; written by Robert Dillon; director of photography, Ralph Woolsey; film editor, Harold F. Kress; music by Henry Mancini; released by 20th Century-Fox. At the Victoria, Broadway and 46th Street; Liberty 42d Street, UA Academy of Music and West End Theatres. Also in the Bronx, Brooklyn, Queens, Nassau, Suffolk, Westchester, Rockland, upstate New York and New Jersey. Running time: 98 minutes. (This film has been rated PG.)

Harry Crown ....Richard Harris
Uncle Frank ....Edmond O'Brien
Big Eddie ....Bradford Dillman
Buffy ....Ann Turkel
Marvin (the Claw) ....Chuck Connors

A lot of talent has gone into making "99 and 44/100% Dead" the sort of movie that wants to have its cake and eat it, too.

The film, playing on Broadway at the Victoria and at other theaters in and around the city, is directed by John Frankenheimer, boasts a sardonic score by Henry Mancini and has a cast headed by Richard Harris, Edmond O'Brien, Bradford Dillman and Chuck Connors.

On one level it is a shoot-'em-up of comic-strip proportions. Mr. Harris as the granite-visaged Harry Crown and Mr. Connors as Marvin (The Claw) Zuckerman, equipped with an artificial left arm fitted with a hilarious array of implements, play the professional killers who are the champions in a gang war between Mr. O'Brien (Uncle Frank) and Mr. Dillman (Big Eddie).

On this level "99" overflows with corpses in cement pedestals, black-suited, black-hatted henchmen, ambushes, gunplay and wholesale killing, chases and the plentiful trashing of expensive cars, to say almost nothing of the presence of a copious supply of beautiful women, who make handy sex objects and hostages.

On another level, "99" mocks the whole genre, and some of the touches are superb: Marvin's artificial arm, with its shiny scissors, its whip, its feather duster; an excursion through a sewer where those legendary alligators flushed down toilets have grown to full length: an underwater gardens of corpses; a final shoot-out in a laundry, where all the workers go about their business as though nothing extraordinary were happening.

Moviegoers who insist on utter fealty to the demands of the shoot-'em-up are going to be disturbed by the strong undercurrent of irreverence. Those who find the shoot-'em-up immoral in the first place won't be satisfied by the injection of humor as an antidote.

It may not be dumb enough to be the flawless action movie and it may not be sharp enough to be a sparkling spoof, but in a summer when so much witless trash is being dumped on the movie market, "99" merits praise for its ambitiousness more than derision for its shortcomings.

LAWRENCE VAN GELDER

1974 Ag 30, 22:1

Ann Turkel and Richard Harris

What Do They See in 'Death Wish'?

By JUDY KLEMESRUD

"DEATH WISH," a highly controversial film about a respectable upper middle-class New Yorker who turns vigilante after muggers murder his wife and rape his daughter, has become the most discussed and debated film in these parts since "The Exorcist."

Despite its very mixed reviews (6 vehement yes's, 6 mixed and 6 vehement no's from the major New York critics), crowds have flocked to the two Loew's theaters where it is playing, breaking box office records. At the Ciné, at 86th Street and Third Avenue, the first week's gross of $70,359 even topped the previous house record set there by "The Godfather."

There is, of course, talk of a sequel.

The moviegoers, who pay $4 to see "Death Wish," don't just sit there in their seats calmly munching popcorn. They applaud and cheer wildly whenever Charles Bronson, playing a wooden-faced, once liberal-minded architect named Paul Kersey, dispatches a mugger with his trusty .32 pistol. And perhaps one of the reasons that no race riots have broken out in the theaters is that Bronson is no racist: the victims of his mission to rid Manhattan of all muggers

Women applaud the vigilante actions more than men.

are black, white and Puerto Rican.

When I saw the film, on a Sunday night in the Astor Plaza theater in Times Square, a black man sitting alone in front of me led the cheers in my section. "Get the mothers," he frequently

Judy Klemesrud is a staff reporter for The Times.

uttered, with no regard for the muggers' race. It is easy to get caught up in the spirit of things—I found myself applauding several times, too—even though I know that New York would probably turn into a Wild West shoot-'em-up town if private citizens started toting guns and taking the law into their own hands.

"Death Wish" is a particularly violent film, showing in excruciatingly graphic detail Bronson's point-blank shooting of several muggers, both in Riverside Park and on a New York subway train; his beating of another mugger with a sock filled with rolls of coins; the brutal stomping by three young thugs of his wife and the rape of his daughter, who, as a result, becomes psychotic.

The critics who dislike the film have complained that it exploits fear irresponsibly; that it gives an exaggerated picture of crime in New York; that it glorifies vigilantism; that it endorses violence as a solution to violence, and that it was made by out-of-towners with a distorted vision of New York. (The producer, Dino De Laurentiis, is from Italy; the director, Michael Winner, is from England, and the writer, Wendell Mayes, is from the West Coast.)

However, in random interviews I had with people coming out of the two theaters where "Death Wish" is playing, I found it hard to find anyone who was critical of the film. Of the 30 people I talked to, only four objected to the film. The others loved it.

"It's great—this is the second time I've seen it," said George Flynn, a 47-year-old Manhattanite who describes himself as a poet. "It's very entertaining and very lively, and tremendously well done. I don't necessarily agree with the vigilante philosophy, but the movie is so entertaining that I don't bother with the morality."

Several of the moviegoers said they went to see "Death Wish" only because of Charles Bronson, the ugly American who made it big in Europe after flopping in Hollywood. Today, he is said to be the world's highest paid actor. "I go to a movie to see Bronson, and not so much for the story," said Dan Lamantain-Leatherman, 36, of Paris, Calif., who manufactures motion picture equipment. "His movies are pretty much the same, but what I like to watch is how he portrays his character. He's kind of rough and rugged, an individualist. He does things *his* way."

The crowds at both theaters were a mixture of well-dressed older people and casually dressed youths. The number of moviegoers over 40 seemed to be higher than is usual these days. Whites outnumbered blacks greatly at both theaters, with more blacks and working class people at the Astor Plaza theater.

"I think it's lovely, a very *comfortable* picture," said Anne Mitchell, a white-haired 62-year-old secretary from Queens, who saw the movie alone. "I like Charles Bronson. I don't approve of killing, but at least the people he killed were not good people. I'm glad the police let him go at the end."

Two couples who walked out of the Astor Plaza theater at the same time had widely differing opinions of the film. "Not at any time was it racist," said Lorenzo Powell, a black 23-year-old teacher's assistant from Brooklyn. His date, also black, Gail Gordon, 23, of Brooklyn, agreed.

*

Behind them, Joseph Delon, 30, of Brooklyn, an Oriental who described his occupation as "bum," shouted so people entering the theater could hear: "This is the worst picture I've ever seen in my life. A white man can get away with anything in America. I've never seen so much racism in a movie —six blacks get killed for every white."

His 30-year-old black wife, Vonnie, who was carrying their month-old daughter, Nia, added, "This picture stinks. I wish we had our $8 back."

Joe Brennan, a 20-year-old security guard at Macy's objected to "Death Wish" on the grounds that its plot was not credible. "I think it's untrue of the New York I know," the Brooklyn native said. "I realize movies have the poetic license to exaggerate, but they stretched it a bit. I never come across those situations in the New York I know."

"Technically tacky," was the verdict of a curly-haired, 23-year-old film student at the University of Southern California, who was spending the summer in New York. He added, "If it weren't for the fact that it exploits peoples' fears of mugging, it would stand only half a chance as a 'B' movie on the drive-in circuit."

Many, but not all, of the women interviewed defended Bronson's vigilante actions more than the men did. One reason, perhaps, is that the scene in which Bronson's wife is murdered and his daughter raped is one of the most bloody and violent of its kind ever to appear on film.

"I think what Bronson did is right— no one else is doing *anything*," said Mrs. Dorothy Weiss, 30, of Brooklyn, who was eight months' pregnant. "Our system just isn't working today. So you've got to protect your own self."

Mrs. Karen Lieberman, a 26-year-old dancer who has been mugged four times in Manhattan, said: "I can certainly go along with the Bronson character's reaction to the whole thing. If I were the kind of person to carry a gun, I might do the same thing—out of protection.

"But I don't walk around spooked out at the city," she added. "I'll never leave this city, even after the four incidents. My parents live in Oklahoma City, and out there they mug people from cars, rather than on the streets."

Her husband, Ira, a 28-year-old chiropractor, said he thought everyone should see "Death Wish" in order to have his consciousness raised. "We should all know what's going on around us," he said.

Several moviegoers said they thought that crime in the city would decrease— in "Death Wish" the number of weekly muggings falls from 950 to 470 after

Bronson starts his rampage—if people started taking the law into their own hands.

"If we had more people like Bronson, we would have less crime," said Al Heidler, 43, a stocky blond advertising salesman. "I would like to do something like Bronson, but I don't see how I would get away with it."

William Maisto, manager of the Astor Plaza theater, said he had heard many of the moviegoers talking about buying guns as they left the theater. "It's mostly said in jest—I think," he added.

Does this mean, then, that "Death Wish" is going to inspire people to pick up guns and take the law into their own hands? Will criminals become fair game in this city? Even before "Death Wish" came out, examples of vigilantism were making headlines all over the city: "Four Men Attack and Knife an Alleged Rapist"..."Store Owner Chases and Kills Hold-Up Man"..."Passersby Chase and Capture Purse Snatcher."

Three mental health professionals I talked to were not terribly worried about the film's possible effects. "This kind of movie plays out the fantasy of getting even," said Dr. Harvey Schlossberg, director of psychological services for the New York City Police Department. "It's not dangerous; it's the kind of thing people cheer when the bad guy gets his come-uppance. It's a fantasy release, something we all want to do. For most people, it's the equivalent of a very satisfying dream."

He added, however, that the movie might give "really disturbed people" an idea that they didn't have before. "But this is a really slim possibility," he said.

Dr. James A. Brussel, a Manhattan psychiatrist who carries a licensed .32 revolver, "even when I go to the bathroom," said he thought that "Death Wish" would not arouse any psychotic drives or obsessions to kill.

Dr. Brussel, who in the past has been a consultant to various law enforcement agencies, including the F.B.I., said

he thought private citizens should be allowed to carry guns under two conditions: That they were "reputable citizens with normal mentality," and that they knew "how to use the damn things."

Dr. Edwin H. Church, a Manhattan psychiatrist, said he had never had a patient who had been affected by what he or she saw in the movies or on television, "although I wondered what would happen with 'The Exorcist.'

"No, I don't think there's anything to worry about," he said. "But if you had a mind that's in a delicate balance, 'Death Wish' could tip it a bit. The thing is, we just don't know enough yet about the media's effect on individuals."

Both the producer and the star of "Death Wish," besides being ecstatic over the box-office receipts and the film's general acceptance, had a few things to say about the controversy surrounding "Death Wish."

Producer De Laurentiis, who was vacationing in Monte Carlo, said through a spokesman that with "Death Wish," he wanted to offer a message and that he believes he has reached his objective. "The film addresses all law enforcement agencies and lawmakers, and slaps them in the face with the reality of violence in the streets," he said.

"In no way is the film an invitation to take to the streets with a gun," he added. "But it is an invitation—an open invitation to the authorities to come up with remedies to the problem of urban

violence, and fast. I do not want people to become Paul Kerseys. I want the proper authorities to take care of the problem."

When asked if he thought that New York was really as much of a jungle as it is portrayed in "Death Wish," he said, "Violence is not typical of New York alone. Singapore, Amsterdam, Tokyo, Detroit, London, Chicago, Paris and Rome are all plagued by the same problem. All big cities are jungles. New York is the symbol of all the metropolitan areas of our planet."

De Laurentiis refused to confirm rumors that a sequel was in the offing, saying, "Personally, I dislike sequels. I always prefer to turn to new areas. But the fact that you ask the question reinforces the feeling that I should consider a sequel . . ."

Bronson, who was making a movie called "Breakout" in California, said through a spokesman that he felt no personal identification with the character of Paul Kersey, and that he himself believed in the law.

The 53-year-old actor added, however, that if someone in his family were mugged, he would "probably start out looking for the one directly responsible."

As to critics' charges that "Death Wish" exploits fear irresponsibly, Bronson, whose films have never been too highly praised in America, said: "We don't make movies for critics, since they don't pay to see them anyhow."

1974 S 1, II:1:5

In 'Death Wish' middle-class architect Charles Bronson turns vigilante and slays a series of muggers. Although the film got mixed reviews, it's drawing crowds to local theaters.

NEW FILMS FOCUS ON CALIFORNIA AND CALIFORNIANS

By NORA SAYRE

JUST when Hollywood has been releasing the sludge of the season —namely, dumb action pictures for the drive-in trade—it's cheering to celebrate two very American pictures: Robert Altman's "California Split" and Roman Polanski's "Chinatown." California itself is a leading character in both films, complete with all its craziness, its contradictions, the charms and brutalizing fantasies. (As a New Yorker, I return from every visit to California convinced that Manhattan is the most peaceful and rational of communities.) In their utterly different ways, both Altman and Polanski evoke the state where I once heard a dashboard radio triumphantly announcing nationwide car crashes as though they were football scores: "Massachusetts—12; New York —17; and California is *still leading* with 24 road deaths!"

Altman's California emerges through its citizens; indeed, this director has a marvelous sense of all kinds of Americans—particularly those with fragmented lives. (Though his movies differ deeply from one another, you can see the kinship among the rebel spirits and nomads in "M*A*S*H" and "The Long Goodbye" and "Thieves Like Us." His Californians are revealed especially through what strangers say to one another in public: the man who reasonably admonishes, "Lady, you don't throw oranges on an escalator;" the hostile woman in a bar who complains to the air about her dog fouling the floor; the bus-rider who worries that the passenger next to him may throw up; the doctor who's so addicted to cards that it's observed that "he'd rather lose a patient than a hand." And then there are the glimpses of random natives: the bulky young man in a mauve undershirt with a flower floating on his paunch, the infinite old women playing poker, and two dulcet prostitutes, one of whom is always searching for her TV Guide.

George Segal, as a taut depressive who can also relish his moments of pleasure, and Elliott Gould, as a cosy clown with a vein of malice, are both at their best as two fanatical gamblers who'll bet on anything from craps to horses. (Now we can forget that Segal was corny and clumsy in "A Touch of Class" and "Blume In Love" and that Gould was downright mongoloid in "SPYS.") While gambling, Segal has a way of sucking his teeth behind closed lips which distills immense anxiety. His drawn and chalky face can suddenly age 10 years when things go wrong— and then shed that decade just as swiftly. Sometimes, the pugnacious thrust of his chin disguises a genial nature. Gould is the jester who can lighten Segal's angst. Chewing imaginary gum or sucking a real toothpick, he appears as a bright person playing dumb.

Gould's casual loopiness both exasperates and beguiles Segal. And, while we've seen infinite movies about boyish bonding in the last year, this picture is really concerned with friendship —

Nora Sayre is a movie critic for The Times and the author of "Sixties Going on Seventies."

in a way that's rare on screen. When Segal and Gould first meet in a poker club, a paranoid wrongly accuses them of working together. Yet their accuser was prophetic, since they were destined to become partners. Much of the time, Segal comes on as an adolescent, while Gould is a huge child. But Gould becomes a soothing parent-figure when Segal tenses up before playing a big game. After Segal wins abundantly, dejection sets in—he's one of those people who has trouble with success, who can suspect that good fortune means bad luck. The exultant Gould asks, "You always take a big win this hard?"

At moments, they're rather flirtatious —as though Altman were experimenting with a metaphor for friendship. Some years ago, I heard a kindly man sneer at the relationship between Jake Barnes and Bill Gorton in "The Sun Also Rises." He said that the fishing sequence was unrealistic, sentimental, and added that most men wouldn't want to show affection—even so indirectly—in private. Today, the attachment between characters like the ones played by Segal and Gould needn't be inhibited—because others no longer assume that demonstrative behavior between men means that they're homosexual. But few filmmakers have actually explored such sympathies as yet.

Like "M*A*S*H," "California Split" moves at such speed that you couldn't follow it if you were stoned—as some of my neighbors in the theater were. In Altman's world, things happen suddenly: milk overwhelms a bowl of Froot Loops just as rapidly as strangers attack one another in parking lots. As in most of Altman's other films, voices overlap on the soundtrack: words are deliberately sacrificed to the mood, and peo-

ple's preoccupations are emphasized instead of their utterances.

Gambling may be the theme of "California Split," but the individuals run away with the movie. Segal and Gould are comic versions of the wanderers— often failures—whom you constantly meet in California, the stragglers who swarm through motels and drive-ins and Pizzaburgers. Meanwhile the Boom State withholds its promise from them, and references to the Gold Rush seem like the reverberations of a real estate flack's lies.

There are no friendships in "Chinatown." Yet this movie also dwells on loyalties: detective Jack Nicholson's loyalty to the truth, to finding facts, to learning what simply happened — and his belated loyalty to Faye Dunaway, the widow whom he finally comes to respect, once he knows that she didn't kill her husband.

Polanski's 1930's California is characterized through its landscape—rather than its inhabitants. In this thriller concerning the manipulation of property rights, the stress is on the crimes that some will commit in order to control the land, to make it yield the promises of the early days, when the West seemed to guarantee riches. Throughout, there's the dramatic use of water; as it gushes over the screen, we learn that that lucid stuff is a political weapon, worth a murder or two.

Elliott Gould had a bandaged nose in "California Split," rather like the one that Polanski has given Jack Nicholson. There, the parallel ends. "Chinatown" is about cover-ups—not merely of noses —but of corrupt politics, crooked real estate, smears, the harassment of enemies, and other familiarities. Nothing is what it seems—not even for the

moviegoer. At first, we don't realize that either Nicholson or Dunaway is a likable (or even decent) person. He appears tough, sarcastic—just a hack doing a routine job—and she seems snotty and guilty: her nervous reflexes and fishy tales help to harden the case against her. (Later, both prove to be quite admirable —in a flawed way which makes them touching.) Dunaway's late husband seemed to be a cheater—but he wasn't. John Huston (the villain) is rather childlike, benign. Layers of deception mount, until Nicholson's reminded of his stint as a cop in Los Angeles' Chinatown, where it was hard to "tell what's going on." In two different scenes, dull sunlight falls in bars through venetian blinds, and that striped light and shadow seems like an image for obscurity.

*

Risking his skin near reservoirs, in orange groves, beaten up for his tenacity as an investigator, the detective realizes that he doesn't even know what he was hired for. (You can't help thinking of several of the original Watergate burglars —Barker, Sturgis, Gonzalez and Martinez—and how little they knew about the basis of their errand.) Nicholson's wonderfully supple and subtle performance evokes a man who feels confident enough to make some hideous mistakes—to be trapped into doing the opposite of what he wanted to.

To begin with, Faye Dunaway's accent was puzzling: the broad a's, an inflection that sounded German or Scandinavian. Then it became clear that someone (probably Polanski) had been thinking of Dietrich and Garbo. Not just the shaved eyebrows or

Elliott Gould and George Segal, two gung-ho gamblers, place their bets in "California Split." As in "Chinatown," California itself is a major character.

Did Polanski have Garbo in mind when he directed Dunaway?

the manner of smoking—when Dunaway bends forward to light a cigarette from a candle, that's Dietrich. But there's a tinge of insolence, a style of smouldering, that recalls both actresses. She strives for the dignity that Garbo had under fire—and doesn't quite make it. But the character does develop from an apparent luxury item to a brave and resourceful victim.

*

Nothing's what it seems—except, perhaps, Polanski himself: self-cast as the gleeful little sadist who slits Nicholson's nostril. He makes the blood stream—as he did in his "Macbeth." Maybe more of his post-Manson movies will be irrigated by Polanski's revenge: certainly, the climax of "Chinatown" is punishing for the public.

I can easily agree with those who object to the ending of the movie. We've now heard that the Dunaway character was allowed to escape in Robert Towne's original script. And a mass audience which mainly expects entertainment from a movie of this kind may be especially unprepared for the profoundly pessimistic conclusion: that the detective was wrong to chase after truth or justice, that effort and commitment are pointless, that it's best to do nothing. The movie states that tragedy can occur simply because facts are often elusive, and that it can be fatal to function in the dark. It's not a viewpoint that you'd want to hang on your wall. But it is, after all, part of this director's vision.

1974 S 1, II:9:1

THE BLACK GODFATHER, directed and produced by John Evans; written by Mr. Evans; music, Martin Yarbrough; a Cougnar Production; distributed by Cinemation Industries. At neighborhood theaters. Running time: 97 minutes. This film has been classified R. With: Rod Perry, Damu King, Don Chastain, Diane Sommerfield and Jimmy Witherspoon.

By NORA SAYRE

There's been a lull in the field of black exploitation movies, but "The Black Godfather" reverts to the formula that some black leaders criticized a few years ago. The movie opened yesterday at neighborhood theaters.

A clever young operator (Rod Perry) gains control of all the organized crime in his neighborhood — except narcotics. Determined to drive a powerful white drug dealer off the turf, Mr. Perry and his gang unleash a lot of bullets along with such pious statements as "The essence of our struggle is independence," and "Money buys dignity—power is a crime," or "We're sick and tired of being exploited." Compliments are exchanged among the gunmen for "protecting the brothers on the street" (by

killing white pushers), and someone even says "Power to the people."

The black and white hoods ice each other with unflagging enthusiasm; the whites are the most sadistic, though the blacks do enjoy the enemy's humiliation. The movie drags because so much of the action requires the characters to take messages to and from one another. The performances aren't too bad, but the karate is negligible.

1974 S 4, 52:1

'Murdered House' Has Grisly Inhabitants

By NORA SAYRE

If you have a soft spot for ruined grandeur, for romantic decay, you'll be captivated by the opening shots of "The Murdered House," a Brazilian movie that is playing today and tomorrow at the First Avenue Screening Room. The picture focuses on an elegant family ravaged with debts; their mansion is falling to pieces—and so (on a grand scale) are they.

•

The movie, which is intensely operatic, begins well; two members of this oppressive tribe detest the entire clan and are eager to humiliate it. One is a defiant transvestite, who says that he's possessed by the soul of his dead aunt, and the other is the beautiful, restless wife of one of the glum sons. (Norma Bengell—who bears a stunning resemblance to Jeanne Moreau — brings strength and subtlety to a complex part.) Although the Brazilian director, Paulo Cesar Saraceni, has studied with Bernardo Bertolucci and Marco Bellochio, his extravagent personas seems more akin to those of Federico Fellini.

About halfway through the movie—after a botched suicide and a successful one—the narrative suddenly jumps 17 years and becomes thoroughly confusing. The characters haven't aged at all (although some of them have grown quite crazy). There's some incest afoot, but—due to the fact that a baby or two were born off camera—it's terribly hard to tell which mother is making out with whose son, and who did or didn't sleep with the gardener.

However, the most impassioned couple hits the sack in such a public spot that their relatives needn't miss a single motion. (Despite the lack of privacy, this scene is extraordinarily erotic.) But much of the acting declines into gusts of bitter laughter and stagey declamations, as hatred becomes the motivation for almost everything. Two characters rend their

The Cast
THE MURDERED HOUSE (A Casa Assasinada), directed by Paulo Cesar Saraceni; script (Brazilian with English subtitles) by Mr. Saraceni, based on the novel by Lucio Cardoso; produced by Sergio Saraceni; music, Antonio Carlos Jobim; photography, Mario Carneiro; distributed by Creative Film Services. At the First Avenue Screening Room, at 61st Street. Running time: 100 minutes. At noon and midnight.
With: Norma Bengell, Tete Medina, Carlos Kroeber, Nelson Dantas.

clothes in rapid succession, a corpse gets its face slapped—finally, we're in a realm beyond tragedy or lunacy, and the emotions have become too exotic to follow.

The photography is magnificent throughout: the browns, blacks, and whites of the landscape simmer in contrast to the lush green gardens, and there's a daring shot of a lifeless body that recalls Mantegna's foreshortned view of the dead Christ. Although the movie doesn't fulfill the promise of its first scenes, let's hope that more of Mr. Saraceni's films are shown in this country.

1974 S 6, 22:3

'A Face in the Crowd' Speaks of Watergate

By NORA SAYRE

BEFORE we all drown in post-Watergate euphoria, there should be a widespread revival of "A Face in the Crowd," which was written by Budd Schulberg, directed by Elia Kazan, and released in 1957. (It was shown recently at the annual Filmmakers of the Hamptons Festival.) The movie focuses on a guitar-punishing primitive (Andy Griffith), who's first discovered in an Arkansas jail by Patricia Neal, a venturesome Sarah Lawrence graduate. She puts him on a local radio station, and is then sucked into his career—as a media monster known as Lonesome Rhodes.

Initially, the country slicker does have a gift for touching a public nerve. As he spiels away to his listeners, he beguiles exhausted housewives with sympathy for their tasks—"cleanin' the grease outa the sink. Or wipin' outa the oven the beef gravy or the apple juice that sizzles over the side of the dish onto yer grill." The mixture of outrageous corn and charm fuels his rapid success. Winsomely insisting that he's "just a country boy," this hulk becomes a television star and acquires prodigious force in advertising. Even when he spoofs the commercials, the sales for the products jump. Meanwhile, his character alters: oozing with sham sincerity, he comes to share the values that he once ridiculed.

Soon, he's coaching politicians on how to sell themselves on television; he points out that people don't buy products which they "respect"—instead a politician must be "loved." Even pets can enhance a Presidential image: "One pitch with a hound is worth ten thousand words. That mutt didn't do Roos-e-velt any harm, did it? Or Dick Nixon either." No longer a mere entertainer, this folksy fraud gathers political momentum until he chortles with the expectation of being "the power behind the President."

Then—at the end of a television program, when he thinks he's off the air—he abuses the audience, calling them "trained seals": "I toss 'em a dead fish and they flap their flippers." Climaxing with "Good night you stupid idiots. Good night you miserable slobs," he's destroyed by the nationwide exposure

Nora Sayre is a movie critic for The Times and the author of "Sixties Going on Seventies."

of his own hypocrisy—in fact, by the medium which made him. And if the scenario sounds familiar, remember that it's over 17 years old.

Along with the theme of conformity (a valid obsession of the 1950's), the stress is on manipulation and mind control. From the comic passages — in which some useless pills are packaged to sound like a marvelous aphrodisiac—to the queasier moments, when a Senator packaged by Rhodes decries Social Security as "coddling—from the cradle to the grave," the potentialities of advertising and television were explored to a degree that was prophetic. And, though the movie had good reviews in 1957, a few thought its viewpoint exaggerated. No one would say that now.

Throughout this acutely American picture, Elia Kazan drew the best out of the cast. From the first shot of Andy Griffith being kicked in the ribs on the jailhouse floor while his hands strangle the air, to the final scene where his shadow rages over a white table cloth as he screams from a balcony to his lost audience, the actor made a stunning screen debut. The volcanic energies of the character, the gut-spilling laugh that makes his body jack-knife forward, the pious intensity with which he exclaims "Moly Hoses!," the gleeful slobbishness—all convey the monomaniac who ruins himself. There are a couple of details that recall Marlon Brando in Mr. Kazan's "Streetcar"—the hefty sweating torso in the worn undershirt, or Lonesome yelling "Marcia!" to Patricia Neal at the pitch in which Stanley Kowalski cried "Stella!" — but Andy Griffith isn't derivative. We're merely aware that the two had the same director.

Patricia Neal's sensitivity builds throughout her performance, as she loses her early confidence and spunk while growing more vulnerable to the ogre she helped to create. Few actresses can show uncertainty or worry or confusion as subtly as she does. (Today, due to the new consciousness, her role seems extraordinarily masochistic —undoubtedly more so than was intended at the time.) Walter Matthau, as a disgruntled writer whom Lonesome derides for his college degree (Vanderbilt, '44), and Anthony Franciosa—all teeth and glitter as Lonesome's agent—are also exhilarating. And Lee Remick (in her first movie part) as a high school drum majorette, excels at mindless smiles and laughter.

After the movie was screened in East Hampton, Budd Schulberg described how he and Elia Kazan prepared for the movie, which had developed out of his novel, "Arkansas Traveller." In the summer of 1955, they saturated themselves in Madison Avenue, attending meetings and studying the art of "playing a magnificent organ of lies." Then they went to Washington and questioned politicians (including Lyndon Johnson and Stuart Symington) about the use of television—at a time when the general public hadn't given the subject much thought. But the candidates "were already thinking a lot about it. A typical remark was: 'You've got to watch yourself, keep your eyes steady—don't shift your eyes or they'll say you're shifty.'"

In 1956, Mr. Kazan wrote in his introduction to the published screenplay of "Face," "We talked of how much more powerful Huey Long would have been if he had had television at his disposal. We

talked about the famous Nixon broadcast, when the question of his financial backers turned somehow into a defense of his children's dog."

Mr. Schulberg explained that they were also particularly concerned with Joseph McCarthy: "The fact that he'd used television to destroy people—and finally it destroyed him. He forgot that when he and Roy Cohn were whispering behind their hands, they were being watched by the entire country, and they looked like another kind of conspiracy—and that was going to finish them."

The East Hampton audience asked him to discuss Watergate parallels—which of course are irresistible. Mr. Schulberg referred to "Nixon saying that he wanted a thorough investigation of the truth. And every time he would announce a new truth, it became so contradictory that all but the die-hards came to feel that he was lying in his teeth." Back in the fifties, a primary interest of both writer and director was

"television as a way of *exposing* evil—of turning the guns around the other way."

Although Lonesome Rhodes may seem like a redneck relative of Mr. Schulberg's Sammy Glick in "What Makes Sammy Run?," the writer said that the specific character drew on traits of Will Rogers, Walter Winchell, Arthur Godfrey, and Don Carney (radio's "Uncle Don")—as well as Huey Long. Will Rogers, the entertainer who began by "swinging his lasso and philosophizing at the same time" became very influential politically. Mr. Schulberg, who went to school with Rogers' son, was struck even in childhood by the contrast between public and private: "the Oklahoma cowboy and the rich man in his mansion whose friends were bankers and powerful politicians. He was a conservative in the guise of a [deleted] kicking populist—a familiar type. He would oppose recognizing the Soviet

voice.") He also kidded the commercials he had to deliver. Uncle Don, whose cloying childrens' program was a seething success, was called "a saint, an oracle, and a pal" to infinite children by "Radio Guide" in 1931. It was widely believed that — after caroling "Good night, little friends, good night!" —he once concluded a broadcast with "I guess that'll hold the little bastards." That legend has been disputed. At any rate, it was fodder for the plot of "A Face in the Crowd." Moreover, Lonesome shows an occasional kinship with Elvis Presley, although the latter wasn't a direct influence.

Lonesome sneers at education — as personified by Patricia Neal and Walter Matthau. Reflecting on the contemporary qualities of his character — with some references to George Wallace and to populism—Mr. Schulberg remarked, "We still like to think of ourselves as woodsy. . . . It's so easy to attack students or professors — because you mustn't be too intelligent or too far ahead of the mass. Other societies have tried to raise the intelligence of the public—but we seem to be afraid of it, more comfortable with a figure like Dwight Eisenhower.Even Rocky plays down instead of up — 'Hi, fella' — pretending to be the common man. We think we're going to stay with the poor-but-honest—but what we wind up with are the John Waynes of this world."

Still, he spoke of the post-Watergate, Bicentennial period as an opportunity for reassessment — "and I hope we won't recover from Watergate too lightly, forget it easily." He added cheerfully that "finally, with a bit of luck, television seems to be able to catch up with the tyrants"—as it did with Lonesome Rhodes.

1974 S 8, II:1:5

Andy Griffith, a folksy fraud, dreams of controlling the President in the 1957 film "A Face in the Crowd." Maybe we should see it again, says a critic.

This movie about a TV star with political ambitions was thought to be exaggerated in 1957. No one would say that now.

Union, or state his faith in self-sufficiency at the time when the New Deal public works policies seemed necessary to pull us out of a depression."

Mr. Schulberg added that Rogers "wasn't as ominous as Lonesome Rhodes. But there were elements of the same kind of deception—talking the language of the little people while sharing the life of the big people. Nixon did that just the other day: when he was talking about the poverty of his parents, and forgetting that what he really relates to are multimillionaires."

Walter Winchell, whose column and radio show thrived in the thirties, forties and early fifties, was also a model for Lonesome: "If Winchell touted a stock, it could go way up—if he knocked it, it went down. Finally, he was able to affect the economy and political careers. He could do it with just a question like: 'What's going on at General Electric? Huh?' Then the three dots . . . He didn't have to say anything—people would think: he must know something. Sometimes he wouldn't even name the company—he'd say, 'A certain firm with a Detroit post-office box is wondering whether to kick their president upstairs or downstairs.' He was interesting in terms of politics: in the thirties and during the war, he was pro-Roosevelt, ardently New Deal. After the war, he became a Roosevelt-hater."

Arthur Godfrey, who made unknowns into stars or turned books into best sellers by pushing them on the air, contributed some of the folksiness of Lonesome Rhodes. (Fred Allen once called Godfrey "the man with the barefoot

New 'Jewish Films'

By DAN ISAAC

IN coming months millions of Americans will be laughing with— and possibly at—Jews. That is, if they go to the movies and see "The Mad Adventures of 'Rabbi' Jacob" and "The Apprenticeship of Duddy Kravitz." But one's reaction will be quite different should he chance to see another new film, Susan Sontag's "Promised Lands," dealing as it does with the political problems confronting the state of Israel.

This then seems an ideal time to explore some of the problems involved in putting the Jewish experience on film. A mythic people and a mythic medium. Thousands of years. Larger than life. The complexity and variety of that experience—involving the evolution of a religious tradition in a multitude of countries and cultures—is reflected in

Dan Isaac is a rabbi and the film archivist for the Jewish Museum.

these three current "Jewish films": a wild farce, an occasionally comic melodrama, and a very sober documentary.

Let us begin with what are perhaps the funniest moments in "Duddy Kravitz" and "Rabbi Jacob." And let us also ask if it is only a coincidence that the high point of hilarity in each film involves a bar mitzvah scene.

In "Duddy Kravitz," which tells the story of a young Canadian Jew on the make, satire is accomplished with a film within a film, a documentary of a boy's bar mitzvah that the ever-hustling Duddy hopes to sell for $2,000 to the boy's father, the richest Jewish junk dealer in Montreal. But to make the film, Duddy Kravitz has had to hire a black-listed director whose interest in the boy and his father is minimal. His chief aim is to create a documentary of Jewish rituals that will reveal primitive tribal rites and the racial unconscious.

*

The resulting film-within-a-film is an anthropological work in the underground tradition, a film so super-serious that the boy's parents and relatives and the rabbi sit in open-mouthed astonishment as it unreels in a screening room. The poor little boy enters the synagogue looking like a lamb being led to slaughter. The background music sets the tone with the opening notes of Beethoven's Fifth Symphony, quickly followed by a solemn voice-over narrative reminiscent of the March of Time newsreels of the thirties and forties: "Older than the banks of the Nile; not so cruel as the circumcision rites of the Zulu. This is a story of one Hebrew babe and how he was accepted by his tribe."

Then comes the visual signature of the underground film, the fast montage —including intercuts of bloody circumcision rites, Zulu tribesmen dancing, and Hitler's marching hordes. When the last ludicrous image fades away and the lights go up in the screening room, we get the final joke of this scene: a desperate silence prevails, and the boy's parents look nervously to the rabbi for the definitive word on this dubious documentary. When the rabbi declares the film a work of art, the family applauds and insists on seeing "Bernie's Bar Mitzvah" again.

The bar mitzvah scene in "The Mad Adventures of 'Rabbi' Jacob" employs less sophistication but more slapstick. In one of the most complicated mistaken-identity chase plots in the history of filmic farce, Louis De Funes plays the part of an anti-semitic businessman who has somehow fallen into the middle of a gang war between two groups of terrorist revolutionaries. In his effort to escape, De Funes disguises himself as a Hasidic rabbi and is promptly picked up at Orly airport by a Parisian Jewish family expecting Rabbi Jacob from America. Rushed off to the Jewish community, where his arrival has been awaited with the fervor usually reserved for the coming of the messiah, Rabbi Jacob is to be the honored guest at a bar mitzvah. Mugging and genuflecting his way through the Jewish service, the bigot pretending to be a holy rabbi can do not wrong in the eyes of the adoring congregation.

All very funny. Yet one cannot help

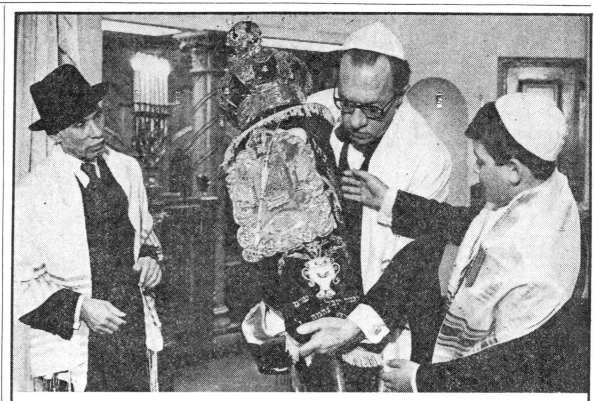

"Is it only a coincidence that the high point of hilarity in both 'The Apprenticeship of Duddy Kravitz,' above, and 'The Mad Adventures of Rabbi Jacob,' below, involves a bar mitzvah scene?" asks a rabbi.

but suspect that the bar mitzvah has been seized upon, not merely because it is a relatively well-known and therefore recognizable Jewish ritual, but because the creators of these films believed that in the bar mitzvah ceremony Jews were somehow vulnerable, perhaps even laughable. This suspicion prompts a further inquiry into these films.

"The Mad Adventures of 'Rabbi' Jacob" is relatively easy to analyze. The action is placed in a crazy world of intrigue where not only capitalists and police carry on secret wars with underground revolutionaries, but revolutionaries with other revolutionaries. In such a mad world, says this frantic French farce, the sanest policy for self-preser-

vation is to go in Jewish drag looking like a Hasidic rabbi, payos flapping in the breeze. In such an absurd world, Jewishness, like everything else, is equally absurd. A naive fantasy? Perhaps. But this film is filled with naive fantasies, ending as it does with a wedding that unites the daughter of a capitalist factory owner with a political revolutionary who has just been named President of an Arab nation.

The film seems more revealing, however, when the real Rabbi Jacob stands on a street corner in his old Parisian neighborhood and wistfully observes that nothing has changed in 30 years. Just as the benevolent rabbi finishes uttering this sentiment, a sack is thrown over his head and he is dragged away. Why is this so funny? Because the rabbi suddenly becomes the classic fool, too simple to realize that if nothing has truly changed in Europe in 30 years, a Jew would still be subject to persecution and abduction. That is indeed the fate he suffers, but not because of the correctness of his observation that nothing has changed; it is rather because of a farcical case of mistaken identity. And that inspires laughter.

But we know, thirty years after Hitler, everything *has* changed. The Jew has become a mythic symbol for ethnic survival—and at the same time, a politically engaged figure crucially concerned with the survival of the state of Israel. "The Mad Adventures of 'Rabbi Jacob'" chooses to de-politicize the Jew and see him simply as a holy man who is innocent and good and uninvolved in larger conflicts. The film itself wants merely to play with political and ideological problems, supplying simplistic happy answers. Which, after all, may be one of the therapeutic functions of comedy: the creation of mock anxiety which dissolves in bliss with the traditional happy ending. In the interest of farce, "The Mad Adventures of 'Rabbi Jacob'" trivializes the controversial and holy significance of the Jew. Of course, the insane madcap world of this film trivializes everything else, too.

"The Apprenticeship of Duddy Kravitz" is a more complicated case. We laugh with Duddy Kravitz when he is able to sell the bar mitzvah "documentary," because Duddy is a scrappy kid from an impoverished family putting one over on his *nouveau riche* brethren. But when Duddy asks his epileptic friend Virgil to drive a truck—an unscrupulous request which results in an accident that leaves Virgil permanently paralyzed from the waist down—and then forges Virgil's name to a check in order to close a deal for the purchase of land, our plucky hero becomes a despicable character.

Now that we have "The Apprenticeship of Duddy Kravitz," we can forget about "The Merchant of Venice." Indeed, the film itself links Duddy with Shylock. For it is Duddy's movie-director friend—played with just the right edge of drunken aloofness by Denholm Elliott—who asks the wheeling-and-dealing Duddy at one point if he has come for his pound of flesh.

✳

Mordecai Richler, the author of both the book and the screenplay, must have been very sensitive to the possibility of complaints about such an unflattering portrait of a young Jewish boy hustling and conniving for monetary success and recognition. For Richler plants speeches in the mouths of other Jewish characters repudiating the behavior of Duddy

Kravitz. Early in the film, at a Jewish resort, one of his fellow waiters says: "It's little money-grubbers like Kravitz that cause anti-Semitism."

And Duddy's Uncle Benjy, on his death bed, tells Duddy that he is nothing more than "a little Jew boy on the make." The movie seems to be straining to say: "Make no mistake about it! We do not condone the behavior of Duddy Kravitz. Nor do we submit that he is representative of Jews in general."

✳

At least that is what the movie says out of one side of its mouth. From the other side, it seems to be making devastating revelations about its central character whom many will regard as a generic.

The other members of Duddy's family and circle of friends with whom we become acquainted do little to alter this highly negative perception. Duddy's father, Max, is a garrulous, loving hard-nosed taxi driver who does a little pimping on the side. A great story-teller who can command the attention of his aging peer group in any bar or restaurant, Max continually sings the praises of the Boy Wonder, a pushy neighborhood kid who parlayed used streetcar transfers into a fortune. The Boy Wonder: a magic name, a mythic hero for emulation. In the middle of the film Duddy finally meets the Boy Wonder and discovers him to be a fat, balding, crippled gangster who uses Duddy to smuggle dope across the border into New York.

The one person in the film possessing even a hint of religious piety is Duddy's bearded grandfather, whose only words of advice to his grandson are, "A man without land is nobody." Duddy takes these words so seriously that when the one woman of his life shows him a secret lake nestled in wooded hills, Duddy doesn't want to swim in it—he wants to buy it.

Duddy's warped sense of morality is most tellingly revealed in his treatment of Virgil, a sweet epileptic kid who happens to have money. And the most crucial scene in the whole movie—crucial to those concerned with moral values—takes place in a Turkish bath. It is Farber the junk dealer who takes Duddy there and tells him that he must get his friend Virgil to sign a release that will remove Duddy from liability for the accident. Farber argues that when you come to this new world with only two cents in your pocket, you have to lie and cheat. This tough-as-nails junk dealer relates in his deep gravel voice how he let his own partner be sent to jail rather than shoulder his own responsibility for the death of a worker in his yard. "It's war, Duddy, it's war. If you want to be a saint, go to Israel and plant orange trees." Coming from one of the most lovable characters in the film, this message is chilling in its ruthless pragmatism—a grim vision of the world in

terms of "them" and "us."

For those who want to grow orange trees in Israel, Susan Sontag's "Promised Lands" is required viewing. It will both enlighten and disillusion.

Esthetically, the film is a masterpiece of visual argument; yet many critics have rejected it precisely because it has a point of view. And, surprisingly, a point of view that is neither New Left nor Zionistic. Using Israeli novelist Yoram Kaniuk as a spokesman, the film looks at things through the eyes of the alienated Israeli intellectual. Miss Sontag brilliantly juxtaposes a cross on the dome of a church with the intricate criss-crossings of TV aerials —a striking symbol of the conflict between the ancient and the modern. Two street signs, one reading "Street of Prophets" and the other "Street of Paratroopers," capture all the pain and ambiguity of modern Israel with a single shot.

"Promised Lands" is most powerfully about the competing claims of two people for the same slice of land. "Jews have never understood tragedy," says Yoram Kaniuk in a long interview. "The Arabs are right and we are right. The Palestinian Arabs are the brightest and smartest among the Arab people. They deserve more than a piece of land no bigger than Long Island."

But Kaniuk also asserts the right of Israel to the land. "The deed is a mystical deed." And Sontag's film proceeds to show us how all of Israel is a memory theater for the Jewish people with the Wailing Wall at the center of the stage.

The essence of the Jewish experience, then, can be located within the dynamic tension of exile—a life without a land of one's own for 2,000 years. Seen from this point of view, Duddy Kravitz' hysterical quest for a piece of property becomes a stunning example of how the thwarted religious aspirations of the tribe can be viciously secularized within an individual who has lost touch with the roots of tradition. And a rabbi Jacob who journeys from America to visit his homeland —*Paris, France!*—is a splendid reminder that it makes little difference for many Jews exactly where they live, so long as there is a synagogue and a community of pious scholars. Place is not primary because they live inside their heads.

"Promised Lands" is superior to the other films because it is crucially concerned with the essential problems and begins to probe for answers. Dramatizing the

tragedy and pathos of people locked into an escalating conflict, Miss Sontag's film is drenched with scenes of death and mourning. And this is just one among many reasons why it will not receive widespread commercial distribution. The chief reason is that the film is a *documentary*.

America likes fiction, adventure, fantastic tales of individual striving, but Susan Sontag's film forces us to think and remember.

And to this point the Baal Shem Tov, the founding saint of the Hasidic movement, is quoted to great effect in "Promised Lands": "Forgetfulness leads to exile. Remembrance is the secret of redemption."

1974 S 8, II:13:1

THE HENRY MILLER ODYSSEY, a documentary directed and produced by Robert. Snyder; photography, Baylis Glascock; editor, Ray Laurent; released by Grove Press. Running time: 110 minutes. This film has not been classified. Showings today and tomorrow at noon and midnight at the First Avenue Screening Room.

By NORA SAYRE

Today, Henry Miller's name triggers a reflex—you can't disassociate it from the gleeful humiliation of the women in his books. But Robert Snyder's excellent 1969 documentary, "The Henry Miller Odyssey," illustrates that Mr. Miller has far more to offer a contemporary audience than his sexual politics (which aren't reflected in this movie). The film is playing today and tomorrow at the First Avenue Screening Room. Don't miss it—if you care at all about writers or writing, it will raise your morale.

In many fascinating flashbacks, the movie details a writer's apprenticeship on the road from Brooklyn to Big Sur, while Mr. Miller narrates in his hoarse, nasal voice. In high school, he volunteered that his vocation might be clowning—an impulse that's recalled when we see him (aged 78) laughing at his own long, rubbery face in a mirror. Early on, he worked in his father's tailor shop, then became the employment manager of Western Union, and edited the catalogue of a mail-order house. Then he quit all jobs to write: "I walked up Broadway feeling like the happiest man on earth"—since he planned to be his own boss forever. "Then began 10 years of misery"—when he doubted his ability and couldn't sell his work—followed by the exhilaration of Paris, "where I found my voice," which surfaced in "Tropic of Cancer."

Although Mr. Miller scorns all conventional work and celebrates play, a sense of his own enormous industry surges through the film. He also exults over the freedom that youthful poverty can give a writer—while the camera ogles windows full of succulent French food that he couldn't afford in the thirties. It was invigorating to have "no crutch of any kind," to learn to be "a bird of prey, an animal." Though he stresses his lifelong interest in the occult, his worship of the arts, and his studies of

dreams, his romanticism is usually cut with comedy—it's rather as though Huck Finn had been an urban esthete.

The movie jumps most skillfully between past and present, between California and France. At one moment, the writer is treading water and talking about his mother, who consulted him (aged 4)

about having a wart removed. She got blood poisoning and blamed him for it—for which he never forgave her. Soon, he's cheerfully discussing suicide with Lawrence Durrell. Both agree that it was much more tempting when they were young.

•

There are fond visits with his old friends, including Anaïs Nin. He also reads a very moving passage about a favorite relative, an aunt who lost her mind. As an adolescent, he had to take her to the asylum; on that journey, she saw blue and green cows, whose names she knew. His rage at the society that insisted on confining her

sounds like fuel for his future rebellions.

In the last shot, Mr. Miller vanishes on a bicycle. All in all, he has some of the gaiety that Yeats attributed to sages, and it's a privilege to see it on the screen.

1974 S 13, 31:1

From Aldrich and Peckinpah— Two Films About Men of Action

By VINCENT CANBY

SOMEWHERE towards the end of "The Longest Yard," Robert Aldrich's new bone-crusher of a movie, Burt Reynolds, as a convict being blackmailed by a power-mad prison warden, asks an ancient con named Pop: "That time you hit Hazen (the prison warden who was then a guard) in the mouth—was it worth it? Was it worth 30 years?"

Pop thinks a moment, grins toothlessly and says it was. He says in effect that one slug to the jaw three decades earlier provided such long-range satisfaction that the subsequent years of degradation, waste, pain and humiliation have been as nothing in comparison.

Ultimately it all depends on what turns you on.

At one point in "Bring Me The Head of Alfredo Garcia," Sam Peckinpah's latest exercise in manic machismo, Warren Oates throws a couple of more bullets into a newly dead gangster just "because it felt so goddam good." By the time that film ends, Oates has been responsible, directly and indirectly, for a couple of dozen murders and though he has nothing much to show for them, we must assume that his life has had more than its share of major pleasures.

Both "The Longest Yard" and "Alfredo Garcia" make half-hearted attempts to support the violent action with moral principles, but what these two movies say is never as convincing as what they demonstrate: the irrevocable action taken without thought of consequence is what makes a man truly heroic, perhaps sublime. This is sit-com Sartre of the sort that could justify the pushing of the nuclear button. The world might go up in a soundless, bright-blue puff, but think of a President's ineffable joy during that final fraction of the second while the button was in process of being pushed. It'd beat all hollow hearing "Hail to the Chief" for the first time, knowing that it was for you.

I suspect that Robert Aldrich sees the fallacy in all this, which is what makes "The Longest Yard" such an entertaining film in spite of itself, in spite of its constant emphasis on a man's groin as the seat of his life as well as of his sensibility, and in spite of the near vacuum in the center of the film caused by the presence of its star.

Burt Reynolds, who may possibly be the phoniest love object to be foisted

on the American public since the late Jayne Mansfield, seems to have no personality of his own. It's not his fault that he looks so much like the early Marlon Brando, but it is a reflection on

his talent as an actor that no matter how close the camera gets to him, he finds it difficult to convince you that he's thinking about anything except how to throw away the next line the

way one does on late-night talk shows.

The film itself is an essentially harmless movie equivalent to Sunday afternoon pro-football games on television, an analogy I'd make even if the climactic sequence had to do with a wrestling match rather than a football game.

In "The Longest Yard," the football game is between a team put together by the guards, which the warden, beautifully played by an impeccably tailored Eddie Al-

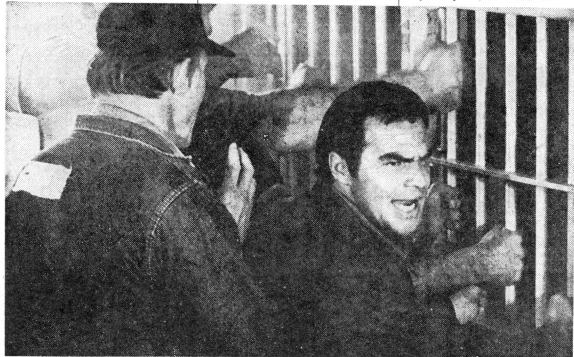

Robert Aldrich, right, is the director of "The Longest Yard," with Burt Reynolds, above, as a battling convict. The film, according to Vincent Canby, is "entertaining in spite of itself."

bert, hopes will win a semi-pro title, and a team fielded by the inmates, coached and captained by Reynolds, with the idea of giving the guards a little practice.

The way Aldrich and his script writer, Tracy Keenan Wynn, see prison, it's a sort of Boy's Town grown up and gone wrong. People in this Boy's Town don't pie beds. Instead they inject a little gasoline into a lightbulb so that when it's turned on, the victim (or jokee) is turned into a human torch. The guards are sadistic, but so are a lot of the cons, which more or less balances things during the football game that concludes the film. It's to Aldrich's credit that this game manages to be hugely suspenseful even when you're aware of being manipulated by clever cutting and by a soundtrack that makes every collision between two players sound as if the Titanic were again plunging into its iceberg.

The hole in the film-as-entertainment is Reynolds both as an actor and as fictional character. It's about

impossible to accept him as a guy who, after being bounced out of the majors for shaving points and after living for years as a second-rate gigolo, would suddenly get religion in prison to the extent that he would risk transforming his 18-month term to life imprisonment for humiliating the warden and the warden's hopes for glory. I couldn't buy it, but if you can, the movie makes a certain amount of conventional sense.

Aldrich is a much more sophisticated and witty film director than a lot of his earlier macho-mayhem movies ("The Dirty Dozen," "Emperor of The North Pole") suggest. At times, "The Longest Yard" seems almost to be a comment on those films, as when Reynolds goes into a crucial huddle during the final football game and suggests they win "for Granny, Nate and the Caretaker" (fellow cons who have been dishonestly incapacitated by one means and another), thus recalling the old Gipper scene from "Knute Rockne—All American." Also I would

think that there is less irony than high comic spirits suggested by the music heard during the film's closing credits: "You Got To Be A Football Hero (to get along with the beautiful girls)."

There are very few redeeming things in "Bring Me The Head of Alfredo Garcia," which is about the scramble of various misfits to find Alfredo Garcia, responsible for making pregnant the young daughter of a rich Mexican landowner. The landowner has offered $1,000,000 in cash for the head of the unfortunate Garcia who, it turns out, has conveniently died in a drunken auto accident, thus making his decapitation less grisly than it might have been were he still alive.

Among the good things in the film is the performance of Warren Oates ("The Wild Bunch," "Badlands"), cast as a seedy, down-at-the-heel American piano player, expatriated in Mexico, a man who wears a mustache and dark glasses that give him more than a passing resemblance to Peckinpah. This fact may

allow the film to be read as some kind of crazy comment by Peckinpah on Peckinpah's adventures as an innocent among the wolves of Hollywood. I'm not sure, though the film doesn't make a great deal of sense read any other way.

"Alfredo Garcia" opens beautifully and ambiguously, in the father's confrontation of his wayward daughter in a Mexico that would seem to be in mid-19th century. "Bring me the head of Alfredo Garcia," he shouts in a mixture of Spanish and English, and you're sure you're in an earlier time and in a far-off place. Suddenly, however, Peckinpah cuts to limousines roaring out of hacienda gates and jet planes taking off from international airdromes. The shock sums up just about everything the film has to say of any importance.

The rest is so witless you can't believe it was made by the man who directed "The Wild Bunch" and "The Ballad of Cable Hogue" and even "Straw Dogs," but then you remember that Peckinpah also was responsible for "The Getaway" and "Pat Garrett and Billy The Kid," in which the violence seemed as frivolous as the toughness was fraudulent.

1974 S 15, II:1:5

tained within the head of a pin.

In "Scenes From a Marriage," Mr. Bergman is examining the molecular structure of a human relationship. You think you've seen it before, but every time you see it, it's new, which is one of the things about love. Like a laboratory model of a molecule, the design is complex and beautiful in a purely abstract way, but the film is also intensely, almost unbearably moving.

●

The look of the film has something to do with this. The two-hour, 48-minute movie, which opened yesterday at the Cinema I, is Mr. Bergman's theatrical version of a five-hour production he made for Swedish television last year. The director has not only edited the six original 50-minute installments down to the present length, but he has blown up the 16-mm. negative to 35-mm., which gives a kind of pointillist effect.

Then, too, the television film was mostly photographed (by Sven Nykvist) in tight close-ups that the masking of the theatrical screen, which is less square than the TV screen, emphasizes by cutting off chins and the tops of heads. A film maker really can't get much closer to his actors without using surgery.

Most ordinary films made for television seem empty when seen in a theater. There simply isn't enough visual and emotional detail to keep the mind occupied. It's like looking at a photomural in Grand Central Terminal, one of those elephantine enlargments of an Instamatic snap.

The absolute opposite is true of "Scenes From a Marriage." Although we seldom see more than two persons at a time, and usually only one, the theater screen is bursting with information, associations and contradictory feelings.

Mr. Bergman tells the story of Johan (Mr. Josephson) and Marianne (Miss Ullmann) in six seemingly arbitrary "chapters" that have titles such as "Innocence and Panic," "The Art of Sweeping Under the Rug" and "In the Middle of the Night in a Dark House."

When we first see them, Johan and Marianne are being interviewed about the perfection of their 10-year marriage as material for a drippy women's magazine. Johan appears to be smug, self-mocking. Marianne is uneasy. When pressed, she says that she thinks Johan is "awfully nice."

They've reached a kind of windless plateau in their marriage Johan has a satisfying career as a university professor. Marianne is a lawyer specializing in family problems. They have two daughters (who always remain offscreen), in-laws who are fondly demanding, and an unstated agreement

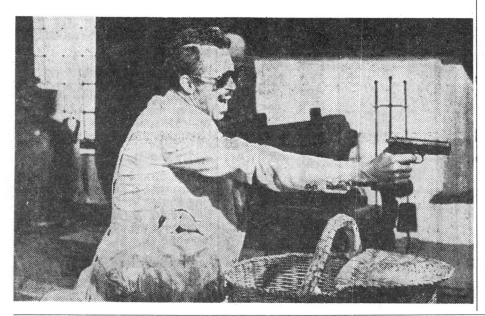

Sam Peckinpah, left, directed "Bring Me the Head of Alfredo Garcia," with Warren Oates, below. Vincent Canby calls the gory film an "exercise in manic machismo."

Santi Visalli/Photoreporters

SCENES FROM A MARRIAGE, directed and written (in Swedish with English subtitles) by Ingmar Bergman; executive producer, Lars-Owe Carlberg; director of photography, Sven Nykvist; editor, Siv Lundgren; a Cinematograph AB production, distributed by Cinema V. Running time: 168 minutes. At the Cinema I Theater, Third Avenue near 60th Street. This film has not been rated.
Marianne .... Liv Ullmann
Johan .... Erland Josephson
Katarina .... Bibi Andersson
Peter .... Jan Malmsjo
Mrs. Palm .... Anita Wall
Eva .... Gunnel Lindblom
Mrs. Jacobi ..... Barbro Hiort AF Ornas

By VINCENT CANBY

Ingmar Bergman's "Scenes From a Marriage," starring the incomparable Liv Ullmann and Erland Josephson as lovers who don't always know it, is the first major film event of the autumn season. It's a movie of such extraordinary intimacy that it has the effect of breaking into mysterious components many things we ordinarily accept without thought, familiar and banal objects, faces, attitudes and emotions, especially love.

A smile is a composite of pain, anger, affection and creeping boredom. The surface of a double bed is a linen batetleground. Later the rumpled white sheets suggest an abandoned Arctic landscape on a planet in a universe that might be con-not to discuss real problems, including the fact that they no longer satisfy each other sexually. Marianne seems cold and at one point says that "sex isn't everything," but with hindsight we are able to recognize her desperation.

It is Johan who flies the coop — with an irritable, hugely jealous girl in her 20's named Paula, who also remains offscreen. In succeeding chapters of the film covering 10 more years, "Scenes From a Marriage" tells of the divorce of Johan and Marianne, of the remarriage of each to other partners and of their continuing meetings. They eventually forge a new relationship that isn't necessarily happy, although it marks a profound development in their capacities to understand and care for each other.

I suspect that if we met Johan or Marianne in real life neither would seem to be especially interesting. It is the accomplishment of the director and his actors that they reveal these humdrum characters in ways that usually aren't possible except in first-person prose, in ways that make them unique and important.

Under Mr. Bergman's direction and with his material, Miss Ullmann again establishes herself as one of the most fascinating actresses of our time, and if she seems to have the edge over her costar, it may well be because of the director's fascination with women. He can't help paying tribute to them.

•

Mr. Josephson gives an equally complex performance, but Johan seems to have been conceived with a certain amount of guilt. He's a not-quite-admirable character. As Marianne liberates herself, Johan drifts into unspectacular failure. Yet this is to oversimplify Bergman, and nothing in this film is cut and dried.

Toward the end, Johan and Marianne are having an illicit weekend at a country cabin. It is 20 years since they met, and Marianne still wonders whether she can love anyone. Johan cradles her as they sit in bed. After 20 years Johan is sleepy but not yet exhausted. He says: "I think I love you in my imperfect and rather selfish way. And I think you love me in your stormy, emotional way. In fact, I think that you and I love one another. In an earthly and imperfect way."

It is a happy ending, almost. And a superb film.

1974 S 16, 41:1

REED: INSURGENT MEXICO, directed by Paul Leduc; screenplay (Spanish with English subtitles) by Juan Tofar and Mr. Leduc; from John Reed's book "Mexico Insurgents"; photography, Alexis Grivas; editors, Rafael Castanieda and Giovanni Korporaal; released by New York Films. At the Regency Theater, Broadway between 67th and 68th Streets. Running time: 110 minutes. This film has not been classified.
John Reed .... Claudio Obregon
General Urbina .. Eduardo Lopez Rojas
Pablo Seanez .... Ernesto Gomez Cruz
Julian Reyes .... Juan Angel Martinez

By NORA SAYRE

How can you film a revolution—without conveying the specific issues and individuals that set it off? It's not enough to show that people are poor, nor to have them talk of "liberty," nor simply to show them fighting. Political fuzziness is the main flaw of Paul Leduc's "Reed: Insurgent Mexico," a movie about John Reed, the American journalist, and his experiences in the Mexican Revolution in 1913-14, when he followed the troops of Gen. Tomas Urbina and Pancho Villa. (The film is based on Reed's own book, "Mexico Insurgente.") But Reed—who later reported on the Russian Revolution, wrote "Ten Days That Shook the World," and formed the American Communist Workers' party—was too complex a figure for this kind of fictionalized account. The movie is playing today at the Regency Theater.

However, the movie is worth seeing for its thoughtful evocation of old-fashioned warfare, when fighting was a slow and clumsy process. Heavy donkey-drawn carts were carefully loaded with explosives, and it was an effort simply to reach the battle itself. Even sparse troops did not have enough horses for everyone, hence some soldiers with cumbersome weapons stumbled after their mounted colleagues.

The movie is shot in sepia to give it a period flavor, and the device does work. The worn faces of civilians and soldiers appear to emerge from another era. And there are many vivid details, such as the general who loves being photographed (he poses with his Victrola at his side), the scenes of soldiers chatting casually or trading insults, and the moments when the troops stare at a calm field—waiting for it to erupt with bullets and bombs.

Claudio Obrégon, who plays John Reed, looks too Latin for the part—hence he seems like a mere outsider, rather than a creature from a totally alien culture. Still, his subtle performance succeeds in evoking a reporter troubled by the familiar question of participation. Since he supports the revolution, he feels guilty at being a mere spectator and thinks he ought to fight, yet admits his personal fear of doing so. At times, he wondered why he was in Mexico at all, when he felt that he should be back in the United States, "fighting the rich." His dilemma is well-served by this movie—even if the Mexican revolution is not.

1974 S 17, 40:6

ANTONIA: A PORTRAIT OF THE WOMAN, directed by Judy Collins and Jill Godmilow; photographed by Coulter Wall; edited by Miss Godmilow; produced by Miss Collins for Rocky Mountain Productions. Running time: 58 minutes. LIGHT, a short film by Jordan Belson, 7 minutes; distributed by Pyramid Films. At the Whitney Museum of American Art, Madison Avenue at 75th Street. Through Oct. 1.

Antonia Brico conducting in the documentary about her life

By NORA SAYRE

The headlines refer to "triumphs." But the tone is patronizing: "Yankee Girl Startles Berlin Critics" (The New York Times, 1930.) Along with the acclaim for a deeply serious conductor, there's the lurch of astonishment at the mere fact of her sex. "Antonia," a superb documentary about conductor Antonia Brico, details the achievements and the struggles that began for a child who was first taught piano because she bit her nails—and continue for the 73-year-old who now leads a community orchestra in Denver.

The film, directed by Judy Collins, singer, and Jill Godmilow, film maker, who was co-director of the documentary "Tales," opened yesterday at the Whitney Museum of American Art and will run through Oct. 1.

•

When she was 28, critics called Dr. Brico a great conductor. After directing the Berlin Philharmonic, she twice conducted the Metropolitan Opera. Ovations ensued, but she was denied a third concert because John Charles Thomas, the baritone, wouldn't work with a woman. Between 1934 and 1937, she assembled and conducted a women's symphony, which thrived until she tried to convert it into an ensemble of both sexes—"I want people to mix in symphonies as they do in life." But the project was rejected by the board of directors at Carnegie Hall because the concept was undramatic. The press had eagerly quoted Dr. Brico when she said that "Art is sexless," or when José Iturbi sneered at women musicians. But when she simply performed as an artist, she wasn't sizzling copy.

•

In the film's most searing moment, Dr. Brico tells Judy Collins (who was her piano student) that she has only about 5 performances a year — when she has the energy for 4 or 5 a month. While a soloist can play a piece for herself, a conductor needs the whole ensemble, along with

the audience. Dr. Brico says, "I cannot play my instrument — which is the orchestra," adding that she rarely confides this "perpetual heartbreak" to anyone. Such a personal revelation is terribly rare on screen — clearly, it's due to Dr. Brico's friendship with Miss Collins. Also, the latter is a good listener — which is no surprise.

Recently, we heard Henry Miller (in Robert Snyder's documentary) reminisce about his early frustrations as a writer. But he was able to look back on those youthful difficulties after years of recognition. Dr. Brico has known no such luxury. Told by many that it was ridiculous for a woman to think of conducting, she admits, "I felt that I'd never forgive myself if I didn't try." And the pain and deprivation which she has known all her life are overshadowed in this film by her ebullient, forthright warmth.

The narrative of her life alternates with glimpses of her at work—rehearsing or teaching. She also reflects on the emotional experience of conducting (including the acute separation pangs that follow a concert, evaluates the work of other conductors, and evokes the strong support that she had from Jean Sibelius, Sir Adrian Boult, and Albert Schweitzer—who telegraphed "Courage Love Success" before a major performance.

"Antonia" is biographical cinema at its best, and it will also encourage many women in fields other than music, thanks to Dr. Brico's determination, her refusal to be defeated. The film ends, as it should, with bravos and applause.

Also on the program is Jordan Belson's "Light"—7 minutes of beautifully shifting images that change radically in intensity and color. At moments the elusive patterns suggest stars, sand, water, or the sun. The results make the concept of psychedelia seem old-fashioned —even though the film appears as a highly sophisticated descendant of that movement.

1974 S 19, 50:1

CORRECTION

An article in The New York Times yesterday incorrectly identified the photographer of the motion picture "Antonia: A Portrait of the Woman." He is Coulter Watt.

1974 S 20, 41:7

KASHIMA PARADISE, a documentary directed by Benie Deswarte and Yann le Masson; director of cinematography, Mrs. le Masson; film editors, Isabelle Rathery and Sarah Matton; music, Hiroshi Hara; Japanese with English subtitles; a Tricontinental Film Center release. Running time: 110 minutes. Showings today and tomorrow at noon and midnight at the First Avenue Screening Room.

With its sometimes tinny soundtrack, its poorly positioned subtitles that frequently require more from the imagination than the eye, its leisurely pace and its cloyingly sincere tone of Marxist didacticism, "Kashima Paradise" is a less than wholly satisfying film.

But despite its obvious shortcomings, this French documentary, playing today and tomorrow at noon and midnight at the First Avenue Screening Room is, at times, a work of considerable visual impact and of engrossing delineation of the fabric of Japanese relationships.

Produced and directed by Benie Deswarte and Yann le Masson, "Kashima Paradise" dwells principally on the effects of encroaching industrialization on a rural community of 450 people 50 miles from Tokyo and—in particular—on the impact of a huge complex of steel and petrochemical plants on the life of a farmer.

It is a story by now all too familiar—of broken promises, ways of life ended forever, terrible clashes between the future and the past.

"Kashima Paradise" is chiefly memorable for the excellence of its camerawork. Its scenes of the Kashima complex, looming out of the wasteland it has created, are a chill vision of progress sprouted from destruction.

This is a documentary in which the camera seems unobtrusive and natural, even in the presence of tranquility. We have grown used to the camera as an accompaniment to disruption, as it is here, in part. But there are also moments in "Kashima Paradise" when the camera functions skillfully on other aspects of life—on a farm, in a school, at a wedding, at a funeral—and reminds us again of what a wise and warm instrument it can be.

LAWRENCE VAN GELDER

1974 S 20, 31:1

The Cast

AMARCORD (I Remember), directed by Federico Fellini; screenplay (Italian with English subtitles) and story by Mr. Fellini and Tonino Guerra; produced by Franco Cristaldi; director of photography, Giuseppe Rotunno; editor, Ruggero Mastroianni; music, Nino Rota; an Italian-French co-production of F. C. Productions (Rome) and P.E.C.F. (Paris), distributed by Roger Corman/New World Pictures. Running time: 127 minutes. At the Plaza Theater, 58th Street, east of Madison Avenue. This film has been rated R.

Gradisca	Magali Noel
Titta	Bruno Zanin
Titta's mother	Pupella Maggio
Father	Armando Brancia
Grandfather	Giuseppe Lanigro
Palaca	Nando Orfei
Uncle Teo	Ciccio Ingrassia
The Lawyer	Luigi Rossi
Bisein	Gennaro Ombra
Volpina	....
Tobacconist	Antonietta Beluzzi

By VINCENT CANBY

"Amarcord," which opened yesterday at the Plaza Theater, may possibly be Federico Fellini's most marvelous film. It's an extravagantly funny, sometimes dreamlike evocation of a year in the life of a small Italian coastal town in the nineteen-thirties, not as it literally was, perhaps, but as it is recalled by a director with a superstar's access to the resources of the Italian film industry and a piper's command over our imaginations.

When Mr. Fellini is working in peak condition, as he is in "Amarcord" (the vernacular for "I remember" in Romagna), he somehow brings out the best in us. We become more humane, less stuffy, more appreciative of the profound importance of attitudes that in other circumstances would seem merely eccentric if not lunatic.

•

"Amarcord" has close associations to Mr. Fellini's last two films, "The Clowns" and "Roma," both memoirs of a sort, but the likeness turns out to be superficial on closer inspection. This new production combines the free form and make-believe splendor of those two films with the comic, bittersweet feeling for character and narrative we remember from some of his best films of the nineteen-fifties—"Variety Lights," "The White Sheik," "I Vitelloni" and "Nights of Cabiria."

"Amarcord" has a sort of narrator-host-master-of-ceremonies who watches over everything. He's called The Lawyer (Luigi Rossi) and is a scholarly, pedantic fellow with a fondness for historical dates that establish links between the present and a past that can be traced with some certainty to 268 B.C. From time to time The Lawyer turns up to talk to us directly, occasionally being pelted with vegetables or tin cans by the town loafers who find all his talk a bore.

The town in the film is not unlike the Adriatic resort inhabited by the young men in "I Vitelloni," based on Rimini, where Mr. Fellini grew up. Yet there is now something magical, larger-than-life about the town, its citizens and many of the things that happen to them.

•

There is no single central character, but an uproariously unruly procession of them. There are Titta (Bruno Zanin), a boy in his teens who could be the young Fellini; Titta's father (Armando Brancia), a terrible-tempered construction foreman who insists on wearing his Socialist tie every time the Fascists hold a local rally; Gradisca (Magali Noel), the town hairdresser, a silly, pretty, immaculately groomed (she even wears her saucy red beret to bed) femme fatale who dreams of Gary Cooper but settles down with a stodgy policeman.

There are also Titta's grandfather (Giuseppe Lanigro), a cheerful, foul-mouthed old man who remembers the joys of intercourse the way someone else might remember football scores, and Titta's crazy uncle (Ciccio Ingrassia), who, while on a picnic away from the asylum, climbs to the top of a tree and calls out his need for a woman. He is finally retrieved by one — a midget nun.

•

The movie is awash in the kind of poetic artifice that Mr. Fellini loves and that has become increasingly rare these days when most directors insist on working in actual locations.

Mr. Fellini is fascinated by movie studios, by make-up, by sets, by the work of the special-effects men, all of which are the materials of his kind of movie-making. One of the most marvelous moments in "Amarcord" is also one of its most frankly fake, a scene in which the townspeople keep watch at night in rowboats and small cruisers, in what looks to be a cellophane sea, to herald the maiden voyage of the old Rex, which, when it appears, looms like some magnificent stage prop. We see what everyone else has been imagining.

This style has the effect of softening the edges of history, which is one of the things that memory also does. The arrogance and cruelty of the town's Fascists are certainly not diminished, but they are set at a distance, as if to be contemplated. A death is not made less poignant but it becomes a heartbreaking fact that has already been accepted.

"Amarcord" is as full of tales as Scherherazade, some romantic, some slapstick, some elegiacal, some bawdy, some as mysterious as the unexpected sight of a peacock flying through a light snowfall. It's a film of exhilarating beauty.

1974 S 20, 32:1

The Screen

"The Promised Land" (La Tierra Prometida) was shown in the "New Directors" series at the Museum of Modern Art. The following excerpt is from A. H. Weiler's review, which appeared in The New York Times last April 8. The film, which ran 120 minutes, has been edited extensively since its first showing. It will be shown for two weeks starting today, at the First Avenue Screening Room, at 61st Street.

Miguel Littin, the Chilean writer-director of "The Promised Land," states his case against Latin-American oppression with the fervor of an unvanquished revolutionary. But if his love of the land and its enfranchisement is as heartfelt as his impassioned rhetoric, his highly stylized drama is less than convincing in its treatment of the Establishment and foreign exploiters.

The 31-year-old movie maker, who completed his film last year when he was still head of the studio that was an official part of the overthrown, left-wing Allende Government, is obviously autobiographical in his treatment of a group of 1930, Depression-afflicted, homeless, wandering peasants who founded and cooperatively worked a village called Palmillo (the director's birthplace).

The tragedy of injustice is strikingly apparent, but its impact is lessened by a plethora of loving declamatory scenes and diffuse religious symbolism that tend to confuse, rather than impress, an uninitiated observer. It is easy to feel the irony and reality of the off-screen narration of the aged peasant who survived doleful things past. The symbolism, however, is still distracting, and a viewer can't help wonder if the estate owners, businessmen and the religious figures were as one-dimensional as they are depicted to be.

1974 S 20, 32:4

The Program

MINAMATA, a documentary directed by Noriaki Tsuchimoto; Japanese with English subtitles; distributed by Monument Films. At the Film Forum, 256 West 88th Street. Running time: 105 minutes. Showing today through Sunday and Sept. 26 through Sept. 29, 8 P.M.

By A. H. WEILER

"Minamata," the Japanese-made documentary that opened the Film Forum's fall season last night, is persuasive and often shocking evidence of the present dangers of pollution. Although the feature occasionally might call for fuller explanations, the awesome, sometimes death-dealing blight that struck Minamata, the fishing and manufacturing town on the island of Kyushu, is a sobering, forceful case history that leaves little doubt as to the dire results of man's current approach to the disposal of modern-living wastes.

•

For the record, Minamata can point to its simple fishermen who have worked its waters for centuries, a large, modern fertilizer factory and, for the last two decades or so, to the sad distinction of being the home of "Minamata disease." This is attributed to the mercury-poisoned effluvia from that factory that made the cycle from fish to humans whom it incapacitated—or killed—in various ways.

Noriaki Tsuchimoto, the director of "Minamata," who is a stranger to this observer, and a fairly large complement of associates shot their black-and-white footage in Minamata, its environs and Osaka in 1971, largely in question-and-answer sessions with victims or their survivors.

The results are either dolefully factual or pitiably tearful but nearly always painfully arresting. Dedication and devotion are obvious in the help given by affected families, friends and hospital personnel to children and grown ups afflicted by cerebral palsy-like retardation, paralysis, blindness or deafness.

•

If these touching scenes in a major portion of the film are subdued, "Minamata," nevertheless, strongly implies and occasionally illustrates what appears to be big industry and governmental apathy before it builds to a literally riotous climax as the diseased and their sympathizers descend on a meeting in Osaka of the impassive president and board of directors of the Chisso company, operators of the plant, to demand reparations and justice.

One would like to read more details in the literal English subtitles such as the specifics of the infection or the newspaper accounts of last July, which listed 428 victims, 69 of whom died. An epilogue points out that the Chisso company paid about £1.5-million to 138 victims last year.

On the basis of the bleak record poignantly and pointedly presented in "Minamata," that statistic doesn't seem to be the answer to the terrible, perhaps portentous, problem of pollution.

1974 S 20, 35:1

A scene from the movie, "Amarcord" (I Remember), directed by Federico Fellini

Ingmar Bergman and The Battle of the Sexes

By VINCENT CANBY

EVERYONE reads relations between men and women in a different way. In a Thurber cartoon a giantess peers down on her husband who comes up to her instep. She's not unfriendly, just dangerously large. Rodgers and Hart decided that love, in spite of all the self-deceptions required to believe a lie, was better than the absence of it. They celebrated conjugal mayhem: "The broken dates/"The endless waits/"The conversations with the broken plates." Ibsen brooded about a non-erotic form of female bondage and Strindberg gave every impression of loathing women.

In Scenes From A Marriage" Ingmar Bergman studies 10 years in the lives of Jonan (Erland Josephson) and Marianne (Liv Ullmann), a happily married, upper-middle-class Swedish couple with two children, a flat in town, a house in the country, and what turns out to be a nearly fatal agreement not to pry into half-lit disappointments and desires. Never before has this extraordinary Swedish director-writer explored relations between the sexes with such compassion and humor, and sometimes in such harrowing detail. But in Bergman there are no villains, male or female.

The film more or less begins with the collapse of the perfect marriage when Johan falls in love with a girl almost 20 years his junior. In succeeding scenes of what is virtually a two-character film, Johan and Marianne reverse positions of dominance and dependence, marry other partners, have other affairs, and continue to circle back to each other, each time getting a little closer to a truth that may remain forever elusive, though that doesn't make the quest any less important or urgent.

"Scenes From A Marriage" seems to be the simplest, most lucid, most spare film that Bergman has ever made. It lacks the visual richness of "Cries and Whispers," the theological associations of "The Passion of Anna," the apocalyptic melodrama of "Shame" and the psychological poetry of "Persona" and "The Silence." One could easily describe it as "A Tragicomedy of Banality," which was the subtitle given "The Lie," the Bergman teleplay about another floundering marriage that was done on CBS last year.

Yet "Scenes From A Marriage" is such a precise work, seemingly so uncomplicated, that it has the impact of one of those laws of physics that are so fundamental you can't understand why it was thousands of years before someone discovered it. One knows, however, that such a scientific breakthrough as the theory of relativity is no more an accidental discovery than is any great music, painting or film. Einstein worked very hard, very long, with immense discipline to discover it.

I find myself slipping into hyperbole here to emphasize the particularity of Bergman's achievement in "Scenes From A Marriage." The film that is now at the Cinema I was originally six 50-minute episodes made by Bergman for Swedish television. The director has edited the material down to its present two-hour, 48-minute length and, in doing so, made what appears to be a quite different film. I've not seen the five-hour version but I have read the script, recently published by Pantheon Books. Although a good deal of subsidiary information about Johan and Marianne has been left out of the present version, as well as some few characters, the result has been to heighten the drama by stripping away a lot of realistic non-essential details. I don't mean to say that the film is not realistic — it is — but it also hugely theatrical in ways that don't often work in movies.

Because the film was made for television, it has been mostly photographed (by Sven Nykvist) in such tight close-ups that the screen is often occupied by no more than one or two faces. Such close-ups are ordinarily the first things to give away second-rate filmmakers and actors. The nanny-like camera gives you no choice but to notice that the movie is about nothing in particular and that the actors have been chosen for the cut of the jaw or the tilt of a nose.

Bergman is one of the few directors who can make this enforced intimacy work. The screenplay of "Scenes From A Marriage" is first-rate and he has two superlative actors interpreting it.

Erland Josephson, who played the architect in "The Passion of Anna" and the doctor in "Cries and Whispers," has what seems to be the more difficult, less appealing role as the husband who takes the initiative to break up the perfect marriage. When we first meet him in the film, when he and Marianne are being interviewed about the perfection they've achieved in their marriage, he appears to be smug and self-assured. It's only as the film progresses that we realize that he has been mocking himself, that his awareness of the emptiness of their marriage has given him a perspective on desolation that Marianne entirely lacks.

It's not news that Miss Ullmann is a sensationally beautiful, complex woman in Bergman films and "Scenes From A Marriage" offers her one of her best Bergman roles as Marianne, who changes in the course of the film from a fearful wife and career woman into an individual of robust appetites, determination and understanding.

There are times when "Scenes From A Marriage" seems to be getting very close to the kind of banalities that soap opera deals in. Somewhere near the middle of the film — when Johan leaves Marianne for his unpleasant mistress — there are moments when you think Bergman really is only reworking the tired old formula about the nice, dumb schnook of a husband who is actually no match for his all-wise, all-seeing Earth Mother of a wife. Since Marianne is played by Miss Ullmann, whom we all adore, it's impossible to believe that any man in his right mind would walk out on her.

This is one of the limitations that Bergman has set himself by keeping almost everyone else off-screen. Yet Bergman continually recoups. The roles are not stereotypes. There are times when Marianne is a full-fledged bitch, a bore, a dumb slave to idiotic social conventions. There are also times when the happiness or the agony that floods across her face transforms her into a

Liv Ullmann and Erland Josephson play a tormented couple in "Scenes From a Marriage." As usual in Bergman films, says Vincent Canby, Miss Ullmann is a "sensationally beautiful, complex woman."

creature of the sort of contradictions seldom met outside of written fiction.

It is curious that at this point in history — when there is so much talk about sexual equality, so many books written about role-playing, so much trendy trash spoken on the talk shows — so few filmmakers should give serious consideration to what men and women mean to each other. In documentary detail that would do credit to the first manned space shot to Jupiter. It is fascinating.

1974 S 22, II:1:1

THE SUDDEN WEALTH OF THE POOR PEOPLE OF KOMBACH, directed and produced by Volker Schlondorff; screenplay (German with English subtitles) by Mr. Schlondorff and Margarethe von Trotta; director of photography, Franz Rath; editor, Claus von Boro; music, Klaus Doldinger; a Hallelujah Films production, distributed by New Yorker Films. Running time: 94 minutes. At the Regency Theater, Broadway at 67th Street. This film has not been rated.

Hans Jacob Geiz ....Georg Lehn
Heinrich Geiz ....Reinhard Hauff
Jacob Geiz ....Karl-Josef Cramer
David Briel ....Wolfgang Bachler

By VINCENT CANBY

Volker Schlondorff's 1970 West German film, "The Sudden Wealth of the Poor People of Kombach," is based on a true story about seven peasants who, in 1821, robbed a tax collector's wagon and were subsequently caught, tried and executed for their crime. The prosecutor didn't have too much difficulty catching the thieves: those who were not informed on, or who didn't reveal themselves by spending money, gave themselves up to expiate their sins.

The thieves, according to the director, were doomed from the start — by their bondage to the land and to their Christian ideals. That is, all except one, the poor Jewish peddler who conceived the robbery and who was not as encumbered as his ignorant friends by feudal social and religious traditions. When last seen in the film the peddler is starting his journey to America.

•

"The Sudden Wealth," which was originally shown here at the Museum of Modern Art in a 1972 series devoted to the New German Cinema, began a limited engagement at the Regency Theater yesterday. Its director has already been represented in New York by "Young Torless" released in 1968, and "A Free Woman," reviewed last June.

Mr. Schlondorff is the sort of director who masks his passionate feelings by keeping his subjects at a distance, as if he's afraid to slip into sentimentality. This worked well enough in "Young Torless," about brutality in a boy's boarding school, but it has the effect of putting the events in "The Sudden Wealth" at such a far remove they would seem quaint except for the role of the Jewish peddler. Mr. Schlondorff seems to admire the peddler for some of the very characteristics that have burdened the Jew of stereotype through the centuries, including a weasel-like cleverness and an ability to persuade others to take the risks.

•

I can't believe that this is what Mr. Schlondorff intended, but it is one of the things suggested by a film that insists on maintaining such detachment from its characters. Much like a documentary, and sometimes much like a black-and-white newsreel, even to the occasional use of the hand-held camera, "The Sudden Wealth" reveals its characters entirely in terms of event, supplemented by occasional voice-over narration.

At one point the narrator tells us that the peasants' only solution to their crushing poverty was "to emigrate, poach or hunt for treasure," even if it happened to be the tax collector's. The film is so sober-sided that even its ironies become solemn.

1974 S 26, 24:1

Ozu's Modest Classic Seems Utterly Fresh

By NORA SAYRE

He feels stifled: by his marriage, his dreary white collar job—above all, by the fact that his life is unlikely ever to change. The scenario would be appropriate for an American or European movie of the seventies, but it happens to be set in Tokyo in 1956. Despite the Western clothes of that period—the women's long flaring skirts, high heels, pony tails, and abundant lipstick, the men's trim slacks and T-shirts—the late Yasujiro Ozu's magnificent "Early Spring" seems utterly fresh and contemporary. This modest classic also conveys the claustrophobia of office life better than any other film I've seen. The movie opened yesterday at the New Yorker theater.

The quiet disgust with daily life is rapidly established as the young clerical worker (Ryo Ikebe) lights a bleak pre-breakfast cigarette before facing the commuters' train. He's an austere, intensely reserved person; his wife (Chikage Awashima) is neat, practical, efficient — and almost as stoical as he is. Theirs was a love match, but now they seem quite indifferent to one another—talking across an empty space that widens steadily.

The husband's colleagues assert that their office is a jail; hence they seize at small pleasures: a joke, a hike, a noodle supper. Any change is important to them. Almost inevitably, the husband — who's hardly a swinger—gets briefly entangled with a young woman (Keiko Kishi) who's brimming over with the gaiety and animation that his life lacks. She's typecast by others as the office flirt, but Ozu has given her a much wider dimension than

The Cast

EARLY SPRING, directed by Yasujiro Ozu; script (Japanese with English subtitles) by Mr. Ozu and Kogo Noda; photography, Yushun Atsuta; music, Takanobu Saito; art direction, Tatsuo Hamada; released by New Yorker Films. At the New Yorker Theater, Broadway and 89th Street. Running time: 144 minutes. This film has not been classified.

Shoji Sugiyama ....Ryo Ikebe
Masako, his wife .....Chikage Awashima
Chiyo Kaneko ....Keiko Kishi
Taizo Aoki ....Teiji Takahashi
Kiichi Onodera ....Chishu Ryu

that: she's the only character who feels free to express strong feelings. Cheerfully, she admits that she's jealous of the wife, while her lover is glum and guilty. Meanwhile, the office staff gossips and intrudes on the affair, thinking it's their business—which it's not.

Throughout, Ozu finds dramatic depths in quiet, ordinary lives. And during the time that you spend with these people—the span of the movie—you really feel that you've come to know them well, to understand why their relationships do or don't develop. Their emotions or hidden instincts are brilliantly revealed through small details: embraced by his girl friend, the husband secretly rings a bell for a waitress, in order to break the clinch; later, the wife's suppressed anger is distilled in the gesture with which she switches off a light.

Despite the self control that most of these individuals strive for, several repeat that they're very "confused" —a condition that appears to accompany the relentless economic worries of even the employed during the mid-fifties in Japan, when the war still seemed recent, and the boom was yet to come. With subtle precision, Ozu shows how personal and national anxieties seep through infinite lives. Yet this impeccably acted movie is far from depressing, since the filmmaker stresses that mistakes aren't irreversible.

1974 S 26, 26:1

THE MUTATIONS, directed by Jack Cardiff; screenplay by Robert D. Weinbach and Edward Mann; director of photography, Paul Beesen; music, Basil Kirchin; produced by Mr. Weinbach; a Getty Picture Corporation, Ltd., Film; released by Columbia Pictures. At neighborhood theaters. Running time: 92 minutes. This film is classified R.

Dr. Nolter ....Donald Pleasence
Lynch ....Tom Baker
Brian ....Brad Harris
Hedi ....Julie Ege
Burns ....Michael Dunn
Tony ....Scott Antony
Lauren ....Jill Haworth
Bridget ....Olga Anthony

The scientist whose genius is evil even though his intentions are as good as aspirin is back with us again to no earthshaking effect in "The Mutations," which landed in local theaters yesterday. If these British-made science-fiction capers appear to be as up-to-date as genetic research, the end results are as basically familiar—or convincing—as a Boris Karloff going berserk in an underground laboratory.

•

Jack Cardiff, the talented former cinematographer and director of such notable films as "Sons and Lovers," and his writers, seem to be torn between their predilection for freaks and their driven London scientist, Donald Pleasence, who is desperate to "induce mutations" of plants and animals for a combined, efficient "new species." They are, for the record, more successful with freaks—authentic dwarfs, a bearded lady and the like—a couple of whom our researcher uses to capture human guinea pigs from among the students in his college classes.

Tom Baker, playing the facially deformed co-owner (with Michael Dunn) of a sideshow, is the dastardly hunter because, you see, he has been promised a cure by Professor Pleasence. The fact is, despite the professor's collection of animal-devouring plant hybrids and all his talk about DNA and nucleic acids, his victims, Olga Anthony and Scott Antony, turn out to look more like cabbages than humans, and, more important, don't survive his far-out experiments.

•

As might be expected, neither does Mr. Pleasence nor Mr. Baker, who is a good deal more villainous than the largely pedantic "Professor." Mr. Pleasence seems to be more dedicated than malignantly inclined toward science. And Brad Harris and Julie Ege as lovers, and Jill Haworth as Mr. Scott's fiancée, are merely decorative in these unlikely situations.

"I'm sure there's a logical explanation," one of the mystified students observes after Miss Anthony disappears. Logic, unfortunately isn't one of the attributes of "The Mutations."

A. H. WEILER

1974 S 26, 26:2

11 HARROWHOUSE, directed by Aram Avakian; screenplay, Jeffrey Bloom; adaptation, Charles Grodin; based on the novel by Gerald A. Browne; editor, Anne V. Coates; music, Michael J. Lewis; director of photography, Arthur Ibbetson; produced by Elliott Kastner; released by 20th Century-Fox Film Corporation. At the Trans-Lux East Theater, Third Avenue and 58th Street. Running time: 96 minutes. This film has been classified PG.

Chesser ....Charles Grodin
Maren ....Candice Bergen
Watts ....James Mason
Clyde Massey.............Trevor Howard
Meecham ....John Gielgud
Lady Bolding..............Helen Cherry

By NORA SAYRE

Today, you rarely see what the English call a romp (or sometimes a prank) from an American director—the form seems particularly British, dating back to the old Ealing comedies. Aram Avakian's "11 Harrowhouse" appears as a Yankee stepgrandchild of that tradition.

Here, Charles Grodin and Candice Bergen decide to steal $12-billion of rocks from an international clearing house of diamonds in London. He's a reluctant robber, but she thinks him too docile, and her enthusiasm spurs him on. The movie, a weightless antic rather than a thriller, opened yesterday at the Trans-Lux East.

•

John Gielgud plays the haughty director of the diamond center, and it's a pleasure just to watch him pulling off his gloves. He's gifted, as always, at looking aloof or pained, or at shooting ironic glances over his spectacles, and few actors can deliver a line like "You're trying my patience" with such taut exasperation.

Trevor Howard, as a wicked millionaire, is affably reptilian, deceptively benign. James Mason—a sad stoic—comes through with that unctuous whisper and the muted anxiety that have graced a number of his performances. All in all, the three Englishmen adorn this movie more brightly than the sought-after gems.

•

Mr. Grodin narrates the soundtrack rather nicely, but he's fairly wooden on screen, and Miss Bergen is both feisty and fetching, though she has little to do beyond driving very badly. This elegant movie is somewhat short on suspense, but there's an amusing, preposterous car chase in which horsemen gallop after a fleeing van. While "11 Harrowhouse" won't bring the blood to your head or your feet, it's an amiable distraction.

1974 S 27, 49:1

DON'T CRY WITH YOUR MOUTH FULL (Pleure Pas la Bouche Pleine), directed by Pascal Thomas; screenplay (French with English subtitles) by Mr. Thomas, Roland Duval and Suzanne Schiffman; director of photography, Christian Bachmann; executive producer, Claude Berri; editor, Helene Plemianikov; music, Michel Choquet; produced by Renn Productions and Les Films du Chef-Lieu-O.R.T.F. Running time: 116 minutes. At the New York Film Festival at Avery Fisher Hall in Lincoln Center, Broadway at 65th Street. This film has not been rated.

Annie.........................Annie Cole
Father........................Jean Carmet
Mother..................Christiane Chamaret
Grandmother..............Helene Dieudonne
Uncle......................Daniel Ceccaldi
Aunt...................Claudine Paringaux
Sister.............................Friquette
Alexander..................Bernard Menez
Frederic......................Frederic Duru

By VINCENT CANBY

Annie (Annie Colé) is in her mid-teens and of a physical ripeness so strong it seems to create an invisible force around her, like a magnetic field. Annie is aware of this and she enjoys it, but she is too sweet-spirited to turn that force into a weapon. Annie inhabits an idealized provincial landscape where everything is in bloom, and where the only aggressions are of natural origin — and over and done with as quickly and as harmlessly as a summer thunderstorm.

Annie is the heroine of Pascal Thomas's bucolic, lazily funny, gently bawdy French film, "Don't Cry With Your Mouth Full" ("Pleure Pas la Bouche Pleine"), which last night opened the 12th New York Film Festival at Avery Fisher Hall in Lincoln Center.

For the first time that I can remember, the New York Film Festival has chosen as its opening night presentation a film by a virtually unknown director. "Don't Cry With Your Mouth Full" is the second film by Mr. Thomas, 28 years old, whose first film, "Les Zozos," was shown last year in the Museum of Modern Art's "New Directors/New Films" series.

Mr. Thomas may be virtually unknown here, but the men whose work seems most to have influenced him certainly are not—Jean Renoir, François Truffaut, and perhaps even Marcel Pagnol, though Mr. Pagnol's name is no longer so fashionable to invoke.

"Don't Cry With Your Mouth Full" is about one summer in Annie's life, set in a small town that would seem to be somewhere southwest of Paris and not too far from the sea. It's the kind of town where there's no great differentiation between village and countryside.

Annie's father (Jean Carmet), a carpenter, has a fine sprawling garden and keeps chickens, which are, I assume, the charges of her mother (Christiane Chamaret).

●

Completing the household are Annie's younger sister, Friquette (whose real name is Friquette), and her grandmother (Hélène Dieudonné), a wise, self-contained old woman who is likely to toss the morning paper aside saying that "the obituaries are dull today" or to cry out in her sleep at night for her mother.

The film's focus is Annie, whom Miss Colé plays with marvelous, un-self-conscious humor. Miss Colé is a very pretty young woman but she's not an idealized beauty. She always seems to have small bruises on her arms and legs, as if on the few occasions when she has pulled herself together to practice

a more elegant walk, she has bumped into chairs and tables.

Her Annie is a delightful character, and the men in her life are no match for her. The men are Frédéric (Frédéric Duru), a nice country boy who, if pressed, would rather win a cross-country bike race than roll in the haystack with Annie, and Alexandre (Bernard Menez), the town lothario, a handsome young man with a hawklike nose that inevitably reduces all his man-of-the-world mannerisms to their comic components.

Mr. Menez, who played the prop boy in Mr. Truffaut's "Day for Night" and has since become one of France's most popular young actors, is a very funny performer, full of the kind of fanaticism (about bedding Annie) that was so appealing about Charles Denner's rat-catcher in "Such a Gorgeous Kid Like Me."

All the performances have a bit of this slightly mad, comic purpose, which is, I suspect, one of the reasons Mr. Thomas's work is compared with that of Renoir and Truffaut. Although "Don't Cry With Your Mouth Full" is a finely disciplined film, which doesn't seek the easy laugh or ask for gratuitous sentiment, it never suggests the dark void beyond the sunlight, something that distinguishes the work of Renoir and Truffaut and sets their films apart from all others.

This is not something that can be tacked onto a film or inserted into it, as an isolated gesture, like the scene in which Annie's father, doubling as undertaker, must dress the nude body of an old woman for burial. The scene is fine in itself but it's not enough to enrich the somewhat too sunny nature of the movie with the sort of intimations that separate good films from great ones.

1974 S 28, 25:1

Let Us Now Praise—Not Overpraise—Altman

By STEPHEN FARBER

ROBERT ALTMAN is the most highly praised American director presently working. Four years ago "M*A*S*H" opened without much publicity and went on to become a critical and commercial triumph; but then Altman received only mixed reviews on "Brewster McCloud," "Images," and even "McCabe & Mrs. Miller," which remains his most haunting and memorable film. With his next two films — "The Long Goodbye" and "Thieves Like Us"—Altman returned to favor and captivated all but one or two skeptical critics.

His newest movie "California Split," a rambling, hollow collection of skits about gambling, has been greeted as if it were the equal of a late Yeats poem or Picasso painting; it also looks as if it may be Altman's first box-office success since "M*A*S*H." Critics, like audiences, are extremely fickle, but when they

Stephen Farber is a freelance critic and the author of "The Movie Rating Game"

find an idol, they aren't troubled by doubts or reservations; they scream out their superlatives in bold face blurbs that make a mockery of criticism, and of the artists they exalt. Altman deserves attention, but his adoring critics are losing all perspective. The release of "California Split" offers an opportunity to review his career, and try to balance his achievements and his failures.

It isn't difficult to understand the reasons for Altman's high standing with the critics. At a time when most American directors are making formula pictures, Altman manages to direct movies that do not have the mechanical quality of products constructed on an assembly line. He stubbornly refuses to make concessions to the studio bosses, and given the cowardly climate of today's Hollywood, his integrity should not be underestimated.

Like many European directors, Altman is discarding conventional story-telling techniques and refining his own idiosyncratic style. It doesn't take more than a few minutes to recognize the trademarks of an Altman movie—the over-

lapping dialogue, the throwaway humor, the wealth of visual detail, the homely, eccentric faces of his company of actors.

The problem with Altman's films is that sometimes style takes precedence over substance. "California Split" (written by Joseph Walsh) is rich in atmosphere; the look and sound of casinos, poker clubs, smoky bars and seedy apartments are precisely caught. But all the careful touches around the edges can't conceal the hole at the center of the movie. Watching "California Split," one has the feeling that Altman became so absorbed in background details that he never got around to asking what the movie was about, or why he wanted to make it.

Following his characters from the racetrack to the poker tables, Altman delineates an intriguing underworld, but he hasn't given us enough information to draw any conclusions about the people who inhabit it. The film centers on the friendship between two very different gamblers — Charlie (Elliott Gould), a cool, easygoing bum who follows his hunches and doesn't really care

if he wins or loses; and Bill (George Segal), a nervous middle-class magazine editor to whom gambling has become an uncontrollable obsession.

Unfortunately, the characters are established but never explored. The film does not give the slightest indication of why Bill is sacrificing his marriage, his job and his sanity to this compulsion. Altman obviously didn't want to present a neat Freudian explanation for Bill's self-destructiveness, but he hasn't even provided any meaningful or provocative hints; the character is simply incomprehensible. Similarly, we can't begin to guess what drives the more nonchalant Charlie, and so Elliott Gould pulls out some of his familiar shticks—his comic shuffle, his stream-of-conciousness mumble, his mournful sheepdog glances—to fill in the role. The character never takes on an independent life, partly because the idea of such a spontaneous, serene hipster-gambler seems terribly romantic, and essentially false.

As if terrified of revealing too much, Altman ends up revealing too little. The

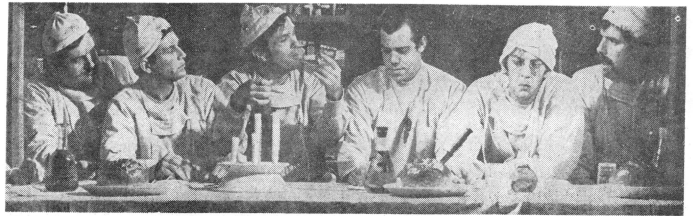

The irreverent "last supper" scene was a high point of "M*A*S*H," Altman's first film to win critical acclaim.

New Yorker's Pauline Kael, his most enthusiastic champion, once wrote that Altman "probably works closer to his unconscious than any other American director." Altman makes movies the way Elliott Gould gambles in "California Split"—in a relaxed, slipshod, slightly stoned style; he plays all his crazy hunches, and enjoys each moment for its own sake, without worrying too much about where he's heading.

In interviews Altman has boasted that he rewrites scripts in the middle of shooting them, and gives the actors great freedom to improvise. The advantage of this loose improvisatory style is that Altman is responsive to happy accidents on the set. He has a shrewd instinct for casting, and he helps actors to discover the shadings in their

roles. For example, the marvelous rapport between Keith Carradine and Shelley Duvall in "Thieves Like Us" intensified the poignancy of what might have been a standard movie romance of a depression bank robber and his moll. With a more rigid, conventional director the actors would never have had the chance to build such a finely-detailed relationship.

Most of Altman's movies, however, could use less improvisation and more control. Because Altman doesn't always think through what he's doing, his films are highly uneven, and they have some embarrassing lapses. Altman has a weakness for chic effects—the reality-illusion tricks in "Images," a muddled subjective record of a woman's mental breakdown; Leonard Cohen's pretentious songs in "McCabe & Mrs. Miller"; Elliott Gould's little dance at the end of "The Long Goodbye"; some of the radio excerpts from programs of the thirties, and the banal use of slow motion at the climax of "Thieves Like Us."

To give a more detailed example of how Altman's approach can misfire, consider the scene in "California Split" in which Charlie and Bill pose as vice cops and surprise an aging transvestite (Bert Remsen) who has come to visit the two hookers with whom Charlie lives. The scene is wacky and startling, but also uncomfortable; the jokes made at "Helen's" expense are really rather cruel. Charlie and Bill have a good time intimidating and abusing their unsuspecting victim, and much of the audience whoops with delight. But it isn't actually very funny to watch the humiliation of a defenseless character.

I'm sure Altman didn't intend to exploit the bigotry that is built into this scene; he probably just wanted to get maximum mileage out of a kinky routine, and he played it for easy laughs. But since he hasn't thought out the implications of the scene, it degenerates into vicious, smug, surprisingly low-brow comedy—like some of the bully-boy antics in "M*A*S*H."

This scene is only the most glaring example of the insecure tone that keeps undermining "California Split." Altman has said that he wanted to make a "celebration" of gambling, but many people have interpreted the movie as a condemnation; Vincent Canby, for example, wrote "the world it depicts is as bleak as a landscape composed entirely of used-car lots." Your interpretation probably depends on whatever preconceptions you bring to the movie.

But if Altman actually meant to "celebrate" gambling, he should have built more exhilarating suspense during the heroes' final winning streak. On the other hand, the film is too breezy and light-hearted to qualify as an expose. It has no impact of any kind; Altman hasn't communicated his own point of view.

Altman probably sensed that the movie wasn't quite expressive enough, for he ends it with a pretentious effort. The mood changes without warning: Bill has hit the jackpot in Reno and won $82,-000, but instead of feeling relieved or excited, he suddenly feels tired and forlorn, overwhelmed by the meaninglessness of all the action. That undercurrent of despair is not implicit in the rest of the movie; it's simply tacked on to the

final reel, in order to inflate a very slight, pointless story.

Altman almost always has difficulty with endings. If a director doesn't know how to end his movies, that is probably because he never thought them out in advance. Altman's most notoriously misconceived ending was in "The Long Goodbye," when detective Philip Marlowe murdered his best friend; it was startling, but completely inconsistent with the character. Altman tries to use shock endings for a bit of last-minute profundity.

All artists achieve many of their most tantalizing effects by intuition, but the greatest art has intellectual rigor as well as emotional resonance. Along with a great many American filmmakers, Altman seems to have the naive notion that intellectual discipline is an impediment to creativity. He once told an interviewer that he hoped to draw an audience that would "see the film and understand the movie's intention without being able to articulate it . . . the audience will sit back and accept the film rather than anticipate it, will simply let the film wash over them."

Altman's movies do express a distinct vision of experience—haphazard, quirky; unexpectedly brutal, vaguely melancholy—and they are full of wit and invention, but most of them are too inarticulate to be absolutely first-rate. Themes are never quite brought into focus; his films give the illusion of complexity when they are sometimes only confused. As Jay Cocks, in his Time magazine review of "Thieves Like Us," wrote: "There is a consistent aloofness in all of Altman's work, as well as a casualness and vagueness about ideas. The suspicion is that whatever interpretation one might bring to 'Thieves Like Us,' Altman would agree with it." One has the same suspicion about "California Split."

Unless artists develop self-awareness —which means an awareness of their intentions, and also of their failings— they have no chance to grow; they keep making the same mistakes. Directors should reflect on the career of Sam Peckinpah, a classic example of an American artist who operates on intuition alone; as he continued to rework the same obsessive fantasies without ever working through them, his movies —from "The Wild Bunch" to "Bring Me the Head of Alfredo Garcia"—have degenerated into self-parody.

Altman isn't at that point yet, but I find it discouraging that "California Split" has some weaknesses that he seemed to have already outgrown. The new film has the same facile, self-congratulatory hipness as "M*A*S*H," and the same adolescent view of women. In the interim Altman created such extraordinary female characters as Julie Christie's Mrs. Miller, a tough-minded, fiercely independent, opium-smoking frontier madam—one of the most complex heroines in American movies of the last decade. By contrast, "California Splits's" whores-with-hearts-of-gold are sentimentalized, two-dimensional characters. The danger of Altman's instinctive, improvisatory approach is that he travels in circles, regressing when he should be progressing.

The hopeful thing about Altman is

Carl Samrock

*Robert Altman's 'California Split' has the same facile, self-congratulatory hipness as his 'M*A*S*H,' says a critic, 'and the same adolescent view of women.'*

"McCabe & Mrs. Miller," starring Julie Christie and Warren Beatty, is Altman's "most haunting and memorable film."

Elliott Gould and George Segal team in "California Split," which some critics treat as if it were "a Picasso painting."

that he keeps working (two movies a year) and experimenting. There is no way of predicting what he'll do next. "California Split" seems a dead end, but his next movie, "Nashville," a study of pop singers and country music, could be the breakthrough he's been groping toward. Altman is trying to clean away all the stale conventions of Hollywood movies and start fresh. Although his quest is hazardous, he is one of the only contemporary American directors who has the potential to make original contributions to the still underdeveloped art of film.

His talent is unmistakable, but he will not fulfill his promise until he asks himself some tougher questions and begins to test himself more ruthlessly. For all of its incidental felicities, "California Split" is the work of a lazy artist, and the critics who have prematurely acclaimed Altman as the savior of American cinema are only encouraging that laziness.

1974 S 29, II:1:1

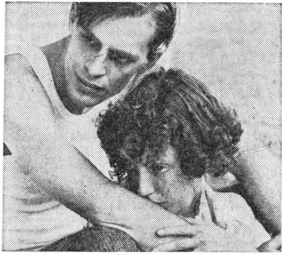

Altman gave Keith Carradine and Shelley Duvall a chance to build a finely detailed relationship in "Thieves Like Us."

Still, they often showed wit, style, sophistication and an unerring instinct for attention-grabbing lines and situations.

If the typical veteran Hollywood writer is a balding man with a well-bitten pipe and a bottle of bourbon at his elbow, the typical wunderkind of today is a bearded, bejeaned, extremely wealthy 28-year-old living in fashionably simulated poverty, with a rustic cottage, a refrigerator stuffed with health foods, a waterbed and a live-in girlfriend. He is a movie buff who can quote lines from "Casablanca," "Now Voyager," "The Maltese Falcon" and other vintage movies, many of which were written by men who can't find jobs today.

It would be nice to say that the young writers—a surprising number of whom are graduates of film schools, most notably those at U.S.C., U.C.L.A. and the American Film Institute—have succeeded in creating an artistic New Wave. But it would also be wrong. What they have brought about is a new kind of commercialism: whatever fresh artistic talent they may have possessed is rapidly being corrupted by a destructive system of agents, producers and distributors. Lost in a welter of business negotiations, fighting for percentages of properties, a young artist can swiftly become as slick and tough as a young attorney.

Even ruthless, successful writers can lose large portions of advances to tough producers who package and sell their scripts, while the producers, in turn, are forced to surrender much of their share to backers, many of whom are in the Texas oil business. In a world ruled by box-office returns, a long-haired, slender, smoky-eyed boy puffing pot in a woodsy attic begins to sound—after a few minutes of conversation—alarmingly like Sammy Glick.

The secret of success in this small provincial jungle is an ability to create charismatic big parts for stars. Despite claims to the contrary, only the interest and involvement of a Nicholson, a Newman, a McQueen, a Redford, a Minnelli, a Streisand—or one of the very few "star" directors, who include Francis Ford Coppola ("The Godfather") and

New Wave of Writers

By CHARLES HIGHAM

LOS ANGELES

IS there a new breed of writer in Hollywood? Lately, there has been a lot of fervent talk about a school of fresh, innovative screenwriters taking over the movie capital; yet it is quite possible that these hotshot authors of the seventies are just as commercial-minded as their assembly-line predecessors ever were.

There are differences, to be sure. The earlier generation of writers who came to Hollywood at the outset of the talkies and remained here decade after decade were mostly newspapermen or playwrights—cynics who set out to get rich by slumming in Hollywood. Most of them promised to go back to New York once they had made their pile; few kept their promise. They grew drunken and bitter, churning out high-priced pap.

Charles Higham, a freelance writer, is the author of "The Art of the American Film" and "The Films of Orson Welles."

Paul Schrader became disillusioned when his script was altered to fit Robert Mitchum.

Roman Polanski ("Chinatown")—can guarantee a´ script's development beyond the option stage. When a young independent producer like Michael Gruskoff or a producing team like Michael and Julia Phillips decide to take a gamble on the first draft of a screenplay, they pay a minimum advance for it and then take it to a big-name star. If the star is interested, the writer will rework it, tailoring it to the star's specifications. After that, a studio's curiosity can be piqued. Otherwise, the battle is long, grueling and uphill.

Take, for example, the case of the talented husband and wife team of Willard Huyck and Gloria Katz, creators of the clever, idiomatic script for the surprisingly successful "American Graffiti." They recently turned over a screenplay called "Lucky Lady"—about a female rum runner—to Michael Gruskoff, who sold it to 20th Century-Fox for $400,000, plus percentages. After film school—Willard went to U.S.C. and Gloria to U.C.L.A.—they wanted to direct films, but found no takers. Eventually, director Francis Ford Coppola took an interest in them and hired them to work for his American Zoetrope Company, centered in San Francisco, but then the company folded. So, for six years, the couple lived on the edge of poverty, writing—but not selling—12 scripts. Obtaining funds from Texas sources, they managed to produce and direct a horror film which turned out to be so horrible that it was never distributed.

Finally, director George Lucas, who wanted to make a movie about growing up in the early 1960's, hired them to write "American Graffiti." The script was turned down by nearly everybody, and it was only after Francis Ford Cop-

Writers Willard Huyck and Gloria Katz made it with "American Graffiti."

pola — shrewdly sensing "Graffiti's" box-office potential—offered to put his name on the picture as co-producer, that Universal decided to take a gamble.

And it took some time before they realized how handsomely that gamble was going to pay off. "Universal didn't know what to do with the movie," Willard Huyck says. "They pushed it into a tiny theater and didn't promote it much. But the public discovered it—young people went crazy with identification, and people who had been teen-agers in the 1950's bathed in the nostalgia. It paid off."

Today, Huyck and Katz—both of whom have reached the ripe old age of 28—are generally considered to be the hottest young writing talents in town, able to command eye-popping sums for their work. Oddly enough, they look enough alike to pass for brother and sister—slender, delicate and fair-skinned. Huyck, however, is subdued and cool, while his wife tends to bubble over with laughter.

Like most of their contemporaries in Hollywood, they seem obsessed with the past, and their home is a riotous ex-

David S. Ward, author of "The Sting," may have made compromises, but he can now afford the house—and horse—of his dreams.

ample of Art Deco, even down to the glassware. Their choice of cinematic subject matter, too, attests to their love of the long-ago: "Lucky Lady," which pairs Liza Minnelli with Burt Reynolds under the direction of Stanley Donen, is set in the thirties, as will be the Huycks' upcoming thriller for George Lucas, "Radioland Murders." After that, they'll be dipping into several generations of a wine-growing dynasty in "The Napa Valley Story."

The Huycks' closest rival—in terms of youth, influence and bankability—is David S. Ward, the tall, slender, bearded, 28-year-old, Oscar-winning author of "The Sting," which has grossed $25-million in the domestic market to date. Ward received a comparatively small sum (about $90,000) for "The Sting," but, luckily, his contract includes a percentage-of-the-profits clause—a clause which will make him a millionaire. His new script, "San Joaquin," about the struggle between the railroad and the landowners in turn-of-the-century California, will probably fetch a figure equal to that being paid to the Huycks for "Lucky Lady."

Born in a Cleveland slum, Ward was so poor he had to drop out of U.S.C. and take a job cutting pictures at night so he could get through his courses at the much cheaper U.C.L.A. His script for a militantly anti-war picture called "Steelyard Blues" was peddled for over a year before Michael and Julia Phillips and their associate, occasional actor Tony Bill, managed to land Donald Sutherland, who later persuaded Jane Fonda to co-star with him in the movie. With both stars set—and only then—Warners agreed to distribute the picture which, in the end, emerged as a travesty of Ward's original concept.

But Ward stuck to his typewriter, ultimately turning out "The Sting," a tale of two thirties con-men. The Phillipses and Bill bought it; producers Richard D. Zanuck and David Brown at Universal backed it; and the script proved enticing to both Paul Newman and Robert Redford, who were searching for a follow-up to their previous lark about lovable bandits, "Butch Cassidy and the Sundance Kid." Not too surprisingly, the screenplay was rewritten to accommodate the special talents of this pair of surefire box-office stars, a fact which may have brought a small measure of grief to "The Sting's" ambitious young author. Ward was also disappointed to hear that George Roy Hill, director of "Butch Cassidy and the Sundance Kid," would once again be guiding Newman and Redford through their capers. He had envisioned himself in that role.

If Ward has had to compromise, he has at least been handsomely compensated. His dream of becoming a movie director has not yet come true, but his dream home has. He lives lavishly in funky-rural Topanga Canyon, and he has even bought a horse. Although he dresses in the obligatory Californian uniform of jeans and loose denim shirt—and might, at first glance, be mistaken for a run-of-the-mill hippie—he is in fact fast approaching millionaire status.

One of the most vigorous aspirants to the thrones of Huyck, Katz and Ward is a somber 27-year-old former movie critic named Paul Schrader. Because of a repressive Calvinist background, Schrader did not see his first movie until he was 18. He managed to catch up with the other movie buffs of his generation, however, by seeing several films a day for four years. When a scholarly book he had written about movie directors failed to sell, he realized that a career of specialized criticism would mean a life of poverty, so he set out to write tough commercial scripts. But he was tortured by a feeling of guilt for having sold out. Unlike Huyck, Katz and Ward, he is not a cheerful supplier of saleable material; he is a moody man who would like to be an artist, caught in the

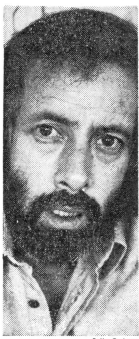

Betty Graham

Since the success of his "Chinatown," Robert Towne gets $400,000 per script.

sweet life of the Hollywood system like a fly in a jar of honey.

Schrader, like his contemporaries, has suffered through a long and exhausting struggle for success. The pressure was intense and at one point he began drinking heavily. Seemingly on the verge of coming apart, he submitted to intensive psychiatric treatment when his script about pipeline crews in Canada failed to find a buyer. Finally, he set out to make money in a hurry. Virtually bankrupt, he found material for a script in stories supplied to him by his brother, a teacher in Japan. He assembled a script about the Tokyo gangster mobs known as the Yazuka, one packed with commercial violence—with a few touches of downbeat Schrader poetry thrown in for good measure. His agents managed to secure a commitment from Warner Brothers, earning Schrader and his brother a whopping $300,000. Robert Mitchum was cast as the star, and everything seemed to be coming up roses and dollar bills.

But then Schrader had the painful experience of seeing "The Yakuza" altered to fit Mitchum by Hollywood's busiest young script doctor—38-year-old Robert Towne, who is in the $400,000 class himself, due to the success of his screenplay for the popular "Chinatown." Disillusioned and angry, Schrader fought desperately to have Towne's name removed from the credits of "The Yakuza," but the Writers' Guild of America West insisted that the names of both writers appear on the finished draft. Schrader, a dark and muscular man with brooding eyes, seems more tension-ridden than ever about his painful but lucrative progress as a Hollywood screenwriter. An uneasy offspring of the unholy marriage between God and mammon, he has now written several other six-figure scripts. The first of his screenplays set for production is "Taxi Driver," written for Martin Scorsese, director of "Mean Streets." Robert De Niro, who achieved stardom last year with "Mean Streets" and "Bang the Drum Slowly," will play a cab driver obsessed with the idea of political assassination.

In a few cases, Hollywood's infatuation with young, unknown writers has led to conspicuous disaster. There is the case of Marc Norman, for instance. His agent offered Norman's script, "Oklahoma Crude," to all the major Hollywood studios on a Friday, asking for bids by the following Monday. Amazingly, there were several bids, the highest being that of producer-director Stanley Kramer and Columbia Pictures. They paid the stunning sum of $300,000 and confidently enlisted the torrid box-office team of George C. Scott and Faye Dunaway. They opened the movie, sat back, and waited for the money to roll in. They're still waiting.

Twentieth Century-Fox, too, seems to have taken a loss on an item called "The Insurance Company." Two years ago, they shelled out $200,000 for young Gerald Di Pego's script. Today, it remains unproduced, because no star took a shine to it. No doubt, there are scores of scripts by youthful writers collecting dust in studio vaults.

Still, the list of young authors making it big in Hollywood is impressive. In their twenties—or early thirties—and going strong are: Colin Higgins, the author of "Harold and Maude," who has just been signed to do the movie version of "Hair" for a six-figure sum; Walter Hill, who wrote the Steve McQueen-Ali MacGraw vehicle, "The Getaway," and is now at work on a Charles Bronson thriller; Carole Eastman, acclaimed for "Five Easy Pieces" and soon to be represented by "The Fortune," a comedy directed by Mike Nichols and tailored to the talents of Jack Nicholson and Warren Beatty; John Milius, who fetched a handsome $300,000 for his "The Life and Times of Judge Roy Bean" and who recently received somewhere in the neighborhood of $400,000 for "The Wind and the Lion," an action movie starring Sean Connery and Candice Bergen; Terence Malick, author of "Pocket Money" and "Badlands"; W. D. Richter, who penned the James Caan-Sally Kellerman suspense comedy, "Slither"; and Tracy Keenan Wynn (son of actor Keenan Wynn), who turned out the screenplay for Burt Reynolds' "The Longest Yard."

The agent, of course, plays a major role in negotiating contracts for these much-in-demand writers, and one of the most powerful agents in the field today is John Ptak. How old is he? Thirty—and his record for pushing his clients into the $400,000 class is the envy of many a fiftyish agent.

How did Ptak achieve his super-agent status? He began, unceremoniously enough, as an employe of the American Film Institute; his task was to make sure that film equipment was in good shape. Later, he worked as a theater manager. In both of these jobs, he came to know and to become close friends with a number of hungry young writers.

His next job proved to be the crucial break. He was appointed assistant to the powerful agent Mike Medavoy at International Famous Agency, and when Medavoy left to become head of production at United Artists, Ptak got his position at I.F.A. Which is where he can now be found, wheeling and dealing expertly among the hot properties of such prized clients as the no-longer-hungry Willard Huyck, Gloria Katz and Paul Schrader.

So Ptak—and virtually all of Hollywood— is thinking young. The question is, will anything of enduring value emerge from this fashionable New Wave?

"It's enormously difficult," says Paul Schrader. "We're trying to make the money so that we can direct and write pictures of artistic merit; given our record of commercial success, perhaps the major studios will give us a chance to create our own personal, poetic films."

One other question remains: In achieving financial viability, are Hollywood's young writers falling into the same trap as their predecessors?

1974 S 29, II:15:1

Fellini Again At the Top Of His Form

By VINCENT CANBY

"AMARCORD" ("I remember" in the vernacular of Romagna) is Federico Fellini's 13th feature and as full of marvels as anything he's ever done. It takes place in the early 1930's in a small Adriatic resort town that seems to be Fellini's recollection of Rimini, where he was born and grew up, although it's sometimes as exotic as the ancient Rome of "Satyricon" and as familiar as the Rimini Fellini remembered in "I Vitelloni."

"Amarcord" is a haunting, funny, beautiful work that makes most other recent movies, with the exception of Ingmar Bergman's "Scenes From a Marriage," look as drab as winter fields without snow. What's more startling —and almost unforgivable—is the way in which it exposes the small, toll-taker souls of some critics (myself included) who have been fussing at Fellini about his last two films, "The Clowns" and "Roma," those visually spectacular, free-form memoirs that didn't seem to test his talents. A lot of us thought he was loafing—rerunning old scenes—and we expressed ourselves with the kind of sadness that usually accompanies a line like "this hurts me more than it does you." We needn't have worried as, I'm sure, he didn't.

Like "The Clowns" and "Roma," Fellini's new film is a sort of memoir, and it is sometimes as splendid to look at as a light show designed simply to surprise, dazzle and make the eyes blink. Yet "Amarcord" is often as emotionally implicating as "Nights of Cabiria" or "8½." The free form has been combined with Fellini's insatiable curiosity about and fondness for the human animal, especially those who maintain only the most tenuous holds on their dignity or sanity.

"Amarcord" is not a single narrative in the conventional sense and thus, I'm sure, may be incorrectly described as a film without a story. It doesn't have a single narrative. It has dozens. There is one for nearly every character who turns up on the screen, plus the story of Fellini himself, not only the Fellini who is represented in the film by a firm-jawed, decently rebellious teen-ager named Titta (Bruno Zanin), nor the Fellini surrogate called The Lawyer (Luigi Rossi), who turns up in the film from time to time as a kind of tour guide.

Fellini himself is never actually in the movie, as he was in "The Clowns" and "Roma," but he is all over it. "Amarcord" is his memory of a year in the life of Rimini, or a town much like it, and for Fellini memory has a lot in common with dream. It needn't be what literally happened but what he wanted to believe, or perhaps what time has forced him to believe.

One of the off-screen stories in "Amarcord" is that of the young man from the provinces who went to Rome to become a hugely successful film director. Forty years later he looks back, recalling the events of one year not as a novelist might but more like a poet, or a filmmaker who has enormous studio resources at his command and a small boy's love for the circus that provided Fellini with his sense of theater.

"Amarcord" has the circus's pace, drive, good spirits, fascination with costume and masquerade (sometimes grotesque) and abundance of

Magali Noel inflames the imagination of every man and boy in Fellini's "Amarcord."

events. The characters tumble onto the screen one after another, as if there weren't going to be enough time to get through all the acts.

Among these are Gradisca (Magali Noel), the town's pretty, romantic femme fatale, a hairdresser who so inflames the imaginations of every man and boy that on evening strolls around the piazza she must be escorted by two not-as-pretty women who act as human fenders; Titta's father (Armando Brancia), a construction foreman of terrible temper, abiding love for his family (which is constantly being tested) and hatred for the Fascists, who more or less force honor upon him; Titta's crazy Uncle Teo (Ciccio Ingrassia); his rummy old grandfather (Giuseppe Lanigro) who looks like something carved out of wood to be used as a bottle stopper; the Tobacconist (Antonietta Beluzzi), a hefty woman with such formidable breasts that she almost smothers Titta in one of his initial forays into sex (he tries to lift her off the floor).

Some of the stories are both magical and funny, such as the one we are told about Gradisca and her encounter with an important prince to explain how she got her name (translated as "Please do"). Some are bawdy and some elegiacal. Throughout the film, uproarious comedy is punctuated with images that foretell feelings of isolation and loss: a small boy walks stoically to school through a pea-soup fog, scared out of his wits; a terminally ill woman sits on a hospital bed and fiddles with her wedding ring that is now too big.

There are also images so mysterious that they defy simple categorization, such as the one of the peacock who comes out of the sky to land in the piazza during a snowfall, interrupting a snowball fight when he suddenly spreads his extraordinary tail.

One of Fellini's greatest gifts is his ability to communicate a sense of wonder, which has the effect of making us all feel much younger than we have any right to. Fellini's is a very special, personal kind of cinema and in "Amarcord" he is in the top of his form.

1974 S 29, II:1:6

Belmondo at His Best in Resnais Creation

STAVISKY, directed by Alain Resnais; screenplay (French with English subtitles) by Jorge Semprun; photography, Sacha Vierny; editor, Albert Jurgenson; music, Stephen Sondheim; executive producers, Alexandre Mnouchkine and Georges Dancigers; production companies, Ariane Films/Cerito Films/Euro International (Italy). At the New York Film Festival at Alice Tully Hall, Lincoln Center. Running time: 117 minutes.
Alexandre Stavisky....Jean-Paul Belmondo
Arlette Stavisky............Anny Duperey
Baron Raoul..............Charles Boyer
Borelli..................Francois Perier
Montalvo................Roberto Bisaco
Dr. Mezy...............Michel Lonsdale
Bonny....................Claude Rich
Henriel...................Gigi Balista

By NORA SAYRE

The difficulty of knowing what is true, of discovering what really happened, ripples throughout Alain Resnais's "Stavisky" — a spell-casting mood piece that is also factually frustrating. Ideally, it should be possible to relish this fascinating movie on its own. But, since so little French history of the nineteen-thirties is provided, it's likely to send you flying to the library. ("Stavisky" isn't perplexing just to Americans; a colleague reports that a Parisian audience was also bewildered.) The movie opened last night at the New York Film Festival and will be repeated tonight. It doesn't yet have a commercial release—but it will be startling if it's denied one.

Briefly, the real Stavisky was an entrepreneur, an impresario and an accomplished swindler who bribed politicians, the police, the courts and the press; he also squandered all of his own wealth. When he flooded France with fake vouchers in 1932, the banks were closed. As a result, there were violent street riots early in 1933, in which a number of persons were shot by the police. The Government could no longer rely on the loyalty of the army or the police, and Premiere Edouard Daladier was forced to resign. (Stavisky himself appears to have been an apo-

Charles Boyer, left, and Jean-Paul Belmondo

litical adventurer, although he had a megalomaniacal belief that he could solve the economic problems of Europe—and also end unemployment. Apparently, the press dwelled on the fact that he was a Russian Jew, and the fascist agents in France exploited the anti-Semitic issue by insisting that foreign crooks were out to ruin the nation.

The movie mutes the last point, but the characterization of Stavisky seems very faithful to the accounts of the period. He appears as a dual personality: a graceful bon vivant who luxuriates in every conceivable pleasure and an acute melancholic. There's a charming moment when he explains the difference between happiness and pleasure: he says that happiness can occur in a single moment, but that pleasure requires a huge investment of time — and that it's available only to the rich. He's also obsessed by suicides and by mysterious deaths. He was once a scruffy hood, but his friends remark that his present self despises his past one.

As Stavisky, whom a journalist of the thirties called "a gentleman among gangsters and a gangster among gentlemen," Jean-Paul Belmondo is at his best. Despite the tycoon's grandeur, he still breaks into a mobster's strut: arms swinging, wearing his shoulders high, he lunges forward with his torso aslant, while his respectable companions walk erect. Mr. Belmondo has all the authority and the gaiety of the man who refused to believe that he could make a mistake. But although others later call him crazy, we don't really see that aspect of his nature — perhaps because of the stubborn sanity that Mr. Belmondo brings to even his loopier roles.

Charles Boyer is effortlessly elegant and supple as a baron who enjoyed Stavisky's company. The eyebrows rise delicately above those knowing eyes, and it's a treat to watch him playing with Mr. Belmondo: They seem to greet each other across the span of movie history. Anny Duperey at first appears as a brittle, expensive moll; she then emerges as a sympathetic person. The teasing, troubling musical score by Stephen Sondheim and the stunning art deco interiors suit the subject to perfection. There is also an engaging use of the theater: A reading from Jean Giradoux's "Intermezzo" and a performance of "Coriolanus" gently distil the themes of disorder and death.

•

As usual, Mr. Resnais flirts with time: Here, there are many flash-forwards—mainly to a parliamentary committee, where witnesses testify about the Stavisky case. Most of these leaps into the future work very well, although there are a few too many of them. Less successful is the insertion of Leon Trotsky. Both he and Stavisky were exiles, but since their lives never touched, the revolutionary's appearance in the movie is unsettling. (Also, one wishes that the riots had been filmed — but perhaps they were omitted due to expense.) Meanwhile, despite its mystifications, "Stavisky" is one of the most rewarding films I've seen this year—and also one of the most intelligent.

1974 S 30, 51:5

LIEBELEI, directed by Max Ophuls; screenplay (German with English subtitles by Hans Wilhelm and Curt Alexander) from the play "Liebelel" by Arthur Schnitzler; photography, Franz Planer; editor, Friedel Buchott; music, Theo Mackeben; executive producer, Fred Lissa; production company, Elite Tonfilm Productions; print is courtesy of the National Film Archive of the British Film Institute and Serge Silberman. At the New York Film Festival, Alice Tully Hall, Lincoln Center. Running time: 88 minutes.

Fritz Lobheimer ....Wolfgang Liebeneiner
Christine Weiring ..... Magda Schneider
Mitzi Schlager ....Luise Ullrich
Theo Kaiser ....Willy Eichberger
Hans Weiring ....Paul Hoerbiger
Baron Eggerdorff ....Gustaf Gruendgens
Baroness Eggerdorff ...Olga Tschechowa

The conviction that the past can be canceled out, that it "doesn't count" any more, is one of the illusions that feed romantic tragedy That notion is beautifully illustrated in Max Ophuls's adaptation of Arthur Schnitzler's "Liebelei," which was shown at the 12th New York Film Festival last Friday. As elsewhere, Schnitzler also stressed the importance of living in the present, of savoring what may be suddenly snuffed out.

The movie, made in 1932 and set in Vienna, 1910, focuses on a touching love affair between a shy singer (Magda Schneider) and a vulnerable young officer (Wolfgang Liebeneiner) whose feelings surface most sensitively, despite all his strict military training. Before they met, he was involved with a married baroness. He breaks with his mistress—but although the liaison is over, her husband kills him in a duel. Evidently, being punished for the wrong thing—or paying for a chapter of life that's past—were recurrent themes of Schnitzler's. And meeting the right person after you've spent too long with the wrong one was the kind of irony that the playwright was fond of exploring.

"Liebelei" embodies what Edmund Wilson defined as Schnitzler's gift for "lightly handled tragedy," and Ophuls's own lightness of style is as beguiling here as it later was in Schnitzler's "La Ronde." Amid the waltzes, the cafes, the elaborate staircases and winding back streets, the moments of emotional consequence are marvelously detailed. When the Baron (Gustaf Gruendgens) learns of his wife's adultery, he runs through his own palatial home and glares at the rooms where the couple met in a manner that's truly frightening; later, when he discovers that one of her keys fits her lover's door, he grinds it to and fro in the lock with outraged bitterness.

Ophuls was at his best when he caused climates of feeling to build or change. As the singer and the officer begin to fall in love, their mutual absorption is subtly conveyed as they dance very slowly to rapid, noisy music —they don't know that they're not with the rhythm. This scene is cleverly contrasted by the next one, in which the officer dances correctly but unenthusiastically with the woman whom he no longer wants. When the hero—celebrating his freedom from the Baroness—romps and fools about with his friends before a party, he and they seem particularly childlike and innocent; hence they (and we) are utterly unprepared for the Baron's sudden, threatening entrance.

The movie makes the code of "honor" appear very stupid — and when another youthful officer protests that any shot that isn't fired in self-defense is "criminal," his rebellion against the military is a denunciation of all senseless duels. All in all, it's a privilege to see a movie that is romantic without being sentimental. Since that distinction is rarely respected now, it's exhilarating to learn what Ophuls achieved more than 40 years ago.

NORA SAYRE

1974 S 30, 51:5

THE NIGHT OF THE SCARECROW (A Noite do Espantalho), directed by Sergio Ricardo; screenplay (Portuguese with English subtitles) by Mr. Ricardo, Maurice Capovilla, Jean-Claude Bernadet, Plineo Pacheco and Nilson Barbosa; photography, Dib Luffi; editor, Sylvio Renoldi; music, Mr. Ricardo; production companies, Zen Producoes Cinematograf/Otto Engel. At the New York Film Festival. Running time: 92 minutes.

Maria do Grotao ....Rejane Medeiros
Ze do Cao ....Jose Pimentel
Ze Tulao ....Gilson Moura
The Scarecrow ....Alceu Valenca
Colonel ....Emmanuel Cavalcanti
Dragon ....Fatima Batista
Josue .... Luis Gomes Correa

Any movie maker who sets out to tell the story of his people, to pit good against evil and cowboy against hired gun, to mix in local myths and Christian symbolism, to match reality with fantasy, to inveigh against the evils of capitalism, to tell a story of tortured love—and, what's more, do it all as a musical — had better bring in a masterpiece.

Sérgio Ricardo, a Brazilian singer, composer and movie maker, set out to do all of these things in a film called "The Night of the Scarecrow," shown last weekend at the 12th New York Film Festival.

It is not a masterpiece.

It is, instead, a lavish and self-indulgent film so encumbered with ambitiousness and artistic and intellectual baggage, and committed in so many directions, that it can manage only sporadic and somewhat frenzied efforts at the full realization of any of its goals.

Stripped of its burden of pretension, "The Night of the Scarecrow" is the story of impoverished Brazilian peasants exploited by the greasy landowner whose parched fields they work. The peasants are championed by a cowboy figure; the landlord, by a pack of hired, motorcycle-riding soldier-gunmen. Drawn to the peasants' champion and the leader of the gunmen, and torn between the two, is a peasant woman.

Upon this basic structure have been piled the Scarecrow, part Christ figure, part minstrel; a bosomy dragon representing evil; the landowner's bourgeois retinue — given to clown make-up or satanic garb, whichever best serves the demands of the moment's symbolism; a mad holy man; a peasant chorus, and a set of insect-wing motorcycles and cycling costumes that appear to have come out of "The Wild One" by way of Attila the Hun and Tinker Bell.

However many its faults, "Night of the Scarecrow" is too busy a film to be accused of dullness. At its best, this revolutionary pop opera is full of color and movement; and some of its music—pulsing with rhythm or wailing with despair—is captivating, although the lyrics, at least in their English translation, seem less accomplished.

Set beside the exceptionally good "Os Fuzis" ("The Guns"), a Brazilian film by Ruy Guerra, shown last June at the First Avenue Screening Room, that deals with essentially the same subject matter in the same locale from the same viewpoint, "The Night of the Scarecrow" comes off as a case of egregious bloat.

LAWRENCE VAN GELDER

1974 S 30, 51:6

LACOMBE, LUCIEN, directed and produced by Louis Malle; screenplay (French with English subtitles) by Mr. Malle and Patrick Modiano; director of photography, Tonino Delli Colli; editor, Suzanne Baron; music, Django Reinhardt and the Quintet from the Hot-Club of France; distributed by 20th Century-Fox Films. Running time: 114 minutes. At the New York Film Festival at Alice Tully Hall in Lincoln Center, Broadway at 65th Street. This film has been rated R.

Lucien ....Pierre Blaise
France ....Aurore Clement
Albert Horn.............Holger Lowenadler
Bella Horn...................Therese Gieshe
Jean-Bernard de Beisin....Stephane Bouy
Betty Beaulieu...........Loumi Iacobesco
Faure ....Rene Bouloc
Aubert ....Pierre Decazes
Tonin ....Jean Rougerie
Madame Lacombe..........Gilberte Rivet
Monsieur Laborit..........Jacques Rispal
Monsieur Laborit..........Jacques Rispal

By VINCENT CANBY

"Lacombe, Lucien," the title of Louis Malle's fine, uncompromising new film, is a statistic, a name on a list, someone unknown, without identity. Which is pretty much the way Lucien Lacombe, aged 17, sees himself in June, 1944.

Lucien (Pierre Blaise) is a strong, square-jawed, none-too-bright country boy living in southwest France during the Nazi occupation. He scrubs floors in the hospital of a small provincial city and makes occasional visits to his home, a farm now run by the landlord who has become his mother's lover while his father is a prisoner of war.

•

Lucien is a hunter, usually by necessity and now and then for sport. He shoots rabbits and wrings the necks of chickens, which are food for the dinner table, but sometimes he can't resist going after a yellow warbler with his slingshot. The bird means nothing to him. Proving the excellence of his aim does.

In "Lacombe, Lucien, Mr. Malle asks us to contemplate Lucien as he chooses, it seems accidentally, his course toward destruction. After being turned down for membership in the Underground in his native village because he's too young, Lucien more or less slips into total collaboration with the French arm of the German police, the only club that will accept him, at just that point in history when it's apparent to even the densest minds that the Germans are beaten.

The film, which was shown at Alice Tully Hall on Saturday and Sunday evenings, will open in a theater here in mid-October.

"Lacombe, Lucien" is Mr. Malle's toughest, most rueful, least sentimental film. Like the extraordinary Marcel Ophuls documentary, "The Sorrow and the Pity," the film refuses to identify heroes and villains with certainty. That, Mr. Malle seems to say, is to oversimplify issues and to underrate the complexity of the human experience.

Mr. Malle is adamant on these points. It's very difficult for anyone of my (World War II) generation to understand a collaborationist, which the director-writer underscores by allowing Lucien scarcely any saving graces. When hunting rabbits, he has the impassive face of a killer. Once taken into the police force, he becomes as impossibily arrogant as only the ignorant can be. He coolly witnesses torture procedures as if the system had nothing to do with him.

•

Instinctively, however, he finds himself attracted to the household of a once-famous, rich Paris tailor, an aristocratic Jew named Albert Horn (Holger Lowenadler), who is in hiding with his ancient mother and pretty daughter, France (Aurore Clement), in Lucien's town.

Armed with a machine gun, his official police passes and gifts such as confiscated champagne, as well as with a monumental insensitivity, Lucien invites himself into the lives of these refugees. Lucien bullies them, makes a

Pierre Blaise plays a French youth who aids the Germans

fool of himself and suddenly falls in love with France.

The difficulty of the task that Mr. Malle has set for himself by focusing on Lucien is manifest in two magnificent scenes that are the highlights of the film. In one, Mr. Horn turns his elegant, exhausted eyes on Lucien and warns that he doesn't need Lucien to make him appreciate his daughter. "We're both fragile," he says. In the other scene, France clings to Lucien, who doesn't come up to her instep in any way, and damns the fact of being a Jew. Her degradation is complete.

•

A more sentimental director would, I'm sure, have made this film the story of the Horns. They are marvelous, gallant creatures, and both Mr. Lowenadler and Miss Clément are superb.

By fixing the sights of the film on Lucien, Mr. Malle and Patrick Modiano, who worked with him on the screenplay, force us to considerations of more agonizing import. We never know how Lucien got that way, only that the times made possible his short, disastrous season in the sun. With the liberation, Lucien once again becomes a statistic.

"Lacombe, Lucien" is easily Mr. Malle's most ambitious, most provocative film, and if it is not as immediately affecting as "The Fire Within" or even the comic "Murmur of the Heart," it's because—to make his point—he has centered it on a character who must remain forever mysterious, forever beyond our sympathy.

1974 S 30, 52:1

A Bresson 'Spectacle' Inspired by Malory

By VINCENT CANBY

It's said that at one time or another every film director yearns to make a spectacle, one of those multi-million-dollar epics with lots of horses, costumes and extras, the sort of film that has to be directed from a raised platform with an electronic voice-magnifying system. To the extent that "Lancelot of The Lake" has horses, costumes and extras (a few), and to the extent that it's inspired by some of the tales in Malory's "Morte D'arthur," it may be called Robert Bresson's spectacle, but it's unlike any conventional film spectacle, you've ever seen.

•

The film, which was shown last night at Alice Tully Hall in the New York Film Festival, will be repeated Thursday evening.

"Lancelot of The Lake" is about the last days of King Arthur's Round Table when, after the bloody, fruitless quest for the Holy Grail, the knights return to a fading Camelot and fall out among one another.

The age of chivalry is over but no one knows why. Arthur suspects that God has been provoked. He urges his knights to forget their enmities and to better themselves.

Lancelot, who once was allowed a vision of the Grail, thinks God is punishing them all for his being Guinevere's lover. When he asks her to release him from his vows to her and to surrender to God, she refuses. "If I surrender," she says, "it will be to you not God."

Although Mr. Bresson ("Diary of a Country Priest," "Au Hazard, Balthazar," "La Femme Douce," etc.) is not

especially interested in visual spectacle, he has made a stunning-looking movie that often pares down spectacle to what seems to be an irreducible minimum. Virtually an entire tournament is photographed with the camera's eye focused between the horse's hoofs and midsection.

Mr. Bresson once said that the true calling of cinema "is first to be exact, and then to be interior — rather than exterior or decorative."

"Lancelot" could never be called decorative, but it is sometimes breathtaking in its exterior details, which is not the same as being realistic. The concluding sequence of the film, after chivalry's final upheaval, is one of the most beautiful and strange the director has ever done:

A riderless horse charges aimlessly through a twilight forest as the world's last knight, wounded and dying, staggers slowly toward the bodies of other armor-clad knights. It looks simultaneously mysterious, like the remains of the civilization on another planet, and banal, like a pile of damaged gasoline pumps.

What's missing from the film is any urgent interior meaning, and this it may be because of the distractions of the exterior details. It may also be because the conflicts that rage within Lancelot — between duty and desire, courtly love and physical love — simply aren't complex enough to bring out the best in Mr. Bresson. There are times, too, when the armor seems to get in the way of ideas or any sense of passion. There's something essentially comic about the sight of a knight impetuously trying to tear off his gear for a quick roll in the loft.

The Cast

LANCELOT OF THE LAKE (Lancelot du Lac), directed by Robert Bresson; screenplay (French with English subtitles) by Mr. Bresson; produced by Jean-Pierre Rassam and Francois Rochas; director of photography, Pasqualino de Santis; editor, Germaine Lamy; music, Philippe Sarde; a French-Italian co-production of Mara Films/ORTF/Laser Productions/Gerico Sound. Running time: 85 minutes. At the New York Film Festival at Alice Tully Hall in Lincoln Center, Broadway at 65th Street. This film has not been rated.
Lancelot .... Luc Simon
Guinevere ..... Laura Duke Condominas
Gawain .... Humbert Balsan
King Arthur .... Vladimir Antolek-Oresek
Mordred .... Patrick Bernard
Lionel .... Arthur de Montalembert

As usual in a Bresson film, the actors are unknowns or nonprofessionals, chosen by the director for their faces and their willingness to be drilled into that state of somnambulance by which he is best able to create his interior visions.

Laura Duke Condominas is a lovely, young, girlish Guinevere, who is both passionate and demanding. Luc Simon also looks right as a Lancelot who is no longer young, and whose trials have given a firm set to ascetic features that, in youth, would have seemed soft.

In "Lancelot of the Lake," which the director first announced in 1957, the style is intact but the content is missing.

1974 O 1, 33:1

ROME WANTS ANOTHER CAESAR (Roma Rivuole Cesare), directed by Miklos Jancso; screenplay (Italian) with English subtitles) by Mr. Jancso and Giovanna Gagliardo; director of photography, Janos Kende; editor, Giuliano Mattioli; music, Uberta Bertacca; produced by RAI/Films S.P.A. Running time: 100 minutes. At the New York Film Festival at Alice Tully Hall in Lincoln Center. This film has not been rated.
Claudius .... Daniel Olbrychski
Attavius .... Hiram Keller
Proconsul .... Lino Troisi
First Republican .... Gino Lavagetto

By VINCENT CANBY

"Rome Wants Another Caesar," which was shown at the New York Film Festival last night and will be repeated this evening, comes quite close to being a hysterically funny bad film, a movie of such ridiculous pretentions that it restores a lofty reputation to philistinism.

It is an Italian production directed by Miklos Jancso, the Hungarian who once made two good films, "The Roundup" and "The Red and The White," which seemed to be pioneering a new kind of epic film making. What impressed many of us about those two early films was the director's extraordinary ability to turn complex historical events into personal political dramas of intense lyricism.

•

In his recent films, Mr. Jancso has pursued his spectacular camera techniques to a point of no return. The only memorable thing about "Winter Wind," shown here in 1970, was that the entire film consisted of 12 takes (compared to a couple of hundred in an ordinary film). "Red Psalm," shown at the 1972 New York Film Festival, was done in 26 takes. The style added nothing to the movie. It was the movie.

"Rome Wants Another Caesar" looks not quite so inhibited, but it may be Mr. Jancso's most sincerely witless work. It's about some Roman revolutionaries in Numidia in North Africa during the last days of the Roman republic, plotting to assassinate the Roman proconsul and arguing among themselves.

That is what it is about, but what we see is a kind of junior high school pageant with a dozen European actors on location in Tunisia, wearing funny looking costumes and carrying swords as if they were eels. That is, awkwardly. Holding hands and dancing around statues of Caesar, they get off such mind-benders as "The wise man knows that without enemies it's impossible to create friends."

Mr. Jancso isn't really much interested in ancient Rome. He keeps making lugubrious parallels between revolutionaries then and now. Instead of illuminating his subject, he buries it in sand. What the movie is doing in the New York Film Festival, I can't imagine. It is to serious film making what knitting is to a benched football player. It's fooling around.

1974 O 2, 58:1

THE NIGHT PORTER, directed by Liliana Cavani; screenplay by Miss Cavani and Italo Moscati; story by Miss Cavani, Barbara Alberti and Amedeo Pagani; editor, Franco Arcalli; director of photography, Alfio Contini; music, Daniele Paris; produced by Robert Gordon Edwards. Released by Avco Embassy Pictures. At the Baronet Theater, Third Avenue at 59th Street. Running time: 117 minutes. This film is classified R.
Max .... Dirk Bogarde
Lucia .... Charlotte Rampling
Klaus .... Philippe Leroy
Hans .... Gabriele Ferzetti
Stumm .... Giuseppe Addobbati
Countess Stein .... Isa Miranda

By NORA SAYRE

If you don't love pain, you won't find "The Night Porter" erotic—and by now, even painbuffs may be satiated with Nazi decadence. The movie, which opened yesterday at the Baronet, reunites a former SS officer (Dirk Bogarde) and a young woman (Charlotte Rampling) who was raped by him during her adolescence in a concentration camp. In Vienna, in 1957, they enthusiastically resume their old sadomasochistic relationship, which includes a taste for broken glass.

Since the director, Liliana Cavani, made a four-hour documentary on the Third Reich for Italian television, she has a robust background in fascism. Yet her new movie is romantic about abuse. The anguish of the prisoners in the camps is exploited simply for the sake of sensationalism—given the sexual motifs of the film, their suffering is almost made to seem chic. And when Mr. Bogarde and Miss Rampling relive their common past in flashbacks, the titillating build-up to the rape scene is accompanied by "The Magic Flute," which both characters are hearing: Pamina and Tamino sing pledges of undying love while the cruelties grow more intricate. If the friends of Mozart decide to picket on his behalf, I'll be among them.

•

Is this slab of opulent claptrap worth any serious consideration? Yes, because of the talents involved—mainly Mr. Bogarde's. Sensuality and austerity meet and mingle in the face of this impeccable authoritarian, and his silken moments alternate with harsh ones. He's best when he's reserved—his outbursts aren't always successful—and there are a few too many sly, slow smiles. But he's skilled at hiding his feelings from the characters around him while revealing all of his emotions to the audience. When it occurs to him to murder someone, his rigid poise lapses, and he becomes socially awkward — slightly embarrassed and ingratiating at the same time. Occasionally, you recall his performance in "The Servant," but his range is much wider here.

Miss Rampling's elegant sternness and low, bitter voice are suitable for her role, but she's a one-dimensional actress who can't convey much beyond tension.

Dirk Bogarde

Charlotte Rampling

Toward the end, she produces, one sulky scowl that makes you grateful for a new facial expression. Also, she has the world's most unconvincing laugh — especially when making love. Credibility is a problem throughout the picture—partly because of Miss Rampling's styles of response. In a scene where she's literally fettered, someone tries to break into her lover's apartment, and she rattles her chains like an apprehensive hostess — just as a nervous partygiver may

fidget with her jewelry before the guests arrive.

•

"The Night Porter" is handsomely filmed in dark, rich tones. But the movie's visual virtues are negated by infinite absurdities—particularly by the sentimentality with which the director views this luckless couple. Near the finish, we even catch a whiff of an old Hollywood formula, which asks us to regard these lovers as poignant — because the

world won't allow them to enjoy each other in peace. All in all, the image that recurs is that of sucking a wound. Meanwhile, if you're in the market for masochism, see Luis Buñuel's "Belle de Jour" again, or revisit Bernardo Bertolucci's "The Conformist" for fascist decay. Granted that both are classics. But that's why "The Night Porter" shouldn't be allowed to ride on their reputation.

1974 O 2, 58:1

THE GAMBLER, directed by Karel Reisz; screenplay by James Toback; produced by Irwin Winkler and Robert Chartoff; director of photography, Victor J. Kemper; music, Jerry Fielding; editor, Roger Spottiswoode; distributed by Paramount Pictures. Running time: 111 minutes. At Loews Tower East Theater, Third Avenue near 72d Street. This film has been rated R.

Axel ....James Caan
Hips ....Paul Sorvino
Billie ....Lauren Hutton
A. R. Lowenthal ......Morris Carnovsky
Naomi ....Jacqueline Brooks
Carmine ....Burt Young

By VINCENT CANBY

Axel Freed (James Caan), the young New York English professor, the hero of Karel Reisz's "The Gambler," has a ravenous monkey on his back. Axel loves to gamble. He'll bet on anything for staggering stakes. More than winning he likes the uncertainty, the threat of disaster that, ultimately, is death or its reasonable facsimile.

At the beginning of the film, Axel has just lost $44,-000, which he doesn't have, and by the time the film ends he's even worse off, though he may be happy because, momentarily, anyway, he's achieved the terrible humiliation he's apparently been seeking all along.

•

"The Gambler," which opened yesterday at Loews Tower East Theater, was written by James Toback who, in his first film, becomes the author of some of

James Caan

the most disabling dialogue to be imposed on any serious movie in years. But more about that later.

Compulsive gamblers are very special cases. Mr. Reisz, the director of several notable English films ("This Sporting Life," "Morgan," "Isadora"), and Mr. Toback have no special interest in treating Axel as a psychoanalytic case, though they provide some basic information if anyone else wants to go into that.

Axel's father is nowhere on the family scene. His mother, Naomi (Jacqueline Brooks), is a successful medical doctor, a self-sufficient, liberated sort of woman who might have had man-to-man talks with her son when he was 12 years old.

Observing the family from a walled-in compound in Riverdale is Axel's grandfather, A. R. Lowenthal (Morris Carnovsky), a self-made millionaire (a chain of furniture stores) who is probably a good deal less kind than the movie would want us to believe.

The movie prefers to consider Axel almost romantically, as a kind of artist whose misspent life is his work-in-progress. Axel himself brushes aside all efforts of friends and family to make him see himself as sick. "My god, Axel," his mother says at one point, in a line that Woody Allen might have written for laughs, "have I been such a failure as a mother that I've raised a son with the morals of a snake?" Says Axel's girlfriend (Lauren Hutton), "I don't understand any of it." Replies Axel: "It's just something I like to do." The movie follows Axel's downward path with such care that you keep thinking there must be some illuminating purpose, but there isn't. "The Gambler" is a very small movie, sometimes with embarrassing delusions of

grandeur as when Axel quotes E. E. Cummings ("Buffalo Bill's defunct") or lectures his class on William Carlos Williams and Dostoyevsky. Mr. Toback writes as if he were a literature groupie, snatching at bits and pieces of other men's ideas for the loose-leaf album that eventually became his screenplay.

His original inspirations tend to a particular awfulness. Early in the film there's a scene in which Axel accompanies his mother to the bank where she wants to withdraw money to pay Axel's debts. The bank man insists on two pieces of identification, though Naomi has only her driver's license. At this point Axel grabs the bank man and shouts: "Look, I came out of her womb and I'm telling you she's Naomi Freed!"

Each one of us, I suppose, is someone else's I.D. card, but that's not what "The Gambler" is all about.

Mr. Reisz and Mr. Toback reportedly worked a couple of years putting the screenplay into this shape, which is lifeless. The physical production, shot mostly in New York, looks good and Mr. Caan is generally convincing, except in those classroom scenes, but all of the other actors, with the exception of James Sorvino who plays a sympathetic bookie, seem defeated by the quality of the material.

1974 O 3, 50:1

THE TAKING OF PELHAM ONE TWO THREE, directed by Joseph Sargent; screenplay, Peter Stone, based on the novel by John Godey; director of photography, Owen Roizman; editors, Gerald Greenberg and Robert Q. Lovett; music, David Shire; producers, Edgar J. Scherick and Gabriel Katzka; released by United Artists; a Palomar Pictures and Palladium Productions presentation. At the Criterion Theater, Broadway at 45th Street, and the 86th Street East Theater at Third Avenue. Running time: 102 minutes. This film is classified R.

Lieutenant Garber........Walter Matthau
Blue ....Robert Shaw
Green ....Martin Balsam
Green ....Hector Elizondo
Gray ....Earl Hindman
Brown ....James Broderick
Denny Doyle ....Lee Wallace
The Mayor...................

It's been a while since we've had a movie that really catches the mood of New York and New Yorkers. The crisis mentality of what Henry James called "the vast hot pot"—which was revealed when numerous natives were convinced that they alone had caused the great November blackout of 1965—or the New York brand of logic that surfaced when a taxi driver shouted, "If we can get rid of Lindsay, we can get rid of the traffic!" is reflected in "The Taking of Pelham One Two Three." The picture, directed by Joseph Sargent, opened yesterday at the 86th Street East and the Criterion Theater.

Four highly efficient hoods hijack an IRT subway car and hold 18 people hostage for a million dollars; if the city doesn't pay within an hour, one hostage will be shot a minute. The Transit Authority, the Police Department, the Mayor and his colleagues all go into frenzied but coordinated action, while the film cuts most expertly between the stalled car and its passengers, the T.A. Command Center, Gracie Mansion and the city streets. Of course the subway system is soon backed up to the Bronx.

•

Walter Matthau's best caustic energies erupt as a Transit Authority lieutenant, and Peter Stone's script abounds with dialogue that's just right for this actor's benign bad temper. (Surely no one can say "Gesundheit!" to a sneezer quite so aggressively as Mr. Matthau.) Martin Balsam and Robert Shaw—one glazed with a sleazy regret, the other endowed with a calm brutality —are all too likely as your typical rush-hour hijackers. Lee Wallace makes a pleasing, indecisive slob of a Mayor—aware that he'll be booed by any random crowd —and Tom Pedi is particularly good as an outraged official who can't tolerate a mess or a mystery in the subway. The bullying Deputy Mayor (Tony Roberts) unleashes a line that does sound just like home: "We're trying to run a city, not a goddam democracy!"

•

Throughout, there's a skillful balance between the vulnerability of New Yorkers and the drastic, provocative sense of comedy that thrives all over our sidewalks. And the hijacking seems like a perfectly probable event for this town. (Perhaps the only element of fantasy is the implication that the city's departments could function so smoothly together.) Meanwhile, the movie adds up to a fine piece of reporting— and it's the only action picture I've seen this year that has a rousing plot.

NORA SAYRE

1974 O 3, 50:1

PART-TIME WORK OF A DOMESTIC SLAVE (Gelegenheitsarbeit Einer Sklavin), directed by Alexander Kluge; screenplay (German with English subtitles) by Hans Drawe and H. D. Muller; photography, Thomas Mauch; editor, Beate Mainka-Jellinghaus; production companies, Kairos Film/Film Verlag der Autoren. At the New York Film Festival, Alice Tully Hall, Lincoln Center. Running time: 88 minutes.

Roswitha Bronski ....Alexandra Kluge
Franz Bronski.............Franz Bronski
Sylvia....................Sylvia Gartmann
Dr. Genee................Traugott Buhre
                   and

THE BENCH OF DESOLATION, directed by Claude Chabrol; adapted by Roger Grenier from Henry James's "The Bench of Desolation" (French with English subtitles); photography, Jean Rabier; editor, Jacques Gaillard; art director, Guy Littaye. Produced by Philippe Barauc. An O.R.T.F. Cosmovision Technicolor Production, in cooperation with Scott Free Enterprises of London. At the New York Film Festival, Alice Tully Hall, Lincoln Center. Running time: 52 minutes.

Herbert Dodd.........Michel Duchaussoy
Kate Cookham.........Catherine Samie
Nan Drury..............Thalie Fruges
Guest appearance.........Michel Piccoli

By NORA SAYRE

She drops the plates, he glowers, the children wail, he says the house is a pigsty. He even reproaches her for the kind of bread she buys. He's furious when she leaves the house for work, and the children tend to build dangerous little fires in her absence. There's no apparent friendliness in this marriage —the man and woman seem to share only a nose-wrinkling disgust. As a chemist who prefers research to wage-earning, he lets her support him by performing abortions —which he deplores.

●

From the content, you might think that Alexander Kluge's "Part-Time Work of a Domestic Slave"—which played Tuesday and last night at the New York Film Festival—is sympathetic to women's issues. And I suspect that the director may fancy himself a male feminist. However, "Slave" manages to be reactionary in several ways — partly because you can't possibly like either of these one-note characters: the wife (Alexandra Kluge, the director's sister) is presented as a dreary clod, and the husband (Franz Bronski) is just a grouch. The shallowness of the characterization, combined with the pretentious bleakness that runs throughout, results in a paralyzing pessimism that makes the lives depicted seem contemptible.

There's an exceptionally grim abortion that should please the Friends of the Foetus — especially since this foetus quivers after it's removed. (Program notes state that the operation was simulated.) The patient appears to be dressed for a festive occasion (indeed, who would wear an off-the-shoulder blouse to her abortion?). It's hard to know what this scene is supposed to prove— unless it's a device to establish the director's toughness.

The husband reluctantly takes a job, and the wife becomes a political activist. Most of the time, she's hopelessly inefficient, naive, and ineffective. Her social concerns are made to appear faddish, until she manages to rally the workers at her husband's firm against the management. Hence her husband —who doesn't like her politics—is fired. The conclusion implies that the effort for change is useless. All in all, the movie would be depressing if it weren't so dull.

Also on the program is a marvelous adaptation of Henry James's "The Bench of Desolation," directed by Claude Chabrol for television. A fastidious man is faced with a breach of promise suit by a woman who eventually makes him pay a sum that plummets him into a lifetime of debt and destroys his marriage. Years later, the woman reappears and offers to repay him—with interest. Her love and her revenge took the same form: of making money for him (and out of him), and of creating his need for her. She has blighted his life so that she may later have the chance to comfort him—that is, if he no longer loathes her.

The James tale respects the pain of both characters—the rejected woman and the crippled man—while stressing her appalling ruthlessness and condemning the aptitude for suffering plus the dread of vulgarity that made him unable to defy her. (She's also the kind of controlling, semi-maternal figure that frightened James himself.)

The movie is faithful to the original, and it's admirably performed. Catherine Samie achieves an extraordinary shift of character: early on, she's formidable, threatening in her upright posture; later, she's extremely touching, also acrid and sensitive by turns. Meanwhile, the contrast between Michel Duchaussoy's cautious glares and his moments of raw suffering fully express his sense of a wasted life. These people even have the pallor that James described, and the film is merely a small triumph for Mr. Chabrol.

1974 O 3, 50:2

Ullmann, Finch in Life of Queen Christina

By NORA SAYRE

Someone should give a crash course on how distinguished actors and actresses choose their scripts, since it's one of the queasier mysteries of the movie business. What, for example, persuaded two such particularly intelligent performers as Liv Ullmann and Peter Finch to appear in Anthony Harvey's "The Abdication"? Was it the legend of Greta Garbo in "Queen Christina" in 1933? But that was one of Garbo's creakiest vehicles, which fully justified Graham Greene's complaint that she was often "badly served . . . by writers and producers . . . in compensation they treat her with deathly reverence: she is like a Tudor mansion set up again brick by numbered brick near Philadelphia."

Miss Ullmann should also beware of reverence—not the deathly brand, but the sort that packages her as an awesome property. It's discomforting to see her in "The Abdication" (which opened yesterday at the Sutton Theater) so soon after her magnificent performance in Ingmar Bergman's "Scenes From a Marriage."

●

The setting and the camerawork in this movie are among the handsomest we've seen in years. If only the visual sophistication didn't emphasize the verbal and psychological naiveté of the script. Christina—who abandoned her 17th-century Swedish throne after she had been converted to Roman Catholicism — is presented here as a love-starved waif who needs only a great passion to wash out all her early traumas.

Her sexual ambiguities are swept aside when she falls for Peter Finch, who plays Cardinal Azzolino. He interrogates her in order to determine the sincerity of her conversion—and to learn if she's really "the harlot of the northern hemisphere." The sun sets obligingly behind them when she declares her love.

The Cast

THE ADDICATION, directed by Anthony Harvey; screenplay by Ruth Wolff, based on Miss Wolff's play; director of photography, Geoffrey Unsworth; editor, John Bloom; music by Nino Rota; produced by Robert Fryer and James Cresson; released by Warner Bros. At the Sutton Theater, Third Avenue and 57th Street. Running time: 103 minutes. This film is classified PG.
Azzolino .... Peter Finch
Queen Christina .... Liv Ullmann
Oxenstierna .... Cyril Cusack
Altieri .... Paul Rogers
Dwarf .... Michael Dunn

Soggy lyrical flashbacks establish that Christina had an unhappy girlhood, that she couldn't bear being pressured to marry. In these evocations of the past, those gripped by emotion tend to whirl about in circles while holding their arms aloft, or else to run about like agitated poultry. Stormy or wistful music surges up on cue, and the dialogue would make a fossil weep: Question: "What's the matter; can't you sleep?" Answer: "Sleep is the refuge of idiots."

●

Yet, despite the abundant whimsey, the movie has some surprisingly solid moments—entirely thanks to Miss Ullmann and Mr. Finch (although both seem completely contemporary, and we just can't think of them as historical figures). True, this is far from Miss Ullmann's best work: She's even embarrassing at times, as when—right after her abdication — she bursts into chuckles and lets down her hair while running through a wheatfield, which matches that hair, or when she melts into glowing affability in reference to God. But her imperious or flippant responses are fine, and she's gifted at rebellion.

Mr. Finch is equally formidable and meticulous as a person who loves power so intensely that he can't imagine why a queen would give it up. And he can even bring dignity to such lines as: "God spare me from the common mind . . . God spare me from myself." The ironic play between him and Miss Ullmann does salvage some passages of this preposterous movie, and Paul Rogers is pleasantly scathing as one of the Cardinal's colleagues.

1974 O 4, 30:1

A BIGGER SPLASH, directed and produced by Jack Hazan; screenplay by Mr. Hazan and David Mingay; director of photography, Mr. Hazan; editor, Mr. Mingay; music, Patrick Gowers and Greg Bailey; a Buzzy Enterprises Ltd. production. Running time: 105 minutes. At the New York Film Festival at Alice Tully Hall in Lincoln Center.
Painter .... David Hockney
Painter's friend .... Peter Schlesinger
Dress designer .... Ossie Clark
Designer's wife .... Celia Birtwell
Friend .... Mo McDermott
Collector .... Henry Geldzahler
Dealer .... Kasmin

By VINCENT CANBY

"A Bigger Splash," which was shown at the New York Film Festival last night, is a fiction film about David Hockney, one of the more successful and durable of the English pop artists to come out of the nineteen-sixties, in which Mr. Hockney and his friends play themselves in situations that may or may not have happened in life.

A note in the festival program draws a parallel between what Jack Hazan, the director-cameraman-producer of this film, is doing in "A Bigger Splash" and what Mr. Hockney's paintings do when the artist takes details from life, strips them to their essential lines and colors, then projects them into larger-than-life reality onto huge canvases.

Perhaps because most movie screens, including the one at Alice Tully Hall (where the film will be repeated tonight), are already larger than life, the effect of this fragmented, often self-conscious film is to make the subject seem sort of small and drab, a fact that is immediately denied whenever we are given a chance to look at the paintings themselves.

There is a kind of story line to the film, which, we're told, was three years in the making. It's about Mr. Hockney's inability to finish a painting when his lover for the last five years, another artist named Peter Schlesinger, walks out on him. His friends worry about him. They worry about a forthcoming show, and they worry about the décor of his house. "It looks like a waiting room now," says Celia Birtwell, a beautiful young woman who looks a lot like Andy Warhol's Viva. Another friend says, "When love goes wrong, it's more than two people suffer."

In these moments, there's a suggestion of the satire that is almost always evident in Mr. Hockney's paintings, but the film's Hockney-like gags are mostly blunt, as when Henry Geldzahler of the Metropolitan Museum of Art is "discovered" striking the pose in which Mr. Hockney once painted him.

The manner of making the film—in London, Geneva, California and New York, whenever the artist's schedule permitted—has as much to do with the non-content of the film as with its style. There are only the slightest traces of the outrageous self-promotion and put-on that once were so much a part of the pop scene. "A Bigger Splash" is unforgivably solemn, something that Andy Warhol and Paul Morrissey would never have allowed.

1974 O 4, 31:2

5 Shorts at Whitney

"Transformations" is the blanket title covering a well-organized exhibition of five short films exploring motion pictures as the vehicle of expression of pure art. The exhibition opened yesterday for a week's run in the New American Filmmakers Series at the Whitney Museum of American Art.

Of the five, which range in length from 6 to 35 minutes, the least imaginative was "Birds of Paradise," by Mike Lovell, in which the soaking of film in bleach produced whitened patterns washing across repetitive shots of caged vultures.

More active and successful in working out thematic variations were Steve Osborn with "Polyphemus," a piece of cinematic choreography that makes the camera and a mirror partners in a contredanse; Sheldon Brown's "Clean Gate!!," fugal in the increasing complexity of its patterns; Mr. Brown's "Frame/Rate Declension" in which juxtaposed vertical film strips moving at changing speeds provide a tapestry of images, and David Hykes's "Moving Parts," a combination of eerie sound and colored particles that form a kaleidoscopic universe, at once pastoral and nightmarish.

LAWRENCE VAN GELDER

1974 O 4, 31:4

Screen: New Sjoman

Vilgot Sjoman, who was effectively serious about sex, politics and sundry other matters in his controversial "I Am Curious (Yellow)" and "I Am Curious (Blue)," is impishly curious only about sex in "'Til Sex Do Us Part," which opened this week at the Ciné Malibu and Cinema Village. But if the Swedish director and his cast appear to be having a fine old raunchy time, their farce, unfortunately, is as thin as a negligee and as obvious as its good measure of nudity and couplings.

The Swedish feature, completed in 1971, or some four years after the "Curious" tandem, is concerned with the adventures of a zany but loving young couple who have avoided sex because they're terrified that it would literally kill them.

Solveig Ternstron and Borje Ahlstedt, as the young marrieds with the old hang-up, are, clothed or otherwise, properly wacky and photogenic in their tongue-in-cheek approach to offbeat situations. Equally energetic are Margaretha Bystrom and Frej Lindquist as their married friends, who seemingly destroy themselves in demonstrating the ecstasies of sex rampant.

Music lovers should know that Mr. Sjoman also appears to have set a movie precedent in having, as the credits state, "members of the Royal Swedish Opera Company" grapple in an uninhibited orgy while lustily vocalizing the quartet from "Rigoletto."

A. H. WEILER

1974 O 5, 17:1

French Films Dominate The New York Festival

By VINCENT CANBY

FRENCHMEN may not know it but filmmaking is flourishing in France. That, at least, is the impression given by the selection committee for the 12th New York Film Festival, now in progress at Lincoln Center. Of the 21 programs, eight are French, including Jean-Pierre Melville's 1949 film adaptation of Jean Cocteau's "Les Enfants Terribles," which is being given a retrospective showing at Alice Tully Hall tomorrow night (Oct. 7).

Because the festival's two entries by Jacques Rivette add up to 7½ hours of film ("Out One/Spectre" is 4¼ hours and "Céline and Julie Go Boating" is 3¼ hours), one might be able to prove that the French are occupying almost 50 per cent of the festival's total screen time. Which seems like a lot of time to devote to the films of one country when the United States and England are represented by only one entry each and Russia by none.

At this writing—two days after the festival's start—it's still too early to tell whether this extraordinary emphasis on French films constitutes the sort of revelation that the figures promise, or whether it is simply another example of the favor that the New York Festival has shown toward French films down through the years.

However, the first two French films seen indicate that the selection committee could have done a lot worse. The opening night spot, which in the past has been given to films by directors of the order of Buñuel, Truffaut and Godard, this year was given to a film by a virtually unknown (here, anyway) young French director, 28-year-old Pascal Thomas. "Don't Cry With Your Mouth Full," his second feature, is not exactly a revelation but because of the directors whose work it recalls (Renoir, Truffaut, Pagnol), the film evokes important heritages. It's almost as if the festival felt that since it's now in its 12th year, it ought to show us what the youngsters have learned from their elders.

"Don't Cry With Your Mouth Full" is a pastoral comedy of today (which some might consider to be frivolous if not a downright contradiction in terms) about one summer in the life of a robust 15-year-old girl growing up in a small town in the provinces. Annie, beautifully played by Annie Colé, an actress with a remarkable ability to appear simultaneously cheerful, self-absorbed and loving, is as ripe as the landscape she inhabits. She loves one young man, who leaves to do his military service, but without any fuss she gives her virginity to another young man, more or less because she feels it's time and because he makes her laugh. Bernard Menez plays this role with great comic effect, coming across as a sort of fussy, fraudulent Don Juan.

"Don't Cry With Your Mouth Full" is too resolutely charming to be as deeply affecting as the films of Renoir and Truffaut it recalls. I think particularly of Truffaut's "Stolen Kisses," whose lightest moments are never unaffected by tragic possibilities. Renoir's comedies are sunlit patches of activity encircled by darkness. He—and we—are always aware that there are places that the sun cannot reach, which is one of the things that enriches the meaning of his comedies.

I probably wouldn't quibble in this fashion about the Thomas film if it hadn't come to us under the comparatively solemn auspices of the festival. It's more fun than most such movies.

This year only four of the festival entries already are set for American release, which should put an end to those suspicions that in recent years the festival was tending to become a kind of posh, pre-release showcase for movies opening up the next day in conventional theaters. One of the festival's purposes has always been to provide us with films—one assumes, good films—that we wouldn't otherwise be able to see. Another purpose is to give recognition to films considered both good and important even though they might already have local distribution outlets.

Such a film was the second French film to be seen at the festival, Louis Malle's fine, tough, unsentimental drama, "Lacombe, Lucien," which will open Friday at the 68th St. Playhouse. The film arrives here having already been labeled—unfortunately, I think—a masterpiece in Paris. It's a beautifully considered, complex, disquieting film but I think to go around calling it a masterpiece may well set up audiences to expect something they aren't going to get,

something more finished, more like a last word on an Important Subject. Malle's film really isn't neat enough to be a masterpiece. It's almost open-ended.

"Lacombe, Lucien" is about a strong-shouldered, none-too-bright, 17-year-old French farm boy who joins the Gestapo in a small provincial town just four months before the collapse of the German occupation of France in October, 1944. Thus, for a few swaggering months he enjoys the power and the prestige of the conquerors.

Lucien (Pierre Blaise) is a kind of cold, cloudy prism through which we see reflected the terrible psychological dislocations of a very special time and place.

Malle never means for us to sympathize with Lucien in any facile way, yet like the aristocratic Jewish tailor from Paris whom Lucien tries to befriend, much as if the tailor were an animal to be trained with whip and sugar, we find it very hard to hate him.

The crux of the film is Lucien's relationship with the tailor, played by Holger Lowenadler, a Swedish stage actor, and the tailor's fragile daughter (Aurore Clement), with whom he carries on a belligerent love affair that apparently satisfies some need in her as much it does in him.

Malle is, I think, one of the most underrated (under-exploited?) of France's fine directors, largely because his preoccupations are not clearly seen from film to film, and because his style is so resolutely in the service of whatever material he's doing. It's impossible to think of a "Malle subject" or a "Malle shot" or a "Malle mood" when one thinks back over his various films from "The Lovers" to "The Fire Within" and "Murmur of The Heart."

*

"Lacombe, Lucien" is not a decisive last word about war or even about Frenchmen under the German occupation. It meditates upon some of the horrors, which, in this cool vision, include not only divided loyalties but no loyalties at all. Lucien is not dumb enough to be an obvious tool of the Gestapo, but not sensitive or sophisticated enough to have developed a moral code that is in any way outraged by what he does. He simply joins the club that will have him and does what he has to do until the bottom drops out.

To call the film a masterpiece is to suggest that it leaves the viewer with a single overwhelming impression, and probably with a feeling of exaltation. It doesn't. You come out of the theater so disturbed you don't want to believe it. You see war not in terms of grand gestures but as waste, misunderstanding, petty opportunism.

The movie itself, however, is full of its own grand gestures, including the sequence in which the tailor puts on his fanciest Paris clothes, leaves the apartment where he's been hiding and goes to the French Gestapo headquarters to advise Lucien to stop seeing his daughter. It's his suicide. There's also a marvelous moment near the end of the film when Lucien, the tailor's daughter and her ancient grandmother are hiding in an abandoned farmhouse, living a temporary idyll while France seethes with liberation. The grand-

mother walks slowly through the yard and suddenly hears a cricket. For just a second she bends over and studies the cricket on the leaf of a bush, as if the cricket were the most exotic creature she'd ever seen.

Like all great artists, Malle views life with the kind of deep focus that allows horizons to be just as distinct as things seen in tight close-up.

1974 O 6, II:1:5

Fassbinder Explores Racial Prejudice

By VINCENT CANBY

One of the most encouraging things about Rainer Werner Fassbinder, the young German writer-director-actor, is his extraordinary productivity, not that productivity is much help to someone without talent. There's no question that Mr. Fassbinder, whose "Ali" was shown at the New York Film Festival on Saturday and yesterday evenings, has a great deal of talent, so much that he seems driven by it in the healthiest sense.

Since 1969 he has made at least 11 films, written several plays for the theater, acted in others and written and directed an eight-part television drama. I mention all this because such a large part of a film director's life these days must be devoted either to deal-making or to rewriting and polishing scripts for the approval of people who have easier access to money than to any artistic sensibility.

●

Mr. Fassbinder obviously works fast. He doesn't fool around getting things perfect. He tries something difficult, and if it works, fine. If not, he'll do it better the next time around. Shakespeare worked this way. So, I'm sure, did a lot of the people in Hollywood in what are called the good old days. Experience doesn't accumulate like dust. You simply can't sit around waiting for it to settle on you. You have to work to get it.

Mr. Fassbinder is neither Shakespeare nor an old-time Hollywood type. In addition to his talent and tremendous energy, he has absolutely no fear that he might be off on the wrong track making a fool of himself. His most recent films seen over here, "The Merchant of Four Seasons" and "The Bitter Tears of Petra Von Kant," have been both praised and ridiculed in the kind of extravagant terms that make one pay attention, even when not agreeing.

●

I particularly liked one of his early works (if one can decently call a film by someone who's not yet 30 an early work). "Recruits in Ingolstadt," which was an effectively stylized screen adaptation of a 1929 Brechtian theater piece, shown at the 1971 New York Film Festival.

I like "Ali" even more because it seems to take even greater risks. Its story is the cinematic equivalent of a piece of pop art: Emmi (Brigitte Mira) is a late-fiftyish German charwoman, a widow

The Cast

ALI, directed and produced by Rainer Werner Fassbinder; screenplay (German with English subtitles) by Mr. Fassbinder; director of photography, Jurgen Jurges; editor, Thea Eymes; a production of Tango Film and Filmverlag der Autorn, distributed by New Yorker Films. Running time: 93 minutes. At the New York Film Festival at Alice Tully Hall in Lincoln Center. This film has not been rated.

Emmi .... Brigitte Mira
Ali .... El Hedi Ben Salem
Barbara .... Barbara Valentin
Krista .... Irm Hermann
Bruno .... Peter Gauhe
Albert .... Karl Scheydt
Eugen .... Rainer Werner Fassbinder

whose children have grown up and into proper middle-class prigs. Emmi is no femme fatale. She's short and dumpy and has a too-great willingness to please, a quality she shares with many of the world's lonely and insecure.

Quite by chance, Emmi meets Ali, a young, virile Moroccan who has come to Germany to earn a living as a garage mechanic. They are both lonely. Emmi's friendliness and her common sense, as well as her apartment, beckon Ali. They get married for their own satisfaction and to the horror of family and friends.

The careful detail with which Mr. Fassbinder dramatizes the couple's subsequent ostracism, and the rampant racial prejudice they face, is a deadpan cover for the film's real concerns, which, as I read the film, are the many disguises of love. In one of the several twists that Mr. Fassbinder gives the story, it's Emmi who, once secure in Ali's love, reverts to type, becoming small-minded and in her own way thoroughly heartless.

•

The presence of the director is so dominant in Mr. Fassbinder's films that it's difficult to judge their individual parts. I'm not sure whether Miss Mira and El Hedi Ben Salem, who plays Ali, are especially good actors but they look right. Although they have their idiosyncracies they are primarily types.

The entire film, in fact, has a kind of posterlike blandness to it, something that at times is made visual. When Emmi and Ali go outside, other people are seldom seen, unless they are characters in the film. There are no extras in the background to convince you this is photographed reality, which it most certainly is not.

"Ali" is not an easy movie to warm up to. It's no May-December romance that tugs at the heart. It is, rather, another quite courageous attempt by Mr. Fassbinder to develop a film style free of the kind of realistic conventions that sentimentalize life's mysteries.

1974 O 7, 55:1

The Cast

THE MIDDLE OF THE WORLD (Le Milieu du Mondel), directed by Alain Tanner; screenplay (French with English subtitles) by John Berger and Mr.. Tanner; photography, Renato Berta; editor Brigitte Sousseller; music, Patrick Moray; executive producers Yves Gasser and Yves Peyrot; production companies, Action Films, Citel Films. At the New York Film Festival, Alice Tully Hall, Lincoln Center. Running time: 115 minutes.

Adriana .... Olimpia Carlisi
Paul .... Philippe Leotard
Juliet .... Juliet Berto

By NORA SAYRE

While most American movies continue to dodge the relations between the sexes, some of the European directors are surging ahead in that area. Such totally dissimilar films as Ingmar Bergman's "Scenes From a Marriage," Lina Wertmuller's "The Seduction of Mimi" and now, Alain Tanner's "The Middle of the World"—are exploring emotional territory in ways that we have rarely seen. (Even the best of the recent American movies have only shown couples throbbing or fighting—there's little sense of what happens after a seething scene.)

Mr. Tanner, who made "La Salamandre" and "Le Retour d'Afrique," brings an extraordinary sensitivity to one pair's experiences in "The Middle of the World"—which was shown Saturday and yesterday at the New York Film Festival. A married engineer who's running for parliament in Switzerland becomes obsessed by a waitress whom he glimpses at a railroad café. He pursues her, they revel in their sexual affinities, he loses the election (but doesn't care), he wants to marry her, and she leaves him.

•

Among the film's many virtues is the tranquil build-up to passion. The engineer is reserved, almost stolid. He and the waitress become acquainted on country walks, where they don't touch; he dispenses bits of information about the Doppler effect, or how to get rabbits to nurse their young.

Then, his excitement becomes exciting, and the urgency of their intimacy produces some of the more erotic scenes I've seen of late—even though they are briskly edited. At moments, the film suddenly cuts from wintery Switzerland to shots of yellow summer fields—which appear to be images for this couple's happiness in bed.

Meanwhile, the woman—who is gentle, earthy, affectionate—wonders if they will change each other while he pressures her to quit her job and to leave the room she lives in (which appalls him by its simplicity). His colleagues remark that "she has him in a trance," that "he's lost his mind." He's boyish and playful when they are together, while she grows more remote—mutely rejecting the materialistic life and the swank technology that he cherishes.

Throughout, the movie stresses the concept of "normalization"—whereby contact between the economic classes, or countries such as the United States and the Soviet Union, or the sexes, is acceptable "as long as nothing changes" in the power structure.

The movie takes a profound, though subtle, stand against treating women as objects; it really is a feminist statement. The woman repeats that her lover doesn't know her, that he never listens; she adds that men think they know a woman if they've seen her naked—also, that a man feels that anyone who has seen his genitals can read his mind. Although their physical pleasure is immense, she calmly retreats from his need for authority, his determination to create a second wife, a second middle-class home.

•

Both of these people are very likable, because of the sympathetic performances of Olimpia Carlisi and Philippe Leotard. Yet the director's attitude toward his male character is much sterner than mine would be—even though his feelings have no dimension beyond the sexual. But the woman has been so passive, so inexpressive of herself, that neither her lover nor the audience can guess what she's like. In fact, the movie's one flaw is that her character is so undeveloped. (Also, to American eyes, she doesn't seem like a working person, although the film emphasizes that this kind of bourgeois man could only fall for a waitress.)

However, it was also Mr. Tanner's intention to keep his characters somewhat elusive, so that the spectator might flesh out each portrait. And in its pensive way, this is a very radical movie. By portraying inequality so quietly, the theme has all the more impact—and the film goes on echoing in your mind well after you have seen it.

1974 O 7, 55:1

'Out One/Spectre,' Is Long and Frustrating

By NORA SAYRE

Unheard melodies may be sweet, but unsolved mysteries are about as satisfying as a windowful of succulent food that you can't afford. Jacques Rivette's "Out One/Spectre"—which played Saturday and Sunday at the New York Film Festival—is frustrating for two reasons: first, because $4\frac{1}{2}$ hours of hidden motivations is hard on the soul; second, because some of the characterizations and performances are tantalizingly good — hence you really want to understand these people and what drives them. (The movie has been edited down from a 13-hour version that was —and then wasn't —intended for television.)

Most of Mr. Rivette's actors were invited to invent their own roles. Not a word of script was written, and —as you can easily guess during the first half-hour— the actors didn't know the outcome of the film. (There's no plot, although there is a flow of interwoven relationships.) For an American audience, there's much that seems old-fashioned here — mainly due to a plethora of footage spent on a theater group that suggests a Living Theater manqué. This ensemble's writhing and moaning and declaiming take us back to Off Off Broadway in 1966 or 1967, to a style that's quite conventional for New York. But the exercises are filmed as though we'd never seen that kind of performing before.

•

Two Parisian strays set off a wave of tête-à-têtes and tremors among people who are strangers to them. Jean-Pierre Léaud suspects the existence of a secret society, and he tries to detect its pur-

The Cast

OUT ONE/SPECTRE, directed by Jacques Rivette; photography, Pierre William Glenn; editor, Nicole Lubtchanscky; executive producer, Stephane Tchalgadjieff (French with English subtitles);; production company, Sunchild Productions; distributed in the United States by New York Films. At the New York Film Festival, Lincoln Center, Alice Tully Hall. Running time: 270 minutes.

Sarah .... Bernadette Lafont
Colin .... Jean-Pierre Leaud
Thomas .... Michel Lonsdale
Pauline-Emilie .... Bulle Ogier
Balzac Scholar .... Eric Rohmer
Frederique .... Juliet Berto

poses through clues from Balzac's "Story of the 13" and Lewis Carroll's "The Haunting of the Snark." Meanwhile, Juliet Berto—a nimble con person and sponge—steals some letters that concern the mysterious conspirators. We never learn the function of the society, though there's a woolly hint that it might solve "problems."

If this binge of obscurity makes you turns on your heel, let me hastily stress that there are many intriguing scenes within the movie. Miss Berto has a rich gift for unpredictability; here, as a headlong, rueful thief and professional charmer, she appears in a very amusing episode where she slides into the house of a chess-playing stranger and convinces him that she wants to learn the game — which doesn't interest her at all.

Mr. Léaud begins very well; he pretends to be a deaf-mute (and I suspect that he revisited Jean-Louis Barrault's "Les Enfants du Paradis" for this part). Later, he's both frenetic and austere —also infantile and grandiose in the manner that he's used so often, and he postures more than necessary. Still, he plays nicely with Bulle Ogier, whom he attempts to seduce while she remains deeply absorbed in bookkeeping. Françoise Fabian — amused and affirmative as usual—teams skillfully with Miss Berto who is trying to blackmail her. Bernadette Lafont, a blocked writer, and Michel Lonsdale have an engaging scene, which fully conveys the ease of intimate, long-term friendship. Also, the director Eric Rohmer makes a pleasing Balzac scholar.

My own interest in the movie was sustained for about three hours — until it was obvious that the puzzles would never be worked out. Then, most of the scenes themselves began to appear like actors' exercises—improvisations for a tale that didn't exist. Eventually, the cast itself seemed like a secret society—or like people who've gone underground when they don't need to. While the leisurely pace of the movie seems justifed by the characters' development in the first half, it finally weighs on you because—despite all the worry and concern and concentration expressed — there are very few strong emotions in the movie.

•

The editing appears as the most deliberate aspect of the film. Many scenes are fragmented to mingle with one another; the narrative leaps in and out of continuing conversations, and it's often interrupted by black and white stills, accompanied by a low buzz. Apparently, the stills evoke parts of the 13-hour version, or are meant to remind us of characters we've seen briefly.

Almost certainly, this film was more rewarding for Mr. Rivette and his cast than it can be for the spectators. Yet I will remember the particular acting styles of some of the performers when I see them in future roles. The movie unquestionably reveals their potentialities and their individual talents in a way that's educational for critics and for dedicated students of the cinema.

1974 O 8, 38:1

The Cast

CELINE AND JULIE GO BOATING (Celine et Julie Vont en Bateau), directed by Jacques Rivette; screenplay (French with English subtitles) by Mr. Rivette, Eduardo di Gregorio, Juliet Berto, Dominique Labourier, Bulle Ogier and Marie-France Pisier; photography, Jacques Renard and Michel Cenet; editors, Nicole Lubtchansky and Chris Tullio-Altan; music, Jean Marie Senia; executive producer, Barbet Schroeder; production companies, Les Films du Losange/Les Films 7/ Renn Productions/SAGA/SIMAR/ V. M. Productions/Action Films/Les Films Christian Fechner. At the New York Film Festival, Lincoln Center, Alice Tully Hall. Running time: 193 minutes.

Celine .... Juliet Berto
Julie .... Dominique Labourier
Camille .... Bulle Ogier
Sophie .... Marie-France Pisier
Olivier .... Barbet Schroeder
Guilou .... Philippe Clevenot

The riddles and delusions of Jacques Rivette's "Céline and Julie Go Boating" are much more accessible than the enigmas of his "Out One/Spectre". "Céline," the later movie, has the dotty logic of dreams, and the characters' rational solemnity while talking nonsense does succeed in evoking Lewis Carroll. The movie played last night at the New York Film Festival and will be repeated on Friday.

There's a beguiling opening, as Juliet Berto (Céline) dashes past Dominique Labourier—Julie, a librarian who's reading on a park bench—dropping her possessions and conveying the desperate haste of the White Rabbit. A droll chase ensues; eventually, the two young women meet and become flirtatious friends—it's not clear if there's a sexual relationship, although the possibility is suggested.

•

Céline—a professional magician—is also a true spellcaster. Inventing a story about a mystifying household, she soon inspires her friend to visit the site of her fantasies. Proustian flashbacks, set off by bits of candy or memory potions, enable both of them to review various events within the house; thus, they become spectators of a film within a film, and they can even rerun the footage as though they were using a moviola.

Inside the house, two women compete over a widower who had promised his dying wife that (for the sake of their child) he would never remarry—a scenario that indirectly alludes to Henry James's "The Other House" (which was itself influenced by "Hedda Gabler" and several of Ibsen's plays). These imaginary beings are stagey in their manner, rather like zombies oozing with grandeur. Bulle Ogier manages to be aggressively ethereal in what almost seems to be a spoof on a bad Ophelia. Finally, Céline and Julie participate in the drama; they take turns playing a nurse, while rehearsing and forgetting their lines, messing up the dialogue and signaling wildly to the other characters like incompetent amateur actresses.

There's some delightful slapstick afoot as the two run amok, and the last section of the movie is on a par with the comedy of the beginning. In between, there are some marshy passages, mainly due to relentless whimsey. As in "Out One/Spectre," the actresses invented their own parts (although the scenes in the house were scripted). In both movies, there are leading characters who are obsessed with solving a mystery; as they become detectives, the audience is invited to do likewise. We're also supposed to create our own plotline for what's actually occurring in that house.

Miss Berto, as a defiant, ruthless clown, simply runs away with this movie. She brings an intense concentration to everything she does, and also excels at horseplay. At times, she shows an extraordinary resemblance to Jeanne Moreau — minus a couple of decades—but she's in no way derivative. Miss Labourier was clearly cast and directed as a contrast for Miss Berto, but her more pedestrian part lacks the agility and wit that Miss Berto scatters all over the screen. Still, Miss Labourier can alternate glowering with giggling or turn clumsy in a way that's often appealing.

Céline and Julie complain that their interior film is full of holes, like a Swiss cheese —and of course that's what Mr. Rivette intended for his own 3¼-hour feature. When this movie sags, it becomes a series of skits, but the best parts do achieve the spontaneity and impudent freshness that this director relishes.

NORA SAYRE

1974 O 8, 38:1

Kitsch and Camp Clash in Story of Singer

By NORA SAYRE

LA PALOMA, directed by Daniel Schmid; screenplay (French with English subtitles) by Mr. Schmid; photography, Renato Berta; editor Ila von Hungsberg; executive producer, Yves Gasser; production companies, Citel Films/ARTCO Films/Les Films du Losange. Running time: 112 minutes. At the New York Film Festival, Lincoln Center, Alice Tully Hall.

Viola Schlump .... Ingrid Caven
Count Isidor Palewski .... Peter Kern
Raoul .... Peter Chatel
Countess Palewski .... Bulle Ogier

When you play with clichés, you have to be very careful that they don't backfire; the little things have a way of maiming almost everything around them.

Daniel Schmid's "La Paloma" — which was shown last night and to be repeated tonight at the New York Film Festival — is intentionally crammed with cultural chestnuts, and also makes a heavy pass at the plots of "Camille" and "La Traviata." Kitsch and camp collide in this storm of pity and terror and wonder, which seethes with boundless love, burning glances, and unfathomable revenge. Nestling within this Swiss movie are some humorous intentions gone astray; it's also what they call dreamlike, although the dreams I've been watching lately have been funnier.

•

A glum nightclub singer—Ingrid Caven, who's tricked out like a caricature of Dietrich — is ailing with some nameless rot. She permits a wealthy young admirer (Peter Kern) to cosset her, cure her, and finally marry her. It's repeated that she doesn't love him, but she cherishes his passion for her. Then she falls for his best friend and wants to decamp with him; her husband selfishly refuses to finance the expedition. Therefore, she dies slowly and even more tidily than Ali McGraw in "Lovy Story."

Her deathbed wish forces her husband to exhume and dismember her three years later; the corpse chuckles as he moans while converting it into cutlets. By then, since I was into the swing of the movie, I expected poisonous fumes to rise from the coffin and wipe out the suffering spouse—and was rather embarrassed when they didn't.

Some obligatory decadence trickles through the nightclub scenes—but mercifully, the movie is set in 1952, so there aren't any Nazis around. The soundtrack endows the actors with theme-tunes; occasionally, they even flower into song, and the incidental music ranges from an opera by Erich Korngold to "Don't Sit Under the Apple Tree." Just after the couple are married, there's a soaring duet on a mountaintop. Suddenly, a transparent apparition floats over their heads: the thing grins jovially while its draperies flap in a breeze that doesn't even ruffle their coiffures.

•

You can't really discuss "La Paloma" in terms of acting; the performers stalk rigidly about, exchanging long, brooding stares or significant smirks, and the result is a failed parody of the grand manner. (It was probably meant to be some sort of pantomime.) They also speak their lines very, very slowly — as though one another's reflexes were impaired.

The ultimate astonishment is the appearance of Bulle Ogier as the husband's mother. Looking younger than her offspring, she doesn't seem to be on good terms with her cane. If only Elaine May had directed "La Paloma" — the brisk deadpan delivery that she can draw out of actors might have been marvelous for this material.

1974 O 9, 52:1

ALICE IN THE CITIES (Alice in den Stadten), directed by Wim Wenders; screenplay (German with English subtitles) by Mr. Wenders and Veith von Furstenberg; photography, Robby Muller and Martin Schafer; editor, Pater Przygodda; music, Can; executive producer, Peter Genee; production companies, Produktionl/Filverlag der Autoren. Running time: 110 minutes. At the New York Film Festival, Lincoln Center, Alice Tully Hall.

Phillip .... Rudiger Vogeler
Alice .... Yella Rottlander
Lisa .... Elisabeth Kreuzer

If you are searching for a fine, tightly controlled, intelligent and ultimately touching film, one will be shown tonight at 9:30 P.M. at Alice Tully Hall at Lincoln Center as part of the 12th New York Film Festival.

Its title is "Alice in the Cities" ("Alice in den Stadten"), and it is a West German film directed and, in part, written by Wim Wenders, a young German who received praise here two years ago when his second feature, "The Anxiety of the Goalie at the Penalty Kick," was shown at the Museum of Modern Art in the New Directors/New Films series.

•

Ostensibly, "Alice in the Cities," filmed in black and white, tells what happens when a footloose 31-year-old German journalist suddenly finds himself saddled with a well-traveled 9-year-old girl on a journey from the United States back to Europe.

To suggest that this is a foreign version of "Paper Moon" is like fostering the belief that Otto Soglow's Little King is creative kin to Shakespeare's Hamlet because both, after all, share a preoccupation with royalty.

"Alice in the Cities" is a film with a great deal to say about Europe and America, about the exhaustion of dreams and the homogenization of nations, about roots and the awareness of time, about sterility and creativity, about vicarious and real adventure and, eventually, about the possibilities of the future.

At the outset, Phillip, the journalist, played with a seemingly effortless skill by Rudiger Vogeler, is an emotionally and creatively exhausted man caught up in and overwhelmed by a standardized ugly America of roadside stands, gasoline stations, car radios blaring time, weather and rock; motel rooms that look like all the rooms of the nights before; and television sets relentlessly emitting old movies and commercials.

He is reduced to snapping pictures with his Polaroid; unable to write, he misses the deadline for a story about America and decides to return home, only to discover that an airline strike has grounded all flights to Germany. At the airport, he meets Lisa, who has decided to abandon her husband and return to Germany, and her daughter, Alice. Alice is 9, the same age as Tatum O'Neal when she starred in "Paper Moon," but the eyes of Yella Rottlander, who plays this little girl, are light years older. Lisa abandons Alice with Phillip and tells him she will meet them in a couple of days in Amsterdam, but she fails to turn up. After a time, Phillip and Alice go looking for her grandmother.

•

Arrival in Europe unfolds the lovely symmetry of this film — beginning with the change of time. There is, too, the contrast of music from the radio, the slackening of photography and the increase in writing, a seemingly idle bedtime story that sounds a note first struck in New York and is not very idle at all; the abandonment of old homes; the contrast between the German women who refuse to sleep with Phillip in New York and the one who will in Germany.

"Alice in the Cities" is not sentimental about its people. Better than that, it is concerned about what is to become of all of us.

LAWRENCE VAN GELDER

1974 O 9, 52:2

Farce Slides Between Humor and Despair

By VINCENT CANBY

Ivan Passer's "Law and Disorder" is a gentle, touching, sometimes disruptively funny movie about—among other things — ignorance, prejudice, rape, larceny, the failure of small dreams, about people trying desperately to cope and often coming apart.

It stars Carroll O'Connor as a taxicab driver and Ernest Borgnine as an ex-Marine, who is a hairdresser with a passion for guns. They are the nucleus of a small group of outraged tenants of a housing project called Co-op Village, set on the Lower East Side of a New York City that bears some superficial resemblance to the setting of the inexecrable "Death Wish."

The Cast

LAW AND DISORDER, directed by Ivan Passer; screenplay by Mr. Passer, William Richert and Kenneth Harris Fishman; executive producers, Michael Medwin and Edgar J. Sherick; produced by Mr. Richert; music, Andy Badale; director of Photography, Arthur J. Ornitz; editor, Anthony Protenza; distributed by Columbia Pictures. Running time: 99 minutes. At the Coronet Theater, Third Avenue at 55th Street, and Little Carnegie Theater, 57th Street east of Seventh Avenue. This film has been rated R.

Willie .... Carroll O'Connor
Cy .... Ernest Borgnine
Sally .... Ann Wedgeworth
Irene .... Anita Dangler
Karen .... Leslie Ackerman
Gloria .... Karen Black
Elliott .... Jack Kehoe
Bobby .... David Spielberg
Pete .... Joe Ragno

•

"Law and Disorder," which opened yesterday at the Coronet and Little Carnegie theaters, is the second American film by Mr. Passer (his first was "Born to Win") whose "Intimate Lighting" is regarded as one of the major achievements of the brief, mysterious renaissance of Czechoslovak films in the nineteen-sixties.

His new film is a poet's appreciation of lives lived on the edge of the precipice by people whose finger-holds are giving out.

Willie (Mr. O'Connor) and Cy (Mr. Borgnine) and their friends are threatened as much by the onset of barren middle age as they are by the collapse of civil order. Thus, when they form a police auxiliary unit to protect their neighborhood, they are as invigorated by the opportunity to wear uniforms as they are by the opportunity to bring peace to the community.

Perhaps more so. The uniforms define purpose. They recall a more innocent time. say World War II, when there was never any question as to who was right and who was wrong.

The ultimate failure of Willie, Cy and the others is less a comment on their inadequacies, often hilariously detailed, than on the overwhelming complexity of the urban problems they face. It's this awareness on the part of Mr. Passer, as well as on the part of William Richert and Kenneth Harris Fishman, who collaborated with the director on the script, that separates "Law and Disorder" from exploitation junk like "Death Wish."

It also dictates the mood of a film that slides between farce and melodrama, between high good humor and enervating despair. Some of Mr. Passer's characters, like Willie, continue to try to improve things. Willie dreams of a new career. He wants to sell his taxi medallion and buy a lunch counter, much to his wife's horror. Says Willie in desperation: "I ain't a failure, Sally. I just ain't on time."

Cy, the hairdresser, is a hunter. He keeps an entire stuffed deer in the bedroom and has a piranha fish in a tank in the living room. He doesn't hunt people, however, and he hasn't quite arrived at the point occupied by most of the other citizens of the city whose motto, repeatedly expressed, is an obscene two-word imperative.

The film is not perfect but I couldn't care less. A number of characters are as dimly seen as faces across a subway car. The sense of alienation that grips the city at times seizes the film itself, though almost always in fascinating ways. A film of less consistent intelligence would probably be destroyed by a scene so pricelessly funny it's almost a specialty number, when the auxiliary policemen and their wives attend a lecture on rape by "the author of the best-selling book, 'Sexual Deviations of the Seventies,'"

•

"Law and Disorder" is full of eccentric things, one of the most marvelous being Karen Black, who plays a lasciviously lunatic beautician who simply can't keep her tongue in place. Mr. O'Connor reins in his familiar Archie Bunker personality to give a fine, controlled performance as the stalwart Willie, while Mr. Borgnine is inspired casting as the unhappy hairdresser.

"Law and Disorder" has none of the vicarious thrills of "Death Wish." It's thoughtful about people, even vicious hoods. It's also very, very funny.

1974 O 10, 62:1

SHANKS, directed by William Castle; written by Ranald Graham; director of photography, Joe Biroc; editor, David Berlatsky; music, Alex North; produced by Steven North; released by Paramount Pictures. At the Beekman Theater, Second Avenue and 65th Street.

Running time: 93 minutes. This film is classified PG.
Malcolm Shanks/.........Marcel Marceau
Old Walker
Mrs. Barton ....Tsilla Chelton
Mr. Barton ....Philippe Clay
Celia ....Cindy Eilbacher
Mata Hari ....Helena Kallianiotes
Napoleon ....Larry Bishop

If Marcel Marceau, the greatest of mimes, and William Castle, the prolific producer of such spellbinding horrors as "Rosemary's Baby" and "The House on Haunted Hill," are an obviously off-beat team, "Shanks," their first joint effort, which opened yesterday at the Beekman, makes a decidedly strange combination of their talents. They and their company are as unusual as might be expected but they leave a viewer uncommitted, if not confused, by their largely far-out, somber fiction.

The script by Ranald Graham, a young newcomer to films, is described as "a grim fairy tale," and it is just that. It involves Mr. Marceau in the dual roles of a mute puppeteer and as his employer, an odd, aged inventor, Old Walker, of gadgets, who can revive the dead. These improbable, but handy, tools enable him to animate Old Walker, his wicked sister-in-law and her drunken husband and a young girl who adores him, after they have died, to successfully fight the forces of evil represented by a gang of wild motorcyclists.

•

Mr. Marceau, who has been seen in several films including "Barbarella," does not achieve the remarkable illusions he has created on stage. But his silent performances as the wistful, badgered Shanks and the wonderfully made-up senile Old Walker are, nevertheless, strikingly charming pantomimes on screen.

He is ably abetted by Tsilla Chelton and Philippe Clay, French mime artists who are making their movie debuts here as the relatives with as much dedication as Mr. Marceau, and Cindy Eilbacher, a newcomer from TV, as the wide-eyed youngster in love with the puppeteer's magic.

But the magic here is diffused. The succession of grim, cute or gimmicky approaches to this "fairy story" make it an extraordinary but only intermittently edifying fable.

A. H. WEILER

1974 O 10, 62:1

Olmi Work Is Shown at Film Festival

By VINCENT CANBY

"La Circostanza" (The Circumstance), which was shown at the New York Film Festival last night and will be repeated there, is another unsuccessful attempt by Ermanno Olmi, the Italian director, to rise above the banality of the subjects that have occupied him in recent years.

The film is about one summer in the lives of the members of an upper-middle-class Milan family, each of whom faces his or her teeny-weeny crisis with the kind of gravity that a more idiosyncratic, less schematic film maker might have made seem important, maybe even funny. Middle-class life is wretched, says Mr. Olmi. It's dehumanizing. We're almost like cattle, he goes on to say, showing us scenes in the stockyards in which cattle are led up ramps, then slaughtered. Mr. Olmi is not a director to let a cliché die peacefully.

•

He makes movies with a petty file clerk's love for the nonessential detail and a bad

The Cast

LA CIRCOSTANZA (The Circumstance), directed by Ermanno Olmi; written (Italian with English subtitles), photographed and edited by Mr. Olmi; an Italnoleggio Cinematografico/RAI production. Running time: 90 minutes. At the New York Film Festival at Alice Tully Hall in Lincoln Center, Broadway at 65th Street. This film has not been rated.
Mother ....Ada Savelli
Father ....Gaetano Porro
Daughter ....Raffaella Bianchi
Elder Son ....Mario Sireci
Elder Son's Wife.........Barbara Pezzuto
Younger Son............Massimo Tabak
Blind Boy ....Giorgio Roncaglia

writer's total inability to fabricate spontaneity. The festival program describes Mr. Olmi's editing technique in "La Circostanza" as "more aggressive" than it's been in the past, in his earlier, much better films, like "Il Posto" and "The Fiancés."

I don't know if it's really more aggressive or just film-school fancy. There are lots of fragmented flashbacks and flash-forwards, but they don't add anything. It just takes one a little longer to realize fully the film's complete lack of excitement.

1974 O 11, 25:1

Australian Sex Comedy at Two Theaters

Alvin Purple is the playboy of the southern world, an unprepossessing young Australian who, for absolutely no reason brought forth by the makers of the movie that bears his name, is irresistible to women.

As a 16-year-old schoolboy, the hero of "Alvin Purple," which opened yesterday at the New Embassy and the Eastside Cinema, is the sex object of a pack of female schoolmates who lie in wait for him after classes until the 28-year-old wife of one of his teachers rescues him for purposes of her own.

Later, selling water beds, Alvin finds himself constantly in the presence of women (and one transvestite) who want to mix his business

with their pleasure. Eventually, he has recourse to a female psychiatrist, whom he finds resistible, and her charlatan of an associate, who sets Alvin up as a sex therapist, while using him as the unwitting star of pornographic films. The result is a sensational trial. Through it all, Tina, the one girl Alvin really seems to care about, finds him resistible.

The Cast

ALVIN PURPLE, directed by Tim Burstall; screenplay by Alan Hopgood; camera, John Seale; music, Brian Cadd; produced by Mr. Burstall; presented by Bi-Jay Films; distributed by the Sands Film Company. At the New Embassy Theater, Broadway and 46th Street, and the Eastside Cinema, Third Avenue and 55th Street. Running time: 92 minutes. This film is classified R.
Alvin Purple ....Graeme Blundell
Dr. McBurney ....George Whaley
Dr. Liz Sort......Penne Hackforth-Jones
Tina Donovan................Elli Maclure
Judge ....Noel Ferrier
Mrs. Horwood ....Jill Foster

The principals — Graeme Blundell as Alvin, George Whaley as the fraudulent Dr. McBurney, Penne Hackforth-Jones as the resistible psychiatrist and Elli Maclure as Tina—give this movie their best efforts.

But that isn't enough. Although it is an attractive production, filmed in Melbourne, "Alvin Purple" is an essentially juvenile romp, lighthearted but not truly funny, reliant on double entrendre for sniggers, a kind of pubescent's idea of sexual heaven.

Word is that in Australia, "Alvin Purple" has outdrawn "The Godfather," "The Sting" and "The Exorcist." If true, that word does not say as much about differences in taste between here and there as it does about differences in needs.

LAWRENCE VAN GELDER

1974 O 12, 21:1

'Porter' Is Romantic Pornography

By VINCENT CANBY

LET us now consider a piece of junk. Soberly. Without snickering. Which is not easy to do when the movie is about the ups and downs of a hectic love affair involving a former concentration camp officer and the little Jewish girl he raped, tortured and knocked about, humiliating her in those funny, thoughtful little ways that only she understood as the gestures of a fully ripened affection.

The movie is called "The Night Porter." It was directed by Liliana Cavani whose first film to be seen here, "The Cannibals," was a sort of updated version of "Antigone" set in a Milan where half the citizens seemed to have caught ptomaine poisoning at precisely the same instant. There were bodies everywhere and Antigone wanted desperately to clean up the streets, to bury some of the bodies, including her brother's.

The Times critic who reviewed "The Cannibals" in 1970, calling it dreadful, couldn't possibly have imagined the dizzy heights of nonsense to which Miss Cavani would aspire in "The Night Porter." Apparently with some success. People are standing two abreast outside the Baronet Theater these days. Although they want to be shocked, they more often wind up in advanced stages of giggles. There's no other way to react sanely to a movie that recalls the concentration camp as Our Blue Heaven.

The night porter of the title is good old Max (Dirk Bogarde) who, when the film opens in 1957 in Vienna, minds his switchboard and tends to the needs of the hotel guests. These include the Countess (Isa Miranda), who has a taste for rough young men and whose balloon-like shape suggests she also likes to sniff helium, and Bert (Amadeo Amodio), one of Max's former S.S. comrades. Bert likes to hire a room at the hotel and give private dance recitals for Max, who then rewards him with an injection in the buttocks of something that looks suspiciously habit-forming, though we never know exactly what it is (which is the level of the subtleties that "The Night Porter" deals in.)

For reasons that soon become understandable Max has been keeping a low profile since the war. He seems happy enough, spending his days in his tiny flat with a well-behaved Siamese cat, at night carrying on like a fussy madame in a Jean Genet whorehouse, running out to fetch a fellow for the Countess or stage-managing a fantasy for Bert. Max's past then suddenly catches up with him, much as pasts do.

It's not so bad that some of his old S.S. buddies want to stage a mock trial, just to find out whether or not there's any evidence that could be used against him by various war crimes tribunals, though Max finds the whole procedure a silly intrusion. "I just want to be left in peace," he says with some frequency, often lifting one eyebrow to drive the point dramatically home. What is worse is the appearance of the beautiful Lucia (Charlotte Rampling), the wife of a famous American conductor who has come to Vienna to conduct "The Magic Flute." Lucia turns out to be—are you

sitting down?—the pretty little Jewish girl whom Max so brutalized years ago that she can hardly wait to resume their relationship, which they do in short order, Lucia having told her husband that she wants to stay on in Vienna for a little shopping.

I realize that my synopsis of the film is much too chronological. This is not really the way the movie unfolds. It sort of tumbles out as a montage of contemporary events and flashbacks that overlap to form a cinematic style you might call gossipy. It doesn't tell you much but hints at a lot. The concentration camp remembered by both Max and Lucia looks like a sort of depressed Club Mediterranée where everyone runs around doing his thing, Max taking his pleasure with the scared Lucia, while Lucia spends most of the time either on the floor or sinking slowly to it. Among the film's various definitions of decadence is a strong preference to do on a floor what most other people would do on a chair, table or bed.

So far, so bad. But it gets worse. Such as the scene in which Max confides to the Countess that he's found his little girl "from the old days," though he doesn't say that at that very moment she's waiting for him back in the flat, in chains. "Oh, Max," says the Countess,

beaming, "I've never seen you so much in love. What a romantic story!" Max, however, thinks it's more Biblical than romantic, if only because he once presented Lucia with the severed head of another prisoner who had been pestering her.

There may possibly be some way of using the sort of sado-masochistic relationship of Max and Lucia as a metaphor for the terrible interdependencies of torturer and victim in the concentration camps. Possibly, though I doubt it. Miss Cavani is less interested in the banality of evil or its psychology than in what she tries to picture as the eroticism of it. What a kinky turn-on! Apparently the only inmates who didn't have any fun were the senior citizens, the golden age group, but then (as Miss Cavani shows us) they were always allowed to stand around and watch.

One might be able to become outraged with "The Night Porter" if it weren't so vulnerable in every way. It is loaded with built-in self-destruct mechanisms, mostly in the form of dialogue of a witlessness unheard on the screen since "The Agony and The Ecstasy," when a droopy Charlton Heston was approached by a worried admirer who demanded:

"Michelangelo, are you or are you not going to finish that ceiling?"

The acting is atrocious. Bogarde seems to have reverted to the mannerisms of his juvenile days, two in all, the lifted eyebrow and the self-satisfied smirk, which aren't really adequate to cover the range of feelings that Miss Cavani would have us believe are passing through him. Or even nearby. Miss Rampling has a magnificent profile but very tiny passions, like a boy's.

The major blame is Miss Cavani's. The world she pictures is no upside-down vision of a would-be revolutionary like Sade or Genet. It is, instead, a world of romantic pornography. Almost any two sequences in Bergman's "Scenes From A Marriage" are more revealing about the shifting needs involved in sadomasochism than the whole of "The Night Porter," in spite of all its simulated blood, beatings, ground glass and such. If you don't allow Miss Cavani's monumental chutzpah to antagonize you too much, and if you find the pretentions as funny as I do, you can hear a familiar refrain ringing through many of the scenes: the high cheerful voice of a Victorian bawd screaming with pleasure: "Ain't we beasts!"

1974 O 13, II: 1:6

The Cast

LE FANTOME DE LA LIBERTE (The Specter of Freedom), directed by Luis Buñuel; screenplay (French with English subtitles) by Mr. Buñuel with the collaboration of Jean-Claude Carrière; produced by Serge Silberman; director of photography, Edmond Richard; editor, Helene Plemianikov; a Greenwich Film production, distributed by 20th Century-Fox. Running time: 104 minutes. At the New York Film Festival at Alice Tully Hall in Lincoln Center, Broadway at 65th Street. This film has not been rated.

Prefct's Sister .... Adrianna Asti
First Prefect .... Julien Bertheau
Mr. Foucauld ....Jean-Claude Brialy
Dr. Legendre ....Adolfo Celi
Inkeeper .... Paul Frankeur
Hatter .... Michel Lonsdale
Policeman Gerard ..... Pierre Maguelon
Professor .... Francois Maistre
Aunt ....Helen Perdriere
Second Prefect .... Michel Piccoli
Commissioner .... Claude Piéplu
Lost Girl's Father ....Jean Rochefort
Captain .... Bernard Verley
Nurse .... Milena Vukotic
Mrs. Foucauld ....Monica Vitti

By VINCENT CANBY

After 17 days of good, bad, and mostly indifferent films, the 12th annual New York Film Center at Lincoln Center closed triumphantly last night with the American premiere of Luis Buñuel's brilliant, anarchic new comedy, "Le Fantôme de la Liberté" (The Specter of Freedom"), which will begin its commercial run at the Paris Theater here on Oct. 27.

The premiere of "Fantôme" came the day after the festival's homage to Mr. Buñuel in the form of the retrospective showing of four of his earlier works, "L'Age D'Or" (1930), made in collaboration with Salvador Dali, "The Exterminating Angel" (1962), "The Milky Way" (1969) and "The Discreet Charm of the Bourgeoisie" (1972). This had the effect of italicizing what we have all been saying for years: the Buñuel talent has continued to grow and refine itself at that period in a film maker's life when he is ordinarily expected to taper off,

Jean-Claude Brialy and Monica Vitti

if not retire to campus or swimming pool.

•

Mr. Buñuel must be awfully tired of people going on and on about his age. (He'll be 75 nex February.) Yet the subject is pertinent when so few film makers have endured long enough to give us the benefit of the wit and wisdom that come only from living through decades of changing fashions. Writers, painters, musicians and composers survive into creative old age. Film makers have a way of wearing out too soon, like American automobiles. Not Luis Buñuel.

In "Le Fantôme de la Liberté" Mr. Buñuel and Jean-Claude Carrière, who has collaborated with the director on all of his feature films since "Diary of a Chambermaid" (1964), contemplate man's survival in spite of his idiocies. I'm not at all sure the film has as much to do with specific ideas about freedom as the title would imply. Rather, I suspect, the concept of freedom as touched upon in the film is just another in the system of reversals—one of dozens of dumbfounding paradoxes — that so fascinate and amuse this most free yet most disciplined of film makers.

"Le Fantôme de le Liberté" is not for people who see movies as butterflies, trophies to be netted, pinned down, then pulled apart with tweezers. The movie can't be pinned down. There's no single correct way to read it, which is not a rationale for its ambiguities, but a rigor-

ous instruction to those who would enjoy all that is most marvelous and poetic in surrealism at its best.

•

The film opens in Toledo in 1808 as Napoleon's soldiers attempt to liberate Spain and summarily shoot all citizens who refuse to be liberated. "Down with liberty!" is the heroic cry of one of the victims standing before a Goya-like firing squad.

Thereupon the camera follows a French officer who, being slightly drunk on communion wine and stuffed with communion wafers, becomes enchanted by the beauty of the statue of a knight's wife on a sepulcher in the cathedral they're then violating. As the officer bends to kiss the statue, the stone hand of the knight's figure gives the officer a terrific swat, so enraging the officer he vows to take his pleasure with the dead lady, whose coffin, they find, is filled with paraphernalia.

•

"Paraphernalia?" asks a woman sitting in a park in modern-day Paris. "What is par-a-pher-na-lia?" The woman, a nanny, has been reading aloud to a friend the story we've been watching, at which point "Le Fantôme" moves into another story, that of the nanny, her small charge, a little girl who is given what seem to be obscene postcards by a strange man, and the girl's parents, who are so outraged by the postcards (pictures of Nôtre Dame, Sacré Coeur and the like) that they sack the nanny on the spot.

"Le Fantôme de la Liberté" is dozens of stories that lead

from one to another with a dreamlike logic, and a dream-like way of never quite arriving at a neatly satisfactory conclusion. Among the characters who turn up are a courteous sniper, who shoots a couple of dozen people from the top of Montparnasse skyscraper at the edge of Paris and becomes a celebrity; a group of poker - playing monks, a little girl who vanishes from school but is able to accompany her parents to the police station where she gives her own vital statistics, even though no one acknowledges her presence.

More than any other Buñuel film "Le Fantôme" recalls "L'Age D'Or" with its riddles, jokes, outrageous associations, contradictions and dim view of reason's power. "Le Fantôme" is no less dense with symbols (for those who care about such things), but the style is more precise, less heavy, much funnier, no less mysterious, yet so economical that when he ridicules the arbitrariness of a social convention, like table manners, he manages also to make a few pithy observations on ecology.

•

The physical production is stunning to look at. The cast is large, first-rate, but the presence that dazzles us is that of the Old Master, just off screen, mercilessly testing our senses of sanity and humor.

1974 O 14, 39:1

The Cast

A WOMAN UNDER THE INFLUENCE, directed by John Cassavetes; screenplay by Mr. Cassavetes; photography, Mitch Breit; editors, Bob Heffernan and Tom Cornwell; music, Bo Harwood; executive producer, Sam Shaw; production company, Faces International Films, Inc. At the New York Film Festival, Lincoln Center, Alice Tully Hall. Running time: 155 minutes.

Nick Longhetti	Peter Falk
Mabel Longhetti	Gena Rowlands
Mama Longhetti	Katherine Cassavetes
Martha Mortensen	Lady Rowlands
George Mortensen	Fred Draper

By NORA SAYRE

When a husband and wife need to keep saying how much they love each other, something's apt to be awfully wrong. That nervous repetition is one of the danger signals in John Cassavetes's "A Woman Under the Influence," and it contains all the warning urgency of a siren. The movie played on Saturday at the New York Film Festival.

Throughout, the film dwells on the abrasions of daily living, centered in the domestic world where each individual grinds on the other's nerves. Gena Rowlands plays a woman adrift. Her manic, likable, hard-hat husband (Peter Falk) quite hysterically keeps assuring her that everything's fine. Meanwhile, she looks to him for her identity, asking him to tell her "what" to be, insisting that she'll "be anything" he wants. Later, he punctuates a horrendous uproar by shouting "Just be yourself!" But she hardly has a self—beyond the bundle of symptoms that make up her hectic public persona.

Miss Rowlands unleashes an extraordinary characterization of a harried, anxious creature, who's convinced that she "makes a jerk of" herself every day. (The actresses' style of performing sometimes shows a kinship with that of the early Kim Stanley or the recent Joanne Woodward, but the notes of desperation are emphatically her own.) Despair lurks behind her smile—which often collapses suddenly—as she jabbers, hums or retreats to a little-girl manner. Pantomime is one of her defenses. She mugs with exasperation, working her jaw and rolling her eyes when she's annoyed or throwing indignant punches into the air. When frenzy gives way to apology, her mouth tightens with resentment, which then yields to a miserable leer. With her three small children, she's wildly demonstrative—she seems to be pleading for their affection, trying to be a fellow-child who plays their games.

A troubled person, yes, and certainly an insecure one. But she doesn't seem sick or crazed enough to justify the crack-up that's awaiting her, nor to spend six months in a sanitarium. And that's the hitch in the movie: you can't really tell how the director regards this character. Mr. Cassavetes is unquestionably sympathetic to the rootless state of the middle-American housewife. (Moreover, the hospitalization is meant to seem like a betrayal by the husband.)

•

But—perhaps unintentionally—he has made the man appear much crazier than his wife; are we supposed to assume that his frantic nature has driven her over the edge? Or are we meant to see madness as contagious? Ultimately, the essential problems of this woman remain unclear: we're shown her behavior, but not what inspired it.

The movie is also a study in embarrassment—since that's the dominant emotion shared by everyone who encounters this headlong person. There's also a conscientious effort to show a continuing relationship, but the picture doesn't touch a common nerve in the way that Ingmar Bergman's "Scenes From a Marriage" does—because a number of moments that could be moving or touching are made to be farcical.

•

Peter Falk gives a rousing performance as the man who lives at a perpetual bursting point, and the children are very well directed. But the movie didn't need to be 2 hours and 35 minutes long: there's too much small talk, which doesn't really reveal character. Still, the most frightening scenes are extremely compelling, and this is a thoughtful film that does prompt serious discussion.

1974 O 14, 39:1

The Cast

THE WIDOW COUDERC, directed by Pierre Granier-Deferre; screenplay (French with English subtitles) by Mr. Granier-Deferre and Pascal Jardin; adapted from a novel by George Simeon; director of photography, Walter Wottitz; music, Phillipe Sarde; produced by Raymond Danon; a co-production from Lira Films (Paris) and Pegaso Films (Rome); presented by H G Entertainment. At the Playboy Theater, 110 West 57th Street, Running time: 92 minutes. This film has not been classified.

Jean	Alain Delon
La Veuve Couderc	Simone Signoret
Felicie	Ottavia Piccolo

Since Simone Signoret appears in all too few movies these days, it's so good to see her on the screen that one tends to be almost undemanding of the picture—which, in this case, is a modest film of high quality that never quite gets off the ground, despite its many fine details and a beautiful evocation of the French countryside.

In Pierre Granier-Deferre's "The Widow Couderc," which opened yesterday at the Playboy Theater, Miss Signoret is a widowed farm woman who shelters a murderer on the lam (Alain Delon). With deft, swift movements, she conveys the authority of a person who has wrenched a living out of the land. Cutting hay, digging or hoeing, washing laundry in a stream, slicing meat, she makes us momentarily forget all the worldly or urban roles that she has played so superbly—here, she's the total peasant.

•

Hard work and hard times have armored the widow against almost any form of indulgence. Hence Miss Signoret is also very touching as a stern, aging woman who falls reluctantly in love with a footloose young man. As in some of her other movies, there's the hopeful half-smile that appears when she likes someone, or the wistful appreciation that she reveals after making love.

The man also sleeps with a mindless adolescent (Ottavia Piccolo—very good.) Then the widow's in-laws, who hate her, identify him to the police. The movie was adapted from a novel by Georges Simenon; the director is respectful of its characters, and their situation might even have the stuff of tragedy. However, Mr. Delon's role and his performance are too thin and elusive—so we can't care greatly when his life's in jeopardy.

The actor just doesn't use the vitality that he has brought to some of his earlier parts; instead, he's almost phlegmatic, and—not for the first time—he seems to be thinking of James Dean. (A nice thought, admittedly, but one that's hardly rooted in the French working class.) Since Miss Signoret has all the strength to move us, it's worth wishing that the director had made her opposite number more substantial.

NORA SAYRE

1974 O 14, 39:3

AMERICA'S POP COLLECTOR: ROBERT C. SCULL. "Conceptualized and coordinated" by E. J. Vaughn and John Schott; edited by Leah Siegel and Mr. Schott; filmed by Susan and Alan Raymond and Ron Dorfman; originated and produced by Mr. Vaughn. Running time: 72 minutes. EUPHORIA by Vincent Collins, 4 minutes. At the Whitney Museum of American Art, Madison Avenue and 75th Street. Through Tuesday.

By NORA SAYRE

Many people are going to enjoy "America's Pop Collector: Robert C. Scull—Contemporary Art at Auction," but I especially recommend it to publishers and movie makers—since this documentary makes the book or film industries look pure and pastoral in comparison to the art world. The movie, which was "conceptualized and coordinated" by E. J. Vaughn and John Schott, and filmed by Susan and Alan Raymond, opened yesterday at the Whitney Museum of American Art and will run until Tuesday.

•

Once you've witnessed the October, 1973, auction of 50 works of art from the collection of the taxi tycoon Robert Scull—the sale brought him $2,240,900—you may be glad that you don't paint, sculpture, own, sell, or buy contemporary art—which appears to addle many who come in contact with it. In fact, the movie makes the audience feel superior to those on screen—a sensation that's always pleasing, whether it's justified or not.

The sale included works by Willem de Kooning, Frank Stella, Robert Rauschenberg, Franz Kline, Barnett Newman, Larry Poons, Andy Warhol and James Rosenquist. When asked why he chose to sell his possessions, Mr. Scull answers repeatedly that the exhibition at Parke Bernet was the only way that he could see these paintings, sculptures and constructions together; he emphasizes the lack of space in his apartment, remarking that many pieces had been in storage. (Apparently, he had to part with these things in order to look at them.) He adds that owning art is "a different kind of high." Others criticize him for loving publicity, though he's also credited for his adventurousness in buying difficult works when they weren't popular, and Robert Rauschenberg stresses that the Sculls helped artists at a period "when there wasn't enough activity to support them."

Meanwhile, some are distressed at seeing these works leave the country. And although the question of artists' royalties isn't discussed in this film, it does raise the issue of a collector's making such gargantuan profits when the artists receive none. (Mr. Scull, who dodges queries about art as an investment, gets quite huffy about profits; he insists that he's raising the artists' price for their future work.) Throughout, he comes through as jovial and benign; though the film mocks him, he's allowed to appear likable.

In this documentary, the works of art are definitely treated as objects—they're filmed very casually, without perception or respect. It's hard to tell if this was totally intentional — if the film makers deliberately presented paintings and sculptures in the spirit of the market place, or if they were also somewhat insensitive. However, it's gripping to see the stuff handled about as tenderly as the airlines treat your luggage: a Larry Poons painting slips while it's being hung, and two Jasper Johns beer cans are shoved around as though they came straight from Ballantine's. All in all, there's a sense of no deposit, no return.

•

Some of the best parts of the film are the preparations for the auction; the ushers are instructed to "be forceful without being rude" and to make people sit in their assigned seats—which were "thoroughly researched" in light o most individuals' bidding records. The film is a very amusing putdown of an occasion that doesn't inspire reverence. Of course it's an easy target. But since the artists' talent or diligence are made to seem irrelevant, our laughter at those who were enriched by their work can refresh us in fierce economic times.

1974 O 17, 55:3

The Cast

GOLD, directed by Peter Hunt; screenplay by Wilbur Smith and Stanley Price, based on the novel by Mr. Smith; produced by Michael Kinger; director of photography, Ousama Rawi; music, Elmer Bernstein; editor, John Glen; distributed by Allied Artists. Running time: 120 minutes. At the National Theater, Broadway at 44th Street; Fine Arts, 56th Street, east of Park Avenue, and 34th Street East, 34th Street near Second Avenue. This film has been rated PG.

Rod Slater	Roger Moore
Terry Steyner	Susannah York
Hurry Hirschfeld	Ray Milland
Manfred Steyner	Bradford Dillman
Farrell	John Gielgud
Big King	Simon Sabela
Stephen Marais	Tony Beckley
Kowalski	Bernard Horsfall

By VINCENT CANBY

"Gold," which opened at three theaters here yesterday, is an overwritten, overacted, overdirected, overproduced adventure film that, like many much better, much simpler B-movies of the nineteen-thirties and forties, is about men doing a job. This time the job is goldmining in South Africa, where most of the film was made with, I suspect, lots of cooperation.

The story is about an evil plan to control the international price of gold by sabotaging one of the country's largest gold mines by flooding it with an underground sea. The plan is nicked in the last reel by Roger Moore, standing up to his neck in swirling mineshaft waters, with the help of Simon Sabela, who plays his trusted black friend. Because "Gold" has the social conscience of a dim-witted ostrich, you expect Mr. Moore at any minute to refer to Mr. Sabela as a good darkie.

In addition to Mr. Moore and Mr. Sabela, the cast includes Ray Milland, as the kind, crusty old white millionaire who owns the mine and is called "Pops" by his bored, beautiful granddaughter, Susannah York, who is married to cold, mean Bradford Dillman, one of the chief plotters along with elegant, detached John Gielgud, an international tycoon not above a little murder. Without exception they all are dreadful.

The movie was directed by Peter Hunt, who directed "On Her Majesty's Secret Service," the worst Bond film ever. Mr. Hunt's sense of style is summed up in his decision to photograph the beginning of one scene through a brandy glass. It could have been, of course, that he was only embarrassed by the content of the film and trying his best to hide it.

1974 O 17, 57:1

DODES'KA-DEN, directed by Akira Kurosawa; screenplay (Japanese wtih English subtitles) by Mr. Kurosawa, Hideo Oguni and Shinobu Hashimoto, based on "The Town Without Seasons" by Shugoro Yamamoto; photography, Tawao Saito and Yasumichi Fukuzawa; music, Toro Takemitsu; produced by Yonki-no-Kai Taho Company, Ltd.; released by Janus Films. At the First Avenue Screening Room, at 61st Street. Running time: 140 minutes. This film has not been classified.

Roku-shan .... Yoshitaka Zuxhi
Shima-san .... Junzaburo Ban
Shima-san's wife .... Kiyoko Tange
Laborers ... Hisashi Igawa and Kunie Tanaka

Never having read Shugoro Yamamoto's "The Town Without Seasons," I cannot be too certain how faithfully Akira Kurosawa has followed its text in his adaptation, "Dodes'ka-den," now playing at the First Avenue Screening Room.

But judging by what is visible on screen, the novel must have been a rather slick, episodic work, one of those "good reads" that pokes its nose behind closed doors into the lives of "little people" to sniff out a heady mixture of scandal, sentiment and spiritual uplift.

•

These, certainly, are the principal findings of "Dodes-'ka-den" ("The Song of the Trolley), as it weaves its way through a shanty town sprouting out of a wasteland of refuse. Among the characters in the forefront is the demented boy who spends his days commanding an imaginary trolley into and out of the town; the father and son who inhabit the shell of a car and plan a dream house; the wise and compassionate old artisan who is kind to burglars and confounding to enraged drunks; the two drunken laborers who swap wives; and the cuckold who illustrates the distinction between parenthood and fatherhood.

•

There is also the spiritually dead man who will never forgive his wife her indiscretion; the deformed, tic-ridden clerk and his surly wife; and the frail, unhappy girl who makes artificial flowers and is abused by her stepfather And, out in the midst of all the shanties, a group of women spending all day at the communal water spigot acts the role of a chorus.

The unifying image is that of the trolley, and the trolley is on a shuttle run. Like the people in the movie, it is going nowhere. All are anchored in their poverty. Some are oblivious to it; some dream t heir way above it; some are afflicted with more distracting—even more agonizing—burdens.

"Dodes'ka-den" is smooth, Mr. Kurosawa's first color film, and he is clearly enchanted by its possibilities, drenching the screen with hues, using them to establish mood and identify characters; to transport the audience into surreal realms dominated by dreams and death.

"Dodes'ka-den is smooth, handsome and well-acted. Those are its virtues. Its overriding fault is an acceptance of superficiality. In place of profundity, it gives us gossip.

LAWRENCE VAN GELDER

1974 O 18, 28:1

Great Battle' Opens

"The Great Battle," now playing at the Trans-Lux West and Columbia 1 Theaters, is an hour-and-41-minute condensation of a nearly five-hour Russian film recreating the defense of Kursk and the liberation of Kiev from the German armies in 1943.

It has the manner of a noisy pageant, punctuated from time to time by quieter scenes, in which heavily made-up actors portray the likes of Stalin, Hitler, Mussolini and Marshal Georgi K. Zhukov. The Russians speak idiomatic American dialogue. The Germans speak German translated into English by a narrator, and Stalin is treated with the majesty due Mother Russia's thoughtful, pipe-smoking Uncle Joe.

The film was directed by Yuri Ozerov and produced by Mosfilm. It looks like a chopped-up souvenir of the pre-Khrushchev era.

VINCENT CANBY.

1974 O 18, 28:1

FILMS FROM APPALACHIA: VISITING WITH DARLENE by P. J. O'Connell and Lisa Marshall, 44 minutes; NATURE'S WAY by John Long and Elizabeth Barrett, 20 minutes; TRADITION by Billy Hatton and Tony Stone, 20 minutes. At the Film Forum, 256 West 88th Street. Through Saturday and Oct. 24-27, 8 P.M.

By A. H. WEILER

It's hardly a secret that a fair proportion of rural Americans are not idyllic figures in a Grandma Moses picture of bucolic bliss. And "Films From Appalachia," the newly arrived collection of documentaries at the Film Forum, make it starkly clear that our affluent society also includes sadly impressive poverty and isolation as well as quaint, largely unchanged folkways.

Since all the subjects were shot by local film makers, a mutual respect for people and customs and an unslanted approach are obvious in each of the films depicted mostly by the principals involved. This is especially notable in "Visiting With Darlene," which was filmed in 1971 in a hilly, wooded, remote corner of Pennsylvania for showing on public television outlets.

•

Although this interview tends to be loquacious and static, it makes its points in simple, sober truths. A viewer needs little convincing that the film's titular young mother of four preschool children, whose absent husband is of little help, is, despite her casual recital, underlining hopelessness, loneliness and nagging fear. The evidence is there in her grim job of trying to pay $33 per month for a three-room shack with no running water, a bathroom or adequate heat and the frightening possibility that the youngsters she loves might be turned over to welfare authorities.

The Kentucky section of Appalachia is equally impressive in the two films made this year by Appashop, Inc., a cooperative group formed five years ago and based in Whitesburg, Ky. The mountaineer moonshiner of "Tradition" is not a Hollywood caricature. He's an admittedly rough-hewn, unlettered, poor man, who's been in and out of jail. And, as the federal revenue officer stresses, he is typical of the proud hill folk who return to their illegal whisky stills because poverty, too, is traditional and it's the only way of life that will keep them off welfare.

•

Pride and tradition, if not always poverty, are the basic elements of "Nature's Way" in which local "healers" demonstrate homes cures for virtually everything from sores to cancer. The most believable, however, is an elderly, kindly midwife who is shown delivering twins, the latest addition to the more than 5,000 she says she has helped add to Kentucky's population in two years. She performs with the dedication of a big city obstetrical team. "Sometimes they pay me," she notes placidly," but I always feel good." The Appalachians introduced here always affect a viewer even if they don't make him feel good.

1974 O 18, 35:5

Thriller About Secret SS Society Opens

By NORA SAYRE

When a thriller is built entirely around one star, you know that he's not going to vanish, that he simply can't get bumped off—hence the suspense sags. And that's one of the many flaws in Ronald Neame's "The Odessa File," which opened yesterday at Loews State, Loews Orpheum, and Cinema 2. The movie is so dependent on Jon Voight's presence that he's hardly allowed off the screen. So the threats to his life are no more exciting than watching a shopper being elbowed at a January white sale.

•

The picture—set in Germany in 1963, and based on Frederick Forsyth's novel—is concerned with a secret society of former SS men. Equipped with new identities, they're conspiring to produce rockets that will destroy Israel. Mr. Voight, a German journalist obsessed with tracking down a sadistic war criminal, finally infiltrates

The Cast

THE ODESSA FILE, directed by Ronald Neame, screenplay by Kenneth Ross and George Markstein, based on the novel by Frederick Forsyth; director of photography, Oswald Morris; film editor, Ralph Kemplen; music, Andrew Lloyd Webber, produced by John Woolf; released by Columbia Pictures. At Loews State 1, Broadway and 45th Street; Loews Orpheum, 86th Street at Third Avenue, and Cinema 2, Third Avenue at 60th Street. Running time: 140 Minutes. This film is classified PG.

Peter Miller .... Jon Voight
Edward Roschmann .. Maximilian Schell
Frau Miller .... Maria Schell
Sigi .... Mary Tamm
Klaus Wenzer .... Derek Jacobi
Gustav MacKensen .... Klaus Lowitsch •

the organization by masquerading as an alumnus of the SS. (He's asked if he's willing to risk his life to crack the case. Whenever that demand is made of a reporter in a movie, I picture trouble at the story conference.) Naturally, the villains are eager to erase him—unlike the audience, they don't know that he's unkillable, or that every trap set for him has to fizzle.

The film makes its points methodically, almost academically. It also drags because there are many unnecessary transitional passages, devoted to moving the characters from one situation to another. Almost every occurrence is predictable. But at least there are no cabaret scenes; these Nazis don't have as much fun as those in "The Night Porter."

Mr. Voight is not at his best—he's just too thoughtful a performer for a mere action part, which offers too little scope for the variety of his talents. He hasn't much to do beyond conveying worry, weariness and patience; he's rarely allowed to smile—and it's a deprivation not to see this actor smile. He's quite skillful at impersonating a 40-year-old Nazi—but throughout, his German accent comes out Chermann.

•

Maximilian Schell does transcend the banality of the script; he's very good indeed as the dexterous survivor who was once the concentration camp butcher. Mary Tamm, as Mr. Voight's girlfriend, is colorless in a colorless part; almost her only function is to chide him for living dangerously. Meanwhile, moviegoers who crave dazzling suspense should see Claude Pintoteau's "Escape to Nowhere" instead of "The Odessa File."

1974 O 19, 36:1

AIRPORT 1975, directed by Jack Smight; screenplay by Don Ingalls; inspired by the film "Airport," based on the novel by Arthur Hailey; produced by William Frye; executive producer, Jennings Lang; director of photography, Philip Lathtrop; editor, J. Terry Williams; music, John Cacavas; distributed by Universal Pictures. Running time: 107 minutes. At Loews State 2, Broadway at 45th Street; Loews Cine, 86th Street at Third Avenue, and the Murray Hill Theater, 34th Street near Third Avenue. This film has been rated PG.

Murdock .... Charlton Heston
Nancy .... Karen Black
Patroni .... George Kennedy
Stacy .... Efrem Zimbalist Jr.
Mrs. Patroni .... Susan Clark
Sister Ruth .... Helen Reddy
Janice .... Linda Blair
Scott Freeman .... Dana Andrews
Urias .... Roy Thinnes
Barney .... Sid Caesar
Mrs. Davaney .... Myrna Loy
Gloria Swanson .... Gloria Swanson

By VINCENT CANBY

"Airport 1975," which opened at three theaters yesterday, is a silly, jumbo-size sequel to the original film adaptation of Arthur Hailey's "Airport," which was about the trials of a Boeing 707 that had the misfortune to have a mad bomber aboard. The two films are very much alike; only the planes and the names of the characters have been changed to amuse the innocent.

Like its predecessor, "Airport 1975" is carefully designed not to bring up any subject as touchy as air safety and traffic control, even though it's about a mid-air collision. A great deal is made of the fact that the collision is a result of what might be called a private failing, and that, anyway, the 747 is "the best aircraft ever made."

•

The crisis in "Airport 1975" occurs when the pilot of a private plane has a heart attack and plunges his small craft into the cockpit of a 747 en route from Washington to Los Angeles, either killing or maiming the members of the jetliner's flight crew.

Who is left aboard the big plane to handle the controls until some sort of help can arrive?

Who will be able to steer it, more or less, through mountain passes, receiving her instructions through the headphones of the damaged radio, looking distraught from time to time, but game and pretty throughout?

By golly, you've guessed it, but I shouldn't give away any more of the plot. He who gives away the plot of a movie like this gives away its soul.

Karen Black plays the spunky stewardess, and Charlton Heston plays her boyfriend, the man who saves the day in a daring plane-to-plane pilot transfer that prompts someone to say in all seriousness: "This is plain suicide, sir!"

There are a lot of exclamation points in this movie, which is also extremely polite, even in its crises. Worse failings are its smugness ("The public's right to know gives me huge pain in the ——," says a righteous airline executive of a pushy TV reporter) and a total lack of awareness of how comic it is when it's attempting to be most serious.

•

The supporting characters include a little girl en route to a kidney transplant (played by Linda Blair with all of the naïveté of a Vegas showgirl); a singing nun (Helen Reddy), a lady who drinks with two fists (Myrna Loy), another nun who doesn't sing (Martha Scott) and Gloria Swanson (played by Gloria Swanson in what amounts to ferocious self-parody).

The screenplay was written by Don Ingalls, and Jack Smight was the director. The plane is by Boeing.

1974 O 19, 63:4

Luis Bunuel— Much of the Fun Is in Surprise

FILM VIEW

VINCENT CANBY

"Le Fantôme De La Liberté" (The Spectre of Freedom) is Luis Buñuel's 30th feature film and one of his most glorious assaults on the world of what passes for reason—the world we assume we see with our own eyes—since "L'Age D'Or," his first feature film made in 1930. At the age of 74 Buñuel has outlived the Surrealist movement, with which he once identified himself, to create a cinema all his own, simultaneously classic and a little vulgar, always contemporary yet always somewhat dated, if only because this most passionate of film poets, having very early mastered the basics of filmmaking, has resolutely refused to clutter his movies with gratuitous style.

"Fantôme," which was the closing night attraction at the 12th New York Film Festival (and pulled that mostly hum-drum festival's chestnuts off the fire), will open at the Paris Theater next Sunday. I can't imagine that it will ever be very long out of release, at least as long as there are people seriously concerned with having fun, with movies, with the anguish of supposedly being civilized.

Don't let the title throw you, and don't be misled by the New York Festival program note that suggested the film's theme is the fear of freedom and the fascination of enslavement. This title, I suspect, is as much a Buñuelian joke as it is a marvelous title (not quite as good as "The Discreet Charm of The Bourgeoisie," but

The New York Times/Jack Manning

At 74, Luis Bunuel has reached an artistic peak.

"Le Fantôme De La Liberté," the latest triumph from Luis Bunuel.

almost) chosen for its own sake. "Le Fantôme De La Liberté" does have to do with freedom, from time to time, anyway, but it's mostly a very funny meditation upon the irrationalities of existence.

•   •   •

Nowhere except in films can such irrationalities be so vividly demonstrated, whether by a cow lounging on a Louis XV bed ("L'Age D'Or") or by an ostrich picking its way across the bedroom of Jean-Claude Brialy and Monica Vitti ("Fantôme"). It couldn't happen but there it is, and the act of reconciling the film image, which amounts to fact, with actual experience stretches the mind. It forces one to reconsider all sorts of verities, like gravity, the blessedness of being meek, or the communion of saints, all of which have been questioned at one time or another by Buñuel.

"The Spectre of Liberty" might be more accurately if less poetically titled "The Spectre of Reason," for it is misconceptions of reason, perversions of common sense, that run through the film's very freely associated episodes.

These begin with the Napoleonic occupation of Spain in 1808, when French soldiers shoot all Spaniards who refuse to be liberated, thus recalling some more recent massacres in the name of freedom and liberation. "Down with liberty!" shouts a heroic Spaniard just before he faces the firing squad, and "Le Fantôme De La Liberté" is off and running through a series of tales that are hot-foots to sanity.

Buñuel is an intractable old moralist and social critic, a revolutionist who believes that virtually every idea, belief and custom of the bourgeoisie should be tested with a little T.N.T. New orders cannot be built without destroying old ones. Sometimes Buñuel's outrage has been clearly apparent, as in "L'Age D'Or," "Los Olvidados," "Viridiana" and the immaculately beautiful "Tristana," which is a first cousin to "Viridiana."

Sometimes it has been successfully disguised to make a cerebrally funny film like "The Exterminating Angel" and hugely funny ones like "The Discreet Charm of The Bourgeoise" and "La Fantôme De La Liberté," although all three of these films are filled with portents of doom and death. Only Buñuel could, I'm sure, get a laugh out of the scene in "Fantôme" in which a man has just been told he has terminal cancer. The patient's reaction? He slugs the doctor. Not necessarily because of the bad news but because the doctor has been unconscionably sloppy in reading the X-rays and patronizing in his attitude to the victim.

In Buñuel's films, all passions are suspect, whether they have to do with sex, love, rage, religious beliefs or, as in "The Discreet Charm," with a sense of decorum. Sometimes we never know the basis of the passion. One of the more marvelous (and mysterious) episodes in "Fantôme" has to do with the outrage expressed by Jean-Claude Brialy and Monica Vitti when they discover that a nasty old deviate has cornered their young daughter in a playground and given her a set of picture postcards. "Unbelievable," says the appalled Brialy as he holds up a picture postcard of the Acropolis. "This is going too far," says Miss Vitti, turning her eyes away from a view of Sacré Couer. The nanny who was responsible for the girl's protection is sacked on the spot.

I won't attempt to synopsize the new film more than I already have. A great deal of its fun is in surprise, though by now we're all familiar with most of Buñuel's historic concerns that turn up in the movie—with fetishists, with public servants operating according to their own lunatic values, with the Roman Catholic Church, with unexpected encounters and magical events that dumbfound us but scarcely raise an eyebrow on any of the characters involved. You get the idea that if Buñuel's characters were in a theater looking at us on a screen, they'd be just as amused and mystified as we are.

A word about the Buñuel style: although he so often deals in the fantastic, in the surreal, Buñuel never betrays his intentions by letting the techniques come between us and the subject. No dramatic camera movements. No music unless it's within the scene itself. No dissolves that might allow us to catch our breath. Only quick, clean cuts. As Buñuel and his writing collaborator, Jean-Claude Carrière, eschew high-toned literary allusions, so are there no technical gimmicks in his films. It's the work of a man who knows precisely what he's doing, and does it simply, which is why watching his films is such a tonic, no matter how tough the subject.

1974 O 20, II:17:1

The Bettmann Archives

Above: "The Exterminating Angel," a Bunuelian beauty from the past.

PHASE IV, directed by Saul Bass; screenplay, Mayo Simon; director of photography, Dick Bush; editor, Willy Kemplen; music, Brian Gascolgne; produced by Paul Radin; released by Paramount Pictures. At neighborhood theaters. Running time: 83 minutes. This film is classified PG.

Hubbs .... Nigel Davenport
Kendra .... Lynne Frederick
Lesko .... Michael Murphy
Mr. Eldridge .... Alan Gifford
Mrs. Eldridge .... Helen Horton
Clete .... Robert Henderson

The ominous possibility of insects threatening to dominate and perhaps destroy man is again posed in "Phase IV," which opened at local theaters last Friday. The adversary—in this case, it's the familiar, highly coordinated and indomitable ant—is less a threat than a problem created by a concept and a script that is initially spellbinding but then quickly turns into mystifying vacil-lations between fact and largely unconvincing fiction.

"Phase IV" is reminiscent of, say, those sobering ant sagas, "Them!" and "The Hellstrom Chronicle," and Stanley Kubrick's futuristic "2001" space odyssey. Elements of all are evident here as a couple of dedicated scientists do their learned best to combat various species of ants that, because of a vague interplanetary disturbance, have joined forces to cause a "biological imbalance" in a remote corner of the Arizona desert.

•

In making his feature directorial debut after a succession of distinguished film titles, graphics and short subjects, Saul Bass, with the aid of special insect photography by Ken Middleham ("Hellstrom Chronicle"), has fashioned a pictorially persuasive adventure. His ants — in close-up and otherwise — make their awesome potential terrifyingly real, even if his principals—Nigel Davenport and Michael Murphy, as the scientists, and Lynne Frederick, as the frightened young woman—are merely one-dimensional figures registering surface emotions.

It's ungallant to reveal the dénouement but, like a good deal of "Phase IV," it's beclouded by enigmas. For all of its good, scientific and human intentions, "Phase IV" cries for a Phase V of fuller explanations.

A. H. WEILER

1974 O 21, 48:6

Timothy Bottoms Plays Mad for Laughs

By NORA SAYRE

The charms of mental illness and the superiority conferred by psychic wounds are celebrated almost as whimsically in Arthur Hiller's "The Crazy World of Julius Vrooder" as in Phillippe de Broca's horribly winsome "King of Hearts." Timothy Bottoms plays a Vietnam veteran who frolics all over his hospital, convinced that he's far saner than the doctors who pronounce him "psychiatrically impaired." The movie—which drowns its antiwar theme in a cataract of cuteness—opened last Friday at neighborhood theaters.

Mr. Bottoms is a beguiling actor, but here he has been directed to be elfin; with eyebrows perpetually raised, he seems in peril of turning into

The Cast

THE CRAZY WORLD OF JULIUS VROODER, directed by Arthur Hiller; associate producer and writer, Daryl Henry; director of photography, David M. Walsh; music, Bob Alcivar; film editor, Robert C. Jones; produced by Edward Rissien and Mr. Hiller; executive producer, Hugh M. Hefner; released by 20th Century-Fox Film Corporation. At 59th Street 1, east of Third Avenue; 86th Street 1, at Lexington Avenue, and the Beacon, Broadway and 74th Street. Running time: 100 minutes. This film is classified PG.
Julius Vrooder..........Timothy Bottoms
Zanni Willis...........Barbara Seagull
Dr. Melvin Passki....Lawrence Pressman
Anthony Vrooder:.....Richard A. Dysart

Peter Pan. He loves a dimwit nurse (Barbara Seagull), who specializes in an amused maternal gaze and adoring smiles. They plan to escape the crassness of American society by snuggling into a little cabin in the woods, where their children will live off the land. The movie, which was produced by Hugh M. Hefner of Playboy, contains one of the silliest wedding scenes I've seen; hasn't Mr. Hefner heard that marriage is outmoded?

1974 O 21, 48:6

Hungarian Import Is at Screening Room

By NORA SAYRE

Although a certain radiant obscurity permeates parts of Zoltan Huszark's "Sindbad," this Hungarian movie, made in 1970, is well worth the attention of film makers (and others) who are concerned with the use of imagery on film. "Sindbad" is playing today and tomorrow at noon and midnight at the First Avenue Screening Room. The movie explores an aging roué's memories and reveries about the women he was involved with, circa 1900. In some cases, he revisits them in person—in others, in his fantasies. His old flames are grateful or reproachful or nostalgic or indignant, according to characterizations that are left deliberately vague. Two themes concur: the rueful man alternates between admiring and loathing himself, until his lack of self-respect overrides the impulse of self-congratulation; also, he confesses that "women were always good" to him just because he never pretended that he loved them —although he occasionally scatters that message around. Throughout, there's the consciousness of death: he clings to the past because he senses the brevity of the present.

The atmosphere of this movie may sound banal—but it isn't, because of the extraordinary (and very beautiful) images that pour over the screen, intensified by rapid cuts. Sap leaking from bark gives way to the faces of those remembered; a piece of raw cauliflower evokes a split lip; a red shawl stiff with ice, dragged from a river, is then seen on the shoulders of the person who drowned herself. There's a marvelous scene in a restaurant where the privileged Sindbad luxuriates in a fine meal while he both stimulates and discourages the waiter in describing his private life — a conversation that results in the discovery that both were once married to the same young woman. Actually, this movie treats

The Program

SINDBAD (SZINDBAD), directed by Zoltan Huszarik; screenplay by Zoltan Huszarik based on the novels of Gyula Krudy; director of photography, Sandor Sara; music, Zoltan Jeney. With Zoltan Latinovits, Margit Dayka, and Eva Ruttkay. A Maflim Studio production; distributed by Hungarofilm, Budapest. At First Avenue Screening Room. Running time: 98 minutes.

food more seductively than most I've seen; perhaps intentionally, eating comes through more pungently than sex. All in all, the visual enchantments of the film outweigh the very old-fashioned romanticism—which isn't exactly what one expects from Hungary.

1974 O 25, 24:1

The Casts

FRANKENSTEIN AND THE MONSTER FROM HELL, directed by Terence Fisher; screenplay by John Elder; produced by Roy Skeggs; director of photography, Brian Probyn; editor, James Needs; music, James Bernard; a Hammer production, distributed by Paramount Pictures. Running time: 93 minutes. This film has been rated R.
Baron Frankenstein ...... Peter Cushing
Simon .... Shane Briant
Sarah .... Madeleine Smith
Monster .... Dave Prowse
and
CAPTAIN KRONOS: VAMPIRE HUNTER, directed and written by Brian Clemens; produced by Albert Fennell and Mr. Clemens; director of photography, Ian Wilson; music, Laurie Johnson; editor, James Needs; a Hammer production, distributed by Paramount Pictures. Running time: 91 minutes. At the Liberty Theater, 42d Street west of Seventh Avenue, and other theaters. This film has been rated R.
Capt. Kronos .... Horst Janson
Dr. Marcus .... John Carson
Paul Durward .... Shane Briant
Carla .... Caroline Munro
Grost .... John Cater

By VINCENT CANBY

"Frankenstein and the Monster From Hell" and "Captain Kronos: Vampire Hunter," the new double bill from the Hammer horror-film factory in England, presents something of a problem. Anyone with a grain of sense shouldn't care less about them, but anyone who has a grain of sense as well as a fondness for horror films, especially the expensive-looking, mostly deadpan Hammer kind, can't afford to miss them.

The two movies, which opened yesterday at the Liberty Theater and other houses around town, are foolish but fun in quite respectable ways.

Of the two, "Captain Kronos" is easily the more foolish, and the more elaborately produced. The film introduces into movie vampire lore a superman of fine Nordic good looks, a slight German accent and a vow to go wherever evil is to be fought. To those of us of the World War II generation, a superman like Kronos (Horst Janson) is possibly a scarier concept than plain old bloodsucking, which may be beside the point to people who have doted on the comic-strip exploits of Captain Marvel and Clark Kent.

I have a personal preference for conventional vampire movies in which every vampire shrinks before the sign of the cross, goes invisible in mirrors and can be efficiently dispatched with a stake through the heart. In this film, written and directed by Brian Clemens, there are, to quote the screenplay, as many varieties of vampire as beasts of prey. It takes all of Kronos's energies before he finally traps the fiends who have been ravaging a magnificent English countryside, stripping pretty little girls of their youth and leaving them in heaps of wrinkled flesh, washed up, at 15 or 16. The acting is terrible.

Good old Peter Cushing, his hair blonder and more spit-curled than ever, shows up once again as the visionary doctor, the 19th-century father of body-part transplants, in "Frankenstein and the Monster From Hell." The setting is a hospital for the criminally insane run by Baron Frankenstein, who persists in trying to put people together in eccentric combinations God never intended.

The Baron has learned a few things since the last time I saw him in the fastidious dress and manner of Mr. Cushing. There's now a good deal of dialogue about a patient whose head is rejecting the brain newly placed in it.

Late in the story the Baron suggests, with a marvelously woeful sigh, that perhaps his career's ups and downs are the result of his always having relied too much on surgery and not enough on biochemistry.

The film, written by John Elder and directed by Terence Fisher, is not without its intentional giggles. Compared with "Andy Warhol's Frankenstein," however, it is very straight and solemn, chock full of the old horror film values we don't see much of any more.

1974 O 31, 48:1

The Program

RIVERS OF SAND, a documentary photographed, edited, written and directed by Robert Gardner; translating, I. K. Eikeberians, Ivo Strecker and Jean Strecker; music, editing and composition, Michel Chalufour. At the Whitney Museum of American Art, Madison Avenue at 75th Street. Running time: 83 minutes. Through Tuesday.

By NORA SAYRE

Robert Gardner's stunning documentary, "Rivers of Sand," operates on two levels at once: It educates us about the daily life of the Hamar people of southwestern Ethiopia, and, while exploring an utterly alien culture the narrative also dwells on a phenomenon that everyone knows well—that is, male supremacy. The film opened yesterday at the Whitney Museum of American Art and will run through Tuesday.

A woman who seems ironically at ease with the camera explains that Hamar wives are always beaten by their husbands. She adds, "It's a custom, so how can it be bad?" Yet she also evokes fear and demoralization. Women are simply men's servants, and they do most of the work that sustains this small tribe. Adornment, in the form of heavy leg irons or decorative scars, is necessary to prove a woman's worth. The narrator —who looks young though worn—says that she accepts all of these traditions. Yet, at moments, there seems to be a tinge of caustic defiance in her gaze.

She compares a wife's role to one stone's being ground by another occasionally, a fly roams over her face, and it takes her a while to brush it away—obviously, she's used to much greater irritations or problems. The film maker also observes that the Hamar men are victims "of their own tyranny," which feeds idleness and self-doubt. Throughout, the movie makes powerful points about inequality without ever lecturing the audience.

A great deal of time must have been invested in gaining the trust of the Hamar, and the film is totally respectful of the people in it. The women harvest and grind grain, fetch water and milk goats, while the men arrange one another's elaborate clay coiffures, drink and hunt down an occasional ostrich. In a way, the American work ethic is oddly reinforced by this movie, since the industrious women do look far more cheerful than the rather indolent men.

The ceremonies essential to a burial, a hunt or a boy's coming of age are filmed with acute sensitivity. These people rely on rain water, and, when a huge storm builds, the camera conveys the enormous importance of those thunderclouds. Since "Rivers of Sand" was completed, the Hamar have experienced the drought and famine that have ravaged much of Africa. Hence this very beautiful film may already be an epitaph.

1974 O 31, 48:1

2 Documentaries Raise Issues About Justice

By NORA SAYRE

Two impressive documentaries at the Film Forum both excel at dispensing complex information about the legal experiences of black radicals. "Frame-Up! The Imprisonment of Martin Sostre," by the Pacific Street Film Collective, and "Mangrove Nine," by Franco Rosso, are truly educational films, which raise grim questions about the system of justice in America and Great Britain. The program is running through Sunday and Nov. 7-10 at 256 West 88th Street.

Martin Sostre, a black Puerto Rican who spent 12 years at Attica, is considered the most successful prisoner to litigate for prisoners' rights in this country. At 51, he's also a very important figure for other prisoners, for whom he symbolizes resistance to injustices in prison. Because of his efforts as a jailhouse lawyer, Black Muslim prisoners won the right to practice their religion in prison. At Green Haven prison, he was put in solitary for "practicing law without a license"; after he filed a suit, Federal Judge Constance Baker Motley ordered his release from solitary and awarded him $13,020 in punitive damages. He also organized a prisoners' union to improve working conditions at Walkill State Prison.

In 1967, when he owned two Afro-Asian bookstores in Buffalo, the local authorities accused him of being a leader of upheavals in the ghetto. He was arrested on a charge of selling $15 worth of heroin and sentenced to 25 to 30 years in jail. However, the charges of riot and arson that had been brought against him were dropped for lack of evidence.

In 1971, the prosecution witness, a former addict named Arto Williams, said that he had cooperated with the police to frame Mr. Sostre to attain probation for himself. Admitting that he had already possessed the heroin that he said he had bought from Mr. Sostre, Mr.

The Program

FRAME-UP! THE IMPRISONMENT OF MARTIN SOSTRE, a documentary produced by the Pacific Street Film Collective (Howard Blatt, Steve Fishler and Joe Sucher); running time: 30 minutes, and **MANGROVE NINE,** a documentary by Franco Rosso; distributed by Monument Films; running time: 40 minutes. At the Film Forum, 256 West 88th Street. Through Sunday and Nov. 7-10, 8 P.M.

Williams recanted his testimony. In March, 1974, Mr. Sostre's appeal for a new trial was rejected. The case is now on appeal, and Mr. Sostre is back in solitary for refusing to submit to rectal examinations, which he defines as rituals of humiliation.

The documentary includes interviews with Buffalo officials, and a dialogue about cell conditions between Mr. Sostre and a prison warden. (The latter looks far more defensive than the prisoner.) Mr. Williams also appears, explaining why he lied and how he volunteered to change his testimony. Amnesty International and P.E.N. American Center declare their commitment to the case of Mr. Sostre—whose own resilience and humor seem to be unwavering.

•

"Mangrove Nine" focuses on the lives of black people in England—where until a few years ago, many liberals belittled the existence of racism. Nine very articulate West Indians who were arrested and tried on varying charges after a demonstration in London's Notting Hill Gate discuss the relationship between police brutality and the slum housing and unemployment experienced by black citizens all over the world. They also say that most defense lawyers fail to understand the issues that concern them, and that the structure of the British court system tends to cause the jury to identify with the judge. The film also includes some unintentionally hilarious excerpts from an elderly British Broadcasting Corporation documentary about lawyers, in which taking snuff appears to be almost as serious a task as representing the clients.

All in all, this is one of the best programs on the quality of inequality that we've seen in a long time.

1974 N 1, 32:1

The Cast

PARACELSUS, directed by G. W. Pabst; screenplay (German with English subtitles) by Kurt Heuser; director of photography, Bruno Stephan; music, Herbert Windt; editor, Lena Newmann; distributed by Transworld Films. Running time: 105 minues. At the First Avenue Screening Room, First Avenue near 61st Street. This film has not been rated.

Paracelsus .... Werner Krauss
U. V. Hutten .... Mathias Wieman
Fliegenbein .... Harald Kreutzberg

By VINCENT CANBY

"Paracelsus," which was shown at the First Avenue Screening Room last Sunday and will be repeated there at noon and midnight today and tomorrow, is a very special footnote to film and political history. Never before released in New York, it is the second film made by the great, supposedly left-wing German director, G. W. Pabst, after he returned to Nazi Germany just in time for World War II.

Pabst, who died at the age of 82 in 1967, is a fascinating character, known as "the red Pabst" (Papst means pope in German) until he went back to Hitler's new German empire. His best films, including the silent "Joyless Street" with Greta Garbo and "The Threepenny Opera" (1931), are rather uproarious amalgams of stark realism, wild melodrama and pure poetry. Lots of elements in his films look dated today but also there is usually something that looks totally new and surprising.

•

"Paracelsus," considering when it was made (1943) and under what conditions, is a remarkably interesting film, though full of not especially well disguised propaganda. It's the story of Paracelsus, the 16th-century Swiss healer whose reputation took on a new vogue in the Germany of the early nineteen-forties. Nazi writers and intellectuals began to attribute all sorts of Nazi ideals to the mystic healer who had been ridiculed and oppressed for choosing to write in German instead of Latin and who had challenged the authority of vested (feudal) interests.

With the exception of Werner Krauss, who plays Paracelsus as a sort of medieval Dr. Gillespie, crusty but kind, the acting is operatic. The screenplay is full of noble opinions about the German character and its ability to triumph over the ignorance of its enemies.

•

The physical production, however, is astonishingly handsome. In addition, the movie contains one of Pabst's most magical scenes, in which Death, in the person of a juggler, enters a town in the siege of plague and invites the citizens to join him in a celebratory dance. Realism moves into fantasy (and back again) with less awkwardness than most other directors display when making a simple cut between two scenes in the same style.

A further footnote to this footnote to history: after the war, Pabst went on to make other films, including "The Trial" (1949), about anti-Semitism in Hungary in 1882, but Werner Krauss was blacklisted, largely for his participation in the notorious "Jud Süiss."

1974 N 1, 32:1

PHANTOM OF THE PARADISE, directed and written by Brian De Palma; produced by Edward R. Pressman; executive producer, Gustave Berne; director of photography Larry Pizer; editor, Paul Hirsch; music, Paul Williams; a Pressman-Williams production, distributed by 20th Century-Fox. Running time: 92 minutes. At the Trans-Lux East Theater, Third Avenue at 58th Street. This film has been rated PG.

Swan .... Paul Williams
Winslow Leach .... William Finley
Phoenix .... Jessica Harper
Philbin .... George Memmoli
Beef .... Gerrit Graham

By VINCENT CANBY

Brian De Palma's "Phantom of the Paradise" is a very busy movie.

Among other things it attempts to be a put-on of "Faust," "The Phantom of the Opera," "The Picture of Dorian Gray," rock music, the rock music industry, rock music movies and horror movies.

The problem is that since all of these things, with the possible exception of "Faust" (and I'm not really sure about "Faust"), already contain elements of self-parody, there isn't much that the outside parodist can do to make the parody seem funnier or more absurd than the originals already are.

•

"Phantom of the Paradise," which opened yesterday at the Trans-Lux East, is about an evil, pint-size rock music impresario named Swan (Paul Williams), who has sold his soul for eternal youth and an exclusive franchise on the soul-buying business in the music industry. It's also about an innocent young composer named Winslow Leach (William Finley), whose music is stolen by Swan and who becomes the murderous phantom of Swan's new rock palace, the Paradise, after his head gets badly mashed in a record-pressing machine.

At one point or another just about everybody in the film sells his soul to Swan (with much signing of heavy, thick legal documents in blood), including a pretty rock singer (Jessica Harper), the girl the Phantom loves and cherishes from afar.

Mr. De Palma is a very funny man, as he has shown in marvelously eccentric comedies such as "Greetings" and "Hi, Mom," and even in his more conventional films, "Get to Know Your Local Rabbit" and "Sisters." Compared with even the least of these, "Phantom of the Paradise" is an elaborate disaster, full of the kind of facetious humor you might find on bumper stickers and cocktail coasters.

•

The movie spends much too much time just laying out the plot, which is fatal to parody of any sort. It also becomes quite enchanted with its own special photograpic effects, as well as with its bizarre sets, which, because there's very little of interest going on within them, become the mildly amusing surrogate subjects of the film.

Almost redeeming the movie is the rock score, by Mr. Williams, and the comic orchestrations that trace the evolution of rock from the duck-tailed, surfing nineteen-fifties and sixties to the seventies and the triumphant emergence of androgyny. The concert scenes—filled with pandemonium, blinking lights and extraordinary sounds—are well staged but hardly seem worth the terrific time and effort that must have been required. Almost any A.I.P. "Beach" picture or Vincent Price horror film, being the real thing, is funnier.

1974 N 2, 16:3

A Film of Dull Sadism at Neighborhoods

By NORA SAYRE

Perhaps there are only two kinds of sadism: lively or dull. Peter Collinson's "Open Season's," which arrived yesterday at neighborhood theaters, features the phlegmatic sort and includes some of the most sluggish shootouts we've seen in ages. Three youngish war veterans indulge in a yearly ritual of kidnapping, abusing, then releasing and hunting down a random couple; one of them explains, "After you've hunted men, animals just don't rate." However, animals also get their due in this movie, when a child's wavery voice sings "All things bright and beautiful, all creatures great and small" while the veterans gun down the furred and feathered beings of the woods.

•

The movie may be meant to strike a blow for humanity, but the message is drowned out by the laughter of the lawless trio—in fact, the picture is an anthology of yuks. Cackling, giggling, whooping, gurgling, checking and howling, the old buddies appear to have harvested a sense of the ridiculous from the battlefield. Peter Fonda's talents are wasted throughout. He manages to look formidable at moments, but he mainly behaves like the jovial entertainment director at a resort camp, and he soon runs out of variations on the hahas and the o-ho-hos and the heh-heh-hehs.

William Holden appears briefly in an early scene; you then spend the rest of the movie waiting for him to come back. Perhaps he was just visiting the set or taking a shortcut on his way to an appointment on the lot. A hundred minutes pass until you see his face again, although there are a few shots of his boots.

•

Cornelia Sharpe is as bad at screaming as she is at running, and only Albert Mendoza—as the male victim—

The Cast

OPEN SEASON, directed by Peter Collinson; screenplay by David Osborn and Liz Charles-Williams; director of photography, Fernando Arribas; editor, Alan Pattillo; music, Ruggero Cini; produced by Jose S. Vicuna; released by Columbia Pictures. At neighborhood theaters. Running time: 104 minutes. This film is classified R.

Ken .... Peter Fonda
Nancy .... Cornelia Sharpe
Greg .... John Phillip Law
Art .... Richard Lynch
Martin .... Albert Mendoza
Wolkowski .... William Holden

acts with any conviction; his bitter reserve does seem just right for the part. Without betraying the plot, it seems safe to voice the suspicion that a couple of the actors had clauses written into their contracts that permitted them to die quite slowly in close-up. Still, although "Open Season" is innocent of all suspense, it's not the very worst movie I've seen this year.

1974 N 2, 16:3

The Cast

AMAZING GRACE, directed by Stan Lathan; written and produced by Matt Robinson; director of photography, Sol Negrin; distributed by United Artists. Running time: 99 minutes. At the Cinerama Theater, Broadway at 47th Street, RKO 86th Street Twin 2 Theater, near Lexington Avenue, and 55th Street Twin 2 Theater, near Third Avenue. This film has been rated G.

Grace .... Moms Mabley
Forthwith Wilson .... Slappy White
Welton J. Waters .... Moses Gunn
Creola Waters .... Rosalind Cash
Jim Annenberg .... Jim Karen
Cousin Lincoln .... Stepin Fetchit
Clarine .... Butterfly McQueen

Moms Mabley, one of the most durable resources of American humor, is treated like a holy relic in "Amazing Grace," a comedy about an old black woman of such grit and gumption she almost single-handedly masterminds the successful campaign of a black candidate for Mayor of Baltimore.

Like Moms, whose age is somewhere in the 70's, the movie sort of shambles along from one scene to another, sometimes mugging outrageously, though it never displays (or allows Mom to display) a lack of respect for anything except safe targets (blacks who deny their blackness, crooked politicians).

Moms has come to triumph over the years not through the force of her wit but through her candor. When someone says that something is too highly complicated, her most likely response is, "I'll highly complicate you on the seat of your pants."

•

It wouldn't be funny if anyone else said it, but we laugh with Moms in appreciation of her implacable, firmly unbudgeable stand in favor of common sense. The people around her never come up to her instep.

"Amazing Grace," which opened at three theaters yesterday, keeps Moms on screen almost constantly, but it doesn't provide her with much material. Sometimes the camera just silently follows her as she moves around her house, or walks down a sidewalk, as if hoping she'll come up with a line or a bit of business that will save the day. She doesn't, and it seems rude of the film makers to have put her in such a spot.

Two black performers associated with an earlier movie age—Stepin Fetchit and Butterfly McQueen—turn up in cameo roles that are unrewarding, both to us and to them.

VINCENT CANBY.

1974 N 2, 16:5

'Amarcord' and 'Lacombe, Lucien': Illuminations of Things Past

By STEPHEN FARBER

The two best European films of the past year are both studies of provincial life just before and during World War II. Federico Fellini's "Amarcord" is set in the thirties, when Mussolini was at the height of his influence; Louis Malle's "Lacombe, Lucien" covers a few months in 1944, shortly before the Allied liberation of France.

Like Marcel Ophuls's "The Sorrow and the Pity," both films explode the neat dichotomies of good and evil that characterized Hollywood's wartime melodramas. Instead of portraying the Fascist as psychotic monster, Fellini and Malle probe the guilt of ordinary people whose passive acquiescence gave the dictators their real power. Although they tackle similar themes, these two movies illustrate contrasting approaches to filmmaking. "Lacombe, Lucien" is a straightforward, naturalistic work, an old fashioned narrative developed with meticulous logic. "Amarcord" is in Fellini's distinctive dreamlike, freeform style, and it is a far more audacious cinematic experiment. They make intriguing companion pieces.

"Lacombe, Lucien," the story of a 17-year-old French peasant boy who joins the Gestapo, adapts the documentary techniques of "The Sorrow and the Pity" to a fictional narrative. Malle has cast the movie with many non-actors, and his style is carefully understated, virtually free of melodrama and sentimentality. Hannah Arendt's thesis of the banality of evil is familiar by now, but I have never seen a film that so convincingly and concretely dramatizes that abstract thesis. The French workers in Gestapo headquarters—a converted hotel

Stephen Farber is a freelance critic and the author of "The Movie Rating Game."

Henri Dauman

Federico Fellini's "Amarcord" is an "audacious cinematic experiment."

Lawrence Fried

Louis Malle's "Lacombe, Lucien" is "full of surprising insights."

—are indistinguishable from office bureaucrats. The screams of a Resistance leader being tortured punctuate the sounds of a Ping-Pong match in the game room downstairs.

On his way to bed Lucien stops to peek into the room where the interrogations are conducted. There are no exotic tortures; one of the French Gestapo agents is holding his victim's head under water in a bathtub, while the interrogator's girlfriend laughs that he is splashing his expensive pants. These homely, prosaic, almost comical images are somehow more shocking than the lurid sadistic images that we are used to seeing in movies about Nazis. When torture insinuates itself into the everyday domestic world, we understand how easily people can assimilate brutality.

The film is very perceptive in documenting how haphazardly Lucien falls into the Gestapo. First planning to join the Resistance but rejected, he is picked up by the Vichy police on his way back

to his menial job in a hospital. They bully him a little, and when he tells them where to find the Resistance leader in his village, they offer him a job. Lucien feels as if he is being initiated into a splendid, aristocratic club. Riding around in a fancy car, wearing an elegant Parisian suit, and carrying a gun, he is able to live out some of his comic-book fantasies of power and glamour. Lucien is completely apolitical, and it is by accident that he ends up on the wrong side in the summer of 1944.

"Lacombe, Lucien" is full of surprising insights. The portrait of the Jewish family with whom Lucien becomes involved is a masterly study in the psychology of defeat and abasement. Albert Horn (superbly played by Holger Lowenadler), the Jewish tailor who once worked for the Paris aristocracy, now lives in obscurity under a false name; he sits inside all day, in his pajamas and robe, his spirit broken by the loss of identity, and by the deference he must show his persecutors. Degraded and

ashamed, he tries to pretend that he can still take pride in his work; he washes his hands carefully before touching the fine wool he uses to make suits for the Gestapo thugs. One day, no longer able to keep up the charade, he gets dressed, goes out for a walk, and ends up at Gestapo headquarters. This suicidal gesture is convincingly tentative and unheroic, the last possible assertion of dignity for a man consumed with self-disgust.

Horn's lovely daughter France is amused by Lucien's naivete and his childlike gestures of bravado, and she allows herself to be swept along by her sexual attraction to him. Also, because the Nazis have taught her to hate herself, she succumbs to Lucien, who is everything she is not; on the most elemental level he offers her a chance to belong.

France's acquiescence to Fascism seems even more disturbing than Lucien's. She is more intelligent, yet too weak to resist. Lucien is simply insensitive—totally insensitive. He feels no pity, no fear, no remorse. Movies have conditioned us to believe that heroes are always capable of a change of heart, but Lucien remains unthinking and unfeeling from start to finish. He is a child of nature, and in Malle's view, nature is innately, incomprehensibly cruel. Lucien has about the same capacity for moral awareness as the animals he so blithely kills.

Unfortunately, Lucien's impassivity turns the film from a potentially rich, tragic drama into a textbook case history. Although Malle deliberately chose a protagonist incapable of change or growth, it may be that this choice was a conceptual mistake. Although Lucien frightens us because he is absolutely unreachable, we can never see ourselves in him, or imagine ourselves acting like him, and this does diminish the film's impact. A character with greater complexity—a character who was capable of feeling remorse, who had flickerings of self-awareness, but *still* surrendered to the seductive power of Fascism—might have been infinitely more disturbing, because then we would not have had the luxury of detachment. Watching "Lacombe, Lucien," we are interested, but never implicated.

In comparing "Lacombe, Lucien," intelligent and provocative though it is, with Fellini's "Amarcord," one's first temptation is to say that the difference between them is the difference between the French and Italian temper-

ament. Malle's movie is cool, rational, cerebral, while Fellini's is warm and lyrical, urgent and passionate. On first glance "Amarcord" is less overtly political; it is a personal memoir, a recreation of a year in the life of Rimini, the small town Fellini grew up. But Fellini is such an economical filmmaker that in one 15-minute segment explicitly dealing with the town's Fascist regime, he manages to say a good deal of what "Lacombe, Lucien" says in 140 minutes.

The scene in "Amarcord" in which the young hero's father is arrested for playing the Socialist anthem during a Fascist rally suggests the paranoia of petty bureaucrats and the banality of torturers; his crazy, ineffectual protest is an unsentimental emblem of the stubborn human defiance that Fascism cannot quite suppress—much like Horn's suicidal stroll into Gestapo headquarters. The preceding scene of the Fascist parade held in honor of a visiting dignitary mocks the pomposity of the Brown Shirts and, at the same time, demonstrates the appeal of this spurious spectacle and military panoply; the townspeople respond as if they were watching a circus or a football game.

This sequence is perhaps the most crucial in a film full of stunning set-pieces, for it colors everything else we see. The remarkable thing about "Amarcord" is its double-edged vision of the past. Fellini makes us feel a profound longing for the recreated world on screen, the spirit of affectionate community that has disappeared in the age of urban sprawl. We marvel at the beauty of simple seasonal changes, the richness of Rimini's folklore, mythology and ritual, the shared fantasies, and the communal adventures—like the journey of the entire town out to sea to watch a giant ocean liner pass.

As a nostalgic portrait of smalltown life, "Amarcord" is unequaled in the history of cinema. But the dream of community that Fellini celebrates is qualified by persistent, ominous reminders of the citizens' apathy and docility. We are not permitted to forget that Fascism fed on the insularity and solidarity of towns like Rimini. Watching "Amarcord," we realize how easy it is to be mesmerized by the day-to-day rituals, how tempting it is to surrender to the pageant and ignore the larger political world beyond the movie house and the luxury hotel. Fellini *involves* us in his meditation on the past, and forces us to recognize our own complicity.

These two films are extraordinary records of a vanished time. If I finally prefer the Fellini movie, that is because it touches the imagination and the emotions as well as the intellect. Both "Lacombe, Lucien" and "Amar-cord" succeed at what they set out to do: they illuminate the past. The fundamental difference between them is the difference between prose and poetry. ∎

1974 N 3, II:15:1

FILM VIEW

VINCENT CANBY

Was the New York Festival Necessary?

It's easier to take film festivals seriously in some years than in others. This year was not one of them. The recently concluded 12th annual New York Film Festival at Lincoln Center was much less festive than desperate, a conclusion that may have less to do with observable fact than with accumulated feeling. In the same way that several superior films from unexpected sources can lend excitement and tone to an entire festival, so can a nearly uninterrupted series of ordinary films make one fear that filmmaking everywhere has gone to pieces.

All film festivals, including the New York festival (which is one of the more respectable), are to a large extent artificial and arbitrary. The New York festival people like to tell us that their aim is to present what the members of the program committee believe to be the best, the most interesting, and possibly the most innovative films of the year, chosen largely from the entries at other film festivals held earlier in the year.

What they know and admit readily enough when pressed is that the New York festival shows only those films it can get its hands on. The fact is that many of the better films of any year are never shown because (1) they've already been released commercially, or (2) their producers don't want them in the festival.

The New York festival got off to a very poor start this year even before it started. That is, when Ingmar Bergman's "Scenes From A Marriage" and Federico Fellini's "Amarcord" opened theatrical engagements a week ahead of the festival. Because "Scenes From A Marriage" and "Amarcord" are two of the best films by two of the world's greatest filmmakers, their (I assume) coincidental openings had the effect of making the festival an anti-climax a week or so before the festival's opening night.

• • •

The festival later recouped to some extent by presenting the American premieres of Louis Malle's "Lacombe, Lucien" and Luis Buñuel's "Le Fantôme De La Liberté," yet both of these films, like the Bergman and the Fellini, were already set to open in local theaters anyway. There's nothing wrong with the festival's presenting films already set for commercial release since the festival has a certain obligation to present—or try to present—the best films available. This year, however, more than any earlier year that I can remember, the air of anti-climax hung over the New York festival, transforming into 17 days of hard slogging what should have been (and has been in the past) two weeks or so of mostly first-rate movie-going.

There are some years, you see, when festivals aren't necessary.

What else can be said when the New York festival could only come up with two American programs out of 21? I mention this because Richard Roud, the festival director, took the opportunity of an article in the festival program to call the re-emergence of the American film "one of the

most exciting developments in world cinema in the last two years."

It's so exciting that the only American entries he could find for the Lincoln Center affair were one feature, John Cassavetes's "A Woman Under the Influence," and a program of four short films billed under the collective title of "Roots."

This is not to blame Roud and his program committee but to underscore the artificiality of a festival that for one reason and another doesn't have access even to the American films shown at this year's Cannes festival, including Francis Ford Coppola's "The Conversation" (which took the grand prize), and Robert Altman's "Thieves Like Us."

Perhaps no American films this year have achieved the idiosyncratic splendor of "Scenes From A Marriage," "Amarcord" and "Le Fantôme De La Liberté," but there have been at least a dozen (don't ask me to name them here) that would deserve a place in a festival long before Miklos Jancso's Italian TV film, "Rome Wants Another Caesar" (described in the festival program as "a choreographic essay on power in which ceremonial movement buttresses logical argument"), or the Wim Wenders German film, "Alice in The Cities," a rather drab exploration of an identity crisis. Jack Hazan's "A Bigger Splash," in which English Pop painter David Hockney and his friends act out a fiction about themselves, has been more exuberantly done by Andy Warhol and Paul Morrissey in almost any number of funnier, less pretentious films.

The pickings for the New York festival were thin this year—which raises the question of whether or not there has to be a festival every year even when the films available don't warrant festival presentation. Couldn't we just skip a year?

We probably could, but by so doing the impression would be given that filmmaking in general has been substandard, even though it hasn't been. There's also the problem of keeping a festival organization together. You can't organize a film festival on a few months' notice. You have to have people working on it throughout the year. The New York Film Festival has gotten itself into the American auto maker's bind: it must come out with a new model every year or perish. It has to do with economics.

• • •

The vaporousness of so many of this year's festival selections rubbed off on a half-dozen or so other entries, films that I might have looked at with more tolerance under more exciting circumstances.

I suppose any film by Robert Bresson deserves a place at the New York festival but this year's "Lancelot du Lac" came close to being a parody of Bresson. Here is a film by a director, known for the impassive acting style he imposes on his performers, in which a great deal of the "acting" is done inside suits of armor with faces hidden? I was irritated—perhaps unnecessarily so—by the ambiguous cross-references to Trotsky in Alain Resnais' "Stavisky," and inclined to be impatient with Jacques Rivette's "Céline and Julie Go Boating" (3¼ hours) and Cassavetes's "A Woman Under The Influence" (2½ hours), both being films in which the directors indulge themselves and their actors with the freedom to mould and shape the films as they are being made.

Although I prefer films that always know where they're going, I'm sure I'd have happier memories of both "Céline" and "A Woman Under The Influence" had the festival that presented them known where it was going. This year's festival was marking time.

1974 N 3, II:15:1

The Cast

THE NADA GANG, directed by Claude Chabrol; script (French with English subtitles) based on the novel "Nada" by Jean-Patrick Manchette; adaptation and dialogue by Mr. Chabrol and Mr. Manchette; photography, Jean Rabier; executive producer, Andre Genoves; a Franco-Italian co-production: Les Films la Boetie (Paris); Italian International Film (Rome); a New Line Cinema Release. At the Playboy Theater, 110 West 57th Street. Running time: 110 minutes. This film has not been classified.
Diaz .... Fabio Testi
Cash .... Mariangela Melato
Epaulard .... Maurice Garrel
Treuffais .... Michel Duchaussoy
Goemond .... Michel Aumont

By NORA SAYRE

Why do anarchists in contemporary movies have to wear black broadbrimmed hats? Solving that minor mystery is essential to understanding the defects of Claude Chabrol's "The Nada Gang," a muddled yet sometimes rewarding movie, which opened yesterday at the Playboy Theater.

In Paris, a group of youthful terrorists kidnap the United States Ambassador to France, and the French Government responds with a scenario of overkill. The movie condemns the state even more fiercely than it does the outlaws; when the authorities consider sacrificing the hostage's life so that the public will lose its sympathy for the Left, the film thoroughly fulfills Mr. Chabrol's own conviction that "the state prefers terrorism to revolution."

•

There are many fine scenes throughout the movie—each enhanced by impeccable camerawork—as when the stolid Ambassador is seized at a posh brothel while watching a barely veiled prostitute ape Salome, or when a getaway car overturns in a field of rippling wheat. And there are several good performances—notably, Maurice Garrel as an aging professional revolutionary, a rueful cynic who alternates between being vulnerable or ruthless, wistful or hardheaded.

But the trouble with the movie—and here comes that again—is that the pivotal character, the anarchist, is a joke figure. Played by Fabio Testi, he's all burning glances, flaring nostrils, and operatic gestures. Whereas the murderous police officer (Michel Aumont) is thoroughly believable, the Nada gang is mainly ludicrous. To portray them, the director grasps at clichés: those on the Left simply have to oversleep, guzzle booze in the morning and keep untidy homes.

Although Mr. Chabrol deplores the group's tactics, he has some sympathy for its intentions. Yet he makes its members into political idiots; for example, the ransom demanded for the Ambassador serves no revolutionary purpose, it's just for "the cause." Also, because the script is sloppy, the film seems to equate dissidence with terrorism.

•

Meanwhile, Mariangela Melato plays a creature who's almost obligatory in a movie of this kind: a rebellious swinger who has joined the revolution for sex, not politics, and who dramatizes her own self-hate by boasting that she's a whore. The actress, who doesn't equal her performances in Lina Wertmuller's films, does salvage moments of this hackneyed role with the ironic, level-eyed gaze that she used in "The Seduction of Mimi."

Mr. Chabrol has chosen a milieu that's just too alien for him, as the absurdity of the film's conclusion proves. While most of his terrorists are middle class, they're too far removed from the bourgeoisie that he understands so well. Still, he has achieved an elegant blast at corrupt authority, even though he has muffed the characterization of its enemies or critics.

1974 N 7, 56:5

The Program

HORIZONS, 80 minutes and HARMONICA, 10 minutes, films by Larry Gottheim. At the Whitney Museum of American Art, Madison Avenue and 75th Street. Through Tuesday.

The American scene, which too often is a vagrant, passing vision, has been captured in arresting style by Larry Gottheim in his silent but decidedly colorful feature, "Horizons," which began a week's stand yesterday at the Whitney Museum of American Art. If his compilation of vignettes tends to become redundant eventually, the over-all documentation of seasonal changes is as varied and beautiful as nature itself.

•

As the latest entry in the museum's New American Filmmakers series, "Horizons" is, according to a program note, the results of the 37-year-old movie-maker's "endless waiting and wandering" on rural sites in upstate New York over a two-year period ending last year. And in focusing on those horizons in varying perspectives he has recorded the timelessness of the countryside's appearances rather than a formal film structure.

The light and then darker greens of spring and summer are crystalized in a succession of vistas from moving cars of meadows, hillsides, woods, grazing horses, cattle, sheep, birds, clouds, streams and occasional people, trains and planes. And, autumn and winter are viewed in panoramas of russet-hued trees and fields, snowfalls, icy ponds, children sledding, a red barn on a snowscape or solitary horses or cows gazing toward those distant horizons.

•

Mr. Gottheim also is diverting in his accompanying short, "Harmonica," made in 1971, in which a player inside a speeding car turns from the blues to some inventive experiments with the wind's effects on his harmonica. "Horizons" is not that simple, of course, but Mr. Gottheim, who seems to dote on repeated, similar shots of livestock and clothes flapping on outdoor lines, nevertheless has managed to make most of his affection for the pastoral scene lovely and worthwhile.

A. H. Weiler

1974 N 7, 56:6

An Exasperating Film at the Music Hall

By VINCENT CANBY

"The Little Prince," based on the late Antoine de Saint-Exupéry's fable, is a very exasperating experience. It's the kind of movie that refers to adults as grown-ups to show us where it means its sympathies to be. Yet it's too abstract and sophisticated to be of interest to most children, and too simple-mindedly mystic and smug to charm even the most indulgent adult. You don't have to be W.C. Fields to want to swat it.

More exasperating is that it's the first film musical in years to be directed by Stanley Donen, who has made some of the best ("Seven Brides for Seven Brothers," "Singin' in the Rain," "Funny Face"), and its book and lyrics are by Alan Jay Lerner and its music is by Frederick Loewe. This score, the first Lerner-Loewe collaboration since "Gigi" and "Camelot," is full of lovely things that are a total waste in these barren circumstances.

The film opened yesterday at the Radio City Music Hall.

I doubt that anyone could make a really satisfactory movie out of the tiny Saint Exupéry book, a fable about a pilot who crash-lands in the Sahara where, while he repairs his plane, he is befriended by a small extraterrestrial boy who happens to be on a sight-seeing tour of the universe.

The pilot and the Little Prince talk at great length. The Little Prince reports on his own planet (which is the size of a house) and his earlier encounters on other planets with facetious caricatures, (all of which we see), but nothing much happens. So little happens, in fact, that the movie, which is stretched out with the Lerner-Loewe music, lasts only 88 minutes and seems at least five times that long.

Even though "The Little Prince" is virtually a two-man musical supplemented by specialty numbers by a handful of other performers, it's been given the big movie-musical treatment (including a location trip to Tunisia), which simply emphasizes the coyness of its philosophy and the desperation of actors who never seem to know what kind of movie they're making.

•

When Richard Kiley, who plays the pilot, races across the Sahara singing (in very good voice) a new Lerner-Loewe love song, Mr. Donen photographs him from what

seems to have been a swooping helicopter. The song will sound great in the soundtrack album, but the actor, seen alternately in long shots and close-ups, appears to have lost his mind.

Steven Warner, who plays the Little Prince, is a sweet-looking child who bears a strong resemblance to the original Saint-Exupéry illustrations (the best things in the book), but since he is never more than a sweet-looking child of 6, it's difficult to understand how he could prompt the stereophonic passions of the score. He has a delightful laugh, but the way things are done

Steven Warner

The Cast

THE LITTLE PRINCE, directed and produced by Stanley Donen; screenplay and lyrics by Alan Jay Lerner; music by Frederick Loewe; based on the story by Antoine de Saint-Exupery; director of photography, Christopher Challis; editors, Peter Boita, John Guthridge; distributed by Paramount Pictures. Running time: 88 minutes. At Radio City Music Hall. This film has been rated G.
The Pilot .... Richard Kiley
The Little Prince .... Steven Warner
The Snake .... Bob Fosse
The Fox .... Gene Wilder
The King .... Joss Ackland
The Businessman .... Clive Revill
The Historian .... Victor Spinetti
The General .... Graham Crowden
The Rose .... Donna McKechnie

these days I wondered if it might be Mercedes McCambridge.

Bob Fosse, an extraordinarily talented actor-director-dancer-choreographer, shows up in one sequence as the personification of the poisonous snake who finally provides the Little Prince with transportation home. What a child might make of this scene I can't imagine; Mr. Fosse, dressed like a 19th-century Chicago pimp, dances around the Sahara in those marvelously eccentric movements that look great when done by Gwen Verdon but embarrassing in this context.

•

Less peculiar but not much more effective is Gene Wilder as a fox who hands on to the Little Prince one of the nuggets of wisdom that is supposed to make the movie

meaningful. What is essential, says the fox, is invisible to the eye. Another variation is that "it's only with the heart that one can see clearly."

This is the sort of gimcracky wisdom that only a self-absorbed adult could conceive of as being comprehensible to a child. When children imagine things, they see them. There is no nonsense about it. The imagined things are invisible only to jaded adults who patronize children and childhood, either because the real world is too much for them or because they don't know better.

In addition to the score, particularly a song called "I've Never Loved a Rose," there are some other isolated good things in the movie, including the opening sequence in which a small boy tries to convince his elders that a picture he has drawn is not of a hat but the silhouette of a snake that has swallowed an elephant.

There are lots of pleasures that children and adults can share: zoos, circuses, "Alice in Wonderland," Charlie Brown, roller coasters, hot dogs between meals. "The Little Prince" is not one of them.

1974 N 8, 24:1

Japanese Import Opens at Screening Room

By NORA SAYRE

A romance involving dismemberment may seem about as likely as a caper concerning castration, but the first half of Yasuzo Masumura's "Warehouse," which is playing today and tomorrow at the First Avenue Screening Room, sustains an eerie interest. In Tokyo, a blind sculptor and his mother keep her prisoner in a warehouse adorned with his sculptures of gigantic eyes, mouths, noses, breasts, arms, legs, and torsos—all of which he re-created from the bodies that he handled as a professional masseur.

This movie recalls "The Collector," especially when the kidnapper is enraged by the frantic victim's efforts to escape. He wants to sculpture her through touch; after infinite struggles, she capitulates, while taunting him for his virginity and for being his "mother's toy." The frightening sensitivity of the blind man is well conveyed, along with the claustrophobia induced by his huge darkened studio. And the respectable appearance of his portly mother—who abets his every lunacy — bestows a background of normalcy that strengthens the obsessions of the picture.

The Cast

WAREHOUSE (MOJU—Blind Beast), directed by Yasuzo Masumura; screenplay (Japanese with English subtitles) by Yoshio Shirasuka; original story by Ranpo Edogawa; photography, Setsuo Kobayashi; produced by Daiei; released in the United States by Roninfilm, Inc. At the First Avenue Screening Room, at 61st Street. Running time: 86 minutes. This film has not been classified.
Michio .... Eiji Funakoshi
Aki Shima .... Mako Midori
Shino .... Noriko Sengoku

However, the film turns lowlsh toward its conclusion, when the ill-mated pair become lovers, then take bites out of each other's shoulders and hack each other up with knives. (All this occurs on a 70-foot reclining rubber nude.) The woman becomes a raving pain buff, and the movie eventually suggests an Oriental parody of "The Night Porter." Subtitles enhance the action: "Listen, I have a dandy idea!", she exclaims—and then urges her rather reluctant admirer to chop off her arms and legs. He quite rationally says, "Why?"

•

The camera is tactfully averted from the ensuing carpentry: we simply hear some heavy thumps and ecstatic howls as she's converted to a torso. He asks if she's happy, while in a voiceover narration, she praises "the world of the actual sense." "Warehouse," which was called "Blind Beast" in Japan, may not grip your emotions, but it certainly clutches your attention. Still, it's a trifle hard to know just whom this movie will satisfy—apart from sentimental surgeons.

1974 N 8, 24:1

Romy Schneider Stars in French Import

By VINCENT CANBY

Philomene (Romy Schneider) and Catherine (Mascha Gomska) are sisters, two beautiful German girls trying to make their way in southern France in what appears to be the early nineteen-thirties. George Sarret (Michel Piccoli) is a former World War I hero, now a lawyer with a way of seizing the unexpected opportunity at a moment's notice.

When Philomene and Catherine enter his life, George begins to plan things with care. He premeditates. He is the architect of what becomes their (mostly) astonishing good fortune. Their game: insurance fraud and murder.

•

"Le Trio Infernal," which opened yesterday at the Little Carnegie Theater, is an elegantly acted, handsome-looking French film, a macabre comedy with serious intentions that ultimately prevent it from being as funny as one longs for it to be.

Philomene and George are made for each other, both being ambitious, calculating, venal and, when the occasion requires, horrendously vicious. Compared with these two, Catherine, the younger sister, is an old-fashioned sentimentalist.

She doesn't mind sharing George with Philomene, and she doesn't object to George's marrying each of them off in turn to an elderly husband who is then quickly injured and dispatched in one way or another.

However, Catherine does become all weepy on Christmas Eve, when George, strictly according to plan, shoots their two dinner guests, a pushy, opinionated, overfed pawnbroker (Andrea Ferreol) and the pawnbroker's timid lover (Hubert Deschamps).

•

Catherine becomes so upset she can hardly help lug the bodies up to the bathroom, where they are to be dissolved in sulphuric acid. A couple of days later, when it's time to ladle the contents out of each bathtub, Catherine gets sick to her stomach. In

The Cast

LE TRIO INFERNAL, directed by Francis Girod; screenplay (French with English subtitles) by Mr. Girod and Jacques Rouffio, based on the novel by Solange Fasquelle; produced by Raymond Danon and Jacques Dorfman; music, Ennio Morricone; director of photography, Andreas Winding; distributed by Levitt-Pickman Film Corp. Running time: 106 minutes. At the Little Carnegie Theater, 57th Street, east of Seventh Avenue. This film has not been rated.
Philomene .... Romy Schneider
George Sarret .... Michel Piccoli
Catherine .... Mascha Gomska
Noemie .... Andrea Ferreol
Magali .... Monica Fiorentini
Chambon .... Hubert Deschamps

the context of these goings-on, Catherine is a silly goose.

"Le Trio Infernal" is the first feature to be directed by a new French director named Francis Girod, who also collaborated with Jacques Rouffio on the screenplay, adapted from a novel by Solange Fasquelle. He clearly is a director of talent, though not just because the film looks so good.

After "The Conformist," "Stavisky," "Love and Anarchy" and "Amarcord," all thirties movies are beginning to look alike, if only because of the marceled hair, the slashing red lipstick and the vintage motor cars.

Mr. Girod scores his success with his actors. For the first time in years, I was convinced that Romy Schneider is an actress of wit, capable of expressing all kinds of feelings simultaneously. Mr. Piccoli may have played this sort of role before, but he has never done it with such cold, comic, vain precision. Miss Gomska, who looks enough like Miss Schneider really to be her sister, expresses a kind of vestigial decency that finally seems to be what the film is all about.

That is, if the film is about

anything at all, and I'm not sure it is.

•

Because of the emphasis the director places on grotesque though not really shocking details, he seems to be inviting us to interpret the film as some kind of extravagant comment on France (or Europe) midway between two extraordinary cataclysms. These details aren't funny. Neither are they interesting enough clinically to justify their inclusion in the movie. The tone is confused rather than ambiguous in the way that would allow us to appreciate it on several levels at once.

1974 N 9, 24:1

The Cast

CONFESSIONS OF A WINDOW CLEANER, directed by Val Guest; screenplay by by Christopher Wood and Mr. Guest; film editor, Bill Lenny; director of photography, Norman Warwick; music, Sam Sklair; produced by Greg Smith; released by Columbia Pictures. At neighborhood theaters. Running time: 90 minutes. This film is classified R.
Timothy Lea .... Robin Askwith
Mrs. Lea .... Dandy Nichols
Mr. Lea .... Bill Maynard

By NORA SAYRE

Since the British film industry has been gutted by the economy and so very few English movies are being

made at all, it's painful to report that Val Guest's "Confessions of a Window Cleaner" should be avoided. Oozing with a horrible jauntiness, this feeble sex farce is also very old-fashioned. Set in a world of birds and dollies, it reeks of something that Time magazine once called Swinging London, and even the miniskirts are out of date. The movie opened yesterday at neighborhood theaters.

A winsome window washer (Robin Askwith), who has a lovable tendency to shatter glass, manages to hit the hay with most of his female clients while wrestling with the difficulties of seducing a voluptuous young policewoman. The script strains hard for wit, as when someone brings home a stuffed moose head and all his relatives say "Oh, God." Then they promptly name it Clarence. But of course it falls off the wall. Even so, the picture would be no more than momentarily depressing if the cast didn't include some veteran English character actors, such as John le Mesurier, Dandy Nichols and Richard Wattis. Their dignified presence yields a bleak reminder that movie work is scarce in England now.

1974 N 9, 24:2

FILM VIEW

VINCENT CANBY

New York's Woes Are Good Box Office

As reflected in good movies and bad, serious ones as well as forthrightly foolish, New York City has become a metaphor for what looks like the last days of American civilization. The metaphor is there for all to see in Ivan Passer's gently chaotic comedy, "Law and Disorder," which is about a team of bumbling auxiliary policemen, in Michael Winner's vicious "Death Wish," in Joseph Sargent's cheerful underground caper movie, "The Taking of Pelham One Two Three" (in which an IRT subway train is hijacked), and in any number of cop movies, from Sidney Lumet's angry, obsessed "Serpico" to the nonsense of something like "The Super Cops." It's even there in a farce of the order of Barbra Streisand's "For Pete's Sake."

New York City is a mess, say these films. It's run by fools. Its citizens are at the mercy of its criminals who, as often as not, are protected by an unholy alliance of civil libertarians and crooked cops. The air is foul. The traffic is impossible. Services are diminishing and the morale is such that ordering a cup of coffee in a diner can turn into a request for a fat lip.

New York City is a mess, though most filmmakers tend to overdramatize the effects while oversimplifying the causes. It's also getting worse all the time. New York City is a mess but it has been for much of its history, as anyone familiar with some of its problems in the 19th century must know. Being the most fanatic

kind of New Yorker (that is, one who converted comparatively late in life), I'm not as worried about the city's bad notices as I am curious as to why the matter has suddenly become of interest to filmmakers. Is being a mess box office?

There must be a cab driver somewhere who will want to blame former Mayor Lindsay. It was Lindsay, after all, who first set up an office at City Hall to entice filmmakers to New York by winning the cooperation of the labor unions and facilitating location shooting permits. When filmmakers arrived to work here in quantity, they began to make movies that weren't simply set in New York but were also about New York. The cabbie would probably say that that is exactly what he means. Lindsay should never have allowed the filmmakers into the city. It was encouraging the foxes to enter the henhouse.

• • •

This is not quite the entire story. The image of New York in contemporary movies has as much to do with changes in the American film industry over the last 20 years as it has to do with the continuing collapse of New York. It has to do with the decline of the Hollywood studios—physically and psychologically, with the conviction of an increasing number of filmmakers that movies should be made on location as often as possible (one result of the influence of foreign films of the fifties), and with the emergence of what might be called the regional or environmental American film, the film in which the locale may be as important as plot.

The opening of Passer's "Law and Disorder" exemplifies the difference between the New York film of today and the New York film of the thirties or forties. Passer starts his film with a long, leisurely, horizontal pan shot along the New York skyline, then cuts to a series of uproariously outrageous crimes taking place within that city. The oldtime movie about New York might open with a stockshot of Manhattan seen from the air, followed by a slow pan down the side of a tall building (sometimes the Empire State Building), ending with a quick dissolve to a California studio and a familiar, much-used, city street set.

Passer eases directly into a real New York in his film, which is less about individual character than about coping nowhere else but in New York City.

The earlier films almost literally dropped into their stories, which were set in a mythical Big Town, U.S.A. The Big Town could as easily be Chicago or Detroit or Kansas City as New York. I doubt whether the oldtime studio filmmakers consciously denatured locations to obtain this kind of universality. It was more likely the automatic result of working in a studio. The lack of emphasis on geography produced a quite different kind of movie from what we're getting today, in some ways better, in some ways worse.

The old films had nothing if not stories. They may not have been very good but they did have beginnings, middles and ends. Directors working in studios didn't have the time, facilities or interest to "discover" their characters within environments. As much of the environment that was to be important to the film had already been built on the backlot. As a result the characters often seem to exist in limbo, which is not necessarily bad, only when the characters are unrealized. We don't usually feel the need for more geographical information in "King Lear."

• • •

"Law and Disorder," which attempts to capture the desperation, humor, squalor, confusion and frustration of living in New York, could not have been conceived as a studio film. Nor could have Martin Scorsese's "Mean Streets" (though I understand that he shot a number of his New York street scenes on the streets of Los Angeles). In this fashion the *availability* of New York City, for better or worse, is having a direct influence on the content of what we're seeing in movie theaters. It's also influencing the style of movies like "Law and Disorder" and "Mean Streets," in which character and accumulated incident replace more conventional plots.

I suspect that this availability also encourages the production of conventionally structured movies that would be too expensive to do in a studio. "Death Wish" is probably one. "The Taking of Pelham One Two Three" is another.

The construction in a Hollywood studio of the elaborate subway sets would have made the cost of "Pelham" prohibitive. Compared to the general run of New York City films, "Pelham" is practically a tonic, a good-humored, often witty suspense melodrama in which the representatives of law and decency triumph without bending the rules. Of course, if you have to take any form of public transport to and from the theater where it's playing, you may find its conclusions wildly improbable.

1974 N 10, II:1:1

LENNY, directed by Bob Fosse; screenplay by Julian Barry, based on his stage play; produced by Marvin Worth; executive producer, David V. Picker; editor, Alan Heim; director of photography, Bruce Surtees; distributed by United Artists. Running time: 112 minutes. At the Cinema One Theater, Third Avenue near 60th Street. This film has been rated R.

Lenny Bruce	Dustin Hoffman
Honey Bruce	Valerie Perrine
Sally Marr	Jan Miner
Artie Silver	Stanley Beck
Sherman Hart	Gary Morton
Aunt Mema	Rashel Novikoff
Jack Goldstein	Guy Rennie

By VINCENT CANBY

"Lenny," Bob Fosse's film version of Julian Barry's Broadway play about the life, assorted trials and death in 1966 of Lenny Bruce, looks to be about three-fourths dramatized biography and one-fourth recreated stage performances.

These scenes trace Lenny's progression from the early nineteen-fifties, when he was a strip-joint comic (Customer: "Do you sell alligator shoes?" Salesman: "What size does your alligator wear?"), to Lenny's last exhausted years, when, after successive police busts for drugs and obscenity, he had reduced his nightclub act to obsessive readings from the court records.

This one-fourth of the film is so brilliant—and so brilliantly acted by Dustin Hoffman—that it helps cool one's impatience with the rest of the film, which is much more fancily edited and photographed but no more profound than those old movie biographies Jack L. Warner used to grind out about people like George Gershwin, Mark Twain and Dr. Ehrlich. In movies, now as then, genius is principally defined by the amount of time spent dealing with disappointment.

●

"Lenny," which opened yesterday at the Cinema One, has the advantage of being able to present a lot of the original Lenny Bruce material, even the material that just a few years ago got him arrested here and in San Francisco. The movie also has an advantage in that much of this material still has some shock value in its dependence on rude 4-letter and 10-letter words and on rude allusions to sacred events (the Crucifixion) and sacred people (Eleanor Roosevelt, Pope John XIII).

However, "Lenny" is never very precise about what happened to Lenny or why. Unless you've read the Albert Goldman-Lawrence Schiller biography, "Ladies and Gentlemen, Lenny Bruce!!" you might get the impression from the film that the desperation of Lenny's last years, as well as his death, were the exclusive result of harassment by the police and the courts and that Lenny had no role in his own collapse.

Ironically the form of the movie only serves to emphasize this fuzziness. Mr. Barry's screenplay is in the shape of a series of overlapping interviews with Lenny's former wife, Honey (Valerie Perrine); his mother, Sally Marr (Jan Miner), and his agent (Stanley Beck), which, in turn, cue in the flashbacks.

●

These interviews are full of phony, simulated cinéma vérité-type irrelevancies in speech and manner that you never for a minute believe, any more than you believe that Lenny was just a sweet brilliant fellow who had some hard luck.

The movie makes no point of Lenny's terrible childhood or his ambivalent feelings toward his father. His mother, the sometimes nightclub comic and emcee, is, as played by Miss Miner, a good deal less bizarre than Portnoy's, and Honey, as played by Miss Perrine, is about as voracious as a Goldilocks with a big habit for porridge.

Honey's affairs with other women, accepted and sometimes encouraged by Lenny, are touched upon so gently as to seem of little imporance, as is Lenny's dependence on drugs, taken in such massive doses that he seems to have been a mental as well as physical wreck toward the end.

Such vagueness, probably prompted by the producer's necessity to have the legal approval of both Honey and Sally Marr, denies the actors a lot of material that would have enriched their performances. Mr. Hoffman is such an interesting actor that he goes a long way toward filling in the gaps, but the others are not so fortunate. Miss Perrine is immensely effective in individual scenes but the character remains a cipher. Miss Miner is the gold-hearted stereotype.

●

Mr. Fosse, the director of "Cabaret," is also inhibited here. The production, photographed in glorious black-and-white, has a fine, seedy look but this, after all, is just more description. Was Lenny truly some kind of mad prophet or simply an accidental product of his times, which, though he died in 1966, were really the gung-ho nineteen-forties and the uptight fifties? It's to the film's credit that it raises this question, though it doesn't supply us with much information with which to answer it.

1974 N 11, 40:1

The Cast

THE TRIAL OF BILLY JACK, directed by Frank Laughlin; screenplay by Frank and Teresa Christina; produced by Joe Cramer; director of photography, Jack A. Marta; music, Elmer Bernstein; editors, Tom Rolf, Michael Economou, George Grenville, Miehael Karr and Jules Nayfack; a Taylor-Laughlin Distribution Company presentation. Running time: 170 minutes. At the Penthouse Theater, Broadway at 47th Street, and other theaters. This film has been rated PG.

Billy Jack	Tom Laughlin
Jean Roberts	Delores Taylor
Doc	Victor Izay
Carol	Teresa Laughlin
National Guardsman	William Wellman Jr.
Posner	Riley Hill
Sheriff Cole	Sparky Watt
Blue Elk	Gus Graymountain
Patsy Littlejohn	Sacheen Littlefeather
Danny	Michael Bolland

By VINCENT CANBY

"The Trial of Billy Jack" is nearly three hours of naiveté merchandised and marketed with the not-so-innocent vengeance that I associate with religious movements that take leases on places like the Houston Astrodome.

The film, which opened at theaters around town yesterday, is the sequel to the hugely successful "Billy Jack" and is more or less a rerun of the kind of things that happened in that 1971 film. It's part pageant, part kung fu action film, part Western, part earnest civics lesson, part Show Boat melodrama, part recollection of the various horrors of the late nineteen-sixties and early nineteen-seventies updated (sometimes desperately) to make contact with today.

Like "The Little Prince," it places a heavy philosophical load on the old ticker. "That's the trouble," says a character at one point, "you always try to understand with your head. You don't listen to your heart." Brains are getting it in the neck in the new movies.

●

"The Trial of Billy Jack," like the original film, is about the good-doing Indian half-breed, Billy Jack (Tom Laughlin), who has a lot of Bruce Lee, Robin Hood, Cochise and Jesus in him. (It's no accident that the film contains a song that asks "Are You Dying Just for Me, Billy Jack?" and seems to expect an affirmative reply.)

It's also about Jean Roberts (Delores Taylor), who is beloved (usually from afar) by Billy Jack and runs the Freedom School, somewhere near Arizona's Monument Valley, where flower children left over from the sixties edit "Nader-like periodicals and newspapers" that expose Big Government and Big Business.

The narrative, which has a gargantuan clumsiness to it that some critics have professed to find endearing, though it strikes me as aggressively dumb, picks up the story of Billy Jack where the first film left off. Billy Jack gets out of prison and returns to the Freedom School, which has had such success with its exposés that not only the local bigots but also the rascals in Washington try to crush the school. In between rap sessions on child abuse and the rights of American Indians, the melodrama accumulates (it certainly doesn't *mount*), climaxing in a Kent State-like attack on the school by members of the National Guard.

●

It would be easier to accept the film's good intentions if the movie weren't so schizoid that one can't be at all sure what its intentions really are.

Though it means to preach nonviolence, the only scenes of any interest are the violent ones, and always violence shows up as the only meaningful way to deal with evil.

We are told that the Freedom School kids have successfully exposed the oil industry's influence on Washington, yet the kids we see and hear would have difficulty exposing anything more complicated than a Baby Ruth bar. Senator Sam J. Ervin Jr. and Representative Peter W. Rodino Jr. didn't get to the bottom of Watergate by sitting around and listening to their hearts, for heaven's sake.

The movie is very, very long. It lurches towards obligatory scenes that turn up in no special order, and it is spotted here and there with topical references that are so arbitrary they prompt laughter ("With Ford and Rockefeller, nothing will change much"). It's also shot through with Indian (American) mysticism and self-improvement suggestions that evoke shades of Moral Re-Armament, which was never a hotbed for radical political thinkers.

●

Even the scenery becomes offensive after a while; it's such a waste of magnificent backgrounds we have long associated with the great John Ford films.

In addition to Mr. Laughlin and Miss Taylor (Mrs. Laughlin in private life), the cast includes Teresa Laughlin, their 16-year-old daughter, in a prominent supporting role, while 19-year-old Frank Laughlin, their son, is given directorial credit. None of them is terrific. The screenplay was written by Frank and Teresa Christina, who, I understand, are actually Pa and Ma Laughlin. If this film has even half of the success of the first film, "Billy Jack" could well become Hollywood's first one-family, multimillion-dollar cottage industry.

1974 N 14, 58:1

The Program

LET THE CHURCH SAY AMEN!, a documentary by St. Clair Bourne. Running time: 78 minutes. At the Whitney Museum of American Art, Madison Avenue and 75th Street. Through Tuesday.

By NORA SAYRE

"I know I want to be a minister and I know I've got to be black": the discoveries and the dilemmas of a young seminarian are evoked in St. Clair Bourne's "Let the Church Say Amen!", a thoughtful and skillfully made documentary which opened yesterday at the Whitney Museum of American Art and will run through Tuesday.

●

We first encounter the young man on the campus of the Interdenominational Theological Center in Atlanta, where it's stated that "religion has been one of the basic elements of black life . . .from the church, many progressive movements have sprung." One student remarks, "I don't think we deal with challenging the white man's conception of God." Before participating in a field interneship program, the future minister says that the choice of a denomination doesn't matter greatly to him, but that he's particularly interested in the ghetto church. However, an adviser suggests that he become acquainted with a rural church.

The film follows him to a Baptist church in Mound Bayou, Miss., where he confers with an old country preacher about the intensity of religious feeling in that community. Next, he spends time at a Methodist church in Chicago, where the urban congregation airs some generational conflicts. He also visits a group of teen-agers whom a youth organizer encourages to talk about their attitudes toward death, suicide—"Is is a cop-out?"—and the assassinations of black leaders. A member of the church later objects that the organizer "teaches them too much black."

●

Finally, the seminarian returns to Atlanta; the film then intercuts between a Christian minister's sermon and a discussion with some Black Muslims who are standing outside the chapel. The minister stresses the tangible realities of black life—including the children who suffer from malnutrition "while the politicians thrive"—and he warns against an overly mystical approach to religion. Especially because the camera never seems to be intrusive, the film yields a strong sense of the varieties of religious experience that one young man has been exposed to, and the breadth of choice that confronts him. Since the different roles of the contemporary church are so sensitively explored, the documentary should be equally enlightening for those who do or don't belong to the church itself.

1974 N 14, 58:1

'Introduction to Enemy' From Jane Fonda

By NORA SAYRE

Patience may never become one of our national characteristics. But we could take some lessons from the Vietnamese. Rebuilding and rebirth are the themes of "Introduction to the Enemy," which was made collectively by Jane Fonda, Tom Hayden, Haskell Wexler, and others; it depicts their travels through North and South Vietnam last spring. The documentary is playing today and tomorrow at the First Avenue Screening Room. Anyone who was or is concerned with the war should see it—along with those who think that the war is over.

Throughout this quiet, modest film, in which scrap metal from American airplanes is made into bicycles, and an old man explains that he rebuilt his house 12 times (on five occasions after the French bombings, and seven times after the American raids) and misty green crops rise from filled-in craters, it is stressed that the Vietnamese do not hate Americans, that they want to know more about us. Again and again, different Vietnamese citizens say that they distinguish between a population and its political leaders: they repeat that they do not blame Americans at large for the destruction of their country. Yet the wounds of their continuing experience are as tangible as the unexploded mine that goes off and kills a man during the filming.

The film seethes with small children; it seems quite amazing that there are so many Vietnamese children left alive, or that smiles of all ages should be turned toward the camera. Miss Fonda and Mr. Hayden function as unobtrusive guides. They journey from Hanoi to the South, crossing the demilitarized zone to the Quang Tri province. Miss Fonda interviews people about their work, asking why one chose to become an actress, or a translator, or a member of the resistance. The answers are thoughtful, decisive — as much personal as political.

Another recurrent theme is that Vietnam is one country —that the artificial division of the North and the South is not accepted by the Vietnamese. It's remarked that most families have relatives living in both areas; an editor adds, "The North and the South have always shared moments of joy as well as moments of sorrow and tragedy." Moreover, "American leaders are constantly reminding us that the bombing could be renewed." A very old man says he'd be happy to die if he could see one day of reunification.

Though the Paris Peace Agreements have not been fulfilled, a restrained optimism surges through this documentary. The mood of the film is distilled when someone asserts that "the needs of peace are greater than the needs of war"—meaning that rebuilding schools and hospitals and homes and entire cities demands resources and energies that simply aren't available in wartime. All in all, this pensive and moving film serves as a chapter of our own education about the Vietnamese past and the rhythm of life in that country now.

The Cast

INTRODUCTION TO THE ENEMY, a documentary about Vietnam from The Indochina Peace Campaign by Christine Burrill, Jane Fonda, Tom Hayden, Haskell Wexler and Bill Yahraus; photography, Mr. Wexler with the assistance of Pham Viet Tung; edited by Christine Burrill and Mr. Yahraus; sound, Cao Xuan Nghia; translation, Tram Minh Quoc with the assistance of Vietnamese students in the United States. At the First Avenue Screening Room, at 61st Street. Running time: 60 minutes. Showings today and tomorrow at noon and midnight.

1974 N 15, 32:1

The Cast

EARTHQUAKE, directed and produced by Mark Robson; written by George Fox and Mario Puzo; director of photographic effects, Albert Whitlock; special effects, Frank Brendel; film editor, Dorothy Spencer; music, John Williams; in Sensurround; released by Universal Pictures. At the Ziegfeld Theater, Avenue of the Americas and 54th Street, and neighborhood theaters. Running time: 129 minutes. This film is classified PG.

Graff	Charlton Heston
Remy	Ava Gardner
Slade	George Kennedy
Denise	Genevieve Bujold
Miles	Richard Roundtree
Jody	Marjoe Gortner

By NORA SAYRE

Although no one has yet produced the feelies that Aldous Huxley evoked in "Brave New World" — in which a love scene on a bearskin rug transmitted every hair of the bear, and there were aromas of newmown hay and kidney pudding, while a kiss on the lips or a blow on the skull were felt by everyone in the audience — Mark Robson's "Earthquake" makes an awesome stab in that direction. The dam breaking, floods rising, bodies falling, towers crashing or burning, the earth heaving, pavements parting and the random explosions are all enhanced by Sensurround: special vibrations on the soundtrack cause your spine and your throat to tingle. (You may also wonder if they curdle the brain cells.) It seems greedy to wish that "Earthquake" were in 3-D. At any rate, the whole experience opened yesterday at the Ziegfeld Theater.

The deadpan delivery of key lines informs us when the worst is coming. Such as: "I know you'll laugh, but—I think we're going to have a really big quake." Or (to a child on his way to the playground): "Just be careful crossing that bridge." And (to those fleeing from a cellar that's about to be flooded): "Relax! there's lots of time!" The impulse to shout advice to the screen—get out! go away! don't enter that building—is quite powerful, so this does rank as a participatory movie.

•

While the exertions that the cast goes through can't really be called acting, Ava Gardner (looking magnificent), Charlton Heston (a bit less wooden than usual), Genevieve Bujold (brisk and beguiling), Marjoe Gortner (a righteous psychotic) and George Kennedy (a nimble cop) do convey an exhilarating amount of panic. There's also a pleasing glimpse of Walter Matthau as an imperturbable drunk; he's listed under his true name, Walter Matuschanskavasky. Although the special effects are staggeringly realistic, I'll go along with the psychologists who say that the disaster movies manage to assert that it couldn't happen to you—because it's happening to movie stars.

"Earthquake" is far less sophisticated than "Juggernaut," but much more so than "Airport 75"—a really rotten movie that's entertaining just because it's so bad. (There, it would be nice to see the Charlton Heston and Karen Black roles reversed, so that an experienced woman pilot would guide a sobbing male steward at the controls: "Take a left turn, honey." "Oh God I *can't*." "Now, now.") "Earthquake" also includes a skyscraper bursting into flames — no doubt in order to steal a march on "The Towering Inferno," which won't open until next month. While the quake isn't gory, it's the most harrowing of these movies so far, hence it mightn't be appropriate for anyone under 10. But for those who have a soft spot for calamity pictures, there's a sense of ritual cleansing afterward. And for some reason, it also made me hungry.

1974 N 16, 20:2

The Screen: 'Hindered'

By A. H. WEILER

Having chosen a decidedly unusual, if slightly improbable but altogether touching subject, Steve Dwoskin demonstrates delicate artistry in "Hindered," which had its American premiere last night at the Film Forum. The 35-year-old, New York-born moviemaker - artist, reportedly completed his feature in recent months for showing on German television. He has made a liaison between an Angst-ridden girl and her disabled, crutch and braces-encumbered young man into a microscopically fine and sensitive dissection of the tenderness and pain of an extraordinary involvement.

Mr. Dwoskin, who was represented here last year by another absorbing feature, "Dyn Amo," exhibits an almost exhausting predilection for close-ups of eyes, noses, hands, feet and faces to dramatize, ever so slowly, the feeling of his star-crossed principals. **But if a viewer is nagged by a need for explanations, the cumulative effect of their personal drama is both bittersweet and moving.**

The film, whose sparse German dialogue is translated by literal English subtitles, projects a special kind of poignancy since, as a program note mentions, it is basically autobiographical and Mr. Dwoskin, who also plays the young man, seems also to be handicapped. But to his credit, his color camera focuses mostly on the object of his affection, Carola Regnier, a newcomer to this observer, who uses her expressive, if not beautiful face and body to affect a powerful, controlled tour de force.

Her detailed fascination with his disability, her precise, sensitive reactions to growing anxieties, her mounting indecision and her final wrenching decision to leave him are interlaced, glowing cameos of authentic emotion and meaning.

Mr. Dwoskin's comparatively rare appearances are self-effacing but equally realistic. At one point, Mr. Dwoskin, a long-haired, laconic, seemingly unemotional type, comforts his perturbed girl. "Don't worry. You think too much about it." Mr. Dwoskin's forthright and unsentimental drama not only gives us something to think about but also stirs the heart.

1974 N 15, 33:1

THE SAVAGE IS LOOSE, directed and produced by George C. Scott; written by Max Ehrlich and Frank De Felitta; executive producer, Robert E. Relyea; director of photography, Alex Phillips Jr.; editor, Michael Kahn; music, Gil Melle; distributed by Campbell Devon Productions. Running time: 114 minutes. At the Rivoli Theater, Broadway at 49th Street, and other theaters. This film has been rated R.

John	George C. Scott
Maida	Trish Van Devere
David	John David Carson
Young David	Lee H. Montgomery

By VINCENT CANBY

"The Savage Is Loose," produced, directed and distributed by George C. Scott, who also stars in it with his wife, Trish Van Devere, is one of those desert-island movies in which the members of the audience, more often than the characters within the film, keep searching the horizon in hopes that a ship will pass by.

The film, which opened yesterday at the Rivoli and other theaters, is a three-character, four-actor melodrama about a scientist, his much younger wife and their son who are shipwrecked on a tropical isle early in this century. What begins as a kind of tab show version of "The Swiss Family Robinson" quickly disintegrates into a muddled meditation upon the survival of the human race, but under conditions so special that the film's primal concerns eventually become ludicrous.

A heavily portentous line spoken early in the film by the son (played as an adolescent by Lee H. Montgomery) points the way: "Mother, when I grow up, can we get married?"

Trouble erupts 10 years later when the son, now played by John David Carson, has started to court his mother in earnest. He leaves orchids by her coconut-shell soup bowl and asks pointed questions on the order of: "Who was Cain's wife?" When Mom and Dad make love, he likes to peek.

Says Mom to Dad in the semi-privacy of their bamboo-walled bedroom: "We've got a lusting male with no outlet." That is, no *satisfactory* outlet. Mom has found that the boy has constructed a curious substitute woman, apparently out of the all-purpose coconut shells, in a jungle hideaway.

It isn't long before things come to a showdown, largely because Dad has allowed himself to get cranky and go to wrack and ruin (Mr. Scott at this point looks like a cross between the Biblical Abraham and Raymond Duncan) and seemingly because the life force is so strong that Mom's resistance to her son begins to run out.

Someone might very well have made a plausible Oedipal metaphor out of this story, but not Max Ehrlich and Frank De Felitta Jr., who wrote the screenplay and stuffed it with unequal alternatives.

A major point is made at the beginning of the film of the conflict between the parents. The mother wants to raise the boy as a civilized child who can read and write, while the father feels the boy must be taught to dominate his environment. This supposedly has the effect of turning him into the savage of the title, though why he couldn't also have learned to read and write is never properly explained.

By reducing the Oedipal conflict to such a basic confrontation, the movie has the effect of making a common psychological conflict seem as remote to most of us as the emotional lives of Siamese twins.

•

"The Savage Is Loose" works neither as an adventure film, as a psychological exploration, nor, heaven help us, as a family melodrama. Although I think that Mr. Scott has been talking through his hat in recent public statements that the movie is not about incest, the subject is so genteelly handled that I can't imagine children seeing the film would be anything but confused and probably bored.

The production, photographed entirely on location south of Puerto Vallarta,

Mexico, looks pretty and has the studied blandness of a film directed according to a 50-year-old textbook on movie making. What force it has comes entirely from the performances of Mr. Scott and Miss Van Devere, though the banality of the script has a way of letting them seem overwrought when they mean to be believably passionate. The less said about the other performances, the better.

1974 N 16, 21:1

FILM VIEW

VINCENT CANBY

'The Little Prince' Is An Important Disappointment

Stanley Donen's first musical film in years, "The Little Prince," is a fairly impossible movie to sit through — often coyly cute, sometimes blank and boring, and full of the sort of Antoine de Saint Exupéry philosophy that better belongs in fortune cookies. "What is essential is invisible to the eye," and "It's only with the heart that one can see clearly" are two of its zingers.

I wouldn't go so far as to call this level of anti-intellectualism dangerous and reactionary. I suspect it's harmless and no more simplistic than a lot of the stuff that is so piously pronounced in "The Trial of Billy Jack." Yet where "The Trial of Billy Jack" is just more of the same "Billy Jack" that we know enough about to avoid if we want to, "The Little Prince" is an important disappointment.

It's a disappointment because the subject matter —a fable about a neurotic aviator and the extra-terrestrial boy who teaches him about life and love— is not the sort of thing designed to bring out the best in Mr. Donen. He's a bright, clever, sophisticated director ("Seven Brides for Seven Brothers," "Singin' in The Rain," "Two for The Road") whose talent looks most strained, most phony really, when he wants to be most simple and sincere. "The Little Prince" seems to have been as fated for foolish results from the start as Marie Antoinette's attempts to get close to the soil by dressing up as a milkmaid at the Little Trianon.

● ● ●

Yet "The Little Prince" is not without importance and deserving of our attention, if only aural. It is the first new musical score by Alan Jay Lerner and Frederick Loewe since "Camelot" and their first original film score since "Gigi." "New" may be a somewhat misleading word. The Lerner (lyrics) and Loewe (music) collaboration hit its stride in the mid-fifties with "My Fair Lady" and the team is still writing in that style—melodic, romantic, and witty in the way of writers for whom words are as much shape and sound as meaning.

The score of "The Little Prince" is a sheer delight, a recollection of a kind of expertise that is, in its way, as ageless as Chaplin's. I wouldn't be

at all surprised if some of the same people who found Chaplin's "A Countess From Hong Kong" old-fashioned, simply because he dared make a movie that wasn't according to contemporary fashions, will also call "The Little Prince" score old-fashioned. However, it's a throwback to a Broadway idiom that Lerner and Loewe still know best, and which, when they are in top form, makes no call on fad or fashion.

We don't have so many film musicals that we can dismiss something like "The Little Prince" simply because the book (by Lerner, based on Saint Exupéry) is so frail, a series of philosophic confrontations between the aviator (Richard Kiley) and the Little Prince (six-year-old Steven Warner), and between the Little Prince and characters designated as The King, The Fox, The Snake and The Rose. It's this film's hardly unique discovery that civilization is full of idiocies, and it's the manner of this film to label the idiocies so generally (war, greed, pride) that only a dim-witted toad could disagree.

While watching and listening to "The Little Prince" I kept wishing that Lerner and Loewe and Donen had tackled some other subject and left this not really modern fairy tale to the Disney organization, which would probably know better than to touch it. (Irrelevant historical footnote: Hedy Lamarr once announced that she was going to make a film of the Saint Exupéry book.)

● ● ●

Some time ago, while writing about "That's Entertainment," I inclined to the idea that film musicals had become an all but lost art form because of economics and a lack of contemporary talent to compare with people like Dietz and Schwartz, Cole Porter, Jerome Kern and the others who were responsible for the great M-G-M films of the forties and fifties. "The Little Prince" shows us that economics need not be an important barrier and that, indeed, the talent is still around. However, the talent does seem to get sidetracked on the wrong projects.

As Lerner and Loewe were sidetracked on "The Little Prince," so was Burt Bacharach sidetracked by "Lost Horizon." Bacharach, the best of the comparatively new composers, can do original, first-rate work ("Promises, Promises"), but Hollywood hasn't yet given him an opportunity to do much more than theme songs that are intended to become singing commercials for individual films. The Paul Williams rock score for Brian De Palma's "Phantom of The Paradise" may be good but it's difficult to tell in the context of the film since so much time is devoted to arrangements parodying various rock styles.

Movie musicals are still an endangered if not quite extinct species, but movie music is more pervasive than ever. Currently being promoted are the original soundtrack albums for such things as "Airport 1975," "The Trial of Billy Jack," "Lenny," a single record for "The Odessa File" and the original soundtrack album for "Earthquake," which might be called music to fall through the floor by.

1974 N 17, II:17:1

Film: 'Under Influence'

"A Woman Under the Influence" was shown at the 12th New York Film Festival. The following excerpt is from Nora Sayre's review, which appeared in The New York Times on Oct. 14. The film is being shown at the Columbia 1 and 2 Theaters, Second Avenue and 64th Street. Running time: 155 minutes. This film has not been classified.

When a husband and wife need to keep saying how much they love each other, something's apt to be awfully wrong. That nervous repetition is one of the danger signals in John Cassavetes's

"A Woman Under the Influence," and its contains all the warning urgency of a siren.

●

Throughout, the film dwells on the abrasions of daily living, centered in the domestic world where each individual grinds on the other's nerves. Gena Rowlands plays a woman adrift. Her manic, likable, hard-hat husband (Peter Falk) quite hysterically keeps assuring her that everything's fine. Meanwhile, she looks to him for her identity, asking him

to tell her "what" to be, insisting that she'll "be anything" he wants. Later, he punctuates a horrendous uproar by shouting "Just be yourself!" But she hardly has a self—beyond the bundle of symptoms that make up her hectic public persona.

Miss Rowlands unleashes an extraordinary characterization of a harried, anxious creature, who's convinced that she "makes a jerk of" herself every day. (The actress's style of performing sometimes shows a kinship with that of the early Kim Stanley or the recent Joanne Woodward, but the notes of desperation are emphatically her own.) Despair lurks behind her smile—which often collapses suddenly—as she jabbers, hums or retreats to a little-girl manner. Pantomime is one of her defenses. She mugs with exasperation, working her jaw and rolling her eyes when she's annoyed or throwing indignant punches into the air.

A troubled person, yes, and certainly an insecure one. But she doesn't seem sick or crazed enough to justify the crack-up that's awaiting her, nor to spend six months in a sanitarium. And that's the hitch in the movie: you can't really tell how the director regards this character. Mr. Cassavetes is unquestionably sympathetic to the rootless state of the middle-American housewife. (Moreover, the hospitalization is meant to seem like a betrayal by the husband.)

But—perhaps unintentionally—he has made the man appear much crazier than his wife; are we supposed to assume that his frantic nature has driven her over the edge? Or are we meant to see madness as contagious? Ultimately, the essential problems of this woman remain unclear: we're shown her behavior, but not what inspired it.

1974 N 19, 52:1

Clumsy Adaptation of the Novel by Huie

By VINCENT CANBY

"The Klansman" is one of those rare films that are not as bad as they seem when you're watching them. That's a warning to be disregarded only by lunatics, but the point should be made that it's not an uninteresting film to think about afterward.

The movie, which opened yesterday at Loews Astor Plaza, is a thoroughly clumsy adaptation of William Bradford Huie's novel set against the racial confrontations that destroy a large part of the population of a small Alabama town in the nineteen-sixties.

It's about the town's would-be-humané sheriff (Lee Marvin), a card-carrying Ku Klux Klanner who apparently joined the Klan for the same reason one joins organizations en masse in any small town—that is, to get elected—and it's about the town's most respectable eccentric (Richard Burton), the last member of an aristocratic family (eight generations on the same ground) who finds the Klan ridiculous and abhorrent but who is only slightly less out of touch with reality than the black-baiting redneck farmers.

●

To the extent that the rather primitively written script allows, Mr. Marvin and Mr. Burton are effective as these complex, contradictory characters (though Mr. Burton's accent seems to have less to do with geography than with partial paralysis of the mouth muscles).

The characters are valid and the events that bring about the final bloody shootout (an accumulation of rapes and murders and an invasion by Northern liberals who want to aid a voter registration drive) are not without a certain relation to recent history.

Terence Young, the director, and the writers, Millard Kaufman and Samuel Fuller

The Cast

THE KLANSMAN, directed by Terence Young; screenplay by Millard Kaufman and Samuel Fuller, based on the novel by William Bradford Huie; produced by William Alexander; executive producer, Bill Shiffrin; editor, Gene Milford; director of photography, Lloyd Ahern; music, Dale O. Warren and Stu Gardner; distributed by Paramount Pictures. Running time: 112 minutes. At Loews Astor Plaza Theater, 44th Street west of Broadway. This film has been rated R.
Sheriff Bascomb .... Lee Marvin
Breck Stancill .... Richard Burton
Butt Cut Cates .... Cameron Mitchell
Garth ....O. J. Simpson
Loretta Sykes .... Lola Falana
Mayor Hardy ......David Huddleston
Trixie ....Luciana Paluzzi
Nancy Poteet ....Linda Evans

(himself a director known for his almost cartoon-like bluntness), effectively defuse the very real drama by so lovingly depicting the horrors that one comes to suspect their motives. As the movie progresses, the events come to seem less and less urgent and particular to a specific time and place, and more and more like the automatic responses to the demands of cheap, easy movie melodrama.

●

The subject — and Mr. Huie's tough, journalistic novel — should have been much better served.

The supporting cast includes Cameron Mitchell as an especially vicious Klansman, the football star O.J. Simpson as the town's single black radical and Lola Falana, as a beautiful black local girl who loves Mr. Burton wisely but not so well that he ever touches her.

1974 N 21, 54:1

MIXED COMPANY, produced and directed by Melville Shavelson; written by Mr. Shavelson and Mort Lachman; director of photography, Stan Lazan; film editors, Walter Thompson and Ralph James Hall; music, Fred

Karlin; released by United Artists. At the Thalia Theater, Broadway and 95th Street and neighborhood theaters. Running time: 109 minutes. This film is classified PG.
Kathy ....Barbara Harris
Pete ....Joseph Bologna
Al ....Tom Bosley

By NORA SAYRE

As everyone knows a woman's tears can work wonders, and the wonders in Melville Shavelson's "Mixed Company" add up to the adoption of a small Vietnamese girl, a black boy and a Hopi moppet by a suburban couple who can't even cope with their own three children. The movie opened yesterday at the Thalia.

The immense talents of Barbara Harris and Joseph Bologna are wasted throughout this dreary farce, which is tempered with ominously perky music, some liberal intentions run amok, cozy jokes about bedwetting, and an attempt at hipness that puts racist lines into the children's mouths. The film struggles so hard against sentimentality that it comes full circle, and each wave of sentiment is lusher than the last.

Mr. Bologna is cast as a lovable bigot (whom we know will see the light); confronted with the black child he's made to say, "Why don't we adopt Eldridge Cleaver?" Most of the time, he just has to keep yelling, "I don't believe this! I don't believe it!" Miss Harris has no scope for the level, wry alertness that is her specialty. Her voice trembles as though she were ready to weep over her lines, which range from "You promised me a baby" to "I thought I was gaining a child, I'm losing a husband" and "Get my Vietnamese dictionary." There are ghastly moments when the whole family kneels down and pretends to cry together. Spectators who came in hopes of comedy could always join them.

1974 N 21, 54:2

11 Short Films Shown at the Whitney

Walt Disney has passed to his reward with justifiable earthly rewards for the likes of "Mickey Mouse" and "Snow White." But as deviators from the estimable, literal norm he set, the avant-garde as represented by the shorts in "Animation," which opened yesterday at the Whitney Museum of American Art, are similarly dedicated to this genre. If this collection of 11 subjects made over the last two years tends to be too experimental and unusual for one sitting, it is, nevertheless, generally impressive evidence of talent aimed at art, not commerce.

●

As expert hands in the complex techniques of inte-

grating the computer and animation, Lillian Schwartz and Ken Knowlton make fascinating use of exotic, flowing forms, colors and electronic music in "Metamorphosis" and "Metathesis." And among the more striking shorts that run from 3 to 8 minutes each is Jules Engel's "Train Landscape," which captivatingly projects sights and sounds from an accelerating train.

His associate at the California Institute of Arts, Adam Beckett, is imaginative in quickly developing lines and figures in three films best exemplified by the eroti-

The Program

ANIMATION: BRAIN FIELD, 7 minutes, by Robert Russett; NEURON, 5 minutes, by Mr. Russett; TRAIN LANDSCAPE by Jules Engel, 5 minutes; SPACE FOR ONE SELF by Lorraine Bubar, 5 minutes; TANGRAM by Alan Slasor, 2.5 minutes; METATHESIS and METAMORPHOSIS by Lillian Schwartz and Ken Knowlton, 8 minutes; SAUSAGE CITY, 5.5 minutes, by Adam Beckett; FLESH FLOWS, 6.5 minutes, by Mr. Beckett; EVOLUTION OF THE RED STAR, 7 minutes, by Mr. Beckett; PANDORA'S BOX by Steve Sega, 7 minutes. At the Whitney Museum of American Art, Madison Avenue and 75th Street, through Dec. 3.

cally accented "Flesh Flows." On the other hand, Robert Russett's "Neuron" and "Brain Field" evolve as somewhat confusing abstract exercises in design.

●

If these are decidedly serious efforts, a sense of humor is apparent in three of the offerings. Alan Slasor's combinations of geometric cutouts which become a dog, cat, horse and man in "Tangram," are whimsical and cute. Steven Segal's more ambitious "Pandora's Box," which emits self-devouring boxes, people, shapes and live action, is both inventive and funny. And Lorraine Bubar's "Space for One Self" amusingly focuses on a tiny, man-like figure grappling with a succession of aggressively moving lines and squares.

"Animation" makes an interesting, occasionally creative, package even if the whole is not equal to some of its shining parts.

A. H. WEILER

1974 N 21, 54:3

The Program

SIMABADDHA (The Target), directed by Satyajit Ray; screenplay dialogue with English subtitles) by Mr. Ray, based on a story by Shankar; music, Mr. Ray; produced by Bharat Shamsher and Jang Bahadur Rana. Running time: 112 minutes. This film has not been classified. At the First Avenue Screening Room, at 61st Street. Today and tomorrow at noon and midnight. With: Baru Chanda.

By NORA SAYRE

In this country, we're rather schizoid about ambition; although that drive is often harshly criticized, so are the individuals who lack it, and those who don't partake of the native work ethic are usually considered more alarming than the hustlers. Satyajit Ray's "Simabaddha" ("The Target"), made in 1971, is enormously interest-

ing on this subject. The movie is playing today and tomorrow at the First Avenue Screening Room.

The film doesn't condemn ambition per se; instead, Mr. Ray shows how far someone can go once his ambitions have anesthetized the rest of his nature. A pleasant but desperately conventional young Indian is a sales manager in a British firm in Calcutta, and he longs to be the next director. When a shipment of merchandise for export proves to be defective, he precipitates a strike among the factory workers to cover up the errors. During the strike, a bomb is set and badly burns a watchman—while the schemer is soon rewarded with a promotion. Blowing smoke rings of satisfaction at one moment, haunted by his duplicity at others, he exaults in winning yet suffers the loss of self-respect.

●

This is an extremely subtle portrait of a tainted person; although the film deplores his actions, we're allowed to sympathize with his severe anxieties. He's also a victim of the values that the British left behind in Calcutta: the obsequious snobberies of the nouveau riche, the numbing materialism, and the indifference to the poverty of countless Indians. His glossy apartment, the golf he plays with senior colleagues, the deft power ploys and the musty British slang that he carefully uses—"jolly good" or "touch wood"—are all essential to assure him of his worth.

The corrosion of this man's character is seen through the eyes of his intelligent young sister-in-law, who's neither a moralist nor a prude. One of the film's most extraordinary achievements is the headlong attraction between them: intimacy mounts and simmers, and there are spells of almost hostile flirtation. If this were a Western movie, they would suddenly hurtle into bed. But these two very traditional people are unlikely to act on impulse. Will they or won't they? The suspense is acute, and this movie — which is impeccably acted — conveys unspoken sexual excitement in a way that's rare on screen. Throughout, Mr. Ray uses close-ups that enable us to read the characters' minds: when their gaze rests on one another's faces, we know exactly what they're thinking.

"The Target" completes Mr. Ray's Calcutta trilogy, which includes "Days and Nights in the Forest" and "The Adversary." Like much of his other work, this movie is pensive, reflective — built on details that reveal people's obsessions or their pleasures or defenses. This director is able to wring dramatic intensity out of material that may not sound dramatic, and there's a fine, nervy balance between the tensions that the protagonist experiences at the office and at home. Although "The Target" isn't quite in the league with Mr. Ray's greatest films, all of his admirers should be sure to see it.

1974 N 22, 30:1

FILM VIEW

VINCENT CANBY

Brace Yourself, Here Come the 'Splat' Movies

In this year of the Big Splat, otherwise known as the disaster movie, it may be difficult to find one as wish-fulfilling, as technically ingenious and as classically nutty as "Earthquake," written by George Fox and Mario Puzo, and directed by Mark Robson. It's the biggest, corniest, most spectacular calamity movie since Merian C. Cooper's "The Last Days of Pompeii," which goes all the way back to 1935, but then "The Last Days of Pompeii" (Cooper's, not Bulwer-Lytton's) didn't have the brain-bending accompaniment of Sensurround (patent pending).

Though it will probably have limited application except in films dealing with earthquakes, Sensurround seems to be the last word in audience participation gimmicks. It beats 3-D, CinemaScope and the smellies by being a kind of elaboration of stereophonic sound to produce what Aldous Huxley predicted would be the feelies.

Sensurround is low-frequency sound vibrations, emitted from speakers near the screen and at the back of the theater, that act on the eardrums like thousands of angry Magic Fingers. Instead of putting one to sleep, they help convince you that everything is becoming physically unhinged, thus augmenting the visual evidence in "Earthquake" to such an extent that you may want to glance at the ceiling of the theater just to make sure that the chandelier isn't swaying.

Disaster movies—end-of-the-world movies, really—have long been hugely popular with members of the mass audience who go to them, I suspect, with the same kind of anticipation with which they get onto roller coasters and enter musées of wax. Unlike "Juggernaut" and "Airport 1975," which aren't, strictly speaking, disaster movies since there is ultimately no disaster (the people at Boeing have enough problems to cope with without encouraging movies about plane crashes), "Earthquake" is one of those disaster movies in which the worst actually happens.

And, being about an earthquake, one that levels much of present-day Los Angeles, it encompasses all sorts of other disasters caused by the earthquake, including a fire in a glass-and-steel skyscraper (a disaster that will be explored at somewhat more depth or height next month in "The Towering Inferno"), a shattered dam and a flood, and a variation on the one about people-trapped-in-a-mine-shaft. There are a few but not many disasters that "Earthquake" doesn't treat, at least peripherally.

•   •   •

Having thus rigorously disciplined themselves, the writers and director of "Earthquake" have still managed to make two points essential to our enjoyment of disaster movies: (1) that the people caught in the disaster have somehow flaunted God's physical laws, and (2) that God is punishing the victims for sexually misbehaving.

No big deal is made of either point. The movie doesn't have the Biblical underpinnings of Robert Aldrich's "The Last Days of Sodom and Gomorrah," but both points are made quite clearly, as when Charlton Heston, the Los Angeles architect responsible for a lot of the city's new high-rises, says in the middle of the quake, while sheets of glass are falling off buildings like pieces of icing off a stale birthday cake: "Buildings 40 stories tall shouldn't be built—at least here." What he means is that if God had intended 40-story buildings to be built on the San Andreas fault, He would have built them Himself.

Point two is covered by the fact that on the day the quake occurs in the movie, Heston has just begun a deliriously happy but adulterous affair with Genevieve Bujold. That will teach him.

Some kinds of disasters are more photogenic than others. Earthquakes, volcanic eruptions, fires, tidal waves and hurricanes (or typhoons) do well in movies, principally, I guess, because they either last a longish time or their after-effects do.

Movies about bubonic plague, typhus, cholera, etc., tend to be serious. There isn't much spectacle in seeing someone simply faint in a street or die in his bed, no matter how blue or scabrous his face. Tornadoes don't last long enough to justify the cost of the special effects, which means that when you see a tornado in a movie, it's usually just a plot device, as is the wreck of some means of public transportation, such as a train or an airplane.

The great thing about the earthquake in "Earthquake" is that it does go on and on, beginning with the first tremors that lead to the quake itself, followed by the after-shocks, at which time the city is in flames and other disasters have caught our attention.

Since the end of World War II, I'd begun to think that Japanese moviemakers had cornered the special effects market as they turned out mostly foolish monster movies in which, however, the final cataclysms (usually the destruction of Tokyo) were often very cleverly done. "Earthquake" shows that the Hollywood technicians have not lost the touch.

One may well wonder why we're getting this plague of disaster movies right now and why they're so popular. Do they take our minds off the Middle East and stories about unsafe atomic reactors? Perhaps. Disaster movies are seldom about real, everyday problems. Have you ever seen a disaster movie about inflation? And the characters who inhabit these calamitous fables are seldom more than easily recognized stereotypes. The more so the

better. Idiosyncratic characters would get in the way of our appreciation of the broad view of things these films take.

•   •   •

We don't want to be emotionally shattered by disaster movies. We want to be invigorated, as much by the excitement as by the fact that the victims on the screen suffer instead of us. Then, too, I suspect that many moviegoers are sophisticated enough in the ways that movies are made to enjoy seeing how well the film technicians can create the illusion of some horrendous event that couldn't possibly be photographed in life. When and if the world comes to an end, few of us are going to be able to appreciate the display.

1974 N 24, II:1:1

GUEST VIEW

JOHN SIMON

THOSE whom the Catholic Church did not prevent from seeing Rossellini's "The Miracle" (the ban on it was reversed by the Supreme Court, but the film has been shown very little, all the same) will remember the mute figure of the Stranger, a handsome, delicate-faced, sensitive-looking man whom the heroine, a simple peasant woman guarding the villagers' sheep, could understandably mistake for St. Joseph. His visage had rare dignity and subtlety, and the mysteriously ironic expression with which he responded to the adoration of the shepherdess was worthy of the Mona Lisa's countenance. That tall, slender man, who was none other than the not-yet-director Federico Fellini, was in every way the antithesis of the gross sensualist—double-chinned and bulging-bellied, though still in his early fifties—Fellini of today, the has-been director. It is not so much that he was younger and had dyed his hair blond for the film; it is rather that there was no vulgarity in his appearance or demeanor.

But if the physical change was great, how much greater yet is that between the earlier Fellini films, starting with "Variety Lights" (1950), and the later Fellini films, culminating in the current, critically overpraised "Amarcord," made by that grotesque yet idolized figure wearing vaguely "artistic" apparel, and seen lording it all over Rome followed by a sizable, sycophantic entourage. "I want to surround myself with acrobats, storytellers, and jesters, as in a medieval court, but there will be no despotism," Fellini declared 13 years ago in an interview in Films and Filming magazine. A retinue of servile clowns may not be the

creation of a despot—it may even be that the despot is the creation of his toadying followers—but Fellini "the King of Rome," as the late, highly respected critic Charles Thomas Samuels described him, is too crudely despotic a creature to have much of the artist left about him.

Looking back over Fellini's career, one can see that in a sense he has always made the same film, because, as he has often remarked, all his films are autobiographical in spirit, sometimes indeed in their letter. This need not be a drawback if only the basic themes undergo sufficient variations, and if they are not so self-centered as to exclude awareness of other people. If, in short, the films are concerned with transmuting felt life into art. This was the

John Simon is film critic for Esquire and drama critic for New York magazine.

case, to a greater or lesser extent, with all of Fellini's films through "The Nights of Cabiria" (1956), and including even a number of scenes in "La Dolce Vita" (1959), where some episodes were already tainted with dishonest sleight-of-hand, bathetic pretentiousness, pseudo-intellectual attitudinizing, and a kind of bloated self-imitation. Thus the latter's phony miracle episode was only a more melodramatic reworking of the pilgrimage sequence from "Cabiria"; the various orgies were more diffuse revampings of the New Year's Eve party in "Il Bidone" (1955); and "La Dolce Vita's" structure was so overextended and rambling as to be rather more than the largely passive central figure, the quasi-autobiographical Marcello, could hold together.

Fellini was already cheating. True, there may have been something contrived even in "Cabiria," what with the one seemingly devoted man in the prostitute-heroine's life turning out to be the biggest crook of all, and her unduly speedy arousal from blackest despair to dancing jocundity by the rather too fortuitous appearance of a band of merry revelers. But at least the transformations occurred on camera, and were there for us to believe or disbelieve on ocular evidence. In "La Dolce Vita," Marcello's deterioration takes place between the film's episodes, and must be taken entirely on faith—the

In his earlier films, Fellini was "always drawn to the baroque and bizarre. He nevertheless handled it with taste and control."

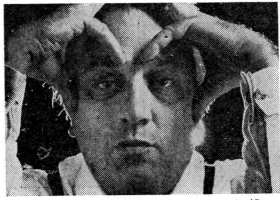

Henri Dauman

filmmaker's tendentious bad faith.

There followed a series of ever more frantic, garish, and unsatisfying films, with the partial exception of "8½" (1962), which, though also overloaded, posturing, and intellectually confused, had at least the virtue of admitting, in scarcely disguised autobiographical outspokenness, that Fellini had nothing more to say, no more films to make. For "8½" was a film about a great director's spiritual and physical paralysis, about his inability to make the film he is supposed to be making, and his incapacity to make decisions or choices in art and life. In every possible way the protagonist, Guido Anselmi, was equated with Fellini, and the film would have been a perfect confession of present, and presage of future, impotence, had it not been enshrouded in an opaque, hocus-pocusy *mise en scène* and furbished with one of the most dishonest endings in the history of cinema: a circular procession of all the characters—creatures from the hero's past and present, and anonymous additional figures—all led by a band of clown-musicians in a capering parade of bustle for its own sake, of what the Canadian critic Peter Harcourt has called "the impulse toward life without demanding why."

But aside from the glaring schematism with which this was staged, there was its total incredibility. Although partly yet another fantasy of Anselmi's, it was, like other fantasy scenes in the film, meant to function also on the level of truth; but it was a truth unearned by anything that preceded it. Why the demanding mistress and the dissatisfied wife, the dead parents and the morally rigid, exacting, and possibly fraudulent churchmen, and all the other ghosts and bugbears, victims and tormentors in the protagonist's life should suddenly turn into a tractable, docilely cavorting roundelay could be explained only as the meretricious concoction of an arbitrary happy ending.

The tragic deterioration of Fellini's talent—indeed, genius—can be traced in his handling of any one of the recurrent motifs on which his films are based. In several of Fellini's works, for example, we encounter the town simpleton, Giudizio, who first appears in Fellini's masterpiece, "I Vitelloni" (1953), as a harmless halfwit, a fisherman whom the young provincial idlers sometimes watch at his work. When the leader of the gang of *vitelloni* (fatted calves, i.e., drifters) steals and tries unsuccessful-ly to sell the statue of an angel—a piece of cheap, mass-produced religious art—he ends up leaving the angel with the ecstatically worshipful Giudizio. We now get a lovely shot of Giudizio carrying this vapid-looking angel out to the beach, squatting down beside him, fondling him with his hands and eyes, and raptly murmuring the one word, "Angel." In a world of turmoil and frustration, Giudizio is an image of simple-hearted contentment.

But look at this same Giudizio in "The Clowns" (1970). He has become a mere grotesque, the typical village idiot, whom Fellini's camera examines with cold curiosity as one of those malformations by means of which everyday life impinges on the circus. Finally, in the current "Amarcord," Giudizio has become a laughing stock, a poor harebrain whom the crowd at a spring festival entrap on top of the pyre on which the effigy of winter is about to be burned. They scare Giudizio out of his remaining wits by pretending they'll immolate him, too, and his fear only heightens their hilarity. Notice how Fellini's heart has hardened—not only toward Giudizio, but also, and more importantly, toward his and Fellini's own fellow human beings.

•

Take another festivity: the outdoor wedding feast, a meal consumed somewhere in the open countryside under an awning, or in front of a farmhouse, where a long table is set up, and food and drink are liberally ingested in honor of the newlyweds. "Amarcord" concludes with such a scene, but all it tells us is that the town belle, getting long in the tooth (or, because we are in Italy, broad in the beam), finally marries the likeliest available man: a plain and dull *carabiniere* who, at least, sports a fine uniform. Nothing happens during this entire scene except chitchat, teasing, and a little horseplay; finally the married couple and most of the guests take off, leaving behind a few stragglers, and allowing Fellini to end with a facilely bittersweet dying fall. In "La Strada" (1954), there was a similar al fresco wedding feast, but it served as backdrop to the activities of the main characters, to reveal their troubled, nomadic lives in counterpoint and contrast to the texture of busy yet normal, stationary existence.

Granted, Fellini was always drawn to the excessive, the baroque and bizarre, he nevertheless handled it with taste and control. Take the figure of the fat woman that seems to have haunted his childhood and, apparently, affects him still. I am not thinking of such comic fat women as appear, for instance, in that early comic masterpiece, "The White Sheik" (1952), but of La Saraghina, the woman-mountain, seated before whose rhumba-dancing form the schoolboys of "8½" get their first intimations of female flesh in action. But in "8½" the heaving of that ultra-Rubensian flesh is not dwelt on in extreme close-up, and our noses are not figuratively rubbed in it as the nose of the autobiographical boy-hero of "Amarcord" literally is. In the latter, the fat woman inundates the wide screen with her bared mammoth mammae, between which she imprisons the boy's head, nearly suffocating him as well as nauseating the civilized filmgoer, while around him *hoi polloi* laugh their heads off.

The difference is obvious: La Saraghina was, as Fellini told Charles Thomas Samuels, "sex (as) seen by a child . . . grotesque, but also seductive"; in "Amarcord," her counterpart is merely good for a few belly laughs from those whose stomachs remain unturned. And, furthermore, she becomes an object for kids to masturbate over, in a scene that is particularly tasteless and, in more than one way, heavy-handed. But one can go to any one of Fellini's later films for unending parades of ghastly grotesques, which preponderate especially in "Juliet of the Spirits," "Satyricon," and "Toby Dammit," though such a sequence as the outdoor diners wolfing down their food in "Roma" should not be overlooked either. And this living wax museum of horrors does not even serve a symbolic purpose.

There is in "I Vitelloni" a marvelously funny and humane carnival sequence in which the most clownish of the five drifters, superbly played by Alberto Sordi, gotten up in drag, drunkenly drags after him a huge papier-mâché clown's head. "Come, my beloved *testone*," he apostrophizes it, and the audio-visual pun is perfect. *Testone* means large head, blockhead, and obstinate fellow, all of which Alberto is without facing up to it, and the image of him dragging the symbol of his own folly through the dust behind him is funny and moving without being patronizing or vulgar.

•

But by 1969, in "Satyricon," Fellini allows us to glimpse several times an enor-mous marble head that has no other meaning than its own oddity; in "Amarcord," we get an immense head of Mussolini, a kind of float made of flowers, which, in the fantasy of a porcine boy, opens its flowery mouth to promise him a glorious future. A motif that had a sound psychological, dramatic, and even symbolic raison d'être in an early film is dragged in, later, merely for show, for visual grandiloquence; and, still later, just for a corny gag. If these three heads symbolize anything to me, it is the pitiful decline of Fellini's mind and sensibility.

Quite rightly Peter Harcourt speaks about the "imaginative emptiness of Fellini's later films," of which "Amarcord" is the perfect example. Take, for instance, the much-lauded scene in which the family takes an insane uncle' out of the asylum for an afternoon in the country. The scene has possibilities, but Fellini makes nothing of them. The humor is either, as in much of the rest of the film, puerilely scatological-obscene, or virtually non-existent. Thus the carriage in which they are riding must stop for the uncle to urinate in a field. The comic grandfather (he has earned his comedic stripes earlier by breaking wind and illustrating his sexual prowess with suggestive gestures) joins him in the act, but notices that his son, having failed to unbutton his fly, has befouled himself. There is much pseudo-comic to-do about this, and when the coach finally moves on, we are shown that the horse, too, has left behind a large memento. Now though the audience laps it all up—and the sequence may, indeed, be worthy of the wretched films of a Mel Brooks—does it deserve being called by some reviewers equal or superior to scenes from Fellini's early masterworks?

Is any part of the film worthy of such kudos? When the mad uncle climbs up a tree, keeps shouting he wants a woman, and pelts those who would remove him with pebbles, I begin to wonder by what ingenious and humanly significant device the fellow will be brought down to earth. But the best Fellini can come up with is a midget nun who climbs up into the tree, utters a banality, and, pronto, down comes uncle like a lamb. True, the midget nun is played by a man, as certain normal-size nuns in early Fellini films were played, but does this, even so, make any kind of usable comment? At most, it makes nuns look ridiculous, which is neither germane nor humane.

And so it goes throughout this crude, unfunny film, in which the father, in moments of frenzy, beats his head or tramples his hat, something I thought went out with Chester Conklin or, at the latest, Leon Errol. "Amarcord" is even considered by some misguided souls to make a deep comment on Fascists, by showing them as nothing more than petty, spiteful, and ludicrous; but since just about everyone else in the film is mean and risible, the Fascists end up no different from the good guys. Because both "I Vitelloni" and "Amarcord" deal with the provincial life of Rimini, where Fellini grew up, some reviewers have sacrilegiously bracketed the two films. Yet they are as different as bread and mudpies, the early film dealing sympathetically with human beings, however fallible, and allowing the funny-sad life of the town to emerge through their stories, while the recent movie starts with some abstract notion of The Town, and, as in "Roma" (1972), slaps together some warmed-over autobiography and a few burlesque set pieces into a stillborn self-parody.

Yet the worst thing about "Amarcord" and its immediate predecessors is that the chief joke is human ugliness. Whether it is obese women displaying their behinds on bicycles, a ridiculous-looking uncle (another one) making himself more obviously repugnant by sporting a hairnet, a female Goliath using her naked bosom as a weapon, a family dinner scene in which almost all the faces, even those of the youngsters, are profoundly unprepossessing, a school in which every teacher is some kind of puppet or gargoyle, a town populated mostly with freaks, or saddest of all, a little schoolgirl whose homeliness is paraded about as a source of delicious mirth—the joke is always on humanity, and almost always on the easiest, cheapest, and, finally, most witless level.

There is no denying that witty satire thrives on savaging mankind, but where in "Amarcord" is there witty satire? Alternatively, where is compassion? Even the figure of the whore, whom Fellini used to depict with almost excessive, often sentimental, sympathy, has become a ghoulish, nymphomaniacal madwoman, wallowing in a crude parody of autoeroticism. Time was when Fellini could tell the journalist Anita Pensotti that he had to make movies in an atmosphere of fun, confidence, and enthusiasm. More recently, he told Charles Thomas Sam-

Magali Noel acts the town temptress in "Amarcord."

uels that his films were tormenting imps to be got rid of, that "the sign I have to make a film is given by my hatred of it." The hatred, alas, extends to all humankind, and, lacking the wit of a Swift or Voltaire, the best Fellini can look forward to is equaling the dismal record of Ken Russell.

And to think that this once great artist is still only 54; an age at which one hasn't even earned the right to the excuse of senility.

1974 N 24, II:17:1

THE THREE STOOGES FOLLIES: "Violent Is the Word for Curly" (1936); "Yes, We Have No Bonanza" (1934) and "You Natzy Spy" (1941) with Moe Howard, Larry Pine and Curly Howard. Also the Krazy Kat Cartoon "Crystal Gazabo", (1931), Vera Vague in "Strife of the Party" (1946); Buster Keaton in "Nothing but Pleasure" (1938); "Batman," Chapter One (1943) and "America Sings With Kate Smith" (1943). Edited for theatrical presentation by Columbia Pictures. At the Sutton Theater, Third Avenue and 57th Street.

By NORA SAYRE

Old boffolas are apt to age well—partly because the slapstick of previous periods almost always seems endearingly naive, and that makes an audience feel worldly, even superior. While the Three Stooges weren't our leading national wits, it's a pleasure to see them bashing skulls and tweaking noses while falling about like small children unaccustomed to ice skates. "The Three Stooges Follies," which includes other shorts of the nineteen-thirties and forties, is now playing at the Sutton Theater.

Many of the gags in brief movies depend on desperate or urgent situations that must be coped with immediately—such as restoring a drunken stranger to her Hide-a-Bed, or having to knock your neighbors out with a frying pan or building a fire under a friend who's been frozen stiff. Lines essential to the action are "Gentlemen, I demand an explanation!" and "What's the meaning of this?"

The Stooges tended toward jokes about mothers-in-law, mustard plasters, stingy Scottish landlords, creamy pies, Mexican jumping beans, bubble gum, belches, baggy pants vs. tall silk hats, liquids that get squirted in all directions and Hitler. "You Natzy Spy" (1941) is perhaps their best; it begins with rich businessmen who own munitions plants, complaining, "There's no money in peace. We must start a war!" and builds to some inspired goose-stepping. And I'll remain indebted to the Stooges for the intelligence that "cackle fruit"

meant eggs, and for one particular exchange: "Why have we no lions?" "Because there's no bones in ice cream."

A Krazy Kat cartoon (1931) also dwells on the theme of outfoiling others, and a similar struggle for survival is reflected in "Nothing but Pleasure" (1938), in which Buster Keaton is more animated than usual. (Who else could assure his skeptical wife that life is about to become delightful with such a sprightly lack of conviction?) It's not his greatest performance, but he tumbles over and among large stationary objects with his usual grace and makes a casserole to which he adds a pumpkin and a bunch of grapes but pensively extracts a kitten.

Vera Vague is equally disaster-prone in "Strife of the Party," (1946); her fingers stick in locks, appliances knock her to the ground, and she has an affinity for collapsible laundry racks. In fact, throughout "Follies," Americans appear to be the most incompetent, uncoordinated people on earth, and there's an exhilarating glimpse of Batman and Robin fighting clumsily in their capes. Though their teamwork was meant to "strike terror to the heart of many a swaggering denizen of the underworld," they seem much less formidable than the Stooges.

The awkward duo battles with "shifty-eyed Japs"—who plan to free the "enslaved American people" and then re-enslave them—in a flurry of racist propaganda that could never pass the censor now. And there's a subsidiary fascination in

parts of this program: Lines or images projected in the name of wartime patriotism reek of a crudity that's quite astounding today. In "America Sings With Kate Smith," shots of marching helmets and bayonets accompany her renditions of "The Caissons Go Rolling Along" and "From the Halls of Montezuma." In conclusion, she sings "America, I love you . . . Just like a little baby—Climbing its mother's knee." An infant symbolizing our nation promptly appears on the screen; as Miss Smith's glowing affirmation envelops us all, you can't help wondering what that baby's up to now.

1974 N 25, 37:6

MURDER ON THE ORIENT EXPRESS, directed by Sidney Lumet; screenplay by Paul Dehn, based on the novel by Agatha Christie; produced by John Brabourne and Richard Goodwin; edited by Anne V. Coates; director of photography, Geoffrey Unsworth; music, Richard Rodney Bennett; distributed by Paramount Pictures. Running time: 127 minutes. At the Coronet Theater Third Avenue near 59th Street. This film has been rated PG.
Hercule Poirot..............Albert Finney
Mrs. Hubbard...........Lauren Bacall
Bianchi..................Martin Balsam
Greta Ohlsson...........Ingrid Bergman
Countess Andrenyi.....Jacqueline Bisset
Pierre Paul Michael...Jean-Pierre Cassel
Colonel Arbuthnot.........Sean Connery
Beddoes................John Gielgud
Princess Dragomiroff......Wendy Hiller
Hector McQueen.......Anthony Perkins
Mary Debenham .....Vanessa Redgrave
Hildegarde Schmidt.....Rachel Roberts
Ratchett...........Richard Widmark
Count Andrenyi............Michael York
Hardman................Colin Blakely
Dr. Constantine.......George Coulouris
Foscarelli................Denis Quilley

By VINCENT CANBY

Had Dame Agatha Christie's "Murder on the Orient Express" been made into a movie 40 years ago (when it was published here as "Murder on

the Calais Coach"), it would have been photographed in black-and-white on a back lot in Burbank or Culver City, with one or two stars and a dozen character actors and studio contract players. Its running time would have been around 67 minutes and it could have been a very respectable B-picture.

"Murder on the Orient Express" wasn't made into a movie 40 years ago, and after you see the Sidney Lumet production that opened yesterday at the Coronet, you may be both surprised and glad it wasn't. An earlier adaptation could have interfered with plans to produce this terrifically entertaining super-valentine to a kind of whodunit that may well be one of the last fixed points in our inflationary universe.

●

The new film, directed by Mr. Lumet and written by Paul Dehn, was made mostly in Britain and on location in France and Turkey. It was shot in color. It runs a bit over two never-flagging hours. And it has the kind of all-star cast that only M-G-M could have afforded 40 years ago.

Like the lovely, extravagantly overemphasized nineteen-thirties' costumes and production designed by Tony Walton, "Murder on the Orient Express" is much less a literal re-creation of a type of thirties movie than an elaborate and witty tribute that never for a moment condescends to the subject.

Setting the tone for the film is Albert Finney's extraordinary performance as Hercule Poirot, Dame Agatha's Belgian detective whose smug, unflappable brilliance

Albert Finney, playing Herculte Poirot, questioning suspects in "Murder on the Orient Express." From left: Jean-Pierre Cassel, Anthony Perkins, Vanessa Redgrave.

Sean Connery, Ingrid Bergman, George Coulouris, Rachel Roberts, Wendy Hiller, Denis Quilley, Michael York, Jacqueline Bisset, Lauren Bacall and Martin Balsam.

makes Sherlock Holmes seem like a hysterical freak. When Hercule first appears in the film, dining with dainty disgust in an Istanbul hotel, one can't even be sure it's really Mr. Finney, so transformed is he by black, patent-leather hair, waxed mustache, portly, middle-aged physique and a musical-comedy French accent that comes and goes, much like the accent of Hercule Poirot in Dame Agatha's books.

The performance is made up of the sort of wildly theatrical overstatements that heretofore only Laurence Olivier, Marlon Brando and, occasionally, Maggie Smith have gotten away with. It's a performance of exaggeration, which is fun to watch both for the goals achieved and the risks taken.

Though to a lesser extent almost all the other stars come on strong and take similar risks: Lauren Bacall as a pushy, garrulous American widow, Ingrid Bergman as a virtually psychotic Swedish nurse-missionary, Rachel Roberts as a very weird German maid, Sean Connery as a stuffy British Army officer, Jacqueline Bisset as a beautiful, preoccupied Hungarian countess, Wendy Hiller as a Russian princess and Jean-Pierre Cassel as an unlikely sleeping-car conductor.

Everyone in the film is very, very busy acting (which is about the only clue one should give about the plot), and one shouldn't be put off by the fact that some of the actors have acted similar roles before, especially Anthony Perkins (as a possibly homicidal man of indeterminate youth), John Gielgud (as a fastidious valet), Vanessa Redgrave (as a coolly passionate English beauty) and Richard Widmark (as a ruthless American millionaire).

For the record I must say how much I also liked Martin Balsam, Michael York, Colin Blakely, George Coulouris and Denis Quilley. It's a movie in which everyone is important to its success.

Some purposely vague details about the story: the time is the mid-nineteen-thirties, five years after a notorious case of kidnapping on Long Island (detailed in a fine precredit sequence), and it is set aboard the Orient Express, the crack train that went from Istanbul to Calais, with stops at Zagreb, Trieste and other points in between. The murder, which is committed the second night out, is solved by Hercule Poirot in the time it takes to dig the train out of a huge Balkan snowdrift but not before absolutely everyone has come under suspicion and all identities have been scrambled.

In addition to being the sort of mystery that treats death as a largely goreless inconvenience, an intellectual riddle to be solved as politely as possible, clue by clue, "Murder on the Orient Express" recalls that innocent, pre-Amtrak time when the Orient was still mysterious and railroad travel was full of exotic possibilities. (I suspect that because it took so long to get from one place to another on trains in those days, the places arrived at were invested with a magic that has since been lost, but that's another subject entirely.)

My only quarrel with the film is a minor one: There is too much music on the soundtrack. Especially when the train is under way I miss hearing, loud and clear, the rhythmical, monotonous, wheel-on-rail clickety-clack that I associate with such great moments of childhood as "The Lady Vanishes" and my first overnight trip in a Pullman berth.

1974 N 25, 38:1

The Program

NEW AMERICAN DOCUMENTARIES: 5 PORTRAITS OF MEN: EDDIE by Laurence Salzmann and Peter Barton, 16 minutes; **HAMPTON** by Paul Justman and Andrew Dintenfass, 29 minutes; **EL MOJADO** by Danny Lyon, 20 minutes; **WILD YEAST** by Roger Phenix, 8 minutes; **QUARRY** by Richard Rogers, 11 minutes. At the Film Forum, 256 West 88th Street. Showings: tomorrow through Sunday and Dec. 5-8 at 8 P.M.

By NORA SAYRE

The lives depicted in "New American Documentaries: 5 Portraits of Men" range from the miseries of helpless destitution to the pleasures of a voluntary vagabond. This very rewarding program, which concentrates on outcasts and outlaws, opens with the grimmest material and ends with the most cheerful; because of the sequence, the films all enhance one another. The documentaries are playing at the Film Forum at 256 West 88th Street tomorrow through Sunday and Dec. 5-8.

"Eddie," by Laurence Salzmann and Peter Barton, follows an elderly Irish alcoholic who's about to be evicted from his room in a welfare residency hotel on Manhattan's Upper West Side. At moments, he's sarcastic, self-mocking—at others, lost and weeping. His slurred voice explains that he has nowhere to go. Ejected, rejected, he panhandles and totters through the streets; he protests that he doesn't want to die, even though "I don't want to stomach any more."

•

"Hampton," by Paul Justman and Andrew Dintenfass, dwells on a survivor: an old black plumber living in a neighborhood of Philadelphia that's being demolished around him. Battered and half toothless, he still has a wry resiliency. The film makers, whose approach is cautious, almost timid, also interview others who dwell amid the rubble, and there's a fine passage in which young boys discuss how aging men become "bums"—while the latter hunch over fires in empty lots. Hampton, in the thick of his poverty, speaks very touchingly of his dead wife, with whom he "lived like a king"; she was "the best thing I ever had. Money don't mean as much as she did to me."

"El Mojado" (meaning "The Wetback") by Danny Lyon, focuses on a Mexican laborer in this country, and the efforts of the border patrol to trap illegal entrants. (One official enthusiastically says that it's like being a hunter, "but you're stalking human beings, and that's a lot more fun.") The film skillfully records the tension of the interviews at the border, and the surprisingly high spirits that radiate from some Mexicans who are living and working here now.

•

"Quarry," by Richard Rogers, evokes the atmosphere around a former marble quarry in Quincy, Mass., a refuge where young men and boys swim, play cards, chat and unwind. Rather like a neighborhood pub, it's a place to gather, relax, and drink beer—only it happens to be out of doors. Some recall fighting "Charlie Cong" in Vietnam, others muse on work and marriage. Beautiful shots of their diving bodies float in slow motion to music from transistors; the songs of the mid-sixties, such as "Hang On, Snoopy" and "Gonna Get Married" remind us that psychedelia and the antiwar movement were still utterly remote from youthful working-class people. This is a sympathetic view of mid-America, and the attitude is subtly reinforced by the elegant sensitivity of the camera work.

"Wild Yeast," by Roger Phenix, concerns a wanderer (Keith Yingling) who writes and sings the exuberant songs that grace the soundtrack; he's also a countryside garbage collector. Relishing the footloose life, which relies on some voluntary austerity, he also jokes about renting a South Sea island and living in a mansion with gold doorknobs. On the lam from the middle class, he reflects that "It's hard to be honest and not be a fugitive." His ease and lightness echo with the freedoms that seemed so accessible a few years ago, before the economic angst descended, and the movie makes you hope that he's still unfettered.

1974 N 28, 45:1

Glossy Thriller Arrives at New Yorker

When Alfred Hitchcock discussed cinematic logic with Francois Truffaut, he referred to certain plots that provoke "that old complaint: 'But why didn't he tell the police about it?'" Etienne Perier's "A Murder . . . Is a Murder," which opened yesterday at the New Yorker Theater, is one of those pictures where you grow exasperated because the hero is so police-shy — to a degree that isn't justified by the threadbare script. It's the old was - it - accident - or - murder formula, but the very predictable alternatives are ungripping.

Jean-Claude Brialy is liberated and enriched by the sudden death of his unpleasant wife, but his relief is brief, since her nearly identical sister promptly moves into his house, calls him a killer, impersonates the dead woman and proceeds to go bananas. Meanwhile, he's blackmailed by a man who claims to have "executed" the departed. No wonder there are so few smiles throughout this glum and glossy French thriller. Mr. Brialy conveys taut marital loathing and then bitterly asserts his innocence mainly by narrowing his eyes and clenching his jaw; since he plays a colorless person, you can't feel much for him.

Stephane Audran is miscast in the dual role of wife and sister. Lunacy is simply not her style, and whether she's being stern and dour, or spiteful and hysterical, she remains wooden. Robert Hossein, as the blackmailer, is by far the best in this distinguished but ill-served cast: although he has been directed to unleash too many knowing smiles, he's deft at masquerading, which is his technique for manipulating others.

The plot carries more than a whiff of Hitchcock's "Strangers on a Train," and it powerfully reeks of the influence of Claude Chabrol's movies. There's a small, endearingly self-conscious appearance by Mr. Chabrol, who seems compelled to mug all over the screen.) But the narrative is innocent of surprises, and even the props are clichés: a wheelchair gleams and squeaks with mechanical menace, and thick leather gloves inform you of sinister intentions. The incredibly raucous soundtrack is probably intended to supply the excitement that's otherwise lacking: telephones and doorbells and car horns ring the roof down, and that wheelchair is even noisier than the late Third Avenue El.

NORA SAYRE

The Cast

A MURDER IS A MURDER . . . IS A MURDER, directed by Etienne Perier; screenplay (French with English subtitles) by Dominique Fabre and Mr. Perier; photographer, Marcel Grignon; music, Paul Misraki; produced by J-C Roblin and Adolphe Viezzi; a Peel Properties Associates Presentation; distributed by the Levitt-Pickman Film Corporation. At the New Yorker Theater, Broadway and 88th Street. Running time: 90 minutes. This film has not been classified.

Paul	Jean-Claude Brialy
Marie-Anne	Stephane Audran
Carouse	Robert Hossein
The Commissaire	Michel Serrault
Francoise	Catherine Spaak

1974 N 28, 47:2

THE ALIENIST (O Alienista), directed and produced by Nelson Pereira Dos Santos; screenplay (Portuguese with English subtitles) by Mr. Dos Santos, based on the novel by Machado De Assis; director of photgorphy, Dib Luffi; editor, Rafael Valverde; music, Guicherme Magalhaes Vaz; distributed by New Yorker Films. Running time: 88 minutes. At the First Avenue Screening Room, near 61st Street. This film has not been rated.

Priest	Nildo Parente
Dona Evarista	Isabel Ribeiro
Druggist's wife	Leila Diniz

By VINCENT CANBY

Nelson Pereira Dos Santos, at the age of 46, can be called the grand old man of Brazil's now largely defunct Cinema Novo, that movement of socially and politically conscious young film makers that flourished so briefly in the nineteen-sixties. Mr. Dos Santos's "The Alienist," which was made in 1970, belongs to the final phase of Cinema Novo in style if not in fact (his 1971 film, "How Tasty Was My Little Frenchman," was shown here last year).

•

"The Alienist" is like many other Cinema Novo films, made after the right-wing swing of the Brazilian Government forced the militant film makers to adopt forms that could be called more truly nationalistic and that were also, conveniently, so disguised within metaphors that their content would elude almost everybody.

"The Alienist," which will be shown at noon and midnight at the First Avenue Screening Room today and tomorrow, is not uninterest-

'Green Hornet,' From Bruce Lee Series

"The Green Hornet," which opened yesterday at the New Amsterdam and other theaters, is three installments of the mid-sixties TV series stitched together and prefaced with footage from the late Bruce Lee's screen test.

Mr. Lee, who played Kato, the kung fu artist and faithful houseboy to the Green Hornet (Van Williams), gets star billing now as the result of the huge popularity of the kung fu films he made in Hong Kong before his death last year.

He looks very young, very clean-cut and very American (in an oriental sort of way), and he does his kung fu stuff with grace. The three narratives are low camp, lacking the verve and humor that often distinguished the "Batman" series. The program is 83 minutes long and rated PG. Twentieth Century-Fox is the distributor.

VINCENT CANBY.

1974 N 28, 47:2

ing to look at but it is less interesting to read than the installation instructions that come with a pair of traverse curtain rods. The movie's Portuguese dialogue is translated by English subtitles that, I assume, do not do justice to the original, but I have no real way of knowing.

The film seems to be about what happens to a small Brazilian town in the early 19th century when an obsessed young priest decides to study lunacy to be able to relate lunacy to reason, which he describes as the pearl within the shell of the skull. Little by little he succeeds in luring just about everybody into his asylum. There are then reversals of reversals, when it is decided the sane world should be in the asylum, and the lunatics outside.

The asylum is, I suspect, Brazil and the idiocies, dangerously well-meaning, of the alienist - priest may make sense to someone familiar with Brazilian social and political history. To an outsider, the form of the film is unbearably facetious.

Mr. Dos Santos, known here principally for the poetic realism of his "Vidas Secas," composes this film as a fantastic carnival, with lots of splashy costumes, discordant music, Fellini - like processions and windy confrontations that are probably meant to be both comic and significant, though they struck me as neither.

1974 N 29, 48:1

FILM VIEW

VINCENT CANBY

Who Ever Thought Lenny Would Be Respectable?

Don't take away my words." The plea comes somewhere near the end of "Lenny" when Lenny Bruce (Dustin Hoffman), America's most revolutionary "name" comic, is almost at obscenity bust and so obsessed with the idiocies the end of his rope, fighting still another of the world that he succeeds in merely sabotaging his own defense. "Don't take away my words," Lenny says almost tearfully to the judge and Lenny's goose is cooked. He is finished. Washed up. Ready to O.D. Lenny's words had somehow gotten out of hand. They were no longer symbols of casual irreverence, rudeness, and disaffection, things to be strung together to make banners for the alienated, passports to underground cultures.

Words—four-letter, five-letter, 10-letter—had become weapons, and to make them weapons there had to be a certain amount of collusion on the part of Lenny and the people who were out to put him away. They had to *agree* that words could hurt, that they were dangerous. There had to be collusion between Lenny and his time.

We once used to think that ideas could be dangerous. Lenny found—as did the demonstrators in Chicago in 1968—that words had replaced ideas. Sometimes the words were the shorthand for ideas. Most of the time they were simply the hieroglyphs for positions taken, displayed like bumper stickers and T-shirts.

•   •   •

This helps to explain, I think, why Lenny Bruce, who died in 1966 two months before his 41st birthday, is now becoming something of a mass-market hero.

Nothing I've read about him ("Ladies and Gentlemen, Lenny Bruce!!", the full-scale biography by Albert Goldman and Lawrence Schiller, as well as dozens of reminiscences by people who knew him when), nothing I've heard by him, including the recordings of his nightclub acts and his Carnegie Hall show, and nothing I've seen, including "Lenny" and the "Lenny Bruce Performance Film," a filmed record of one of his last nightclub

appearances, can easily explain the phenomenon that now seems to be taking place.

Lenny Bruce was a very funny, very talented stand-up comedian but he was never a great wit. His targets weren't too different from other comedians', including Mort Sahl's (whom Lenny found terribly square) and his manner of freely associating ideas is primitive alongside Woody Allen's. The man himself hardly comes across as lovable, though his involvement with narcotics agents to the extent that he was forced to squeal on pushers and dealers and may have turned in his own wife (something seldom talked about) gives his story a truly tragic shape, the sort, however, that isn't likely to make him a mass-market hero.

What is making Lenny more or less respectable today?

Dustin Hoffman as "Lenny," and the real Lenny Bruce with his family

I suspect it's those words that the court was trying to take away from him.

In some ways times have changed radically since Lenny's obscenity trials in the early sixties and in other ways not at all. We have pornographic films playing freely in many parts of the country. Some of the words that so offended police officers in San Francisco and New York when Lenny said them can now be heard in movies rated PG. They are heard so frequently that even though they may not be printed very often in newspapers, they have been effectively defused as weapons. Defused they are but they continue to carry impact as the still-warm shell-casings of ammunition fired in a battle not very long ago. That battle is so respectable now it's almost forgotten.

In 1966, the year Lenny died, the guardians of public morals feared the worst with the release of the film version of "Who's Afraid of Virginia Woolf?" Well, a lot

Four-letter words were his weapon.

of them said (wrongly, of course), this is one film that will never be seen on television! That was in the last days of the old Production Code, which had to be so wrenched to accommodate the film that it was abandoned two years later.

In December of 1966, Andy Warhol's "The Chelsea Girls" opened in New York and demonstrated that not even subversive language combined with subversive images would bring down the wrath of the blue-coats if they weren't goaded into action. More importantly, "The Chelsea Girls" made a lot of money, something duly noted by the kind of respectable movie producers who fight for the freedom of the screen when it suits their purposes.

Lenny made a big thing about the gap between public morality and private morality, and the sad thing about his last, harassed years is that they were already much closer together than anyone would have believed. As late as three years ago former President Nixon was shaking his head sadly that such a wonderful movie as "Love Story" would have to be tainted by Ali MacGraw's use of "that word," which subsequently turned up with some frequency in the Watergate tapes. However, in language as in politics, Nixon was one of the last to understand just what the public was on to.

"Lenny" is probably the perfect popular movie for this time and place. The language and subject matter of Lenny's routines are just raunchy enough to titillate without inspiring real fury. Furthermore Dustin Hoffman is superb in these "on-stage" sections of the film, not imitating Lenny so much as creating the essential myth of the man. (Just how good he is can be seen in comparing Hoffman's Lenny with Lenny's Lenny in the fascinating "Lenny Bruce Performance Film." The two don't clash but complement each other.)

"Lenny" is otherwise a fairly unfocused film biography, skirting Lenny's drug problems so delicately that one might get the idea he died solely because of his obscenity busts. The supporting performances by Valerie Perrine as Lenny's wife, Honey, and Jan Miner as his mother, Sally Marr, are straitjacketed by material that treats the characters as hardly more than somewhat eccentric. Bob Fosse, the director, makes effective use of the sleezy backstage atmosphere, but atmosphere doesn't make an entire movie.

In compensation we have those on-stage sequences, which account for about one-fourth of the film. They are important and timely. They remind us of the mysterious properties of words.

1974 D 1, II:17:1

Text of the Wedekind Play Is Butchered

By NORA SAYRE

Occasionally, there's a movie that almost bestows a lifelong allergy to close-ups. After watching the huge faces awash with repressed emotions or the great meaningless grins and mild scowls in Stephen Dwoskins's "Death and Devil," you may never again want to see a mug that's larger than your own. The movie, which opened yesterday at the Whitney Museum of American Art and will run through Tuesday, is "based on" the play by Frank Wedekind (1864-1918). Aside from butchering the text, the director has achieved a style of camerawork that results in a riot of dullness.

During the film, a woman debates the historical oppression of women with a mysterious elderly man; she denounces sex, he extols it, From time to time, the camera visits another woman who's referred to as a joyful sensualist; however, she says that she has never found happiness in love.

The whole exercise remains stolidly obscure, until you consult Wedekind's play itself—which reveals that the action occurs in a brothel, that the man is a pimp, that much of the discussion is actually about prostitution, that both women are masochists, and above all, that Mr. Dwoskin has garbled

The Program

DEATH AND DEVIL, a film by Stephen Dwoskin; based on the play "Tod und Teufel" by Frank Wedekind; distributed by Monument Film Corporation. Running time: 90 minutes. This film has not been classified. At the Whitney Museum of American Art, Madison Avenue and 75th Street. Through Tues. WITH: Carola Regnier, Charles Regnier, Ulla Larrson, Mathias von Spallart.

many lines out of context. (He's cut a few details as well, such as a climactic suicide and a passionate declaration of love.)

Such a garrulous play needs to be acted at high speed, but Mr. Dwoskin has directed his zombified performers to pause between each sentence. Although the delivery of the dialogue is triumphantly static, the film's at its worst when the talking heads fall silent.

Throughout, the camera rarely stops moving, though its pace is sluggish; it wanders over the vast faces, isolating a few features at a time. Pores and nostrils are carefully examined, and Mr. Dwoskin has an affection for collarbones and foreheads. For variation, we finally get a shot of an ear. In a speechless sequence, one character opens and closes her mouth very slowly, and it's a dramatic event when someone blinks.

There's a lot of human humming and metallic whining on the soundtrack, noises

that may be intended to suggest fulfillment or frustration. Meanwhile, it's safe to assume that the director is interested in women; however, his interest isn't interesting.

1974 D 5, 57:1

Molinaro Directs an Action Thriller

By NORA SAYRE

Building apprehension in an audience requires a particular skill; quite often, we need to be nervous about the combination of personalities and their sudden responses to one another, their capacity for violence of craziness, in order to give a hoot about who gets chased or shot. Edouard Molinaro's "The Hostages," playing today and tomrrow at the First Avenue Screening Room, is an unusually intelligent action picture, partly because it stresses how dangerous a self-destructive persons can be.

The movie is based on a recent case in France. A drifter with a fearfully short fuse falls in and out of

The Program

THE HOSTAGES (La Gang des Hostages), directed by Edouard Molinaro; written (French with English subtitles) by Alphonse Boudard; photographed by Raoul Coutard; music, Michel Legrand; produced by Gaumont Distribution. At the First Avenue Screening Room, at 61st Street. Running time: 90 minutes. This film has not been classified. Showings today and tomorrow at noon and midnight. WITH: Bulle Ogier, Daniel Cauchy and Gilles Segal.

prison; between assaults and armed robberies, he marries a call girl and the hold-ups continue until they're arrested. Then, they take a judge hostage to bargain for their release. Their ruthless teamwork has none of the sentimentally that oozed through "Bonnie and Clyde." Here, the tension between the hard-headed practicality and the extreme carelessness of the outlaws yields an intriguing characterization.

Daniel Cauchy and Bulle Ogier are first-rate as the pair on the prowl. His forlorn yet ominous stare, or the fey, ingratiating smiles that surface when he pulls a weapon or gets nabbed, established the deadly unpredictability of his character. Meanwhile, she's deceptively cherubic; that sweet little face masks a completely brutal nature. This beguiling waif is even more lethal than her husband, even though he's crazed and she is not.

The plot thins in invention toward the end, so the suspense is muted. But there are many fine details, including a scene where some hoods devastate a bar with gaudy spray paint, to punish the proprietor. And I liked the man who's reluctant to surrender his beloved new car to the famous fugitives; as he protests that it's not broken in, that the monthly payments aren't finished, it's clear that his wheels are more important to him than his life. It's that kind of deft absurdity that gives "The Hostages" its special dimensions.

1974 D 6, 32:1

FILM VIEW

VINCENT CANBY

The Thirties Through Rose-Colored Glasses

The nineteen-thirties *did* exist. At long last moviemakers have gotten around to certifying this fact, and with a vengeance. It used to be that people who were responsible for the production of films were only at ease in period films if they were about the Roaring Twenties and the Gay Nineties. Then they loosened up. They began to remember the Forties, the Fifties and even the Sixties. The Thirties were always there, of course, but except for isolated films, the Thirties were years most filmmakers avoided.

It was the Dim Decade of the Depression, bread lines, unemployment, the short-lived National Recovery Act, the Spanish Civil War, and saying in farewell not "so long" but "Abyssinia," thus jauntily to acknowledge the collapse of Ethiopia as well as of the League of Nations, though nobody much cared at the time.

Now, more or less suddenly, the Thirties have become fashionable. Romantic, really, and to anyone who remembers them at all vividly, it's a little like listening to someone describe the flyswatter as a piece of folk art.

I suspect that this phenomenon actually began with the critical and boxoffice triumph of Arthur Penn's "Bonnie and Clyde," the first film that simultaneously dealt honestly with the Thirties and put them at such a distance that we could feel some kind of romantic identification that was not threatening or depressing. We had to be sort of *eased* into the Thirties, however. It's no accident that Faye Dunaway's Bonnie looks a lot less like someone out of the Thirties than Faye Dunaway's mysterious widow in "Chinatown," one of this year's batch of Thirties movies. In 1967—the year of "Bonnie and Clyde"—no actress in her right mind would be caught dead wearing the frizzled Thirties look. Today it's chic.

Just how far we've come in accepting the Thirties (and, in so doing, distorting them to fit our current mood) is apparent in Sidney Lumet's hugely successful, all-star screen version of Dame Agatha Christie's "Murder on The Orient Express," a whodunit set in its own time (the mid-Thirties when it was first published) with a lavishness of talent and an eye for period detail heretofore reserved for epics on the order of "Dr. Zhivago."

When you go see "Murder on The Orient Express" I doubt very much if you'll be reminded of bank holidays, Samuel Insull, marathon dance contests or the rise of Mussolini and Hitler. You may remember the Lindberg kidnapping (a fictional variation on which is used as the plot's point of departure), but mostly you'll remember Hollywood's Golden Age of super stars acting in movies of total escapism. Twenty or maybe even 10 years ago, a film production of "Murder on The Orient Express" would have been yanked out of the Thirties and somehow wrenched into the shape of a (probably idiotic) movie of the Fifties or Sixties.

• • •

The success of Bernardo Bertolucci's "The Conformist" (1970) may well have had something to do with our new willingness to accept films of the Thirties. Behind the political bleakness and the economic frustrations of the Thirties, Bertolucci discovered sexual decadence and made it look marvelously photogenic. It was also so classily done that we didn't have to compromise our critical faculties to see it all as a metaphor for the rise of fascism in Mussolini's Italy.

The way European directors have shot films about the Thirties, the period has come to look remarkably lush, even erotic, which has as much to do with the quality of the color (very rich, brilliant reds, as in the lipstick worn by the actresses, glowy whites and silvers, as in the hair of women imitating Jean Harlow's dye job) as it has to do with costumes, props and the art deco interiors. Though they are very different sorts of films, Federico Fellini's "Amarcord," Alain Resnais'. "Stavisky" and Lina Wertmuller's "Love and Anarchy" really do look alike. The similarity between "Amarcord" and "Love and Anarchy" may be explained by the fact that both were photographed by Giuseppe Rotunno, but I think the real point is that moviemakers have found that they (and we) can only accommodate the truths of the Thirties by presenting them as romantically as possible. This works best in the Fellini film, which is designed to have the softened contours of a dream.

• • •

There is something of this same dreamlike quality in the Thirties as seen in George Roy Hill's "The Sting." The film is so dreamlike, in fact, that the period details suggest the Twenties and the pre-World War I Teens as easily as the Thirties. When filmmakers have emphasized the bitterness and hopelessness of the times, as Robert Altman did in "Thieves Like Us" and Sydney Pollack did in "They Shoot Horses, Don't They," the public hasn't been as keen to respond. Only one successful American film I can think of, Peter Bogdanovich's "Paper Moon," had the physical look of the Thirties as I remember them, but that hardluck landscape was effectively rendered benign by the sentimental activities that took place within it.

Bacall, Dunaway and 30's chic

"Murder on The Orient Express" looks no more like any movie actually made in the Thirties than a 747 looks like a DC-3. It is, instead, a terrifically entertaining homage to a classic kind of fiction so popular in the Thirties, the largely bloodless murder-mystery involving a small group of people temporarily isolated from the rest of the world. It's a movie of disguises, accumulated clues, sudden changes of identity and bigger-than-life gestures (including those of the very busy actors, especially Albert Finney as Hercule Poirot, Lauren Bacall, Ingrid Bergman, Anthony Perkins, Jacqueline Bisset, Vanessa Redgrave and Sean Connery). It's superb fun, but I'd caution anyone who sees it and sheds a tear for the, dear departed innocent Thirties to remember the Santayana line, quoted in the preface to "Lacombe, Lucien": "Those who cannot remember the past are condemned to repeat it." Could that possibly be what we're doing now?

1974 D 8, II:15:1

A FILM ABOUT A WOMAN WHO .. Directed and written by Yvonne Rainer; photogra her, Babette Mangolte. At the Whitney Museum of American Art, Madison Avenue and 75th Street. Running time: 105 minutes. This film has not been classified. Through Dec 17.

By NORA SAYRE

Themes of seduction and death, jealousy and rejection, swirl through Yvonne Rainer's "Film About A Woman Who. . . ." along with sexual fantasies and frustrations, and the movie dwells on failures of all stripes. Miss Rainer, known for her "postmodern" choreography and performance pieces, seems less at home with the medium of film. Narrated by a woman and a man, whose voices are often assisted by printed titles, the movie unleashes a series of woolly images and brief scenes. The work has all the earnestness of some of the early happenings of years ago, on those occasions when comedy or absurdity was absent. The film opened yesterday at the Whitney Museum of American Art and will run through Dec. 17.

•

There's a stolidity about this movie—the free associations don't manage to be very free. The highlights include some rather stately love making, a rerun of stills (plus a denunciation) of Janet Leigh's murder in "Psycho," a couple who very, very slowly undress a passive woman, many hostile moments, and a long close-up of a woman's face pasted over with bits of newspaper paragraphs—which turn out to be Angela Davis's letters to George Jackson. (What a fate for your private correspondence: to wind up on some stranger's cheeks and chin, while a disembodied voice reads your sentences aloud.) Miss Davis's words are the only ones that convey any enthusiasm about love in this pessimistic movie, which is somberly lit and filmed in stark black and white.

There are some thunderstorms and some beach scenes; Miss Rainer has a nice taste in thunder, which helps to cut through the tedium. Such statements as "In the morning, she is hugely depressed," and "If I were wiser, life might be unbearable," or "She grieves for herself" reinforce the rampant narcissism. No doubt making the film was gratifying for the participants, who include Miss Rainer, but there's little here for an audience to share or experience.

1974 D 12, 58:1

The Cast

THE GODFATHER, PART II, directed and produced by Francis Ford Coppola; screenplay by Mr. Coppola and Mario Puzo, based on Mr. Puzo's novel, "The Godfather"; co-produced by Gary Frederickson and Fred Roos; director of photography, Gordon Willis; music, Nino Rota; editors, Peter Zinner, Barry Malkin, Richard Marks; distributed by Paramount Pictures. Running time: 200 minutes. At Loews State 1 and 2, Broadway at 45th Street, Loews Orpheum and Cine Theaters, 86th Street at Third Avenue, and Loew's Tower East, Third Avenue near 72d Street. This film has been rated R.

Michael	Al Pacino
Tom Hagen	Robert Duvall
Kay	Diane Keaton
Vito Corleone	Robert De Niro
Fredo Corleone	John Cazale
Connie Corleone	Talia Shire
Hyman Roth	Lee Strasberg
Frankie Pentangeli	Michale V. Gazzo
Senator Pat Geary	G. D. SSpradlin
Al Nerl	Richard Bright
Fanucci	Gaston Moschin
Young Clemenza	B. Kirby Jr.
Mama Corleone	Morsana King
Sonny	James Caan

By VINCENT CANBY

The only remarkable thing about Francis Ford Coppola's "The Godfather, Part II" is the insistent manner in which it recalls how much better his original film was. Among other things, one remembers

"The Godfather's" tremendous narrative drive and the dominating presence of Marlon Brando in the title role, which, though not large, unified the film and transformed a super-gangster movie into a unique family chronicle.

"Part II," also written by Mr. Coppola and Mario Puzo, is not a sequel in any engaging way. It's not really much of anything that can be easily defined.

It's a second movie made largely out of the bits and pieces of Mr. Puzo's novel that didn't fit into the first. It's a Frankenstein's monster stitched together from leftover parts. It talks. It moves in fits and starts but it has no mind of its own. Occasionally it repeats a point made in "The Godfather" (organized crime is just another kind of American business, say) but its insights are fairly lame at this point.

"The Godfather, Part II," which opened yesterday at five theaters, is not very far along before one realizes that it hasn't anything more to say. Everything of any interest was thoroughly covered in the original film, but like many people who have nothing to say, "Part II" won't shut up.

•

Not the least of its problems is its fractured form. "Part II" moves continually back and forth in time between two distinct narratives. It's the story of the young Vito Corleone (who grew up to be played by Marlon Brando in the first movie) seen first around the turn of the century in Sicily and then in 1917 in New York, where he's played by Robert De Niro, and it's the story of Vito's son, Michael, played again by Al Pacino, the new Mafia don who sets out to control Las Vegas in the late nineteen-fifties.

One story doesn't necessarily illuminate the other. It's just additional data, like footnotes. I can't readily imagine what Mr. Coppola and Mr. Puzo were trying to do, except to turn their first film into a long parenthesis that would fit between the halves of the new movie.

Even if "Part II" were a lot more cohesive, revealing and exciting than it is, it probably would have run the risk of appearing to be the self-parody it now seems.

Looking very expensive but spiritually desperate, "Part II" has the air of a very long, very elaborate revue sketch. Nothing is sacred. The photography by Gordon Willis, so effective originally, is now comically fancy—the exteriors are too bright and glowy while the interiors are so dark you wonder if these Mafia chiefs can't afford to buy bigger light bulbs.

Nino Rota's old score keeps thumping away like a heavenly juke box. The performers, especially those repeating their original roles, seem locked into waxily rigid attitudes. Mr. Pacino, so fine the

first time out, goes through the film looking glum, sighing wearily as he orders the execution of an old associate or a brother, winding up very lonely and powerful, which is just about the way he wound up before. Mr. De Niro, one of our best young actors, is interesting as the young Vito until, toward the end of his section of the film, he starts giving a nightclub imitation of Mr. Brando's elderly Vito.

•

There are a couple of nottble exceptions. Lee Strasberg, the head of the Actors Studio, makes an extraordinarily effective screen debut as Hyman Roth, the powerful Jewish mobster (reportedly modeled on Meyer Lansky) with whom Michael attempts to take over the Havana rackets under the Battista regime. Mr. Strasberg's Roth is a fascinating mixture of lust, ruthlessness and chicken soup. Michael V. Gazzo, the

playwright ("A Hatful of Rain"), is also superb as a Corleone captain who crosses the Family. Another more or less nonpro, G. D. Spradlin (a former politician, according to publicity sources) is absolutely right as a crooked, very WASPish United States Senator from Nevada.

The plot defies any rational synopsis, but it allows Mr. Coppola, in his role as director, to rework lots of scenes that were done far better the first time: family reunions, shoot-outs, ambushes and occasional dumb exchanges between Don Michael Corleone and his square, long-suffering wife, Kay (Diane Keaton). "Oh, Michael," says the slow-to-take-offense Kay when Michael is about to sew up the Vegas rackets, "seven years ago you told me you'd be legitimate in five years."

"Part II's" dialogue often sounds like cartoon captions.

1974 D 13, 58:1

FILM VIEW

VINCENT CANBY

Home-Made Movie Makes Millions

The average American is a sucker for anything described as home-made. Slap that label on candy, cookies, ice cream, canned soups and even though the American consumer is aware the product was turned out in a kitchen the size of Kankakee, and distributed by an organization as large and complex as General Motors, he'll buy it, no matter what it tastes like. "Home-made" answers a kind of longing. It evokes earlier, safer times when food preservatives didn't cause cancer, when moral codes were supposedly uncomplicated and when it seemed to be possible to get a definite fix on the identities of heroes and villains.

Which helps to explain, I suspect, the staggering response first to "Billy Jack" and now to its sequel, "The Trial of Billy Jack," a blindingly dumb and joyless movie that, according to Variety, earned in the neighborhood of $11,000,000 in its first week of national release in something more than 1,000 theaters.

In at least one respect, "The Trial of Billy Jack" really is home-made. It stars Tom Laughlin in the title role of the Indian half-breed, an amalgam of Jesus, Robin Hood, Cochise and Bruce Lee, and his wife, Delores Taylor, as Billy Jack's long-suffering love, Jean Roberts, the head of the controversial Freedom School. The Laughlins' 16-year-old daughter, Teresa, plays the principal ingenue role, and Frank Laughlin, their 19-year-old son, is listed in the credits as the film's director. The screenplay was written by Frank and Teresa Christina, said to be pseudonyms for the elder Laughlins, and the Taylor-Laughlin Distribution Company is handling the film's initial engagements.

The only thing the Laughlins aren't doing is making the popcorn being sold in the theaters, but I wouldn't be surprised if they're getting a percentage of the sales. Since "The Trial of Billy Jack" runs only slightly less than three hours, the consumption of popcorn should be conspicuous.

The fact that "The Trial of Billy Jack" is a home-made movie does not in itself explain its huge theatrical success, though the film doesn't exactly encourage coherent thinking. How can one easily explain—for example—the tremendous response to "Billy Jack" in its first release in 1971 and in its subsequent reissues at just about the time that President

'Billy Jack and fine-feathered friend

Nixon was winning his landslide victory for reelection in the 1972 campaign? Were the people who were going to see "Billy Jack" also the people who were voting for Nixon?

If so, the country is more schizoid than most of us might have suspected. Or perhaps this is its secret. One of the most important properties of both "Billy Jack" films is the ability to preach simultaneously two or more contradictory messages.

•   •   •

Like the first film, "The Trial of Billy Jack" is a violent film in the cause of non-violence, a revolutionary film that attacks Big Business and Big Government but labels as sophomoric slogans about the class struggle, a film that means to stress the importance of free will though most of the characters are faceless automatons who babble clichés in what are intended to be exchanges of ideas.

The story of the film is almost identical with that of "Billy Jack," though everything has been made bigger and is more ferociously calculated to appeal to people who would like to live in the best of all possible worlds without thinking how to achieve it.

"The Trial of Billy Jack" is told largely in flashback by Miss Taylor who, as Jean Roberts, lies paralyzed in her hospital bed after her school has been attacked by the National Guard in an event meant to recall Kent State. The movie doesn't hesitate to purloin actual events for its own ends, including a Mylai-like massacre, witnessed in a flashback to Vietnam, in which the camera is more concerned with Billy Jack's sadness than with the fate of the villagers.

In the four years since the end of the first film, Miss Taylor tells us, her Freedom School, located on the edge of Arizona's Monument Valley, launched "Nader-like periodicals and newspapers" that so successfully exposed the rascals in business in government that everyone from a local millionaire named Posner to the C.I.A. and the people in the White House joined in a concerted effort to destroy the school.

Chief among the causes of the Freedom School students, who seem to spend even less time in class than did the students in any Mickey Rooney-Judy Garland musical, are child abuse and the rights of American Indians.

The structure of the film is loose enough to allow for short, sincere and nearly always muddled editorials on behalf of these causes, episodes of pure violence, a long, idiotic sequence in which we follow Billy Jack as he goes through an Indian rite to attain his "inner vision" (requiring him to wear, on different occasions, vermillion body paint and royal blue body paint), and several kung fu demonstrations. There's also some folk-singing ("Are you dying just for me, Billy Jack?" asks one of the lyrics).

It's mysticism mixed up with Moral Re-Armament.

The dialogue is sometimes hilariously awful. Some of my favorite lines: "Beware the red-eyed demon" (said to Billy Jack at the beginning of his initiation); "Dr. Ailand, you're a dentist. You took an oath. How can you enjoy this?" (said to a man watching an Indian about to be lynched); and my favorite, which is an exchange between an enquiring reporter and the Freedom School's headmistress. Reporter: "I bet you remember the day Billy Jack got out of prison." Miss Roberts: "I sure do. It was the day we had our first international seminar on child abuse."

What's offensive about the film, however, is something far more subtle—a clean-cut, self-righteous smugness, as well as a pious anti-intellectualism that sometimes sounds suspiciously like the texts parrotted so long by defenders of the now discredited Nixon-Agnew Administration.

1974 D 15, II:19:1

The Cast

LES VIOLONS DU BAL, written, directed and produced by Michel Drach (in French with English subtitles); photography, Yann le Masson and William Lubtchansky; music, Jean Manuel de Scarano and Jacques Monty; a Violons Associates, Ltd., presentation; distributed by Levitt-Pickman Film Corporation. At the Regency Theater, Broadway between 67th and 68th Streets. Running time: 110 minutes. This film has not been classified.

Michel's wife and mother	Marie-Josee Nat
Michel	Jean-Louis Trintignant
The Grandmother	Gabrielle Doulcet
Himself	Michel Drach
Michel, the boy	David Drach
Michel's brother	Christian Rist
Michel's sister	Nathalie Roussel

By NORA SAYRE

For over a year, many movies have been insisting that the past was prettier than the present. But Michel Drach's "Les Violons du Bal"—which nearly drowns you in a cataract of facile charm—is the first picture that seems downright nostalgic about World War II. The film, which was the official French entry at the 1974 Cannes Film Festival, is a huge hit in France. Perhaps the French are grateful for this idylic view of their history, after the painful abrasions of Marcel Ophuls's "The Sorrow and the Pity," Louis Malle's "Lacombe, Lucien," and Michel Mitrani's "Black Thursday," all of which dwell on collaboration with the Germans. The movie opened yesterday at the Regency Theater.

•

The film focuses on the director's childhood during the German occupation of France, when his Jewish family tried to live in hiding and then escaped to Switzerland. Misty shots of handsome people moving gracefully through pastel landscapes make it almost impossible to believe these are fugitives fleeing for their lives. The elegant camera angles, the lovely clothes, the comely faces and the lush colors combine to cancel out the suffering of the French Jews: the movie's style is just too lyrical to convey their desperation or pain. Since their survival seems as miraculous as a fairytale — instead of being rooted in human experience—we can't fear for them when the Germans approach, or when the bullets fly.

In fact, the trouble with this sensitive but shallow movie is that it has bags of style but very little content. And the often-pleasing device of a film within a film only serves to weaken the material: the theme of a director who's determined to make a movie about his boyhood gives the wary potential investor some trenchant lines. The latter is meant to be appallingly commercial when he protests that this movie won't work. He's a cliché figure when he says that it needs to be livelier, that some sex and death would supply the vitality that's lacking. But he happens to be right when he complains about the lack of substance.

Mr. Drach begins by playing himself as the frustrated director; he then does a life-swap with Jean-Louis Trintignant, while Marie-Josée Nat (who's married to Mr. Drach) is cast as his mother as well as herself, and their small son plays Mr. Drach as a child. The present is filmed in cinema vérité style in black and white, and the past wells up in color. Mr. Trintignant has almost no acting to do: he merely responds to "his" memories with sad or fond expressions.

•

Miss Nat, who won the Best Actress award at Cannes for her performance as the totally beloved, utterly magical mother, is very beguiling in a liquid way. But her role is so idealized that we just can't swallow such perfection. The child is engaging: however he has been directed to be too poignant and too winsome, as well as wise beyond his years. All in all, "Les Violons" is one of those movies that's so tasteful it makes you feel boorish—and that's not a useful context for reflecting any kind of war.

1974 D 16, 46:1

The Cast

EMMANUELLE, direced by Just Jaeckin; screenplay (French with English subtitles) by Jean-Louis Richard, based on the novel by Emmanuelle Arsan; director of photography, Richard Suzuki; film editor, Claudine Bouchet; produced by Yves Rousset-Rouard; a co-production of Trinacra Film and Orphee Productions; released by Columbia Pictures in the United States and Canada. At the Paris Theater, 4 West 58th Street. Running time: 92 minutes. This film is classified X.

Emmanuelle	Sylvia Kristel
Mario	Alain Cuny
Bee	Marika Green
Jean	Daniel Sarky
Ariane	Jeanne Colletin
Marie-Ange	Christine Boisson

By A. H. WEILER

Having arrived in a wave of eroticism-as-art fanfare, "Emmanuelle," France's top box-office blockbuster and the first X-rated feature released here by Columbia, doesn't say a great deal for great expectations. It had its premiere at the Paris Theater yesterday.

As a study of a young wife's amours in high and low Bangkok society, "Emmanuelle" is a fluffy consignment of romantic, slick, soft-core, sexual simulations that is largely uninspired and hardly a revelation to enthusiasts long exposed to the genre.

For the record, "Emmanuelle" stems from the novel of 1957 by Emmanuelle Arsan, whose real identity is still secret. The book was banned by the de Gaulle Government, but eventually it was made available to the public. The film, too, survived a banning by President Georges Pompidou and was released in France last August. And "Emmanuelle" is the first movie made by Just Jaeckin, the director, a 34-year-old former fashion photographer, and Yves Rousset-Rouard, his producer.

Filmed in superb color mostly in and around Bangkok, the script centers on the pretty wife of a young member of the French Embassy. It's difficult to discern whether ennui, the weather, dull diplomatic parties or life at home with her husband in their tropical Xanadu-like estate make her so sexually inquisitive. But Emmanuelle, after recalling a couple of quick liaisons aboard the plane bringing her to Thailand, spends nearly all of her time in a variety of couplings.

You see, Daniel Sarky, as her husband, is a handsome, loving worldly type who has encouraged her to broaden her horizons. So, amid a good deal of nudity, there's a succession of lesbian bouts with Jeanne Colletin as a fading blonde who is her squash partner and whom she doesn't love, and Marika Green, as a statuesque, dominant blond archeologist she adores, but who doesn't really love her.

•

Her husband, on the other hand, is, it seems, a mite jealous too. So, after a trip to a bordello and a rough, sexy encounter with Miss Colletin, he introduces her to Alain Cuny, the elderly but leading sexual educator in French circles. His courses include a trip to an opium den where she is raped, then to a prizefight where she is the prize for the winner and, eventually, to his place where he reveals that sex is best with a third party involved.

Sylvia Kristel, a cherubfaced, leggy Dutch newcomer, is decorative as the seemingly confused but love-hungry Emmanuelle, who, like the other bare women, works diligently at simulating the ecstasies of sex. Unfortunately, Mr. Cuny's tensely serious portrayal of her mentor, awash in a sea of banal philosophizing about love, eroticism and personal relationships, underlines the superficiality of most of what meets the ear and eye.

An exception should be noted, however. The Thai countryside, a vision of authentically exotic greenery, waterfalls and canals raucously alive with native activity, makes a fleeting triumph of reality over fiction.

1974 D 16, 47:5

YOUNG FRANKENSTEIN, directed by Mel Brooks; screenplay by Gene Wilder and Mr. Brooks; produced by Michael Gruskoff; director of photography, Gerald Hirschfeld; music, John Morris; editor, John Howard; distributed by 20th Century-Fox. Running time: 104 minutes. At the Sutton Theater, 57th Street east of Third Avenue. This film has been rated PG.

Dr. Frankenstein	Gene Wilder
Monster	Peter Boyle
Igor	Marty Feldman
Elizabeth	Madeline Kahn
Frau Blucher	Cloris Leachman
Inga	Teri Garr
Inspector Kemp	Kenneth Mars
Herr Falkenstein	Richard Hadyn
Blindman	Gene Hackman

By VINCENT CANBY

He's young. He's clean-cut. He's all-American. You are certain he uses the correct deodorants and after-shave lotions. He has a fiancée who's so fussy about her make-up that when they say good-by, they don't kiss, they gently rub elbows. The young man is a brain surgeon named Dr. Frankenstein, but when a medical student calls him that, he has a fit. "No, no," he screams, "it's pronounced Fron-ken-shteen!" He doesn't want to be confused with his infamous grandfather.

As played by Gene Wilder in Mel Brooks's funniest, most cohesive comedy to date, this Dr. Frankenstein is a marvelous addled mixture of young Tom Edison, Winnie-the-Pooh and your average Playboy reader with a keen appreciation of beautiful bosoms.

•

At this point in time it isn't easy to make fun of Mary Shelley's durable old chestnut about the visionary doctor and the monster to whom he gave life. All of the jokes would seem to have been told. Hammer Productions' "Frankenstein," movies employ deadpan humor. "Andy Warhol's Frankenstein," released this year, was an all-out assault that used wild anachronisms and grotesque special effects.

It would be misleading to describe "Young Frankenstein," written by Mr. Wilder and Mr. Brooks, as astoundingly witty, but it's a great deal of low fun of the sort that Mr. Brooks specializes in. Although it hasn't as many roof-raising boffs as "Blazing Saddles," it is funnier over the long run because it is more disciplined. The anarchy is controlled. Mr. Brooks sticks to the subject, recalling the clichés of horror films of the nineteen-thirties as lovingly as someone remembering the small sins of youth.

Perhaps the nicest thing about "Young Frankenstein" is that one can laugh with it and never feel as if the target film, James Whale's 1931 classic that starred Boris Karloff, is being rudely used.

The new movie, which has Young Frankenstein returning to the family castle and bringing to life a monster played by Peter Boyle, is a horror film compared almost entirely of hilarious interruptions, including the doctor's near-fatal encounter with one of those mysterious bookcases that hides a secret door. It keeps turning around and hitting him in the back.

The doctor is helped in his endeavors by his loyal hunchback servant, Igor pronounced Eye-gor), played by a nervily funny newcomer to films named Marty Feldman; by a pretty blond laboratory assistant (Teri Garr) who recalls (intentionally) every blond starlet who never quite made the big time and, of course, by Mr. Boyle in monster-drag.

Madeline Kahn, one of the best things in "Blazing Saddles," is in top form as the doctor's bossy fiancée who eventually finds sexual fulfillment in the arms of the monster, and Gene Hackman turns up in a pricelessly funny bit as the blind man who befriends the monster and after offering him a cigar carefully lights the monster's thumb.

The high point of the film is a sequence in which the young doctor takes his monster to a medical convention in Bucharest and demonstrates his accomplishment by joining the monster for several choruses of "Puttin' On the Ritz," both dressed nattily in white tie and tails.

"Young Frankenstein," which opened yesterday at the Sutton, was photographed in black and white with fastidious attention to the kind of slightly fake details you'll find only in a studio-made movie over which tremendous care has been taken. It has an affectionate look to it, especially in the laboratory equipment that is said to be a reproduction of the stuff used in the Whale film.

Some of the gags don't work, but fewer than in any previous Brooks film that I've seen, and when the jokes are meant to be bad, they are riotously poor. What more can one ask of Mel Brooks?

1974 D 16, 48:1

THE FRONT PAGE, directed by Billy Wilder; screenplay by Mr. Wilder and I. A. L. Diamond, based on the play by Ben Hecht and Charles MacArthur; produced by Paul Monash; executive producer, Jennings Lang; director of photography, Jordan S. Cronenweth; editor, Ralph E. Winters; music adaptation, Billy May; distributed by Uni-

Jack Lemmon, left, and Walter Matthau

versal Pictures. Running time: 105 minutes. At the Coronet Theater, Third Avenue near 59th Street, and Little Carnegie Theater, 57th Street east of Seventh Avenue. This film has been rated PG.

Hildy Johnson	Jack Lemmon
Walter Burns	Walter Matthau
Mollie Malloy	Carol Burnett
Peggy Grant	Susan Sarandon
Sheriff	Vincent Gardenia
Bensinger	David Wayne
Kruger	Allen Garfield
Earle Williams	Austin Pendleton
Murphy	Charles Durning
Schwartz	Herbert Edelman
Dr. Eggelhofer	Martin Gabel
Mayor	Harold Gould
Jacobi	Cliff Osmond
Rudy Keppler	Jon Korkes
Jennie	Dora Merande

By VINCENT CANBY

It had to happen sooner or later that Billy Wilder, one of the most astringent wits of the American cinema, would make a movie out of "The Front Page," the great nineteen-twenties Chicago newspaper farce by Ben Hecht and Charles MacArthur. No matter that it's been very well made before—in 1931 by Lewis Milestone and in 1940 by Howard Hawks, who turned the play into his own movie classic.

The property is a natural for Mr. Wilder and his screenwriting collaborator, I.A.L. Diamond, who, despite all their comparatively "nice" hits ("Love in the Afternoon," "Some Like It Hot," "The Apartment," and "The Private Life of Sherlock Holmes"), have a special (and, to my mind, very appealing) appreciation for vulgar, brilliant con artists of monumental tackiness.

●

This appreciation has resulted in at least one Wilder movie of such bad taste that its gaffs became its gaudy style ("Kiss Me, Stupid") and in another movie that ranks among their very best, "The Fortune Cookie."

"The Front Page," which opened yesterday at the Coronet and Little Carnegie Theaters, falls somewhere between these two extremes. Even though the mechanics and demands of movie-making slow what should be the furious tempo, this "Front Page" displays a giddy bitterness that is rare in any films except those of Mr. Wilder. It is also, much of the time, extremely funny.

The orginal place and time (Chicago in the late twenties) have been preserved, as well as the principal setting, the press room in Chicago's ancient Criminal Courts Building. The Wilder - Diamond screenplay updates and makes somewhat rougher the original tough-guy dialogue and wisecracks, but the story has not been violated. It's still about the efforts of Chicago's most brilliant, most ruthless managing editor, Walter Burns (Walter Matthau) to keep his star reporter, Hildy Johnson (Jack Lemmon), on the job long enough to cover the impending execution of a poor, shy left - wing innocent whom Chicago's yellow press has turned into a Red Menace from Moscow.

The film contains at least two marvelous performances, Mr. Matthau's snarling, mon-omaniacal editor ("I picked you up when you were nothing—covering Polack weddings on the South Side!") and Austin Pendleton as the condemned revolutionary who got his start stuffing fortune cookies with messages demanding freedom for Sacco and Vanzetti.

Mr. Lemmon is comparatively reserved as the flamboyant Hildy, never quite letting go of his familiar comic personality to become dominated by the lunacies of the farce. He always remains a little outside it, acting.

Carol Burnett has an even tougher time as Molly Malloy, the self-described $2 Clark Street whore who loves Mr. Pendleton. This role may well be impossible, however, since it requires the actress to play for straight melodrama while everyone around her is going for laughs. Two lines sum up the difficulty of the role as they define the spirit of the movie. When Molly, in a desperate effort to save her lover, jumps out the courthouse window to what could be her death, one reporter shakes his head and says, "All whores are a little goofy," while another races to his telephone to report, "Shady lady leaps for love!"

Mr. Wilder has great fun with the period newspaper detail—such as human interest stories about Admiral Byrd and penguins—and admires his various supporting actors to such an extent that he allows them to play as broadly as they could possibly desire. Some are better than others.

I particularly liked Vincent Gardenia as an inefficient sheriff, Martin Gabel as a mad Viennese alienist and David Wayne as a prissy Chicago Tribune reporter, a performance that may bring down the wrath of the Gay Activists Alliance though it seems as much a comment on what was considered funny in the twenties as it is a replayed homosexual stereotype.

The hysteria is not as consistent as one might wish, nor, indeed, as epic as in Mr. Wilder's own "One, Two, Three." The cohesive force is, instead, the director's fondness for frauds, which, I suspect, is really an admiration for people who barrel on through life completely intimidating those who should know better.

1974 D 19, 58:1

THE MAN WITH THE GOLDEN GUN, directed by Guy Hamilton; screenplay by Richard Maibaum and Tom Mankiewicz; editor, Roy Poulton; directors of photography, Ted Moore and Ossie Morris; music, John Barry; produced by Albert R. Broccoli and Harry Saltzman; released by United Artists Corporation. At the Cinerama Theater, Broadway at 47th Street; 86th Street Twin 2, west of Lexington Avenue, and the 59th Street Twin 1 and 2, east of Third Avenue. Running time: 125 minutes. This film is classified PG.

James Bond	Roger Moore
Scaramanga	Christopher Lee
Mary Goodnight	Britt Ekland
Nick Nack	Herve Villechaize

By NORA SAYRE

The throbbing information that "the energy crisis is still with us" isn't what you need or want to learn from a James Bond picture. But that poverty of invention and excitement characterizes Guy Hamilton's "The Man With the Golden Gun," which opened yesterday at neighborhood theaters.

The movie, which also explains that "coal and oil will soon be depleted," sets Bond in pursuit of a missing device that converts solar energy into electricity Bored already? That was predictable, Even Kingsley Amis, a great admirer of the late Ian Fleming, spoke of "the over-all inferiority" of the writer's last novel, and this movie is doggishly faithful to its model.

There's a male villain with three nipples, but you can't milk much plot out of that— or them. Amid the general lack of gumption, Roger Moore's large rigid figure appears to be wheeled about on tiny casters I always have a soft spot for statues that turn out to be alive, and there are a couple in this film.

But an actor who appears to have been cast in clay is another matter, and Mr. Moore functions like a vast garden ornament. Pedantic, sluggish on the uptake, incapable of even swaggering, he's also clumsy at innuendo. (While Sean Connery wasn't the wit of the century, he did manage to be impudent, and there were those pleasing moments of self-parody.) But whether Mr. Moore is twisting a woman's arm to discover a fact that he already knows, or nuzzling an abdomen without enthusiasm he merely makes you miss his predecessor.

The script trundles out such lines as "Your steam bath is ready" or "A mistress cannot serve two masters" between the dullest car chase of the decade and a very routine explosion. The only energetic moments are provided by Herve Villechaize, as a midget gifted with mocking authority, and Christopher Lee as the golden gunman— both have a sinister vitality that cuts through the narrative dough. (Yet if I were a midget, I'd rebel against the perky bass music that bubbles up at every entrance; cute bassoons did the same for the dwarf in "The Abdication." Can't small persons be filmed without coy theme tunes?) The movie also includes some beautiful glimpses of Thailand. But if you enjoyed the early Bond films as much as I did, you'd better skip this one.

1974 D 19, 60:5

TWO PORTRAITS: NANA, MOM AND ME, produced and directed by Amalie R. Rothschild; edited by Bronwen Sennish and Miss Rothschild; photography, Daniel Drasin and Miss Rothschild; sound by John K. Chester; music, Randolph S. Rothschild; distributed by New Day Films. Running time: 17 minutes. OLD FASHIONED WOMAN, produced, directed and edited by Martha Coolidge; cinematography, Arthur Albert; original music by Lucy Coolidge; distributed by Films Inc.; Running time: 49 minutes. At the Whitney Museum of American Art, Madison Avenue and 75th Street. Through Dec. 28.

In delving into their roots, Martha Coolidge and Amalie R. Rothschild, the young movie makers responsible, respectively, for "Old Fashioned Woman" and "Nana, Mom and Me," the documentaries that arrived yesterday at the Whitney Museum of American Art, vividly illustrate the idea that personal history need not be a bore. If traces of self-indulgence occasionally surface in these family portraits, they depict meaningful personalities lovingly exposed by deeply concerned relatives.

●

In both instances, the protagonists, as well as the film makers, largely speak for themselves in forthright, sometimes understated and occasionally funny terms that point up the color, joys and hardships of their backgrounds. Miss Coolidge's grandmother and Miss Rothschild's grandmother and parents evolve as people worthy of the attention they are being paid.

Martha Tilton Coolidge, her granddaughter admits, "has been a small but intimidating old-fashioned woman." But in "Old Fashioned Woman," which, incidentally, had a screening at the recent New York Film Festival, the 86-year-old subject about whom she is so curious emerges, in a brilliant but gently hued cameo, as a charming, resolute Yankee who is old only in years.

The tragedies and fulfillments of a life distilled from the past that dates back to Colonial days have enabled her to take time, life, family, friends and issues, old and new, such as abortion and morality, in stride and wisdom. Her grandmother comes across as much of a comfort to a viewer as she obviously did to her sensitively inquisitive granddaughter.

●

Equally illuminating is Miss Rothschild's inspection of her antecedents, who, she says in a program footnote, helped her in "self-discovery." They also, it is almost immediately obvious, show an observer the subtle but definite influence they had on the dedicated researcher who focused color cameras and sound on them. Miss Rothschild's "Nana" is, like Miss Coolidge's grandmother, a forthright 86-year-old who, unfortunately, is not too willing to submit to questioning. But her parents, an artist-mother and an equally loving lawyer-musician father, indicate that the roots are strong and effective.

The generation gaps in both films are made into bridges to an affectionate, perhaps biased, but always edifying look at unheralded individualists whose lives and values are worthwile and stir the heart and mind.

A. H. WEILER

1974 D 19, 60:5

out in real theaters, with his 48-year-old's face and his 14-year-old's confusions, is a cruelty I suspect Mr. Haines never intended.

LAWRENCE VAN GELDER

1974 D 19, 60:5

The Cast

STEPPENWOLF, directed and written by Fred Haines; director of photography, Tom Pinter; editor, Irving Lerner; music, George Gruntz; produced by Melvin Fishman and Richard Herland; a D/R Films, Inc., release. At the Eastside Cinema, Third Avenue between 55th and 56th Streets. Running time: 105 minutes. This film has been classified R.

Harry .... Max von Sydow
Hermine ....Dominique Sanda
Pablo .... Pierre Clementi
Maria .... Carla Romanelli
Goethe .... Alfred Bailloux

The recent vogue enjoyed by "Steppenwolf," particularly among the young, seems unlikely to be expanded by the film version of the 1927 Hermann Hesse novel that opened yesterday at the Eastside Cinema.

Fred Haines, who wrote the screenplay and directed the movie, has approached the Nobel Prize-winning German author's exploration of the spiritual and sensual elements of human personality with the all-too-familiar translational reverence that preserves literature while creating stillborn cinema.

•

But he has not failed for want of trying. And he has succeeded in keeping at least one wolf — utter boredom — from the door by recruiting the screen's most ascetic-looking actor, Max von Sydow, to impersonate the tortured, aging writer Harry Haller; and the screen's most enigmatic woman, Dominique Sanda, to portray Hermine, Harry's alter ego and cicerone to the unconventional.

Mr. Haines has also marshaled an impressive battery of special effects — animation, Daliesque art, television superimpositions and color synthesizers—that divert the eye, while the mind and the emotions remain uncaptivated.

Neither the stars nor the special effects can disguise the fact that "Steppenwolf" is a wordy, talky movie, stubbornly rooted in its printed origins.

This might be tolerable if the talk were interesting or if Harry Haller's sufferings managed to evoke sympathy. The truth is that the talk ranges from the silly to the sententious, the philosophy is simpleminded, and Harry emerges as an insufferable case of attenuated adolescence.

He probably should have been left forever to the printed page, an actor both in Hesse's "Magic Theater for Madmen Only" and in the inexhaustible theater of readers' imaginations. To trot him

THE TOWERING INFERNO, directed by John Guillermin; screenplay by Sterling Silliphant, based on the novels "The Tower" by Richard Martin Stern and "The Glass Inferno" by Thomas N. Scortia and Frank M. Robinson; produced by Irwin Allen; action sequences directed by Mr. Allen; director of photography, Fred Koenekamp; director of action-sequence photography, Joseph Biroc; editors, Harold F. Kress and Carl Kress; music, John Williams; distributed by 20th Century-Fox (domestic) and Warner Bros. (foreign). Running time: 160 minutes. At the National Theater, Broadway at 44th Street, and Trans-Lux East Theatre, Third Avenue at 58th Street. This film has been rated PG.

Michael O'Hallorhan......Steve McQueen
Doug Roberts............ Paul Newman
James Duncan.........William Holden
Susan Franklin............Faye Dunaway
Harlee Claiborne........... Fred Astaire
Patty Simmons........... Susan Blakely
Roger Simmons....Richard Chamberlain
Lisolette Mueller........Jennifer Jones
Jernican.................O.J. Simpson
Senator Gary Parker.....Robert Vaughn
Dan Bigelow...........Robert Wagner
Lorrie...................Susan Flannery

By VINCENT CANBY

"The Towering Inferno" is a nearly three-hour suspense film for arsonists, firemen, movie-technology buffs, building inspectors, worry warts.

The film, which opened yesterday at the National and Trans-Lux East Theaters, is a gigantic cautionary tale for people who want the worst to happen. It's this year's best end-of-the-world movie—the world in this case being represented by a 138-story, glass-and-steel San Francisco skyscraper that, on the night of its dedication, becomes history's biggest Roman candle. It doesn't burn down, just up.

It's not a movie that bothers too much about the specifics of *how* it happened (something about cheap wiring). It's mainly concerned with what happens during the holocaust, that is with an almost interminable succession of rescue episodes involving lovers, frauds, villains, a little girl, a small cat, a mayor and his wife and other assorted characters whose life spans conform roughly to their billing: actors at the head of the cast live longest.

•

Granting that end-of-the-world movies are not designed to test the intellect but, rather, to provide second-hand thrills of a visceral sort, "The Towering Inferno" must be everything its producer (Irwin Allen) and its two distribution companies (20th Century-Fox and Warner Bros., paired in a one-shot marriage-of-convenience to finance the film) could have possibly desired.

The special effects are smashing, better than those in "Earthquake" even without the brain-bending Sensurround effect of "Earthquake." The technological work is old-fashioned Hollywood make-believe at its painstaking best.

A battle for a rescue car in "The Towering Inferno"

I have absolutely no idea which scenes of crematory horror were filmed in life-size studio mockups, in real locations or in miniatures — and I don't particularly want to know. The fun in a movie like this is in being fooled by the talents of the stuntmen, the production designers and especially by the editors, the men who fit all the pieces together without the seams showing.

"The Towering Inferno" has an advantage over most movies of this sort in that it has a really classy cast. Though the actors are not required to do much except behave well according to type, their presence upgrades a secondary form of movie melodrama.

They include Paul Newman (the architect), Faye Dunaway (the editor of a woman's magazine who goes through the entire fire in a dress so sheer but indestructible that it becomes an engineering feat in itself), Steve McQueen (the heroic fire chief), William Holden (the building's developer-builder), Richard Chamberlain (the man responsible for the faulty wiring who is also a cad to his wife, which may or may not be something to think about), Robert Vaughn (a United States Senator) and Robert Wagner (the building's public-relations man who gets somewhat more coverage than he dared hope for).

Fred Astaire also shows up, benignly, as an old con artist out to bilk a rich, middle-aged woman played by Jennifer Jones, and O.J. Simpson is on hand as the building's security chief.

•

Sterling Silliphant's screenplay, based on two different but similar novels ("The Tower" and "The Glass Inferno"), probably reads like a traffic control report, but it succeeds in presenting dozens of incidents without noticeable overlaps or collisions. The dialogue, espe-

cially at the beginning, is full of those portentous hints of things to come that make the audience giggle in nervous anticipation. "You forget," someone says early on, "the many modern safety devices we have today."

John Guillermin directed the film, but it's difficult to know exactly what he might have done aside from suggesting a few line readings, perhaps. Movies like "The Towering Inferno" appear to have been less directed than physically constructed. This one is overwrought and silly in its personal drama, but the visual spectacle is first rate. You may not come out of the theater with any important ideas about American architecture or enterprise, but you will have had a vivid, completely safe nightmare.

1974 D 20, 20:1

Arctic Isle Is Focus of Children's Tale

By NORA SAYRE

A civilized movie for children, Robert Stevenson's "Island at the Top of the World" is a Jules Vernish adventure fantasy, concerning a small group that voyages by airship to the Arctic in 1907. They wind up on a mysterious volcanic island, among the furry descendants of a lost Viking expedition. There are pleasing glimpses of polar bears, whales, and reindeer,

and some quite stunning shots of the airship maneuvering between canyons of ice. The movie opened yesterday at neighborhood theaters.

Pursued by hostile Vikings, lava flows, floods and killer whales, the cast emits the high seriousness and the mock authority common to adults performing for children. Donald Sinden, as a bossy aristocrat, brings some lush classical delivery to lines like "I can offer you nothing but hardship and danger, except for your place in history," and he makes the most of the "p" in "Poppycock!" and the "t" in "Tomryrot!"

The Cast

ISLAND AT THE TOP OF THE WORLD, directed by Robert Stevenson; screenplay by John Whedon, based on "The Lost Ones" by Ian Cameron; director of photography, Frank Phillips; film editor, Robert Stafford; music, Maurice Jarre; produced by Winston Hibler; released by Buena Vista Distribution Company, Inc.; a Walt Disney Productions presentation. At neighborhood theaters. Running time: 94 minutes. This film is classified G.

Professor Ivarsson........David Hartman
Sir Anthony Ross.........Donald Sinden
Captain Brieux.........Jacques Marin
Comiak ....Mako
Donald Ross..............David Gwillim
Freyja..................Agneta Eckemyr

At moments, the Scandinavian actors seem slightly hampered by having to speak so much old Norse, but their dragon ships are first rate. And the small children in the audience—who broadcasted their responses and opinions throughout — enjoyed the movie loudly.

Also on the program is "Winnie the Pooh and Tigger Too," an animated short.

1974 D 21, 18:6

FILM VIEW

VINCENT CANBY

'The Godfather, Part II': One Godfather Too Many

I f Francis Ford Coppola were a less intelligent and less talented filmmaker, one might indulge the failed aspirations of "The Godfather, Part II"—if not the thick fog of boredom that settles in before the film is even one hour old. Clumsy directors may not be entitled but because their gaffs are not exactly unexpected, they are more easily accommodated. We snicker and laugh at multi-million-dollar dreadfuls like "The Valachi Papers" and "Crazy Joe." Our good spirits remain intact since there's no particular surprise or sorrow. The earnest confusions of "The Godfather, Part II" are something else again. They look like the solemn attempts to rip-off one of the best, most successful commercial American movies ever made, Coppola's original screen adaptation of Mario Puzo's "The Godfather."

Rip-off is an unkind word and, in this case, not really accurate since it implies a willingness to take the easy way, to exploit in the most obvious, cheapest manner an earlier success. Now I hardly think that Coppola, Puzo (who collaborated with him on the new screenplay) and Paramount Pictures did not hope to make a bundle on "Part II," but it's apparent in the physical scope (New York, Las Vegas, Sicily, the Caribbean), expense and shape of the new film that this was meant to be something more than a sequel, something more than a revisit to a planet of murderous, vengeful apes.

Well it is and it isn't.

•　　　•　　　•

It's actually two films cross-cut into each other. The first is the story of young Vito Corleone (who grew up to be the Mafia don played by Marlon Brando in "The Godfather"), from his early days in Sicily when his father was murdered by the Black Hand to his first rather nobly motivated criminal triumphs in New York's Little Italy in 1917. The second is the story of Michael Corleone (Al Pacino), who inherited the Corleone Family control from old Vito at the end of "The Godfather" and here goes on to win a Las Vegas gambling empire, with time out for an aborted attempt to take over the rackets in Cuba just before the Castro revolution.

"Part II" is as stuffed with material as a Christmas goose. It's a mass (sometimes mess) of plots, subplots, characters, alliances, betrayals, ambushes, renunciations, kisses of death, you name it. Much of the time it's next to impossible to figure out who's doing what to whom, not, I suspect, because its mode is ambiguity, but because it's been cut and edited in what looks to have been desperation, a quality that "Part II" shares with another Coppola film, "The Conversation."

There are dozens of narratives going on more or less simultaneously in "Part II," a couple of which give every sign of being material enough for an interesting, self-sustaining individual film if lifted out of this fractured epic. One has to do with the first forays into crime by young Vito, played with a fascinating, reserved

passion by Robert De Niro until the shadow of Brando's earlier performance falls over it and turns it into what amounts to an impersonation.

Another promising sequence has to do with Michael's uneasy alliance with a Jewish mob king, Hyman Roth (played by Lee Strasberg, the head of the Actors Studio, in what becomes the dominant performance of the picture), and the efforts of the pair to seize control of Havana with Battista's cooperation.

"We're bigger than U.S. Steel," Hyman says genially to Michael as they sit sunning themselves on the terrace of a Havana (actually Santo Domingo) hotel. The most chilling moment of the film has nothing to do with mob vengeance, with family betrayals or with virtue corrupted. It is a street scene in Havana when Michael watches impassively as Battista's police round up some revolutionaries, one of whom blows himself up with a hand grenade. You suddenly realize not only how isolated from the real world Michael has become, but also how isolated are the concerns of the rest of the film.

One of the most remarkable qualities of the original "The Godfather" was the manner in which it suggested all

Robert De Niro, as the Don, poses with the Corleone clan.

sorts of sad truths about American life, business, manners, goals, entirely within a headlong narrative in which character was defined almost entirely in terms of action. The relentless forward motion of the film was as much the content of the film as the gang wars it seemed to be about. The ending was inevitable and tragic.

The cross-cutting in the new film gives it a contemplative air, but the truths it contemplates about fate, family and feuds seem hardly worth all the fuss and time (three hours and 20 minutes).

• • •

I've been told that one of Coppola's intentions in "Part II" was to de-romanticize "The Godfather," which some critics had accused (wrongly, I think) of glorifying crime. At the end of "The Godfather," Michael Corleone, the once sensitive Ivy League student who has become the new don, is left lonely in his new authority. At the end of Part II he is still lonely,though we are asked to believe that he is now a more ruthless, more wracked man who suspects enemies everywhere around him and as easily orders the execution of a brother as he cooperated in the execution of a brother-in-law in the first film. The difference between Michael in the first film and "Part II" is not one of real substance but of degree.

Coppola also seems intent on contrasting the comparatively noble criminality of Michael's father Vito, in his early days in Little Italy, with Michael's use of power for its own sake later on. The idea that old-time criminals were somehow less vicious and venal than today's is, however, as romantic as any notion that turned up in the original film. "Part II" doesn't illuminate or enrich the original film. It simply brackets it with additional information that may not make too much sense unless you've seen the first one.

It also seems to have been written by writers wearing wooly mittens—the dialogue is that clumsy. You get the idea when Kay, Michael's middle-class, WASP wife, admits that what Michael thought was a miscarriage wasn't. "It was an abortion, Michael," says Kay who, though grieving, has a way with words, "just like our marriage is an abortion."

"The Godfather, Part II," directed by Francis Ford Coppola and starring Al Pacino, Robert De Niro, Robert Duvall, Diane Keaton, John Cazale and Lee Strasberg. At Loews State 1 and 2, Orpheum, Cine and Tower East.

1974 D 22, II:19:7

The Cast

STAVISKY, directed by Alain Resnais; screenplay (French with English subtitles) by Jorge Semprun; photograph, Sacha Vierny; editor, Albert Jurgenson; music, Stephen Sondheim; executive producers, Alesandre Mnouchkine and Georges Dancigers; production companies, Arlane Films/Cerito Films/Euro International (Italy). Running time: 117 minutes. This film is classified PG.

Alexandre Stavisky...Jean-Paul Belmondo
Arlette Stavisky...Anny Duperey
Baron Raoul...Charles Boyer
Borelli...Francois Perier
Montalvo...Roberto Bisaco
Dr. Mezy...Michel Lonsdale

"Stavisky" was shown this year at the 12th New York Film Festival. The following excerpt is from Nora Sayre's review, which appeared in The New York Times on Sept. 30. The film, released by Cinemation Industries, is being shown at the Cinema II Theater, Third Avenue at 60th Street.

Alain Resnais's "Stavisky" is a spell-casting mood piece that is also factually frustrating. Ideally, it should be possible to relish this fascinating movie on its own. But, since so little French history of the nineteen-thirties is provided, it's likely to send you flying to the library.

Briefly, the real Stavisky was an entrepreneur, an impresario and an accomplished swindler who bribed politicians, the police, the courts and the press; he also squandered all of his own wealth. When he flooded France with fake vouchers in 1932, the banks were closed. As a result, there were violent street riots early in 1934, in which a number of persons were shot by the police. The Government could no longer rely on the loyalty of the army or the police and Premier Edouard Daladier was forced to resign. (Stavisky himself appears to have been an apolitical adventurer, although he had a megalomaniacal belief that he could solve the economic problems of Europe — and also end unemployment.) Apparently, the press dwelled on the fact that he was a Russian Jew, and the fascist agents in France exploited the anti-Semitic issue by insisting that foreign crooks were out to ruin the nation.

•

The movie mutes the last point, but the characterization of Stavisky seems very faithful to the accounts of the period. He appears as a dual personality: a graceful bon vivant who luxuriates in every conceivable pleasure and an acute melancholic. He's also obsessed by suicides and by mysterious deaths. He was once a scruffy hood, but his friends remark that his present self despises his past one.

As Stavisky, whom a journalist of the thirties called "a gentleman among gangsters and a gangster among gentlemen," Jean-Paul Belmondo is at his best. Despite the tycoon's grandeur, he still breaks into a mobster's strut: arms swinging, wearing his shoulders high, he lunges forward with his torso aslant, while his respectable companions walk erect. Mr. Belmondo has all the authority and the gaiety of the man who refused to believe that he could make a mistake. But although others later call him crazy, we don't really see that aspect of his nature — perhaps because of the stubborn sanity that Mr. Belmondo brings to even his loopier roles.

Charles Boyer is effortlessly elegant and supple as a baron who enjoyed Stavisky's company. The eyebrows rise delicately above those knowing eyes, and it's a treat to watch him playing with Mr. Belmondo: They seem to greet each other across the span of movie history. Meanwhile, despite its mystifications, "Stavisky" is one of the most rewarding films I've seen this year—and also one of the most intelligent.

1974 D 23, 32:2

The Cast

THAT'LL BE THE DAY, directed by Claude Whatham; story and screenplay by Ray Connolly; photographed by Peter Suschitzky; editor, Michael Bradsell; music, Neil Aspinall and Keith Moon; produced by David Puttnam and Sanford Liebersen; an Anglo EMI Film Goodtimes Enterprises production; a Mayfair Films release. At the Cine Malibu, 59th Street between Second and Third Avenues and the Cinema Village, 12th Street east of Fifth Avenue. Running time: 90 minutes. This film is classified PG.

Jim MacLaine...David Essex
Mike...Ringo Starr
Mrs. MacLaine...Rosemary Leach
Stormy Tempest...Billy Fury

By NORA SAYRE

Movies about boredom aren't ever likely to make the blood leap, and "That'll Be the Day" proves that there's no such thing as a rousing soporific. Set in the late nineteen-fifties, this English movie —which opened yesterday at the Cine Malibu and the Cinema Village—is lazily concerned with the ennui of a young provincial who balks at taking his university exams, leaves home to work at odd jobs, writes whimsical pop lyrics, and pines to enter the rock world. He also makes out with bland young women who beg him not to tell anyone. Eventually, he marries a hairdresser who blinks a lot, and the result is just as boring for us as it is for him.

As the soundtrack churns out some elderly (even whiskery) rock music, this tame rebel without claws seems like a ghost of the defiant, adventurous English film heroes of the early sixties, when such splendid actors as Albert Finney in "Saturday Night and Sunday Morning" and Tom Courtney in "The Loneliness of the Long Distance Runner" conveyed the impassioned energy that sprang from claustrophobia.

It's a bit forlorn to think of David Essex, who plays the rock fan, as their descendant. He's rather beautiful but has been directed to be utterly passive: for him, acting takes the form of long, slow elfin smiles and dreamy stares, and he struggles to reproduce a particular English accent that's been scarce on screen of late: "fink" for think, "flay" for slay, "frow up" for upchuck.

Ringo Starr makes a phlegmatic appearance—he looks a bit sheepish, as though apologizing for making no music at all. As a titillating conclusion for the movie, the young man buys a guitar; a sequel is promised. Let's hope that many strong stimulants were administered to everyone involved with the next picture.

1974 D 23, 32:3

BLACK THURSDAY, directed by Michel Mitrani; screenplay (French with English subtitles) by Albert Cossery and Mr. Mitrani, based on the novel "Les Guichets du Louvre" by Roger Boussinot; produced by Carole Weisweiller and Roger Fleytoux; music, Mort Shuman; a Louvre Associates, Ltd., presentation, distributed by Levitt-Pickman Film Corporation. Running time: 92 minutes. At the New Yorker Theater, Broadway at 89th Street. This film has not been rated.

Jeanne...Christine Pascal
Paul...Christian Rist
Old Lady...Alice Sapritch
Mr. Edmond...Michel Auclair
Mrs. Ash...Judith Magre
Cousin...Michel Robin

By VINCENT CANBY

"Black Thursday," the new French film that opened yesterday at the New Yorker Theater, solemnly commemorates one of the bleakest chapters in the history of Paris during the German occupation. On July 16, 1942, 9,000 French policemen rounded up 13,000 Jews, including 4,500 children, hustled them aboard city buses and carted them off on the first leg of a journey that eventually led to the Nazi death camps.

For the most part, everything was extremely orderly. There was no panic. The policemen were, after all, French not German. The Jews, too, were polite. They were mostly French nationals and they had faith in the Republic. Also, there were no more hiding places. Some policemen were glad to see the Jews go. If at all conscience-stricken they could tell themselves their victims were simply being sent off to work in factories somewhere. Like in '14-'18.

•

"Black Thursday" is based on the haunted memoir, "Les Guichets du Louvre" (The Gates of the Louvre), by Roger Boussinot, published in France in 1960. At the time of the all-day roundup, Mr. Boussinot was a 20-year-old student at the Sorbonne. Having obtained advance warning of the raids, he spent that day in the Right Bank Jewish quarter, trying unsuccessfully to persuade Jews to hide, or to flee with him to the labyrinths of the Left Bank's student quarter, or just to remove the gold Stars of David they wore on their breasts.

He was notably unsuccessful. He was a fresh-faced kid. He might be in the pay of the police. One preferred to take one's chances with one's family rather than to go off on a wild goose chase. A handsome Jewish woman in a pastry shop thanked him with a smile but pointed out that she really didn't know him well enough. She had heard stories about the wild lives the students led. He could have been inviting her to an orgy.

Only one person listened to him, though reluctantly: a pretty girl who first found that her mother and younger sister had been arrested, and then watched as the policemen led away all the employes at the furrier's where she worked.

"Black Thursday" is the story of the efforts of the young man, named Paul in the film and played by Christian Rist, to persuade the girl (Christine Pascal) to save herself if not to let him save her. It's an agonizing film, both because of the complex emotions it evokes and because it so often slips into clumsily romantic movie attitudes that don't do justice to the subject.

Michel Mitrani, the director, seems at times to be making one of those old Gerard Philippe tearjerkers of the late nineteen-forties, with lots of music on the soundtrack, swoopy, circular camera movements, and actors who look more like idealizations than real people. Everything suggests a softer kind of fiction than this really is.

•

Miss Pascal is an exception. She has an irregular beauty that never denies or gets in the way of the successive waves of fear, hope, resignation and despair she experiences during her day-long flight to nowhere. She is especially fine in the film's quietest, most terrifying scene, when she at last allows a friend to snip the stitches attaching the Star of David to her coat. She has suddenly become anonymous.

Like Marcel Ophuls's "The Sorrow and The Pity" and Louis Malle's "Lacombe, Lucien," "Black Thursday" examines a moment in history that most Frenchmen have preferred to ignore until now. It's not very interesting movie-making, but I suspect that for many (including the French) the subject itself is transforming enough.

1974 D 23, 34:1

ABBY. Directed by William Girdler; screenplay by G. Cornell Layne from a story by Mr. Girdler and Mr. Layne; produced by Mr. Girdler, Mr. Layne and Mike Henry and released by American International Pictures. At the Penthouse Theater, Broadway and 47th Street, and the RKO 86th Street Theater at Lexington Avenue. Running time: 91 minutes. This film has been classified R.

Rev. Dr. Garnet Williams	W. Marshall
Abby Williams	Carol Speed
Rev. Emmett Williams	Terry Carter
Cass Potter	Austin Stoker
Mamma Potter	Juanita Moore
Doctor Hennings	Charles Kissinger
Russell	Elliott Moffitt

If "The Exorcist" luridly indicated that a white girl plagued by demons could be a problem, "Abby," which landed unsteadily at the Penthouse and RKO 86th Street theaters yesterday, illustrates that a black girl, if not an amused moviegoer, can also be unsettled by dire manufactured powers. As "the story of a woman possessed" who is finally cleansed of those devils, "Abby" is more silly than shocking even if it seems to take itself seriously.

Blame all the ersatz deviltry on William Marshall, as the film's imposingly learned minister-archeologist who unwittingly looses evil forces by digging up an ancient religious artifact in Nigeria that invades the body of his young, lovely, decent daughter-in-law back home in Louisville, Ky. And, of course, Carol Speed, as Abby, his daughter-in-law, begins to behave more and more like a rampaging hooker than a loving bride, churchwoman and dedicated community worker.

Her personal poltergeist—which sets off a series of mysterious sounds and furies, including slamming doors and flying furniture, as well as sexual and physical assaults—threatens to send the family, a hospital staff and the cops off the deep end. But not before Mr. Marshall, wearing exotic garb and intoning an exotic religious ritual, steps in climactically to exorcise and save the plagued Abby from her destructive alter ego.

Mr. Marshall does manage to be dignified despite the mumbo-jumbo he's involved with. But Miss Speed, whose lips turn purple and whose voice turns basso profundo in spewing obscenities in her "possessed" state, is energetic, if unconvincing, as the afflicted Abby. Terry Carter

and Austin Stoker are believably confused and frightened as her minister husband and cop brother, respectively.

As her distraught mother, Juanita Moore delivers one of the film's most intelligent lines. She comforts her ailing daughter at one point with: "I'm gonna get you a cold towel for your head. It'll make you feel better." A cold towel could help a viewer, too.

A. H. WEILER

1974 D 26, 53:1

FREEBIE AND THE BEAN, directed and produced by Richard Rush; screenplay by Robert Kaufman, based on a story by Floyd Mutrux; executive producer, Mr. Mutrux; director of photography, Laszlo Kovacs; editors, Frederic Steinkamp and Michael McLean; distributed by Warner Brothers. Running time: 113 minutes. At the Criterion Theater, Broadway at 45th Street; Beekman Theater, Second Avenue at 65th Street, and 86th Street East, near Third Avenue. This film has been rated R.

Bean	Alan Arkin
Freebie	James Caan
District Attorney	Alex Rocco
Bean's wife	Valerie Harper
Meyer's wife	Loretta Swit
Red Meyers	Jack Kruschen
Lieutenant Rosen	Mike Kellin
Freebie's girl	Linda Marsh
Whitey	Paul Koslo
Chauffeur	John Garwood

By VINCENT CANBY

"Freebie and the Bean," this year's final cop comedy, seems the worst of the lot, probably because it has a cast of otherwise good actors doing bits of business (sometimes called acting) as if they thought they could upstage all of the movie's automobiles, which are seldom still. Cars tail one another endlessly. Sometimes they race and every now and then there's a very complicated, very dumb, all-out chase. Even a single parked car becomes something of a plot point.

You finally get the feeling that a car directed the picture —its as sensitive as a door knob and as witty as a bumper sticker — and maybe one did, though the title credits list Richard Rush. He is the man who directed the worst of the campus-revolution movies, "Getting Straight" (1970). Before that disaster Mr. Rush had earned a name in Hollywood for directing low-budget motorcycle films.

The stars of the film are Alan Arkin, who plays Bean, a sensitive Mexican-born policeman who suspects his beautiful wife of infidelity, and James Caan, who plays Bean's all-American partner, Freebie. The best performance is that of Valerie Harper (television's Rhoda), who is seen briefly as Bean's wife. For a few minutes there is something very funny about the movie when Bean confronts his wife with his suspicions: the intensity of Miss Harper's tolerance of Bean's suspicions and the answers

she has for every charge against her exactly matches Mr. Arkin's fury.

The rest of the time the movie is serio-comic trash. It was written by Robert Kaufman and what story there is —about two lawmen trying to capture the Mr. Big of the rackets'—is not at all dissimilar to "Busting," the much better Peter Hyams cop film seen earlier in the year. "Freebie and the Bean" opened yesterday at the Criterion, Beekman and 86th Street East Theaters.

1974 D 26, 59:1

THE SHADOW CATCHER: Edward S. Curtis and the North American Indian, produced and directed by T. C. McLuhan; written by Mr. McLuhan and Dennis Wheeler; cinematography, Robert M. Flore; edited by Charlotte Zwerin; distributed by Shadow catcher, Inc. At the Whitney Museum of American Art, Madison Avenue and 75th Street. Running time: 88 minutes. This film has not been classified.

Voice of Edward S. Curtis	D. Southerland
Narrator	Patrick Watson

By NORA SAYRE

A dead man's obsession seeps over the screen throughout T. C. McLuhan's "The Shadow Catcher," and that fixation casts as strong a spell as the evocations of the North American Indians he studied.

Between 1896 and 1930, the photographer and anthropologist Edward S. Curtis dedicated his life to recording the customs of more than 80 tribes, convinced that these "dispossessed people" were losing their way of life as rapidly as he could film them. This superb documentary, which recreates the years that Curtis spent among the Navajo, the Hopi, the Kwakiutl, the Eskimos and others, opened yesterday at the Whitney Museum of American Art and will run until Jan. 7.

Theodore Roosevelt was impressed by Curtis's work, and J. P. Morgan agreed to finance some of the field work that resulted in 20 volumes and portfolios of photogravure plates, plus many 35-mm. films. Meanwhile, as you watch the dances of thanksgiving or supplication, or learn that the Hopi associated the movements of snakes with lightning flashes (hence the snake dance was a prayer for rain), the political sensitivity of this film emerges: Long ago, when the Indians' culture was sacrificed in the name of "progress," Curtis felt that the destruction of their traditions showed "that there was something wrong with the American dream."

Careful not to violate the Indians' privacy, Curtis nonetheless succeeded in participating in some of their rituals. He was also a dexterous

2 Films About Rock Star Find Loneliness at Top

By JOHN ROCKWELL

"That'll Be the Day" and "Stardust" are two British films that between them tell the story of a rock star's rise from provincial adolescence to lonely splendor at the top. Whatever their appeal for general moviegoers, the films should be of great interest to rock fans.

Both pictures star David Essex and share some supporting actors, although they have different directors and are being distributed in this country by different organizations. "That'll Be the Day," after a spotty release pattern in a few cities around the country, is at the Cine Malibu and the Cinema Village. "Stardust" opens here in about a month and will presumably be publicized more lavishly.

"Stardust" is the flashier effort, mostly because "That'll Be the Day" ends just as the hero, Jim MacLaine, has decided to buy his first electric guitar. That leaves all the glamour and excitement to the sequel—the first gigs in scruffy clubs, the rise to fame with the first American tour, the hysterical crowd scenes, the tensions within the band and confrontations with rapacious money men and the final isolation of the star and his ultimate denouement, by then the world's most idolized rocker and a drugged psychotic recluse in his forbidding Spanish castle.

The trouble with "Stardust" is that everything is too jumpy and too melodramatically, cynically sensationalistic. The screenwriters and the director, Michael Apted, have tried to squeeze a decade into two hours, and the result is a series of sketchy tableaus. Some of the tableaus look and sound very real — unlike the performers in Brian De Palma's "Phan-

tom of the Paradise," these are people you actually believe could earn all that adulation. (And some of them have, since Keith Moon is Mr. Essex's drummer, and Mr. Essex himself is a rising star in Britain even now.) But for all its pleasures as a "cinéma à clef" — which band's history was that bit based on? — "Stardust" ends up inconclusive and unsatisfying.

"That'll Be the Day," which was directed by Claude Whatham, tells us less of Jim MacLaine's story but tells it with far greater depth and seriousness. The film has been criticized on the ground that not enough happens. It is a realistic picture like "Room at the Top" or "Saturday Night and Sunday Morning," yet there is precious little outward incident, and Mr. Essex, pretty and passive, creates a far less extroverted character than, say, Albert Finney or Richard Harris.

And yet for anybody who cares about rock 'n' roll, the movie rings wonderfully true. Lots of teen-agers who love rock do seem passive, especially to their parents, yet still have an inner intensity that expresses itself in music. Mr. Essex, moodily kicking about the Isle of Wight and, along with Ringo Starr, staring wistfully up at the likes of Billy Fury and Mr. Moon, says more than any other fictional character I have seen about what it was like to be a trapped young man with ambitions toward the kind of glamour that rock alone promised to bring. "That'll Be the Day" is very British, but it owes the universality of its appeal to fidelity to its roots.

1974 D 27, 14:1

interviewer. If an individual didn't want to talk with him, Curtis would discuss theology and deliberately make an error, so that the Indian would correct him, and that would lead to further conversation.

Donald Sutherland becomes Curtis's voice, narrating from the journals and letters of 30 years. Mr. Sutherland conveys the delights of discovery, the fatigue, the discouragement and the determination that drove the man until his marriage, and then his health, collapsed. Intercut with Curtis's magnificent photographs and excerpts from "In the Land of the Head Hunters," his 1914 film on the Kwakiutl, there are

modern sequences that focus on the landscapes and the descendants of the people he knew.

Now and then, his stills pass too quickly, and occasionally the contemporary passages in color break the sepia mood of the past. But it's fascinating to hear three elderly Indians recalling how they performed in Curtis's film for 50 cents an hour. Subtly, the movie says as much about white America as it does about the Indians, and it also distills the nature of another kind of vanishing American: a person who loved his work.

1974 D 30, 37:1

Film Critics Cite 'Amarcord' and Fellini

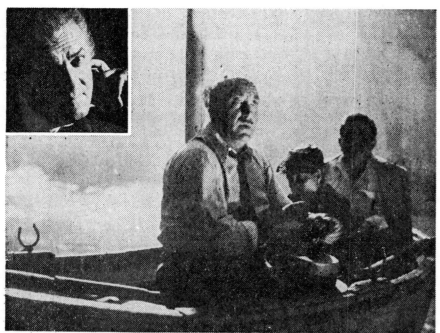

Scene from "Amarcord," directed by Federico Fellini, inset. At right, from top: Jack Nicholson, Liv Ullmann, Charles Boyer and Valerie Perrine, winners of acting awards.

By A. H. WEILER

"Amarcord" ("I Remember"), the Italian-made comedy-drama that evoked a year in the life of an Italian town in the nineteen-thirties, was judged the year's best film and Federico Fellini the top director of 1974 for his work on that import, in the 40th annual poll yesterday of the New York Film Critics Circle.

The critics also bestowed two awards on Ingmar Bergman's sensitive dissection of marital relations, "Scenes From a Marriage." The director's own script for the Swedish drama originally made for television was voted the prize for the year's best screen writing. And Liv Ullmann, a previous winner (1971) of the critics award for Mr. Bergman's "Cries and Whispers," was named the year's outstanding actress.

Jack Nicholson won handily as the year's top actor. He achieved the honor, by garnering 32 votes each for his performances as a wacky sailor in "The Last Detail" and the tough private eye in "Chinatown." In closely contested canvassing, the veteran Charles Boyer was judged the best supporting actor for his characterization of a friend of the swindler "Stavisky" in the French drama of that title.

Valerie Perrine won easily as the year's top supporting actress for her portrayal of the stripper-wife of the tormented night-club performer, played by Dustin Hoffman, in "Lenny."

The critics also voted a special citation to Fabiano Canosa for his innovative

programing that brought many new films to the First Avenue Screening Room.

Although "Amarcord" competed against 17 other films, only "Scenes From a Marriage" proved to be a tough contender. "Amarcord" topped "Scenes" on a second ballot by a vote of 43 to 38. Runners-up included "The Godfather, Part II" (17), "The Conversation" (12), and "Chinatown" (10).

Mr. Fellini, who previously won foreign-language film awards for "Juliet of the Spirits" (1965), "8½" (1963), and "La Strada" (1956), was a strong winner in the directorial category. His 40 votes topped the 25 votes gathered by Ingmar Bergman ("Scenes").

In snagging the best actor prize, Jack Nicholson with 32 votes each for "The Last Detail" and "Chinatown" was far ahead of the 17 performers he was opposing. Second place with 19 votes each went to Gene Hackman for his portrayal of the tortured wiretapper in "The Conversation" and to Richard Dreyfuss as the titular schemer in "The Apprenticeship of Duddy Kravitz."

Miss Ullmann was a clear victor with 52 votes to top the 42 votes for Gena Rowlands for her sensitive performance of the disturbed wife in "A Woman Under the Influence."

The supporting actor category resulted in one of the closest contests with more than 20 performers in competition. Mr. Boyer's 43 votes topped the 35 cast for Robert De Niro ("The Godfather, Part II"). Mr. De Niro won the supporting actor honor last year for "Mean Streets." Among

the others competing were Lee Strasberg ("The Godfather, Part II") 16 votes; and Holger Lowenadler ("Lacombe, Lucien") and Randy Quaid ("The Last Detail") with 12 votes each.

In amassing 45 votes, Valerie Perrine outdistanced Bibi Andersson ("Scenes") with 20 tallies in the supporting actress category, which teemed with more than 20 entries. Madeleine Kahn ("Young Frankenstein") 18 votes and Ellen Burstyn's 10 votes for her work in "Harry and Tonto" were the closest runners-up Mr. Bergman's script for "Scenes From a Marriage" won with 45 votes. Following in order were the scripts for "Chinatown" (32), "The Conversation" (30) and "The Apprenticeship of Duddy Kravitz" and "Badlands" with 10 votes each.

Plaques will be presented to the winners at Sardi's Restaurant on Jan. 26.

The voting critics were: Roger Greenspun, Penthouse magazine, chairman of the group; Howard Kissel, Women's Wear Daily; Judith Crist, New York magazine; Pauline Kael and Penelope Gilliatt, The New Yorker magazine; Jay Cocks, Time magazine; Joy Gould Boyum, The Wall Street Journal; Kathleen Carroll, Ann Guarino, Rex Reed and Jerry Oster, The Daily News; Bernard Drew, Gannett Newspapers; Paul Zimmerman, Newsweek magazine; Joseph Gelmis, Newsday; Archer Winsten and Frances Herridge, The New York Post; Andrew Sarris and Molly Haskell, The Village Voice; Frances Taylor, The Long Island Daily Press; William Wolf and Donald Mayerson, Cue magazine; Robert Salmaggi, WINS Radio; Bruce Williamson, Playboy magazine; Hollis Alpert, Saturday Review/World magazine; James P. Murray, New York Amsterdam News, and Vincent Canby, Nora Sayre, Howard Thompson and A. H. Weiler, The New York Times.

1974 D 31, 12:1

FILM VIEW

VINCENT CANBY

Critic's Choice: The Eleven Best Films of 1974

It needn't always be The Ten Best Films of the Year. Some years there may only be three, other years seven, or, as I choose to think in 1974, 11. It wasn't one of those years that will go down in history as exceptional but it was, in retrospect, a very good year, especially for American films.

The truly remarkable films of the year were all European (six of my list of 11 are foreign), yet one of these was made in 1966 and another in 1969, meaning that 1974's American films were competing with the best European films representing virtually a decade of work.

If there were no American films last year to compare with "Amarcord" and "Scenes From A Marriage," there were dozens that in one way and another raised one's hopes for the future of American production. It's no coincidence that box-office receipts at American theaters soared toward the end of the year. A lot of the money was being earned by junk ("The Trial of Billy Jack," "Airport 1975"), but some of this money was going to what the film trade calls "audience pictures" of a very respectable sort like "The Towering Inferno."

I'd be hard-pressed to put "The Towering Inferno" on any list of best films, or even a list of runners-up, but it may be some kind of special effects classic. Dustin Hoffman's fine performance gives "Lenny" legitimate importance though it may not make it a film for the ages. Francis Ford Coppola's "Godfather II" must be acknowledged for its ambitions and John Cassavetes's

"A Woman Under the Influence" must be noted for its all-stops-out performance by Gena Rowlands, though the film itself is chaos. These are not movies that anyone need be ashamed of.

•   •   •

I feel the same way about two such dissimilar films as "Law and Disorder," directed by a brilliant filmmaker (Ivan Passer) and "Uptown Saturday Night," directed by an actor (Sidney Poitier) who has a lot of talented friends. Even the serious pretentions of Karel Reisz's "The Gambler" and the farcical ones of Barbra Streisand's "For Pete's Sake" (actually directed by Peter Yates) are

encouraging in a special way: the American film industry continues to display vitality even in films that fail for one reason or another.

My choices of the 11 best films of 1974, winnowed from a list of 20 and listed in alphabetical order, are as follows:

"Amarcord," directed by Federico Fellini; screenplay (Italian with English subtitles) and story by Mr. Fellini and Tonino Guerra; produced by Franco Cristaldi; distributed by Roger Corman/New World Films. Fellini's beautiful, moving reminiscence of his youth in a small town in Fascist Italy combines the concerns of his early, neo-realist

A

B

A Critic's Choice

A. "Scenes From a Marriage"
B. "Lacombe, Lucien"
C. "Badlands"
D. "Harry & Tonto"
E. "Claudine"
F. "California Split"
G. "Le Petit Théatre de Jean Renoir"
H. "Daisy Miller"
I. "Amarcord"
J. "The Phantom of Liberté"
K. "Man Is Not a Bird"

C

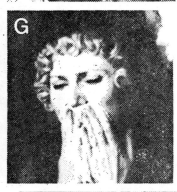

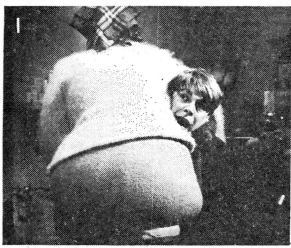

goals, if only by chance.

"Claudine," directed by John Berry; screenplay by Lester and Tina Pine; produced by Hannah Weinstein; a Third World Cinema production distributed by 20th Century-Fox. The best American comedy of the year—also the best black film—is anything but a black comedy. "Claudine" is an ordinary television situation comedy transformed into meaningful social comedy through the blunt honesty of its script, by the direction that skirts clichés as if they were condemned buildings, and by the superb performances of Diahann Carroll as a Harlem Welfare mother, James Earl Jones as her suitor, and Tamu as her edgy, 15-year-old daughter.

• • •

"Daisy Miller," directed and produced by Peter Bogdanovich; screenplay by Frederic Raphael, based on the Henry James story; distributed by Paramount. The total effect of this film is that of an illustrated introduction to a literary classic, but it's been done so beautifully, with such lightness and wit, and with such a lack of (usually fatal) self-importance, that one responds to it with easy warmth. Cybill Shepherd seems absolutely right as the beautiful Daisy, who has a brain pan the size of a small white kid glove, and receives excellent support from Barry Brown, Cloris Leachman and Mildred Natwick.

"Harry & Tonto," directed and produced by Paul Mazursky; screenplay by Mr. Mazursky and Josh Greenfeld; distributed by 20th Century-Fox. Paul Mazursky, director and co-author of "Bob & Carol & Ted & Alice" and author-director of "Blume in Love," is getting better and better and "Harry & Tonto" is his best. It's

comedies with the fantastic style of his later films to produce one of this director's most loving, most imaginative movies.

"Badlands," directed, written and produced by Terrence Malick; a Pressman-Williams production distributed by Warner Brothers. This first film to be directed by Terrence Malick, a former Rhodes Scholar and philosophy instructor, is the toughest, most original American film of the year, a clear-eyed look at the American civilization in mid-20th century as represented by 25-year-old, Mid-western garbage collector and the 15-year-old girl who accompanies him on a cross-country murder spree. The story, inspired by the Charlie Starkweather case, is set in the nineteen-fifties but it seems to have closer associations to a world further along in the TV age, a society in which there are no meaningful consequences, only commercial breaks. It's a ferocious and scary film, beautifully acted by Martin Sheen and Sissy Spacek as the lovers, and by Warren Oates as the girl's father.

"California Split," directed by Robert Altman; screenplay by Joseph Walsh; produced by Mr. Altman and Mr. Walsh; distributed by Columbia Pictures. Robert Altman's best film of the year (his other film, "Thieves Like Us," is almost as good) is supposed to be about gambling as it follows the driven journey of two dissimilar gamblers, Elliott Gould and George Segal, from Los Angeles betting parlors and race tracks to the big time casinos in Reno. But because Altman can't make a simple movie, "California Split" also manages to suggest a lot of things about ambition, friendship, the quality of American middle-class life and what might happen should we attain our paltry

the picaresque tale of a 72-year-old New Yorker traveling across America with his large, ailing orange cat. Brilliantly acted by Art Carney, the film is equally unafraid of real sentiment and the seamier prospects for a society whose younger generation is at such loose ends.

"Lacombe, Lucien," directed and produced by Louis Malle; screenplay (French with English subtitles) by Mr. Malle and Patrick Modiano; distributed by 20th Century-Fox. A precise, rueful film about a young French farm boy who, seemingly by chance, joins the German police during the last months of the Nazi occupation of France. Malle does not attempt to pinpoint reasons. He rivets us by saying simply that this is the way it was.

"Man Is Not A Bird," directed by Dusan Makavejev; screenplay (Serbo-Croatian with English subtitles) by Mr. Makavejev; produced by Avala Film; distributed by Grove Press. The first film (made in 1966) by the Yugoslav director (best known here for his mixed-up political-sexual farce, "WR—Mysteries of The Organism"), "Man Is Not A Bird" is one of the two most original, sophisticated and complex films to come out of a Communist society (the other is the Cuban "Memories of Underdevelopment"). The story centers on a moody, introspective engineer who, against his better judgment, has an affair with a pretty, much younger barber in a factory town. The real subject, however, is Tito's Great Experiment.

"Le Petit Théâtre de Jean Renoir," directed, produced and narrated by Jean Renoir; screenplay (French with English subtitles) by Mr. Renoir; distributed by Phoenix Films. Three short films, plus a between-the-acts song by Jeanne Moreau, become a kind of graceful farewell performance by this greatest of French directors. The style is simultaneously delicate and firm, ageless and full of the vigor of youth, detached but compassionate.

• • •

"The Phantom of Liberté," directed by Luis Buñuel; screenplay (French with English subtitles) by Mr. Buñuel and Jean-Claude Carrière; produced by Serge Silberman; distributed by 20th Century-Fox. The Golden Age of Buñuel continues into his eighth decade as the 74-year-old director returns to the surreal form of his "L'Age D'Or," made in 1930. A dazzling collection of loosely related tales acknowledging the paradoxes of politics, religion, love and what is taken for good taste.

"Scenes From A Marriage," directed and written (in Swedish with English subtitles) by Ingmar Bergman; a Cinematograph AB production distributed by Cinema V. Bergman's five-hour TV drama edited into a 168-minute theatrical epic about the losses and achievements in a 20-year love affair. Liv Ullmann's performance is one of the best of this or any other year.

For the record, the runners-up, in no special order of preference, were:

Rainer Werner Fassbinder's "Ali," Hal Ashby's "The Last Detail," Robert Altman's "Thieves Like Us," Francis Ford Coppola's "The Conversation," Cinda Firestone's "Attica," Ted Kotcheff's "The Apprenticeship of Duddy Kravitz," Roman Polanski's "Chinatown," Billy Wilder's "The Front Page" and Sidney Lumet's "Murder on The Orient Express."

That's not a bad year at all.

1975 Ja 5, II:1:7

National Society of Film Critics Hails 'Scenes From a Marriage'

"Scenes From a Marriage," written and directed by Ingmar Bergman, has been judged the best movie of 1974 in the eighth annual poll of the National Society of Film Critics.

The representatives of 24 newspapers and magazines also cited Mr. Bergman for the year's top screenplay. In addition, Liv Ullmann, who portrays the troubled wife in the drama, was named the year's outstanding actress, and Bibi Andersson, who plays a friend of the couple, was voted best supporting actress.

Francis Ford Coppola won best-director honors for "The Godfather, Part II" and "The Conversation." Mr. Bergman and Federico Fellini, who directed the Italian "Amarcord," were tied as close runners-up in this category.

Jack Nicholson was named the year's best actor for his roles as the private eye in "Chinatown" and the wacky sailor in "The Last Detail." The top supporting actor award went to Holger Lowenadler, the harried tailor in the French drama "Lacombe, Lucien."

Gordon Willis was voted best cinematographer for both "The Godfather, Part II" and "The Parallax View." Jean Renoir was given a special award for his achievements over a long career as a director.

Although the society did not disclose voting statistics, "Amarcord" ("I Remember"), Mr. Fellini's comedy-drama about life in an Italian town in the nineteen-thirties, which last week was named the best film of 1974 by the New York Film Critics Circle, was the runner-up to "Scenes" as the year's best film.

Penelope Gilliatt of The New Yorker was elected chairman of National Society of Film Critics, succeeding Andrew Sarris of The Village Voice. Scrolls will be mailed to the award winners.

1975 Ja 6, 33:1

'Godfather, Part II' Wins 7 Oscars

By JON NORDHEIMER
Special to The New York Times

LOS ANGELES, April 8— "The Godfather, Part II," the sequel to the Oscar-winning Mafia film of two years ago, "The Godfather," continued the family tradition tonight by sweeping seven top honors at the 47th annual Academy Awards presentations.

The film, which continued the underworld saga of the Vito Corleone family, was named best picture and won the directing award for Francis Ford Coppola, the bearded wunderkind of Hollywood who in a few short years has become one of the few dominant figures in the film industry. It was the first time in the history of the awards that a sequel to a major film won the next picture honor.

Carney and Miss Burstyn

Best acting awards went to Art Carney for his portrayal of an aging widower in a transcontinental search in "Harry and Tonto," and to Ellen Burstyn for her role in "Alice Doesn't Live Here Anymore," a film that is seen as part of a trend toward greater realism in the Hollywood depiction of women.

In keeping with the trend for using the Oscar ceremony as a political platform, the winners of the best achievement in documentary production, Peter Davis and Bert Schneider for the film "Hearts and Minds," a con-

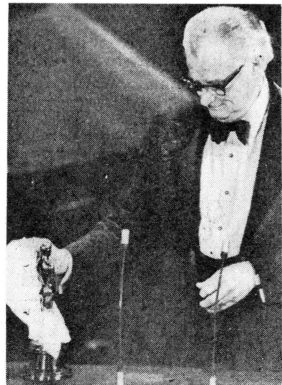

United Press International
Art Carney, best actor, playfully dusting his Oscar

United Press International
Ingrid Bergman after being named best supporting actress last night.

troversial report on the Vietnam war, read "greetings of friendship" from a North Vietnamese Communist leader to the star-studded audience and 65 million television viewers.

The local outlet for the

National Broadcasting Company, which carried the national telecast, was "swamped

with outraged calls" from hundreds of local viewers who strongly objected to the use of the airwaves "for Communist propaganda," an NBC spokesman reported.

Before the end of the telecast, Frank Sinatra, one of the hosts read a statement that sought to disassociate the Academy of Motion Picture Arts and Sciences from the views of Mr. Davis and Mr. Schneider. "We are not responsible for any political statements made on this program and it does not reflect the attitude of the academy," said the statement, which academy officials said had been dictated by Bob Hope, another host.

Mr. Hope and Mr. Sinatra had been closely associated with support of the policies of former President Nixon, and their statement evoked a mixed sprinkling of mild applause and catcalls from the audience at the Dorothy Chandler Pavilion of the Los Angeles Music Center. The brief expressions made by Mr. Davis and Mr. Schneider while they were accepting the award before the television cameras had been politely applauded.

Surprise on 'Chinatown'

Aside from the political fireworks, the Oscar show produced a number of surprises in the usually predictable awards. Most notable was the paucity of honors for "Chinatown," unsentimental study of power and corruption in the nineteen-thirties, which had been considered a frontrunner in several major categories. It captured the award for best original screenplay for Robert Towne, but nothing else, another disappointment for Jack Nicholson, who played the hardbitten detective, J. J. Gettis, in the film. It was the actor's third nomination for best actor without a victory.

Robert De Niro, who portrayed the brooding young Mafia chieftain Vito Corleone in 'The Goodfather, Part II," won the Academy Award for best supporting actor.

It was the same underworld character role for which Marlon Brando won the award for best acting two years ago in "The Godfather," an award that Mr. Brando refused to accept personally in a protest over the treatment of American Indians.

Ingrid Bergman won the Oscar as the best supporting actress of 1974 for her work as one of the suspects in "Murder On the Orient Express." Miss Bergman won the best actress awards in 1944 for "Gaslight" and in 1956 for "Anastasia." She joins Helen Hayes as the only actress to have won Oscars in both the best actress and best supporting actress categories.

"The Godfather" film, the sequel to the annals of a crime dynasty written by Mr. Coppola and Mario Puzo, won the Oscar for the best script adapted from other material.

Ellen Burstyn
Best Actress

"Amarcord," the Italian comedy-drama that evoked a year in the life of an Italian town in the nineteen-thirties, was named the best foreign-language film. The import previously won the New York Film Critics prize as the year's best movie.

Hollywood's élite gathered for the ceremonies under threatening, rainy skies, the product of an unseasonal cold spell. Stars, starlets,

Francis Ford Coppola
Best Director

producers and other film industry royalty stood gathered in the Dorothy Chandler Pavilian before show time.

Four Special Awards

In addition to the competitive awards, the academy gave four special awards during the evening.

Jean Renoir, the veteran French director, was honored for his achievements over

Robert De Niro
Best Supporting Actor

the years; the film "Earthquake" received a visual effects award; the director Howard Hawks received an honorary award for his outstanding work, and Arthur B. Krim, chairman of United Artist, was given the Jean Hersholt Humanitarian Award for his charitable work.

Other awards follow:
Documentary feature: "Hearts and Minds," Touchstone-Aud-

jeff-BBS Prods. Howard Zucker/Henry Jaglom-Rainbow Pictures presentation, Peter Davis and Bert Schneider, producers.

Documentary short subject: "Don't," R. A. Films, Robin Lehman, producer.

Short subjects—live: "One-Eyed Men Are Kings, CAPAC Prods. (Paris). Produced by Paul Claudon and Edmond Sechan.

Short subjects — animated: "Closed Mondays," Lighthouse Prods. Will Vinton and Bob Gardiner, producers.

Song: "We May Never Love Like This Again" from "The Towering Inferno." Music and lyrics by Al Kasha and Joel Hirshhorn.

Sound: "Earthquake," by Ronald Pierce and Melvin Metcalfe Sr.

Original dramatic score: "The Godfather, Part II," by Nino Rota and Carmine Coppola.

Film editing: "The Towering Inferno," Harold F. Kress, Carl Kress. 20th Century - Fox and Warner Bros.

Cinematography: "The Towering Inferno," Fred Koenekamp, Joseph Biroc. 20th Century-Fox and Warner Bros.

Costume: "The Great Gatsby," Theoni V. Aldredge. Paramount.

Scoring: "The Great Gatsby," Nelson Riddle.

Art direction and set decoration: "The Godfather, Part II," a Coppola-Paramount production; Dean Tavoularis and Angelo Graham, art direction; George R. Nelson, set direction.

1975 Ap 9, 28:1

How To Use Index

This index covers all the film reviews included in this volume. It is divided into three sections: Titles, Persons, and Corporations.

The Title Index lists each film reviewed by title. The Persons Index lists by name every performer, producer, director, screenwriter, etc. mentioned in the reviews, with the function in parentheses following the name, and the titles of the movies with which the person was connected, in chronological order. The Corporations Index lists all producing, distributing and otherwise participating companies mentioned in the reviews by name, again with the function in parentheses following the name, and the titles of the movies with which they were associated, in chronological order.

Citations in this index are by year, month, day, section of newspaper (if applicable), page and column; for example, 1973 Ja 11, II: 12:1. Since the reviews appear in chronological order, the date is the key locator. The citations also serve to locate the reviews in bound volumes and microfilm editions of The Times.

In the citations, the months are abbreviated as follows:

Ja—January	My—May	S—September
F—February	Je—June	O—October
Mr—March	Jl—July	N—November
Ap—April	Ag—August	D—December

TITLE INDEX

All films reviewed are listed alphabetically by title. Titles are inverted only if they begin with an article ("Doctor Glas" is listed under D, not G; but "The Graduate" is listed under G, not T). Titles beginning with a number are alphabetized as though the number were spelled out. Wherever possible, foreign films are entered under both the English and foreign-language title. Titles given incorrectly in the review appear correctly here. Films reviewed more than once and films with identical titles are given multiple listings.

PERSONS INDEX

All persons included in the credits are listed alphabetically, last name first. Their function in the films is listed after the name in parentheses, such as director, producer, screenwriter, etc. In entries where no such qualifier appears, the person was a performer (actor, actress, singer). A person with multiple functions will have multiple entries; for example, an actor who later turned producer or director will have two listings. A person having two functions in the same film will also have two listings. Functions that are very uncommon or are given imprecisely in the reviews are designated miscellaneous (misc).

Names beginning with Mc are alphabetized as though spelled Mac.

Entries under each name are by title of film, in chronological order.

CORPORATIONS INDEX

All companies mentioned in reviews as involved in the production or distribution of the film or in some other major function connected with it are listed here alphabetically. Company names are not inverted unless they start with a personal surname (for example, J Arthur Rank Organization is listed as Rank, J Arthur, Organization). The function of the company is given in parentheses after the name, abbreviated as follows:

Prod—Producer
Distr—Distributer
Misc—Miscellaneous

Misc is used when the function is uncommon or not precisely defined in the review. A company that has more than one function is given more than one listing; thus a user who has completed scanning a long listing under RKO (Distr) will then find an additional listing under RKO (Prod).

Abbreviations in names are alphabetized as though they were words (RKO as Rko).

Entries under each company name are by title of film, in chronological order.

A

Aaron, Jack
Spook Who Sat by the Door, The 1973,S 22,18:1
Aarsted, Turid
Snapshots 1973,D 14,57:1
Abel, Robert (Director)
Let the Good Times Roll 1973,My 26,18:1
Elvis on Tour 1973,Je 7,54:1
Let the Good Times Roll 1973,Jl 8,II,8:1
Abel, Robert (Miscellaneous)
Elvis on Tour 1973,Je 17,II,1:1
Abel, Robert (Producer)
Elvis on Tour 1973,Je 7,54:1
Abelino, Dino
Sambizanga 1973,N 22,50:2
Abplanalp, Armand
Tear in the Ocean, A 1973,O 1,45:2
Abramson, Zivit
But Where Is Daniel Vax? 1974,Ap 1,42:1
Abroms, Edward M (Miscellaneous)
Sugarland Express, The 1974,Mr 30,20:1
Abzug, Bella
Year of the Woman 1973,O 20,27:2
Ackerman, Leslie
Law and Disorder 1974,O 10,62:1
Ackland, Joss
England Made Me 1973,N 19,53:1
Black Windmill, The 1974,My 18,18:4
Little Prince, The 1974,N 8,24:1
Adachi, Masao
Death by Hanging (Koshikel) 1974,F 15,23:1
Adachi, Masao (Screenwriter)
Diary of a Shinjuku Burglar 1973,Jl 6,7:1
Adams, Lillian
Heavy Traffic 1973,Ag 9,30:1
Adams, Maud
Christian Licorice Store, The 1974,Ap 5,27:4
Adams, Richard L (Screenwriter)
Slams, The 1973,S 27,45:1
Addams, Dawn
Vault of Horror, The 1973,Mr 17,17:1
King in New York, A 1973,D 22,11:1
King in New York, A 1974,Ja 20,II,1:1
Addison, John (Composer)
Luther 1974,F 5,30:1
Addobbati, Giuseppe
Night Porter, The 1974,O 2,58:1
Adidge, Pierre (Director)
Elvis on Tour 1973,Je 7,54:1
Let the Good Times Roll 1973,Jl 8,II,8:1
Adidge, Pierre (Miscellaneous)
Elvis on Tour 1973,Je 17,II,1:1
Adidge, Pierre (Producer)
Elvis on Tour 1973,Je 7,54:1
Adler, Luther
Crazy Joe 1974,F 16,36:2
Adorf, Mario
Italian Connection, The 1973,N 1,48:1
Advis, Luis (Composer)
Promised Land, The (La Tierra Prometida)
1974,Ap 8,43:1
Agostini, Claude (Cinematographer)
Sambizanga 1973,N 22,50:2
Aguila, Rigoberto
First Charge of the Machete (La Primera Carga al
Machete) 1974,Jl 5,11:1
Ahern, Lloyd (Cinematographer)
Klansman, The 1974,N 21,54:1
Ahlstedt, Borge
You're Lying 1973,My 5,25:3
'Til Sex Do Us Part 1974,O 5,17:1
Aidman, Charles
Dirty Little Billy 1973,My 19,28:1
Aimimi, Jean-Claude
Adieu Philippine 1973,My 17,56:4
Akins, Claude
Battle for the Planet of the Apes 1973,Jl 13,9:1
Akira, Kurosawa (Director)
Sanshiro Sugata 1974,Ap 29,49:1
Akutagawa, Yasushi (Composer)
Scarlet Camellia, The (Goben No Tsubaki)
1973,S 27,45:1
Alarcon, Lucho
Que Hacer 1973,S 29,22:1
Alarcon, Luis
Chacal de Nahueltoro, El (The Jackal of
Nahueltoro) 1974,Ap 13,18:1
Albee, Edward (Original Author)
Delicate Balance, A 1973,D 11,52:1
Delicate Balance, A 1974,Ja 27,II,1:7

Albee, Edward (Screenwriter)
Delicate Balance, A 1973,D 11,52:1
Albert, Arthur (Cinematographer)
Old Fashioned Woman 1974,D 19,60:5
Albert, Eddie
Heartbreak Kid, The 1973,S 9,II,1:3
MCQ 1974,F 7,46:1
Longest Yard, The 1974,Ag 22,28:1
Longest Yard, The 1974,S 15,II,1:5
Albert, Edward
40 Carats 1973,Je 29,14:1
Albert, Marvin H (Original Author)
Don Is Dead, The 1973,N 15,58:3
Albert, Marvin H (Screenwriter)
Don Is Dead, The 1973,N 15,58:3
Albert, Ross (Screenwriter)
Erotic Cinema (Kiss) 1974,My 10,24:3
Alberti, Barbara (Original Author)
Night Porter, The 1974,O 2,58:1
Alberti, Guido
What? 1973,O 4,57:1
Albertson, Eric (Miscellaneous)
From the Mixed-Up Files of Mrs Basil E
Frankweiler 1973,S 28,25:1
Albertson, Jack
Poseidon Adventure, The 1973,Ja 14,II,1:6
Poseidon Adventure, The 1973,Ja 21,II,13:6
Alcan, Gerard (Director)
Second Gun, The 1973,O 9,43:1
Alcan, Gerard (Miscellaneous)
Second Gun, The 1973,O 9,43:1
Alcan, Gerard (Producer)
Second Gun, The 1973,O 9,43:1
Alcan, Gerard (Screenwriter)
Second Gun, The 1973,O 9,43:1
Alcivar, Bob (Composer)
Crazy World of Julius Vrooder, The 1974,O 21,48:6
Alderton, John
Zardoz 1974,F 7,46:1
Aldous, Lucette
Don Quixote 1973,N 3,25:1
Aldrich, Robert (Director)
Emperor of the North Pole 1973,My 25,23:1
Emperor of the North Pole 1973,Je 3,II,1:3
Longest Yard, The 1974,Ag 22,28:1
Longest Yard, The 1974,S 15,II,1:5
Alea, Tomas Gutierrez (Director)
Memories of Underdevelopment (Memorias del
Subdesarrollo) 1973,My 18,28:1
Memories of Underdevelopment (Memorias del
Subdesarrollo) 1974,Ja 6,II,1:2
Memories of Underdevelopment 1974,Ja 7,38:3
Memories of Underdevelopment 1974,F 17,II,1:1
Alea, Tomas Gutierrez (Screenwriter)
Memories of Underdevelopment (Memorias del
Subdesarrollo) 1973,My 18,28:1
Memories of Underdevelopment (Memorias del
Subdesarrollo) 1974,Ja 6,II,1:2
Alexander, Curt (Screenwriter)
Liebelei 1974,S 30,51:5
Alexander, Edward
Saphead, The 1974,Ag 28,16:1
Alexander, Larry (Screenwriter)
Stoolie, The 1974,My 22,36:2
Alexander, Peter (Director)
Divine Mr J, The 1974,My 25,16:2
Alexander, Peter (Producer)
Divine Mr J, The 1974,My 25,16:2
Alexander, William (Producer)
Klansman, The 1974,N 21,54:1
Alfi, Volfango (Cinematographer)
Villeggiatura, La (Black Holiday) 1974,Ap 9,37:1
Alfredson, Hans
New Land, The 1973,O 27,17:1
Ali, Muhammad
Fighters, The 1974,Ja 5,34:4
Alice, Mary
Education of Sonny Carson, The 1974,Jl 18,32:1
Allan, Valerie
Disney on Parade 1973,Ag 1,49:3
Allen, Dede (Miscellaneous)
Serpico 1973,D 6,61:1
Allen, George
Soul of Nigger Charley, The 1973,My 17,54:1
Allen, Irwin (Director)
Towering Inferno, The 1974,D 20,20:1
Allen, Irwin (Producer)
Towering Inferno, The 1974,D 20,20:1
Allen, Jay (Original Author)
40 Carats 1973,Je 29,14:1
Allen, Penny
Scarecrow 1973,Ap 12,56:1

Allen, Rex
Charlotte's Web 1973,F 23,18:1
Allen, Woody
Sleeper 1973,D 18,52:1
Sleeper 1973,D 23,II,3:7
Sleeper 1974,Ja 6,II,1:2
Allen, Woody (Director)
Sleeper 1973,D 18,52:1
Sleeper 1973,D 23,II,3:7
Sleeper 1974,Ja 6,II,1:2
Allen, Woody (Screenwriter)
Sleeper 1973,D 18,52:1
Sleeper 1973,D 23,II,3:7
Sleeper 1974,Ja 6,II,1:2
Allin, Michael (Screenwriter)
Enter the Dragon 1973,Ag 18,26:1
Truck Turner 1974,Je 27,54:4
Almagor, Gila
House on Chelouche Street, The 1974,Ap 18,51:1
Alonzo, John (Cinematographer)
Wattstax 1973,F 16,17:1
Get to Know Your Rabbit 1973,S 21,49:1
Conrack 1974,Mr 28,33:1
Alonzo, John A (Cinematographer)
Hit 1973,S 19,38:3
Chinatown 1974,Je 21,26:1
Altman, Robert (Director)
Long Goodbye, The 1973,O 28,II,1:1
Long Goodbye, The 1973,O 29,42:1
Long Goodbye, The 1973,N 18,II,1:1
Long Goodbye, The 1974,Ja 6,II,1:2
Long Goodbye, The 1974,Ja 13,II,13:1
Thieves Like Us 1974,F 12,41:1
Thieves Like Us 1974,Ap 7,II,1:6
California Split 1974,Ag 8,28:1
California Split 1974,S 1,II,9:1
California Split 1974,S 29,II,1:1
Altman, Robert (Producer)
California Split 1974,Ag 8,28:1
Altman, Robert (Screenwriter)
Thieves Like Us 1974,F 12,41:1
Amendola, Mario (Screenwriter)
Battle of the Amazons 1973,N 22,51:2
America, Paul
Ciao! Manhattan 1973,Ap 20,15:1
Amico, Gianni (Director)
Ritorno 1973,O 1,44:3
Amico, Gianni (Screenwriter)
Ritorno 1973,O 1,44:3
Partner 1974,F 7,46:1
Lion Has Seven Heads, The 1974,F 8,17:1
Amin, Abbas (Miscellaneous)
Flesh Gordon 1974,Jl 31,20:1
Ammann, Peter (Director)
Red Train, The 1974,Mr 30,20:1
Ammann, Peter (Producer)
Red Train, The 1974,Mr 30,20:1
Ammann, Peter (Screenwriter)
Red Train, The 1974,Mr 30,20:1
Amodio, Amadeo
Night Porter, The 1974,O 13,II,1:6
Amos, John
World's Greatest Athlete, The 1973,F 5,25:1
Amour, Yvette Brind
Pyx, The 1974,Mr 28,34:1
Anders, Luana
Last Detail, The 1974,F 11,50:1
Anderson, Bill (Producer)
Charley and the Angel 1973,Je 28,58:1
Anderson, Carl
Jesus Christ Superstar 1973,Ag 8,28:1
Anderson, Edward (Original Author)
Thieves Like Us 1974,F 12,41:1
Thieves Like Us 1974,Ap 7,II,1:6
Anderson, Esther
Warm December, A 1973,My 24,53:1
Anderson, Georges (Composer)
Soleil-o 1973,Mr 15,55:3
Anderson, John
Executive Action 1973,N 8,60:1
Anderson, Ken (Screenwriter)
Robin Hood 1973,N 9,29:1
Anderson, Lindsay (Director)
O Lucky Man! 1973,Je 14,58:1
O Lucky Man! 1973,Je 24,II,1:3
O Lucky Man! 1973,Jl 8,II,8:1
Anderson, Lindsay (Producer)
O Lucky Man! 1973,Je 14,58:1
Anderson, Maxwell (Original Author)
Lost in the Stars 1974,My 7,54:1
Anderson, Michael (Cinematographer)
Jail, The 1974,F 8,20:3

C

8

Dunn, Liam
Blazing Saddles 1974,F 8,21:1
Dunn, Michael
Mutations, The 1974,S 26,26:2
Addication, The 1974,O 4,30:1
Dunning, George (Miscellaneous)
Maggot, The 1974,Ja 9,22:1
Duparc, Marguerite (Cinematographer)
ReJeanne Padovani 1973,O 2,56:3
Duparc-Lefebvre, Marguerite (Producer)
ReJeanne Padovani 1973,O 2,56:3
Duperey, Anny
Stavisky 1974,S 30,51:5
Stavisky 1974,D 23,32:2
Durand, Claude (Miscellaneous)
Adieu Philippine 1973,My 17,56:4
Durante, Jimmy
That's Entertainment 1974,Jl 7,II,1:6
Duras, Marguerite (Director)
Femme Du Gange, La (Woman of the Ganges)
1974,Je 7,23:1
Duras, Marguerite (Screenwriter)
Femme Du Gange, La (Woman of the Ganges)
1974,Je 7,23:1
Durell, Marina
Badge 373 1973,Jl 26,43:1
Durham, Marilyn (Original Author)
Man Who Loved Cat Dancing, The 1973,Je 29,17:1
Durning, Charles
Sisters 1973,S 27,44:4
Sting, The 1973,D 26,60:1
Front Page, The 1974,D 19,58:1
Duru, Frederic
Don't Cry With Your Mouth Full (Pieure Pas la
Bouche Pleine) 1974,S 28,25:1
Dusay, Marj
Breezy 1973,N 19,53:2
Dusenberry, Phil (Original Author)
Hail to the Chief 1973,Jl 28,16:1
Dusenberry, Phil (Screenwriter)
Hail to the Chief 1973,Jl 28,16:1
Dussollier, Andre
Such a Gorgeous Kid Like Me 1973,Mr 26,55:1
Dutta, Ahim (Producer)
Adversary, The (Pratidwandi) 1973,Jl 20,14:1
Dutta, Dulai (Miscellaneous)
Adversary, The (Pratidwandi) 1973,Jl 20,14:1
Distant Thunder (Ashani Sanket) 1973,O 12,32:1
Nyak-The Hero 1974,Jl 19,24:1
Dutte, Nepal (Producer)
Adversary, The (Pratidwandi) 1973,Jl 20,14:1
Duune, Dominick (Producer)
Ash Wednesday 1973,N 22,50:2
Duval, Roland (Screenwriter)
Don't Cry With Your Mouth Full (Pieure Pas la
Bouche Pleine) 1974,S 28,25:1
Duvall, Robert
Badge 373 1973,Jl 26,43:1
Lady Ice 1973,Ag 3,19:1
Outfit, The 1974,Ap 25,48:2
Godfather, Part II, The 1974,D 13,58:1
Godfather: Part II, The 1974,D 22,II,19:7
Duvall, Shelley
Thieves Like Us 1974,F 12,41:1
Thieves Like Us 1974,Ap 7,II,1:6
Dvornik, Boris
Man Is Not a Bird (Covek Nile Tijka)
1974,F 1,12:1
Dwoskin, Stephen (Cinematographer)
Dyn Amo 1973,Ap 28,21:1
Dwoskin, Stephen (Director)
Dyn Amo 1973,Ap 28,21:1
Dwoskin, Stephen (Miscellaneous)
Dyn Amo 1973,Ap 28,21:1
Dwoskin, Stephen (Screenwriter)
Death and Devil 1974,D 5,57:1
Dwoskin, Steve (Director)
Hindered 1974,N 15,33:1
Dylan, Bob
Pat Garrett and Billy the Kid 1973,My 24,53:1
Pat Garrett and Billy the Kid 1973,Je 3,II,1:3
Pat Garrett and Billy the Kid 1973,Je 17,II,13:4
Pat Garrett and Billy the Kid 1973,Jl 8,II,8:1
Dylan, Bob (Composer)
Pat Garrett and Billy the Kid 1973,My 24,53:1
Pat Garrett and Billy the Kid 1973,Je 17,II,13:4
Pat Garrett and Billy the Kid 1973,Jl 8,II,8:1
Dynam, Jacques
Petit Theatre de Jean Renoir, Le (The Little
Theater of Jean Renoir) 1974,My 3,46:1
Petit Theatre de Jean Renoir, Le (The Little
Theater of Jean Renoir) (The Electric Waxer)
1974,My 3,46:1
Dysart, Richard A
Terminal Man, The 1974,Je 20,47:2
Crazy World of Julius Vrooder, The 1974,O 21,48:6
Dzienisiewicz-Olbrychska, Monika
Illumination 1973,O 1,45:3

E

Eager, Brenda Lee
Save the Children 1973,S 19,40:2
East, Jeff
Tom Sawyer 1973,Mr 15,28:1
Huckleberry Finn 1974,My 25,16:1
Eastman, Carole (Screenwriter)
Fortune, The 1974,S 29,II,15:1
Five Easy Pieces 1974,S 29,II,15:1
Eastman, Charles (Director)
All-American Boy, The 1973,O 25,56:1
Eastman, Charles (Screenwriter)
All-American Boy, The 1973,O 25,56:1
Eastman, George
Scalawag 1973,N 15,58:7
Eastwood, Clint
High Plains Drifter 1973,Ap 20,21:1
Magnum Force 1973,D 26,60:1
Thunderbolt and Lightfoot 1974,My 24,23:3
Eastwood, Clint (Director)
High Plains Drifter 1973,Ap 20,21:1
Breezy 1973,N 19,53:2
Ebbinghouse, Bernard (Composer)
Tales That Witness Madness 1973,N 1,48:1
Eckemyr, Agneta
Island at the Top of the World 1974,D 21,18:6
Economou, Michael (Miscellaneous)
Five on the Black Hand Side 1973,O 26,51:1
Deadly Trackers, The 1973,D 22,11:1
Trial of Billy Jack, The 1974,N 14,58:1
Eda-Young, Barbara
Serpico 1973,D 6,61:1
Eddington, Paul
Baxter 1973,Mr 5,23:4
Ede, H S (Original Author)
Savage Messiah 1973,Ja 7,II,1:8
Edell, Nancy (Screenwriter)
Eroticism and Exploitation: (Charlie Company)
1973,Mr 2,23:1
Edelman, Herbert
Way We Were, The 1973,O 18,68:1
Front Page, The 1974,D 19,58:1
Edelman, Randy (Composer)
Executive Action 1973,N 8,60:1
Edogawa, Ranpo (Original Author)
Warehouse (Moju-Blind Beast) 1974,N 8,24:1
Edwards, Blake (Director)
Tamarind Seed, The 1974,Jl 12,41:1
Tamarind Seed, The 1974,Jl 21,II,1:1
Tamarind Seed, The 1974,Jl 28,II,1:1
Edwards, Blake (Screenwriter)
Tamarind Seed, The 1974,Jl 12,41:1
Tamarind Seed, The 1974,Jl 21,II,1:1
Edwards, Robert Gordon (Producer)
Ludwig 1973,Mr 9,27:1
Night Porter, The 1974,O 2,58:1
Edwards, Stephanie
Maurie 1973,Ag 2,31:1
Efron, Marshall
Bang the Drum Slowly 1973,Ag 27,35:1
Efroni, Yehudah
Kazablan 1974,My 9,54:1
Egan, Eddie
Badge 373 1973,Jl 26,43:1
Egan, Martin (Composer)
POW, The 1973,My 11,30:1
Egan, Peter
Hireling, The 1973,Je 11,45:1
Ege, Julie
Mutations, The 1974,S 26,26:2
Egea, Jose Luis (Director)
Challenges, A Trilogy, The: (Part II)
1973,Ap 13,48:2
Egleton, Clive (Original Author)
Black Windmill, The 1974,My 18,18:4
Egorova, Elena
Happiness 1973,My 25,24:1
Eguino, Antonio (Cinematographer)
Blood of the Condor 1973,Jl 27,19:3
Ehrenborg, Lennart (Producer)
Ra Expeditions, The 1974,Ag 15,25:1
Ehrlich, Max (Screenwriter)
Savage Is Loose, The 1974,N 16,21:1
Eichberger, Willy
Liebelei 1974,S 30,51:5
Eiji Okada
Face of Another 1974,My 8,36:3
Eikeberians, I K (Miscellaneous)
Rivers of Sand 1974,O 31,48:1
Ekland, Britt
Baxter 1973,Mr 5,23:4
Man With the Golden Gun, The 1974,D 19,60:5
Elam, Jack
Pat Garrett and Billy the Kid 1973,My 24,53:1
Elbacher, Cindy
Shanks 1974,O 10,62:1
Elcar, Dana
Sting, The 1973,D 26,60:1

Elder, John (Screenwriter)
Frankenstein and the Monster From Hell
1974,O 31,48:1
Eliash, Arie
Kazablan 1974,My 9,54:1
Elic, Josip
Dirty Little Billy 1973,My 19,28:1
Stoolie, The 1974,My 22,36:2
Elizondo, Hector
Taking of Pelham One Two Three, The
1974,O 3,50:1
Elkins, Hillard (Producer)
Doll's House, A 1973,My 23,38:1
Eller, Carl
Black Six, The 1974,Mr 14,42:1
Elliman, Yvonne
Jesus Christ Superstar 1973,Ag 8,28:1
Ellinger, Mark (Screenwriter)
Spring Potpourri: (Boggy Depot) 1974,My 10,24:5
Elliot, J Arthur (Producer)
I Am a Dancer 1973,Mr 29,41:1
Elliot, Stephen
Death Wish 1974,Jl 25,27:1
Elliott, Denholm
Vault of Horror, The 1973,Mr 17,17:1
Doll's House, A 1973,My 23,38:1
Doll's House, A 1973,Je 3,II,1:3
Apprenticeship of Duddy Kravitz, The
1974,Jl 15,31:4
Apprenticeship of Duddy Kravitz, The
1974,Jl 28,II,1:1
Apprenticeship of Duddy Kravitz, The
1974,Ag 25,II,11:1
Elliott, Jack (Composer)
Get to Know Your Rabbit 1973,S 21,49:1
Elliott, William
Coffy 1973,Je 16,13:3
Ellsworth, Scott
Girls Are for Loving 1973,My 26,19:1
Elwenspoek, Hans
Hunters Are the Hunted, The (Jagdszenen aus
Niederbayern) 1973,My 31,48:4
Embassahy, Eduardo
How Tasty Was My Little Frenchman
1973,Ap 17,34:1
Emi, Sanee
Lake of Dracula 1973,S 1,14:3
Emmich, Cliff
Payday 1973,F 23,22:1
Payday 1973,Mr 11,II,13:7
Emotions, The
Wattstax 1973,F 16,17:1
Emshwiller, Ed (Miscellaneous)
Painters Painting 1973,Mr 20,30:1
Engel, Jules (Screenwriter)
Animation: (Train Landscape) 1974,N 21,54:3
Engel, Susan
Butley 1974,Ap 9,34:1
Englund, Robert
Buster and Billie 1974,Ag 22,28:1
Engstrom, Stig
You're Lying 1973,My 5,25:3
Equarzina, Luigi
Mattei Affair, The 1973,My 21,40:1
Erdmann, Hans (Composer)
Testament of Dr Mabuse, The 1973,D 6,61:1
Testament of Dr Mabuse, The 1974,Ag 27,25:4
Erice, Victor (Director)
Challenges, A Trilogy, The: (Part III)
1973,Ap 13,48:2
Erickson, Carl (Screenwriter)
Black Fury 1973,Jl 1,II,9:1
Eriksson, Bengt Gunnar (Miscellaneous)
Ra Expeditions, The 1974,Ag 15,25:1
Erlich, Jacques (Miscellaneous)
But Where Is Daniel Vax? 1974,Ap 1,42:1
Erlichman, Martin (Producer)
For Pete's Sake 1974,Je 27,54:2
Ernryd, Bengt (Composer)
New Land, The 1973,O 27,17:1
Ernst, Donald W (Miscellaneous)
Heavy Traffic 1973,Ag 9,30:1
Ernst, Ole
First Circle, The 1973,Ja 13,17:3
Erwitt, Elliott (Cinematographer)
American Dreams and Nightmares: (Beauty Knows
No Pain) 1973,Ja 5,14:2
Erwitt, Elliott (Director)
American Dreams and Nightmares: (Beauty Knows
No Pain) 1973,Ja 5,14:2
Red White and Bluegrass 1974,Ap 16,44:1
Erwitt, Elliott (Producer)
American Dreams and Nightmares: (Beauty Knows
No Pain) 1973,Ja 5,14:2
Escorel, Lauro (Cinematographer)
All Nudity Shall Be Punished (Todo Nudez Sera
Castigada) 1974,Ap 1,42:1
Esheto, Debebe
Shaft in Africa 1973,Je 21,53:1
Espinosa, Julio Garcia (Screenwriter)
First Charge of the Machete (La Primera Carga al
Machete) 1974,Jl 5,11:1

15

G

Gerdt, Zinovi
Golden Calf, The (If I Had One Million Rubies)
1974,Je 14,19:1
Germain, Gregoire
Soleil-o 1973,Mr 15,55:3
Germi, Pietro (Director)
Alfredo Alfredo 1973,D 18,54:1
Germi, Pietro (Original Author)
Alfredo Alfredo 1973,D 18,54:1
Germi, Pietro (Screenwriter)
Alfredo Alfredo 1973,D 18,54:1
Gershe, Leonard (Screenwriter)
40 Carats 1973,Je 29,14:1
Gershfeld, Burton (Producer)
Prison Girls 1973,Ja 25,51:6
Gershwin, Jerry (Producer)
Your Three Minutes Are Up 1974,Mr 28,34:1
Gerstad, Harry (Miscellaneous)
Walking Tall 1974,F 9,18:1
Gettinger, Peter (Producer)
I Love You Rosa 1973,F 17,39:2
Ghia, Fernando (Producer)
Lady Caroline Lamb 1973,F 12,24:4
Gholson, Julie
Where the Lilies Bloom 1974,Je 8,18:4
Ghostley, Alice
Ace Eli and Rodger of the Skies 1974,Mr 2,22:5
Giacobino, Giuseppe (Miscellaneous)
Villeggiatura, La (Black Holiday) 1974,Ap 9,37:1
Giagni, Daniel
First Position 1973,Je 2,19:1
Gianini, Giulio (Director)
Frederick 1974,Ap 5,27:5
Giannini, Giancarlo
Love and Anarchy 1974,Ap 15,41:1
Seduction of Mimi, The (Mimi Metallurgico ferito
nell'onore) 1974,Je 19,40:3
Love and Anarchy 1974,Je 23,II,13:1
Gibbs, Ann
Private Parts 1973,F 2,16:1
Gibbs, Antony (Miscellaneous)
Ragman's Daughter, The 1974,Mr 25,39:1
Black Windmill, The 1974,My 18,18:4
Gibbs, Mark
Sweet Jesus, Preacher Man 1973,My 26,27:2
Gibney, Sheridan (Screenwriter)
I Am a Fugitive From a Chain Gang
1973,Jl 1,II,9:1
Gibson, Henry
Charlotte's Web 1973,F 23,18:1
Long Goodbye, The 1973,O 29,42:1
Long Goodbye, The 1973,N 18,II,1:1
Gibson, Richard M (Producer)
Childhood II 1973,F 26,28:1
Gielgud, John
Lost Horizon 1973,Mr 15,58:1
Lost Horizon 1973,Mr 18,II,1:6
11 Harrowhouse 1974,S 27,49:1
Gold 1974,O 17,57:1
Murder on the Orient Express 1974,N 25,38:1
Gieshe, Therese
Lacombe, Lucien 1974,S 30,52:1
Giffard, Ellen (Director)
Christo's Valley Curtain 1974,Mr 15,20:1
Gifford, Alan
Phase IV 1974,O 21,48:6
Gilbert, Edmund
Howzer 1973,O 19,58:1
Giler, David (Screenwriter)
Parallax View, The 1974,Je 20,47:1
Gilford, Jack
Save The Tiger 1973,F 15,53:1
Save the Tiger 1973,Mr 25,II,13:1
Save the Tiger 1973,S 9,II,1:3
Gilic, Vlatko (Director)
Power 1974,Ja 18,25:1
To Love 1974,Ja 18,25:1
One Day More 1974,Ja 18,25:1
Continuo, In 1974,Ja 18,25:1
Gilic, Vlatko (Producer)
Continuo, In 1974,Ja 18,25:1
To Love 1974,Ja 18,25:1
Power 1974,Ja 18,25:1
One Day More 1974,Ja 18,25:1
Gill, Beverly
Scream Blacula Scream 1973,Jl 19,31:1
Gilliam, Burton
Paper Moon 1973,My 17,53:1
Gillis, Ivry (Composer)
Tear in the Ocean, A 1973,O 1,45:2
Ging, Jack
Sssssss 1973,Ag 2,31:1
That Man Bolt 1973,D 24,21:1
Giorgio, Tony
Harry in Your Pocket 1973,S 24,39:1
Giovanelli, Franco
Spider's Stratagem, The 1973,Ja 6,21:1
Girard, Daniele
Such a Gorgeous Kid Like Me 1973,Mr 26,55:1
Giraud, Claude
Phedre 1973,Mr 30,34:1
Mad Adventures of "Rabbi" Jacob, The
1974,Jl 18,32:1

Girdler, William (Director)
Abby 1974,D 26,53:1
Girdler, William (Original Author)
Abby 1974,D 26,53:1
Girdler, William (Producer)
Abby 1974,D 26,53:1
Girod, Francis (Director)
Trio Infernal, Le 1974,N 9,24:1
Girod, Francis (Screenwriter)
Trio Infernal, Le 1974,N 9,24:1
Girotti, Massimo
Baron Blood 1973,F 8,36:3
Girouard, Tina (Director)
Dissolve 1973,F 1,41:1
Giurato, Blasco (Cinematographer)
Seduction of Mimi, The (Mimi Metallurgico ferito
nell'onore) 1974,Je 19,40:3
Gizzi, Claudio (Composer)
What? 1973,O 4,57:1
Andy Warhol's Frankenstein 1974,My 16,52:1
Gladwell, David (Miscellaneous)
O Lucky Man! 1973,Je 14,58:1
Glaeser, Henri
Tear in the Ocean, A 1973,O 1,45:2
Glaeser, Henri (Director)
Tear in the Ocean, A 1973,O 1,45:2
Glaeser, Henri (Producer)
Tear in the Ocean, A 1973,O 1,45:2
Glaeser, Henri (Screenwriter)
Tear in the Ocean, A 1973,O 1,45:2
Glasberg, Jimmy (Cinematographer)
Red Train, The 1974,Mr 30,20:1
Glascock, Baylis (Cinematographer)
Anais Nin Observed 1974,Je 28,20:1
Henry Miller Odyssey, The 1974,S 13,31:1
Gleckler, Gayle (Screenwriter)
Lords of Flatbush, The 1974,My 2,61:5
Glen, John (Miscellaneous)
Pulp 1973,F 9,32:1
Doll's House, A 1973,My 23,38:1
Gold 1974,O 17,57:1
Glenn, Pierre William (Cinematographer)
Such a Gorgeous Kid Like Me 1973,Mr 26,55:1
State of Siege 1973,Ap 14,39:1
Day for Night (La Nuit Amercaine) 1973,S 29,22:1
Out One/Spectre 1974,O 8,38:1
Glissand, Gabriel
Soleil-o 1973,Mr 15,55:3
Globus, Yoram (Producer)
I Love You Rosa 1973,F 17,39:2
Gloria, Darlene
All Nudity Shall Be Punished (Todo Nudez Sera
Castigada) 1974,Ap 1,42:1
Glouner, Richard C (Cinematographer)
Soul of Nigger Charley, The 1973,My 17,54:1
Glover, Bruce
Walking Tall 1974,F 9,18:1
Godard, Jean-Luc (Director)
Tout Va Bien 1973,F 17,39:1
Tout Va Bien (Just Great) 1973,F 25,II,1:1
Godard, Jean-Luc (Screenwriter)
Tout Va Bien 1973,F 17,39:1
Tout Va Bien (Just Great) 1973,F 25,II,1:1
Letter to Jane 1974,Ap 12,18:3
Godey, John (Original Author)
Taking of Pelham One Two Three, The
1974,O 3,50:1
Godin, Jacques
Pyx, The 1974,Mr 28,34:1
Godmilow, Jill (Director)
Antonia: A Portrait of the Woman 1974,S 19,50:1
Godmilow, Jill (Miscellaneous)
Antonia: A Portrait of the Woman 1974,S 19,50:1
Golan, Menahem (Director)
Kazablan 1974,My 9,54:1
Golan, Menahem (Producer)
I Love You Rosa 1973,F 17,39:2
Goldberg, Bart (Screenwriter)
American Dreams and Nightmares: (The Chromium
Horse) 1973,Ja 5,14:2
Goldberg, Leonard (Producer)
California Split 1974,Ag 8,28:1
Golden, John (Producer)
Saphead, The 1974,Ag 28,16:1
Goldenberg, Billy (Composer)
Last of Sheila, The 1973,Je 15,24:1
Busting 1974,F 28,33:1
Goldman, Danny
World's Greatest Athlete, The 1973,F 5,25:1
Goldsmith, Jerry (Composer)
Shamus 1973,F 1,41:1
Don Is Dead, The 1973,N 15,58:3
Papillon 1973,D 17,59:1
Ace Eli and Rodger of the Skies 1974,Mr 2,22:5
Chinatown 1974,Je 21,26:1
Goldsmith, Paul
Snapshots 1973,D 14,57:1
Goldsmith, Paul (Cinematographer)
Jeremy 1973,Ag 2,28:1
Goldsmith, Silvianna (Screenwriter)
Women Artists As Filmmakers, Part One: (The
Transformation of Persephone) 1973,Ja 29,25:1

Goldstein, Neal (Composer)
POW, The 1973,My 11,30:1
Goldstein, William (Composer)
Stoolie, The 1974,My 22,36:2
Goldstein, William (Miscellaneous)
Dr Phibes Rises Again 1973,Ja 11,35:1
Gomska, Mascha
Trio Infernal, Le 1974,N 9,24:1
Good, Jack (Producer)
Catch My Soul 1974,Mr 23,20:1
Good, Jack (Screenwriter)
Catch My Soul 1974,Mr 23,20:1
Goodfellow, Joan
Lolly-Madonna XXX 1973,F 22,30:1
Buster and Billie 1974,Ag 22,28:1
Goodier, Robert
Apprenticeship of Duddy Kravitz, The
1974,Jl 15,31:4
Goodis, David (Original Author)
..And to Hope to Die 1973,Ja 7,II,1:8
Goodman, David Zelag (Screenwriter)
Man on a Swing 1974,F 28,33:1
Goodman, Jesse (Cinematographer)
Attica 1974,Ap 12,18:1
Goodrow, Garry
Steelyard Blues 1973,F 1,41:1
Goodwin, Angela
Come Have Coffee With Us 1973,Ap 6,28:1
Goodwin, Richard (Producer)
Murder on the Orient Express 1974,N 25,38:1
Goofy
Disney on Parade 1973,Ag 1,49:3
Gora, Claudio
Confessions of a Police Captain 1974,Ag 16,18:2
Goraguer, Alain (Composer)
Fantastic Planet 1973,D 19,54:2
Gordon, Carl
Gordon's War 1973,Ag 10,26:2
Gordon, Don
Mack, The 1973,Ap 5,51:2
Papillon 1973,D 17,59:1
Education of Sonny Carson, The 1974,Jl 18,32:1
Gordon, Leo
My Name Is Nobody 1974,Jl 18,30:1
Gordon, Ruth
Harold and Maude 1974,My 26,II,1:4
Gorin, Jean-Pierre (Director)
Tout Va Bien 1973,F 17,39:1
Gorin, Jean-Pierre (Screenwriter)
Tout Va Bien 1973,F 17,39:1
Tout Va Bien (Just Great) 1973,F 25,II,1:1
Letter to Jane 1974,Ap 12,18:3
Gorman, Cliff
Cops and Robbers 1973,Ag 16,40:1
Cops and Robbers 1973,S 23,II,1:6
Cops and Robbers 1974,Ja 20,II,1:4
Gorman, Gayle
Cops and Robbers 1973,Ag 16,40:1
Gortchev, Anton
Goat's Horn, The 1974,Ag 23,16:4
Gortner, Marioe
Earthquake 1974,N 16,20:2
Gossett, Dion
Tough 1974,Jl 25,27:1
Gossett, Lou
Laughing Policeman, The 1973,D 21,46:1
White Dawn, The 1974,Jl 22,41:1
White Dawn, The 1974,Jl 28,II,1:1
Gottheim, Larry (Screenwriter)
Horizons 1974,N 7,56:6
Harmonica 1974,N 7,56:6
Gottlieb, Gordon (Composer)
Very Natural Thing, A 1974,Je 28,22:1
Gottlieb, Linda (Producer)
Limbo 1973,Ja 27,17:1
Gould, Elliott
Long Goodbye, The 1973,O 28,II,1:1
Long Goodbye, The 1973,O 29,42:1
Long Goodbye, The 1973,N 18,II,1:1
Busting 1974,Ja 20,II,1:4
M*A*S*H 1974,Ja 20,II,1:4
S*P*Y*S 1974,Ja 20,II,1:4
Busting 1974,F 28,33:1
California Split 1974,Ag 8,28:1
Touch, The 1974,Ag 11,II,1:1
S*P*Y*S 1974,Ag 11,II,11:1
California Split 1974,S 1,II,9:1
California Split 1974,S 29,II,1:1
Gould, Harold
Sting, The 1973,D 26,60:1
Front Page, The 1974,D 19,58:1
Gowers, Patrick (Composer)
Bigger Splash, A 1974,O 4,31:2
Graf, Josef
If I Had a Gun 1973,Ja 19,23:1
Grafton, Sue (Original Author)
Lolly-Madonna XXX 1973,F 22,30:1
Grafton, Sue (Screenwriter)
Lolly-Madonna XXX 1973,F 22,30:1
Graham, Gerrit
Phantom of the Paradise 1974,N 2,16:3
Graham, Ranald (Screenwriter)
Shanks 1974,O 10,62:1

Hinnant, Skip
Plastic Dome of Norma Jean, The 1974,Jl 12,44:1
Hinton, James E (Cinematographer)
Ganja & Hess 1973,Ap 21,19:2
Hinton-Jacobs, Lawrence
Claudine 1974,Ap 23,34:3
Hinzman, S William (Cinematographer)
Crazies, The 1973,Mr 24,20:1
Hipp, Paul E (Cinematographer)
Sweet Jesus, Preacher Man 1973,My 26,27:2
Hiroshi Teshigahara (Director)
Face of Another 1974,My 8,36:3
Hirsch, Paul (Miscellaneous)
Sisters 1973,S 27,44:4
Phantom of the Paradise 1974,N 2,16:3
Hirschfield, Gerald (Cinematographer)
Summer Wishes, Winter Dreams 1973,O 22,46:1
Young Frankenstein 1974,D 16,48:1
Hirschmuller, Hans
Merchant of Four Seasons, The 1973,N 17,26:1
Hirtz, Dagmar
Pedestrian, The 1974,Mr 1,16:1
Hirtz, Dagmar (Miscellaneous)
Pedestrian, The 1974,Mr 1,16:1
Hiss, Nicole
Femme Du Gange, La (Woman of the Ganges)
1974,Je 7,23:1
Hitzig, Rupert (Original Author)
Electra Glide in Blue 1973,Ag 20,21:1
Ho Cheng Chang (Director)
Five Fingers of Death 1973,Mr 22,54:3
Ho Lang Shang (Cinematographer)
Return of the Dragon 1974,Ag 8,30:1
Hoberman, James (Director)
Rocky Raccoon 1973,D 21,45:1
Hochman, Sandra
Year of the Woman 1973,O 20,27:2
Hochman, Sandra (Director)
Year of the Woman 1973,O 20,27:2
Year of the Woman, The 1973,O 28,II,1:1
Year of the Woman 1973,D 30,II,1:1
Hochman, Sandra (Producer)
Year of the Woman 1973,D 30,II,1:1
Hochman, Sandra (Screenwriter)
Year of the Woman 1973,O 20,27:2
Hock, Louis (Screenwriter)
Chicagofilm: (Silent Reversal) 1974,Ja 6,57:2
Hockney, David
Bigger Splash, A 1974,O 4,31:2
Hodges, Michael (Director)
Pulp 1973,F 9,32:1
Hodges, Michael (Screenwriter)
Pulp 1973,F 9,32:1
Hodges, Mike (Director)
Terminal Man, The 1974,Je 20,47:2
Hodges, Mike (Producer)
Terminal Man, The 1974,Je 20,47:2
Hodges, Mike (Screenwriter)
Terminal Man, The 1974,Je 20,47:2
Hodgson, Brian (Composer)
Legend of Hell House, The 1973,Je 16,14:5
Hoenig, Dov (Miscellaneous)
I Love You Rosa 1973,F 17,39:2
Hoerbiger, Paul
Liebelei 1974,S 30,51:5
Hoey, Michael A (Miscellaneous)
Class of '44 1973,Ap 11,41:1
Hoffman, Dustin
Straw Dogs 1973,S 30,II,1:4
Papillon 1973,D 17,59:1
Alfredo Alfredo 1973,D 18,54:1
Midnight Cowboy 1974,Ja 20,II,1:4
Papillon 1974,Ja 20,II,1:4
Lenny 1974,N 11,40:1
Lenny 1974,D 1,II,17:1
Hoffman, Hans
Painters Painting 1973,Mr 20,30:1
Hoffman, Jane
Up the Sandbox 1973,Ja 21,II,13:1
Hoffman, Peter (Screenwriter)
Narrative Cinema-Part Two: (Pilgrims)
1974,Mr 23,20:1
Hogg, Patricia
Hireling, The 1973,Je 11,45:1
Holbrook, Hal
Magnum Force 1973,D 26,60:1
Girl From Petrovka, The 1974,Ag 23,16:1
Holcombe, Harry
Foxy Brown 1974,Ap 6,16:2
Holden, William
Breezy 1973,N 19,53:2
Open Season 1974,N 2,16:3
Towering Inferno, The 1974,D 20,20:1
Holder, Geoffrey
Live and Let Die 1973,Je 28,56:1
Holdridge, Lee (Composer)
Jeremy 1973,Ag 2,28:1
Jonathan Livingston Seagull 1973,O 25,59:1
Holemder, Adam (Cinematographer)
Man on a Swing 1974,F 28,33:1
Hollar, Lloyd
Crazies, The 1973,Mr 24,20:1

Holly, Ellen
Cops and Robbers 1973,Ag 16,40:1
Holm, Celeste
Tom Sawyer 1973,Mr 15,28:1
Tom Sawyer 1973,Mr 25,II,1:2
Holm, Ian
Homecoming, The 1973,N 13,53:1
Homecoming, The 1974,Ja 6,II,1:2
Holmes, Chris (Miscellaneous)
Dirty Mary Crazy Larry 1974,Jl 11,27:1
Holmes, Christopher (Miscellaneous)
Slaughter's Big Ripoff 1973,S 1,14:3
All-American Boy, The 1973,O 25,56:1
Holmes, John W (Miscellaneous)
Showdown 1973,N 22,51:1
Holmes, Rich
Tough 1974,Jl 25,27:1
Holt, Nancy (Director)
Swamp 1973,F 1,41:1
Holzer, Jane
Ciao! Manhattan 1973,Ap 20,15:1
Homel, Bob
Boy Who Cried Werewolf, The 1973,Ag 2,31:1
Homel, Bob (Screenwriter)
Boy Who Cried Werewolf, The 1973,Ag 2,31:1
Homoika, Oscar
Tamarind Seed, The 1974,Jl 12,41:1
Honda, Shozo (Cinematographer)
Zatoichi's Conspiracy 1974,Ap 16,44:1
Hondo, Med (Director)
Soleil-o 1973,Mr 15,55:3
Hondo, Med (Screenwriter)
Soleil-o 1973,Mr 15,55:3
Hooks, Robert
Trouble Man 1973,Ja 7,II,1:8
Hopf, Heinz
They Call Her One Eye 1974,Je 6,49:7
Hopgood, Alan (Screenwriter)
Alvin Purple 1974,O 12,21:1
Hopkins, Anthony
Doll's House, A 1973,My 23,38:1
Doll's House, A 1973,Je 3,II,1:3
Girl From Petrovka, The 1974,Ag 23,16:1
Hopkins, Bo
Man Who Loved Cat Dancing, The 1973,Je 29,17:1
White Lightning 1973,Ag 9,30:2
Hopkins, John (Screenwriter)
Offence, The 1973,My 12,19:1
Offence, The 1973,Je 3,II,11:1
Hopper, Dennis
Kid Blue 1973,O 1,45:2
Hopper, Dennis (Director)
Last Movie, The 1974,Ja 13,II,1:1
Hora, John (Cinematographer)
Maurie 1973,Ag 2,31:1
Hordern, Michael
Theater of Blood 1973,My 12,19:1
Mackintosh Man, The 1973,Jl 26,44:1
England Made Me 1973,N 19,53:1
Horger, John C (Miscellaneous)
Thief Who Came to Dinner, The 1973,Mr 2,22:1
Battle for the Planet of the Apes 1973,Jl 13,9:1
Hornish, Rudy
POW, The 1973,My 11,30:1
Horsfall, Bernard
Gold 1974,O 17,57:1
Horton, Helen
Phase IV 1974,O 21,48:6
Hossein, Robert
Murder Is a Murder...Is a Murder, A
1974,N 28,47:2
Hotaka, Minoru
Sasuke Against the Wind 1973,S 6,43:1
Hotchkis, Joan
Breezy 1973,N 19,53:2
Hough, John (Director)
Legend of Hell House, The 1973,Je 16,14:5
Dirty Mary Crazy Larry 1974,Jl 11,27:1
Hough, Stan (Producer)
Emperor of the North Pole 1973,My 25,23:1
Houseman, John
Paper Chase, The 1973,O 28,II,1:1
Paper Chase, The 1973,N 4,II,1:6
Paper Chase, The 1974,Ap 3,36:1
Housman, John
Paper Chase, The 1973,O 17,55:1
Houston, Donald
Tales That Witness Madness 1973,N 1,48:1
Houston, James (Original Author)
White Dawn, The 1974,Jl 22,41:1
White Dawn, The 1974,Jl 28,II,1:1
Houston, James (Screenwriter)
White Dawn, The 1974,Jl 22,41:1
Houwer, Rob (Producer)
Hunters Are the Hunted, The (Jagdszenen aus
Niederbayern) 1973,My 31,48:4
Howard, Curly
Three Stooges Follies, The: (You Natzy Spy)
1974,N 25,37:6
Howard, Harry
Carry on Doctor 1973,F 8,36:3
Howard, Harry (Miscellaneous)
Super Cops, The 1974,Mr 21,51:1

Howard, Harry (Miscellaneous)—Cont
Education of Sonny Carson, The 1974,Jl 18,32:1
Howard, John (Miscellaneous)
Scalawag 1973,N 15,58:7
Blazing Saddles 1974,F 8,21:1
Young Frankenstein 1974,D 16,48:1
Howard, Mel (Director)
Snapshots 1973,D 14,57:1
Howard, Mel (Screenwriter)
Snapshots 1973,D 14,57:1
Howard, Moe
Three Stooges Follies, The: (You Natzy Spy)
1974,N 25,37:6
Howard, Rance
Where the Lilies Bloom 1974,Je 8,18:4
Howard, Rita
Ragman's Daughter, The 1974,Mr 25,39:1
Howard, Ron
Happy Mothers' Day, Love George
1973,Ag 18,26:1
Spikes Gang, The 1974,My 2,61:4
Howard, Ronny
American Graffiti 1973,Ag 5,II,1:4
American Graffiti 1973,Ag 13,21:1
American Graffiti 1973,S 16,II,1:1
American Graffiti 1973,D 2,II,13:1
American Graffiti 1974,Ja 6,II,1:2
Howard, Sanford (Producer)
Neptune Factor, The 1973,Ag 4,19:1
Howard, Trevor
Ludwig 1973,Mr 9,27:1
Ludwig 1973,Mr 18,II,1:6
Offence, The 1973,My 12,19:1
Doll's House, A 1973,O 2,54:1
11 Harrowhouse 1974,S 27,49:1
Hrusinsky, Rudolf
Cremator, The 1973,Ap 11,39:1
Hrzan, Jiri
Prison Guard 1973,Jl 13,19:1
Hsiang-ting, Ke
Deadly China Doll 1973,S 27,45:1
Hsiao-pei, Chou (Director)
Deadly China Doll 1973,S 27,45:1
Hsin-mei, Siao (Miscellaneous)
Deadly China Doll 1973,S 27,45:1
Hsing, Chen
Triple Irons 1973,S 25,37:1
Hsiung, Chao
Five Fingers of Death 1973,Mr 22,54:3
Hsun, Nan-Kung
Five Fingers of Death 1973,Mr 22,54:3
Huanca, Benedicta Mendoza
Blood of the Condor 1973,Jl 27,19:3
Huang, Carter
Deadly China Doll 1973,S 27,45:1
Hubbs, Gilbert (Cinematographer)
Enter the Dragon 1973,Ag 18,26:1
Golden Needles 1974,Jl 18,32:1
Hubley, Season
Lolly-Madonna XXX 1973,F 22,30:1
Catch My Soul 1974,Mr 23,20:1
Huddleston, David
MCQ 1974,F 7,46:1
Blazing Saddles 1974,F 8,21:1
Klansman, The 1974,N 21,54:1
Huddleston, Floyd (Composer)
Robin Hood 1973,N 9,29:1
Hudson, Fred (Screenwriter)
Education of Sonny Carson, The 1974,Jl 18,32:1
Hudson, Rock
Showdown 1973,N 22,51:1
Hughes, Barnard
Sisters 1973,S 27,44:4
Hughes, Tresa
Lolly-Madonna XXX 1973,F 22,30:1
Summer Wishes, Winter Dreams 1973,O 22,46:1
Hugo, Michael (Cinematographer)
Spook Who Sat by the Door, The 1973,S 22,18:1
Hugo, Michel (Screenwriter)
Artists at Work: (Sort of a Commercial for an
Icebag) 1974,Mr 18,39:8
Huie, William Bradford (Original Author)
Klansman, The 1974,N 21,54:1
Huillet, Daniele (Producer)
History Lessons 1973,O 1,45:2
Huillet, Daniele (Screenwriter)
History Lessons 1973,O 1,45:2
Huke, Bob (Cinematographer)
Under Milk Wood 1973,Ja 22,20:1
Hume, Alan (Cinematographer)
Legend of Hell House, The 1973,Je 16,14:5
Hume, Edward (Screenwriter)
Reflection of Fear, A 1973,F 13,25:5
Hundman, Earl
Parallax View, The 1974,Je 20,47:1
Hunnicutt, Arthur
Spikes Gang, The 1974,My 2,61:4
Harry and Tonto 1974,Ag 13,24:2
Hunnicutt, Gayle
Scorpio 1973,Ap 19,52:1
Legend of Hell House, The 1973,Je 16,14:5
Hunning, Carter
Lady Kung-Fu 1973,S 6,43:1

Hunt, Peter (Director)
Gold 1974,O 17,57:1
Hunter, Ross (Director)
Lost Horizon 1973,Mr 18,II,1:6
Hunter, Ross (Producer)
Lost Horizon 1973,Mr 15,58:1
Lost Horizon 1973,D 30,II,1:1
Huppert, Isabelle
Going Places 1974,My 14,31:1
Hussein, Waris (Director)
Henry VIII and His Six Wives 1973,D 14,57:1
Hussey, Olivia
Lost Horizon 1973,Mr 15,58:1
Lost Horizon 1973,Mr 18,II,1:6
Summertime Killer 1973,O 24,38:3
Huston, Christopher (Composer)
Prison Girls 1973,Ja 25,51:6
Huston, John
Battle for the Planet of the Apes 1973,Jl 13,9:1
Chinatown 1974,Je 21,26:1
Chinatown 1974,Jl 28,II,1:1
Chinatown 1974,Ag 11,II,11:1
Chinatown 1974,Ag 18,II,1:1
Chinatown 1974,S 1,II,9:1
Huston, John (Director)
Mackintosh Man, The 1973,Jl 26,44:1
Mackintosh Man, The 1973,Jl 29,II,1:3
Huston, Walter
Mission to Moscow 1973,Jl 1,II,9:1
Huszarik, Zoltan (Director)
Sindbad (Szindbad) 1974,O 25,24:1
Huszarik, Zoltan (Screenwriter)
Sindbad (Szindbad) 1974,O 25,24:1
Hutch, Willie (Composer)
Mack, The 1973,Ap 5,51:2
Foxy Brown 1974,Ap 6,16:2
Hutchinson, Robert (Screenwriter)
Spring Potpourri: (The Prodigal Wiener)
1974,My 10,24:5
Spring Potpourri: (The Mating Habits of the
Northern Pacific Kelp) 1974,My 10,24:5
Hutton, Brian G (Director)
Night Watch 1973,Ag 10,26:1
Hutton, Lauren
Gambler, The 1974,O 3,50:1
Hutton, Peter (Cinematographer)
Hippodrome Hardware 1973,F 17,39:1
Huyck, Willard (Screenwriter)
American Graffiti 1973,Ag 5,II,1:4
American Graffiti 1973,Ag 13,21:1
American Graffiti 1973,S 16,II,1:1
American Graffiti 1974,Ja 6,II,1:2
American Graffiti 1974,Ja 7,38:3
American Graffiti 1974,Ja 9,24:1
Radioland 1974,S 29,II,15:1
Napa Valley Story, The 1974,S 29,II,15:1
American Graffiti 1974,S 29,II,15:1
Lucky Lady 1974,S 29,II,15:1
Hyams, Peter (Director)
Busting 1974,F 28,33:1
Our Time 1974,Ap 11,31:1
Hyams, Peter (Screenwriter)
Busting 1974,F 28,33:1
Hykes, David (Director)
Moving Parts 1974,O 4,31:4
Hyman, Kenneth (Producer)
Emperor of the North Pole 1973,My 25,23:1

I

Iacobesco, Loumi
Lacombe, Lucien 1974,S 30,52:1
Ibbetson, Arthur (Cinematographer)
Doll's House, A 1973,My 23,38:1
11 Harrowhouse 1974,S 27,49:1
Ibsen, Henrik (Original Author)
Doll's House, A 1973,My 23,38:1
Doll's House, A 1973,Je 3,II,1:3
Doll's House, A 1973,O 2,54:1
Ichikawa, Kon (Director)
Visions of Eight 1973,Ag 11,25:3
Ifukube, Akira (Composer)
Zatoichi's Conspiracy 1974,Ap 16,44:1
Igawa, Hisashi
Dodes'Ka-Den 1974,O 18,28:1
Ignez, Helena
Priest and the Girl, The 1973,F 26,28:1
Ikebe, Ryo
Pale Flower 1974,My 13,36:8
Early Spring 1974,S 26,26:1
Ikehiro (Director)
Trail of Blood 1974,My 3,47:1
Ilf (Original Author)
Golden Calf, The (If I Had One Million Rubies)
1974,Je 14,19:1
Illig, Rolf (Narrator)
Land des Schweigens und der Dunkelheit (Land of
Silence and Darkness) 1973,O 9,43:1
Imafuku, Masao
Demons 1974,Ja 18,22:1
Ingalls, Don (Screenwriter)
Airport 1975 1974,O 19,63:4

Ingram, Luther
Wattstax 1973,F 16,17:1
Ingrassia, Ciccio
Amarcord (I Remember) 1974,S 20,32:1
Amarcord 1974,S 29,II,1:6
Intillimani Group (Miscellaneous)
Promised Land, The (La Tierra Prometida)
1974,Ap 8,43:1
Ionesco, Eugene (Original Author)
Rhinoceros 1974,Ja 22,30:3
Rhinoceros 1974,Ja 27,II,1:7
Irikawa, Yasunori
Sasuke Against the Wind 1973,S 6,43:1
Irvine, Louva (Screenwriter)
Spring Potpourri: (Rain) 1974,My 10,24:5
Irving, Richard (Producer)
Newman's Law 1974,Ag 22,28:1
Isasi, Antonio (Director)
Summertime Killer 1973,O 24,38:3
Isasi, Antonio (Producer)
Summertime Killer 1973,O 24,38:3
Isenberg, Gerald I (Producer)
Let the Good Times Roll 1973,My 26,18:1
Ishida, Toshiro
Death by Hanging (Koshikei) 1974,F 15,23:1
Ito, Yunosuke
Day the Sun Rose, The 1973,Ag 30,26:3
Iwasa, Toshie (Miscellaneous)
Funeral Parade of Roses 1973,Je 8,47:1
Iwasaki, Kaneko
Long Darkness, The 1973,Ag 18,26:1
Iwashita, Shima
Autumn Afternoon, An 1973,My 8,39:1
Day the Sun Rose, The 1973,Ag 30,26:3
Scarlet Camellia, The (Goben No Tsubaki)
1973,S 27,45:1
Izay, Victor
Trial of Billy Jack, The 1974,N 14,58:1

J

Jabara, Paul
Lords of Flatbush, The 1974,My 2,61:5
Jabor, Arnaldo (Director)
All Nudity Shall Be Punished (Todo Nudez Sera
Castigada) 1974,Ap 1,42:1
Jabor, Arnaldo (Screenwriter)
All Nudity Shall Be Punished (Todo Nudez Sera
Castigada) 1974,Ap 1,42:1
Jack, Wolfman
American Graffiti 1973,Ag 13,21:1
Jacks, Jeff (Original Author)
Black Eye 1974,My 18,18:4
Jackson, Glenda
Mary Queen of Scots 1973,Ja 7,II,1:8
Nelson Affair, The 1974,Ap 19,52:1
Touch of Class, A 1973,Je 21,52:1
Triple Echo 1973,N 1,48:1
Nelson Affair, The 1973,D 30,II,1:1
Touch of Class, A 1974,Ap 3,36:1
Jackson, Horace (Director)
Tough 1974,Jl 25,27:1
Jackson, Horace (Producer)
Tough 1974,Jl 25,27:1
Jackson, Horace (Screenwriter)
Tough 1974,Jl 25,27:1
Jackson, J J (Composer)
Badge 373 1973,Jl 26,43:1
Jackson, Jesse (Rev)
Save the Children 1973,S 19,40:2
Jackson, Kate
Limbo 1973,Ja 27,17:1
Jackson, Leonard
Ganja & Hess 1973,Ap 21,19:2
Five on the Black Hand Side 1973,O 26,51:1
Jackson, Merrell
Godspell 1973,Mr 22,52:1
Jackson Five
Save the Children 1973,S 19,40:2
Jacobi, Derek
Day of the Jackal, The 1973,My 17,53:1
Three Sisters 1974,Mr 12,34:4
Odessa File, The 1974,O 19,36:1
Jacobs, Alexander (Screenwriter)
Seven-Ups, The 1973,D 22,11:2
Jacobs, Allan (Miscellaneous)
Cleopatra Jones 1973,Jl 5,24:6
Jacobs, Arnold (Producer)
Marketa Lazarova 1974,Ag 30,19:1
Jacobs, Arthur J (Producer)
Battle for the Planet of the Apes 1973,Jl 13,9:1
Jacobs, Arthur P (Producer)
Tom Sawyer 1973,Mr 15,28:1
Huckleberry Finn 1974,My 25,16:1
Jacobs, Paul (Cinematographer)
Jail, The 1974,F 8,20:3
Jacobs, Paul (Director)
Jail, The 1974,F 8,20:3
Jacobs, Paul (Producer)
Jail, The 1974,F 8,20:3

Jacobs, Paul (Screenwriter)
Ann Arbor Film Festival: (Zombies In a House of
Madness) 1973,My 13,59:1
Jacoby, Joseph (Director)
Hurry Up, or I'll Be 30 1973,N 15,58:5
Jacoby, Joseph (Original Author)
Hurry Up, or I'll Be 30 1973,N 15,58:5
Jacoby, Joseph (Producer)
Hurry Up, or I'll Be 30 1973,N 15,58:5
Jacoby, Joseph (Screenwriter)
Hurry Up, or I'll Be 30 1973,N 15,58:5
Jacoby, Scott
Baxter 1973,Mr 5,23:4
Jacques, Hattie
Carry on Doctor 1973,F 8,36:3
Jae, Han
Lady Kung-Fu 1973,S 6,43:1
Jaeckel, Richard
Pat Garrett and Billy the Kid 1973,My 24,53:1
Pat Garrett and Billy the Kid 1973,Je 3,II,1:3
Outfit, The 1974,Ap 25,48:2
Chosen Survivors 1974,My 23,52:1
Jaeckin, Just (Director)
Emmanuelle 1974,D 16,47:5
Jaffe, Howard B (Producer)
Reflection of Fear, A 1973,F 13,25:5
Man on a Swing 1974,F 28,33:1
Jaffe, Pat (Miscellaneous)
Friends of Eddie Coyle, The 1973,Je 27,68:1
Jaggs, Alan L (Miscellaneous)
Battle for the Planet of the Apes 1973,Jl 13,9:1
Jahra, Howard
POW, The 1973,My 11,30:1
Jaime de Mora y Aragon, Don
Love and Pain and the Whole Damned Thing
1973,Ap 20,14:1
James, Clifton
Live and Let Die 1973,Je 28,56:1
Live and Let Die 1973,Jl 15,II,1:6
Kid Blue 1973,O 1,45:2
Last Detail, The 1974,F 11,50:1
Bank Shot 1974,Ag 1,18:6
Buster and Billie 1974,Ag 22,28:1
James, David (Screenwriter)
Narrative Cinema-Part Two: (My Weakness)
1974,Mr 23,20:1
James, Henry (Original Author)
Daisy Miller 1974,My 23,52:1
Daisy Miller 1974,Je 16,II,1:5
Daisy Miller 1974,Je 30,II,5:1
Bench of Desolation, The 1974,O 3,50:2
James, Sydney
Carry on Doctor 1973,F 8,36:3
King in New York, A 1974,Ja 20,II,1:1
Janeso, Miklos (Director)
Red Psalm 1973,Je 15,28:1
Rome Wants Another Caesar (Roma Rivusie
Cesare) 1974,O 2,58:1
Rome Wants Another Caesar 1974,N 3,II,15:1
Janeso, Miklos (Screenwriter)
Rome Wants Another Caesar (Roma Rivusie
Cesare) 1974,O 2,58:1
Janina
Save The Tiger 1973,F 15,53:1
Janni, Joseph (Producer)
Deaf Smith & Johnny Ears 1973,Jl 26,43:1
Jansen, Pierre (Composer)
Rupture, La (The Breakup) 1973,O 5,19:1
Juste Avant la Nuit (Just Before Nightfall)
1973,O 9,42:1
Wedding in Blood 1974,My 23,52:1
Ophelia 1974,Ag 8,30:1
Janson, Horst
Captain Kronos: Vampire Hunter 1974,O 31,48:1
Janzilli, Rosana
Amarcord (I Remember) 1974,S 20,32:1
Japrisot, Sebastian (Screenwriter)
..And to Hope to Die 1973,Ja 7,II,1:8
Jardin, Pascal (Screenwriter)
Widow Couderc, The 1974,O 14,39:3
Jarnow, Al (Screenwriter)
Owl and the Pussycat, The 1973,F 17,39:1
Painting and Scratching on Film 1973,F 17,39:1
Rotations 1973,F 17,39:1
Visor 1973,F 17,39:1
Jarnow, Jill (Screenwriter)
Owl and the Pussycat, The 1973,F 17,39:1
Jarre, Maurice (Composer)
Mackintosh Man, The 1973,Jl 26,44:1
Ash Wednesday 1973,N 22,50:2
Island at the Top of the World 1974,D 21,18:6
Jarrell, Andy
Bang the Drum Slowly 1973,Ag 27,35:1
Jarrott, Charles (Director)
Mary Queen of Scots 1973,Ja 7,II,1:8
Lost Horizon 1973,Mr 15,58:1
Jarva, Risto (Director)
Worker's Diary 1973,S 27,44:1
Worker's Diary 1974,Ag 9,22:4
Jarva, Risto (Screenwriter)
Worker's Diary 1974,Ag 9,22:4
Jarvis, Barbara (Director)
Lambing 1974,F 15,23:1

Karras, Alex
Blazing Saddles 1974,F 8,21:1
Blazing Saddles 1974,Mr 17,II,15:5
Kasmin
Bigger Splash, A 1974,O 4,31:2
Kass, Katyana
Optimists, The 1973,O 19,58:1
Kastner, Elliott (Producer)
Cops and Robbers 1973,Ag 16,40:1
Long Goodbye, The 1973,O 29,42:1
11 Harrowhouse 1974,S 27,49:1
Katcha, Vahe (Screenwriter)
Death of a Jew 1973,Ja 18,47:1
Kates, Bernard
Super Cops, The 1974,Mr 21,51:1
Kato, Go
Long Darkness, The 1973,Ag 18,26:1
Scarlet Camellia, The (Goben No Tsubaki)
1973,S 27,45:1
Kato, Tai (Director)
Theater of Life 1974,My 21,51:1
Kato, Tai (Screenwriter)
Theater of Life 1974,My 21,51:1
Kato, Yoshi
Scarlet Camellia, The (Goben No Tsubaki)
1973,S 27,45:1
Katselas, Milton (Director)
40 Carats 1973,Je 29,14:1
Katsu, Shintaro
Zatoichi's Conspiracy 1974,Ap 16,44:1
Hoodlum Soldier (Heitai Yakuza) 1974,Je 20,47:1
Katsu, Shintaro (Producer)
Zatoichi's Conspiracy 1974,Ap 16,44:1
Katz, Gloria (Screenwriter)
American Graffiti 1973,Ag 5,II,1:4
American Graffiti 1973,Ag 13,21:1
American Graffiti 1973,S 16,II,1:1
American Graffiti 1974,Ja 6,II,1:2
American Graffiti 1974,Ja 7,38:3
American Graffiti 1974,Ja 9,24:1
Napa Valley Story, The 1974,S 29,II,15:1
Lucky Lady 1974,S 29,II,15:1
Radioland 1974,S 29,II,15:1
American Graffiti 1974,S 29,II,15:1
Katz, Peter (Producer)
Don't Look Now 1973,D 10,56:1
Katz, Robert (Original Author)
Massacre in Rome 1973,O 25,59:1
Katz, Robert (Screenwriter)
Massacre in Rome 1973,O 25,59:1
Katz, Sidney (Miscellaneous)
Life Study 1973,Ja 26,42:4
Summer Wishes, Winter Dreams 1973,O 22,46:1
Man on a Swing 1974,F 28,33:1
Katz, Stephen M (Cinematographer)
Your Three Minutes Are Up 1974,Mr 28,34:1
Katzka, Gabriel (Producer)
Parallax View, The 1974,Je 20,47:1
Taking of Pelham One Two Three, The
1974,O 3,50:1
Kauffman, Shirley
Arnold's Wrecking Co 1973,S 21,48:1
Kaufman, Joseph
Heavy Traffic 1973,Ag 9,30:1
Kaufman, Maurice
Hero, The 1973,Mr 9,27:2
Kaufman, Millard (Screenwriter)
Klansman, The 1974,N 21,54:1
Kaufman, Philip (Director)
White Dawn, The 1974,Jl 22,41:1
Kaufman, Robert (Screenwriter)
Freebie and the Bean 1974,D 26,59:1
Kawamato, Ko (Cinematographer)
Scarlet Camellia, The (Goben No Tsubaki)
1973,S 27,45:1
Kawarazaki, Kenzo
Ceremony, The (Gishiki) 1974,F 8,18:1
Kay, Alan (Producer)
Ben-Gurion Remembers 1973,O 8,40:4
Kay, Barry (Miscellaneous)
Don Quixote 1973,N 3,25:1
Kayama, Yoshiko
Theater of Life 1974,My 21,51:1
Kayama, Yuzo
Battle of Okinawa 1973,S 12,41:1
Kazama, Ken
That Man Bolt 1973,D 24,21:1
Kazan, Elia (Director)
Face in the Crowd, A 1974,S 8,II,1:5
Keach, Stacy
Luther 1974,F 5,30:1
Gravy Train, The 1974,Je 17,25:5
Keach, Stacy (Screenwriter)
Group of Experimental Films, A: (The Repeater)
1973,F 3,19:1
Keane, Basil
Harder They Come, The 1973,F 9,32:3
Kearney, Philip (Screenwriter)
Private Parts 1973,F 2,16:1
Keating, John (Composer)
Innocent Bystanders 1973,Ja 25,51:6
Keating, Kevin (Cinematographer)
Attica 1974,Ap 12,18:1

Keaton, Buster
Saphead, The 1974,Ag 28,16:1
Three Stooges Follies, The: (Nothing But Pleasure)
1974,N 25,37:6
Keaton, Diane
Sleeper 1973,D 18,52:1
Sleeper 1973,D 23,II,3:7
Sleeper 1974,Ja 6,II,1:2
Godfather: Part II, The 1974,D 13,58:1
Godfather: Part II, The 1974,D 22,II,19:7
Keats, Steve
Death Wish 1974,Jl 25,27:1
Keats, Steven
Friends of Eddie Coyle, The 1973,Je 27,68:1
Kehoe, Jack
Serpico 1973,D 6,61:1
Keitel, Harvey
Mean Streets 1973,O 3,38:1
Mean Streets 1973,O 14,II,1:1
Mean Streets 1974,Ja 6,II,1:2
Kelber, Michel (Cinematographer)
Phedre 1973,Mr 30,34:1
Keljan, Bob (Director)
Scream Blacula Scream 1973,Jl 19,31:1
Keller, Frank (Miscellaneous)
For Pete's Sake 1974,Je 27,54:2
Keller, Hiram
Rome Wants Another Caesar (Roma Rivusie
Cesare) 1974,O 2,58:1
Keller, Sheldon (Screenwriter)
Cleopatra Jones 1973,Jl 5,24:6
Kellerman, Sally
Reflection of Fear, A 1973,F 13,25:5
Slither 1973,Mr 8,32:2
Lost Horizon 1973,Mr 15,58:1
Lost Horizon 1973,Mr 18,II,1:6
Slither 1973,Mr 18,II,1:6
Slither 1974,S 29,II,15:1
Kelley, Fred
Three the Hard Way 1974,Jl 28,II,1:1
Kellin, Mike
Freebie and the Bean 1974,D 26,59:1
Kelly, Fred
Three the Hard Way 1974,Je 27,55:1
Kelly, Gene
40 Carats 1973,Je 29,14:1
That's Entertainment 1974,Jl 7,II,1:6
Kelly, Jim
Enter the Dragon 1973,Ag 18,26:1
Black Belt Jones 1974,Ja 29,21:1
Golden Needles 1974,Jl 18,32:1
Three the Hard Way 1974,Jl 28,II,1:1
Kelly, Paula
Three Tough Guys 1974,Mr 16,16:3
Lost in the Stars 1974,My 7,54:1
Uptown Saturday Night 1974,Je 17,25:1
Kelly, Walt (Director)
We Have Met the Enemy and It Is Us
1973,D 21,45:1
Kemeny, John (Producer)
Apprenticeship of Duddy Kravitz, The
1974,Jl 15,31:4
Kemmering, Warren
Hit 1973,S 19,38:3
Kemp, Valli
Dr Phibes Rises Again 1973,Ja 11,35:1
Kemper, Victor J (Cinematographer)
Shamus 1973,F 1,41:1
Friends of Eddie Coyle, The 1973,Je 27,68:1
From the Mixed-Up Files of Mrs Basil E
Frankweiler 1973,S 28,25:1
Gambler, The 1974,O 3,50:1
Kemplen, Ralph (Miscellaneous)
Day of the Jackal, The 1973,My 17,53:1
Odessa File, The 1974,O 19,36:1
Kemplen, Willy (Miscellaneous)
Under Milk Wood 1973,Ja 22,20:1
Siddhartha 1973,Jl 19,31:1
Kemplen (Miscellaneous)
Phase IV 1974,O 21,48:6
Kemr, Josef
Marketa Lazarova 1974,Ag 30,19:1
Kendall, Nancy (Screenwriter)
Cine-Dance: (Almira) 1973,Ja 6,22:1
Women Artists As Filmmakers, Part One: (Almira)
1973,Ja 29,25:1
Kendall, Suzy
Fear Is the Key 1973,Mr 15,55:6
Tales That Witness Madness 1973,N 1,48:1
Kende, Janos (Cinematographer)
Rome Wants Another Caesar (Roma Rivusie
Cesare) 1974,O 2,58:1
Kennedy, Burt (Director)
Train Robbers, The 1973,F 8,36:3
Kennedy, Burt (Screenwriter)
Train Robbers, The 1973,F 8,36:3
Kennedy, Florynce
Year of the Woman 1973,O 20,27:2
Year of the Woman 1973,O 28,II,1:1
Kennedy, George
Lost Horizon 1973,Mr 15,58:1
Thunderbolt and Lightfoot 1974,My 24,23:3
Airport 1975 1974,O 19,63:4

Kennedy, George—Cont
Earthquake 1974,N 16,20:2
Kennedy, Patrick (Composer)
Cinderella Liberty 1973,D 19,54:2
Kercheval, Ken
Seven-Ups, The 1973,D 22,11:2
Kern, Peter
Paloma, La 1974,O 9,52:1
Kerr, Anita (Composer)
Limbo 1973,Ja 27,17:1
Kershner, Irvin (Director)
SPYS 1974,Ag 11,II,11:1
Kershner, Irving (Director)
Up the Sandbox 1973,Ja 21,II,13:1
Kerwin, Maureen
Inheritor, The 1973,O 18,63:1
Kessler, Catherine
Dyn Amo 1973,Ap 28,21:1
Kestelman, Sara
Zardoz 1974,F 7,46:1
Ketchum, David
Your Three Minutes Are Up 1974,Mr 28,34:1
Keyes, Joe Jr (Original Author)
Willie Dynamite 1974,Ja 24,45:1
Kezich, Tulio (Screenwriter)
Come Have Coffee With Us 1973,Ap 6,28:1
Kiboine, Gilbert (Miscellaneous)
Emitai 1973,F 10,22:1
Kidder, Margot
Sisters 1973,S 27,44:4
Kido, Shiro (Producer)
Scarlet Camellia, The (Goben No Tsubaki)
1973,S 27,45:1
Kien, Shih
Enter the Dragon 1973,Ag 18,26:1
Kier, Udo
Andy Warhol's Frankenstein 1974,My 16,52:1
Andy Warhol's Dracula 1974,Jl 14,II,11:1
Kietel, Harvey
Mean Streets 1974,Ja 20,II,1:4
Kikushima, Ryuzo (Screenwriter)
Hoodlum Soldier (Heitai Yakuza) 1974,Je 20,47:1
Kilafa
Emitai 1973,F 10,22:1
Kilar, Wojciech (Composer)
Illumination 1973,O 1,45:3
Kiley, Richard
Little Prince, The 1974,N 8,24:1
Little Prince, The 1974,N 17,II,17:1
King, Albert
Wattstax 1973,F 16,17:1
King, Damu
Sweet Jesus, Preacher Man 1973,My 26,27:2
Black Godfather, The 1974,S 4,52:1
King, Mabel
Ganja & Hess 1973,Ap 21,19:2
King, Morgana
Godfather, Part II, The 1974,D 13,58:1
King, Perry
Lords of Flatbush, The 1974,My 2,61:5
King, Richard (Screenwriter)
Looking Forward, Looking Back: (The Thirties)
1974,My 24,23:2
King, Rick (Screenwriter)
New American Cinema: (Jeffrey) 1973,Ap 15,59:1
King, Tony
Gordon's War 1973,Ag 10,26:2
King, Zaiman
Some Call It Loving 1973,N 17,26:1
Kinger, Michael (Producer)
Gold 1974,O 17,57:1
Kingsley, Ben
Fear Is the Key 1973,Mr 15,55:6
Kinsky, Klaus
Vampir 1973,My 26,27:1
Kippen, Manart
Mission to Moscow 1973,Jl 1,II,9:1
Kirby, Bruce Jr
Harrad Experiment, The 1973,My 12,19:1
Cinderella Liberty 1973,D 19,54:2
Godfather, Part II, The 1974,D 13,58:1
Kirchin, Basil (Composer)
Mutations, The 1974,S 26,26:2
Kirk, David
Hurry Up, or I'll Be 30 1973,N 15,58:5
Kirtsis, George
Days of 36 (Meres Tou 36) 1974,Ap 3,38:1
Kishi, Keiko
Early Spring 1974,S 26,26:1
Kissinger, Charles
Abby 1974,D 26,53:1
Kita, Ryuji
Autumn Afternoon, An 1973,My 8,39:1
Kiuge, Alexander (Director)
Part-Time Work of a Domestic Slave
(Gelegenheitsarbeit Einer Sklavin) 1974,O 3,50:2
Kleckner, Susan (Screenwriter)
New Consciousness, A: (Birth Film) 1973,F 16,17:2
Klein-Rogge, Rudolph
Testament of Dr Mabuse, The 1973,D 6,61:1
Kline, Richard H (Cinematographer)
Harrad Experiment, The 1973,My 12,19:1
Battle for the Planet of the Apes 1973,Jl 13,9:1
Don Is Dead, The 1973,N 15,58:3

Kline, Richard H (Cinematographer)—Cont
Terminal Man, The 1974,Je 20,47:2
Klinger, Michael (Producer)
Pulp 1973,F 9,32:1
Klingman, Larry (Miscellaneous)
Dreams and Nightmares 1974,Ap 26,30:1
Klingman, Larry (Producer)
Dreams and Nightmares 1974,Ap 26,30:1
Klocksiem, Steve (Screenwriter)
Spring Potpourri: (Musa Paradisiaca Sapientum)
1974,My 10,24:5
Klosinski, Edward (Cinematographer)
Illumination 1973,O 1,45:3
Kluge, Alexandra
Part-Time Work of a Domestic Slave
(Gelegenheitsarbeit Einer Sklavin) 1974,O 3,50:2
Knight, Gladys and the Pips
Save the Children 1973,S 19,40:2
Knoop, John (Screenwriter)
Erotic Cinema (Norien Ten) 1974,My 10,24:3
Knopf, Christopher (Screenwriter)
Emperor of the North Pole 1973,My 25,23:1
Emperor of the North Pole 1973,Je 3,II,1:3
Knowlton, Ken (Director)
Apotheosis 1973,D 21,45:1
Knowlton, Ken (Screenwriter)
Animation: (Metathesis) 1974,N 21,54:3
Animation: (Metamorphosis) 1974,N 21,54:3
Knudson, Robert (Miscellaneous)
Exorcist, The 1974,Ap 3,36:1
Kobayashi, Keiju
Battle of Okinawa 1973,S 12,41:1
Kobayashi, Setsuo (Cinematographer)
Hoodlum Soldier (Heitai Yakuza) 1974,Je 20,47:1
Warehouse (Moju-Blind Beast) 1974,N 8,24:1
Kobo Abe (Original Author)
Face of Another 1974,My 8,36:3
Kobo Abe (Screenwriter)
Face of Another 1974,My 8,36:3
Kocela, Paul (Screenwriter)
American Dreams and Nightmares: (The End of
One) 1973,Ja 5,14:2
Koch, Howard (Screenwriter)
Mission to Moscow 1973,Jl 1,II,9:1
Koch, Howard W (Director)
Badge 373 1973,Jl 26,43:1
Koch, Howard W (Producer)
Badge 373 1973,Jl 26,43:1
Koenekamp, Fred (Cinematographer)
Harry in Your Pocket 1973,S 24,39:1
Papillon 1973,D 17,59:1
Towering Inferno, The 1974,D 20,20:1
Koenekamp, Fred J (Cinematographer)
Uptown Saturday Night 1974,Je 17,25:1
Koenig, Klaus (Cinematographer)
Pedestrian, The 1974,Mr 1,16:1
Koenig, Raymond (Original Author)
Scream Blacula Scream 1973,Jl 19,31:1
Koenig, Raymond (Screenwriter)
Scream Blacula Scream 1973,Jl 19,31:1
Kogura, Michiyo
Flavor of Green Tea Over Rice, The
1973,Ja 25,51:6
Kohn, John (Producer)
Theater of Blood 1973,My 12,19:1
Kohoe, Jack
Law and Disorder 1974,O 10,62:1
Koike, Kazuo (Screenwriter)
Sword of Vengeance 1973,Ag 24,18:1
Kolarov, Dimo (Cinematographer)
Goat's Horn, The 1974,Ag 23,16:4
Kolden, Scott
Charley and the Angel 1973,Je 28,58:1
Koldhoffer, Rene
Lion Has Seven Heads, The 1974,F 8,17:1
Kombinat, Moskino (Producer)
Happiness 1973,My 25,24:1
Konigsburg, E L (Original Author)
From the Mixed-Up Files of Mrs Basil E
Frankweiler 1973,S 28,25:1
Koo, Joseph (Composer)
Deadly China Doll 1973,S 27,45:1
Kopapik, Simonie
White Dawn, The 1974,Jl 22,41:1
Kopkins, Bo
American Graffiti 1973,Ag 13,21:1
Korkes, Jon
Day of the Dolphin, The 1973,D 20,57:1
Front Page, The 1974,D 19,58:1
Korman, Harvey
Blazing Saddles 1974,F 8,21:1
Blazing Saddles 1974,Mr 17,II,15:5
Huckleberry Finn 1974,My 25,16:1
Kornbluh, Ken
Limbo 1973,Ja 27,17:1
Kornbluh, Laura
Limbo 1973,Ja 27,17:1
Korporaal, Giovanni (Miscellaneous)
Reed: Insurgent Mexico 1974,S 17,40:6
Korshaki, Harry (Producer)
Hit 1973,S 19,38:3
Kosio, Paul
Freebie and the Bean 1974,D 26,59:1

Kosleck, Martin
Confessions of a Nazi Spy 1973,Jl 1,II,9:1
Koslo, Paul
Lolly-Madonna XXX 1973,F 22,30:1
Kosma, Vladimir (Composer)
Tall Blond Man With One Black Shoe, The
1973,Ag 31,10:1
Kosugi, Massao (Cinematographer)
Sasuke Against the Wind 1973,S 6,43:1
Pale Flower 1974,My 13,36:8
Kotcheff, Ted (Director)
Apprenticeship of Duddy Kravitz, The
1974,Jl 15,31:4
Apprenticeship of Duddy Kravitz, The
1974,Jl 28,II,1:1
Apprenticeship of Duddy Kravitz, The
1974,Ag 18,II,1:1
Apprenticeship of Duddy Kravitz, The
1974,Ag 25,II,11:1
Kotto, Yaphet
Live and Let Die 1973,Je 28,56:1
Live and Let Die 1973,Jl 15,II,1:6
Truck Turner 1974,Je 27,54:4
Kovac, Roland (Composer)
Jonathan 1973,Je 16,13:1
Kovacs, Laszio (Cinematographer)
Huckleberry Finn 1974,My 25,16:1
For Pete's Sake 1974,Je 27,54:2
Kovacs, Laszlo (Cinematographer)
Steelyard Blues 1973,F 1,41:1
Reflection of Fear, A 1973,F 13,25:5
Slither 1973,Mr 8,32:2
Paper Moon 1973,My 17,53:1
Freebie and the Bean 1974,D 26,59:1
Kowalski, Bernard L (Director)
Sssssss 1973,Ag 2,31:1
Kowalski, Frank (Original Author)
Bring Me the Head of Alfredo Garcia
1974,Ag 15,28:1
Koyama Aiko
Ceremony, The (Gishiki) 1974,F 8,18:1
Death by Hanging (Koshikel) 1974,F 15,23:1
Kozen, Nishioica (Producer)
Zatoichi's Conspiracy 1974,Ap 16,44:1
Kozuch, Michal
Marketa Lazarova 1974,Ag 30,19:1
Krainin, Julian (Cinematographer)
Princeton: A Search for Answers 1974,Mr 23,20:1
Krainin, Julian (Director)
Princeton: A Search for Answers 1974,Mr 23,20:1
Krainin, Julian (Producer)
Princeton: A Search for Answers 1974,Mr 23,20:1
Princeton: A Search for Answers 1974,Ap 3,36:1
Kramer, Hilton
Painters Painting 1973,Mr 20,30:1
Kramer, Larry (Screenwriter)
Lost Horizon 1973,Mr 15,58:1
Lost Horizon 1973,Mr 18,II,1:6
Kramer, Stanley (Director)
Oklahoma Crude 1973,Jl 4,8:4
Oklahoma Crude 1973,Jl 24,28:3
Oklahoma Crude 1973,S 29,II,15:1
Kramer, Stanley (Producer)
Oklahoma Crude 1973,Jl 4,8:4
Krantz, Steve (Producer)
Heavy Traffic 1973,Ag 9,30:1
Heavy Traffic 1974,Ja 6,II,1:2
Nine Lives of Fritz the Cat, The 1974,Je 28,21:1
Kratina, Dick (Cinematographer)
Super Cops, The 1974,Mr 21,51:1
Kraushaar, Raoul (Composer)
Dirty O'Neil 1974,Je 6,49:7
Krauss, Werner
Paracelsus 1974,N 1,32:1
Kreines, Jeff (Screenwriter)
Chicagofilm: (Ricky and Rocky) 1974,Ja 6,57:2
Kreis, Anne
Such a Gorgeous Kid Like Me 1973,Mr 26,55:1
Kress, Carl (Miscellaneous)
Towering Inferno, The 1974,D 20,20:1
Kress, Harold (Miscellaneous)
Iceman Cometh, The 1973,O 30,36:1
Towering Inferno, The 1974,D 20,20:1
Kress, Harold F (Miscellaneous)
99 and 44/100% Dead 1974,Ag 30,22:1
Kreutzberg, Harald
Paracelsus 1974,N 1,32:1
Kreuzer, Elisabeth
Alice in the Cities (Alice in den Stadten)
1974,O 9,52:2
Krisman, Nino E (Producer)
Crazy Joe 1974,F 16,36:2
Kristel, Sylvia
Emmanuelle 1974,D 16,47:5
Kristofferson, Kris
Pat Garrett and Billy the Kid 1973,My 24,53:1
Pat Garrett and Billy the Kid 1973,Je 3,II,1:3
Pat Garrett and Billy the Kid 1973,Je 17,II,13:4
Blume in Love 1973,Je 18,37:1
Pat Garrett and Billy the Kid 1973,Jl 8,II,8:1
Blume in Love 1973,Ag 12,II,11:1
Blume in Love 1973,S 9,II,1:3

Kroeber, Carlos
Murdered House, The (A Casa Assasinada)
1974,S 6,22:3
Kroner, Ludevit
If I Had a Gun 1973,Ja 19,23:1
Krudy, Gyula (Original Author)
Sindbad (Szindbad) 1974,O 25,24:1
Kruger, Christiane
Little Mother 1973,Ja 6,25:1
Little Mother 1973,F 4,II,1:6
Kruger, David
Claudine 1974,Ap 23,34:3
Krugman, Saul J (Producer)
All-American Boy, The 1973,O 25,56:1
Krumins, Diana (Screenwriter)
Ten Personal Films: (The Divine Miracle)
1973,F 23,22:2
Krumm, Paul Albert
Jonathan 1973,Je 16,13:1
Kruschen, Jack
Freebie and the Bean 1974,D 26,59:1
Ku Chia Hui (Composer)
Return of the Dragon 1974,Ag 8,30:1
Kuam Chih Chung (Producer)
Return of the Dragon 1974,Ag 8,30:1
Kuang, I (Screenwriter)
Triple Irons 1973,S 25,37:1
Kuchar, George (Screenwriter)
Brothers Kuchar, The: (The Sunshine Sisters)
1973,Mr 31,41:2
Kuchar, Mike (Screenwriter)
Brothers Kuchar, The: (Variations 15)
1973,Mr 31,41:3
Brothers Kuchar, The: (Aqua Circus)
1973,Mr 31,41:3
Brothers Kuchar, The: (Abode of the Snows)
1973,Mr 31,41:3
Brothers Kuchar, The: (Far Away Places)
1973,Mr 31,41:3
Brothers Kuchar, The: (Tales of the Bronx)
1973,Mr 31,41:3
Kudo, Mitsumu (Producer)
Funeral Parade of Roses 1973,Je 8,47:1
Kueveillier, Luigi (Cinematographer)
Andy Warhol's Frankenstein 1974,My 16,52:1
Kulchewsky, Mireya
Promised Land, The (La Tierra Prometida)
1974,Ap 8,43:1
Kulik, Andrei
First Position 1973,Je 2,19:1
Kulik, Buzz (Director)
Shamus 1973,F 1,41:1
Kumai, Kei (Director)
Long Darkness, The 1973,Ag 18,26:1
Kumai, Kei (Screenwriter)
Long Darkness, The 1973,Ag 18,26:1
Kumar, Uttam
Nyak-The Hero 1974,Jl 19,24:1
Kung-hsun, Nan
Deadly China Doll 1973,S 27,45:1
Kunkele, Ilse
Jonathan 1973,Je 16,13:1
Kunstmann, Doris
Hitler: The Last Ten Days 1973,My 10,57:1
Kuperman, Howard (Miscellaneous)
Soul of Nigger Charley, The 1973,My 17,54:1
Kuralev, Leonid
Golden Calf, The (If I Had One Million Rubies)
1974,Je 14,19:1
Kurihara, Komaki
Long Darkness, The 1973,Ag 18,26:1
Kuroda, Klyami (Cinematographer)
Long Darkness, The 1973,Ag 18,26:1
Kurosawa, Akira (Director)
Dodes'Ka-Den 1974,O 18,28:1
Kurosawa, Akira (Screenwriter)
Dodes'Ka-Den 1974,O 18,28:1
Kurtz, Marcia Jean
Stoolie, The 1974,My 22,36:2
Kymlicka, Milan (Composer)
Wedding in White 1973,Ap 30,26:1
Kyo, Machiko
Face of Another 1974,My 8,36:3
Kyokai, Nihon Eiga Fukko (Producer)
Day the Sun Rose, The 1973,Ag 30,26:3
Kyoko Kishida
Face of Another 1974,My 8,36:3

L

I-feng, Yen
Deadly China Doll 1973,S 27,45:1
La Loggia, Danika
Alfredo Alfredo 1973,D 18,54:1
LaBour, Fred (Screenwriter)
Spring Potpourri: (The Vanguard Story)
1974,My 10,24:5
Labourier, Dominique
Petit Theatre de Jean Renoir, Le (The Little
Theater of Jean Renoir) (Le Roi d'Yvetot)
1974,My 3,46:1

M

N

P

Shuman, Mort (Composer)
  Black Thursday 1974,D 23,34:1
Shveitser, Mikhail (Director)
  Golden Calf, The (If I Had One Million Rubies)
    1974,Je 14,19:1
Shveitser, Mikhail (Miscellaneous)
  Golden Calf, The (If I Had One Million Rubies)
    1974,Je 14,19:1
Shveitser, Mikhail (Producer)
  Golden Calf, The (If I Had One Million Rubies)
    1974,Je 14,19:1
Sibesalang
  Emitai 1973,F 10,22:1
Sicart, Manuel
  POW, The 1973,My 11,30:1
Siciliano, Antonio (Miscellaneous)
  Confessions of a Police Captain 1974,Ag 16,18:2
Sidney, Sylvia
  Summer Wishes, Winter Dreams 1973,O 22,46:1
Siegel, Don (Director)
  Charlie Varrick 1973,O 20,27:1
  Charley Varrick 1973,O 21,II,13:1
  Charley Varrick 1973,O 28,II,1:1
  Black Windmill, The 1974,My 18,18:4
Siegel, Don (Miscellaneous)
  Charley Varrick 1974,Ja 6,II,1:2
Siegel, Don (Producer)
  Charlie Varrick 1973,O 20,27:1
  Black Windmill, The 1974,My 18,18:4
Siegel, Leah (Miscellaneous)
  America's Pop Collector: Robert C Scull
    1974,O 17,55:3
Siegel, Lois (Screenwriter)
  Ten Personal Films: (Spectrum in White)
    1973,F 23,22:2
Siegel, Stan (Miscellaneous)
  Lords of Flatbush, The 1974,My 2,61:5
Sierra, Gregory
  Thief Who Came to Dinner, The 1973,Mr 2,22:1
Signoret, Simone
  Widow Couderc, The 1974,O 14,39:3
Silano, George (Cinematographer)
  Last American Hero, The 1973,Jl 28,16:1
Silberg, Yoel (Screenwriter)
  Kazablan 1974,My 9,54:1
Silberman, Serge (Miscellaneous)
  Liebelei 1974,S 30,51:5
Silberman, Serge (Producer)
  Fantome de la Liberte, Le (The Spector of
    Freedom) 1974,O 14,39:1
Silliphant, Stirling (Screenwriter)
  Poseidon Adventure, The 1973,Ja 14,II,1:6
  Shaft in Africa 1973,Je 21,53:1
  Towering Inferno, The 1974,D 20,20:1
Sillitoe, Alan (Original Author)
  Ragman's Daughter, The 1974,Mr 25,39:1
Sillitoe, Alan (Screenwriter)
  Ragman's Daughter, The 1974,Mr 25,39:1
Silva, Helio (Cinematographer)
  Razor in the Flesh (A Navalha Na Carne)
    1974,Ja 24,44:2
Silva, Henry
  Italian Connection, The 1973,N 1,48:1
Silver, Joan (Original Author)
  Limbo 1973,Ja 27,17:1
Silver, Joan (Screenwriter)
  Limbo 1973,Ja 27,17:1
Silver, Jody (Screenwriter)
  Birth of the Big Mamoo, The 1973,F 17,39:1
Silver, Joe
  Rhinoceros 1974,Ja 22,30:3
  Apprenticeship of Duddy Kravitz, The
    1974,Jl 15,31:4
  Apprenticeship of Duddy Kravitz, The
    1974,Ag 25,II,11:1
Silverheels, Jay
  Man Who Loved Cat Dancing, The 1973,Je 29,17:1
Silverman, Ron (Producer)
  Buster and Billie 1974,Ag 22,28:1
Silvi, Robert (Miscellaneous)
  Massacre in Rome 1973,O 25,59:1
Sim, Gerald
  Dr Phibes Rises Again 1973,Ja 11,35:1
Simeon, George (Original Author)
  Widow Couderc, The 1974,O 14,39:3
Simmons, Anthony (Director)
  Optimists, The 1973,O 19,58:1
Simmons, Anthony (Original Author)
  Optimists, The 1973,O 19,58:1
Simmons, Anthony (Screenwriter)
  Optimists, The 1973,O 19,58:1
Simon, Luc
  Lancelot of the Lake (Lancelot du Lac)
    1974,O 1,33:1
Simon, Mayo (Screenwriter)
  Phase IV 1974,O 21,48:6
Simon, Neil (Screenwriter)
  Heartbreak Kid, The 1973,F 18,II,1:1
  Heartbreak Kid, The 1973,S 9,II,1:3
Simpson, O J
  Klansman, The 1974,N 21,54:1
  Towering Inferno, The 1974,D 20,20:1

Simpson, Robert L (Miscellaneous)
  Cahill, United States Marshal 1973,Jl 12,46:1
Sims, Joan
  Carry on Doctor 1973,F 8,36:3
Sims, Nelson
  Together Brothers 1974,Ag 8,30:1
Sims, Sylvia
  Tamarind Seed, The 1974,Jl 12,41:1
Sinatra, Frank
  That's Entertainment 1974,Jl 7,II,1:6
Sinatra, Frank (Miscellaneous)
  That's Entertainment 1974,Jl 28,II,1:1
Sinclair, Andrew (Director)
  Under Milk Wood 1973,Ja 22,20:1
  Under Milk Wood 1973,F 4,II,1:6
Sinclair, Andrew (Screenwriter)
  Under Milk Wood 1973,Ja 22,20:1
Sinclair, Madge
  Conrack 1974,Mr 28,33:1
  Conrack 1974,Ap 21,II,1:1
Sinden, Donald
  Day of the Jackal, The 1973,My 17,53:1
  Island at the Top of the World 1974,D 21,18:6
Singer, Loren (Original Author)
  Parallax View, The 1974,Je 20,47:1
Sireci, Mario
  Circostanza, La (The Circumstance) 1974,O 11,25:1
Sirola, Joseph
  Hail to the Chief 1973,Jl 28,16:1
  Super Cops, The 1974,Mr 21,51:1
Sissia, Jean-Noel
  Phedre 1973,Mr 30,34:1
Sit, Nancy
  Lady Kung-Fu 1973,S 6,43:1
Sivo, Gyorgy (Miscellaneous)
  Love 1973,Mr 23,22:1
Sjoman, Vilgot
  You're Lying 1973,My 5,25:3
Sjoman, Vilgot (Director)
  You're Lying 1973,My 5,25:3
  'Til Sex Do Us Part 1974,O 5,17:1
Sjowall, Maj (Original Author)
  Laughing Policeman, The 1973,D 21,46:1
Skeggs, Roy (Producer)
  Frankenstein and the Monster From Hell
    1974,O 31,48:1
Skerritt, Tom
  Thieves Like Us 1974,F 12,41:1
Skiar, Michael
  Amour, L' 1973,My 11,26:1
Sklair, Sam (Composer)
  Confessions of a Window Cleaner 1974,N 9,24:2
Skotnicki, Jan
  Illumination 1973,O 1,45:3
Slade, Betsy
  Our Time 1974,Ap 11,31:1
Slasor, Alan (Screenwriter)
  Animation: (Tangram) 1974,N 21,54:3
Slater, Barney (Original Author)
  Cahill, United States Marshal 1973,Jl 12,46:1
Slattery, Richard X
  Walking Tall 1974,F 9,18:1
Slem, El Hedi Ben
  All 1974,O 7,55:1
Slim, Iceberg (Original Author)
  Trick Baby 1973,Ja 27,15:1
Sliwinska, Urszula (Miscellaneous)
  Illumination 1973,O 1,45:3
Sloane, Patricia (Screenwriter)
  Women Artists As Filmmakers, Part One:
    (Painting) 1973,Ja 29,25:1
Slocombe, Douglas (Cinematographer)
  Great Gatsby, The 1974,Mr 28,32:1
Slywan, Kari
  Cries and Whispers 1973,Ja 14,II,13:1
Small, Ed (Screenwriter)
  Group of Experimental Films, A: (In Progress)
    1973,F 3,19:1
Small, Marya
  Sleeper 1973,D 18,52:1
Small, Michael (Composer)
  Love and Pain and the Whole Damned Thing
    1973,Ap 20,14:1
  Parallax View, The 1974,Je 20,47:1
Smight, Jack (Director)
  Airport 1975 1974,O 19,63:4
Smirnov, Edward (Director)
  Taming of Fire, The 1973,Je 23,18:1
Smirnov, Edward (Screenwriter)
  Taming of Fire, The 1973,Je 23,18:1
Smith, Bud (Miscellaneous)
  Rhinoceros 1974,Ja 22,30:3
Smith, Charles Martin
  American Graffiti 1974,Ja 6,II,1:2
Smith, Charlie Martin
  American Graffiti 1973,Ag 5,II,1:4
  American Graffiti 1973,Ag 13,21:1
  American Graffiti 1973,S 16,II,1:1
  Spikes Gang, The 1974,My 2,61:4
Smith, Elizabeth
  Castaway Cowboy, The 1974,Ag 15,25:1
Smith, Greg (Producer)
  Confessions of a Window Cleaner 1974,N 9,24:2

Smith, John Victor (Miscellaneous)
  Harder They Come, The 1973,F 9,32:3
  Offence, The 1973,My 12,19:1
  Delicate Balance, A 1973,D 11,52:1
  Three Musketeers, The 1974,Ap 4,52:1
Smith, Madeleine
  Frankenstein and the Monster From Hell
    1974,O 31,48:1
Smith, Maggie
  Love and Pain and the Whole Damned Thing
    1973,Ap 20,14:1
Smith, Maria
  Lords of Flatbush, The 1974,My 2,61:5
Smith, Patricia
  Save The Tiger 1973,F 15,53:1
Smith, Ray
  Under Milk Wood 1973,Ja 22,20:1
Smith, Terrence L (Original Author)
  Thief Who Came to Dinner, The 1973,Mr 2,22:1
Smith, Wilbur (Original Author)
  Gold 1974,O 17,57:1
Smith, Wilbur (Screenwriter)
  Gold 1974,O 17,57:1
Smith, William
  Sweet Jesus, Preacher Man 1973,My 26,27:2
  Deadly Trackers, The 1973,D 22,11:1
  Black Samson 1974,Ag 15,25:1
Smith, Winchell (Original Author)
  Saphead, The 1974,Ag 28,16:1
Smith, Winchell (Producer)
  Saphead, The 1974,Ag 28,16:1
Smith, Winchell (Screenwriter)
  Saphead, The 1974,Ag 28,16:1
Smithers, Jan
  Where the Lilies Bloom 1974,Je 8,18:4
Smithers, William
  Papillon 1973,D 17,59:1
Smithson, Robert (Director)
  Swamp 1973,F 1,41:1
Smothers, Tom
  Get to Know Your Rabbit 1973,S 21,49:1
Snee (Mr) (Screenwriter)
  Free Life, The 1974,F 5,30:1
Snyder, Robert (Director)
  World of Buckminster Fuller, The 1974,Je 20,49:1
  Henry Miller Odyssey, The 1974,S 13,31:1
Snyder, Robert (Producer)
  Henry Miller Odyssey, The 1974,S 13,31:1
Snyder, Robert (Screenwriter)
  Anais Nin Observed 1974,Je 28,20:1
Soffin, Alan (Cinematographer)
  Confessor 1974,Mr 15,20:1
Soffin, Alan (Director)
  Confessor 1974,Mr 15,20:1
Soffin, Alan (Miscellaneous)
  Confessor 1974,Mr 15,20:1
Soffin, Alan (Producer)
  Confessor 1974,Mr 15,20:1
Solas, Humberto (Director)
  Lucia 1974,Mr 1,16:1
Solinas, Franco (Screenwriter)
  State of Siege 1973,Ap 14,39:1
  State of Siege 1973,Ap 22,II,1:4
Solomon (Composer)
  Arnold's Wrecking Co 1973,S 21,48:1
Solonitzine, Anatoll
  Andrei Rublev 1973,O 10,43:1
Solzhenitsyn, Aleksandr I (Original Author)
  First Circle, The 1973,Ja 13,17:3
  First Circle, The 1973,F 4,II,1:6
Sommer, Elke
  Baron Blood 1973,F 8,36:3
Sommerfield, Diane
  Black Godfather, The 1974,S 4,52:1
Sondheim, Stephen (Composer)
  Stavisky 1974,S 30,51:5
  Stavisky 1974,D 23,32:2
Sondheim, Stephen (Screenwriter)
  Last of Sheila, The 1973,Je 15,24:1
  Last Sheila, The 1973,Jl 29,II,1:3
  Last of Sheila, The 1973,Jl 29,II,7:1
Sontag, Susan (Director)
  Promised Lands 1974,Jl 12,41:1
  Promised Lands 1974,S 8,II,13:1
Sopanen, Jeri (Cinematographer)
  I Could Never Have Sex With Anyone Who Has
    So Little Regard for My Husband 1973,Jl 21,21:4
  Promised Lands 1974,Jl 12,41:1
Sorbas, Elga
  Little Mother 1973,Ja 6,25:1
Sordi, Alberto
  I Vitelloni 1974,N 24,II,17:1
Soria, Oscar (Screenwriter)
  Blood of the Condor 1973,Jl 27,19:3
Sorvino, Paul
  Touch of Class, A 1973,Je 21,52:1
  Day of the Dolphin, The 1973,D 20,57:1
  Gambler, The 1974,O 3,50:1
Sothern, Ann
  Golden Needles 1974,Jl 18,32:1
Soul, David
  Magnum Force 1973,D 26,60:1

York, Michael—Cont
Three Musketeers, The 1974,Ap 14,II,13:1
Murder on the Orient Express 1974,N 25,38:1
York, Susannah
Gold 1974,O 17,57:1
Yorkin, Bud (Director)
Thief Who Came to Dinner, The 1973,Mr 2,22:1
Yorkin, Bud (Producer)
Thief Who Came to Dinner, The 1973,Mr 2,22:1
Yoshimura, Jitsuko
Sasuke Against the Wind 1973,S 6,43:1
Yoshio Kosugi
Sanshiro Sugata 1974,Ap 29,49:1
Yoshioka, Yasuhiro (Cinematographer)
Diary of a Shinjuku Burglar 1973,Jl 6,7:1
Death by Hanging (Koshikel) 1974,F 15,23:1
Yoshiro Harada
Trail of Blood 1974,My 3,47:1
Young, Burt
Cinderella Liberty 1973,D 19,54:2
Gambler, The 1974,O 3,50:1
Young, Freddie (Cinematographer)
Tamarind Seed, The 1974,Jl 12,41:1
Young, Gig
Bring Me the Head of Alfredo Garcia
1974,Ag 15,28:1
Young, Otis
Last Detail, The 1974,F 11,50:1
Last Detail, The 1974,F 24,II,1:2
Young, Roderick (Cinematographer)
Wattstax 1973,F 16,17:1
Young, Terence (Director)
Klansman, The 1974,N 21,54:1
Youssov, Vadim (Cinematographer)
Andrei Rublev 1973,O 10,43:1
Yu, Wang
Screaming Tiger 1973,N 8,58:6
Yuasa, Joji (Composer)
Funeral Parade of Roses 1973,Je 8,47:1
Yukiko Todoroki
Sanshiro Sugata 1974,Ap 29,49:1
Yun, Yun-Do
Death by Hanging (Koshikel) 1974,F 15,23:1
Yung-lung, Wang (Miscellaneous)
Five Fingers of Death 1973,Mr 22,54:3
Yunghuang, Chen (Composer)
Triple Irons 1973,S 25,37:1
Yursky, Sergei
Golden Calf, The (If I Had One Million Rubies)
1974,Je 14,19:1
Yust, Larry (Director)
Trick Baby 1973,Ja 27,15:1
Yust, Larry (Screenwriter)
Trick Baby 1973,Ja 27,15:1

Z

Zanin, Bruno
Amarcord (I Remember) 1974,S 20,32:1
Amarcord 1974,S 29,II,1:6
Zanuck, Darryl (Producer)
I Am a Fugitive From a Chain Gang
1973,Jl 1,II,9:1
Zanuck, Richard D (Producer)
Sssssss 1973,Ag 2,31:1
Sting, The 1973,D 26,60:1
Willie Dynamite 1974,Ja 24,45:1
Sugarland Express, The 1974,Mr 30,20:1
Girl From Petrovka, The 1974,Ag 23,16:1
Sting, The 1974,S 29,II,15:1
Zanussi, Krzysztof (Director)
Illumination 1973,O 1,45:3
Zanussi, Krzysztof (Screenwriter)
Illumination 1973,O 1,45:3
Zardi, Dominique
Tear in the Ocean, A 1973,O 1,45:2
Juste Avant la Nuit (Just Before Nightfall)
1973,O 9,42:1
Zebrowski, Edward
Illumination 1973,O 1,45:3
Zeffirelli, Franco (Director)
Brother Sun, Sister Moon 1973,Ap 9,48:1
Zeffirelli, Franco (Original Author)
Brother Sun, Sister Moon 1973,Ap 9,48:1
Zeffirelli, Franco (Screenwriter)
Brother Sun, Sister Moon 1973,Ap 9,48:1
Zelenovic, Srdjan
Andy Warhol's Frankenstein 1974,My 16,52:1
Andy Warhol's Frankenstein 1974,Je 30,II,1:5
Zeljenka, Ilia (Composer)
If I Had a Gun 1973,Ja 19,23:1
Zemke, Ken (Miscellaneous)
Elvis on Tour 1973,Je 7,54:1
Zenor, Suzanne
Get to Know Your Rabbit 1973,S 21,49:1
Zerbe, Anthony
Papillon 1973,D 17,59:1
Laughing Policeman, The 1973,D 21,46:1
Zettering, Mal (Director)
Visions of Eight 1973,Ag 11,25:3
Zetterlund, Monica
New Land, The 1973,O 27,17:1
Zevko, Esther
But Where Is Daniel Vax? 1974,Ap 1,42:1
Zieff, Howard (Director)
Slither 1973,Mr 8,32:2
Slither 1973,Mr 18,II,1:6

Ziegler, William (Miscellaneous)
MCQ 1974,F 7,46:1
Ziehm, Howard (Cinematographer)
Flesh Gordon 1974,Jl 31,20:1
Ziehm, Howard (Director)
Flesh Gordon 1974,Jl 31,20:1
Ziehm, Howard (Producer)
Flesh Gordon 1974,Jl 31,20:1
Zihlmann, Max (Original Author)
Over Night (Uber Nacht) 1974,Ap 9,37:1
Zimbalist, Efrem Jr
Airport 1975 1974,O 19,63:4
Zindel, Paul (Original Author)
Effect of Gamma Rays on Man-in-the-Moon
Marigolds, The 1973,Ja 28,II,13:1
Effect of Gamma Rays on Man-in-the-Moon
Marigolds, The 1973,Ap 8,II,15:1
Zindel, Paul (Screenwriter)
Up the Sandbox 1973,Ja 21,II,13:1
Mame 1974,Mr 8,18:1
Zingg, David Drew (Cinematographer)
Memories of Helen (Memoria de Helena)
1974,Mr 29,25:1
Zinnemann, Fred (Director)
Day of the Jackal, The 1973,My 17,53:1
Zinner, Peter (Miscellaneous)
Crazy Joe 1974,F 16,36:2
Godfather, Part II, The 1974,D 13,58:1
Zinoviev, Piotr
Happiness 1973,My 25,24:1
Ziska
Life Study 1973,Ja 26,42:4
Zoghby, Emil Dean (Composer)
Catch My Soul 1974,Mr 23,20:1
Zorich, Louis
Don Is Dead, The 1973,N 15,58:3
For Pete's Sake 1974,Je 27,54:2
Newman's Law 1974,Ag 22,28:1
Zsigmond, Vilmos (Cinematographer)
Scarecrow 1973,Ap 12,56:1
Scarecrow 1973,My 13,II,13:1
Long Goodbye, The 1973,O 29,42:1
Long Goodbye, The 1973,N 18,II,1:1
Cinderella Liberty 1973,D 19,54:2
Long Goodbye, The 1974,Ja 7,38:3
Sugarland Express, The 1974,Mr 30,20:1
Girl From Petrovka, The 1974,Ag 23,16:1
Zulauf, Benedikt
History Lessons 1973,O 1,45:2
Zulema
Save the Children 1973,S 19,40:2
Zuxhi, Yoshitaka
Dodes'Ka-Den 1974,O 18,28:1
Zwerin, Charlotte (Miscellaneous)
Shadow Cather, The: Edward S Curtis and the
North American Indian 1974,D 30,37:1
Zwerling, Darrell
Chinatown 1974,Je 21,26:1

Jean Renoir Company (Prod.)—Cont

Petit Theatre de Jean Renoir, Le (The Little Theater of Jean Renoir) (The Last Christmas Dinner) 1974,My 3,46:1
Jina Films Production (Prod.)
Tough 1974,Jl 25,27:1
Joko Films Inc (Prod.)
Imagine 1973,Ja 13,17:1

K

K-S Production (Prod.)
Groove Tube, The 1974,Je 24,25:1
Kairos Film/Film Verlag der Autoren (Prod.)
Part-Time Work of a Domestic Slave (Gelegenheitsarbeit Einer Sklavin) 1974,O 3,50:2
Kelly-Jordan Enterprises Inc (Distr.)
Ganja & Hess 1973,Ap 21,19:2
Krainin/Sage Productions (Distr.)
Princeton: A Search for Answers 1974,Mr 23,20:1

L

LA Express (Misc.)
Nine Lives of Fritz the Cat, The 1974,Je 28,21:1
Laboratoire Vitfer (Misc.)
Israel Why 1973,O 8,40:1
Leisure Media Inc (Prod.)
I Love You Rosa 1973,F 17,39:2
Les Films du Carosse (Prod.)
Such a Gorgeous Kid Like Me 1973,Mr 26,55:1
Day for Night (La Nuit Amercaine) 1973,S 29,22:1
Les Films du Chef-Lieu-ORTF (Prod.)
Don't Cry With Your Mouth Full (Pieure Pas la Bouche Pleine) 1974,S 28,25:1
Les Films du Losange/Les Films 7 (Prod.)
Celine and Julie Go Boating (Celine et Julie Vont en Bateau) 1974,O 8,38:1
Les Films du Losangeand Simar Film (Prod.)
Mother and the Whore, The (La Maman et La Putain) 1973,O 6,17:1
Les Films la Boetie (Paris) (Prod.)
Nada Gang, The 1974,N 7,56:5
Les Films La Boetie (Prod.)
Rupture, La (The Breakup) 1973,O 5,19:1
Juste Avant la Nuit (Just Before Nightfall) 1973,O 9,42:1
Wedding in Blood 1974,My 23,52:1
Levine, Joseph E, and Brut Productions (Prod.)
Night Watch 1973,Ag 10,26:1
Levitt-Pickman Film Corp (Dist.)
Tear in the Ocean, A 1973,O 1,45:2
Henry VIII and His Six Wives 1973,D 14,57:1
Groove Tube, The 1974,Je 24,25:1
Trio Infernal, Le 1974,N 9,24:1
Murder Is a Murder...Is a Murder, A 1974,N 28,47:2
Violons du Bal, Les 1974,D 16,46:1
Black Thursday 1974,D 23,34:1
Lido Films/Empire Films (Prod.)
Tout Va Bien 1973,F 17,39:1
Lira Films (Paris) (Prod.)
Widow Couderc, The 1974,O 14,39:3
Lobo Films Production (Prod.)
Que Hacer 1973,S 29,22:1
Louvre Associates Ltd (Prod.)
Black Thursday 1974,D 23,34:1

M

M-G-M (Prod.)
Outfit, The 1974,Ap 25,48:2
Mafilm, Studio 1 (Prod.)
Love 1974,Ja 6,II,1:2
Mafilm, Studio 1, Budapest (Prod.)
Love 1973,Mr 23,22:1
Mafilm Studio (Prod.)
Sindbad (Szindbad) 1974,O 25,24:1
Magnus Films (Prod.)
Razor in the Flesh (A Navalha Na Carne) 1974,Ja 24,44:2
Malpaso Company (Prod.)
Thunderbolt and Lightfoot 1974,My 24,23:3
Mammouth Films (Distr.)
Flesh Gordon 1974,Jl 31,20:1
Mapa Films (Prod.)
Memories of Helen (Memoria de Helena) 1974,Mr 29,25:1
Mara Film-Capitolina (Prod.)
Grande Bouffe, La (The Big Feast) 1973,S 20,64:3
Mara Films/ORTF/Laser Productions/Gerico Sound /(Misc.)
Lancelot of the Lake (Lancelot du Lac) 1974,O 1,33:1
Maron Films Ltd (Distr.)
Ciao! Manhattan 1973,Ap 20,15:1
Matsumoto (Prod.)
Funeral Parade of Roses 1973,Je 8,47:1
Matsumoto Productions (Prod.)
Demons 1974,Ja 18,22:1

Mayfair Films (Distr.)
That'll Be the Day 1974,D 23,32:3
Maysles Films (Distr.)
Christo's Valley Curtain 1974,Mr 15,20:1
Maysles Films (Prod.)
Christo's Valley Curtain 1974,Mr 15,20:1
Memorial-Sam (Prod.)
O Lucky Man! 1973,Je 14,58:1
Metro-Goldwyn-Mayer (Distr.)
Super Cops, The 1974,Mr 21,51:1
Private Parts 1973,F 2,16:1
Lolly-Madonna XXX 1973,F 22,30:1
Slither 1973,Mr 8,32:2
Ludwig 1973,Mr 9,27:1
Pat Garrett and Billy the Kid 1973,My 24,53:1
Elvis on Tour 1973,Je 7,54:1
Wicked, Wicked 1973,Je 14,56:1
Shaft in Africa 1973,Je 21,53:1
Man Who Loved Cat Dancing, The 1973,Je 29,17:1
Deaf Smith & Johnny Ears 1973,Jl 26,43:1
Deadly China Doll 1973,S 27,45:1
Slams, The 1973,S 27,45:1
Westworld 1973,N 22,51:1
Metromedia Producers Corp (Prod.)
Let the Good Times Roll 1973,My 26,18:1
Min-On of America (Distr.)
Battle of Okinawa 1973,S 12,41:1
Mirisch Corporation (Prod.)
Spikes Gang, The 1974,My 2,61:4
Mogens Skot-Hansen (Prod.)
First Circle, The 1973,Ja 13,17:3
Montage Creations (Prod.)
Very Natural Thing, A 1974,Je 28,22:1
Monument Film Corp (Distr.)
Minamata 1974,S 20,35:1
Mangrove Nine 1974,N 1,32:1
Death and Devil 1974,D 5,57:1
Greece of the Christian Greeks 1974,Ap 26,30:1
Mosfilm Production (Prod.)
Andrei Rublev 1973,O 10,43:1
Mosfilm Sorexport Film Production (Prod.)
Golden Calf, The (If I Had One Million Rubies) 1974,Je 14,19:1
Musemorphoses, The (Misc.)
Very Natural Thing, A 1974,Je 28,22:1
Museum of Modern Art (Prod.)
Over Night (Uber Nacht) 1974,Ap 9,37:1

N

Nader, Richard, Production (Prod.)
Let the Good Times Roll 1973,My 26,18:1
NASA (Misc.)
Looking Forward, Looking Back: (The Search Begins) 1974,My 24,23:2
National Board of Canada (Prod.)
Cry of the Wild 1974,Ja 3,45:1
National Film Archive of the British Film Institute /(Misc.)
Liebelei 1974,S 30,51:5
National Film Board of Canada (Distr.)
Ordinary Tenderness (La Tendresse Ordinaire) 1974,Ap 6,16:1
National Film Board of Canada (Misc.)
Family That Dwelt Apart, The 1974,Ja 9,22:1
National Film Board of Canada (Prod.)
Ordinary Tenderness (La Tendresse Ordinaire) 1974,Ap 6,16:1
National General Pictures (Distr.)
Baxter 1973,Mr 5,23:4
Fists of Fury 1973,My 5,25:3
Extreme Close-Up 1973,My 18,33:3
Warm December, A 1973,My 24,53:1
Maurie 1973,Ag 2,31:1
Lady Kung-Fu 1973,S 6,43:1
Triple Irons 1973,S 25,37:1
Man Called Noon, The 1973,S 25,37:1
Second Gun, The 1973,O 9,43:1
Massacre in Rome 1973,O 25,59:1
Executive Action 1973,N 8,60:1
Christian Licorice Store, The 1974,Ap 5,27:4
National Theater Company of Great Britain (Prod.)
Three Sisters 1974,Mr 12,34:4
NEF (Paris) (Prod.)
Retour D'Afrique, Le (Return From Africa) 1973,S 17,41:1
New Day Films (Distr.)
Two Portraits: Nana, Mom and Me 1974,D 19,60:5
New Line Cinema (Distr.)
Wedding in Blood 1974,My 23,52:1
Very Natural Thing, A 1974,Je 28,22:1
Ophelia 1974,Ag 8,30:1
New Line Cinema (Prod.)
Seduction of Mimi, The (Mimi Metallurgico ferito nell'onore) 1974,Je 19,40:3
New World Picture (Prod.)
Fantastic Planet 1973,D 19,54:2
New World Pictures Inc (Distr.)
Harder They Come, The 1973,F 9,32:3
New Yorker Films (Distr.)
Late Autumn 1973,O 17,55:1
Reed: Insurgent Mexico 1974,S 17,40:6

New Yorker Films (Distr.)—Cont

Out One/Spectre 1974,O 8,38:1
Flavor of Green Tea Over Rice, The 1973,Ja 25,51:6
Emitai 1973,F 10,22:1
Tout Va Bien 1973,F 17,39:1
Priest and the Girl, The 1973,F 26,28:1
Soleil-o 1973,Mr 15,55:3
Painters Painting 1973,Mr 20,30:1
How Tasty Was My Little Frenchman 1973,Ap 17,34:1
Autumn Afternoon, An 1973,My 8,39:1
Adieu Philippine 1973,My 17,56:4
Retour D'Afrique, Le (Return From Africa) 1973,S 17,41:1
History Lessons 1973,O 1,45:2
Sambizanga 1973,N 22,50:2
David Holzman's Diary 1973,D 7,34:1
Partner 1974,F 7,46:1
Ceremony, The (Gishiki) 1974,F 8,18:1
In the Name of the Father 1974,Mr 21,51:1
Memories of Helen (Memoria de Helena) 1974,Mr 29,25:1
Villeggiatura, La (Black Holiday) 1974,Ap 9,37:1
Diary of a Yunbogi Boy 1974,Ap 12,18:3
Dreams and Nightmares 1974,Ap 26,30:1
Free Woman, A 1974,Je 18,31:1
Promised Lands 1974,Jl 12,41:1
Sudden Wealth of the Poor People of Kombach, The 1974,S 26,24:1
Early Spring 1974,S 26,26:1
All 1974,O 7,55:1
Alienist, The (O Alienista) 1974,N 29,48:1
New Yorker Films (Prod.)
Happiness 1973,My 25,24:1
Jonathan 1973,Je 16,13:1

O

Orphee Productions (Prod.)
Emmanuelle 1974,D 16,47:5
ORTF (Prod.)
Femme Du Gange, La (Woman of the Ganges) 1974,Je 7,23:1
ORTF Cosmovision Technisoner Production (Prod.)
Bench of Desolation, The 1974,O 3,50:2

P

P I C (Prod.)
Day for Night (La Nuit Americaine) 1974,Ja 6,II,1:2
P I C (Rome) (Prod.)
Day for Night (La Nuit Amercaine) 1973,S 29,22:1
Pacific Film Industries (Misc.)
Prison Girls 1973,Ja 25,51:6
Pacific Street Film Collective (Prod.)
Frame-Up! The Imprisonment of Martin Sostre 1974,N 1,32:1
Palladium Productions (Prod.)
Taking of Pelham One Two Three, The 1974,O 3,50:1
Palomar Pictures (Prod.)
Taking of Pelham One Two Three, The 1974,O 3,50:1
Panasia Film Production (Prod.)
Deadly China Doll 1973,S 27,45:1
Parafrance (Prod.)
Israel Why 1973,O 8,40:1
Paramount Pictures (Distr.)
Super Fly TNT 1973,Je 16,13:1
Conversation, The 1974,Ap 8,44:3
First Circle, The 1973,Ja 13,17:3
Innocent Bystanders 1973,Ja 25,51:6
Save The Tiger 1973,F 15,53:1
Charlotte's Web 1973,F 23,18:1
Fear Is the Key 1973,Mr 15,55:6
Brother Sun, Sister Moon 1973,Ap 9,48:1
Charley-One-Eye 1973,Ap 19,52:1
Hitler: The Last Ten Days 1973,My 10,57:1
Paper Moon 1973,My 17,53:1
Soul of Nigger Charley, The 1973,My 17,54:1
Mattei Affair, The 1973,My 21,40:1
Doll's House, A 1973,My 23,38:1
Friends of Eddie Coyle, The 1973,Je 27,68:1
Badge 373 1973,Jl 26,43:1
Bang the Drum Slowly 1973,Ag 27,35:1
Hit 1973,S 19,38:3
Save the Children 1973,S 19,40:2
Optimists, The 1973,O 19,58:1
Tales That Witness Madness 1973,N 1,48:1
Scalawag 1973,N 15,58:7
Ash Wednesday 1973,N 22,50:2
Serpico 1973,D 6,61:1
Don't Look Now 1973,D 10,56:1
Alfredo Alfredo 1973,D 18,54:1
Man on a Swing 1974,F 28,33:1
Three Tough Guys 1974,Mr 16,16:3
Great Gatsby, The 1974,Mr 28,32:1
Daisy Miller 1974,My 23,52:1
Malizia (Malice) 1974,Je 6,49:7
Parallax View, The 1974,Je 20,47:1

H
ce
an
in
did
the
"tha
alley
small
bad"
t'